917.3
Bo   Boyer, Richard
      Places rated almanac. 2nd
      edition

DATE DUE

SE 1 8 86	10-3-87		
SE 29 86	SEP. 27 1997		
OC 20 '86			
DE 10 '86			
JA 26 '87			
NO 22 '88			
AP 13 '90			
JA 1 1 '92			
JE 23 '92			
MY 28 93			
SE 15 '93			
MAY 3 1 98			

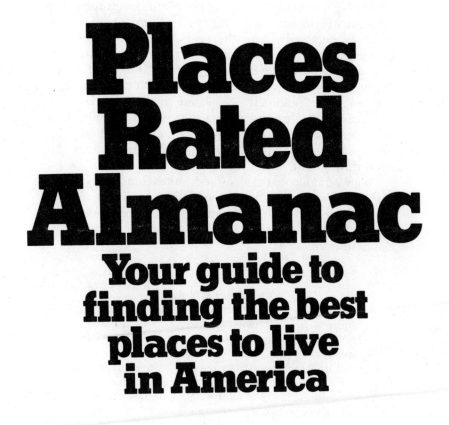

Places Rated Almanac

Your guide to finding the best places to live in America

Richard Boyer & David Savageau

Rand McNally & Company

Chicago • New York • San Francisco

Acknowledgments

Each time we produce a volume in the *Places Rated* series, we realize that the book could not have been written but for the help we've gotten from so many sources.

We are indebted to scores of people in government and with private organizations, many of whom we have come to know personally over the years. They have not only kept our research pointed in proper directions, but more than a few times have blocked our turns into blind alleys. Many of the improvements in this edition of *Places Rated Almanac* were originally suggested by them. Thanks to their generosity, pertinent data that would not otherwise have seen daylight are published here for the first time. These sources, along with other of their publications, are cited throughout.

We would like to thank our editors at Rand McNally for their many contributions at every step of the way. Special mention should also be made of Karyl Savageau and Donna Seymour for their valuable assistance in preparing the manuscript.

Publisher's Note

This book contains information provided by many sources. It is published for general reference and not as a substitute for independent verification by users when circumstances warrant. Although care and diligence have been used in its preparation, the publisher does not guarantee the accuracy of the information. The interpretation of the data and the views expressed are the authors' and not necessarily those of Rand McNally & Company.

Printed in the United States of America
Library of Congress Catalog Card No.: 84–43149

First printing, February 1985
Second printing, March 1985
Third printing, April 1985
Fourth printing, May 1985
Fifth printing, October 1985

Contents

Introduction

Why do you live where you do? Are you there because of family ties? A job commitment? A sentimental attachment to hometown turf? Will you spend the rest of your life there?

Much has been made of Americans moving. From time to time a majority of those polled by the Gallup Organization say they would prefer to live somewhere else. Most of us will change our address several times during our lives, but we will do it simply by moving from one neighborhood to another nearby. Each year, however, six million Americans move to another state. They may count six million different reasons among them for relocating a long distance, but they do have one thing in common—the need for information.

The response to the first edition of *Places Rated Almanac*, published in 1981, confirmed that people are indeed eager for a reliable, practical source of information about places. This new edition takes the same general approach as its predecessor but has been thoroughly updated, revised, and expanded. In 1977, when we began research for the first edition, there were 277 federally defined metropolitan areas in the United States. Now, as a result of population growth revealed by the 1980 census, our *Places Rated* universe has grown to 329. Besides the greatly expanded list of places, this edition introduces a number of new features and improvements, many based on the suggestions of experts in government, academia, and private organizations.

Like its predecessor, this edition of *Places Rated Almanac* is meant for people who are thinking of moving as well as for armchair travelers who enjoy finding out about American cities and towns and what they have to offer. As an almanac, it provides thousands of facts about 329 U.S. metropolitan areas, where 75 percent of Americans live. You won't find this information in standard guidebooks or blandishments from the chamber of commerce. In what other single source, for instance, can you find out which place has the best public transit, the least earthquake risk, and the most good restaurants per capita? But *Places Rated Almanac* is more than a collection of interesting, odd, and useful information about metro areas, for it also rates and ranks them on nine factors that greatly influence the quality of life: climate, housing, health care, crime, transportation, education, the arts, recreation, and economics.

Places Rated Almanac might be considered a self-help book with a difference: Instead of pointing the way toward upward mobility, as most such books do, it helps you determine whether geographical mobility might be the route to a more satisfying life. Where you live can significantly affect your happiness and personal success; it just may be that your current location doesn't match your needs and preferences. After all, given the incredible variety offered throughout the country, what are the odds that the place where you happen to live is the right one for you?

After using *Places Rated Almanac*, your hunch that you've never had it so good might well be confirmed. On the other hand, you may be in for a surprise. And if you're part of the discontented majority identified by pollsters, you may find yourself asking: What am I waiting for?

RATING PLACES—AN AMERICAN TRADITION

"The tradition of hating New York started long before it began asking the rest of us to pay its bills while condescendingly viewing us as amusing rustics," Mike Royko wrote in a Chicago *Sun-Times* column back in 1978. "Actually, I like New York," he continued. "There are better reasons to hate cities like Cleveland or Indianapolis or Detroit or Dallas. But I do dislike New Yorkers. . . ."

It may seem the height of effrontery, this business of judging American places. Yet we all do it, privately. Some lump Baltimore, Buffalo, Cleveland, Pittsburgh, and all of New Jersey together as object lessons in where the sins of free enterprise ultimately get you. Others suspect that living in Des Moines or Omaha couldn't be duller, that life in Chicago is spent avoiding shoot-outs, that Seattle is fog-bound and rain-soaked, and that residents of Los Angeles spend most of their time behind a steering wheel.

Passing judgment on different locales isn't just a current pastime; Americans have been at it for quite a while. To entice seventeenth-century colonists to pick Maryland over Virginia, promoters assembled figures showing heavier turkeys, more plentiful deer, and fewer deaths from foul summer diseases and Indian massacres, all yours if you settled in the northern reaches of Chesapeake Bay. In the nineteenth century, many northern observers connected the South's slave-holding and rebellious ways with the region's broilingly hot climate and an overabundance of lunatics, drunkards, and wastrels per capita.

In our own century, the process of comparing places has borrowed a great deal from statistical methods. One of America's education pioneers, E. L. Thorndike, in the late 1930s devised a "goodness index" drawn from 39 indicators for measuring a city's day-to-day living. Since then, others have jumped into the rating game. In 1983, Prof. Murray Straus, a sociologist at the University of New Hampshire, selected factors such as divorce, mortgage foreclosures, high school dropouts, personal bankruptcies, abortions, and new welfare cases to determine the most "stressful" states. Nevada and Alaska were numbers one and two on the stress list. And the most laid-back state, according to the indicators? Nebraska.

The Ways Places Are Rated

Places Rated Almanac, we believe, is more useful than any system that limits its evaluations to the 50 states because statewide averages can hide local realities. For mobile people, there may be more differences between the Texas metro areas of San Antonio and San Angelo than there are between the Lone Star State and Florida. This guide is also more objective than the opinions travelers may exchange in an airport bar or at a rest stop on the Interstate highway. Each of the 329 metro areas is rated by criteria that most people thinking of moving would deem important.

- Climate is rated on mildness; that is, how close temperatures remain to 65 degrees Fahrenheit throughout the year.
- Housing is compared in terms of dollar costs. We look at prices for single homes, plus the taxes and utilities a would-be homeowner can expect to pay. We also note the supply of apartments, mobile homes, and condominiums, as well as rental costs.
- Health care is evaluated on the basis of the supply of general health care facilities and special options available.
- Crime is measured by the annual number of violent and property crimes per 100,000 population.
- Transportation measures both assets and performance, including local commuting time, public transit, and the supply of intercity travel options by way of air, rail, and Interstate highway.
- Education ratings are based on each metro area's elementary and secondary school systems as well as options in higher education.
- The chapter on the arts compares cultural assets, among them museums and libraries, opera companies and symphony orchestras.
- Recreation also rates assets, from good restaurants to public golf courses, zoos, professional sports teams, inland lakes, and national parks acreage.
- Economics looks at local living costs, household income, tax bites, and the metro area's recent track record for job and income growth.

Some readers may fault *Places Rated*'s criteria. Some of the standards for rating health care, recreational and cultural life, and education, for example, tend to favor big metro areas. On the other hand, the methods for scoring climate, safety from crime, economic health, and affordable housing have nothing to do with population size; in fact, many smaller metro areas lead in these categories.

You may not agree with our rating system. If you like, you can devise your own method using the vast array of data presented. You may rule out metro areas with more than one million people. As long as summers aren't hot, you may not care a hoot for relative humidity, wind speed, and rainfall. You may have little interest in wildlife refuges or ocean shorelines but place a premium on good public schools. For you, a medium-sized metro area with good public transit and a record of job expansion may be more desirable than one with an abundant supply of performing arts and professional sports attractions.

We have tried to put together the most up-to-date facts for all 329 metro areas. In most instances, our information is as fresh as 1984; in a few isolated cases, the most recent statistics predate 1980. Our sources, which we document throughout the book, are principally different agencies of the federal government, but pertinent private sources have also been tapped.

Places Rated Almanac is like a snapshot of a moving target; metro areas are dynamic and won't always sit still for their statistical portraits. A continued turn-around in the automobile industry can improve the job and income prospects of more than a few Great Lakes metro areas, just as a prolonged cold snap and a natural gas shortage can markedly increase the costs of owning a Maryland home. With so much in life that can't be predicted, it's necessary to supplement *Places Rated Almanac* with your own independent verification.

But for now you can be sure that you'll find more affordable homes in Joplin, Missouri, than in Joliet, Illinois; public golf courses in greater supply in Akron than in Atlanta; more flights out of Denver's airport than Detroit's; and more acres of national public parkland in Fort Collins–Loveland, Colorado, than in Fort Pierce, Florida.

Why Have the Rankings Changed?

If you compare a metro area's ranks in this edition with its ranks in the previous one, you'll find that many have improved while others have slipped. There are several reasons.

First, of course, is simply that more places—329 instead of 277—are being rated; thus, a metro area might receive a lower absolute rank and still maintain the same *relative* position in the ratings. Besides there being a greater number of places, their geographic definitions, as established by the U.S. Office of Management and Budget, or OMB (more on this below), have changed. Only 166 of the 329 metro areas are exactly the same geographic entities they were in *Places Rated*'s 1981 edition (and 21 of these now have different names). For the rest, many have either gained or lost component counties, others were created by the merger of previously separate metro areas or by the partition of large ones, and 44 are entirely new areas that have qualified for metropolitan status because of their recent population growth.

Statistics have changed over the past few years, too. Figures for average household income, violent and property crimes, tax rates, golf courses, and airline departures are just a few of many that have been brought up to date for this edition. The upgrading of a symphony orchestra or the departure of a pro sports team could also cause a change in a metro area's ranking.

In many chapters, the criteria for rating the metro areas have undergone modification. Some of the factors have been weighted differently: The number of days when the outdoor thermometer hits 90 degrees Fahrenheit, for example, counts as a greater penalty against a metro area in this edition of *Places Rated* than it did in its predecessor. New scoring factors have been added in several chapters, such as a hospitalization/

Finding Your Way in the Chapters

Places Rated Almanac contains thousands of useful facts and many descriptive sections, and it is organized so that readers can find specific items that interest them. Each of its nine chapters has four parts:

- The **introductory section** gives basic information on the chapter's topic, interspersed with facts and figures to help you evaluate metro areas. We also describe the system used to rate and rank the 329 metro areas for that particular topic. At the end of this section, two metro areas are selected for a sample comparison to show why one place performs better than another in the ratings.
- **Places Rated:** This part ranks the 329 metro areas. They are listed first in their rank order, from best to worst, along with their score. (Metro areas that receive the same score are assigned the same rank and are listed in alphabetical order.) An alphabetical list with individual rankings follows so that you can quickly find the ranks of specific places.
- **Place Profiles:** Arranged alphabetically by metro area, these capsule comparisons cover all the elements used to rate the metro areas and usually give additional data. The Place Profiles can be columns of information (like the recreation profiles) or page-wide charts (like the economics profiles); the climate profiles have their own special format. All are designed to help you see differences among metro areas at a glance.
- **Et Cetera:** This section expands on the quality-of-life features mentioned in the introductory section. It contains information on other topics as well. These can range all the way from lists of metro area professional sports championships, state-by-state high school graduation requirements, and metro area Fortune 500 headquarters, to essays on water shortages and contradictory traffic laws.

The final chapter, "Putting It All Together," adds up the ranks to identify America's best all-around metro areas and discusses the good and bad points of the top 20. Here we also weigh the pros and cons of living in big and small metro areas, and give examples of how using personal preferences to devise your own scoring system can lead to different rankings.

insurance costs index in the Health Care chapter and a whole new category called Outdoor Recreation Assets in the Recreation chapter. And other scoring factors have been dropped, such as data for hospital beds, which were excluded from a metro area's health care rating because they are no longer regarded as the critical measurement for health care supply they once were. As much as is practical, we have tried to point out such scoring changes in each chapter.

Finally, a major scoring innovation has been made to reflect the fact that certain major assets—such as theme parks, pro sports arenas, large symphony orchestras, airports, and major medical centers—are frequently enjoyed or used in one metro area by residents of another. The federal government, in its classification of metropolitan areas for statistical purposes, has given some expression to this reality by grouping certain closely related metro areas into Consolidated Metropolitan Statistical Areas (CMSAs). Seventy-six of the 329 metro areas in *Places Rated Almanac* are included in 22 CMSA complexes. The Los Angeles–Anaheim–Riverside CMSA, for example, includes four metropolitan areas: Anaheim–Santa Ana, Los Angeles–Long Beach, Oxnard–Ventura, and Riverside–San Bernardino. (A complete list of CMSAs and their component metro areas is in the Appendix).

In its chapters rating health care, transportation, cultural assets, and recreational opportunities, *Places Rated* now recognizes the importance of shared assets by awarding bonus points to metro areas that are members of CMSAs. The way these CMSA Access points are calculated is explained in detail in each of the affected chapters. The impact of the CMSA Access factor on the rankings of some member metro areas is pronounced.

METROPOLITAN AREAS

Certainly this second edition of *Places Rated Almanac* offers readers a wide range of places for research and consideration. Whether your motivation is personal relocation, plant expansion, personnel placement, or mere curiosity, the 329 metro areas presented here— from Abilene, Texas, to Yuba City, California; from huge New York (pop. 8,274,961) to tiny Enid, Oklahoma (pop. 62,820); from Anchorage to Miami–Hialeah— cover the entire spectrum of American cities. There are agricultural centers and fashion markets; mill towns and bedroom communities; financial centers and small college towns. You'll find resort communities, entertainment meccas, and cultural havens right next to ports of entry, rail centers, and industrial giants.

What is a metropolitan area? Standard metropolitan area definitions were first developed and issued about 35 years ago by the OMB for use by all federal agencies compiling general statistical data, including census statistics on population, housing, industry trade, current employment and payroll data, and local

housing market and labor market analyses. In 1981, when the first edition of *Places Rated Almanac* was published, the OMB nomenclature for these statistical entities was Standard Metropolitan Statistical Areas (SMSAs), and these were the basic entities we compared throughout the book.

On June 30, 1983, as a result of periodic government review of metropolitan area definitions, a new three-tiered system of designations went into effect: Metropolitan Statistical Areas (MSAs), Primary Metropolitan Statistical Areas (PMSAs), and Consolidated Metropolitan Statistical Areas (CMSAs). For all practical purposes, the units now referred to as MSAs and PMSAs are the equivalent of the former SMSAs, and it is these units that are compared in this book and referred to as metro areas. Of the 329 metro areas, 253 are MSAs and 76 are PMSAs. The main difference between MSAs and PMSAs is that MSAs are "standalone" metro areas, whereas PMSAs are metropolitan entities that are also joined with other PMSAs in the megalopolitan complexes designated CMSAs.

Metropolitan statistical areas are defined according to detailed federal standards. The general concept underlying these definitions is that of a geographic area consisting of a large population nucleus together with adjacent communities that have a high degree of economic and social integration with that nucleus. Broadly speaking, an area qualifies as a metropolitan area in one of two ways: if there is a city with a population of at least 50,000, or an urbanized area (embracing one or more towns) of at least 50,000 located in a county or counties with a total population of at least 100,000 (75,000 in New England). In either case, for statistical purposes the metropolitan area's boundaries coincide with the boundaries of the surrounding county or counties (except in New England, where towns and cities are the basis of OMB designations). Most metro areas are within single states; 34 of them, however, cross state boundaries. Metropolitan Cincinnati, for example, includes three counties in Ohio, three in Kentucky, and one in Indiana; Memphis takes in two counties in Tennessee, plus one in Arkansas and one in Mississippi. (Puerto Rico has six metro areas, but *Places Rated* confines its comparisons to places within the United States.)

There is a good reason for focusing on these entities rather than on cities, counties, or states. Thanks to the automobile, cities, counties, and states have become less relevant to an individual's daily personal geography. Commonly, we live in one community, such as the suburb of a large city; commute to a job in another; patronize the restaurants, shopping centers, and recreation assets of all the towns around; and every two years approve or disapprove of our district's congressional representative. We pay taxes or fees to water, sewer, park, and school districts that often cross city lines. The perimeters of metro areas supersede the anachronistic political boundaries of incorporated areas and include not only the frequently troubled and depressed older city cores but also the newer suburbs with their sleek new malls, office parks, factories, and choice residential districts. For example, metropolitan Newark includes affluent Morris County; the Cleveland metro area includes Shaker Heights; and the Boston area, with its 106 cities and towns, takes in a wealthy fringe of high-tech industries.

The list below provides the county definitions of the metropolitan areas rated in this edition of *Places Rated Almanac* (metro areas classified as PMSAs are identified by an asterisk). The number of metro areas is constantly on the rise. Recently, two additional areas —Naples, Florida, and Santa Fe, New Mexico—were designated MSAs. Whatever their number, the chances are good that you, like three of every four Americans, live in one of the official metropolitan areas surveyed here.

The Places We Rate: 329 Metropolitan Areas

Metro Areas and Component Counties	Population 1980	Population 1970	Population Change, 1970–1980	Metro Areas and Component Counties	Population 1980	Population 1970	Population Change, 1970–1980
Abilene, TX Taylor County	110,932	97,853	+13.4%	**Atlanta, GA** Barrow, Butts, Cherokee, Clayton, Cobb, Coweta, De Kalb, Douglas, Fayette, Forsyth, Fulton, Gwinnett, Henry, Newton, Paulding, Rockdale, Spalding, and Walton counties	2,138,231	1,684,200	+27.0%
Akron, OH* Portage and Summit counties	660,328	679,239	− 2.8				
Albany, GA Dougherty and Lee counties	112,402	96,683	+16.3				
Albany–Schenectady–Troy, NY Albany, Greene, Montgomery, Rensselaer, Saratoga, and Schenectady counties	835,880	811,113	+ 3.1	**Atlantic City, NJ** Atlantic and Cape May counties	276,385	234,597	+17.8
				Augusta, GA–SC Columbia, McDuffie, and Richmond counties, GA; Aiken County, SC	345,918	291,063	+18.8
Albuquerque, NM Bernalillo County	419,700	315,774	+32.9				
Alexandria, LA Rapides Parish	135,282	118,078	+14.6	**Aurora–Elgin, IL*** Kane and Kendall counties	315,607	277,379	+13.8
Allentown–Bethlehem, PA–NJ Carbon, Lehigh, and Northampton counties, PA; Warren County, NJ	635,481	594,382	+ 6.9	**Austin, TX** Hays, Travis, and Williamson counties	536,688	360,463	+48.9
Alton–Granite City, IL* Jersey and Madison counties	268,229	269,403	− 0.4	**Bakersfield, CA** Kern County	403,089	330,234	+22.1
Altoona, PA Blair County	136,621	135,356	+ 0.9	**Baltimore, MD** Baltimore city; Anne Arundel, Baltimore, Carroll, Harford, Howard, and Queen Annes counties	2,199,531	2,089,438	+ 5.3
Amarillo, TX Potter and Randall counties	173,699	144,396	+20.2				
Anaheim–Santa Ana, CA* Orange County	1,932,709	1,421,233	+36.0	**Bangor, ME** Parts of Penobscot and Waldo counties	83,919	79,933	+ 5.0
Anchorage, AK Anchorage Borough	174,431	126,385	+38.0	**Baton Rouge, LA** Ascension, East Baton Rouge, Livingston, and West Baton Rouge parishes	494,151	375,628	+31.6
Anderson, IN Madison County	139,336	138,522	+ 0.6				
Anderson, SC Anderson County	133,235	105,474	+26.3	**Battle Creek, MI** Calhoun County	141,557	141,963	− 0.3
Ann Arbor, MI* Washtenaw County	264,748	234,103	+13.1	**Beaumont–Port Arthur, TX** Hardin, Jefferson, and Orange counties	375,497	347,568	+ 8.0
Anniston, AL Calhoun County	119,761	103,092	+16.2	**Beaver County, PA*** Beaver County	204,441	208,418	− 1.9
Appleton–Oshkosh–Neenah, WI Calumet, Outagamie, and Winnebago counties	291,369	276,948	+ 5.2	**Bellingham, WA** Whatcom County	106,701	81,983	+30.2
Asheville, NC Buncombe County	160,934	145,056	+10.9	**Benton Harbor, MI** Berrien County	171,276	163,940	+ 4.5
Athens, GA Clarke, Jackson, Madison, and Oconee counties	130,015	107,702	+20.7	**Bergen–Passaic, NJ*** Bergen and Passaic counties	1,292,970	1,357,930	− 4.8

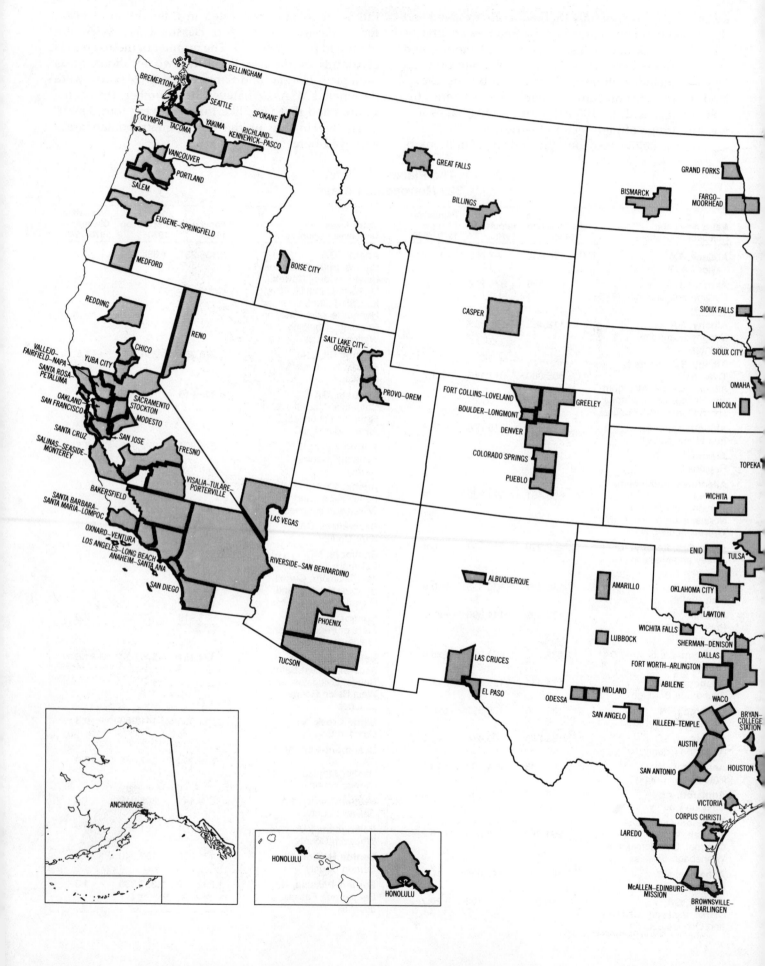

Places Rated Almanac
329 Metropolitan Areas

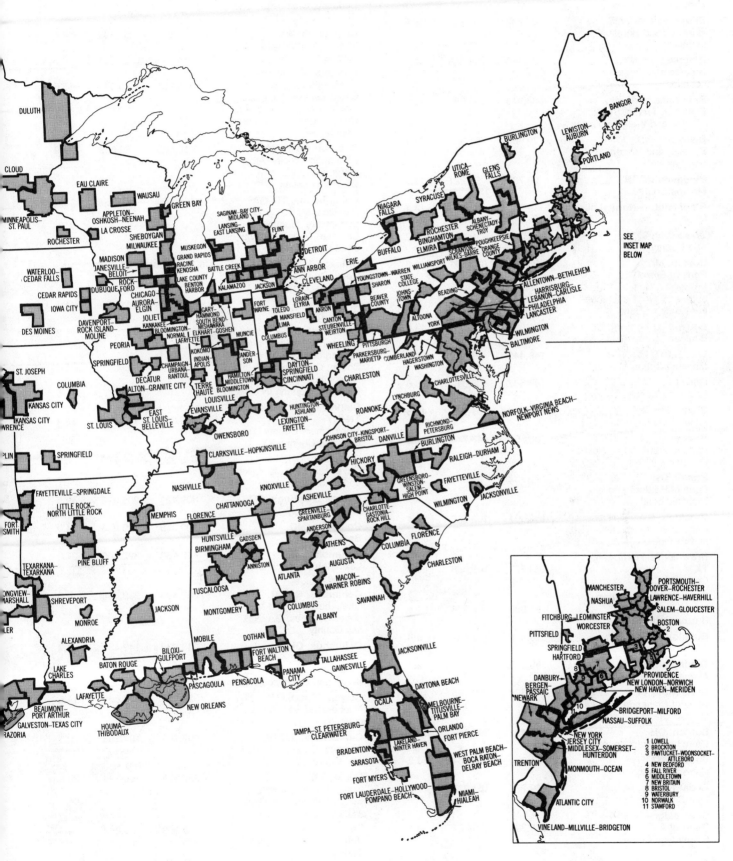

Metro Areas and Component Counties	Population 1980	Population 1970	Population Change, 1970–1980	Metro Areas and Component Counties	Population 1980	Population 1970	Population Change, 1970–1980
Billings, MT Yellowstone County	108,035	87,367	+23.7%	**Charleston, SC** Berkeley, Charleston, and Dorchester counties	430,462	336,036	+28.1%
Biloxi–Gulfport, MS Hancock and Harrison counties	182,202	151,969	+19.9	**Charleston, WV** Kanawha and Putnam counties	269,595	257,140	+ 4.4
Binghamton, NY Broome and Tioga counties	263,460	268,328	− 1.8	**Charlotte–Gastonia–Rock Hill, NC–SC** Cabarrus, Gaston, Lincoln, Mecklenburg, Rowan, and Union counties, NC; York County, SC	971,391	840,347	+15.6
Birmingham, AL Blount, Jefferson, St. Clair, Shelby, and Walker counties	883,946	794,083	+11.3				
Bismarck, ND Burleigh and Morton counties	79,988	61,024	+31.1	**Charlottesville, VA** Charlottesville city; Albemarle, Fluvanna, and Greene counties	113,568	89,529	+26.9
Bloomington, IN Monroe County	98,785	85,221	+15.9	**Chattanooga, TN–GA** Hamilton, Marion, and Sequatchie counties, TN; Catoosa, Dade, and Walker counties, GA	426,540	370,857	+19.0
Bloomington–Normal, IL McLean County	119,149	104,389	+14.1				
Boise City, ID Ada County	173,036	112,230	+54.2				
Boston, MA* Parts of Bristol, Essex, Middlesex, Norfolk, Plymouth, and Worcester counties; Suffolk County	2,805,911	2,887,191	− 2.8	**Chicago, IL*** Cook, Du Page, and McHenry counties	6,060,387	6,093,287	− 0.5
				Chico, CA Butte County	143,851	101,969	+41.1
Boulder–Longmont, CO* Boulder County	189,625	131,889	+43.8	**Cincinnati, OH–KY–IN*** Clermont, Hamilton, and Warren counties, OH; Boone, Campbell, and Kenton counties, KY; Dearborn County, IN	1,401,491	1,387,207	+ 1.3
Bradenton, FL Manatee County	148,442	97,115	+52.9				
Brazoria, TX* Brazoria County	169,587	108,312	+56.6				
Bremerton, WA Kitsap County	147,152	101,732	+44.6	**Clarksville–Hopkinsville, TN–KY** Montgomery County, TN; Christian County, KY	150,220	118,945	+33.4
Bridgeport–Milford, CT* Parts of Fairfield and New Haven counties	438,557	443,714	− 1.2				
Bristol, CT* Parts of Hartford and Litchfield counties	73,762	69,878	+ 5.6	**Cleveland, OH*** Cuyahoga, Geauga, Lake, and Medina counties	1,898,825	2,063,729	− 8.0
Brockton, MA* Parts of Bristol, Norfolk, and Plymouth counties	182,891	162,750	+12.4	**Colorado Springs, CO** El Paso County	309,424	235,972	+39.5
				Columbia, MO Boone County	100,376	80,935	+24.0
Brownsville–Harlingen, TX Cameron County	209,727	140,368	+49.4	**Columbia, SC** Lexington and Richland counties	410,088	322,880	+27.0
Bryan–College Station, TX Brazos County	93,588	57,978	+61.4	**Columbus, GA–AL** Chattahoochee and Muscogee counties, GA; Russell County, AL	239,196	238,584	+ 0.3
Buffalo, NY* Erie County	1,015,472	1,113,491	− 8.8				
Burlington, NC Alamance County	99,319	96,502	+ 2.9	**Columbus, OH** Delaware, Fairfield, Franklin, Licking, Madison, Pickaway, and Union counties	1,243,833	1,149,432	+ 8.2
Burlington, VT Parts of Chittenden, Franklin, and Grand Isle counties	115,308	99,145	+16.3				
Canton, OH Carroll and Stark counties	404,421	393,789	+ 2.7	**Corpus Christi, TX** Nueces and San Patricio counties	326,228	284,832	+14.5
Casper, WY Natrona County	71,856	51,264	+40.2	**Cumberland, MD–WV** Allegany County, MD; Mineral County, WV	107,782	107,153	+ 0.6
Cedar Rapids, IA Linn County	169,775	163,213	+ 4.0	**Dallas, TX*** Collin, Dallas, Denton, Ellis, Kaufman, and Rockwall counties	1,957,378	1,556,324	+25.8
Champaign–Urbana–Rantoul, IL Champaign County	168,392	163,281	+ 3.1				
				Danbury, CT* Parts of Fairfield and Litchfield counties	170,369	136,462	+24.9

Metro Areas and Component Counties	Population 1980	Population 1970	Population Change, 1970–1980	Metro Areas and Component Counties	Population 1980	Population 1970	Population Change, 1970–1980
Danville, VA Danville city and Pittsylvania County	111,789	105,180	+ 6.3%	**Fayetteville–Springdale, AR** Washington County	100,494	77,370	+29.9%
Davenport–Rock Island–Moline, IA–IL Scott County, IA; Henry and Rock Island counties, IL	383,958	362,638	+ 5.9	**Fitchburg–Leominster, MA** Parts of Middlesex and Worcester counties	94,018	93,732	+ 0.3
Dayton–Springfield, OH Clark, Greene, Miami, and Montgomery counties	942,083	974,927	− 3.4	**Flint, MI** Genesee County	450,449	445,589	+ 1.1
Daytona Beach, FL Volusia County	258,762	169,487	+52.7	**Florence, AL** Colbert and Lauderdale counties	135,065	117,743	+14.7
Decatur, IL Macon County	131,375	125,010	+ 5.1	**Florence, SC** Florence County	110,163	89,636	+22.9
Denver, CO* Adams, Arapahoe, Denver, Douglas, and Jefferson counties	1,428,836	1,106,384	+29.2	**Fort Collins–Loveland, CO** Larimer County	149,184	89,900	+65.9
Des Moines, IA Dallas, Polk, and Warren counties	367,561	339,647	+ 8.2	**Fort Lauderdale–Hollywood–Pompano Beach, FL*** Broward County	1,018,200	620,100	+64.2
Detroit, MI* Lapeer, Livingston, Macomb, Monroe, Oakland, St. Clair, and Wayne counties	4,488,072	4,554,266	− 1.5	**Fort Myers, FL** Lee County	205,266	105,216	+95.1
Dothan, AL Dale and Houston counties	122,453	109,569	+11.8	**Fort Pierce, FL** Martin and St. Lucie counties	151,196	78,871	+91.7
Dubuque, IA Dubuque County	93,745	90,609	+ 3.5	**Fort Smith, AR–OK** Crawford and Sebastian counties, AR; Sequoyah County, OK	162,813	128,284	+26.9
Duluth, MN–WI St. Louis County, MN; Douglas County, WI	266,650	265,350	+ 0.5	**Fort Walton Beach, FL** Okaloosa County	109,920	88,187	+24.6
East St. Louis–Belleville, IL* Clinton and St. Clair counties	300,148	313,906	− 4.4	**Fort Wayne, IN** Allen, De Kalb, and Whitley counties	354,156	334,687	+ 5.8
Eau Claire, WI Chippewa and Eau Claire counties	130,932	114,936	+13.9	**Fort Worth–Arlington, TX*** Johnson, Parker, and Tarrant counties	973,138	795,244	+22.4
El Paso, TX El Paso County	479,899	359,291	+33.6	**Fresno, CA** Fresno County	514,621	413,329	+24.5
Elkhart–Goshen, IN Elkhart County	137,330	126,529	+ 8.5	**Gadsden, AL** Etowah County	103,057	94,144	+ 9.5
Elmira, NY Chemung County	97,656	101,537	− 3.8	**Gainesville, FL** Alachua and Bradford counties	171,371	119,389	+43.5
Enid, OK Garfield County	62,820	56,343	+11.5	**Galveston–Texas City, TX*** Galveston County	195,940	169,812	+15.4
Erie, PA Erie County	279,780	263,654	+ 6.1	**Gary–Hammond, IN*** Lake and Porter counties	642,781	633,367	+ 1.5
Eugene–Springfield, OR Lane County	275,226	215,401	+27.8	**Glens Falls, NY** Warren and Washington counties	109,649	102,127	+ 7.4
Evansville, IN–KY Posey, Vanderburgh, and Warrick counties, IN; Henderson County, KY	276,252	254,515	+ 8.5	**Grand Forks, ND** Grand Forks County	66,100	61,102	+ 8.2
Fall River, MA–RI* Parts of Bristol County, MA; parts of Newport County, RI	157,222	152,361	+ 3.2	**Grand Rapids, MI** Kent and Ottawa counties	601,680	539,225	+11.6
Fargo–Moorhead, ND–MN Cass County, ND; Clay County, MN	137,574	120,261	+14.4	**Great Falls, MT** Cascade County	80,696	81,804	− 1.4
Fayetteville, NC Cumberland County	247,160	212,042	+16.6	**Greeley, CO** Weld County	123,438	89,297	+38.2
				Green Bay, WI Brown County	175,280	158,244	+10.8

Metro Areas and Component Counties	Population 1980	Population 1970	Population Change, 1970–1980	Metro Areas and Component Counties	Population 1980	Population 1970	Population Change, 1970–1980
Greensboro–Winston-Salem–High Point, NC Davidson, Davie, Forsyth, Guilford, Randolph, Stokes, and Yadkin counties	851,851	742,984	+14.7%	**Johnson City–Kingsport–Bristol, TN–VA** Carter, Hawkins, Sullivan, Unicoi, and Washington counties, TN; Bristol city and Scott and Washington counties, VA	433,638	373,591	+16.1%
Greenville–Spartanburg, SC Greenville, Pickens, and Spartanburg counties	569,066	473,454	+20.2	**Johnstown, PA** Cambria and Somerset counties	264,506	262,822	+ 0.6
Hagerstown, MD Washington County	113,086	103,829	+ 8.9	**Joliet, IL*** Grundy and Will counties	355,042	274,360	+29.4
Hamilton–Middletown, OH* Butler County	258,787	226,207	+14.4	**Joplin, MO** Jasper and Newton counties	127,513	112,833	+13.0
Harrisburg–Lebanon–Carlisle, PA Cumberland, Dauphin, Lebanon, and Perry counties	555,158	510,170	+ 8.8	**Kalamazoo, MI** Kalamazoo County	212,378	201,550	+ 5.4
Hartford, CT* Parts of Hartford, Litchfield, Middlesex, New London, and Tolland counties	715,923	710,926	+ 0.7	**Kankakee, IL** Kankakee County	102,926	97,250	+ 5.8
Hickory, NC Alexander, Burke, and Catawba counties	202,711	170,703	+18.8	**Kansas City, KS*** Johnson, Leavenworth, Miami, and Wyandotte counties	519,031	479,512	+ 8.3
Honolulu, HI Honolulu County	762,565	630,528	+20.9	**Kansas City, MO*** Cass, Clay, Jackson, Lafayette, Platte, and Ray counties	914,427	893,634	+ 2.3
Houma–Thibodaux, LA Lafourche and Terrebonne parishes	176,876	144,990	+22.0	**Kenosha, WI*** Kenosha County	123,137	117,917	+ 4.4
Houston, TX* Fort Bend, Harris, Liberty, Montgomery, and Waller counties	2,735,766	1,891,004	+44.6	**Killeen–Temple, TX** Bell and Coryell counties	214,656	159,794	+34.3
Huntington–Ashland, WV–KY–OH Cabell and Wayne counties, WV; Boyd, Carter, and Greenup counties, KY; Lawrence County, OH	336,410	306,785	+ 9.7	**Knoxville, TN** Anderson, Blount, Grainger, Jefferson, Knox, Sevier, and Union counties	565,970	476,538	+18.8
Huntsville, AL Madison County	196,966	186,540	+ 5.6	**Kokomo, IN** Howard and Tipton counties	103,715	99,848	+ 3.9
Indianapolis, IN Boone, Hamilton, Hancock, Hendricks, Johnson, Marion, Morgan, and Shelby counties	1,166,575	1,111,352	+ 5.0	**La Crosse, WI** La Crosse County	91,056	80,468	+13.2
Iowa City, IA Johnson County	81,717	72,127	+13.3	**Lafayette, IN** Tippecanoe County	121,702	109,378	+11.3
Jackson, MI Jackson County	151,495	143,274	+ 5.7	**Lafayette, LA** Lafayette and St. Martin parishes	190,231	144,096	+32.0
Jackson, MS Hinds, Madison, and Rankin counties	362,038	288,643	+25.4	**Lake Charles, LA** Calcasieu Parish	167,223	145,415	+15.0
Jacksonville, FL Clay, Duval, Nassau, and St. Johns counties	722,252	612,585	+17.9	**Lake County, IL*** Lake County	440,372	382,638	+15.0
Jacksonville, NC Onslow County	112,784	103,126	+ 9.4	**Lakeland–Winter Haven, FL** Polk County	321,652	228,515	+40.8
Janesville–Beloit, WI Rock County	139,420	131,970	+ 5.6	**Lancaster, PA** Lancaster County	362,346	320,079	+13.2
Jersey City, NJ* Hudson County	556,972	607,839	− 8.4	**Lansing–East Lansing, MI** Clinton, Eaton, and Ingham counties	419,750	378,423	+10.9
				Laredo, TX Webb County	99,258	72,859	+36.2
				Las Cruces, NM Dona Ana County	96,340	69,773	+38.1
				Las Vegas, NV Clark County	463,087	273,288	+69.5

Metro Areas and Component Counties	Population 1980	Population 1970	Population Change, 1970–1980
Lawrence, KS Douglas County	67,640	57,932	+16.8%
Lawrence–Haverhill, MA–NH* Parts of Essex County, MA; parts of Rockingham County, NH	339,090	300,943	+12.7
Lawton, OK Comanche County	112,456	108,144	+ 4.0
Lewiston–Auburn, ME Parts of Androscoggin County	84,690	80,135	+ 5.7
Lexington–Fayette, KY Bourbon, Clark, Fayette, Jessamine, Scott, and Woodford counties	317,629	266,701	+19.1
Lima, OH Allen and Auglaize counties	154,795	149,746	+ 3.4
Lincoln, NE Lancaster County	192,884	167,972	+14.8
Little Rock–North Little Rock, AR Faulkner, Lonoke, Pulaski, and Saline counties	474,484	381,123	+24.5
Longview–Marshall, TX Gregg and Harrison counties	151,752	120,770	+25.7
Lorain–Elyria, OH* Lorain County	274,909	256,843	+ 7.0
Los Angeles–Long Beach, CA* Los Angeles County	7,477,503	7,041,980	+ 6.2
Louisville, KY–IN Bullitt, Jefferson, Oldham, and Shelby counties, KY; Clark, Floyd, and Harrison counties, IN	956,756	906,752	+ 5.5
Lowell, MA–NH* Parts of Middlesex County, MA; parts of Hillsborough County, NH	243,142	225,447	+ 7.8
Lubbock, TX Lubbock County	211,651	179,295	+18.1
Lynchburg, VA Lynchburg city; Amherst and Campbell counties	141,289	124,960	+13.1
Macon–Warner Robins, GA Bibb, Houston, Jones, and Peach counties	263,591	234,550	+12.4
Madison, WI Dane County	323,545	290,272	+11.5
Manchester, NH Parts of Hillsborough, Merrimack, and Rockingham counties	129,305	115,225	+12.2
Mansfield, OH Richland County	131,205	129,997	+ 0.9
McAllen–Edinburg–Mission, TX Hidalgo County	283,229	181,535	+56.1
Medford, OR Jackson County	132,456	94,533	+40.1
Melbourne–Titusville–Palm Bay, FL Brevard County	272,959	230,006	+18.7

Metro Areas and Component Counties	Population 1980	Population 1970	Population Change, 1970–1980
Memphis, TN–AR–MS Shelby and Tipton counties, TN; Crittenden County, AR; De Soto County, MS	913,472	834,103	+ 9.5%
Miami–Hialeah, FL* Dade County	1,625,781	1,267,792	+28.2
Middlesex–Somerset–Hunterdon, NJ* Hunterdon, Middlesex, and Somerset counties	886,383	851,903	+ 4.1
Middletown, CT* Parts of Middlesex County	81,582	73,769	+10.6
Midland, TX Midland County	82,636	65,433	+26.3
Milwaukee, WI* Milwaukee, Ozaukee, Washington, and Waukesha counties	1,397,143	1,403,884	− 0.5
Minneapolis–St. Paul, MN–WI Anoka, Carver, Chisago, Dakota, Hennepin, Isanti, Ramsey, Scott, Washington, and Wright counties, MN; St. Croix County, WI	2,137,133	1,981,951	+ 7.8
Mobile, AL Baldwin and Mobile counties	443,536	376,690	+17.8
Modesto, CA Stanislaus County	265,900	194,506	+36.7
Monmouth–Ocean, NJ* Monmouth and Ocean counties	849,211	670,319	+26.7
Monroe, LA Ouachita Parish	139,241	115,387	+20.7
Montgomery, AL Autauga, Elmore, and Montgomery counties	272,687	225,911	+20.7
Muncie, IN Delaware County	128,587	129,219	− 0.5
Muskegon, MI Muskegon County	157,589	157,426	+ 0.1
Nashua, NH* Parts of Hillsborough and Rockingham counties	142,527	100,011	+42.1
Nashville, TN Cheatham, Davidson, Dickson, Robertson, Rutherford, Sumner, Williamson, and Wilson counties	850,505	699,271	+21.4
Nassau–Suffolk, NY* Nassau and Suffolk counties	2,605,813	2,555,868	+ 1.9
New Bedford, MA Parts of Bristol and Plymouth counties	166,699	158,682	+ 5.0
New Britain, CT* Parts of Hartford County	142,241	145,269	− 2.1
New Haven–Meriden, CT Parts of Middlesex and New Haven counties	500,474	488,732	+ 2.4
New London–Norwich, CT–RI Parts of New London and Windham counties, CT; parts of Washington County, RI	250,839	242,624	+ 3.4

Metro Areas and Component Counties	Population 1980	Population 1970	Population Change, 1970–1980	Metro Areas and Component Counties	Population 1980	Population 1970	Population Change, 1970–1980
New Orleans, LA Jefferson, Orleans, St. Bernard, St. Charles, St. John The Baptist, and St. Tammany parishes	1,256,256	1,099,833	+14.0%	**Pensacola, FL** Escambia and Santa Rosa counties	289,782	243,075	+19.0%
New York, NY* Bronx, Kings, New York, Putnam, Queens, Richmond, Rockland, and Westchester counties	8,274,961	9,076,568	− 8.8	**Peoria, IL** Peoria, Tazewell, and Woodford counties	365,864	341,979	+ 6.9
Newark, NJ* Essex, Morris, Sussex, and Union counties	1,878,959	1,936,624	− 3.0	**Philadelphia, PA–NJ*** Bucks, Chester, Delaware, Montgomery, and Philadelphia counties, PA; Burlington, Camden, and Gloucester counties, NJ	4,716,818	4,824,110	− 2.2
Niagara Falls, NY* Niagara County	227,354	235,720	− 3.5	**Phoenix, AZ** Maricopa County	1,509,052	971,228	+55.4
Norfolk–Virginia Beach– Newport News, VA Chesapeake, Hampton, Newport News, Norfolk, Poquoson, Portsmouth, Suffolk, Virginia Beach, and Williamsburg cities; Gloucester, James City, and York counties	1,160,311	1,058,764	+ 9.5	**Pine Bluff, AR** Jefferson County	90,718	85,329	+ 6.3
				Pittsburgh, PA* Allegheny, Fayette, Washington, and Westmoreland counties	2,218,870	2,347,611	− 5.5
Norwalk, CT* Parts of Fairfield County	126,692	127,595	− 0.7	**Pittsfield, MA** Parts of Berkshire County	83,490	88,094	− 5.2
Oakland, CA* Alameda and Contra Costa counties	1,761,759	1,627,562	+ 8.2	**Portland, ME** Parts of Cumberland and York counties	193,831	171,870	+12.7
Ocala, FL Marion County	122,488	69,030	+77.4	**Portland, OR*** Clackamas, Multnomah, Washington, and Yamhill counties	1,105,699	918,889	+20.3
Odessa, TX Ector County	115,374	92,660	+24.3				
Oklahoma City, OK Canadian, Cleveland, Logan, McClain, Oklahoma, and Pottawatomie counties	860,969	718,737	+19.6	**Portsmouth–Dover– Rochester, NH–ME** Parts of Rockingham and Strafford counties, NH; part of York County, ME	190,938	161,199	+18.4
Olympia, WA Thurston County	124,264	76,894	+61.6	**Poughkeepsie, NY** Dutchess County	245,055	222,295	+10.1
Omaha, NE–IA Douglas, Sarpy, and Washington counties, NE; Pottawattamie County, IA	585,122	555,956	+ 5.2	**Providence, RI*** Parts of Bristol, Kent, Newport, Providence, and Washington counties	618,514	612,362	+ 1.0
Orange County, NY* Orange County	259,603	221,657	+17.0	**Provo–Orem, UT** Utah County	218,106	137,776	+58.3
Orlando, FL Orange, Osceola, and Seminole counties	700,055	453,270	+54.4	**Pueblo, CO** Pueblo County	125,972	118,238	+ 6.5
Owensboro, KY Daviess County	85,949	79,486	+ 8.1	**Racine, WI*** Racine County	173,132	170,838	+ 1.0
Oxnard–Ventura, CA* Ventura County	529,174	378,497	+39.8	**Raleigh–Durham, NC** Durham, Franklin, Orange, and Wake counties	561,222	446,074	+25.6
Panama City, FL Bay County	97,740	75,283	+29.5	**Reading, PA** Berks County	312,509	296,382	+ 5.4
Parkersburg–Marietta, WV–OH Wood County, WV; Washington County, OH	157,914	143,978	+ 9.6	**Redding, CA** Shasta County	115,715	77,640	+49.0
Pascagoula, MS Jackson County	118,015	87,975	+34.1	**Reno, NV** Washoe County	193,623	121,068	+59.9
Pawtucket–Woonsocket– Attleboro, RI–MA* Parts of Providence County, RI; parts of Bristol, Norfolk, and Worcester counties, MA	307,403	300,694	+ 2.2	**Richland–Kennewick– Pasco, WA** Benton and Franklin counties	144,469	93,356	+54.8
				Richmond–Petersburg, VA Colonial Heights, Hopewell, Petersburg, and Richmond cities; Charles City, Chesterfield, Dinwiddie, Goochland, Hanover, Henrico, New Kent, Powhatan, and Prince George counties	761,311	676,351	+12.6

Metro Areas and Component Counties	Population 1980	Population 1970	Population Change, 1970–1980	Metro Areas and Component Counties	Population 1980	Population 1970	Population Change, 1970–1980
Riverside–San Bernardino, CA* Riverside and San Bernardino counties	1,558,182	1,139,149	+36.8%	**Savannah, GA** Chatham and Effingham counties	220,553	201,448	+ 9.5%
Roanoke, VA Roanoke and Salem cities; Botetourt and Roanoke counties	220,393	199,629	+10.4	**Scranton–Wilkes-Barre, PA** Columbia, Lackawanna, Luzerne, Monroe, and Wyoming counties	728,796	696,078	+ 4.7
Rochester, MN Olmsted County	92,006	84,104	+ 9.3	**Seattle, WA*** King and Snohomish counties	1,607,469	1,424,605	+12.7
Rochester, NY Livingston, Monroe, Ontario, Orleans, and Wayne counties	971,230	961,516	+ 1.0	**Sharon, PA** Mercer County	128,299	127,225	+ 0.8
Rockford, IL Boone and Winnebago counties	279,514	272,063	+ 2.7	**Sheboygan, WI** Sheboygan County	100,935	96,660	+ 4.4
Sacramento, CA El Dorado, Placer, Sacramento, and Yolo counties	1,099,814	847,626	+29.5	**Sherman–Denison, TX** Grayson County	89,796	83,225	+ 7.9
Saginaw–Bay City–Midland, MI Bay, Midland, and Saginaw counties	421,518	400,851	+ 5.1	**Shreveport, LA** Bossier and Caddo parishes	333,079	296,061	+12.5
St. Cloud, MN Benton, Sherburne, and Stearns counties	163,256	134,585	+21.4	**Sioux City, IA–NE** Woodbury County, IA; Dakota County, NE	117,457	116,189	+ 1.1
St. Joseph, MO Buchanan County	87,888	86,915	+ 1.1	**Sioux Falls, SD** Minnehaha County	109,435	95,209	+14.9
St. Louis, MO–IL* St. Louis city and Franklin, Jefferson, St. Charles, and St. Louis counties, MO; Monroe County, IL	1,808,621	1,846,067	− 2.0	**South Bend–Mishawaka, IN** St. Joseph County	241,617	244,827	− 1.3
Salem, OR Marion and Polk counties	249,895	186,658	+33.9	**Spokane, WA** Spokane County	341,835	287,487	+18.9
Salem–Gloucester, MA* Parts of Essex County	258,175	262,687	− 1.7	**Springfield, IL** Menard and Sangamon counties	187,789	171,020	+ 9.8
Salinas–Seaside–Monterey, CA Monterey County	290,444	247,450	+17.2	**Springfield, MA** Parts of Hampden and Hampshire counties	515,259	528,072	− 2.4
Salt Lake City–Ogden, UT Davis, Salt Lake, and Weber counties	910,222	683,913	+32.8	**Springfield, MO** Christian and Greene counties	207,704	168,053	+23.6
San Angelo, TX Tom Green County	84,784	71,047	+19.1	**Stamford, CT*** Parts of Fairfield County	198,854	206,340	− 3.6
San Antonio, TX Bexar, Comal, and Guadalupe counties	1,071,954	888,179	+20.5	**State College, PA** Centre County	112,760	99,267	+13.6
San Diego, CA San Diego County	1,861,846	1,357,854	+37.1	**Steubenville–Weirton, OH–WV** Jefferson County, OH; Brooke and Hancock counties, WV	163,099	166,385	− 1.6
San Francisco, CA* Marin, San Francisco, and San Mateo counties	1,488,871	1,481,687	+ 0.5	**Stockton, CA** San Joaquin County	347,342	291,073	+19.3
San Jose, CA* Santa Clara County	1,295,071	1,065,313	+21.4	**Syracuse, NY** Madison, Onondaga, and Oswego counties	642,971	636,596	+ 1.0
Santa Barbara–Santa Maria–Lompoc, CA Santa Barbara County	298,694	264,324	+12.9	**Tacoma, WA*** Pierce County	485,643	412,344	+17.8
Santa Cruz, CA* Santa Cruz County	188,141	123,790	+51.5	**Tallahassee, FL** Gadsden and Leon counties	190,220	142,231	+33.7
Santa Rosa–Petaluma, CA* Sonoma County	299,681	204,885	+46.3	**Tampa–St. Petersburg–Clearwater, FL** Hernando, Hillsborough, Pasco, and Pinellas counties	1,613,603	1,105,553	+44.2
Sarasota, FL Sarasota County	202,251	120,413	+68.5	**Terre Haute, IN** Clay and Vigo counties	137,247	138,461	− 0.9

Metro Areas and Component Counties	Population 1980	Population 1970	Population Change, 1970–1980	Metro Areas and Component Counties	Population 1980	Population 1970	Population Change, 1970–1980
Texarkana, TX– Texarkana, AR Bowie County, TX; Miller County, AR	113,067	102,294	+10.5%	Manassas Park cities, VA; Arlington, Fairfax, Loudoun, Prince William, and Stafford counties, VA			
Toledo, OH Fulton, Lucas, and Wood counties	616,864	606,344	+ 1.7	**Waterbury, CT** Parts of Litchfield and New Haven counties	204,968	196,134	+ 4.5%
Topeka, KS Shawnee County	154,916	155,322	− 0.3	**Waterloo–Cedar Falls, IA** Black Hawk and Bremer counties	162,781	155,653	+ 4.6
Trenton, NJ* Mercer County	307,863	304,116	+ 1.2	**Wausau, WI** Marathon County	111,270	97,457	+14.1
Tucson, AZ Pima County	531,443	351,667	+51.1	**West Palm Beach–Boca Raton–Delray Beach, FL** Palm Beach County	576,863	348,993	+65.3
Tulsa, OK Creek, Osage, Rogers, Tulsa, and Wagoner counties	657,173	525,852	+25.0	**Wheeling, WV–OH** Marshall and Ohio counties, WV; Belmont County, OH	185,566	181,954	+ 2.0
Tuscaloosa, AL Tuscaloosa County	137,541	116,029	+18.5	**Wichita, KS** Butler and Sedgwick counties	411,313	389,352	+ 5.6
Tyler, TX Smith County	128,366	97,096	+33.2	**Wichita Falls, TX** Wichita County	121,082	120,563	+ 0.4
Utica–Rome, NY Herkimer and Oneida counties	320,180	340,477	− 6.0	**Williamsport, PA** Lycoming County	118,416	113,296	+ 4.5
Vallejo–Fairfield–Napa, CA* Napa and Solano counties	334,402	251,129	+33.2	**Wilmington, DE–NJ–MD*** New Castle County, DE; Salem County, NJ; Cecil County, MD	523,221	499,493	+ 4.8
Vancouver, WA* Clark County	192,227	128,454	+49.6	**Wilmington, NC** New Hanover County	103,471	82,996	+24.7
Victoria, TX Victoria County	68,807	53,766	+28.0	**Worcester, MA** Parts of Worcester County	402,918	399,682	+ 0.8
Vineland–Millville–Bridgeton, NJ* Cumberland County	132,866	121,374	+ 9.5	**Yakima, WA** Yakima County	172,508	145,212	+18.8
Visalia–Tulare–Porterville, CA Tulare County	245,738	188,322	+30.5	**York, PA** Adams and York counties	381,255	329,540	+15.7
Waco, TX McLennan County	170,755	147,553	+15.7	**Youngstown–Warren, OH** Mahoning and Trumbull counties	531,350	537,124	− 1.1
Washington, DC–MD–VA District of Columbia; Calvert, Charles, Frederick, Montgomery, and Prince Georges counties, MD; Alexandria, Fairfax, Falls Church, Manassas, and	3,250,822	3,040,307	+ 6.9	**Yuba City, CA** Sutter and Yuba counties	101,979	86,671	+17.7

Source: U.S. Office of Management and Budget, 1983.

*An asterisk identifies a Primary Metropolitan Statistical Area.

The list above includes Metropolitan Statistical Areas and Primary Metropolitan Statistical Areas as defined by the Office of Management and Budget as of June 30, 1983.

Places Rated Almanac

Climate & Terrain:

Fundamental Considerations

Have you given much thought to what kind of climate you'd like to live in? Most Americans prefer (or say they prefer) mild, sunny climates. Yet when asked where the mild climates are, they are likely to answer that the "good, warm" weather is in the South. In fact, many of America's best climates are located north of the Mason-Dixon line, some in places that might surprise you.

Americans have an enormous variety of climates to choose from. There are northern maritime climates, extremely mild Mediterranean climates, southerly mountain climates, lowland desert climates, tropical "paradise" climates, desert highland climates, rugged northern continental climates, windward slope climates, leeward slope climates, humid subtropical climates—in fact, just about every kind of climate on the face of the earth. You name it, you can probably find it somewhere in the United States.

The weather events that make up a place's climate —rain, snow, heat, cold, drought, wind—can vary, sometimes dramatically, from year to year. But climate cannot be bought, built, remodeled, or relocated. A place's climate is there for keeps, and patterns of weather and climate have a profound effect on our lives. The economic impact of climate, for example, seems greater each year as heating and cooling costs continue to rise. Air-conditioning is almost always more expensive than home heating. Thus, people who

assumed they'd save on utility bills by moving to the Sun Belt might well be mistaken. A better bet for these people could be a milder climate in such middle-latitude states as Arkansas or North Carolina. The financial considerations for companies putting up large office buildings or warehouses, which are extremely expensive to heat and cool, are even more compelling. In fact, the site for a corporate building or relocation may hinge more on climate than on proximity to major transportation facilities.

Most of us have found that weather profoundly affects our moods and emotions. Long, snowy winters that confine people indoors can have adverse emotional effects; many people become irritable when the weather gets so hot they cannot sleep. We are cheered by brisk, sunny weather but sobered by cloudy, rainy days or very cold temperatures.

Relative humidity, barometric pressure, and altitude are just a few factors related to climate or terrain that can influence your physical well-being. There is no proven link between longevity and climate, although the three places on the globe whose populations have the highest percentage of centenarians—the Caucasus Mountains of the Soviet Union, the mountains of Bolivia, and northwestern India—are all in southerly latitudes at high elevations. But in America, where careful records have been kept for generations, a similar situation does not exist. In fact, most of the

1

highest average life spans occur in states with severe climates—Minnesota, North Dakota, and Iowa, for example.

It has been shown, however, that people with certain chronic diseases or disorders are far more comfortable in some climates than others. Asthmatics generally do best in warm, dry places that have a minimum of airborne allergens and no molds. People with rheumatism or arthritis find comfort in warm, moist, southerly climates where the weather is fairly constant and the atmospheric pressure undergoes the least daily change. Those who suffer from lung disorders such as tuberculosis or emphysema seem to do best in mountainous locales with lots of clear air and sunshine.

FACTORS THAT DETERMINE CLIMATE

Five factors have a major influence on the climate of a particular area: water, latitude, elevation, prevailing winds, and mountain ranges.

Water, especially in large bodies like oceans, has a moderating effect on temperatures. Water warms up slowly, holds much more heat than does land, and cools more slowly. Therefore, places near or surrounded by large bodies of water tend to be cooler in summer and warmer in winter than others far from water. Marine climates are thus by definition relatively mild. San Francisco, with water on three sides, has one of the most even climates on the continent.

On the other hand, places located in the middle of large land masses, away from the moderating effects of water, experience large swings of temperature. The tendency is for this kind of climate—called continental—to be more rigorous in the higher latitudes. The closer to the poles one moves, the more exaggerated are the seasonal shifts, because polar (and very northerly) locations undergo the greatest seasonal variation in the amount and intensity of sunlight. In Fairbanks, Alaska, for example, the average "day" (the period between the sun's rising and setting) in December is only four hours long. But in late June, each day receives more than 18 hours of sun, and the heat is intense. Places in the North and Far North, then, can experience not only bitterly cold winters but broiling summers as well!

Elevation, or height above sea level, has the same general effect as a higher latitude. Each 1,000 feet of elevation lowers the average temperature by 3.3 degrees Fahrenheit. Places that combine high altitudes with southerly latitudes seem to get the best of both North and South, enjoying the mild, short winters of

Climatic Regions of the United States

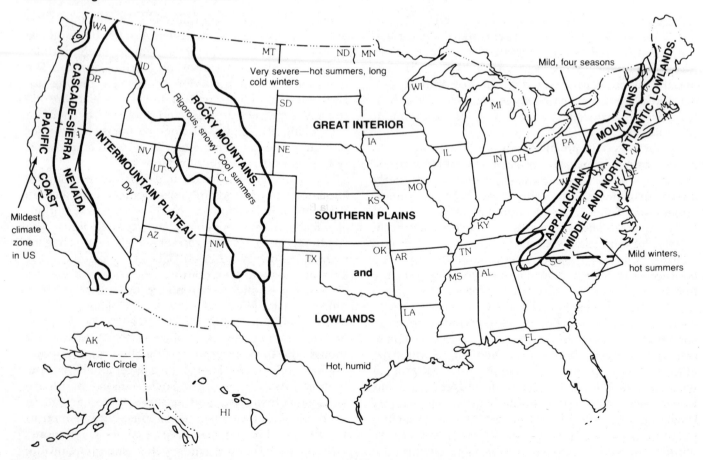

the South and the cooler nights and crisp falls of the North. Locations in the southern Appalachian Mountains and in the mountains of the Southwest have long been known for their mild, four-season climates.

To understand how prevailing winds influence climate, we have only to look at a pair of metro areas: Portland, Oregon, and Portland, Maine. Each is located at a rather northerly latitude. Both are also situated on ocean coasts. Thus one would naturally suppose that the two Portlands would have roughly the same type of climate. Why, then, is Portland, Oregon, so much milder? The answer lies in the prevailing winds that sweep across our continent. America's prevailing winds blow from west to east. Places along the West Coast receive the full impact of winds that have moved thousands of miles over water; cities even hundreds of miles inland still feel some of the beneficial effects of the Pacific winds. But inland cities in the East feel few consequences of the Atlantic save on those rare occasions when the prevailing wind direction *doesn't* prevail. And, sad to say, this reversal of wind direction often means a storm.

Mountain ranges help determine climate and weather because they act as giant barriers that deflect and channel winds and weather. The weather—and also climate—on one side of a mountain range is often radically different from that on the other. Because of this, mountain ranges are natural dividing points between climate zones.

AMERICA'S MAJOR CLIMATIC REGIONS

Mountain ranges delineate the seven major climatic regions of the continental United States. The Pacific Coast is the mildest of these regions, and the northern portion of the Great Interior is the most rigorous. The Intermountain Plateau (which is also called the Great Basin), lying between the Sierra Nevada to the west and the Rocky Mountains to the east, is noted primarily for its dryness. Some of the best climates for variety and mildness are found in the southern portion of this area. The southern half of the Appalachian Mountains region also offers climates that are both mild and variable.

Most Americans live in the large climatic zone that includes the Great Interior, Southern Plains, and Lowlands regions. This zone, ironically, also happens to be the least desirable as far as mildness and human comfort are concerned. Those who live in its northern part are plagued by severe winters and hot, humid summers with very short springs and autumns. In the southern portion, winters are mild while springs and autumns are longer, but the steam-bath summers are very uncomfortable and debilitating. The climate of the East Coast, called the Middle and North Atlantic Lowlands, is similar to that of the Great Interior, but milder and somewhat damper. Right on the coast, winters are milder and summers are noticeably cooler.

The 8 Coldest Metro Areas

	Zero-Degree Days per Year	Freezing Days per Year
Fargo–Moorhead, ND–MN	54	181
Duluth, MN–WI	51	187
Bismarck, ND	51	186
Anchorage, AK	41	192
Rochester, MN	35	165
Minneapolis–St. Paul, MN–WI	34	158
Sioux Falls, SD	33	171
Waterloo–Cedar Falls, IA	31	159

Listed above are those metro areas described in the Place Profiles that combine more than 30 zero-degree days per year with more than 150 freezing days.

The 12 Hottest Metro Areas

	90-Degree Days per Year	July Noon Relative Humidity
San Antonio, TX	111	55%
Fort Myers, FL	106	65
Orlando, FL	104	65
Brownsville–Harlingen, TX	102	55
Austin, TX	101	55
Corpus Christi, TX	96	65
Tallahassee, FL	87	65
Shreveport, LA	87	55
Jacksonville, FL	82	65
Mobile, AL	81	65
Tampa–St. Petersburg–Clearwater, FL	81	65
Houston, TX	81	60

Listed above are those metro areas described in the Place Profiles that combine 80 or more 90-degree days with a July noon relative humidity of 55 percent or higher. Three metro areas have more than 130 ninety-degree days per year—Phoenix, AZ (164); Tucson, AZ (139); and Las Vegas, NV (131)—but all of them have a July relative humidity of less than 30 percent.

The 10 Sunniest Metro Areas ... and the 11 Drizzliest

	Clear Days per Year		Precipitation Days per Year
Chico, CA	219	Saginaw–Bay City–Midland, MI	181
Las Vegas, NV	216	Buffalo, NY	168
Phoenix, AZ	214	Syracuse, NY	168
Bakersfield, CA	202	Binghamton, NY	163
Fresno, CA	200	Olympia, WA	163
Tucson, AZ	198	Seattle, WA	160
El Paso, TX	194	Cleveland, OH	156
Sacramento, CA	193	Akron, OH	153
Santa Barbara–Santa Maria–Lompoc, CA	177	Burlington, VT	153
Santa Rosa–Petaluma, CA	176	Pittsburgh, PA	152
		Portland, OR	152

Listed above are those metro areas described in the Place Profiles that have more than 175 clear days per year or more than 150 precipitation days per year. A precipitation day is one on which at least .01 inch of precipitation falls.

There are some excellent climates to be found in this region, especially in coastal locations.

The high-altitude regions that include the Rocky Mountains, the Cascades and Sierra Nevada, and the northern half of the Appalachian Mountains are resort areas because they all have cool, crisp, sunny summers with cold nights, and winters that provide plenty of snow for outdoor sports. These places are popular with people who enjoy a stimulating yet not too mild climate.

The Alaskan climate varies from bitterly cold in the northern tundra area—about one fifth of the state lies north of the Arctic Circle—to relatively mild temperatures in the interior and southern regions. The southern area experiences abundant rainfall, the Aleutian Islands chain being one of the stormiest regions in the world.

Hawaii is the only state situated in the tropical zone. The islands undergo relatively small temperature changes, with summer temperatures averaging only 4 degrees to 8 degrees higher than those in winter. Moisture-bearing trade winds from over the Pacific have a moderating effect on the heat associated with a tropical climate.

JUDGING CLIMATE MILDNESS

Temperature affects human comfort and our daily range of activities more than any other climate-related variable. Bioclimatologists—scientists who study the connection between weather and health—generally agree that an average temperature of 65 degrees Fahrenheit with 65 percent humidity is ideal for work, play, and general well-being. *Places Rated* uses 65 degrees Fahrenheit as a standard for mildness in the discussions that follow.

Because most people tend to favor mild, sunny climates, *Places Rated* compares the 329 metro areas on the basis of climate mildness, using a combination of temperature and humidity factors. "Mild," as we use the term, does not necessarily mean warm but simply refers to the absence of great variations or extremes of temperature. A mild climate is characterized by cool summers and warm winters, with long falls and springs. *Places Rated* defines the mildest climates as those whose mean temperatures remain closest to 65 degrees Fahrenheit for the greatest percentage of time. Any deviations from this mean are labeled negative indicators, and are scored as such. Each place's final score indicates its climate mildness.

Nearly all climate and weather data presented in this chapter are from the National Oceanic and Atmospheric Administration (NOAA), the National Climatic Center, Asheville, North Carolina, and its two-volume publication *Local Climatological Data*. The National Climatic Center houses the world's largest climate data bank, with the equivalent of 25 miles of shelf space devoted solely to worldwide climate and weather data and research.

Some of the figures we present are referred to by the NOAA as 30-year normals—mean averages collected over three decades. Each ten years, the data for the new decade are added into the normal, and the data for the earliest ten years are dropped. Data are collect-

ed and averaged over this rather long period to flatten out irregularities and weather extremes. Atypical events such as blizzards and heat waves have little overall effect on a 30-year normal. Other figures are the means of annual records kept for periods ranging from a few years to more than 100 years. Mean temperatures are the average of the highest and lowest readings during a given period. For example, to determine the mean temperature for a particular month, the mean maximum temperature (the average of the highest daily readings during the month) and the mean minimum temperature (the average of the lowest) are averaged.

Each metro area is given a base number of 1,000 points, from which points are subtracted according to the following indicators, based on yearly averages:

1. *Very hot and very cold months.* Ten points are subtracted for each month in which the mean temperature is above 70 degrees or below 32. An additional 10 points are subtracted, for a total of 20 points, if the mean temperature is above 80 degrees or below 20.
2. *Seasonal temperature variation.* The difference in degrees Fahrenheit between the summer mean maximum temperature and the winter mean minimum is subtracted from the base score.
3. *Heating- and cooling-degree days.* The total number of these days per year is divided by 50, and the result is subtracted from the score. The base temperature for arriving at heating- and cooling-degree days is 65 degrees, the standard established by the American gas industry. If, for example, the average temperature on a summer day is 66 degrees, 1 degree of cooling is necessary, which counts as 1 cooling-degree day. Similarly, if the average temperature on a particular winter day is 55 degrees, 10 degrees of heating are needed, yielding 10 heating-degree days.
4. *Freezing days.* One point is subtracted for each day on which the average temperature is 32 degrees or below.
5. *Zero-degree days.* Five additional points are subtracted for each day the temperature drops to zero or below.
6. *Ninety-degree days.* Since relative humidity has a profound effect on felt heat and daily temperature range, points are subtracted in accordance with each location's mean relative humidity at noon in July, when high temperatures are most likely to occur (see the map on page 59). For each day with a high of at least 90 degrees, 4 points are subtracted if the metro area's July relative humidity is more than 60 percent, 3 points if relative humidity is 51 percent to 60 percent, 2 points if relative

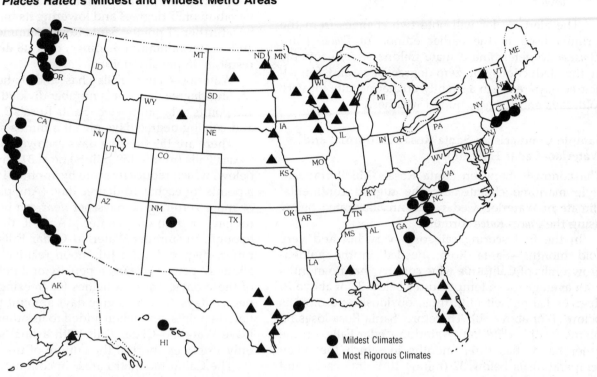

Places Rated's Mildest and Wildest Metro Areas

● Mildest Climates
▲ Most Rigorous Climates

Mild and Wild

With such a large variety of climates in the United States, a mix of places around the country qualify for the descriptions "mild" and "wild."

The area of greatest mildness is the Pacific Coast, as the map "*Places Rated*'s Mildest and Wildest Metro Areas" illustrates. This region contains 23 of the 35 top-ranked climates. The California metro areas owe their high ratings in part to their southerly locations, but all 23 (as well as the Honolulu metro area) are indebted to the moderating influence of the Pacific, which reduces their seasonal shifts to a minimum and practically rules out any zero-degree or 90-degree days.

The second mildest region in America is located in the southern Appalachian Mountains, in sections of Georgia, North and South Carolina, Tennessee, and Virginia. Here, southerly latitudes provide mild winters and long springs and falls, while high elevations offer relief from the hot, muggy summers that plague most other southern locations.

Other mild areas are to be found along the Atlantic coast in New York and Connecticut, and in the southern tip of the Rocky Mountains, near Albuquerque. This mountain region resembles the southern Appalachians, except that it is noticeably drier.

The climates of America's most rigorous metro areas are characterized by great swings in temperature from season to season and from day to day. They have either a winter that is cold and long, a summer that is long, hot, and humid, or both. Most of these rigorous places are located inside the wide band stretching up the center of the continent that is known as the Great Interior.

Besides the northern and southern extremes of the Great Interior, rigorous climates are found in Alaska, northern New England, the northern Rockies, and the Florida peninsula. A characteristic of all these places is an excessive number of 90-degree days and/or zero-degree days.

In a few areas, good and bad weather bump up against each other. Metro areas located in northern New England experience long, cold, snowy winters and a lot of cloudiness, and thus we find Burlington, Vermont, and Manchester, New Hampshire, near the bottom of the *Places Rated* climate list. However, not far from up-country New Hampshire are the coastal waters of Cape Ann, Massachusetts, and the mild climate of Salem–Gloucester.

Similarly, although the neighboring Texas metro areas of Victoria and McAllen–Edinburg–Mission have rigorous climates because of the excessive heat and humidity during the summer, nearby Galveston–Texas City, with its coastal location and sea breezes, ranks as one of America's mildest metro areas.

humidity is 41 percent to 50 percent, and 1 point if relative humidity is 40 percent or lower.

(The alert reader will note two changes from the formula used in the earlier edition of *Places Rated Almanac* to determine climate mildness. Adjustments in the deductions for zero-degree days and for 90-degree days result in a slightly greater penalty for very cold days and for hot, humid weather.)

Sample Comparison: Santa Rosa, California, and Waterloo–Cedar Falls, Iowa

The contrasts between Santa Rosa's Mediterranean-style maritime climate and the rugged continental climate of Waterloo–Cedar Falls are illustrated below using the *Places Rated* formula.

In the first scoring category—very hot and very cold months—Santa Rosa, nestled in the golden-brown hills of California wine country, has no months with average mean temperatures below 32 or above 70 degrees Fahrenheit (and thus, obviously, no months below 20 or above 80). Therefore, Santa Rosa loses no points for this criterion. Waterloo–Cedar Falls, on the other hand, has three months in which the mean temperature is below 32 (minus 10 points each) and one month with a mean temperature below 20 (minus 20 points). Furthermore, this metro area on Iowa's northern plains has warm summers, with two months whose average mean temperatures top 70 degrees (minus 20 points). Waterloo–Cedar Falls is penalized a total of 70 points in this category.

The average maximum summer temperature in Waterloo–Cedar Falls is 84, and its minimum winter temperature is 7, amounting to a seasonal temperature variation of 77 degrees and lowering its mildness score by a further 77 points. Santa Rosa's summer maximum and winter minimum readings, only 48 degrees apart, result in 48 penalty points.

Waterloo–Cedar Falls has 8,090 heating- and cooling-degree days. This number divided by 50 yields 162 points to be subtracted. Santa Rosa's 3,900 heating- and cooling-degree days give it a minus score of 78.

There are 159 freezing days each year in Waterloo–Cedar Falls (minus 159 points), and 31 days at zero or below, which reduce its score by another 155 points, or 5 points for each zero-degree day. (Any place with ten or more zero-degree days per year can be considered to have a rigorous winter.) And if that isn't bad enough, in summer Waterloo–Cedar Falls also has 15 ninety-degree days; a July noon relative humidity of about 47 percent means a penalty of 2 points for each of these days. These penalties for freezing days, zero-degree days, and 90-degree days amount to a substantial 344 points, and when added to its other deductions leave Waterloo–Cedar Falls with a final score of 347, only 18 places short of the bottom of the ranking list.

The California metro area, in contrast, has only 43 freezing days (for minus 43 points) and no zero-degree days. However, it does have 33 ninety-degree days, losing 3 points for each one due to a summer humidity of 55 percent. When all its deductions are totaled, Santa Rosa finishes with a mildness score of 732, or 19th out of the 329 metro areas.

Places Rated: Metro Areas Ranked for Climate Mildness

Six criteria are used to determine a score for climate mildness: (1) very hot and very cold months, (2) seasonal temperature variation, (3) heating- and cooling-degree days, (4) freezing days, (5) zero-degree days, and (6) ninety-degree days.

Because the NOAA publication *Local Climatological Data* does not provide specific data for all metro areas, the scores for some places are calculated from data for the nearest substation (this information appears in the *NOAA Series 20*). Scores arrived at in this way are enclosed in parentheses. Metro areas that receive tie scores are given the same rank and are listed in alphabetical order.

Those metro areas described in the Place Profiles later on in this chapter are shown in boldface type in the lists below.

Metro Areas from Best to Worst

Places Rated Rank	Places Rated Score	Places Rated Rank	Places Rated Score	Places Rated Rank	Places Rated Score
1. Oakland, CA	(910)	5. **Los Angeles–Long Beach, CA**	885	9. Salinas–Seaside–Monterey, CA	(843)
1. **San Francisco, CA**	910			9. Santa Cruz, CA	(843)
3. **San Diego, CA**	903	7. **Santa Barbara–Santa Maria–Lompoc, CA**	855		
4. Oxnard–Ventura, CA	(890)			11. Vallejo–Fairfield–Napa, CA	(821)
5. Anaheim–Santa Ana, CA	885	8. San Jose, CA	(850)	12. Bremerton, WA	(808)

Places Rated Rank	Places Rated Score
12. **Seattle, WA**	808
12. Tacoma, WA	(808)
15. Bellingham, WA	(772)
16. **Portland, OR**	768
16. Vancouver, WA	(768)
18. **Eugene–Springfield, OR**	741
19. **Santa Rosa–Petaluma, CA**	(732)
20. **Galveston–Texas City, TX**	(727)
21. **Olympia, WA**	726
22. **Honolulu, HI**	717
23. Salem, OR	716
24. **Atlanta, GA**	696
25. **Asheville, NC**	694
26. **Knoxville, TN**	670
27. Redding, CA	(664)
27. Richland–Kennewick–Pasco, WA	(664)
29. **Johnson City–Kingsport–Bristol, TN–VA**	663
30. **Albuquerque, NM**	659
31. Nassau–Suffolk, NY	(656)
32. **Greenville–Spartanburg, SC**	655
33. **Roanoke, VA**	652
34. Bridgeport–Milford, CT	648
34. Norwalk, CT	(648)
34. Stamford, CT	(648)
37. **Raleigh–Durham, NC**	647
38. **Charlotte–Gastonia–Rock Hill, NC–SC**	644
38. Salem–Gloucester, MA	(644)
40. Fall River, MA–RI	(643)
40. **New Bedford, MA**	(643)
42. Lynchburg, VA	642
43. Modesto, CA	(639)
44. **New York, NY**	638
45. Burlington, NC	(637)
46. Huntington–Ashland, WV–KY–OH	636
46. Trenton, NJ	(636)
48. **Lexington–Fayette, KY**	635
49. **Miami–Hialeah, FL**	634
50. **Norfolk–Virginia Beach–Newport News, VA**	632
51. **Washington, DC–MD–VA**	631
52. **Philadelphia, PA–NJ**	630
53. **Charleston, WV**	627
54. Greensboro–Winston-Salem–High Point, NC	626
55. Stockton, CA	625
56. **Boston, MA**	623
56. Hickory, NC	(623)
58. Charlottesville, VA	(618)
59. Parkersburg–Marietta, WV–OH	617
60. **Louisville, KY–IN**	616
61. **Atlantic City, NJ**	615
61. Monmouth–Ocean, NJ	(615)
61. Riverside–San Bernardino, CA	(615)
61. Vineland–Millville–Bridgeton, NJ	(615)
65. Reading, PA	(614)
66. **Birmingham, AL**	612
67. **Medford, OR**	611
68. **Amarillo, TX**	609

Places Rated Rank	Places Rated Score
69. Yuba City, CA	(608)
70. Erie, PA	605
71. **Lubbock, TX**	604
72. **Chico, CA**	(603)
72. **Midland, TX**	603
72. Odessa, TX	(603)
75. Fort Pierce, FL	(602)
76. Athens, GA	601
76. Jersey City, NJ	(601)
76. Newark, NJ	601
79. **Huntsville, AL**	600
79. **Nashville, TN**	600
81. Wilmington, DE–NJ–MD	597
82. Middletown, CT	(593)
83. **Boise City, ID**	592
83. **El Paso, TX**	592
85. Anderson, SC	(591)
85. **Cumberland, MD–WV**	(591)
87. **Tucson, AZ**	589
88. Beaver County, PA	(586)
88. Pawtucket–Woonsocket–Attleboro, RI–MA	(586)
88. **Pittsburgh, PA**	586
88. Providence, RI	586
92. **Richmond–Petersburg, VA**	585
93. **Biloxi–Gulfport, MS**	(584)
93. **Cincinnati, OH–KY–IN**	584
93. Pascagoula, MS	(584)
96. New Haven–Meriden, CT	(583)
96. New London–Norwich, CT–RI	(583)
98. Melbourne–Titusville–Palm Bay, FL	(582)
99. Joplin, MO	(580)
99. Muskegon, MI	580
101. **Cleveland, OH**	579
101. Lorain–Elyria, OH	(579)
103. **Chattanooga, TN–GA**	576
103. **Sacramento, CA**	576
105. **Akron, OH**	575
105. Brockton, MA	(575)
105. Canton, OH	(575)
105. Scranton–Wilkes-Barre, PA	575
105. **State College, PA**	(575)
110. **Spokane, WA**	574
111. Fort Lauderdale–Hollywood–Pompano Beach, FL	(572)
112. **Buffalo, NY**	571
113. Sharon, PA	(570)
113. Youngstown–Warren, OH	570
115. **Charleston, SC**	569
115. Danbury, CT	(569)
115. Waterbury, CT	(569)
118. Hagerstown, MD	(568)
119. **Baltimore, MD**	567
120. Benton Harbor, MI	(566)
121. Jacksonville, NC	(564)
121. **Wilmington, NC**	564
123. Worcester, MA	562
124. Altoona, PA	(561)
124. Daytona Beach, FL	561
124. Fayetteville, NC	(561)
127. Anniston, AL	(560)

Places Rated Rank	Places Rated Score
127. **Bakersfield, CA**	560
129. **Allentown–Bethlehem, PA–NJ**	559
129. Bergen–Passaic, NJ	(559)
129. **Fresno, CA**	559
129. Lancaster, PA	559
129. Middlesex–Somerset–Hunterdon, NJ	(559)
134. Bloomington, IN	(558)
134. **Columbus, OH**	558
134. Mansfield, OH	558
134. Williamsport, PA	558
138. **Indianapolis, IN**	557
138. Terre Haute, IN	(557)
140. **Harrisburg–Lebanon–Carlisle, PA**	(556)
140. **Las Vegas, NV**	556
142. Niagara Falls, NY	(554)
142. **Oklahoma City, OK**	554
144. Florence, SC	(552)
144. Las Cruces, NM	(552)
146. **Binghamton, NY**	550
146. **Evansville, IN–KY**	550
148. Fayetteville–Springdale, AR	(549)
148. **Kansas City, KS**	549
148. Kansas City, MO	549
151. Lawrence–Haverhill, MA–NH	(548)
151. **Syracuse, NY**	548
151. Utica–Rome, NY	(548)
154. Johnstown, PA	(547)
155. Ann Arbor, MI	(546)
155. Florence, AL	(546)
157. Danville, VA	(545)
157. South Bend–Mishawaka, IN	(545)
159. Clarksville–Hopkinsville, TN–KY	(544)
159. **Dallas, TX**	544
159. Dayton–Springfield, OH	544
159. **Springfield, MO**	544
163. Visalia–Tulare–Porterville, CA	(543)
164. Hamilton–Middletown, OH	(542)
164. **Savannah, GA**	542
164. Steubenville–Weirton, OH–WV	(542)
164. Wheeling, WV–OH	(542)
168. **Columbia, MO**	(541)
168. **Salt Lake City–Ogden, UT**	541
170. Flint, MI	540
170. York, PA	(540)
172. Nashua, NH	(538)
173. Alton–Granite City, IL	(537)
173. East St. Louis–Belleville, IL	537
173. **St. Louis, MO–IL**	537
176. **Detroit, MI**	536
176. Fort Walton Beach, FL	(536)
176. Panama City, FL	536
176. Pensacola, FL	536
176. **Phoenix, AZ**	536
176. Rochester, NY	536
182. **Reno, NV**	535
182. **Yakima, WA**	535
184. **Augusta, GA–SC**	534
185. Anderson, IN	(530)

Places Rated Rank	Places Rated Score
185. Muncie, IN	(530)
185. **Tulsa, OK**	530
188. Fort Worth–Arlington, TX	(528)
189. Battle Creek, MI	(527)
189. Kalamazoo, MI	(527)
191. **Colorado Springs, CO**	526
191. **Columbia, SC**	526
191. Gadsden, AL	(526)
191. Lowell, MA–NH	526
195. Champaign–Urbana–Rantoul, IL	(525)
196. Owensboro, KY	(524)
196. Sherman–Denison, TX	(524)
196. **Springfield, IL**	524
199. Lima, OH	(522)
200. **Abilene, TX**	521
200. **Denver, CO**	521
200. Elkhart–Goshen, IN	(521)
203. **Alexandria, LA**	520
204. Jackson, MI	(518)
204. **Toledo, OH**	518
206. **Columbus, GA–AL**	(517)
207. Bristol, CT	(516)
207. **Hartford, CT**	516
207. New Britain, CT	(516)
210. **Saginaw–Bay City–Midland, MI**	(515)
211. **Chicago, IL**	514
211. Lake County, IL	514
211. **Memphis, TN–AR–MS**	514
214. **Grand Rapids, MI**	513
214. Lawrence, KS	(513)
216. Kokomo, IN	(512)
217. **Fort Wayne, IN**	509
217. Orange County, NY	(509)
217. West Palm Beach–Boca Raton–Delray Beach, FL	509
220. Shreveport, LA	508
221. Fitchburg–Leominster, MA	(507)
222. Topeka, KS	501
223. Longview–Marshall, TX	(500)
223. Provo–Orem, UT	(500)
223. Tyler, TX	(500)
226. **New Orleans, LA**	498
227. **Little Rock–North Little Rock, AR**	497
227. Pueblo, CO	497
229. Kenosha, WI	(496)
229. Racine, WI	(496)
231. Lafayette, IN	(494)
231. **Wichita, KS**	494
233. **Peoria, IL**	491
234. Fort Collins–Loveland, CO	(490)
234. Greeley, CO	(490)
234. Lewiston–Auburn, ME	(490)
237. Poughkeepsie, NY	(488)
237. **San Angelo, TX**	488
239. Bloomington–Normal, IL	(487)
240. Gary–Hammond, IN	(483)
240. Kankakee, IL	(483)
240. **Montgomery, AL**	483
240. **Portland, ME**	483
244. **Fort Smith, AR–OK**	482
244. Pittsfield, MA	(482)
246. Decatur, IL	(480)
246. Lansing–East Lansing, MI	480
248. Joliet, IL	(479)
248. Lawton, OK	(479)
250. **Albany–Schenectady–Troy, NY**	476
250. Glens Falls, NY	(476)
252. St. Joseph, MO	(475)
253. Aurora–Elgin, IL	(474)
254. Tuscaloosa, AL	(470)
255. Lake Charles, LA	469
255. Portsmouth–Dover–Rochester, NH–ME	(469)
257. Albany, GA	(468)
258. Elmira, NY	(467)
258. Texarkana, TX–Texarkana, AR	(467)
260. Janesville–Beloit, WI	(466)
260. **Rockford, IL**	466
262. Pine Bluff, AR	(463)
263. Enid, OK	(461)
264. **Milwaukee, WI**	460
265. Boulder–Longmont, CO	(459)
266. **Jacksonville, FL**	457
266. Orlando, FL	457
268. Wichita Falls, TX	456
269. Monroe, LA	(455)
270. Springfield, MA	(453)
271. **Billings, MT**	452
272. **Bangor, ME**	(451)
273. Macon–Warner Robins, GA	(447)
274. **Des Moines, IA**	444
275. **Mobile, AL**	442
275. Sheboygan, WI	(442)
277. Bradenton, FL	(440)
277. **Brownsville–Harlingen, TX**	440
277. **Davenport–Rock Island–Moline, IA–IL**	440
277. **Omaha, NE–IA**	440
277. **Tampa–St. Petersburg–Clearwater, FL**	440
282. **Austin, TX**	435
283. Cedar Rapids, IA	(434)
283. Iowa City, IA	(434)
285. Lafayette, LA	(429)
286. Baton Rouge, LA	427
286. Houma–Thibodaux, LA	(427)
288. **Houston, TX**	424
288. Laredo, TX	(424)
290. Beaumont–Port Arthur, TX	423
290. Brazoria, TX	(423)
292. Dubuque, IA	419
293. **Jackson, MS**	412
293. Waco, TX	412
295. **Great Falls, MT**	410
296. **Manchester, NH**	(404)
296. **Tallahassee, FL**	404
298. Gainesville, FL	(402)
299. **Casper, WY**	401
300. **Lincoln, NE**	398
300. **San Antonio, TX**	398
302. Appleton–Oshkosh–Neenah, WI	(396)
303. Sarasota, FL	(391)
304. **Sioux City, IA–NE**	385
305. Bryan–College Station, TX	(383)
305. **Burlington, VT**	383
307. **Madison, WI**	378
308. **Green Bay, WI**	367
309. Killeen–Temple, TX	(365)
310. **Corpus Christi, TX**	362
311. **La Crosse, WI**	352
312. **Waterloo–Cedar Falls, IA**	(347)
313. **Fort Myers, FL**	(342)
314. Dothan, AL	(336)
314. Victoria, TX	336
316. Ocala, FL	(333)
317. **Rochester, MN**	308
317. Wausau, WI	(308)
319. Lakeland–Winter Haven, FL	(307)
320. **Minneapolis–St. Paul, MN–WI**	293
321. **Sioux Falls, SD**	276
322. Eau Claire, WI	257
323. McAllen–Edinburg–Mission, TX	(238)
324. **Anchorage, AK**	195
324. St. Cloud, MN	(195)
326. **Duluth, MN–WI**	193
327. **Bismarck, ND**	149
328. **Fargo–Moorhead, ND–MN**	148
329. Grand Forks, ND	(105)

Place Profiles: Climate and Terrain of 140 Selected Weather Stations

The pages that follow are brief profiles of 140 weather stations, which were carefully selected to present a sampling of reports from weather stations all over the country. The figures given in each profile are taken from extensive government data tables. The narrative summaries, describing climate and terrain, are condensations of those that appear in the NOAA publication *Local Climatological Data*.

These summaries provide brief descriptions of each location and point out important or distinctive features of the climate and the local terrain. When terrain is described in the profiles, it is usually in connection with the effect—if any—it has on the climate in the immediate area. But few people would deny that terrain is an important element in its own right; to many it's as important as climate. Some people prefer mountains or seacoast, others rolling plains or forest. Rather than attempt to judge, rate, or score terrain, *Places Rated* simply describes it briefly and lets you decide.

The table of average temperatures on the right-hand side of each profile is a detailed and extremely useful set of data, from which you can get a clear idea of the temperature ranges, averages, and extremes of each place. For example, if you want to know how hot it gets in Albuquerque in July, simply look at the table in Albuquerque's profile. There you'll see that in July the daily high temperatures (which usually occur in midafternoon) average 92.2 degrees Fahrenheit. That sounds hot, and it is. But note that the average low, or minimum, temperature for the same month is only 65.2 degrees. The minimum temperature generally occurs in the early hours of the morning. Therefore,

even a quick glance at these temperatures tells us that Albuquerque in the summer has hot days and cool nights, with a mean temperature of less than 80 degrees (78.7). This is in keeping with Albuquerque's dry, desert location and altitude of about 5,000 feet.

Rounding out the weather picture of each locale are data such as wind speed, amount of snow and rain, number of heating- and cooling-degree days, clear and cloudy days, storms, very hot and cold days, and precipitation days (days on which there is at least .01 inch of precipitation). To derive the greatest benefit from these assorted indicators, compare two or more metro areas. Which has more snow? More rain? More 90-degree days? Comparing two places you're interested in may lead to your deciding which to visit first.

A unique visual device in each profile is the circular graph showing the length of each season. These graphs are prepared from a formula developed by *Places Rated* and reflect the theory that seasonal change should be defined and measured by weather conditions, human activities, and growth or dormancy of plant life rather than by the calendar. In *Places Rated Almanac*, the seasons are defined as follows: Summer begins when the mean monthly temperature rises above 60 degrees Fahrenheit; summer ends when it falls below 60. Winter begins when the average daily low falls below 32 degrees and ends when it rises above that mark. The remaining portions of the year constitute fall and spring. (In the seasonal graphs, winter is shown by the black segments, spring and fall appear as gray, and summer is white.)

A star preceding a metro area's name highlights it as one of the top 25 places for climate mildness.

Abilene, TX

Terrain: Rolling plains, treeless except for mesquite, broken by low hills to the south and west. Land rises gently to the south and east. Primarily cattle-grazing terrain, with some dry-land cotton and feed.

Climate: Lies roughly midway between the humid climate of East Texas and the semiarid climate to the west and north. Most rain occurs in thunderstorms during April, May, June, September, and October. Severe storms or tornadoes are rare. Summer brings hot days and cool nights, with temperatures dropping to the 60s or 70s most nights. High summer temperatures are usually associated with clear skies, southwesterly winds, and dry air. Low relative humidity, however, makes the climate comfortable. The region receives almost 70% of possible sunshine over the year. Rapid temperature changes occur in winter, as polar air replaces warm, moist tropical air. Temperatures may fall 30 degrees in one hour. Strongest winds come from the north and often bring cold and severe weather.

Pluses: Warm, sunny, and dry.

Minuses: Hot summer days; can be dusty.

Places Rated Score: 521

Places Rated Rank: 200

Elevation: 1,790 feet

Relative Humidity: 59%
Wind Speed: 12.2 mph

Seasonal Change

Annual Rainfall 24 in

Annual Snowfall 5 in

Clear 148 days   Partly Cloudy 98 days   Cloudy 119 days

Precipitation Days: 65   Storm Days: 42

Average Temperatures			
	Daily High	Daily Low	Monthly Mean
January	55.7	31.7	43.7
February	59.9	35.9	47.9
March	67.3	41.7	54.5
April	77.7	52.7	65.2
May	83.9	60.8	72.4
June	91.6	69.0	80.3
July	95.3	72.4	83.9
August	95.3	71.9	83.6
September	87.5	64.6	76.1
October	78.0	54.2	66.1
November	66.2	42.0	54.1
December	58.2	34.5	46.4

Zero-Degree Days: 0
Freezing Days: 56
90-Degree Days: 89
Heating- and Cooling-Degree Days: 5,076

Akron, OH

Terrain: Rolling, with highest elevations almost 1,300 feet above sea level. Many small lakes provide water for local industry as well as recreation for the densely populated region. The area is mainly industrial; the number of agricultural operations has diminished rapidly in recent years.

Climate: Lake Erie has a considerable effect on area weather, tempering cold air masses during the winter and contributing to brief but heavy snow squalls until the lake freezes over. Snowfall is much heavier north of the weather station near the lake, in the area commonly referred to as the Snow Belt. Spring comes late here. Summers are moderately warm, though humid. September, October, and November are pleasant, but there is considerable morning fog. Average date of last freeze: April 30. First freeze: October 22.

Pluses: Pleasant falls.

Minuses: Cold, wet winters with heavy snowfalls; damp and cloudy.

Places Rated Score: 575

Places Rated Rank: 105

Elevation: 1,027 feet

Relative Humidity: 71%
Wind Speed: 9.9 mph

Seasonal Change

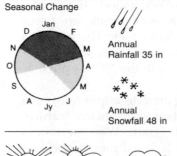

Annual Rainfall 35 in

Annual Snowfall 48 in

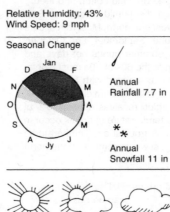

Clear 70 days
Partly Cloudy 101 days
Cloudy 194 days

Precipitation Days: 153   Storm Days: 40

Average Temperatures			
	Daily High	Daily Low	Monthly Mean
January	33.9	18.6	26.3
February	36.0	19.4	27.7
March	45.4	26.9	36.2
April	59.3	37.7	48.5
May	69.8	47.5	58.7
June	79.4	57.1	68.3
July	82.6	60.8	71.7
August	81.3	59.3	70.3
September	74.7	52.7	63.7
October	63.7	42.8	53.3
November	48.6	32.7	40.7
December	36.5	22.2	29.4

Zero-Degree Days: 5
Freezing Days: 128
90-Degree Days: 7
Heating- and Cooling-Degree Days: 6,858

Albany–Schenectady–Troy, NY

Terrain: On the west bank of the Hudson River 150 miles north of New York City and 8 miles south of the confluence of the Hudson and Mohawk rivers. The point at which the city meets the river is only a few feet above sea level. Eleven miles west, the Helderberg escarpment rises to between 1,400 and 1,800 feet. To the east is a rugged valley floor rising to hills 1,600 to 2,000 feet high. The valley floor on which the city is located is gently rolling.

Climate: Harsh continental but subject to some moderating influences from the Atlantic, to the south. Winters are cold and occasionally severe. Maximum temperatures during cold months often do not rise above 32° F. In the warmer months, temperatures rise quickly during the day to moderate levels, then fall rapidly at night to moderate to cool. Occasional hot spells of a week or so occur during the summer. The growing season is about 160 days, long for a city in this latitude. Average date of last freeze: April 27. First freeze: October 13.

Pluses: Cool summer nights.

Minuses: Cold, snowy winters.

Places Rated Score: 476

Places Rated Rank: 250

Elevation: 292 feet

Relative Humidity: 71%
Wind Speed: 8.9 mph

Seasonal Change

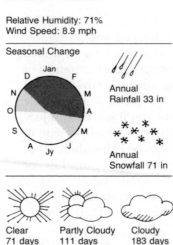

Annual Rainfall 33 in

Annual Snowfall 71 in

Clear 71 days
Partly Cloudy 111 days
Cloudy 183 days

Precipitation Days: 135   Storm Days: 28

Average Temperatures			
	Daily High	Daily Low	Monthly Mean
January	30.4	12.5	21.5
February	32.7	14.3	23.5
March	42.6	24.2	33.4
April	58.0	35.7	46.9
May	69.7	45.7	57.7
June	79.4	55.6	67.5
July	83.9	60.1	72.0
August	81.4	57.8	69.6
September	73.7	50.1	61.9
October	62.8	40.0	51.4
November	48.1	31.1	39.6
December	34.1	17.7	25.9

Zero-Degree Days: 17
Freezing Days: 155
90-Degree Days: 8
Heating- and Cooling-Degree Days: 7,462

Albuquerque, NM

Terrain: Rests in the Rio Grande Valley 55 miles southwest of Santa Fe, and is surrounded by mountains, most of them to the east. These mountainous areas receive more precipitation than does the city proper. With an annual rainfall of 8 inches, only the most hardy desert flora can grow. However, successful farming—primarily fruit and produce—is carried out in the valley by irrigation.

Climate: Arid continental. No muggy days. Half the moisture falls between July and September in the form of brief but severe thunderstorms. Long drizzles are unknown. These storms do not greatly interfere with outdoor activities, and they have a moderating effect on the heat. The hottest month is July, with temperatures reaching 90° F almost constantly. However, the low humidity and cool nights make the heat much less felt.

Pluses: Sunny and dry, with mild winters.

Minuses: Dust storms.

Places Rated Score: 659

Places Rated Rank: 30

Elevation: 5,314 feet

Relative Humidity: 43%
Wind Speed: 9 mph

Seasonal Change

Annual Rainfall 7.7 in

Annual Snowfall 11 in

Clear 172 days
Partly Cloudy 111 days
Cloudy 82 days

Precipitation Days: 59   Storm Days: 43

Average Temperatures			
	Daily High	Daily Low	Monthly Mean
January	46.9	23.5	35.2
February	52.6	27.4	40.0
March	59.2	32.3	45.8
April	70.1	41.4	55.8
May	79.9	50.7	65.3
June	89.5	59.7	74.6
July	92.2	65.2	78.7
August	89.7	63.4	76.6
September	83.4	56.7	70.1
October	71.7	44.7	58.2
November	57.1	31.8	44.5
December	47.5	24.9	36.2

Zero-Degree Days: 1
Freezing Days: 123
90-Degree Days: 61
Heating- and Cooling-Degree Days: 5,608

Alexandria, LA

Terrain: Located along the Red River in the geographic center of the state. The area is heavily wooded and is the site of the Kisatchie National Forest. The river is lined by high levees, which protect the surrounding land and cities from floods. The terrain is mostly flat.
Climate: Generally subtropical and humid. The winter months are mild, with short cold spells that occur when severely cold air moving across the Plains and the Mississippi Valley invades the city. Snowfall here is negligible, averaging less than an inch a year. Rainfall is heavy in all seasons. Summers are hot, humid, and uncomfortable, but temperatures in April, May, and especially late September through November are pleasant. Severe storms, including hailstorms and tornadoes, occur in all seasons.

Pluses: Mild winters.

Minuses: Hot and humid; stormy.

Places Rated Score: 520

Places Rated Rank: 203

Elevation: 118 feet

Relative Humidity: 77%
Wind Speed: 6.2 mph

Seasonal Change

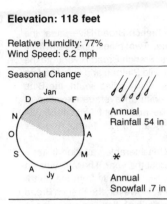

Annual Rainfall 54 in

Annual Snowfall .7 in

Clear 110 days Partly Cloudy 109 days Cloudy 146 days

Precipitation Days: 106 Storm Days: 69

Average Temperatures			
	Daily High	Daily Low	Monthly Mean
January	58.6	36.7	47.7
February	61.8	39.2	50.5
March	68.3	44.3	56.3
April	76.9	54.1	65.5
May	83.7	60.8	72.3
June	89.6	67.5	78.6
July	91.4	70.4	80.9
August	91.8	69.6	80.7
September	87.0	64.0	75.5
October	79.6	51.9	65.8
November	68.6	42.5	55.6
December	61.0	37.8	49.4

Zero-Degree Days: 0
Freezing Days: 43
90-Degree Days: 75
Heating- and Cooling-Degree Days: 4,393

Amarillo, TX

Terrain: Located in the heart of the Panhandle, Amarillo sits on the cap rock, or High Plains, of the Southwest. The area, which includes part of Oklahoma and northern Mexico, has often been called the Dust Bowl. It is a plateau with scrubby growth; cotton and sorghum are the primary crops. Amarillo lies between the Canadian and Red rivers.
Climate: The area is generally dry, but thunderstorms occur between April and September. This, however, can vary greatly from year to year, and droughts are fairly frequent. The area is subject to rapid and great temperature changes, especially in winter, when cold air comes down from the Plains and the Rocky Mountains at high speed. Nearness to paths of moving pressure systems causes strong winds, especially in March and April. Though summer days are hot, the low humidity lessens the felt heat and makes for pleasant mornings and nights.

Pluses: Sunny, dry, and mild, with distinct seasons.

Minuses: Hot; can be dusty.

Places Rated Score: 609

Places Rated Rank: 68

Elevation: 3,604 feet

Relative Humidity: 55%
Wind Speed: 13.7 mph

Seasonal Change

Annual Rainfall 20 in

Annual Snowfall 14.4 in

Clear 163 days Partly Cloudy 102 days Cloudy 100 days

Precipitation Days: 67 Storm Days: 48

Average Temperatures			
	Daily High	Daily Low	Monthly Mean
January	49.4	22.5	36.0
February	53.0	26.4	39.7
March	60.0	31.2	45.6
April	70.9	42.1	56.5
May	79.2	51.9	65.6
June	88.0	61.2	74.6
July	91.4	65.9	78.7
August	90.4	64.7	77.6
September	82.9	56.7	69.8
October	72.9	46.1	59.5
November	60.0	32.5	46.3
December	51.5	25.5	38.5

Zero-Degree Days: 2
Freezing Days: 108
90-Degree Days: 63
Heating- and Cooling-Degree Days: 5,616

Anchorage, AK

Terrain: Situated in a broad valley with adjacent narrow bodies of water. Terrain rises gradually to the east with marshes interspersed with glacial moraines, depressions, streams, and knolls. Beyond this area, the Chugach Mountains rise sharply to between 4,000 feet and 5,000 feet, with some peaks 8,000 feet to 10,000 feet high. These mountains block the warm air and the moisture from the Gulf of Alaska. Approximately 100 miles north lies the Alaska Range, which keeps much of the very cold air from the interior. Consequently, when temperatures in the interior are −50° F or −60° F, they will be −15° F to −30° F in Anchorage. The two ranges can also act as a trap, stalling very cold air when winds are light.
Climate: The four seasons are well marked in Anchorage, though in length and other characteristics they differ considerably from the standards of the middle latitudes. The rivers and lakes thaw in mid-April to early May. Snow arrives in October, leaves in mid-April.

Pluses: Well-defined, four-season climate.

Minuses: Rigorous.

Places Rated Score: 195

Places Rated Rank: 324

Elevation: 132 feet

Relative Humidity: 71%
Wind Speed: 6.7 mph

Seasonal Change

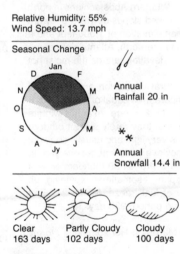

Annual Rainfall 14 in

Annual Snowfall 70 in

Clear 64 days Partly Cloudy 67 days Cloudy 234 days

Precipitation Days: 113 Storm Days: 1

Average Temperatures			
	Daily High	Daily Low	Monthly Mean
January	20.0	3.5	11.8
February	26.6	8.9	17.8
March	32.8	14.6	23.7
April	43.8	26.8	35.3
May	55.2	37.2	46.2
June	62.9	46.2	54.6
July	65.6	50.1	57.9
August	63.8	48.0	55.9
September	55.7	40.4	48.1
October	41.8	27.8	34.8
November	28.3	13.9	21.1
December	20.6	5.3	13.0

Zero-Degree Days: 41
Freezing Days: 192
90-Degree Days: 12
Heating- and Cooling-Degree Days: 10,911

★ Asheville, NC

Terrain: Located on both banks of the French Broad River, near the center of the basin of the same name. Two miles upstream from Asheville, the Swannanoa River joins the French Broad River from the east. The entire valley is called the Asheville Plateau and is flanked on the east and west by mountain ranges. Thirty miles south, the Blue Ridge Mountains form an escarpment, with an average elevation of 2,700 feet. Tallest peaks near Asheville are Mount Mitchell (6,684 feet), 20 miles northeast, and Big Pisgah (5,721 feet), 16 miles southwest.

Climate: Temperate but invigorating. Considerable variation in temperature occurs from day to day throughout the year. The valley has a pronounced effect on wind direction, which is mostly from the northwest. Destructive weather events are rare. However, the French Broad Valley is subject to flooding, with especially high flooding occurring in 12-year cycles.

Pluses: Long spring, beginning early.

Minuses: Drizzly, flood-prone.

Places Rated Score: 694

Places Rated Rank: 25

Elevation: 2,207 feet

Relative Humidity: 77%
Wind Speed: 7.8 mph

Seasonal Change

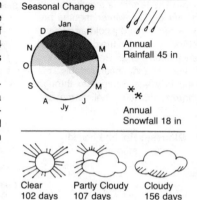

Annual Rainfall 45 in

Annual Snowfall 18 in

Clear 102 days   Partly Cloudy 107 days   Cloudy 156 days

Precipitation Days: 128   Storm Days: 49

Average Temperatures			
	Daily High	Daily Low	Monthly Mean
January	48.4	27.3	37.9
February	50.6	28.2	39.4
March	58.3	33.5	45.9
April	69.4	42.4	55.9
May	76.8	50.6	63.7
June	82.5	58.7	70.6
July	84.3	62.6	73.5
August	83.8	61.8	72.8
September	78.0	55.4	66.7
October	69.1	44.5	56.8
November	58.2	34.3	46.3
December	49.3	28.1	38.7

Zero-Degree Days: 1
Freezing Days: 106
90-Degree Days: 5
Heating- and Cooling-Degree Days: 5,109

★ Atlanta, GA

Terrain: Located in the foothills of the southern Appalachians in north central Georgia. Terrain is rolling to hilly and slopes downward toward the east, west, and south. With a mean elevation of 1,000 feet and a location on a plateau with mountains to the north, Atlanta's exposure to the cold north air is blocked, and its elevation retards the moist hot air from the Gulf of Mexico.

Climate: Abundant rainfall fosters natural vegetation and growth of crops. In summer, afternoon high temperatures equal or exceed 90° F one day in five, but a temperature of 100° F is rare. Atlanta's winters are mild: Cold spells are not unusual, but they rarely disrupt outdoor activities for extended periods. Snow is very light and usually does not stay on the ground long. Ice storms, however, occur about one year in ten and cause heavy damage. Atlanta averages 50 thunderstorms a year, which occur mostly in the spring, sometimes spinning off destructive tornadoes. Average date of last freeze: March 24. First freeze: November 12. Average growing period: 233 days.

Pluses: Mild, sunny, pleasant.

Minuses: Hot summers, stormy.

Places Rated Score: 696

Places Rated Rank: 24

Elevation: 1,034 feet

Relative Humidity: 70%
Wind Speed: 9.1 mph

Seasonal Change

Annual Rainfall 48 in

Annual Snowfall 2 in

Clear 108 days   Partly Cloudy 111 days   Cloudy 146 days

Precipitation Days: 116   Storm Days: 50

Average Temperatures			
	Daily High	Daily Low	Monthly Mean
January	51.4	33.4	42.4
February	54.5	35.5	45.0
March	61.1	41.1	51.1
April	71.4	50.7	61.1
May	79.0	59.2	69.1
June	84.6	66.6	75.6
July	86.5	69.4	78.0
August	86.4	68.6	77.5
September	81.2	63.4	72.3
October	72.5	52.3	62.4
November	61.9	40.8	51.4
December	52.7	34.3	43.5

Zero-Degree Days: 0
Freezing Days: 59
90-Degree Days: 19
Heating- and Cooling-Degree Days: 4,684

Atlantic City, NJ

Terrain: Located on a sand island south of Absecon Inlet on the southeast coast of New Jersey. Surrounding terrain, composed of tidal marshes and beach sand, is flat and lies slightly above sea level.

Climate: Continental, but the moderating influence of the Atlantic Ocean is apparent throughout the year. Summers are relatively cooler, winters warmer than those of other places at the same latitude. During the warm season, sea breezes in the late morning and afternoon prevent excessive heat. On occasion, sea breezes may lower the temperature between 15 degrees and 20 degrees within a half hour. Temperatures of 90° F or higher are recorded only about three times a year here. Fall is long, lasting until almost mid-November. On the other hand, warming is somewhat delayed in the spring. Ocean temperatures range from an average near 37° F in winter to 72° F in August. Precipitation is moderate and well distributed throughout the year, but great variation is seen from year to year in precipitation during the late summer and early fall (August, September, and October).

Pluses: Moderate temperatures.

Minuses: Late springs.

Places Rated Score: 615

Places Rated Rank: 61

Elevation: 10 feet

Relative Humidity: 73%
Wind Speed: 10.7 mph

Seasonal Change

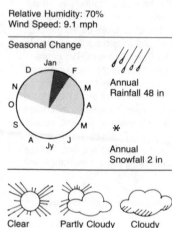

Annual Rainfall 46 in

Annual Snowfall 16 in

Clear 96 days   Partly Cloudy 108 days   Cloudy 161 days

Precipitation Days: 112   Storm Days: 25

Average Temperatures			
	Daily High	Daily Low	Monthly Mean
January	41.4	24.0	32.7
February	42.9	24.9	33.9
March	50.7	31.5	41.1
April	62.3	41.0	51.7
May	72.4	50.7	61.6
June	80.8	59.7	70.3
July	84.7	65.4	75.1
August	83.0	63.8	73.4
September	77.3	56.8	67.1
October	67.5	45.9	56.7
November	55.9	36.1	46.0
December	44.2	26.0	35.1

Zero-Degree Days: 1
Freezing Days: 15
90-Degree Days: 16
Heating- and Cooling-Degree Days: 5,810

Augusta, GA–SC

Terrain: Located in eastern Georgia on the Savannah River, which forms part of the boundary between Georgia and South Carolina. The dividing line between the Piedmont Plateau and the Coastal Plain, which is known as the fall line, passes through the Savannah River basin in a northeast-southwest direction near Augusta. The terrain consists of low hills to the western half of the city and swampland immediately to the north and east.

Climate: Warm and mild, with occasional hot spells. In the winter, measurable snow is a rarity and remains on the ground only a short time. In 100 years of weather records, a temperature of zero or colder has never been reached. The growing season averages 241 days, from March 16 to November 16, although frosts have been reported as late as April 21 and as early as October 17. Although Augusta is protected from flooding of the Savannah River by two multipurpose dams, the potential for flooding still exists in some low-lying areas.

Pluses: Very brief winters.

Minuses: Can be hot, flood-prone.

Places Rated Score: 534

Places Rated Rank: 184

Elevation: 136 feet

Relative Humidity: 72%
Wind Speed: 6.6 mph

Seasonal Change

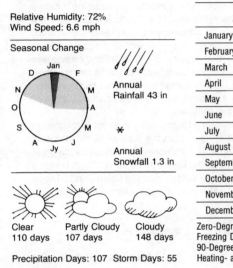

Annual Rainfall 43 in

Annual Snowfall 1.3 in

Clear 110 days | Partly Cloudy 107 days | Cloudy 148 days

Precipitation Days: 107   Storm Days: 55

Average Temperatures			
	Daily High	Daily Low	Monthly Mean
January	56.7	34.0	45.8
February	60.5	36.1	48.3
March	67.1	42.0	54.6
April	76.9	50.7	63.8
May	84.2	59.1	71.7
June	89.6	66.7	78.2
July	90.8	69.9	80.4
August	90.2	69.0	79.6
September	85.2	63.2	74.2
October	77.0	51.2	64.1
November	67.1	40.2	53.7
December	58.7	34.1	46.4

Zero-Degree Days: 0
Freezing Days: 59
90-Degree Days: 63
Heating- and Cooling-Degree Days: 4,542

Austin, TX

Terrain: Located on the Colorado River where it crosses the Balcones escarpment, which separates the Texas hill country from the blackland prairies of East Texas. Elevations within the city limits vary from 400 feet to 900 feet above sea level. Native trees include cedar, oak, walnut, mesquite, and pecan.

Climate: Subtropical. Although summers are hot, the nights are a bit cooler, with temperatures usually dropping into the 70s. Winters are mild, with below-freezing temperatures on fewer than 25 days; strong northers may bring cold spells, but these rarely last more than a few days. Precipitation is well distributed but heaviest in late spring, with a secondary rainfall peak in September. With summer come heavy thunderstorms; in winter, the rain tends to be slow and steady. Snowfall (1 inch per year) is inconsequential. Prevailing winds are southerly. Destructive weather is infrequent. Freeze-free season: 270 days. Average date of last freeze: March 3. First freeze: November 28.

Pluses: Mild winters.

Minuses: Hot.

Places Rated Score: 435

Places Rated Rank: 282

Elevation: 570 feet

Relative Humidity: 67%
Wind Speed: 9.4 mph

Seasonal Change

Annual Rainfall 33 in

Annual Snowfall 1 in

Clear 115 days | Partly Cloudy 116 days | Cloudy 134 days

Precipitation Days: 82   Storm Days: 41

Average Temperatures			
	Daily High	Daily Low	Monthly Mean
January	60.0	39.3	49.7
February	63.8	42.8	53.3
March	70.7	48.2	59.5
April	79.0	58.2	68.6
May	85.2	65.1	75.2
June	91.7	71.4	81.6
July	95.4	73.7	84.6
August	95.9	73.5	84.7
September	89.4	68.4	78.9
October	81.3	58.9	70.1
November	70.2	48.0	59.1
December	63.0	41.6	52.3

Zero-Degree Days: 0
Freezing Days: 23
90-Degree Days: 101
Heating- and Cooling-Degree Days: 4,645

Bakersfield, CA

Terrain: Situated in the extreme southern end of the great San Joaquin Valley, the city is partially surrounded by a horseshoe-shaped rim of mountains with an opening at the northwest. The Sierra Nevada to the northeast block much of the cold air that flows southward over the country in the winter. This range also catches and stores snow, which is used for irrigation in the valley below. The valley is suited for Mediterranean and specialized forms of agriculture.

Climate: Because of the surrounding topography, there are three different climates within short distances of each other: valley, mountain, and desert. The overall climate, however, is warm and semiarid. Ninety percent of the precipitation falls between October and April, typical of the southern half of California. Thunderstorms and snow are rare in the valley. Summers are hot, cloudless, and dry but occasionally relieved by ocean breezes from the west. Winters are mild. Average growing season: 265 days.

Pluses: Dry; mild winters.

Minuses: Hot summers.

Places Rated Score: 560

Places Rated Rank: 127

Elevation: 492 feet

Relative Humidity: 52%
Wind Speed: 6.4 mph

Seasonal Change

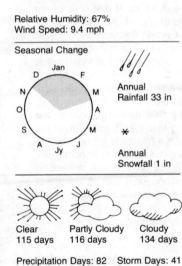

Annual Rainfall 6 in

Annual Snowfall 0 in

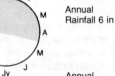

Clear 202 days | Partly Cloudy 79 days | Cloudy 84 days

Precipitation Days: 36   Storm Days: 3

Average Temperatures			
	Daily High	Daily Low	Monthly Mean
January	57.5	37.4	47.5
February	63.3	41.4	52.4
March	68.6	44.5	56.6
April	75.5	49.9	62.7
May	83.6	56.0	69.8
June	91.5	62.3	76.9
July	99.1	68.7	83.9
August	96.5	66.6	81.6
September	91.1	62.1	76.6
October	80.5	53.3	66.9
November	67.8	44.2	56.0
December	57.4	38.4	47.9

Zero-Degree Days: 0
Freezing Days: 11
90-Degree Days: 110
Heating- and Cooling-Degree Days: 4,364

Baltimore, MD

Terrain: Baltimore lies in a region about midway between the rigorous climates of the North and the mild ones of the South. It is also adjacent to the modifying influences of Chesapeake Bay and the Atlantic Ocean. Since this region is near the usual path of the low-pressure systems that move across the country, shifts in wind direction are frequent and contribute to the changeable character of the weather. The net effect of the Appalachian Mountains to the west and the ocean to the east is to produce an equable climate compared with other locations farther inland at the same latitude.

Climate: Rainfall is fairly uniform throughout the year but is greatest in late summer and early fall. This is also the time of hurricanes and severe thunderstorms. In summer, Baltimore is influenced by the great high-pressure system known as the Bermuda High. This high brings a constant flow of warm, humid air masses from the Deep South. These air masses, as well as the proximity of water, account for the high humidity here.

Pluses: Mild for its latitude.

Minuses: Humid, stormy.

Places Rated Score: 567

Places Rated Rank: 119

Elevation: 155 feet

Relative Humidity: 67%
Wind Speed: 9.5 mph

Seasonal Change

Annual Rainfall 40 in

Clear 106 days
Partly Cloudy 109 days
Cloudy 150 days

Precipitation Days: 112 Storm Days: 26

Average Temperatures			
	Daily High	Daily Low	Monthly Mean
January	41.9	24.9	33.4
February	43.9	25.7	34.8
March	53.0	32.5	42.8
April	65.2	42.4	53.8
May	74.8	52.5	63.7
June	83.2	61.6	72.4
July	86.7	66.5	76.6
August	85.1	64.7	74.9
September	79.0	57.9	68.5
October	68.3	46.4	57.4
November	56.1	36.0	46.1
December	43.9	26.6	35.3

Zero-Degree Days: 0
Freezing Days: 100
90-Degree Days: 31
Heating- and Cooling-Degree Days: 5,837

Bangor, ME

Terrain: Located in east-central Maine at the navigable head of the Penobscot River, about 80 miles northeast of the state capital, Augusta. By means of the Penobscot River, Bangor links the vast timber forests of Maine's northern interior with Penobscot Bay, to the south. It has always been an important trading and commercial center, especially for the lumber industry.

Climate: Decidedly continental in character; summers are pleasant, with cool nights, and winters are moderately severe and fairly long. The extremes of weather caused by this northerly location are somewhat modified by Bangor's setting less than 50 miles from the Atlantic Ocean. The tempering effect of the Atlantic is felt most during the summer, when southerly winds bring ocean-cooled air northward. In the winter, westerly and northerly winds predominate, enhancing the cold. Precipitation is dependable and abundant, with an average of 43 inches of rain and almost 100 inches of snow each year.

Pluses: Comfortable summers.

Minuses: Long, cold winters.

Places Rated Score: 451

Places Rated Rank: 272

Elevation: 202 feet

Relative Humidity: 74%
Wind Speed: 8.8 mph

Seasonal Change

Annual Rainfall 43 in

Annual Snowfall 97 in

Clear 107 days
Partly Cloudy 98 days
Cloudy 160 days

Precipitation Days: 136 Storm Days: 17

Average Temperatures			
	Daily High	Daily Low	Monthly Mean
January	26.9	9.8	18.4
February	29.5	10.4	20.0
March	38.0	21.3	29.7
April	50.8	32.5	41.7
May	63.4	42.3	52.9
June	73.3	52.3	62.8
July	77.7	57.6	67.7
August	76.0	55.8	65.9
September	67.9	47.9	57.9
October	57.3	39.0	48.2
November	44.6	30.2	37.4
December	31.3	15.8	23.6

Zero-Degree Days: 18
Freezing Days: 157
90-Degree Days: 3
Heating- and Cooling-Degree Days: 8,113

Billings, MT

Terrain: Situated on the border between the Great Plains and the Rocky Mountains, and located on the west bank of the Yellowstone River. Billings is the center of a vast, rich agricultural belt; irrigation and sufficient rain during early spring and fall make it possible to raise a variety of crops here.

Climate: Takes on the character of both the Plains and the Rockies but is classified as semiarid. About a third of the yearly total of 14 inches of rain falls during May and June. The winter is usually dry and cold, although heavy snows can occur anytime during the winter months. The heaviest snows come either in spring or fall, when the temperature may take an unexpected drop. Blizzard conditions are expected. Severe cold spells are sometimes relieved by the Chinook, or "drainage," winds moving down Yellowstone Valley and bringing warm Pacific air. Springs: changeable, cloudy, cool. Summers: mild, dry, sunny, with cool to cold nights.

Pluses: Cool summers.

Minuses: Fairly rugged.

Places Rated Score: 452

Places Rated Rank: 271

Elevation: 3,570 feet

Relative Humidity: 55%
Wind Speed: 11.5 mph

Seasonal Change

Annual Rainfall 14 in

Annual Snowfall 56 in

Clear 90 days
Partly Cloudy 116 days
Cloudy 159 days

Precipitation Days: 95 Storm Days: 29

Average Temperatures			
	Daily High	Daily Low	Monthly Mean
January	31.2	12.5	21.9
February	37.1	17.7	27.4
March	42.1	23.1	32.6
April	55.8	33.4	44.6
May	65.7	43.3	54.5
June	73.7	51.5	62.6
July	85.6	58.0	71.8
August	83.8	56.3	70.1
September	71.3	46.5	58.9
October	61.0	37.5	49.3
November	45.0	26.4	35.7
December	35.8	17.7	26.8

Zero-Degree Days: 18
Freezing Days: 152
90-Degree Days: 28
Heating- and Cooling-Degree Days: 7,763

Biloxi–Gulfport, MS

Terrain: In speaking of the Mississippi Gulf Coast, one usually thinks of the thickly settled area stretching from St. Louis Bay at Pass Christian to Biloxi Bay and Ocean Springs. This area is climatologically homogeneous, and a summary of any town (in this case, Biloxi–Gulfport) is applicable to the others. The terrain is flat, consisting of low-lying delta floodplains sloping down to sand beaches and rather shallow harbors and bays.

Climate: The Gulf waters have a modifying effect on the local climate that is not felt farther inland. Temperatures of 90° F or higher occur only half as often here as they do in Hattiesburg, 60 miles north. However, there is no such reverse effect on cold air moving down from the north in winter. Rainfall is plentiful and is heaviest in July, with totals in March and September following close behind. Damage from hurricanes and tropical storms can occur six to seven times a year.

Pluses: Warm, mild beach climate.

Minuses: Winters relatively chilly; hurricane-prone.

Places Rated Score: 584

Places Rated Rank: 93

Elevation: 15 feet

Relative Humidity: 77%
Wind Speed: 9.1 mph

Seasonal Change

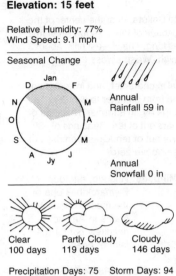

Annual Rainfall 59 in

Annual Snowfall 0 in

Clear 100 days Partly Cloudy 119 days Cloudy 146 days

Precipitation Days: 75 Storm Days: 94

Average Temperatures			
	Daily High	Daily Low	Monthly Mean
January	61.7	45.5	53.6
February	63.6	47.2	55.4
March	68.2	52.0	60.1
April	75.0	59.6	67.3
May	82.4	67.2	74.8
June	87.9	73.2	80.6
July	89.3	74.5	81.9
August	89.6	74.2	81.9
September	85.9	70.3	78.1
October	79.1	60.7	69.9
November	68.8	50.4	59.6
December	62.6	46.2	54.4

Zero-Degree Days: 0
Freezing Days: 11
90-Degree Days: 52
Heating- and Cooling-Degree Days: 3,652

Binghamton, NY

Terrain: Binghamton, in south-central New York State, lies in a narrow valley at the confluence of the Susquehanna and Chenango rivers. Within a radius of approximately 5 miles around the city, hills rise to some 1,400 feet to 1,600 feet. In the spring, melting snow and rains sometimes cause flooding along the riverbanks.

Climate: Representative of the humid area of the northeastern United States and decidedly continental in character. Since the area is adjacent to the so-called St. Lawrence Valley storm track and is also subject to intruding Arctic air masses that approach from the west and north, the local weather undergoes frequent and rapid changes. Winters are cold but usually not severe. However, moisture-laden winds from the Great Lakes bring much snow. Summers are pleasantly cool and invigorating.

Pluses: Nice summers.

Minuses: Cloudy, snowy.

Places Rated Score: 550

Places Rated Rank: 146

Elevation: 1,590 feet

Relative Humidity: 74%
Wind Speed: 10.3 mph

Seasonal Change

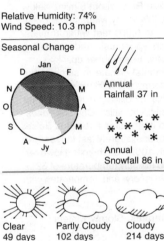

Annual Rainfall 37 in

Annual Snowfall 86 in

Clear 49 days Partly Cloudy 102 days Cloudy 214 days

Precipitation Days: 163 Storm Days: 31

Average Temperatures			
	Daily High	Daily Low	Monthly Mean
January	28.7	15.2	22.0
February	30.1	15.4	22.8
March	38.9	23.7	31.3
April	54.0	35.3	44.7
May	65.0	45.2	55.1
June	74.5	55.1	64.8
July	78.5	59.6	69.1
August	76.8	57.8	67.3
September	69.4	50.9	60.2
October	59.2	41.4	50.3
November	44.5	31.8	38.2
December	31.3	19.4	25.4

Zero-Degree Days: 8
Freezing Days: 147
90-Degree Days: 2
Heating- and Cooling-Degree Days: 7,654

Birmingham, AL

Terrain: Hilly and located in a valley between a ridge of hills, extending from the northeast to the west, and the Red Mountain ridge, covering the east to the southwest. This valley is 8 miles long and 2 miles to 4 miles wide. The Red Mountain ridge approaches a height of 600 feet above the valley floor. Rolling terrain extends to the southwest and west. The hills in the Birmingham area, which extend to the northeast and north, are the foothills of the Appalachians and the Cumberland Plateau.

Climate: Ideal solar radiation and cold-air drainage produce extreme temperature inversions and low minimum temperatures. Located 300 miles from the Gulf of Mexico, Birmingham is safe from the direct effects of tropical hurricanes, although it does receive heavy rains from these storms. Birmingham occasionally receives very low temperatures. Average growing season: 239 days.

Pluses: Mild winters.

Minuses: Humid, rainy.

Places Rated Score: 612

Places Rated Rank: 66

Elevation: 630 feet

Relative Humidity: 72%
Wind Speed: 7.4 mph

Seasonal Change

Annual Rainfall 53 in

Annual Snowfall 1 in

Clear 99 days Partly Cloudy 111 days Cloudy 155 days

Precipitation Days: 118 Storm Days: 58

Average Temperatures			
	Daily High	Daily Low	Monthly Mean
January	54.3	34.1	44.2
February	57.7	36.1	46.9
March	64.8	41.8	53.3
April	75.3	51.0	63.2
May	82.5	58.4	70.5
June	88.4	66.4	77.4
July	90.3	69.5	79.9
August	89.7	68.7	79.2
September	84.7	63.0	73.9
October	75.8	50.8	63.3
November	64.0	40.1	52.1
December	55.5	34.9	45.2

Zero-Degree Days: 0
Freezing Days: 60
90-Degree Days: 39
Heating- and Cooling-Degree Days: 4,772

Bismarck, ND

Terrain: Located in south central North Dakota, near the center of the North American land mass, on the east bank of the Missouri River in a shallow basin 7 miles wide and 11 miles long. The closest hills, about 3 miles away, are 200 feet or 300 feet high. West, across the river, the land is hilly and considerably higher.

Climate: Semiarid, typically continental in character, and invigorating. The normal average temperature range from summer to winter is 135 degrees, typical of the northern Great Plains. In summer, readings of 100° F or more may be expected six years out of ten. Readings of −30° F in winter are experienced seven years out of ten. On seven days of the year, the temperature does not rise above zero.

Pluses: Invigorating, variable.

Minuses: Rugged, rigorous; Bismarck has one of the most extreme climates in America— definitely *not* for the faint of heart.

Places Rated Score: 149

Places Rated Rank: 327

Elevation: 1,660 feet

Relative Humidity: 66%
Wind Speed: 10.6 mph

Seasonal Change

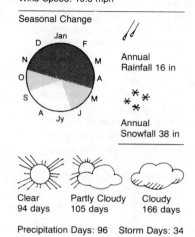

Annual Rainfall 16 in

Annual Snowfall 38 in

Clear 94 days   Partly Cloudy 105 days   Cloudy 166 days

Precipitation Days: 96   Storm Days: 34

	Average Temperatures		
	Daily High	Daily Low	Monthly Mean
January	19.1	−2.8	8.2
February	24.5	2.4	13.5
March	35.4	14.7	25.1
April	54.8	31.1	43.0
May	67.1	41.7	54.4
June	75.8	51.8	63.8
July	84.3	57.3	70.8
August	83.5	54.9	69.2
September	71.3	43.7	57.5
October	60.3	33.2	46.8
November	39.4	18.3	28.9
December	26.0	5.2	15.6

Zero-Degree Days: 51
Freezing Days: 186
90-Degree Days: 22
Heating- and Cooling-Degree Days: 9,531

Boise City, ID

Terrain: Cradled in the valley of the Boise River about 8 miles below the mouth of a mountain canyon, where this valley widens. The Boise Mountains rise to a height of 5,000 feet to 6,000 feet within 8 miles. Their slopes are partially mantled with sagebrush and chaparral, changing to stands of fir, spruce, and pine trees higher up.

Climate: Almost a typical upland continental climate in summer but one tempered by periods of cloudy or stormy and mild weather during almost every winter. The cause of this modification in the winter months is the flow of warm, moist Pacific air, called Chinook winds. While this air is considerably moderated by the time it reaches Boise, its effect is nonetheless felt. Summer hot spells rarely last longer than a few days, but temperatures may reach 100° F each year. However, due to the low humidity, the average 5:00 PM July temperature of 62° F is comfortable. In general, the climate is dry and temperate, with enough variation to be stimulating.

Pluses: Mild; low humidity.

Minuses: Stormy winters.

Places Rated Score: 592

Places Rated Rank: 83

Elevation: 2,868 feet

Relative Humidity: 57%
Wind Speed: 9 mph

Seasonal Change

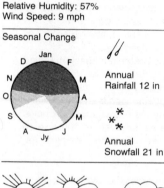

Annual Rainfall 12 in

Annual Snowfall 21 in

Clear 124 days   Partly Cloudy 90 days   Cloudy 151 days

Precipitation Days: 91   Storm Days: 15

	Average Temperatures		
	Daily High	Daily Low	Monthly Mean
January	36.5	21.4	29.0
February	43.8	27.2	35.5
March	51.6	30.5	41.1
April	61.4	36.5	49.0
May	70.6	44.1	57.4
June	78.3	51.2	64.8
July	90.5	58.5	74.5
August	87.6	56.7	72.2
September	77.6	48.5	63.1
October	64.7	39.4	52.1
November	48.9	30.7	39.8
December	39.1	25.0	32.1

Zero-Degree Days: 2
Freezing Days: 124
90-Degree Days: 43
Heating- and Cooling-Degree Days: 6,547

Boston, MA

Terrain: Located in Massachusetts Bay at the mouths of the Mystic and Charles rivers. The western section of Massachusetts Bay is called Boston Bay, and its innermost part is called Boston Harbor, a large, sheltered body of water studded with many small islands, known as the Harbor Islands. Sections of Boston are rolling; two of the more famous hills are Beacon Hill in Boston and Bunker Hill in Charlestown.

Climate: Boston's proximity to the ocean greatly influences its climate —roughly described as damp, changeable, and relatively mild, considering its northern location. Sea breezes from the Atlantic do a great deal to moderate the temperature in both summer and winter. Hot summer afternoons as well as winter cold snaps (which may be severe and aggravated by high winds) are frequently relieved by these breezes. Rain is plentiful and well distributed throughout the year. Boston receives a great amount of snow, although in the city proper and to the south it often falls as sleet with no accumulation.

Pluses: Great variety, frequent changes.

Minuses: Rainy, snowy.

Places Rated Score: 623

Places Rated Rank: 56

Elevation: 29 feet

Relative Humidity: 67%
Wind Speed: 12.6 mph

Seasonal Change

Annual Rainfall 43 in

Annual Snowfall 42 in

Clear 99 days   Partly Cloudy 106 days   Cloudy 160 days

Precipitation Days: 128   Storm Days: 19

	Average Temperatures		
	Daily High	Daily Low	Monthly Mean
January	35.9	22.5	29.2
February	37.5	23.3	30.4
March	44.6	31.5	38.1
April	56.3	40.8	48.6
May	67.1	50.1	58.6
June	76.6	59.3	68.0
July	81.4	65.1	73.3
August	79.3	63.3	71.3
September	72.2	56.7	64.5
October	63.2	47.5	55.4
November	51.7	38.7	45.2
December	39.3	26.6	33.0

Zero-Degree Days: 1
Freezing Days: 99
90-Degree Days: 12
Heating- and Cooling-Degree Days: 6,282

Brownsville–Harlingen, TX

Terrain: Situated at the extreme southern tip of Texas, on the Mexican border, and on the alluvial soils of the Rio Grande. The only more southerly city in America is Key West, Florida. The Gulf of Mexico is 18 miles to the east, and more than half the land toward the coast consists of tidal marshlands, which have the net effect of "moving" the coast 10 miles nearer to the city.

Climate: Humid subtropical. It's always summer here, accounting for the area's agricultural importance in growing citrus fruits, cotton, and warm-weather vegetables. Part of the climate is man-made: Irrigation, used for all the crops, adds considerably to the humidity. Summer temperatures follow a predictable pattern of lower 90s in the day and middle 70s at night. Gulf breezes help temper the summer heat. This is a popular tourist spot in the winter months. The normal daily January minimum temperature is 51° F.

Pluses: Long growing season.   **Minuses:** Hot.

Places Rated Score: 440   **Places Rated Rank: 277**

Elevation: 20 feet

Relative Humidity: 76%
Wind Speed: 11.8 mph

Seasonal Change

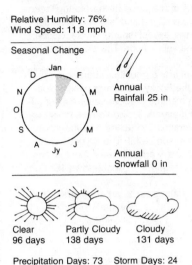

Annual Rainfall 25 in

Annual Snowfall 0 in

Clear 96 days   Partly Cloudy 138 days   Cloudy 131 days

Precipitation Days: 73   Storm Days: 24

Average Temperatures			
	Daily High	Daily Low	Monthly Mean
January	69.5	51.0	60.3
February	72.7	54.1	63.4
March	76.6	58.8	67.7
April	83.1	66.7	74.9
May	87.1	71.4	79.3
June	90.6	75.0	82.8
July	92.8	75.9	84.4
August	93.0	75.7	84.4
September	89.9	73.2	81.6
October	84.7	66.6	75.7
November	77.5	58.7	68.1
December	72.3	53.3	62.8

Zero-Degree Days: 0
Freezing Days: 2
90-Degree Days: 102
Heating- and Cooling-Degree Days: 4,524

Buffalo, NY

Terrain: The surrounding country is comparatively low and level to the west, and gently rolling to the east and south, rising to pronounced hills within 12 miles to 18 miles, and to 1,000 feet above Lake Erie at a point 35 miles south-southeast of the city. The eastern end of Lake Erie is 9 miles to the west-southwest, and Lake Ontario is 25 miles to the north. The two lakes are connected by the Niagara River and the famous falls of the same name.

Climate: The weather here is varied and changeable. Wide seasonal swings of temperature are tempered somewhat by the surrounding lakes. Spring comes late, primarily because of the ice buildup and cold water on Lake Erie. Summers are mild, with more sun here than anywhere else in the state. Thunderstorms are infrequent. Autumn has long, dry periods and is frost-free until mid-October. Winters are famous for snow: 90 inches are expected each year.

Pluses: Pleasant summers.   **Minuses:** Snowy, cloudy.

Places Rated Score: 571   **Places Rated Rank: 112**

Elevation: 706 feet

Relative Humidity: 73%
Wind Speed: 12.3 mph

Seasonal Change

Annual Rainfall 36 in

Annual Snowfall 90 in

Clear 55 days   Partly Cloudy 104 days   Cloudy 206 days

Precipitation Days: 168   Storm Days: 31

Average Temperatures			
	Daily High	Daily Low	Monthly Mean
January	29.8	17.6	23.7
February	31.0	17.7	24.4
March	39.0	25.2	32.1
April	53.3	36.4	44.9
May	64.3	45.9	55.1
June	75.1	56.3	65.7
July	79.5	60.7	70.1
August	77.6	59.1	68.4
September	70.8	52.3	61.6
October	60.2	42.7	51.5
November	46.1	33.5	39.8
December	33.6	22.2	27.9

Zero-Degree Days: 5
Freezing Days: 137
90-Degree Days: 2
Heating- and Cooling-Degree Days: 7,364

Burlington, VT

Terrain: Located on the eastern shore of Lake Champlain at the widest part of that lake. About 35 miles to the west lie the highest peaks of the Adirondacks; the foothills of the Green Mountains begin 10 miles to the east and southeast.

Climate: Burlington's northerly latitude assures the variety and vigor of a true New England climate. Lake Champlain, however, has a tempering effect; during the winter months, temperatures along the lakeshore often run from 5 degrees to 10 degrees warmer than those at the airport 3.5 miles away. The summer, while not long compared with most, is quite pleasant, with only four 90-degree days per year on the average. Fall is cool, extending through October. Winters are cold, with intense cold snaps (usually not lasting long) formed by high-pressure systems moving down from central Canada and Hudson Bay. Because of its location in the path of the St. Lawrence Valley storm track and the effects of the lake, Burlington is one of the cloudiest cities in the United States.

Pluses: Cool summers.   **Minuses:** Long, cold winters.

Places Rated Score: 383   **Places Rated Rank: 305**

Elevation: 340 feet

Relative Humidity: 71%
Wind Speed: 8.8 mph

Seasonal Change

Annual Rainfall 33 in

Annual Snowfall 79 in

Clear 58 days   Partly Cloudy 103 days   Cloudy 204 days

Precipitation Days: 153   Storm Days: 25

Average Temperatures			
	Daily High	Daily Low	Monthly Mean
January	25.9	7.6	16.8
February	28.2	8.9	18.6
March	38.0	20.1	29.1
April	53.3	32.6	43.0
May	66.1	43.5	54.8
June	76.5	53.9	65.2
July	81.0	58.5	69.8
August	78.3	56.4	67.4
September	70.0	48.6	59.3
October	58.7	38.8	48.8
November	44.3	29.7	37.0
December	30.3	14.8	22.6

Zero-Degree Days: 28
Freezing Days: 163
90-Degree Days: 5
Heating- and Cooling-Degree Days: 8,272

Casper, WY

Terrain: Located in the central part of the state in the North Platte River valley. The nearby countryside is rolling and hilly with considerable flat prairie land in all directions except south, where Casper Mountain rises 3,500 feet above the valley floor. The prairie land is used mostly for grazing.

Climate: Rather dry due to the effective moisture barrier of the Cascades, the Sierra Nevada, and the Rocky Mountains, which block most of the moist Pacific winds. Summertime precipitation is almost all in the form of thunderstorms, which generally provide ample moisture for grasslands. Annual snowfall averages 77 inches, but the winter season is not severe, contrary to common belief. The dryness of the air prevents discomfort during both the warm summer months and winter cold snaps. Summer highs average 84° F, winter lows 15° F.

Pluses: Invigorating.

Minuses: Short summers, long winters.

Places Rated Score: 401

Places Rated Rank: 299

Elevation: 5,338 feet

Relative Humidity: 56%
Wind Speed: 13 mph

Seasonal Change

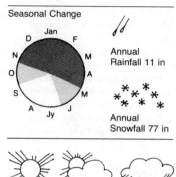

Annual Rainfall 11 in

Annual Snowfall 77 in

Clear 109 days   Partly Cloudy 110 days   Cloudy 146 days

Precipitation Days: 93   Storm Days: 34

Average Temperatures			
	Daily High	Daily Low	Monthly Mean
January	33.6	12.7	23.2
February	37.7	15.9	26.8
March	42.6	19.4	31.0
April	55.5	29.9	42.7
May	66.1	39.3	52.7
June	76.3	47.4	61.9
July	87.1	54.9	71.0
August	85.6	53.5	69.6
September	74.1	43.3	58.7
October	61.4	33.9	47.7
November	44.8	22.9	33.9
December	36.2	16.2	26.2

Zero-Degree Days: 21
Freezing Days: 185
90-Degree Days: 25
Heating- and Cooling-Degree Days: 8,013

Charleston, SC

Terrain: Before the expansion begun in 1960, Charleston was limited to the peninsula bounded on the west and south by the Ashley River, on the east by the Cooper River, and on the southeast by a spacious harbor that contains historic Fort Sumter. The terrain is generally level and the soil sandy to sandy loam. Because of the low elevation, a portion of the city and nearby coastal islands are vulnerable to tidal flooding.

Climate: Generally temperate, modified considerably by the ocean. Summer is warm and humid, but temperatures over 100° F are infrequent. Most rain—41% of the annual total—occurs then. The fall passes from an Indian summer to the prewinter cold spells that begin in November. From late September to early November, the weather is very pleasant, being cool and sunny. Winters are mild; temperatures of 20° F or less are very unusual. Spring is warm, windy, and changeable. Most storms occur then.

Pluses: Pleasant falls, mild winters.

Minuses: Hot, humid, stormy.

Places Rated Score: 569

Places Rated Rank: 115

Elevation: 48 feet

Relative Humidity: 76%
Wind Speed: 8.8 mph

Seasonal Change

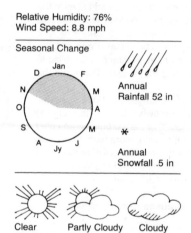

Annual Rainfall 52 in

Annual Snowfall .5 in

Clear 101 days   Partly Cloudy 113 days   Cloudy 151 days

Precipitation Days: 115   Storm Days: 56

Average Temperatures			
	Daily High	Daily Low	Monthly Mean
January	59.8	37.3	48.6
February	61.9	39.0	50.5
March	67.8	45.1	56.5
April	76.2	53.0	64.6
May	83.1	61.1	72.1
June	87.7	68.1	77.9
July	89.1	71.2	80.2
August	88.6	70.6	79.6
September	84.5	65.9	75.2
October	77.1	55.1	66.1
November	68.4	44.1	56.3
December	60.8	37.7	49.3

Zero-Degree Days: 0
Freezing Days: 36
90-Degree Days: 47
Heating- and Cooling-Degree Days: 4,224

Charleston, WV

Terrain: Situated in the western foothills of the Appalachians at the junction of the Kanawha and Elk rivers.

Climate: Characterized by sharp temperature contrasts, both seasonal and day-to-day. May through September is generally warm; November through March moderately cold. April and October are months of rapid transition. Cold spells occur on the average of two or three times each winter, but they seldom last longer than several days. Ample precipitation is well distributed throughout the year, with a maximum in July and a minimum in October. Because of the conditions of terrain and air flow, Charleston experiences 111 fog days per year, more than any other major city in the United States.

Pluses: Changeable climate.

Minuses: Foggy, rainy.

Places Rated Score: 627

Places Rated Rank: 53

Elevation: 951 feet

Relative Humidity: 70%
Wind Speed: 6.5 mph

Seasonal Change

Annual Rainfall 41 in

Annual Snowfall 32 in

Clear 59 days   Partly Cloudy 116 days   Cloudy 190 days

Precipitation Days: 149   Storm Days: 43

Average Temperatures			
	Daily High	Daily Low	Monthly Mean
January	43.6	25.3	34.5
February	46.2	26.8	36.5
March	55.2	33.8	44.5
April	67.9	43.8	55.9
May	76.6	52.3	64.5
June	83.4	60.6	72.0
July	85.6	64.3	75.0
August	84.4	62.8	73.6
September	79.0	55.9	67.5
October	69.1	44.8	57.0
November	55.8	35.0	45.4
December	45.2	27.2	36.2

Zero-Degree Days: 1
Freezing Days: 101
90-Degree Days: 21
Heating- and Cooling-Degree Days: 5,645

Charlotte–Gastonia–Rock Hill, NC–SC

Terrain: Charlotte is located in the southern Piedmont, an area of rolling country between the mountains to the west and the Coastal Plain to the east. The mountains extend from southwest to northeast, being about 80 miles to 90 miles from the city to the west and north. The ocean is approximately 160 miles to the southeast. The mountains have a moderating effect on winter temperatures, causing appreciable warming of cold air coming from the west and northwest. The ocean is too distant to affect summer weather, but it moderates winter weather.

Climate: Moderate, characterized by cool winters and summers that are quite warm. Winter weather is changeable, alternating between mild and cool spells, with occasional cold periods. Extreme cold is rare. Snow is infrequent, occurring, on the average, once a month from December through March. Summers are long and warm, with afternoon temperatures frequently in the 90s. Nights are cooler, with temperatures dropping into the low 70s even in the warmest months.

Pluses: Moderate, mild winters.

Minuses: Long summers.

Places Rated Score: 644

Places Rated Rank: 38

Elevation: 769 feet

Relative Humidity: 69%
Wind Speed: 7.6 mph

Seasonal Change

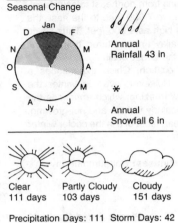

Annual Rainfall 43 in

Annual Snowfall 6 in

Clear 111 days Partly Cloudy 103 days Cloudy 151 days

Precipitation Days: 111   Storm Days: 42

Average Temperatures			
	Daily High	Daily Low	Monthly Mean
January	52.1	32.1	42.1
February	54.9	33.1	44.0
March	62.2	39.0	50.6
April	72.7	48.9	60.8
May	80.2	57.4	68.8
June	86.4	65.3	75.9
July	88.3	68.7	78.5
August	87.4	67.9	77.7
September	82.0	61.9	72.0
October	73.1	50.3	61.7
November	62.4	39.6	51.0
December	52.5	32.4	42.5

Zero-Degree Days: 0
Freezing Days: 71
90-Degree Days: 31
Heating- and Cooling-Degree Days: 4,814

Chattanooga, TN–GA

Terrain: Local topography is complex, with the difference in elevation between minor valleys and ridges being as much as 500 feet. The city is located in the southern portion of the Great Valley of the Tennessee, an area of the Tennessee River between the Cumberland Mountains to the west and the Appalachian Mountains to the east. Most of the city lies south of the river. In winter the Cumberlands have a moderating influence on the local climate, retarding the flow of cold air from the north and west.

Climate: Moderate, characterized by cool winters and summers that are quite warm. Winter weather is changeable and alternates between cool spells and an occasional cold period. Extreme or prolonged cold is rare. Summer temperatures average in the high 80s or low 90s. Most afternoon summer temperatures are modified by brief thundershowers, which cause the mercury to drop 10 degrees to 15 degrees.

Pluses: Mild winters.

Minuses: Can be hot and muggy.

Places Rated Score: 576

Places Rated Rank: 103

Elevation: 665 feet

Relative Humidity: 72%
Wind Speed: 6.2 mph

Seasonal Change

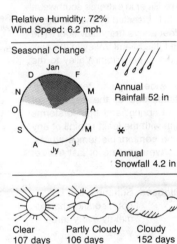

Annual Rainfall 52 in

Annual Snowfall 4.2 in

Clear 107 days Partly Cloudy 106 days Cloudy 152 days

Precipitation Days: 121   Storm Days: 56

Average Temperatures			
	Daily High	Daily Low	Monthly Mean
January	49.9	30.5	40.2
February	53.4	32.3	42.9
March	61.2	38.4	49.8
April	72.9	48.1	60.5
May	81.0	56.0	68.5
June	87.5	64.5	76.0
July	89.5	68.1	78.8
August	89.0	67.0	78.0
September	83.4	60.4	71.9
October	73.5	48.1	60.8
November	60.7	37.1	48.9
December	50.9	31.4	41.2

Zero-Degree Days: 0
Freezing Days: 75
90-Degree Days: 49
Heating- and Cooling-Degree Days: 5,141

Chicago, IL

Terrain: Sprawls along the southwest shore of Lake Michigan on a plain that, for the most part, is only some tens of feet above the lake. Topography does not significantly affect air flow in or near the city, except that lower frictional drag over Lake Michigan permits winds to be frequently stronger along the lakeshore. Terrain is basically flat.

Climate: Predominantly continental, with warm to hot summers and cold winters. The climate of the city proper is modified by the lake, with summer temperatures near the shore often 10 degrees cooler than elsewhere. Summer hot spells—an uncomfortable combination of high temperature and high humidity—may last for several days, then end abruptly with a shift of winds to the north or northwest. They are often accompanied by thunderstorms. The normal heating season lasts from mid-September to early June. The air-conditioning season lasts from mid-June to early September.

Pluses: Changeable; pleasant falls.

Minuses: Hot summers, cold winters, cloudy.

Places Rated Score: 514

Places Rated Rank: 211

Elevation: 623 feet

Relative Humidity: 67%
Wind Speed: 10.4 mph

Seasonal Change

Annual Rainfall 34 in

Annual Snowfall 40 in

Clear 94 days Partly Cloudy 103 days Cloudy 168 days

Precipitation Days: 123   Storm Days: 40

Average Temperatures			
	Daily High	Daily Low	Monthly Mean
January	31.5	17.0	24.3
February	34.6	20.2	27.4
March	44.6	29.0	36.8
April	59.3	40.4	49.9
May	70.3	49.7	60.0
June	80.5	60.3	70.5
July	84.4	65.0	74.7
August	83.3	64.1	73.7
September	75.8	56.0	65.9
October	65.1	45.6	55.4
November	48.1	32.6	40.4
December	35.3	21.6	28.5

Zero-Degree Days: 7
Freezing Days: 119
90-Degree Days: 21
Heating- and Cooling-Degree Days: 7,052

Chico, CA

Terrain: Lies in the northern third of the Sacramento River valley in the foothills of the Sierra Nevada. The city itself is about 6 miles east of the Sacramento River. The lower slopes of the nearby Sierra foothills are cut by well-defined canyons draining from northeast to southwest. To the west the Coast Ranges rise up to 7,000 feet; to the east, the peaks of the Sierra Nevada reach as high as 9,000 feet. Thus Chico and the other towns of the upper valley are sheltered from ocean breezes and the extreme dryness of the Great Basin.

Climate: As a result of its inland location, Chico experiences a considerable range of temperature. However, even in winter the average low temperature is not below freezing, which enhances the region's agricultural productivity, particularly in fruit- and nut-growing. Chico receives 26 inches of rain per year, most of it in the cooler winter months.

Pluses: Mild, sunny, variable.   **Minuses:** Hot summer days.

Places Rated Score: 603   **Places Rated Rank: 72**

Elevation: 230 feet

Relative Humidity: 68%
Wind Speed: 8 mph

Seasonal Change

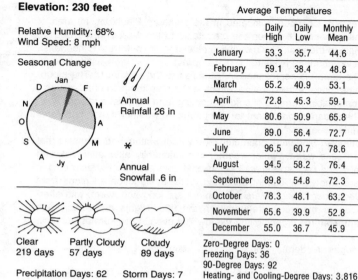

Annual Rainfall 26 in

Annual Snowfall .6 in

Clear 219 days   Partly Cloudy 57 days   Cloudy 89 days

Precipitation Days: 62   Storm Days: 7

Average Temperatures			
	Daily High	Daily Low	Monthly Mean
January	53.3	35.7	44.6
February	59.1	38.4	48.8
March	65.2	40.9	53.1
April	72.8	45.3	59.1
May	80.6	50.9	65.8
June	89.0	56.4	72.7
July	96.5	60.7	78.6
August	94.5	58.2	76.4
September	89.8	54.8	72.3
October	78.3	48.1	63.2
November	65.6	39.9	52.8
December	55.0	36.7	45.9

Zero-Degree Days: 0
Freezing Days: 36
90-Degree Days: 92
Heating- and Cooling-Degree Days: 3,816

Cincinnati, OH–KY–IN

Terrain: Located on the bank of the Ohio River in extreme southwestern Ohio. It extends over two ranges of hills bisected by the Mill Creek Valley, with hills extending some 400 feet above the valley floor. The city incorporates the lower portion of the Little Miami Valley to the east and extends to within 5 or 6 miles of the Great Miami Valley to the west.

Climate: Basically continental, with a wide range in temperature. Subject to frequent changes in weather due to the passage of numerous cyclonic storms in winter and spring, and thunderstorms during the summer. Fall is very pleasant, with the least rainfall of any season, an abundance of sunshine, and comfortable temperatures. Average freeze-free period: 198 days. Average date of last freeze: April 10. First freeze: October 25.

Pluses: Milder version of continental climate.   **Minuses:** Summers can be hot; flooding approximately every three years.

Places Rated Score: 584   **Places Rated Rank: 93**

Elevation: 869 feet

Relative Humidity: 70%
Wind Speed: 7.1 mph

Seasonal Change

Annual Rainfall 40 in

Annual Snowfall 19 in

Clear 80 days   Partly Cloudy 97 days   Cloudy 188 days

Precipitation Days: 131   Storm Days: 50

Average Temperatures			
	Daily High	Daily Low	Monthly Mean
January	39.8	24.3	32.1
February	42.9	25.8	34.4
March	52.2	33.5	42.9
April	65.5	44.6	55.1
May	75.2	53.6	64.4
June	83.6	62.5	73.1
July	86.6	65.8	76.2
August	86.0	64.1	75.1
September	79.8	57.0	68.4
October	68.8	46.7	57.8
November	53.0	36.2	44.6
December	41.8	27.1	34.4

Zero-Degree Days: 2
Freezing Days: 98
90-Degree Days: 28
Heating- and Cooling-Degree Days: 6,032

Cleveland, OH

Terrain: Situated on the south shore of Lake Erie, with a lake frontage of 31 miles. The surrounding terrain is mostly level, except for a ridge of the southeastern edge of the city rising some 500 feet above shore level. A rather deep north-south valley, in which flows the Cuyahoga River, approximately bisects the city. Local topography is of minor importance to the climate.

Climate: In the winter, Cleveland lies in the path of many cold air masses advancing south and east out of Canada, but the low temperatures are somewhat modified by the air having passed over the comparatively warm water of the lake. But this also means considerable winter cloudiness and frequent snows. Spring is generally a brief transition period. Summer heat is moderated somewhat by the lake, since breezes are felt a considerable distance inland. Fall is the most pleasant season, with mild, sunny weather often extending into November or even early December. Average growing season: 195 days.

Pluses: Long, sunny falls.   **Minuses:** Cloudy, snowy.

Places Rated Score: 579   **Places Rated Rank: 101**

Elevation: 805 feet

Relative Humidity: 72%
Wind Speed: 10.8 mph

Seasonal Change

Annual Rainfall 35 in

Annual Snowfall 52 in

Clear 70 days   Partly Cloudy 98 days   Cloudy 197 days

Precipitation Days: 156   Storm Days: 36

Average Temperatures			
	Daily High	Daily Low	Monthly Mean
January	33.4	20.3	26.9
February	35.0	20.8	27.9
March	44.1	28.1	36.1
April	58.0	38.5	48.3
May	68.4	48.1	58.3
June	78.2	57.5	67.9
July	81.6	61.2	71.4
August	80.4	59.6	70.0
September	74.2	53.5	63.9
October	63.6	43.9	53.8
November	48.8	34.4	41.6
December	36.4	24.1	30.3

Zero-Degree Days: 5
Freezing Days: 125
90-Degree Days: 8
Heating- and Cooling-Degree Days: 6,767

Colorado Springs, CO

Terrain: At an elevation of more than 6,000 feet, Colorado Springs is located in relatively flat semiarid country on the eastern slope of the Rocky Mountains. Immediately to the west, the mountains rise abruptly to heights ranging from 10,000 feet to 14,000 feet. To the east lies the gently undulating prairie land of eastern Colorado. The land slopes upward to the north, reaching an average height of 8,000 feet within 20 miles, at the top of Palmer Lake Divide.

Climate: The terrain of the area, particularly its wide range of elevations, helps to give Colorado Springs the pleasant plains-and-mountain mixture of climate that has established it as a desirable place to live. Precipitation is generally light, with 80% of it falling between April 1 and September 30. Heavy downpours accompany summer thunderstorms. Temperatures are on the mild side for a city in this latitude and at this elevation.

Pluses: Dry, sunny, variable. **Minuses:** Long winters.

Places Rated Score: 526   **Places Rated Rank: 191**

Elevation: 6,170 feet

Relative Humidity: 49%
Wind Speed: 10.4 mph

Seasonal Change

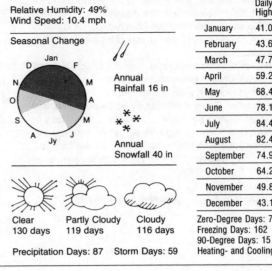

Annual Rainfall 16 in

Annual Snowfall 40 in

Clear 130 days   Partly Cloudy 119 days   Cloudy 116 days

Precipitation Days: 87   Storm Days: 59

Average Temperatures			
	Daily High	Daily Low	Monthly Mean
January	41.0	16.1	28.6
February	43.6	18.9	31.3
March	47.7	22.8	35.3
April	59.2	33.1	46.2
May	68.4	42.6	55.5
June	78.1	51.1	64.6
July	84.4	57.0	70.7
August	82.4	55.8	69.1
September	74.9	46.9	60.9
October	64.2	36.8	50.5
November	49.8	25.1	37.5
December	43.1	18.9	31.0

Zero-Degree Days: 7
Freezing Days: 162
90-Degree Days: 15
Heating- and Cooling-Degree Days: 6,934

Columbia, MO

Terrain: Columbia is located on the broad, gently rolling plains of northern Missouri in the valley of the Missouri River. Its elevation is almost 900 feet, and its location dictates a continental climate.

Climate: With its interior location, Columbia experiences moderately cold winters and warm, often humid summers. Each summer brings some temperatures over 100° F, and winter lows reach zero an average of eight times annually. Yet summer hot spells are relieved by thunderstorms, and winter cold snaps are often interrupted by days that are almost balmy, with temperatures as high as the 50s and 60s. The late spring and early summer months are the rainiest, but by late summer the rain diminishes so that by middle or late August, the moisture in the top two feet of soil is often depleted. The last spring freeze is usually on April 9; first autumn frost is October 24.

Pluses: Variable, sunny. **Minuses:** Tornado-prone.

Places Rated Score: 541   **Places Rated Rank: 168**

Elevation: 887 feet

Relative Humidity: 69%
Wind Speed: 9.8 mph

Seasonal Change

Annual Rainfall 37 in

Annual Snowfall 24 in

Clear 100 days   Partly Cloudy 91 days   Cloudy 174 days

Precipitation Days: 109   Storm Days: 51

Average Temperatures			
	Daily High	Daily Low	Monthly Mean
January	38.0	20.6	29.3
February	42.7	24.5	33.6
March	51.3	32.0	41.7
April	65.3	44.6	55.0
May	74.5	54.3	64.4
June	82.7	63.3	73.0
July	87.4	67.1	77.3
August	86.4	65.5	76.0
September	79.4	57.2	68.3
October	69.2	46.7	58.0
November	53.6	34.2	43.9
December	41.1	24.5	32.8

Zero-Degree Days: 8
Freezing Days: 108
90-Degree Days: 39
Heating- and Cooling-Degree Days: 6,352

Columbia, SC

Terrain: Located on the Congaree River in the center of the state, near the confluence of the Broad and Saluda rivers. The fall line, or division between the Piedmont and the Coastal Plain, is near Columbia. The soil ranges from sand to clay loam. Terrain is rolling, sloping from about 350 feet above sea level in the northern part of the city to about 200 feet at the city's southeastern edge.

Climate: Although the Appalachian chain to the north shields the city from northern cold fronts in the winter, the surrounding gently rolling terrain offers little moderating effect on summer heat. Summers are long and hot, with high temperatures from May to September. Temperatures will surpass 100° F an average of six times a year. Winters are mild: Only about a third of the days have freezing temperatures. Snow accumulation is very rare. Spring is changeable and may bring some violent weather. Fall is cool, pleasant, and very sunny. Some grazing crops are grown year-round. Average growing period: 217 days.

Pluses: Cool, sunny falls. **Minuses:** Long, hot summers.

Places Rated Score: 526   **Places Rated Rank: 191**

Elevation: 225 feet

Relative Humidity: 73%
Wind Speed: 6.9 mph

Seasonal Change

Annual Rainfall 46 in

Annual Snowfall 2 in

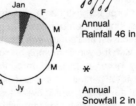

Clear 120 days   Partly Cloudy 103 days   Cloudy 142 days

Precipitation Days: 111   Storm Days: 54

Average Temperatures			
	Daily High	Daily Low	Monthly Mean
January	56.9	33.9	45.4
February	59.7	35.5	47.6
March	66.5	41.9	54.2
April	76.9	51.3	64.1
May	84.5	59.6	72.1
June	90.3	67.2	78.8
July	92.0	70.3	81.2
August	91.0	69.4	80.2
September	85.4	63.5	74.5
October	77.1	51.3	64.2
November	66.9	40.6	53.8
December	57.9	34.1	46.0

Zero-Degree Days: 0
Freezing Days: 60
90-Degree Days: 64
Heating- and Cooling-Degree Days: 4,685

Columbus, GA–AL

Terrain: Located on the Chattahoochee River at the western boundary of Georgia, about 225 miles west of the Atlantic and 170 miles north of the Gulf of Mexico. Elevation ranges from between 200 feet to 500 feet. The terrain is basically level, and effects of terrain on climate are therefore negligible.

Climate: Humid and warm, with pronounced maritime effects at some periods and equally pronounced continental effects at others. Rainfall averages an abundant 51 inches a year; the wettest months are March and July, the driest October. Snow is rare but by no means unknown, with each winter usually bringing at least a few flakes. Most days in June, July, and August will see a high of 90° F or higher, with accompanying high humidity. The unpleasant effects of this heat are perhaps balanced by the mild winters, during which temperatures seldom drop below 20° F.

Pluses: Very mild winters.

Minuses: Hot summers; humid.

Places Rated Score: 517

Places Rated Rank: 206

Elevation: 445 feet

Relative Humidity: 73%
Wind Speed: 6.8 mph

Seasonal Change

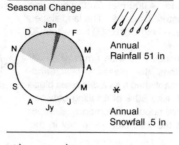

Annual Rainfall 51 in

Annual Snowfall .5 in

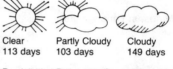

Clear 113 days
Partly Cloudy 103 days
Cloudy 149 days

Precipitation Days: 111   Storm Days: 58

Average Temperatures			
	Daily High	Daily Low	Monthly Mean
January	57.8	35.9	46.9
February	60.9	37.8	49.4
March	67.4	43.3	55.4
April	77.3	51.8	64.4
May	84.7	60.0	72.4
June	89.9	67.5	78.7
July	90.8	70.4	80.6
August	90.8	69.8	80.3
September	85.8	65.1	75.5
October	77.4	53.4	65.4
November	66.8	41.9	54.4
December	59.0	36.3	47.7

Zero-Degree Days: 0
Freezing Days: 46
90-Degree Days: 74
Heating- and Cooling-Degree Days: 4,521

Columbus, OH

Terrain: Situated in the center of the state and in the drainage area of the Ohio River. Four small rivers—the Scioto, Alum, Big Walnut, and Olentangy—flow through and near the city.

Climate: The city is located in an area of changeable weather. Cold air masses from central and northwest Canada frequently invade the region. Tropical Gulf masses often reach central Ohio during the summer but to a much lesser extent in fall and winter. Columbus's four rivers provide variations in the microclimate of the area, contributing to the formation of shallow ground fog at daybreak in the summer and fall.

Pluses: Changeable climate.

Minuses: Cold spells.

Places Rated Score: 558

Places Rated Rank: 134

Elevation: 833 feet

Relative Humidity: 70%
Wind Speed: 8.7 mph

Seasonal Change

Annual Rainfall 37 in

Annual Snowfall 28 in

Clear 75 days
Partly Cloudy 106 days
Cloudy 184 days

Precipitation Days: 136   Storm Days: 42

Average Temperatures			
	Daily High	Daily Low	Monthly Mean
January	36.4	20.4	28.4
February	39.2	21.4	30.3
March	49.3	29.1	39.2
April	62.8	39.5	51.2
May	72.9	49.3	61.1
June	81.9	58.9	70.4
July	84.8	62.4	73.6
August	83.7	60.1	71.9
September	77.6	52.7	65.2
October	66.4	42.0	54.2
November	50.9	32.4	41.7
December	38.7	22.7	30.7

Zero-Degree Days: 4
Freezing Days: 122
90-Degree Days: 15
Heating- and Cooling-Degree Days: 6,511

Corpus Christi, TX

Terrain: Located on Corpus Christi Bay, an inlet in the Gulf of Mexico. It is in the southern part of the Texas Gulf coastline, roughly halfway between Galveston to the north and Brownsville to the south. Padre Island National Seashore adjoins the city. Climate and abundant beaches make the area a major resort center.

Climate: Although located on the Gulf, Corpus Christi has a climate midway between humid subtropical conditions to the northeast along the Gulf Coast and the semiarid ones to the west and southwest. Peak rainfall months are May and September, with the winter months being the driest. Tropical storms, which may occur from June through November, add a large portion to the total rainfall. There is little variation in the summer temperature from day to day, which averages in the high 80s or low 90s. But nights are cooler, even pleasant, with temperatures dropping into the low 70s because of sea breezes.

Pluses: Winter vacation spot.

Minuses: Storms.

Places Rated Score: 362

Places Rated Rank: 310

Elevation: 44 feet

Relative Humidity: 77%
Wind Speed: 12 mph

Seasonal Change

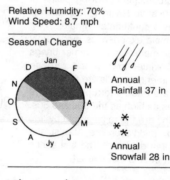

Annual Rainfall 29 in

Annual Snowfall 0 in

Clear 104 days
Partly Cloudy 118 days
Cloudy 143 days

Precipitation Days: 77   Storm Days: 31

Average Temperatures			
	Daily High	Daily Low	Monthly Mean
January	66.5	46.1	56.3
February	69.8	49.3	59.6
March	75.5	54.2	64.9
April	82.1	63.4	72.8
May	86.6	69.1	77.9
June	91.2	73.6	82.4
July	94.4	75.2	84.8
August	94.8	75.4	85.1
September	90.0	72.0	81.0
October	84.1	63.7	73.9
November	75.2	54.6	64.9
December	69.3	48.9	59.1

Zero-Degree Days: 0
Freezing Days: 7
90-Degree Days: 96
Heating- and Cooling-Degree Days: 4,404

Cumberland, MD–WV

Terrain: Cumberland, the seat of Allegany County and Maryland's third largest city, is located in what is called the Ridge and Valley Physiographic Province, with the valleys and ridges running from northeast to southwest. The valleys drain southward into the Potomac Basin and vary from narrow, steep-sided trenches to broad, gently sloping valleys. Most of Cumberland lies on the valley floor, but nearby elevations range from 600 feet to 900 feet. The surrounding terrain is fairly rugged.

Climate: A variable continental-type climate on the mild side. The ridge-and-valley terrain exerts strong influences on local weather, with considerable variation observed over short distances. The annual rainfall of 37 inches is evenly distributed throughout the year. June is usually the wettest month and November the driest. Prevailing winds are from the northwest. There are about 35 thunderstorms a year on the average.

Pluses: Mild and variable.   **Minuses:** Cloudy.

Places Rated Score: 591   **Places Rated Rank: 85**

Elevation: 945 feet

Relative Humidity: 70%
Wind Speed: 8 mph

Seasonal Change

Annual Rainfall 37 in

Annual Snowfall 33 in

Clear 102 days   Partly Cloudy 114 days   Cloudy 149 days

Precipitation Days: 122   Storm Days: 35

Average Temperatures			
	Daily High	Daily Low	Monthly Mean
January	40.8	23.6	32.2
February	43.8	25.3	34.6
March	51.2	30.8	41.0
April	64.8	41.3	53.1
May	75.7	50.0	62.9
June	82.7	57.5	70.1
July	86.5	61.3	73.9
August	84.8	60.3	72.6
September	78.4	53.3	65.9
October	68.6	43.4	56.0
November	53.2	34.3	43.8
December	41.2	25.0	33.1

Zero-Degree Days: 1
Freezing Days: 114
90-Degree Days: 27
Heating- and Cooling-Degree Days: 5,788

Dallas, TX

Terrain: Located in north central Texas, about 250 miles north of the Gulf of Mexico, near the headwaters of the Trinity River. This hilly area marks the upper boundary of the Coastal Plain. Grasses, live oaks, and coniferous trees compose most of the local vegetation.

Climate: Humid, subtropical, with hot summers. It is also continental, characterized by a wide range in annual temperature. Winters tend to be mild, but "northers" occur, bringing cold air masses down from the Great Plains and the Rocky Mountains. These cold snaps are not prolonged, however. Much of the rain falls at night; downpours may accompany thunderstorms during April and May. July and August are relatively dry. Hail falls about two or three times a year. Snowfall is slight and doesn't accumulate. Average freeze-free growing period: 249 days.

Pluses: Wide range of weather.   **Minuses:** Hot summers.

Places Rated Score: 544   **Places Rated Rank: 159**

Elevation: 596 feet

Relative Humidity: 67%
Wind Speed: 11 mph

Seasonal Change

Annual Rainfall 32 in

Annual Snowfall 3 in

Clear 138 days   Partly Cloudy 95 days   Cloudy 132 days

Precipitation Days: 79   Storm Days: 46

Average Temperatures			
	Daily High	Daily Low	Monthly Mean
January	55.7	33.9	44.8
February	59.8	37.6	48.7
March	66.6	43.3	55.0
April	76.3	54.1	65.2
May	82.8	62.1	72.5
June	90.8	70.3	80.6
July	95.5	74.0	84.8
August	96.1	73.7	84.9
September	88.5	66.8	77.7
October	79.2	56.0	67.6
November	67.5	44.1	55.8
December	58.7	37.0	47.9

Zero-Degree Days: 0
Freezing Days: 39
90-Degree Days: 88
Heating- and Cooling-Degree Days: 4,969

Davenport–Rock Island–Moline, IA–IL

Terrain: Located on the banks of the Mississippi River. Topography characterized by rolling agricultural prairie. Close to the river there is considerable truck gardening and dairying. Field production of grains and livestock is greater in rolling prairie, away from the large streams.

Climate: Temperate continental, with a wide temperature range throughout the year. Some intensely hot, usually humid periods in summer and severely cold periods in winter. Proximity to major storm tracks brings substantial weather changes, frequently occurring at three- or four-day intervals. Maxima of 90° F or higher have occurred as frequently as 55 days a year (1936), but in 1882 there were none. Readings of zero or below have been made during every winter, ranging from 37 times in 1874–75 to one time during four other winters.

Pluses: Variable climate with average growing season and even precipitation.

Minuses: Unpredictable climate, long winters, hot summer stretches.

Places Rated Score: 440   **Places Rated Rank: 277**

Elevation: 594 feet

Relative Humidity: 70%
Wind Speed: 9.9 mph

Seasonal Change

Annual Rainfall 36 in

Annual Snowfall 30 in

Clear 101 days   Partly Cloudy 101 days   Cloudy 163 days

Precipitation Days: 112   Storm Days: 47

Average Temperatures			
	Daily High	Daily Low	Monthly Mean
January	30.0	13.0	21.5
February	34.3	17.0	25.7
March	45.0	26.4	35.7
April	61.3	39.8	50.6
May	72.0	50.2	61.1
June	81.4	60.2	70.8
July	85.2	63.8	74.5
August	83.8	62.0	72.9
September	76.0	53.2	64.6
October	66.0	42.8	54.4
November	48.1	30.2	39.2
December	34.6	18.5	26.6

Zero-Degree Days: 16
Freezing Days: 136
90-Degree Days: 22
Heating- and Cooling-Degree Days: 7,288

Denver, CO

Terrain: The Mile-High City rests on the eastern slope of the Rocky Mountains. It is far from any source of moisture and is isolated from the Pacific Ocean by three mountain ranges: the Coastal Ranges, the Sierra Nevada, and the Rockies.

Climate: A mild, sunny, semiarid climate, reaching over much of the central Rocky Mountain region. This tempered climate lacks the extremely cold winter mornings of the high elevations and remote mountain valleys, as well as the hot summer afternoons of lower altitudes. There is little humidity or precipitation, and lots of sunshine. During the cold months, invasion of cold air from the north can be abrupt and severe. Yet many of these air masses from Canada are too low to reach Denver and so are deflected off to the east by the mountains. For this reason, Denver often has milder winters than cities of comparable latitude on the Great Plains. Spring is wet, cloudy, and windy. Summers are cool. Fall is the most pleasant season.

Pluses: Sunny; dry; comparatively mild winters.

Minuses: Cold snaps in winter, stormy springs.

Places Rated Score: 521

Places Rated Rank: 200

Elevation: 5,332 feet

Relative Humidity: 53%
Wind Speed: 9.1 mph

Seasonal Change

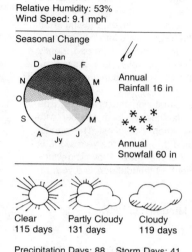

Annual Rainfall 16 in

Annual Snowfall 60 in

Clear 115 days   Partly Cloudy 131 days   Cloudy 119 days

Precipitation Days: 88   Storm Days: 41

Average Temperatures			
	Daily High	Daily Low	Monthly Mean
January	43.5	16.2	29.9
February	46.2	19.4	32.8
March	50.1	23.8	37.0
April	61.0	33.9	47.5
May	70.3	43.6	57.0
June	80.1	51.9	66.0
July	87.4	58.6	73.0
August	85.8	57.4	71.6
September	77.7	47.8	62.8
October	66.8	37.2	52.0
November	53.3	25.4	39.4
December	46.2	18.9	32.6

Zero-Degree Days: 10
Freezing Days: 163
90-Degree Days: 32
Heating- and Cooling-Degree Days: 6,641

Des Moines, IA

Terrain: Located close to the center of Iowa, and roughly in the geographic center of the continental United States. The terrain is flat to gently rolling prairie, ideally suited to agriculture. Most of the soil in Iowa is dark, rich, sandy loam with good drainage. The state has the highest rate of agricultural production per acre in the nation.

Climate: Situated in the center of the country far from any large body of water, Des Moines, not surprisingly, has a continental climate, characterized by rather long, cold winters, hot summers, and short springs and falls. Winter cold is often intensified by the winds that sweep over the flat land.

Pluses: Sunny falls.

Minuses: Climate tending toward rigorous.

Places Rated Score: 444

Places Rated Rank: 274

Elevation: 963 feet

Relative Humidity: 69%
Wind Speed: 11.1 mph

Seasonal Change

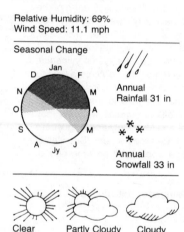

Annual Rainfall 31 in

Annual Snowfall 33 in

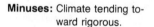

Clear 103 days   Partly Cloudy 96 days   Cloudy 166 days

Precipitation Days: 106   Storm Days: 50

Average Temperatures			
	Daily High	Daily Low	Monthly Mean
January	27.5	11.3	19.4
February	32.5	15.8	24.2
March	42.5	25.2	33.9
April	59.7	39.2	49.5
May	70.9	50.9	60.9
June	79.8	61.1	70.5
July	84.9	65.3	75.1
August	83.2	63.4	73.3
September	74.6	54.0	64.3
October	64.9	43.6	54.3
November	46.4	29.2	37.8
December	32.8	17.2	25.0

Zero-Degree Days: 16
Freezing Days: 137
90-Degree Days: 21
Heating- and Cooling-Degree Days: 7,638

Detroit, MI

Terrain: Detroit is located in the southeastern corner of the state, across the St. Clair River from Windsor, Ontario. Consequently, it is one of the few metro areas that cross international boundaries. Detroit lies on an important waterway that connects Lake Huron to Lake Erie. Nearly flat land slopes up gently from the water's edge northwestward for about 10 miles, then gives way to increasingly rolling terrain. The Irish Hills, about 40 miles northwest, are more than 1,000 feet high.

Climate: The winters, while cold, are modified by the Great Lakes, which warm and moisten the cold Arctic air that passes over the northern Plains. As a result, however, the area is quite cloudy, especially in the winter. Summers in the city are warm and sunny. Brief showers usually occur every few days but often fall on only part of the city. Winter storms may bring rain, snow, or both. Freezing rain and sleet are common. Though cloudy, Detroit's proximity to the Great Lakes helps give it a milder climate than one would expect in a place so far north.

Pluses: Mild for its latitude.

Minuses: Cold winters, cloudy.

Places Rated Score: 536

Places Rated Rank: 176

Elevation: 664 feet

Relative Humidity: 72%
Wind Speed: 10.4 mph

Seasonal Change

Annual Rainfall 32 in

Annual Snowfall 39 in

Clear 75 days   Partly Cloudy 110 days   Cloudy 180 days

Precipitation Days: 133   Storm Days: 33

Average Temperatures			
	Daily High	Daily Low	Monthly Mean
January	31.9	17.3	24.6
February	34.3	18.8	26.6
March	43.8	26.7	35.3
April	58.1	37.3	47.7
May	69.1	47.0	58.1
June	79.4	57.2	68.3
July	83.4	61.1	72.3
August	82.0	59.5	70.8
September	74.8	52.3	63.6
October	64.1	42.1	53.1
November	47.8	32.3	40.1
December	35.4	21.5	28.5

Zero-Degree Days: 7
Freezing Days: 139
90-Degree Days: 11
Heating- and Cooling-Degree Days: 7,073

Duluth, MN–WI

Terrain: Located at Lake Superior's western tip, Duluth lies at the base of a range of hills that rise abruptly to between 600 feet and 800 feet above the lake level. Two or 3 miles back from the waterfront, however, the country assumes the character of a slightly rolling plateau. Directly opposite, on the flats occupying the east banks of St. Louis Bay, lies the city of Superior, Wisconsin. These two cities are referred to as the Twin Ports.

Climate: Rugged continental in character. Winters are long and quite cold. Snow comes early and remains on the ground until springtime. While the airport area receives more than 75 inches of snow a year, the city proper receives only about 55 inches. Summers are seldom hot, due to the northerly latitude and proximity of Lake Superior.

Pluses: Cool summers, rugged four-season climate.

Minuses: Cold.

Places Rated Score: 193   **Places Rated Rank: 326**

Elevation: 1,417 feet

Relative Humidity: 71%
Wind Speed: 11.4 mph

Seasonal Change

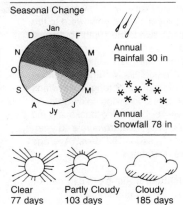

Annual Rainfall 30 in

Annual Snowfall 78 in

Clear 77 days   Partly Cloudy 103 days   Cloudy 185 days

Precipitation Days: 135   Storm Days: 35

Average Temperatures			
	Daily High	Daily Low	Monthly Mean
January	17.6	–.6	8.5
February	22.1	2.0	12.1
March	32.6	14.4	23.5
April	47.8	29.3	38.6
May	60.0	38.8	49.4
June	69.7	48.3	59.0
July	76.4	54.7	65.6
August	74.4	53.7	64.1
September	64.0	44.8	54.4
October	54.3	36.2	45.3
November	35.3	21.4	28.4
December	22.5	6.3	14.4

Zero-Degree Days: 51
Freezing Days: 187
90-Degree Days: 2
Heating- and Cooling-Degree Days: 9,932

El Paso, TX

Terrain: Located at the extreme western tip of Texas at an elevation of 3,700 feet. Across the Rio Grande to the south lies Ciudad Juárez, Mexico. The Franklin Mountains begin within the city limits and extend northward for about 16 miles. Some of these peaks reach as high as 4,500 feet to 5,000 feet above sea level. The general terrain is composed of mountains and mesas characteristic of western Texas and New Mexico.

Climate: Dry and sunny. Summer temperatures are high but not extreme. The very low relative humidity (39%) lessens the felt heat. The winter is mild, typical of arid areas at low altitudes. Rainfall is scarce year-round and fosters only scrublike desert vegetation. Irrigation is necessary for crops, gardens, and lawns. Winter nights can be cold, but the days are warm, averaging in the 50s. Similarly, summer days are hot but the nights cool, averaging in the 60s.

Pluses: Mild winters, low humidity.

Minuses: Dust storms and sandstorms.

Places Rated Score: 592   **Places Rated Rank: 83**

Elevation: 3,700 feet

Relative Humidity: 39%
Wind Speed: 9.6 mph

Seasonal Change

Annual Rainfall 8 in

Annual Snowfall 5 in

Clear 194 days   Partly Cloudy 100 days   Cloudy 71 days

Precipitation Days: 45   Storm Days: 36

Average Temperatures			
	Daily High	Daily Low	Monthly Mean
January	57.0	30.2	43.6
February	62.5	34.3	48.4
March	68.9	40.3	54.6
April	78.5	49.3	63.9
May	87.2	57.2	72.2
June	94.9	65.7	80.3
July	94.6	69.9	82.3
August	92.8	68.2	80.5
September	87.4	61.0	74.2
October	78.5	49.5	64.0
November	66.1	37.0	51.6
December	57.8	30.9	44.4

Zero-Degree Days: 0
Freezing Days: 64
90-Degree Days: 103
Heating- and Cooling-Degree Days: 4,776

★ Eugene–Springfield, OR

Terrain: Situated at the southern end of the fertile Willamette Valley. This valley is bounded on both sides by mountain ranges: the Cascades to the east and the Coast Ranges to the west. To the north, the valley widens and levels out. Hills of the rolling, wooded Coast Ranges begin about 5 miles west of the airport and rise to between 1,500 feet and 2,000 feet midway between the city and the Pacific, 50 miles to the west. The Cascades, 75 miles east, reach heights of 10,000 feet. These sheltering ranges and the proximity of the ocean contribute heavily to Eugene's extremely mild climate. This is one of the nation's most important agricultural and lumbering areas.

Climate: Very mild maritime climate. Temperature minima below 20° F occur only five times a year. The temperature rarely reaches the mid-90s. Seasonal change is gradual, with intermediate seasons being as long as summer and winter.

Pluses: Mild; gradual change of seasons.

Minuses: Cloudy, damp.

Places Rated Score: 741   **Places Rated Rank: 18**

Elevation: 373 feet

Relative Humidity: 77%
Wind Speed: 7.6 mph

Seasonal Change

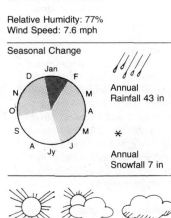

Annual Rainfall 43 in

Annual Snowfall 7 in

Clear 77 days   Partly Cloudy 81 days   Cloudy 207 days

Precipitation Days: 137   Storm Days: 5

Average Temperatures			
	Daily High	Daily Low	Monthly Mean
January	45.6	33.1	39.4
February	51.7	35.2	43.5
March	55.2	36.5	45.9
April	61.2	39.4	50.3
May	67.8	43.7	55.8
June	74.1	48.7	61.4
July	82.6	51.1	66.9
August	81.3	50.9	66.1
September	76.5	47.4	62.0
October	64.0	42.3	53.2
November	53.1	38.1	45.6
December	47.4	35.6	41.5

Zero-Degree Days: 0
Freezing Days: 54
90-Degree Days: 15
Heating- and Cooling-Degree Days: 4,739

Evansville, IN–KY

Terrain: Located on the Ohio River near the juncture of Indiana, Illinois, and Kentucky. The country around Evansville ranges from level to rolling. Dress Regional Airport, where weather observations have been made since 1940, is in a shallow valley with low hills to the east and west that run parallel to the valley but slope downward to the south. The open end of this valley slopes down to the south-southwest toward Evansville and the Ohio River.

Climate: Prevailing wind here is from the south, and, although Evansville is 550 miles from the Gulf of Mexico, its weather generally resembles that of its neighbors to the south. Strong cold winds sometimes blow from the north and northwest following cold fronts. As soon as the high-pressure ridge moves by, the wind backs around again from the south. Snowfall varies a great deal from year to year; accumulation is rare. Average growing season: 199 days. Average date of last freeze: April 7. First freeze: October 23.

Pluses: Influenced by Gulf winds.

Minuses: Summers can be hot and humid.

Places Rated Score: 550

Places Rated Rank: 146

Elevation: 388 feet

Relative Humidity: 70%
Wind Speed: 8.3 mph

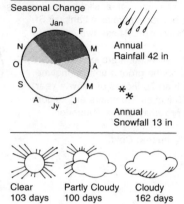

Annual Rainfall 42 in

Annual Snowfall 13 in

Clear 103 days   Partly Cloudy 100 days   Cloudy 162 days

Precipitation Days: 114   Storm Days: 45

Average Temperatures			
	Daily High	Daily Low	Monthly Mean
January	41.5	23.7	32.6
February	45.4	26.4	35.9
March	54.6	34.0	44.3
April	67.9	45.5	56.7
May	77.0	54.4	65.7
June	86.0	63.4	74.7
July	88.9	66.7	77.8
August	88.0	64.4	76.2
September	81.4	56.7	69.1
October	71.2	45.2	58.2
November	55.2	34.5	44.9
December	44.0	26.5	35.3

Zero-Degree Days: 3
Freezing Days: 103
90-Degree Days: 39
Heating- and Cooling-Degree Days: 5,993

Fargo–Moorhead, ND–MN

Terrain: Moorhead, Minnesota, and Fargo, North Dakota, are twin cities in the Red River valley of the north. This river flows between the two cities and is part of the Hudson Bay drainage area. The river has no effect on the climate but does cause occasional severe spring flooding. Surrounding terrain is flat and open.

Climate: Summers are generally comfortable, with a few days of hot and humid weather; nights are cool. Winter months are cold and dry, with maximum temperatures rising above freezing only six times per month. At night, the temperature drops below zero half the time. With the flat terrain, surface friction has little slowing effect on the wind, contributing to the legendary Dakota blizzards. Strong winds with even light snowfall cause heavy snowdrifts. Surprisingly, the area averages only 35 inches of snow per year.

Pluses: Pleasant, dry summers.

Minuses: Extremely rigorous; ranks next to last in mildness of the 329 metro areas.

Places Rated Score: 148

Places Rated Rank: 328

Elevation: 899 feet

Relative Humidity: 71%
Wind Speed: 12.7 mph

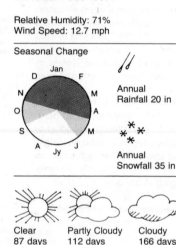

Annual Rainfall 20 in

Annual Snowfall 35 in

Clear 87 days   Partly Cloudy 112 days   Cloudy 166 days

Precipitation Days: 102   Storm Days: 33

Average Temperatures			
	Daily High	Daily Low	Monthly Mean
January	15.4	–3.6	5.9
February	20.6	.8	10.7
March	33.5	14.9	24.2
April	52.6	31.9	42.3
May	66.8	42.3	54.6
June	75.9	53.4	64.7
July	82.8	58.6	70.7
August	81.6	56.8	69.2
September	69.6	46.2	57.9
October	58.4	35.5	47.0
November	37.2	20.0	28.6
December	21.9	4.1	13.0

Zero-Degree Days: 54
Freezing Days: 181
90-Degree Days: 15
Heating- and Cooling-Degree Days: 9,744

Fort Myers, FL

Terrain: Located on the south bank of the Caloosahatchee River, about 15 miles from the Gulf of Mexico, Fort Myers sits on land that is level and low, with lush greenery.

Climate: Subtropical, with temperature extremes of both summer and winter checked by the influence of the Gulf. The average annual mean temperature is a warm 74° F, with averages ranging from the low 60s in January to the low 80s in the summer months. Winters are mild, with many bright, warm days and moderately cool nights. Maximum temperatures average in the low 90s from June through the first part of September, with daily highs of 90° F or greater on 80% of the days. Rainfall averages more than 50 inches annually, with two thirds of this total coming between June and September. Most rain falls as late afternoon or early evening thunderstorms, which in the summer bring welcome relief from the heat and occur almost every day.

Pluses: Mild, sunny winters.

Minuses: Hot, humid, stormy.

Places Rated Score: 342

Places Rated Rank: 313

Elevation: 15 feet

Relative Humidity: 76%
Wind Speed: 8.2 mph

Annual Rainfall 54 in

Annual Snowfall 0 in

Clear 103 days   Partly Cloudy 161 days   Cloudy 101 days

Precipitation Days: 112   Storm Days: 93

Average Temperatures			
	Daily High	Daily Low	Monthly Mean
January	74.7	52.3	63.5
February	76.0	53.3	64.7
March	79.7	57.3	68.5
April	84.8	61.8	73.3
May	89.0	66.4	77.7
June	90.5	71.7	81.1
July	91.1	73.8	82.5
August	91.5	74.1	82.8
September	89.8	73.4	81.6
October	85.3	67.5	76.4
November	79.9	58.8	69.4
December	75.9	53.6	64.8

Zero-Degree Days: 0
Freezing Days: 1
90-Degree Days: 106
Heating- and Cooling-Degree Days: 4,168

Fort Smith, AR–OK

Terrain: Located at the confluence of the Poteau and Arkansas rivers. About 20 miles to the northwest are the Cookson Hills, which have an elevation of 1,500 feet. To the northeast are the Boston Mountains (in the Ozark region of Arkansas), 2,700 feet high. To the west, south, and east, the terrain is broken hills separated by creek- and river-bottom land. The bottomlands are very fertile and produce large yields of hay, beans, and spinach. Small wild game is plentiful; lakes and streams have an abundance of game fish.

Climate: Well suited to raising fruits and berries. The climate is generally mild, except during the summer, which can be hot.

Pluses: Mild.

Minuses: Hot summers.

Places Rated Score: 482

Places Rated Rank: 244

Elevation: 463 feet

Relative Humidity: 68%
Wind Speed: 7.6 mph

Seasonal Change

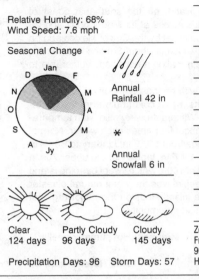

Annual Rainfall 42 in

Annual Snowfall 6 in

Clear 124 days

Partly Cloudy 96 days

Cloudy 145 days

Precipitation Days: 96   Storm Days: 57

Average Temperatures			
	Daily High	Daily Low	Monthly Mean
January	49.9	28.0	39.0
February	54.6	32.0	43.3
March	62.1	38.5	50.3
April	74.2	50.2	62.2
May	81.3	58.8	70.1
June	89.0	67.0	78.0
July	93.8	70.5	82.2
August	93.5	69.3	81.4
September	86.3	61.7	74.0
October	76.5	49.9	63.2
November	62.7	38.0	50.4
December	52.2	30.8	41.5

Zero-Degree Days: 0
Freezing Days: 80
90-Degree Days: 65
Heating- and Cooling-Degree Days: 5,358

Fort Wayne, IN

Terrain: Located at the junction of the St. Mary's, St. Joseph, and Maumee rivers in northeastern Indiana. Terrain is generally level south and east of the city. Southwest and west, the land is somewhat rolling, while to the northwest and north it becomes slightly hilly. The highest point in the area is 40 miles north, near the town of Angola, where the elevation is 1,060 feet above sea level.

Climate: Similar to that of other midwestern cities at the same latitude. Precipitation is well distributed throughout the year, varying from a monthly rate of 2 inches in February to 4 inches in May. Damaging hailstorms may be expected twice a year. Snow usually covers the ground for 30 days each winter, but heavy snowstorms are rare. Average date of last freeze: April 26. First freeze: October 17.

Pluses: Milder version of Great Interior climate.

Minuses: Cold winters, hot summers.

Places Rated Score: 509

Places Rated Rank: 217

Elevation: 828 feet

Relative Humidity: 72%
Wind Speed: 10.3 mph

Seasonal Change

Annual Rainfall 36 in

Annual Snowfall 31 in

Clear 77 days

Partly Cloudy 105 days

Cloudy 183 days

Precipitation Days: 131 Storm Days: 41

Average Temperatures			
	Daily High	Daily Low	Monthly Mean
January	32.6	17.9	25.3
February	35.5	19.7	27.6
March	45.1	27.9	36.5
April	59.5	39.0	49.3
May	70.2	48.9	59.6
June	80.1	58.8	69.5
July	83.6	62.4	73.0
August	82.2	60.4	71.3
September	75.9	53.0	64.5
October	64.6	42.5	53.6
November	48.3	32.0	40.2
December	35.7	21.4	28.6

Zero-Degree Days: 10
Freezing Days: 134
90-Degree Days: 14
Heating- and Cooling-Degree Days: 6,957

Fresno, CA

Terrain: Rests in the middle of the San Joaquin Valley, near its eastern edge. The valley runs northwest to southeast and is about 225 miles long, with an average width of about 50 miles. The terrain around Fresno is generally level, with an abrupt upward slope 15 miles eastward to the foothills of the Sierra Nevada. This mountain range lies 50 miles to the east and has elevations from 12,000 feet to 14,000 feet. Forty-five miles to the west lie the foothills of the Coast Ranges.

Climate: Dry and sunny. Winters are mild, summers are hot. Ninety percent of the city's precipitation falls between November and April. Summers are virtually rainless. Because of the great amount of sunshine the valley receives, and the blockage of cooler moist air from the Pacific, daily maximum temperatures in July climb to the upper 90s. But on summer afternoons, the relative humidity is only 5% to 8%; on winter mornings, it is 90%.

Pluses: Sunny; nice springs and falls.

Minuses: Hot summers.

Places Rated Score: 559

Places Rated Rank: 129

Elevation: 327 feet

Relative Humidity: 61%
Wind Speed: 6.3 mph

Seasonal Change

Annual Rainfall 10 in

Annual Snowfall 0 in

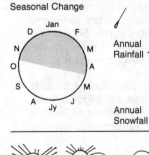

Clear 200 days

Partly Cloudy 71 days

Cloudy 94 days

Precipitation Days: 44   Storm Days: 6

Average Temperatures			
	Daily High	Daily Low	Monthly Mean
January	54.8	35.8	45.3
February	60.8	39.0	49.9
March	66.6	41.2	53.9
April	74.3	46.2	60.3
May	82.9	51.9	67.4
June	90.3	57.5	73.9
July	98.2	62.9	80.6
August	96.0	60.6	78.3
September	91.0	56.5	73.8
October	79.8	48.6	64.2
November	66.1	40.8	53.5
December	54.6	36.9	45.8

Zero-Degree Days: 0
Freezing Days: 29
90-Degree Days: 107
Heating- and Cooling-Degree Days: 4,321

★ Galveston–Texas City, TX

Terrain: Located on Galveston Island, off the southeast coast of Texas. The island is nearly 3 miles across at its widest point and 29 miles long. It is bounded on the southeast by the Gulf of Mexico and on the northwest by Galveston Bay, which is about 3 miles wide at this point. The island's low-lying terrain makes it especially vulnerable to tidal surges.

Climate: Predominantly marine, with periods of modified continental influence during the colder months, when cold fronts from the Northwest sometimes reach the coast. Winters are very mild, with temperatures below 34° F recorded only about four times each winter. Normal daily maximum temperatures range from 60° F in January to 88° F in August, while minima range from 48° F in January to the upper 70s in the summer. The Great Hurricane of 1900, which swept over the island and killed approximately 6,000 people, was the worst natural disaster in American history. It also made inland Houston the major regional city, relegating Galveston to a resort community.

Pluses: Mild maritime climate.   **Minuses:** Hot summer spells.

Places Rated Score: 727   **Places Rated Rank: 20**

Elevation: 7 feet

Relative Humidity: 78%
Wind Speed: 11 mph

Seasonal Change

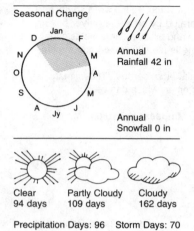

Annual
Rainfall 42 in

Annual
Snowfall 0 in

Clear
94 days

Partly Cloudy
109 days

Cloudy
162 days

Precipitation Days: 96   Storm Days: 70

Average Temperatures			
	Daily High	Daily Low	Monthly Mean
January	59.4	48.3	53.9
February	61.5	50.9	56.2
March	66.0	55.9	61.0
April	73.3	65.0	69.2
May	80.0	71.8	75.9
June	85.2	77.4	81.3
July	87.4	79.0	83.2
August	87.6	78.9	83.3
September	84.6	75.3	80.0
October	78.0	68.1	73.1
November	68.8	58.2	63.5
December	62.7	51.5	57.1

Zero-Degree Days: 0
Freezing Days: 4
90-Degree Days: 11
Heating- and Cooling-Degree Days: 4,228

Grand Rapids, MI

Terrain: Located in the Grand River valley 30 miles east of Lake Michigan. The Grand River, Michigan's largest stream, bisects the city. The valley has tall hills and bluffs rising on all sides, ranging in elevation from 600 feet to 1,000 feet. The area is known for fruit growing, especially peaches and cherries.

Climate: Largely determined by the proximity of Lake Michigan. In spring, the cooling effect of the lake retards the growth of vegetation until the danger of frost is past. In the fall, the warming effect holds off frost until the crops have matured. Summer days are warm and pleasant, with cooler nights. Winters are snowy and cold, but extremely cold temperatures or prolonged cold spells are rare because of the warm lake breeze. Average growing season: 170 days. Average date of last freeze: April 25. First freeze: October 12.

Pluses: Pleasant summers, temperatures moderated by Lake Michigan.   **Minuses:** Very cloudy, lots of snow.

Places Rated Score: 513   **Places Rated Rank: 214**

Elevation: 803 feet

Relative Humidity: 73%
Wind Speed: 9.9 mph

Seasonal Change

Annual
Rainfall 32 in

Annual
Snowfall 77 in

Clear
67 days

Partly Cloudy
96 days

Cloudy
202 days

Precipitation Days: 144   Storm Days: 37

Average Temperatures			
	Daily High	Daily Low	Monthly Mean
January	30.3	16.0	23.2
February	32.6	16.4	24.5
March	42.0	24.2	33.1
April	57.3	35.6	46.5
May	68.8	45.4	57.1
June	79.1	55.6	67.4
July	83.3	59.6	71.5
August	81.9	58.1	70.0
September	73.9	50.8	62.4
October	63.1	40.8	52.0
November	46.2	31.1	38.7
December	33.9	20.8	27.4

Zero-Degree Days: 8
Freezing Days: 149
90-Degree Days: 11
Heating- and Cooling-Degree Days: 7,376

Great Falls, MT

Terrain: Located astride the main stem of the Missouri River at its confluence with the Sun River. Except to the north and northeast, the valley is bordered by mountain ranges, which lie about 30 miles away from east to south, 40 miles to the southwest, and 60 miles to 100 miles from west to northwest. Terrain plays an important part in the climate here: The Continental Divide to the west and the Big Belt and Little Belt mountains to the south are major factors in producing the frequent wintertime Chinook winds blowing through this part of the state.

Climate: Semiarid. Summers are cool, sunny, and pleasant. Seventy percent of the annual rainfall occurs between April and September, the growing season. Winters are cold but continually modified by Chinook winds, which bear warm air from the Pacific, causing rapid warming and preventing accumulation of snow.

Pluses: Good, rigorous climate.   **Minuses:** Long winters.

Places Rated Score: 410   **Places Rated Rank: 295**

Elevation: 702 feet

Relative Humidity: 55%
Wind Speed: 13.1 mph

Seasonal Change

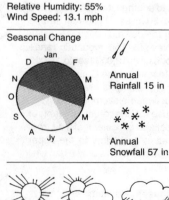

Annual
Rainfall 15 in

Annual
Snowfall 57 in

Clear
81 days

Partly Cloudy
106 days

Cloudy
178 days

Precipitation Days: 100   Storm Days: 26

Average Temperatures			
	Daily High	Daily Low	Monthly Mean
January	29.3	11.6	20.5
February	35.9	17.2	26.6
March	40.4	20.6	30.5
April	54.5	32.3	43.4
May	65.0	41.5	53.3
June	72.1	49.5	60.8
July	83.7	54.9	69.3
August	81.8	53.0	67.4
September	70.0	44.6	57.3
October	59.4	37.1	48.3
November	43.4	25.7	34.6
December	34.7	18.2	36.5

Zero-Degree Days: 28
Freezing Days: 156
90-Degree Days: 22
Heating- and Cooling-Degree Days: 7,991

Green Bay, WI

Terrain: Located at the mouth of the Fox River, which empties into the southernmost end of Green Bay, a long and narrow bay off Lake Michigan in northeastern Wisconsin. The comparatively small temperature variation and the fact that the majority of precipitation falls during the growing periods contribute to successful dairy farming, as well as large acreages of vegetables, grown mostly for canning. Apple and cherry orchards predominate locally, with potatoes grown widely farther west.

Climate: Continental, modified somewhat by the proximity of Lake Superior to the northwest and Lake Michigan and Green Bay to the east. Summers are pleasant, with cool evenings and nights. Winters tend to be long and cold. Has a moderate amount of snow for a city in this region and latitude.

Pluses: Cool summers.   **Minuses:** Long winters.

Places Rated Score: 367   **Places Rated Rank: 308**

Elevation: 702 feet

Relative Humidity: 73%
Wind Speed: 10.2 mph

Seasonal Change

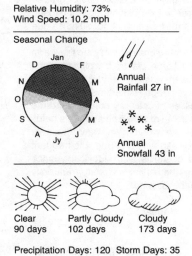

Annual
Rainfall 27 in

Annual
Snowfall 43 in

Clear 90 days   Partly Cloudy 102 days   Cloudy 173 days

Precipitation Days: 120   Storm Days: 35

Average Temperatures			
	Daily High	Daily Low	Monthly Mean
January	23.9	6.9	15.4
February	27.2	8.8	18.0
March	37.1	20.1	28.6
April	54.1	33.5	43.8
May	65.8	43.1	54.5
June	75.8	53.2	64.5
July	80.7	57.7	69.2
August	79.1	56.3	67.7
September	69.8	48.0	58.9
October	59.6	38.7	49.2
November	41.8	26.4	34.1
December	28.6	13.2	20.9

Zero-Degree Days: 29
Freezing Days: 163
90-Degree Days: 7
Heating- and Cooling-Degree Days: 8,484

Greenville–Spartanburg, SC

Terrain: Located on the Piedmont Plateau, on the eastern slope of the southern Appalachian Mountains. It is rolling country with the first ridge of mountains about 20 miles to the northwest. These mountains usually protect the area from the full force of the cold air masses that move southeastward from central Canada during the winter.

Climate: The area's elevation is conducive to cool nights, even during the summer months. The temperature rises to 90° F or above on almost half of the days during the summer but usually falls to 70° F or lower at night. Winters are mild and pleasant, with the temperature falling below freezing during daylight hours only several times annually, though the nights are colder. There are usually two freezing rainstorms and two or three small snowstorms each winter. Rainfall is abundant and well distributed throughout the year. The region is fairly stormy, but tornadoes are infrequent. Average growing season: 225 days.

Pluses: Mildness coupled with variety.   **Minuses:** Hot summers.

Places Rated Score: 655   **Places Rated Rank: 32**

Elevation: 971 feet

Relative Humidity: 70%
Wind Speed: 6.8 mph

Seasonal Change

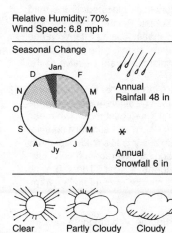

Annual
Rainfall 48 in

Annual
Snowfall 6 in

Clear 117 days   Partly Cloudy 104 days   Cloudy 144 days

Precipitation Days: 119   Storm Days: 44

Average Temperatures			
	Daily High	Daily Low	Monthly Mean
January	51.6	33.0	42.3
February	54.1	34.7	44.4
March	61.6	40.2	50.9
April	72.0	49.9	61.0
May	79.9	58.3	69.1
June	85.9	65.9	75.9
July	87.6	69.0	78.3
August	86.8	68.1	77.5
September	81.0	62.3	71.7
October	72.4	50.9	61.7
November	61.8	40.1	51.0
December	52.4	33.3	42.9

Zero-Degree Days: 0
Freezing Days: 68
90-Degree Days: 29
Heating- and Cooling-Degree Days: 4,736

Harrisburg–Lebanon–Carlisle, PA

Terrain: Situated on the east bank of the Susquehanna River in the Great Valley formed by the eastern foothills of the Appalachian chain and about 60 miles southeast of the state's geographic center. It is nestled in a saucerlike depression 8 miles to 10 miles south of the Blue Mountains. This serves as a barrier to severe winter weather experienced 50 miles to 100 miles to the north and west. Although Harrisburg is too far inland (150 miles) to derive full benefits of the coastal climate, it does receive precipitation produced when warm, maritime air from the Atlantic is forced upslope to cross the Blue Ridge Mountains.

Climate: Although the saucer-shaped valley protects the area from generally severe winter weather, it often traps cool air, which causes the accumulation of heavy fog and industrial smoke. Fortunately, the weather is changeable enough so that this trapped air does not remain for long. Average growing season: 201 days.

Pluses: Relatively mild winters, changeable weather.   **Minuses:** Damp, foggy.

Places Rated Score: 556   **Places Rated Rank: 140**

Elevation: 351 feet

Relative Humidity: 67%
Wind Speed: 7.7 mph

Seasonal Change

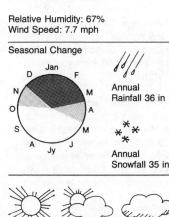

Annual
Rainfall 36 in

Annual
Snowfall 35 in

Clear 86 days   Partly Cloudy 107 days   Cloudy 172 days

Precipitation Days: 125   Storm Days: 33

Average Temperatures			
	Daily High	Daily Low	Monthly Mean
January	37.7	22.5	30.1
February	40.5	24.0	32.3
March	50.7	31.2	41.0
April	64.1	41.5	52.8
May	74.5	51.6	63.1
June	83.0	61.0	72.0
July	86.8	65.4	76.1
August	84.6	63.2	73.9
September	78.0	56.0	67.0
October	66.9	44.6	55.8
November	52.9	34.7	43.8
December	40.1	25.0	32.6

Zero-Degree Days: 1
Freezing Days: 107
90-Degree Days: 24
Heating- and Cooling-Degree Days: 6,249

Hartford, CT

Terrain: Located on the Connecticut River on a slight rise of ground between north-south mountain ranges whose heights do not exceed 1,200 feet. It is near the state's geographic center, about 30 miles due north of Long Island Sound.

Climate: Varies from the cold continental climate in winter to the warm maritime air of summer. Hartford's latitude places it well within the northern temperate climate zone, with westerly winds bearing the majority of weather systems. The average wintertime polar front, which is the boundary between masses of cold, dry polar air and the warm, moist air of the tropics, is just south of New England. This helps explain the great changeability of the weather in New England, characterized by rapidly shifting winds and temperatures, and frequent storms. Hartford's proximity to the ocean is also significant, since many storms move upward along the Atlantic Coast, frequently producing strong and persistent northeast winds.

Pluses: Changeable, varied, yet relatively mild.

Minuses: Stormy.

Places Rated Score: 516

Places Rated Rank: 207

Elevation: 179 feet

Relative Humidity: 68%
Wind Speed: 9 mph

Seasonal Change

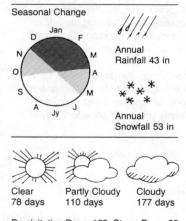

Annual Rainfall 43 in

Annual Snowfall 53 in

Clear 78 days
Partly Cloudy 110 days
Cloudy 177 days

Precipitation Days: 128   Storm Days: 22

Average Temperatures			
	Daily High	Daily Low	Monthly Mean
January	33.4	16.1	24.8
February	35.7	17.9	26.8
March	44.6	26.6	35.6
April	58.9	36.5	47.7
May	70.3	46.2	58.3
June	79.5	56.0	67.8
July	84.1	61.2	72.7
August	81.9	58.9	70.4
September	74.5	51.0	62.8
October	64.3	40.8	52.6
November	50.6	31.9	41.3
December	36.8	19.6	28.2

Zero-Degree Days: 6
Freezing Days: 36
90-Degree Days: 20
Heating- and Cooling-Degree Days: 6,934

★ Honolulu, HI

Terrain: Oahu, the island on which Honolulu is located, is the third largest of the Hawaiian Islands. The Koolau Range, at an average height of 2,000 feet, parallels the northeast coast. The Waianae Mountains, somewhat higher in elevation, parallel the west coast. Much of the city lies along the coastal plain, leeward (relative to the trade winds) of the Koolaus.

Climate: Mild marine tropical. Honolulu shows the least seasonal temperature change of any American city: The difference between the mean January minimum temperature and the August maximum mean temperature is only about 22 degrees. Honolulu's location just south of the Tropic of Cancer in the Pacific Ocean assures this mildness. It has no snow, fog, or freezing weather, and an average of only nine 90-degree days and seven thunderstorms a year. There are no heating-degree days here. Although it can be uncomfortably warm occasionally, the persistent trade winds give relief.

Pluses: Extremely mild.

Minuses: A bit monotonous.

Places Rated Score: 717

Places Rated Rank: 22

Elevation: 15 feet

Relative Humidity: 67%
Wind Speed: 11.8 mph

Seasonal Change

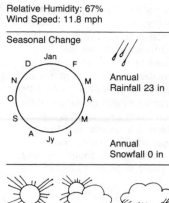

Annual Rainfall 23 in

Annual Snowfall 0 in

Clear 90 days
Partly Cloudy 174 days
Cloudy 101 days

Precipitation Days: 102   Storm Days: 7

Average Temperatures			
	Daily High	Daily Low	Monthly Mean
January	79.3	65.3	72.3
February	79.2	65.3	72.3
March	79.7	66.3	73.0
April	81.4	68.1	74.8
May	83.6	70.2	76.9
June	85.6	72.2	78.9
July	86.8	73.4	80.1
August	87.4	74.0	80.7
September	87.4	73.4	80.4
October	85.8	72.0	78.9
November	83.2	69.8	76.5
December	80.3	67.1	73.7

Zero-Degree Days: 0
Freezing Days: 0
90-Degree Days: 9
Heating- and Cooling-Degree Days: 4,221

Houston, TX

Terrain: Located in the flat Coastal Plain of the state, about 50 miles inland from the Gulf of Mexico and 25 miles from Galveston Bay. The surrounding numerous small streams and bayous, together with the bay, favor the development of both ground and advective fogs. The land is low and flat and, since it receives almost 50 inches of rain a year, is ideal for agriculture—especially fruit farming—and livestock raising.

Climate: Predominantly marine. Temperatures are modified by winds from the Gulf. Winters are mild. Summer days are hot and humid, though the evenings are relatively cool. Polar air penetrates the area frequently enough to provide some stimulating variety. Although temperatures dip below freezing occasionally, they never remain there long, accounting for a year-round growing season. Destructive windstorms are fairly infrequent, but thunderstorms and hurricanes occur occasionally.

Pluses: Mild winters.

Minuses: Hot and humid.

Places Rated Score: 424

Places Rated Rank: 288

Elevation: 108 feet

Relative Humidity: 77%
Wind Speed: 6.1 mph

Seasonal Change

Annual Rainfall 48 in

Annual Snowfall 0 in

Clear 94 days
Partly Cloudy 109 days
Cloudy 162 days

Precipitation Days: 107   Storm Days: 69

Average Temperatures			
	Daily High	Daily Low	Monthly Mean
January	62.6	41.5	52.1
February	66.0	44.6	55.3
March	71.8	49.8	60.8
April	79.4	59.3	69.4
May	85.9	65.6	75.8
June	91.3	70.9	81.1
July	93.8	72.8	83.3
August	94.3	72.4	83.4
September	90.1	68.2	79.2
October	83.5	58.3	70.9
November	73.0	49.1	61.1
December	65.8	43.4	54.6

Zero-Degree Days: 0
Freezing Days: 24
90-Degree Days: 81
Heating- and Cooling-Degree Days: 4,323

Huntsville, AL

Terrain: The city is almost surrounded by the foothills of the Appalachian Mountains. The Tennessee River winds its way westward about 7 miles south of the city, and the broad and fertile Tennessee Valley, with flat to gently rolling terrain, extends to the west.

Climate: Cold air masses from the north predominate during the winter, but at times mild air from the Gulf of Mexico, spreading northward to Huntsville and beyond, may persist for several days. There are very few severely cold days. Temperatures drop below zero on an average of once a year. Springs are variable and can be stormy as cold polar air and warm Gulf air meet. Summers are hot and humid, relieved only by the showers that come about every three days. Falls are dry, cooler, and pleasant. The length of the growing season, 241 days, and high rainfall make the area suitable for truck farming.

Pluses: Mild yet variable winter through spring.

Minuses: Hot, humid summers.

Places Rated Score: 600   **Places Rated Rank: 79**

Elevation: 644 feet

Relative Humidity: 73%
Wind Speed: 8 mph

Seasonal Change

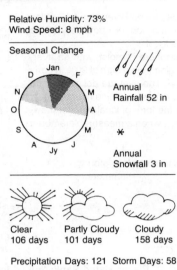

Annual Rainfall 52 in

Annual Snowfall 3 in

Clear 106 days   Partly Cloudy 101 days   Cloudy 158 days

Precipitation Days: 121   Storm Days: 58

Average Temperatures			
	Daily High	Daily Low	Monthly Mean
January	50.5	31.3	40.9
February	54.0	33.2	43.6
March	61.7	39.8	50.8
April	73.1	50.2	61.7
May	80.9	58.3	69.6
June	87.9	65.9	76.9
July	90.2	68.8	79.5
August	90.2	67.7	79.0
September	84.2	61.6	72.9
October	74.5	49.8	62.2
November	61.6	38.9	50.3
December	52.1	32.7	42.4

Zero-Degree Days: 0
Freezing Days: 65
90-Degree Days: 38
Heating- and Cooling-Degree Days: 5,110

Indianapolis, IN

Terrain: Located in the central part of the state on mostly level or slightly rolling terrain. The greater part of the city lies east of the White River, which flows approximately from north to south. From Weir Cook Airport, 7 miles southwest of the city, the terrain slopes gradually downward to the city, then upward again past the city to the east.

Climate: Continental. Rather warm summers, moderately cold winters, and occasional wide variations in temperatures, especially during the cold season. Snowfalls of 3 inches or more occur about three times annually. Periods of muggy weather can occur in summer, although usually air masses from the Gulf of Mexico are soon replaced by cooler air from the northern Plains and Great Lakes. Occasionally, hot dry winds from the Southwest prevail. Late spring and fall are the most pleasant seasons. Precipitation, well distributed throughout the year, is normally adequate for good crops. Several flood-control reservoirs protect most formerly flood-prone areas.

Pluses: Pleasant springs and falls.

Minuses: Humid spells in summer, cold winters.

Places Rated Score: 557   **Places Rated Rank: 138**

Elevation: 808 feet

Relative Humidity: 73%
Wind Speed: 9.7 mph

Seasonal Change

Annual Rainfall 39 in

Annual Snowfall 21 in

Clear 90 days   Partly Cloudy 101 days   Cloudy 174 days

Precipitation Days: 122   Storm Days: 45

Average Temperatures			
	Daily High	Daily Low	Monthly Mean
January	36.0	19.7	27.9
February	39.3	22.1	30.7
March	49.0	30.3	39.7
April	62.8	41.8	52.3
May	72.9	51.5	62.2
June	82.3	61.1	71.7
July	85.4	64.6	75.0
August	84.0	62.4	73.2
September	77.7	54.9	66.3
October	67.0	44.3	55.7
November	50.5	32.8	41.7
December	38.7	23.1	30.9

Zero-Degree Days: 7
Freezing Days: 122
90-Degree Days: 15
Heating- and Cooling-Degree Days: 6,551

Jackson, MS

Terrain: Jackson is about 45 miles east of the Mississippi River on the west bank of the Pearl River and about 150 miles north of the Gulf of Mexico. The terrain is gently rolling, with no local topographic features that appreciably influence the weather. Alluvial plains up to 3 miles wide extend along the river near Jackson. Some levees have been built on both sides of the river.

Climate: Significantly humid during most of the year, with one short cold season and one long warm one. In summer, the southerly winds and accompanying warm Gulf air masses predominate, resulting in a warm, humid maritime climate. Summer days are hot and humid, and often so are the nights. In winter, colder northern air occasionally invades the area, causing rapid and sometimes dramatic temperature shifts. Average freeze-free period: 235 days.

Pluses: Long summers.

Minuses: Hot, humid, stormy.

Places Rated Score: 412   **Places Rated Rank: 293**

Elevation: 331 feet

Relative Humidity: 75%
Wind Speed: 7.6 mph

Seasonal Change

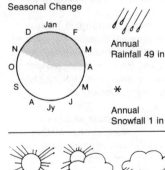

Annual Rainfall 49 in

Annual Snowfall 1 in

Clear 109 days   Partly Cloudy 108 days   Cloudy 148 days

Precipitation Days: 112   Storm Days: 65

Average Temperatures			
	Daily High	Daily Low	Monthly Mean
January	58.4	35.8	47.1
February	61.7	37.8	49.8
March	68.7	43.4	56.1
April	78.2	53.1	65.7
May	85.0	60.4	72.7
June	91.0	67.7	79.4
July	92.7	70.6	81.7
August	92.6	69.8	81.2
September	88.0	64.0	76.0
October	80.1	51.5	65.8
November	68.5	42.0	55.3
December	60.5	37.3	48.9

Zero-Degree Days: 0
Freezing Days: 47
90-Degree Days: 78
Heating- and Cooling-Degree Days: 4,621

Jacksonville, FL

Terrain: Jacksonville, located on the St. Johns River about 16 miles inland from the Atlantic Ocean, is near the northern boundary of the trade winds. The surrounding terrain is level.

Climate: Humid subtropical. The atmosphere is moist, with an average relative humidity of about 75%, ranging from a high of 90% in early morning to about 55% in late afternoon. The average daily sunshine ranges from five and one-half hours in December to nine hours in May. The greatest amount of rain, mostly in the form of local thundershowers, falls during the last summer months, when a measurable amount can be expected every other day.

Pluses: Pleasant winters.   **Minuses:** Hot, stormy summers.

Elevation: 31 feet

Relative Humidity: 75%
Wind Speed: 8.5 mph

Seasonal Change

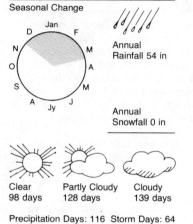

Annual Rainfall 54 in

Annual Snowfall 0 in

Clear 98 days   Partly Cloudy 128 days   Cloudy 139 days

Precipitation Days: 116   Storm Days: 64

Average Temperatures			
	Daily High	Daily Low	Monthly Mean
January	64.6	44.5	54.6
February	66.9	45.7	56.3
March	72.2	50.1	61.2
April	79.0	57.1	68.1
May	84.6	63.9	74.3
June	88.3	70.0	79.2
July	90.0	72.0	81.0
August	89.7	72.3	81.0
September	86.0	70.4	78.2
October	79.2	61.7	70.5
November	71.4	51.0	61.2
December	65.6	45.1	55.4

Zero-Degree Days: 0
Freezing Days: 12
90-Degree Days: 82
Heating- and Cooling-Degree Days: 3,923

Places Rated Score: 457   **Places Rated Rank: 266**

Johnson City–Kingsport–Bristol, TN–VA

Terrain: This tri-city area is located in the extreme upper east Tennessee Valley. Mountain ranges begin about 10 miles to the southeast and 15 miles to the west and north, with many peaks and ridges rising to 4,000 feet, and some to 6,000 feet in the southeast.

Climate: The topography has considerable influence on the weather changes peculiar to this area. Moist easterly air flow in the lower levels of the atmosphere is more or less blocked on the eastern slopes of the mountains, thus producing an abundance of precipitation in these higher ridges and reaching the tri-city area drier and slightly warmer. Although average annual rainfall is 41 inches in the vicinity, annual amounts of 80 inches have been recorded in mountainous sections to the east and south. Snowfall seldom begins before November and rarely remains on the ground more than a few days. Mountainous regions to the southeast, however, are frequently blanketed for long periods.

Pluses: Mild winters.   **Minuses:** Can be drizzly.

Elevation: 1,525 feet

Relative Humidity: 72%
Wind Speed: 5.6 mph

Seasonal Change

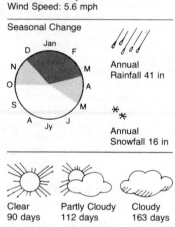

Annual Rainfall 41 in

Annual Snowfall 16 in

Clear 90 days   Partly Cloudy 112 days   Cloudy 163 days

Precipitation Days: 134   Storm Days: 45

Average Temperatures			
	Daily High	Daily Low	Monthly Mean
January	46.0	26.7	36.4
February	48.9	28.4	38.7
March	57.1	34.5	45.8
April	68.3	44.2	56.3
May	77.1	52.6	64.9
June	84.0	60.7	72.4
July	85.9	64.4	75.2
August	85.3	63.1	74.2
September	80.4	56.6	68.5
October	70.4	45.3	57.9
November	56.9	34.5	45.7
December	47.3	28.0	37.7

Zero-Degree Days: 1
Freezing Days: 96
90-Degree Days: 13
Heating- and Cooling-Degree Days: 5,413

Places Rated Score: 663   **Places Rated Rank: 29**

Kansas City, KS

Terrain: Kansas City is very near the geographic center of the United States. The surrounding terrain is gently rolling. Its continental climate is modified by a lack of natural obstructions to the free sweep of air currents from all directions.

Climate: Early spring brings a period of frequent and rapid fluctuations of weather, tapering off as spring progresses. Summer days are warm, sometimes hot, but nights are mild with moderate humidity. As with so many locations in America's heartland, fall is the most pleasant season, characterized by many mild sunny days and cool nights. Average date of last freeze: April 7. First freeze: October 26.

Pluses: Sunny; good four-season climate.   **Minuses:** Variable weather in early spring; winters can be cold, summers hot.

Elevation: 1,025 feet

Relative Humidity: 68%
Wind Speed: 10.3 mph

Seasonal Change

Annual Rainfall 37 in

Annual Snowfall 20 in

Clear 132 days   Partly Cloudy 85 days   Cloudy 148 days

Precipitation Days: 97   Storm Days: 47

Average Temperatures			
	Daily High	Daily Low	Monthly Mean
January	36.2	19.3	27.8
February	41.9	24.2	33.1
March	50.5	31.8	41.2
April	64.8	45.1	55.0
May	74.3	55.7	65.0
June	82.6	65.2	73.9
July	88.0	69.6	78.8
August	86.7	68.1	77.4
September	78.8	58.8	68.8
October	68.9	48.3	58.6
November	52.7	34.5	43.6
December	40.4	24.1	32.3

Zero-Degree Days: 5
Freezing Days: 105
90-Degree Days: 40
Heating- and Cooling-Degree Days: 6,581

Places Rated Score: 549   **Places Rated Rank: 148**

Knoxville, TN

Terrain: Located in a broad valley between the Cumberland Mountains to the northwest and the Great Smoky Mountains to the southeast. The Cumberland Mountains serve to retard and weaken the force of the cold winter air moving down from the northern Plains during the colder months, and the Smoky Mountains shelter Knoxville from much of the hot, humid tropical air that moves northward during the summertime.

Climate: Moderate, thanks to the sheltering effects of the two mountain ranges. Though summers are long, the nights are almost always cool, with the average diurnal variation being about 20 degrees. The mean daytime temperature for July is 81° F, but nighttime temperatures are in the mid-70s.

Pluses: Mild mountain climate.

Minuses: Somewhat stormy in summer.

Places Rated Score: 670

Places Rated Rank: 26

Elevation: 980 feet

Relative Humidity: 71%
Wind Speed: 7.3 mph

Seasonal Change

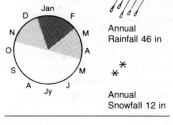

Annual Rainfall 46 in

Annual Snowfall 12 in

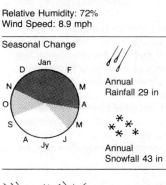

Clear 95 days   Partly Cloudy 107 days   Cloudy 163 days

Precipitation Days: 128   Storm Days: 47

Average Temperatures			
	Daily High	Daily Low	Monthly Mean
January	48.9	32.2	40.6
February	52.0	33.5	42.8
March	60.4	39.4	49.9
April	72.0	48.6	60.3
May	79.8	56.9	68.4
June	86.1	64.8	75.5
July	88.0	68.3	78.2
August	87.3	67.2	77.3
September	82.0	61.2	71.6
October	71.8	50.0	60.9
November	58.9	39.4	49.2
December	49.8	33.1	41.5

Zero-Degree Days: 1
Freezing Days: 71
90-Degree Days: 19
Heating- and Cooling-Degree Days: 5,047

La Crosse, WI

Terrain: Situated on the east bank of the Mississippi River at the confluence of the Mississippi, Black, and La Crosse rivers. The town is on a level, sandy plain, but steep-sided hills with narrow valleys are characteristic of most of the surrounding area. The leading field crops are corn, hay, and oats. Dairying is the principal farm activity.

Climate: The location of the city in a natural bowl between the hills results in colder temperatures at night due to air drainage and in valley fogs that often persist through forenoon. The continental climate means frequent variations in temperature. Winters are cold and humid; snows are frequent. Summers are warm and moderately humid. Most of the annual precipitation falls during the main growing season extending from May to September.

Pluses: Five-month growing season with above-average rainfall.

Minuses: Long, cold winters with frequent snow.

Places Rated Score: 352

Places Rated Rank: 311

Elevation: 672 feet

Relative Humidity: 72%
Wind Speed: 8.9 mph

Seasonal Change

Annual Rainfall 29 in

Annual Snowfall 43 in

Clear 95 days   Partly Cloudy 97 days   Cloudy 173 days

Precipitation Days: 109   Storm Days: 40

Average Temperatures			
	Daily High	Daily Low	Monthly Mean
January	25.0	7.1	16.1
February	29.7	10.3	20.0
March	40.0	22.1	31.1
April	57.8	37.4	47.6
May	69.3	48.7	59.0
June	78.4	58.5	68.5
July	83.0	62.5	72.8
August	81.7	61.0	71.4
September	71.8	51.8	61.8
October	61.8	41.7	51.8
November	43.0	27.8	35.4
December	29.6	14.0	21.8

Zero-Degree Days: 26
Freezing Days: 152
90-Degree Days: 16
Heating- and Cooling-Degree Days: 8,112

Las Vegas, NV

Terrain: Situated near the center of a broad desert valley surrounded by mountains ranging from 2,000 feet to 10,000 feet higher than the valley's floor. These mountains act as effective barriers to moisture-laden storms moving eastward from the Pacific Ocean, so that Las Vegas sees very few overcast or rainy days.

Climate: Summers are typical of a desert climate—low humidity with maximum temperatures in the 100-degree levels. Nearby mountains contribute to relatively cool nights, with minimums between 70° F and 75° F. Springs and falls are ideal: Outdoor activities are rarely interrupted by adverse weather conditions. Winters, too, are mild, with daytime averages of 60° F, clear skies, and warm sunshine.

Pluses: Mild year-round climate with especially pleasant springs and falls.

Minuses: High winds, though infrequent, bring dust and sand.

Places Rated Score: 556

Places Rated Rank: 140

Elevation: 2,180 feet

Relative Humidity: 29%
Wind Speed: 9 mph

Seasonal Change

Annual Rainfall 4 in

Annual Snowfall 1.5 in

Clear 216 days   Partly Cloudy 84 days   Cloudy 65 days

Precipitation Days: 24   Storm Days: 15

Average Temperatures			
	Daily High	Daily Low	Monthly Mean
January	55.7	32.6	44.2
February	61.3	36.9	49.1
March	67.8	41.7	54.8
April	77.5	50.0	63.8
May	87.5	59.0	73.3
June	97.2	67.4	82.3
July	103.9	75.3	89.6
August	101.5	73.3	87.4
September	94.8	65.4	80.1
October	81.0	53.1	67.1
November	65.7	40.8	53.3
December	56.7	33.7	45.2

Zero-Degree Days: 0
Freezing Days: 41
90-Degree Days: 131
Heating- and Cooling-Degree Days: 5,547

Lexington–Fayette, KY

Terrain: Located in the heart of the Kentucky Bluegrass region on a gently rolling plateau with varying elevations of 900 feet to 1,050 feet. The surrounding country is noted for its beauty, fertile soil, excellent grass, stock farms, and burley tobacco. There are no bodies of water nearby that are large enough to have an effect on climate.

Climate: Decidedly continental, temperate, yet subject to sudden large but brief changes in temperature. Precipitation is evenly distributed throughout the winter, spring, and summer, with an average of 12 inches falling in each of these seasons. Snowfall is variable, but the ground does not retain snow for more than a few days at a time. The months of September and October are the most pleasant of the year; they have the least precipitation, the most clear days, and generally comfortable temperatures.

Pluses: Temperate, four-season climate with pleasant falls.

Minuses: Large diurnal temperature range.

Places Rated Score: 635   **Places Rated Rank: 48**

Elevation: 989 feet

Relative Humidity: 70%
Wind Speed: 9.7 mph

Seasonal Change

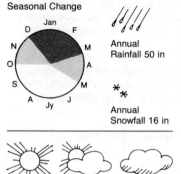

Annual Rainfall 50 in

Annual Snowfall 16 in

Clear 95 days   Partly Cloudy 102 days   Cloudy 168 days

Precipitation Days: 130   Storm Days: 47

Average Temperatures			
	Daily High	Daily Low	Monthly Mean
January	41.3	24.5	32.9
February	44.3	26.2	35.3
March	53.4	33.7	43.6
April	66.0	44.6	55.3
May	75.5	53.8	64.7
June	83.5	62.5	73.0
July	86.4	65.9	76.2
August	85.5	64.4	75.0
September	79.6	57.6	68.6
October	68.8	46.8	57.8
November	53.9	35.3	44.6
December	43.7	27.2	35.5

Zero-Degree Days: 2
Freezing Days: 97
90-Degree Days: 16
Heating- and Cooling-Degree Days: 5,926

Lincoln, NE

Terrain: Lies on rolling prairie in southeastern Nebraska beyond the edge of the tornado and hail belt.

Climate: The majority of winter outbreaks of severely cold air from Canada move over the Lincoln area. However, the centers of some cold air masses move so far to the east that their full effect is not felt here. The Chinook effect often produces rapid rises in temperature during the winter, with a shift of the wind to westerly. An average winter brings 26 inches of snow, most of which doesn't melt until spring. The crop season, April through September, receives three fourths of the yearly precipitation. Nighttime showers occur mostly in the summer. There is much sunshine—Lincoln receives an average of 64% of possible sunlight—with humidity at a comfortable level, except for short periods during the summer.

Pluses: Varied but not too rigorous continental climate.

Minuses: Occasional high winds and high temperature combinations; long winters.

Places Rated Score: 398   **Places Rated Rank: 300**

Elevation: 1,189 feet

Relative Humidity: 68%
Wind Speed: 10.5 mph

Seasonal Change

Annual Rainfall 29 in

Annual Snowfall 26 in

Clear 115 days   Partly Cloudy 97 days   Cloudy 153 days

Precipitation Days: 88   Storm Days: 48

Average Temperatures			
	Daily High	Daily Low	Monthly Mean
January	32.8	11.7	22.2
February	38.3	17.4	27.9
March	47.0	26.0	36.5
April	63.4	39.2	51.3
May	73.4	50.6	62.0
June	83.1	60.9	72.0
July	88.9	65.7	77.3
August	87.0	64.2	75.6
September	77.5	53.6	65.6
October	67.6	44.2	54.9
November	50.3	27.8	39.0
December	37.7	16.9	27.3

Zero-Degree Days: 17
Freezing Days: 146
90-Degree Days: 43
Heating- and Cooling-Degree Days: 7,366

Little Rock–North Little Rock, AR

Terrain: Located on the Arkansas River near the geographic center of the state. To the west lie the Ouachita Mountains and to the east the flat lowlands of the Mississippi River valley.

Climate: Modified four-season continental climate. The area is exposed to all North American air-mass types, but the Gulf of Mexico gives the summer season prolonged periods of warm and humid weather. Sixty-two percent of the normal annual precipitation occurs during the growing season, averaging 233 days. Winters are mild, but polar and Arctic outbreaks are not uncommon. Glaze and ice storms, though infrequent, can be severe.

Pluses: Negligible snow, long growing season, sufficient precipitation.

Minuses: Long periods of warm, humid days in summer.

Places Rated Score: 497   **Places Rated Rank: 227**

Elevation: 265 feet

Relative Humidity: 70%
Wind Speed: 8.2 mph

Seasonal Change

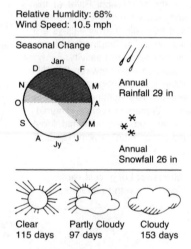

Annual Rainfall 49 in

Annual Snowfall 5 in

Average Temperatures			
	Daily High	Daily Low	Monthly Mean
January	50.1	28.9	39.5
February	53.8	31.9	42.9
March	61.8	38.7	50.3
April	73.5	49.9	61.7
May	81.4	58.1	69.8
June	89.3	66.8	78.1
July	92.6	70.1	81.4
August	92.6	68.6	80.6
September	85.8	60.8	73.3
October	76.0	48.7	62.4
November	62.4	38.1	50.3
December	52.1	31.1	41.6

Zero-Degree Days: 0
Freezing Days: 63
90-Degree Days: 70
Heating- and Cooling-Degree Days: 5,279

★ Los Angeles–Long Beach, CA

Terrain: Predominating influences on the climate of Los Angeles are the Pacific Ocean, 3 miles to the west, and the southern California coastal mountain ranges, which line the inland side of the coastal plain of the city and act as buffers to the more extreme conditions of the interior.

Climate: The most characteristic features of this mild, two-season climate are low clouds at night and morning, and sunny afternoons that prevail during the spring and summer and occur often during the remainder of the year. Combined with a sea breeze, the coastal cloudiness is associated with mild temperatures throughout the year. Pronounced differences in temperature, humidity, fog, sunshine, and rain occur over fairly short distances on the coastal plains and adjoining foothills. Temperature ranges are least and humidity higher close to the coast; precipitation increases with elevation.

Pluses: Positive benefits from Pacific Ocean and surrounding foothills.

Minuses: Frequent haze, fog, and smoke; dry Santa Ana winds.

Places Rated Score: 885

Places Rated Rank: 5

Elevation: 104 feet

Relative Humidity: 71%
Wind Speed: 7.4 mph

Seasonal Change

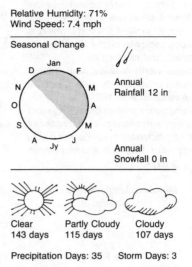

Annual Rainfall 12 in

Annual Snowfall 0 in

Clear 143 days
Partly Cloudy 115 days
Cloudy 107 days

Precipitation Days: 35   Storm Days: 3

Average Temperatures			
	Daily High	Daily Low	Monthly Mean
January	63.5	45.4	54.5
February	64.1	47.0	55.6
March	64.3	48.6	56.5
April	65.9	51.7	58.8
May	68.4	55.3	61.9
June	70.3	58.6	64.5
July	74.8	62.1	68.5
August	75.8	63.2	69.5
September	75.7	61.6	68.7
October	72.9	57.5	65.2
November	69.6	51.3	60.5
December	66.5	47.3	56.9

Zero-Degree Days: 0
Freezing Days: 0
90-Degree Days: 5
Heating- and Cooling-Degree Days: 2,437

Louisville, KY–IN

Terrain: Located on the south bank of the Ohio River, about 400 miles southwest of Pittsburgh. The eastern part of the city is residential and consists of rolling hills and plateaus. The western, industrial part lies on the river's floodplain. A low range of hills on the Indiana bank provides a partial barrier to icy blasts of winter.

Climate: Continental, but more variable because of its position in midlatitudes, in the belt of westerly winds, not completely shut off from the Gulf of Mexico. Winters are moderately cold. Snows, although seldom heavy, are a usual occurrence from November through March. Summers are quite warm, with high relative humidity and rainstorms of high intensity common during both springs and summers.

Pluses: Well-defined seasons with good precipitation.

Minuses: Humid summers, intense rainfalls.

Places Rated Score: 616

Places Rated Rank: 60

Elevation: 488 feet

Relative Humidity: 69%
Wind Speed: 8.4 mph

Seasonal Change

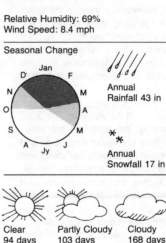

Annual Rainfall 43 in

Annual Snowfall 17 in

Clear 94 days
Partly Cloudy 103 days
Cloudy 168 days

Precipitation Days: 124   Storm Days: 45

Average Temperatures			
	Daily High	Daily Low	Monthly Mean
January	42.0	24.5	33.3
February	45.0	26.5	35.8
March	54.0	34.0	44.0
April	66.9	44.8	55.9
May	75.6	53.9	64.8
June	83.7	62.9	73.3
July	87.3	66.4	76.9
August	86.8	64.9	75.9
September	80.5	57.7	69.1
October	70.3	45.9	58.1
November	54.9	35.1	45.0
December	44.1	27.1	35.6

Zero-Degree Days: 2
Freezing Days: 92
90-Degree Days: 24
Heating- and Cooling-Degree Days: 5,908

Lubbock, TX

Terrain: Located in a plateau area of northwestern Texas that is often referred to as the South Plains region. It is an essentially level area with numerous small playas, small stream valleys, and low hummocks. There are no appreciable terrain features that affect wind flow across the plateau.

Climate: Semiarid, transitional between desert conditions to the west and humid climates to the east. Normal precipitation is 18 inches per year, with maximum precipitation occurring during May, June, and July, when warm tropical air is carried inland from the Gulf of Mexico. This air mass produces moderate to heavy afternoon and evening convective thunderstorms, sometimes with hail. Dry daytime winds help alleviate summer heat.

Pluses: Generally pleasant climate year-round.

Minuses: During dry spells, high winds cause dusty conditions.

Places Rated Score: 604

Places Rated Rank: 71

Elevation: 3,241 feet

Relative Humidity: 56%
Wind Speed: 10.8 mph

Seasonal Change

Annual Rainfall 18 in

Annual Snowfall 9.6 in

Clear 164 days
Partly Cloudy 103 days
Cloudy 98 days

Precipitation Days: 60   Storm Days: 45

Average Temperatures			
	Daily High	Daily Low	Monthly Mean
January	53.4	24.8	39.1
February	57.0	28.3	42.7
March	63.8	34.0	48.9
April	74.8	45.1	60.0
May	82.5	54.5	68.5
June	90.6	63.6	77.1
July	92.4	66.9	79.7
August	91.3	65.5	78.4
September	83.8	58.2	71.0
October	74.7	47.3	61.0
November	63.1	34.4	48.8
December	55.2	27.4	41.3

Zero-Degree Days: 0
Freezing Days: 98
90-Degree Days: 77
Heating- and Cooling-Degree Days: 5,192

Madison, WI

Terrain: Madison sits on a narrow isthmus of land between Lakes Mendota (15 square miles) and Monona (5 square miles). Normally these lakes are frozen from December 17 to April 5. Most farming is dairying, with field crops mainly of corn, oats, and alfalfa. The majority of fruits grown are apples, strawberries, and raspberries.

Climate: Continental, typical of interior North America, with a large annual temperature range and frequent short periods of temperature changes. The absolute temperature range is from 107° F to −37° F. Winter temperatures average 20° F and summer ones 68° F. The most common air masses are of polar origin, with occasional outbreaks of Arctic air during the winter. Much of the precipitation falls between May and September. Lighter winter precipitation falls over a longer period of time. Average growing season: 175 days.

Pluses: Pleasant summers with moderate growing season; even precipitation.

Minuses: Long, severe winters.

Places Rated Score: 378

Places Rated Rank: 307

Elevation: 866 feet

Relative Humidity: 73%
Wind Speed: 9.9 mph

Seasonal Change

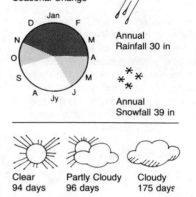

Annual Rainfall 30 in

Annual Snowfall 39 in

Clear 94 days Partly Cloudy 96 days Cloudy 175 days

Precipitation Days: 117 Storm Days: 40

Average Temperatures			
	Daily High	Daily Low	Monthly Mean
January	25.4	8.2	16.8
February	29.5	11.1	20.3
March	39.2	21.2	30.2
April	56.0	34.6	45.3
May	67.3	44.6	56.0
June	76.9	54.6	65.8
July	81.4	58.8	70.1
August	80.0	57.3	68.7
September	70.9	48.5	59.7
October	60.9	38.9	49.9
November	43.0	26.4	34.7
December	29.8	14.0	21.9

Zero-Degree Days: 25
Freezing Days: 164
90-Degree Days: 12
Heating- and Cooling-Degree Days: 8,190

Manchester, NH

Terrain: Surrounded by hills, with many lakes and ponds. Manchester is situated on the Merrimack River near the geographic center of the New England region. The countryside is generously wooded, most of it land that was formerly used for farming Mount Washington, the highest peak in the Presidential Chain of the White Mountains (and the site of perhaps the most violent weather in the continental United States), is 75 miles north.

Climate: Northwesterly winds prevail here, bringing cold, dry air during the winter and pleasantly cool, dry air in the summer. Although the winters here are long, cold, and snowy, the summers are ideal, with warm sunny days and cool nights. Thus the Manchester area and New Hampshire in general offer year-round recreation: Ski areas and other resorts dot the countryside. Agriculture is limited to freeze-resistant crops, such as potatoes and apples, and to forage crops for the dairy industry.

Pluses: Good rugged climate, pleasant summers.

Minuses: Long, cold, snowy winters.

Places Rated Score: 404

Places Rated Rank: 296

Elevation: 346 feet

Relative Humidity: 73%
Wind Speed: 6.7 mph

Seasonal Change

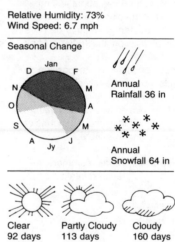

Annual Rainfall 36 in

Annual Snowfall 64 in

Clear 92 days Partly Cloudy 113 days Cloudy 160 days

Precipitation Days: 125 Storm Days: 21

Average Temperatures			
	Daily High	Daily Low	Monthly Mean
January	31.3	9.9	20.6
February	33.8	11.3	22.6
March	42.4	22.1	32.3
April	56.7	31.7	44.2
May	68.6	41.5	55.1
June	77.7	51.6	64.7
July	82.6	56.7	69.7
August	80.1	54.2	67.2
September	72.4	46.5	59.5
October	62.3	36.3	49.3
November	47.9	28.1	38.0
December	34.6	14.9	24.8

Zero-Degree Days: 26
Freezing Days: 176
90-Degree Days: 11
Heating- and Cooling-Degree Days: 7,709

Medford, OR

Terrain: Located in a mountain valley formed by the famous Rogue River and one of its tributaries, Bear Creek. Most of the valley ranges in elevation from 1,300 feet to 1,400 feet above sea level. The valley's outlet to the ocean 80 miles west is the narrow canyon of the Rogue.

Climate: Moderate, with marked seasonal characteristics. Late fall, winter, and early spring are cloudy, damp, and cool. The remainder of the year is warm, dry, and sunny. The rain shadow afforded by the Siskiyous and the Coast Ranges results in relatively light rainfall, most of which falls in the wintertime. Snowfalls are very light and seldom remain on the ground more than 24 hours. Winters are mild, with the temperatures just dipping below freezing during December and January. Summer days can reach 90° F, but nights are cool. The climate is ideal for truck and fruit farming, and the area is dotted with orchards.

Pluses: Very mild four-season climate; sunny summers.

Minuses: Half the year is damp and cloudy.

Places Rated Score: 611

Places Rated Rank: 67

Elevation: 1,298 feet

Relative Humidity: 67%
Wind Speed: 4.8 mph

Seasonal Change

Annual Rainfall 21 in

Annual Snowfall 8 in

Clear 117 days Partly Cloudy 79 days Cloudy 169 days

Precipitation Days: 101 Storm Days: 9

Average Temperatures			
	Daily High	Daily Low	Monthly Mean
January	44.2	29.0	36.6
February	51.8	30.7	41.3
March	56.7	32.8	44.8
April	63.8	36.6	50.2
May	71.7	42.8	57.3
June	79.4	49.1	64.3
July	89.5	53.8	71.7
August	87.8	52.9	70.4
September	82.1	46.7	64.4
October	67.4	39.1	53.4
November	52.7	34.2	43.5
December	44.2	31.1	37.7

Zero-Degree Days: 0
Freezing Days: 90
90-Degree Days: 54
Heating- and Cooling-Degree Days: 5,492

Memphis, TN–AR–MS

Terrain: Located on the east bank of the Mississippi River in slightly rolling topography, across from the level alluvial area on the Arkansas side. Major crops are cotton, corn, peaches, apples, and vegetables. The climate is favorable for dairying and for raising cattle and hogs.
Climate: Though not in the normal paths of storms coming from the Gulf of Mexico or from Canada, Memphis is affected by both and therefore has comparatively frequent changes in weather. Extremes in highs and lows are relatively rare; the average annual temperature is in the low 60s and varies from the low 40s in January to the low 80s in July. Average growing season: 230 days.

| **Pluses:** Short winters, long summers, moderate temperature variation. | **Minuses:** Frequent weather changes, occasional humid periods in summer. |

Places Rated Score: 514   **Places Rated Rank: 211**

Elevation: 284 feet

Relative Humidity: 69%
Wind Speed: 9.2 mph

Seasonal Change

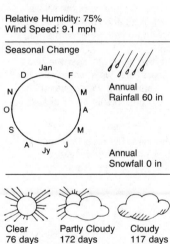

Annual Rainfall 49 in

Annual Snowfall 6 in

Clear 118 days   Partly Cloudy 99 days   Cloudy 148 days

Precipitation Days: 106   Storm Days: 53

	Daily High	Daily Low	Monthly Mean
January	49.4	31.6	40.5
February	53.1	34.4	43.8
March	60.8	41.1	51.0
April	72.7	52.3	62.5
May	81.2	60.6	70.9
June	88.7	68.5	78.6
July	91.6	71.5	81.6
August	90.6	70.1	80.4
September	84.3	62.8	73.6
October	74.9	51.1	63.0
November	61.5	40.3	50.9
December	51.7	33.7	42.7

Zero-Degree Days: 0
Freezing Days: 59
90-Degree Days: 64
Heating- and Cooling-Degree Days: 5,256

Miami–Hialeah, FL

Terrain: Located on the lower east coast of Florida. To the east lies Biscayne Bay, and east of it Miami Beach. The surrounding countryside is level and sparsely wooded.
Climate: Essentially subtropical marine, characterized by a long, warm summer with abundant rainfall and a mild, dry winter. The Atlantic Ocean greatly influences the city's small range of daily temperature and aids the rapid warming of colder air masses that pass to the east of the state. During the early morning hours, more rainfall occurs at Miami Beach than at the airport (9 miles inland), while during the afternoon the reverse is true. Even more striking is the difference in the annual number of days over 90° F: at Miami Beach, 15 days; at the airport, 60. Freezing temperatures occur occasionally in surrounding farming districts but almost never near the ocean. In 1977, for the first time in Miami's history, traces of snow were reported. Tropical hurricanes affect the area and are most frequent in early fall.

| **Pluses:** Single-season, sub-tropical climate. | **Minuses:** Hurricanes, frequent thunderstorms. |

Places Rated Score: 634   **Places Rated Rank: 49**

Elevation: 12 feet

Relative Humidity: 75%
Wind Speed: 9.1 mph

Seasonal Change

Annual Rainfall 60 in

Annual Snowfall 0 in

Clear 76 days   Partly Cloudy 172 days   Cloudy 117 days

Precipitation Days: 129   Storm Days: 75

	Daily High	Daily Low	Monthly Mean
January	75.6	58.7	67.2
February	76.6	59.0	67.8
March	79.5	63.0	71.3
April	82.7	67.3	75.0
May	85.3	70.7	78.0
June	88.0	73.9	81.0
July	89.1	75.5	82.3
August	89.9	75.8	82.9
September	88.3	75.0	81.7
October	84.6	71.0	77.8
November	79.9	64.5	72.2
December	76.6	60.0	68.3

Zero-Degree Days: 0
Freezing Days: 0
90-Degree Days: 30
Heating- and Cooling-Degree Days: 4,244

Midland, TX

Terrain: Located on the southern extension of the South Plains region of Texas. Topography is level, with only slight and infrequent undulations. Vegetation consists mainly of grasses, and there are very few trees in the area, most of them mesquite.
Climate: Semiarid. Droughts occur with monotonous frequency, resulting in dust storms so severe that suspended dust remains in the air several days after the storm has passed. Though summer afternoon temperatures are frequently above 90° F, low humidity and rapid evaporation have a cooling effect. The climate is generally pleasant, with the most disagreeable weather concentrated in late winter and spring.

| **Pluses:** Short winters; long, pleasant summers and falls. | **Minuses:** Severe drought conditions, frequent dust storms. |

Places Rated Score: 603   **Places Rated Rank: 72**

Elevation: 2,862 feet

Relative Humidity: 53%
Wind Speed: 10.8 mph

Seasonal Change

Annual Rainfall 14 in

Annual Snowfall 3.5 in

Clear 167 days   Partly Cloudy 97 days   Cloudy 101 days

Precipitation Days: 51   Storm Days: 36

	Daily High	Daily Low	Monthly Mean
January	57.8	29.4	43.6
February	62.1	33.5	47.8
March	69.4	39.2	54.3
April	79.1	49.4	64.3
May	86.5	58.1	72.3
June	92.8	66.9	79.9
July	95.0	69.5	82.3
August	94.4	69.1	81.8
September	87.9	62.8	75.4
October	79.2	52.4	65.8
November	67.5	39.1	53.3
December	60.1	31.6	45.9

Zero-Degree Days: 0
Freezing Days: 65
90-Degree Days: 89
Heating- and Cooling-Degree Days: 4,871

Milwaukee, WI

Terrain: Milwaukee is situated on the west shore of Lake Michigan, 50 miles north of Chicago.

Climate: Influenced by storms that move eastward across the upper Ohio River valley and the Great Lakes region. Large high-pressure systems moving southeastward out of Canada also have an effect, and it is seldom that two or three days will pass without a distinct change in the weather, particularly during winter and spring. The major influence on the climate is Lake Michigan, which has a particularly marked effect when the temperature of the water differs considerably from that of the air. Generally, the lake cools the shoreline in summer and warms it in winter. Thunderstorms occur less frequently in Milwaukee than in areas to the south and west. Winters are cloudy. Summers are usually clear, receiving an average of 70% of possible sunshine.

Pluses: Lake Michigan has a moderating effect on temperature extremes.

Minuses: Subject to severe winter storm systems.

Places Rated Score: 460

Places Rated Rank: 264

Elevation: 693 feet

Relative Humidity: 73%
Wind Speed: 11.8 mph

Seasonal Change

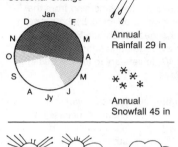

Annual Rainfall 29 in

Annual Snowfall 45 in

Clear 96 days	Partly Cloudy 99 days	Cloudy 170 days

Precipitation Days: 122   Storm Days: 36

Average Temperatures			
	Daily High	Daily Low	Monthly Mean
January	27.3	11.4	19.4
February	30.3	14.6	22.5
March	39.4	23.4	31.4
April	54.6	34.7	44.7
May	65.0	43.3	54.2
June	75.3	53.6	64.5
July	80.4	59.3	69.9
August	79.7	58.7	69.2
September	71.5	50.7	61.1
October	61.4	40.6	51.0
November	44.4	28.5	36.5
December	31.5	16.8	24.2

Zero-Degree Days: 16
Freezing Days: 146
90-Degree Days: 9
Heating- and Cooling-Degree Days: 7,894

Minneapolis–St. Paul, MN–WI

Terrain: The Twin Cities are located at the confluence of the Mississippi and Minnesota rivers over the heart of an artesian water basin. The topography is flat or gently rolling with numerous lakes that are small, shallow, and ice-covered in winter.

Climate: Predominantly continental (the two cities are near the geographic center of North America). There are wide variations in temperature, ample summer rainfall, and scanty winter precipitation. In general, there exists a tendency toward extremes in almost all climatic features.

Pluses: Changeable weather that many find stimulating and invigorating.

Minuses: Extreme weather features; severe, long winters.

Places Rated Score: 283

Places Rated Rank: 320

Elevation: 838 feet

Relative Humidity: 69%
Wind Speed: 10.5 mph

Seasonal Change

Annual Rainfall 26 in

Annual Snowfall 46 in

Clear 100 days	Partly Cloudy 100 days	Cloudy 165 days

Precipitation Days: 113   Storm Days: 36

Average Temperatures			
	Daily High	Daily Low	Monthly Mean
January	21.2	3.2	12.2
February	25.9	7.1	16.5
March	36.9	19.6	28.3
April	55.5	34.7	45.1
May	67.9	46.3	57.1
June	77.1	56.7	66.9
July	82.4	61.4	71.9
August	80.8	59.6	70.2
September	70.7	49.3	60.0
October	60.7	39.2	50.0
November	40.6	24.2	32.4
December	26.6	10.6	18.6

Zero-Degree Days: 34
Freezing Days: 158
90-Degree Days: 15
Heating- and Cooling-Degree Days: 8,744

Mobile, AL

Terrain: Located at the head of Mobile Bay, approximately 30 miles from the Gulf of Mexico.

Climate: Although Mobile has not had a destructive hurricane since 1926, this seems to be due more to chance than to location. The area is subject to hurricanes from the West Indies and the Gulf of Mexico. The normal annual rainfall is among the highest in the United States. It is evenly distributed throughout the year, with a slight maximum at the height of the summer thunderstorm season (there are thunderstorms every other day during July and August). Most of these storms are showers; long periods of continuous rain are rare. The growing season averages 274 days, enough for citrus fruit to be grown in the area.

Pluses: Mild winters, ample and even precipitation.

Minuses: Summers are hot and muggy with frequent thunderstorms, area prone to hurricanes.

Places Rated Score: 442

Places Rated Rank: 275

Elevation: 221 feet

Relative Humidity: 73%
Wind Speed: 9.2 mph

Seasonal Change

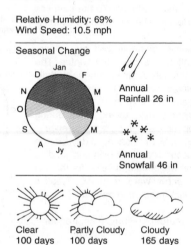

Annual Rainfall 67 in

Clear 100 days	Partly Cloudy 117 days	Cloudy 148 days

Precipitation Days: 124   Storm Days: 80

Average Temperatures			
	Daily High	Daily Low	Monthly Mean
January	61.1	41.3	51.2
February	64.1	43.9	54.0
March	69.5	49.2	59.4
April	78.0	57.7	67.9
May	85.0	64.5	74.8
June	89.8	70.7	80.3
July	90.5	72.6	81.6
August	90.6	72.3	81.5
September	86.5	68.4	77.5
October	79.7	58.0	68.9
November	69.5	47.5	58.5
December	63.0	42.8	52.9

Zero-Degree Days: 0
Freezing Days: 19
90-Degree Days: 81
Heating- and Cooling-Degree Days: 4,261

Montgomery, AL

Terrain: Located in a gently rolling area of southern Alabama. No local topographic features appreciably influence climate.

Climate: From June through September, humidity and temperature conditions show little daily change. During summer, 100-degree readings are infrequent. From April through September, all precipitation is from local heat thundershowers in the afternoon. Rain is abundant and includes all types and intensities from December through March. During the coldest months (December, January, and February), there are frequent shifts between mild, moist air from the Gulf of Mexico and dry, cool continental air. Hard freezes are infrequent during winter; snow is rare enough to be a curiosity.

Pluses: Mild, two-season climate with abundant rainfall.

Minuses: Humid summers and falls, lots of cloudy days.

Places Rated Score: 483

Places Rated Rank: 240

Elevation: 202 feet

Relative Humidity: 73%
Wind Speed: 6.8 mph

Seasonal Change

Annual Rainfall 50 in

Annual Snowfall .2 in

Clear 107 days   Partly Cloudy 109 days   Cloudy 149 days

Precipitation Days: 109   Storm Days: 62

Average Temperatures			
	Daily High	Daily Low	Monthly Mean
January	57.9	37.1	47.5
February	61.4	39.7	50.6
March	67.7	45.2	56.5
April	76.8	53.6	65.2
May	83.6	61.2	72.4
June	89.2	68.6	78.9
July	90.5	71.5	81.0
August	90.7	70.7	80.7
September	86.5	65.5	76.0
October	78.0	53.5	65.8
November	67.2	42.7	55.0
December	59.3	37.7	48.5

Zero-Degree Days: 0
Freezing Days: 39
90-Degree Days: 66
Heating- and Cooling-Degree Days: 4,507

Nashville, TN

Terrain: Located on the Cumberland River in the northwestern corner of the Nashville Basin, near the escarpment of the Highland Rim. The rim rises 400 feet above the mean elevation of the basin, forming an amphitheater around the city from the southwest to the southeast.

Climate: Moderate temperatures. Extremes of heat or cold are rare, yet fairly frequent changes give variety. The humidity is moderate compared with other locations east of the Mississippi River and south of the Ohio River. The city is not in the most highly traveled path of general storm systems that cross the country; however, it is in a zone that experiences thunderstorms moderately often. Average growing season: 211 days.

Pluses: Fairly mild four-season climate, long summers.

Minuses: Relatively few clear days.

Places Rated Score: 600

Places Rated Rank: 79

Elevation: 605 feet

Relative Humidity: 71%
Wind Speed: 7.9 mph

Seasonal Change

Annual Rainfall 46 in

Annual Snowfall 10.7 in

Clear 103 days   Partly Cloudy 107 days   Cloudy 155 days

Precipitation Days: 119   Storm Days: 55

Average Temperatures			
	Daily High	Daily Low	Monthly Mean
January	47.6	29.0	38.3
February	50.9	31.0	41.0
March	59.2	38.1	48.7
April	71.3	48.8	60.1
May	79.8	57.3	68.5
June	87.5	65.7	76.6
July	90.2	69.0	79.6
August	89.2	67.7	78.5
September	83.5	60.5	72.0
October	73.2	48.6	60.9
November	59.0	37.7	48.4
December	49.6	31.1	40.4

Zero-Degree Days: 1
Freezing Days: 75
90-Degree Days: 37
Heating- and Cooling-Degree Days: 5,390

New Bedford, MA

Terrain: New Bedford, one of America's most famous whaling ports, lies at the mouth of the Acushnet River in Buzzards Bay. The terrain is relatively flat and low-lying, which makes New Bedford especially vulnerable to tidal hurricane surges. Because of severe hurricanes that have struck the area over the last 50 years, huge floodgates have been installed around the city and remain an interesting sight.

Climate: Although this fishing port and manufacturing center is only an hour and a half south of Boston, there's a great difference between the climates of the two cities. New Bedford, located on the northern portion of Rhode Island Sound in a large bay, is almost surrounded by ocean. Thus, it enjoys a modified maritime climate characterized by cool summer ocean breezes and warm ocean air in the wintertime. When Boston is in the midst of a blizzard, New Bedford is usually experiencing rain or sleet that melts away in a few days. Similarly, when Boston and points north simmer in a summer heat wave, New Bedford is usually cooler.

Pluses: Mild maritime climate.

Minuses: Ice storms.

Places Rated Score: 643

Places Rated Rank: 40

Elevation: 60 feet

Relative Humidity: 76%
Wind Speed: 10 mph

Seasonal Change

Annual Rainfall 45 in

Annual Snowfall 36 in

Clear 97 days   Partly Cloudy 114 days   Cloudy 154 days

Precipitation Days: 79   Storm Days: 14

Average Temperatures			
	Daily High	Daily Low	Monthly Mean
January	36.3	21.6	29.0
February	38.4	22.7	30.6
March	45.2	29.6	37.4
April	56.8	38.5	47.7
May	67.3	47.6	57.5
June	76.6	57.6	67.1
July	81.7	63.8	72.8
August	80.3	62.4	71.3
September	73.4	55.2	64.3
October	63.3	45.7	54.5
November	51.0	36.3	43.7
December	40.2	25.8	33.1

Zero-Degree Days: 0
Freezing Days: 110
90-Degree Days: 5
Heating- and Cooling-Degree Days: 6,373

New Orleans, LA

Terrain: The metropolitan area is surrounded by water: Lake Pont-chartrain (610 square miles) to the north; the Mississippi River to the east and south; bayous, lakes, and marshy delta land to the west and south. Elevations in the city vary from a few feet above mean sea level to a few feet below. A massive levee system offers protection from river flooding and tidal surges.

Climate: Best described as humid with surrounding water modifying the temperature and decreasing the range of temperatures. Heavy and frequent rains are typical, and there are daily afternoon thunder-storms from mid-June through September. From December to March, precipitation is likely to be steady rain of two or three days' duration, instead of showers. During winter and spring, cold rain forms fogs that inhibit air and river transportation. The city has been hard hit by three hurricanes since 1900.

Pluses: Tropical climate moderated by water.

Minuses: Hot and humid, heavy rains and fogs, hurricanes.

Places Rated Score: 498

Places Rated Rank: 226

Elevation: 30 feet

Relative Humidity: 77%
Wind Speed: 8.4 mph

Seasonal Change

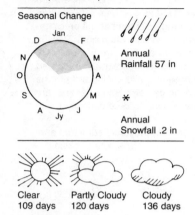

Annual Rainfall 57 in

Annual Snowfall .2 in

Clear 109 days | Partly Cloudy 120 days | Cloudy 136 days

Precipitation Days: 113 Storm Days: 68

Average Temperatures			
	Daily High	Daily Low	Monthly Mean
January	62.3	43.5	52.9
February	65.1	46.0	55.6
March	70.4	50.9	60.7
April	78.4	58.8	68.6
May	84.9	65.3	75.1
June	89.6	71.2	80.4
July	90.4	73.3	81.9
August	90.6	73.1	81.9
September	86.6	69.7	78.2
October	79.9	59.6	69.8
November	70.3	49.8	60.1
December	64.2	45.3	54.8

Zero-Degree Days: 0
Freezing Days: 13
90-Degree Days: 67
Heating- and Cooling-Degree Days: 4,171

New York, NY

Terrain: Located on the Atlantic Coastal Plain at the mouth of the Hudson River. Topography is diversified by numerous waterways: All but one of the city's five boroughs are situated on islands.

Climate: Close to the path of most storm and frontal systems that move across the continent. Therefore, weather conditions affecting the city approach from a westerly direction. New York City can thus experience higher temperatures in summer and lower ones in winter than would otherwise be expected in a coastal area. However, the frequent passage of weather systems often helps reduce the length of warm and cold spells and also keeps periods of air stagnation brief. Although continental influence is dominant, ocean influence is by no means absent. Sea breezes moderate the afternoon heat of summer and delay the advent of winter snows. The Atlantic's influence is also measured in the length of the frost-free season—more than 200 days.

Pluses: Moderating ocean influence, mild summers and falls.

Minuses: Coastal storms bring record snow and rain.

Places Rated Score: 638

Places Rated Rank: 44

Elevation: 87 feet

Relative Humidity: 65%
Wind Speed: 9.4 mph

Seasonal Change

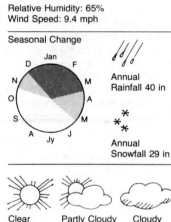

Annual Rainfall 40 in

Annual Snowfall 29 in

Clear 107 days | Partly Cloudy 125 days | Cloudy 133 days

Precipitation Days: 121 Storm Days: 20

Average Temperatures			
	Daily High	Daily Low	Monthly Mean
January	38.5	25.9	32.2
February	40.2	26.5	33.4
March	48.4	33.7	41.1
April	60.7	43.5	52.1
May	71.4	53.1	62.3
June	80.5	62.6	71.6
July	85.2	68.0	76.6
August	83.4	66.4	74.9
September	76.8	59.9	68.4
October	66.8	50.6	58.7
November	54.0	40.8	47.4
December	41.4	29.5	35.5

Zero-Degree Days: 0
Freezing Days: 81
90-Degree Days: 16
Heating- and Cooling-Degree Days: 5,916

Norfolk–Virginia Beach–Newport News, VA

Terrain: Located on low level land, with Chesapeake Bay immediately to the north, Hampton Roads to the west, and the Atlantic Ocean to the east.

Climate: The metro area is in a favorable geographic position, being north of the track of hurricanes and tropical storms and south of high-latitude storm systems. Winters are mild. Springs and falls are especially pleasant. Summers, though, are warm, humid, and long. A temperature of zero has never been recorded here, although there is occasional snow.

Pluses: Four-season climate suited for year-round outdoor activities.

Minuses: Long, humid summers.

Places Rated Score: 632

Places Rated Rank: 50

Elevation: 30 feet

Relative Humidity: 71%
Wind Speed: 10.6 mph

Seasonal Change

Annual Rainfall 45 in

Annual Snowfall 7 in

Clear 110 days | Partly Cloudy 102 days | Cloudy 153 days

Precipitation Days: 115 Storm Days: 37

Average Temperatures			
	Daily High	Daily Low	Monthly Mean
January	48.8	32.2	40.5
February	50.0	32.7	41.4
March	57.3	38.9	48.1
April	67.7	47.9	57.8
May	76.2	57.2	66.7
June	83.5	65.5	74.5
July	86.6	69.9	78.3
August	84.9	68.9	76.9
September	79.6	63.9	71.8
October	70.1	53.3	61.7
November	60.5	42.6	51.6
December	50.6	34.0	42.3

Zero-Degree Days: 0
Freezing Days: 54
90-Degree Days: 30
Heating- and Cooling-Degree Days: 4,929

Oklahoma City, OK

Terrain: Situated along the North Canadian River at the geographic center of the state. The countryside is rolling, with the nearest hills, the Arbuckles, 80 miles south.

Climate: Although some influence is exerted at times by warm, moist air from the Gulf of Mexico, the climate of the city falls mainly under continental controls characteristic of the Great Plains. The continental effect produces pronounced daily and seasonal temperature changes and considerable variation in seasonal and annual precipitation. Summers are long and usually hot. Winters are comparatively mild and short.

Pluses: Clear days, mild winters.

Minuses: Long, hot summers; tornadoes.

Places Rated Score: 554   **Places Rated Rank: 142**

Elevation: 1,304 feet

Relative Humidity: 65%
Wind Speed: 12.8 mph

Seasonal Change

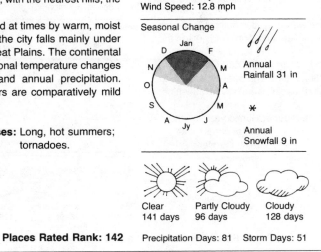

Annual Rainfall 31 in

Annual Snowfall 9 in

Clear 141 days   Partly Cloudy 96 days   Cloudy 128 days

Precipitation Days: 81   Storm Days: 51

Average Temperatures			
	Daily High	Daily Low	Monthly Mean
January	47.6	26.0	36.8
February	52.6	30.0	41.3
March	59.8	36.5	48.2
April	71.6	49.1	60.4
May	78.7	57.9	68.3
June	87.0	66.6	76.8
July	92.6	70.4	81.5
August	92.5	69.6	81.1
September	84.7	61.3	73.0
October	74.2	50.6	62.4
November	60.9	37.4	49.2
December	50.7	29.2	40.0

Zero-Degree Days: 0
Freezing Days: 80
90-Degree Days: 64
Heating- and Cooling-Degree Days: 5,571

★ Olympia, WA

Terrain: The capital of the state of Washington, Olympia lies at the southernmost end of Puget Sound, some 60 miles south-southwest of Seattle. The Olympic Peninsula, with its fine remnants of the Pacific Northwest rain forests, active glaciers, and alpine meadows, lies to the northwest. The city and vicinity are well protected by the Coast Ranges from the strong south and southwest winds accompanying many Pacific storms during the fall and winter.

Climate: Characterized by warm, generally dry summers and wet, mild winters. Fall rains begin in October and continue with few interruptions until spring. During the rainy season there is little variation in temperature, with days in the 40s and 50s and nights in the 30s, and constant cloud cover. The summer highs are between 60° F and 80° F, with up to 20 days without rain. The summer is marked by clear skies at night and frequent morning fog.

Pluses: Mild winters, dry summers.

Minuses: Cloudy, damp, rainy.

Places Rated Score: 726   **Places Rated Rank: 21**

Elevation: 195 feet

Relative Humidity: 71%
Wind Speed: 6.7 mph

Seasonal Change

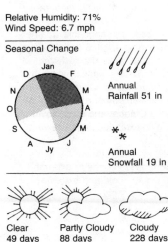

Annual Rainfall 51 in

Annual Snowfall 19 in

Clear 49 days   Partly Cloudy 88 days   Cloudy 228 days

Precipitation Days: 163   Storm Days: 5

Average Temperatures			
	Daily High	Daily Low	Monthly Mean
January	44.0	30.4	37.2
February	49.0	32.4	41.0
March	53.6	32.8	43.2
April	59.9	36.5	48.2
May	67.2	40.8	54.0
June	71.9	45.9	58.9
July	78.4	48.7	63.6
August	77.2	48.4	62.8
September	72.1	45.0	58.6
October	61.2	40.0	50.6
November	51.3	35.2	43.3
December	45.8	33.1	39.5

Zero-Degree Days: 0
Freezing Days: 89
90-Degree Days: 6
Heating- and Cooling-Degree Days: 5,631

Omaha, NE–IA

Terrain: Situated on the west bank of the Missouri River among rolling hills that rise 300 feet above the riverbank.

Climate: Typically continental, with relatively warm summers and cold, dry winters. It is situated midway between two climates, those of the humid East and the dry West, and receives weather conditions characteristic of both. Omaha is also affected by most storms, or "lows," that cross the country. This causes periodic and rapid changes in weather, especially during the winter.

Pluses: Moderate growing season with adequate rainfall.

Minuses: Long, cold winters.

Elevation: 982 feet

Relative Humidity: 68%
Wind Speed: 10.9 mph

Seasonal Change

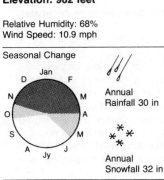

Annual Rainfall 30 in

Annual Snowfall 32 in

Clear 113 days   Partly Cloudy 107 days   Cloudy 145 days

Precipitation Days: 99   Storm Days: 48

Average Temperatures			
	Daily High	Daily Low	Monthly Mean
January	32.7	12.4	22.6
February	38.5	17.4	28.0
March	47.7	26.4	37.1
April	64.4	40.1	52.3
May	74.4	51.5	63.0
June	83.1	61.3	72.2
July	88.6	65.8	77.2
August	87.2	64.0	75.6
September	78.6	54.0	66.3
October	69.1	42.6	55.9
November	50.9	29.1	40.0
December	37.8	18.1	28.0

Zero-Degree Days: 13
Freezing Days: 138
90-Degree Days: 38
Heating- and Cooling-Degree Days: 7,222

Orlando, FL

Terrain: Located in the central section of the Florida peninsula, almost surrounded by lakes. The countryside is flat, with no natural barriers to exterior weather systems.

Climate: Because of the surrounding water, relative humidity remains high year-round, hovering near 90% at night and dipping to 50% in the afternoon. The rainy season extends from June through September; afternoon thundershowers occur daily. Rain is light during the winter, and snow and sleet are rare. Winter temperatures may drop to freezing at night, but days are usually pleasant, with brilliant sunshine.

Pluses: Mild.

Minuses: Humid year-round; hot summers with daily thunder-showers.

Places Rated Score: 457   **Places Rated Rank: 266**

Elevation: 106 feet

Relative Humidity: 74%
Wind Speed: 8.7 mph

Seasonal Change

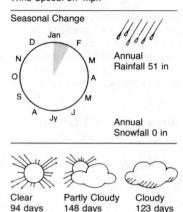

Annual Rainfall 51 in

Annual Snowfall 0 in

Clear 94 days   Partly Cloudy 148 days   Cloudy 123 days

Precipitation Days: 116   Storm Days: 81

Average Temperatures			
	Daily High	Daily Low	Monthly Mean
January	70.5	50.0	60.3
February	71.8	51.2	61.5
March	76.0	55.7	65.9
April	81.5	61.1	71.3
May	86.7	66.1	76.4
June	89.3	71.1	80.2
July	89.8	72.9	81.4
August	90.0	73.5	81.8
September	87.9	72.3	80.1
October	82.5	66.0	74.3
November	76.2	56.9	66.6
December	71.5	51.5	61.5

Zero-Degree Days: 0
Freezing Days: 2
90-Degree Days: 104
Heating- and Cooling-Degree Days: 3,959

Peoria, IL

Terrain: Located on the Illinois River, with gently rising topography extending to level tableland.

Climate: Typically continental, characterized by changeable weather and a wide range of temperatures. For example, 1936 had 17 days with temperatures of 100° F or higher in July, while the early part of that same year had 26 days within a 31-day period when the temperature was zero. The same year had the absolute maximum record of 113° F, set on July 15. June and September are usually the most pleasant months of the year. During October and early November, residents enjoy Indian summer, with its extended period of warm, dry weather.

Pluses: Invigorating continental climate, with especially pleasant falls.

Minuses: Periods of extreme cold and extreme heat.

Places Rated Score: 491   **Places Rated Rank: 233**

Elevation: 662 feet

Relative Humidity: 72%
Wind Speed: 10.3 mph

Seasonal Change

Annual Rainfall 35 in

Annual Snowfall 23 in

Clear 97 days   Partly Cloudy 100 days   Cloudy 168 days

Precipitation Days: 111   Storm Days: 49

Average Temperatures			
	Daily High	Daily Low	Monthly Mean
January	31.9	15.7	23.8
February	36.0	19.3	27.7
March	46.5	28.1	37.3
April	61.7	40.8	51.3
May	72.3	50.7	61.5
June	81.7	60.9	71.3
July	85.5	64.6	75.1
August	84.0	62.9	73.5
September	76.4	54.6	65.5
October	65.9	44.0	55.0
November	48.7	31.1	39.9
December	35.7	20.3	28.0

Zero-Degree Days: 11
Freezing Days: 132
90-Degree Days: 17
Heating- and Cooling-Degree Days: 7,066

Philadelphia, PA–NJ

Terrain: Situated on the Schuylkill and Delaware rivers on the eastern border of Pennsylvania. The Appalachian Mountains to the west and the Atlantic Ocean to the east have a moderating effect on the city's climate.

Climate: Sustained periods of very high or very low temperatures seldom last for more than three or four days. Occasionally during the summer, the area becomes engulfed in marine air, so that high humidity adds to the discomfort of warm temperatures. Precipitation is evenly distributed throughout the year, with maximum amounts during late summer. Snowfall often is considerably higher in the northern suburbs than in the city, where sometimes rain will fall instead. Winters often bring high winds, accompanying cold air after the passage of a deep low-pressure system.

Pluses: Four-season climate moderated by the proximity of the Atlantic Ocean.

Minuses: Humid summer periods; high winter winds accentuate the cold.

Places Rated Score: 630   **Places Rated Rank: 52**

Elevation: 28 feet

Relative Humidity: 67%
Wind Speed: 9.6 mph

Seasonal Change

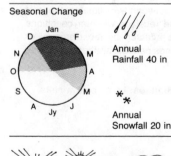

Annual Rainfall 40 in

Annual Snowfall 20 in

Clear 92 days   Partly Cloudy 113 days   Cloudy 160 days

Precipitation Days: 116   Storm Days: 27

Average Temperatures			
	Daily High	Daily Low	Monthly Mean
January	40.1	24.4	32.3
February	42.2	25.5	33.9
March	51.2	32.5	41.9
April	63.5	42.3	52.9
May	74.1	52.3	63.2
June	83.0	61.6	72.3
July	86.8	66.7	76.8
August	84.8	64.7	74.8
September	78.4	57.8	68.1
October	67.9	46.9	57.4
November	55.5	36.9	46.2
December	43.2	27.2	35.2

Zero-Degree Days: 0
Freezing Days: 101
90-Degree Days: 19
Heating- and Cooling-Degree Days: 5,969

Phoenix, AZ

Terrain: Located in the center of the Salt River valley, on a broad, oval, nearly flat plain. To the south, west, and north are nearby mountain ranges, and 35 miles to the east are the famous Superstition Mountains, which rise to 5,000 feet.

Climate: Typical desert; with low annual rainfall and low humidity. Daytime temperatures are high throughout the summer. Winters are mild, but nighttime temperatures frequently drop below freezing during December, January, and February. The valley floor is generally free of wind except during the thunderstorm season, in July and August, when local gusts flow from the east. The majority of days are clear and sunny, except for July and August; then, considerable afternoon cloudiness builds up over nearby mountains.

Pluses: Dry, two-season desert climate.

Minuses: Hot summers.

Places Rated Score: 536　　**Places Rated Rank: 176**

Elevation: 1,107 feet

Relative Humidity: 36%
Wind Speed: 6.2 mph

Seasonal Change

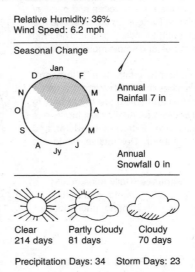

Annual Rainfall 7 in

Annual Snowfall 0 in

Clear 214 days　Partly Cloudy 81 days　Cloudy 70 days

Precipitation Days: 34　Storm Days: 23

Average Temperatures			
	Daily High	Daily Low	Monthly Mean
January	64.8	37.6	51.2
February	69.3	40.8	55.1
March	74.5	44.8	59.7
April	83.6	51.8	67.7
May	92.9	59.6	76.3
June	101.5	67.7	84.6
July	104.8	77.5	91.2
August	102.2	76.0	89.1
September	98.4	69.1	83.8
October	87.6	56.8	72.2
November	74.7	44.8	59.8
December	66.4	38.5	52.5

Zero-Degree Days: 0
Freezing Days: 32
90-Degree Days: 164
Heating- and Cooling-Degree Days: 5,060

Pittsburgh, PA

Terrain: Lies at the foothills of the Allegheny Mountains at the confluence of the Allegheny and Monongahela rivers, forming the Ohio. The city is approximately 100 miles south of Lake Erie.

Climate: Humid, continental type, modified only slightly by its nearness to the Atlantic Seaboard and the Great Lakes. The predominant air is of polar origin from Canada and moves in by way of storm tracks, which vary in origin from Hudson Bay to the Rockies. There are frequent inversions of air from the Gulf of Mexico during the summer, resulting in spells of warm, humid weather. Precipitation is well distributed; during the winter, one fourth of it is snow, and there is a 50% chance of measurable precipitation on any given day.

Pluses: Variable continental climate.

Minuses: Cloudy, wet, cold winters; occasional humid summer days.

Places Rated Score: 586　　**Places Rated Rank: 88**

Elevation: 1,223 feet

Relative Humidity: 68%
Wind Speed: 9.4 mph

Seasonal Change

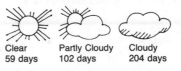

Annual Rainfall 36 in

Annual Snowfall 45 in

Clear 59 days　Partly Cloudy 102 days　Cloudy 204 days

Precipitation Days: 152　Storm Days: 36

Average Temperatures			
	Daily High	Daily Low	Monthly Mean
January	35.3	20.8	28.1
February	37.3	21.3	29.3
March	47.2	29.0	38.1
April	60.9	39.4	50.2
May	70.8	48.7	59.8
June	79.5	57.7	68.6
July	82.5	61.3	71.9
August	80.9	59.4	70.2
September	74.9	52.7	63.8
October	63.9	42.4	53.2
November	49.3	33.3	41.3
December	37.3	23.6	30.5

Zero-Degree Days: 5
Freezing Days: 124
90-Degree Days: 7
Heating- and Cooling-Degree Days: 6,577

Portland, ME

Terrain: Located on a hilly section of the southern coast of Maine, some 45 miles southeast of the White Mountains.

Climate: As a rule, the city has very pleasant summers and falls, cold winters with frequent thaws, and disagreeable springs. Autumn has the greatest number of sunny days. Winters are severe: They begin late but extend deep into what is normally considered springtime, and temperatures well below zero are recorded frequently. Normal monthly precipitation is uniform throughout the year, but heavy snowfalls, sometimes totaling more than 100 inches per year, do occur.

Pluses: Northern marine setting with extremely pleasant summers and falls.

Minuses: Severe winters, with heavy snows, extending well into normal springtime.

Places Rated Score: 483　　**Places Rated Rank: 240**

Elevation: 63 feet

Relative Humidity: 74%
Wind Speed: 8.8 mph

Seasonal Change

Annual Rainfall 41 in

Annual Snowfall 74 in

Clear 107 days　Partly Cloudy 98 days　Cloudy 160 days

Precipitation Days: 127　Storm Days: 18

Average Temperatures			
	Daily High	Daily Low	Monthly Mean
January	31.2	11.7	21.5
February	33.3	12.5	22.9
March	40.8	22.8	31.8
April	52.8	32.5	42.7
May	63.6	41.7	52.7
June	73.2	51.1	62.2
July	79.1	56.9	68.0
August	77.6	55.2	66.4
September	69.9	47.4	58.7
October	60.2	38.0	49.1
November	47.5	29.7	38.6
December	34.9	16.4	25.7

Zero-Degree Days: 15
Freezing Days: 160
90-Degree Days: 5
Heating- and Cooling-Degree Days: 7,750

★ Portland, OR

Terrain: Situated 65 miles inland from the Pacific Ocean and midway between the northerly oriented low Coast Ranges on the west and the higher Cascade Range on the east, each 30 miles distant. The long growing season, with its mild temperatures and ample moisture, favors local nursery and seed industries.

Climate: A rain climate in winter, marked by relatively mild temperatures and cloudy skies. Summers are pleasantly mild with northwesterly winds and very little precipitation. Fall and spring are transitional in nature. Fog occurs frequently in fall and winter. At all times, incursions of marine air are a moderating influence. Extremes in winter and summer come from the continental interior. Destructive winds are infrequent.

Pluses: Short winters; long, pleasant summers; ample precipitation.

Minuses: Daily rains during winter and part of spring; often cloudy.

Places Rated Score: 768

Places Rated Rank: 16

Elevation: 39 feet

Relative Humidity: 74%
Wind Speed: 7.8 mph

Seasonal Change

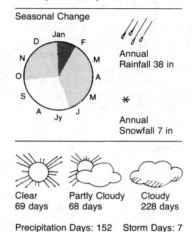

Annual Rainfall 38 in

Annual Snowfall 7 in

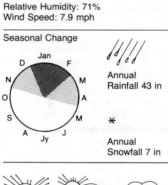

| Clear 69 days | Partly Cloudy 68 days | Cloudy 228 days |

Precipitation Days: 152   Storm Days: 7

Average Temperatures			
	Daily High	Daily Low	Monthly Mean
January	43.6	32.5	38.1
February	50.1	35.5	42.8
March	54.3	37.0	45.7
April	60.3	40.8	50.6
May	67.0	46.3	56.7
June	72.1	51.8	62.0
July	79.0	55.2	67.1
August	78.1	55.0	66.6
September	73.9	50.5	62.2
October	62.9	44.7	53.8
November	52.1	38.5	45.3
December	46.0	35.3	40.7

Zero-Degree Days: 0
Freezing Days: 44
90-Degree Days: 10
Heating- and Cooling-Degree Days: 5,092

Raleigh–Durham, NC

Terrain: Situated in the transition zone between the Coastal Plain and the Piedmont Plateau of North Carolina. The surrounding topography is rolling, with elevations from 200 feet to 500 feet within a 10-mile radius.

Climate: Because it is located between mountains to the west and the Atlantic Coast to the east and south, the metro area enjoys a favorable climate. The mountains form a partial barrier to cold air masses moving eastward from the nation's interior, so that there are very few days in the heart of the winter when the temperature falls below 20° F. Tropical air is present over the eastern and central sections of North Carolina during much of the summer, bringing warm temperatures and high humidity. In midsummer, afternoon temperatures reach 90° F or higher on an average of every fourth day. Rainfall is well distributed throughout the year. July has, on the average, the greatest amount of rainfall, and November the least.

Pluses: Mild four-season climate.

Minuses: Long, humid summers.

Places Rated Score: 647

Places Rated Rank: 37

Elevation: 441 feet

Relative Humidity: 71%
Wind Speed: 7.9 mph

Seasonal Change

Annual Rainfall 43 in

Annual Snowfall 7 in

| Clear 113 days | Partly Cloudy 107 days | Cloudy 145 days |

Precipitation Days: 112   Storm Days: 46

Average Temperatures			
	Daily High	Daily Low	Monthly Mean
January	51.0	30.0	40.5
February	53.2	31.1	42.2
March	61.0	37.4	49.2
April	72.2	46.7	59.5
May	79.4	55.4	67.4
June	85.6	63.1	74.4
July	87.7	67.2	77.5
August	86.8	66.2	76.5
September	81.5	59.7	70.6
October	72.4	48.0	60.2
November	62.1	37.8	50.0
December	51.9	30.5	41.2

Zero-Degree Days: 0
Freezing Days: 82
90-Degree Days: 25
Heating- and Cooling-Degree Days: 4,908

Reno, NV

Terrain: Located at the west edge of Truckee Meadows in a semiarid plateau lying in the lee of the Sierra Nevada. To the west, this range rises to elevations of 9,000 feet to 10,000 feet, and hills to the east reach 6,000 feet to 7,000 feet. The Truckee River, flowing from the Sierra Nevada eastward through Reno, drains into Pyramid Lake to the northeast.

Climate: Sunshine is abundant throughout the year. Temperatures are mild, but the daily range may exceed 45 degrees. Even when afternoons reach the upper 90s, a light jacket is needed shortly after sunset. Nights with a minimum temperature over 60° F are rare. Afternoon temperatures are moderate, and only about ten days a year fail to reach a level above freezing. Humidity is very low during the summer months and moderately low during winter.

Pluses: Mild, sunny climate in alpine setting.

Minuses: Considerable daily temperature variation, little precipitation.

Places Rated Score: 535

Places Rated Rank: 182

Elevation: 4,400 feet

Relative Humidity: 50%
Wind Speed: 6.3 mph

Seasonal Change

Annual Rainfall 7 in

Annual Snowfall 27 in

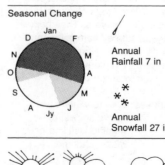

| Clear 165 days | Partly Cloudy 90 days | Cloudy 110 days |

Precipitation Days: 49   Storm Days: 13

Average Temperatures			
	Daily High	Daily Low	Monthly Mean
January	45.4	18.3	31.9
February	51.1	23.0	37.1
March	56.0	24.6	40.3
April	64.0	29.6	46.8
May	72.2	37.0	54.6
June	80.4	42.5	61.5
July	91.1	47.4	69.3
August	89.0	44.8	66.9
September	81.8	38.6	60.2
October	70.0	30.5	50.3
November	56.3	23.9	40.1
December	46.4	19.6	33.0

Zero-Degree Days: 3
Freezing Days: 189
90-Degree Days: 52
Heating- and Cooling-Degree Days: 6,351

Richmond–Petersburg, VA

Terrain: Located in east-central Virginia at the head of navigation on the James River between Tidewater Virginia and the Piedmont. The Blue Ridge Mountains lie about 90 miles to the west and the Chesapeake Bay 60 miles to the east.

Climate: Water- and mountain-modified continental, with warm, humid summers and generally mild winters. The mountains to the west act as a barrier to outbreaks of cold, continental air in winter; the open waters of the Chesapeake Bay and the Atlantic also contribute to mild winters and to humid summers. Coldest weather usually occurs in late December and in January, with a normal temperature range from 20° F to 50° F. Precipitation is uniformly distributed throughout the year, though dry periods do occur in the autumn, when long periods of pleasant, mild weather are most common.

Pluses:	Minuses:
Modified continental climate with long growing season.	Humid summers, severe thunderstorms, hurricanes.

Places Rated Score: 585   **Places Rated Rank: 92**

Elevation: 177 feet

Relative Humidity: 72%
Wind Speed: 7.5 mph

Seasonal Change

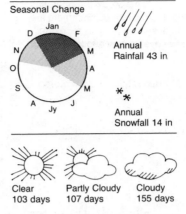

Annual Rainfall 43 in

Annual Snowfall 14 in

Clear 103 days   Partly Cloudy 107 days   Cloudy 155 days

Precipitation Days: 113   Storm Days: 37

Average Temperatures			
	Daily High	Daily Low	Monthly Mean
January	47.4	27.6	37.5
February	49.9	28.8	39.4
March	58.2	35.5	46.9
April	70.3	45.2	57.8
May	78.4	54.5	66.5
June	85.4	62.9	74.2
July	88.2	67.5	77.9
August	86.6	65.9	76.3
September	80.9	59.0	70.0
October	71.2	47.4	59.3
November	60.6	37.3	49.0
December	49.1	28.8	39.0

Zero-Degree Days: 0
Freezing Days: 85
90-Degree Days: 41
Heating- and Cooling-Degree Days: 5,292

Roanoke, VA

Terrain: Located in the part of the Great Valley that runs from the northernmost part of Virginia southwest to Scott County. The Blue Ridge Mountains are to the west, the Allegheny Mountains to the north.

Climate: Mild. The mountain barrier moderates cold air from the north before it reaches the area. The elevation of the city usually produces cool summer nights. Rainfall is well distributed throughout the year, with an average of 23 inches in the warm season. Snow usually falls each winter, with extremes ranging from a trace to 60 inches.

Pluses:	Minuses:
Invigorating, but rare extremes of temperature do occur.	Roanoke River liable to flood.

Places Rated Score: 652   **Places Rated Rank: 33**

Elevation: 1,176 feet

Relative Humidity: 65%
Wind Speed: 8.3 mph

Seasonal Change

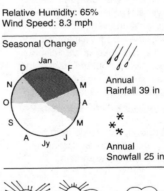

Annual Rainfall 39 in

Annual Snowfall 25 in

Clear 103 days   Partly Cloudy 114 days   Cloudy 148 days

Precipitation Days: 121   Storm Days: 38

Average Temperatures			
	Daily High	Daily Low	Monthly Mean
January	45.6	27.2	36.4
February	47.9	28.3	38.1
March	56.3	34.3	45.3
April	67.9	43.9	55.9
May	76.1	52.7	64.4
June	83.0	60.4	71.7
July	85.9	64.4	75.2
August	84.9	63.3	74.1
September	79.5	56.5	68.0
October	69.9	45.6	57.8
November	57.6	35.8	46.7
December	46.6	28.1	37.4

Zero-Degree Days: 0
Freezing Days: 92
90-Degree Days: 20
Heating- and Cooling-Degree Days: 5,337

Rochester, MN

Terrain: Located in the Zumbro River valley in southeastern Minnesota amid rolling farmland.

Climate: Continental weather pattern with four definite seasons. Winters are cold, but summers are pleasant, with temperatures reaching as high as 90° F on only seven days in an average summer. Thunderstorms (sometimes heavy downpours) occur about once every three days, on the average, during the growing season. These storms often cause high winds. About four times each year, hail will fall. Tornadoes are rare but do occur. Heavy fog occurs 35 times a year on the average.

Pluses:	Minuses:
Invigorating four seasons with especially pleasant summers.	Cold winters lasting at least five months.

Places Rated Score: 308   **Places Rated Rank: 317**

Elevation: 1,320 feet

Relative Humidity: 74%
Wind Speed: 12.7 mph

Seasonal Change

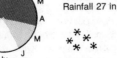

Annual Rainfall 27 in

Annual Snowfall 44 in

Clear 91 days   Partly Cloudy 96 days   Cloudy 178 days

Precipitation Days: 115   Storm Days: 41

Average Temperatures			
	Daily High	Daily Low	Monthly Mean
January	21.9	3.9	12.9
February	26.4	7.4	16.9
March	36.5	19.1	27.8
April	54.9	34.1	44.5
May	67.1	45.3	56.2
June	76.4	55.5	66.0
July	80.7	59.5	70.1
August	79.4	57.7	68.6
September	70.2	48.3	59.3
October	60.4	38.7	49.6
November	40.9	24.2	32.6
December	26.9	10.9	18.9

Zero-Degree Days: 35
Freezing Days: 165
90-Degree Days: 7
Heating- and Cooling-Degree Days: 8,701

Rockford, IL

Terrain: Located northwest of the Chicago area in rolling prairie.
Climate: When winter winds blow from Lake Michigan, cloudiness is often increased, and temperatures are somewhat higher than those to the west around the Mississippi. The lake can also be a moderating influence in summer, sometimes lowering temperatures. Summers are usually hot, however, but oppressive heat seldom prevails for extended periods. Winters are cold, and snow cover is continuous from late December through February.

Pluses: Adequate snow cover for diversified winter sports.

Minuses: Long, cold winters; hot summers.

Elevation: 743 feet

Relative Humidity: 72%
Wind Speed: 9.9 mph

Seasonal Change

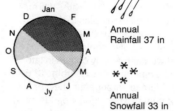

Annual Rainfall 37 in

Annual Snowfall 33 in

Clear 96 days   Partly Cloudy 100 days   Cloudy 169 days

Precipitation Days: 114   Storm Days: 42

Average Temperatures			
	Daily High	Daily Low	Monthly Mean
January	28.9	11.5	20.2
February	32.6	15.3	24.0
March	43.1	25.0	34.1
April	59.1	37.3	48.2
May	70.3	47.2	58.8
June	79.9	57.7	68.8
July	84.2	61.4	72.8
August	82.8	60.1	71.5
September	74.7	51.8	63.3
October	64.3	41.1	52.7
November	46.5	28.7	37.6
December	33.1	16.7	24.9

Zero-Degree Days: 16
Freezing Days: 142
90-Degree Days: 13
Heating- and Cooling-Degree Days: 7,559

Places Rated Score: 466   **Places Rated Rank: 260**

Sacramento, CA

Terrain: Located in the heart of a broad, flat valley between California's Coast Ranges and the Sierra Nevada. The land is tabletop-flat and, when irrigated, perfect for growing fruits and vegetables.
Climate: The two mountain ranges shelter the area from many storms and violent weather, thus adding to the mildness of the climate. Occasionally, however, northerly winds, called northers, reach the valley over the Siskiyou Mountains, causing heat waves. Summers are sunny and hot, but low humidity lessens the felt heat. Winters are mild, and snow is rare enough to not be regarded a climatic feature.

Pluses: Sunny, mild.

Minuses: Hot winds from the north on occasion, hot summers.

Elevation: 25 feet

Relative Humidity: 66%
Wind Speed: 8.3 mph

Seasonal Change

Annual Rainfall 17 in

Annual Snowfall .1 in

Clear 193 days   Partly Cloudy 72 days   Cloudy 100 days

Precipitation Days: 57   Storm Days: 5

Average Temperatures			
	Daily High	Daily Low	Monthly Mean
January	53.0	37.1	45.1
February	59.1	40.4	49.8
March	64.1	41.9	53.0
April	71.3	45.3	58.3
May	78.8	49.8	64.3
June	86.4	54.6	70.5
July	92.9	57.5	75.2
August	91.3	56.9	74.1
September	87.7	55.3	71.5
October	77.1	49.5	63.3
November	63.6	42.4	53.0
December	53.3	38.3	45.8

Zero-Degree Days: 0
Freezing Days: 17
90-Degree Days: 77
Heating- and Cooling-Degree Days: 4,002

Places Rated Score: 576   **Places Rated Rank: 103**

Saginaw–Bay City–Midland, MI

Terrain: Located south of the tip of Saginaw Bay on the Saginaw River, which flows into the bay. To the west, the land is level and sandy; to the east, it is heavy and fertile lake-bed clay. The metro area is far enough from the bay (and Lake Huron) to be considered an inland location. However, these bodies of water do moderate the climate somewhat.
Climate: The highest temperature ever recorded here was 111° F on July 13, 1936. The coldest was –18° F on February 9, 1934. However, the area averages only five zero-degree days per year, which is low for a location this far north away from an ocean. On the other hand, there are 16 ninety-degree days each summer, on average. Heaviest rainfall is in May. Cloud cover is most frequent in November but is generally less so than that in other places in the state nearer Lake Michigan. The driest month is usually January.

Pluses: Pleasant summers with cool nights.

Minuses: Long winters, cloudy.

Elevation: 662 feet

Relative Humidity: 76%
Wind Speed: 10 mph

Seasonal Change

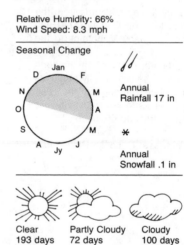

Annual Rainfall 29 in

Annual Snowfall 47 in

Clear 67 days   Partly Cloudy 96 days   Cloudy 202 days

Precipitation Days: 181   Storm Days: 38

Average Temperatures			
	Daily High	Daily Low	Monthly Mean
January	30.4	16.5	23.5
February	31.3	16.1	23.7
March	40.1	24.4	32.3
April	54.9	34.6	44.8
May	67.5	45.1	56.3
June	78.1	55.6	66.9
July	83.8	59.8	71.8
August	81.2	57.9	69.6
September	72.7	50.7	61.7
October	61.4	40.8	51.1
November	45.1	30.7	37.9
December	33.5	20.9	27.2

Zero-Degree Days: 5
Freezing Days: 147
90-Degree Days: 16
Heating- and Cooling-Degree Days: 7,362

Places Rated Score: 515   **Places Rated Rank: 210**

St. Louis, MO–IL

Terrain: Located at the confluence of the Missouri and Mississippi rivers and slightly east of the geographic center of the United States. The surrounding terrain is gently rolling, with occasional high bluffs characteristic of parts of the Mississippi Valley.

Climate: Modified continental. St. Louis is in the enviable position of having a changeable, four-season climate without prolonged periods of extreme cold, heat, or humidity. To the south is the warm, moist air of the Gulf of Mexico and to the north the region of cold polar air masses. Alternating invasions by these influences, and the conflict along the frontal zones where they meet, produce a great variety of weather conditions, but none lasting long enough to become monotonous. Winters are brisk but seldom severe. Snowfall averages less than 20 inches per season. Summers are quite warm, often uncomfortably so when coupled with high humidity. These oppressive spells usually are relieved by storms.

Pluses: Changeable weather, relatively mild winters.

Minuses: Hot, humid summers.

Places Rated Score: 537

Places Rated Rank: 173

Elevation: 564 feet

Relative Humidity: 70%
Wind Speed: 9.5 mph

Seasonal Change

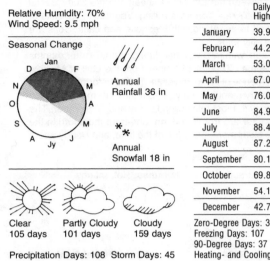

Annual Rainfall 36 in

Annual Snowfall 18 in

Clear 105 days
Partly Cloudy 101 days
Cloudy 159 days

Precipitation Days: 108   Storm Days: 45

Average Temperatures			
	Daily High	Daily Low	Monthly Mean
January	39.9	22.6	31.3
February	44.2	26.0	35.1
March	53.0	33.5	43.3
April	67.0	46.0	56.5
May	76.0	55.5	65.8
June	84.9	64.8	74.9
July	88.4	68.8	78.6
August	87.2	67.1	77.2
September	80.1	59.1	69.6
October	69.8	48.4	59.1
November	54.1	35.9	45.0
December	42.7	26.5	34.6

Zero-Degree Days: 3
Freezing Days: 107
90-Degree Days: 37
Heating- and Cooling-Degree Days: 6,225

Salt Lake City–Ogden, UT

Terrain: Spectacular setting. To the east, the Wasatch Mountains rise from heights of 8,000 feet to 12,000 feet; to the southwest, the Oguirrh Mountains climb to 10,000 feet.

Climate: Though by no means mild, it is modified by the surrounding mountains, which deflect stormy weather elsewhere. There are four well-defined seasons, including a long winter. Summers are hot, but the dry air lessens felt heat, and nights are cool. Winters are cold but not severe. Most of the precipitation is snow, with accumulations staying on the ground for most of the winter. Fall is short, with spring longer and sometimes stormy. Nearby Great Salt Lake also helps modify the climate.

Pluses: Scenic setting, good rigorous climate.

Minuses: Cold, snowy winters.

Elevation: 4,227 feet

Relative Humidity: 54%
Wind Speed: 8.7 mph

Seasonal Change

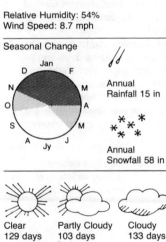

Annual Rainfall 15 in

Annual Snowfall 58 in

Clear 129 days
Partly Cloudy 103 days
Cloudy 133 days

Precipitation Days: 88   Storm Days: 35

Average Temperatures			
	Daily High	Daily Low	Monthly Mean
January	37.4	18.5	28.0
February	43.4	23.3	33.4
March	50.8	28.3	39.6
April	61.8	36.6	49.2
May	72.4	44.2	58.3
June	81.3	51.1	66.2
July	92.8	60.5	76.7
August	90.2	58.7	74.5
September	80.3	43.3	64.8
October	66.4	38.4	52.4
November	50.0	28.1	39.1
December	39.0	21.5	30.3

Zero-Degree Days: 3
Freezing Days: 134
90-Degree Days: 58
Heating- and Cooling-Degree Days: 6,910

Places Rated Score: 541

Places Rated Rank: 168

San Angelo, TX

Terrain: Lies on the northern edge of the Edwards Plateau. The land is flat, sometimes slightly rolling, and is classified as semiarid, or steppe, covered with grass, thorny bush, and cacti.

Climate: San Angelo is situated between the humid climate of eastern Texas and the dry High Plains and the Basin and Range region of western Texas. It is hot, though usually dry. However, uncomfortable hot spells with humid air permeate the area occasionally. The wind is brisk, modifying summer heat. Summers are long, winters short and mild.

Pluses: Dry sunny climate, long summers, short winters.

Minuses: Can be dusty; humid hot spells.

Elevation: 1,908 feet

Relative Humidity: 59%
Wind Speed: 10.5 mph

Seasonal Change

Annual Rainfall 18 in

Annual Snowfall 3 in

Clear 157 days
Partly Cloudy 97 days
Cloudy 111 days

Precipitation Days: 57   Storm Days: 37

Average Temperatures			
	Daily High	Daily Low	Monthly Mean
January	59.1	33.6	46.4
February	63.2	37.5	50.4
March	70.7	43.5	57.1
April	80.4	54.0	67.2
May	86.5	62.4	74.5
June	93.4	69.8	81.6
July	96.9	72.4	84.7
August	96.9	72.0	84.5
September	88.4	65.1	76.8
October	79.6	54.7	67.2
November	68.5	42.5	55.5
December	61.4	35.2	48.3

Zero-Degree Days: 0
Freezing Days: 52
90-Degree Days: 109
Heating- and Cooling-Degree Days: 4,942

Places Rated Score: 488

Places Rated Rank: 237

San Antonio, TX

Terrain: Located between the Edwards Plateau and the Gulf Coastal Plain of south central Texas. Terrain is rolling. Vegetation consists of grasses and live oak trees, along with mesquite and cacti. Soils are blackland clay and silty loam.

Climate: Two-season, with mild weather during normal winter months and a long, hot summer. Though 140 miles from the Gulf of Mexico, the city feels the influence of its hot moist air. Thunderstorms and rains have occurred in every month of the year, but they are most common during the summer, with most rain falling in May and September. The winds during the winter are from the north, and from the south in the summer. Skies are clear more than 30% of the time, and cloudy about 30%.

Pluses: No winter, attractive terrain.

Minuses: Hot, muggy summers.

Places Rated Score: 398

Places Rated Rank: 300

Elevation: 794 feet

Relative Humidity: 67%
Wind Speed: 9.3 mph

Seasonal Change

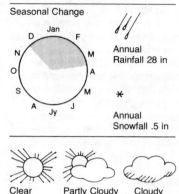

Annual Rainfall 28 in

Annual Snowfall .5 in

Clear 110 days   Partly Cloudy 117 days   Cloudy 138 days

Precipitation Days: 81   Storm Days: 36

Average Temperatures			
	Daily High	Daily Low	Monthly Mean
January	61.6	39.8	50.7
February	65.6	43.4	54.5
March	72.5	49.1	60.8
April	80.3	58.8	69.6
May	86.2	65.7	76.0
June	92.4	72.0	82.2
July	95.6	73.8	84.7
August	95.9	73.4	84.7
September	89.8	68.8	79.3
October	81.8	59.2	70.5
November	71.1	48.2	59.7
December	64.4	41.8	53.2

Zero-Degree Days: 0
Freezing Days: 22
90-Degree Days: 111
Heating- and Cooling-Degree Days: 4,564

★ San Diego, CA

Terrain: Located on San Diego Bay in the southwest corner of California near the Mexican border. Its coastal location is backed by coastal foothills and mountains to the east.

Climate: One of the mildest in North America: typically marine, sometimes called Mediterranean. There are no freezing days and an average of only three 90-degree days each year. San Diego has abundant sunshine and mild sea breezes. Only two seasons occur here: a dry, mild summer and a spring that is cooler, with some rain. Storms are practically unknown, though there is considerable fog along the coast, and many low clouds in early morning and evening during the summer.

Pluses: One of the best climates for sun and mildness.

Minuses: Paradise climate lacking variety and seasonal contrasts.

Places Rated Score: 903

Places Rated Rank: 3

Elevation: 28 feet

Relative Humidity: 68%
Wind Speed: 6.7 mph

Seasonal Change

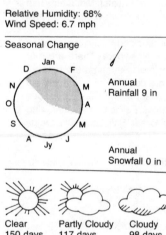

Annual Rainfall 9 in

Annual Snowfall 0 in

Clear 150 days   Partly Cloudy 117 days   Cloudy 98 days

Precipitation Days: 41   Storm Days: 3

Average Temperatures			
	Daily High	Daily Low	Monthly Mean
January	64.6	45.8	55.2
February	65.6	47.8	56.7
March	66.0	50.1	58.1
April	67.6	53.8	60.7
May	69.4	57.2	63.3
June	71.1	59.9	65.5
July	75.3	63.9	69.6
August	77.3	65.4	71.4
September	76.5	63.2	69.9
October	73.8	58.4	66.1
November	70.1	51.5	60.8
December	66.1	55.4	62.9

Zero-Degree Days: 0
Freezing Days: 0
90-Degree Days: 3
Heating- and Cooling-Degree Days: 2,229

★ San Francisco, CA

Terrain: Unique location—at the northern end of a narrow peninsula that separates San Francisco Bay from the Pacific Ocean and forms the southern shore of the Golden Gate Bridge—causes San Francisco to be known as the Air-Conditioned City.

Climate: Two-season climate: a cool, pleasant summer and a mild spring. Flowers bloom throughout the year, and warm clothing is needed every month. Sea fogs and associated low stratus clouds are a striking characteristic of the city's climate. On the average, though, the sun shines during 66% of the daylight hours. There are wide contrasts in climate within short distances of the bay; nearby communities of Marin County, to the north across the Golden Gate and sheltered from the prevailing winds by high peaks and ridges of the Coast Ranges, enjoy warmer and sunnier weather than the city.

Pluses: Mild, springlike weather ten months of the year; ranks first among the 329 metro areas.

Minuses: Invariable climate patterns; fogs and cloudy days.

Places Rated Score: 910

Places Rated Rank: 1

Elevation: 155 feet

Relative Humidity: 75%
Wind Speed: 8.7 mph

Seasonal Change

Annual Rainfall 21 in

Annual Snowfall 0 in

Clear 162 days   Partly Cloudy 103 days   Cloudy 100 days

Precipitation Days: 67   Storm Days: 2

Average Temperatures			
	Daily High	Daily Low	Monthly Mean
January	55.3	41.2	48.3
February	58.6	43.8	51.2
March	61.0	44.9	53.0
April	63.5	47.0	55.3
May	66.6	49.9	58.3
June	70.2	53.0	61.6
July	70.9	54.0	62.5
August	71.6	54.3	63.0
September	73.6	54.5	64.1
October	70.3	51.6	61.0
November	63.3	47.2	55.3
December	56.5	42.9	49.7

Zero-Degree Days: 0
Freezing Days: 0
90-Degree Days: 1
Heating- and Cooling-Degree Days: 3,119

★ Santa Barbara–Santa Maria–Lompoc, CA

Terrain: Located in the Santa Maria Valley 150 miles north of Los Angeles and 250 miles south of San Francisco. The valley is flat and fertile, opening onto the Pacific Ocean at its widest point and tapering inland at a distance of 30 miles from the coast. It is bounded by the foothills of the San Rafael Mountains, the Solomon Hills, and the Casmalia Hills.

Climate: Rainfall season, typical of the California coast, is winter. During the rest of the year, particularly from June to October, there is little or no precipitation. Clear, sunshiny afternoons prevail on most days. At night and in the morning, however, the California stratus and fog appear.

Pluses: Year-round mildness moving through gradual transitions.

Minuses: No distinct seasonal changes, night and morning fogs.

Places Rated Score: 855

Places Rated Rank: 7

Elevation: 238 feet ·

Relative Humidity: 74%
Wind Speed: 7 mph

Seasonal Change

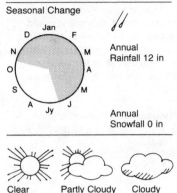

Annual Rainfall 12 in

Annual Snowfall 0 in

Clear 177 days | Partly Cloudy 108 days | Cloudy 80 days

Precipitation Days: 45   Storm Days: 2

Average Temperatures			
	Daily High	Daily Low	Monthly Mean
January	62.7	38.3	50.5
February	63.6	40.3	52.0
March	64.3	41.3	52.8
April	66.0	43.7	54.9
May	67.4	46.7	57.1
June	69.7	49.5	59.6
July	71.8	52.4	62.1
August	72.1	52.5	62.3
September	73.9	51.2	62.6
October	73.3	47.5	60.4
November	69.2	42.9	56.1
December	64.2	39.3	51.8

Zero-Degree Days: 0
Freezing Days: 24
90-Degree Days: 6
Heating- and Cooling-Degree Days: 3,137

★ Santa Rosa–Petaluma, CA

Terrain: Located in the east-central portion of the Petaluma–Santa Rosa–Russian River valley, which extends northwestward from San Pablo Bay, about 45 miles from the Golden Gate Bridge. This valley runs parallel to the Pacific Coast, with only low hills (300 feet to 500 feet) between it and the ocean 25 miles southwest. Higher hills rise to the east of the metro area, with greater elevations about 10 miles farther east, in the foothills of the Coast Ranges.

Climate: The nearness of the ocean and the surrounding topography join with the prevailing westerly circulation to produce a predominantly southerly air flow year-round. However, the area is sufficiently far inland to assure it a more varied climate than San Francisco's. Summers are warmer, winters cooler, and there is more daily temperature shift, as well as less fog and drizzle.

Pluses: Mild, yet sunnier and warmer than coastal locations; ideal retirement climate.

Minuses: Some hot weather.

Places Rated Score: 732

Places Rated Rank: 19

Elevation: 167 feet

Relative Humidity: 70%
Wind Speed: 7 mph

Seasonal Change

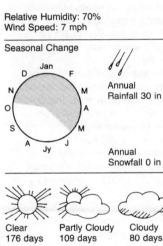

Annual Rainfall 30 in

Annual Snowfall 0 in

Clear 176 days | Partly Cloudy 109 days | Cloudy 80 days

Precipitation Days: 47   Storm Days: 4

Average Temperatures			
	Daily High	Daily Low	Monthly Mean
January	57.1	35.7	46.4
February	62.3	37.9	50.1
March	66.6	39.5	53.1
April	70.1	40.1	55.1
May	75.0	44.6	59.8
June	80.2	49.2	64.1
July	83.6	48.8	66.4
August	83.4	48.8	66.1
September	83.3	47.7	65.5
October	77.7	44.3	61.0
November	67.7	39.2	53.5
December	58.4	37.0	47.7

Zero-Degree Days: 0
Freezing Days: 43
90-Degree Days: 33
Heating- and Cooling-Degree Days: 3,900

Savannah, GA

Terrain: Surrounded by flat land, low and marshy to the north and east, rising to several feet above sea level to the west and south. About half the land to the west and south is clear of trees; the other half is woods, much of which lie in swamp.

Climate: Temperate with a seasonal mean temperature of 51° F in winter, 64° F in spring, 80° F in summer, and 66° F in autumn. Summer temperatures are moderated by thundershowers almost every afternoon. Sunshine is adequate in all seasons; seldom are there more than two or three days in succession without it. The long growing season is accompanied by abundant rain.

Pluses: Mild winters, pleasant autumns.

Minuses: Low, marshy terrain; humid summers.

Places Rated Score: 542

Places Rated Rank: 164

Elevation: 51 feet

Relative Humidity: 74%
Wind Speed: 8.1 mph

Seasonal Change

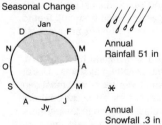

Annual Rainfall 51 in

Annual Snowfall .3 in

Clear 104 days | Partly Cloudy 113 days | Cloudy 148 days

Precipitation Days: 112   Storm Days: 64

Average Temperatures			
	Daily High	Daily Low	Monthly Mean
January	61.1	38.7	49.9
February	63.6	40.5	52.1
March	69.5	46.4	58.0
April	77.8	54.3	66.1
May	84.8	61.8	73.3
June	89.3	68.8	79.1
July	90.8	71.3	81.1
August	90.3	70.9	80.6
September	85.4	66.9	76.2
October	78.2	55.9	67.1
November	69.3	44.9	57.1
December	62.1	38.7	50.4

Zero-Degree Days: 0
Freezing Days: 35
90-Degree Days: 54
Heating- and Cooling-Degree Days: 4,269

★ Seattle, WA

Terrain: Located on Puget Sound on the northwest Pacific coast of Washington. The Cascade Range and the Olympic Mountains serve as barriers to easterly and northerly weather systems.

Climate: Midlatitude coast climate, characterized by moderate temperatures, a pronounced though not sharply defined rainy season, and considerable cloudiness, particularly during the winter. Occasionally, severe winter storms come in from the north. Summers are very pleasant, and winters are relatively mild, with prevailing temperatures in the 40s. Summer heat and winter cold are modified by the nearness of the ocean.

Pluses: Mild temperatures, especially pleasant summers and autumns.

Minuses: Wet winters, ground fogs, lots of drizzle.

Places Rated Score: 808

Places Rated Rank: 12

Elevation: 450 feet

Relative Humidity: 74%
Wind Speed: 9.3 mph

Seasonal Change

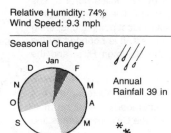

Annual Rainfall 39 in

Annual Snowfall 15 in

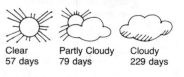

Clear 57 days
Partly Cloudy 79 days
Cloudy 229 days

Precipitation Days: 160   Storm Days: 7

Average Temperatures			
	Daily High	Daily Low	Monthly Mean
January	43.4	33.0	38.2
February	48.5	36.0	42.3
March	51.5	36.6	44.1
April	57.0	40.3	48.7
May	64.1	45.6	54.9
June	69.0	50.6	59.8
July	75.1	53.8	64.5
August	73.8	53.7	63.8
September	68.7	50.4	59.6
October	59.4	44.9	52.2
November	50.4	38.8	44.6
December	45.4	35.5	40.5

Zero-Degree Days: 0
Freezing Days: 32
90-Degree Days: 3
Heating- and Cooling-Degree Days: 5,314

Shreveport, LA

Terrain: Located on the west bank of the Red River opposite Bossier City, in the northwestern section of the state, some 30 miles south of Arkansas and 15 miles east of the Texas state line. Part of the city is situated in the Red River bottomlands and the remainder in the gently rolling hills that begin a mile west of the river.

Climate: Transitional between the humid subtropical climate prevalent to the south and the continental climates of the Great Plains and Middle West to the north. Winter months are normally mild, with cold spells generally of short duration. The typical pattern is a drop in temperature the first day, minimum temperatures the second day, and gradual warming on the third. Summers are hot and humid, relieved only by the thunderstorms that come about eight times per month during that season. April and May are pleasant. Fall, which lasts from late September until December, is delightful for outdoor activities.

Pluses: Mild winters, long falls.

Minuses: Hot, steamy summers; occasional flooding.

Places Rated Score: 508

Places Rated Rank: 220

Elevation: 259 feet

Relative Humidity: 71%
Wind Speed: 8.8 mph

Seasonal Change

Annual Rainfall 45 in

Annual Snowfall 1 in

Clear 118 days
Partly Cloudy 99 days
Cloudy 148 days

Precipitation Days: 97   Storm Days: 54

Average Temperatures			
	Daily High	Daily Low	Monthly Mean
January	56.6	37.8	47.2
February	60.4	40.6	50.5
March	67.3	46.2	56.8
April	76.9	55.9	66.4
May	83.6	63.1	73.4
June	90.1	70.2	80.2
July	93.5	72.8	83.2
August	93.8	72.5	83.2
September	87.9	66.8	77.4
October	79.3	55.7	67.5
November	67.2	45.2	56.2
December	58.9	39.4	49.2

Zero-Degree Days: 0
Freezing Days: 1
90-Degree Days: 87
Heating- and Cooling-Degree Days: 4,705

Sioux City, IA–NE

Terrain: Sioux City is located along the Missouri River at a point where Iowa touches both Nebraska and South Dakota. The terrain is rolling, except for the river valleys and bottomlands. The Sioux City business district lies in the river valley, and the residential sections, for the most part, are spread over the hills, which range from 100 feet to 200 feet higher. Corn, small grains, and grazing grasses are products of abundant rainfall here.

Climate: Typically continental and largely determined by the movement and interaction of the large-scale weather systems. Under normal conditions, winters are cold and summers warm, with most rain falling between April and September. Except for an occasional dry year, rain is plentiful. There is considerable fluctuation in temperature and precipitation from season to season and year to year, as elsewhere in the northern Plains. Average growing season: 160 days. The first freeze is in early October and the last in late April.

Pluses: Variable.

Minuses: Rugged continental.

Places Rated Score: 385

Places Rated Rank: 304

Elevation: 1,103 feet

Relative Humidity: 69%
Wind Speed: 10.9 mph

Seasonal Change

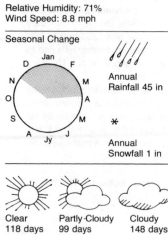

Annual Rainfall 26 in

Annual Snowfall 31 in

Clear 107 days
Partly Cloudy 103 days
Cloudy 155 days

Precipitation Days: 98   Storm Days: 45

Average Temperatures			
	Daily High	Daily Low	Monthly Mean
January	28.2	7.7	18.0
February	33.3	13.4	23.4
March	42.9	23.4	33.2
April	61.3	37.4	49.4
May	72.5	49.3	60.9
June	81.3	59.3	70.3
July	86.7	63.9	75.3
August	84.8	62.1	73.5
September	75.3	51.4	63.4
October	65.8	40.4	53.1
November	47.0	25.6	36.3
December	33.3	13.6	23.5

Zero-Degree Days: 22
Freezing Days: 150
90-Degree Days: 24
Heating- and Cooling-Degree Days: 7,885

Sioux Falls, SD

Terrain: Located in the Big Sioux River valley in the southeastern portion of South Dakota. Surrounding terrain is gently rolling. Within a 100-mile radius of the city, the land slopes upward 300 feet to 400 feet in the north and northwest and downward in the southeast. There is little change in elevation in the other directions.

Climate: Invigorating continental. Cold air masses from the north often move in very rapidly, causing strong, gusty winds for several hours. During late fall and winter, these cold fronts sometimes bring temperature drops of 20 degrees to 30 degrees in a day. Severe cold spells rarely last more than a few days. During a cold winter, frost may penetrate the ground to a depth of 3 feet to 4 feet unless there is heavy snow cover to protect the ground. There are usually one to two very heavy snowstorms each winter. Summer temperatures may climb over 100° F once or twice a year. Thunderstorms are frequent, especially during June and July. Occasional tornadoes and floods.

Pluses: Vigorous four-season climate.

Minuses: Extremes in temperature, snowy winters.

Places Rated Score: 276

Places Rated Rank: 321

Elevation: 1,427 feet

Relative Humidity: 69%
Wind Speed: 11.2 mph

Seasonal Change

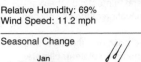

Annual Rainfall 25 in

Annual Snowfall 39 in

Clear 105 days | Partly Cloudy 105 days | Cloudy 155 days

Precipitation Days: 93   Storm Days: 43

	Average Temperatures		
	Daily High	Daily Low	Monthly Mean
January	24.6	3.7	14.2
February	29.7	9.0	19.4
March	39.7	20.2	30.0
April	57.8	34.4	46.1
May	69.7	45.7	57.7
June	78.9	56.3	67.6
July	85.1	61.5	73.3
August	83.8	59.8	71.8
September	73.0	48.7	60.9
October	62.7	37.6	50.2
November	43.5	22.7	33.1
December	29.6	10.4	20.0

Zero-Degree Days: 33
Freezing Days: 171
90-Degree Days: 28
Heating- and Cooling-Degree Days: 8,557

Spokane, WA

Terrain: Spokane lies on the eastern edge of the broad Columbia Basin area of Washington, which is bounded by the Cascade Range on the west and the Rocky Mountains to the east. The elevations in eastern Washington vary from less than 400 feet above sea level near Pasco to 5,000 feet in the extreme eastern edge of the state. Spokane is in the upper plateau area, where the long, gradual slope from the Columbia River meets the sharp rise of the Rockies.

Climate: Combines some of the characteristics of the damp coastal climate with the arid interior climate. Most air masses are brought from the west or southwest and lose most of their moisture passing over the Coast and Cascade ranges. Sometimes dry, continental air masses from the east invade the area, bringing high temperatures with low humidity in the summer and subzero temperatures in the winter. Generally, Spokane has a mild, arid climate during summer and a cold, coastal climate during winter.

Pluses: Mild, dry summers.

Minuses: Damp winters.

Places Rated Score: 574

Places Rated Rank: 110

Elevation: 2,365 feet

Relative Humidity: 63%
Wind Speed: 8.7 mph

Seasonal Change

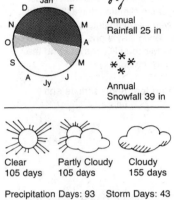

Annual Rainfall 17 in

Annual Snowfall 53 in

Clear 89 days | Partly Cloudy 87 days | Cloudy 189 days

Precipitation Days: 114   Storm Days: 11

	Average Temperatures		
	Daily High	Daily Low	Monthly Mean
January	31.9	19.6	25.4
February	39.0	25.3	32.2
March	46.2	28.8	37.5
April	57.0	35.2	46.1
May	66.5	42.8	54.7
June	73.6	49.4	61.5
July	84.3	55.1	69.7
August	81.9	54.0	68.0
September	72.5	46.7	59.6
October	58.1	37.5	47.8
November	41.8	29.2	35.5
December	33.9	24.0	29.0

Zero-Degree Days: 5
Freezing Days: 141
90-Degree Days: 21
Heating- and Cooling-Degree Days: 7,225

Springfield, IL

Terrain: Surrounding country is nearly level. There are no large hills in the area, but rolling terrain is found near the Sangamon River and Spring Creek.

Climate: Typically continental in character, with warm to hot summers and cold winters. Monthly average temperatures range from the upper 20s in January to the upper 70s in July. Considerable variation takes place frequently within each season. Although summer weather is often uncomfortably warm and humid, winters are less severe than those farther to the north, although prairie winds may accentuate the cold. Summers are sunny.

Pluses: Changeable climate.

Minuses: Hot summers, rather cold winters.

Places Rated Score: 524

Places Rated Rank: 196

Elevation: 613 feet

Relative Humidity: 71%
Wind Speed: 11.4 mph

Seasonal Change

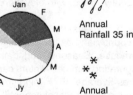

Annual Rainfall 35 in

Annual Snowfall 22 in

Clear 108 days | Partly Cloudy 92 days | Cloudy 165 days

Precipitation Days: 112   Storm Days: 50

	Average Temperatures		
	Daily High	Daily Low	Monthly Mean
January	34.8	18.6	26.7
February	38.9	21.8	30.4
March	48.7	30.1	39.4
April	63.6	42.6	53.1
May	74.1	52.6	63.4
June	83.3	62.5	72.9
July	86.6	65.6	76.1
August	85.0	63.7	74.4
September	78.7	55.6	67.2
October	68.1	45.0	56.6
November	51.0	32.7	41.9
December	38.2	22.7	30.5

Zero-Degree Days: 8
Freezing Days: 119
90-Degree Days: 28
Heating- and Cooling-Degree Days: 6,674

Springfield, MO

Terrain: Located on very gently rolling tableland, almost atop the crest of the Missouri Ozark Plateau. The average elevation of the city proper is just over 1,300 feet above sea level.

Climate: As a result of this advantageous position, the city and surrounding countryside enjoy what is described as a plateau climate. The area possesses the mild and changeable climate often associated with high places in southerly latitudes, with warmer winters and cooler summers than other parts of the state at lower elevations. The city sits astride two major drainage systems: the Missouri River system to the north and the White-Mississippi system to the south.

Pluses: Mild, changeable.

Minuses: Short springs and falls.

Elevation: 1,270 feet

Relative Humidity: 70%
Wind Speed: 11.2 mph

Seasonal Change

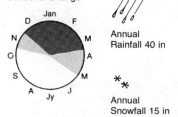

Annual Rainfall 40 in

Annual Snowfall 15 in

Clear 117 days — Partly Cloudy 99 days — Cloudy 149 days

Precipitation Days: 107   Storm Days: 58

Average Temperatures			
	Daily High	Daily Low	Monthly Mean
January	43.2	22.6	32.9
February	47.5	26.5	37.0
March	55.1	32.8	44.0
April	68.0	45.0	56.5
May	76.1	54.0	65.1
June	84.2	62.9	73.6
July	89.0	66.5	77.8
August	88.9	65.2	77.1
September	81.2	57.3	69.3
October	71.1	46.8	59.0
November	56.4	34.5	45.5
December	45.7	26.3	36.0

Zero-Degree Days: 3
Freezing Days: 105
90-Degree Days: 40
Heating- and Cooling-Degree Days: 5,952

Places Rated Score: 544   **Places Rated Rank: 159**

State College, PA

Terrain: Located in Centre County, the geographic center of Pennsylvania. The orientation of the ridges and valleys of the Appalachian Mountains is northeast to southwest. Elevations within Centre County vary from 977 feet to 2,400 feet. The largest valley in the area is Nittany Valley, much of which is under cultivation. The surrounding higher elevations are covered with second-growth forests.

Climate: A composite of the relatively dry midwestern continental climate and the more humid climate characteristic of the eastern seaboard. Prevailing westerly winds carry weather disturbances from the interior of the country into the area. Coastal storms occasionally affect the local weather as they move toward the northeast, but generally the Atlantic is too distant to have a noticeable effect on the climate. Winters are cold and relatively dry, with thick cloud cover. Summer and fall are the most pleasant seasons of the year.

Pluses: Nice falls and summers.

Minuses: Humid, lots of cloudy days.

Elevation: 1,200 feet

Relative Humidity: 67%
Wind Speed: 7.8 mph

Seasonal Change

Annual Rainfall 37 in

Annual Snowfall 48 in

Clear 66 days — Partly Cloudy 114 days — Cloudy 185 days

Precipitation Days: 122   Storm Days: 35

Average Temperatures			
	Daily High	Daily Low	Monthly Mean
January	34.2	19.8	27.0
February	36.1	20.2	28.2
March	45.4	27.7	36.5
April	59.2	38.9	49.1
May	70.2	48.8	59.3
June	78.7	57.3	68.0
July	82.6	61.1	71.9
August	80.7	59.1	69.9
September	73.5	52.0	62.8
October	62.9	42.5	52.7
November	48.7	33.2	41.0
December	36.3	22.9	29.6

Zero-Degree Days: 4
Freezing Days: 132
90-Degree Days: 8
Heating- and Cooling-Degree Days: 6,797

Places Rated Score: 575   **Places Rated Rank: 105**

Syracuse, NY

Terrain: Located at approximately the geographic center of New York State. Gently rolling terrain stretches northward for about 30 miles to the eastern end of Lake Ontario. Oneida Lake lies about 8 miles northeast of the city. Five miles to the south, hills rise to about 1,500 feet. Immediately to the west, terrain is gently rolling, with elevations 500 feet to 800 feet above sea level.

Climate: Continental and comparatively humid. Nearly all cyclonic systems moving from the interior of the country and passing through the St. Lawrence Valley will affect Syracuse. Seasonal and daily changes are marked and produce an invigorating climate. Winters can be cold and severe; daytime temperatures average 35° F, nighttime lows around 18° F. Autumn, winter, and spring show great changeability. Summer nights generally are cool, but days can be uncomfortable because of the humidity. The area is overcast, and the cloudiest months are December, January, and February.

Pluses: Changeable weather.

Minuses: Snowy, cloudy, rigorous in general.

Elevation: 408 feet

Relative Humidity: 73%
Wind Speed: 9.8 mph

Seasonal Change

Annual Rainfall 36 in

Annual Snowfall 109 in

Clear 64 days — Partly Cloudy 100 days — Cloudy 201 days

Precipitation Days: 168   Storm Days: 29

Average Temperatures			
	Daily High	Daily Low	Monthly Mean
January	31.4	15.8	23.6
February	32.7	16.5	24.6
March	41.5	24.8	33.2
April	56.5	36.4	46.5
May	67.6	46.0	56.8
June	77.7	56.1	66.9
July	82.0	61.0	71.5
August	80.2	59.2	69.7
September	73.3	52.3	62.8
October	62.4	42.5	52.5
November	48.3	33.6	41.0
December	35.0	21.2	28.1

Zero-Degree Days: 9
Freezing Days: 138
90-Degree Days: 6
Heating- and Cooling-Degree Days: 7,229

Places Rated Score: 548   **Places Rated Rank: 151**

Tallahassee, FL

Terrain: Located in flat topography in northwest Florida about 20 miles from the Gulf of Mexico.

Climate: Average year-round temperatures compare with those of southern portions of California, Brazil, China, and Australia. The yearly average of 68° F has varied from 64° F to 71° F. In contrast to the southern part of Florida, there is a more definite march of the four seasons here, with considerable winter rainfall and much less winter sunshine. Summer is the least pleasant time of the year; thunderstorms occur on the average of every other day. High humidities and high temperatures cause discomfort. Maxima of 90° F or higher occur on an average of almost 90 days per year, with readings as high as 95° F on 22 of those days.

Pluses: Warm winters, sufficient rainfall.

Minuses: Long, humid summers; few clear days relative to the rest of the state.

Places Rated Score: 404

Places Rated Rank: 296

Elevation: 68 feet

Relative Humidity: 76%
Wind Speed: 7.0 mph

Seasonal Change

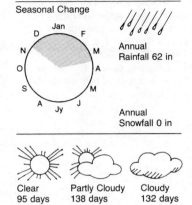

Annual Rainfall 62 in

Annual Snowfall 0 in

Clear 95 days   Partly Cloudy 138 days   Cloudy 132 days

Precipitation Days: 119   Storm Days: 86

Average Temperatures			
	Daily High	Daily Low	Monthly Mean
January	64.2	41.0	52.6
February	66.5	43.0	54.8
March	72.1	48.4	60.3
April	80.1	55.7	67.9
May	86.7	62.8	74.8
June	90.4	69.6	80.0
July	90.6	71.6	81.1
August	90.5	71.7	81.1
September	87.4	68.7	78.1
October	80.6	57.9	69.3
November	71.4	46.4	58.9
December	65.1	41.3	53.2

Zero-Degree Days: 0
Freezing Days: 36
90-Degree Days: 87
Heating- and Cooling-Degree Days: 4,126

Tampa–St. Petersburg–Clearwater, FL

Terrain: Located in flat topography on the Gulf coast of Florida.

Climate: An outstanding feature is the summer thunderstorm season. On the average, there are 88 days of thundershowers per year, occurring mostly in the afternoons in July, August, and September. The resulting temperature drop from 90° F to 70° F produces an agreeable physiologic reaction. Temperature throughout the year is modified by the waters of the Gulf of Mexico and surrounding bays. Snowfall is negligible, and freezing temperatures are rare; during the cooling season, however, night ground fogs occur frequently because of the flat terrain.

Pluses: Mild Gulf climate.

Minuses: Gulf hurricanes, regular summer thundershowers.

Places Rated Score: 440

Places Rated Rank: 277

Elevation: 11 feet

Relative Humidity: 74%
Wind Speed: 8.8 mph

Seasonal Change

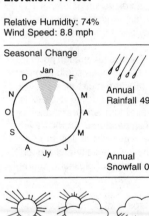

Annual Rainfall 49 in

Annual Snowfall 0 in

Clear 98 days   Partly Cloudy 140 days   Cloudy 127 days

Precipitation Days: 107   Storm Days: 88

Average Temperatures			
	Daily High	Daily Low	Monthly Mean
January	70.6	50.1	60.4
February	71.9	51.7	61.8
March	76.1	55.9	66.0
April	82.4	61.6	72.0
May	87.5	66.9	77.2
June	89.9	72.0	81.0
July	90.1	73.7	81.9
August	90.4	74.0	82.2
September	89.0	72.6	80.8
October	83.9	65.5	74.7
November	77.1	56.4	66.8
December	72.0	51.2	61.6

Zero-Degree Days: 0
Freezing Days: 4
90-Degree Days: 81
Heating- and Cooling-Degree Days: 4,084

Toledo, OH

Terrain: Located on the western end of Lake Erie at the mouth of the Maumee River, on flat ground. The city has excellent harbor facilities, making it a large transportation center for rail, water, and motor freight. Generally rich agricultural land is found in the surrounding area, especially up the Maumee River toward the Indiana state line.

Climate: Nearness to Lake Erie has a moderating effect on temperature, and extremes are seldom recorded. Humidity is high, and there is an excessive amount of cloudiness. In the winter months, the sun shines during only 30% of the daylight hours; December and January, the cloudiest months, sometimes receive as little as 16% of the possible amount of sunshine.

Pluses: Lakefront location moderates extreme temperatures.

Minuses: Humid, cloudy.

Places Rated Score: 518

Places Rated Rank: 204

Elevation: 692 feet

Relative Humidity: 72%
Wind Speed: 9.5 mph

Seasonal Change

Annual Rainfall 32 in

Annual Snowfall 37 in

Clear 71 days   Partly Cloudy 110 days   Cloudy 184 days

Precipitation Days: 136   Storm Days: 40

Average Temperatures			
	Daily High	Daily Low	Monthly Mean
January	32.4	17.2	24.8
February	35.2	18.9	27.1
March	45.0	26.6	35.8
April	59.5	37.2	48.4
May	70.5	47.1	58.8
June	80.5	57.2	68.9
July	83.8	60.8	72.3
August	82.4	59.1	70.8
September	75.7	51.8	63.8
October	64.8	41.2	53.0
November	48.0	31.1	39.6
December	35.4	20.5	28.0

Zero-Degree Days: 8
Freezing Days: 145
90-Degree Days: 13
Heating- and Cooling-Degree Days: 7,066

Tucson, AZ

Terrain: Lies at the foot of the Catalina Mountains in a flat to gently rolling valley floor in southern Arizona.

Climate: Desert, characterized by a long, hot season beginning in April and ending in October. Temperature maxima above 90° F are the rule during this period; on 41 days each year, on the average, the temperature reaches 100° F. These high temperatures are modified by low humidity, reducing discomfort. Tucson lies in the zone receiving more sunshine than any other in the United States. Clear skies or very thin, high clouds permit intense surface heating during the day and active radiational cooling at night, a process enhanced by the characteristic atmospheric dryness.

Pluses: Clear, warm, dry.

Minuses: Intense summer heat.

Places Rated Score: 589

Places Rated Rank: 87

Elevation: 2,555 feet

Relative Humidity: 38%
Wind Speed: 8.2 mph

Seasonal Change

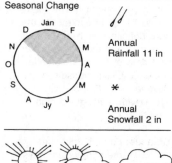

Annual Rainfall 11 in

Annual Snowfall 2 in

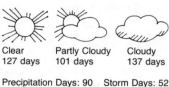

Clear 198 days   Partly Cloudy 89 days   Cloudy 78 days

Precipitation Days: 50   Storm Days: 40

Average Temperatures			
	Daily High	Daily Low	Monthly Mean
January	63.5	38.2	50.9
February	67.0	39.9	53.5
March	71.5	43.6	57.6
April	80.7	50.3	65.5
May	89.6	57.5	73.6
June	97.9	66.2	82.1
July	98.3	74.2	86.3
August	95.3	72.3	83.8
September	93.1	67.1	80.1
October	83.8	56.4	70.1
November	72.2	44.8	58.5
December	64.8	39.1	52.0

Zero-Degree Days: 0
Freezing Days: 21
90-Degree Days: 139
Heating- and Cooling-Degree Days: 4,566

Tulsa, OK

Terrain: Lies along the Arkansas River at an elevation of almost 700 feet above sea level. The surrounding terrain is gently rolling. There are no natural formations—such as mountains or large water surfaces—that influence its climate.

Climate: At a latitude of 30 degrees north, Tulsa is far enough north to escape long periods of heat in summer, yet far enough south to miss the extreme cold of winter. The influence of warm moist air from the Gulf of Mexico is often felt in the high humidity, but the climate is essentially continental, characterized by rapid temperature changes. Generally, the winter months are mild. Temperatures of 100° F or higher are frequently experienced from the latter part of July to early September but are usually accompanied by low humidity and a good southerly breeze. Fall is long, with a great number of pleasant, sunny days and cool, bracing nights.

Pluses: Four-season climate with long summers and pleasant falls.

Minuses: Hot periods during summer months, tornadoes.

Places Rated Score: 530

Places Rated Rank: 185

Elevation: 676 feet

Relative Humidity: 67%
Wind Speed: 10.6 mph

Seasonal Change

Annual Rainfall 37 in

Annual Snowfall 9 in

Clear 127 days   Partly Cloudy 101 days   Cloudy 137 days

Precipitation Days: 90   Storm Days: 52

Average Temperatures			
	Daily High	Daily Low	Monthly Mean
January	47.0	26.1	36.6
February	52.2	30.2	41.2
March	59.7	36.9	48.3
April	71.8	49.7	60.8
May	79.2	58.4	68.8
June	87.3	67.3	77.3
July	92.8	71.4	82.1
August	92.7	70.0	81.4
September	84.8	61.7	73.3
October	75.0	50.8	62.9
November	60.8	38.0	49.4
December	50.1	29.5	39.8

Zero-Degree Days: 1
Freezing Days: 85
90-Degree Days: 70
Heating- and Cooling-Degree Days: 5,629

Washington, DC–MD–VA

Terrain: Situated at the western edge of the Middle Atlantic Coastal Plain, 50 miles east of the Blue Ridge Mountains and 35 miles west of Chesapeake Bay at the junction of the Potomac and Anacostia rivers.

Climate: Summers are warm and humid, winters mild; generally pleasant weather prevails in the spring and autumn. The coldest weather occurs in late January and early February, and the warmest month is July. There are no pronounced wet and dry seasons. Thunderstorms, during the summer, often bring sudden and heavy showers and damaging winds, hail, or lightning. In winter, snow accumulations of more than 10 inches are rare.

Pluses: Pleasant springs and autumns, relatively mild winters.

Minuses: Humid summers, heavy thunderstorms.

Places Rated Score: 631

Places Rated Rank: 51

Elevation: 65 feet

Relative Humidity: 64%
Wind Speed: 9.3 mph

Seasonal Change

Annual Rainfall 39 in

Annual Snowfall 16 in

Clear 101 days   Partly Cloudy 106 days   Cloudy 158 days

Precipitation Days: 111   Storm Days: 29

Average Temperatures			
	Daily High	Daily Low	Monthly Mean
January	43.5	27.7	35.6
February	46.0	28.6	37.3
March	55.0	35.2	45.1
April	67.1	45.7	56.4
May	76.6	55.7	66.2
June	84.6	64.6	74.6
July	88.2	69.1	78.7
August	86.6	67.6	77.1
September	80.2	61.0	70.6
October	69.8	49.7	59.8
November	57.2	38.8	48.0
December	45.2	29.5	37.4

Zero-Degree Days: 0
Freezing Days: 75
90-Degree Days: 37
Heating- and Cooling-Degree Days: 5,626

Waterloo–Cedar Falls, IA

Terrain: Situated on the banks of the Cedar River in northeast Iowa, this area is far removed from the moderating influences of any large body of water. The terrain is level to very gently rolling and is ideally suited to agriculture. The flat, open topography has no influence on climate other than the fact that it offers little resistance to winds, which in the winter can greatly enhance the windchill factor.

Climate: Definitely continental in character, with hot summers, cold winters, and short springs and falls. The average annual rainfall is 34 inches, with 71% of this total falling in the April-to-September crop season. As befits its landlocked, northerly location, the temperature range in Waterloo–Cedar Falls is large: January's mean temperature is 16° F, July's 73° F. The lowest and highest temperatures ever recorded here are –34° F and 112° F. Bitterly cold days of zero or below average 31 in number. The mercury hits 90° F or above on an average of 15 days a year, including two 100-degree days.

Pluses: Sunny falls.

Minuses: Hot summers, cold winters.

Places Rated Score: 347

Places Rated Rank: 312

Elevation: 868 feet

Relative Humidity: 72%
Wind Speed: 10.7 mph

Seasonal Change

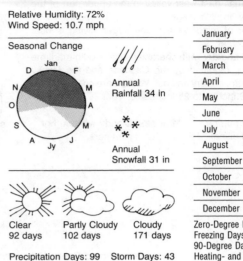

Annual Rainfall 34 in

Annual Snowfall 31 in

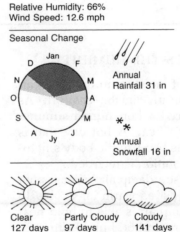

Clear 92 days   Partly Cloudy 102 days   Cloudy 171 days

Precipitation Days: 99   Storm Days: 43

Average Temperatures			
	Daily High	Daily Low	Monthly Mean
January	25.7	6.9	16.3
February	30.2	11.3	20.8
March	40.6	22.3	31.5
April	58.5	36.3	47.4
May	70.0	47.5	58.8
June	79.4	57.6	68.5
July	83.6	61.5	72.6
August	82.1	59.5	70.8
September	73.3	49.8	61.6
October	63.5	39.7	51.6
November	44.6	25.6	35.1
December	30.6	12.9	21.8

Zero-Degree Days: 31
Freezing Days: 159
90-Degree Days: 15
Heating- and Cooling-Degree Days: 8,090

Wichita, KS

Terrain: Located in gentle sloping topography. There are no large bodies of water nearby to affect the city's climate.

Climate: Because it lies in the path of alternate masses of warm, moist air moving northward from the Gulf of Mexico and cold, dry air from the polar regions, the city is subject to frequent and often abrupt weather changes. Summers are usually warm and occasionally hot (there are more than 60 days over 90° F during that time). Winters are mild, and snowfalls are light, averaging 16 inches a year.

Pluses: Four-season Great Plains climate with mild winters.

Minuses: Tornadoes, long summers that can be hot.

Elevation: 1,340 feet

Relative Humidity: 66%
Wind Speed: 12.6 mph

Seasonal Change

Annual Rainfall 31 in

Annual Snowfall 16 in

Clear 127 days   Partly Cloudy 97 days   Cloudy 141 days

Precipitation Days: 84   Storm Days: 55

Average Temperatures			
	Daily High	Daily Low	Monthly Mean
January	41.4	21.2	31.3
February	47.1	25.4	36.3
March	55.0	32.1	43.6
April	68.1	45.1	56.6
May	77.1	55.0	66.1
June	86.5	65.0	75.8
July	91.7	69.6	80.7
August	91.0	68.3	79.7
September	81.9	59.2	70.6
October	71.3	47.9	59.6
November	55.8	33.8	44.8
December	44.3	24.6	34.5

Zero-Degree Days: 2
Freezing Days: 114
90-Degree Days: 62
Heating- and Cooling-Degree Days: 6,360

Places Rated Score: 494

Places Rated Rank: 268

Wilmington, NC

Terrain: Located in the Tidewater section of southeastern North Carolina, near the Atlantic Ocean. The city proper is built adjacent to the east bank of the Cape Fear River. The surrounding terrain, typical of the state's Coastal Plain, is low-lying (the average elevation is less than 40 feet) and level. There are many rivers, creeks, and lakes nearby, most with considerable swampy growth surrounding them. Large tracts of woods alternate with cultivated fields.

Climate: Wilmington's climate shows a strong maritime influence. Summers are quite warm and humid, but excessive heat is rare. During the colder part of the year, polar air masses reach the coastal areas, causing sharp drops in temperature. However, much of the coldness of these air masses has diminished by the time they reach the Wilmington area. Rainfall is ample and well distributed, with most occurring in summer in the form of thundershowers. In winter, rain may fall steadily for several days. Snowfall is very slight.

Pluses: Warm, moist, mild.

Minuses: Hot and muggy in summertime.

Elevation: 30 feet

Relative Humidity: 75%
Wind Speed: 8.9 mph

Seasonal Change

Annual Rainfall 54 in

Annual Snowfall 1.8 in

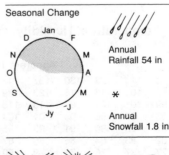

Clear 113 days   Partly Cloudy 106 days   Cloudy 146 days

Precipitation Days: 117   Storm Days: 46

Average Temperatures			
	Daily High	Daily Low	Monthly Mean
January	56.6	36.2	46.4
February	58.7	37.5	48.1
March	64.9	43.7	54.3
April	74.3	52.2	63.3
May	81.4	60.9	71.2
June	86.8	68.2	77.5
July	88.8	72.0	80.4
August	88.0	71.0	79.5
September	83.5	65.9	74.7
October	75.4	55.1	65.3
November	66.8	44.3	55.6
December	58.2	36.7	47.5

Zero-Degree Days: 0
Freezing Days: 45
90-Degree Days: 45
Heating- and Cooling-Degree Days: 4,397

Places Rated Score: 564

Places Rated Rank: 121

Yakima, WA

Terrain: Located in a small east-west valley in the upper part of the irrigated Yakima Valley in Washington. The local topography is complex, with a number of minor valleys and ridges giving a local elevation as high as 500 feet.

Climate: Relatively mild and dry, with characteristics of both maritime and continental climates, modified by the Cascade and the Rocky Mountain ranges. Summers are dry and hot. Winters are cool with only light snowfall, usually 20 inches to 25 inches per year.

Pluses: Combination of marine and continental climatic features.

Minuses: Cloudy winters, hot summers.

Places Rated Score: 535

Places Rated Rank: 182

Elevation: 1,066 feet

Relative Humidity: 60%
Wind Speed: 7.2 mph

Seasonal Change

Annual Rainfall 8 in

Annual Snowfall 25 in

Clear 112 days   Partly Cloudy 90 days   Cloudy 163 days

Precipitation Days: 67   Storm Days: 7

Average Temperatures			
	Daily High	Daily Low	Monthly Mean
January	36.4	18.6	27.5
February	46.1	25.2	35.7
March	54.8	28.8	41.8
April	64.1	34.8	49.5
May	73.1	42.6	57.9
June	79.7	49.3	64.5
July	88.1	53.3	70.7
August	85.9	51.2	68.6
September	78.3	44.3	61.3
October	64.7	35.4	50.1
November	48.5	28.3	36.4
December	39.1	23.5	31.3

Zero-Degree Days: 4
Freezing Days: 150
90-Degree Days: 33
Heating- and Cooling-Degree Days: 6,488

Et Cetera

IT'S NOT THE HEAT, IT'S THE HUMIDITY

Humidity, or the amount of moisture in the air, is an extremely important factor in climatic comfort. As anyone who has experienced a hot, humid summer knows, humidity intensifies heat. A hot day that is also humid is uncomfortable because the body's natural cooling process of evaporation is retarded.

But there is another reason damp air increases felt heat in the summertime. Just as warm air is able to hold more moisture, so damp air is able to hold heat better, and longer. Therefore, in hot, humid climates, heat is retained in the damp air even after the sun goes down, resulting in nights that are almost as hot as the days. In contrast, dry climates offer greater comfort not only during hot summer days but also during the nights, which can be cool and sometimes even chilly.

Excessive humidity can aggravate certain types of arthritis and rheumatism and, combined with low temperatures, can have a harmful effect on those suffering from pulmonary diseases. Very moist air also encourages the growth of a wide variety of bacteria and molds, thus increasing the chances of infection.

Low humidity can also have undesirable consequences. When the humidity falls below 50 percent, most of us experience dry nasal passages and perhaps a dry, tickling throat. In some areas of the Southwest where the relative humidity can drop to 20 percent or below, many people suffer from nosebleeds, flaking skin, and a constant sore throat.

The table "Temperature, Humidity, and Apparent Temperature" examines the relationship between rela-

Temperature, Humidity, and Apparent Temperature

Apparent Temperature

Air Temperature (°F)	0	5	10	15	20	25	30	35	40	45	50	55	60	65	70	75	80	85	90	95	100
110	99	102	105	108	112	117	123	130	137	143	150										
105	95	97	100	102	105	109	113	118	123	129	135	142	149								
100	91	93	95	97	99	101	104	107	110	115	120	126	132	138	144						
95	87	88	90	91	93	94	96	98	101	104	107	110	114	119	124	130	136				
90	83	84	85	86	87	88	90	91	93	95	96	98	100	102	106	109	113	117	122		
85	78	79	80	81	82	83	84	85	86	87	88	89	90	91	93	95	97	99	102	105	108
80	73	74	75	76	77	77	78	79	79	80	81	81	82	83	85	86	86	87	88	89	91
75	69	69	70	71	72	72	73	73	74	74	75	75	76	76	77	77	78	78	79	79	80
70	64	64	65	65	66	66	67	67	68	68	69	69	70	70	70	70	71	71	71	71	72

Relative Humidity (%)

July Noon Average Relative Humidity

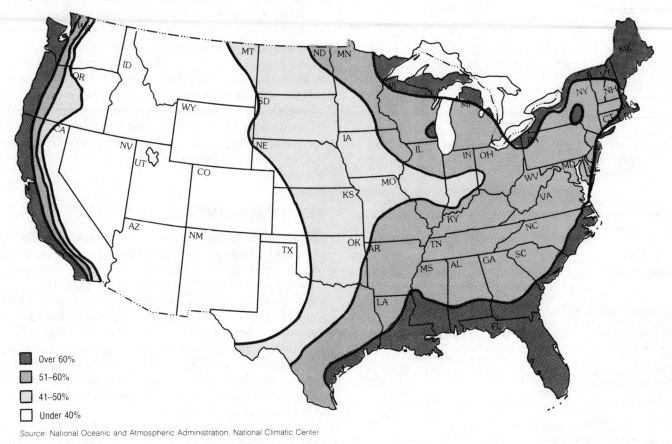

■ Over 60%

▨ 51–60%

▧ 41–50%

□ Under 40%

Source: National Oceanic and Atmospheric Administration, National Climatic Center

tive`humidity and temperature. Relative humidity is the ratio of the amount of water vapor present in the air to the greatest possible amount of water vapor air can hold at that temperature. To find the apparent temperature, locate the air temperature at the left and the relative humidity along the bottom. The intersection of the horizontal row of figures opposite the temperature with the vertical row above the relative humidity is the apparent temperature. For example, an air temperature of 85 degrees Fahrenheit feels like 89 degrees at 55 percent relative humidity but like 102 when the humidity is 90 percent.

GOING TO EXTREMES

Many people gripe about the weather in the places they live. True, extreme weather does occur routinely in some of the rugged climates of North America. But how bad is your local climate compared with some really nasty places? Below are some ridiculous extremes.

Mount Washington, New Hampshire. New England's highest peak, Mount Washington claims justifiably to have the world's worst weather. Here, even in midsummer, the temperature may drop 50 or 60 de-

grees Fahrenheit in a matter of minutes. People visiting the summit are warned to bring parkas with them, even in July. Despite these warnings, deaths occur every year on Mount Washington. The weather station on the summit (which provides data for the NOAA's *Local Climatological Data*) reports winds in excess of 100 miles per hour with dismal regularity. On April 12, 1934, a gust traveling at 231 miles per hour was recorded here. This is the greatest wind speed—excluding those of tornado funnel clouds—ever measured on the earth's surface. In fact, the winds are so severe on Mount Washington's summit that a standard anemometer, which consists of three rotating metal cups, cannot survive. Instead, the station must employ a pitot tube, a wind-measuring device used on aircraft. Fingers of ice, called rime ice, form very rapidly here on buildings and vehicles during icy weather and often measure up to two or three feet in length.

Meteorologically speaking, the summit of Mount Washington is an arctic island in an otherwise temperate zone. It is surrounded by clouds or fog on at least 300 days each year, the average annual snowfall is 242 inches, and the average year-round temperature is 27 degrees.

The 10 Snowiest Metro Areas

	Inches per Year
Syracuse, NY	109
Bangor, ME	97
Buffalo, NY	90
Binghamton, NY	86
Burlington, VT	79
Duluth, MN–WI	78
Casper, WY	77
Grand Rapids, MI	77
Portland, ME	74
Albany–Schenectady–Troy, NY	71

. . . and the 11 Stormiest

	Storm Days per Year
Biloxi–Gulfport, MS	94
Fort Myers, FL	93
Tampa–St. Petersburg–Clearwater, FL	88
Tallahassee, FL	86
Orlando, FL	81
Mobile, AL	80
Miami–Hialeah, FL	75
Galveston–Texas City, TX	70
Alexandria, LA	69
Houston, TX	69
New Orleans, LA	68

Listed above are those metro areas described in the Place Profiles that have more than 70 inches of snow per year or more than 65 storm days per year.

The 8 Dampest Metro Areas

	Relative Humidity
Galveston–Texas City, TX	78%
Alexandria, LA	77
Asheville, NC	77
Biloxi–Gulfport, MS	77
Corpus Christi, TX	77
Eugene–Springfield, OR	77
Houston, TX	77
New Orleans, LA	77

. . . and the 7 Driest

	Relative Humidity
Las Vegas, NV	29%
Phoenix, AZ	36
Tucson, AZ	38
El Paso, TX	39
Albuquerque, NM	43
Colorado Springs, CO	49
Reno, NV	50

Listed above are those metro areas described in the Place Profiles with an average relative humidity greater than 76 percent or lower than 51 percent.

How would Mount Washington score according to the *Places Rated* formula? With, among other things, 66 zero-degree days, 243 freezing days, 13,878 heating-degree days, and many months during which the mean temperature is below 20 degrees, Mount Washington receives a climate mildness score of minus 19.

Greenland Ranch, Death Valley, California. So you think it gets hot where you live? Try Greenland Ranch, in California's Death Valley. They didn't name it Death Valley just for effect, you know. There is no weather station here recording data for the NOAA's *Local Climatological Data*, so the best we can do is roughly estimate the climate score. Suffice it to say that America's all-time heat record of 134 degrees Fahrenheit was set in Greenland Ranch. This is only 2 degrees lower than the highest temperature ever recorded on the face of the earth, at Al Aziziyah, Libya, in 1922. The exact number of 90-degree days in Greenland Ranch is not recorded, but data show that during five months the mean daily temperature exceeds 80 degrees. In July, the mean daily temperature is above 100. The mean maximum temperature for the months of May through September are as follows: 99.2, 109.2, 116.1, 113.6, and

105.5. Think about it the next time you complain about summer heat.

Barrow, Alaska. The settlement of Barrow is located on the northern coastline of Alaska, well above the Arctic Circle. The monthly mean temperatures are below zero during six months of the year. The average daily maximum temperature in the hottest month, July, is only 44 degrees. Yet Barrow does record three 90-degree days thanks to its very long "summer" days. It has an average of 323 freezing days a year and 170 zero-degree days. It also has more than 20,000 heating-degree days. Barrow's *Places Rated* climate score? Minus 829!

ARE WE RUNNING OUT OF WATER?

Climate and terrain have an importance far more profound than simple considerations of pleasant weather and attractive surroundings. They also determine an area's access to one of America's most precious natural resources: the abundance of fresh water found in lakes, rivers, and streams, and in the underground aquifers that feed our wells. The Great Lakes, which the United States shares with Canada, contain more than one fifth of the world's supply of surface fresh water. By any reckoning, these giant inland seas of usable, drinkable water are among the most valuable resources on the planet.

And yet we hear increasing cries of alarm concerning our supplies of fresh water. Some areas of the nation appear to be rapidly depleting both surface water and groundwater. In other areas, serious pollution threatens. Even in regions like New England, where water is plentiful, growing numbers of metro areas are faced with shortages due to antiquated water delivery systems and purification plants. The situation is further complicated by growing competition for water between farmers on the one hand and urban residents and industry on the other, and by the efforts of American Indians to recapture water rights taken from them more than a hundred years ago.

So is America really faced with a water shortage? No and yes.

No. America has plenty of water. The national supply of renewable fresh water is about 1,400 billion gallons of water per day. Of this total, about 380 billion gallons per day is withdrawn for use by the nation's homes, farms, and industry. Of the 380 billion gallons withdrawn, about 280 billion gallons per day is returned to lakes and streams. Although a large percentage of the country's waste is carried by this return flow, much of the returned water is usable. Withdrawn water that is not returned to lakes or streams (either due to evaporation or ingestion by humans and livestock) is termed consumed water. On any given day, then, some 100 billion gallons of water is consumed, or only about one fourteenth of the total amount of water available.

Yes. Although the total average supply is more than plentiful, the problem arises from the uneven distribution of that supply. Most places in America have adequate water supplies. Some have much more than they can ever use. And a few are already facing a water crisis. Predictably, the majority of areas that suffer most from lack of water are those that receive scant rainfall. The Great Basin area receives the least precipitation since it is located between two high mountain ranges, which block moisture-laden air. In Nevada, Arizona, and New Mexico, the southern part of this region, the water problem is greatest. Several other parts of the West and Southwest are also troubled by shortages.

Where Our Water Comes From

There are two main sources of water, those on the surface of the earth (rivers, lakes, and streams) and those below the surface. We're all familiar with the aboveground sources, and many people assume they represent all our water resources. Actually, 80 percent of U.S. water reserves are located below ground in aquifers. Aquifers are composed of water-permeable rock or gravel through which groundwater percolates from the earth's surface. Since the water flows through many layers of sand, gravel, and rock, it is usually cleaned by this natural filter as it flows. Therefore wells, which often tap aquifers, are known for the purity and high mineral content of their water. Unless otherwise polluted, well water is good water.

But as water is pumped out, the aquifer becomes depleted. It will refill with water if left alone for a while; its water level, or table, will rise again. The time required for the aquifer's water table to return to its normal level is called the recharge rate. If the rate of depletion exceeds the recharge rate, the aquifer will continue to be depleted, and its water table will continue to fall. This process is called groundwater mining.

Many aquifers are located directly below, or nearby, big lakes or rivers that feed them. However, many of our biggest aquifers fortunately lie under dry ground, so they can supply water to what would otherwise be water-starved places.

One such formation is the huge High Plains aquifer, which lies deep below Texas, Oklahoma, New Mexico, Kansas, Colorado, Nebraska, South Dakota, and Wyoming, and covers 177,000 square miles. If it were on the surface instead of below ground, it would be the largest lake in the world (the largest is the Caspian Sea, at 152,084 square miles). For decades, this giant underground cistern has provided irrigation and drinking water for the eight states mentioned above. There are about 170,000 wells tapping the High Plains aquifer, watering 14.3 million acres of farmland that produce 15 percent of America's corn, wheat, sorghum, and cotton, and nourish 38 percent of its livestock. But the aquifer's water table is falling rapidly. Water is being pumped out of it eight times faster than it can recharge itself. If groundwater mining continues at the present rate, experts predict, the aquifer (which took at least 10,000 years to form) could begin to dry up around the year 2000.

Water-Resource Regions

The U.S. Geological Survey has divided the nation into 20 water-resource regions, based on their water systems and named accordingly. Thus there are the Great Lakes, the Missouri, and the Arkansas-Red-White regions, the last named for the system of rivers that feeds Oklahoma, northern Texas, and parts of New Mexico and Colorado.

The map "Water-Resource Regions" presents a vivid summary of water availability and rates of groundwater mining in America. The unshaded regions are in no danger of depleting their renewable supplies of water. The lightly shaded areas are at some risk of running short, but this probably will not happen in the immediate future unless there are several severe drought years in a row. The darker areas represent water-resource regions that are consuming more than 40 percent of their renewable water supplies. The region with the darkest shading, the Lower Colorado (so named for the Colorado River, whose lower section flows through Arizona and forms the boundary between Arizona and California), is using more than 100 percent of its supplies and is mining its groundwater reserves.

Metro Areas with Water Problems

Not only do areas of the country differ in the amount of water readily available to them; they also differ in the quality and purity of their water. The list below pinpoints the major water problems in 269 metro areas. Data are from the 1984 report from the U.S. Geological Survey entitled *Water-Supply Paper 2250.* Metro areas that do not appear on the list—a total of 60—have no significant water troubles.

The major problems delineated are: groundwater mining; insufficient surface water; decreased streamflow, or water in the stream channel, which reduces the water supply; hazardous wastes in groundwater; radioactive wastes in groundwater; pollution of groundwater and/or surface water; flooding; saline-water intrusion in aquifers; sedimentation, which can restrict shipping, increase the potential for flooding, and reduce the capacities of reservoirs; chemical-industrial wastes; wetlands depletion; rising groundwater tables; eutrophication of lakes (the process by which waters become enriched with plant nutrients from the addition of sewage, fertilizers, or wastes, thus upsetting the ecological balance, destroying plant and animal life, and rendering the water unusable for

**Water-Resource Regions, Showing Average Consumptive
Use As a Percentage of Renewable Water Supply**

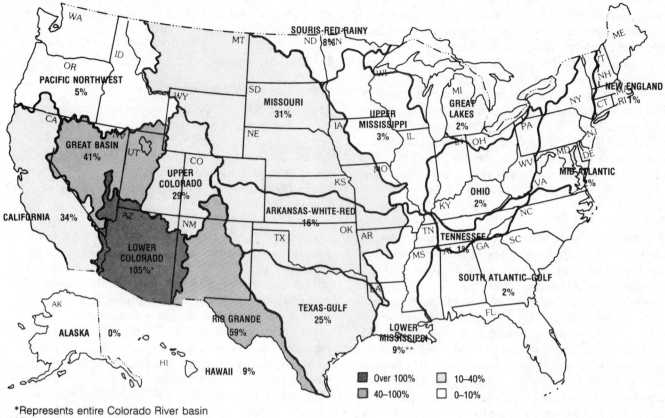

*Represents entire Colorado River basin
**Represents entire Mississippi River basin

Source: U.S. Geological Survey, *Water-Supply Paper 2250,* "National Water Summary 1983—Hydrologic Events and Issues."

public consumption or recreation); and acid rain (a more detailed discussion of acid rain is found in the chapter "Health Care & Environment").

In some instances, problems arising from management of water resources are mentioned. For example, resource development, or the extracting of minerals from the earth, is considered hazardous by the U.S. Geological Survey because the water needed to mine and process minerals may reduce water supplies and because wastes that result from such mining can contaminate surface water and groundwater. In those metro areas where resource development is taking place, the kinds of mining under way are listed.

Metro areas that *Places Rated* deems especially prone to water problems, based on the U.S. Geological Survey paper, are preceded by one, two, or three

triangles (▲), depending on the severity of the situation, with three triangles indicating the worst problems. Of the 269 metro areas described, 41 receive one triangle, 21 two triangles, and only 9 three triangles: Bakersfield, California; Fresno, California; Las Vegas, Nevada; Modesto, California; Norfolk–Virginia Beach–Newport News, Virginia; Phoenix, Arizona; Sacramento, California; Tucson, Arizona; and Visalia–Tulare–Porterville, California.

It should be noted that *Water-Supply Paper 2250* points out situations that may not now be causing damage but that will probably do so in the next few years. These problems should not discourage you from considering a move to a certain metro area. You should, however, make inquiries about the local water situation before reaching a final decision.

Metro Areas with Water Problems, by State

ALABAMA
Dothan: Groundwater mining.
Florence: Sinkholes.
Huntsville: Sinkholes.
Mobile: Pollution and increased sedimentation of Mobile River and Mobile Bay.
(See also Georgia, Columbus)

ALASKA
Anchorage: Current systems cannot meet projected demands, some septic pollution.

ARIZONA
▲▲▲ Phoenix: Groundwater pollution, hazardous wastes, severe groundwater mining.
▲▲▲ Tucson: Groundwater mining, hazardous wastes.

ARKANSAS
Fayetteville–Springdale: Surface-water pollution.
Fort Smith (AR–OK): Surface-water pollution.
Little Rock–North Little Rock: Surface-water pollution.
Pine Bluff: Groundwater mining.
(See also Tennessee, Memphis; Texas, Texarkana)

CALIFORNIA
▲ Anaheim–Santa Ana: Groundwater mining, saline-water intrusion.
▲▲▲ Bakersfield: Groundwater mining.
▲▲▲ Fresno: Groundwater mining, land subsidence.
▲ Los Angeles–Long Beach: Groundwater mining, saline-water intrusion.
▲▲▲ Modesto: Groundwater mining.
▲ Oakland: Decreased streamflow, some heavy-metal pollution.
▲ Oxnard–Ventura: Groundwater mining, saline-water intrusion.
Redding: Hazardous wastes.
Riverside–San Bernardino: Hazardous wastes.*
▲▲▲ Sacramento: Groundwater mining, hazardous wastes.
▲ Salinas–Seaside–Monterey: Groundwater mining, saline-water intrusion.
▲ San Diego: Groundwater mining.
▲ San Francisco: Decreased streamflow, some heavy-metal pollution.
▲▲ San Jose: Groundwater mining, saline-water intrusion.
▲ Santa Cruz: Groundwater mining, saline-water intrusion.
Santa Rosa–Petaluma: Hazardous wastes.
▲▲ Stockton: Groundwater mining, decreased streamflow.

Vallejo–Fairfield–Napa: Decreased streamflow, hazardous wastes.
▲▲▲ Visalia–Tulare–Porterville: Groundwater mining, land subsidence.
Yuba City: Some groundwater mining.

COLORADO
Boulder–Longmont: Hazardous wastes.
▲ Denver: Hazardous wastes, eutrophication, pollution.

CONNECTICUT
Bridgeport–Milford: Groundwater mining.
Danbury: Groundwater mining.
Hartford: Surface-water pollution.
Middletown: Surface-water pollution.
New Haven–Meriden: Groundwater mining, surface-water pollution.
New London–Norwich (CT–RI): Groundwater mining, surface-water pollution.
Norwalk: Groundwater mining.
Stamford: Groundwater mining.

DELAWARE
▲ Wilmington (DE–NJ–MD): Groundwater mining, flooding, hazardous wastes.

FLORIDA
▲ Bradenton: Groundwater mining, saline-water intrusion.
Daytona Beach: Groundwater mining.
▲ Fort Lauderdale–Hollywood–Pompano Beach: Groundwater mining, hazardous wastes, saline-water intrusion.
Fort Myers: Groundwater mining.
Fort Pierce: Groundwater mining.
Fort Walton Beach: Groundwater mining.
▲ Jacksonville: Groundwater mining, hazardous wastes.
▲▲ Lakeland–Winter Haven: Groundwater mining, hazardous wastes, phosphate mining.
Melbourne–Titusville–Palm Bay: Groundwater mining.
▲▲ Miami–Hialeah: Groundwater mining, surface-water pollution, saline-water intrusion, hazardous wastes.
Ocala: Sinkholes.
Orlando: Groundwater mining.
▲ Pensacola: Groundwater mining, hazardous wastes.
Sarasota: Groundwater mining, saline-water intrusion.
Tallahassee: Some groundwater mining, sinkholes.
▲▲ Tampa–St. Petersburg–Clearwater: Groundwater mining, saline-water intrusion, hazardous wastes.
▲ West Palm Beach–Boca Raton–Delray Beach: Groundwater mining, saline-water intrusion, surface-water pollution.

GEORGIA
▲ Albany: Groundwater mining, pesticide pollution, sinkholes.
Athens: Surface-water shortages.
Atlanta: Surface-water pollution, some surface-water shortages.
Columbus (GA–AL): Groundwater mining.

Macon–Warner Robins: Surface-water pollution.
▲ Savannah: Groundwater mining, saline-water intrusion.
(See also Tennessee, Chattanooga)

HAWAII
▲▲ Honolulu: Groundwater mining, surface-water pollution, saline-water intrusion.

IDAHO
Boise City: Groundwater pollution, hazardous wastes.

ILLINOIS
Alton–Granite City: Rising groundwater tables.
Aurora–Elgin: Groundwater mining, flooding.
Champaign–Urbana–Rantoul: Surface-water pollution.
Chicago: Groundwater mining, flooding.
Decatur: Surface-water pollution.
East St. Louis–Belleville: Rising groundwater tables.
Joliet: Groundwater mining, flooding.
Kankakee: Surface-water pollution, hazardous wastes.
▲ Lake County: Groundwater mining, flooding, hazardous wastes.
Peoria: Surface-water pollution.
▲ Rockford: Surface-water pollution, hazardous wastes.
Springfield: Surface-water pollution.
(See also Iowa, Davenport–Rock Island–Moline; Missouri, St. Louis)

INDIANA
Anderson: Surface-water pollution.
Bloomington: Surface-water pollution, hazardous wastes in groundwater.
Elkhart–Goshen: Flooding, groundwater and surface-water pollution.
Fort Wayne: Hazardous wastes in groundwater.
▲▲ Gary–Hammond: Surface-water and groundwater pollution, hazardous wastes.
▲ Indianapolis: Extensive surface-water pollution.
Kokomo: Surface-water pollution.
Lafayette: Groundwater mining.
Muncie: Surface-water pollution.
▲ South Bend–Mishawaka: Flooding, surface-water and groundwater pollution, hazardous wastes.
Terre Haute: Surface-water pollution.
(See also Ohio, Cincinnati)

IOWA
Davenport–Rock Island–Moline (IA–IL): Surface-water pollution.
Des Moines: Surface-water and groundwater pollution, hazardous wastes.
Dubuque: Pollution in groundwater.
Sioux City (IA–NE): Surface-water scarcity.

KANSAS
Kansas City: Hazardous wastes in surface water and groundwater.

---

*According to a University of California study released in August 1984, seepage from a toxic waste pit near Riverside threatens major contamination of the Chino Basin aquifer, which supplies drinking water to half a million people in this region. The extent of contamination and the effectiveness of preventive action will not be known for many months.

Topeka: Surface-water pollution.
▲ Wichita: Saline-water intrusion in surface water and groundwater, hazardous wastes.

KENTUCKY
Lexington–Fayette: Surface-water scarcity.
(See also Ohio, Cincinnati; Tennessee, Clarksville–Hopkinsville; West Virginia, Huntington–Ashland)

LOUISIANA
Alexandria: Hazardous wastes in groundwater.
Baton Rouge: Groundwater mining.
Houma–Thibodaux: Wetlands and estuaries threatened.
Lafayette: Groundwater mining.
Lake Charles: Groundwater mining.
Monroe: Groundwater mining.
▲ New Orleans: Wetlands and estuaries threatened, potential for radioactive wastes in groundwater.

MAINE
Lewiston–Auburn: Groundwater and surface-water shortages.
Portland: Hazardous wastes in surface water and groundwater.
(See also New Hampshire, Portsmouth–Dover–Rochester)

MARYLAND
▲▲ Baltimore: Hazardous wastes in groundwater, acid rain, Chesapeake Bay threatened by nutrient enrichment (the first step in eutrophication), hazardous wastes, and a decrease in important submerged aquatic vegetation.
Cumberland (MD–WV): Pollution from coal mining.
Hagerstown: Acid rain, hazardous wastes in groundwater.
(See also Delaware, Wilmington)

MASSACHUSETTS
Boston: Not enough fresh water for peak demand.
Fall River (MA–RI): Hazardous wastes in groundwater.
Fitchburg–Leominster: Hazardous wastes in surface water and groundwater.
Lawrence–Haverhill (MA–NH): Hazardous wastes in surface water and groundwater.
Lowell (MA–NH): Hazardous wastes and highway deicing salts in groundwater.
Worcester: Highway deicing salts in surface water and groundwater.
(See also Rhode Island, Pawtucket–Woonsocket–Attleboro)

MICHIGAN
Benton Harbor: Hazardous wastes in surface water.
Detroit: Hazardous wastes in surface water.
Flint: Hazardous wastes in surface water.
Kalamazoo: Hazardous wastes in surface water.
Lansing–East Lansing: Hazardous wastes in surface water.

Muskegon: Hazardous wastes in surface water (Lake Michigan).
Saginaw–Bay City–Midland: Hazardous wastes in surface water (Saginaw River and Saginaw Bay).

MINNESOTA
▲ Duluth (MN–WI): Natural salinity of groundwater, waste sites or landfills that contain hazardous materials, acid rain, erosion and sedimentation.
▲ Minneapolis–St. Paul (MN–WI): Groundwater mining, eutrophication, hazardous wastes.
Rochester: Nitrates in groundwater.
St. Cloud: Acid rain.
(See also North Dakota, Fargo–Moorhead)

MISSISSIPPI
Biloxi–Gulfport: Groundwater mining and surface-water depletion.
Jackson: Groundwater mining and surface-water depletion, flooding, saline-water intrusion.
Pascagoula: Groundwater mining and surface-water depletion.
(See also Tennessee, Memphis)

MISSOURI
Columbia: Some saline-water intrusion.
▲ Joplin: Dioxin in surface water and groundwater, resource development (lead and zinc mining).
Kansas City: Resource development (coal mining).
St. Joseph: Erosion and sedimentation, saline-water intrusion.
St. Louis (MO–IL): Dioxin in surface water and groundwater, possible depletion of river surface water.
▲ Springfield: Dioxin in surface water and groundwater, sinkholes, groundwater mining.

MONTANA
Great Falls: Erosion and sedimentation of surface water.

NEBRASKA
(See Iowa, Sioux City)

NEVADA
▲▲▲ Las Vegas: Surface-water depletion and groundwater mining, land subsidence, surface-water pollution, radioactive wastes and chemicals in groundwater.
Reno: Surface-water depletion and pollution, some groundwater mining.

NEW HAMPSHIRE
Manchester: Surface-water and stream pollution.
Nashua: Hazardous wastes in surface water and groundwater.
Portsmouth–Dover–Rochester (NH–ME): Hazardous wastes in surface water and groundwater.
(See also Massachusetts, Lawrence–Haverhill and Lowell)

NEW JERSEY
▲ Atlantic City: Pollution of estuaries, flooding, saline-water intrusion, acid rain.

▲ Bergen–Passaic: Surface-water scarcity, surface-water pollution, flooding.
▲ Jersey City: Surface-water pollution and scarcity, pollution of estuaries, flooding.
▲ Middlesex–Somerset–Hunterdon: Surface-water pollution and scarcity, acid rain.
▲▲ Monmouth–Ocean: Surface-water scarcity, saline-water intrusion, pollution of estuaries, acid rain.
▲ Newark: Surface-water pollution and scarcity, flooding.
▲▲ Trenton: Surface-water pollution and scarcity, pollution of estuaries, flooding, acid rain.
▲ Vineland–Millville–Bridgeton: Saline-water intrusion, acid rain.
(See also Delaware, Wilmington; Pennsylvania, Allentown–Bethlehem and Philadelphia)

NEW MEXICO
▲▲ Albuquerque: Groundwater mining, nitrates and hazardous wastes in groundwater.

NEW YORK
Albany–Schenectady–Troy: Acid rain.
Glens Falls: Acid rain.
▲▲ Nassau–Suffolk: Bacteria in surface water, groundwater mining, saline-water intrusion, radioactive wastes in groundwater.
New York: Rising groundwater, some saline-water intrusion.
Niagara Falls: Rising groundwater levels.
Orange County: Some groundwater mining.
Rochester: Eutrophication.

NORTH CAROLINA
Asheville: Surface-water scarcity and pollution.
Burlington: Surface-water pollution.
Charlotte–Gastonia–Rock Hill (NC–SC): Surface-water pollution.
Greensboro–Winston-Salem–High Point: Surface-water pollution.
Hickory: Surface-water pollution.
Jacksonville: Groundwater mining.
Raleigh–Durham: Surface-water scarcity, surface-water pollution.

NORTH DAKOTA
▲ Bismarck: Resource development (lignite mining), wetlands drainage, eutrophication.
Fargo–Moorhead (ND–MN): Flooding, surface-water scarcity and pollution.
Grand Forks: Flooding, surface-water pollution.

OHIO
Akron: Resource development (coal mining and oil and gas production), erosion and sedimentation.
Canton: Resource development (coal mining and oil and gas production), erosion and sedimentation.
Cincinnati (OH–KY–IN): Erosion and sedimentation, hazardous wastes in groundwater.
Cleveland: Erosion and sedimentation, resource development (oil and gas production).

Water Wars

Although many small conflicts arising from water usage, pollution, and diversion exist throughout the nation, the biggest battles for water are being fought in the Southwest.

Arizona. Of all the states in the nation, this one is in the most danger of facing a water crisis. Arizonans now pump twice as much groundwater from their aquifers as is being replaced by natural recharge. Large, fast-growing metro areas like Phoenix and Tucson are headed for trouble. However, a recent U.S. Supreme Court decision has granted Arizona the right to tap the lower Colorado River, which it shares with California as a common boundary. By 1985, Phoenix will receive this river water through a series of aqueducts and canals, thus easing the strain on the underground aquifers; Tucson is slated to do the same as of 1989. But this is not a total solution, since the water Arizona will get is now going to Southern California.

California. This state is hurting for water in two areas: the 20,000-square-mile Central Valley and the metro areas of Southern California. In the Central Valley, where almost half of America's fruits and vegetables are grown on land that is fertile, flat, and totally irrigated for year-round productivity, the groundwater supplies are being pumped dry at an alarming rate. According to the U.S. Geological Survey's *Water-Supply Paper 2250,* "National Water Summary 1983—Hydrologic Events and Issues," this valley is probably the most heavily pumped area in the nation. The report warns that not only groundwater mining but land subsidence, or sinking, is a direct result of this heavy pumping. In the future, if alternative supplies are not developed, the amount of farming in the Central Valley will be drastically reduced. This could have serious implications for California's economy.

The giant metro areas of Los Angeles–Long Beach and San Diego have always had water scarcities. As they have grown explosively over the last 30 years, the problem has increased. Southern California has depended on diverted water from the lower Colorado for half its water needs. Soon the Colorado water will also go to Phoenix and Tucson, thus aggravating the problem. The only viable solution is to pipe water from moisture-rich Northern California, which receives about 60 percent of the state's rainfall and has only 40 percent of the population. Plans for this massive undertaking are still in the preliminary stage.

The Southwest and High Plains. Eastern New Mexico, northwestern Texas, Oklahoma, and the states to the north of these make up the area known as the High Plains. This huge region is rife with dissent over water. New Mexico is bitter about the "piracy" of water by El Paso, Texas, from New Mexico's Elephant Butte Reservoir. The Land of Enchantment has also locked horns with Colorado over use of the Vermejo River, which rises in Colorado and flows through New Mexico.

Texas, a huge state growing like Topsy, has water woes that are becoming grave. Even in the Texas Gulf region, which receives plenty of rain, extensive groundwater mining has led to the intrusion of salt water in freshwater aquifers and to land subsidence. Those "mysterious" sinkholes you see on the evening news are actually easily explained: They're the result of water being sucked out of underlying rock strata. West Texas and North Texas continually face drought. When the High Plains aquifer begins to go dry, an alternative source will be as far away as the Mississippi River or the Great Lakes—and extremely costly.

The High Plains region, which has increased its agricultural yields dramatically in the past 20 years as a direct result of irrigation, faces long-term groundwater mining. The importance of the High Plains aquifer cannot be overemphasized. When that gigantic underground sea is drained, the entire region will be in considerable trouble.

Columbus: Erosion and sedimentation, resource development (oil and gas production).

Dayton–Springfield: Erosion and sedimentation.

Hamilton–Middletown: Erosion and sedimentation, hazardous wastes in groundwater.

Lima: Erosion and sedimentation.

Lorain–Elyria: Erosion and sedimentation.

Mansfield: Erosion and sedimentation, resource development (oil and gas production).

Steubenville–Weirton (OH–WV): Resource development (coal mining and oil and gas production).

Toledo: Erosion and sedimentation.

▲ Youngstown–Warren: Hazardous wastes in groundwater, resource development (coal mining and oil and gas production).

(*See also* West Virginia, Huntington–Ashland, Parkersburg–Marietta, and Wheeling)

OKLAHOMA
Oklahoma City: Surface-water pollution, hazardous wastes in groundwater.

Tulsa: Natural salinity of surface water. (*See also* Arkansas, Fort Smith)

OREGON
Eugene–Springfield: Acid rain.

Medford: Acid rain, degradation of aquatic habitats in surface water.

Portland: Groundwater mining, hazardous wastes in groundwater.

Salem: Hazardous wastes in groundwater.

PENNSYLVANIA
Allentown–Bethlehem (PA–NJ): Hazardous wastes in groundwater, sinkholes, landslide-prone areas.

Erie: Hazardous wastes in groundwater.

Harrisburg–Lebanon–Carlisle: Sinkholes.

Lancaster: Agricultural runoff (fertilizers and organic or chemical wastes) in surface water and groundwater, sinkholes.

▲▲ Philadelphia (PA–NJ): Sinkholes, erosion and sedimentation, hazardous wastes and industrial wastes in groundwater.

▲ Pittsburgh: Hazardous wastes in groundwater, landslide-prone areas, inadequate river water.

Scranton–Wilkes-Barre: Hazardous wastes in groundwater.

State College: Sinkholes, hazardous wastes in groundwater.

York: Hazardous wastes in groundwater.

RHODE ISLAND

Pawtucket–Woonsocket–Attleboro (RI–MA): Groundwater insufficiency, hazardous wastes in groundwater.
Providence: Groundwater insufficiency, hazardous wastes in groundwater.
(*See also* Connecticut, New London–Norwich; Massachusetts, Fall River)

SOUTH CAROLINA

Anderson: Hazardous wastes in river water.
Charleston: Surface-water scarcity, excess fluoride and chloride in groundwater.
Columbia: Saline-water intrusion, excess fluoride and chloride in groundwater.
Florence: Excess fluoride and chloride in groundwater, saline-water intrusion.
Greenville–Spartanburg: Surface-water scarcity.
(*See also* North Carolina, Charlotte–Gastonia–Rock Hill)

SOUTH DAKOTA

Sioux Falls: Eutrophication, groundwater mining.

TENNESSEE

Chattanooga (TN–GA): Resource development (coal mining), sinkholes, surface-water pollution, hazardous wastes in groundwater.
Clarksville–Hopkinsville (TN–KY): Surface-water pollution, sinkholes.
Johnson City–Kingsport–Bristol (TN–VA): Sinkholes, surface-water pollution.
Knoxville: Sinkholes, radioactive wastes in groundwater.
Memphis (TN–AR–MS): Surface-water pollution, hazardous wastes in groundwater.
▲ **Nashville:** Surface-water scarcity, sinkholes, surface-water pollution.

TEXAS

Abilene: Groundwater pollution.
▲▲ **Amarillo:** Groundwater mining and pollution, eutrophication, natural salinity of surface water.
Austin: Groundwater and surface-water pollution.
▲ **Beaumont–Port Arthur:** Groundwater mining, surface-water pollution, hazardous wastes in groundwater.
▲▲ **Brazoria:** Groundwater mining, land subsidence, hazardous wastes in groundwater, surface-water pollution.
Brownsville–Harlingen: Pollution of groundwater and surface water.
Bryan–College Station: Pollution of groundwater, resource development (lignite mining).
Corpus Christi: Groundwater mining and pollution.
▲ **Dallas:** Groundwater mining, hazardous wastes in groundwater, groundwater pollution, eutrophication.
El Paso: Groundwater mining, surface-water pollution, water disputes with New Mexico and Mexico.
▲▲ **Fort Worth–Arlington:** Groundwater mining and pollution, hazardous wastes

and eutrophication in groundwater, surface-water pollution.
▲▲ **Galveston–Texas City:** Groundwater mining, saline-water intrusion, land subsidence, hazardous wastes in groundwater, surface-water pollution.
▲▲ **Houston:** Groundwater mining, saline-water intrusion, land subsidence, hazardous wastes in groundwater, surface-water pollution.
Killeen–Temple: Groundwater mining, surface-water pollution.
Longview–Marshall: Groundwater pollution, resource development (lignite mining).
Lubbock: Groundwater mining.
McAllen–Edinburg–Mission: Surface-water and groundwater pollution.
Midland: Groundwater mining and pollution.
Odessa: Groundwater mining and pollution.
San Angelo: Groundwater pollution.
▲ **San Antonio:** Groundwater mining and pollution, surface-water pollution.
Sherman–Denison: Groundwater mining, eutrophication.
Texarkana, TX–Texarkana, AR: Resource development (lignite mining).
Tyler: Groundwater pollution, resource development (lignite mining).
Waco: Groundwater mining, eutrophication.
Wichita Falls: Groundwater pollution, natural salinity of surface water.

UTAH

▲▲ **Provo–Orem:** Surface-water and groundwater shortages, landslides, flooding.
▲▲ **Salt Lake City–Ogden:** Groundwater depletion, acid rain, surface-water pollution, flooding.

VERMONT

▲ **Burlington:** Flooding, eutrophication, hazardous wastes in surface water and groundwater.

VIRGINIA

Charlottesville: Radioactivity in groundwater, flooding.
Danville: Radioactivity in groundwater.
Lynchburg: Radioactivity in groundwater.
▲▲▲ **Norfolk–Virginia Beach–Newport News:** Eutrophication, surface-water depletion, groundwater mining, pollution of surface water and bottom sediments, hazardous wastes in surface water and groundwater, bacteria and chemical elements in groundwater.
Richmond–Petersburg: Bacteria and chemical elements in groundwater, radioactivity in groundwater.
Roanoke: Flooding, hazardous wastes in surface water and groundwater.
(*See also* Tennessee, Johnson City–Kingsport–Bristol)

WASHINGTON

Bellingham: Groundwater mining, saline-water intrusion, volcanic danger.*

Bremerton: Saline-water intrusion, groundwater mining.
Olympia: Pollution of bottom sediments.
Richland–Kennewick–Pasco: Natural salinity of groundwater.
Seattle: Hazardous wastes in groundwater, volcanic danger.*
Spokane: Nitrates in, and natural salinity of, groundwater.
Tacoma: Pollution of bottom sediments, volcanic danger.*
Vancouver: Hazardous wastes in groundwater.
Yakima: Hazardous wastes in, and natural salinity of, groundwater.

WEST VIRGINIA

▲▲ **Charleston:** Resource development (coal mining), surface-water pollution, surface-water scarcity, possibility of unsafe dams.
Huntington–Ashland (WV–KY–OH): Resource development (coal mining), hazardous wastes in surface water and groundwater, surface-water scarcity.
Parkersburg–Marietta (WV–OH): Hazardous wastes in surface water and groundwater, surface-water scarcity.
Wheeling (WV–OH): Resource development (coal mining), surface-water scarcity, possibility of unsafe dams.
(*See also* Maryland, Cumberland; Ohio, Steubenville–Weirton)

WISCONSIN

Appleton–Oshkosh–Neenah: Groundwater mining, surface-water pollution.
Eau Claire: Acid rain.
Green Bay: Groundwater mining, surface-water pollution.
Janesville–Beloit: Surface-water pollution.
Kenosha: Groundwater mining, surface-water pollution.
La Crosse: Surface-water pollution.
Madison: Surface-water and groundwater pollution.
Milwaukee: Groundwater mining, surface-water pollution.
Racine: Groundwater mining, surface-water pollution.
Sheboygan: Groundwater mining, surface-water pollution.
Wausau: Acid rain, surface-water pollution.
(*See also* Minnesota, Duluth and Minneapolis–St. Paul)

WYOMING

Casper: Resource development (mining of coal, oil shale, and uranium, and oil and gas production), eutrophication, insufficient drainage.

---

*According to the U.S. Geological Survey paper, a large eruption of any of the five active volcanoes in Washington—Glacier Peak, Mount Adams, Mount Baker (near Bellingham), Mount Rainier (near Seattle and Tacoma), and Mount St. Helens—could have "devastating consequences." The intrusion of fresh and salt water in molten magma could cause massive flooding from mudflows as well as huge steam explosions.

NATURAL HAZARDS

We're all familiar—even if only through television or newspapers—with the awesome destruction that nature can unleash. Perhaps no sight in recent memory was more dramatic than the eruption of Mount St. Helens in 1980, an initial blast equivalent to 10 million tons of TNT, which blew off the topmost 1,300 feet of the mountain. Volcanic eruptions can wipe out lives and property in an instant. Fortunately, however, volcanoes usually give warning of impending activity, as did Mount St. Helens. Even more fortunately, the places where volcanic activity is a potential hazard are very few. A number of violent natural events are much more common and widespread, and although they may be less cataclysmic than a full-blown volcanic eruption, they can cause great damage and threaten lives. Many of these natural hazards follow definite geographic patterns within the United States, and some metro areas are at much greater risk than others.

The Sun Belt Is Also a Storm Belt

Many if not most severe storms occur in the southern half of the nation. For this reason, you might say that the Sun Belt is also a storm belt.

Thunderstorms and Lightning. Thunderstorms are common and don't usually cause death. But lightning kills 200 Americans a year. It remains the most common and frequent natural danger. At any given moment there are about 2,000 thunderstorms in progress around the globe; in the time it takes you to read this paragraph, lightning will have struck the earth 700 times.

Florida, the Sunshine State, is actually the country's stormiest state, with three times as much thunder and lightning as any other. California, on the other hand, is one of the most storm-free states along with Oregon and Washington. In a typical year, coastal California towns will average between two and five thunderstorm episodes. Most American towns average between 35 and 50. Fort Myers, Florida, averages 128. (A thunderstorm episode represents the presence of a single storm cell; a place like Fort Myers can register four or five episodes in a single day.)

The Place Profiles earlier in this chapter tell how many thunderstorm days each place can expect in an average year. The southeastern quadrant of our country generally receives more rain and thunderstorms than the rest, although the thunderstorms of the Great Plains are awesome spectacles.

Tornadoes. While they are not nearly as large or long-lived as hurricanes and release much less total force, tornadoes have more destructive ·and killing power concentrated in a small area than any other storm known. For absolute ferocity and wind speed, a tornado has no rival.

The hallmark of this vicious inland storm is the huge, snakelike funnel cloud that sweeps and bounces along the ground, destroying buildings, sweeping up cars, trains, livestock, and trees, and sucking them up hundreds of feet into the whirling vortex. Wind speeds close to 300 miles per hour have been recorded.

Although no one can tell for certain just where a particular tornado might touch down, their season, origin, and direction of travel are fairly predictable. Tornado season reaches its peak in late spring and early summer, and most storms originate in the central and southern Great Plains, in the states of Oklahoma, Texas, Arkansas, Kansas, and Missouri. After forming in the intense heat and rising air of the Plains, these storms proceed toward the northeast at speeds averaging 25 to 40 miles per hour. Most tornadoes do not last very long or travel very far. Half of all tornadoes reported travel less than five miles on the ground; a few have been tracked for more than 200 miles.

Metro areas in Oklahoma, eastern Texas, Arkansas, northern Louisiana and Mississippi, eastern Tennessee, Kansas, Missouri, and parts of Nebraska, Iowa, and Illinois have a high potential for tornado damage and danger. Nearly one third of all tornadoes ever reported in the United States have occurred within the boundaries of Kansas, Oklahoma, and Texas.

Hurricanes. Giant tropical cyclonic storms that originate at sea, hurricanes are unmatched for sheer power over a very large area. Hurricanes last for days, measure hundreds of miles across, and release tremendous energy in the form of high winds, torrential rains, lightning, and tidal surges. They usually occur from June through November and strike the Gulf states and southern segments of the Atlantic Coast primarily, though they will also strike locations farther north. Like thunderstorms, hurricanes are much less frequent and less severe on the Pacific Coast.

Hurricanes usually originate in the tropical waters of the Atlantic Ocean. Most of them occur toward summer's end because it takes that long for the water temperature and evaporation rate to rise sufficiently to begin the cyclonic, counterclockwise rotation of a wind system around a low-pressure system. When the wind velocities are less than 39 miles per hour, this cyclone is called a tropical depression; when wind velocities are between 39 and 74 miles per hour, the cyclone is called a tropical storm. And when the winds reach 74 miles per hour, the storm becomes a hurricane.

Often the greatest danger and destruction from hurricanes are due not to the winds but to the tidal surges that can sweep ashore with seas 15 or more feet higher than normal high tides. Although Florida and the southern coasts are most vulnerable to hurricanes, locations as far north as Cape Cod and the coast of Maine are by no means immune.

Earthquake Risks

The cause of an earthquake is the pressure building between two contiguous masses of rock—called plates —that are moving slowly but inexorably toward each

Tornado and Hurricane Risk Areas

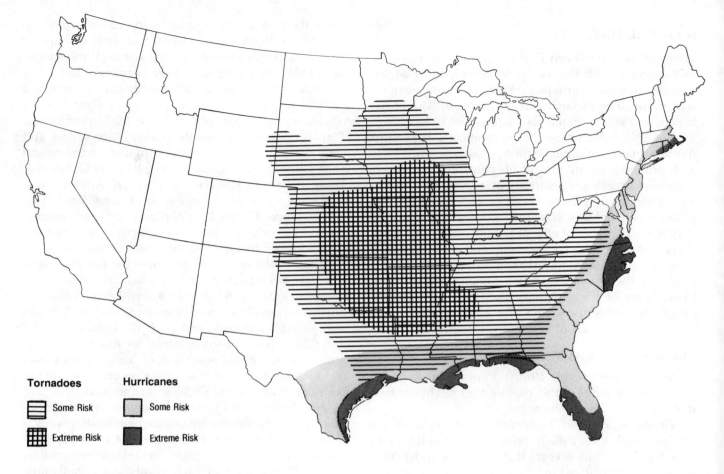

Tornadoes

▦ Some Risk

▦ Extreme Risk

Hurricanes

░ Some Risk

▓ Extreme Risk

Earthquake Hazard Zones

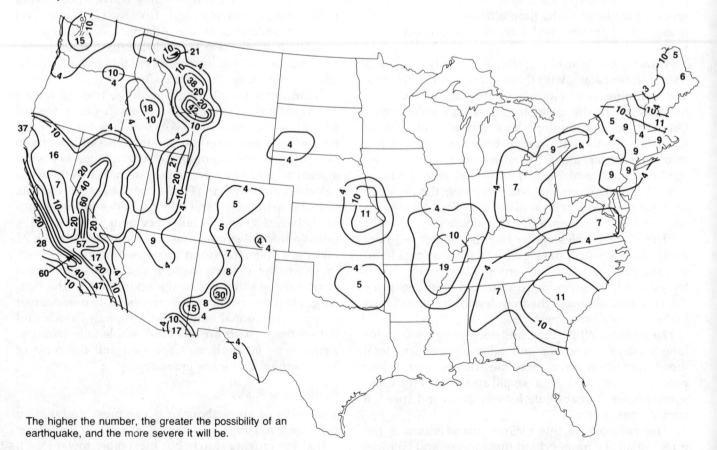

The higher the number, the greater the possibility of an earthquake, and the more severe it will be.

Source: U.S. Geological Survey Open-File Report 76-416, 1976.

other in slightly different directions. When the pressure becomes too great for the rock substance to hold, it shears suddenly. This shearing, along with the consequent shuddering, swaying, and even shifting of immense masses of underground rock, is experienced on the earth's surface as an earthquake.

Those conditions necessary to cause an earthquake exist only in certain areas. The entire area ringing the Pacific Ocean is earthquake-prone, from western South America to Central America, North America's Pacific states, and Alaska, through the Aleutian chain across to Japan, down through China, and ending in New Zealand (which has more earthquakes than any other place in the world).

According to the map "Earthquake Hazard Zones," although huge stretches of America are free from the threat of earthquakes, some areas appear to be resting on powder kegs. (U.S. Geological Survey seismologists warn that the map is still experimental and that its predictions cannot be guaranteed.)

Northeast. There is a good deal of disagreement among geologists concerning earthquake risk in the Northeast. A number of theories about seismic trends have been advanced, and attempts have been made to relate these trends to various fault systems. The best known of these systems is the Boston-Ottawa trend, shown on the map as a continuous area from the Atlantic coast of Massachusetts to the St. Lawrence River valley, encompassing the two cities for which it is named. Most people are unaware that Boston suffered a severe earthquake in the 1700s and that it remains earthquake-prone today.

Southeast. One theory about earthquake risk is that possible earthquake epicenters (the points of origin of ground tremors) are not randomly distributed but occur in zones. In the Southeast, these zones run both parallel to and across the Appalachian Mountains. The greatest shock recorded east of the Mississippi occurred in Charleston, South Carolina, in 1886. The present hazard in South Carolina and eastern Georgia is as high as in the Boston-Ottawa trend.

Midwest and Rocky Mountains Regions. The zone of greatest hazard in the Mississippi Valley lies around the side of the cataclysmic series of quakes that occurred near New Madrid, Missouri. The biggest city in this zone is Memphis. The risk of seismic activity is greater in the Rocky Mountains region. The three biggest mountain cities—Denver, Albuquerque, and Salt Lake City—all lie within risk zones.

Pacific Northwest. The Puget Sound area near Seattle has experienced two major shocks within the past 30 years, both causing considerable damage. And in 1964, an earthquake in Anchorage registered 8.4 on

America's Other Earthquake Hazard

Most people know that California is the most earthquake-ridden state in America. Three major faults, or unstable cracks in the earth's surface, contribute to continual and severe seismic activity there. The most destructive earthquake in U.S. history in terms of property and casualties occurred in San Francisco in 1906, killing 452 people and destroying 28,000 buildings through tremors and resulting fire.

But what was probably the most powerful earthquake ever to strike in America took place in another danger zone, one less well known than the quake-prone Golden State—the Mississippi Valley. This earthquake hit on February 7, 1812, in New Madrid, Missouri, and its tremors cracked pavement and rang church bells as far away as Washington, D.C., about 700 miles distant. Its force has been estimated at 8.6 on the Richter scale (the San Francisco earthquake has been estimated at 8.3). This was one of a series of severe quakes over the winter of 1811–12 that changed the course of the Mississippi River and created nearby Reelfoot Lake. Yet another major earthquake followed in 1895, striking the area with a Richter force of 6.5.

All these quakes have been attributed to the New Madrid Fault, which runs along the western border of Tennessee. According to a statement made by the Federal Emergency Management Agency in early 1984, scientists believe it is likely that increasing pressure on the fault will lead to a recurrence before the year 2000, one that could cause thousands of deaths and up to $60 billion in damage. Such a quake could register as high as 7.5, experts say, and affect 21 states, from Kansas east to Pennsylvania and from Illinois south to Louisiana.

the Richter scale (a nine-point span on a seismograph used to express the relative magnitude of an earthquake).

California and Nevada. Much more seismic activity (and, therefore, more research and data) is present in California and Nevada than anywhere else in America. The greatest hazards in the United States are found in the San Andreas, Owens Valley, and Garlock fault systems, which are shown on the map as zones numbered as high as 60. All the metro areas in California are affected by these faults, particularly (in alphabetical order) Bakersfield, Los Angeles–Long Beach, Oakland, San Francisco, and San Jose. These places, most of which have mild climates and pleasant terrain, are in real danger.

Housing:

Affording the American Dream

Have you heard the story about the two California contractors who bumped into each other at the lumberyard? It is now being retold in other parts of the United States, with local emphasis.

"Congratulate me, Ralph," one of them says. "I've just sold my first $150,000 house!"

"Holy breezeway, Earl, last time we talked you were building $80,000 houses."

"I still am, but now I get $150,000 for them."

The question is, Who can afford these houses? As the average price of a new house reached an all-time high of $101,000 in May 1984, up from $20,000 in 1965, more prospective buyers got edged out of the market. The average U.S. family now puts 33 percent of its income toward monthly house payments, compared with the 25 percent necessary eight years ago. These figures mean that fewer than three of every ten Americans can afford current mortgage rates and building costs.

The 1980s may well be the era of making do, doubling up with parents, buying a house with several people unrelated to you, making dollhouses livable, learning creative financing tactics, budgeting up to 40 percent of your gross income for shelter costs—or, yes, simply getting used to renting indefinitely.

Most of us change our address several times during

our lives. In most metro areas the options are an apartment, a single home, a condominium, or a mobile home. The choices often fall within common life stages and income levels. Here are several possibilities:

- *You are eighteen to twenty-one,* carefully looking at a college or graduate school in Big Ten country. Unless you take a room in a dormitory, the odds are you'll rent an apartment. Small metro areas dominated by a major university tend to have an oversupply of structures with five or more rental units.

- *You are twenty to twenty-five,* single, with a minimum of responsibilities, diligently working at your first job but willing to change employers and move anywhere for a better opportunity. If moving in with Mom and Dad is not your preference, you could take the common tack of renting a studio or one-bedroom apartment; your commitment lasts only as long as the term of the lease.

- *You are twenty-five to thirty-five,* married, with two small children and an offer for a better job in a distant and unfamiliar metro area. Renting a house for a year or so may give you an opportunity to become thoroughly acquainted with the new area before you invest in a home of your own. You might also consider buying an inexpensive condominium that can easily be resold or rented once you find a house and neighborhood that are right for you.

- *You are thirty-five to forty-five,* married, with children, and have recently taken a promotion in another city with a fat relocation bonus and corresponding pay increase. If you're selling a home, the odds are you'll trade up for a larger house in the suburbs.
- *You are well into your sixth decade,* your children have scattered like tumbleweeds in the wind, and you have an ark of a home that you plan to sell. Your options are wider than those of other age groups: You can rent an apartment or buy a smaller home, condo, or mobile home in town or in another metro area, perhaps one with a milder climate and a lower cost of living.

MAJOR HOUSING CHOICES

If you're thinking of moving to a metro area hundreds of miles distant, it would help to know what kinds of local shelter choices are available, what the average costs would be for renting, and—because two thirds of us eventually end up buying a single-family home—what are the average homeowner costs you'll encounter there.

Single Houses

If you walk through the front door of the typical American home, you'll find yourself in a structure that was built in 1964 and has a single-level, 1,600-square-foot floor plan enclosing five rooms (three bedrooms, one bath, a complete kitchen), no basement, and an insulated attic and storm windows to conserve the heat from its gas-fired, warm-air furnace. This house is kept cool during hot spells by a central air-conditioning unit. It is also connected to city water and sewerage lines.

So much for national composites. Among the 57 million single houses in the United States (and particularly among the newer suburban homes), a buyer can choose from many building styles—Cape Cods and Cape Anns, mountain A-frames, cabins of peeled pine log, desert adobes, Greek revivals, American and Dutch colonials, Puget Sounds, catslides, exotic glass solaria, futuristic earth berms, Victorians, plantation cottages, and ubiquitous split-levels and California bungalows.

In the metro areas, the portion of single homes you'll actually find among all the other options—apartments, condos, duplexes, triplexes, and mobile homes—can vary considerably.

The Silent Housing Boom

With all the talk about squeezes, shortages, and crises in American housing, one can easily overlook some remarkable things that happened during the 1970s.

Only 58 of the nation's 3,100 counties lost housing units between 1970 and 1980, and almost all of the net loss was in Bronx and Kings counties, in the New York metro area.

While our population was growing at the second slowest rate per decade in history, housing grew faster than during any decade since 1900. Americans managed to erect 20 million new housing units in those ten years, which amounts to almost one new housing unit for each new person added to the population. These 20 million homes, apartments, condos, and mobile homes exceed the total housing stock of either Canada or Mexico as well as the total number of housing units in Italy, France, or Britain.

Single Houses in the Metro Areas

Most Single Houses	As % of All Units	Fewest Single Houses	As % of All Units
1. Joplin, MO	84	1. Jersey City, NJ	12%
2. Enid, OK	83	2. New York, NY	17
Huntsville, AL	83	3. Boston, MA	22
3. Anderson, SC	82	4. Lewiston–Auburn, ME	41
Gadsden, AL	82	5. Chicago, IL	46
Lynchburg, VA	82	5. Lawrence–Haverhill, MA–NH	46
Parkersburg-Marietta, WV–OH	82	7. Anchorage, AK	48
4. Anderson, IN	81	7. Fall River, MA–RI	48
Dayton-Springfield, OH	81	9. Fort Lauderdale–Hollywood–Pompano Beach, FL	50
Muskegon, MI	81	9. Honolulu, HI	50
Sherman-Denison, TX	81	9. Miami–Hialeah, FL	50
South Bend, IN	81		

Source: U.S. Bureau of the Census, *1980 Census of Population and Housing.*

The national average for single houses as a percentage of all occupied units is 71%.

Condominiums

"Condominium" was nothing more than an obscure Latin word before a new legal concept for owning real estate was imported from Puerto Rico to the U.S. mainland in 1960. Under the arrangement, you could own outright an apartment, townhouse, or single house in a multiple-unit development. You could also sell, lease, bequeath, and furnish that legally described cube of air space independent of other unit owners.

Moreover, you owned the elevators, heating plant, streets, parking spaces, garden landscaping, tennis courts, swimming pool, lights, and walkways in common with the rest of the development's residents.

Throughout most of the 1970s, condominiums were heavily promoted to either newlywed or nearly dead buyers, as some brokers called them. Indeed, young couples and singles making their way out of the rental market and retired couples who wanted to unload a large house for a smaller one were major reasons for the number of condominium units growing from zero in 1960 to more than 2.5 million today.

If you've been reluctantly tearing rental payments from your checkbook and are weighing the purchase of a home for the first time, you might consider a condominium as a compromise between apartment living and the tax advantages of owning a single-family home. With a condominium, you have freedom from house and yard maintenance, a ready-made social life, and common recreation facilities. You also receive the tax advantages of ownership, often at a lower cost than buying a house would entail.

On the minus side, condo owners sometimes complain of ticky-tacky construction, parking problems, thin party walls, and living cheek by jowl with renters or other unfamiliar neighbors.

Condos can be high-rise (vertical) or low-rise (horizontal), depending on local zoning laws and available land. You'll find residential condominiums in metro areas where land is scarce and where the prices of single detached homes are out of reach for people looking to buy a first home. This form of real estate is most common in the resort-and-vacation metro areas.

Condominiums in the Metro Areas

Most Condominiums	As % of All Units
1. West Palm Beach–Boca Raton–Delray Beach, FL	33%
2. Fort Lauderdale–Hollywood–Pompano Beach, FL	32
3. Honolulu, HI	24
4. Sarasota, FL	20
5. Fort Myers, FL	18
6. Bradenton, FL	16
7. Fort Pierce, FL	14
7. Miami–Hialeah, FL	14
9. Anaheim–Santa Ana, CA	11
10. Reno, NV	10

Source: U.S. Bureau of the Census, *1980 Census of Population and Housing.* (All percent figures are rounded.)

The national average for condominiums as a percentage of all occupied units is 3%. Sixty-eight metro areas have no condominiums.

Mobile Homes

As you struggle to scrape up the down payment for a suburban ranch or a town house close to work, you may already have the $21,000 needed to buy an average mobile home outright.

The major advantage of a mobile home is price. It takes a typical contractor's crew several months to build a typical three-bedroom house, whereas a mobile home takes 80 to 100 hours. In 1983, when the average cost of building a conventional home was $45 per square foot, exclusive of land, the cost of manufacturing a mobile home was $21 per square foot.

This doesn't mean that mobile homes lack quality. Since World War II, when many defense workers were housed in 300-square-foot sheet-metal boxes with ersatz cooking facilities and no plumbing, mobile homes have gradually shaken their reputation for tackiness. Mobile homes now are at least 14 feet wide. Seventy-foot-long Double Wides can enclose three bedrooms, two baths, a living room, dining room, kitchen, and closets. New mobile homes are usually sold complete; appliances, furniture, draperies, lamps, and carpeting are all included in the price, as are built-in plumbing, heating, air-conditioning, and electrical systems.

Among the attractions of a mobile home are its availability (there are 410 factories around the country where you can buy one) and its affordability (the purchase price is low, and one can be easily financed through a personal property loan or a conventional 30-year VA or FHA loan). It's simple to transport and install at the owner's private acreage or at a well-run park, and inexpensive to maintain.

The value of a mobile home, however, may depreciate in many areas where conventional homes increase in value. Arbitrary evictions from mobile home parks are not uncommon in many states, nor are restrictive zoning laws that confine this kind of housing to the urban/rural fringe.

The only time the mobile home is actually mobile is when it leaves the factory and is towed by a truck in one or more sections to a concrete foundation, whether on the owner's acreage or at one of 24,000 trailer parks in the country. When it arrives, the wheels, axle, and towing tongue are removed, and all that still resembles a trailer is the I-beamed chassis, which quickly becomes hidden structural reinforcement once the unit is winched onto the foundation and plumbed. After that, the mobile home becomes more or less permanent; no more than 3 percent of them are ever moved again.

Last year, half of all new mobile homes were trucked to just eight states: California, Florida, Georgia, Louisiana, North Carolina, Oklahoma, South Carolina, and Texas. You're more likely, in general, to find permissive zoning regulations and a wider choice of mobile home parks in smaller metro areas of the Sun Belt. You're less likely to find them in large metro areas where the high cost of residential land offsets any economic benefits of owning a mobile home.

Mobile Homes in the Metro Areas

Most Mobile Homes	As % of All Units
1. Ocala, FL	20%
2. Jacksonville, NC	18
2. Redding, CA	18
4. Bradenton, FL	17
5. Las Cruces, NM	16
6. Fort Myers, FL	15
7. Lakeland–Winter Haven, FL	14
8. Casper, WY	13
8. Chico, CA	13
8. Fort Pierce, FL	13

Source: U.S. Bureau of the Census, *1980 Census of Population and Housing.* (All percent figures are rounded.)

The national average for mobile homes as a percentage of all occupied units is 5%. Sixteen metro areas have no mobile homes.

Renting an Apartment

Looking for digs close to work, with reasonable rent, tenants similar to yourself, a pleasant landlord, off-street parking, ambience, and all the other items on your checklist might turn out to be a quest that stops when the lease is signed but starts up again on the lease's anniversary. Still, for most newcomers to a metro area, renting is the main style of housing tenure.

As a renter you remain flexible, since you need not stay in an apartment beyond the term of the lease should your income slump or your job take you to another part of the country. You don't need to come up with a down payment; taxes, insurance, repairs, and sometimes utilities are the landlord's headaches.

But you also miss out on such ownership benefits as growing equity, property appreciation, and tax deductions for mortgage interest, while being subject to condo conversion or arbitrary rent hikes in times of low vacancy rates.

Many of us tend to think that apartments are available only in blocks of large, high-rise tower complexes near a large metro area's central business district. In fact, only one out of 50 apartments is in a building of 13 stories or more, and only one out of ten is in a building higher than three stories. Moreover, apartments make up as large a part of occupied housing in smaller metro areas dominated by state universities as they do in metro areas that are much larger in population.

According to the Census Bureau, an apartment is simply a rental unit in a structure with five or more rental units, which excludes rental duplexes, triplexes, and fourplexes.

Apartments in the Metro Areas

Most Apartments	As % of All Units	Fewest Apartments	As % of All Units
1. New York, NY	56%	1. Anderson, SC	4%
2. Austin, TX	43	1. Florence, SC	4
3. Jersey City, NJ	41	1. Hickory, NC	4
4. Washington, DC–MD–VA	34	4. Anderson, IN	5
5. Los Angeles–Long Beach, CA	30	4. Burlington, NC	5
5. Miami–Hialeah, FL	30	4. Dothan, AL	5
5. Oakland, CA	30	4. Florence, AL	5
8. Ann Arbor, MI	28	4. Gadsden, AL	5
8. Honolulu, HI	28	4. Joplin, MO	5
8. Iowa City, IA	28	4. Ocala, FL	5

Source: U.S. Bureau of the Census, *1980 Census of Population and Housing.* (All percent figures are rounded.)

The national average for apartments as a percentage of all occupied units is 15%.

BUYING THAT SINGLE-FAMILY HOME . . .

Despite the growing number of options in housing, the single-family house seems to be the most common (87 percent of homeowner units are single-family homes) and the most popular (in a 1983 poll, 81 percent of current owners and 70 percent of renters expecting to move within five years said they planned to buy a detached home). In fact, two thirds of us eventually buy a single-family home.

Where are the best markets for prospective buyers? You might guess that a consequence of the country's west-by-south population shift would be dramatically inflated home prices in the same direction. But some of the highest prices estimated for 1984 are found in places where homes have always been expensive: Anchorage, Honolulu, New York City and its suburbs in Connecticut and New Jersey, the District of Columbia and its environs, and, since 1975, California metro areas.

We may never again experience the explosive 178 percent inflation in market values seen in this country during the 1970s, however. In May of 1984, according to the National Association of Realtors, an existing single house carried a price tag of $87,600. Prices rose 31 percent between 1980 and 1984 in the rebounding East, 28 percent in the South, only 18 percent in the slower-growing North Central states, and 17 percent in the West, where values were historically high. These increases don't mean that an $87,600 house can't be found for half that much. It can, in smaller metro areas of Alabama, Indiana, Missouri, and Texas.

Average Single-Family House Prices

Highest		Lowest	
1. Stamford, CT	$200,000	1. Joplin, MO	$37,600
2. Norwalk, CT	168,400	2. McAllen–Edinburg–Mission, TX	39,800
3. Honolulu, HI	163,400	3. Terre Haute, IN	40,200
4. San Francisco, CA	154,500	4. St. Joseph, MO	40,900
5. San Jose, CA	143,900	5. Brownsville–Harlingen, TX	41,100
6. Anaheim–Santa Ana, CA	142,300	6. Battle Creek, MI	41,500
7. Santa Barbara–Santa Maria–Lompoc, CA	138,100	7. Muskegon, MI	41,900
8. Santa Cruz, CA	127,300	8. Danville, VA	42,100
9. San Diego, CA	123,503	9. Gadsden, AL	43,400
10. Salinas–Seaside–Monterey, CA	122,900	10. Pine Bluff, AR	43,500
11. Oxnard–Ventura, CA	122,800	11. Altoona, PA	43,600
		11. Sherman–Denison, TX	43,600

Source: U.S. Bureau of the Census, *1980 Census of Population and Housing,* and the National Association of Realtors, 1984.

. . . AND REBUYING IT WITH PROPERTY TAXES

In recent years, homeowners who banded together to protest confiscatory property taxes likened them to a ransom that they were forced to pay to keep their shelter off the local tax assessor's auction block. Using this analogy, homeowners in Islip, New York, buy their homes back from the town every 22 years, since the effective tax rate (a tax on the home's full value) is 4.63 percent. Down in Mobile County, Alabama, on the other hand, the "ransom" period is 526 years because of an extremely low effective rate of 0.19 percent. The difference in these figures illustrates the wide variation in property taxes around the country.

Locally, too, property taxes can vary enormously and be madly confusing to homeowners. In California, two houses on the same block with identical price tags and physical characteristics can have substantially different, yet legally impeccable tax bills if one of them was sold before the approval of Proposition 13 and the other after. In Texas, a home's value can be assessed at different levels at different times of the year by different assessors.

Although residential property taxes aren't collected by metro areas (that is done by 13,527 cities, townships, counties, school districts, sanitary districts, hospital districts, and other special districts), statewide average property tax rates are useful in estimating local property tax bills. Clearly, homeowners in Connecti-

cut, Massachusetts, New Jersey, and New York have good reason for envying their counterparts in Alabama and Louisiana.

House Property Tax Bills

Highest			Lowest	
1. Stamford, CT	$3,061		1. Alexandria, LA	$ 75
2. Bergen–Passaic, NJ	2,777		2. Monroe, LA	82
3. Newark, NJ	2,695		3. Shreveport, LA	88
4. Norwalk, CT	2,576		4. Lake Charles, LA	92
5. New York, NY	2,462		5. Houma–Thibodaux, LA	97
6. Middlesex–Somerset–Hunterdon, NJ	2,253		6. Baton Rouge, LA	111
6. Monmouth–Ocean, NJ	2,253		7. New Orleans, LA	118
8. Ann Arbor, MI	2,132		8. Lafayette, LA	119
9. Salem–Gloucester, MA	2,066		9. Gadsden, AL	178
10. Danbury, CT	1,779		10. Anniston, AL	184

Source: Places Rated estimates based on average market values multiplied by each state's average effective property tax rate as reported by the Advisory Commission on Intergovernmental Relations, *Significant Features of Fiscal Federalism*, 1984.

WHAT A DIFFERENCE AGE MAKES

Anyone watching the speed at which houses can be put up on pricey lots in suburbia or in cheap-jack developments near the industrial fringe might well agree with old-timers who have seen large, balloon-framed homes built with a good deal of craftsmanship. "They don't build them the way they used to," some of them might mutter.

No, they don't. Wraparound porches are rarely found. A porch is now merely a recessed space at the entrance of a house. The ten-foot interior ceilings common before World War II have been replaced with the eight-foot standard. The kind of formal stairway with well-turned balusters and waxed rails that Andy Hardy used to slide down are no longer necessary—most new homes are built on a single level. Milled red oak fascias and moldings have become too expensive for common use; walls are envelopes of three-eighths inch gypsum board nailed to studs rather than the old "mud jobs" of plaster on lath; and solid six-panel doors have lost out to hollow-core flush doors of hemlock veneer.

On the other hand, copper and polyvinyl chloride water pipes have replaced galvanized iron plumbing; knob-and-tube wiring has surrendered to safer electrical circuitry; cast-iron radiators no longer interfere with furniture arrangement; pressure-treated wood has eliminated termite and dry-rot risks; and the seasonal problem of cellar flooding arises less often because there aren't many cellars being excavated. Indeed, as much as 20 percent of a new home's breathtaking price tag is due to vastly superior building materials, according to a recent Prudential Insurance Company study.

One useful indication of the quality of a metro area's housing stock is the percent of homes put up

---

The Ground Factor

Any real estate broker touting a suburban ranch or condo can tick off the basic factors that play a part in the price tags for housing. Aside from seller's greed, the factors are quality of original construction, turnover rate in the neighborhood, current upkeep, and location. But all these are of secondary importance to local supply and demand.

Cut off a slice of a tract development in suburban Topeka, Kansas, and drop it in the middle of New Jersey's Morris County, and you can see supply and demand at work. The transplanted homes will double in market value, not because they are roomier and are made with better materials, but because of the more intense competition for housing around much of New York City's periphery. You can find well-cared-for three-bedroom ranches in the Kansas capital for $60,000 and nearly identical homes in suburban Newark for $150,000. The local demand for housing, then, is the single best determinant of a home's price.

Based on Federal Housing Authority data, the value of the ground on which a typical existing house is built represents 22 percent of the price of the home if it were to be sold immediately. The figure varies considerably depending on where in the country this typical house is found. In Hawaii, the true cost of the site is more than half the price of the house; in California, it's 34 percent. Elsewhere, in Michigan or Georgia, for example, it's only 14 percent and 15 percent respectively.

Land Costs As Percent of House Prices

Highest			Lowest	
1. Hawaii	51%		1. Michigan	14%
2. California	34		2. Georgia	15
3. Oregon	29		2. Indiana	15
4. Connecticut	26		2. South Carolina	15
4. Florida	26		5. Alabama	16
4. Washington	26		5. Kansas	16
7. Utah	25		5. Pennsylvania	16
8. Nevada	24		5. South Dakota	16

Source: Federal Housing Authority, Property Characteristics, One-Family Homes, by States, 1983.

before 1940. Although an older house isn't necessarily on the verge of tumbling down, age can signal functional obsolescence and looming maintenance headaches. Clapboards do need scraping and repainting every three years, clogged sewer drains must be snaked, furnaces do wear out, and storm windows must be retrofitted. These tasks can mean both dollars and difficulties.

Old and New Metro Areas

Newest	Houses Built Before 1940	Oldest	Houses Built Before 1940
1. Anchorage, AK	1.1%	1. Jersey City, NJ	60.2%
2. Las Vegas, NV	1.5	2. Scranton–Wilkes-Barre, PA	56.6
3. Fort Lauderdale–Hollywood–Pompano Beach, FL	1.7	3. Fall River, MA–RI	55.2
4. Melbourne–Titusville–Palm Bay, FL	3.1	4. Pittsfield, MA	54.1
		5. Altoona, PA	54.0
5. Fort Walton Beach, FL	3.4	6. New Bedford, MA	53.8
6. Odessa, TX	3.6	7. Lewiston–Auburn, ME	52.9
7. Anaheim–Santa Ana, CA	3.7	8. Cumberland, MD–VA	52.8
8. Midland, TX	3.8	9. Salem–Gloucester, MA	52.4
9. Fort Myers, FL	3.9	10. Glens Falls, NY	51.5
10. Sarasota, FL	4.0	10. Johnstown, PA	51.5

Source: U.S. Bureau of the Census, *1980 Census of Population and Housing.*

The median age of the nation's housing is 23 years, the same as it was in 1970.

HOME ENERGY REQUIREMENTS

After mortgage interest rates, fuel and electricity for the home have been the fastest-rising items on the Consumer Price Index since 1967. What was once a minor and predictable expense, averaging less than 1 percent of a household's budget 15 years ago, may now amount to more than the cost of medical care or clothing.

There are three reasons for the $656 difference between the annual average residential utility bills in Chicago and Huntsville, Alabama: climate, the form of energy used to maintain comfortable temperatures in the house, and the source of this energy.

Counting the Hours

Texans say that their Gulf Coast, from Brownsville–Harlingen to Corpus Christi and beyond to Beaumont–Port Arthur, is a place where air-conditioning is a necessity like food and water, without which all mankind becomes delirious, withers, and dies. Here, a meteorologist measuring humidity with a psychrometer whenever the temperature climbs over 80 degrees Fahrenheit will count nearly 2,500 hours every year when the instrument's bulb stays wet from moist air. New Delhi records similar numbers, and so does Kinshasa, capital of Zaire. These 2,500-odd hours are the equivalent of more than 200 days per year with

Older Isn't Always Cheaper

Most people live in homes built years ago that were bought, lived in, and sold by a succession of owners. We all confirm the "filtering theory" of housing, which states that houses filter down from high-income first owners to middle-income buyers to lower-income owners. To put it another way, many high-income families live in newer homes, and most lower-income households occupy older homes.

So what else is new?

Just that when the weekend real estate sections of the *Boston Globe, Washington Post, Chicago Tribune,* or *San Francisco Chronicle* list old homes in "upscale" neighborhoods on the market for $100,000 or more, you're looking at big exceptions to this theory. Nowhere is this more apparent than in Connecticut's Fairfield County. Stamford and Norwalk homes carry some of the biggest price tags in the country, and most of them were built long before World War II.

Nevertheless, the filtering theory holds true for most of America's 329 metro areas: The older the housing, the lower the price.

uncomfortable, sweaty, 12-hour periods of high humidity.

In such desert metro areas as Las Vegas, Phoenix, and Tucson, the days are much drier, but the number of hours there when the temperature is more than 80 degrees Fahrenheit is even greater than the number found on the Texas Gulf Coast. These hours were first counted by U.S. Defense Department building engineers in the late 1940s and updated in 1978 for a worldwide inventory of air and naval bases, supply depots, and weather stations. Not only are these hours useful for gauging how hot a given place is over time, they are also good indicators of how often your home's air conditioner may be humming.

Counting the Days

In 1915, Eugene P. Milener, an engineer with the Gas Company of Baltimore, made a discovery for which he received little recognition outside of his industry: The amount of natural gas needed to keep buildings warm can be accurately predicted for every degree that the outdoor temperature falls below 65 degrees. Natural gas utilities still use this measurement, called a degree day, to estimate consumption patterns among their customers.

A heating-degree day is the number of degrees the daily average temperature is below 65. Heating your home isn't usually necessary when the temperature outdoors is more than 65, but furnaces are fired up when the outdoor temperature falls below that mark. Thus, a heating-degree day indicates the number of degrees of heating required to keep a house at 65. If, for example, the temperature on a winter day is 35, that day has 30 heating-degree days, meaning that 30 degrees of heating are called for.

The average for annual heating-degree days (total heating-degree days over one year) in the United States is 4,671, ranging among *Places Rated* metro areas from zero in Honolulu to 10,911 in Anchorage. The number of annual degree days in a given place tells you how cold it gets and also how often you'll need to run a home's heating system to keep the indoors comfortable.

Household Energy Geography

In the early 1950s, the rumbling of coal trucks along their delivery routes was a familiar urban street sound. Three-dollar-a-ton black anthracite was the dominant home heating fuel everywhere east of the Mississippi except for Florida and New England. The blue flame of piped-in natural gas, the major heating fuel today, was just starting to burn in new refrigerators, stoves, clothes dryers, and in furnaces in new homes. Electric utilities were just beginning to encourage construction of total-electric homes.

Today, coal has virtually disappeared from the home energy scene. In spite of the heavy marketing of airtight coal stoves as an auxiliary means of heating houses, the number of homes burning this fuel declined by more than one million over the past decade. The major options now, from most expensive to least, are electric power, residual fuel oil or kerosene, and piped-in natural gas. And, in some timber country metro areas, there's wood.

Electricity. In 1950, the only place where most of the homes were all-electric was the small desert town of Las Vegas, seat of Nevada's Clark County. The power there was the cheapest in the country, simply because it was generated by falling water at the new Boulder Canyon hydroelectric project some 25 miles southeast. It still is cheap, relative to nuclear-generated or fossil fuel–generated power that home-owners pay for elsewhere in the country. So is the power that heats and lights homes in the Pacific Northwest and in certain Alabama and Tennessee metro areas close to TVA projects.

Although most American homes are heated with natural gas, electricity is gaining fast. Between 1970 and 1980, the number of all-electric homes increased by more than 200 percent. The reason: It costs much less to wire a new house for electric resistance heat than to install a gas or oil furnace with piping and sheet-metal hot-air conduits. All-electric homes pre-dominate in 50 of the 329 metro areas. The U.S. Department of Energy surveys average annual house-hold energy consumption and prices, and the following are its figures for electricity in 1983:

- Typical Consumption: 17,287 kilowatt-hours per year
- Average Bill: $1,186 per year
- Cost per Million Btus: $18.51

Air-Conditioning Needs: The Top 11 Hot-Weather Metro Areas

Metro Area	More than 80° F per Year
1. Phoenix, AZ	2,845 hrs
2. Laredo, TX	2,736
3. Galveston–Texas City, TX	2,639
4. Corpus Christi, TX	2,531
5. Tucson, AZ	2,445
6. Miami–Hialeah, FL	2,388
7. Las Vegas, NV	2,360
8. Dallas, TX	2,304
8. Sherman–Denison, TX	2,304
10. Brownsville–Harlingen, TX	2,295
10. McAllen–Edinburg–Mission, TX	2,295

Source: U.S. Department of Defense, *Engineering Weather Data*, 1978.

The above range of hours is the equivalent of between 94 and 119 full days of temperatures of 80 degrees Fahrenheit or higher.

Heating Needs: The Top 10 Cold-Weather Metro Areas

Metro Area	Degree Days
1. Anchorage, AK	10,911
2. Grand Forks, ND	9,876
3. Duluth, MN–WI	9,757
4. Fargo–Moorhead, ND–MN	9,271
5. Bismarck, ND	9,044
6. St. Cloud, MN	8,868
7. Bangor, ME	8,648
8. Wausau, WI	8,586
9. Eau Claire, WI	8,388
10. Minneapolis–St. Paul, MN–WI	8,310

Source: National Oceanic and Atmospheric Administration, *Substation Summaries*, 1951 to date.

Oil and Kerosene. Though their prices have stabilized because of the current world oil glut, number-two heating oil and kerosene were the only items on the Consumer Price Index to sextuple in cost between 1967 and 1980 (since surpassed by mortgage interest costs). This explains why the number of homes heated with fuel oil or kerosene declined by more than two million since 1970. You won't find the price varying greatly by location, but you will find these distillates of imported crude to be the most common heating fuel in 61 metro areas, most of them in New England and Mid-Atlantic states. The Department of Energy gives these figures for 1983 consumption and prices:

- Typical Consumption: 1,043 gallons per year
- Average Bill: $1,237 per year
- Cost per Million Btus: $8.53

Natural Gas. In 228 metro areas, the major source for heating a house is a by-product of oil drilling that for many years flamed at the wellhead for lack of a market. Natural gas, a fossil fuel, has meant inexpensive heat for most householders, mainly because the federal government has regulated its interstate price. It is slowly being deregulated and quickly becoming expensive; some experts predict that its cost per million Btus will equal that of fuel oil or kerosene by 1990.

Natural gas has never been cheap to homeowners at the end of the continental transmission lines that begin in Louisiana and Texas gas fields, however. This explains why natural gas isn't preferred in New England or Mid-Atlantic homes, where oil is the least expensive of fuels; or in the Pacific Northwest, where hydroelectric power costs the least. The Department of Energy provides these figures for natural gas usage in 1983:

- Typical Consumption: 13,100 cubic feet per year
- Average Bill: $724 per year
- Cost per Million Btus: $5.53

Wood. Anyone who feeds a wood stove has heard the proverb about this fuel: It warms you twice, first when you cut and stack it, and second when you watch it burn. From Rocky Mountain piñon to hickory and ash from Ozark forests, it is the main heating fuel in 2.6 million homes (up from less than one million in 1970). Among metro areas today, only a small percentage of homes—10 percent or so—in Maine, Oregon, and Vermont burn wood exclusively. The U.S. Forest Service determines energy content for various kinds of wood; consumption and price figures for 1983 come from the Department of Energy:

- Typical Consumption: 2.8 cords per year
- Average Bill: $350 per year
- Cost per Million Btus: $5.34 (hardwood)

Keeping It All Going

Ever since the Arab oil embargo of late 1973, home energy bills—for heating and cooling, lighting, and running appliances—have skyrocketed. During the winter, this expense is borne mostly by northerners, though many residents of the Sun Belt need winter heat as well. The brunt of energy expenses takes a southerly shift during the summer because of air-conditioning.

If you'd like to dodge both winter heating and summer air-conditioning bills, move to Hawaii. You'll still be writing checks to the local public utility, however. Although Honolulu is the only metro area in the United States with no heated homes and also a place where air-conditioning is considered extravagant, you'll still pay the Hawaiian Electric Company nearly $80 a month to keep your water hot, food cool, and lamps lit.

JUDGING HOMEOWNING COSTS

On the average, are single homes more expensive in Danbury, Dayton, or Duluth? When it comes to paying property taxes, might you be better off in Birmingham than in Boston? Would a February relocation to a warm metro area haunt you in August when you realize how much air-conditioning costs?

To help you answer these questions, *Places Rated* tallies the three biggest dollar expenses of buying and maintaining a single-family home: utility bills, local property taxes, and mortgage payments. The sum of these three items equals the amount you can expect to pay each year for the basics of homeownership. It also represents each metro area's score. Because the single-family home is the type of housing most commonly bought by Americans, we use it here as the basis of our examination of homeowning costs.

Property taxes and mortgage payments are based on the average market value of owner-occupied single homes within each metro area as reported by the *1980 Census of Population and Housing*. These were owners' estimates of what their home would be worth if they decided to sell immediately. To show realistic 1984 prices, *Places Rated* updated these estimates with regional inflation factors reported by the National Association of Realtors.

Each metro area starts with a base score of zero. Points are added according to the following indicators:

1. *Utility bills.* The utility bills are estimated for a home that uses natural gas for space heating, water heating, and cooking because this fuel is available everywhere and is the most frequently chosen in most of the metro areas. Also included in the utility bills are the costs of electricity for lighting, running appliances, and air-conditioning based on local bills for 750 kilowatt-hours of consumption as reported by the Department of Energy. In metro areas where total-electric homes predominate, utility bills are estimates of annual residential all-electric costs, also from the Department of Energy.
2. *Property taxes.* Property taxes are calculated by multiplying the average market value of a house by the state's average effective tax rate for residential property. For example, the property tax bill in Phoenix of $435 is derived from a 1984 house value of $77,700 times Arizona's effective tax rate of 0.56 percent.
3. *Mortgage payments.* Annual mortgage payments are based on a 12 percent, 25-year loan on the average price of a house, after a one-quarter down payment has been made.

Sample Comparison: Joplin, Missouri, and Stamford, Connecticut

Does anyone recall J. Blandings? Cary Grant played him in the 1948 movie "Mr. Blandings Builds His Dream House." The film tells the story of a New York City couple, tired of living in a crowded apartment, who one day discover a rambling old house for sale on 50 bucolic acres in nearby Connecticut. They fall in love with the place and take a $10,000 plunge to join the suburban gentry.

The ensuing comedy of Mr. Blandings and his trials with country carpenters, stonemasons, and well-diggers may be familiar to homeowners today who buy a "fixer-upper" and then get into money trouble. At the end of the film, Mr. Blandings adds up what he spent to "put the place in shape" and learns that he is out more than $50,000. He might have been better off with a new Cape Cod–style home then being built on the potato patches of Long Island in a place called Levittown.

Or would he? Today, 50 residential-zoned acres close to New York City would be worth millions, and a restored farmhouse in a good location would bring more than half a million all by itself. Nowhere is this more apparent than in Stamford, a metro area that includes the towns of Greenwich, Darien, and New Canaan. The average market value of local homes in Stamford is $200,000. Utility bills average $1,617, property taxes $3,061, and mortgage payments another $18,962, all of which adds up to an incredible annual housing score of 23,640.

In contrast to Stamford, the lowest basic homeowner costs in metropolitan America are found some 1,100 miles west in the environs of Joplin, a pleasant city in Missouri's southeast Ozark corner. As in Stamford, many of the homes were built before World War II, and most are owned by the people living in them.

But unlike the pricey New York City suburbs of Connecticut, Joplin can boast an average market value for homes of $37,600. Through the 1970s, new homes were added to the local housing stock at a faster rate than in many other places in Missouri. Existing houses now range from nineteenth-century farmhouses in rural sections to fine Victorian homes in town and newer brick-and-frame bi-levels and ranches out along U.S. 71. Estimated utility bills in Joplin amount to $1,156, property taxes $440, and mortgage payments $3,563, totaling a score of 5,159 for homeowning costs, the lowest among the metro areas.

Housing Winners and Losers

Least Expensive Metro Areas	Places Rated Score	Most Expensive Metro Areas	Places Rated Score
1. Joplin, MO	5,159	1. Stamford, CT	23,640
2. McAllen–Edinburg–Mission, TX	5,345	2. Norwalk, CT	20,151
3. Brownsville–Harlingen, TX	5,376	3. San Francisco, CA	17,158
4. Gadsden, AL	5,382	4. Honolulu, HI	17,021
5. Terre Haute, IN	5,527	5. San Jose, CA	16,048
6. Anniston, AL	5,530	6. Anaheim–Santa Ana, CA	16,047
7. St. Joseph, MO	5,589	7. Santa Barbara–Santa Maria–Lompoc, CA	15,547

It's dryly said in California that the only way to make a killing on the sale of your home is to sell it for what it will bring and then skip back East, where you can find twice the home at half the price. The kicker is that you have to live in the cold, cold East.

In fact, a mobile Californian choosing to live in Connecticut's Fairfield County may end up losing money on the move. House prices are higher in this part of the Northeast, as are household energy costs and property taxes.

Although sky-high shelter costs don't always indicate desirable housing, they do indicate the pitch of local supply and demand in desirable locations. The irony is that house prices in these locations are beyond the reach not only of most U.S. households but of most households in the area. A quick look at household incomes in the Economics Place Profiles (later on in this book) shows that the average market values for houses in Southern California, Hawaii, and New York City suburbs are between three and five times the annual household incomes there. So much for the rule of shopping only for homes that cost about two and a half times your gross income.

Smaller metro areas located in the slow-growing Midwest and in historically poor parts of the Sun Belt, on the other hand, are ranked at the top when it comes to affordable houses. Market values in these places are only one and a half to two times local household income. The tired maxim of the real estate broker—Location, location, location—applies not only to neighborhoods but to metro areas across the nation as well.

Places Rated: Metro Areas Ranked for Homeowning Costs

Three criteria are used to rank the 329 metropolitan areas for basic costs of owning a house over one year: (1) annual average utility bills, (2) annual average property taxes, and (3) annual average mortgage payments. The sum of these three items represents the score for each metropolitan area. Places that receive tie scores are given the same rank and are listed in alphabetical order.

Metro Areas from Least to Most Expensive

Places Rated Rank	Places Rated Score	Places Rated Rank	Places Rated Score	Places Rated Rank	Places Rated Score
1. Joplin, MO	5,159	3. Brownsville–Harlingen, TX	5,376	6. Anniston, AL	5,530
2. McAllen–Edinburg–Mission, TX	5,345	4. Gadsden, AL	5,382	7. St. Joseph, MO	5,589
		5. Terre Haute, IN	5,527	8. Pine Bluff, AR	5,674

Places Rated Rank	Places Rated Score	Places Rated Rank	Places Rated Score	Places Rated Rank	Places Rated Score
9. Anderson, IN	5,704	66. Pueblo, CO	6,637	125. Williamsport, PA	7,284
10. Dothan, AL	5,708	67. Parkersburg–Marietta, WV–OH	6,657	126. Vineland–Millville–Bridgeton, NJ	7,295
11. Danville, VA	5,709	68. Lakeland–Winter Haven, FL	6,680	127. Tyler, TX	7,298
12. Texarkana, TX–Texarkana, AR	5,717	69. Fayetteville–Springdale, AR	6,686	128. Canton, OH	7,332
13. Sherman–Denison, TX	5,722	70. Odessa, TX	6,689	129. Albany, GA	7,339
14. Anderson, SC	5,725			130. El Paso, TX	7,343
15. Fort Smith, AR–OK	5,784	71. Athens, GA	6,691		
		72. Knoxville, TN	6,692		
16. Muncie, IN	5,800	73. Scranton–Wilkes-Barre, PA	6,697	131. Saginaw–Bay City–Midland, MI	7,368
17. Columbus, GA–AL	5,817	73. Sharon, PA	6,697	132. Gainesville, FL	7,388
18. Alexandria, LA	5,819	75. Mobile, AL	6,704	133. Decatur, IL	7,395
19. Lawton, OK	5,850			134. Charleston, SC	7,402
20. South Bend–Mishawaka, IN	5,938	76. Asheville, NC	6,722	135. Tampa–St. Petersburg–Clearwater, FL	7,442
		77. Fort Wayne, IN	6,733		
21. Florence, AL	5,962	78. Evansville, IN–KY	6,743		
22. Clarksville–Hopkinsville, TN–KY	6,007	79. Utica–Rome, NY	6,744	136. Janesville–Beloit, WI	7,447
		80. Ocala, FL	6,750	137. Roanoke, VA	7,476
23. Duluth, MN–WI	6,040			138. Lawrence, KS	7,497
24. Cumberland, MD–WV	6,054	81. Montgomery, AL	6,754	139. Tulsa, OK	7,498
25. Waco, TX	6,106	82. Hickory, NC	6,760	140. Columbia, SC	7,519
		82. Owensboro, KY	6,760		
26. Jacksonville, NC	6,111	84. Benton Harbor, MI	6,761	141. Fort Walton Beach, FL	7,554
27. Johnson City–Kingsport–Bristol, TN–VA	6,119	85. Jackson, MI	6,794	142. Rockford, IL	7,584
28. Laredo, TX	6,152			143. St. Louis, MO–IL	7,605
29. Burlington, NC	6,179	86. Birmingham, AL	6,811	144. Reading, PA	7,614
30. Chattanooga, TN–GA	6,189	87. Louisville, KY–IN	6,812	145. Dayton–Springfield, OH	7,635
		88. Enid, OK	6,829		
31. Monroe, LA	6,190	89. Wilmington, NC	6,858	146. Gary–Hammond, IN	7,641
32. Altoona, PA	6,191	90. Lewiston–Auburn, ME	6,876	147. Wausau, WI	7,642
33. Abilene, TX	6,200			148. Syracuse, NY	7,670
34. Macon–Warner Robins, GA	6,235	91. Mansfield, OH	6,881	149. Niagara Falls, NY	7,686
35. Pascagoula, MS	6,248	92. Savannah, GA	6,896	150. Columbia, MO	7,702
		93. San Antonio, TX	6,898		
36. Fayetteville, NC	6,274	94. Lake Charles, LA	6,921	151. Erie, PA	7,715
37. Huntsville, AL	6,283	95. Spokane, WA	6,927	152. Hagerstown, MD	7,763
38. Beaumont–Port Arthur, TX	6,288			153. Galveston–Texas City, TX	7,767
39. Augusta, GA–SC	6,292	96. Corpus Christi, TX	6,929	153. Toledo, OH	7,767
40. San Angelo, TX	6,321	97. Lynchburg, VA	6,934	155. Tacoma, WA	7,770
		98. Las Cruces, NM	6,962		
41. Greenville–Spartanburg, SC	6,336	99. Lima, OH	6,986	156. Cedar Rapids, IA	7,774
42. Battle Creek, MI	6,342	100. Lubbock, TX	6,990	157. Lafayette, IN	7,778
43. Springfield, MO	6,343			157. Visalia–Tulare–Porterville, CA	7,778
44. Panama City, FL	6,373	101. Indianapolis, IN	7,012	159. Grand Rapids, MI	7,780
45. Muskegon, MI	6,391	102. Memphis, TN–AR–MS	7,015	160. Charleston, WV	7,789
		103. Youngstown–Warren, OH	7,021		
46. Wichita Falls, TX	6,404	104. Bloomington, IN	7,056	161. Nashville, TN	7,800
47. Yakima, WA	6,440	105. Wichita, KS	7,061	162. Pittsfield, MA	7,807
48. Biloxi–Gulfport, MS	6,458			163. Beaver County, PA	7,866
49. Killeen–Temple, TX	6,463	106. Greensboro–Winston-Salem–High Point, NC	7,064	164. Yuba City, CA	7,875
50. Tuscaloosa, AL	6,464	107. Kansas City, MO	7,076	165. Appleton–Oshkosh–Neenah, WI	7,877
		108. Eau Claire, WI	7,078		
51. Pensacola, FL	6,479	108. Elmira, NY	7,078	166. Waterloo–Cedar Falls, IA	7,881
52. Alton–Granite City, IL	6,487	110. Houma–Thibodaux, LA	7,094	167. Springfield, IL	7,882
53. East St. Louis–Belleville, IL	6,501			168. Harrisburg–Lebanon–Carlisle, PA	7,891
54. Florence, SC	6,508	111. Topeka, KS	7,110	169. Grand Forks, ND	7,898
55. Johnstown, PA	6,524	112. Glens Falls, NY	7,120	170. Lansing–East Lansing, MI	7,907
		113. Omaha, NE–IA	7,128		
56. Sioux City, IA–NE	6,528	114. Great Falls, MT	7,143	171. Albany–Schenectady–Troy, NY	7,908
57. Shreveport, LA	6,534	114. Victoria, TX	7,143	172. Kalamazoo, MI	7,919
58. Amarillo, TX	6,546			173. Wilmington, DE–NJ–MD	7,927
59. Elkhart–Goshen, IN	6,573	116. Charlotte–Gastonia–Rock Hill, NC–SC	7,169	174. Fort Worth–Arlington, TX	7,956
60. Wheeling, WV–OH	6,576	117. Oklahoma City, OK	7,186	175. Sioux Falls, SD	7,983
		118. Daytona Beach, FL	7,203		
61. Steubenville–Weirton, OH–WV	6,578	119. Flint, MI	7,204	176. Dubuque, IA	7,993
62. Longview–Marshall, TX	6,608	120. Kankakee, IL	7,230	177. Des Moines, IA	8,028
63. Kokomo, IN	6,616			178. Tallahassee, FL	8,029
64. Jacksonville, FL	6,626	121. St. Cloud, MN	7,235	179. Springfield, MA	8,039
65. Huntington–Ashland, WV–KY–OH	6,632	122. Jackson, MS	7,245	180. Buffalo, NY	8,064
		123. Little Rock–North Little Rock, AR	7,270		
		124. Bangor, ME	7,277		

Places Rated Rank	Places Rated Score	Places Rated Rank	Places Rated Score	Places Rated Rank	Places Rated Score
181. Bakersfield, CA	8,068	232. Chico, CA	8,587	281. Orange County, NY	10,173
182. Baton Rouge, LA	8,083	233. Rochester, NY	8,609	282. Milwaukee, WI	10,176
182. Davenport–Rock Island–		234. Champaign–Urbana–		283. Seattle, WA	10,183
Moline, IA–IL	8,083	Rantoul, IL	8,627	284. New London–Norwich, CT–RI	10,218
184. New Bedford, MA	8,087	235. Modesto, CA	8,630	285. Miami–Hialeah, FL	10,267
185. Columbus, OH	8,093				
		236. Lancaster, PA	8,631	286. Aurora–Elgin, IL	10,384
186. Pittsburgh, PA	8,099	237. Bloomington–Normal, IL	8,654	287. Lawrence–Haverhill, MA–NH	10,414
187. Portland, ME	8,100	238. Midland, TX	8,672	288. Vallejo–Fairfield–Napa, CA	10,503
188. Sheboygan, WI	8,121	239. Worcester, MA	8,715	289. New Britain, CT	10,509
189. Kansas City, KS	8,126	240. Melbourne–Titusville–		290. West Palm Beach–Boca	
190. Akron, OH	8,138	Palm Bay, FL	8,721	Raton–Delray Beach, FL	10,512
191. Cincinnati, OH–KY–IN	8,143	241. Jersey City, NJ	8,810	291. Trenton, NJ	10,616
192. Fargo–Moorhead, ND–MN	8,168	242. Austin, TX	8,831	292. Nashua, NH	10,757
193. Orlando, FL	8,196	243. Fort Pierce, FL	8,842	293. Denver, CO	10,789
194. Greeley, CO	8,218	244. Phoenix, AZ	8,921	294. Fort Lauderdale–Hollywood–	
195. Boise City, ID	8,221	245. Racine, WI	8,943	Pompano Beach, FL	10,810
				295. Chicago, IL	10,913
196. Hamilton–Middletown, OH	8,227	246. Medford, OR	9,008		
197. Bryan–College Station, TX	8,228	247. Vancouver, WA	9,015	296. Ann Arbor, MI	11,014
198. Raleigh–Durham, NC	8,230	248. Fall River, MA–RI	9,017	297. Atlantic City, NJ	11,074
199. Bradenton, FL	8,242	249. Bremerton, WA	9,060	298. Nassau–Suffolk, NY	11,138
200. Fitchburg–Leominster, MA	8,252	250. Baltimore, MD	9,148	299. New Haven–Meriden, CT	11,460
				300. Boston, MA	11,609
201. Lincoln, NE	8,256	251. Cleveland, OH	9,168		
202. Binghamton, NY	8,257	252. Rochester, MN	9,193	301. Salem–Gloucester, MA	11,622
203. Brockton, MA	8,263	253. Providence, RI	9,274	302. Hartford, CT	11,652
203. Olympia, WA	8,263	254. Fresno, CA	9,291	302. Middletown, CT	11,652
205. Allentown–Bethlehem, PA–NJ	8,288	255. Fort Myers, FL	9,298	304. Monmouth–Ocean, NJ	11,660
				305. Boulder–Longmont, CO	11,914
206. Lorain–Elyria, OH	8,309	256. Dallas, TX	9,318		
207. La Crosse, WI	8,310	257. Provo–Orem, UT	9,321	306. Middlesex–Somerset–	
207. Philadelphia, PA–NJ	8,310	258. Joliet, IL	9,327	Hunterdon, NJ	12,135
209. Billings, MT	8,315	259. Eugene–Springfield, OR	9,370	307. Anchorage, AK	12,175
210. Atlanta, GA	8,316	260. Iowa City, IA	9,429	308. Reno, NV	12,449
				309. Santa Rosa–Petaluma, CA	12,931
211. Bellingham, WA	8,329	261. Pawtucket–Woonsocket–		310. Oakland, CA	13,135
212. Lexington–Fayette, KY	8,340	Attleboro, RI–MA	9,462		
213. Richmond–Petersburg, VA	8,343	262. Salt Lake City–Ogden, UT	9,466	311. Lake County, IL	13,282
214. Bismarck, ND	8,365	263. Charlottesville, VA	9,531	312. New York, NY	13,358
215. York, PA	8,371	264. Minneapolis–St. Paul,		313. Bridgeport–Milford, CT	13,429
		MN–WI	9,559	314. Washington, DC–MD–VA	13,724
216. Salem, OR	8,378	265. Sarasota, FL	9,560	315. Salinas–Seaside–Monterey,	
217. Peoria, IL	8,388			CA	13,838
218. Albuquerque, NM	8,393	266. Lowell, MA–NH	9,640		
219. Brazoria, TX	8,394	267. Burlington, VT	9,673	316. Los Angeles–Long Beach,	
220. Green Bay, WI	8,401	268. Riverside–San Bernardino,		CA	13,868
		CA	9,754	317. Oxnard–Ventura, CA	14,000
221. State College, PA	8,405	269. Houston, TX	9,760	318. Newark, NJ	14,220
222. Richland–Kennewick–		270. Casper, WY	9,839	319. Santa Cruz, CA	14,303
Pasco, WA	8,461			320. Danbury, CT	14,420
223. Stockton, CA	8,474	271. Sacramento, CA	9,855		
224. Colorado Springs, CO	8,509	272. Manchester, NH	9,860	321. San Diego, CA	14,465
225. New Orleans, LA	8,515	273. Madison, WI	9,897	322. Bergen–Passaic, NJ	14,607
		274. Las Vegas, NV	9,906	323. Santa Barbara–Santa	
226. Kenosha, WI	8,516	275. Portland, OR	9,912	Maria–Lompoc, CA	15,547
227. Detroit, MI	8,525			324. Anaheim–Santa Ana, CA	16,047
228. Tucson, AZ	8,548	276. Fort Collins–Loveland, CO	9,951	325. San Jose, CA	16,048
229. Norfolk–Virginia Beach–		277. Portsmouth–Dover–Rochester,			
Newport News, VA	8,568	NH–ME	9,966	326. Honolulu, HI	17,021
230. Lafayette, LA	8,572	278. Poughkeepsie, NY	9,981	327. San Francisco, CA	17,158
		279. Waterbury, CT	10,024	328. Norwalk, CT	20,151
231. Redding, CA	8,584	280. Bristol, CT	10,041	329. Stamford, CT	23,640

Metro Areas Listed Alphabetically

Metro Area	Places Rated Rank	Metro Area	Places Rated Rank	Metro Area	Places Rated Rank
Abilene, TX	33	Charleston, WV	160	Galveston–Texas City, TX	153
Akron, OH	190	Charlotte–Gastonia–Rock Hill, NC–SC	116	Gary–Hammond, IN	146
Albany, GA	129	Charlottesville, VA	263	Glens Falls, NY	112
Albany–Schenectady–Troy, NY	171	Chattanooga, TN–GA	30		
Albuquerque, NM	218	Chicago, IL	295	Grand Forks, ND	169
				Grand Rapids, MI	159
Alexandria, LA	18	Chico, CA	232	Great Falls, MT	114
Allentown–Bethlehem, PA–NJ	205	Cincinnati, OH–KY–IN	191	Greeley, CO	194
Alton–Granite City, IL	52	Clarksville–Hopkinsville, TN–KY	22	Green Bay, WI	220
Altoona, PA	32	Cleveland, OH	251		
Amarillo, TX	58	Colorado Springs, CO	224	Greensboro–Winston-Salem–High Point, NC	106
				Greenville–Spartanburg, SC	41
Anaheim–Santa Ana, CA	324	Columbia, MO	150	Hagerstown, MD	152
Anchorage, AK	307	Columbia, SC	140	Hamilton–Middletown, OH	196
Anderson, IN	9	Columbus, GA–AL	17	Harrisburg–Lebanon–Carlisle, PA	168
Anderson, SC	14	Columbus, OH	185		
Ann Arbor, MI	296	Corpus Christi, TX	96	Hartford, CT	302
				Hickory, NC	82
Anniston, AL	6	Cumberland, MD–WV	24	Honolulu, HI	326
Appleton–Oshkosh–Neenah, WI	165	Dallas, TX	256	Houma–Thibodaux, LA	110
Asheville, NC	76	Danbury, CT	320	Houston, TX	269
Athens, GA	71	Danville, VA	11		
Atlanta, GA	210	Davenport–Rock Island–Moline, IA–IL	182	Huntington–Ashland, WV–KY–OH	65
				Huntsville, AL	37
Atlantic City, NJ	297	Dayton–Springfield, OH	145	Indianapolis, IN	101
Augusta, GA–SC	39	Daytona Beach, FL	118	Iowa City, IA	260
Aurora–Elgin, IL	286	Decatur, IL	133	Jackson, MI	85
Austin, TX	242	Denver, CO	293		
Bakersfield, CA	181	Des Moines, IA	177	Jackson, MS	122
				Jacksonville, FL	64
Baltimore, MD	250	Detroit, MI	227	Jacksonville, NC	26
Bangor, ME	124	Dothan, AL	10	Janesville–Beloit, WI	136
Baton Rouge, LA	182	Dubuque, IA	176	Jersey City, NJ	241
Battle Creek, MI	42	Duluth, MN–WI	23		
Beaumont–Port Arthur, TX	38	East St. Louis–Belleville, IL	53	Johnson City–Kingsport–Bristol, TN–VA	27
				Johnstown, PA	55
Beaver County, PA	163	Eau Claire, WI	108	Joliet, IL	258
Bellingham, WA	211	El Paso, TX	130	Joplin, MO	1
Benton Harbor, MI	84	Elkhart–Goshen, IN	59	Kalamazoo, MI	172
Bergen–Passaic, NJ	322	Elmira, NY	108		
Billings, MT	209	Enid, OK	88	Kankakee, IL	120
				Kansas City, KS	189
Biloxi–Gulfport, MS	48	Erie, PA	151	Kansas City, MO	107
Binghamton, NY	202	Eugene–Springfield, OR	259	Kenosha, WI	226
Birmingham, AL	86	Evansville, IN–KY	78	Killeen–Temple, TX	49
Bismarck, ND	214	Fall River, MA–RI	248		
Bloomington, IN	104	Fargo–Moorhead, ND–MN	192	Knoxville, TN	72
				Kokomo, IN	63
Bloomington–Normal, IL	237	Fayetteville, NC	36	La Crosse, WI	207
Boise City, ID	195	Fayetteville–Springdale, AR	69	Lafayette, IN	157
Boston, MA	300	Fitchburg–Leominster, MA	200	Lafayette, LA	230
Boulder–Longmont, CO	305	Flint, MI	119		
Bradenton, FL	199	Florence, AL	21	Lake Charles, LA	94
				Lake County, IL	311
Brazoria, TX	219	Florence, SC	54	Lakeland–Winter Haven, FL	68
Bremerton, WA	249	Fort Collins–Loveland, CO	276	Lancaster, PA	236
Bridgeport–Milford, CT	313	Fort Lauderdale–Hollywood–Pompano Beach, FL	294	Lansing–East Lansing, MI	170
Bristol, CT	280	Fort Myers, FL	255		
Brockton, MA	203	Fort Pierce, FL	243	Laredo, TX	28
				Las Cruces, NM	98
Brownsville–Harlingen, TX	3	Fort Smith, AR–OK	15	Las Vegas, NV	274
Bryan–College Station, TX	197	Fort Walton Beach, FL	141	Lawrence, KS	138
Buffalo, NY	180	Fort Wayne, IN	77	Lawrence–Haverhill, MA–NH	287
Burlington, NC	29	Fort Worth–Arlington, TX	174		
Burlington, VT	267	Fresno, CA	254	Lawton, OK	19
				Lewiston–Auburn, ME	90
Canton, OH	128	Gadsden, AL	4	Lexington–Fayette, KY	212
Casper, WY	270	Gainesville, FL	132	Lima, OH	99
Cedar Rapids, IA	156			Lincoln, NE	201
Champaign–Urbana–Rantoul, IL	234				
Charleston, SC	134				

Metro Area	Places Rated Rank	Metro Area	Places Rated Rank	Metro Area	Places Rated Rank
Little Rock–North Little Rock, AR	123	Panama City, FL	44	Seattle, WA	283
Longview–Marshall, TX	62	Parkersburg–Marietta, WV–OH	67	Sharon, PA	73
Lorain–Elyria, OH	206	Pascagoula, MS	35	Sheboygan, WI	188
Los Angeles–Long Beach, CA	316				
Louisville, KY–IN	87	Pawtucket–Woonsocket–Attleboro, RI–MA	261	Sherman–Denison, TX	13
		Pensacola, FL	51	Shreveport, LA	57
Lowell, MA–NH	266	Peoria, IL	217	Sioux City, IA–NE	56
Lubbock, TX	100	Philadelphia, PA–NJ	207	Sioux Falls, SD	175
Lynchburg, VA	97	Phoenix, AZ	244	South Bend–Mishawaka, IN	20
Macon–Warner Robins, GA	34				
Madison, WI	273	Pine Bluff, AR	8	Spokane, WA	95
		Pittsburgh, PA	186	Springfield, IL	167
Manchester, NH	272	Pittsfield, MA	162	Springfield, MA	179
Mansfield, OH	91	Portland, ME	187	Springfield, MO	43
McAllen–Edinburg–Mission, TX	2	Portland, OR	275	Stamford, CT	329
Medford, OR	246				
Melbourne–Titusville–Palm Bay, FL	240	Portsmouth–Dover–Rochester, NH–ME	277	State College, PA	221
		Poughkeepsie, NY	278	Steubenville–Weirton, OH–WV	61
Memphis, TN–AR–MS	102	Providence, RI	253	Stockton, CA	223
Miami–Hialeah, FL	285	Provo–Orem, UT	257	Syracuse, NY	148
Middlesex–Somerset–Hunterdon, NJ	306	Pueblo, CO	66	Tacoma, WA	155
Middletown, CT	302				
Midland, TX	238	Racine, WI	245	Tallahassee, FL	178
		Raleigh–Durham, NC	198	Tampa–St. Petersburg–Clearwater, FL	135
Milwaukee, WI	282	Reading, PA	144	Terre Haute, IN	5
Minneapolis–St. Paul, MN–WI	264	Redding, CA	231	Texarkana, TX–Texarkana, AR	12
Mobile, AL	75	Reno, NV	308	Toledo, OH	153
Modesto, CA	235				
Monmouth–Ocean, NJ	304	Richland–Kennewick–Pasco, WA	222	Topeka, KS	111
		Richmond–Petersburg, VA	213	Trenton, NJ	291
Monroe, LA	31	Riverside–San Bernardino, CA	268	Tucson, AZ	228
Montgomery, AL	81	Roanoke, VA	137	Tulsa, OK	139
Muncie, IN	16	Rochester, MN	252	Tuscaloosa, AL	50
Muskegon, MI	45				
Nashua, NH	292	Rochester, NY	233	Tyler, TX	127
		Rockford, IL	142	Utica–Rome, NY	79
Nashville, TN	161	Sacramento, CA	271	Vallejo–Fairfield–Napa, CA	288
Nassau–Suffolk, NY	298	Saginaw–Bay City–Midland, MI	131	Vancouver, WA	247
New Bedford, MA	184	St. Cloud, MN	121	Victoria, TX	114
New Britain, CT	289				
New Haven–Meriden, CT	299	St. Joseph, MO	7	Vineland–Millville–Bridgeton, NJ	126
		St. Louis, MO–IL	143	Visalia–Tulare–Porterville, CA	157
New London–Norwich, CT–RI	284	Salem, OR	216	Waco, TX	25
New Orleans, LA	225	Salem–Gloucester, MA	301	Washington, DC–MD–VA	314
New York, NY	312	Salinas–Seaside–Monterey, CA	315	Waterbury, CT	279
Newark, NJ	318				
Niagara Falls, NY	149	Salt Lake City–Ogden, UT	262	Waterloo–Cedar Falls, IA	166
		San Angelo, TX	40	Wausau, WI	147
Norfolk–Virginia Beach–Newport News, VA	229	San Antonio, TX	93	West Palm Beach–Boca Raton–Delray Beach, FL	290
Norwalk, CT	328	San Diego, CA	321	Wheeling, WV–OH	60
Oakland, CA	310	San Francisco, CA	327	Wichita, KS	105
Ocala, FL	80				
Odessa, TX	70	San Jose, CA	325	Wichita Falls, TX	46
		Santa Barbara–Santa Maria–Lompoc, CA	323	Williamsport, PA	125
Oklahoma City, OK	117	Santa Cruz, CA	319	Wilmington, DE–NJ–MD	173
Olympia, WA	203	Santa Rosa–Petaluma, CA	309	Wilmington, NC	89
Omaha, NE–IA	113	Sarasota, FL	265	Worcester, MA	239
Orange County, NY	281				
Orlando, FL	193	Savannah, GA	92	Yakima, WA	47
		Scranton–Wilkes-Barre, PA	73	York, PA	215
Owensboro, KY	82			Youngstown–Warren, OH	103
Oxnard–Ventura, CA	317			Yuba City, CA	164

Place Profiles: Housing Features of 329 Metro Areas

The following pages summarize local housing features in each metro area, dividing them into the categories of Local Choices, Houses, Energy Requirements, and Annual Costs.

Data in the first category, Local Choices, show the mix of occupied single houses, condominiums, mobile homes, and apartments (defined here as a rented housing unit in a building with five or more rental units) in each metro area. The sums of these percentages (which are rounded) are not always 100; the balance represents renter-occupied duplexes, triplexes, and fourplexes. Data on average monthly rent come from the *1980 Census of Population and Housing* and are boosted by regional inflation factors as reported in the Bureau of Labor's *Consumer Price Index* for April 1984.

In the Houses category, information on the average price for all owner-occupied houses comes from the *1980 Census of Population and Housing* and is adjusted for inflation with 1984 regional data from the National Association of Realtors. Property taxes are based on statewide average residential rates taken from the 1984 issue of *Significant Features of Fiscal Federalism*, an annual publication of the Advisory Commission on Intergovernmental Relations. The percentages of houses built before 1940 also come from the *1980 Census of Population and Housing.*

The heating season, listed under Energy Requirements, is given in terms of heating-degree days per year, and is derived from NOAA's *Substation Summaries.* The number of hours given for air-conditioning represents the normal number of hours per year when the outside temperature climbs over 80 degrees Fahrenheit. These figures come from the Department of Defense manual *Engineering Weather Data.*

The dollar amounts given for the entry Mortgage and Taxes are the annual sum of property taxes and mortgage payments. Utilities, too, are annual dollar amounts. Typical bills for residential natural gas by state come from the Energy Information Administration's unpublished figures for 1983. The Department of Energy's 1983 publication *Typical Electric Bills* details electricity consumption and cost for each metro area. To reflect realistic 1984 energy costs, data from these sources are adjusted for inflation using the Bureau of Labor's Consumer Price Index for April 1984.

A star preceding a metro area's name highlights it as one of the best 25 places for homeowning costs.

Abilene, TX
Local Choices
79% houses, 5% mobile homes, 9% apartments (rent $300/month)
Houses
Price: $47,900
Property Taxes: $671
Built Before 1940: 16.3%
Energy Requirements
Heating Season: 2,610 degree days
Major Source: Natural gas/Electricity
Air-conditioning: 2,005 hours
Annual Costs
Mortgage and Taxes: $5,213
Utilities: $987
Places Rated Score: 6,200
Places Rated Rank: 33

Akron, OH
Local Choices
74% houses, 2% condos, 2% mobile homes, 12% apartments (rent $305/month)
Houses
Price: $62,200
Property Taxes: $715
Built Before 1940: 29.3%
Energy Requirements
Heating Season: 6,224 degree days
Major Source: Natural gas/Electricity
Air-conditioning: 416 hours
Annual Costs
Mortgage and Taxes: $6,608
Utilities: $1,530
Places Rated Score: 8,138
Places Rated Rank: 190

Albany, GA
Local Choices
67% houses, 7% mobile homes, 10% apartments (rent $275/month)
Houses
Price: $60,200
Property Taxes: $729
Built Before 1940: 7.2%
Energy Requirements
Heating Season: 1,872 degree days
Major Source: Natural gas/Electricity
Air-conditioning: 420 hours
Annual Costs
Mortgage and Taxes: $6,439
Utilities: $900
Places Rated Score: 7,339
Places Rated Rank: 129

Albany–Schenectady–Troy, NY
Local Choices
58% houses, 4% mobile homes, 12% apartments (rent $305/month)
Houses
Price: $55,200
Property Taxes: $1,418
Built Before 1940: 46.9%
Energy Requirements
Heating Season: 6,888 degree days
Major Source: Natural gas/Electricity
Air-conditioning: 420 hours
Annual Costs
Mortgage and Taxes: $6,649
Utilities: $1,259
Places Rated Score: 7,908
Places Rated Rank: 171

Albuquerque, NM
Local Choices
67% houses, 2% condos, 7% mobile homes, 17% apartments (rent $335/month)
Houses
Price: $69,900
Property Taxes: $650
Built Before 1940: 6.7%
Energy Requirements
Heating Season: 4,292 degree days
Major Source: Natural gas/Electricity
Air-conditioning: 1,130 hours
Annual Costs
Mortgage and Taxes: $7,276
Utilities: $1,117
Places Rated Score: 8,393
Places Rated Rank: 218

★ Alexandria, LA
Local Choices
79% houses, 1% condos, 6% mobile homes, 6% apartments (rent $265/month)
Houses
Price: $50,100
Property Taxes: $75
Built Before 1940: 14.8%
Energy Requirements
Heating Season: 2,200 degree days
Major Source: Natural gas/Electricity
Air-conditioning: 1,721 hours
Annual Costs
Mortgage and Taxes: $4,820
Utilities: $999
Places Rated Score: 5,819
Places Rated Rank: 18

Allentown–Bethlehem, PA–NJ
Local Choices
   74% houses, 1% condos, 2% mobile homes, 11% apartments (rent $310/month)
Houses
   Price: $62,800
   Property Taxes: $1,024
   Built Before 1940: 44.8%
Energy Requirements
   Heating Season: 5,827 degree days
   Major Source: Oil/Electricity
   Air-conditioning: 509 hours
Annual Costs
   Mortgage and Taxes: $6,981
   Utilities: $1,307
Places Rated Score: 8,288
Places Rated Rank: 205

Alton–Granite City, IL
Local Choices
   79% houses, 4% mobile homes, 6% apartments (rent $275/month)
Houses
   Price: $47,700
   Property Taxes: $758
   Built Before 1940: 30.2%
Energy Requirements
   Heating Season: 4,840 degree days
   Major Source: Natural gas/Electricity
   Air-conditioning: 1,223 hours
Annual Costs
   Mortgage and Taxes: $5,278
   Utilities: $1,209
Places Rated Score: 6,487
Places Rated Rank: 52

Altoona, PA
Local Choices
   76% houses, 6% mobile homes, 7% apartments (rent $270/month)
Houses
   Price: $43,600
   Property Taxes: $705
   Built Before 1940: 54.0%
Energy Requirements
   Heating Season: 6,121 degree days
   Major Source: Oil/Electricity
   Air-conditioning: 351 hours
Annual Costs
   Mortgage and Taxes: $4,806
   Utilities: $1,385
Places Rated Score: 6,191
Places Rated Rank: 32

Amarillo, TX
Local Choices
   77% houses, 4% mobile homes, 12% apartments (rent $310/month)
Houses
   Price: $50,500
   Property Taxes: $707
   Built Before 1940: 11.3%
Energy Requirements
   Heating Season: 4,183 degree days
   Major Source: Natural gas/Electricity
   Air-conditioning: 1,176 hours
Annual Costs
   Mortgage and Taxes: $5,496
   Utilities: $1,050
Places Rated Score: 6,546
Places Rated Rank: 58

Anaheim–Santa Ana, CA
Local Choices
   63% houses, 11% condos, 4% mobile homes, 20% apartments (rent $510/month)
Houses
   Price: $142,300
   Property Taxes: $1,466
   Built Before 1940: 3.7%
Energy Requirements
   Heating Season: 1,675 degree days
   Major Source: Natural gas/Electricity
   Air-conditioning: 888 hours
Annual Costs
   Mortgage and Taxes: $14,953
   Utilities: $1,094
Places Rated Score: 16,047
Places Rated Rank: 324

Anchorage, AK
Local Choices
   48% houses, 6% condos, 10% mobile homes, 21% apartments (rent $520/month)
Houses
   Price: $111,400
   Property Taxes: $702
   Built Before 1940: 1.1%
Energy Requirements
   Heating Season: 10,911 degree days
   Major Source: Natural gas/Electricity
   Air-conditioning: 6 hours
Annual Costs
   Mortgage and Taxes: $11,261
   Utilities: $914
Places Rated Score: 12,175
Places Rated Rank: 307

★ Anderson, IN
Local Choices
   81% houses, 1% condos, 4% mobile homes, 5% apartments (rent $265/month)
Houses
   Price: $43,600
   Property Taxes: $519
   Built Before 1940: 32.4%
Energy Requirements
   Heating Season: 5,580 degree days
   Major Source: Natural gas/Electricity
   Air-conditioning: 745 hours
Annual Costs
   Mortgage and Taxes: $4,653
   Utilities: $1,051
Places Rated Score: 5,704
Places Rated Rank: 9

★ Anderson, SC
Local Choices
   82% houses, 1% condos, 9% mobile homes, 4% apartments (rent $245/month)
Houses
   Price: $46,100
   Property Taxes: $424
   Built Before 1940: 19.9%
Energy Requirements
   Heating Season: 2,900 degree days
   Major Source: Total electric
   Air-conditioning: 1,262 hours
Annual Costs
   Mortgage and Taxes: $4,793
   Utilities: $932
Places Rated Score: 5,725
Places Rated Rank: 14

Ann Arbor, MI
Local Choices
   60% houses, 3% condos, 2% mobile homes, 28% apartments (rent $385/month)

Houses
   Price: $79,600
   Property Taxes: $2,132
   Built Before 1940: 20.5%
Energy Requirements
   Heating Season: 6,306 degree days
   Major Source: Natural gas/Electricity
   Air-conditioning: 511 hours
Annual Costs
   Mortgage and Taxes: $9,673
   Utilities: $1,341
Places Rated Score: 11,014
Places Rated Rank: 296

★ Anniston, AL
Local Choices
   77% houses, 10% mobile homes, 7% apartments (rent $250/month)
Houses
   Price: $44,900
   Property Taxes: $184
   Built Before 1940: 16.6%
Energy Requirements
   Heating Season: 2,820 degree days
   Major Source: Natural gas/Electricity
   Air-conditioning: 1,251 hours
Annual Costs
   Mortgage and Taxes: $4,441
   Utilities: $1,089
Places Rated Score: 5,530
Places Rated Rank: 6

Appleton–Oshkosh–Neenah, WI
Local Choices
   76% houses, 1% condos, 2% mobile homes, 8% apartments (rent $275/month)
Houses
   Price: $57,200
   Property Taxes: $1,150
   Built Before 1940: 36.2%
Energy Requirements
   Heating Season: 7,665 degree days
   Major Source: Natural gas/Electricity
   Air-conditioning: 388 hours
Annual Costs
   Mortgage and Taxes: $6,574
   Utilities: $1,303
Places Rated Score: 7,877
Places Rated Rank: 165

Asheville, NC
Local Choices
   73% houses, 1% condos, 12% mobile homes, 9% apartments (rent $270/month)
Houses
   Price: $53,100
   Property Taxes: $515
   Built Before 1940: 23.1%
Energy Requirements
   Heating Season: 4,237 degree days
   Major Source: Oil/Electricity
   Air-conditioning: 610 hours
Annual Costs
   Mortgage and Taxes: $5,546
   Utilities: $1,176
Places Rated Score: 6,722
Places Rated Rank: 76

Athens, GA
Local Choices
   64% houses, 1% condos, 11% mobile homes, 14% apartments (rent $265/month)
Houses
   Price: $53,300

Property Taxes: $645
Built Before 1940: 15.7%
Energy Requirements
Heating Season: 2,822 degree days
Major Source: Natural gas/Electricity
Air-conditioning: 1,122 hours
Annual Costs
Mortgage and Taxes: $5,699
Utilities: $992
Places Rated Score: 6,691
Places Rated Rank: 71

Atlanta, GA
Local Choices
66% houses, 2% condos, 3% mobile homes, 21% apartments (rent $330/month)
Houses
Price: $68,500
Property Taxes: $829
Built Before 1940: 10.3%
Energy Requirements
Heating Season: 3,095 degree days
Major Source: Natural gas/Electricity
Air-conditioning: 1,151 hours
Annual Costs
Mortgage and Taxes: $7,324
Utilities: $992
Places Rated Score: 8,316
Places Rated Rank: 210

Atlantic City, NJ
Local Choices
67% houses, 4% condos, 2% mobile homes, 13% apartments (rent $355/month)
Houses
Price: $79,800
Property Taxes: $2,034
Built Before 1940: 29.4%
Energy Requirements
Heating Season: 4,946 degree days
Major Source: Oil/Electricity
Air-conditioning: 473 hours
Annual Costs
Mortgage and Taxes: $9,596
Utilities: $1,478
Places Rated Score: 11,074
Places Rated Rank: 297

Augusta, GA–SC
Local Choices
76% houses, 1% condos, 8% mobile homes, 8% apartments (rent $275/month)
Houses
Price: $49,600
Property Taxes: $600
Built Before 1940: 13.2%
Energy Requirements
Heating Season: 2,547 degree days
Major Source: Natural gas/Electricity
Air-conditioning: 1,431 hours
Annual Costs
Mortgage and Taxes: $5,300
Utilities: $992
Places Rated Score: 6,292
Places Rated Rank: 39

Aurora–Elgin, IL
Local Choices
72% houses, 2% condos, 1% mobile homes, 13% apartments (rent $350/month)
Houses
Price: $81,400
Property Taxes: $1,295

Built Before 1940: 28.8%
Energy Requirements
Heating Season: 6,551 degree days
Major Source: Natural gas/Electricity
Air-conditioning: 549 hours
Annual Costs
Mortgage and Taxes: $9,015
Utilities: $1,369
Places Rated Score: 10,384
Places Rated Rank: 286

Austin, TX
Local Choices
64% houses, 2% condos, 4% mobile homes, 22% apartments (rent $360/month)
Houses
Price: $73,100
Property Taxes: $1,024
Built Before 1940: 9.2%
Energy Requirements
Heating Season: 1,737 degree days
Major Source: Natural gas/Electricity
Air-conditioning: 2,243 hours
Annual Costs
Mortgage and Taxes: $7,955
Utilities: $876
Places Rated Score: 8,831
Places Rated Rank: 242

Bakersfield, CA
Local Choices
73% houses, 2% condos, 8% mobile homes, 10% apartments (rent $340/month)
Houses
Price: $68,000
Property Taxes: $700
Built Before 1940: 11.5%
Energy Requirements
Heating Season: 2,185 degree days
Major Source: Natural gas/Electricity
Air-conditioning: 1,648 hours
Annual Costs
Mortgage and Taxes: $7,147
Utilities: $921
Places Rated Score: 8,068
Places Rated Rank: 181

Baltimore, MD
Local Choices
69% houses, 2% condos, 1% mobile homes, 18% apartments (rent $330/month)
Houses
Price: $73,000
Property Taxes: $1,001
Built Before 1940: 27.7%
Energy Requirements
Heating Season: 4,101 degree days
Major Source: Natural gas/Electricity
Air-conditioning: 833 hours
Annual Costs
Mortgage and Taxes: $7,925
Utilities: $1,223
Places Rated Score: 9,148
Places Rated Rank: 250

Bangor, ME
Local Choices
60% houses, 8% mobile homes, 11% apartments (rent $295/month)
Houses
Price: $55,600
Property Taxes: $845
Built Before 1940: 49.7%

Energy Requirements
Heating Season: 8,648 degree days
Major Source: Oil/Electricity
Air-conditioning: 181 hours
Annual Costs
Mortgage and Taxes: $6,114
Utilities: $1,163
Places Rated Score: 7,277
Places Rated Rank: 124

Baton Rouge, LA
Local Choices
73% houses, 2% condos, 6% mobile homes, 14% apartments (rent $325/month)
Houses
Price: $74,000
Property Taxes: $111
Built Before 1940: 8.3%
Energy Requirements
Heating Season: 1,670 degree days
Major Source: Natural gas/Electricity
Air-conditioning: 1,723 hours
Annual Costs
Mortgage and Taxes: $7,128
Utilities: $955
Places Rated Score: 8,083
Places Rated Rank: 182

Battle Creek, MI
Local Choices
77% houses, 1% condos, 4% mobile homes, 9% apartments (rent $280/month)
Houses
Price: $41,500
Property Taxes: $1,111
Built Before 1940: 38.2%
Energy Requirements
Heating Season: 6,720 degree days
Major Source: Natural gas/Electricity
Air-conditioning: 511 hours
Annual Costs
Mortgage and Taxes: $5,041
Utilities: $1,301
Places Rated Score: 6,342
Places Rated Rank: 42

Beaumont–Port Arthur, TX
Local Choices
80% houses, 1% condos, 6% mobile homes, 8% apartments (rent $315/month)
Houses
Price: $47,800
Property Taxes: $669
Built Before 1940: 14.3%
Energy Requirements
Heating Season: 1,518 degree days
Major Source: Natural gas/Electricity
Air-conditioning: 1,807 hours
Annual Costs
Mortgage and Taxes: $5,201
Utilities: $1,087
Places Rated Score: 6,288
Places Rated Rank: 38

Beaver County, PA
Local Choices
77% houses, 1% condos, 4% mobile homes, 8% apartments (rent $290/month)
Houses
Price: $58,400
Property Taxes: $952
Built Before 1940: 37.4%

Energy Requirements
Heating Season: 4,865 degree days
Major Source: Natural gas/Electricity
Air-conditioning: 461 hours
Annual Costs
Mortgage and Taxes: $6,491
Utilities: $1,375
Places Rated Score: 7,866
Places Rated Rank: 163

Bellingham, WA
Local Choices
73% houses, 2% condos, 6% mobile homes, 13% apartments (rent $350/month)
Houses
Price: $74,100
Property Taxes: $748
Built Before 1940: 27.4%
Energy Requirements
Heating Season: 5,738 degree days
Major Source: Total electric
Air-conditioning: 40 hours
Annual Costs
Mortgage and Taxes: $7,770
Utilities: $559
Places Rated Score: 8,329
Places Rated Rank: 211

Benton Harbor, MI
Local Choices
77% houses, 1% condos, 4% mobile homes, 8% apartments (rent $295/month)
Houses
Price: $45,700
Property Taxes: $1,224
Built Before 1940: 29.9%
Energy Requirements
Heating Season: 6,296 degree days
Major Source: Natural gas/Electricity
Air-conditioning: 465 hours
Annual Costs
Mortgage and Taxes: $5,555
Utilities: $1,206
Places Rated Score: 6,761
Places Rated Rank: 84

Bergen–Passaic, NJ
Local Choices
54% houses, 1% condos, 13% apartments (rent $415/month)
Houses
Price: $108,900
Property Taxes: $2,777
Built Before 1940: 35.8%
Energy Requirements
Heating Season: 5,350 degree days
Major Source: Natural gas/Electricity
Air-conditioning: 592 hours
Annual Costs
Mortgage and Taxes: $13,099
Utilities: $1,508
Places Rated Score: 14,607
Places Rated Rank: 322

Billings, MT
Local Choices
70% houses, 1% condos, 8% mobile homes, 10% apartments (rent $330/month)
Houses
Price: $69,400
Property Taxes: $791
Built Before 1940: 17.3%
Energy Requirements
Heating Season: 7,265 degree days

Major Source: Natural gas/Electricity
Air-conditioning: 515 hours
Annual Costs
Mortgage and Taxes: $7,367
Utilities: $948
Places Rated Score: 8,315
Places Rated Rank: 209

Biloxi–Gulfport, MS
Local Choices
74% houses, 1% condos, 6% mobile homes, 12% apartments (rent $280/month)
Houses
Price: $53,200
Property Taxes: $404
Built Before 1940: 11.6%
Energy Requirements
Heating Season: 1,496 degree days
Major Source: Natural gas/Electricity
Air-conditioning: 2,052 hours
Annual Costs
Mortgage and Taxes: $5,442
Utilities: $1,016
Places Rated Score: 6,458
Places Rated Rank: 48

Binghamton, NY
Local Choices
62% houses, 6% mobile homes, 10% apartments (rent $285/month)
Houses
Price: $58,100
Property Taxes: $1,493
Built Before 1940: 44.6%
Energy Requirements
Heating Season: 7,285 degree days
Major Source: Natural gas/Electricity
Air-conditioning: 225 hours
Annual Costs
Mortgage and Taxes: $6,999
Utilities: $1,258
Places Rated Score: 8,257
Places Rated Rank: 202

Birmingham, AL
Local Choices
74% houses, 1% condos, 6% mobile homes, 13% apartments (rent $290/month)
Houses
Price: $57,900
Property Taxes: $237
Built Before 1940: 19.0%
Energy Requirements
Heating Season: 2,844 degree days
Major Source: Natural gas/Electricity
Air-conditioning: 1,380 hours
Annual Costs
Mortgage and Taxes: $5,722
Utilities: $1,089
Places Rated Score: 6,811
Places Rated Rank: 86

Bismarck, ND
Local Choices
57% houses, 2% condos, 12% mobile homes, 15% apartments (rent $285/month)
Houses
Price: $66,800
Property Taxes: $735
Built Before 1940: 19.8%
Energy Requirements
Heating Season: 9,044 degree days
Major Source: Natural gas/Electricity
Air-conditioning: 439 hours

Annual Costs
Mortgage and Taxes: $7,067
Utilities: $1,298
Places Rated Score: 8,365
Places Rated Rank: 214

Bloomington, IN
Local Choices
59% houses, 2% condos, 8% mobile homes, 25% apartments (rent $275/month)
Houses
Price: $54,600
Property Taxes: $649
Built Before 1940: 17.6%
Energy Requirements
Heating Season: 4,905 degree days
Major Source: Natural gas/Electricity
Air-conditioning: 848 hours
Annual Costs
Mortgage and Taxes: $5,822
Utilities: $1,234
Places Rated Score: 7,056
Places Rated Rank: 104

Bloomington–Normal, IL
Local Choices
68% houses, 2% condos, 5% mobile homes, 15% apartments (rent $315/month)
Houses
Price: $65,300
Property Taxes: $1,038
Built Before 1940: 34.7%
Energy Requirements
Heating Season: 5,648 degree days
Major Source: Natural gas/Electricity
Air-conditioning: 848 hours
Annual Costs
Mortgage and Taxes: $7,226
Utilities: $1,428
Places Rated Score: 8,654
Places Rated Rank: 237

Boise City, ID
Local Choices
75% houses, 2% condos, 8% mobile homes, 8% apartments (rent $365/month)
Houses
Price: $72,100
Property Taxes: $750
Built Before 1940: 12.8%
Energy Requirements
Heating Season: 5,833 degree days
Major Source: Total electric
Air-conditioning: 706 hours
Annual Costs
Mortgage and Taxes: $7,583
Utilities: $638
Places Rated Score: 8,221
Places Rated Rank: 195

Boston, MA
Local Choices
22% houses, 2% condos, 23% apartments (rent $375/month)
Houses
Price: $84,300
Property Taxes: $2,047
Built Before 1940: 50.6%
Energy Requirements
Heating Season: 5,621 degree days
Major Source: Oil/Electricity
Air-conditioning: 420 hours

Annual Costs
Mortgage and Taxes: $10,033
Utilities: $1,576
Places Rated Score: 11,609
Places Rated Rank: 300

Boulder–Longmont, CO
Local Choices
66% houses, 5% condos, 5% mobile
homes, 19% apartments (rent
$440/month)
Houses
Price: $102,200
Property Taxes: $1,033
Built Before 1940: 12.4%
Energy Requirements
Heating Season: 5,540 degree days
Major Source: Natural gas/Electricity
Air-conditioning: 667 hours
Annual Costs
Mortgage and Taxes: $10,725
Utilities: $1,189
Places Rated Score: 11,914
Places Rated Rank: 305

Bradenton, FL
Local Choices
60% houses, 16% condos, 17% mobile
homes, 7% apartments (rent
$350/month)
Houses
Price: $67,700
Property Taxes: $697
Built Before 1940: 7.0%
Energy Requirements
Heating Season: 597 degree days
Major Source: Total electric
Air-conditioning: 2,154 hours
Annual Costs
Mortgage and Taxes: $7,110
Utilities: $1,132
Places Rated Score: 8,242
Places Rated Rank: 199

Brazoria, TX
Local Choices
72% houses, 1% condos, 12% mobile
homes, 12% apartments (rent
$385/month)
Houses
Price: $67,600
Property Taxes: $946
Built Before 1940: 5.3%
Energy Requirements
Heating Season: 1,434 degree days
Major Source: Natural gas/Electricity
Air-conditioning: 1,763 hours
Annual Costs
Mortgage and Taxes: $7,350
Utilities: $1,044
Places Rated Score: 8,394
Places Rated Rank: 219

Bremerton, WA
Local Choices
74% houses, 1% condos, 6% mobile
homes, 10% apartments (rent
$350/month)
Houses
Price: $81,000
Property Taxes: $819
Built Before 1940: 18.3%
Energy Requirements
Heating Season: 4,350 degree days
Major Source: Total electric
Air-conditioning: 64 hours

Annual Costs
Mortgage and Taxes: $8,501
Utilities: $559
Places Rated Score: 9,060
Places Rated Rank: 249

Bridgeport–Milford, CT
Local Choices
56% houses, 5% condos, 11%
apartments (rent $360/month)
Houses
Price: $107,200
Property Taxes: $1,641
Built Before 1940: 34.2%
Energy Requirements
Heating Season: 5,461 degree days
Major Source: Oil/Electricity
Air-conditioning: 302 hours
Annual Costs
Mortgage and Taxes: $11,806
Utilities: $1,623
Places Rated Score: 13,429
Places Rated Rank: 313

Bristol, CT
Local Choices
62% houses, 1% condos, 13%
apartments (rent $315/month)
Houses
Price: $76,500
Property Taxes: $1,171
Built Before 1940: 29.9%
Energy Requirements
Heating Season: 6,130 degree days
Major Source: Oil/Electricity
Air-conditioning: 292 hours
Annual Costs
Mortgage and Taxes: $8,424
Utilities: $1,617
Places Rated Score: 10,041
Places Rated Rank: 280

Brockton, MA
Local Choices
54% houses, 1% condos, 1% mobile
homes, 16% apartments (rent
$330/month)
Houses
Price: $57,100
Property Taxes: $1,388
Built Before 1940: 42.0%
Energy Requirements
Heating Season: 6,517 degree days
Major Source: Oil/Electricity
Air-conditioning: 133 hours
Annual Costs
Mortgage and Taxes: $6,802
Utilities: $1,461
Places Rated Score: 8,263
Places Rated Rank: 203

★ Brownsville–Harlingen, TX
Local Choices
71% houses, 2% condos, 6% mobile
homes, 12% apartments (rent
$260/month)
Houses
Price: $41,100
Property Taxes: $575
Built Before 1940: 12.3%
Energy Requirements
Heating Season: 650 degree days
Major Source: Natural gas/Electricity
Air-conditioning: 2,295 hours
Annual Costs
Mortgage and Taxes: $4,466
Utilities: $910

Places Rated Score: 5,376
Places Rated Rank: 3

Bryan–College Station, TX
Local Choices
56% houses, 1% condos, 7% mobile
homes, 25% apartments (rent
$350/month)
Houses
Price: $64,900
Property Taxes: $908
Built Before 1940: 7.4%
Energy Requirements
Heating Season: 1,658 degree days
Major Source: Natural gas/Electricity
Air-conditioning: 1,194 hours
Annual Costs
Mortgage and Taxes: $7,058
Utilities: $1,170
Places Rated Score: 8,228
Places Rated Rank: 197

Buffalo, NY
Local Choices
55% houses, 1% condos, 1% mobile
homes, 10% apartments (rent
$290/month)
Houses
Price: $56,600
Property Taxes: $1,454
Built Before 1940: 43.4%
Energy Requirements
Heating Season: 6,927 degree days
Major Source: Natural gas/Electricity
Air-conditioning: 347 hours
Annual Costs
Mortgage and Taxes: $6,818
Utilities: $1,246
Places Rated Score: 8,064
Places Rated Rank: 180

Burlington, NC
Local Choices
80% houses, 8% mobile homes, 5%
apartments (rent $260/month)
Houses
Price: $48,500
Property Taxes: $470
Built Before 1940: 19.8%
Energy Requirements
Heating Season: 3,810 degree days
Major Source: Oil/Electricity
Air-conditioning: 916 hours
Annual Costs
Mortgage and Taxes: $5,067
Utilities: $1,112
Places Rated Score: 6,179
Places Rated Rank: 29

Burlington, VT
Local Choices
59% houses, 3% condos, 5% mobile
homes, 14% apartments (rent
$355/month)
Houses
Price: $75,000
Property Taxes: $1,200
Built Before 1940: 32.9%
Energy Requirements
Heating Season: 7,876 degree days
Major Source: Oil/Electricity
Air-conditioning: 263 hours
Annual Costs
Mortgage and Taxes: $8,309
Utilities: $1,364
Places Rated Score: 9,673
Places Rated Rank: 267

Canton, OH
Local Choices
   77% houses, 3% mobile homes, 8% apartments (rent $280/month)
Houses
   Price: $56,500
   Property Taxes: $650
   Built Before 1940: 32.2%
Energy Requirements
   Heating Season: 6,224 degree days
   Major Source: Natural gas/Electricity
   Air-conditioning: 416 hours
Annual Costs
   Mortgage and Taxes: $6,004
   Utilities: $1,328
Places Rated Score: 7,332
Places Rated Rank: 128

Casper, WY
Local Choices
   66% houses, 1% condos, 13% mobile homes, 10% apartments (rent $445/month)
Houses
   Price: $88,700
   Property Taxes: $426
   Built Before 1940: 16.1%
Energy Requirements
   Heating Season: 7,553 degree days
   Major Source: Natural gas/Electricity
   Air-conditioning: 559 hours
Annual Costs
   Mortgage and Taxes: $8,836
   Utilities: $1,003
Places Rated Score: 9,839
Places Rated Rank: 270

Cedar Rapids, IA
Local Choices
   74% houses, 1% condos, 4% mobile homes, 14% apartments (rent $315/month)
Houses
   Price: $59,300
   Property Taxes: $972
   Built Before 1940: 29.3%
Energy Requirements
   Heating Season: 6,601 degree days
   Major Source: Natural gas/Electricity
   Air-conditioning: 340 hours
Annual Costs
   Mortgage and Taxes: $6,593
   Utilities: $1,181
Places Rated Score: 7,774
Places Rated Rank: 156

Champaign–Urbana–Rantoul, IL
Local Choices
   60% houses, 2% condos, 6% mobile homes, 23% apartments (rent $320/month)
Houses
   Price: $65,000
   Property Taxes: $1,033
   Built Before 1940: 21.0%
Energy Requirements
   Heating Season: 5,631 degree days
   Major Source: Natural gas/Electricity
   Air-conditioning: 788 hours
Annual Costs
   Mortgage and Taxes: $7,193
   Utilities: $1,434
Places Rated Score: 8,627
Places Rated Rank: 234

Charleston, SC
Local Choices
   67% houses, 2% condos, 7% mobile homes, 11% apartments (rent $320/month)
Houses
   Price: $60,700
   Property Taxes: $559
   Built Before 1940: 11.9%
Energy Requirements
   Heating Season: 2,146 degree days
   Major Source: Natural gas/Electricity
   Air-conditioning: 1,252 hours
Annual Costs
   Mortgage and Taxes: $6,314
   Utilities: $1,088
Places Rated Score: 7,402
Places Rated Rank: 134

Charleston, WV
Local Choices
   75% houses, 1% condos, 8% mobile homes, 7% apartments (rent $280/month)
Houses
   Price: $67,500
   Property Taxes: $250
   Built Before 1940: 25.5%
Energy Requirements
   Heating Season: 4,417 degree days
   Major Source: Natural gas/Electricity
   Air-conditioning: 779 hours
Annual Costs
   Mortgage and Taxes: $6,644
   Utilities: $1,145
Places Rated Score: 7,789
Places Rated Rank: 160

Charlotte–Gastonia–Rock Hill, NC–SC
Local Choices
   72% houses, 1% condos, 7% mobile homes, 12% apartments (rent $305/month)
Houses
   Price: $59,200
   Property Taxes: $574
   Built Before 1940: 15.4%
Energy Requirements
   Heating Season: 3,218 degree days
   Major Source: Natural gas/Electricity
   Air-conditioning: 1,138 hours
Annual Costs
   Mortgage and Taxes: $6,188
   Utilities: $981
Places Rated Score: 7,169
Places Rated Rank: 116

Charlottesville, VA
Local Choices
   65% houses, 1% condos, 5% mobile homes, 17% apartments (rent $375/month)
Houses
   Price: $75,400
   Property Taxes: $1,086
   Built Before 1940: 21.3%
Energy Requirements
   Heating Season: 4,162 degree days
   Major Source: Natural gas/Electricity
   Air-conditioning: 826 hours
Annual Costs
   Mortgage and Taxes: $8,237
   Utilities: $1,294
Places Rated Score: 9,531
Places Rated Rank: 263

Chattanooga, TN–GA
Local Choices
   74% houses, 1% condos, 6% mobile homes, 8% apartments (rent $290/month)
Houses
   Price: $50,600
   Property Taxes: $627
   Built Before 1940: 17.7%
Energy Requirements
   Heating Season: 3,505 degree days
   Major Source: Total electric
   Air-conditioning: 1,250 hours
Annual Costs
   Mortgage and Taxes: $5,419
   Utilities: $770
Places Rated Score: 6,189
Places Rated Rank: 30

Chicago, IL
Local Choices
   46% houses, 9% condos, 1% mobile homes, 27% apartments (rent $325/month)
Houses
   Price: $86,000
   Property Taxes: $1,367
   Built Before 1940: 34.7%
Energy Requirements
   Heating Season: 6,497 degree days
   Major Source: Natural gas/Electricity
   Air-conditioning: 727 hours
Annual Costs
   Mortgage and Taxes: $9,519
   Utilities: $1,394
Places Rated Score: 10,913
Places Rated Rank: 295

Chico, CA
Local Choices
   67% houses, 1% condos, 13% mobile homes, 11% apartments (rent $325/month)
Houses
   Price: $73,000
   Property Taxes: $751
   Built Before 1940: 12.9%
Energy Requirements
   Heating Season: 2,865 degree days
   Major Source: Natural gas/Electricity
   Air-conditioning: 1,410 hours
Annual Costs
   Mortgage and Taxes: $7,666
   Utilities: $921
Places Rated Score: 8,587
Places Rated Rank: 232

Cincinnati, OH–KY–IN
Local Choices
   63% houses, 1% condos, 2% mobile homes, 19% apartments (rent $270/month)
Houses
   Price: $63,900
   Property Taxes: $735
   Built Before 1940: 30.3%
Energy Requirements
   Heating Season: 4,844 degree days
   Major Source: Natural gas/Electricity
   Air-conditioning: 849 hours
Annual Costs
   Mortgage and Taxes: $6,791
   Utilities: $1,352
Places Rated Score: 8,143
Places Rated Rank: 191

★ Clarksville–Hopkinsville, TN–KY
Local Choices
>   70% houses, 1% condos, 8% mobile
>   homes, 9% apartments (rent
> $290/month)

Houses
>   Price: $48,700
>   Property Taxes: $604
>   Built Before 1940: 10.5%

Energy Requirements
>   Heating Season: 3,757 degree days
>   Major Source: Total electric
>   Air-conditioning: 1,260 hours

Annual Costs
>   Mortgage and Taxes: $5,222
>   Utilities: $785

Places Rated Score: 6,007
Places Rated Rank: 22

Cleveland, OH
Local Choices
>   63% houses, 3% condos, 1% mobile
>   homes, 19% apartments (rent
> $300/month)

Houses
>   Price: $70,800
>   Property Taxes: $814
>   Built Before 1940: 32.8%

Energy Requirements
>   Heating Season: 6,154 degree days
>   Major Source: Natural gas/Electricity
>   Air-conditioning: 523 hours

Annual Costs
>   Mortgage and Taxes: $7,523
>   Utilities: $1,645

Places Rated Score: 9,168
Places Rated Rank: 251

Colorado Springs, CO
Local Choices
>   67% houses, 3% condos, 4% mobile
>   homes, 19% apartments (rent
> $330/month)

Houses
>   Price: $72,600
>   Property Taxes: $734
>   Built Before 1940: 12.5%

Energy Requirements
>   Heating Season: 6,473 degree days
>   Major Source: Natural gas/Electricity
>   Air-conditioning: 644 hours

Annual Costs
>   Mortgage and Taxes: $7,619
>   Utilities: $890

Places Rated Score: 8,509
Places Rated Rank: 224

Columbia, MO
Local Choices
>   60% houses, 1% condos, 9% mobile
>   homes, 15% apartments (rent
> $305/month)

Houses
>   Price: $60,100
>   Property Taxes: $704
>   Built Before 1940: 14.1%

Energy Requirements
>   Heating Season: 5,078 degree days
>   Major Source: Natural gas/Electricity
>   Air-conditioning: 1,066 hours

Annual Costs
>   Mortgage and Taxes: $6,405
>   Utilities: $1,297

Places Rated Score: 7,702
Places Rated Rank: 150

Columbia, SC
Local Choices
>   71% houses, 2% condos, 7% mobile
>   homes, 13% apartments (rent
> $320/month)

Houses
>   Price: $61,800
>   Property Taxes: $569
>   Built Before 1940: 9.7%

Energy Requirements
>   Heating Season: 2,347 degree days
>   Major Source: Natural gas/Electricity
>   Air-conditioning: 1,359 hours

Annual Costs
>   Mortgage and Taxes: $6,431
>   Utilities: $1,088

Places Rated Score: 7,519
Places Rated Rank: 140

★ Columbus, GA–AL
Local Choices
>   70% houses, 1% condos, 4% mobile
>   homes, 15% apartments (rent
> $245/month)

Houses
>   Price: $45,100
>   Property Taxes: $546
>   Built Before 1940: 14.6%

Energy Requirements
>   Heating Season: 2,378 degree days
>   Major Source: Natural gas/Electricity
>   Air-conditioning: 1,511 hours

Annual Costs
>   Mortgage and Taxes: $4,825
>   Utilities: $992

Places Rated Score: 5,817
Places Rated Rank: 17

Columbus, OH
Local Choices
>   68% houses, 2% condos, 2% mobile
>   homes, 16% apartments (rent
> $290/month)

Houses
>   Price: $62,300
>   Property Taxes: $716
>   Built Before 1940: 24.7%

Energy Requirements
>   Heating Season: 5,702 degree days
>   Major Source: Natural gas/Electricity
>   Air-conditioning: 759 hours

Annual Costs
>   Mortgage and Taxes: $6,618
>   Utilities: $1,475

Places Rated Score: 8,093
Places Rated Rank: 185

Corpus Christi, TX
Local Choices
>   73% houses, 2% condos, 3% mobile
>   homes, 14% apartments (rent
> $320/month)

Houses
>   Price: $54,300
>   Property Taxes: $761
>   Built Before 1940: 9.0%

Energy Requirements
>   Heating Season: 930 degree days
>   Major Source: Natural gas/Electricity
>   Air-conditioning: 2,531 hours

Annual Costs
>   Mortgage and Taxes: $5,911
>   Utilities: $1,018

Places Rated Score: 6,929
Places Rated Rank: 96

★ Cumberland, MD–WV
Local Choices
>   77% houses, 4% mobile homes, 6%
>   apartments (rent $230/month)

Houses
>   Price: $45,000
>   Property Taxes: $617
>   Built Before 1940: 52.8%

Energy Requirements
>   Heating Season: 5,916 degree days
>   Major Source: Natural gas/Electricity
>   Air-conditioning: 596 hours

Annual Costs
>   Mortgage and Taxes: $4,885
>   Utilities: $1,169

Places Rated Score: 6,054
Places Rated Rank: 24

Dallas, TX
Local Choices
>   67% houses, 2% condos, 2% mobile
>   homes, 23% apartments (rent
> $360/month)

Houses
>   Price: $76,600
>   Property Taxes: $1,073
>   Built Before 1940: 8.6%

Energy Requirements
>   Heating Season: 2,290 degree days
>   Major Source: Natural gas/Electricity
>   Air-conditioning: 2,304 hours

Annual Costs
>   Mortgage and Taxes: $8,338
>   Utilities: $980

Places Rated Score: 9,318
Places Rated Rank: 256

Danbury, CT
Local Choices
>   62% houses, 3% condos, 7%
>   apartments (rent $420/month)

Houses
>   Price: $116,300
>   Property Taxes: $1,779
>   Built Before 1940: 25.0%

Energy Requirements
>   Heating Season: 6,250 degree days
>   Major Source: Oil/Electricity
>   Air-conditioning: 476 hours

Annual Costs
>   Mortgage and Taxes: $12,803
>   Utilities: $1,617

Places Rated Score: 14,420
Places Rated Rank: 320

★ Danville, VA
Local Choices
>   78% houses, 1% condos, 8% mobile
>   homes, 7% apartments (rent
> $225/month)

Houses
>   Price: $42,100
>   Property Taxes: $607
>   Built Before 1940: 24.8%

Energy Requirements
>   Heating Season: 3,702 degree days
>   Major Source: Oil/Electricity
>   Air-conditioning: 600 hours

Annual Costs
>   Mortgage and Taxes: $4,602
>   Utilities: $1,107

Places Rated Score: 5,709
Places Rated Rank: 11

Davenport–Rock Island–Moline, IA–IL
Local Choices
74% houses, 1% condos, 3% mobile homes, 12% apartments (rent $315/month)
Houses
Price: $62,500
Property Taxes: $1,025
Built Before 1940: 30.3%
Energy Requirements
Heating Season: 6,395 degree days
Major Source: Natural gas/Electricity
Air-conditioning: 703 hours
Annual Costs
Mortgage and Taxes: $6,951
Utilities: $1,132
Places Rated Score: 8,083
Places Rated Rank: 182

Dayton–Springfield, OH
Local Choices
81% houses, 2% condos, 2% mobile homes, 11% apartments (rent $285/month)
Houses
Price: $57,300
Property Taxes: $659
Built Before 1940: 26.0%
Energy Requirements
Heating Season: 5,641 degree days
Major Source: Natural gas/Electricity
Air-conditioning: 679 hours
Annual Costs
Mortgage and Taxes: $6,092
Utilities: $1,543
Places Rated Score: 7,635
Places Rated Rank: 145

Daytona Beach, FL
Local Choices
69% houses, 7% condos, 10% mobile homes, 11% apartments (rent $325/month)
Houses
Price: $57,800
Property Taxes: $595
Built Before 1940: 9.4%
Energy Requirements
Heating Season: 987 degree days
Major Source: Total electric
Air-conditioning: 1,597 hours
Annual Costs
Mortgage and Taxes: $6,071
Utilities: $1,132
Places Rated Score: 7,203
Places Rated Rank: 118

Decatur, IL
Local Choices
78% houses, 4% mobile homes, 10% apartments (rent $300/month)
Houses
Price: $54,000
Property Taxes: $859
Built Before 1940: 32.9%
Energy Requirements
Heating Season: 5,344 degree days
Major Source: Natural gas/Electricity
Air-conditioning: 867 hours
Annual Costs
Mortgage and Taxes: $5,981
Utilities: $1,414
Places Rated Score: 7,395
Places Rated Rank: 133

Denver, CO
Local Choices
66% houses, 7% condos, 3% mobile homes, 21% apartments (rent $370/month)
Houses
Price: $91,500
Property Taxes: $924
Built Before 1940: 14.4%
Energy Requirements
Heating Season: 6,016 degree days
Major Source: Natural gas/Electricity
Air-conditioning: 659 hours
Annual Costs
Mortgage and Taxes: $9,600
Utilities: $1,189
Places Rated Score: 10,789
Places Rated Rank: 293

Des Moines, IA
Local Choices
72% houses, 1% condos, 3% mobile homes, 16% apartments (rent $335/month)
Houses
Price: $60,900
Property Taxes: $999
Built Before 1940: 29.4%
Energy Requirements
Heating Season: 6,710 degree days
Major Source: Natural gas/Electricity
Air-conditioning: 738 hours
Annual Costs
Mortgage and Taxes: $6,773
Utilities: $1,255
Places Rated Score: 8,028
Places Rated Rank: 177

Detroit, MI
Local Choices
74% houses, 3% condos, 2% mobile homes, 13% apartments (rent $330/month)
Houses
Price: $59,100
Property Taxes: $1,583
Built Before 1940: 24.1%
Energy Requirements
Heating Season: 6,228 degree days
Major Source: Natural gas/Electricity
Air-conditioning: 498 hours
Annual Costs
Mortgage and Taxes: $7,184
Utilities: $1,341
Places Rated Score: 8,525
Places Rated Rank: 227

★ Dothan, AL
Local Choices
76% houses, 10% mobile homes, 5% apartments (rent $260/month)
Houses
Price: $48,000
Property Taxes: $197
Built Before 1940: 11.3%
Energy Requirements
Heating Season: 958 degree days
Major Source: Total electric
Air-conditioning: 1,406 hours
Annual Costs
Mortgage and Taxes: $4,750
Utilities: $958
Places Rated Score: 5,708
Places Rated Rank: 10

Dubuque, IA
Local Choices
71% houses, 4% mobile homes, 9% apartments (rent $280/month)
Houses
Price: $61,200
Property Taxes: $1,004
Built Before 1940: 42.6%
Energy Requirements
Heating Season: 7,277 degree days
Major Source: Natural gas/Electricity
Air-conditioning: 381 hours
Annual Costs
Mortgage and Taxes: $6,804
Utilities: $1,189
Places Rated Score: 7,993
Places Rated Rank: 176

★ Duluth, MN–WI
Local Choices
70% houses, 5% mobile homes, 12% apartments (rent $265/month)
Houses
Price: $46,900
Property Taxes: $361
Built Before 1940: 47.3%
Energy Requirements
Heating Season: 9,757 degree days
Major Source: Oil/Electricity
Air-conditioning: 132 hours
Annual Costs
Mortgage and Taxes: $4,810
Utilities: $1,230
Places Rated Score: 6,040
Places Rated Rank: 23

East St. Louis–Belleville, IL
Local Choices
73% houses, 1% condos, 9% mobile homes, 8% apartments (rent $285/month)
Houses
Price: $47,600
Property Taxes: $757
Built Before 1940: 26.4%
Energy Requirements
Heating Season: 4,486 degree days
Major Source: Natural gas/Electricity
Air-conditioning: 941 hours
Annual Costs
Mortgage and Taxes: $5,273
Utilities: $1,228
Places Rated Score: 6,501
Places Rated Rank: 53

Eau Claire, WI
Local Choices
75% houses, 4% mobile homes, 8% apartments (rent $280/month)
Houses
Price: $50,700
Property Taxes: $1,020
Built Before 1940: 35.5%
Energy Requirements
Heating Season: 8,388 degree days
Major Source: Oil/Electricity
Air-conditioning: 496 hours
Annual Costs
Mortgage and Taxes: $5,829
Utilities: $1,249
Places Rated Score: 7,078
Places Rated Rank: 108

El Paso, TX
Local Choices
68% houses, 2% condos, 3% mobile homes, 21% apartments (rent $260/month)
Houses
Price: $57,800
Property Taxes: $809
Built Before 1940: 11.0%
Energy Requirements
Heating Season: 2,678 degree days
Major Source: Natural gas/Electricity
Air-conditioning: 1,860 hours
Annual Costs
Mortgage and Taxes: $6,288
Utilities: $1,055
Places Rated Score: 7,343
Places Rated Rank: 130

Elkhart–Goshen, IN
Local Choices
77% houses, 6% mobile homes, 8% apartments (rent $280/month)
Houses
Price: $50,900
Property Taxes: $606
Built Before 1940: 32.1%
Energy Requirements
Heating Season: 6,272 degree days
Major Source: Natural gas/Electricity
Air-conditioning: 534 hours
Annual Costs
Mortgage and Taxes: $5,432
Utilities: $1,141
Places Rated Score: 6,573
Places Rated Rank: 59

Elmira, NY
Local Choices
70% houses, 4% mobile homes, 8% apartments (rent $275/month)
Houses
Price: $48,300
Property Taxes: $1,241
Built Before 1940: 47.2%
Energy Requirements
Heating Season: 6,642 degree days
Major Source: Natural gas/Electricity
Air-conditioning: 420 hours
Annual Costs
Mortgage and Taxes: $5,820
Utilities: $1,258
Places Rated Score: 7,078
Places Rated Rank: 108

Enid, OK
Local Choices
83% houses, 5% mobile homes, 6% apartments (rent $320/month)
Houses
Price: $58,000
Property Taxes: $429
Built Before 1940: 25.4%
Energy Requirements
Heating Season: 3,718 degree days
Major Source: Natural gas/Electricity
Air-conditioning: 1,521 hours
Annual Costs
Mortgage and Taxes: $5,925
Utilities: $904
Places Rated Score: 6,829
Places Rated Rank: 88

Erie, PA
Local Choices
70% houses, 1% condos, 5% mobile homes, 8% apartments (rent $290/month)

Houses
Price: $57,100
Property Taxes: $930
Built Before 1940: 40.1%
Energy Requirements
Heating Season: 6,851 degree days
Major Source: Natural gas/Electricity
Air-conditioning: 769 hours
Annual Costs
Mortgage and Taxes: $6,338
Utilities: $1,377
Places Rated Score: 7,715
Places Rated Rank: 151

Eugene–Springfield, OR
Local Choices
70% houses, 1% condos, 8% mobile homes, 14% apartments (rent $355/month)
Houses
Price: $76,800
Property Taxes: $1,581
Built Before 1940: 10.8%
Energy Requirements
Heating Season: 4,739 degree days
Major Source: Total electric
Air-conditioning: 441 hours
Annual Costs
Mortgage and Taxes: $8,857
Utilities: $513
Places Rated Score: 9,370
Places Rated Rank: 259

Evansville, IN–KY
Local Choices
76% houses, 1% condos, 4% mobile homes, 10% apartments (rent $275/month)
Houses
Price: $52,700
Property Taxes: $627
Built Before 1940: 31.6%
Energy Requirements
Heating Season: 4,624 degree days
Major Source: Natural gas/Electricity
Air-conditioning: 1,195 hours
Annual Costs
Mortgage and Taxes: $5,622
Utilities: $1,121
Places Rated Score: 6,743
Places Rated Rank: 78

Fall River, MA–RI
Local Choices
48% houses, 1% mobile homes, 16% apartments (rent $245/month)
Houses
Price: $63,400
Property Taxes: $1,542
Built Before 1940: 55.2%
Energy Requirements
Heating Season: 5,774 degree days
Major Source: Natural gas/Electricity
Air-conditioning: 164 hours
Annual Costs
Mortgage and Taxes: $7,556
Utilities: $1,461
Places Rated Score: 9,017
Places Rated Rank: 248

Fargo–Moorhead, ND–MN
Local Choices
59% houses, 4% condos, 5% mobile homes, 23% apartments (rent $285/month)
Houses
Price: $65,500

Property Taxes: $721
Built Before 1940: 25.8%
Energy Requirements
Heating Season: 9,271 degree days
Major Source: Oil/Electricity
Air-conditioning: 409 hours
Annual Costs
Mortgage and Taxes: $6,931
Utilities: $1,237
Places Rated Score: 8,168
Places Rated Rank: 192

Fayetteville, NC
Local Choices
72% houses, 1% condos, 10% mobile homes, 9% apartments (rent $300/month)
Houses
Price: $49,700
Property Taxes: $482
Built Before 1940: 5.7%
Energy Requirements
Heating Season: 3,073 degree days
Major Source: Total electric
Air-conditioning: 1,260 hours
Annual Costs
Mortgage and Taxes: $5,194
Utilities: $1,080
Places Rated Score: 6,274
Places Rated Rank: 36

Fayetteville–Springdale, AR
Local Choices
74% houses, 7% mobile homes, 11% apartments (rent $280/month)
Houses
Price: $53,900
Property Taxes: $765
Built Before 1940: 14.9%
Energy Requirements
Heating Season: 3,839 degree days
Major Source: Natural gas/Electricity
Air-conditioning: 1,207 hours
Annual Costs
Mortgage and Taxes: $5,873
Utilities: $813
Places Rated Score: 6,686
Places Rated Rank: 69

Fitchburg–Leominster, MA
Local Choices
55% houses, 1% mobile homes, 18% apartments (rent $295/month)
Houses
Price: $55,900
Property Taxes: $1,359
Built Before 1940: 48.2%
Energy Requirements
Heating Season: 6,475 degree days
Major Source: Oil/Electricity
Air-conditioning: 297 hours
Annual Costs
Mortgage and Taxes: $6,659
Utilities: $1,593
Places Rated Score: 8,252
Places Rated Rank: 200

Flint, MI
Local Choices
78% houses, 1% condos, 5% mobile homes, 11% apartments (rent $320/month)
Houses
Price: $48,500
Property Taxes: $1,301
Built Before 1940: 21.7%

Energy Requirements
Heating Season: 7,041 degree days
Major Source: Natural gas/Electricity
Air-conditioning: 509 hours
Annual Costs
Mortgage and Taxes: $5,903
Utilities: $1,301
Places Rated Score: 7,204
Places Rated Rank: 119

★ Florence, AL
Local Choices
58% houses, 6% mobile homes, 5% apartments (rent $265/month)
Houses
Price: $51,800
Property Taxes: $213
Built Before 1940: 14.3%
Energy Requirements
Heating Season: 836 degree days
Major Source: Total electric
Air-conditioning: 1,431 hours
Annual Costs
Mortgage and Taxes: $5,126
Utilities: $836
Places Rated Score: 5,962
Places Rated Rank: 21

Florence, SC
Local Choices
76% houses, 1% condos, 12% mobile homes, 4% apartments (rent $260/month)
Houses
Price: $52,200
Property Taxes: $480
Built Before 1940: 12.8%
Energy Requirements
Heating Season: 2,669 degree days
Major Source: Total electric
Air-conditioning: 1,210 hours
Annual Costs
Mortgage and Taxes: $5,430
Utilities: $1,078
Places Rated Score: 6,508
Places Rated Rank: 54

Fort Collins–Loveland, CO
Local Choices
67% houses, 4% condos, 8% mobile homes, 14% apartments (rent $375/month)
Houses
Price: $83,700
Property Taxes: $845
Built Before 1940: 13.9%
Energy Requirements
Heating Season: 6,599 degree days
Major Source: Natural gas/Electricity
Air-conditioning: 647 hours
Annual Costs
Mortgage and Taxes: $8,778
Utilities: $1,173
Places Rated Score: 9,951
Places Rated Rank: 276

Fort Lauderdale–Hollywood–Pompano Beach, FL
Local Choices
49% houses, 32% condos, 3% mobile homes, 16% apartments (rent $425/month)
Houses
Price: $92,100
Property Taxes: $949
Built Before 1940: 1.7%

Energy Requirements
Heating Season: 244 degree days
Major Source: Total electric
Air-conditioning: 2,342 hours
Annual Costs
Mortgage and Taxes: $9,678
Utilities: $1,132
Places Rated Score: 10,810
Places Rated Rank: 294

Fort Myers, FL
Local Choices
60% houses, 18% condos, 13% mobile homes, 8% apartments (rent $370/month)
Houses
Price: $77,700
Property Taxes: $800
Built Before 1940: 3.9%
Energy Requirements
Heating Season: 457 degree days
Major Source: Total electric
Air-conditioning: 1,863 hours
Annual Costs
Mortgage and Taxes: $8,166
Utilities: $1,132
Places Rated Score: 9,298
Places Rated Rank: 255

Fort Pierce, FL
Local Choices
63% houses, 14% condos, 13% mobile homes, 9% apartments (rent $350/month)
Houses
Price: $75,000
Property Taxes: $773
Built Before 1940: 4.8%
Energy Requirements
Heating Season: 503 degree days
Major Source: Total electric
Air-conditioning: 2,276 hours
Annual Costs
Mortgage and Taxes: $7,885
Utilities: $957
Places Rated Score: 8,842
Places Rated Rank: 243

★ Fort Smith, AR–OK
Local Choices
80% houses, 6% mobile homes, 8% apartments (rent $245/month)
Houses
Price: $45,000
Property Taxes: $640
Built Before 1940: 18.1%
Energy Requirements
Heating Season: 3,336 degree days
Major Source: Natural gas/Electricity
Air-conditioning: 1,534 hours
Annual Costs
Mortgage and Taxes: $4,912
Utilities: $872
Places Rated Score: 5,784
Places Rated Rank: 15

Fort Walton Beach, FL
Local Choices
71% houses, 8% condos, 11% mobile homes, 9% apartments (rent $310/month)
Houses
Price: $63,800
Property Taxes: $657
Built Before 1940: 3.4%
Energy Requirements
Heating Season: 1,361 degree days

Major Source: Natural gas/Electricity
Air-conditioning: 1,788 hours
Annual Costs
Mortgage and Taxes: $6,706
Utilities: $848
Places Rated Score: 7,554
Places Rated Rank: 141

Fort Wayne, IN
Local Choices
76% houses, 1% condos, 4% mobile homes, 10% apartments (rent $285/month)
Houses
Price: $52,200
Property Taxes: $621
Built Before 1940: 30.2%
Energy Requirements
Heating Season: 6,209 degree days
Major Source: Natural gas/Electricity
Air-conditioning: 607 hours
Annual Costs
Mortgage and Taxes: $5,567
Utilities: $1,166
Places Rated Score: 6,733
Places Rated Rank: 77

Fort Worth–Arlington, TX
Local Choices
75% houses, 1% condos, 4% mobile homes, 14% apartments (rent $350/month)
Houses
Price: $63,700
Property Taxes: $892
Built Before 1940: 10.2%
Energy Requirements
Heating Season: 2,382 degree days
Major Source: Natural gas/Electricity
Air-conditioning: 2,095 hours
Annual Costs
Mortgage and Taxes: $6,932
Utilities: $1,024
Places Rated Score: 7,956
Places Rated Rank: 174

Fresno, CA
Local Choices
71% houses, 2% condos, 4% mobile homes, 16% apartments (rent $335/month)
Houses
Price: $79,700
Property Taxes: $820
Built Before 1940: 12.6%
Energy Requirements
Heating Season: 2,650 degree days
Major Source: Natural gas/Electricity
Air-conditioning: 1,364 hours
Annual Costs
Mortgage and Taxes: $8,370
Utilities: $921
Places Rated Score: 9,291
Places Rated Rank: 254

★ Gadsden, AL
Local Choices
82% houses, 7% mobile homes, 5% apartments (rent $235/month)
Houses
Price: $43,400
Property Taxes: $178
Built Before 1940: 18.9%
Energy Requirements
Heating Season: 3,059 degree days
Major Source: Natural gas/Electricity
Air-conditioning: 1,401 hours

Annual Costs
Mortgage and Taxes: $4,293
Utilities: $1,089
Places Rated Score: 5,382
Places Rated Rank: 4

Gainesville, FL
Local Choices
59% houses, 1% condos, 11% mobile homes, 20% apartments (rent $335/month)
Houses
Price: $60,600
Property Taxes: $624
Built Before 1940: 8.5%
Energy Requirements
Heating Season: 1,081 degree days
Major Source: Total electric
Air-conditioning: 1,724 hours
Annual Costs
Mortgage and Taxes: $6,366
Utilities: $1,022
Places Rated Score: 7,388
Places Rated Rank: 132

Galveston–Texas City, TX
Local Choices
73% houses, 1% condos, 5% mobile homes, 14% apartments (rent $335/month)
Houses
Price: $61,800
Property Taxes: $865
Built Before 1940: 15.6%
Energy Requirements
Heating Season: 1,224 degree days
Major Source: Natural gas/Electricity
Air-conditioning: 2,639 hours
Annual Costs
Mortgage and Taxes: $6,723
Utilities: $1,044
Places Rated Score: 7,767
Places Rated Rank: 153

Gary–Hammond, IN
Local Choices
71% houses, 1% condos, 4% mobile homes, 12% apartments (rent $300/month)
Houses
Price: $57,700
Property Taxes: $687
Built Before 1940: 22.7%
Energy Requirements
Heating Season: 6,165 degree days
Major Source: Natural gas/Electricity
Air-conditioning: 525 hours
Annual Costs
Mortgage and Taxes: $6,160
Utilities: $1,481
Places Rated Score: 7,641
Places Rated Rank: 146

Glens Falls, NY
Local Choices
71% houses, 6% mobile homes, 6% apartments (rent $295/month)
Houses
Price: $48,800
Property Taxes: $1,253
Built Before 1940: 51.5%
Energy Requirements
Heating Season: 6,421 degree days
Major Source: Oil/Electricity
Air-conditioning: 277 hours

Annual Costs
Mortgage and Taxes: $5,874
Utilities: $1,246
Places Rated Score: 7,120
Places Rated Rank: 112

Grand Forks, ND
Local Choices
54% houses, 4% condos, 6% mobile homes, 24% apartments (rent $270/month)
Houses
Price: $63,400
Property Taxes: $698
Built Before 1940: 24.3%
Energy Requirements
Heating Season: 9,876 degree days
Major Source: Oil/Electricity
Air-conditioning: 652 hours
Annual Costs
Mortgage and Taxes: $6,709
Utilities: $1,189
Places Rated Score: 7,898
Places Rated Rank: 169

Grand Rapids, MI
Local Choices
74% houses, 2% condos, 4% mobile homes, 9% apartments (rent $295/month)
Houses
Price: $53,300
Property Taxes: $1,428
Built Before 1940: 29.5%
Energy Requirements
Heating Season: 6,801 degree days
Major Source: Natural gas/Electricity
Air-conditioning: 420 hours
Annual Costs
Mortgage and Taxes: $6,479
Utilities: $1,301
Places Rated Score: 7,780
Places Rated Rank: 159

Great Falls, MT
Local Choices
67% houses, 2% condos, 8% mobile homes, 13% apartments (rent $280/month)
Houses
Price: $58,300
Property Taxes: $665
Built Before 1940: 24.6%
Energy Requirements
Heating Season: 7,652 degree days
Major Source: Natural gas/Electricity
Air-conditioning: 286 hours
Annual Costs
Mortgage and Taxes: $6,195
Utilities: $948
Places Rated Score: 7,143
Places Rated Rank: 114

Greeley, CO
Local Choices
67% houses, 1% condos, 10% mobile homes, 13% apartments (rent $315/month)
Houses
Price: $67,400
Property Taxes: $681
Built Before 1940: 22.4%
Energy Requirements
Heating Season: 6,639 degree days
Major Source: Natural gas/Electricity
Air-conditioning: 647 hours

Annual Costs
Mortgage and Taxes: $7,073
Utilities: $1,145
Places Rated Score: 8,218
Places Rated Rank: 194

Green Bay, WI
Local Choices
71% houses, 2% mobile homes, 11% apartments (rent $285/month)
Houses
Price: $62,100
Property Taxes: $1,248
Built Before 1940: 24.5%
Energy Requirements
Heating Season: 8,098 degree days
Major Source: Natural gas/Electricity
Air-conditioning: 264 hours
Annual Costs
Mortgage and Taxes: $7,136
Utilities: $1,265
Places Rated Score: 8,401
Places Rated Rank: 220

Greensboro–Winston-Salem–High Point, NC
Local Choices
74% houses, 1% condos, 7% mobile homes, 10% apartments (rent $280/month)
Houses
Price: $58,200
Property Taxes: $565
Built Before 1940: 15.9%
Energy Requirements
Heating Season: 3,825 degree days
Major Source: Oil/Electricity
Air-conditioning: 916 hours
Annual Costs
Mortgage and Taxes: $6,083
Utilities: $981
Places Rated Score: 7,064
Places Rated Rank: 106

Greenville–Spartanburg, SC
Local Choices
76% houses, 1% condos, 8% mobile homes, 9% apartments (rent $275/month)
Houses
Price: $52,000
Property Taxes: $478
Built Before 1940: 16.1%
Energy Requirements
Heating Season: 3,095 degree days
Major Source: Total electric
Air-conditioning: 1,094 hours
Annual Costs
Mortgage and Taxes: $5,404
Utilities: $932
Places Rated Score: 6,336
Places Rated Rank: 41

Hagerstown, MD
Local Choices
71% houses, 1% condos, 4% mobile homes, 11% apartments (rent $275/month)
Houses
Price: $61,200
Property Taxes: $838
Built Before 1940: 40.0%
Energy Requirements
Heating Season: 5,152 degree days
Major Source: Natural gas/Electricity
Air-conditioning: 702 hours

Annual Costs
    Mortgage and Taxes: $6,634
    Utilities: $1,129
Places Rated Score: 7,763
Places Rated Rank: 152

Hamilton–Middletown, OH
Local Choices
    74% houses, 2% condos, 4% mobile
        homes, 11% apartments (rent
        $300/month)
Houses
    Price: $65,300
    Property Taxes: $751
    Built Before 1940: 23.1%
Energy Requirements
    Heating Season: 5,015 degree days
    Major Source: Natural gas/Electricity
    Air-conditioning: 928 hours
Annual Costs
    Mortgage and Taxes: $6,940
    Utilities: $1,287
Places Rated Score: 8,227
Places Rated Rank: 196

Harrisburg–Lebanon–Carlisle, PA
Local Choices
    72% houses, 1% condos, 5% mobile
        homes, 12% apartments (rent
        $315/month)
Houses
    Price: $59,300
    Property Taxes: $966
    Built Before 1940: 36.3%
Energy Requirements
    Heating Season: 5,224 degree days
    Major Source: Oil/Electricity
    Air-conditioning: 744 hours
Annual Costs
    Mortgage and Taxes: $6,584
    Utilities: $1,307
Places Rated Score: 7,891
Places Rated Rank: 168

Hartford, CT
Local Choices
    70% houses, 6% condos, 1% mobile
        homes, 20% apartments (rent
        $350/month)
Houses
    Price: $91,100
    Property Taxes: $1,395
    Built Before 1940: 27.1%
Energy Requirements
    Heating Season: 6,350 degree days
    Major Source: Oil/Electricity
    Air-conditioning: 476 hours
Annual Costs
    Mortgage and Taxes: $10,035
    Utilities: $1,617
Places Rated Score: 11,652
Places Rated Rank: 302

Hickory, NC
Local Choices
    50% houses, 12% mobile homes, 4%
        apartments (rent $265/month)
Houses
    Price: $54,100
    Property Taxes: $524
    Built Before 1940: 15.8%
Energy Requirements
    Heating Season: 3,831 degree days
    Major Source: Oil/Electricity
    Air-conditioning: 1,040 hours

Annual Costs
    Mortgage and Taxes: $5,648
    Utilities: $1,112
Places Rated Score: 6,760
Places Rated Rank: 82

Honolulu, HI
Local Choices
    48% houses, 24% condos, 28%
        apartments (rent $450/month)
Houses
    Price: $163,400
    Property Taxes: $588
    Built Before 1940: 8.4%
Energy Requirements
    Heating Season: 0 degree days
    Major Source: Total electric
    Air-conditioning: 1,342 hours
Annual Costs
    Mortgage and Taxes: $16,075
    Utilities: $946
Places Rated Score: 17,021
Places Rated Rank: 326

Houma–Thibodaux, LA
Local Choices
    75% houses, 11% mobile homes, 6%
        apartments (rent $290/month)
Houses
    Price: $64,400
    Property Taxes: $97
    Built Before 1940: 12.3%
Energy Requirements
    Heating Season: 1,215 degree days
    Major Source: Natural gas/Electricity
    Air-conditioning: 1,727 hours
Annual Costs
    Mortgage and Taxes: $6,205
    Utilities: $889
Places Rated Score: 7,094
Places Rated Rank: 110

Houston, TX
Local Choices
    64% houses, 4% condos, 3% mobile
        homes, 24% apartments (rent
        $390/month)
Houses
    Price: $80,100
    Property Taxes: $1,122
    Built Before 1940: 6.9%
Energy Requirements
    Heating Season: 1,434 degree days
    Major Source: Natural gas/Electricity
    Air-conditioning: 1,894 hours
Annual Costs
    Mortgage and Taxes: $8,716
    Utilities: $1,044
Places Rated Score: 9,760
Places Rated Rank: 269

Huntington–Ashland, WV–KY–OH
Local Choices
    72% houses, 8% mobile homes, 6%
        apartments (rent $260/month)
Houses
    Price: $55,700
    Property Taxes: $206
    Built Before 1940: 29.5%
Energy Requirements
    Heating Season: 4,073 degree days
    Major Source: Natural gas/Electricity
    Air-conditioning: 979 hours
Annual Costs
    Mortgage and Taxes: $5,487
    Utilities: $1,145
Places Rated Score: 6,632
Places Rated Rank: 65

Huntsville, AL
Local Choices
    83% houses, 1% condos, 4% mobile
        homes, 12% apartments (rent
        $280/month)
Houses
    Price: $56,100
    Property Taxes: $230
    Built Before 1940: 7.3%
Energy Requirements
    Heating Season: 738 degree days
    Major Source: Total electric
    Air-conditioning: 1,240 hours
Annual Costs
    Mortgage and Taxes: $5,545
    Utilities: $738
Places Rated Score: 6,283
Places Rated Rank: 37

Indianapolis, IN
Local Choices
    72% houses, 1% condos, 3% mobile
        homes, 16% apartments (rent
        $290/month)
Houses
    Price: $55,100
    Property Taxes: $655
    Built Before 1940: 24.9%
Energy Requirements
    Heating Season: 5,577 degree days
    Major Source: Natural gas/Electricity
    Air-conditioning: 763 hours
Annual Costs
    Mortgage and Taxes: $5,873
    Utilities: $1,139
Places Rated Score: 7,012
Places Rated Rank: 101

Iowa City, IA
Local Choices
    54% houses, 1% condos, 7% mobile
        homes, 28% apartments (rent
        $320/month)
Houses
    Price: $74,600
    Property Taxes: $1,224
    Built Before 1940: 23.3%
Energy Requirements
    Heating Season: 6,404 degree days
    Major Source: Natural gas/Electricity
    Air-conditioning: 615 hours
Annual Costs
    Mortgage and Taxes: $8,297
    Utilities: $1,132
Places Rated Score: 9,429
Places Rated Rank: 260

Jackson, MI
Local Choices
    78% houses, 1% condos, 5% mobile
        homes, 7% apartments (rent
        $300/month)
Houses
    Price: $45,200
    Property Taxes: $1,211
    Built Before 1940: 38.3%
Energy Requirements
    Heating Season: 6,755 degree days
    Major Source: Natural gas/Electricity
    Air-conditioning: 511 hours
Annual Costs
    Mortgage and Taxes: $5,493
    Utilities: $1,301
Places Rated Score: 6,794
Places Rated Rank: 85

Jackson, MS

Local Choices
74% houses, 1% condos, 6% mobile homes, 13% apartments (rent $310/month)

Houses
Price: $61,400
Property Taxes: $467
Built Before 1940: 8.8%

Energy Requirements
Heating Season: 2,300 degree days
Major Source: Natural gas/Electricity
Air-conditioning: 1,611 hours

Annual Costs
Mortgage and Taxes: $6,288
Utilities: $957

Places Rated Score: 7,245
Places Rated Rank: 122

Jacksonville, FL

Local Choices
68% houses, 2% condos, 8% mobile homes, 15% apartments (rent $325/month)

Houses
Price: $52,400
Property Taxes: $540
Built Before 1940: 11.3%

Energy Requirements
Heating Season: 1,327 degree days
Major Source: Total electric
Air-conditioning: 1,725 hours

Annual Costs
Mortgage and Taxes: $5,507
Utilities: $1,119

Places Rated Score: 6,626
Places Rated Rank: 64

Jacksonville, NC

Local Choices
70% houses, 1% condos, 18% mobile homes, 6% apartments (rent $295/month)

Houses
Price: $48,400
Property Taxes: $470
Built Before 1940: 4.8%

Energy Requirements
Heating Season: 2,975 degree days
Major Source: Total electric
Air-conditioning: 1,020 hours

Annual Costs
Mortgage and Taxes: $5,062
Utilities: $1,049

Places Rated Score: 6,111
Places Rated Rank: 26

Janesville–Beloit, WI

Local Choices
76% houses, 2% mobile homes, 8% apartments (rent $285/month)

Houses
Price: $53,900
Property Taxes: $1,083
Built Before 1940: 37.4%

Energy Requirements
Heating Season: 6,563 degree days
Major Source: Natural gas/Electricity
Air-conditioning: 234 hours

Annual Costs
Mortgage and Taxes: $6,193
Utilities: $1,254

Places Rated Score: 7,447
Places Rated Rank: 136

Jersey City, NJ

Local Choices
12% houses, 2% condos, 41% apartments (rent $305/month)

Houses
Price: $60,700
Property Taxes: $1,548
Built Before 1940: 60.2%

Energy Requirements
Heating Season: 5,238 degree days
Major Source: Oil/Electricity
Air-conditioning: 592 hours

Annual Costs
Mortgage and Taxes: $7,302
Utilities: $1,508

Places Rated Score: 8,810
Places Rated Rank: 241

Johnson City–Kingsport–Bristol, TN–VA

Local Choices
79% houses, 1% condos, 11% mobile homes, 8% apartments (rent $250/month)

Houses
Price: $50,300
Property Taxes: $624
Built Before 1940: 19.1%

Energy Requirements
Heating Season: 4,306 degree days
Major Source: Total electric
Air-conditioning: 850 hours

Annual Costs
Mortgage and Taxes: $5,392
Utilities: $727

Places Rated Score: 6,119
Places Rated Rank: 27

Johnstown, PA

Local Choices
74% houses, 6% mobile homes, 6% apartments (rent $260/month)

Houses
Price: $46,300
Property Taxes: $755
Built Before 1940: 51.5%

Energy Requirements
Heating Season: 5,724 degree days
Major Source: Natural gas/Electricity
Air-conditioning: 467 hours

Annual Costs
Mortgage and Taxes: $5,147
Utilities: $1,377

Places Rated Score: 6,524
Places Rated Rank: 55

Joliet, IL

Local Choices
77% houses, 3% condos, 2% mobile homes, 10% apartments (rent $335/month)

Houses
Price: $71,900
Property Taxes: $1,143
Built Before 1940: 22.2%

Energy Requirements
Heating Season: 6,180 degree days
Major Source: Natural gas/Electricity
Air-conditioning: 632 hours

Annual Costs
Mortgage and Taxes: $7,958
Utilities: $1,369

Places Rated Score: 9,327
Places Rated Rank: 258

★ Joplin, MO

Local Choices
84% houses, 5% mobile homes, 5% apartments (rent $220/month)

Houses
Price: $37,600
Property Taxes: $440
Built Before 1940: 37.2%

Energy Requirements
Heating Season: 4,188 degree days
Major Source: Natural gas/Electricity
Air-conditioning: 1,171 hours

Annual Costs
Mortgage and Taxes: $4,003
Utilities: $1,156

Places Rated Score: 5,159
Places Rated Rank: 1

Kalamazoo, MI

Local Choices
70% houses, 2% condos, 3% mobile homes, 16% apartments (rent $310/month)

Houses
Price: $54,400
Property Taxes: $1,459
Built Before 1940: 27.1%

Energy Requirements
Heating Season: 6,281 degree days
Major Source: Natural gas/Electricity
Air-conditioning: 311 hours

Annual Costs
Mortgage and Taxes: $6,618
Utilities: $1,301

Places Rated Score: 7,919
Places Rated Rank: 172

Kankakee, IL

Local Choices
73% houses, 5% mobile homes, 9% apartments (rent $310/month)

Houses
Price: $52,700
Property Taxes: $837
Built Before 1940: 28.4%

Energy Requirements
Heating Season: 5,980 degree days
Major Source: Natural gas/Electricity
Air-conditioning: 659 hours

Annual Costs
Mortgage and Taxes: $5,829
Utilities: $1,401

Places Rated Score: 7,230
Places Rated Rank: 120

Kansas City, KS

Local Choices
77% houses, 2% condos, 2% mobile homes, 11% apartments (rent $360/month)

Houses
Price: $66,600
Property Taxes: $646
Built Before 1940: 19.0%

Energy Requirements
Heating Season: 5,161 degree days
Major Source: Natural gas/Electricity
Air-conditioning: 1,092 hours

Annual Costs
Mortgage and Taxes: $6,956
Utilities: $1,170

Places Rated Score: 8,126
Places Rated Rank: 189

Kansas City, MO

Local Choices
69% houses, 1% condos, 2% mobile

homes, 16% apartments (rent
$305/month)
Houses
Price: $53,200
Property Taxes: $623
Built Before 1940: 27.1%
Energy Requirements
Heating Season: 5,161 degree days
Major Source: Natural gas/Electricity
Air-conditioning: 1,092 hours
Annual Costs
Mortgage and Taxes: $5,667
Utilities: $1,409
Places Rated Score: 7,076
Places Rated Rank: 107

Kenosha, WI
Local Choices
70% houses, 1% condos, 3% mobile
homes, 10% apartments (rent
$295/month)
Houses
Price: $62,800
Property Taxes: $1,262
Built Before 1940: 32.9%
Energy Requirements
Heating Season: 6,765 degree days
Major Source: Natural gas/Electricity
Air-conditioning: 358 hours
Annual Costs
Mortgage and Taxes: $7,213
Utilities: $1,303
Places Rated Score: 8,516
Places Rated Rank: 226

Killeen–Temple, TX
Local Choices
65% houses, 1% condos, 7% mobile
homes, 15% apartments (rent
$290/month)
Houses
Price: $50,400
Property Taxes: $706
Built Before 1940: 9.5%
Energy Requirements
Heating Season: 2,039 degree days
Major Source: Natural gas/Electricity
Air-conditioning: 2,194 hours
Annual Costs
Mortgage and Taxes: $5,484
Utilities: $979
Places Rated Score: 6,463
Places Rated Rank: 49

Knoxville, TN
Local Choices
75% houses, 1% condos, 6% mobile
homes, 12% apartments (rent
$280/month)
Houses
Price: $55,100
Property Taxes: $683
Built Before 1940: 16.5%
Energy Requirements
Heating Season: 3,478 degree days
Major Source: Total electric
Air-conditioning: 1,094 hours
Annual Costs
Mortgage and Taxes: $5,907
Utilities: $785
Places Rated Score: 6,692
Places Rated Rank: 72

Kokomo, IN
Local Choices
80% houses, 1% condos, 5% mobile
homes, 7% apartments (rent
$280/month)

Houses
Price: $50,400
Property Taxes: $600
Built Before 1940: 35.3%
Energy Requirements
Heating Season: 5,585 degree days
Major Source: Natural gas/Electricity
Air-conditioning: 700 hours
Annual Costs
Mortgage and Taxes: $5,382
Utilities: $1,234
Places Rated Score: 6,616
Places Rated Rank: 63

La Crosse, WI
Local Choices
70% houses, 4% mobile homes, 11%
apartments (rent $285/month)
Houses
Price: $61,500
Property Taxes: $1,235
Built Before 1940: 36.5%
Energy Requirements
Heating Season: 7,417 degree days
Major Source: Oil/Electricity
Air-conditioning: 401 hours
Annual Costs
Mortgage and Taxes: $7,061
Utilities: $1,249
Places Rated Score: 8,310
Places Rated Rank: 207

Lafayette, IN
Local Choices
64% houses, 1% condos, 5% mobile
homes, 19% apartments (rent
$290/month)
Houses
Price: $61,300
Property Taxes: $730
Built Before 1940: 26.0%
Energy Requirements
Heating Season: 5,603 degree days
Major Source: Natural gas/Electricity
Air-conditioning: 1,807 hours
Annual Costs
Mortgage and Taxes: $6,544
Utilities: $1,234
Places Rated Score: 7,778
Places Rated Rank: 157

Lafayette, LA
Local Choices
74% houses, 1% condos, 12% mobile
homes, 10% apartments (rent
$355/month)
Houses
Price: $79,100
Property Taxes: $119
Built Before 1940: 9.8%
Energy Requirements
Heating Season: 1,551 degree days
Major Source: Natural gas/Electricity
Air-conditioning: 1,807 hours
Annual Costs
Mortgage and Taxes: $7,617
Utilities: $955
Places Rated Score: 8,572
Places Rated Rank: 230

Lake Charles, LA
Local Choices
77% houses, 4% condos, 9% mobile
homes, 7% apartments (rent
$310/month)
Houses
Price: $61,200

Property Taxes: $92
Built Before 1940: 10.9%
Energy Requirements
Heating Season: 1,498 degree days
Major Source: Natural gas/Electricity
Air-conditioning: 1,807 hours
Annual Costs
Mortgage and Taxes: $5,895
Utilities: $1,026
Places Rated Score: 6,921
Places Rated Rank: 94

Lake County, IL
Local Choices
74% houses, 5% condos, 2% mobile
homes, 12% apartments (rent
$375/month)
Houses
Price: $107,300
Property Taxes: $1,707
Built Before 1940: 18.8%
Energy Requirements
Heating Season: 6,550 degree days
Major Source: Natural gas/Electricity
Air-conditioning: 599 hours
Annual Costs
Mortgage and Taxes: $11,881
Utilities: $1,401
Places Rated Score: 13,282
Places Rated Rank: 311

Lakeland–Winter Haven, FL
Local Choices
70% houses, 2% condos, 14% mobile
homes, 8% apartments (rent
$295/month)
Houses
Price: $53,500
Property Taxes: $551
Built Before 1940: 11.6%
Energy Requirements
Heating Season: 678 degree days
Major Source: Total electric
Air-conditioning: 1,759 hours
Annual Costs
Mortgage and Taxes: $5,619
Utilities: $1,061
Places Rated Score: 6,680
Places Rated Rank: 68

Lancaster, PA
Local Choices
73% houses, 5% mobile homes, 9%
apartments (rent $310/month)
Houses
Price: $65,900
Property Taxes: $1,075
Built Before 1940: 40.5%
Energy Requirements
Heating Season: 5,283 degree days
Major Source: Oil/Electricity
Air-conditioning: 654 hours
Annual Costs
Mortgage and Taxes: $7,324
Utilities: $1,307
Places Rated Score: 8,631
Places Rated Rank: 236

Lansing–East Lansing, MI
Local Choices
70% houses, 1% condos, 4% mobile
homes, 17% apartments (rent
$330/month)
Houses
Price: $54,500
Property Taxes: $1,459
Built Before 1940: 27.0%

Energy Requirements
Heating Season: 6,904 degree days
Major Source: Natural gas/Electricity
Air-conditioning: 323 hours
Annual Costs
Mortgage and Taxes: $6,618
Utilities: $1,289
Places Rated Score: 7,907
Places Rated Rank: 170

Laredo, TX
Local Choices
75% houses, 1% condos, 7% mobile homes, 9% apartments (rent $250/month)
Houses
Price: $47,200
Property Taxes: $661
Built Before 1940: 16.5%
Energy Requirements
Heating Season: 876 degree days
Major Source: Natural gas/Electricity
Air-conditioning: 2,736 hours
Annual Costs
Mortgage and Taxes: $5,134
Utilities: $1,018
Places Rated Score: 6,152
Places Rated Rank: 28

Las Cruces, NM
Local Choices
65% houses, 1% condos, 16% mobile homes, 9% apartments (rent $285/month)
Houses
Price: $54,500
Property Taxes: $507
Built Before 1940: 10.5%
Energy Requirements
Heating Season: 3,194 degree days
Major Source: Natural gas/Electricity
Air-conditioning: 1,848 hours
Annual Costs
Mortgage and Taxes: $5,675
Utilities: $1,287
Places Rated Score: 6,962
Places Rated Rank: 98

Las Vegas, NV
Local Choices
56% houses, 6% condos, 11% mobile homes, 22% apartments (rent $430/month)
Houses
Price: $87,300
Property Taxes: $673
Built Before 1940: 1.5%
Energy Requirements
Heating Season: 2,601 degree days
Major Source: Total electric
Air-conditioning: 2,360 hours
Annual Costs
Mortgage and Taxes: $8,954
Utilities: $952
Places Rated Score: 9,906
Places Rated Rank: 274

Lawrence, KS
Local Choices
61% houses, 1% condos, 6% mobile homes, 20% apartments (rent $310/month)
Houses
Price: $61,200
Property Taxes: $594
Built Before 1940: 24.2%

Energy Requirements
Heating Season: 4,728 degree days
Major Source: Natural gas/Electricity
Air-conditioning: 1,094 hours
Annual Costs
Mortgage and Taxes: $6,394
Utilities: $1,103
Places Rated Score: 7,497
Places Rated Rank: 138

Lawrence–Haverhill, MA–NH
Local Choices
46% houses, 1% condos, 1% mobile homes, 14% apartments (rent $328/month)
Houses
Price: $74,900
Property Taxes: $1,819
Built Before 1940: 51.3%
Energy Requirements
Heating Season: 6,195 degree days
Major Source: Oil/Electricity
Air-conditioning: 506 hours
Annual Costs
Mortgage and Taxes: $8,916
Utilities: $1,498
Places Rated Score: 10,414
Places Rated Rank: 287

★ Lawton, OK
Local Choices
78% houses, 1% condos, 4% mobile homes, 10% apartments (rent $300/month)
Houses
Price: $48,500
Property Taxes: $359
Built Before 1940: 11.7%
Energy Requirements
Heating Season: 3,147 degree days
Major Source: Natural gas/Electricity
Air-conditioning: 2,047 hours
Annual Costs
Mortgage and Taxes: $4,955
Utilities: $895
Places Rated Score: 5,850
Places Rated Rank: 19

Lewiston–Auburn, ME
Local Choices
41% houses, 4% mobile homes, 18% apartments (rent $250/month)
Houses
Price: $52,900
Property Taxes: $804
Built Before 1940: 52.9%
Energy Requirements
Heating Season: 7,374 degree days
Major Source: Oil/Electricity
Air-conditioning: 298 hours
Annual Costs
Mortgage and Taxes: $5,819
Utilities: $1,057
Places Rated Score: 6,876
Places Rated Rank: 90

Lexington–Fayette, KY
Local Choices
66% houses, 2% condos, 4% mobile homes, 18% apartments (rent $310/month)
Houses
Price: $69,400
Property Taxes: $770
Built Before 1940: 21.0%
Energy Requirements
Heating Season: 4,729 degree days

Major Source: Natural gas/Electricity
Air-conditioning: 954 hours
Annual Costs
Mortgage and Taxes: $7,347
Utilities: $993
Places Rated Score: 8,340
Places Rated Rank: 212

Lima, OH
Local Choices
62% houses, 1% condos, 4% mobile homes, 7% apartments (rent $270/month)
Houses
Price: $51,200
Property Taxes: $589
Built Before 1940: 37.5%
Energy Requirements
Heating Season: 5,838 degree days
Major Source: Natural gas/Electricity
Air-conditioning: 665 hours
Annual Costs
Mortgage and Taxes: $5,443
Utilities: $1,543
Places Rated Score: 6,986
Places Rated Rank: 99

Lincoln, NE
Local Choices
68% houses, 2% condos, 3% mobile homes, 17% apartments (rent $295/month)
Houses
Price: $61,500
Property Taxes: $1,372
Built Before 1940: 25.3%
Energy Requirements
Heating Season: 6,218 degree days
Major Source: Natural gas/Electricity
Air-conditioning: 1,000 hours
Annual Costs
Mortgage and Taxes: $7,205
Utilities: $1,051
Places Rated Score: 8,256
Places Rated Rank: 201

Little Rock–North Little Rock, AR
Local Choices
74% houses, 1% condos, 7% mobile homes, 11% apartments (rent $300/month)
Houses
Price: $58,200
Property Taxes: $826
Built Before 1940: 11.9%
Energy Requirements
Heating Season: 3,354 degree days
Major Source: Natural gas/Electricity
Air-conditioning: 1,545 hours
Annual Costs
Mortgage and Taxes: $6,341
Utilities: $929
Places Rated Score: 7,270
Places Rated Rank: 123

Longview–Marshall, TX
Local Choices
77% houses, 7% mobile homes, 8% apartments (rent $310/month)
Houses
Price: $52,300
Property Taxes: $732
Built Before 1940: 14.9%
Energy Requirements
Heating Season: 2,271 degree days
Major Source: Natural gas/Electricity
Air-conditioning: 1,853 hours

Annual Costs
Mortgage and Taxes: $5,686
Utilities: $922
Places Rated Score: 6,608
Places Rated Rank: 62

Lorain–Elyria, OH
Local Choices
77% houses, 2% condos, 3% mobile homes, 10% apartments (rent $300/month)
Houses
Price: $63,800
Property Taxes: $733
Built Before 1940: 24.1%
Energy Requirements
Heating Season: 5,800 degree days
Major Source: Natural gas/Electricity
Air-conditioning: 523 hours
Annual Costs
Mortgage and Taxes: $6,779
Utilities: $1,530
Places Rated Score: 8,309
Places Rated Rank: 206

Los Angeles–Long Beach, CA
Local Choices
57% houses, 4% condos, 2% mobile homes, 30% apartments (rent $405/month)
Houses
Price: $122,600
Property Taxes: $1,263
Built Before 1940: 17.7%
Energy Requirements
Heating Season: 1,819 degree days
Major Source: Natural gas/Electricity
Air-conditioning: 576 hours
Annual Costs
Mortgage and Taxes: $12,889
Utilities: $979
Places Rated Score: 13,868
Places Rated Rank: 316

Louisville, KY–IN
Local Choices
73% houses, 2% condos, 3% mobile homes, 14% apartments (rent $275/month)
Houses
Price: $54,600
Property Taxes: $606
Built Before 1940: 21.7%
Energy Requirements
Heating Season: 4,640 degree days
Major Source: Natural gas/Electricity
Air-conditioning: 1,041 hours
Annual Costs
Mortgage and Taxes: $5,785
Utilities: $1,027
Places Rated Score: 6,812
Places Rated Rank: 87

Lowell, MA–NH
Local Choices
62% houses, 1% condos, 15% apartments (rent $335/month)
Houses
Price: $68,400
Property Taxes: $1,661
Built Before 1940: 38.5%
Energy Requirements
Heating Season: 6,056 degree days
Major Source: Natural gas/Electricity
Air-conditioning: 506 hours

Annual Costs
Mortgage and Taxes: $8,142
Utilities: $1,498
Places Rated Score: 9,640
Places Rated Rank: 266

Lubbock, TX
Local Choices
71% houses, 1% condos, 4% mobile homes, 16% apartments (rent $335/month)
Houses
Price: $55,000
Property Taxes: $769
Built Before 1940: 6.1%
Energy Requirements
Heating Season: 3,545 degree days
Major Source: Natural gas/Electricity
Air-conditioning: 1,341 hours
Annual Costs
Mortgage and Taxes: $5,979
Utilities: $1,011
Places Rated Score: 6,990
Places Rated Rank: 100

Lynchburg, VA
Local Choices
82% houses, 1% condos, 7% mobile homes, 8% apartments (rent $280/month)
Houses
Price: $52,800
Property Taxes: $760
Built Before 1940: 24.2%
Energy Requirements
Heating Season: 4,233 degree days
Major Source: Oil/Electricity
Air-conditioning: 661 hours
Annual Costs
Mortgage and Taxes: $5,764
Utilities: $1,170
Places Rated Score: 6,934
Places Rated Rank: 97

Macon–Warner Robins, GA
Local Choices
71% houses, 1% condos, 5% mobile homes, 9% apartments (rent $255/month)
Houses
Price: $49,100
Property Taxes: $594
Built Before 1940: 13.3%
Energy Requirements
Heating Season: 2,240 degree days
Major Source: Natural gas/Electricity
Air-conditioning: 1,549 hours
Annual Costs
Mortgage and Taxes: $5,243
Utilities: $992
Places Rated Score: 6,235
Places Rated Rank: 34

Madison, WI
Local Choices
58% houses, 1% condos, 1% mobile homes, 26% apartments (rent $325/month)
Houses
Price: $75,700
Property Taxes: $1,522
Built Before 1940: 23.1%
Energy Requirements
Heating Season: 7,730 degree days
Major Source: Natural gas/Electricity
Air-conditioning: 485 hours

Annual Costs
Mortgage and Taxes: $8,699
Utilities: $1,198
Places Rated Score: 9,897
Places Rated Rank: 273

Manchester, NH
Local Choices
65% houses, 2% condos, 4% mobile homes, 11% apartments (rent $330/month)
Houses
Price: $70,200
Property Taxes: $1,677
Built Before 1940: 40.3%
Energy Requirements
Heating Season: 7,101 degree days
Major Source: Oil/Electricity
Air-conditioning: 506 hours
Annual Costs
Mortgage and Taxes: $8,327
Utilities: $1,533
Places Rated Score: 9,860
Places Rated Rank: 272

Mansfield, OH
Local Choices
77% houses, 4% mobile homes, 8% apartments (rent $260/month)
Houses
Price: $50,300
Property Taxes: $579
Built Before 1940: 30.4%
Energy Requirements
Heating Season: 6,520 degree days
Major Source: Natural gas/Electricity
Air-conditioning: 426 hours
Annual Costs
Mortgage and Taxes: $5,351
Utilities: $1,530
Places Rated Score: 6,881
Places Rated Rank: 91

★ McAllen–Edinburg–Mission, TX
Local Choices
72% houses, 1% condos, 8% mobile homes, 10% apartments (rent $235/month)
Houses
Price: $39,800
Property Taxes: $557
Built Before 1940: 9.0%
Energy Requirements
Heating Season: 696 degree days
Major Source: Natural gas/Electricity
Air-conditioning: 2,295 hours
Annual Costs
Mortgage and Taxes: $4,327
Utilities: $1,018
Places Rated Score: 5,345
Places Rated Rank: 2

Medford, OR
Local Choices
70% houses, 1% condos, 12% mobile homes, 9% apartments (rent $355/month)
Houses
Price: $73,100
Property Taxes: $1,506
Built Before 1940: 13.9%
Energy Requirements
Heating Season: 4,930 degree days
Major Source: Total electric
Air-conditioning: 630 hours

Annual Costs
Mortgage and Taxes: $8,435
Utilities: $573
Places Rated Score: 9,008
Places Rated Rank: 246

Melbourne–Titusville–Palm Bay, FL
Local Choices
69% houses, 8% condos, 10% mobile homes, 12% apartments (rent $355/month)
Houses
Price: $72,200
Property Taxes: $744
Built Before 1940: 3.1%
Energy Requirements
Heating Season: 611 degree days
Major Source: Total electric
Air-conditioning: 2,112 hours
Annual Costs
Mortgage and Taxes: $7,589
Utilities: $1,132
Places Rated Score: 8,721
Places Rated Rank: 240

Memphis, TN–AR–MS
Local Choices
70% houses, 2% condos, 2% mobile homes, 17% apartments (rent $275/month)
Houses
Price: $57,400
Property Taxes: $712
Built Before 1940: 12.6%
Energy Requirements
Heating Season: 3,227 degree days
Major Source: Natural gas/Electricity
Air-conditioning: 1,509 hours
Annual Costs
Mortgage and Taxes: $6,153
Utilities: $862
Places Rated Score: 7,015
Places Rated Rank: 102

Miami–Hialeah, FL
Local Choices
50% houses, 14% condos, 2% mobile homes, 30% apartments (rent $375/month)
Houses
Price: $86,900
Property Taxes: $895
Built Before 1940: 7.3%
Energy Requirements
Heating Season: 206 degree days
Major Source: Total electric
Air-conditioning: 2,388 hours
Annual Costs
Mortgage and Taxes: $9,135
Utilities: $1,132
Places Rated Score: 10,267
Places Rated Rank: 285

Middlesex–Somerset–Hunterdon, NJ
Local Choices
65% houses, 2% condos, 1% mobile homes, 15% apartments (rent $455/month)
Houses
Price: $88,300
Property Taxes: $2,253
Built Before 1940: 24.6%
Energy Requirements
Heating Season: 5,100 degree days
Major Source: Natural gas/Electricity
Air-conditioning: 663 hours

Annual Costs
Mortgage and Taxes: $10,627
Utilities: $1,508
Places Rated Score: 12,135
Places Rated Rank: 306

Middletown, CT
Local Choices
72% houses, 3% condos, 1% mobile homes, 19% apartments (rent $360/month)
Houses
Price: $91,100
Property Taxes: $1,395
Built Before 1940: 31.8%
Energy Requirements
Heating Season: 5,966 degree days
Major Source: Oil/Electricity
Air-conditioning: 476 hours
Annual Costs
Mortgage and Taxes: $10,035
Utilities: $1,617
Places Rated Score: 11,652
Places Rated Rank: 302

Midland, TX
Local Choices
75% houses, 1% condos, 6% mobile homes, 12% apartments (rent $390/month)
Houses
Price: $70,300
Property Taxes: $984
Built Before 1940: 3.8%
Energy Requirements
Heating Season: 2,621 degree days
Major Source: Natural gas/Electricity
Air-conditioning: 1,884 hours
Annual Costs
Mortgage and Taxes: $7,648
Utilities: $1,024
Places Rated Score: 8,672
Places Rated Rank: 238

Milwaukee, WI
Local Choices
59% houses, 2% condos, 17% apartments (rent $320/month)
Houses
Price: $77,200
Property Taxes: $1,552
Built Before 1940: 32.1%
Energy Requirements
Heating Season: 7,444 degree days
Major Source: Natural gas/Electricity
Air-conditioning: 358 hours
Annual Costs
Mortgage and Taxes: $8,873
Utilities: $1,303
Places Rated Score: 10,176
Places Rated Rank: 282

Minneapolis–St. Paul, MN–WI
Local Choices
66% houses, 2% condos, 2% mobile homes, 22% apartments (rent $330/month)
Houses
Price: $80,600
Property Taxes: $621
Built Before 1940: 26.6%
Energy Requirements
Heating Season: 8,310 degree days
Major Source: Natural gas/Electricity
Air-conditioning: 496 hours

Annual Costs
Mortgage and Taxes: $8,265
Utilities: $1,294
Places Rated Score: 9,559
Places Rated Rank: 264

Mobile, AL
Local Choices
77% houses, 1% condos, 6% mobile homes, 9% apartments (rent $270/month)
Houses
Price: $56,800
Property Taxes: $233
Built Before 1940: 11.7%
Energy Requirements
Heating Season: 1,684 degree days
Major Source: Natural gas/Electricity
Air-conditioning: 1,844 hours
Annual Costs
Mortgage and Taxes: $5,615
Utilities: $1,089
Places Rated Score: 6,704
Places Rated Rank: 75

Modesto, CA
Local Choices
77% houses, 1% condos, 5% mobile homes, 10% apartments (rent $340/month)
Houses
Price: $75,200
Property Taxes: $775
Built Before 1940: 13.2%
Energy Requirements
Heating Season: 2,767 degree days
Major Source: Natural gas/Electricity
Air-conditioning: 1,017 hours
Annual Costs
Mortgage and Taxes: $7,907
Utilities: $723
Places Rated Score: 8,630
Places Rated Rank: 235

Monmouth–Ocean, NJ
Local Choices
76% houses, 6% condos, 2% mobile homes, 12% apartments (rent $395/month)
Houses
Price: $88,300
Property Taxes: $2,253
Built Before 1940: 19.2%
Energy Requirements
Heating Season: 5,128 degree days
Major Source: Natural gas/Electricity
Air-conditioning: 592 hours
Annual Costs
Mortgage and Taxes: $10,132
Utilities: $1,528
Places Rated Score: 11,660
Places Rated Rank: 304

Monroe, LA
Local Choices
77% houses, 6% mobile homes, 10% apartments (rent $265/month)
Houses
Price: $54,500
Property Taxes: $82
Built Before 1940: 11.1%
Energy Requirements
Heating Season: 2,311 degree days
Major Source: Natural gas/Electricity
Air-conditioning: 1,846 hours

Annual Costs
Mortgage and Taxes: $5,251
Utilities: $939
Places Rated Score: 6,190
Places Rated Rank: 31

Montgomery, AL
Local Choices
76% houses, 1% condos, 6% mobile homes, 10% apartments (rent $270/month)
Houses
Price: $57,300
Property Taxes: $235
Built Before 1940: 14.1%
Energy Requirements
Heating Season: 2,269 degree days
Major Source: Natural gas/Electricity
Air-conditioning: 1,743 hours
Annual Costs
Mortgage and Taxes: $5,665
Utilities: $1,089
Places Rated Score: 6,754
Places Rated Rank: 81

★ Muncie, IN
Local Choices
78% houses, 4% mobile homes, 8% apartments (rent $265/month)
Houses
Price: $43,700
Property Taxes: $520
Built Before 1940: 31.2%
Energy Requirements
Heating Season: 5,580 degree days
Major Source: Natural gas/Electricity
Air-conditioning: 653 hours
Annual Costs
Mortgage and Taxes: $4,659
Utilities: $1,141
Places Rated Score: 5,800
Places Rated Rank: 16

Muskegon, MI
Local Choices
81% houses, 4% mobile homes, 7% apartments (rent $270/month)
Houses
Price: $41,900
Property Taxes: $1,122
Built Before 1940: 28.4%
Energy Requirements
Heating Season: 6,890 degree days
Major Source: Natural gas/Electricity
Air-conditioning: 247 hours
Annual Costs
Mortgage and Taxes: $5,090
Utilities: $1,301
Places Rated Score: 6,391
Places Rated Rank: 45

Nashua, NH
Local Choices
56% houses, 2% condos, 3% mobile homes, 14% apartments (rent $400/month)
Houses
Price: $77,700
Property Taxes: $1,857
Built Before 1940: 26.4%
Energy Requirements
Heating Season: 7,015 degree days
Major Source: Oil/Electricity
Air-conditioning: 506 hours
Annual Costs
Mortgage and Taxes: $9,224

Utilities: $1,533
Places Rated Score: 10,757
Places Rated Rank: 292

Nashville, TN
Local Choices
69% houses, 2% condos, 4% mobile homes, 15% apartments (rent $310/month)
Houses
Price: $65,700
Property Taxes: $815
Built Before 1940: 14.6%
Energy Requirements
Heating Season: 3,696 degree days
Major Source: Total electric
Air-conditioning: 1,295 hours
Annual Costs
Mortgage and Taxes: $7,046
Utilities: $754
Places Rated Score: 7,800
Places Rated Rank: 161

Nassau–Suffolk, NY
Local Choices
80% houses, 2% condos, 8% apartments (rent $475/month)
Houses
Price: $79,400
Property Taxes: $2,042
Built Before 1940: 19.0%
Energy Requirements
Heating Season: 5,330 degree days
Major Source: Oil/Electricity
Air-conditioning: 648 hours
Annual Costs
Mortgage and Taxes: $9,573
Utilities: $1,565
Places Rated Score: 11,138
Places Rated Rank: 298

New Bedford, MA
Local Choices
51% houses, 1% mobile homes, 11% apartments (rent $260/month)
Houses
Price: $54,800
Property Taxes: $1,332
Built Before 1940: 53.8%
Energy Requirements
Heating Season: 5,395 degree days
Major Source: Natural gas/Electricity
Air-conditioning: 164 hours
Annual Costs
Mortgage and Taxes: $6,528
Utilities: $1,559
Places Rated Score: 8,087
Places Rated Rank: 184

New Britain, CT
Local Choices
52% houses, 1% condos, 2% mobile homes, 18% apartments (rent $305/month)
Houses
Price: $80,000
Property Taxes: $1,236
Built Before 1940: 34.0%
Energy Requirements
Heating Season: 6,140 degree days
Major Source: Oil/Electricity
Air-conditioning: 476 hours
Annual Costs
Mortgage and Taxes: $8,892
Utilities: $1,617
Places Rated Score: 10,509
Places Rated Rank: 289

New Haven–Meriden, CT
Local Choices
57% houses, 3% condos, 2% mobile homes, 18% apartments (rent $355/month)
Houses
Price: $89,400
Property Taxes: $1,367
Built Before 1940: 34.0%
Energy Requirements
Heating Season: 5,793 degree days
Major Source: Oil/Electricity
Air-conditioning: 193 hours
Annual Costs
Mortgage and Taxes: $9,837
Utilities: $1,623
Places Rated Score: 11,460
Places Rated Rank: 299

New London–Norwich, CT–RI
Local Choices
65% houses, 1% condos, 3% mobile homes, 12% apartments (rent $340/month)
Houses
Price: $78,100
Property Taxes: $1,195
Built Before 1940: 34.2%
Energy Requirements
Heating Season: 6,030 degree days
Major Source: Oil/Electricity
Air-conditioning: 292 hours
Annual Costs
Mortgage and Taxes: $8,601
Utilities: $1,617
Places Rated Score: 10,218
Places Rated Rank: 284

New Orleans, LA
Local Choices
62% houses, 1% condos, 3% mobile homes, 15% apartments (rent $315/month)
Houses
Price: $78,700
Property Taxes: $118
Built Before 1940: 21.1%
Energy Requirements
Heating Season: 1,465 degree days
Major Source: Natural gas/Electricity
Air-conditioning: 1,733 hours
Annual Costs
Mortgage and Taxes: $7,576
Utilities: $939
Places Rated Score: 8,515
Places Rated Rank: 225

New York, NY
Local Choices
17% houses, 2% condos, 56% apartments (rent $360/month)
Houses
Price: $95,800
Property Taxes: $2,462
Built Before 1940: 47.8%
Energy Requirements
Heating Season: 4,848 degree days
Major Source: Oil/Electricity
Air-conditioning: 648 hours
Annual Costs
Mortgage and Taxes: $11,544
Utilities: $1,814
Places Rated Score: 13,358
Places Rated Rank: 312

Newark, NJ
Local Choices
 59% houses, 1% condos, 23%
  apartments (rent $365/month)
Houses
 Price: $105,700
 Property Taxes: $2,695
 Built Before 1940: 37.5%
Energy Requirements
 Heating Season: 5,034 degree days
 Major Source: Oil/Electricity
 Air-conditioning: 592 hours
Annual Costs
 Mortgage and Taxes: $12,712
 Utilities: $1,508
Places Rated Score: 14,220
Places Rated Rank: 318

Niagara Falls, NY
Local Choices
 67% houses, 3% mobile homes, 9%
  apartments (rent $280/month)
Houses
 Price: $53,400
 Property Taxes: $1,374
 Built Before 1940: 43.0%
Energy Requirements
 Heating Season: 6,927 degree days
 Major Source: Natural gas/Electricity
 Air-conditioning: 350 hours
Annual Costs
 Mortgage and Taxes: $6,440
 Utilities: $1,246
Places Rated Score: 7,686
Places Rated Rank: 149

**Norfolk–Virginia Beach–
Newport News, VA**
Local Choices
 71% houses, 1% condos, 2% mobile
  homes, 16% apartments (rent
  $340/month)
Houses
 Price: $66,600
 Property Taxes: $959
 Built Before 1940: 12.5%
Energy Requirements
 Heating Season: 3,488 degree days
 Major Source: Natural gas/Electricity
 Air-conditioning: 990 hours
Annual Costs
 Mortgage and Taxes: $7,274
 Utilities: $1,294
Places Rated Score: 8,568
Places Rated Rank: 229

Norwalk, CT
Local Choices
 70% houses, 5% condos, 11%
  apartments (rent $465/month)
Houses
 Price: $168,400
 Property Taxes: $2,576
 Built Before 1940: 29.5%
Energy Requirements
 Heating Season: 5,900 degree days
 Major Source: Oil/Electricity
 Air-conditioning: 345 hours
Annual Costs
 Mortgage and Taxes: $18,534
 Utilities: $1,617
Places Rated Score: 20,151
Places Rated Rank: 328

Oakland, CA
Local Choices
 66% houses, 5% condos, 2% mobile

homes, 20% apartments (rent
  $400/month)
Houses
 Price: $116,200
 Property Taxes: $1,197
 Built Before 1940: 19.7%
Energy Requirements
 Heating Season: 2,909 degree days
 Major Source: Natural gas/Electricity
 Air-conditioning: 360 hours
Annual Costs
 Mortgage and Taxes: $12,214
 Utilities: $921
Places Rated Score: 13,135
Places Rated Rank: 310

Ocala, FL
Local Choices
 68% houses, 2% condos, 20% mobile
  homes, 5% apartments (rent
  $290/month)
Houses
 Price: $52,300
 Property Taxes: $538
 Built Before 1940: 7.1%
Energy Requirements
 Heating Season: 700 degree days
 Major Source: Total electric
 Air-conditioning: 1,824 hours
Annual Costs
 Mortgage and Taxes: $5,493
 Utilities: $1,257
Places Rated Score: 6,750
Places Rated Rank: 80

Odessa, TX
Local Choices
 69% houses, 1% condos, 12% mobile
  homes, 13% apartments (rent
  $345/month)
Houses
 Price: $52,100
 Property Taxes: $729
 Built Before 1940: 3.6%
Energy Requirements
 Heating Season: 2,621 degree days
 Major Source: Natural gas/Electricity
 Air-conditioning: 1,884 hours
Annual Costs
 Mortgage and Taxes: $5,665
 Utilities: $1,024
Places Rated Score: 6,689
Places Rated Rank: 70

Oklahoma City, OK
Local Choices
 76% houses, 1% condos, 3% mobile
  homes, 13% apartments (rent
  $325/month)
Houses
 Price: $61,500
 Property Taxes: $455
 Built Before 1940: 14.1%
Energy Requirements
 Heating Season: 3,457 degree days
 Major Source: Natural gas/Electricity
 Air-conditioning: 1,439 hours
Annual Costs
 Mortgage and Taxes: $6,282
 Utilities: $904
Places Rated Score: 7,186
Places Rated Rank: 117

Olympia, WA
Local Choices
 68% houses, 1% condos, 11% mobile

homes, 12% apartments (rent
  $365/month)
Houses
 Price: $73,300
 Property Taxes: $740
 Built Before 1940: 13.3%
Energy Requirements
 Heating Season: 5,530 degree days
 Major Source: Total electric
 Air-conditioning: 117 hours
Annual Costs
 Mortgage and Taxes: $7,685
 Utilities: $578
Places Rated Score: 8,263
Places Rated Rank: 203

Omaha, NE–IA
Local Choices
 73% houses, 1% condos, 2% mobile
  homes, 19% apartments (rent
  $290/month)
Houses
 Price: $52,100
 Property Taxes: $1,162
 Built Before 1940: 28.8%
Energy Requirements
 Heating Season: 6,049 degree days
 Major Source: Natural gas/Electricity
 Air-conditioning: 901 hours
Annual Costs
 Mortgage and Taxes: $6,101
 Utilities: $1,027
Places Rated Score: 7,128
Places Rated Rank: 113

Orange County, NY
Local Choices
 67% houses, 1% condos, 3% mobile
  homes, 11% apartments (rent
  $355/month)
Houses
 Price: $70,600
 Property Taxes: $1,815
 Built Before 1940: 37.5%
Energy Requirements
 Heating Season: 5,415 degree days
 Major Source: Oil/Electricity
 Air-conditioning: 460 hours
Annual Costs
 Mortgage and Taxes: $8,509
 Utilities: $1,664
Places Rated Score: 10,173
Places Rated Rank: 281

Orlando, FL
Local Choices
 69% houses, 4% condos, 7% mobile
  homes, 15% apartments (rent
  $340/month)
Houses
 Price: $67,600
 Property Taxes: $697
 Built Before 1940: 6.4%
Energy Requirements
 Heating Season: 710 degree days
 Major Source: Total electric
 Air-conditioning: 1,609 hours
Annual Costs
 Mortgage and Taxes: $7,108
 Utilities: $1,088
Places Rated Score: 8,196
Places Rated Rank: 193

Owensboro, KY
Local Choices
 78% houses, 4% mobile homes, 8%
  apartments (rent $260/month)

Houses
Price: $54,900
Property Taxes: $609
Built Before 1940: 19.8%
Energy Requirements
Heating Season: 4,268 degree days
Major Source: Natural gas/Electricity
Air-conditioning: 1,195 hours
Annual Costs
Mortgage and Taxes: $5,813
Utilities: $947
Places Rated Score: 6,760
Places Rated Rank: 82

Oxnard–Ventura, CA
Local Choices
73% houses, 9% condos, 5% mobile homes, 13% apartments (rent $455/month)
Houses
Prices: $122,800
Property Taxes: $1,265
Built Before 1940: 6.2%
Energy Requirements
Heating Season: 2,286 degree days
Major Source: Natural gas/Electricity
Air-conditioning: 124 hours
Annual Costs
Mortgage and Taxes: $12,905
Utilities: $1,095
Places Rated Score: 14,000
Places Rated Rank: 317

Panama City, FL
Local Choices
70% houses, 5% condos, 12% mobile homes, 8% apartments (rent $280/month)
Houses
Price: $50,400
Property Taxes: $519
Built Before 1940: 5.8%
Energy Requirements
Heating Season: 1,388 degree days
Major Source: Total electric
Air-conditioning: 1,884 hours
Annual Costs
Mortgage and Taxes: $5,293
Utilities: $1,080
Places Rated Score: 6,373
Places Rated Rank: 44

Parkersburg–Marietta, WV–OH
Local Choices
82% houses, 7% mobile homes, 6% apartments (rent $265/month)
Houses
Price: $55,300
Property Taxes: $205
Built Before 1940: 49.9%
Energy Requirements
Heating Season: 4,750 degree days
Major Source: Natural gas/Electricity
Air-conditioning: 632 hours
Annual Costs
Mortgage and Taxes: $5,445
Utilities: $1,212
Places Rated Score: 6,657
Places Rated Rank: 67

Pascagoula, MS
Local Choices
78% houses, 1% condos, 7% mobile homes, 7% apartments (rent $305/month)

Houses
Price: $51,100
Property Taxes: $388
Built Before 1940: 6.2%
Energy Requirements
Heating Season: 1,496 degree days
Major Source: Natural gas/Electricity
Air-conditioning: 1,844 hours
Annual Costs
Mortgage and Taxes: $5,232
Utilities: $1,016
Places Rated Score: 6,248
Places Rated Rank: 35

Pawtucket–Woonsocket–Attleboro, RI–MA
Local Choices
59% houses, 2% condos, 15% apartments (rent $305/month)
Houses
Price: $69,300
Property Taxes: $1,338
Built Before 1940: 46.8%
Energy Requirements
Heating Season: 6,199 degree days
Major Source: Oil/Electricity
Air-conditioning: 290 hours
Annual Costs
Mortgage and Taxes: $7,908
Utilities: $1,554
Places Rated Score: 9,462
Places Rated Rank: 261

Pensacola, FL
Local Choices
78% houses, 1% condos, 8% mobile homes, 8% apartments (rent $300/month)
Houses
Price: $51,400
Property Taxes: $529
Built Before 1940: 8.9%
Energy Requirements
Heating Season: 1,578 degree days
Major Source: Total electric
Air-conditioning: 1,884 hours
Annual Costs
Mortgage and Taxes: $5,399
Utilities: $1,080
Places Rated Score: 6,479
Places Rated Rank: 51

Peoria, IL
Local Choices
78% houses, 1% condos, 3% mobile homes, 11% apartments (rent $325/month)
Houses
Price: $62,900
Property Taxes: $1,001
Built Before 1940: 29.1%
Energy Requirements
Heating Season: 6,098 degree days
Major Source: Natural gas/Electricity
Air-conditioning: 617 hours
Annual Costs
Mortgage and Taxes: $6,967
Utilities: $1,421
Places Rated Score: 8,388
Places Rated Rank: 217

Philadelphia, PA–NJ
Local Choices
72% houses, 2% condos, 1% mobile homes, 15% apartments (rent $340/month)

Houses
Price: $61,800
Property Taxes: $1,008
Built Before 1940: 42.8%
Energy Requirements
Heating Season: 4,865 degree days
Major Source: Natural gas/Electricity
Air-conditioning: 702 hours
Annual Costs
Mortgage and Taxes: $6,870
Utilities: $1,440
Places Rated Score: 8,310
Places Rated Rank: 207

Phoenix, AZ
Local Choices
69% houses, 7% condos, 8% mobile homes, 15% apartments (rent $405/month)
Houses
Price: $77,700
Property Taxes: $435
Built Before 1940: 19.1%
Energy Requirements
Heating Season: 1,124 degree days
Major Source: Natural gas/Electricity
Air-conditioning: 2,845 hours
Annual Costs
Mortgage and Taxes: $7,797
Utilities: $1,124
Places Rated Score: 8,921
Places Rated Rank: 244

★ Pine Bluff, AR
Local Choices
79% houses, 6% mobile homes, 7% apartments (rent $245/month)
Houses
Price: $43,500
Property Taxes: $618
Built Before 1940: 15.5%
Energy Requirements
Heating Season: 2,588 degree days
Major Source: Natural gas/Electricity
Air-conditioning: 1,641 hours
Annual Costs
Mortgage and Taxes: $4,745
Utilities: $929
Places Rated Score: 5,674
Places Rated Rank: 8

Pittsburgh, PA
Local Choices
73% houses, 1% condos, 3% mobile homes, 12% apartments (rent $310/month)
Houses
Price: $60,500
Property Taxes: $986
Built Before 1940: 43.4%
Energy Requirements
Heating Season: 5,930 degree days
Major Source: Natural gas/Electricity
Air-conditioning: 471 hours
Annual Costs
Mortgage and Taxes: $6,724
Utilities: $1,375
Places Rated Score: 8,099
Places Rated Rank: 186

Pittsfield, MA
Local Choices
69% houses, 1% condos, 2% mobile homes, 12% apartments (rent $290/month)
Houses
Price: $52,600

Property Taxes: $1,279
Built Before 1940: 54.1%
Energy Requirements
Heating Season: 7,406 degree days
Major Source: Oil/Electricity
Air-conditioning: 199 hours
Annual Costs
Mortgage and Taxes: $6,267
Utilities: $1,540
Places Rated Score: 7,807
Places Rated Rank: 162

Portland, ME
Local Choices
57% houses, 1% condos, 3% mobile homes, 16% apartments (rent $320/month)
Houses
Price: $64,000
Property Taxes: $973
Built Before 1940: 47.0%
Energy Requirements
Heating Season: 7,496 degree days
Major Source: Oil/Electricity
Air-conditioning: 236 hours
Annual Costs
Mortgage and Taxes: $7,043
Utilities: $1,057
Places Rated Score: 8,100
Places Rated Rank: 187

Portland, OR
Local Choices
70% houses, 2% condos, 3% mobile homes, 18% apartments (rent $380/month)
Houses
Price: $80,800
Property Taxes: $1,664
Built Before 1940: 24.5%
Energy Requirements
Heating Season: 4,792 degree days
Major Source: Total electric
Air-conditioning: 208 hours
Annual Costs
Mortgage and Taxes: $9,321
Utilities: $591
Places Rated Score: 9,912
Places Rated Rank: 275

Portsmouth–Dover–Rochester, NH–ME
Local Choices
52% houses, 5% mobile homes, 12% apartments (rent $330/month)
Houses
Price: $71,100
Property Taxes: $1,698
Built Before 1940: 38.0%
Energy Requirements
Heating Season: 7,089 degree days
Major Source: Oil/Electricity
Air-conditioning: 220 hours
Annual Costs
Mortgage and Taxes: $8,433
Utilities: $1,533
Places Rated Score: 9,966
Places Rated Rank: 277

Poughkeepsie, NY
Local Choices
65% houses, 1% condos, 4% mobile homes, 15% apartments (rent $360/month)
Houses
Price: $69,000
Property Taxes: $1,774
Built Before 1940: 30.6%

Energy Requirements
Heating Season: 5,824 degree days
Major Source: Oil/Electricity
Air-conditioning: 623 hours
Annual Costs
Mortgage and Taxes: $8,317
Utilities: $1,664
Places Rated Score: 9,981
Places Rated Rank: 278

Providence, RI
Local Choices
56% houses, 1% condos, 15% apartments (rent $295/month)
Houses
Price: $68,000
Property Taxes: $1,313
Built Before 1940: 49.5%
Energy Requirements
Heating Season: 5,927 degree days
Major Source: Oil/Electricity
Air-conditioning: 316 hours
Annual Costs
Mortgage and Taxes: $7,759
Utilities: $1,515
Places Rated Score: 9,274
Places Rated Rank: 253

Provo–Orem, UT
Local Choices
68% houses, 2% condos, 4% mobile homes, 12% apartments (rent $310/month)
Houses
Price: $80,300
Property Taxes: $739
Built Before 1940: 15.2%
Energy Requirements
Heating Season: 5,463 degree days
Major Source: Natural gas/Electricity
Air-conditioning: 877 hours
Annual Costs
Mortgage and Taxes: $8,351
Utilities: $970
Places Rated Score: 9,321
Places Rated Rank: 257

Pueblo, CO
Local Choices
77% houses, 1% condos, 5% mobile homes, 10% apartments (rent $275/month)
Houses
Price: $51,800
Property Taxes: $523
Built Before 1940: 26.5%
Energy Requirements
Heating Season: 5,394 degree days
Major Source: Natural gas/Electricity
Air-conditioning: 954 hours
Annual Costs
Mortgage and Taxes: $5,436
Utilities: $1,201
Places Rated Score: 6,637
Places Rated Rank: 66

Racine, WI
Local Choices
72% houses, 1% condos, 1% mobile homes, 11% apartments (rent $310/month)
Houses
Price: $66,500
Property Taxes: $1,337
Built Before 1940: 33.9%
Energy Requirements
Heating Season: 6,787 degree days

Major Source: Natural gas/Electricity
Air-conditioning: 358 hours
Annual Costs
Mortgage and Taxes: $7,640
Utilities: $1,303
Places Rated Score: 8,943
Places Rated Rank: 245

Raleigh–Durham, NC
Local Choices
67% houses, 1% condos, 6% mobile homes, 16% apartments (rent $320/month)
Houses
Price: $68,700
Property Taxes: $667
Built Before 1940: 13.1%
Energy Requirements
Heating Season: 3,514 degree days
Major Source: Total electric
Air-conditioning: 1,031 hours
Annual Costs
Mortgage and Taxes: $7,181
Utilities: $1,049
Places Rated Score: 8,230
Places Rated Rank: 198

Reading, PA
Local Choices
75% houses, 1% condos, 3% mobile homes, 10% apartments (rent $300/month)
Houses
Price: $55,500
Property Taxes: $905
Built Before 1940: 49.3%
Energy Requirements
Heating Season: 4,931 degree days
Major Source: Oil/Electricity
Air-conditioning: 788 hours
Annual Costs
Mortgage and Taxes: $6,168
Utilities: $1,446
Places Rated Score: 7,614
Places Rated Rank: 144

Redding, CA
Local Choices
64% houses, 18% mobile homes, 10% apartments (rent $335/month)
Houses
Price: $75,800
Property Taxes: $780
Built Before 1940: 7.4%
Energy Requirements
Heating Season: 2,610 degree days
Major Source: Natural gas/Electricity
Air-conditioning: 1,515 hours
Annual Costs
Mortgage and Taxes: $7,961
Utilities: $623
Places Rated Score: 8,584
Places Rated Rank: 231

Reno, NV
Local Choices
57% houses, 10% condos, 10% mobile homes, 23% apartments (rent $490/month)
Houses
Price: $108,400
Property Taxes: $835
Built Before 1940: 7.7%
Energy Requirements
Heating Season: 6,022 degree days
Major Source: Natural gas/Electricity
Air-conditioning: 647 hours

Annual Costs
  Mortgage and Taxes: $11,113
  Utilities: $1,336
Places Rated Score: 12,449
Places Rated Rank: 308

Richland–Kennewick–Pasco, WA
Local Choices
  66% houses, 2% condos, 11% mobile homes, 14% apartments (rent $410/month)
Houses
  Price: $74,000
  Property Taxes: $747
  Built Before 1940: 5.5%
Energy Requirements
  Heating Season: 4,892 degree days
  Major Source: Total electric
  Air-conditioning: 689 hours
Annual Costs
  Mortgage and Taxes: $7,760
  Utilities: $701
Places Rated Score: 8,461
Places Rated Rank: 222

Richmond–Petersburg, VA
Local Choices
  73% houses, 2% condos, 2% mobile homes, 15% apartments (rent $335/month)
Houses
  Price: $64,600
  Property Taxes: $930
  Built Before 1940: 17.9%
Energy Requirements
  Heating Season: 3,939 degree days
  Major Source: Oil/Electricity
  Air-conditioning: 1,006 hours
Annual Costs
  Mortgage and Taxes: $7,049
  Utilities: $1,294
Places Rated Score: 8,343
Places Rated Rank: 213

Riverside–San Bernardino, CA
Local Choices
  72% houses, 5% condos, 10% mobile homes, 10% apartments (rent $380/month)
Houses
  Price: $83,000
  Property Taxes: $855
  Built Before 1940: 7.6%
Energy Requirements
  Heating Season: 1,919 degree days
  Major Source: Natural gas/Electricity
  Air-conditioning: 1,209 hours
Annual Costs
  Mortgage and Taxes: $8,721
  Utilities: $1,033
Places Rated Score: 9,754
Places Rated Rank: 268

Roanoke, VA
Local Choices
  73% houses, 1% condos, 2% mobile homes, 15% apartments (rent $280/month)
Houses
  Price: $57,700
  Property Taxes: $832
  Built Before 1940: 21.8%
Energy Requirements
  Heating Season: 4,307 degree days
  Major Source: Natural gas/Electricity
  Air-conditioning: 799 hours

Annual Costs
  Mortgage and Taxes: $6,306
  Utilities: $1,170
Places Rated Score: 7,476
Places Rated Rank: 137

Rochester, MN
Local Choices
  67% houses, 3% condos, 5% mobile homes, 15% apartments (rent $315/month)
Houses
  Price: $77,600
  Property Taxes: $597
  Built Before 1940: 22.9%
Energy Requirements
  Heating Season: 8,227 degree days
  Major Source: Natural gas/Electricity
  Air-conditioning: 336 hours
Annual Costs
  Mortgage and Taxes: $7,952
  Utilities: $1,241
Places Rated Score: 9,193
Places Rated Rank: 252

Rochester, NY
Local Choices
  67% houses, 1% condos, 3% mobile homes, 14% apartments (rent $330/month)
Houses
  Price: $59,700
  Property Taxes: $1,534
  Built Before 1940: 39.9%
Energy Requirements
  Heating Season: 6,718 degree days
  Major Source: Natural gas/Electricity
  Air-conditioning: 419 hours
Annual Costs
  Mortgage and Taxes: $7,194
  Utilities: $1,415
Places Rated Score: 8,609
Places Rated Rank: 233

Rockford, IL
Local Choices
  73% houses, 1% condos, 2% mobile homes, 10% apartments (rent $305/month)
Houses
  Price: $58,900
  Property Taxes: $936
  Built Before 1940: 26.2%
Energy Requirements
  Heating Season: 6,845 degree days
  Major Source: Natural gas/Electricity
  Air-conditioning: 583 hours
Annual Costs
  Mortgage and Taxes: $6,215
  Utilities: $1,369
Places Rated Score: 7,584
Places Rated Rank: 142

Sacramento, CA
Local Choices
  61% houses, 3% condos, 4% mobile homes, 14% apartments (rent $350/month)
Houses
  Price: $87,200
  Property Taxes: $898
  Built Before 1940: 9.7%
Energy Requirements
  Heating Season: 2,843 degree days
  Major Source: Natural gas/Electricity
  Air-conditioning: 1,006 hours

Annual Costs
  Mortgage and Taxes: $9,166
  Utilities: $689
Places Rated Score: 9,855
Places Rated Rank: 271

Saginaw–Bay City–Midland, MI
Local Choices
  79% houses, 1% condos, 5% mobile homes, 8% apartments (rent $305/month)
Houses
  Price: $49,900
  Property Taxes: $1,337
  Built Before 1940: 27.8%
Energy Requirements
  Heating Season: 7,143 degree days
  Major Source: Natural gas/Electricity
  Air-conditioning: 392 hours
Annual Costs
  Mortgage and Taxes: $6,067
  Utilities: $1,301
Places Rated Score: 7,368
Places Rated Rank: 131

St. Cloud, MN
Local Choices
  75% houses, 5% mobile homes, 11% apartments (rent $290/month)
Houses
  Price: $58,000
  Property Taxes: $446
  Built Before 1940: 29.0%
Energy Requirements
  Heating Season: 8,868 degree days
  Major Source: Oil/Electricity
  Air-conditioning: 496 hours
Annual Costs
  Mortgage and Taxes: $5,941
  Utilities: $1,294
Places Rated Score: 7,235
Places Rated Rank: 121

★ St. Joseph, MO
Local Choices
  76% houses, 4% mobile homes, 8% apartments (rent $240/month)
Houses
  Price: $40,900
  Property Taxes: $478
  Built Before 1940: 50.0%
Energy Requirements
  Heating Season: 5,440 degree days
  Major Source: Natural gas/Electricity
  Air-conditioning: 1,125 hours
Annual Costs
  Mortgage and Taxes: $4,352
  Utilities: $1,237
Places Rated Score: 5,589
Places Rated Rank: 7

St. Louis, MO–IL
Local Choices
  68% houses, 2% condos, 2% mobile homes, 13% apartments (rent $300/month)
Houses
  Price: $60,500
  Property Taxes: $708
  Built Before 1940: 26.8%
Energy Requirements
  Heating Season: 4,486 degree days
  Major Source: Natural gas/Electricity
  Air-conditioning: 1,131 hours

Annual Costs
Mortgage and Taxes: $6,447
Utilities: $1,158
Places Rated Score: 7,605
Places Rated Rank: 143

Salem, OR
Local Choices
74% houses, 1% condos, 7% mobile homes, 12% apartments (rent $345/month)
Houses
Price: $67,300
Property Taxes: $1,387
Built Before 1940: 15.3%
Energy Requirements
Heating Season: 4,852 degree days
Major Source: Total electric
Air-conditioning: 296 hours
Annual Costs
Mortgage and Taxes: $7,771
Utilities: $607
Places Rated Score: 8,378
Places Rated Rank: 216

Salem–Gloucester, MA
Local Choices
58% houses, 3% condos, 1% mobile homes, 15% apartments (rent $330/month)
Houses
Price: $85,000
Property Taxes: $2,066
Built Before 1940: 52.4%
Energy Requirements
Heating Season: 6,321 degree days
Major Source: Oil/Electricity
Air-conditioning: 152 hours
Annual Costs
Mortgage and Taxes: $10,124
Utilities: $1,498
Places Rated Score: 11,622
Places Rated Rank: 301

Salinas–Seaside–Monterey, CA
Local Choices
66% houses, 4% condos, 4% mobile homes, 18% apartments (rent $415/month)
Houses
Price: $122,900
Property Taxes: $1,266
Built Before 1940: 13.6%
Energy Requirements
Heating Season: 2,959 degree days
Major Source: Natural gas/Electricity
Air-conditioning: 14 hours
Annual Costs
Mortgage and Taxes: $12,917
Utilities: $921
Places Rated Score: 13,838
Places Rated Rank: 315

Salt Lake City–Ogden, UT
Local Choices
72% houses, 4% condos, 3% mobile homes, 12% apartments (rent $345/month)
Houses
Price: $78,500
Property Taxes: $722
Built Before 1940: 16.6%
Energy Requirements
Heating Season: 5,983 degree days
Major Source: Natural gas/Electricity
Air-conditioning: 877 hours

Annual Costs
Mortgage and Taxes: $8,159
Utilities: $1,307
Places Rated Score: 9,466
Places Rated Rank: 262

San Angelo, TX
Local Choices
75% houses, 1% condos, 4% mobile homes, 16% apartments (rent $300/month)
Houses
Price: $48,700
Property Taxes: $682
Built Before 1940: 14.6%
Energy Requirements
Heating Season: 2,240 degree days
Major Source: Natural gas/Electricity
Air-conditioning: 2,082 hours
Annual Costs
Mortgage and Taxes: $5,297
Utilities: $1,024
Places Rated Score: 6,321
Places Rated Rank: 40

San Antonio, TX
Local Choices
74% houses, 1% condos, 3% mobile homes, 15% apartments (rent $290/month)
Houses
Price: $53,800
Property Taxes: $753
Built Before 1940: 13.0%
Energy Requirements
Heating Season: 1,570 degree days
Major Source: Natural gas/Electricity
Air-conditioning: 2,004 hours
Annual Costs
Mortgage and Taxes: $5,850
Utilities: $1,048
Places Rated Score: 6,898
Places Rated Rank: 93

San Diego, CA
Local Choices
62% houses, 9% condos, 5% mobile homes, 22% apartments (rent $410/month)
Houses
Price: $123,503
Property Taxes: $1,272
Built Before 1940: 8.9%
Energy Requirements
Heating Season: 1,507 degree days
Major Source: Natural gas/Electricity
Air-conditioning: 130 hours
Annual Costs
Mortgage and Taxes: $12,979
Utilities: $1,486
Places Rated Score: 14,465
Places Rated Rank: 321

San Francisco, CA
Local Choices
51% houses, 4% condos, 1% mobile homes, 23% apartments (rent $445/month)
Houses
Price: $154,500
Property Taxes: $1,591
Built Before 1940: 34.7%
Energy Requirements
Heating Season: 3,042 degree days
Major Source: Natural gas/Electricity
Air-conditioning: 42 hours

Annual Costs
Mortgage and Taxes: $16,237
Utilities: $921
Places Rated Score: 17,158
Places Rated Rank: 327

San Jose, CA
Local Choices
66% houses, 6% condos, 4% mobile homes, 20% apartments (rent $480/month)
Houses
Price: $143,900
Property Taxes: $1,483
Built Before 1940: 7.4%
Energy Requirements
Heating Season: 3,184 degree days
Major Source: Natural gas/Electricity
Air-conditioning: 157 hours
Annual Costs
Mortgage and Taxes: $15,127
Utilities: $921
Places Rated Score: 16,048
Places Rated Rank: 325

Santa Barbara–Santa Maria–Lompoc, CA
Local Choices
61% houses, 5% condos, 5% mobile homes, 22% apartments (rent $440/month)
Houses
Price: $138,100
Property Taxes: $1,423
Built Before 1940: 13.8%
Energy Requirements
Heating Season: 1,980 degree days
Major Source: Natural gas/Electricity
Air-conditioning: 44 hours
Annual Costs
Mortgage and Taxes: $14,514
Utilities: $1,033
Places Rated Score: 15,547
Places Rated Rank: 323

Santa Cruz, CA
Local Choices
69% houses, 4% condos, 7% mobile homes, 13% apartments (rent $430/month)
Houses
Price: $127,300
Property Taxes: $1,312
Built Before 1940: 18.2%
Energy Requirements
Heating Season: 3,139 degree days
Major Source: Natural gas/Electricity
Air-conditioning: 14 hours
Annual Costs
Mortgage and Taxes: $13,382
Utilities: $921
Places Rated Score: 14,303
Places Rated Rank: 319

Santa Rosa–Petaluma, CA
Local Choices
74% houses, 3% condos, 7% mobile homes, 10% apartments (rent $410/month)
Houses
Price: $114,300
Property Taxes: $1,177
Built Before 1940: 14.8%
Energy Requirements
Heating Season: 3,065 degree days
Major Source: Natural gas/Electricity
Air-conditioning: 770 hours

Annual Costs
Mortgage and Taxes: $12,010
Utilities: $921
Places Rated Score: 12,931
Places Rated Rank: 309

Sarasota, FL
Local Choices
62% houses, 20% condos, 10% mobile
homes, 8% apartments (rent
$390/month)
Houses
Price: $80,700
Property Taxes: $831
Built Before 1940: 4.0%
Energy Requirements
Heating Season: 597 degree days
Major Source: Total electric
Air-conditioning: 2,154 hours
Annual Costs
Mortgage and Taxes: $8,480
Utilities: $1,080
Places Rated Score: 9,560
Places Rated Rank: 265

Savannah, GA
Local Choices
71% houses, 1% condos, 6% mobile
homes, 10% apartments (rent
$280/month)
Houses
Price: $53,100
Property Taxes: $642
Built Before 1940: 17.6%
Energy Requirements
Heating Season: 1,952 degree days
Major Source: Natural gas/Electricity
Air-conditioning: 1,515 hours
Annual Costs
Mortgage and Taxes: $5,675
Utilities: $1,221
Places Rated Score: 6,896
Places Rated Rank: 92

Scranton–Wilkes-Barre, PA
Local Choices
69% houses, 4% mobile homes, 7%
apartments (rent $260/month)
Houses
Price: $48,500
Property Taxes: $791
Built Before 1940: 56.6%
Energy Requirements
Heating Season: 6,114 degree days
Major Source: Oil/Electricity
Air-conditioning: 425 hours
Annual Costs
Mortgage and Taxes: $5,390
Utilities: $1,307
Places Rated Score: 6,697
Places Rated Rank: 73

Seattle, WA
Local Choices
68% houses, 4% condos, 3% mobile
homes, 19% apartments (rent
$400/month)
Houses
Price: $92,800
Property Taxes: $937
Built Before 1940: 20.5%
Energy Requirements
Heating Season: 4,487 degree days
Major Source: Total electric
Air-conditioning: 91 hours
Annual Costs
Mortgage and Taxes: $9,735

Utilities: $448
Places Rated Score: 10,183
Places Rated Rank: 283

Sharon, PA
Local Choices
78% houses, 7% mobile homes, 6%
apartments (rent $290/month)
Houses
Price: $47,900
Property Taxes: $782
Built Before 1940: 43.0%
Energy Requirements
Heating Season: 6,350 degree days
Major Source: Natural gas/Electricity
Air-conditioning: 371 hours
Annual Costs
Mortgage and Taxes: $5,327
Utilities: $1,370
Places Rated Score: 6,697
Places Rated Rank: 73

Sheboygan, WI
Local Choices
71% houses, 2% mobile homes, 6%
apartments (rent $270/month)
Houses
Price: $59,800
Property Taxes: $1,201
Built Before 1940: 47.8%
Energy Requirements
Heating Season: 7,240 degree days
Major Source: Natural gas/Electricity
Air-conditioning: 309 hours
Annual Costs
Mortgage and Taxes: $6,867
Utilities: $1,254
Places Rated Score: 8,121
Places Rated Rank: 188

★ Sherman–Denison, TX
Local Choices
81% houses, 5% mobile homes, 6%
apartments (rent $275/month)
Houses
Price: $43,600
Property Taxes: $610
Built Before 1940: 23.8%
Energy Requirements
Heating Season: 2,864 degree days
Major Source: Natural gas/Electricity
Air-conditioning: 2,304 hours
Annual Costs
Mortgage and Taxes: $4,743
Utilities: $979
Places Rated Score: 5,722
Places Rated Rank: 13

Shreveport, LA
Local Choices
77% houses, 1% condos, 5% mobile
homes, 10% apartments (rent
$270/month)
Houses
Price: $58,800
Property Taxes: $88
Built Before 1940: 14.2%
Energy Requirements
Heating Season: 2,167 degree days
Major Source: Natural gas/Electricity
Air-conditioning: 1,846 hours
Annual Costs
Mortgage and Taxes: $5,659
Utilities: $875
Places Rated Score: 6,534
Places Rated Rank: 57

Sioux City, IA–NE
Local Choices
76% houses, 5% mobile homes, 10%
apartments (rent $285/month)
Houses
Price: $47,000
Property Taxes: $771
Built Before 1940: 46.5%
Energy Requirements
Heating Season: 6,953 degree days
Major Source: Natural gas/Electricity
Air-conditioning: 796 hours
Annual Costs
Mortgage and Taxes: $5,227
Utilities: $1,301
Places Rated Score: 6,528
Places Rated Rank: 56

Sioux Falls, SD
Local Choices
68% houses, 1% condos, 5% mobile
homes, 17% apartments (rent
$275/month)
Houses
Price: $60,900
Property Taxes: $1,077
Built Before 1940: 25.6%
Energy Requirements
Heating Season: 7,838 degree days
Major Source: Natural gas/Electricity
Air-conditioning: 498 hours
Annual Costs
Mortgage and Taxes: $6,847
Utilities: $1,136
Places Rated Score: 7,983
Places Rated Rank: 175

★ South Bend–Mishawaka, IN
Local Choices
81% houses, 1% condos, 2% mobile
homes, 6% apartments (rent
$285/month)
Houses
Price: $45,000
Property Taxes: $535
Built Before 1940: 33.0%
Energy Requirements
Heating Season: 6,462 degree days
Major Source: Natural gas/Electricity
Air-conditioning: 563 hours
Annual Costs
Mortgage and Taxes: $4,797
Utilities: $1,141
Places Rated Score: 5,938
Places Rated Rank: 20

Spokane, WA
Local Choices
73% houses, 1% condos, 5% mobile
homes, 14% apartments (rent
$315/month)
Houses
Price: $61,300
Property Taxes: $619
Built Before 1940: 26.5%
Energy Requirements
Heating Season: 6,835 degree days
Major Source: Total electric
Air-conditioning: 373 hours
Annual Costs
Mortgage and Taxes: $6,425
Utilities: $502
Places Rated Score: 6,927
Places Rated Rank: 95

Springfield, IL
Local Choices
73% houses, 1% condos, 5% mobile homes, 10% apartments (rent $300/month)
Houses
Price: $60,400
Property Taxes: $960
Built Before 1940: 32.9%
Energy Requirements
Heating Season: 5,558 degree days
Major Source: Natural gas/Electricity
Air-conditioning: 867 hours
Annual Costs
Mortgage and Taxes: $6,684
Utilities: $1,198
Places Rated Score: 7,882
Places Rated Rank: 167

Springfield, MA
Local Choices
59% houses, 1% condos, 1% mobile homes, 19% apartments (rent $295/month)
Houses
Price: $54,600
Property Taxes: $1,326
Built Before 1940: 41.1%
Energy Requirements
Heating Season: 5,844 degree days
Major Source: Oil/Electricity
Air-conditioning: 436 hours
Annual Costs
Mortgage and Taxes: $6,499
Utilities: $1,540
Places Rated Score: 8,039
Places Rated Rank: 179

Springfield, MO
Local Choices
78% houses, 5% mobile homes, 10% apartments (rent $260/month)
Houses
Price: $48,400
Property Taxes: $566
Built Before 1940: 21.5%
Energy Requirements
Heating Season: 4,570 degree days
Major Source: Natural gas/Electricity
Air-conditioning: 964 hours
Annual Costs
Mortgage and Taxes: $5,151
Utilities: $1,192
Places Rated Score: 6,343
Places Rated Rank: 43

Stamford, CT
Local Choices
61% houses, 5% condos, 17% apartments (rent $480/month)
Houses
Price: $200,000
Property Taxes: $3,061
Built Before 1940: 31.7%
Energy Requirements
Heating Season: 5,250 degree days
Major Source: Oil/Electricity
Air-conditioning: 345 hours
Annual Costs
Mortgage and Taxes: $22,023
Utilities: $1,617
Places Rated Score: 23,640
Places Rated Rank: 329

State College, PA
Local Choices
60% houses, 1% condos, 7% mobile

---

homes, 23% apartments (rent $350/month)
Houses
Price: $64,900
Property Taxes: $1,057
Built Before 1940: 29.5%
Energy Requirements
Heating Season: 6,132 degree days
Major Source: Oil/Electricity
Air-conditioning: 351 hours
Annual Costs
Mortgage and Taxes: $7,205
Utilities: $1,200
Places Rated Score: 8,405
Places Rated Rank: 221

Steubenville–Weirton, OH–WV
Local Choices
79% houses, 6% mobile homes, 6% apartments (rent $260/month)
Houses
Price: $49,400
Property Taxes: $568
Built Before 1940: 39.2%
Energy Requirements
Heating Season: 5,515 degree days
Major Source: Natural gas/Electricity
Air-conditioning: 471 hours
Annual Costs
Mortgage and Taxes: $5,250
Utilities: $1,328
Places Rated Score: 6,578
Places Rated Rank: 61

Stockton, CA
Local Choices
73% houses, 2% condos, 4% mobile homes, 14% apartments (rent $320/month)
Houses
Price: $71,900
Property Taxes: $740
Built Before 1940: 16.5%
Energy Requirements
Heating Season: 2,806 degree days
Major Source: Natural gas/Electricity
Air-conditioning: 1,017 hours
Annual Costs
Mortgage and Taxes: $7,553
Utilities: $921
Places Rated Score: 8,474
Places Rated Rank: 223

Syracuse, NY
Local Choices
64% houses, 1% condos, 4% mobile homes, 16% apartments (rent $310/month)
Houses
Price: $53,300
Property Taxes: $1,370
Built Before 1940: 40.6%
Energy Requirements
Heating Season: 6,678 degree days
Major Source: Natural gas/Electricity
Air-conditioning: 433 hours
Annual Costs
Mortgage and Taxes: $6,424
Utilities: $1,246
Places Rated Score: 7,670
Places Rated Rank: 148

Tacoma, WA
Local Choices
70% houses, 1% condos, 5% mobile homes, 16% apartments (rent $340/month)

Houses
Price: $70,900
Property Taxes: $716
Built Before 1940: 20.7%
Energy Requirements
Heating Season: 4,835 degree days
Major Source: Total electric
Air-conditioning: 122 hours
Annual Costs
Mortgage and Taxes: $7,432
Utilities: $338
Places Rated Score: 7,770
Places Rated Rank: 155

Tallahassee, FL
Local Choices
61% houses, 1% condos, 10% mobile homes, 18% apartments (rent $320/month)
Houses
Price: $64,700
Property Taxes: $667
Built Before 1940: 7.5%
Energy Requirements
Heating Season: 1,563 degree days
Major Source: Total electric
Air-conditioning: 1,538 hours
Annual Costs
Mortgage and Taxes: $6,802
Utilities: $1,227
Places Rated Score: 8,029
Places Rated Rank: 178

Tampa–St. Petersburg–Clearwater, FL
Local Choices
65% houses, 8% condos, 10% mobile homes, 13% apartments (rent $330/month)
Houses
Price: $59,500
Property Taxes: $613
Built Before 1940: 7.0%
Energy Requirements
Heating Season: 717 degree days
Major Source: Total electric
Air-conditioning: 2,154 hours
Annual Costs
Mortgage and Taxes: $6,254
Utilities: $1,188
Places Rated Score: 7,442
Places Rated Rank: 135

★ Terre Haute, IN
Local Choices
79% houses, 6% mobile homes, 6% apartments (rent $255/month)
Houses
Price: $40,200
Property Taxes: $479
Built Before 1940: 47.2%
Energy Requirements
Heating Season: 5,351 degree days
Major Source: Natural gas/Electricity
Air-conditioning: 834 hours
Annual Costs
Mortgage and Taxes: $4,293
Utilities: $1,234
Places Rated Score: 5,527
Places Rated Rank: 5

★ Texarkana, TX–Texarkana, AR
Local Choices
78% houses, 1% condos, 6% mobile homes, 7% apartments (rent $250/month)

Houses
Price: $44,100
Property Taxes: $617
Built Before 1940: 15.4%
Energy Requirements
Heating Season: 2,362 degree days
Major Source: Natural gas/Electricity
Air-conditioning: 1,730 hours
Annual Costs
Mortgage and Taxes: $4,795
Utilities: $922
Places Rated Score: 5,717
Places Rated Rank: 12

Toledo, OH
Local Choices
73% houses, 1% condos, 4% mobile
homes, 12% apartments (rent
$300/month)
Houses
Price: $58,700
Property Taxes: $675
Built Before 1940: 36.2%
Energy Requirements
Heating Season: 6,381 degree days
Major Source: Natural gas/Electricity
Air-conditioning: 540 hours
Annual Costs
Mortgage and Taxes: $6,241
Utilities: $1,526
Places Rated Score: 7,767
Places Rated Rank: 153

Topeka, KS
Local Choices
74% houses, 2% condos, 4% mobile
homes, 13% apartments (rent
$280/month)
Houses
Price: $57,500
Property Taxes: $558
Built Before 1940: 25.6%
Energy Requirements
Heating Season: 5,243 degree days
Major Source: Natural gas/Electricity
Air-conditioning: 1,154 hours
Annual Costs
Mortgage and Taxes: $6,007
Utilities: $1,103
Places Rated Score: 7,110
Places Rated Rank: 111

Trenton, NJ
Local Choices
69% houses, 1% condos, 18%
apartments (rent $365/month)
Houses
Price: $75,700
Property Taxes: $1,931
Built Before 1940: 36.3%
Energy Requirements
Heating Season: 4,947 degree days
Major Source: Oil/Electricity
Air-conditioning: 448 hours
Annual Costs
Mortgage and Taxes: $9,108
Utilities: $1,508
Places Rated Score: 10,616
Places Rated Rank: 291

Tucson, AZ
Local Choices
66% houses, 5% condos, 11% mobile
homes, 15% apartments (rent
$350/month)

Houses
Price: $75,200
Property Taxes: $421
Built Before 1940: 18.6%
Energy Requirements
Heating Season: 1,002 degree days
Major Source: Natural gas/Electricity
Air-conditioning: 2,445 hours
Annual Costs
Mortgage and Taxes: $7,546
Utilities: $1,002
Places Rated Score: 8,548
Places Rated Rank: 228

Tulsa, OK
Local Choices
75% houses, 1% condos, 5% mobile
homes, 12% apartments (rent
$320/month)
Houses
Price: $64,600
Property Taxes: $478
Built Before 1940: 15.9%
Energy Requirements
Heating Season: 3,680 degree days
Major Source: Natural gas/Electricity
Air-conditioning: 1,420 hours
Annual Costs
Mortgage and Taxes: $6,603
Utilities: $895
Places Rated Score: 7,498
Places Rated Rank: 139

Tuscaloosa, AL
Local Choices
68% houses, 1% condos, 7% mobile
homes, 15% apartments (rent
$265/month)
Houses
Price: $54,400
Property Taxes: $223
Built Before 1940: 12.0%
Energy Requirements
Heating Season: 2,626 degree days
Major Source: Natural gas/Electricity
Air-conditioning: 1,533 hours
Annual Costs
Mortgage and Taxes: $5,375
Utilities: $1,089
Places Rated Score: 6,464
Places Rated Rank: 50

Tyler, TX
Local Choices
79% houses, 6% mobile homes, 9%
apartments (rent $320/month)
Houses
Price: $58,100
Property Taxes: $813
Built Before 1940: 13.7%
Energy Requirements
Heating Season: 1,923 degree days
Major Source: Natural gas/Electricity
Air-conditioning: 1,855 hours
Annual Costs
Mortgage and Taxes: $6,319
Utilities: $979
Places Rated Score: 7,298
Places Rated Rank: 127

Utica–Rome, NY
Local Choices
60% houses, 5% mobile homes, 9%
apartments (rent $265/month)
Houses
Price: $45,600

Property Taxes: $1,173
Built Before 1940: 51.0%
Energy Requirements
Heating Season: 6,520 degree days
Major Source: Natural gas/Electricity
Air-conditioning: 301 hours
Annual Costs
Mortgage and Taxes: $5,498
Utilities: $1,246
Places Rated Score: 6,744
Places Rated Rank: 79

Vallejo–Fairfield–Napa, CA
Local Choices
74% houses, 3% condos, 5% mobile
homes, 11% apartments (rent
$370/month)
Houses
Price: $91,200
Property Taxes: $939
Built Before 1940: 12.2%
Energy Requirements
Heating Season: 3,065 degree days
Major Source: Natural gas/Electricity
Air-conditioning: 588 hours
Annual Costs
Mortgage and Taxes: $9,582
Utilities: $921
Places Rated Score: 10,503
Places Rated Rank: 288

Vancouver, WA
Local Choices
69% houses, 1% condos, 5% mobile
homes, 9% apartments (rent
$390/month)
Houses
Price: $81,700
Property Taxes: $825
Built Before 1940: 12.5%
Energy Requirements
Heating Season: 4,667 degree days
Major Source: Total electric
Air-conditioning: 208 hours
Annual Costs
Mortgage and Taxes: $8,569
Utilities: $446
Places Rated Score: 9,015
Places Rated Rank: 247

Victoria, TX
Local Choices
74% houses, 6% mobile homes, 11%
apartments (rent $330/month)
Houses
Price: $56,300
Property Taxes: $788
Built Before 1940: 10.5%
Energy Requirements
Heating Season: 1,227 degree days
Major Source: Natural gas/Electricity
Air-conditioning: 1,861 hours
Annual Costs
Mortgage and Taxes: $6,125
Utilities: $1,018
Places Rated Score: 7,143
Places Rated Rank: 114

Vineland–Millville–Bridgeton, NJ
Local Choices
73% houses, 1% condos, 6% mobile
homes, 11% apartments (rent
$315/month)
Houses
Price: $48,400
Property Taxes: $1,233
Built Before 1940: 34.1%

Energy Requirements
Heating Season: 4,750 degree days
Major Source: Oil/Electricity
Air-conditioning: 679 hours
Annual Costs
Mortgage and Taxes: $5,817
Utilities: $1,478
Places Rated Score: 7,295
Places Rated Rank: 126

Visalia–Tulare–Porterville, CA
Local Choices
78% houses, 6% mobile homes, 8% apartments (rent $320/month)
Houses
Price: $64,200
Property Taxes: $661
Built Before 1940: 15.1%
Energy Requirements
Heating Season: 2,386 degree days
Major Source: Natural gas/Electricity
Air-conditioning: 1,399 hours
Annual Costs
Mortgage and Taxes: $6,745
Utilities: $1,033
Places Rated Score: 7,778
Places Rated Rank: 157

★ **Waco, TX**
Local Choices
77% houses, 3% mobile homes, 12% apartments (rent $280/month)
Houses
Price: $46,300
Property Taxes: $648
Built Before 1940: 16.5%
Energy Requirements
Heating Season: 2,058 degree days
Major Source: Natural gas/Electricity
Air-conditioning: 2,194 hours
Annual Costs
Mortgage and Taxes: $5,037
Utilities: $1,069
Places Rated Score: 6,106
Places Rated Rank: 25

Washington, DC–MD–VA
Local Choices
58% houses, 7% condos, 1% mobile homes, 31% apartments (rent $415/month)
Houses
Price: $117,800
Property Taxes: $1,360
Built Before 1940: 19.2%
Energy Requirements
Heating Season: 4,260 degree days
Major Source: Natural gas/Electricity
Air-conditioning: 910 hours
Annual Costs
Mortgage and Taxes: $12,530
Utilities: $1,194
Places Rated Score: 13,724
Places Rated Rank: 314

Waterbury, CT
Local Choices
60% houses, 3% condos, 2% mobile homes, 14% apartments (rent $310/month)
Houses
Price: $76,400
Property Taxes: $1,168
Built Before 1940: 33.2%
Energy Requirements
Heating Season: 6,150 degree days
Major Source: Oil/Electricity
Air-conditioning: 344 hours

Annual Costs
Mortgage and Taxes: $8,407
Utilities: $1,617
Places Rated Score: 10,024
Places Rated Rank: 279

Waterloo–Cedar Falls, IA
Local Choices
76% houses, 1% condos, 4% mobile homes, 10% apartments (rent $320/month)
Houses
Price: $59,300
Property Taxes: $973
Built Before 1940: 32.8%
Energy Requirements
Heating Season: 7,415 degree days
Major Source: Natural gas/Electricity
Air-conditioning: 425 hours
Annual Costs
Mortgage and Taxes: $6,594
Utilities: $1,287
Places Rated Score: 7,881
Places Rated Rank: 166

Wausau, WI
Local Choices
77% houses, 4% mobile homes, 6% apartments (rent $280/month)
Houses
Price: $55,500
Property Taxes: $1,116
Built Before 1940: 36.4%
Energy Requirements
Heating Season: 8,586 degree days
Major Source: Natural gas/Electricity
Air-conditioning: 456 hours
Annual Costs
Mortgage and Taxes: $6,377
Utilities: $1,265
Places Rated Score: 7,642
Places Rated Rank: 147

West Palm Beach–Boca Raton–Delray Beach, FL
Local Choices
51% houses, 33% condos, 5% mobile homes, 10% apartments (rent $385/month)
Houses
Price: $89,300
Property Taxes: $919
Built Before 1940: 5.2%
Energy Requirements
Heating Season: 299 degree days
Major Source: Total electric
Air-conditioning: 2,052 hours
Annual Costs
Mortgage and Taxes: $9,380
Utilities: $1,132
Places Rated Score: 10,512
Places Rated Rank: 290

Wheeling, WV–OH
Local Choices
74% houses, 1% condos, 6% mobile homes, 7% apartments (rent $245/month)
Houses
Price: $53,800
Property Taxes: $199
Built Before 1940: 49.9%
Energy Requirements
Heating Season: 5,216 degree days
Major Source: Natural gas/Electricity
Air-conditioning: 471 hours
Annual Costs
Mortgage and Taxes: $5,303

Utilities: $1,273
Places Rated Score: 6,576
Places Rated Rank: 60

Wichita, KS
Local Choices
74% houses, 1% condos, 4% mobile homes, 11% apartments (rent $270/month)
Houses
Price: $56,800
Property Taxes: $551
Built Before 1940: 19.9%
Energy Requirements
Heating Season: 4,687 degree days
Major Source: Natural gas/Electricity
Air-conditioning: 1,280 hours
Annual Costs
Mortgage and Taxes: $5,931
Utilities: $1,130
Places Rated Score: 7,061
Places Rated Rank: 105

Wichita Falls, TX
Local Choices
77% houses, 1% condos, 4% mobile homes, 11% apartments (rent $290/month)
Houses
Price: $49,500
Property Taxes: $692
Built Before 1940: 19.4%
Energy Requirements
Heating Season: 2,904 degree days
Major Source: Natural gas/Electricity
Air-conditioning: 2,047 hours
Annual Costs
Mortgage and Taxes: $5,380
Utilities: $1,024
Places Rated Score: 6,404
Places Rated Rank: 46

Williamsport, PA
Local Choices
71% houses, 7% mobile homes, 8% apartments (rent $275/month)
Houses
Price: $53,800
Property Taxes: $877
Built Before 1940: 49.3%
Energy Requirements
Heating Season: 5,981 degree days
Major Source: Oil/Electricity
Air-conditioning: 549 hours
Annual Costs
Mortgage and Taxes: $5,977
Utilities: $1,307
Places Rated Score: 7,284
Places Rated Rank: 125

Wilmington, DE–NJ–MD
Local Choices
73% houses, 1% condos, 3% mobile homes, 16% apartments (rent $335/month)
Houses
Price: $64,100
Property Taxes: $481
Built Before 1940: 23.3%
Energy Requirements
Heating Season: 4,940 degree days
Major Source: Oil/Electricity
Air-conditioning: 683 hours
Annual Costs
Mortgage and Taxes: $6,556
Utilities: $1,371
Places Rated Score: 7,927
Places Rated Rank: 173

Wilmington, NC
Local Choices
74% houses, 1% condos, 6% mobile homes, 10% apartments (rent $280/month)
Houses
Price: $55,600
Property Taxes: $539
Built Before 1940: 14.9%
Energy Requirements
Heating Season: 2,433 degree days
Major Source: Total electric
Air-conditioning: 683 hours
Annual Costs
Mortgage and Taxes: $5,809
Utilities: $1,049
Places Rated Score: 6,858
Places Rated Rank: 89

Worcester, MA
Local Choices
50% houses, 1% mobile homes, 15% apartments (rent $300/month)
Houses
Price: $60,600
Property Taxes: $1,473
Built Before 1940: 46.8%
Energy Requirements
Heating Season: 6,848 degree days
Major Source: Oil/Electricity
Air-conditioning: 297 hours
Annual Costs
Mortgage and Taxes: $7,217
Utilities: $1,498
Places Rated Score: 8,715
Places Rated Rank: 239

Yakima, WA
Local Choices
74% houses, 1% condos, 8% mobile homes, 9% apartments (rent $300/month)
Houses
Price: $56,200
Property Taxes: $567
Built Before 1940: 24.5%
Energy Requirements
Heating Season: 6,009 degree days
Major Source: Total electric
Air-conditioning: 551 hours
Annual Costs
Mortgage and Taxes: $5,891
Utilities: $549
Places Rated Score: 6,440
Places Rated Rank: 47

York, PA
Local Choices
76% houses, 1% condos, 6% mobile homes, 6% apartments (rent $295/month)
Houses
Price: $62,300
Property Taxes: $1,016
Built Before 1940: 38.4%
Energy Requirements
Heating Season: 5,075 degree days
Major Source: Natural gas/Electricity
Air-conditioning: 744 hours
Annual Costs
Mortgage and Taxes: $6,925
Utilities: $1,446
Places Rated Score: 8,371
Places Rated Rank: 215

Youngstown–Warren, OH
Local Choices
78% houses, 1% condos, 3% mobile homes, 10% apartments (rent $280/month)
Houses
Price: $51,700
Property Taxes: $594
Built Before 1940: 32.0%
Energy Requirements
Heating Season: 6,426 degree days
Major Source: Natural gas/Electricity
Air-conditioning: 388 hours
Annual Costs
Mortgage and Taxes: $5,491
Utilities: $1,530
Places Rated Score: 7,021
Places Rated Rank: 103

Yuba City, CA
Local Choices
68% houses, 1% condos, 8% mobile homes, 14% apartments (rent $295/month)
Houses
Price: $66,200
Property Taxes: $682
Built Before 1940: 12.9%
Energy Requirements
Heating Season: 2,585 degree days
Major Source: Natural gas/Electricity
Air-conditioning: 1,294 hours
Annual Costs
Mortgage and Taxes: $6,954
Utilities: $921
Places Rated Score: 7,875
Places Rated Rank: 164

Et Cetera

HOME FEATURES: WHERE YOU SEE THEM, WHERE YOU GET THEM

Each year, the Federal Housing Authority reports on the characteristics of single-family homes whose mortgages it insures. Here's a geography of eight selected features.

Stories. The use of the word "story" to refer to flights of buildings may have originated with tiers of stained-glass or painted windows that described a special event. The common definition today is the space between the floor and the ceiling, roof, or the floor above, in the case of a multistory home. It has nothing to do with the height of a house; a house that appears from the outside to be two stories may actually be a single-story with a cathedral ceiling. More than 85 percent of new houses have only one story. Older homes with more than one story predominate in Connecticut, Maine, Maryland, Massachusetts, New Jersey, New York, Pennsylvania, and Wisconsin.

Construction and Exterior. In frame construction, the wood frame supports the floors and roof; in masonry construction, the exterior masonry wall serves as the support. Masonry construction using local stone has virtually disappeared in new houses. Concrete block construction, however, is a common technique in Arizona (40 percent of new homes have it) and Florida (85 percent), where the exterior is either spray-painted or stuccoed. Everywhere else, the majority of new houses are of frame construction.

Aluminum siding is the preferred exterior in Maryland and Ohio; wood is the choice in Georgia and Washington. The majority (86 percent) of all homes being built with brick exteriors in the United States are in the southern states. Exteriors of brick or stucco are preferred in California and Nevada.

Basements. The basement is an area of full-story height below the first floor that is not meant for year-round living. Only a third of new houses have basements, because they are expensive to excavate. In six states, however, two out of three new houses come

Taxing the Home: Statewide Averages

Although the dollar amount of your home's recent property tax bills may seem to ratchet upward with each reassessment, there is some slight comfort in knowing that the rate at which your home is being taxed is actually going down.

Over the past ten years, while the prices of existing homes rose dramatically, nationwide average effective property tax rates dropped from 2 percent of these values to less than 1.25 percent. Economists expect the trend downward to continue.

Nowhere in the United States can you own a home and entirely escape property taxes (except in Alaska, where you have to be 65). But homeowners in certain states (like Louisiana, where the statewide average property tax rate is 0.15 percent) shoulder less of a burden than do homeowners in other states (such as Michigan, which has an average tax rate of 2.68 percent).

Property Tax on a $100,000 Home by State

State	Average Effective Rate	Annual Bill	State	Average Effective Rate	Annual Bill	State	Average Effective Rate	Annual Bill
Alabama	0.41%	$ 410	Louisiana	0.15%	$ 150	Ohio	1.15%	$1,150
Alaska	1.35	1,350	Maine	1.52	1,520			
Arizona	0.56	560	Maryland	1.37	1,370	Oklahoma	0.74	740
Arkansas	1.42	1,420				Oregon	2.06	2,060
California	1.03	1,030	Massachusetts	2.43	2,430	Pennsylvania	1.63	1,630
			Michigan	2.68	2,680	Rhode Island	1.93	1,930
Colorado	1.01	1,010	Minnesota	0.77	770	South Carolina	0.92	920
Connecticut	1.53	1,530	Mississippi	0.76	760			
Delaware	0.75	750	Missouri	1.17	1,170	South Dakota	1.77	1,770
Florida	1.03	1,030				Tennessee	1.24	1,240
Georgia			Montana	1.14	1,140	Texas	1.40	1,400
			Nebraska	2.23	2,230	Utah	0.92	920
Hawaii	0.36	360	Nevada	0.77	770	Vermont	1.60	1,600
Idaho	1.04	1,040	New Hampshire	2.39	2,390			
Illinois	1.59	1,590	New Jersey	2.55	2,550	Virginia	1.44	1,440
Indiana	1.19	1,190				Washington	1.01	1,010
Iowa	1.64	1,640	New Mexico	0.93	930	West Virginia	0.37	370
			New York	2.57	2,570	Wisconsin	2.01	2,010
Kansas	0.97	970	North Carolina	0.97	970	Wyoming	0.48	480
Kentucky	1.11	1,110	North Dakota	1.10	1,100			

Source: Advisory Commission on Intergovernmental Relations, *Significant Features of Fiscal Federalism,* 1984.

with some kind of basement, reflecting a pattern of locating the furnace below grade and a preference for extra living space. These states are Illinois, Iowa, Michigan, Minnesota, New York, and Pennsylvania.

Most new houses without basements either have a crawl space (an unfinished, accessible space below the first floor that is usually less than full-story height) or are simply resting on a concrete slab poured on the ground. In the United States, crawl spaces are preferred only in the Pacific Northwest and the Carolinas. Concrete slab footings support almost all new houses in the Sun Belt states of Arizona, Arkansas, Georgia, Louisiana, Mississippi, Oklahoma, and Texas.

Bathrooms. Bathrooms are either full (a tub or shower stall, a sink, and a toilet) or half (just a sink and a toilet). All new houses have at least one full bathroom. You'll find the majority of new homes with both a full bathroom and a half-bathroom only in the states of Alabama, Arkansas, Georgia, Louisiana, Maryland, Mississippi, New Jersey, Oklahoma, South Carolina, and Tennessee.

Fireplaces. Flueless imitation fireplaces, like dinettes and rumpus rooms, are memories of the 1950s. Half of all new American homes now are built with working fireplaces and chimneys. Unfortunately, many fireplaces in these new homes aren't used, because of smoke problems caused by short chimneys. For a good fireplace draft, the chimney cap should be at least 20 feet above the hearth.

Homes with two fireplaces can be found more frequently in the northern timber states of Idaho, Minnesota, Montana, Oregon, and Washington, and also in North Carolina and Pennsylvania.

Enclosed Porches. A porch is a covered addition or recessed space at the entrance of a home. These Main Street lookouts have disappeared from new home markets. You'll find an enclosed porch attached to one out of every 12 older homes in this country. In Connecticut, Iowa, Maine, Massachusetts, New Jersey, and New York, more than one fifth of older homes have them.

Garages and Carports. Garages, as everyone knows, are completely enclosed shelters for automobiles; carports are roofed shelters that aren't completely enclosed. Detached garages are a feature of older homes and were typically built behind the home, invisible from the street. Attached two-car garages, which became a popular feature on new homes during the 1950s, now are a standard feature on half of all newly built homes. Today, six out of ten houses, new and old, have garages; just one in ten has a carport. Only in Arizona, Hawaii, Louisiana, and Mississippi is this pattern reversed.

Swimming Pools. You won't find new tract houses anywhere with in-ground swimming pools. Builders have learned that few buyers shop for shelter *and* a swimming pool at the same time. Moreover, local ordinances can require expensive liability insurance and a four-foot-high fence around the pool's perimeter to prevent accidents.

Among older homes, fewer than 2 percent have in-ground pools. You'll find at least twice that portion in Arizona, California, Florida, Nevada, and surprisingly, Maine, Massachusetts, and New York.

HOW MUCH HOUSE CAN YOU AFFORD?

One way of figuring how much house you can afford is to use the 20/25 lending requirements set by the Federal National Mortgage Association, a major purchaser of mortgages in the secondary mortgage market. According to this rule, a family making a 20 percent down payment can finance the rest as long as no more than 25 percent of their gross income (income before taxes) covers the annual principal and interest.

For example, at the average 1983 mortgage rate of 12.85 percent, a family would need a gross income of $30,000 to handle the $620 monthly principal and interest payments on a $70,000 house.

That's one way of looking at it. A far simpler way is to recall the long-standing rule of thumb handed down from parents to children which states that, if you buy a house that costs much more than two and a half times your gross income, you're headed for trouble. For example, if your gross annual income is $25,000, the price range of houses to shop for is $60,000 to $62,500; if your income is $30,000, you can afford a house costing between $70,000 and $75,000.

Based on either of these rules, can a typical American family afford a typical home? Unfortunately, no. According to the National Association of Realtors, the last time a family with the national median income had exactly enough income to qualify for a mortgage on a home priced at the national median was in December of 1978.

A RENTER'S MISCELLANY

The kind of apartment building you choose to live in definitely makes a difference in your monthly costs. Rents for a typical four-room, 850-square-foot unit are much higher in high-rise elevator buildings (U.S. median $392) than in walk-ups or elevator buildings of three stories or fewer (U.S. median $335), according to

Rent in the Metro Areas

Highest

1.	Anchorage, AK	$520
2.	Anaheim–Santa Ana, CA	510
3.	Reno, NV	490
4.	San Jose, CA	480
4.	Stamford, CT	480
6.	Nassau–Suffolk, NY	475
7.	Norwalk, CT	465
8.	Middlesex–Somerset–Hunterdon, NJ	455
9.	Casper, WY	445
10.	Las Vegas, NV	430
11.	Bergen–Passaic, NJ	415
12.	Richland–Kennewick–Pasco, WA	410
13.	Seattle, WA	400

Lowest

1.	Joplin, MO	$220
2.	Danville, VA	225
3.	Cumberland, MD–WV	230
4.	Gadsden, AL	235
4.	McAllen–Edinburg–Mission, TX	235
6.	St. Joseph, MO	240
7.	Anderson, SC	245
7.	Columbus, GA–AL	245
7.	Fall River, MA–RI	245
7.	Fort Smith, AR–OK	245
7.	Pine Bluff, AR	245
7.	Wheeling, WV–OH	245

Source: U.S. Bureau of the Census, *1980 Census of Population and Housing.*

Above figures represent 1980 rents boosted by Consumer Price Index inflation factors to show realistic 1984 figures. All figures are rounded to the nearest five dollars.

the latest Institute of Real Estate Management survey. The least expensive kind of building is the garden apartment, defined by the institute as a group of low-rise apartment buildings on a large landscaped lot under one manager. The national median monthly rental for this kind of building is $310.

You'll find that the annual turnover rate, defined as newly occupied apartments as a percent of all the apartments in the building in a year's time, also varies by the kind of building. Around the country, high-rise elevator buildings have the lowest turnover rate (U.S. median 22 percent), whereas the turnover rate in walk-ups and elevator buildings of three or fewer stories is twice this (U.S. median 44 percent). The kind of apartment building with the most transient population is the garden apartment, in which 54 percent of tenants moved in within the previous 12 months.

The Rule of 156

One useful way of determining the rent for a house is to divide its market value by 156. This rule of 156 was developed by the city of San Francisco as a way of specifying the fair value of an apartment being converted into a condo for a tenant who had been renting it. As the landlord might put it, the price equals 156 times your monthly rent, take it or leave it.

What the rule implies in reverse is that landlords

can expect a 156-month (or 13-year) payback on houses they rent. Using this rule plus the prices of houses given in the Place Profiles, it isn't difficult to figure roughly what it would cost you to rent a house in a given metro area, assuming that the landlord has realistic expectations for the rate of return on property.

In Miami–Hialeah, the rent would be $557; in San Francisco, $990; in Joplin, Missouri, $241. The rule of 156 may seem unfair to landlords, since there is only an 8 percent return from which maintenance and taxes must be paid. Bear in mind, however, that landlords rarely buy houses for the rental income they may bring; rather, they buy them for their market appreciation and rent them during the interim merely to cover expenses.

The Renter Majority

Today about 60 percent of American households live in urbanized areas, which make up only 1.5 percent of total U.S. land area. Renter households are even more concentrated, with one fourth of total rental units located in just 17 counties, which compose only 0.5 percent of the country's land area. Half of all rental units are found within 84 counties. Yet, of the 3,100 counties in the United States, renters constitute a majority only in the 13 listed below.

Counties with a Majority of Rental Units

County	Rental Units as % of All Units
1. New York County, NY	92.2%
2. Bronx County (New York), NY	85.4
3. Kings County (New York), NY	76.6
4. Hudson County (Jersey City), NJ	71.3
5. Suffolk County (Boston), MA	70.8
6. San Francisco County, CA	66.3
7. Queens County (New York), NY	61.9
8. Orleans Parish (New Orleans), LA	61.3
9. Essex County (Newark), NJ	60.5
10. Fulton County (Atlanta), GA	53.5
11. Baltimore City, MD	52.8
12. Los Angeles County, CA	51.5
13. Honolulu County, HI	50.1

Source: U.S. Bureau of the Census, *1980 Census of Population and Housing.*

LEGAL SAFEGUARDS FOR RENTERS AND CONDO BUYERS

If you're thinking of moving to another state and either renting an apartment or buying a condominium, a knowledge of local laws could save you from some potentially expensive surprises.

Renters' Rights

In many states with large renter populations, laws concerning relations between landlords and tenants give rights to the landlord while imposing obligations on the tenant.

Seventeen states, however, have passed landlord-tenant laws based on the Uniform Residential Land-lord and Tenant Act (1972), a model law drawn up by the National Conference of Commissioners on Uniform State Laws. These states are Alaska, Arizona, Connecticut, Florida, Hawaii, Iowa, Kansas, Kentucky, Michigan, Montana, Nebraska, New Mexico, Oklahoma, Oregon, Tennessee, Virginia, and Washington.

This law defines rights and obligations of both parties to a lease on an apartment or house, and it also specifies the way disputes can be resolved. Among its provisions are:

- If your dispute with a landlord leads you to complain to the local housing board, to join a tenants' group, or to sue your landlord, the landlord cannot retaliate by cutting services, raising your rent, or evicting you.
- If the landlord doesn't make needed repairs, and the cost of the repairs is no more than $100 or half the rent (whichever is greater), you may make the repairs and deduct the expense from your monthly rent.
- After you vacate the apartment or house, any money you've deposited as security must be returned. If there are any deductions from the deposit for damages or other reasons, these deductions must be itemized.
- If your landlord doesn't live up to the lease's terms, you can recover damages in small claims court.

Protection for Condo Buyers

During the 1960s and 1970s, condo buyers had little legal protection when they signed a purchase agreement. Over the past four years, nine states have passed comprehensive laws to deal with condominium ownership based on the Uniform Condominium Act (1980), drawn up by the National Conference of Commissioners on Uniform State Laws. These states are Maine, Minnesota, Missouri, Nebraska, New Mexico, Pennsylvania, Rhode Island, Virginia, and West Virginia.

The Uniform Condominium Act covers owners' associations, developers' activities, eminent domain, separate titles and taxation, and safeguards for condo buyers. It stipulates, among other things, that:

- The developer must provide you with a Public Offering Statement, accurately and fully disclosing a schedule for finishing construction, the total number of units, the bylaws of the owners' association, copies of any contracts or leases that you have to sign, a current balance sheet and projected one-year budget for the owners' association, and a statement of the monthly common assessments you'll have to pay.
- After signing a purchase agreement, you are given 15 days to "cool off," after which you

can either cancel the agreement without penalty or accept conveyance of the property.

- If you buy a condominium without first being given a Public Offering Statement, you're entitled to receive from the developer an amount equal to 10 percent of the sales price of the unit you bought.
- The developer and real estate agent must guarantee that the unit you are buying is free from defective materials, is built to sound engineering and construction standards, and conforms to local codes.

PAYING FOR POWER

Household electric bills around the country vary widely in dollar amounts, for several reasons. Customer density, distance from oil and coal fuel sources, age of the power plant, and the type and size of equipment used in generating electricity all play a part in the charges to consumers. Who owns the company, however, may be the biggest factor in determining the amount of your bill.

The Energy Department's latest nationwide price comparison of electricity shows that, in general, publicly owned (municipal) electric power companies charge much lower rates than their larger, privately owned counterparts.

In communities of 2,500 or more, the ten lowest bills for 750 kilowatt-hours of monthly service range from $203 (Tacoma Department of Public Utilities) to $350 (City of Colorado Springs Department of Public Utilities). In contrast, the ten highest bills for the same service are mailed out by such privately owned giants as Consolidated Edison of New York ($1,318) and Narragansett Electric ($753).

Annual Electric Bills

Highest

1.	Consolidated Edison of New York	$1,318
2.	San Diego Gas and Electric (California)	1,117
3.	Long Island Lighting (New York)	984
4.	Hawaiian Electric	953
5.	United Illuminating (Connecticut)	882
6.	Public Service Electric and Gas (New Jersey)	877
7.	Northern Indiana Public Service	856
8.	Connecticut Light and Power	838
9.	Boston Edison (Massachusetts)	814
10.	Narragansett Electric (Rhode Island)	753

Lowest

1.	City of Tacoma (Washington)	$203
2.	City of Palo Alto (California)	212
3.	City of Seattle (Washington)	221
4.	Washington Water Power	290
5.	City of Eugene (Oregon)	309
5.	Puget Sound Power and Light (Washington)	309
7.	Portland General Electric (Oregon)	324
8.	Pacific Power and Light (Oregon)	328
9.	City of Sacramento (California)	335
10.	City of Colorado Springs (Colorado)	350

Source: U.S. Department of Energy, *Typical Electric Bills*, 1983.

The national average electric bill for 750 kilowatt-hours of monthly service is $665 per year.

NUCLEAR HOT SPOTS: A NATIONWIDE LOCATOR

Would you mind living near a nuclear power plant?

Given the record of the industry after 900 reactor-years of commercial operation in this country, even a proponent of nuclear power would admit that fears about a catastrophic meltdown or low-level environmental contamination are legitimate.

Because of a lower demand for electricity, construction and regulatory delays, skyrocketing costs, and concerns about reactor safety after the 1979 Three Mile Island incident, the growth of nuclear power has slowed considerably in recent years. Utility planners are simply not willing to take the risk of investing billions in a 12- to 14-year process of building a nuclear plant and then face the possibility of not being allowed to operate it. As a result, plans for 76 power plants have been canceled over the past decade, and not one nuclear plant has been ordered since 1978.

During 1983, the 292 billion kilowatt-hours produced by nuclear reactors accounted for 13 percent of total U.S. electrical output. In Vermont, 80 percent of electricity consumed comes from nuclear power; in Maine, 65 percent; in Connecticut and Nebraska, 50 percent or more. The state with the greatest generating capacity, however, is Illinois, partly because Chicago-based Commonwealth Edison has built or plans to build more nuclear power plants than any other utility in the country.

The following list ranks, in order of their total generating capacity, the 34 states in which nuclear power plants are found. The generating capacity, or power output, for a typical reactor is 1,000 megawatts (1 million kilowatts) of electricity, or enough to supply the needs of a city of 600,000 people at any given moment. Each plant listed is either operating (84 of them) or under construction (39) as of June 1984. The date of operation—actual or planned—is also given for each unit, along with its county location. Not included in this list are three reactors that are licensed but shut down indefinitely (Dresden #1 near Joliet, Illinois, and Three Mile Island #1 and #2 near Harrisburg, Pennsylvania), and two reactors each in Indiana, Mississippi, Ohio, Tennessee, and Washington on which construction has been postponed indefinitely.

Nuclear Electric-Generating Units: The States Ranked

1. ILLINOIS: 13,015 megawatts total capacity
De Witt County (Clinton #1), 1986; Grundy County (Dresden #2 and #3), 1970, 1971; Lake County (Zion #1 and #2), 1973, 1974; La Salle County (La Salle #1 and #2), 1982, 1984; Ogle County (Byron #1 and #2), 1984, 1985; Rock Island County (Quad Cities #1 and #2), 1972, 1972; Will County (Braidwood #1 and #2), 1985, 1986.

2. PENNSYLVANIA: 8,025 megawatts total capacity
Beaver County (Beaver Valley #1 and #2), 1976, 1986; Luzerne County (Susquehanna #1 and #2), 1983, 1984; Montgomery

(continued on page 116)

Nuclear Power Plants in the United States

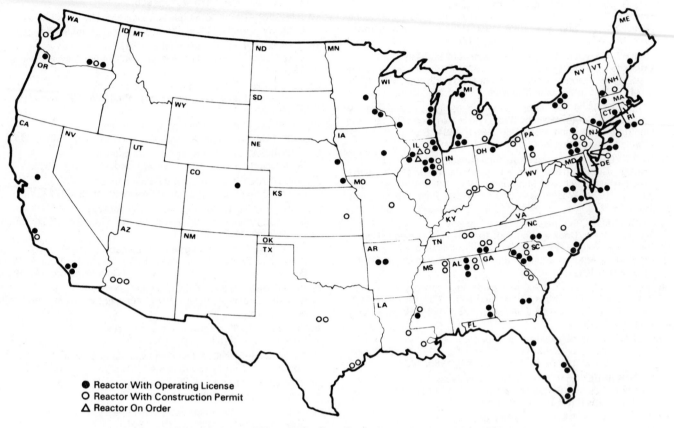

● Reactor With Operating License
O Reactor With Construction Permit
△ Reactor On Order

Source: Atomic Industrial Forum, Inc., January 1984, modified by *Places Rated* to include changes as of August 1984.

Atomic Metro Areas

Metro Area	Nuclear Power Plants	Generating Capacity (Megawatts)	Metro Area	Nuclear Power Plants	Generating Capacity (Megawatts)
Beaver County, PA	2	1,669	Minneapolis–St. Paul, MN–WI	1	545
Benton Harbor, MI	2	2,130	Monmouth–Ocean, NJ	1	650
Boston, MA	1	670	Nassau–Suffolk, NY	2	1,667
Cedar Rapids, IA	1	538	New London–Norwich, CT–RI	3	2,679
Charlotte–Gastonia–Rock Hill, NC–SC	4	4,650			
			New Orleans, LA	1	1,104
			New York, NY	2	1,838
Chattanooga, TN–GA	2	2,296	Philadelphia, PA–NJ	2	2,110
Cleveland, OH	1	1,205	Phoenix, AZ	3	3,810
Davenport–Rock Island– Moline, IA–IL	2	1,578	Raleigh–Durham, NC	1	900
Detroit, MI	1	1,139	Richland–Kennewick–Pasco, WA	2	1,960
Dothan, AL	2	1,720	Rochester, NY	1	470
			Sacramento, CA	1	918
Fort Pierce, FL	2	1,608	Saginaw–Bay City–Midland, MI	2	1,233
Greeley, CO	1	330	San Diego, CA	3	2,636
Joliet, IL	4	3,828			
Lake County, IL	2	2,080	Scranton–Wilkes-Barre, PA	2	2,100
Lawrence–Haverhill, MA–NH	1	1,150	Syracuse, NY	2	1,700
			Washington, DC–MD–VA	2	1,690
Miami–Hialeah, FL	2	1,332	Wilmington, DE–NJ–MD	2	2,205

Source: U.S. Department of Energy, *Inventory of Electric Power Plants in the United States,* 1983.

County (Limerick #1 and #2), 1985, 1988; York County (Peach Bottom #2 and #3), 1974, 1974.

3. ALABAMA: 7,279 megawatts total capacity
Houston County (Farley #1 and #2), 1977, 1981; Jackson County (Bellefonte #1 and #2), 1988, 1990; Morgan County (Browns Ferry #1, #2, and #3), 1974, 1975, 1977.

4. SOUTH CAROLINA: 6,551 megawatts total capacity
Darlington County (Robinson #2), 1971; Fairfield County (Summer), 1984; Oconee County (Oconee #1, #2, and #3), 1973, 1974, 1974; York County (Catawba #1 and #2), 1985, 1987.

5. CALIFORNIA: 5,744 megawatts total capacity
Sacramento County (Rancho Seco), 1975; San Diego County (San Onofre #1, #2, and #3), 1968, 1983, 1984; San Luis Obispo County (Diablo Canyon #1 and #2), 1984, 1985.

6. NEW YORK: 5,668 megawatts total capacity
Oswego County (Nine Mile #1 and #2), 1969, 1986; Suffolk County (FitzPatrick and Shoreham), 1975, 1985; Wayne County (Ginna), 1970; Westchester County (Indian Point #2 and #3), 1973, 1976.

7. MICHIGAN: 5,395 megawatts total capacity
Berrien County (Cook #1 and #2), 1975, 1978; Charlevoix County (Big Rock Point), 1963; Midland County (Midland #1 and #2), 1985, 1985; Monroe County (Fermi #2), 1984; Van Buren County (Palisades), 1971.

8. NORTH CAROLINA: 4,900 megawatts total capacity
Brunswick County (Brunswick #1 and #2), 1975, 1977; Mecklenburg County (McGuire #1 and #2), 1981, 1984; Wake County (Harris #1), 1986.

9. TEXAS: 4,800 megawatts total capacity
Matagorda County (South Texas #1 and #2), 1987, 1989; Somervell County (Comanche Peak #1 and #2), 1985, 1986.

10. TENNESSEE: 4,650 megawatts total capacity
Hamilton County (Sequayah #1 and #2), 1981, 1982; Rhea County (Watts Bar #1 and #2), 1984, 1986.

11. NEW JERSEY: 3,922 megawatts total capacity
Ocean County (Oyster Creek), 1969; Salem County (Salem #1 and #2, Hope Creek), 1977, 1981, 1986.

12. FLORIDA: 3,820 megawatts total capacity
Citrus County (Crystal River #3), 1977; Dade County (Turkey Point #3 and #4), 1972, 1973; St. Lucie County (St. Lucie #1 and #2), 1976, 1983.

13. ARIZONA: 3,810 megawatts total capacity
Maricopa County (Palos Verde #1, #2, and #3), 1984, 1985, 1986.

14. GEORGIA: 3,776 megawatts total capacity
Appling County (Hatch #1 and #2), 1975, 1979; Burke County (Vogtle #1 and #2), 1987, 1988.

15. VIRGINIA: 3,390 megawatts total capacity
Louisa County (North Anna #1 and #2), 1978, 1980; Surry County (Surry #1 and #2), 1972, 1973.

16. CONNECTICUT: 3,261 megawatts total capacity
Middlesex County (Haddam), 1968; New London County (Millstone #1, #2, and #3), 1970, 1975, 1986.

17. MISSISSIPPI: 2,500 megawatts total capacity
Claiborne County (Grand Gulf #1 and #2), 1982, 1990.

18. OHIO: 2,095 megawatts total capacity
Lake County (Perry #1), 1985; Ottawa County (Davis-Besse #1), 1977.

19. LOUISIANA: 2,038 megawatts total capacity
St. Charles Parish (Waterford #3), 1984; West Feliciana Parish (River Bend #1), 1985.

20. WASHINGTON: 1,940 megawatts total capacity
Benton County (Hanford Nuclear and WPSS #2), 1966, 1984.

21. ARKANSAS: 1,762 megawatts total capacity
Pope County (Arkansas Nuclear #1 and #2), 1974, 1980.

22. MARYLAND: 1,690 megawatts total capacity
Calvert County (Calvert Cliffs #1 and #2), 1975, 1977.

23. MINNESOTA: 1,605 megawatts total capacity
Goodhue County (Prairie Island #1 and #2), 1973, 1974; Wright County (Monticello), 1971.

24. WISCONSIN: 1,579 megawatts total capacity
Kewaunee County (Kewaunee), 1974; Manitowoc County (Point Beach #1 and #2), 1970, 1972; Vernon County (La Crosse), 1969.

25. NEBRASKA: 1,256 megawatts total capacity
Nemaha County (Cooper), 1974; Washington County (Fort Calhoun), 1973.

26. KANSAS: 1,150 megawatts total capacity
Coffey County (Wolf Creek), 1985.

26. NEW HAMPSHIRE: 1,150 megawatts total capacity
Rockingham County (Seabrook #1), 1985.

28. OREGON: 1,130 megawatts total capacity
Columbia County (Trojan #1), 1976.

29. MISSOURI: 1,120 megawatts total capacity
Callaway County (Callaway #1), 1984.

30. MAINE: 825 megawatts total capacity
Lincoln County (Maine Yankee), 1972.

31. MASSACHUSETTS: 745 megawatts total capacity
Franklin County (Yankee), 1961; Plymouth County (Pilgrim), 1972.

32. IOWA: 538 megawatts total capacity
Linn County (Arnold #1), 1975.

33. VERMONT: 514 megawatts total capacity
Windham County (Vermont Yankee), 1972.

34. COLORADO: 330 megawatts total capacity
Weld County (Fort St. Vrain), 1979.

Source: Atomic Industrial Forum, *Directory,* 1984, and Energy Information Administration, *Inventory of Electric Power Plants,* 1983.

Health Care & Environment:

Matters of Life & Death

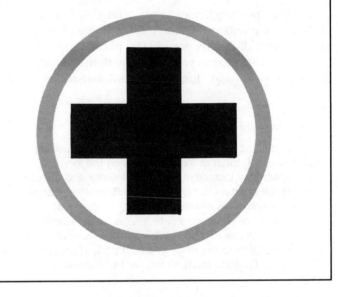

Americans continue to get healthier. Judging by two universal measures of population health, infant mortality and life expectancy, America is healthier now than it was even a few years ago. Why are life expectancy and infant mortality such commonly accepted indications of the health of general populations? First, because data can be found in almost every developed nation in the form of birth and death certificates. Second, the quality of postpartum and infant care available in a nation (or state or town) generally reflects the quality of other important health services as well. As for life expectancy, it remains a very broad but meaningful indicator of a nation's ability to provide lifelong necessities for health, such as sanitary food and drinking water, proper immunization and disease screening, and a basic measure of professional medical attention when needed.

In January 1984, the U.S. Department of Health and Human Services reported that infant mortality in America had dropped to its lowest level ever, with provisional data showing 11.2 deaths per 1,000 live births in 1982. At the same time, life expectancy had risen to 74.5 years in 1982, with girls born that year likely to live 78.2 years and boys 70.8 years. This represented an overall increase of about two years since 1978, when general life expectancy was 72.5 years, and a gain of nearly 30 years since 1900.

Not all Americans share equally in these statistical gains. The mortality rate for black infants is nearly twice that of white infants; and although in recent years life expectancy has increased at a faster rate for blacks than for whites, blacks on average still live about six years less than whites.

You might assume, given this news about our declining infant mortality rate and rising life expectancy, that America is the world's healthiest nation. But the sobering fact is that we lag behind many developed nations in these basic health indicators. In 1978, the most recent date for which comparable data are available, the United States ranked 16th in infant mortality and 15th in life expectancy.

Why does America, land of plenty, finish behind so many other countries? A 1984 article by John McPhee in the *New Yorker*, describing the lives of several young family physicians in rural Maine, may have one answer. McPhee quotes a well-known Boston-based cardiologist, Dr. Roman DeSanctis, as saying: "Canada has a lower death rate than we do, and broader medical care. Canada has doctors everywhere, in all the small towns. Sweden does, too. Meanwhile, we have all these high-tech doctors in cities with their machines."

Despite our great number of physicians, and their advanced training and technical support, the basic problem could be maldistribution of medical care. Many physicians, for example, want to practice near a major hospital and also wish to live in a city large enough to provide them with the amenities their incomes allow. In general, as *Places Rated*'s examination of the metro areas shows, larger, more affluent places such as Boston, New York, and San Francisco have a greater proportion of health care facilities, whereas more sparsely settled areas have increasingly smaller proportions.

AMERICA'S LEADING KILLERS

Given the inevitability of death and taxes, it seems likely that we will always have a death rate. The death rate (number of deaths per 100,000 population) changes slightly from year to year, along with the percentage of deaths each year due to different causes, but the

three most common killers of Americans remain heart disease, cancer, and stroke, which make up about 68 percent of all deaths. Altogether the ten leading causes of death accounted for 85 percent of all deaths in 1980.

The Top 10 Killers

Cause of Death	Estimated Rate per 100,000 People
Heart diseases	336.0
Malignant neoplasms	183.9
Cerebrovascular diseases	75.1
Accidents	46.7
Chronic obstructive pulmonary conditions	24.7
Influenza and pneumonia	24.1
Diabetes mellitus	15.4
Chronic liver conditions and cirrhosis of the liver	13.5
Atherosclerosis	13.0
Suicide	11.9

Source: National Center for Health Statistics, *Monthly Vital Statistics Report, Advanced Data: Final Mortality, 1980,* 1983.

When we speak of death rates, we usually mean the number of people who die every year for every 100,000 people in the general population. Death rates may be either unadjusted (crude) or age-adjusted. The latter allow for the fact that a country, state, or metro area with a generally older population will have a higher death rate than places with younger residents. Florida, for example, has a median age of 34.7 years—the oldest in the nation—and 17.3 percent of its total population is aged 65 or over. Alaska, on the other hand, has a median age of only 26.1 years, which is the nation's lowest, and only 2.9 percent of its population is over age 65. Missouri, Arkansas, New York, and Pennsylvania also have relatively old populations, and states in the West, including the Mountain States, have young ones. The discussions and maps in this chapter generally use age-adjusted figures to compensate for these regional differences.

Heart disease is still our number-one killer. More than 760,000 Americans died of heart disease in 1980, which represented almost four out of every ten deaths. Although the age-adjusted death rate from this leading killer increased 1.3 percent between 1979 and 1980, its incidence has fallen since 1950 due to the strides made in prevention, diagnosis, surgery, and treatment. In 1980, roughly twice the number of men died of heart disease as did women.

Although the percentage of deaths caused by heart disease is decreasing, the proportion of deaths caused by the second greatest killer, cancer, is on the rise and has been since 1950. In 1980, cancer (referred to by the National Center for Health Statistics as malignant neoplasms) was responsible for about two of every ten American deaths, or 416,509 victims. The age-adjusted death rate for cancer in 1980 was 1.5 times greater for men than women.

Cerebrovascular disease, or stroke, remains our third greatest killer, accounting for nearly one out of

---

Life Expectancy in the States

Life expectancy in America's states shows noticeable variation, with most of the states having the longest life expectancy located in the Great Interior and states having the shortest in the Southeast. The listing below shows average life expectancy for 1970, the most recent year for which complete figures are available. Life expectancies in many states are now considerably longer, but due to the delay in compiling and analyzing statistics, final data for 1980 will not be available until 1985.

States Ranked for Life Expectancy

State	Life Expectancy	State	Life Expectancy
1. Hawaii	73.60	26. Missouri	70.69
2. Minnesota	72.96	27. Arkansas	70.66
3. Utah	72.90	27. Florida	70.66
4. North Dakota	72.79	29. Michigan	70.63
5. Nebraska	72.60	30. Montana	70.56
6. Kansas	72.58	31. Arizona	70.55
7. Iowa	72.56	31. New York	70.55
8. Connecticut	72.48	33. Pennsylvania	70.43
8. Wisconsin	72.48	34. New Mexico	70.32
10. Oregon	72.13	35. Wyoming	70.29
11. South Dakota	72.08	36. Maryland	70.22
12. Colorado	72.06	37. Illinois	70.14
13. Rhode Island	71.90	38. Tennessee	70.11
14. Idaho	71.87	39. Kentucky	70.10
15. Massachusetts	71.83	40. Virginia	70.08
16. Washington	71.72	41. Delaware	70.06
17. California	71.71	42. West Virginia	69.48
18. Vermont	71.64	43. Alaska	69.31
19. Oklahoma	71.42	44. North Carolina	69.21
20. New Hampshire	71.23	45. Alabama	69.05
21. Maine	70.93	46. Nevada	69.03
21. New Jersey	70.93	47. Louisiana	68.76
23. Texas	70.90	48. Georgia	68.54
24. Indiana	70.88	49. Mississippi	68.09
25. Ohio	70.82	50. South Carolina	67.96

Source: National Center for Health Statistics, *U.S. Decennial Life Tables for 1969–71, Vol. II,* June 1975.

every ten American deaths and claiming 170,225 lives in 1980. It was the only one of the three leading killers to show a decline (2 percent) between 1979 and 1980, which reflects the general downward trend of deaths from stroke since 1950. The age-adjusted death rate for stroke was 1.2 times higher for men than women, and 1.8 times higher for blacks than for whites.

THE HIGH COSTS OF HEALTH CARE

Life expectancy is rising, but so is the cost of health care. Recent surveys showed that medical costs in the United States climbed to $322.4 billion in 1982, up about 25 percent from the previous year. That 1982 figure amounts to an average of $1,365 per person, or 10.5 percent of the gross national product!

The future promises little improvement. By 1990, government forecasts say, the annual cost of national health care will climb to $756 billion. Standard and Poor's estimates are even higher, putting the total at $480 billion by 1985 and $821 billion by 1990.

One sector of the U.S. business world that gives health care costs particular scrutiny is the insurance industry. For decades, people who have sold health insurance have evaluated the relative health of various parts of the country and the cost of illness care. Every large health insurance company that sells to individuals (and there are fewer and fewer of these companies each year as more and more group plans are sold) issues its agents a rate book, a confidential, in-house tool that enables the agent to quote prices for policies based on the age, health, occupational status, and sex of the proposed insured. In addition to these variables, premiums for policies also vary according to place of residence. Why? Are some places greater health risks?

The answer lies not so much in the varying risks of becoming ill (although the health companies tell us that the frequency with which people get sick *does* vary noticeably around the country) as in the consequent cost of caring for the patient, both in terms of physician's fees and hospital rooms.

Places Rated examined six rate books from major companies specializing in health insurance and found that they agree closely on which places in America are good health insurance risks and which aren't. The best place in America to buy health insurance, for example, is the southeastern corner of Pennsylvania, excluding the Philadelphia metro area. York, Lancaster, Lebanon, and Berks counties are the only ones in the rate books to get top-of-the-line ratings. Immediately following this prime location are South Carolina and South Dakota. Next best are North Carolina and Arkansas. Some of the worst places? New York City and Syracuse, New York.

Based on the listings of these six rate books, *Places Rated* devised a system that classifies the relative insurance/hospitalization costs of the 329 metro areas as either Outstanding, Excellent, Good, Fair, Poor, or Unacceptable. (The costs index for each metro area is given in the Place Profiles.) Twenty metro areas receive Outstanding ratings, whereas 13 are classified as Poor and four as Unacceptable.

Insurance/Hospitalization Costs Index: Best and Worst Metro Areas

Outstanding Costs Index	Poor Costs Index
Anderson, SC	Binghamton, NY
Asheville, NC	Buffalo, NY
Burlington, NC	Elmira, NY
Charleston, SC	Galveston–Texas City, TX
Columbia, SC	Glens Falls, NY
Cumberland, MD–WV	Houston, TX
Fayetteville, NC	Los Angeles–Long Beach, CA
Florence, SC	Miami–Hialeah, FL
Greenville–Spartanburg, SC	Niagara Falls, NY
Hagerstown, MD	Orange County, NY
Harrisburg–Lebanon–Carlisle, PA	Poughkeepsie, NY
Hickory, NC	Rochester, NY
Jacksonville, NC	Utica–Rome, NY
Lancaster, PA	
Owensboro, KY	**Unacceptable Costs Index**
Raleigh–Durham, NC	Albany–Schenectady–Troy, NY
Reading, PA	Nassau–Suffolk, NY
Sioux Falls, SD	New York, NY
Wilmington, NC	Syracuse, NY
York, PA	

ENVIRONMENT AND DAILY HEALTH

It wasn't until the early 1970s that terms like *ecosystem, ecology,* and *environmental hazards* became part of our vocabulary. Before that time, only health specialists and physicians seemed concerned about the potentially lethal effects of pollution, contaminants, and additives. More and more, experts are focusing on environmental factors to explain the distribution and concentration of various ailments and diseases. Where

Rising Hospital Costs

Hospital care accounted for about 42 percent of total health care costs in 1982, followed by doctors' services at 19 percent, nursing home care 9 percent, and dentists 6 percent, according to a 1984 report from the Department of Health and Human Services.

Hospital costs have increased five and a half times since 1965. The average hospital stay, for example, skyrocketed from $316 in 1965 to $1,844 in 1980. (Consumer costs rose two and a half times during the same period.)

The average daily cost for a semiprivate hospital room in 1982 was $165, with prices generally highest in parts of the West, Midwest, and East, and lowest in the South.

Average Daily Hospital Room Rates: The States and District of Columbia Ranked

Place and Rank	Average Daily Room Charge	Place and Rank	Average Daily Room Charge
1. District of Columbia	$233	26. Indiana	$146
2. Alaska	217	26. Minnesota	146
3. California	215	26. Utah	146
4. Illinois	190	26. Wisconsin	146
5. Pennsylvania	186	30. Arizona	145
6. Michigan	185	30. Missouri	145
7. New York	184	32. Florida	140
8. Oregon	182	32. Kansas	140
9. Massachusetts	180	34. Iowa	139
10. Hawaii	177	35. West Virginia	137
10. Ohio	177	36. Nebraska	133
12. Delaware	172	36. Oklahoma	133
12. Washington	172	38. Virginia	132
14. New Jersey	171	39. South Dakota	131
15. Nevada	169	40. Kentucky	130
16. Vermont	168	40. Wyoming	130
17. Colorado	167	42. Alabama	124
17. New Hampshire	167	43. Georgia	123
19. Rhode Island	166	44. North Dakota	122
20. Connecticut	162	45. Texas	119
21. Maine	159	46. Louisiana	116
22. New Mexico	152	47. Arkansas	114
23. Idaho	151	48. Tennessee	111
23. Montana	151	49. North Carolina	110
25. Maryland	148	50. South Carolina	108
		51. Mississippi	94

Source: Health Insurance Association of America, *Source Book of Health Insurance Data,* annual.

Figures are for 1982 cost to patient for semiprivate room.

dumps, chemical spills, insecticides, industrial wastes, and other contaminants.

In the past 15 years, we've made a lot of progress in cleaning up our soil, air, and water. But problem areas do remain, and they can be health hazards. Water pollution and, to some extent, soil pollution are covered in the chapter "Climate & Terrain." The discussion that follows deals with additional water-related matters and with air pollution.

Think About Your Drinking Water

Most people are aware that pollution of drinking water constitutes a serious health problem in many American cities. But we sometimes forget that pollutants are not the only things in the water we drink that can affect our health.

About half of all Americans drink water from nearly 9,500 fluoridated community systems. What is fluoride? It is the salt form of the element fluorine, which, like gold, iron, or magnesium, can occur naturally in our soil and water. Natural traces of fluoride are found in many foods and in about a third of the nation's water. Most parts of Texas, Illinois, Iowa, Oklahoma, and Ohio have water that is naturally fluoridated.

Fluoride is ingested much like iron, which is beneficial to the blood and may be obtained by eating certain foods, drinking water with traces of iron in it, or by taking pills, capsules, or liquids that contain iron compounds. You may already be aware that fluoridation benefits young people, whose teeth are developing, but did you know that it can also be important to retirement-aged people, whose bones need the extra protection fluoridation offers?

Fluoride has nothing to do with the taste of water or with other qualities such as softness, hardness, acidity, and so on. Research indicates that some types of hard water—water with large amounts of dissolved salts and minerals—may be helpful in preventing certain cardiovascular problems, principally coronary heart disease and stroke. For reasons that are not clear, the dissolved substances (salts of calcium and magnesium, especially carbonates, as well as sulfates and chlorides) seem to protect people from cardiovascular disease. So if you move to a place with hard water, check with the local or county health department before you install a water purifier or softener. The minerals causing the hard water may actually be good for you.

Air Quality in the Metro Areas

The bodily harm caused by air pollution has been well documented. Many of us have experienced the watering eyes, shortness of breath, mild chest pain, or burning feeling in throat or lungs that can accompany a day when air pollution is high. Air pollutants have also been known to cause mental retardation, seizures, nerve disorders, damage to heart and lung tissue, and

you live is increasingly a determining factor in what diseases you are susceptible to. It is possible, for example, that drinking chlorinated water (chlorine is used to kill bacteria not only in swimming pools but also in most drinking water) increases the risk of gastrointestinal cancer by between 50 percent and 100 percent. Many birth defects, disorders of the nervous system, and extraordinarily high rates of certain cancers have been linked directly to hazardous waste even death. In 1948, for example, weather conditions trapped polluted air over the city of Donora, Pennsylvania, for nearly a week. Of a population of 8,000, almost 6,000 became ill, complaining of chest pains, headaches, eye irritation, coughing, and dizzy spells, and 20 people died from related causes. Four years later in London, about 4,000 people died from smog that lingered over the city for five days.

In the Place Profiles later in this chapter, *Places Rated* examines the distribution and concentration of the six major air pollutants as defined by the Environmental Protection Agency (EPA).

Total suspended particulates (TSP) is a name for any minute particle or group of particles—such as pollen, soot, asbestos, sand, or dust—borne by the wind. Generally speaking, the concentration of particulates increases as one travels from west to east, since that is the direction of the prevailing winds. Like most other pollutants, particulates are found in the greatest concentrations around cities and industrial centers and in the smallest concentrations in rural areas. The great exception is the dry regions of the Southwest, where dust storms create clouds of TSP. The EPA primary standard—the point at which a pollutant begins to affect human health—is 75 micrograms per cubic meter of air for TSP. (A microgram is a millionth of a gram.)

Pollution Problems

In examining air pollution, *Places Rated* studied the EPA's *Air Quality Data*, 1983, to identify the pollutants for which each metro area's annual mean average exceeded the EPA primary standard. Many metro areas experience problems with total suspended particulates and carbon monoxide, and a few have severe problems with ozone. Below is a list of the 17 metro areas that exceed the EPA primary standard for two or more major pollutants.

Metro Areas with Air Pollution Problems

Metro Area	Pollutants
Albuquerque, NM	TSP, CO
Anaheim–Santa Ana, CA	TSP, CO, O_3, NO_2, Pb
Baltimore, MD	TSP, SO_2, CO
Boise City, ID	TSP, CO
Chicago, IL	TSP, CO
Denver, CO	TSP, CO
Detroit, MI	TSP, CO
El Paso, TX	TSP, CO
Fresno, CA	CO, O_3
Jersey City, NJ	TSP, CO
Los Angeles–Long Beach, CA	TSP, CO, O_3, NO_2, Pb
Minneapolis–St. Paul, MN–WI	CO, Pb
Nashville, TN	CO, NO_2
Phoenix, AZ	TSP, CO
Riverside–San Bernardino, CA	TSP, O_3
Steubenville–Weirton, OH–WV	TSP, SO_2
Tucson, AZ	TSP, CO

Sulfur dioxide (SO_2) is an acrid, corrosive gas produced by the burning of coal (particularly soft coal) that is high in sulfur. Coal burning accounts for 60 percent of the SO_2 in the air. Most of the SO_2 is found, therefore, in the older eastern cities where coal is still used as a major fuel for industry and home heating. The EPA primary standard for concentration of SO_2 is 80 micrograms per cubic meter of air, or roughly 0.03 parts per million.

Carbon monoxide (CO) is especially deadly. When inhaled in great enough concentrations, it enters the bloodstream and chemically prevents the absorption of oxygen, resulting in death. Carbon monoxide is produced by the incomplete combustion of carbon fuels; about 75 percent of it is produced by automobiles. The EPA primary standard for concentration of CO is 10 milligrams per cubic meter of air, or roughly nine parts per million.

Photochemical oxidants are a group of pollutants that combine chemically in the presence of strong sunlight. These chemicals are mostly nitrous oxides, hydrocarbons, and ozone (O_3). The common name for photochemical oxidants is *smog*. Because oxidant pollution involves two things that are beyond the scope of most regulations and constraints—sunshine and automobiles—it is the fastest-spreading and hardest to control of all air pollution problems. The EPA primary standard for ozone is 0.12 parts per million, and pollution severity is measured by the mean number of days over a given time during which the standard is exceeded.

Nitrous oxides (NO_2) are produced when fossil fuels are burned at extremely high temperatures, a process that occurs most often in internal combustion engines. Nitrous oxides are a primary ingredient of photochemical oxidants, or smog. The EPA primary standard for concentration of NO_2 is 100 micrograms per cubic meter of air, or about 0.05 parts per million.

Lead (Pb) is a poisonous element that usually occurs as a metal. However, traces can be found in living tissue, in soil and water, even in the air we breathe. Fortunately, with the advent of unleaded gasoline, the major source of this airborne poison has been largely controlled. The EPA primary standard for this pollutant is 1.5 micrograms per cubic meter of air.

JUDGING HEALTH CARE AND ENVIRONMENT

In this age of euphemism, *health* means not only health but also its exact opposite, illness. A hospital is not really a health care institution; its business is to take care of sick people. The truly healthy need little health care, save for an occasional shot or checkup; the unhealthy need a lot.

The health care facilities of different places cannot be rated with total fairness. The quality of care that a patient receives may be largely the luck of the draw. The skill of the doctor and the training, competence, and dedication of the nursing staff can vary, sometimes greatly. But it is possible to compare the places for relative abundance of facilities. For this reason, *Places Rated Almanac* looks at the availability of certain facilities for "illness care," at relative costs for insurance and hospitalization, and at two environmental factors—fluoridation of drinking water and air pollution—in ranking the metro areas.

The first of *Places Rated*'s scoring indicators, the number of physicians for every 100,000 residents, is a general measure of basic health care supply. Where is the greatest concentration of doctors? As mentioned briefly earlier, many are found in large cities, which have numerous hospitals and other facilities. Surprisingly, the two metro areas with the greatest concentration of physicians in the nation are located about 150 miles apart on the plains of the northern Midwest: Rochester, Minnesota, and Iowa City, Iowa. Both have relatively small resident populations and unusually large proportions of physicians, Rochester due to the Mayo Clinic and Iowa City because of the medical complex associated with the University of Iowa and the Veterans Administration.

The next two variables, teaching hospitals and medical schools, are almost universally accepted as indicators of health care quality as well as health care capacity. Medical schools are scarce indeed; there are only about 150 of them in America, and quite a few of these (such as Dartmouth College Medical School in Hanover, New Hampshire) are not located in metro areas. These schools attract every type of medical talent: physicians, diagnosticians, psychiatrists, nurses, teachers, and hospital specialists. Furthermore, these schools give rise to and are integrated with teaching hospitals, where one can receive care supervised by medical school faculty. This interaction between medical school and teaching hospital encourages the development and use of the latest techniques, equipment, and therapy. Constant review and analysis of cases by faculty and students—a necessary part of the teaching process—help prevent sloppy or inept patient care.

Cardiac rehabilitation centers, comprehensive cancer treatment centers, and hospices constitute the next three variables. Their presence serves as an indicator of the availability of a range of specialized health care services within an area. The cardiac rehabilitation units (CRUs) considered by *Places Rated Almanac* are not cardiac intensive care units, which most sizable hospitals have. These rehabilitation centers are actually programs in physical fitness and conditioning for patients who have suffered one or more heart attacks. Likewise, the cancer treatment centers are not to be confused with the cancer wards of major hospitals. They are similar, but the centers listed in the Place Profiles include both those institutions designated by the National Cancer Institute as truly comprehensive

(there are only 20 of these in the metro areas) as well as a number of slightly less comprehensive clinical cancer centers.

Hospices, or care for the terminally ill, originated in Europe and have recently become one of the fastest-growing forms of health care. It is estimated that there are now more than 1,200 throughout the country. To be considered by *Places Rated Almanac*, hospices may be either independent, allied with a major hospital, or located within a hospital under the direction of a hospice team. Given the unique and valuable service rendered by hospices, they are an important addition to the health care network of any metro area.

Along with availability of such facilities, the affordability of health care is a major concern of many Americans. Consequently, *Places Rated* has included a major new ranking variable, the insurance/hospitalization costs index, derived from the rate books of major health insurers. This costs index serves as a basic indicator of insurance costs, frequency of illness in a given place, and relative cost of hospitalization. When the *Places Rated* costs index falls into the Poor and Unacceptable ranges, it is viewed as a negative indicator.

Fluoridation of drinking water remains somewhat controversial despite evidence that it helps prevent tooth decay and hardens and protects bones. Since the publication of the first edition of *Places Rated Almanac*, many large cities have discontinued fluoridation, but until hard evidence emerges that it is harmful to living tissue, *Places Rated* continues to regard it as a positive health care asset. The other environmental variable, air pollution, counts heavily against a metro area.

It should be noted that a number of modifications to the system for rating metro areas for health care and environment have been introduced in this edition of *Places Rated Almanac*. Two changes are of major importance. The first is the addition of the insurance/hospitalization costs index. The second, and one that is applied in a similar fashion in three other chapters of this book, is the CMSA Access factor. Every metro area receives full credit for scored assets within its boundaries, but each metro area that is part of a Consolidated Metropolitan Statistical Area, or CMSA (a full listing of the 22 CMSAs and their 76 component metro areas is given in the Appendix) is also awarded bonus points, as explained below, in recognition of the fact that certain assets of a given metro area can benefit residents of nearby areas as well. The special health care facilities for which residents of more than one metro area share the benefits are identified by *Places Rated* as teaching hospitals, medical schools, cardiac rehabilitation centers, comprehensive cancer treatment centers, and hospices.

Each metro area starts with a base score of zero, and points are either added or subtracted according to the following indicators:

1. *Physicians per 100,000 residents.* One point is awarded for every physician per 100,000 people living within the metro area.
2. *Teaching hospitals.* Each teaching hospital is worth 200 points. A ceiling of 2,000 points is set for teaching hospitals because there can be many of them attached to each medical school, some only marginally involved in teaching. Also, the number of teaching hospitals usually is in almost direct proportion to city size. To be as fair as possible in rating facilities nationwide, therefore, only the first ten teaching hospitals in each metro area are awarded points (although all are listed in the Place Profiles).
3. *Medical schools.* Each medical school receives 300 points.
4. *Cardiac rehabilitation centers, comprehensive cancer treatment centers, and hospices.* Each of these facilities is worth 100 points, with a 1,000-point ceiling for each type of facility. Cancer treatment centers that meet rigorous standards set by the National Cancer Institute are awarded an additional 50 points apiece; they are identified by a bullet (•) in the Place Profiles.
5. *Costs index.* Based on health insurance rate books, *Places Rated* has classified the metro areas according to their relative health care costs. Points are either added or subtracted according to the following designations: Outstanding = 400 points; Excellent = 200; Good = 100; Fair = 0; Poor = −100; Unacceptable = −200. The designation for each metro area is listed in the Place Profiles.
6. *Fluoridation.* A metro area receives 300 points if all its central cities have fluoridated water, either natural or adjusted. If only one central city in a two-city metro area is fluoridated, the metro area receives 150 points; in a three-city metro area, each city with fluoridated water is worth 100 points.
7. *Air pollution.* One hundred points is subtracted for each pollutant that exceeds the EPA primary standard in its annual mean average. In the case of ozone, the number of days exceeding the standard varies enormously from metro area to metro area. Accordingly, the severity of the ozone problem is highlighted by one or more triangles (▲) in the Place Profiles, and an additional 100 points is subtracted for each triangle.
8. *CMSA Access.* Each of the 76 metro areas that is part of a Consolidated Metropolitan Statistical Area is eligible to receive bonus points based on "shared" facilities: teaching hospitals, medical schools, cardiac rehabilitation

---

What Do the Rankings Mean?

It should be underscored that what is being judged in this chapter is health *care* in each of America's metro areas, not health of the resident population. Moreover, *Places Rated* is judging not health care service but health care facilities. And, finally, we are judging not *all* facilities but rather some of the exceptional ones.

Keeping this in mind will help the reader avoid the mistake of assuming that a low score in this chapter means either (1) that the people in X place are unhealthy and don't live very long, or (2) that if one were to relocate to X place, basic health care—including even such complex emergency surgery as a coronary bypass—would be unavailable or inferior. Both of these conclusions are incorrect. A low score or rank in this chapter does indicate, however, that the emphasis in that metro area is probably on basic health care and that the latest techniques, equipment, and personnel trained to implement them are more likely to be found elsewhere.

Affluent, big-city metro areas generally score higher in our rankings than the more sparsely populated metro areas. But this doesn't mean that a person cannot receive excellent medical care in a rural area or a poor state or, conversely, experience medical care that is bad enough to be life-threatening in even the best of hospitals. The quality of medical and nursing care most people receive depends upon a number of variables, including the patient's ability to pay, blind chance, and human error.

---

centers, comprehensive cancer treatment centers, and hospices. A place receives a bonus of 10 percent of the points accumulated by the *other* metro areas in the CMSA for these facilities. A metro area's *own* points for shared facilities are not considered in calculating its bonus points. Thus, in the Dallas–Fort Worth consolidated area, the Dallas metro area receives a bonus of 40 access points, or 10 percent of the 400 points accumulated by Fort Worth–Arlington, and Fort Worth–Arlington receives 220 access points, based on Dallas's 2,200 points for shared facilities. (Three metro areas receive no access bonus because the other metro area in the CMSA has none of the shared facilities: Buffalo, New York; Pittsburgh; and Portland, Oregon.)

Sample Comparison: New York, New York, and Glens Falls, New York

As it did in the first edition of *Places Rated Almanac*, New York leads the metro areas in health care facilities and environment. The nation's largest metro area, it consequently has an extensive supply of medical institutions to accommodate its millions of inhabitants. Furthermore, many prestigious universities and philanthropic foundations that support the work of these institutions are located in this city, helping to make it one of the leading medical research centers in the world.

The numbers speak for themselves. New York has 370 physicians per 100,000 residents, for 370 points, and 36 teaching hospitals (more than any other metro area; second-place Chicago has 21), good for the maximum possible 2,000 points. Its seven medical schools (again, more than any other metro area) give it another 2,100 points. New York also has 16 cardiac rehabilitation centers (for which it tallies the maximum possible 1,000 points); five cancer treatment centers, two of which receive a 50-point bonus (600 points); and nine hospices (900 points). In the next three categories, the Big Apple loses 200 points for its Unacceptable rating in insurance costs, is awarded 300 points for fluoridated drinking water, and is penalized 100 points for air pollution (for all its great size and traffic, this metro area has a surprisingly small air pollution problem, with only one pollutant—CO).

But New York's scoring does not end here. Under *Places Rated*'s new scoring system, metro areas that compose what the U.S. Bureau of the Census calls Consolidated Metropolitan Statistical Areas share a percentage of the points accumulated by the other members of their CMSA for medical schools, teaching hospitals, cardiac rehabilitation units, cancer treatment centers, and hospices. Altogether 12 metro areas make up the New York–Northern New Jersey–Long Island consolidated area. The points for shared facilities earned by the other 11 metro areas in the CMSA amount to 8,800, resulting in an 880-point bonus for New York. This pushes New York's score to a hefty 7,850 points for an undisputed first place.

About 200 miles north of New York lies the last-place finisher in the health care race, Glens Falls. This metro area has a respectable number of physicians per 100,000 residents, 143, for 143 points. However, that is about all this small, upstate town can boast of in the way of health care. It has no teaching hospitals, medical schools, cardiac rehabilitation centers, comprehensive cancer centers, or hospices. It receives a Poor rating for health insurance costs, which means a loss of 100 points, and it does not fluoridate its water. There is no air pollution in Glens Falls, which is not surprising, considering its location near the 5.6-million-acre Adirondack Park. All this adds up to only 43 points, the lowest score among the metro areas.

It's interesting to note that another New York metro area, Orange County, has a similarly sparse number of health care assets. However, since Orange County is part of the huge New York–Northern New Jersey–Long Island consolidated area, it earns enough bonus points to be propelled into a respectable 79th place.

Places Rated: Metro Areas Ranked for Health Care and Environment

Nine criteria are used in arriving at a score for the quality of health care and environment in a metro area: (1) physicians per 100,000 residents, (2) teaching hospitals, (3) medical schools, (4) cardiac rehabilitation centers, (5) comprehensive cancer treatment centers, (6) hospices, (7) insurance/hospitalization costs index, (8) fluoridation of drinking water, and (9) air pollution.

Metro areas can also be awarded bonus points for shared facilities—teaching hospitals, medical schools, cardiac rehabilitation centers, cancer treatment centers, and hospices—within their Consolidated Metropolitan Statistical Areas.

Places that receive tie scores are given the same rank and are listed in alphabetical order.

Metro Areas from Best to Worst

Places Rated Rank	Places Rated Score	Places Rated Rank	Places Rated Score	Places Rated Rank	Places Rated Score
1. New York, NY	7,850	11. San Francisco, CA	3,726	21. Seattle, WA	2,715
2. Chicago, IL	5,766	12. Baltimore, MD	3,562	22. Bergen–Passaic, NJ	2,661
3. Boston, MA	5,301	13. Raleigh–Durham, NC	3,476	23. Stamford, CT	2,610
4. Philadelphia, PA–NJ	5,158	14. Pittsburgh, PA	3,413	24. Middlesex–Somerset–Hunterdon, NJ	2,589
5. Los Angeles–Long Beach, CA	5,153	15. Atlanta, GA	3,195	25. New Orleans, LA	2,586
6. Washington, DC–MD–VA	4,361	16. Cleveland, OH	3,167	26. Omaha, NE–IA	2,559
7. Detroit, MI	4,142	17. Milwaukee, WI	3,053	27. Bridgeport–Milford, CT	2,550
8. Newark, NJ	4,106	18. Rochester, MN	2,966	28. Denver, CO	2,533
9. Minneapolis–St. Paul, MN–WI	3,934	19. St. Louis, MO–IL	2,850	29. Norwalk, CT	2,530
10. Nassau–Suffolk, NY	3,919	20. Dallas, TX	2,825	30. Hartford, CT	2,521

Places Rated Rank	Places Rated Score	Places Rated Rank	Places Rated Score	Places Rated Rank	Places Rated Score
31. Ann Arbor, MI	2,508	88. Lansing–East Lansing, MI	1,371	144. Boulder–Longmont, CO	962
32. Monmouth–Ocean, NJ	2,482	89. Gary–Hammond, IN	1,364	145. Knoxville, TN	960
33. Houston, TX	2,467	90. Charlottesville, VA	1,348		
33. Providence, RI	2,467			146. Muncie, IN	949
35. Buffalo, NY	2,465	91. San Antonio, TX	1,337	147. Racine, WI	931
		92. Honolulu, HI	1,298	148. Waterloo–Cedar Falls, IA	925
36. Richmond–Petersburg, VA	2,448	93. Grand Rapids, MI	1,274	149. Fargo–Moorhead, ND–MN	920
37. Iowa City, IA	2,437	94. Greenville–Spartanburg, SC	1,260	150. Brockton, MA	916
38. San Diego, CA	2,416	95. Tucson, AZ	1,259		
39. Oakland, CA	2,362			150. Green Bay, WI	916
40. Danbury, CT	2,350	96. Des Moines, IA	1,256	152. Battle Creek, MI	900
		97. Fort Lauderdale–Hollywood–		152. Fall River, MA–RI	900
41. Miami–Hialeah, FL	2,314	Pompano Beach, FL	1,252	152. Lubbock, TX	900
42. Dayton–Springfield, OH	2,253	98. New Britain, CT	1,245	155. Middletown, CT	884
43. Indianapolis, IN	2,243	99. Lake County, IL	1,237		
44. Riverside–San Bernardino, CA	2,201	100. Salem–Gloucester, MA	1,232	156. Huntington–Ashland, WV–KY–OH	875
45. Madison, WI	2,168	101. Scranton–Wilkes-Barre, PA	1,219	157. Fayetteville, NC	872
		102. Waterbury, CT	1,218	158. Beaver County, PA	861
46. Cincinnati, OH–KY–IN	2,138	103. Asheville, NC	1,204	159. Williamsport, PA	860
47. San Jose, CA	2,117	104. Aurora–Elgin, IL	1,203	160. Nashua, NH	853
48. Louisville, KY–IN	2,111	105. Lawrence–Haverhill, MA–NH	1,202		
49. Harrisburg–Lebanon– Carlisle, PA	2,087	106. Tampa–St. Petersburg–		161. Sioux City, IA–NE	846
50. New Haven–Meriden, CT	2,068	Clearwater, FL	1,189	162. Cedar Rapids, IA	837
		107. Peoria, IL	1,184	163. Portland, ME	834
51. Memphis, TN–AR–MS	2,043	108. Jacksonville, FL	1,181	164. Appleton–Oshkosh–	
52. Anaheim–Santa Ana, CA	2,025	109. Duluth, MN–WI	1,159	Neenah, WI	833
53. Rochester, NY	1,969	110. Reading, PA	1,154	164. Columbus, GA–AL	833
54. Columbia, MO	1,951				
55. Kansas City, MO	1,939	111. Johnson City–Kingsport– Bristol, TN–VA	1,152	166. Montgomery, AL	832
		112. Topeka, KS	1,148	167. South Bend–Mishawaka, IN	830
56. Norfolk–Virginia Beach– Newport News, VA	1,932	113. Hamilton–Middletown, OH	1,135	168. Anderson, SC	820
57. Springfield, IL	1,877	114. Pawtucket–Woonsocket–		169. Florence, SC	818
58. Little Rock–North Little Rock, AR	1,861	Attleboro, RI–MA	1,117	169. Hagerstown, MD	818
59. Lexington–Fayette, KY	1,860	115. Davenport–Rock Island– Moline, IA–IL	1,113	169. Wausau, WI	818
60. Albuquerque, NM	1,853			172. Bloomington–Normal, IL	815
		116. Lancaster, PA	1,111	173. Owensboro, KY	812
61. Nashville, TN	1,850	117. Grand Forks, ND	1,109	174. Vineland–Millville–Bridgeton, NJ	807
62. Columbus, OH	1,837	118. Oxnard–Ventura, CA	1,106	175. Wichita, KS	806
63. Burlington, VT	1,809	119. Lorain–Elyria, OH	1,105		
64. Worcester, MA	1,805	120. Wilmington, NC	1,099	176. Bismarck, ND	804
65. Augusta, GA–SC	1,798			177. Sarasota, FL	801
		121. Youngstown–Warren, OH	1,097	178. Eau Claire, WI	798
66. Jackson, MS	1,792	122. Savannah, GA	1,084	179. Wheeling, WV–OH	791
67. Jersey City, NJ	1,759	123. Lowell, MA–NH	1,083	180. Evansville, IN–KY	783
68. Toledo, OH	1,738	124. Vallejo–Fairfield–Napa, CA	1,079		
69. Gainesville, FL	1,731	125. Kenosha, WI	1,067	181. Austin, TX	782
70. Kansas City, KS	1,711			182. Bangor, ME	780
		126. Fort Wayne, IN	1,060	183. Lincoln, NE	775
71. Greensboro–Winston-Salem– High Point, NC	1,694	127. Joliet, IL	1,058	184. Orlando, FL	765
72. Birmingham, AL	1,692	128. Santa Rosa–Petaluma, CA	1,052	185. Cumberland, MD–WV	760
73. Akron, OH	1,656	129. Kalamazoo, MI	1,043		
74. Salt Lake City–Ogden, UT	1,631	130. Sioux Falls, SD	1,041	186. Lewiston–Auburn, ME	759
75. Oklahoma City, OK	1,623			187. Salem, OR	749
		131. Syracuse, NY	1,040	188. Lima, OH	741
76. Portland, OR	1,590	132. Fort Worth–Arlington, TX	1,038	189. Jacksonville, NC	740
77. Phoenix, AZ	1,584	133. Roanoke, VA	1,036	190. Manchester, NH	737
78. Tulsa, OK	1,581	134. Santa Cruz, CA	1,035		
79. Orange County, NY	1,574	135. Sacramento, CA	1,027	191. Decatur, IL	732
80. Mobile, AL	1,469			191. Lynchburg, VA	732
		136. Saginaw–Bay City– Midland, MI	1,022	193. Bloomington, IN	731
81. Charleston, SC	1,463	137. Binghamton, NY	1,007	193. Fort Collins–Loveland, CO	731
82. Shreveport, LA	1,445	138. Hickory, NC	1,006	193. Johnstown, PA	731
82. Wilmington, DE–NJ–MD	1,445	139. Charlotte–Gastonia–Rock Hill, NC–SC	999		
84. Galveston–Texas City, TX	1,437	140. Burlington, NC	994	196. Flint, MI	724
85. Albany–Schenectady– Troy, NY	1,431			197. Daytona Beach, FL	723
		141. Bristol, CT	975	198. Colorado Springs, CO	721
86. Columbia, SC	1,421	142. Rockford, IL	969	199. York, PA	713
87. Trenton, NJ	1,372	143. Alton–Granite City, IL	965	200. Springfield, MA	710
				201. Charleston, WV	708
				202. Greeley, CO	706

Places Rated Rank	Places Rated Score	Places Rated Rank	Places Rated Score	Places Rated Rank	Places Rated Score
203. Janesville–Beloit, WI	700	246. Las Cruces, NM	588	288. Altoona, PA	432
203. Sharon, PA	700	247. Houma–Thibodaux, LA	583	289. Bakersfield, CA	420
205. Muskegon, MI	699	248. Anderson, IN	580	290. Las Vegas, NV	412
		249. Springfield, MO	577		
206. Pittsfield, MA	694	250. Benton Harbor, MI	570	291. Killeen–Temple, TX	398
207. La Crosse, WI	686			292. Sherman–Denison, TX	394
208. Huntsville, AL	685	251. Chattanooga, TN–GA	564	293. Utica–Rome, NY	391
209. Jackson, MI	679	252. Pensacola, FL	563	294. Odessa, TX	384
210. Tuscaloosa, AL	674	253. Elmira, NY	562	295. West Palm Beach–Boca	
		254. New London–Norwich, CT–RI	556	Raton–Delray Beach, FL	375
211. Champaign–Urbana–		255. Wichita Falls, TX	549		
Rantoul, IL	672			296. McAllen–Edinburg–	
211. Tyler, TX	672	256. Lafayette, LA	548	Mission, TX	372
213. Amarillo, TX	669	257. Fort Myers, FL	546	297. Tallahassee, FL	370
214. Great Falls, MT	667	258. Eugene–Springfield, OR	539	298. Fresno, CA	369
215. Parkersburg–Marietta,		258. Tacoma, WA	539	299. Poughkeepsie, NY	355
WV–OH	665	260. Waco, TX	538	300. Salinas–Seaside–Monterey,	
				CA	352
216. Fitchburg–Leominster, MA	655	261. Santa Barbara–Santa Maria–			
216. Lafayette, IN	655	Lompoc, CA	532	301. Modesto, CA	347
218. Alexandria, LA	640	262. Erie, PA	529	302. Casper, WY	345
218. Bryan–College Station, TX	640	263. El Paso, TX	528	303. Texarkana, TX–Texarkana, AR	343
218. Dubuque, IA	640	264. Fort Pierce, FL	527	304. Baton Rouge, LA	342
		265. New Bedford, MA	519	304. Stockton, CA	342
221. Atlantic City, NJ	637				
222. Enid, OK	626	266. Melbourne–Titusville–		306. Olympia, WA	338
223. Gadsden, AL	622	Palm Bay, FL	517	307. Bradenton, FL	333
224. Allentown–Bethlehem, PA–NJ	621	266. Vancouver, WA	517	308. Monroe, LA	331
224. Lawrence, KS	621	268. Longview–Marshall, TX	509	309. Lakeland–Winter Haven, FL	323
		269. Niagara Falls, NY	507	310. Yakima, WA	317
226. Albany, GA	618	270. Steubenville–Weirton,			
227. Pine Bluff, AR	617	OH–WV	505	311. Lake Charles, LA	314
228. Beaumont–Port Arthur, TX	616			312. Bremerton, WA	310
229. Reno, NV	615	271. Joplin, MO	500	313. Mansfield, OH	303
230. State College, PA	612	272. Spokane, WA	497	314. Richland–Kennewick–	
		273. Ocala, FL	489	Pasco, WA	300
231. Kankakee, IL	609	274. Fort Walton Beach, FL	484	315. Redding, CA	274
232. Florence, AL	607	275. Billings, MT	479		
233. Athens, GA	605			316. Victoria, TX	260
234. St. Cloud, MN	603	276. Lawton, OK	477	317. Medford, OR	256
235. Anchorage, AK	601	277. Pueblo, CO	468	318. Chico, CA	243
		278. Fort Smith, AR–OK	466	319. Bellingham, WA	240
236. Anniston, AL	598	279. Laredo, TX	465	320. Abilene, TX	237
237. Elkhart–Goshen, IN	596	280. Corpus Christi, TX	458		
237. Kokomo, IN	596			321. San Angelo, TX	236
237. Portsmouth–Dover–Rochester,		281. Boise City, ID	453	322. St. Joseph, MO	223
NH–ME	596	281. Terre Haute, IN	453	323. Yuba City, CA	212
240. Fayetteville–Springdale, AR	594	283. Clarksville–Hopkinsville,		324. Visalia–Tulare–Porterville, CA	210
		TN–KY	446	325. Panama City, FL	201
241. Danville, VA	593	284. East St. Louis–Belleville, IL	444		
241. Dothan, AL	593	285. Canton, OH	443	326. Provo–Orem, UT	198
241. Macon–Warner Robins, GA	593			327. Midland, TX	97
241. Pascagoula, MS	593	286. Biloxi–Gulfport, MS	441	328. Brownsville–Harlingen, TX	91
241. Sheboygan, WI	593	287. Brazoria, TX	438	329. Glens Falls, NY	43

Metro Areas Listed Alphabetically

Metro Area	Places Rated Rank	Metro Area	Places Rated Rank	Metro Area	Places Rated Rank
Abilene, TX	320	Anaheim–Santa Ana, CA	52	Atlantic City, NJ	221
Akron, OH	73	Anchorage, AK	235	Augusta, GA–SC	65
Albany, GA	226	Anderson, IN	248	Aurora–Elgin, IL	104
Albany–Schenectady–Troy, NY	85	Anderson, SC	168	Austin, TX	181
Albuquerque, NM	60	Ann Arbor, MI	31	Bakersfield, CA	289
Alexandria, LA	218	Anniston, AL	236	Baltimore, MD	12
Allentown–Bethlehem, PA–NJ	224	Appleton–Oshkosh–Neenah, WI	164	Bangor, ME	182
Alton–Granite City, IL	143	Asheville, NC	103	Baton Rouge, LA	304
Altoona, PA	288	Athens, GA	233	Battle Creek, MI	152
Amarillo, TX	213	Atlanta, GA	15	Beaumont–Port Arthur, TX	228

Metro Area	Places Rated Rank	Metro Area	Places Rated Rank	Metro Area	Places Rated Rank
Beaver County, PA	158	Eau Claire, WI	178	Kalamazoo, MI	129
Bellingham, WA	319	El Paso, TX	263		
Benton Harbor, MI	250	Elkhart–Goshen, IN	237	Kankakee, IL	231
Bergen–Passaic, NJ	22	Elmira, NY	253	Kansas City, KS	70
Billings, MT	275	Enid, OK	222	Kansas City, MO	55
				Kenosha, WI	125
Biloxi–Gulfport, MS	286	Erie, PA	262	Killeen–Temple, TX	291
Binghamton, NY	137	Eugene–Springfield, OR	258		
Birmingham, AL	72	Evansville, IN–KY	180	Knoxville, TN	145
Bismarck, ND	176	Fall River, MA–RI	152	Kokomo, IN	237
Bloomington, IN	193	Fargo–Moorhead, ND–MN	149	La Crosse, WI	207
				Lafayette, IN	216
Bloomington–Normal, IL	172	Fayetteville, NC	157	Lafayette, LA	256
Boise City, ID	281	Fayetteville–Springdale, AR	240		
Boston, MA	3	Fitchburg–Leominster, MA	216	Lake Charles, LA	311
Boulder–Longmont, CO	144	Flint, MI	196	Lake County, IL	99
Bradenton, FL	307	Florence, AL	232	Lakeland–Winter Haven, FL	309
				Lancaster, PA	116
Brazoria, TX	287	Florence, SC	169	Lansing–East Lansing, MI	88
Bremerton, WA	312	Fort Collins–Loveland, CO	193		
Bridgeport–Milford, CT	27	Fort Lauderdale–Hollywood–		Laredo, TX	279
Bristol, CT	141	Pompano Beach, FL	97	Las Cruces, NM	246
Brockton, MA	150	Fort Myers, FL	257	Las Vegas, NV	290
		Fort Pierce, FL	264	Lawrence, KS	224
Brownsville–Harlingen, TX	328			Lawrence–Haverhill, MA–NH	105
Bryan–College Station, TX	218	Fort Smith, AR–OK	278		
Buffalo, NY	35	Fort Walton Beach, FL	274	Lawton, OK	276
Burlington, NC	140	Fort Wayne, IN	126	Lewiston–Auburn, ME	186
Burlington, VT	63	Fort Worth–Arlington, TX	132	Lexington–Fayette, KY	59
		Fresno, CA	298	Lima, OH	188
Canton, OH	285			Lincoln, NE	183
Casper, WY	302	Gadsden, AL	223		
Cedar Rapids, IA	162	Gainesville, FL	69	Little Rock–North Little Rock, AR	58
Champaign–Urbana–Rantoul, IL	211	Galveston–Texas City, TX	84	Longview–Marshall, TX	268
Charleston, SC	81	Gary–Hammond, IN	89	Lorain–Elyria, OH	119
		Glens Falls, NY	329	Los Angeles–Long Beach, CA	5
Charleston, WV	201			Louisville, KY–IN	48
Charlotte–Gastonia–Rock Hill,		Grand Forks, ND	117		
NC–SC	139	Grand Rapids, MI	93	Lowell, MA–NH	123
Charlottesville, VA	90	Great Falls, MT	214	Lubbock, TX	152
Chattanooga, TN–GA	251	Greeley, CO	202	Lynchburg, VA	191
Chicago, IL	2	Green Bay, WI	150	Macon–Warner Robins, GA	241
				Madison, WI	45
Chico, CA	318	Greensboro–Winston-Salem–			
Cincinnati, OH–KY–IN	46	High Point, NC	71	Manchester, NH	190
Clarksville–Hopkinsville, TN–KY	283	Greenville–Spartanburg, SC	94	Mansfield, OH	313
Cleveland, OH	16	Hagerstown, MD	169	McAllen–Edinburg–Mission, TX	296
Colorado Springs, CO	198	Hamilton–Middletown, OH	113	Medford, OR	317
		Harrisburg–Lebanon–Carlisle, PA	49	Melbourne–Titusville–Palm Bay, FL	266
Columbia, MO	54				
Columbia, SC	86	Hartford, CT	30	Memphis, TN–AR–MS	51
Columbus, GA–AL	164	Hickory, NC	138	Miami–Hialeah, FL	41
Columbus, OH	62	Honolulu, HI	92	Middlesex–Somerset–Hunterdon, NJ	24
Corpus Christi, TX	280	Houma–Thibodaux, LA	247	Middletown, CT	155
		Houston, TX	33	Midland, TX	327
Cumberland, MD–WV	185				
Dallas, TX	20	Huntington–Ashland, WV–KY–OH	156	Milwaukee, WI	17
Danbury, CT	40	Huntsville, AL	208	Minneapolis–St. Paul, MN–WI	9
Danville, VA	241	Indianapolis, IN	43	Mobile, AL	80
Davenport–Rock Island–Moline,		Iowa City, IA	37	Modesto, CA	301
IA–IL	115	Jackson, MI	209	Monmouth–Ocean, NJ	32
Dayton–Springfield, OH	42	Jackson, MS	66	Monroe, LA	308
Daytona Beach, FL	197	Jacksonville, FL	108	Montgomery, AL	166
Decatur, IL	191	Jacksonville, NC	189	Muncie, IN	146
Denver, CO	28	Janesville–Beloit, WI	203	Muskegon, MI	205
Des Moines, IA	96	Jersey City, NJ	67	Nashua, NH	160
Detroit, MI	7	Johnson City–Kingsport–Bristol,		Nashville, TN	61
Dothan, AL	241	TN–VA	111	Nassau–Suffolk, NY	10
Dubuque, IA	218	Johnstown, PA	193	New Bedford, MA	265
Duluth, MN–WI	109	Joliet, IL	127	New Britain, CT	98
East St. Louis–Belleville, IL	284	Joplin, MO	271	New Haven–Meriden, CT	50

Metro Area	Places Rated Rank	Metro Area	Places Rated Rank	Metro Area	Places Rated Rank
New London–Norwich, CT–RI	254	Reno, NV	229	Stamford, CT	23
New Orleans, LA	25				
New York, NY	1	Richland–Kennewick–Pasco, WA	314	State College, PA	230
Newark, NJ	8			Steubenville–Weirton, OH–WV	270
Niagara Falls, NY	269	Richmond–Petersburg, VA	36	Stockton, CA	304
		Riverside–San Bernardino, CA	44	Syracuse, NY	131
Norfolk–Virginia Beach– Newport News, VA	56	Roanoke, VA	133	Tacoma, WA	258
		Rochester, MN	18		
Norwalk, CT	29			Tallahassee, FL	297
Oakland, CA	39	Rochester, NY	53	Tampa–St. Petersburg– Clearwater, FL	106
Ocala, FL	273	Rockford, IL	142	Terre Haute, IN	281
Odessa, TX	294	Sacramento, CA	135	Texarkana, TX–Texarkana, AR	303
		Saginaw–Bay City–Midland, MI	136	Toledo, OH	68
Oklahoma City, OK	75	St. Cloud, MN	234		
Olympia, WA	306			Topeka, KS	112
Omaha, NE–IA	26	St. Joseph, MO	322	Trenton, NJ	87
Orange County, NY	79	St. Louis, MO–IL	19	Tucson, AZ	95
Orlando, FL	184	Salem, OR	187	Tulsa, OK	78
		Salem–Gloucester, MA	100	Tuscaloosa, AL	210
Owensboro, KY	173	Salinas–Seaside–Monterey, CA	300		
Oxnard–Ventura, CA	118			Tyler, TX	211
Panama City, FL	325	Salt Lake City–Ogden, UT	74	Utica–Rome, NY	293
Parkersburg–Marietta, WV–OH	215	San Angelo, TX	321	Vallejo–Fairfield–Napa, CA	124
		San Antonio, TX	91	Vancouver, WA	266
Pascagoula, MS	241	San Diego, CA	38	Victoria, TX	316
		San Francisco, CA	11		
Pawtucket–Woonsocket–Attleboro, RI–MA	114	San Jose, CA	47	Vineland–Millville–Bridgeton, NJ	174
		Santa Barbara–Santa Maria– Lompoc, CA	261	Visalia–Tulare–Porterville, CA	324
Pensacola, FL	252			Waco, TX	260
Peoria, IL	107	Santa Cruz, CA	134	Washington, DC–MD–VA	6
Philadelphia, PA–NJ	4	Santa Rosa–Petaluma, CA	128	Waterbury, CT	102
Phoenix, AZ	77	Sarasota, FL	177		
				Waterloo–Cedar Falls, IA	148
Pine Bluff, AR	227	Savannah, GA	122	Wausau, WI	169
Pittsburgh, PA	14	Scranton–Wilkes-Barre, PA	101	West Palm Beach–Boca Raton– Delray Beach, FL	295
Pittsfield, MA	206	Seattle, WA	21		
Portland, ME	163	Sharon, PA	203	Wheeling, WV–OH	179
Portland, OR	76	Sheboygan, WI	241	Wichita, KS	175
Portsmouth–Dover–Rochester, NH–ME	237	Sherman–Denison, TX	292	Wichita Falls, TX	255
Poughkeepsie, NY	299	Shreveport, LA	82	Williamsport, PA	159
Providence, RI	33	Sioux City, IA–NE	161	Wilmington, DE–NJ–MD	82
Provo–Orem, UT	326	Sioux Falls, SD	130	Wilmington, NC	120
Pueblo, CO	277	South Bend–Mishawaka, IN	167	Worcester, MA	64
Racine, WI	147	Spokane, WA	272	Yakima, WA	310
Raleigh–Durham, NC	13	Springfield, IL	57	York, PA	199
Reading, PA	110	Springfield, MA	200	Youngstown–Warren, OH	121
Redding, CA	315	Springfield, MO	249	Yuba City, CA	323

Place Profiles: Health Care Facilities and Environmental Features of 329 Metro Areas

In the pages that follow, some of the health care facilities and environmental characteristics of the 329 metro areas are detailed. The information is derived from a number of sources: American Medical Association, *Physician Characteristics and Distribution in the United States,* 1982; U.S. Department of Commerce, Bureau of the Census, *County and City Data Book,* 1983; Anthony Kruzas, *Medical and Health Information Directory,* 1982; American Heart Association, *Directory of Cardiac Rehabilitation,* 1981; American Cancer Society,

Cancer Facts and Figures, 1984; Environmental Protection Agency, *Air Quality Data, 1983;* and U.S. Department of Health and Human Services, *Fluoridation Census,* 1984.

Teaching hospitals that are located in metro areas that have no medical schools are affiliated with schools in other metro areas. Those cancer treatment centers designated as fully comprehensive by the National Cancer Institute are identified by a bullet (•) before their names. The presence of a symbol for a pollutant in the category Air Pollution indicates that this pollutant exceeds the EPA primary standard in its annual mean average. One or more triangles (▲) in this category signal a severe ozone problem. The CMSA Access entry gives the name of the consolidated area to which the metro area belongs and tells how many points it receives for shared assets.

A star preceding a metro area's name highlights it as one of the top 25 places for health care and environment.

Abilene, TX
Physicians per 100,000: 137
Costs Index: Good
Fluoridation: None
Air Pollution: Insignificant
Places Rated Score: 237
Places Rated Rank: 320

Akron, OH
Physicians per 100,000: 176
Teaching Hospitals:
  Akron City Hospital
  Akron General Medical Center
  St. Thomas Hospital Medical Center
Cardiac Rehabilitation Centers:
  Litchfield Rehabilitation Center CRU
Costs Index: Excellent
Fluoridation: Adjusted
Air Pollution: Insignificant
CMSA Access: CLEVELAND–AKRON–
  LORAIN, OH (280)
Places Rated Score: 1,656
Places Rated Rank: 73

Albany, GA
Physicians per 100,000: 118
Costs Index: Excellent
Fluoridation: Adjusted
Air Pollution: Insignificant
Places Rated Score: 618
Places Rated Rank: 226

Albany–Schenectady–Troy, NY
Physicians per 100,000: 231
Teaching Hospitals:
  Albany Medical Center Hospital
  VA Medical Center
Medical Schools:
  Albany Medical College of Union
    University
Cardiac Rehabilitation Centers:
  Albany Medical Center Hospital Exercise
    Test Lab
  St. Mary's Hospital CRU
  Samaritan Hospital Coronary Care and
    Rehabilitation Unit
  VA Medical Center CRU
Hospices:
  Hospice of Schenectady
Costs Index: Unacceptable
Fluoridation: Adjusted (Schenectady and
  Troy only)
Air Pollution: Insignificant
Places Rated Score: 1,431
Places Rated Rank: 85

Albuquerque, NM
Physicians per 100,000: 253
Teaching Hospitals:
  Bernalillo County Medical Center
  Lovelace-Bataan Medical Center
  VA Medical Center
Medical Schools:
  University of New Mexico School of
    Medicine

Cardiac Rehabilitation Centers:
  Lovelace Medical Center CRU
  New Heart, Inc., Rehabilitation Center
Comprehensive Cancer Treatment
  Centers:
  University of New Mexico Cancer
    Research and Treatment Center
Hospices:
  Hospital Home Health Care–Hospice
    Program
Costs Index: Excellent
Fluoridation: Adjusted
Air Pollution: TSP, CO
Places Rated Score: 1,853
Places Rated Rank: 60

Alexandria, LA
Physicians per 100,000: 140
Costs Index: Excellent
Fluoridation: Natural
Air Pollution: Insignificant
Places Rated Score: 640
Places Rated Rank: 218

Allentown–Bethlehem, PA–NJ
Physicians per 100,000: 171
Cardiac Rehabilitation Centers:
  Sacred Heart Hospital CRU
Costs Index: Excellent
Fluoridation: Adjusted (Bethlehem only)
Air Pollution: Insignificant
Places Rated Score: 621
Places Rated Rank: 224

Alton–Granite City, IL
Physicians per 100,000: 85
Cardiac Rehabilitation Centers:
  St. Elizabeth Medical Center CRU
Hospices:
  Hospice of Madison County
  St. Anthony's Hospital–Home Health
    Agency
Costs Index: Excellent
Fluoridation: Adjusted (Alton only)
Air Pollution: Insignificant
CMSA Access: ST. LOUIS–EAST ST.
  LOUIS–ALTON, MO–IL (230)
Places Rated Score: 965
Places Rated Rank: 143

Altoona, PA
Physicians per 100,000: 132
Cardiac Rehabilitation Centers:
  Altoona Hospital Cardiac Rehabilitation
    Program
Costs Index: Excellent
Fluoridation: None
Air Pollution: Insignificant
Places Rated Score: 432
Places Rated Rank: 288

Amarillo, TX
Physicians per 100,000: 169
Cardiac Rehabilitation Centers:
  Amarillo Cardiac Program CRU
Costs Index: Good

Fluoridation: Natural
Air Pollution: Insignificant
Places Rated Score: 669
Places Rated Rank: 213

Anaheim–Santa Ana, CA
Physicians per 100,000: 205
Teaching Hospitals:
  University of California, Irvine, Medical
    Center
Medical Schools:
  California College of Medicine, Irvine
Cardiac Rehabilitation Centers
  Anaheim Memorial Hospital CRU
  Chapman General Hospital CRU
  Fountain Valley Community Hospital
    CRU
  Fullerton Community Hospital CRU
  Hoag Memorial Presbyterian Hospital
    CRU
  Martin Luther Medical Center CRU
  Mercy General Hospital CRU
  Mission Community Hospital CRU
  Orange CTC
  Palm Harbor General Hospital CRU
  St. Joseph's Hospital CRU
  St. Jude Hospital CRU
  Santa Ana–Tustin Community Hospital
    CTC
  University of California, Irvine, Medical
    Center CRU
Hospices:
  Hospice Orange County, Inc.
Costs Index: Fair
Fluoridation: None
Air Pollution: TSP, CO, O₃, NO₂, Pb
CMSA Access: LOS ANGELES–ANAHEIM–
  RIVERSIDE, CA (720)
Places Rated Score: 2,025
Places Rated Rank: 52

Anchorage, AK
Physicians per 100,000: 201
Cardiac Rehabilitation Centers:
  Alaska Treatment Center CRU
Hospices:
  Hospice of Anchorage
Costs Index: Fair
Fluoridation: Adjusted
Air Pollution: CO
Places Rated Score: 601
Places Rated Rank: 235

Anderson, IN
Physicians per 100,000: 80
Costs Index: Excellent
Fluoridation: Adjusted
Air Pollution: Insignificant
Places Rated Score: 580
Places Rated Rank: 248

Anderson, SC
Physicians per 100,000: 120
Costs Index: Outstanding
Fluoridation: Adjusted

Air Pollution: Insignificant
Places Rated Score: 820
Places Rated Rank: 168

Ann Arbor, MI
Physicians per 100,000: 633
Teaching Hospitals:
St. Joseph Mercy Hospital
University Hospital
VA Medical Center
Medical Schools:
University of Michigan Medical School
Cardiac Rehabilitation Centers:
St. Joseph Mercy Hospital CRU
Hospices:
Hospice of Washtenaw
Costs Index: Good
Fluoridation: Adjusted
Air Pollution: Insignificant
CMSA Access: DETROIT–ANN ARBOR,
MI (375)
Places Rated Score: 2,508
Places Rated Rank: 31

Anniston, AL
Physicians per 100,000: 98
Costs Index: Excellent
Fluoridation: Adjusted
Air Pollution: Insignificant
Places Rated Score: 598
Places Rated Rank: 236

Appleton–Oshkosh–Neenah, WI
Physicians per 100,000: 133
Cardiac Rehabilitation Centers:
Appleton Memorial Hospital CRU
St. Elizabeth Hospital CRU
Costs Index: Excellent
Fluoridation: Adjusted
Air Pollution: Insignificant
Places Rated Score: 833
Places Rated Rank: 164

Asheville, NC
Physicians per 100,000: 204
Cardiac Rehabilitation Centers:
St. Joseph Hospital CRU
VA Medical Center
Hospices:
Mountain Area Hospice
Costs Index: Outstanding
Fluoridation: Adjusted
Air Pollution: Insignificant
Places Rated Score: 1,204
Places Rated Rank: 103

Athens, GA
Physicians per 100,000: 105
Costs Index: Excellent
Fluoridation: Adjusted
Air Pollution: Insignificant
Places Rated Score: 605
Places Rated Rank: 233

★ Atlanta, GA
Physicians per 100,000: 195
Teaching Hospitals:
Crawford W. Long Memorial Hospital of
Emory University
Emory University Hospital
Grady Memorial Hospital
Henrietta Egleston Hospital for Children
VA Medical Center (Decatur)
Medical Schools:
Emory University School of Medicine
School of Medicine at Morehouse
College

Cardiac Rehabilitation Centers:
Atlanta Jewish Community Center CRU
Clayton General Hospital CRU
De Kalb General Hospital CRU
Georgia Baptist Medical Center CRU
Grady Memorial Hospital CRU
Northside Hospital CRU
Piedmont Hospital CRU
Hospices:
Grady Hospice of Grady Memorial
Hospital
Hospice Atlanta
Wesley Homes, Inc.
Costs Index: Good
Fluoridation: Adjusted
Air Pollution: Insignificant
Places Rated Score: 3,195
Places Rated Rank: 15

Atlantic City, NJ
Physicians per 100,000: 137
Costs Index: Excellent
Fluoridation: Adjusted
Air Pollution: Insignificant
Places Rated Score: 637
Places Rated Rank: 221

Augusta, GA–SC
Physicians per 100,000: 298
Teaching Hospitals:
Eugene Talmadge Memorial Hospital and
Clinic–Medical College of Georgia
VA Medical Center
Medical Schools:
Medical College of Georgia School of
Medicine
Cardiac Rehabilitation Centers:
Medical College of Georgia CRU
VA Medical Center CRU
Hospices:
St. Joseph's Hospital–Hospice Program
Costs Index: Excellent
Fluoridation: Adjusted
Air Pollution: Insignificant
Places Rated Score: 1,798
Places Rated Rank: 65

Aurora–Elgin, IL
Physicians per 100,000: 123
Costs Index: Excellent
Fluoridation: Natural (Aurora); adjusted
(Elgin)
Air Pollution: Insignificant
CMSA Access: CHICAGO–GARY–LAKE
COUNTY, IL–IN–WI (580)
Places Rated Score: 1,203
Places Rated Rank: 104

Austin, TX
Physicians per 100,000: 182
Hospices:
Girling and Associates–Home Health
Services, Inc.
Girling and Associates–Home Health
Services (Georgetown)
Costs Index: Good
Fluoridation: Adjusted
Air Pollution: Insignificant
Places Rated Score: 782
Places Rated Rank: 181

Bakersfield, CA
Physicians per 100,000: 120
Teaching Hospitals:
Kern Medical Center
Cardiac Rehabilitation Centers:
Mercy Hospital CRU
Costs Index: Good

Fluoridation: None
Air Pollution: TSP
Places Rated Score: 420
Places Rated Rank: 289

★ Baltimore, MD
Physicians per 100,000: 312
Teaching Hospitals:
Baltimore City Hospitals
Johns Hopkins Hospital
Maryland General Hospital
Sinai Hospital of Baltimore
Union Memorial Hospital
University of Maryland Hospital
VA Medical Center
Medical Schools:
Johns Hopkins University School of
Medicine
University of Maryland School of Medicine
Cardiac Rehabilitation Centers:
Church Hospital Corporation CRU
Greater Baltimore Medical Center CRU
Maryland General Hospital CRU
St. Agnes Hospital Cardiology
Department
St. Joseph Hospital CRU
Sinai Hospital–Department of Rehabilitative
Medicine
U.S. Public Health Service Hospital CRU
Comprehensive Cancer Treatment
Centers:
• Johns Hopkins Oncology Center
Hospices:
Church Hospital Corporation–Hospice
Care Program
St. Agnes Hospital Home Care Program
Sinai Hospital Home Care Hospice
Costs Index: Good
Fluoridation: Adjusted
Air Pollution: TSP, SO_2, CO
Places Rated Score: 3,562
Places Rated Rank: 12

Bangor, ME
Physicians per 100,000: 280
Costs Index: Excellent
Fluoridation: Adjusted
Air Pollution: Insignificant
Places Rated Score: 780
Places Rated Rank: 182

Baton Rouge, LA
Physicians per 100,000: 142
Costs Index: Excellent
Fluoridation: None
Air Pollution: Insignificant
Places Rated Score: 342
Places Rated Rank: 304

Battle Creek, MI
Physicians per 100,000: 100
Cardiac Rehabilitation Centers:
Community Hospital Association
Cardiac Evaluation
Hospices:
Good Samaritan Hospice Care
Visiting Nurse Service of Calhoun
County
Costs Index: Excellent
Fluoridation: Adjusted
Air Pollution: Insignificant
Places Rated Score: 900
Places Rated Rank: 152

Beaumont–Port Arthur, TX
Physicians per 100,000: 116
Hospices:
Home Health–Home Care, Inc.

Costs Index: Good
Fluoridation: Adjusted
Air Pollution: Insignificant
Places Rated Score: 616
Places Rated Rank: 228

Beaver County, PA
Physicians per 100,000: 81
Costs Index: Excellent
Fluoridation: Adjusted
Air Pollution: Insignificant
CMSA Access: PITTSBURGH–BEAVER
   VALLEY, PA (280)
Places Rated Score: 861
Places Rated Rank: 158

Bellingham, WA
Physicians per 100,000: 140
Costs Index: Good
Fluoridation: None
Air Pollution: Insignificant
Places Rated Score: 240
Places Rated Rank: 319

Benton Harbor, MI
Physicians per 100,000: 70
Costs Index: Excellent
Fluoridation: Adjusted
Air Pollution: Insignificant
Places Rated Score: 570
Places Rated Rank: 250

★ Bergen–Passaic, NJ
Physicians per 100,000: 211
Teaching Hospitals:
   Hackensack Hospital
Cardiac Rehabilitation Centers:
   Bergen County Heart Association CRU
   Pascack Valley Hospital CRU
   Passaic General Hospital CRU
   YM-YWHA of Bergen County CRU
Hospices:
   Hackensack Hospital–Hospice Program
   Tri-Hospital Home Health–Palliative Care
      Program
   Valley Hospital–Northwest Bergen
      Hospice Program
Costs Index: Good
Fluoridation: None
Air Pollution: Insignificant
CMSA Access: NEW YORK–NORTHERN
   NEW JERSEY–LONG ISLAND,
   NY–NJ–CT (1,450)
Places Rated Score: 2,661
Places Rated Rank: 22

Billings, MT
Physicians per 100,000: 179
Cardiac Rehabilitation Centers:
   St. Vincent Hospital CRU
Costs Index: Excellent
Fluoridation: None
Air Pollution: Insignificant
Places Rated Score: 479
Places Rated Rank: 275

Biloxi–Gulfport, MS
Physicians per 100,000: 141
Cardiac Rehabilitation Centers:
   Keesler Air Force Base Medical
      Center
Costs Index: Excellent
Fluoridation: None
Air Pollution: Insignificant
Places Rated Score: 441
Places Rated Rank: 286

Binghamton, NY
Physicians per 100,000: 207
Teaching Hospitals:
   Charles S. Wilson Memorial Hospital
Cardiac Rehabilitation Centers:
   Binghamton General Hospital CRU
   Our Lady of Lourdes Hospital CRU
   Wilson Memorial Hospital CRU
Hospices:
   Our Lady of Lourdes Memorial
      Hospital–Hospice
Costs Index: Poor
Fluoridation: Adjusted
Air Pollution: Insignificant
Places Rated Score: 1,007
Places Rated Rank: 137

Birmingham, AL
Physicians per 100,000: 242
Teaching Hospitals:
   Children's Hospital
   University of Alabama Hospitals
   VA Hospital
Medical Schools:
   University of Alabama in Birmingham
      School of Medicine
Cardiac Rehabilitation Centers:
   University of Alabama in Birmingham
      CRU
Comprehensive Cancer Treatment
   Centers:
 • University of Alabama in Birmingham–
      Comprehensive Cancer Center
Hospices:
   The Baptist Medical Centers–Hospice
      House Call
Costs Index: Good
Fluoridation: None
Air Pollution: Insignificant
Places Rated Score: 1,692
Places Rated Rank: 72

Bismarck, ND
Physicians per 100,000: 204
Cardiac Rehabilitation Centers:
   St. Alexius Hospital CRU
Costs Index: Excellent
Fluoridation: Adjusted
Air Pollution: Insignificant
Places Rated Score: 804
Places Rated Rank: 176

Bloomington, IN
Physicians per 100,000: 131
Cardiac Rehabilitation Centers:
   YMCA–Bloomington Hospital CRU
Costs Index: Excellent
Fluoridation: Adjusted
Air Pollution: Insignificant
Places Rated Score: 731
Places Rated Rank: 193

Bloomington–Normal, IL
Physicians per 100,000: 115
Cardiac Rehabilitation Centers:
   Brookhaw Hospital CRU
   Mennonite Hospital Cardiac Rehabilitation
      Program
Costs Index: Excellent
Fluoridation: Adjusted
Air Pollution: Insignificant
Places Rated Score: 815
Places Rated Rank: 172

Boise City, ID
Physicians per 100,000: 153

Cardiac Rehabilitation Centers:
   Idaho Elks Hospital Rehabilitation
      Program
   St. Alphonsus Hospital CRU
Hospices:
   Mountain States Tumor Institute
Costs Index: Excellent
Fluoridation: None
Air Pollution: TSP, CO
Places Rated Score: 453
Places Rated Rank: 281

★ Boston, MA
Physicians per 100,000: 471
Teaching Hospitals:
   Beth Israel Hospital
   Boston Hospital for Women
   Children's Hospital Medical Center
   Faulkner Hospital
   Massachusetts Eye and Ear Infirmary
   Massachusetts General Hospital
   McLean Hospital
   New England Deaconess Hospital
   New England Medical Center Hospital
   Peter Bent Brigham Hospital
   Robert B. Brigham Hospital
   University Hospital
   St. Elizabeth's Hospital
   St. Margaret's Hospital for Women
   VA Medical Center (Boston)
   VA Medical Center (West Roxbury)
Medical Schools:
   Boston University School of Medicine
   Harvard Medical School
   Tufts University School of Medicine
Cardiac Rehabilitation Centers:
   Beth Israel Hospital Exercise Lab
   Faulkner Hospital CRU
   Massachusetts General Hospital CRU
   Massachusetts General Hospital Health
      Enhancement Center
   Massachusetts Rehabilitation Hospital
      CRU
   Mount Auburn Hospital CRU
   New England Heart Center
   New England Medical Center Hospital
      CRU
   New England Memorial Hospital CRU
   New England Rehabilitation Hospital
      CRU
   Norwood Hospital CRU
   University Hospital CRU
Comprehensive Cancer Treatment
   Centers:
 • Sidney Farber Cancer Institute
   Tufts–New England Medical Center–Cancer
      Center
Hospices:
   Hospice of the Good Shepherd
   University Hospital–Regional Oncology
      Program
   Youville Rehabilitation and Chronic Disease
      Hospital
Costs Index: Good
Fluoridation: Adjusted
Air Pollution: CO
CMSA Access: BOSTON–LAWRENCE–SALEM,
   MA–NH (80)
Places Rated Score: 5,301
Places Rated Rank: 3

Boulder–Longmont, CO
Physicians per 100,000: 167
Hospices:
   Boulder County Hospice
Costs Index: Excellent
Fluoridation: Adjusted

Air Pollution: Insignificant
CMSA Access: DENVER–BOULDER,
CO (195)
Places Rated Score: 962
Places Rated Rank: 144

Bradenton, FL
Physicians per 100,000: 133
Cardiac Rehabilitation Centers:
L. W. Blake Memorial Hospital CRU
Costs Index: Good
Fluoridation: None
Air Pollution: Insignificant
Places Rated Score: 333
Places Rated Rank: 307

Brazoria, TX
Physicians per 100,000: 53
Costs Index: Good
Fluoridation: Almost none
Air Pollution: Insignificant
CMSA Access: HOUSTON–
GALVESTON–BRAZORIA, TX (285)
Places Rated Score: 438
Places Rated Rank: 287

Bremerton, WA
Physicians per 100,000: 110
Costs Index: Excellent
Fluoridation: None
Air Pollution: Insignificant
Places Rated Score: 310
Places Rated Rank: 312

Bridgeport–Milford, CT
Physicians per 100,000: 220
Teaching Hospitals:
Bridgeport Hospital
St. Vincent's Medical Center
Cardiac Rehabilitation Centers:
Park City Hospital CRU
Progressive Cardiac Care Rehabilitation
Program
Costs Index: Excellent
Fluoridation: Adjusted (Bridgeport only)
Air Pollution: O_3
CMSA Access: NEW YORK–NORTHERN
NEW JERSEY–LONG ISLAND,
NY–NJ–CT (1,480)
Places Rated Score: 2,550
Places Rated Rank: 27

Bristol, CT
Physicians per 100,000: 265
Costs Index: Excellent
Fluoridation: Adjusted
Air Pollution: Insignificant
CMSA Access: HARTFORD–NEW
BRITAIN–MIDDLETOWN, CT (210)
Places Rated Score: 975
Places Rated Rank: 141

Brockton, MA
Physicians per 100,000: 101
Cardiac Rehabilitation Centers:
Brockton Hospital–Old Colony YMCA
CRU
Costs Index: Excellent
Fluoridation: None
Air Pollution: Insignificant
CMSA Access: BOSTON–LAWRENCE–
SALEM, MA–NH (515)
Places Rated Score: 916
Places Rated Rank: 150

Brownsville–Harlingen, TX
Physicians per 100,000: 91
Costs Index: Good
Fluoridation: None
Air Pollution: TSP
Places Rated Score: 91
Places Rated Rank: 328

Bryan–College Station, TX
Physicians per 100,000: 90
Medical Schools:
Texas A & M University College of
Medicine
Costs Index: Good
Fluoridation: Adjusted (Bryan only)
Air Pollution: Insignificant
Places Rated Score: 640
Places Rated Rank: 218

Buffalo, NY
Physicians per 100,000: 215
Teaching Hospitals:
Deaconess Hospital of Buffalo
Erie County Medical Center
Millard Fillmore Hospital
VA Medical Center
Medical Schools:
SUNY at Buffalo School of Medicine
Cardiac Rehabilitation Centers:
Buffalo Cardiac CRU
Buffalo VA Hospital CRU
Deaconess Hospital of Buffalo CRU
DeGraff Memorial Hospital CRU
Erie County Medical Center CRU
Millard Fillmore Hospital Exercise
Laboratory
St. Joseph Intercommunity Hospital
CRU
Comprehensive Cancer Treatment
Centers:
• Roswell Park Memorial Institute–
Comprehensive Cancer Center
Hospices:
Hospice Buffalo
Costs Index: Poor
Fluoridation: Adjusted
Air Pollution: Insignificant
Places Rated Score: 2,465
Places Rated Rank: 35

Burlington, NC
Physicians per 100,000: 94
Cardiac Rehabilitation Centers:
Memorial Hospital of Alamance County
CRU
Hospices:
Hospice of Alamance County
Costs Index: Outstanding
Fluoridation: Adjusted
Air Pollution: Insignificant
Places Rated Score: 994
Places Rated Rank: 140

Burlington, VT
Physicians per 100,000: 509
Teaching Hospitals:
Medical Center Hospital of Vermont
Medical Schools:
University of Vermont College of
Medicine
Cardiac Rehabilitation Centers:
Mary Fletcher Hospital CRU
Comprehensive Cancer Treatment
Centers:
University of Vermont–Vermont Regional
Cancer Center

Hospices:
Visiting Nurse Association of Vermont
Costs Index: Excellent
Fluoridation: Adjusted
Air Pollution: Insignificant
Places Rated Score: 1,809
Places Rated Rank: 63

Canton, OH
Physicians per 100,000: 143
Cardiac Rehabilitation Centers:
Doctors Hospital of Stark County CRU
Costs Index: Excellent
Fluoridation: None
Air Pollution: Insignificant
Places Rated Score: 443
Places Rated Rank: 285

Casper, WY
Physicians per 100,000: 145
Costs Index: Excellent
Fluoridation: None
Air Pollution: Insignificant
Places Rated Score: 345
Places Rated Rank: 302

Cedar Rapids, IA
Physicians per 100,000: 137
Cardiac Rehabilitation Centers:
Community Hospital CRU
Hospices:
Mercy Hospital–Hospice of Mercy
Costs Index: Excellent
Fluoridation: Adjusted
Air Pollution: Insignificant
Places Rated Score: 837
Places Rated Rank: 162

Champaign–Urbana–Rantoul, IL
Physicians per 100,000: 172
Cardiac Rehabilitation Centers:
Carle Foundation Hospital CRU
Hospices:
Mercy Hospice Care Program
Costs Index: Excellent
Fluoridation: Adjusted (Rantoul only)
Air Pollution: Insignificant
Places Rated Score: 672
Places Rated Rank: 211

Charleston, SC
Physicians per 100,000: 263
Teaching Hospitals:
Medical University Hospital of South
Carolina
VA Medical Center
Medical Schools:
Medical University of South
Carolina–College of Medicine
Cardiac Rehabilitation Centers:
South Carolina University Hospital CRU
Costs Index: Outstanding
Fluoridation: None
Air Pollution: Insignificant
Places Rated Score: 1,463
Places Rated Rank: 81

Charleston, WV
Physicians per 100,000: 208
Teaching Hospitals:
Charleston Area Medical Center
Cardiac Rehabilitation Centers:
Charleston Area Medical Center CRU
Costs Index: Excellent
Fluoridation: None
Air Pollution: Insignificant
Places Rated Score: 708
Places Rated Rank: 201

Charlotte–Gastonia–Rock Hill, NC–SC
Physicians per 100,000: 99
Teaching Hospitals:
Charlotte Memorial Hospital and Medical Center
Cardiac Rehabilitation Centers:
Charlotte Rehabilitation Hospital CRU
Hospices:
Hospice at Charlotte
Hospice of Gastonia
Costs Index: Excellent
Fluoridation: Adjusted
Air Pollution: CO
Places Rated Score: 999
Places Rated Rank: 139

Charlottesville, VA
Physicians per 100,000: 648
Teaching Hospitals:
University of Virginia Hospitals
Medical Schools:
University of Virginia School of Medicine
Costs Index: Excellent
Fluoridation: None
Air Pollution: Insignificant
Places Rated Score: 1,348
Places Rated Rank: 90

Chattanooga, TN–GA
Physicians per 100,000: 164
Teaching Hospitals:
Erlanger Medical Center
Cardiac Rehabilitation Centers:
Erlanger Medical Center CRU
Costs Index: Good
Fluoridation: None
Air Pollution: Insignificant
Places Rated Score: 564
Places Rated Rank: 251

★ Chicago, IL
Physicians per 100,000: 226
Teaching Hospitals:
Children's Memorial Hospital
Christ Hospital
Cook County Hospital
Evanston Hospital
Illinois Masonic Medical Center
Little Company of Mary Hospital
Lutheran General Hospital
MacNeal Memorial Hospital
McGaw Hospital–Loyola University Medical Center
Mercy Hospital and Medical Center
Michael Reese Hospital and Medical Center
Mount Sinai Hospital Medical Center
Northwestern Memorial Hospital
Rush–Presbyterian–St. Luke's Medical Center
St. Joseph Hospital
Schwab Rehabilitation Center
University of Chicago Hospitals and Clinics
University of Illinois Hospital
VA Medical Center (Hines)
VA Medical Center (Lakeside)
VA Medical Center (Westside)
Medical Schools:
Loyola University of Chicago–Stritch School of Medicine
Northwestern University Medical School
Rush Medical College
University of Chicago–Pritzker School of Medicine

University of Health Sciences–Chicago Medical School
University of Illinois College of Medicine
Cardiac Rehabilitation Centers:
Alexian Brothers Medical Center CRU
Gottlieb Memorial Hospital–Special Medical Services
Hinsdale Sanitarium CRU
Holy Family Hospital CRU
Lutheran General Hospital CRU
Marianjoy Hospital Rehabilitation Program
Memorial Hospital of DuPage–Physical Medicine Department
Northwestern Memorial Hospital CRU
Oak Forest Hospital–Cardiac Stress Test Lab
St. Anne's Hospital CRU
St. Francis Hospital CRU (Blue Island)
St. Francis Hospital CRU (Evanston)
Skokie Valley Community Hospital CRU
Swedish Covenant Hospital CRU
Westlake Community Hospital CRU
Hospices:
Carestoel Professional Care Center
Hospice of the North Shore
Illinois Masonic Medical Center Hospice Services
Lutheran General Hospital–Cancer Care Unit
St. Barnabas Hospice–Glen Ellyn
St. Barnabas Hospice–Wheaton
Costs Index: Fair
Fluoridation: Adjusted
Air Pollution: TSP, CO
CMSA Access: CHICAGO–GARY–LAKE COUNTY, IL–IN–WI (40)
Places Rated Score: 5,766
Places Rated Rank: 2

Chico, CA
Physicians per 100,000: 143
Costs Index: Good
Fluoridation: None
Air Pollution: Insignificant
Places Rated Score: 243
Places Rated Rank: 318

Cincinnati, OH–KY–IN
Physicians per 100,000: 198
Teaching Hospitals:
Christ Hospital
Cincinnati General Hospital
Good Samaritan Hospital
VA Medical Center
Medical Schools:
University of Cincinnati College of Medicine
Cardiac Rehabilitation Centers:
Bethesda Hospital CRU
Jewish Community Center CRU
Hospices:
Hospice of Cincinnati
Costs Index: Excellent
Fluoridation: Adjusted
Air Pollution: Insignificant
CMSA Access: CINCINNATI–HAMILTON, OH–KY–IN (40)
Places Rated Score: 2,138
Places Rated Rank: 46

Clarksville–Hopkinsville, TN–KY
Physicians per 100,000: 96
Costs Index: Excellent
Fluoridation: Adjusted (Clarksville only)
Air Pollution: Insignificant
Places Rated Score: 446
Places Rated Rank: 283

★ Cleveland, OH
Physicians per 100,000: 267
Teaching Hospitals:
Cleveland Clinic Educational Foundation
Cuyahoga County Hospital
Highland View Hospital
Mount Sinai Hospital of Cleveland
St. Luke's Hospital
University Hospitals of Cleveland
VA Medical Center
Medical Schools:
Case Western Reserve University School of Medicine
Northeastern Ohio Universities College of Medicine
Cardiac Rehabilitation Centers:
Cuyahoga County Hospital CRU
Lakewood Hospital CRU
Marymount Hospital Coronary Step-Up
Parma Community General Hospital CRU
VA Hospital CRU
Costs Index: Good
Fluoridation: Adjusted
Air Pollution: TSP
CMSA Access: CLEVELAND–AKRON–LORAIN, OH (100)
Places Rated Score: 3,167
Places Rated Rank: 16

Colorado Springs, CO
Physicians per 100,000: 121
Cardiac Rehabilitation Centers:
Pikes Peak "Y" CRU
Hospices:
Penrose Hospital–Hospice Program
Costs Index: Excellent
Fluoridation: Natural
Air Pollution: CO
Places Rated Score: 721
Places Rated Rank: 198

Columbia, MO
Physicians per 100,000: 651
Teaching Hospitals:
Harry S. Truman Memorial VA Hospital
University of Missouri Medical Center
Medical Schools:
University of Missouri, Columbia, School of Medicine
Hospices:
John H. Walters Hospice of Central Missouri
Costs Index: Excellent
Fluoridation: Adjusted
Air Pollution: Insignificant
Places Rated Score: 1,951
Places Rated Rank: 54

Columbia, SC
Physicians per 100,000: 221
Medical Schools:
University of South Carolina School of Medicine
Cardiac Rehabilitation Centers:
Baptist Medical Center CRU
Hospices:
South Carolina Baptist Hospital Hospice
Costs Index: Outstanding
Fluoridation: Adjusted
Air Pollution: Insignificant
Places Rated Score: 1,421
Places Rated Rank: 86

Columbus, GA–AL
Physicians per 100,000: 133
Cardiac Rehabilitation Centers:
Martin Army Hospital CRU

The Medical Center CRU
Costs Index: Excellent
Fluoridation: Adjusted
Air Pollution: Insignificant
Places Rated Score: 833
Places Rated Rank: 164

Columbus, OH
Physicians per 100,000: 187
Teaching Hospitals:
Ohio State University Hospitals
Riverside Methodist Hospital
Medical Schools:
Ohio State University College of
Medicine
Cardiac Rehabilitation Centers:
Doctors Hospital CRU
Ohio State University Hospital CRU
Riverside Methodist Hospital CRU
Comprehensive Cancer Treatment
Centers:
• Ohio State University–Comprehensive
Cancer Center
Costs Index: Excellent
Fluoridation: Adjusted
Air Pollution: Insignificant
Places Rated Score: 1,837
Places Rated Rank: 62

Corpus Christi, TX
Physicians per 100,000: 158
Costs Index: Good
Fluoridation: Adjusted
Air Pollution: TSP
Places Rated Score: 458
Places Rated Rank: 280

Cumberland, MD–WV
Physicians per 100,000: 160
Cardiac Rehabilitation Centers:
Memorial Hospital CRU
Sacred Heart Hospital CRU
Costs Index: Outstanding
Fluoridation: None
Air Pollution: Insignificant
Places Rated Score: 760
Places Rated Rank: 185

★ Dallas, TX
Physicians per 100,000: 185
Teaching Hospitals:
Baylor University Medical Center
Methodist Hospital of Dallas
Parkland Memorial Hospital
Presbyterian Hospital of Dallas
St. Paul Hospital
VA Medical Center
Medical Schools:
University of Texas Southwestern
Medical School at Dallas
Cardiac Rehabilitation Centers:
Baylor University Hospital–Hunt Heart
Center
Dallas Cardiac Institute CRU
Dallas County Hospital
Presbyterian Medical Center CRU
St. Paul Hospital CRU
Hospices:
Ann's Haven–Hospice of Denton County
Hospice–VNA Home Health Care
Costs Index: Good
Fluoridation: Adjusted
Air Pollution: Insignificant
CMSA Access: DALLAS–FORT WORTH,
TX (40)
Places Rated Score: 2,825
Places Rated Rank: 20

Danbury, CT
Physicians per 100,000: 220
Cardiac Rehabilitation Centers:
Danbury Hospital CRU
Costs Index: Excellent
Fluoridation: Adjusted
Air Pollution: Insignificant
CMSA Access: NEW YORK–NORTHERN
NEW JERSEY–LONG ISLAND,
NY–NJ–CT (1,530)
Places Rated Score: 2,350
Places Rated Rank: 40

Danville, VA
Physicians per 100,000: 93
Costs Index: Excellent
Fluoridation: Adjusted
Air Pollution: Insignificant
Places Rated Score: 593
Places Rated Rank: 241

Davenport–Rock Island–
Moline, IA–IL
Physicians per 100,000: 113
Cardiac Rehabilitation Centers:
Davenport and Scott County Family "Y"
CRU
Franciscan Medical Center CRU (Rock
Island)
Mercy Hospital CRU
Hospices:
Hospice Care Group, Inc.
Lutheran Hospital–Hospice Program
Costs Index: Excellent
Fluoridation: Adjusted
Air Pollution: Insignificant
Places Rated Score: 1,113
Places Rated Rank: 115

Dayton–Springfield, OH
Physicians per 100,000: 153
Teaching Hospitals:
Good Samaritan Hospital and Health
Center
Kettering Medical Center
Miami Valley Hospital
VA Medical Center
Medical Schools:
Wright State University School of
Medicine
Cardiac Rehabilitation Centers:
Ambulatory Care Center–Grandview
Hospital
Good Samaritan Hospital Cardiac Center
Kettering Medical Center CRU
Hospices:
Christel and Fairborn Manors
Hospice of Dayton
Costs Index: Excellent
Fluoridation: Adjusted
Air Pollution: Insignificant
Places Rated Score: 2,253
Places Rated Rank: 42

Daytona Beach, FL
Physicians per 100,000: 123
Cardiac Rehabilitation Centers:
Halifax Hospital and Medical Center CRU
Hospices:
Hospice of Volusia
Costs Index: Good
Fluoridation: Adjusted
Air Pollution: Insignificant
Places Rated Score: 723
Places Rated Rank: 197

Decatur, IL
Physicians per 100,000: 132
Cardiac Rehabilitation Centers:
Decatur Memorial Hospital CRU
Costs Index: Excellent
Fluoridation: Adjusted
Air Pollution: Insignificant
Places Rated Score: 732
Places Rated Rank: 191

Denver, CO
Physicians per 100,000: 273
Teaching Hospitals:
Colorado General Hospital
Presbyterian Medical Center
VA Medical Center
Medical Schools:
University of Colorado School of
Medicine
Cardiac Rehabilitation Centers:
Denver General Hospital Coronary Care
Unit
Fitzsimmons Army Base Medical Center
Heart-Lung Center CRU
Lutheran Medical Center CRU
St. Joseph Hospital CRU
South Denver Clinic CRU
University of Colorado Health Sciences
Center CRU
Comprehensive Cancer Treatment
Centers:
• Colorado Regional Cancer Center, Inc.
Hospices:
Hospice of Holy Spirit
Hospice of Metro Denver
Costs Index: Excellent
Fluoridation: Adjusted
Air Pollution: TSP, CO
CMSA Access: DENVER–BOULDER,
CO (10)
Places Rated Score: 2,533
Places Rated Rank: 28

Des Moines, IA
Physicians per 100,000: 156
Teaching Hospitals:
Iowa Methodist Medical Center
Cardiac Rehabilitation Centers:
Iowa Lutheran Hospital CRU
Iowa Methodist Medical Center
Mercy Hospital Medical Center CRU
VA Medical Center CRU
Hospices:
Hospice of Central Iowa
Costs Index: Excellent
Fluoridation: Adjusted
Air Pollution: TSP
Places Rated Score: 1,256
Places Rated Rank: 96

★ Detroit, MI
Physicians per 100,000: 182
Teaching Hospitals:
Children's Hospital of Michigan
Detroit General Hospital
Grace Hospital
Harper Hospital
Henry Ford Hospital
Hutzel Hospital
Oakwood Hospital
Providence Hospital
St. John Hospital
St. Joseph Mercy Hospital
Sinai Hospital of Detroit
Wayne County General Hospital
Medical Schools:
Wayne State University School of
Medicine

Cardiac Rehabilitation Centers:
   Annapolis Hospital Cardiac
      Rehabilitation Program
   Bon Secours Hospital CRU
   Downriver Treadmill Team CRU
   Henry Ford Hospital CRU
   Macomb Heart and Rehabilitation
      Institute
   Outer Drive Hospital CRU
   St. Joseph Mercy Hospital CRU
   Sinai Hospital of Detroit CRU
   William Beaumont Hospital CRU
Comprehensive Cancer Treatment
   Centers:
• Comprehensive Cancer Center of
   Metropolitan Detroit
Hospices:
   Cottage Hospital
   Hospice of Southeastern Michigan
   Michigan Cancer Foundation Services
   St. Joseph's Hospital–Hospice Program
Costs Index: Fair
Fluoridation: Adjusted
Air Pollution: TSP, CO
CMSA Access: DETROIT–ANN ARBOR,
   MI (110)
Places Rated Score: 4,142
Places Rated Rank: 7

Dothan, AL
Physicians per 100,000: 93
Costs Index: Excellent
Fluoridation: Adjusted
Air Pollution: Insignificant
Places Rated Score: 593
Places Rated Rank: 241

Dubuque, IA
Physicians per 100,000: 140
Costs Index: Excellent
Fluoridation: Adjusted
Air Pollution: Insignificant
Places Rated Score: 640
Places Rated Rank: 218

Duluth, MN–WI
Physicians per 100,000: 159
Medical Schools:
   University of Minnesota, Duluth, School
      of Medicine
Cardiac Rehabilitation Centers:
   St. Luke's Hospital CRU
   St. Mary's Hospital CRU
Hospices:
   Hospice–Duluth–St. Luke's Hospital
Costs Index: Excellent
Fluoridation: Adjusted
Air Pollution: TSP
Places Rated Score: 1,159
Places Rated Rank: 109

East St. Louis–Belleville, IL
Physicians per 100,000: 84
Costs Index: Excellent
Fluoridation: None
Air Pollution: TSP
CMSA Access: ST. LOUIS–EAST ST.
   LOUIS–ALTON, MO–IL (260)
Places Rated Score: 444
Places Rated Rank: 284

Eau Claire, WI
Physicians per 100,000: 198
Hospices:
   Sacred Heart Hospital Hospice
Costs Index: Excellent
Fluoridation: Adjusted

Air Pollution: Insignificant
Places Rated Score: 798
Places Rated Rank: 178

El Paso, TX
Physicians per 100,000: 128
Cardiac Rehabilitation Centers:
   R. E. Thomason General Hospital CRU
   St. Joseph's Hospital
Costs Index: Good
Fluoridation: Natural
Air Pollution: TSP, CO
Places Rated Score: 528
Places Rated Rank: 263

Elkhart–Goshen, IN
Physicians per 100,000: 96
Costs Index: Excellent
Fluoridation: Adjusted
Air Pollution: Insignificant
Places Rated Score: 596
Places Rated Rank: 237

Elmira, NY
Physicians per 100,000: 162
Cardiac Rehabilitation Centers:
   St. Joseph Hospital CRU
Hospices:
   Southern Tier Hospice
Costs Index: Poor
Fluoridation: Adjusted
Air Pollution: Insignificant
Places Rated Score: 562
Places Rated Rank: 253

Enid, OK
Physicians per 100,000: 126
Costs Index: Excellent
Fluoridation: Adjusted
Air Pollution: Insignificant
Places Rated Score: 626
Places Rated Rank: 222

Erie, PA
Physicians per 100,000: 129
Teaching Hospitals:
   Hamot Medical Center
Costs Index: Excellent
Fluoridation: None
Air Pollution: Insignificant
Places Rated Score: 529
Places Rated Rank: 262

Eugene–Springfield, OR
Physicians per 100,000: 139
Costs Index: Excellent
Fluoridation: Adjusted
Air Pollution: TSP
Places Rated Score: 539
Places Rated Rank: 258

Evansville, IN–KY
Physicians per 100,000: 183
Cardiac Rehabilitation Centers:
   Evansville Internal Medicine Specialists
      CRU
Costs Index: Excellent
Fluoridation: Adjusted
Air Pollution: Insignificant
Places Rated Score: 783
Places Rated Rank: 180

Fall River, MA–RI
Physicians per 100,000: 100
Hospices:
   Hospice Outreach, Inc.
Costs Index: Excellent
Fluoridation: Adjusted

Air Pollution: Insignificant
CMSA Access: PROVIDENCE–PAWTUCKET–
   FALL RIVER, RI–MA (200)
Places Rated Score: 900
Places Rated Rank: 152

Fargo–Moorhead, ND–MN
Physicians per 100,000: 220
Cardiac Rehabilitation Centers:
   Fargo Clinic CRU
   Rehab Medicine Service, Inc.
Costs Index: Excellent
Fluoridation: Adjusted
Air Pollution: Insignificant
Places Rated Score: 920
Places Rated Rank: 149

Fayetteville, NC
Physicians per 100,000: 72
Cardiac Rehabilitation Centers:
   Fayette VA Medical Center CRU
Costs Index: Outstanding
Fluoridation: Adjusted
Air Pollution: Insignificant
Places Rated Score: 872
Places Rated Rank: 157

Fayetteville–Springdale, AR
Physicians per 100,000: 144
Hospices:
   Northwest Arkansas Hospice
      Association
Costs Index: Excellent
Fluoridation: Adjusted (Springdale only)
Air Pollution: Insignificant
Places Rated Score: 594
Places Rated Rank: 240

Fitchburg–Leominster, MA
Physicians per 100,000: 205
Hospices:
   Burbank Hospital Hospice Care
Costs Index: Excellent
Fluoridation: Adjusted (Fitchburg only)
Air Pollution: Insignificant
Places Rated Score: 655
Places Rated Rank: 216

Flint, MI
Physicians per 100,000: 124
Teaching Hospitals:
   Hurley Medical Center
Cardiac Rehabilitation Centers:
   McLaren General Hospital CRU
   St. Joseph Hospital CRU
Hospices:
   Hospice of Flint
Costs Index: Good
Fluoridation: None
Air Pollution: Insignificant
Places Rated Score: 724
Places Rated Rank: 196

Florence, AL
Physicians per 100,000: 107
Costs Index: Excellent
Fluoridation: Adjusted
Air Pollution: Insignificant
Places Rated Score: 607
Places Rated Rank: 232

Florence, SC
Physicians per 100,000: 118
Costs Index: Outstanding
Fluoridation: Adjusted
Air Pollution: Insignificant
Places Rated Score: 818
Places Rated Rank: 169

Fort Collins–Loveland, CO
Physicians per 100,000: 131
Hospices:
    Hospice, Inc., of Larimer County
Costs Index: Excellent
Fluoridation: Adjusted
Air Pollution: Insignificant
Places Rated Score: 731
Places Rated Rank: 193

Fort Lauderdale–Hollywood–
Pompano Beach, FL
Physicians per 100,000: 167
Cardiac Rehabilitation Centers:
    Broward General Medical Center CRU
    Florida Medical Center CRU
    Holy Cross Hospital CRU
    North Ridge General Hospital CRU
    South Broward Cardiac Center
        Rehabilitation Program
Hospices:
    Gold Coast Home Health Services
        Hospice Team
    Hospice of Broward
    Hospice of South Florida
Costs Index: Fair
Fluoridation: Adjusted (Hollywood only)
Air Pollution: Insignificant
CMSA Access: MIAMI–FORT
    LAUDERDALE, FL (185)
Places Rated Score: 1,252
Places Rated Rank: 97

Fort Myers, FL
Physicians per 100,000: 146
Costs Index: Good
Fluoridation: Adjusted
Air Pollution: Insignificant
Places Rated Score: 546
Places Rated Rank: 257

Fort Pierce, FL
Physicians per 100,000: 127
Costs Index: Good
Fluoridation: Adjusted
Air Pollution: Insignificant
Places Rated Score: 527
Places Rated Rank: 264

Fort Smith, AR–OK
Physicians per 100,000: 166
Cardiac Rehabilitation Centers:
    St. Edward Mercy Medical Center CRU
Costs Index: Excellent
Fluoridation: None
Air Pollution: Insignificant
Places Rated Score: 466
Places Rated Rank: 278

Fort Walton Beach, FL
Physicians per 100,000: 84
Costs Index: Good
Fluoridation: Natural
Air Pollution: Insignificant
Places Rated Score: 484
Places Rated Rank: 274

Fort Wayne, IN
Physicians per 100,000: 160
Cardiac Rehabilitation Centers:
    Fort Wayne Cardiac Rehabilitation
        Program
    Northeastern Indiana Hospital CRU
Hospices:
    Hospice of Fort Wayne
    Parkview Hospice
Costs Index: Excellent

Fluoridation: Adjusted
Air Pollution: Insignificant
Places Rated Score: 1,060
Places Rated Rank: 126

Fort Worth–Arlington, TX
Physicians per 100,000: 118
Cardiac Rehabilitation Centers:
    All Saints Episcopal Hospital CRU
    St. Joseph's Hospital CRU
Hospices:
    Community Hospice of St. Joseph
    Trinity Valley Hospice Association
Costs Index: Good
Fluoridation: Adjusted
Air Pollution: TSP
CMSA Access: DALLAS–FORT
    WORTH, TX (220)
Places Rated Score: 1,038
Places Rated Rank: 132

Fresno, CA
Physicians per 100,000: 169
Cardiac Rehabilitation Centers:
    Fresno Community Hospital CRU
    St. Agnes Hospital Cardiac
        Rehabilitation Program
Hospices:
    Hospice of Fresno
Costs Index: Good
Fluoridation: Almost none
Air Pollution: CO, O_3
Places Rated Score: 369
Places Rated Rank: 298

Gadsden, AL
Physicians per 100,000: 122
Cardiac Rehabilitation Centers:
    Baptist Memorial Hospital CRU
Costs Index: Good
Fluoridation: Adjusted
Air Pollution: Insignificant
Places Rated Score: 622
Places Rated Rank: 223

Gainesville, FL
Physicians per 100,000: 531
Teaching Hospitals:
    Shands Teaching Hospital and
        Clinics
    VA Medical Center
Medical Schools:
    University of Florida College of
        Medicine
Cardiac Rehabilitation Centers:
    Alachua General Hospital CRU
Costs Index: Good
Fluoridation: Adjusted
Air Pollution: Insignificant
Places Rated Score: 1,731
Places Rated Rank: 69

Galveston–Texas City, TX
Physicians per 100,000: 412
Teaching Hospitals:
    University of Texas Medical Branch at
        Arlington
Medical Schools:
    University of Texas Medical School at
        Galveston
Comprehensive Cancer Treatment
    Centers:
    University of Texas Medical Branch
        Hospitals–Cancer Center
Costs Index: Poor
Fluoridation: Natural
Air Pollution: Insignificant

CMSA Access: HOUSTON–GALVESTON–
    BRAZORIA, TX (225)
Places Rated Score: 1,437
Places Rated Rank: 84

Gary–Hammond, IN
Physicians per 100,000: 114
Cardiac Rehabilitation Centers:
    Porter Memorial Hospital CRU
    St. Anthony Medical Center CRU
    St. Catherine Hospital CRU
Costs Index: Excellent
Fluoridation: Adjusted
Air Pollution: TSP
CMSA Access: CHICAGO–GARY–LAKE
    COUNTY, IL–IN–WI (550)
Places Rated Score: 1,364
Places Rated Rank: 89

Glens Falls, NY
Physicians per 100,000: 143
Costs Index: Poor
Fluoridation: None
Air Pollution: Insignificant
Places Rated Score: 43
Places Rated Rank: 329

Grand Forks, ND
Physicians per 100,000: 209
Medical Schools:
    University of North Dakota School of
        Medicine
Cardiac Rehabilitation Centers:
    United Hospital CRU
Costs Index: Excellent
Fluoridation: Adjusted
Air Pollution: Insignificant
Places Rated Score: 1,109
Places Rated Rank: 117

Grand Rapids, MI
Physicians per 100,000: 174
Teaching Hospitals:
    Blodgett Memorial Medical Center
    Butterworth Hospital
Cardiac Rehabilitation Centers:
    Butterworth Hospital CRU
Hospices:
    Hospice of Greater Grand Rapids
Costs Index: Excellent
Fluoridation: Adjusted
Air Pollution: Insignificant
Places Rated Score: 1,274
Places Rated Rank: 93

Great Falls, MT
Physicians per 100,000: 167
Costs Index: Excellent
Fluoridation: Natural
Air Pollution: Insignificant
Places Rated Score: 667
Places Rated Rank: 214

Greeley, CO
Physicians per 100,000: 106
Cardiac Rehabilitation Centers:
    Weld County General Hospital CRU
Costs Index: Excellent
Fluoridation: Adjusted
Air Pollution: Insignificant
Places Rated Score: 706
Places Rated Rank: 202

Green Bay, WI
Physicians per 100,000: 116
Cardiac Rehabilitation Centers:
    Bellin Memorial Hospital CRU

St. Vincent Hospital CRU
Hospices:
Carl Kouba Hospice–Bellin Memorial
Hospital
Costs Index: Excellent
Fluoridation: Adjusted
Air Pollution: Insignificant
Places Rated Score: 916
Places Rated Rank: 150

Greensboro–Winston-Salem–High Point, NC

Physicians per 100,000: 194
Teaching Hospitals:
North Carolina Baptist Hospitals, Inc.
Medical Schools:
Bowman Gray School of Medicine of
Wake Forest University
Cardiac Rehabilitation Centers:
Moses Cone Memorial Hospital CRU
Wake Forest Hospital, Department of
Medical and Physical Education
Comprehensive Cancer Treatment
Centers:
Bowman Gray School of Medicine–
Oncology Research Center
Hospices:
Greensboro Hospice
Hospice of Winston-Salem/Forsyth
County, Inc.
Costs Index: Excellent
Fluoridation: Adjusted
Air Pollution: Insignificant
Places Rated Score: 1,694
Places Rated Rank: 71

Greenville–Spartanburg, SC

Physicians per 100,000: 160
Teaching Hospitals:
Greenville Hospital System
Cardiac Rehabilitation Centers:
Greenville Memorial Hospital CRU
Hospices:
Greenville Hospital System–Hospice
Program
Costs Index: Outstanding
Fluoridation: Adjusted
Air Pollution: Insignificant
Places Rated Score: 1,260
Places Rated Rank: 94

Hagerstown, MD

Physicians per 100,000: 118
Costs Index: Outstanding
Fluoridation: Adjusted
Air Pollution: Insignificant
Places Rated Score: 818
Places Rated Rank: 169

Hamilton–Middletown, OH

Physicians per 100,000: 95
Cardiac Rehabilitation Centers:
Fort Hamilton–Hughes Hospital CRU
Middletown Area YMCA CRU
Middletown Hospital CRU
Hospices:
Hospice of Middletown
Costs Index: Excellent
Fluoridation: Adjusted
Air Pollution: Insignificant
CMSA Access: CINCINNATI–HAMILTON,
OH–KY–IN (140)
Places Rated Score: 1,135
Places Rated Rank: 113

Harrisburg–Lebanon–Carlisle, PA

Physicians per 100,000: 187

Teaching Hospitals:
Harrisburg Hospital
Milton S. Hershey Medical Center
Medical Schools:
Pennsylvania State University College of
Medicine
Cardiac Rehabilitation Centers:
Carlisle Hospital CRU
Holy Spirit Hospital CRU
Milton S. Hershey Medical Center CRU
Hospices:
Harrisburg Hospital Hospice Unit
Hospice of Central Pennsylvania
Costs Index: Outstanding
Fluoridation: Adjusted
Air Pollution: Insignificant
Places Rated Score: 2,087
Places Rated Rank: 49

Hartford, CT

Physicians per 100,000: 281
Teaching Hospitals:
Hartford Hospital
Mount Sinai Hospital
St. Francis Hospital and Medical Center
University of Connecticut Health
Center–John Dempsey Hospital
VA Medical Center (Newington)
Medical Schools:
University of Connecticut School of
Medicine
Cardiac Rehabilitation Centers:
Hartford Hospital CRU
Mount Sinai Hospital CRU
St. Francis Hospital CRU
Hospices:
Palliative Care Team
Costs Index: Excellent
Fluoridation: Adjusted
Air Pollution: Insignificant
CMSA Access: HARTFORD–NEW
BRITAIN–MIDDLETOWN, CT (40)
Places Rated Score: 2,521
Places Rated Rank: 30

Hickory, NC

Physicians per 100,000: 106
Cardiac Rehabilitation Centers:
Glenn K. Frye Memorial Hospital CRU
Hospices:
Hospice of Catawba Valley
Costs Index: Outstanding
Fluoridation: Adjusted
Air Pollution: Insignificant
Places Rated Score: 1,006
Places Rated Rank: 138

Honolulu, HI

Physicians per 100,000: 198
Teaching Hospitals:
Queen's Medical Center
Medical Schools:
University of Hawaii–John A. Burns
School of Medicine
Cardiac Rehabilitation Centers:
Central YMCA CRU
Kaukini Medical Center Cardiac Care
Unit
Tripler Army Base Medical Center
Comprehensive Cancer Treatment
Centers:
University of Hawaii at Manoa–Cancer
Center of Hawaii
Hospices:
St. Francis Hospital–Hospice Program
Costs Index: Good
Fluoridation: Almost none

Air Pollution: Insignificant
Places Rated Score: 1,298
Places Rated Rank: 92

Houma–Thibodaux, LA

Physicians per 100,000: 83
Costs Index: Excellent
Fluoridation: Adjusted
Air Pollution: Insignificant
Places Rated Score: 583
Places Rated Rank: 247

Houston, TX

Physicians per 100,000: 207
Teaching Hospitals:
Harris County Hospital District
Hermann Hospital
Texas Children's Hospital
VA Medical Center
Medical Schools:
Baylor College of Medicine
University of Texas Medical School at
Houston
Cardiac Rehabilitation Centers:
Ben Taub General Hospital CRU
Houston Cardiac Rehabilitation Center
CRU
Methodist Hospital Adult Fitness
Program
Rehabilitation Institute CRU
VA Hospital CRU
West Houston Cardiac Rehabilitation
Center CRU
Comprehensive Cancer Treatment
Centers:
• University of Texas Health System
Cancer Center
Hospices:
Houston Institute for Cancer
Costs Index: Poor
Fluoridation: Natural (approximately 50%
of the metro area)
Air Pollution: TSP
CMSA Access: HOUSTON–GALVESTON–
BRAZORIA, TX (60)
Places Rated Score: 2,467
Places Rated Rank: 33

Huntington–Ashland, WV–KY–OH

Physicians per 100,000: 125
Medical Schools:
Marshall University School of Medicine
Cardiac Rehabilitation Centers:
King's Daughters Hospital CRU
(Ashland)
Costs Index: Excellent
Fluoridation: Adjusted (Huntington only)
Air Pollution: Insignificant
Places Rated Score: 875
Places Rated Rank: 156

Huntsville, AL

Physicians per 100,000: 185
Costs Index: Excellent
Fluoridation: Adjusted
Air Pollution: Insignificant
Places Rated Score: 685
Places Rated Rank: 208

Indianapolis, IN

Physicians per 100,000: 243
Teaching Hospitals:
Indiana University Hospitals
Methodist Hospital of Indiana, Inc.
VA Medical Center
William N. Wishard Memorial Hospital

Medical Schools:
  Indiana University School of Medicine
Cardiac Rehabilitation Centers:
  Methodist Hospital of Indiana CRU
  St. Vincent Hospital CRU
  Vital Cardiac Rehabilitation Unit
  Winona Memorial Hospital CRU
Hospices:
  Methodist Hospital Hospice
Costs Index: Excellent
Fluoridation: Adjusted
Air Pollution: CO
Places Rated Score: 2,243
Places Rated Rank: 43

Iowa City, IA
Physicians per 100,000: 1,137
Teaching Hospitals:
  University of Iowa Hospitals and Clinics
  VA Medical Center
Medical Schools:
  University of Iowa School of Medicine
Cardiac Rehabilitation Centers:
  University of Iowa Hospitals and Clinics
    CRU
Costs Index: Excellent
Fluoridation: Adjusted
Air Pollution: Insignificant
Places Rated Score: 2,437
Places Rated Rank: 37

Jackson, MI
Physicians per 100,000: 79
Hospices:
  Hospice of Jackson
Costs Index: Excellent
Fluoridation: Adjusted
Air Pollution: Insignificant
Places Rated Score: 679
Places Rated Rank: 209

Jackson, MS
Physicians per 100,000: 292
Teaching Hospitals:
  University of Mississippi Medical Center
  VA Medical Center
Medical Schools:
  University of Mississippi School of
    Medicine
Cardiac Rehabilitation Centers:
  Mississippi Methodist Hospital CRU
  St. Dominic–Jackson Hospital CRU
  VA Medical Center CRU
Costs Index: Excellent
Fluoridation: Adjusted
Air Pollution: Insignificant
Places Rated Score: 1,792
Places Rated Rank: 66

Jacksonville, FL
Physicians per 100,000: 181
Teaching Hospitals:
  University Hospital of Jacksonville
Cardiac Rehabilitation Centers:
  Baptist Medical Center CRU
  University Hospital of Jacksonville CRU
Hospices:
  Hospice of Northeast Florida
  Methodist Hospital Hospice
  St. Vincent's Medical Center–Home
    Care Program
Costs Index: Good
Fluoridation: Natural
Air Pollution: Pb
Places Rated Score: 1,181
Places Rated Rank: 108

Jacksonville, NC
Physicians per 100,000: 40
Costs Index: Outstanding
Fluoridation: Natural
Air Pollution: Insignificant
Places Rated Score: 740
Places Rated Rank: 189

Janesville–Beloit, WI
Physicians per 100,000: 100
Cardiac Rehabilitation Centers:
  Beloit Memorial Hospital CRU
Costs Index: Excellent
Fluoridation: Adjusted
Air Pollution: Insignificant
Places Rated Score: 700
Places Rated Rank: 203

Jersey City, NJ
Physicians per 100,000: 139
Cardiac Rehabilitation Centers:
  Morristown Memorial Hospital CRU
  St. Mary Hospital CRU
Costs Index: Good
Fluoridation: None
Air Pollution: TSP, CO
CMSA Access: NEW YORK–NORTHERN
  NEW JERSEY–LONG ISLAND,
  NY–NJ–CT (1,520)
Places Rated Score: 1,759
Places Rated Rank: 67

**Johnson City–Kingsport–
Bristol, TN–VA**
Physicians per 100,000: 152
Medical Schools:
  East Tennessee State University College
    of Medicine
Cardiac Rehabilitation Centers:
  Bristol Memorial Hospital CRU
  Memorial Hospital, Inc., CRU
Costs Index: Excellent
Fluoridation: Adjusted
Air Pollution: Insignificant
Places Rated Score: 1,152
Places Rated Rank: 111

Johnstown, PA
Physicians per 100,000: 131
Teaching Hospitals:
  Conemaugh Valley Memorial Hospital
Cardiac Rehabilitation Centers:
  Mercy Hospital of Johnstown CRU
Hospices:
  Mercy Hospital–Hospice Unit
Costs Index: Excellent
Fluoridation: None
Air Pollution: Insignificant
Places Rated Score: 731
Places Rated Rank: 193

Joliet, IL
Physicians per 100,000: 78
Costs Index: Good
Fluoridation: Natural
Air Pollution: Insignificant
CMSA Access: CHICAGO–GARY–LAKE
  COUNTY, IL–IN–WI (580)
Places Rated Score: 1,058
Places Rated Rank: 127

Joplin, MO
Physicians per 100,000: 100
Cardiac Rehabilitation Centers:
  Freeman Hospital CRU

Hospices:
  St. John's Medical Center–Pastoral Care
    Department
Costs Index: Excellent
Fluoridation: None
Air Pollution: Insignificant
Places Rated Score: 500
Places Rated Rank: 271

Kalamazoo, MI
Physicians per 100,000: 243
Cardiac Rehabilitation Centers:
  Borgess Medical Center CRU
  Bronson Methodist Hospital CRU
Hospices:
  Kalamazoo Hospice
Costs Index: Excellent
Fluoridation: Adjusted
Air Pollution: Insignificant
Places Rated Score: 1,043
Places Rated Rank: 129

Kankakee, IL
Physicians per 100,000: 109
Costs Index: Excellent
Fluoridation: Adjusted
Air Pollution: Insignificant
Places Rated Score: 609
Places Rated Rank: 231

Kansas City, KS
Physicians per 100,000: 251
Teaching Hospitals:
  University of Kansas Medical Center
Medical Schools:
  University of Kansas School of Medicine
Cardiac Rehabilitation Centers
  Bethany Medical Center Cardiac
    Rehabilitation Program
  Heart Institute CRU
  Providence–St. Margaret Center CRU
Costs Index: Excellent
Fluoridation: Adjusted
Air Pollution: Insignificant
CMSA Access: KANSAS CITY, MO–KANSAS
  CITY, KS (160)
Places Rated Score: 1,711
Places Rated Rank: 70

Kansas City, MO
Physicians per 100,000: 159
Teaching Hospitals:
  St. Luke's Hospital of Kansas City
  Truman Medical Center
  VA Medical Center
Medical Schools:
  University of Missouri at Kansas City
    School of Medicine
Cardiac Rehabilitation Centers:
  Research Medical Center–Physical
    Medicine and Rehabilitation
  St. Luke's Hospital CRU
  St. Mary's Hospital CRU
  Trinity Lutheran Hospital CRU
  Truman Medical Center–East–Maximum
    Care Unit
Hospices:
  Hospice Care of Mid-America
  Kansas City Hospice
Costs Index: Good
Fluoridation: None
Air Pollution: Insignificant
CMSA Access: KANSAS CITY, MO–KANSAS
  CITY, KS (80)
Places Rated Score: 1,939
Places Rated Rank: 55

Kenosha, WI
Physicians per 100,000: 87
Costs Index: Good
Fluoridation: Adjusted
Air Pollution: Insignificant
CMSA Access: CHICAGO–GARY–LAKE
    COUNTY, IL–IN–WI (580)
Places Rated Score: 1,067
Places Rated Rank: 125

Killeen–Temple, TX
Physicians per 100,000: 198
Cardiac Rehabilitation Centers:
    Teague VA Center CRU
Costs Index: Good
Fluoridation: None
Air Pollution: Insignificant
Places Rated Score: 398
Places Rated Rank: 291

Knoxville, TN
Physicians per 100,000: 160
Cardiac Rehabilitation Centers:
    Fort Sanders Presbyterian Hospital
        Cardiac Rehabilitation Program
    St. Mary's Medical Center CRU
Hospices:
    Fort Sanders Presbyterian
        Hospital–Hospice
Costs Index: Excellent
Fluoridation: Adjusted
Air Pollution: Insignificant
Places Rated Score: 960
Places Rated Rank: 145

Kokomo, IN
Physicians per 100,000: 96
Costs Index: Excellent
Fluoridation: Adjusted
Air Pollution: Insignificant
Places Rated Score: 596
Places Rated Rank: 237

La Crosse, WI
Physicians per 100,000: 286
Cardiac Rehabilitation Centers:
    La Crosse Exercise Program CRU
    La Crosse Lutheran Hospital CRU
Costs Index: Excellent
Fluoridation: None
Air Pollution: Insignificant
Places Rated Score: 686
Places Rated Rank: 207

Lafayette, IN
Physicians per 100,000: 155
Costs Index: Excellent
Fluoridation: Adjusted
Air Pollution: Insignificant
Places Rated Score: 655
Places Rated Rank: 216

Lafayette, LA
Physicians per 100,000: 148
Cardiac Rehabilitation Centers:
    Lafayette General Hospital CRU
    Our Lady of Lourdes Hospital Cardiac
        Rehabilitation Program
Costs Index: Excellent
Fluoridation: None
Air Pollution: Insignificant
Places Rated Score: 548
Places Rated Rank: 256

Lake Charles, LA
Physicians per 100,000: 114
Costs Index: Excellent

Fluoridation: None
Air Pollution: Insignificant
Places Rated Score: 314
Places Rated Rank: 311

Lake County, IL
Physicians per 100,000: 167
Hospices:
    Hospice of Highland Park Hospital
Costs Index: Good
Flouridation: Natural and adjusted
Air Pollution: Insignificant
CMSA Access: CHICAGO–GARY–LAKE
    COUNTY, IL–IN–WI (570)
Places Rated Score: 1,237
Places Rated Rank: 99

Lakeland–Winter Haven, FL
Physicians per 100,000: 123
Hospices:
    Good Shepherd Hospice
Costs Index: Good
Fluoridation: None
Air Pollution: Insignificant
Places Rated Score: 323
Places Rated Rank: 309

Lancaster, PA
Physicians per 100,000: 111
Cardiac Rehabilitation Centers:
    Lancaster General Hospital CRU
    Lancaster Osteopathic Hospital
        CRU
    St. Joseph's Hospital Cardiac Treatment
        Center
Costs Index: Outstanding
Fluoridation: Adjusted
Air Pollution: Insignificant
Places Rated Score: 1,111
Places Rated Rank: 116

Lansing–East Lansing, MI
Physicians per 100,000: 171
Teaching Hospitals:
    Edward W. Sparrow Hospital
Medical Schools:
    Michigan State University College of
        Human Medicine
Cardiac Rehabilitation Centers:
    Ingham Medical Center Cardiac
        Rehabilitation Program
    Lansing General Hospital CRU
Costs Index: Excellent
Fluoridation: Adjusted
Air Pollution: Insignificant
Places Rated Score: 1,371
Places Rated Rank: 88

Laredo, TX
Physicians per 100,000: 65
Costs Index: Good
Fluoridation: Natural
Air Pollution: Insignificant
Places Rated Score: 465
Places Rated Rank: 279

Las Cruces, NM
Physicians per 100,000: 88
Costs Index: Excellent
Fluoridation: Natural
Air Pollution: Insignificant
Places Rated Score: 588
Places Rated Rank: 246

Las Vegas, NV
Physicians per 100,000: 112

Cardiac Rehabilitation Centers:
    Southern Nevada Memorial Hospital
        CRU
    Sunrise Hospital CRU
Hospices:
    Nathan Adelson Memorial Hospice
Costs Index: Fair
Fluoridation: None
Air Pollution: Insignificant
Places Rated Score: 412
Places Rated Rank: 290

Lawrence, KS
Physicans per 100,000: 121
Costs Index: Excellent
Fluoridation: Adjusted
Air Pollution: Insignificant
Places Rated Score: 621
Places Rated Rank: 224

Lawrence–Haverhill, MA–NH
Physicians per 100,000: 147
Cardiac Rehabilitation Centers:
    Lawrence General Hospital–Exercise
        Tolerance Test Lab
Hospices:
    Bon Secours Hospital
Costs Index: Excellent
Fluoridation: Adjusted (Haverhill only)
Air Pollution: Insignificant
CMSA Access: BOSTON–LAWRENCE–
    SALEM, MA–NH (505)
Places Rated Score: 1,202
Places Rated Rank: 105

Lawton, OK
Physicians per 100,000: 77
Costs Index: Excellent
Fluoridation: Adjusted
Air Pollution: TSP
Places Rated Score: 477
Places Rated Rank: 276

Lewiston–Auburn, ME
Physicians per 100,000: 159
Hospices:
    Clover Manor Hospice
Costs Index: Excellent
Fluoridation: Adjusted
Air Pollution: Insignificant
Places Rated Score: 759
Places Rated Rank: 186

Lexington–Fayette, KY
Physicians per 100,000: 360
Teaching Hospitals:
    Albert B. Chandler Medical Center
    VA Medical Center
Medical Schools:
    University of Kentucky College of
        Medicine
Cardiac Rehabilitation Centers:
    Central Baptist Hospital CRU
    Good Samaritan Hospital Cardiac
        Rehabilitation Department
    St. Joseph Hospital CRU
Comprehensive Cancer Treatment
    Centers:
    McDowell Community Cancer Network,
        Inc.
Hospices:
    Community Hospice of Lexington
    McDowell Community Center–Hospice
Costs Index: Excellent
Fluoridation: None

Air Pollution: Insignificant
Places Rated Score: 1,860
Places Rated Rank: 59

Lima, OH

Physicians per 100,000: 141
Cardiac Rehabilitation Centers:
  Lima Memorial Hospital Cardiac
    Treatment Center
Costs Index: Excellent
Fluoridation: Adjusted
Air Pollution: Insignificant
Places Rated Score: 741
Places Rated Rank: 188

Lincoln, NE

Physicians per 100,000: 175
Cardiac Rehabilitation Centers:
  Bryan Memorial Hospital CRU
Costs Index: Excellent
Fluoridation: Adjusted
Air Pollution: Insignificant
Places Rated Score: 775
Places Rated Rank: 183

Little Rock–North Little Rock, AR

Physicians per 100,000: 261
Teaching Hospitals:
  University of Arkansas Hospital
  VA Medical Center
Medical Schools:
  University of Arkansas College of
    Medicine
Cardiac Rehabilitation Centers:
  Human Performance Center CRU
  University of Arkansas Health Sciences
    CRU
  VA Medical Center Cardiology Unit
Hospices:
  Hospice of Arkansas
Costs Index: Excellent
Fluoridation: Adjusted
Air Pollution: Insignificant
Places Rated Score: 1,861
Places Rated Rank: 58

Longview–Marshall, TX

Physicians per 100,000: 109
Costs Index: Good
Fluoridation: Adjusted
Air Pollution: Insignificant
Places Rated Score: 509
Places Rated Rank: 268

Lorain–Elyria, OH

Physicians per 100,000: 85
Cardiac Rehabilitation Centers:
  Elyria Memorial Hospital CRU
  Lorain Family and Community Hospital
    Post-Cardiac Rehabilitation Program
Hospices:
  St. Joseph's Hospital–Hospice Unit
Costs Index: Good
Fluoridation: Adjusted
Air Pollution: Insignificant
CMSA Access: CLEVELAND–AKRON–LORAIN,
  OH (320)
Places Rated Score: 1,105
Places Rated Rank: 119

★ Los Angeles–Long Beach, CA

Physicians per 100,000: 243
Teaching Hospitals:
  Cedars-Sinai Medical Center
  Children's Hospital of Los Angeles
  Hospital of the Good Samaritan
  Huntington Memorial Hospital

Los Angeles County Harbor General
  Hospital
Martin Luther King Jr. General Hospital
Memorial Hospital Medical Center
Ranchos Los Amigos Hospital
UCLA Hospital
USC Medical Center
VA Medical Center (Brentwood)
VA Medical Center (Long Beach)
VA Medical Center (Sepulveda)
VA Medical Center (Wadsworth)
Medical Schools:
  Charles Drew Postgraduate Medical
    School
  UCLA School of Medicine
  USC School of Medicine
Cardiac Rehabilitation Centers:
  Alhambra Community Hospital CRU
  Antelope Valley Hospital CTC
  Beverly Hospital CRU
  Brotman Medical Center CRU
  California Hospital Medical Center
  Cedars-Sinai Medical Center CRU
  Centinela Hospital Medical Center CRU
  Cerritos Gardens General Hospital CRU
  Daniel Freeman Hospital CRU
  Downey Community Hospital CTC
  Foothill Presbyterian Hospital CTC
  Garfield Medical Center CRU
  Glendale Adventist Medical Center CRU
  Greater El Monte Community Hospital
    CRU
  Harbor General Hospital CRU
  Hawthorne Community Hospital CRU
  Hospital of the Good Samaritan CRU
  Huntington Memorial Hospital
  Kaiser Foundation Hospital CRU
  Little Company of Mary Hospital CRU
  Long Beach Community Hospital CRU
  Long Beach Memorial Medical Center
    CRU
  Martin Luther King Jr. Hospital CRU
  Memorial Hospital of Gardena
  Memorial Hospital of Glendale CRU
  Methodist Hospital of Southern
    California CTC
  Pacific Hospital CRU
  Pomona Valley Community Hospital
    CRU
  Presbyterian Hospital Cardiac
    Rehabilitation Program
  Queen of the Valley Hospital Coronary
    Observation Unit
  Rancho Los Amigos Hospital CRU
  Riverside Hospital CRU
  Ross-Loos Medical Center CRU
  St. John's Hospital CRU
  St. Luke's Hospital CRU
  Santa Monica Hospital CRU
  South Bay Hospital CRU
  Torrance Memorial Hospital CRU
  UCLA Medical Center CRU
  Westside Family YMCA CRU
  Whittier Hospital CRU
Comprehensive Cancer Treatment
  Centers:
• UCLA Jonsson Comprehensive Cancer
    Center
• USC–Cancer Research Institute
Hospices:
  Continuity of Life Program
  Granada Hills Hospice
  Hospice in the Home (Visiting Nurse
    Association of Los Angeles)
  Hospice of Pasadena, Inc.
  Hospital Home Health Care
    Agency–Hospice Program

Kaiser Permanente Hospice Program
Long Beach Community
  Hospital–Hospice Program
Los Angeles County–USC Cancer
  Center Hospice Program
Northridge Hospital–Home Health Care
Parkwood Community Hospital–Hospice
  Program
VA Medical Center (Wadsworth)–
  Palliative Treatment Program
Costs Index: Poor
Fluoridation: Adjusted (Long Beach only)
Air Pollution: TSP, CO, O$_3$ ▲▲, NO$_2$, Pb
CMSA Access: LOS ANGELES–ANAHEIM–
  RIVERSIDE, CA (360)
Places Rated Score: 5,153
Places Rated Rank: 5

Louisville, KY–IN

Physicians per 100,000: 211
Teaching Hospitals:
  Jewish Hospital
  Louisville General Hospital
  VA Medical Center
Medical Schools:
  University of Louisville School of
    Medicine
Cardiac Rehabilitation Centers:
  Audubon Hospital CRU
  Highlands Baptist Hospital CRU
  Norton Memorial Infirmary CRU
  St. Anthony Hospital Cardiac Rebound
Hospices:
  Hospice of Louisville and Southern
    Indiana
  Hospice of Southern Indiana
Costs Index: Excellent
Fluoridation: Adjusted
Air Pollution: CO
Places Rated Score: 2,111
Places Rated Rank: 48

Lowell, MA–NH

Physicians per 100,000: 268
Cardiac Rehabilitation Centers:
  St. John's Hospital CRU
Costs Index: Excellent
Fluoridation: None
Air Pollution: Insignificant
CMSA Access: BOSTON–LAWRENCE–SALEM,
  MA–NH (515)
Places Rated Score: 1,083
Places Rated Rank: 123

Lubbock, TX

Physicians per 100,000: 200
Medical Schools:
  Texas Tech University School of
    Medicine
Hospices:
  Hospice of the Good Samaritan
Costs Index: Good
Fluoridation: Natural
Air Pollution: TSP
Places Rated Score: 900
Places Rated Rank: 152

Lynchburg, VA

Physicians per 100,000: 132
Cardiac Rehabilitation Centers:
  Virginia Baptist Hospital CRU
Costs Index: Excellent
Fluoridation: Adjusted
Air Pollution: Insignificant
Places Rated Score: 732
Places Rated Rank: 191

Macon–Warner Robins, GA
Physicians per 100,000: 143
Cardiac Rehabilitation Centers:
  Medical Center of Central Georgia CRU
Costs Index: Excellent
Fluoridation: Adjusted (Warner Robins
  only)
Air Pollution: Insignificant
Places Rated Score: 593
Places Rated Rank: 241

Madison, WI
Physicians per 100,000: 418
Teaching Hospitals:
  Madison General Hospital
  University of Wisconsin Hospitals
  William S. Middleton Memorial VA
    Medical Center
Medical Schools:
  University of Wisconsin School of
    Medicine
Cardiac Rehabilitation Centers:
  Biodynamics Lab–University of
    Wisconsin
  University of Wisconsin Hospital CRP
Comprehensive Cancer Treatment
  Centers:
• University of Wisconsin Medical
    Center–Clinical Cancer Center
Hospices:
  Dane County Hospice, Inc.
Costs Index: Good
Fluoridation: Adjusted
Air Pollution: Insignificant
Places Rated Score: 2,168
Places Rated Rank: 45

Manchester, NH
Physicians per 100,000: 337
Cardiac Rehabilitation Centers:
  Catholic Medical Center CRU
  Easter Seal Rehabilitation Center
Costs Index: Excellent
Fluoridation: None
Air Pollution: Insignificant
Places Rated Score: 737
Places Rated Rank: 190

Mansfield, OH
Physicians per 100,000: 103
Costs Index: Excellent
Fluoridation: None
Air Pollution: Insignificant
Places Rated Score: 303
Places Rated Rank: 313

McAllen–Edinburg–Mission, TX
Physicians per 100,000: 72
Costs Index: Good
Fluoridation: Natural (McAllen and Mission
  only)
Air Pollution: Insignificant
Places Rated Score: 372
Places Rated Rank: 296

Medford, OR
Physicians per 100,000: 156
Costs Index: Excellent
Fluoridation: None
Air Pollution: CO
Places Rated Score: 256
Places Rated Rank: 317

**Melbourne–Titusville–
Palm Bay, FL**
Physicians per 100,000: 117
Hospices:
  Hospice of St. Francis

Hospice of South Brevard
Costs Index: Good
Fluoridation: Adjusted (Melbourne only)
Air Pollution: Insignificant
Places Rated Score: 517
Places Rated Rank: 266

Memphis, TN–AR–MS
Physicians per 100,000: 243
Teaching Hospitals:
  Baptist Memorial Hospital
  City of Memphis Hospital
  VA Medical Center
Medical Schools:
  University of Tennessee College of
    Medicine
Cardiac Rehabilitation Centers:
  University of Tennessee, Memphis,
    Hospital CRU
  VA Hospital CRU
Comprehensive Cancer Treatment
  Centers:
  St. Jude Children's Research
    Hospital–Cancer Center
Hospices
  Health and Hospice Services of
    Memphis
  Hospice of Memphis, Inc.
  Mid-South Comprehensive Home and
    Hospice, Inc.
Costs Index: Good
Fluoridation: Adjusted
Air Pollution: CO
Places Rated Score: 2,043
Places Rated Rank: 51

Miami–Hialeah, FL
Physicians per 100,000: 284
Teaching Hospitals:
  Jackson Memorial Hospital
  Mount Sinai Medical Center
  VA Medical Center
Medical Schools:
  University of Miami School of Medicine
Cardiac Rehabilitation Centers:
  American Hospital Cardiovascular
    Laboratory
  Baptist Hospital of Miami CRU
  Biscayne Medical Center CRU
  Mercy Cardiac Treatment Center CRU
  Mount Sinai Medical Center CRU
  North Miami General Hospital CRU
  Palmetto General Hospital CRU
Comprehensive Cancer Treatment
  Centers:
• University of Miami School of
    Medicine–Comprehensive Cancer
    Center
Hospices:
  Hospice of Miami
Costs Index: Poor
Fluoridation: Adjusted
Air Pollution: CO
CMSA Access: MIAMI–FORT
  LAUDERDALE, FL (80)
Places Rated Score: 2,314
Places Rated Rank: 41

★ **Middlesex–Somerset–Hunterdon, NJ**
Physicians per 100,000: 159
Teaching Hospitals:
  Middlesex General Hospital
Medical Schools:
  College of Medicine and Dentistry of
    New Jersey, Rutgers Medical School
Hospices:
  Somerset County Hospice

Costs Index: Excellent
Fluoridation: Adjusted (approximately 50%
  of the metro area)
Air Pollution: Insignificant
CMSA Access: NEW YORK–NORTHERN
  NEW JERSEY–LONG ISLAND,
  NY–NJ–CT (1,480)
Places Rated Score: 2,589
Places Rated Rank: 24

Middletown, CT
Physicians per 100,000: 184
Cardiac Rehabilitation Centers:
  Middlesex Memorial Hospital CRU
Costs Index: Excellent
Fluoridation: Adjusted
Air Pollution: O_3
CMSA Access: HARTFORD–NEW
  BRITAIN–MIDDLETOWN, CT (200)
Places Rated Score: 884
Places Rated Rank: 155

Midland, TX
Physicians per 100,000: 97
Costs Index: Good
Fluoridation: Almost none
Air Pollution: TSP
Places Rated Score: 97
Places Rated Rank: 327

★ **Milwaukee, WI**
Physicians per 100,000: 233
Teaching Hospitals:
  Milwaukee County Medical Complex
  Mount Sinai Medical Center
  VA Medical Center
Medical Schools:
  Medical College of Wisconsin
Cardiac Rehabilitation Centers:
  Columbia Hospital CRU
  Deaconess Hospital CRU
  Lutheran Hospital CRU
  Milwaukee Regional Medical Center
    Fitness Program
  Mount Sinai Medical Center CRP
  St. Francis Hospital CRU
  St. Luke's Hospital CRU
  St. Mary's Hospital CRU
  Southeastern Wisconsin Regional
    Medical Center Curative Workshop
Comprehensive Cancer Treatment
  Centers:
  Milwaukee Children's Hospital–
    Department of Hematology and
    Oncology
Hospices:
  Hospice of Milwaukee
  Milwaukee Hospice, Inc.
  Mount Sinai Medical Center–Ambulatory
    Oncology
  St. Joseph's Hospital
  St. Mary's Hospital
Costs Index: Good
Fluoridation: Adjusted
Air Pollution: Insignificant
CMSA Access: MILWAUKEE–RACINE,
  WI (20)
Places Rated Score: 3,053
Places Rated Rank: 17

★ **Minneapolis–St. Paul, MN–WI**
Physicians per 100,000: 234
Teaching Hospitals:
  Abbott–Northwestern Hospital, Inc.
  Hennepin County Medical Center
  Mount Sinai Hospital
  St. Paul–Ramsey Medical Center

University of Minnesota Hospitals and
  Clinics
VA Medical Center
Medical Schools:
  University of Minnesota, Minneapolis,
    Medical School
Cardiac Rehabilitation Centers:
  Bethesda Lutheran Medical Center CRU
  Eitel Hospital CRU
  Fairview-Southdale Hospital CRU
  Hennepin County Medical Center CRU
  Methodist Hospital CRU
  Midway Hospital CRU
  North Memorial Medical Center–
    Intervention and Rehabilitation
    Program
  St. John's Hospital CRU
  St. Joseph's Hospital CRU
  St. Paul–Ramsey Medical Center
  University of Minnesota CRU
  VA Medical Center CRU
Hospices:
  Abbott–Northwestern Hospital–Hospice
    Program
  Bethesda Lutheran Medical
    Hospital–Hospice (St. Paul)
  Fairview Community Hospitals–Hospice
    Program (Edina)
  Fairview Community Hospitals–Hospice
    Program (Minneapolis)
  Mercy-Unity Home Health Care
  Methodist Hospital–Hospice Program
  Metropolitan Medical Center–Hospice
    Program
  Midway Hospital Hospice Program
  Minnesota Coalition for Terminal Care
  North Memorial Medical
    Center–Hospice Program
  St. John's Hospital–Hospice Program
  St. Joseph's Hospital–Hospice Program
  St. Mary's Hospital–Hospice Program
Costs Index: Good
Fluoridation: Adjusted
Air Pollution: CO, Pb
Places Rated Score: 3,934
Places Rated Rank: 9

Mobile, AL
Physicians per 100,000: 169
Teaching Hospitals:
  University of South Alabama Medical
    Center
Medical Schools:
  University of South Alabama School of
    Medicine
Cardiac Rehabilitation Centers:
  Operation Bounce Back, Cardiac
    Therapy, Inc.
Hospices:
  The Hospice of Mobile
  Villa Mercy Hospice
Costs Index: Excellent
Fluoridation: Adjusted
Air Pollution: Insignificant
Places Rated Score: 1,469
Places Rated Rank: 80

Modesto, CA
Physicians per 100,000: 147
Hospices:
  Modesto Community Hospice
Costs Index: Good
Fluoridation: None
Air Pollution: Insignificant
Places Rated Score: 347
Places Rated Rank: 301

Monmouth–Ocean, NJ
Physicians per 100,000: 142
Teaching Hospitals:
  Jersey Shore Medical Center–Fitkin
    Hospital
  Monmouth Medical Center
Hospices:
  Community Memorial Hospital–Hospice
    Program
Costs Index: Excellent
Fluoridation: Adjusted (Monmouth only)
Air Pollution: Insignificant
CMSA Access: NEW YORK–NORTHERN
  NEW JERSEY–LONG ISLAND, NY–NJ–CT
  (1,490)
Places Rated Score: 2,482
Places Rated Rank: 32

Monroe, LA
Physicians per 100,000: 131
Costs Index: Excellent
Fluoridation: None
Air Pollution: Insignificant
Places Rated Score: 331
Places Rated Rank: 308

Montgomery, AL
Physicians per 100,000: 132
Cardiac Rehabilitation Centers:
  Baptist Medical Center CRU
Hospices:
  Hospice of Montgomery
Costs Index: Excellent
Fluoridation: Adjusted
Air Pollution: Insignificant
Places Rated Score: 832
Places Rated Rank: 166

Muncie, IN
Physicians per 100,000: 149
Teaching Hospitals:
  Ball Memorial Hospital
Cardiac Rehabilitation Centers:
  Ball Memorial Hospital CRU
Costs Index: Excellent
Fluoridation: Adjusted
Air Pollution: Insignificant
Places Rated Score: 949
Places Rated Rank: 146

Muskegon, MI
Physicians per 100,000: 99
Cardiac Rehabilitation Centers:
  Mercy Hospital CRU
Costs Index: Excellent
Fluoridation: Adjusted
Air Pollution: Insignificant
Places Rated Score: 699
Places Rated Rank: 205

Nashua, NH
Physicians per 100,000: 128
Costs Index: Excellent
Fluoridation: None
Air Pollution: Insignificant
CMSA Access: BOSTON–LAWRENCE–SALEM,
  MA–NH (525)
Places Rated Score: 853
Places Rated Rank: 160

Nashville, TN
Physicians per 100,000: 250
Teaching Hospitals:
  Hubbard Hospital of the Meharry
    College
  St. Thomas Hospital

VA Medical Center
Vanderbilt University Hospital
Medical Schools:
  Meharry Medical College School of
    Medicine
  Vanderbilt University School of Medicine
Cardiac Rehabilitation Centers:
  Park View Hospital Cardiac
    Conditioning Center
  St. Thomas Hospital CRU
Costs Index: Excellent
Fluoridation: None
Air Pollution: CO, NO$_2$
Places Rated Score: 1,850
Places Rated Rank: 61

★ **Nassau–Suffolk, NY**
Physicians per 100,000: 229
Teaching Hospitals:
  Long Island Jewish–Hillside Medical
    Center
  Nassau County Medical Center
  Nassau Hospital
  North Shore University Hospital
  VA Hospital (Northport)
Medical Schools:
  SUNY at Stony Brook–Health Sciences
    Center–School of Medicine
Cardiac Rehabilitation Centers:
  Adult Fitness Program (Garden City)
  Brookhaven CPR Center CRU (Port
    Jefferson)
  Community Hospital–Department of
    Rehabilitative Medicine (Glen Cove)
  Lydia Hall Hospital CRU (Freeport)
  Nassau Cardiac Rehabilitation and
    Diagnostic Service (Mineola)
  Nassau County Medical Center CRU
    (East Meadow)
  North Shore University Hospital Cardiac
    Exercise Center (Manhasset)
  St. Francis Hospital CRU (Roslyn)
  South Nassau Community Hospital
    Cardiac Work Evaluation Unit
    (Oceanside)
  South Shore Cardiac Clinic CRU (North
    Massapequa)
  Southside Hospital CRU (Bay Shore)
  Suffolk Cardiac Pulmonary Associates,
    Inc. (West Islip)
Hospices:
  Mercy Hospital Hospice
  Nassau Hospital–Hospice Program
Costs Index: Unacceptable
Fluoridation: Adjusted (part of Nassau
  County only)
Air Pollution: Insignificant
CMSA Access: NEW YORK–NORTHERN
  NEW JERSEY–LONG ISLAND, NY–NJ–CT
  (1,290)
Places Rated Score: 3,919
Places Rated Rank: 10

New Bedford, MA
Physicians per 100,000: 319
Costs Index: Excellent
Fluoridation: None
Air Pollution: Insignificant
Places Rated Score: 519
Places Rated Rank: 265

New Britain, CT
Physicians per 100,000: 265
Teaching Hospitals:
  New Britain General Hospital
Cardiac Rehabilitation Centers:
  New Britain General Hospital CRU

Costs Index: Excellent
Fluoridation: Adjusted
Air Pollution: Insignificant
CMSA Access: HARTFORD–NEW
    BRITAIN–MIDDLETOWN, CT (180)
Places Rated Score: 1,245
Places Rated Rank: 98

New Haven–Meriden, CT
Physicians per 100,000: 318
Teaching Hospitals:
    Hospital of St. Raphael
    VA Medical Center–West Haven
    Yale–New Haven Hospital
Medical Schools:
    Yale University School of Medicine
Cardiac Rehabilitation Centers:
    VA Medical Center CRU
    Yale–New Haven Medical Center CRU
Comprehensive Cancer Treatment
    Centers:
• Yale University Comprehensive Cancer
    Center
Hospices:
    Connecticut Hospice, Inc.
    Hospice Institute
Costs Index: Good
Fluoridation: Adjusted
Air Pollution: O₃
Places Rated Score: 2,068
Places Rated Rank: 50

New London–Norwich, CT–RI
Physicians per 100,00: 156
Costs Index: Excellent
Fluoridation: Adjusted
Air Pollution: O₃
Places Rated Score: 556
Places Rated Rank: 254

★ New Orleans, LA
Physicians per 100,000: 286
Teaching Hospitals:
    Charity Hospital of New Orleans
    Ochsner Medical Foundation Hospital
    Touro Infirmary
    VA Medical Center
Medical Schools:
    Louisiana State University School of
        Medicine in New Orleans
    Tulane University School of Medicine
Cardiac Rehabilitation Centers:
    East Jefferson General Hospital CRU
    F. E. Herbert Outpatient Cardiovascular
        Therapy Program
    Jo Ellen Smith Memorial Hospital
        In-Patient Cardio-Therapy Program
    Ochsner Foundation Hospital CRU
Hospices
    Hospice of Greater New Orleans
Costs Index: Good
Fluoridation: Adjusted
Air Pollution: Insignificant
Places Rated Score: 2,586
Places Rated Rank: 25

★ New York, NY
Physicians per 100,000: 370
Teaching Hospitals:
    Beth Israel Medical Center
    Booth Memorial Medical Center
    Bronx-Lebanon Medical Center
    Bronx Municipal Hospital Center
    Brookdale Hospital Medical Center
    Brooklyn Hospital
    Catholic Medical Center of Brooklyn
        and Queens

City Hospital Center at Elmhurst
Cumberland Hospital
Harlem Hospital Center
Hospital for Joint Diseases and Medical
    Center
Hospital for Special Surgery
Hospital of the Albert Einstein School of
    Medicine
Jewish Hospital and Medical Center of
    Brooklyn
Kings County Hospital Center
Lenox Hill Hospital
Long Island College Hospital
Lutheran Medical Center
Memorial Hospital for Cancer and Allied
    Diseases
Methodist Hospital
Misericordia Hospital Medical Center
Montefiore Hospital and Medical Center
Mount Sinai Hospital
New York Hospital
New York Medical College Hospitals
New York University Medical Center
Presbyterian Hospital in the City of New
    York
Roosevelt Hospital
St. John's Episcopal Hospital
St. Luke's Hospital Center
St. Vincent's Hospital and Medical
    Center of New York
St. Vincent's Medical Center of
    Richmond
State University Hospital Downstate
    Medical Center
VA Medical Center (Brooklyn)
VA Medical Center (Manhattan)
Westchester County Medical Center
Medical Schools:
    Albert Einstein College of Medicine of
        Yeshiva University
    Columbia University College of
        Physicians and Surgeons
    Cornell University Medical College
    Mount Sinai School of Medicine, CUNY
    New York Medical College
    New York University School of Medicine
    SUNY Downstate Medical Center
        College of Medicine
Cardiac Rehabilitation Centers:
    Beth Israel Medical Center CRU
    Coronary Exercise Lab CRU
    East Side Cardiopulmonary
        Rehabilitation Department
    Kingsbrook Jewish Medical Center
    Long Island Jewish Medical Center
    Methodist Hospital Reconditioning Lab
    Montefiore Hospital Exercise Lab and
        CRU
    New York Hospital–Cornell Medical
        Center CRU
    New York State University Medical
        Center CRC
    Nyack Hospital CRU
    Phelps Memorial Hospital CRU
    Richmond Cardiological Services CRU
    St. John's Episcopal Hospital CRU
    S. I. Diagnostic and Rehabilitation
        Center
    United Hospital CRU
    Victory Memorial Hospital Cardiological
        Services
Comprehensive Cancer Treatment
    Centers:
    Albert Einstein College of
        Medicine–Cancer Research Center
• College of Physicians and
    Surgeons–Columbia University
    Cancer Research Center

• Memorial Sloan-Kettering Cancer Center
    Mount Sinai School of Medicine–
        Department of Neoplastic Diseases
    New York University Medical
        Center–Cancer Center
Hospices:
    Cabrini Hospice–Cabrini Medical Center
    Calvary Hospital
    Hospice of Rockland, Inc.
    Hospice of St. Luke's–Roosevelt
        Hospital
    Hospice of Westchester
    Metropolitan Jewish Geriatric Center
    New York Infirmary–Beekman Downtown
        Hospital–Hospice Program
    St. Rose's Home
    United Hospital Hospice
Costs Index: Unacceptable
Fluoridation: Adjusted
Air Pollution: CO
CMSA Access: NEW YORK–NORTHERN
    NEW JERSEY–LONG ISLAND, NY–NJ–CT
    (880)
Places Rated Score: 7,850
Places Rated Rank: 1

★ Newark, NJ
Physicians per 100,000: 226
Teaching Hospitals:
    Martland Medical Center
    Muhlenberg Hospital
    Newark–Beth Israel Medical Center
    Overlook Hospital
    St. Barnabas Medical Center
    St. Michael's Medical Center
    VA Medical Center (East Orange)
Medical Schools:
    College of Medicine and Dentistry of
        New Jersey–New Jersey Medical
        School
Cardiac Rehabilitation Centers:
    Hospital Center at Orange CRU
    Newark–Beth Israel Medical Center
        Cardiac Rehabilitation Service
    St. Michael's Medical Center CRU
    VA Medical Center CRU (East Orange)
Hospices:
    Hospice, Inc.
    Karen Anne Quinlan Center of Hope
    Muhlenberg Hospital–Home Health Care
        Program
    Overlook Hospital–Hospice Home Care
        Department
    Riverside Hospice
Costs Index: Good
Fluoridation: Almost none
Air Pollution: CO
CMSA Access: NEW YORK–NORTHERN
    NEW JERSEY–LONG ISLAND, NY–NJ–CT
    (1,280)
Places Rated Score: 4,106
Places Rated Rank: 8

Niagara Falls, NY
Physicians per 100,000: 102
Costs Index: Poor
Fluoridation: Adjusted
Air Pollution: Insignificant
CMSA Access: BUFFALO–NIAGARA FALLS,
    NY (205)
Places Rated Score: 507
Places Rated Rank: 269

Norfolk–Virginia Beach–
Newport News, VA
Physicians per 100,000: 132
Teaching Hospitals:
    Medical Center Hospitals

VA Medical Center
Medical Schools:
  Eastern Virginia Medical School
Cardiac Rehabilitation Centers:
  General Hospital of Virginia Beach CRU
  Non-Invasive Cardio Lab CRU
  Norfolk General Hospital CRU
  Riverside Hospital Cardiovascular
    Therapy
Hospices:
  DePaul Hospital
  Edmarc Hospice for Children, Inc.
  Riverside Hospital
Costs Index: Excellent
Fluoridation: Adjusted (Norfolk and
  Newport News only)
Air Pollution: Insignificant
Places Rated Score: 1,932
Places Rated Rank: 56

Norwalk, CT
Physicians per 100,000: 220
Teaching Hospitals:
  Norwalk Hospital
Cardiac Rehabilitation Centers:
  Norwalk Hospital CRU
Costs Index: Excellent
Fluoridation: Adjusted
Air Pollution: Insignificant
CMSA Access: NEW YORK–NORTHERN
  NEW JERSEY–LONG ISLAND,
  NY–NJ–CT (1,510)
Places Rated Score: 2,530
Places Rated Rank: 29

Oakland, CA
Physicians per 100,000: 212
Teaching Hospitals:
  VA Medical Center (Martinez)
Cardiac Rehabilitation Centers:
  Alta Bates Hospital CRU
  Doctors Hospital CRU
  Eden Hospital CRU
  Herrick Memorial Hospital CRU
  Mount Diablo Medical Center CRU
  Peralta Hospital
Hospices:
  Gray Panther Hospice of Berkeley
  Hospice of Contra Costa (Lafayette)
  Hospice of Contra Costa (Walnut
    Creek)
  Kaiser Permanente Hayward Hospice
  Shanti Project
  Vesper Hospice
Costs Index: Fair
Fluoridation: Adjusted
Air Pollution: Insignificant
CMSA Access: SAN FRANCISCO–
  OAKLAND–SAN JOSE, CA (450)
Places Rated Score: 2,362
Places Rated Rank: 39

Ocala, FL
Physicians per 100,000: 89
Costs Index: Good
Fluoridation: Adjusted
Air Pollution: Insignificant
Places Rated Score: 489
Places Rated Rank: 273

Odessa, TX
Physicians per 100,000: 84
Costs Index: Good
Fluoridation: Natural
Air Pollution: TSP
Places Rated Score: 384
Places Rated Rank: 294

Oklahoma City, OK
Physicians per 100,000: 223
Teaching Hospitals:
  University Hospital and Clinics
  VA Medical Center
Medical Schools:
  University of Oklahoma College of
    Medicine
Cardiac Rehabilitation Centers:
  Baptist Medical Center CRU
  Presbyterian Hospital OMRF CRU
  St. Anthony's Hospital–Progressive CV
    Unit
Costs Index: Excellent
Fluoridation: Adjusted
Air Pollution: TSP
Places Rated Score: 1,623
Places Rated Rank: 75

Olympia, WA
Physicians per 100,000: 138
Cardiac Rehabilitation Centers:
  St. Peter Hospital CRU
Costs Index: Good
Fluoridation: None
Air Pollution: Insignificant
Places Rated Score: 338
Places Rated Rank: 306

Omaha, NE–IA
Physicians per 100,000: 259
Teaching Hospitals:
  Creighton–Omaha Regional Health Care
    Corporation
  University of Nebraska Hospital and
    Clinics
  VA Medical Center
Medical Schools:
  Creighton University School of Medicine
  University of Nebraska College of
    Medicine
Cardiac Rehabilitation Centers:
  Archbishop Bergan Hospital CRU
  Bishop Clarkson Memorial Hospital CRU
  Immanuel Medical Center Cardiac
    Recovery Program
  Lutheran Medical Center CRU
  Nebraska Methodist Hospital CRU
  St. Joseph Hospital CRU
Hospices:
  Montclair Nursing Center
  Omaha Hospice Organization
Costs Index: Good
Fluoridation: Adjusted
Air Pollution: CO
Places Rated Score: 2,559
Places Rated Rank: 26

Orange County, NY
Physicians per 100,000: 134
Costs Index: Poor
Fluoridation: Almost none
Air Pollution: Insignificant
CMSA Access: NEW YORK–NORTHERN
  NEW JERSEY–LONG ISLAND, NY–NJ–CT
  (1,540)
Places Rated Score: 1,574
Places Rated Rank: 79

Orlando, FL
Physicians per 100,000: 165
Cardiac Rehabilitation Centers:
  Florida Hospital CRU
Hospices:
  Hospice of Central Florida
Costs Index: Good
Fluoridation: Adjusted

Air Pollution: Insignificant
Places Rated Score: 765
Places Rated Rank: 184

Owensboro, KY
Physicians per 100,000: 112
Costs Index: Outstanding
Fluoridation: Adjusted
Air Pollution: Insignificant
Places Rated Score: 812
Places Rated Rank: 173

Oxnard–Ventura, CA
Physicians per 100,000: 156
Cardiac Rehabilitation Centers:
  St. John's Hospital CRU
Hospices:
  Conejo Hospice, Inc.
  Mercy Hospice of St. John's Hospital
Costs Index: Good
Fluoridation: None
Air Pollution: O$_3$ ▲▲
CMSA Access: LOS ANGELES–
  ANAHEIM–RIVERSIDE, CA (850)
Places Rated Score: 1,106
Places Rated Rank: 118

Panama City, FL
Physicians per 100,000: 101
Costs Index: Good
Fluoridation: None
Air Pollution: Insignificant
Places Rated Score: 201
Places Rated Rank: 325

Parkersburg–Marietta, WV–OH
Physicians per 100,000: 115
Cardiac Rehabilitation Centers:
  Camden–Clark Memorial Hospital CRU
  St. Joseph's Hospital CRU
Costs Index: Excellent
Fluoridation: Adjusted (Parkersburg only)
Air Pollution: Insignificant
Places Rated Score: 665
Places Rated Rank: 215

Pascagoula, MS
Physicians per 100,000: 93
Costs Index: Excellent
Fluoridation: Adjusted
Air Pollution: Insignificant
Places Rated Score: 593
Places Rated Rank: 241

**Pawtucket–Woonsocket–
Attleboro, RI–MA**
Physicians per 100,000: 237
Teaching Hospitals:
  Memorial Hospital
Cardiac Rehabilitation Centers:
  Memorial Hospital CRU
Costs Index: Good
Fluoridation: Adjusted
Air Pollution: Insignificant
CMSA Access: PROVIDENCE–
  PAWTUCKET–FALL RIVER, RI–MA (180)
Places Rated Score: 1,117
Places Rated Rank: 114

Pensacola, FL
Physicians per 100,000: 163
Cardiac Rehabilitation Centers:
  Baptist Hospital CRU
  Heart-Lung Rehabilitation Center
Hospices:
  Hospice of Pensacola

Costs Index: Good
Fluoridation: None
Air Pollution: Insignificant
Places Rated Score: 563
Places Rated Rank: 252

Peoria, IL
Physicians per 100,000: 184
Teaching Hospitals:
St. Francis Hospital–Medical Center
Cardiac Rehabilitation Centers:
Pekin Memorial Hospital CRU
St. Francis Hospital Medical Center
Health Fitness Unit
Hospices:
Methodist Medical Center of
Illinois–Cancer Care Program
Costs Index: Excellent
Fluoridation: Adjusted
Air Pollution: Insignificant
Places Rated Score: 1,184
Places Rated Rank: 107

★ Philadelphia, PA–NJ
Physicians per 100,000: 268
Teaching Hospitals:
Albert Einstein Medical Center
Albert Einstein Medical Center–Daroff
Division
Bryn Mawr Hospital
Children's Hospital of Philadelphia
Cooper Hospital (Camden, NJ)
Crozer-Chester Medical Center
Episcopal Hospital
Graduate Hospital
Hahnemann Medical College and
Hospital of Philadelphia
Hospital of the University of
Pennsylvania
Lankenau Hospital
Medical College of Pennsylvania
Mercy Catholic Medical Center
Pennsylvania Hospital
Presbyterian–University of Pennsylvania
Medical Center
St. Christopher's Hospital for Children
Temple University Hospital
Thomas Jefferson University Hospital
VA Medical Center
Medical Schools:
Hahnemann Medical College
Jefferson Medical College of Thomas
Jefferson University
Medical College of Pennsylvania
Temple University School of Medicine
University of Pennsylvania School of
Medicine
Cardiac Rehabilitation Centers:
Albert Einstein Medical Center CRU
John F. Kennedy Hospital CRU
Naval Regional Medical Center CRU
Pennsylvania Hospital Cardiopulmonary
Rehabilitation Center
Thomas Jefferson University Hospital
CRU
Comprehensive Cancer Treatment
Centers:
• Fox Chase–University of Pennsylvania
Comprehensive Cancer Center
Hospices:
Bryn Mawr Hospital Hospice Program
Paoli Memorial Hospital–Hospice
Program
Pennsylvania Hospital–Hospice Program
Presbyterian–University of Pennsylvania
Medical Center Hospice Program
Costs Index: Excellent

Fluoridation: Adjusted
Air Pollution: CO, Pb
CMSA Access: PHILADELPHIA–WILMINGTON–
TRENTON, PA–NJ–DE–MD (40)
Places Rated Score: 5,158
Places Rated Rank: 4

Phoenix, AZ
Physicians per 100,000: 184
Teaching Hospitals:
Good Samaritan Hospital
Maricopa County General Hospital
St. Joseph's Hospital and Medical
Center
Cardiac Rehabilitation Centers:
Arizona Heart Institute Preventative
Medicine Department
Good Samaritan Hospital CRU
John C. Lincoln Hospital Cardiac
Fitness Program
Mesa Lutheran Hospital CRU
Phoenix General Hospital CRU
Scottsdale Memorial Hospital CRU
Hospices:
Hospice of the Valley (Mesa)
Hospice of the Valley (Phoenix)
St. Joseph's Hospital and Medical
Center–Oncology Life
Enrichment Program
Samaritan Health Service
Costs Index: Fair
Fluoridation: None
Air Pollution: TSP, CO
Places Rated Score: 1,584
Places Rated Rank: 77

Pine Bluff, AR
Physicians per 100,000: 117
Costs Index: Excellent
Fluoridation: Adjusted
Air Pollution: Insignificant
Places Rated Score: 617
Places Rated Rank: 227

★ Pittsburgh, PA
Physicians per 100,000: 213
Teaching Hospitals:
Allegheny General Hospital
Children's Hospital of Pittsburgh
Eye and Ear Hospital of Pittsburgh
Magee–Women's Hospital
Mercy Hospital of Pittsburgh
Montefiore Hospital Association of
Western Pennsylvania
Presbyterian–University Hospital
St. Francis General Hospital
VA Medical Center
Western Pennsylvania Hospital
Western Psychiatric Institute and Clinic
Medical Schools:
University of Pittsburgh School of
Medicine
Cardiac Rehabilitation Centers:
Human Energy Research Lab–University
of Pittsburgh
Pittsburgh Children's Hospital CRU
St. Francis General Hospital CRU
Shadyside Hospital Progressive
Cardiac Care
Hospices:
Forbes Hospice
Costs Index: Excellent
Fluoridation: Adjusted
Air Pollution: SO₂
Places Rated Score: 3,413
Places Rated Rank: 14

Pittsfield, MA
Physicians per 100,000: 194
Teaching Hospitals:
Berkshire Medical Center
Cardiac Rehabilitation Centers:
Pittsfield YMCA Cardiac Rehabilitation
Program
Costs Index: Excellent
Fluoridation: None
Air Pollution: Insignificant
Places Rated Score: 694
Places Rated Rank: 206

Portland, ME
Physicians per 100,000: 334
Teaching Hospitals:
Maine Medical Center
Hospices:
Hospice of Maine
Costs Index: Excellent
Fluoridation: None
Air Pollution: Insignificant
Places Rated Score: 834
Places Rated Rank: 163

Portland, OR
Physicians per 100,000: 290
Teaching Hospitals:
Emanuel Hospital
University of Oregon Health Sciences
Center
Medical Schools:
University of Oregon Health Sciences
Center
Cardiac Rehabilitation Centers:
Cardio and Pulmonary Rehabilitation
Institute
Portland State University Adult Fitness
Program
YMCA Cardiac Therapy
Hospices:
Hospice of Oregon–Good Samaritan
Hospital
Oregon Comprehensive Cancer
Program–Hospice Program
Providence Hospice–Providence
Medical Center
Costs Index: Good
Fluoridation: None
Air Pollution: Pb
Places Rated Score: 1,590
Places Rated Rank: 76

Portsmouth–Dover–Rochester, NH–ME
Physicians per 100,000: 96
Hospices:
Seacoast Hospice
Costs Index: Excellent
Fluoridation: Adjusted (Portsmouth and
Rochester only)
Air Pollution: Insignificant
Places Rated Score: 596
Places Rated Rank: 237

Poughkeepsie, NY
Physicians per 100,000: 155
Costs Index: Poor
Fluoridation: Adjusted
Air Pollution: Insignificant
Places Rated Score: 355
Places Rated Rank: 299

Providence, RI
Physicians per 100,000: 327
Teaching Hospitals:
Miriam Hospital

Rhode Island Hospital
Roger Williams General Hospital
VA Medical Center
Women and Infants Hospital of Rhode
Island
Medical Schools:
Brown University Program in Medicine
Cardiac Rehabilitation Centers:
Rhode Island Cardiac Rehabilitation
Center
St. Joseph Hospital CRU
Comprehensive Cancer Treatment
Centers:
Roger Williams General
Hospital–Cancer Center
Hospices:
Hospice Care of Rhode Island
Costs Index: Good
Fluoridation: Adjusted
Air Pollution: Insignificant
CMSA Access: PROVIDENCE–
PAWTUCKET–FALL RIVER,
RI–MA (40)
Places Rated Score: 2,467
Places Rated Rank: 33

Provo–Orem, UT
Physicians per 100,000: 98
Costs Index: Excellent
Fluoridation: None
Air Pollution: CO
Places Rated Score: 198
Places Rated Rank: 326

Pueblo, CO
Physicians per 100,000: 168
Cardiac Rehabilitation Centers:
St. Mary–Corwin Hospital CRU
Costs Index: Excellent
Fluoridation: None
Air Pollution: Insignificant
Places Rated Score: 468
Places Rated Rank: 277

Racine, WI
Physicians per 100,000: 91
Cardiac Rehabilitation Centers:
St. Luke's Hospital YMCA
St. Mary's Medical Center CRU
Costs Index: Good
Fluoridation: Adjusted
Air Pollution: Insignificant
CMSA Access: MILWAUKEE–RACINE, WI
(240)
Places Rated Score: 931
Places Rated Rank: 147

★ **Raleigh–Durham, NC**
Physicians per 100,000: 526
Teaching Hospitals:
Duke University Hospital
North Carolina Memorial Hospital
VA Medical Center
Wake County Hospital System, Inc.
Medical Schools:
Duke University School of Medicine
University of North Carolina at Chapel
Hill School of Medicine
Cardiac Rehabilitation Centers:
Duke University Medical Center CRU
North Carolina Memorial Hospital CRU
Raleigh Cardiac Foundation CRU
Wake County Medical Center CRU
Comprehensive Cancer Treatment
Centers:
• Duke University Medical Center–
Comprehensive Cancer Center

University of North Carolina–Cancer
Research Center
Hospices:
Hospice of North Carolina, Inc.
Hospice of Wake County
Triangle Hospice
Costs Index: Outstanding
Fluoridation: Adjusted
Air Pollution: CO
Places Rated Score: 3,476
Places Rated Rank: 13

Reading, PA
Physicians per 100,000: 154
Cardiac Rehabilitation Centers:
Community General Hospital CRU
Reading Hospital and Medical Center
CRU
St. Joseph's Hospital CRU
Costs Index: Outstanding
Fluoridation: Adjusted
Air Pollution: Insignificant
Places Rated Score: 1,154
Places Rated Rank: 110

Redding, CA
Physicians per 100,000: 174
Costs Index: Good
Fluoridation: None
Air Pollution: Insignificant
Places Rated Score: 274
Places Rated Rank: 315

Reno, NV
Physicians per 100,000: 215
Medical Schools:
University of Nevada School of Medical
Sciences
Cardiac Rehabilitation Centers:
Washoe Medical Center CRU
Costs Index: Good
Fluoridation: None
Air Pollution: CO
Places Rated Score: 615
Places Rated Rank: 229

Richland–Kennewick–Pasco, WA
Physicians per 100,000: 100
Cardiac Rehabilitation Centers:
Valley General Hospital CRU
Costs Index: Good
Fluoridation: None
Air Pollution: Insignificant
Places Rated Score: 300
Places Rated Rank: 314

Richmond–Petersburg, VA
Physicians per 100,000: 248
Teaching Hospitals:
McGuire VA Medical Center
Medical College of Virginia Hospitals
Medical Schools:
Virginia Commonwealth University–
Medical College of Virginia School
of Medicine
Cardiac Rehabilitation Centers:
Chippenham Hospital Cardiac
Treatment Center
Johnston–Willis Hospital CRU
Medical College of Virginia Hospital
CRU
VA Medical Center CRU
Virginia Heart Institute CRU
Wirt Hatcher Memorial–The Retreat
Hospital

Comprehensive Cancer Treatment
Centers:
Medical College of Virginia–Virginia
Commonwealth University Cancer
Center
Hospices:
American Cancer Society–Virginia
Division, Inc.
Medical College of Virginia–Hospice
Program
St. Mary's Hospital
Costs Index: Excellent
Fluoridation: Adjusted
Air Pollution: Insignificant
Places Rated Score: 2,448
Places Rated Rank: 36

Riverside–San Bernardino, CA
Physicians per 100,000: 191
Teaching Hospitals:
Jerry L. Pettis Memorial VA Hospital
Loma Linda University Medical Center
Riverside General Hospital–University
Medical Center
Medical Schools:
Loma Linda University School of
Medicine
Cardiac Rehabilitation Centers:
Cardiac Therapy CRU
Cardiopulmonary Stress Test and Work
Evaluation Unit
Eisenhower Medical Center CRU
Jerry L. Pettis VA Hospital CRU
Kaiser Foundation Hospital CRU
Riverside General Hospital CRU
St. Bernardine Hospital CRU
San Antonio Community Hospital CRU
Costs Index: Fair
Fluoridation: None
Air Pollution: TSP, O₃▲▲
CMSA Access: LOS ANGELES–ANAHEIM–
RIVERSIDE, CA (710)
Places Rated Score: 2,201
Places Rated Rank: 44

Roanoke, VA
Physicians per 100,000: 236
Cardiac Rehabilitation Centers:
Lewis-Gale Hospital, Inc., CTC
Roanoke Memorial Hospital CRU
Hospices:
Friendship Manor Geriatric Center
Costs Index: Excellent
Fluoridation: Adjusted
Air Pollution: Insignificant
Places Rated Score: 2,201
Places Rated Rank: 44

★ **Rochester, MN**
Physicians per 100,000: 1,516
Teaching Hospitals:
Rochester Methodist Hospital
St. Mary's Hospital of Rochester
Medical Schools:
Mayo Medical School
Cardiac Rehabilitation Centers:
St. Mary's Hospital CRU
Comprehensive Cancer Treatment
Centers:
• Mayo Comprehensive Cancer Center
Costs Index: Excellent
Fluoridation: Adjusted
Air Pollution: Insignificant
Places Rated Score: 2,966
Places Rated Rank: 18

Rochester, NY
Physicians per 100,000: 269

Teaching Hospitals:
  Genesee Hospital
  Highland Hospital of Rochester
  Rochester General Hospital
  Rochester St. Mary's Hospital of the
    Sisters of Charity
  Strong Memorial Hospital of the
    University of Rochester
Medical Schools:
  University of Rochester–School of
    Medicine and Dentistry
Cardiac Rehabilitation Centers:
  Strong Memorial Hospital Cardiac
    Rehabilitation Project
Comprehensive Cancer Treatment
  Centers:
  University of Rochester Cancer Center
Hospices:
  Genesee Region Home Care
    Association
Costs Index: Poor
Fluoridation: Adjusted
Air Pollution: TSP
Places Rated Score: 1,969
Places Rated Rank: 53

Rockford, IL
Physicians per 100,000: 169
Cardiac Rehabilitation Centers:
  Rockford Memorial Hospital CRU
  St. Anthony Medical Center CRU
Hospices:
  Northern Illinois Hospice Association
Costs Index: Excellent
Fluoridation: Adjusted
Air Pollution: Insignificant
Places Rated Score: 969
Places Rated Rank: 142

Sacramento, CA
Physicians per 100,000: 227
Teaching Hospitals:
  University of California,
    Davis–Sacramento Medical Center
Medical Schools:
  University of California, Davis, School of
    Medicine
Cardiac Rehabilitation Centers:
  University of California, Davis, CRU
  University of California, Davis, Pacers
    CRU
Hospices:
  Hospice of Mercy
Costs Index: Good
Fluoridation: None
Air Pollution: Pb
Places Rated Score: 1,027
Places Rated Rank: 135

Saginaw–Bay City–Midland, MI
Physicians per 100,000: 122
Cardiac Rehabilitation Centers:
  Midland Hospital Center CRU
  Saginaw General Hospital CRU
  Saginaw Osteopathic Hospital CRU
Hospices:
  Hospice of Saginaw
  The Visiting Nurse Association of
    Midland
Costs Index: Excellent
Fluoridation: Adjusted
Air Pollution: Pb
Places Rated Score: 1,022
Places Rated Rank: 136

St. Cloud, MN
Physicians per 100,000: 103
Costs Index: Excellent

Fluoridation: Adjusted
Air Pollution: Insignificant
Places Rated Score: 603
Places Rated Rank: 234

St. Joseph, MO
Physicians per 100,000: 123
Cardiac Rehabilitation Centers:
  Methodist Medical Center CRU
Costs Index: Good
Fluoridation: None
Air Pollution: TSP
Places Rated Score: 223
Places Rated Rank: 322

★ St. Louis, MO–IL
Physicians per 100,000: 220
Teaching Hospitals:
  St. John's Mercy Medical Center
  St. Louis Children's
    Hospital–Washington University
  St. Louis University Hospitals
  VA Medical Center
  Washington University Medical Center
Medical Schools:
  St. Louis University School of Medicine
  Washington University School of
    Medicine
Cardiac Rehabilitation Centers:
  Deaconess Hospital CRU
  DePaul Community Health Center CRU
  Normandy Osteopathic Hospital
  St. Louis Medical Center Cardiac
    Rehabilitation Program
  Washington University School of
    Medicine CRU
Hospices:
  Lutheran Medical Center–Continuing
    Care Unit
  St. Luke's Hospitals Hospice
Costs Index: Good
Fluoridation: Adjusted
Air Pollution: Pb
CMSA Access: ST. LOUIS–EAST ST.
  LOUIS–ALTON, MO–IL (30)
Places Rated Score: 2,850
Places Rated Rank: 19

Salem, OR
Physicians per 100,000: 149
Hospices:
  Mid-Willamette Valley Hospice
Costs Index: Excellent
Fluoridation: Adjusted
Places Rated Score: 749
Places Rated Rank: 187

Salem–Gloucester, MA
Physicians per 100,000: 147
Cardiac Rehabilitation Centers:
  Beverly Hospital CRU
  Hunt Memorial Hospital Telemetry
    Department
Hospices:
  Beverly Hospital-Hospice Program
  Hospice of the North Shore
Costs Index: Excellent
Fluoridation: Almost none
Air Pollution: Insignificant
CMSA Access: BOSTON–LAWRENCE–
  SALEM, MA–NH (485)
Places Rated Score: 1,232
Places Rated Rank: 100

Salinas–Seaside–Monterey, CA
Physicians per 100,000: 152
Hospices:
  Hospice of the Monterey Peninsula

Costs Index: Good
Fluoridation: None
Air Pollution: Insignificant
Places Rated Score: 352
Places Rated Rank: 300

Salt Lake City–Ogden, UT
Physicians per 100,000: 231
Teaching Hospitals:
  Latter-Day Saints Hospital
  University of Utah Hospital
  VA Medical Center
Medical Schools:
  University of Utah College of
    Medicine
Cardiac Rehabilitation Centers:
  Latter-Day Saints Hospital CRU
  McKay Dee Hospital
Hospices:
  Hospice of Northern Utah
  Hospice of Salt Lake
Costs Index: Excellent
Fluoridation: None
Air Pollution: CO
Places Rated Score: 1,631
Places Rated Rank: 74

San Angelo, TX
Physicians per 100,000: 136
Costs Index: Good
Fluoridation: None
Air Pollution: Insignificant
Places Rated Score: 236
Places Rated Rank: 321

San Antonio, TX
Physicians per 100,000: 237
Teaching Hospitals:
  Audie L. Murphy Memorial Veterans
    Hospital
  Bexar County Hospital District
  Wilford Hall U.S. Air Force Medical
    Center
Medical Schools:
  University of Texas Medical School at
    San Antonio
Cardiac Rehabilitation Centers:
  Baptist Memorial Hospital CRU
Hospices:
  Hospice–St. Benedict Hospital and
    Nursing Home
Costs Index: Good
Fluoridation: None
Air Pollution: TSP
Places Rated Score: 1,337
Places Rated Rank: 91

San Diego, CA
Physicians per 100,000: 216
Teaching Hospitals:
  Mercy Hospital and Medical Center
  University Hospital–University of
    California, San Diego, Medical Center
  VA Medical Center
Medical Schools:
  University of California, San Diego,
    School of Medicine
Cardiac Rehabilitation Centers:
  Alvarado Community Hospital CRU
  Cardiopulmonary Rehabilitation Center
  El Cajon Valley CPR Rehabilitation
    Center
  Grossmont Hospital CRU
  Mercy Hospital CRU
  San Diego VA Hospital CRU
  Scripps Memorial Hospital CRU
  Sharp Hospital–San Diego Cardiac
    Center

University of California, San Diego,
Medical Center CRU
**Comprehensive Cancer Treatment
Centers:**
University of California, San Diego,
Cancer Center
Hospices:
College Park Hospital–Hospice Program
El Cajon Valley Hospital–Hospice Unit
The Elizabeth Hospice, Inc.
San Diego County Hospice Corporation
Costs Index: Fair
Fluoridation: None
Air Pollution: O₂
Places Rated Score: 2,416
Places Rated Rank: 38

★ San Francisco, CA
Physicians per 100,000: 416
Teaching Hospitals:
Children's Hospital of San Francisco
Kaiser Foundation Hospital
Mount Zion Hospital and Medical
Center
Presbyterian Hospital of the Pacific
Medical Center
University of California, San Francisco,
Hospitals and Clinics
VA Medical Center
Medical Schools:
University of California, San Francisco,
School of Medicine
Cardiac Rehabilitation Centers:
Letterman Army Medical Center CRU
North Bay Cardiac Treatment Center
Novato Community Hospital CRU
Peninsula Hospital CRU
San Francisco Central YM Cardiac
Therapy
San Francisco General Hospital
Cardiology Outpatient
Department YM Cardiac Therapy CRU
Sequoia Hospital–YMCA CRU
Hospices:
Hospice of Marin (Kentfield)
Hospice of Marin (San Rafael)
Hospice of San Francisco
Mission Hospice, Inc., of San Mateo
County
Sequoia Hospital District–Patient
Support Program
Costs Index: Fair
Fluoridation: Adjusted
Air Pollution: Insignificant
CMSA Access: SAN FRANCISCO–OAKLAND–
SAN JOSE, CA (310)
Places Rated Score: 3,726
Places Rated Rank: 11

San Jose, CA
Physicians per 100,000: 247
Teaching Hospitals:
Stanford University Hospital
VA Medical Center (Palo Alto)
Medical Schools:
Stanford University School of Medicine
Cardiac Rehabilitation Centers:
Community Hospital of Los Gatos CRU
El Camino Cardiovascular Institute CRU
YM Cardiac Therapy CRU
Hospices:
Hospice of the Valley
Visiting Nurses of Santa Clara County
Hospice Program
Costs Index: Fair
Fluoridation: Adjusted

Air Pollution: CO
CMSA Access: SAN FRANCISCO–
OAKLAND–SAN JOSE, CA (470)
Places Rated Score: 2,117
Places Rated Rank: 47

Santa Barbara–Santa
Maria–Lompoc, CA
Physicians per 100,000: 232
Cardiac Rehabilitation Centers:
Marian Hospital CRU
Hospices:
Hospice of Santa Barbara
Santa Barbara Visiting Nurse
Association
Costs Index: Good
Fluoridation: None
Air Pollution: TSP
Places Rated Score: 532
Places Rated Rank: 261

Santa Cruz, CA
Physicians per 100,000: 165
Cardiac Rehabilitation Centers:
Dominican Santa Cruz Hospital
CRU
Hospices:
Hospice of Santa Cruz County
Costs Index: Good
Fluoridation: None
Air Pollution: Insignificant
CMSA Access: SAN FRANCISCO–
OAKLAND–SAN JOSE, CA (570)
Places Rated Score: 1,035
Places Rated Rank: 134

Santa Rosa–Petaluma, CA
Physicians per 100,000: 182
Hospices:
Home Hospice of Sonoma County
Valley of the Moon Hospice
Costs Index: Good
Fluoridation: None
Air Pollution: Insignificant
CMSA Access: SAN FRANCISCO–
OAKLAND–SAN JOSE, CA (570)
Places Rated Score: 1,052
Places Rated Rank: 128

Sarasota, FL
Physicians per 100,000: 201
Cardiac Rehabilitation Centers:
Sarasota YMCA Cardiac Rehabilitation
Program
Hospices:
Hospice of Sarasota County
Costs Index: Good
Fluoridation: Natural
Air Pollution: Insignificant
Places Rated Score: 801
Places Rated Rank: 177

Savannah, GA
Physicians per 100,000: 184
Cardiac Rehabilitation Centers:
Chandler General Hospital CRU
Memorial Medical Center CRU
St. Joseph's Hospital CRU
Hospices:
Hospice Savannah
Costs Index: Excellent
Fluoridation: Adjusted
Air Pollution: Insignificant
Places Rated Score: 1,084
Places Rated Rank: 122

Scranton–Wilkes-Barre, PA
Physicians per 100,000: 119
Cardiac Rehabilitation Centers:
Community Medical Center CRU
Mercy Hospital CRU
Moses Taylor Hospital CTC
State General Hospital–Hazleton CPR
Center
Hospices:
Hospice of Pennsylvania
Hospice St. John
Costs Index: Excellent
Fluoridation: Adjusted
Air Pollution: Insignificant
Places Rated Score: 1,219
Places Rated Rank: 101

★ Seattle, WA
Physicians per 100,000: 245
Teaching Hospitals:
Children's Orthopedic Hospital and
Medical Center
University of Washington Hospitals:
Harborview Medical Center
University of Washington Hospitals:
University Hospital
U.S. Public Health Service Hospital
VA Medical Center
Medical Schools:
University of Washington School of
Medicine
Cardiac Rehabilitation Centers:
Capri CRU
Seattle Public Health Hospital CRU
University of Washington Department of
Physio-Nursing
**Comprehensive Cancer Treatment
Centers:**
• Fred Hutchinson Cancer Research
Center
Hospices:
Community Home Health Care
Hospice of Seattle
Hospice of Snohomish County
Costs Index: Excellent
Fluoridation: Adjusted
Air Pollution: CO
CMSA Access: SEATTLE–TACOMA,
WA (20)
Places Rated Score: 2,715
Places Rated Rank: 21

Sharon, PA
Physicians per 100,000: 100
Cardiac Rehabilitation Centers:
Sharon General Hospital CRU
Costs Index: Excellent
Fluoridation: Adjusted
Air Pollution: Insignificant
Places Rated Score: 700
Places Rated Rank: 203

Sheboygan, WI
Physicians per 100,000: 93
Costs Index: Excellent
Fluoridation: Adjusted
Air Pollution: Insignificant
Places Rated Score: 593
Places Rated Rank: 241

Sherman–Denison, TX
Physicians per 100,000: 144
Costs Index: Good
Fluoridation: Natural (Sherman only)
Air Pollution: Insignificant
Places Rated Score: 394
Places Rated Rank: 292

Shreveport, LA
Physicians per 100,000: 245
Teaching Hospitals:
  Louisiana State University Hospital
  VA Medical Center
Medical Schools:
  Louisiana State University School of
    Medicine in Shreveport
Costs Index: Excellent
Fluoridation: Adjusted
Air Pollution: Insignificant
Places Rated Score: 1,445
Places Rated Rank: 82

Sioux City, IA–NE
Physicians per 100,000: 146
Cardiac Rehabilitation Centers:
  Marian Health Center CRU
Hospices:
  Marian Health Center
Costs Index: Excellent
Fluoridation: Adjusted
Air Pollution: Insignificant
Places Rated Score: 846
Places Rated Rank: 161

Sioux Falls, SD
Physicians per 100,000: 241
Cardiac Rehabilitation Centers:
  Sioux Valley Hospital CRU
Costs Index: Outstanding
Fluoridation: Adjusted
Air Pollution: Insignificant
Places Rated Score: 1,041
Places Rated Rank: 130

South Bend–Mishawaka, IN
Physicians per 100,000: 130
Cardiac Rehabilitation Centers:
  Cardiac Treatment Center of South
    Bend, Inc.
  St. Joseph's Hospital
Costs Index: Excellent
Fluoridation: Adjusted
Air Pollution: Insignificant
Places Rated Score: 830
Places Rated Rank: 167

Spokane, WA
Physicians per 100,000: 197
Cardiac Rehabilitation Centers:
  Deaconess Hospital CRU
  Sacred Heart Medical Center CRU
  Spokane CRU
Hospices:
  Hospice Maranatha
Costs Index: Good
Fluoridation: None
Air Pollution: TSP, CO
Places Rated Score: 497
Places Rated Rank: 272

Springfield, IL
Physicians per 100,000: 277
Teaching Hospitals:
  Memorial Medical Center
  St. John's Hospital
Medical Schools:
  Southern Illinois University School of
    Medicine
Cardiac Rehabilitation Centers:
  Cardiac Rehabilitation for Postcardiac
    Patients, Inc.
  St. John's Hospital CRU
  Springfield Community Hospital
    CRU

Hospices:
  St. John's Hospital–Department of
    Family Practice
Costs Index: Excellent
Fluoridation: Adjusted
Air Pollution: Insignificant
Places Rated Score: 1,877
Places Rated Rank: 57

Springfield, MA
Physicians per 100,000: 210
Teaching Hospitals:
  Baystate Medical Center
Cardiac Rehabilitation Centers:
  Baystate Medical Center CRU
Costs Index: Excellent
Fluoridation: None
Air Pollution: Insignificant
Places Rated Score: 710
Places Rated Rank: 200

Springfield, MO
Physicians per 100,000: 177
Cardiac Rehabilitation Centers:
  St. John's Hospital–YMCA CRU
Hospices:
  Hospice of Southwest Missouri
Costs Index: Excellent
Fluoridation: None
Air Pollution: Insignificant
Places Rated Score: 577
Places Rated Rank: 249

★ **Stamford, CT**
Physicians per 100,000: 220
Teaching Hospitals:
  Stamford Hospital
Cardiac Rehabilitation Centers:
  Greenwich Hospital Association CRU
  St. Joseph Hospital CRU
  YMCA Cardiac Rehabilitation Exercise
    Program
Costs Index: Excellent
Fluoridation: Adjusted
Air Pollution: CO
CMSA Access: NEW YORK–NORTHERN
  NEW JERSEY–LONG ISLAND, NY–NJ–CT
  (1,490)
Places Rated Score: 2,610
Places Rated Rank: 23

State College, PA
Physicians per 100,000: 112
Costs Index: Excellent
Fluoridation: Adjusted
Air Pollution: Insignificant
Places Rated Score: 612
Places Rated Rank: 230

Steubenville–Weirton, OH–WV
Physicians per 100,000: 105
Cardiac Rehabilitation Centers:
  St. John Medical Center CRU
Costs Index: Excellent
Fluoridation: Adjusted
Air Pollution: TSP, SO₂
Places Rated Score: 505
Places Rated Rank: 270

Stockton, CA
Physicians per 100,000: 142
Cardiac Rehabilitation Centers:
  San Joaquin Cardiac Clinic
Costs Index: Good
Fluoridation: None
Air Pollution: Insignificant
Places Rated Score: 342
Places Rated Rank: 304

Syracuse, NY
Physicians per 100,000: 240
Teaching Hospitals:
  State University Hospital of the Upstate
    Medical Center
  VA Medical Center
Medical Schools:
  SUNY Upstate Medical Center College
    of Medicine
Costs Index: Unacceptable
Fluoridation: Adjusted
Air Pollution: Insignificant
Places Rated Score: 1,040
Places Rated Rank: 131

Tacoma, WA
Physicians per 100,000: 134
Cardiac Rehabilitation Centers:
  VA Hospital CRU
Hospices:
  Hospice of Tacoma
Costs Index: Good
Fluoridation: None
Air Pollution: CO
CMSA Access: SEATTLE–TACOMA,
  WA (205)
Places Rated Score: 539
Places Rated Rank: 258

Tallahassee, FL
Physicians per 100,000: 170
Cardiac Rehabilitation Centers:
  Tallahassee Physical Therapy Services
    CRU
Costs Index: Good
Fluoridation: None
Air Pollution: Insignificant
Places Rated Score: 370
Places Rated Rank: 297

**Tampa–St. Petersburg–
Clearwater, FL**
Physicians per 100,000: 189
Teaching Hospitals:
  James E. Haley VA Medical Center
Medical Schools:
  University of South Florida College of
    Medicine
Cardiac Rehabilitation Centers:
  Bayfront Medical Center CRU
  Palms of Pasadena Hospital CRU
  Tampa Bay Cardiac Prevention CRU
Hospices:
  Hospice Care, Inc.
Costs Index: Good
Fluoridation: None
Air Pollution: Insignificant
Places Rated Score: 1,189
Places Rated Rank: 106

Terre Haute, IN
Physicians per 100,000: 153
Cardiac Rehabilitation Centers:
  Union Hospital CRU
Costs Index: Excellent
Fluoridation: None
Air Pollution: Insignificant
Places Rated Score: 453
Places Rated Rank: 281

Texarkana, TX–Texarkana, AR
Physicians per 100,000: 143
Costs Index: Excellent
Fluoridation: None
Air Pollution: Insignificant
Places Rated Score: 343
Places Rated Rank: 303

Toledo, OH
Physicians per 100,000: 238
Teaching Hospitals:
  Medical College of Ohio Hospital
Medical Schools:
  Medical College of Ohio at Toledo
Cardiac Rehabilitation Centers:
  Flower Hospital CRU
  Medical College of Ohio CRU
  Riverside Hospital Acute Progressive
    Coronary Care
  St. Vincent's Hospital Cardiac
    Conditioning Program
  University of Toledo CRU
Hospices:
  Northwest Ohio Hospice Association
Costs Index: Good
Fluoridation: Adjusted
Air Pollution: Insignificant
Places Rated Score: 1,738
Places Rated Rank: 68

Topeka, KS
Physicians per 100,000: 248
Cardiac Rehabilitation Centers:
  St. Francis Hospital CRU
  Stormont–Vail Medical Center CRU
  VA Hospital CRU
Hospices:
  Hospice of Topeka
Costs Index: Excellent
Fluoridation: Adjusted
Air Pollution: Insignificant
Places Rated Score: 1,148
Places Rated Rank: 112

Trenton, NJ
Physicians per 100,000: 287
Cardiac Rehabilitation Centers:
  St. Francis Medical Center–Cardiology
    Section
Costs Index: Excellent
Fluoridation: Adjusted
Air Pollution: Insignificant
CMSA Access: PHILADELPHIA–WILMINGTON–
  TRENTON, PA–NJ–DE–MD (485)
Places Rated Score: 1,372
Places Rated Rank: 87

Tucson, AZ
Physicians per 100,000: 259
Teaching Hospitals:
  Tucson Medical Center
  University of Arizona Health Services
    Center
  VA Medical Center
Medical Schools:
  University of Arizona College of
    Medicine
Cardiac Rehabilitation Centers:
  St. Joseph's Hospital CRU
Comprehensive Cancer Treatment
  Centers:
  University of Arizona Cancer Center
Hospices:
  Hillhaven Hospice
Costs Index: Fair
Fluoridation: None
Air Pollution: TSP, CO
Places Rated Score: 1,259
Places Rated Rank: 95

Tulsa, OK
Physicians per 100,000: 181
Medical Schools:
  Oral Roberts University School of
    Medicine

Cardiac Rehabilitation Centers:
  Hillcrest Medical Center CRU
  Oklahoma Osteopathic Hospital
    CRU
  St. Francis Hospital CRU
  St: John's Medical Center Cardiac
    Exercise Lab
  Thornton Family Hospital CRU
Hospices:
  St. Francis Hospital–Hospice Program
Costs Index: Excellent
Fluoridation: Adjusted
Air Pollution: Insignificant
Places Rated Score: 1,581
Places Rated Rank: 78

Tuscaloosa, AL
Physicians per 100,000: 174
Costs Index: Excellent
Fluoridation: Adjusted
Air Pollution: Insignificant
Places Rated Score: 674
Places Rated Rank: 210

Tyler, TX
Physicians per 100,000: 172
Cardiac Rehabilitation Centers:
  Mother Francis Hospital CRU
Costs Index: Good
Fluoridation: Adjusted
Air Pollution: Insignificant
Places Rated Score: 672
Places Rated Rank: 211

Utica–Rome, NY
Physicians per 100,000: 141
Cardiac Rehabilitation Centers:
  St. Luke's Memorial Hospital CRC
Hospices:
  Hospice Care, Inc.
Costs Index: Poor
Fluoridation: Adjusted (Utica only)
Air Pollution: Insignificant
Places Rated Score: 391
Places Rated Rank: 293

Vallejo–Fairfield–Napa, CA
Physicians per 100,000: 199
Hospices:
  Hospice of Napa Valley
Costs Index: Good
Fluoridation: Adjusted (Vallejo only)
Air Pollution: Insignificant
CMSA Access: SAN FRANCISCO–
  OAKLAND–SAN JOSE, CA (580)
Places Rated Score: 1,079
Places Rated Rank: 124

Vancouver, WA
Physicians per 100,000: 87
Costs Index: Good
Fluoridation: Adjusted
Air Pollution: TSP
CMSA Access: PORTLAND–VANCOUVER,
  OR–WA (130)
Places Rated Score: 517
Places Rated Rank: 266

Victoria, TX
Physicians per 100,000: 160
Costs Index: Good
Fluoridation: Almost none
Air Pollution: Insignificant
Places Rated Score: 260
Places Rated Rank: 316

Vineland–Millville–Bridgeton, NJ
Physicians per 100,000: 112
Costs Index: Excellent
Fluoridation: None
Air Pollution: Insignificant
CMSA Access: PHILADELPHIA–
  WILMINGTON–TRENTON,
  PA–NJ–DE–MD (495)
Places Rated Score: 807
Places Rated Rank: 174

Visalia–Tulare–Porterville, CA
Physicians per 100,000: 110
Costs Index: Good
Fluoridation: None
Air Pollution: Insignificant
Places Rated Score: 210
Places Rated Rank: 324

Waco, TX
Physicians per 100,000: 138
Costs Index: Good
Fluoridation: Adjusted
Air Pollution: Insignificant
Places Rated Score: 538
Places Rated Rank: 260

★ Washington, DC–MD–VA
Physicians per 100,000: 511
Teaching Hospitals:
  Children's Hospital National Medical
    Center
  George Washington University Hospital
  Georgetown University Hospital
  Howard University Hospital
  VA Medical Center
  Washington Hospital Center
Medical Schools:
  George Washington University School of
    Medicine
  Georgetown University School of
    Medicine
  Howard University College of Medicine
Cardiac Rehabilitation Centers:
  Arlington Hospital Cardiac Exercise
    Clinic
  Arlington Hospital CRU
  Fairfax Hospital Cardiac Therapy
    Program
  George Washington University Hospital
    CRU
  Georgetown University Medical Center
    CRU
  Greater Southeast Community Hospital
    CRU
  Loudoun Memorial Hospital CTC
  Mount Vernon Hospital Ancillary
    Services
  Orthopedic and Rehabilitation Hospital
    CRC
  Washington Adventist Hospital CRU
Comprehensive Cancer Treatment
  Centers:
• Georgetown University–Howard
    University Comprehensive Cancer
    Center
Hospices:
  Hospice Care of the District of
    Columbia
  The Washington Home Hospice
  Washington Hospice Society, Inc.
Costs Index: Good
Fluoridation: Adjusted
Air Pollution: CO
Places Rated Score: 4,361
Places Rated Rank: 6

Waterbury, CT
Physicians per 100,000: 318
Teaching Hospitals:
    Waterbury Hospital
Cardiac Rehabilitation Centers:
    St. Mary's Hospital CRU
    Waterbury Hospital CRU
Costs Index: Excellent
Fluoridation: Adjusted
Air Pollution: Insignificant
Places Rated Score: 1,218
Places Rated Rank: 102

Waterloo–Cedar Falls, IA
Physicians per 100,000: 125
Cardiac Rehabilitation Centers:
    Allen Memorial Hospital CRU
    St. Francis Hospital CRU
    Schoitz Memorial Hospital
        CRU
Costs Index: Excellent
Fluoridation: Adjusted
Air Pollution: Insignificant
Places Rated Score: 925
Places Rated Rank: 148

Wausau, WI
Physicians per 100,000: 118
Cardiac Rehabilitation Centers:
    Wausau Hospital Center CRU
Hospices:
    Wausau Hospice Program
Costs Index: Excellent
Fluoridation: Adjusted
Air Pollution: Insignificant
Places Rated Score: 818
Places Rated Rank: 169

**West Palm Beach–Boca
Raton–Delray Beach, FL**
Physicians per 100,000: 175
Hospices:
    Hospice of Boca Raton
    Hospice of Palm Beach County
Costs Index: Fair
Fluoridation: None
Air Pollution: Insignificant
Places Rated Score: 375
Places Rated Rank: 295

Wheeling, WV–OH
Physicians per 100,000: 191
Cardiac Rehabilitation Centers:
    Wheeling Hospital CRU
Hospices:
    Clara Welty Hospice Program
Costs Index: Excellent
Fluoridation: Adjusted
Air Pollution: TSP
Places Rated Score: 791
Places Rated Rank: 179

Wichita, KS
Physicians per 100,000: 206

Teaching Hospitals:
    Wesley Medical Center
Cardiac Rehabilitation Centers:
    St. Francis Hospital–Wichita CRU
    St. Joseph Medical Center CRU
    Wesley Medical Center–Wichita
        University CRU
Costs Index: Good
Fluoridation: None
Air Pollution: Insignificant
Places Rated Score: 806
Places Rated Rank: 175

Wichita Falls, TX
Physicians per 100,000: 149
Costs Index: Good
Fluoridation: Adjusted
Air Pollution: Insignificant
Places Rated Score: 549
Places Rated Rank: 255

Williamsport, PA
Physicians per 100,000: 160
Cardiac Rehabilitation Centers:
    Divine Providence Hospital CRU
    Williamsport Hospital CRU
Costs Index: Excellent
Fluoridation: Adjusted
Air Pollution: Insignificant
Places Rated Score: 860
Places Rated Rank: 159

Wilmington, DE–NJ–MD
Physicians per 100,000: 180
Teaching Hospitals:
    Wilmington Medical Center, Inc.
Cardiac Rehabilitation Centers:
    Wilmington Cardiac Treatment
        Center
Costs Index: Excellent
Fluoridation: Adjusted
Air Pollution: Insignificant
CMSA Access: PHILADELPHIA–
    WILMINGTON–TRENTON,
    PA–NJ–DE–MD (465)
Places Rated Score: 1,445
Places Rated Rank: 82

Wilmington, NC
Physicians per 100,000: 199
Cardiac Rehabilitation Centers:
    New Hanover Memorial Hospital CRU
Hospices:
    North Cape Fear Hospice
Costs Index: Outstanding
Fluoridation: Adjusted
Air Pollution: Insignificant
Places Rated Score: 1,099
Places Rated Rank: 120

Worcester, MA
Physicians per 100,000: 205
Teaching Hospitals:
    Memorial Hospital

    St. Vincent Hospital
    University of Massachusetts Teaching
        Hospital
    Worcester City Hospital
Medical Schools:
    University of Massachusetts, Worcester,
        Medical School
Cardiac Rehabilitation Units:
    St. Vincent Hospital CRU
    University of Massachusetts Medical
        Center CRU
Hospices:
    University of Massachusetts Medical
        Center–Palliative Care, Inc.
Costs Index: Excellent
Fluoridation: None
Air Pollution: Insignificant
Places Rated Score: 1,805
Places Rated Rank: 64

Yakima, WA
Physicians per 100,000: 117
Cardiac Rehabilitation Centers:
    Yakima Valley Memorial Hospital CRU
Costs Index: Good
Fluoridation: None
Air Pollution: Insignificant
Places Rated Score: 317
Places Rated Rank: 310

York, PA
Physicians per 100,000: 113
Teaching Hospitals:
    York Hospital
Costs Index: Outstanding
Fluoridation: None
Air Pollution: Insignificant
Places Rated Score: 713
Places Rated Rank: 199

Youngstown–Warren, OH
Physicians per 100,000: 147
Teaching Hospitals:
    St. Elizabeth Hospital Medical Center
    Youngstown Hospital Association
Cardiac Rehabilitation Centers:
    Professional Cardiac
        Rehabilitation–Procare
    Trumbull Memorial Hospital CRU
Hospices:
    Hospice of Youngstown
Costs Index: Excellent
Fluoridaton: Adjusted (Warren only)
Air Pollution: TSP
Places Rated Score: 1,097
Places Rated Rank: 121

Yuba City, CA
Physicians per 100,000: 112
Costs Index: Good
Fluoridation: None
Air Pollution: Insignificant
Places Rated Score: 212
Places Rated Rank: 323

ARE THERE GEOGRAPHIC PATTERNS OF DISEASE?

A glance at the maps depicting the areas with the highest and the lowest mortality rates for heart disease, cancer, and stroke suggests that there are geographical patterns to the three leading killers. For each of these diseases, the states with the highest death rates lie in the central or eastern section of the country, and the states with the lowest death rates lie in the West. Why these apparent patterns exist can be explained in some instances, but in others the pattern remains an interesting puzzle.

Heart Disease and Stroke: Perennial Threats

The map "Death Rates: Heart Disease" reflects age-adjusted death rates for white men aged 35 to 74, who experience a higher mortality rate than the population as a whole (nationally the death rate in 1980 for this group was 480.9). West Virginia experienced the highest death rate, 581.0, whereas Hawaii had the lowest, only 321.7. As noted above, all the states with the highest rates of heart disease are in the eastern half of the continent, and all the states with the lowest rates are in the West. Compared with the West, the eastern United States is generally more thickly populated and more industrialized, and it has more large cities and a life-style that is usually faster paced. Perhaps the less hectic, more exercise-filled life common in the western states may account for some of the difference in death rates, as may the drinking water. Recently, studies have revealed at least a tentative correlation between hard drinking water (water with a high percentage of dissolved salts and minerals) and a lower incidence of heart disease.

Another possible factor is diet. The Southwest, traditionally the region with the lowest rates of heart disease, is marked by a diet that is heavily influenced by Mexico. Red meat is eaten seldom, with beans, grains, and cheese providing most of the protein. Such a diet, high in complex carbohydrates, is generally considered by nutritionists to be near the ideal.

Cerebrovascular disease, or stroke, is closely related to and interconnected with heart disease. Like the number-one killer, stroke is aggravated by excess weight, high blood pressure, stress, and a diet high in sodium. Therefore, you could assume that states with high death rates from heart disease would likewise have high death rates from stroke. But in fact, as the map "Death Rates: Stroke" shows, not a single state has very high rates of both heart disease and stroke. The entire southeastern quadrant of the United States seems plagued by high rates of either heart disease or stroke. The fact that the Deep South states of Tennessee, Mississippi, Alabama, and Georgia have very high

stroke death rates comes as no surprise, since these states have large black populations. Blacks, with their predisposition to hypertension, have always had a high incidence of death from stroke. Moreover, the traditional Southern black diet tends to be very high in sodium.

Tracking the Deadly Cancers

"It's the one John Wayne part nobody wants," mused actor Robert Ryan after learning he had cancer. Certainly none of us wants to get this disease, the number-two killer in America, despite the continual progress that has been made in early diagnosis and effective treatment for most varieties.

Some cancers are not very serious. Skin cancers—with the exception of melanoma—are rarely fatal, and tremendous progress has been made in treating most cancers of the bones and connective tissues. But other forms remain extremely pernicious. Cancer of the esophagus, for example, has a five-year survival rate of only 5 percent. Lung cancer has a five-year survival rate of 12 percent, and the comparable rate for stomach cancer is only 14 percent.

According to the most recent and thoroughly re-

Death Rates: Heart Disease

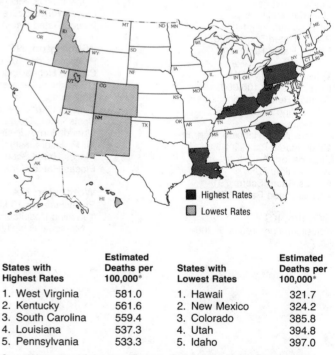

States with Highest Rates	Estimated Deaths per 100,000*	States with Lowest Rates	Estimated Deaths per 100,000*
1. West Virginia	581.0	1. Hawaii	321.7
2. Kentucky	561.6	2. New Mexico	324.2
3. South Carolina	559.4	3. Colorado	385.8
4. Louisiana	537.3	4. Utah	394.8
5. Pennsylvania	533.3	5. Idaho	397.0

Source: Metropolitan Life Insurance Company, *Statistical Bulletin*, July–September 1984.

*Figures represent age-adjusted death rate for white men aged 35 to 74 in 1980.

Death Rates: Stroke

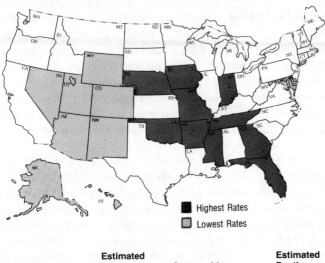

Death Rates: Cancer

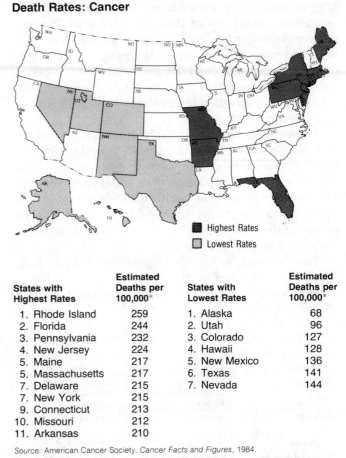

States with Highest Rates	Estimated Deaths per 100,000*	States with Lowest Rates	Estimated Deaths per 100,000*
1. Arkansas	109.8	1. Alaska	18.0
2. Florida	100.2	2. Hawaii	40.3
3. Oklahoma	98.0	3. Utah	45.8
4. Mississippi	97.2	4. New Mexico	50.0
5. Iowa	96.9	5. Colorado	51.2
6. Tennessee	96.0	6. Arizona	51.8
7. Nebraska	92.9	7. Wyoming	54.0
8. Missouri	92.2	8. Maryland	55.0
9. Indiana	90.5	9. Nevada	55.1
10. Georgia	90.1	10. Delaware	55.8

Source: National Center for Health Statistics, *Vital Statistics of the United States, Vol. II: Mortality,* 1982.

*Figures are for 1978.

States with Highest Rates	Estimated Deaths per 100,000*	States with Lowest Rates	Estimated Deaths per 100,000*
1. Rhode Island	259	1. Alaska	68
2. Florida	244	2. Utah	96
3. Pennsylvania	232	3. Colorado	127
4. New Jersey	224	4. Hawaii	128
5. Maine	217	5. New Mexico	136
5. Massachusetts	217	6. Texas	141
7. Delaware	215	7. Nevada	144
7. New York	215		
9. Connecticut	213		
10. Missouri	212		
11. Arkansas	210		

Source: American Cancer Society, *Cancer Facts and Figures,* 1984.

*Figures are projected death rates for 1984 for all cancers.

searched study of cancer incidence yet undertaken, *U.S. Cancer Mortality Rates and Trends—1950–1979,* published by the Environmental Protection Agency and the National Cancer Institute in 1983, there are definite geographic patterns to many cancers. Although research has not yet pinpointed the cause for cancer in general, some environmental risks related to specific toxins called carcinogens (cancer-causing substances) have been documented. Certain factors, such as occupation, environment, personal habits (such as smoking), and diet, have been shown to induce some types of cancer. A number of these risk factors are more prevalent in the heavily urbanized Northeast than they are in the West, especially those related to the environment. The map "Death Rates: Cancer," based on projections for 1984 by the American Cancer Society, bears out this generalization, showing the highest death rates concentrated in the Northeast.

The best-known link between life-style and cancer has been established in the case of lung cancer, a disease that is not only painful and practically incurable but also largely preventable. Lung cancer caused an estimated 13 deaths per 100,000 people in 1950, and that figure reached 42 deaths per 100,000 in 1979. The American Cancer Society claims that cigarette smoking

is responsible for 83 percent of lung cancer cases in men and 43 percent in women.

Some cancers may possibly be linked to nationality. For example, North Dakota and South Dakota have long shown high incidences of stomach cancer. Many of the residents of the Dakotas are descendants of Finns and White Russians. Interestingly enough, the incidence of stomach cancer is elevated in both Finland and the Soviet Union. Likewise, Hawaii's high rates of stomach cancer may be due to the fact that many of its citizens trace their roots to Japan, a country with elevated rates of this cancer. Pure hereditary susceptibility may be involved, although diet is a more plausible explanation.

YOU ARE WHAT YOU EAT, SMOKE, DRINK . . .

Do you subscribe to the when-your-number's-up-it's-up theory of life expectancy? Then you may be surprised to learn that, based on recent trends, experts conclude it's less likely to be a stray bullet or virus that kills you than the way you lead your life.

The most common causes of death at the turn of the century—typhoid fever, cholera, tuberculosis, smallpox, gastroenteritis, and nephritis—have been practically eliminated by scientific advances and improved sanitation. Today, more than 70 percent of the two million Americans who die each year are victims of heart disease, cancer, stroke, cirrhosis of the liver, bronchitis, asthma, and emphysema—the so-called life-style diseases that may be aggravated by such behavior as overeating, heavy drinking, smoking, and lack of exercise.

To see how your daily habits measure up, take a look at the table "How Healthy Is Your Life-Style?" The creators of this table warn that since some risk factors are more important than others, an entirely accurate picture of your health may not emerge from this self-analysis. However, they add, changing your habits so that you qualify for the low-risk ratings will result in a longer life.

The following are some suggestions that can help you reduce your health risks.

Stop smoking and drink only in moderation. Cigarette smokers run twice the risk that nonsmokers do of death from coronary disease. Smoking also contributes to stroke, lung cancer, emphysema, and bronchitis. Likewise, an excess of alcohol can be dangerous, increasing your chances of developing cirrhosis of the liver (this condition is found six times as frequently among alcoholics as among nonalcoholics) and cardiovascular problems. Drinking combined with driving multiplies the risk of dying in an automobile accident; at least half of such accidents in the United States involve drunk drivers.

Eat a balanced diet and watch your weight. Six of the ten leading causes of death have been linked to diet: heart attack, stroke, atherosclerosis, cancer, cirrhosis of the liver, and diabetes. Reducing your intake of refined flour and sugar, salt (which in excess contributes to high blood pressure), and saturated fats (which have been implicated as factors in heart disease and stroke) while choosing from a range of meat, poultry,

How Healthy Is Your Life-Style?

Risk Category	No Risk	Slight Risk	Substantial Risk	Heavy Risk	Dangerous Risk
Smoking	No smoking or stopped for at least 10 years	Less than 10 cigarettes, 5 pipes or cigars a day	Half pack a day	1 pack a day	2 or more packs a day
Alcohol	Nondrinker	Stopped drinker	Fewer than 6 drinks per week	More than 6 drinks per week	More than 2 drinks per day
Trimness	Lean	Slightly plump	Moderately obese	Considerably obese	Grossly obese
Physical activity	Walk more than 2 miles a day or climb 20 or more flights of stairs a day	Walk 1.5–2 miles a day or climb 15–20 flights of stairs a day	Walk only 0.5 to 1.5 miles a day or climb only 5–15 flights of stairs a day	Walk only 2–5 blocks a day or climb 2–4 flights of stairs a day	Walk less than 2 blocks a day or climb less than 2 flights of stairs a day
Prescription drugs	With doctor's consent, following orders carefully	Take medication daily without side effects	Take medication when needed with few side effects	Use sleeping and nerve pills regularly without doctor's supervision	Without doctor's consent, mix with other drugs or alcohol
Nonprescription drugs	Use occasionally only for short periods. Label warnings heeded				Continuing use, drinking or driving despite label warnings
Alcohol and driving —boats, cars, motorcycles, snowmobiles	Never drink. Drive only with safety aids—seat belt, helmet, life jacket	Never drive after drinking without safety aids	Drive after 2 drinks with safety aids	Drive after 2 drinks without safety aids	Drive after more than 2 drinks without safety aids
Motor vehicle safety	Always wear seat belt	Wear seat belt more than half of the time	Wear seat belt as a driver half of the time	Wear seat belt as a passenger half of the time	Wear seat belt less than half of the time
Water safety— swimming and boating	Qualified expert	Know how to swim and the safety rules	Know how to swim and may swim after 1 drink or nerve drug	Do not know how to swim but use life jacket half of the time	Do not know how to swim; never use life jacket
Blood cholesterol	Less than 180	180–220	220–280	280–320	320 and up
Blood pressure	120/80 or less	120/80–140/90	140/90–160/100	160/100–180/105	Above 180/105
Blood sugar	Less than 120 two hours after a meal of syrup and pancakes	Between 110 and 130 two hours after meals; checked each 3 months	Blood sugar more than 150 without diet control	Blood sugar more than 150 without diet control, doctor's care	Diabetes without doctor's care at less than 45 years of age
FOR WOMEN ONLY					
Breast check for lumps	Monthly self-exam and yearly check by physician	Monthly self-exam but no doctor exam	Self-exam 2–3 times a year but no doctor's exam	1 time a year by a doctor	Never
Pap smear	Every year	Every 3 years	Every 4 years	Never	Never; nonmenstrual bleeding

Source: Methodist Hospital of Indianapolis, Inc. Prepared by Pamela Hall under the supervision of Drs. Lewis C. Robbins and Jack H. Hall, developers of the Health Hazard Appraisal System. Used by permission.

fish, fruits, vegetables, and fiber foods is highly recommended. A balanced diet can also help you to lose extra weight, which puts added stress on the heart and organs, aggravating disease conditions.

Get regular exercise. Exercise, now seen almost as a miracle drug, can help you maintain proper weight, keep your body in good operating condition, and relieve stress (which contributes to ulcers and high blood pressure). It's also necessary to prevent premature aging and degeneration of muscles and joints. The use-it-or-lose-it maxim definitely applies here.

Get regular medical care. Be sure to consult your doctor regularly and have whatever checkups or tests he or she recommends, such as a Pap smear or blood pressure tests.

SUICIDE IN AMERICA

Suicide tends to be a phenomenon not of the poor, homeless, and downtrodden, but rather of the well-to-do and highly educated professional, usually male and white. In short, suicide occurs predominantly in the upper middle class. It is not in the slums of New York City, Newark, or Chicago that people kill themselves with greatest frequency; rather, it is in the affluent suburbs and the relatively prosperous, wide-open country of the Mountain States and the West. The highest rates of suicide occur in states without many big cities, such as Wyoming and New Mexico; most of these states also have per capita incomes substantially above the nation's average. In contrast, many of the states with the lowest suicide rates (New Jersey, Massachusetts, New York, and Illinois) have large cities, poverty, high crime, and all the other stress-related problems one would normally associate with despair and self-destruction.

There are several theories about why certain places have higher suicide rates than others. Some people point to the substantial percentage of elderly residents in Arizona and Florida as an explanation for their high suicide records. True, suicide is high among older Americans, many of whom suffer constant pain or irreversible declining health due to a chronic or terminal illness. But many of the states with low suicide rates also have a large number of residents who are over 65.

A more reliable indicator of suicide may be relatively young populations. Most of the suicide-prone states, like Alaska, Arizona, Colorado, and New Mexico, have populations with significant percentages of people under 17. Nevada, the state with by far the highest suicide rate, is the second youngest state after Alaska. However, Nevada's legalized gambling, prostitution, dependence on casinos and the entertainment industry, high rates of alcohol consumption and alcoholism, and transient population probably also contribute to its leading suicide rate.

States Ranked by Suicide Rate

State	Suicides per 100,000 Population	State	Suicides per 100,000 Population
1. New Jersey	7.4	24. Ohio	11.9
2. Massachusetts	8.2	27. Louisiana	12.1
3. Connecticut	8.9	28. Tennessee	12.2
4. Mississippi	9.2	29. Texas	12.3
5. Illinois	9.3	30. Maine	12.5
6. New York	9.5	30. West Virginia	12.5
6. South Carolina	9.5	32. Georgia	12.6
8. Nebraska	10.1	33. South Dakota	12.7
9. Indiana	10.4	34. Kentucky	12.8
10. Maryland	10.8	35. Idaho	13.1
10. Minnesota	10.8	35. Oklahoma	13.1
12. Kansas	10.9	37. Utah	13.2
13. Iowa	11.0	38. Washington	13.3
13. New Hampshire	11.0	39. Virginia	13.4
13. North Dakota	11.0	40. California	14.5
16. Pennsylvania	11.1	40. Montana	14.5
17. Alabama	11.2	42. Oregon	14.6
17. North Carolina	11.2	43. Vermont	14.7
17. Rhode Island	11.2	44. Florida	15.4
20. Hawaii	11.4	45. Wyoming	16.0
21. Michigan	11.5	46. Colorado	16.3
22. Arkansas	11.6	47. Alaska	16.9
23. Wisconsin	11.7	47. Arizona	16.9
24. Delaware	11.9	49. New Mexico	17.4
24. Missouri	11.9	50. Nevada	22.9

Source: National Center for Health Statistics, unpublished data, 1980.

WHAT HAVE THEY DONE TO THE RAIN?

The first noticeable effect was the wearing away of detail on stone and marble monuments around the world—the giant obelisk in St. Peter's square in Rome, the Parthenon in Athens, friezes on buildings in Washington, D.C., the intricate carving on many of Northern Europe's fine Gothic cathedrals. But since the discovery of the phenomenon called acid rain in the late 1960s, increasing evidence has shown the caustic precipitation to be harmful to living creatures as well. In the United States, environmentalists warn, vast stretches of forests, important spawning grounds for fish, even the health of a significant number of people could be in grave danger.

What Is Acid Rain?

Acid rain has been called an insidious form of air pollution, and its poisonous consequences are usually suffered a considerable distance from the source of the problem. The major cause of acid rain is the pollutant sulfur dioxide (SO_2), a principal emission of coal burning; other pollutants are also involved. In the United States, 48 million tons of sulfur and nitrogen fumes was spewed into the air in 1980, most of it coming from 31 states bordering on or east of the Mississippi River. Ohio, Illinois, Indiana, Michigan, Kentucky, Tennessee, and West Virginia have generally been pointed to as the most significant sources of SO_2 pollution.

Acid Rain in the Metro Areas

Most of the country's worst areas for acid rain are in non-metropolitan locations, but according to the U.S. Geological Survey's *Water-Supply Paper 2250*, sixteen metro areas have present or potential problems with acid rain:

Albany–Schenectady–Troy, NY
Atlantic City, NJ
Baltimore, MD
Duluth, MN–WI
Eau Claire, WI
Eugene–Springfield, OR
Glens Falls, NY
Hagerstown, MD
Medford, OR
Middlesex–Somerset–
   Hunterdon, NJ

Monmouth–Ocean, NJ
St. Cloud, MN–WI
Salt Lake City–Ogden,
   UT
Trenton, NJ
Vineland–Millville–
   Bridgeton, NJ
Wausau, WI

Source: U.S. Geological Survey, Water-Supply Paper 2250, 1984.

In measuring acidity of water or soil, the pH scale is used (pH stands for *potential of hydrogen*). This scale has a neutral point of 7; less than 7 means acid, more than 7 means alkaline. The pH scale is logarithmic, so that pH 4.6 is ten times more acid than pH 5.6, and pH 3.6 is 100 times more acidic than pH 4.6. Ordinary rain is somewhat acidic, with a pH of 5.6, but when sulfur and nitrogen oxides react with moisture in the air, they intensify the acidity of rain.

Because of prevailing westerly winds and because most coal burning takes place east of the Mississippi, the effects of acid rain are seen most commonly in the Appalachian Mountains and along the eastern seaboard.

Destructive Effects

The effects of acid rain on forests have long been documented in Europe but only recently observed in America. All along the Appalachian Mountain chain, from Georgia to Maine, the growth rate of mountain trees is slowing. The rate for red spruce, for example, is now only 74 percent of that recorded in 1965, and the decline is not from logging. In the southern half of the Appalachian chain, the new growth of loblolly pine, backbone of the southeastern timber economy, is creeping to a standstill. Such trees as the beech, sugar maple, and hickory are growing deformed limbs, producing weak and brittle wood, and losing their resistance to insects and disease.

Since the pollutants are carried in clouds, the poisoning effect intensifies with altitude. In addition, hilltop trees tend to "comb" damaging particles from the air. Foresters monitoring mountaintop pH levels claim that a pH of 2 exists in some clouds, an acidity greater than that of table vinegar. Mount Mitchell, near Asheville in western North Carolina, the highest peak in the East, is fast becoming a bald mountain.

For more than a decade, sport and commercial fishermen of the Atlantic have witnessed the decline of the East's greatest saltwater sport fish, the striped bass. The rapid decline of this magnificent fish was assumed for a while to be the result of a natural cycle, and the fish was expected to bounce back in a few years. This hasn't happened, and some marine biologists now fear it never will. The reason: rising acidity in the estuaries of the Chesapeake Bay, premier spawning grounds for the striper. Those spawning grounds are now practically barren, not only of the bass but also of shad, herring, perch, and alewife. Why? Biologists have measured the pH of the freshwater streams and rivers (like the Potomac, Rappahannock, James, and York rivers) that flow into the Chesapeake and discovered that the water of these rivers is terribly acidic, with pH readings as low as 3.8. Fish eggs and larvae are sensitive to changes in the pH; the bass especially likes water that is alkaline (a pH of 8). Acid rain, falling on the coastal plain of Maryland, flows into the streams and creates acid surges that kill the eggs and larvae. Even when the river returns to normal alkalinity, the damage has been done.

The problem of acid lakes and rivers is not confined to the Maryland shore. In the Adirondack Mountains of New York, for example, fish have disappeared from more than 200 lakes due to acidification.

Human life may also be at direct risk. In June 1984, the Office of Technological Assessment concluded a three-year study and reported that clouds bearing acid rain and smog from air pollution could be killing as many as 50,000 Americans and Canadians a year. Most threatened, according to the report, are persons with heart and lung ailments. Both the EPA and utilities industries have contested these findings.

Southern California has a problem of its own, acid fog, which some environmental engineers think may have a greater net impact than acid rain. The fog, which is similar to fogs that contributed to more than 12,000 deaths in London during a three-month period in 1952, is most severe in the Los Angeles Basin and San Joaquin Valley.

KEEPING AN EYE ON THE ENVIRONMENT

With the establishment of the EPA in 1970, the U.S. government began an active role in protection of the environment, setting and enforcing standards for the cleanliness of air and water. But how have the states responded to the challenge of safeguarding their natural resources?

According to a 1983 study by the Washington-based Conservation Foundation, the most environment-conscious states are Minnesota, California, New Jersey, Massachusetts, and Oregon, whereas the least are Alabama, Missouri, Mississippi, Idaho, and New Mexico. The report uses 23 criteria to judge the states, among them per capita spending on environmental quality control and parks; land-use planning; congressional voting records of state delegations on environmental and energy issues; and whether a state awards tax breaks for solar energy projects.

In general, the Conservation Foundation concludes, the states of New England, the Great Lakes, and the Pacific Coast deserve the highest marks for their efforts to improve and conserve the environment, and those in the South and the Rocky Mountain states the lowest.

Another finding of the study is that those states with stringent environmental laws are not alienating industry, as had been commonly anticipated; in fact, some have been successful in attracting it. The foundation could find no evidence that strict regulations have led to a "widespread exodus of American industry abroad" or even to other states "in search of pollution havens."

Environmental Effort

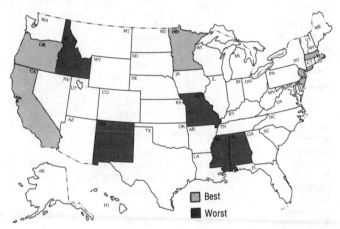

States Ranked for Environmental Effort, from Best to Worst

1. Minnesota	18. Michigan	33. Tennessee
2. California	18. Ohio	
3. New Jersey	18. South Dakota	33. Utah
4. Massachusetts		33. West Virginia
5. Oregon	21. Delaware	33. Wyoming
	21. Iowa	39. Nebraska
6. Washington	23. Illinois	39. Nevada
7. Maryland	23. Pennsylvania	
7. Montana	23. Virginia	39. North Dakota
7. New York		39. Texas
7. Wisconsin	26. Arkansas	43. Louisiana
	27. Colorado	43. New Hampshire
11. Indiana	27. Rhode Island	45. Oklahoma
12. Hawaii	29. Georgia	
12. Kentucky	29. North Carolina	46. New Mexico
14. Connecticut		47. Idaho
14. Maine	29. South Carolina	48. Mississippi
	32. Arizona	49. Missouri
14. Vermont	33. Alaska	50. Alabama
17. Florida	33. Kansas	

Source: Conservation Foundation, 1983.

HAY FEVER SUFFERERS, TAKE NOTE

It doesn't come from hay, and it doesn't cause a fever, but that's not much consolation to the 18 million Americans afflicted with hay fever. Aside from the personal discomfort it causes, various government agencies estimate that it also results in more than five million workdays lost per year, at a price tag of more than $300 million.

Hay fever is any allergic reaction of the eyes, nose, or throat to certain airborne particles. These particles may be either pollen from seed-bearing trees, grasses, and weeds, or spores from certain molds. The term originated in Britain 150 years ago, when people assumed its feverlike symptoms had something to do with the fall haying. Most individuals might think that once they're into adulthood, they already know whether they have hay fever. But if you were to relocate, would you suddenly and mysteriously develop a continual running nose and minor sore throat? Allergy problems aren't always alleviated by relocation, and sometimes a new allergen—absent where you used to live—can turn up to cause you problems with hay fever.

The incidence of hay fever varies around the world. In the Arctic, for example, it doesn't exist. Because of low temperatures and poor soil, arctic plants are small and primitive. In the tropics and subtropics, there is very little hay fever because the plants are generally flowered and produce pollen that is so heavy it cannot become airborne.

It is in the temperate regions that one finds the greatest amounts of irritating pollen. The worst places in America for hay fever are the middle regions, where grasses and trees without flowers predominate. Because farming continually disrupts the soil and therefore encourages the growth of weeds (especially the most troublesome of them, ragweed), America's heartland is the most hay fever–ridden area. It extends from the Rockies to the Appalachian chain, and from the Canadian border down to the states of the mid-South.

Yet no area of the country except Alaska and the southern half of Florida is free from hay fever—it's simply a question of degree. The West Coast is almost ragweed-free, although it has other allergenic pollens.

Some places that were once havens for asthmatics and hay fever sufferers are now less free of allergens. Examples are many of the fast-growing areas of the Southwest. Thirty years ago, Tucson was virtually free of ragweed pollen. Its desert location precluded the growth of the weeds, grasses, and trees that cause hay fever. But as more and more people moved into the area, more trees were planted and lawns seeded. The result? A pollen index that's still good but not as good as it used to be.

The table on the next page shows the ragweed pollen index for a number of places around the country.

Counting All Those Pollen Grains

The American Academy of Allergy has devised the Ragweed Pollen Index to indicate the local severity of the pollen problem. This index is derived from (1) length of the season, (2) concentration of pollen grains in the air at the season's peak, and (3) total pollen catch throughout the season. The higher the index number, the worse the problem; an index greater than 10 means lots of discomfort.

Ragweed Pollen Index for Selected Places

Place	Index	Place	Index	Place	Index	Place	Index
Alabama		Decatur	114.0	**Missouri**		**Oregon**	
Birmingham	49.0	East St. Louis	100.0	Kansas City	109.0	Corvallis	0
Mobile	8.0	Peoria	122.0	St. Louis	78.0	Portland	0.5
Alaska		Quincy	98.0	**Montana**		**Pennsylvania**	
All cities	0	Rockford	96.0	Glacier		Altoona	52.0
Arizona		Springfield	72.0	National Park	0.1	Erie	65.0
Phoenix	0.2	**Indiana**		Yellowstone		Philadelphia	55.0
Tucson	2.0	Evansville	136.0	National Park	0.2	Pittsburgh	90.0
Arkansas		Fort Wayne	107.0	**Nebraska**		**Rhode Island**	
Fort Smith	103.0	Gary	62.0	Lincoln	63.0	Providence	26.0
Little Rock	62.0	Indianapolis	92.0	North Platte	13.0	**South Carolina**	
California		**Iowa**		Omaha	148.0	Charleston	11.0
Alpine	3.0	Cedar Rapids	122.0	Scottsbluff	38.0	Columbia	40.0
Anaheim	0.5	Council Bluffs	148.0	**Nevada**		**South Dakota**	
Los Angeles	0.5	Davenport	113.0	Reno	0.1	Aberdeen	17.0
Sacramento	0.2	Des Moines	69.0	**New Hampshire**		Rapid City	12.0
San Diego	11.0	**Kansas**		Concord	7.0	Sioux Falls	52.0
San Francisco	0.2	Kansas City	101.0	Conway	3.0	**Tennessee**	
Santa Barbara	3.0	Wichita	58.0	Manchester	9.0	Johnson City	51.0
Colorado		**Kentucky**		Nashua	29.0	Knoxville	49.0
Colorado Springs	4.0	Lexington	151.0	**New Jersey**		Memphis	73.0
Denver	19.0	Louisville	99.0	Atlantic City	30.0	Nashville	69.0
Connecticut		**Louisiana**		New Brunswick	60.0	**Texas**	
Bridgeport	23.0	New Orleans	43.0	Newark	18.0	Amarillo	41.0
Hartford	54.0	Tallulah	33.0	Trenton	26.0	Brownsville	24.0
New Haven	25.0	**Maine**		**New Mexico**		Dallas	115.0
Waterbury	27.0	Lewiston	13.0	Albuquerque	7.0	El Paso	15.0
Delaware		Portland	24.0	Roswell	4.0	Galveston	36.0
Wilmington	54.0	Presque Isle	0.4	**New York**		Houston	68.0
District		**Maryland**		Albany	48.0	San Antonio	16.0
of Columbia	42.0	Baltimore	51.0	Binghamton	31.0	**Utah**	
Florida		**Massachusetts**		Buffalo	59.0	Salt Lake City	8.0
Bradenton	4.0	Amherst	25.0	Elmira	43.0	Zion National Park	0.7
Daytona Beach	3.0	Boston	16.0	Manhattan	25.0	**Vermont**	
Fort Lauderdale	9.0	Nantucket	5.0	Rochester	60.0	Burlington	47.0
Fort Myers	0.2	Springfield	20.0	Syracuse	25.0	**Virginia**	
Gainesville	20.0	Worcester	9.0	Tupper Lake	8.0	Charlottesville	35.0
Jacksonville	6.0	**Michigan**		Utica	26.0	Norfolk	54.0
Melbourne	21.0	Ann Arbor	119.0	Yonkers	38.0	Richmond	42.0
Miami	2.0	Bay City	72.0	**North Carolina**		Roanoke	85.0
Orlando	3.0	Charlevoix	21.0	Asheville	57.0	**Washington**	
Panama City	32.0	Detroit	59.0	Charlotte	42.0	Seattle	0
Pensacola	10.0	Escanaba	57.0	Raleigh	28.0	Spokane	0.1
Tallahassee	6.0	Flint	76.0	**North Dakota**		Yakima	0.2
Tampa	6.0	Grand Rapids	126.0	Fargo	125.0	**West Virginia**	
West Palm Beach	5.0	Lansing	94.0	**Ohio**		Charleston	31.0
Georgia		Marquette	12.0	Akron	100.0	**Wisconsin**	
Atlanta	24.0	Saginaw	72.0	Cincinnati	122.0	Eagle River	13.0
Valdosta	8.0	**Minnesota**		Cleveland	56.0	Madison	93.0
Idaho		Duluth	44.0	Columbus	75.0	Milwaukee	86.0
Boise City	5.0	Minneapolis	99.0	Dayton	90.0	Sheboygan	90.0
Illinois		Moorhead	125.0	Toledo	122.0	Superior	44.0
Bloomington	122.0	Rochester	88.0	Youngstown	70.0	**Wyoming**	
Champaign	76.0	**Mississippi**		**Oklahoma**		Lander	23.0
Chicago	62.0	Biloxi	7.0	Oklahoma City	73.0		
		Vicksburg	33.0	Tulsa	65.0		

Source: American Academy of Allergy, 1977.

No figures are given for Hawaii because the academy has no reporting stations there.

Crime:

Safe & Not-So-Safe Places

What are the odds that you'll be a victim of crime in the place you live? Obviously, vulnerability to crime varies enormously from metro area to metro area, just as it does among neighborhoods in the same city. Some places are so safe you couldn't pay someone to assault you, while others are just plain dangerous.

In Wheeling, West Virginia–Ohio, for example, the chances of your encountering violent crime—murder, rape, assault, or robbery—are only one in 806 over a year. But move to New York City and those odds skyrocket to one in 62 over the same period, making the Big Apple 13 times more violent than Wheeling.

Chances are that, for the near term at least, Wheeling will remain a safe place and New York a crime-ridden one. According to the FBI, crime rates do not shift significantly in any given place from year to year. Some of the other patterns in crime observed by the FBI in the past decade are the following:

- Rates of all types of crime are highest in big cities, lower in small and medium-sized towns, and lowest in rural areas.
- Criminal behavior is closely related to the economic status, age, race, and sex of given populations.
- High crime rates are associated with increasing populations and large numbers of transients. Conversely, low crime rates are often linked to steady or decreasing populations, even when coupled with adverse economic conditions.
- Incidence of most crimes peaks during the summer months, especially on weekends.
- Robbery, burglary, and larceny are more prevalent in big cities than elsewhere, and the overwhelming majority of these crimes are committed by people with criminal records.
- Murder and aggravated assault are often committed by people without criminal records, probably because they are usually unpremeditated crimes of passion.

FACTORS LINKED WITH CRIME

What causes crime, and what can be done about it? The FBI has identified several basic factors that are linked with local crime rates:

Population density, as well as the overall size of the area's population. This factor does not appear to affect crime rate directly until population density becomes very high. Thus the high crime rate of a metropolitan area like Miami–Hialeah will be partially attributable to pockets of overcrowding, which can spawn violence. A government booklet entitled "City Size and Quality of Life" points out that most cities become ungovernable when their populations exceed about six million.

Murder in America

The pattern of the murder rate in America, rather than reaching one level or gradually increasing or declining, is one of a wave, alternately rising and falling. What is the reason for this fluctuation?

According to C. Ray Jeffries, professor of criminology at the Criminal Justice School of Florida State University, the explanation can be found in a combination of factors. A great deal of variation in the murder rate can be chalked up to police reporting procedures, for example. As a result of improved reporting methods, more murders are reported now than earlier in the century.

Demography also plays a role in the murder rate, specifically the proportion of young men (aged roughly 16 to 21) to the general population. In times when that proportion is high, violent crime rates will also be high. Jeffries attributes the slight decline in murder over the last few years to a corresponding decline in the size of this violence-prone segment of the population.

Another factor is the social climate. With Prohibition came the rise of bootlegging and organized crime; the Depression meant unemployment, poverty, homelessness, and the destruction of family life and communities. It is not too surprising, then, that the murder rate showed a steady increase throughout the twenties and peaked during the height of the Depression. With World War II, unemployment was almost nonexistent—men were either in uniform or stoking the machine of wartime industry. There were almost no young men at home to boost the murder rate.

During the placid Eisenhower years the murder rate leveled out. But the turbulent sixties, a time of strife resulting from the push for civil rights and the controversy over the Vietnam War, and fueled by a surge in the number of teenaged men born of the baby boom, meant a murder rate that climbed to new heights.

When populations reach this level, the social fabric begins to break down.

Composition of the population, especially in regard to age, race, and sex. Minority-group men between the ages of 15 and 24 commit a large percentage of crimes. Members of this group who are poor or unemployed account for an even greater percentage. If a city has a large proportion of such individuals among its population, its crime rate will usually be high.

Economic status of the population, including job availability. High unemployment, especially when coupled with a large percentage of the population that is unskilled, poor, and uneducated, will result in unacceptably high crime. But unemployment and poverty alone do not predispose a region to crime. Many of the crime-free areas in America are poorer than average, with steady or declining populations. In addition, given similar sets of circumstances, rich people tend to be arrested less frequently than poor ones, especially on suspicion. Once arrested, they are convicted with less frequency. This is especially true in regard to property crimes and crimes committed by juveniles.

Cultural conditions, such as educational level and recreational and religious behavior.

Transience. One of the greatest deterrents to crime appears to be a strong neighborhood in which people know each other well and watch out for each other's safety and property, regardless of the amount of police protection in the area. This is why high transience rates, which indicate strangers living next to each other, are associated with high crime rates.

Climate has a marked relationship with criminal behavior. Crimes increase dramatically during certain weather phases, and violent crime in particular tends to be more frequent in warm climates than cold ones. All crimes except robbery occur most frequently in hot months (July and August) and least frequently in cold ones (January and February). Robbery, the exception, is highest in December, perhaps because during the holiday season pedestrians carrying large amounts of cash and stores doing brisk business make tempting targets.

Other factors the FBI has found to be related to crime rates include strength or weakness of the police force; the policies and attitudes of prosecuting officials, judges, juries, and parole boards; and the attitudes of the community toward crime and its tendency to report crime.

One common misperception about crime and crime prevention is that the safety of a community rises or falls in direct proportion to the size and strength of the local police force. Not so. Police definitely help to fight crime, but most of what police do is after the fact. They respond to complaints or tips; they search for offenders; they apprehend criminals and bring them to trial. A large number of police per capita is usually an

U.S. Homicide Rate, 1900-1980

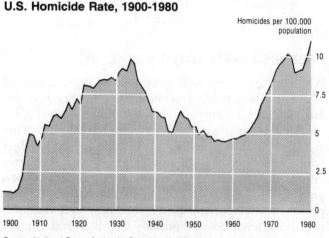

Homicides per 100,000 population

Source: National Center for Health Statistics, *Vital Statistics of the United States.*

indication of a high-crime area rather than an area where crime is being prevented.

The crime rate of an area indicates more than how safe an individual may be there; along with rates of alcoholism, divorce, and suicide, it is one of four social indicators often cited by sociologists that help provide a rough gauge of a place's social solidarity. Areas with high crime rates tend to have a weak social fabric characterized by transience, poverty, and little sense of community. Low-crime areas, whether rich or poor, are generally characterized by some degree of community spirit and, above all, a willingness on the part of residents to watch out for each other's welfare.

KEEPING TRACK OF CRIME

Every year the FBI collects from more than 15,000 police departments around the country the number of arrests for various crimes. Of all the crimes reported, there are eight that, because of their seriousness,

frequency, and likelihood of being reported to the police, have been chosen to serve as an index for determining crime trends across the nation. These compose the FBI's Crime Index:

Violent Crimes	Property Crimes
murder	burglary
forcible rape	larceny-theft
robbery	motor vehicle theft
aggravated assault	arson

Many crimes, of course, are never reported to the police, and this affects the accuracy of the Crime Index. And police departments, in turn, often underreport to the FBI to protect or improve their images. In all, it is estimated that only half of all crimes committed are reported to the FBI.

A necessary distinction to make is that between crime incidence and crime rate. The actual number of occurrences of a crime constitutes its *incidence*. For example, in the Pittsburgh metro area a total of 103 murders were committed in the year 1982 (the latest

Violent vs. Property Crime

Violent crimes, which make up only 10 percent of total crime in the United States, involve bodily injury or the threat of injury. The FBI's Crime Index defines the following offenses as violent crimes: murder, forcible rape (including attempts to commit rape), robbery (which differs from burglary and larceny-theft in that its victims are threatened with harm if they do not surrender their property), and aggravated assault (an attack on a person with intent to kill or cause injury).

Below are the metro areas that in 1982 scored highest and lowest in overall violent crime. Seven of the ten most dangerous metro areas were found in the South or the West, and eight of the safest in the East North Central or West North Central regions.

commit a felony or theft), larceny-theft (which includes such diverse offenses as purse-snatching, pocket-picking, shoplifting, and bicycle theft), motor vehicle theft, and arson. Although arson was designated an Index crime in 1979, data on this crime are not yet available for the metro areas. For this reason *Places Rated Almanac* does not include arson in its survey of crime.

The following metro areas were the winners and losers in overall property crime in 1982. Again we see a preponderance of southern and western metro areas in the Most Dangerous list; mostly Middle Atlantic or East North Central metro areas are found under the heading Safest.

Violent Crime in the Metro Areas

Safest Metro Areas	Violent Crime Rate	Most Dangerous Metro Areas	Violent Crime Rate
1. St. Cloud, MN	47	1. New York, NY	1,782
2. Sheboygan, WI	53	2. Miami–Hialeah, FL	1,589
3. Bismarck, ND	56	3. Los Angeles–Long Beach, CA	1,270
4. Grand Forks, ND	63	4. Baltimore, MD	1,164
5. Eau Claire, WI	87	5. Las Vegas, NV	1,057
6. Rochester, MN	89	6. New Orleans, LA	1,007
7. Binghamton, NY	94	7. West Palm Beach–Boca Raton, FL	995
8. Duluth, MN–WI	101	8. Newark, NJ	977
9. Appleton–Oshkosh–Neenah, WI	106	9. San Francisco, CA	968
9. Nashua, NH	106	10. Orlando, FL	956

Source: FBI, *Crimes by County—1982* (unpublished report), 1984.

The FBI lists four offenses in the category of property crime: burglary (the unlawful entry of a building to

Property Crime in the Metro Areas

Safest Metro Areas	Property Crime Rate	Most Dangerous Metro Areas	Property Crime Rate
1. Johnstown, PA	1,733	1. Atlantic City, NJ	10,849
2. Beaver County, PA	1,810	2. Odessa, TX	10,014
3. Wheeling, WV–OH	1,838	3. Las Cruces, NM	9,271
4. Steubenville–Weirton, OH–WV	2,292	4. Miami–Hialeah, FL	8,701
5. Scranton–Wilkes-Barre, PA	2,356	5. Las Vegas, NV	8,557
6. Danville, VA	2,378	6. West Palm Beach–Boca Raton–Delray Beach, FL	7,882
7. Altoona, PA	2,381	7. Savannah, GA	7,797
8. Sharon, PA	2,528	8. Stockton, CA	7,713
9. Biloxi–Gulfport, MS	2,589	9. Lubbock, TX	7,670
10. Johnson City–Kingsport–Bristol, TN–VA	2,630	10. Tucson, AZ	7,582

Source: FBI, *Crimes by County—1982* (unpublished report), 1984.

Regional Crime Rates

Region	Violent Crime Rates				Property Crime Rates		
	Murder	Forcible Rape	Robbery	Aggravated Assault	Burglary	Larceny-Theft	Motor Vehicle Theft
U.S. National Average	9.1	33.6	231.9	280.8	1,475.2	3,069.8	452.8
Northeast: Maine, New Hampshire, Vermont, Massachusetts, Rhode Island, Connecticut	7.4	25.4	348.5	257.5	1,366.0	2,664.3	626.8
Middle Atlantic: New York, New Jersey, Pennsylvania	8.6	26.4	409.9	266.0	1,375.8	2,648.2	605.8
East North Central: Ohio, Indiana, Illinois, Michigan, Wisconsin	7.2	29.1	185.9	221.2	1,294.4	3,000.9	445.6
West North Central: Minnesota, Iowa, Missouri, North Dakota, South Dakota, Nebraska, Kansas	4.8	21.1	104.2	169.7	1,138.7	2,746.4	238.9
South Atlantic: District of Columbia, Delaware, Maryland, Virginia, West Virginia, North Carolina, South Carolina, Georgia, Florida	10.9	37.4	214.7	376.0	1,503.3	3,201.0	312.3
East South Central: Kentucky, Tennessee, Alabama, Mississippi	10.7	27.6	121.7	220.2	1,197.7	2,279.1	261.2
West South Central: Arkansas, Louisiana, Oklahoma, Texas	14.7	41.2	194.8	302.4	1,687.0	3,047.3	484.0
Mountain: Montana, Idaho, Wyoming, Colorado, New Mexico, Arizona, Utah, Nevada	7.1	37.1	138.8	297.4	1,578.2	3,951.3	341.4
Pacific: Washington, Oregon, California, Alaska, Hawaii	9.7	49.2	313.4	343.3	1,936.2	3,833.7	578.6

Source: FBI, *Crime in the United States*, 1983.

Regions are those defined by the FBI. Figures are crime rates (incidence per 100,000 population) for 1982.

year for which complete FBI data are available). Therefore, Pittsburgh's incidence of murder is 103. Waco, Texas, had only 33 murders in the same year. Judging from these figures, you might think Pittsburgh is far more dangerous than Waco. However, more than two million people live in Pittsburgh, while only about 170,000 live in Waco.

The best way to compare places of different sizes is to look at the crime *rate*, which is the incidence of crime per year per 100,000 people. Calculating by this method yields a murder rate of 4.5 for Pittsburgh and a rate of 17.9 for Waco. The average murder rate for all U.S. metro areas is 10.0, so Pittsburgh, for all its reputation as a tough steel town, is actually twice as safe from murder as the average metro area, whereas Waco is just about twice as dangerous, a characteristic it shares with most metro areas in the Lone Star State.

The distribution of safe and dangerous places follows traditional patterns that any criminologist would recognize immediately. For example, the northern New England states record consistently low crime rates. Wheeling—ranked by *Places Rated* as the safest metro area in the nation—enjoys the generally favorable social indicators found in much of the Middle South.

At the other end of the spectrum, many of the country's most dangerous metro areas are located on the eastern coast from New Jersey southward. The reason? For one thing, all of these coastal areas have shown tremendous growth rates over the past 30 years. New people moving into an area disrupt neighborhoods and social patterns. Florida especially has had explosive increases in population—including many displaced Caribbean islanders—as has Texas. Both now suffer from the instability and crime that such growth can spawn.

But there are other reasons as well. Professional criminals gravitate to places where the living is easy and the pickings bountiful; they don't stay in the declining industrial towns of the North but head South to warm weather, popular resorts, and tourist towns. This is one reason Las Vegas and Miami–Hialeah have been plagued by high crime for decades.

JUDGING SAFETY FROM CRIME

In *Places Rated*'s view, a basic flaw in the FBI's Crime Index totals is that they fail to differentiate adequately between property crimes and the less numerous, but far more serious, violent crimes. The most common crime by far is larceny-theft (stealing hubcaps is an example). Yet according to the FBI's statistical method for determining total crime rate, stealing hubcaps is counted as heavily as first-degree murder. This certainly doesn't allow for a realistic estimate of the relative danger levels in the United States.

Eugene–Springfield, Oregon, for instance, has a total crime rate of 6,504, roughly on a par with Lakeland–Winter Haven, Florida, at 6,510. But are the two metro areas equally dangerous? Not by a long shot. Lakeland–Winter Haven's violent crime rate is more than three times as high as Eugene–Springfield's (802 as compared with 249). Although the Oregon metro area has a relatively high property crime rate, it

nevertheless is a comparatively safe city—something you wouldn't guess from looking at its crime rate as shown in the FBI report.

The formula used to rate the 329 U.S. metro areas for safety is simple: *Places Rated Almanac* uses the FBI *Crimes by County* data for violent and property crimes, but since we consider property crimes much less serious than crimes against people, we give them one-tenth the weight of violent crimes. Each metro area starts with a base score of zero, and points are assigned according to the following indicators:

Crime in the Metro Areas

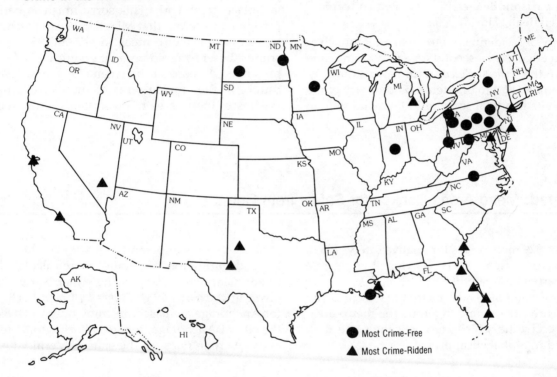

Most Crime-Free Metro Areas	Places Rated Score	Most Crime-Ridden Metro Areas	Places Rated Score
1. Wheeling, WV–OH	308	1. New York, NY	2,498
2. Beaver County, PA	310	2. Miami–Hialeah, FL	2,459
3. Cumberland, MD–WV	337	3. Los Angeles–Long Beach, CA	1,960
4. St. Cloud, MN	343	4. Las Vegas, NV	1,913
5. Johnstown, PA	353	5. Atlantic City, NJ	1,878
6. Scranton–Wilkes-Barre, PA	372	6. West Palm Beach–Boca Raton–Delray Beach, FL	1,783
7. Danville, VA	379	7. Baltimore, MD	1,730
8. Sharon, PA	384	8. Odessa, TX	1,698
9. Altoona, PA	399	9. Orlando, FL	1,671
10. Houma–Thibodaux, LA	400	9. Flint, MI	1,671
10. Utica–Rome, NY	400	11. Gainesville, FL	1,658
12. Grand Forks, ND	401	12. San Francisco, CA	1,619
13. Bismarck, ND	413	13. Savannah, GA	1,614
13. Kokomo, IN	413	14. Lubbock, TX	1,608
13. Lancaster, PA	413	15. New Orleans, LA	1,604

The Places Rated Score is the sum of the violent crime rate and one-tenth the property crime rate.

1. *Violent crime rate.* The rates for all violent crimes—murder, forcible rape, robbery, and aggravated assault—as reported by the FBI are totaled.
2. *Property crime rate.* The FBI rates for burglary, larceny-theft, and motor vehicle theft are added together; the result is divided by 10.

The sum of a metro area's violent crime rate and one-tenth its property crime rate, rounded off, represents the metro area's score. Each metro area's rates for specific crimes are given in the Place Profiles later in this chapter.

Sample Comparison: Beaver County, Pennsylvania, and Miami–Hialeah, Florida

Beaver County, a residential metro area on Pennsylvania's western edge, ranks second for safety from crime according to the *Places Rated* formula. Adding its violent crime rate (129) to one-tenth its property crime rate (181) results in a total score of 310, second only to that of Wheeling, West Virginia–Ohio. In fact, Beaver County is just one of a handful of very safe places found near the junction of Pennsylvania, Ohio, and West Virginia. Altoona, Pennsylvania; Cumberland, Maryland–West Virginia; Johnstown, Pennsylvania; Steubenville–Weirton, Ohio–West Virginia; and Wheeling—all of which rank in the top 95 percent of the *Places Rated* universe—also profit from neighborhoods that are largely working class and untouched by the problems of urban communities.

In contrast, Miami–Hialeah has a crime score of 2,459, the sum of its violent crime rate (1,589) and one-tenth its property crime rate (870). Thus the Florida metro area ends up 328th overall, just ahead of last-place New York. This sorry finish is hardly surprising considering that Miami–Hialeah placed among the ten worst metro areas in six of the seven Index crimes. Beset by rapid population growth—an increase of some 28 percent between 1970 and 1980—and caught in the crosscurrents of the illegal drug trade, this resort metro area has a serious crime problem.

Places Rated: Metro Areas Ranked for Safety from Crime

In ranking the 329 metro areas for relative safety, *Places Rated Almanac* uses two criteria: (1) violent crime rate and (2) property crime rate divided by 10. The sum of these rates, rounded off, is the metro area's score. The higher the score, the more dangerous the metro area. Places that receive tie scores are given the same rank and are listed in alphabetical order.

Those scores in parentheses—for Anchorage, Alaska, and Burlington, Vermont—were calculated by different means since data for these metro areas were not given in the FBI's 1984 *Crimes by County*. The figures for Anchorage are based on crime rates for 1982 within the city of Anchorage, whereas Burlington's represent average crime rates for the state of Vermont.

Metro Areas from Safest to Most Dangerous

Places Rated Rank	Places Rated Score	Places Rated Rank	Places Rated Score	Places Rated Rank	Places Rated Score
1. Wheeling, WV–OH	308	16. Binghamton, NY	415	28. Provo–Orem, UT	485
2. Beaver County, PA	310	17. Steubenville–Weirton, OH–WV	418	29. Duluth, MN–WI	488
3. Cumberland, MD–WV	337	18. Johnson City–Kingsport–Bristol, TN–VA	424	29. Parkersburg–Marietta, WV–OH	488
4. St. Cloud, MN	343	19. Eau Claire, WI	433		
5. Johnstown, PA	353	20. Rochester, MN	437	31. Salem–Gloucester, MA	490
				32. Burlington, VT	(494)
6. Scranton–Wilkes-Barre, PA	372	21. York, PA	440	33. Fargo–Moorhead, ND–MN	503
7. Danville, VA	379	22. Wausau, WI	442	34. Allentown–Bethlehem, PA–NJ	514
8. Sharon, PA	384	23. Sheboygan, WI	450	35. Florence, AL	516
9. Altoona, PA	399	24. Nashua, NH	452		
10. Houma–Thibodaux, LA	400	25. Williamsport, PA	464	36. Reading, PA	522
				37. Elkhart–Goshen, IN	524
10. Utica–Rome, NY	400			38. Appleton–Oshkosh–Neenah, WI	525
12. Grand Forks, ND	401	26. Lafayette, IN	465	39. State College, PA	540
13. Bismarck, ND	413	27. Portsmouth–Dover–Rochester, NH–ME	475	40. Fort Walton Beach, FL	544
13. Kokomo, IN	413				
13. Lancaster, PA	413				

Places Rated Rank	Places Rated Score	Places Rated Rank	Places Rated Score	Places Rated Rank	Places Rated Score
41. Bristol, CT	545	96. Charlottesville, VA	756	153. Kenosha, WI	911
41. Fayetteville–Springdale, AR	545	97. Sioux City, IA–NE	759	154. Santa Rosa–Petaluma, CA	912
43. Danbury, CT	548	98. Lewiston–Auburn, ME	764	155. Peoria, IL	921
44. Sioux Falls, SD	556	99. Hickory, NC	765		
45. Asheville, NC	566	100. Brazoria, TX	768	156. Abilene, TX	923
				157. Huntsville, AL	924
45. Nassau–Suffolk, NY	566	101. Niagara Falls, NY	775	158. Dothan, AL	930
47. Glens Falls, NY	568	102. Madison, WI	779	159. Athens, GA	933
47. Owensboro, KY	568	102. Richland–Kennewick–Pasco, WA	779	160. Louisville, KY–IN	937
49. Dubuque, IA	571	104. Macon–Warner Robins, GA	783		
50. Elmira, NY	582	104. Muncie, IN	783	161. Youngstown–Warren, OH	938
				162. Sarasota, FL	939
51. Green Bay, WI	583	106. Roanoke, VA	784	163. Bridgeport–Milford, CT	943
52. Pascagoula, MS	591	107. Fort Myers, FL	787	164. Chattanooga, TN–GA	946
53. Lorain–Elyria, OH	609	108. Lincoln, NE	789	165. Chico, CA	947
54. Albany–Schenectady–Troy, NY	610	108. Waterbury, CT	789		
55. Knoxville, TN	622	110. Oxnard–Ventura, CA	791	166. Grand Rapids, MI	952
				167. Tyler, TX	955
56. Norwalk, CT	625	111. Great Falls, MT	792	168. Monroe, LA	957
57. Hagerstown, MD	627	112. Orange County, NY	804	169. Santa Cruz, CA	964
58. Joplin, MO	628	113. Billings, MT	810	169. Vallejo–Fairfield–Napa, CA	964
59. Harrisburg–Lebanon–Carlisle, PA	629	113. Biloxi–Gulfport, MS	810		
60. Terre Haute, IN	630	115. Montgomery, AL	815	171. Greensboro–Winston-Salem–High Point, NC	967
				171. Jacksonville, NC	967
61. Manchester, NH	633	116. Lowell, MA–NH	819	173. St. Joseph, MO	969
61. New London–Norwich, CT–RI	633	116. Monmouth–Ocean, NJ	819	173. Salt Lake City–Ogden, UT	969
61. Poughkeepsie, NY	633	118. Columbus, GA–AL	820	175. Albany, GA	970
64. Erie, PA	635	119. Aurora–Elgin, IL	821		
65. Pittsfield, MA	638	120. Lake County, IL	822	176. Buffalo, NY	971
				177. Brownsville–Harlingen, TX	974
66. Lynchburg, VA	643	120. Texarkana, TX–Texarkana, AR	822	178. Anderson, SC	975
67. Middletown, CT	646	122. Portland, ME	823	179. Kankakee, IL	976
68. Canton, OH	650	123. Bellingham, WA	825	179. Longview–Marshall, TX	976
69. Bangor, ME	651	124. Milwaukee, WI	826		
69. Bremerton, WA	651	125. Iowa City, IA	830	181. Cincinnati, OH–KY–IN	978
				182. Raleigh–Durham, NC	981
71. Fitchburg–Leominster, MA	655	126. Davenport–Rock Island–Moline, IA–IL	834	183. Anaheim–Santa Ana, CA	983
72. Bloomington, IN	657	127. Stamford, CT	835	184. Nashville, TN	984
73. Fort Smith, AR–OK	663	128. McAllen–Edinburg–Mission, TX	836	185. Casper, WY	989
74. Huntington–Ashland, WV–KY–OH	665	129. Joliet, IL	837		
75. Bloomington–Normal, IL	673	130. Enid, OK	845	186. Greeley, CO	994
				187. Gary–Hammond, IN	996
76. La Crosse, WI	676	131. Lima, OH	855	188. Norfolk–Virginia Beach–Newport News, VA	997
77. Worcester, MA	680	132. Bergen–Passaic, NJ	857	189. Providence, RI	998
78. Pittsburgh, PA	687	133. Janesville–Beloit, WI	858	189. Toledo, OH	998
79. Syracuse, NY	689	134. Fall River, MA–RI	861		
80. Middlesex–Somerset–Hunterdon, NJ	691	135. Evansville, IN–KY	864	191. Topeka, KS	999
				192. Indianapolis, IN	1,000
81. Waterloo–Cedar Falls, IA	700	136. Spokane, WA	869	193. Omaha, NE–IA	1,008
82. Alton–Granite City, IL	706	137. Augusta, GA–SC	872	194. New Bedford, MA	1,012
83. Burlington, NC	707	138. Eugene–Springfield, OR	874	195. Salem, OR	1,014
84. Fort Wayne, IN	710	139. Anderson, IN	878		
85. Cedar Rapids, IA	714	140. Boise City, ID	880	195. Tuscaloosa, AL	1,014
				197. Bryan–College Station, TX	1,016
86. Charleston, WV	721	141. Akron, OH	886	198. Lawrence, KS	1,018
87. Alexandria, LA	727	142. Honolulu, HI	891	199. Jackson, MI	1,021
88. Medford, OR	728	143. Hamilton–Middletown, OH	892	200. Champaign–Urbana–Rantoul, IL	1,022
89. Killeen–Temple, TX	733	143. Redding, CA	892		
90. Clarksville–Hopkinsville, TN–KY	736	143. Springfield, MO	892	201. Santa Barbara–Santa Maria–Lompoc, CA	1,026
				202. Lafayette, LA	1,030
91. Fort Collins–Loveland, CO	744	146. New Haven–Meriden, CT	893	203. Battle Creek, MI	1,031
91. Pawtucket–Woonsocket–Attleboro, RI–MA	744	147. Lansing–East Lansing, MI	894	204. San Angelo, TX	1,032
93. Gadsden, AL	749	147. Rochester, NY	894	205. Chicago, IL	1,034
94. Olympia, WA	752	149. Decatur, IL	897		
94. Vancouver, WA	752	150. New Britain, CT	903	206. Sherman–Denison, TX	1,035
				207. South Bend–Mishawaka, IN	1,038
		151. Minneapolis–St. Paul, MN–WI	906	208. Melbourne–Titusville–Palm Bay, FL	1,039
		152. Lawrence–Haverhill, MA–NH	909		

Places Rated Rank	Places Rated Score	Places Rated Rank	Places Rated Score	Places Rated Rank	Places Rated Score
209. Des Moines, IA	1,044	250. Wichita, KS	1,164	290. Tucson, AZ	1,400
210. Austin, TX	1,049				
		251. Midland, TX	1,166	291. Fort Pierce, FL	1,422
211. Laredo, TX	1,050	251. Waco, TX	1,166	292. Wilmington, NC	1,423
212. Lexington–Fayette, KY	1,055	253. Pine Bluff, AR	1,169	293. Jersey City, NJ	1,434
212. Racine, WI	1,055	254. Seattle, WA	1,170	294. Las Cruces, NM	1,457
214. Philadelphia, PA–NJ	1,059	255. Wichita Falls, TX	1,179	295. Newark, NJ	1,461
215. Columbia, MO	1,065				
		255. Yuba City, CA	1,179	296. Kansas City, MO	1,468
215. San Jose, CA	1,065	257. Pueblo, CO	1,181	297. Pensacola, FL	1,472
217. Ann Arbor, MI	1,067	257. Trenton, NJ	1,181	298. Riverside–San Bernardino, CA	1,475
218. Saginaw–Bay City–Midland, MI	1,068	259. Greenville–Spartanburg, SC	1,185	299. Albuquerque, NM	1,483
219. Mansfield, OH	1,072	260. Benton Harbor, MI	1,190	299. Fresno, CA	1,483
220. Amarillo, TX	1,073				
		261. San Antonio, TX	1,197	301. Memphis, TN–AR–MS	1,488
221. Richmond–Petersburg, VA	1,076	261. Shreveport, LA	1,197	302. Tampa–St. Petersburg–Clearwater, FL	1,493
222. Tulsa, OK	1,080	263. Jacksonville, FL	1,211	303. Charleston, SC	1,495
223. Colorado Springs, CO	1,086	264. Springfield, MA	1,212	304. Houston, TX	1,499
224. Boulder–Longmont, CO	1,088	265. Galveston–Texas City, TX	1,213	305. Portland, OR	1,504
225. Jackson, MS	1,091				
		266. Boston, MA	1,215	306. Mobile, AL	1,511
226. Columbus, OH	1,092	267. Anchorage, AK	(1,223)	307. Columbia, SC	1,524
226. Victoria, TX	1,092	268. Springfield, IL	1,225	308. Dallas, TX	1,529
228. Bradenton, FL	1,093	269. Phoenix, AZ	1,268	309. Oakland, CA	1,533
228. Lake Charles, LA	1,093	270. Charlotte–Gastonia–Rock Hill, NC–SC	1,273	310. Fort Lauderdale–Hollywood–Pompano Beach, FL	1,536
230. East St. Louis–Belleville, IL	1,096				
231. San Diego, CA	1,099	271. Hartford, CT	1,279	311. Muskegon, MI	1,537
232. Yakima, WA	1,106	272. Oklahoma City, OK	1,297	312. Bakersfield, CA	1,561
233. Salinas–Seaside–Monterey, CA	1,107	273. St. Louis, MO–IL	1,306	313. Baton Rouge, LA	1,565
234. Wilmington, DE–NJ–MD	1,115	274. Atlanta, GA	1,308	314. Detroit, MI	1,587
235. Reno, NV	1,116	275. Beaumont–Port Arthur, TX	1,313	315. New Orleans, LA	1,604
236. Kalamazoo, MI	1,120	276. Washington, DC–MD–VA	1,317	316. Lubbock, TX	1,608
237. Birmingham, AL	1,123	277. El Paso, TX	1,323	317. Savannah, GA	1,614
238. Anniston, AL	1,125	278. Ocala, FL	1,327	318. San Francisco, CA	1,619
239. Visalia–Tulare–Porterville, CA	1,132	279. Little Rock–North Little Rock, AR	1,328	319. Gainesville, FL	1,658
240. Vineland–Millville–Bridgeton, NJ	1,135	280. Florence, SC	1,334	320. Flint, MI	1,671
		281. Corpus Christi, TX	1,335	320. Orlando, FL	1,671
241. Cleveland, OH	1,138	282. Brockton, MA	1,336	322. Odessa, TX	1,698
242. Kansas City, KS	1,142	283. Panama City, FL	1,344	323. Baltimore, MD	1,730
243. Fayetteville, NC	1,150	284. Daytona Beach, FL	1,347	324. West Palm Beach–Boca Raton–Delray Beach, FL	1,783
244. Dayton–Springfield, OH	1,151	285. Fort Worth–Arlington, TX	1,348	325. Atlantic City, NJ	1,878
245. Modesto, CA	1,154				
		286. Sacramento, CA	1,363	326. Las Vegas, NV	1,913
246. Lawton, OK	1,156	287. Denver, CO	1,365	327. Los Angeles–Long Beach, CA	1,960
246. Rockford, IL	1,156	288. Lakeland–Winter Haven, FL	1,373	328. Miami–Hialeah, FL	2,459
248. Tallahassee, FL	1,161	289. Stockton, CA	1,395	329. New York, NY	2,498
249. Tacoma, WA	1,162				

Metro Areas Listed Alphabetically

Metro Area	Places Rated Rank	Metro Area	Places Rated Rank	Metro Area	Places Rated Rank
Abilene, TX	156	Anaheim–Santa Ana, CA	183	Atlantic City, NJ	325
Akron, OH	141	Anchorage, AK	267	Augusta, GA–SC	137
Albany, GA	175	Anderson, IN	139	Aurora–Elgin, IL	119
Albany–Schenectady–Troy, NY	54	Anderson, SC	178	Austin, TX	210
Albuquerque, NM	299	Ann Arbor, MI	217	Bakersfield, CA	312
Alexandria, LA	87	Anniston, AL	238	Baltimore, MD	323
Allentown–Bethlehem, PA–NJ	34	Appleton–Oshkosh–Neenah, WI	38	Bangor, ME	69
Alton–Granite City, IL	82	Asheville, NC	45	Baton Rouge, LA	313
Altoona, PA	9	Athens, GA	159	Battle Creek, MI	203
Amarillo, TX	220	Atlanta, GA	274	Beaumont–Port Arthur, TX	275

Metro Area	Places Rated Rank	Metro Area	Places Rated Rank	Metro Area	Places Rated Rank
Beaver County, PA	2	East St. Louis–Belleville, IL	230	Johnstown, PA	5
Bellingham, WA	123			Joliet, IL	129
Benton Harbor, MI	260	Eau Claire, WI	19	Joplin, MO	58
Bergen–Passaic, NJ	132	El Paso, TX	277	Kalamazoo, MI	236
Billings, MT	113	Elkhart–Goshen, IN	37		
		Elmira, NY	50	Kankakee, IL	179
Biloxi–Gulfport, MS	113	Enid, OK	130	Kansas City, KS	242
Binghamton, NY	16			Kansas City, MO	296
Birmingham, AL	237	Erie, PA	64	Kenosha, WI	153
Bismarck, ND	13	Eugene–Springfield, OR	138	Killeen–Temple, TX	89
Bloomington, IN	72	Evansville, IN–KY	135		
		Fall River, MA–RI	134	Knoxville, TN	55
Bloomington–Normal, IL	75	Fargo–Moorhead, ND–MN	33	Kokomo, IN	13
Boise City, ID	140			La Crosse, WI	76
Boston, MA	266	Fayetteville, NC	243	Lafayette, IN	26
Boulder–Longmont, CO	224	Fayetteville–Springdale, AR	41	Lafayette, LA	202
Bradenton, FL	228	Fitchburg–Leominster, MA	71		
		Flint, MI	320	Lake Charles, LA	228
Brazoria, TX	100	Florence, AL	35	Lake County, IL	120
Bremerton, WA	69			Lakeland–Winter Haven, FL	288
Bridgeport–Milford, CT	163	Florence, SC	280	Lancaster, PA	13
Bristol, CT	41	Fort Collins–Loveland, CO	91	Lansing–East Lansing, MI	147
Brockton, MA	282	Fort Lauderdale–Hollywood– Pompano Beach, FL	310		
Brownsville–Harlingen, TX	177	Fort Myers, FL	107	Laredo, TX	211
Bryan–College Station, TX	197	Fort Pierce, FL	291	Las Cruces, NM	294
Buffalo, NY	176			Las Vegas, NV	326
Burlington, NC	83	Fort Smith, AR–OK	73	Lawrence, KS	198
Burlington, VT	32	Fort Walton Beach, FL	40	Lawrence–Haverhill, MA–NH	152
		Fort Wayne, IN	84		
Canton, OH	68	Fort Worth–Arlington, TX	285	Lawton, OK	246
Casper, WY	185	Fresno, CA	299	Lewiston–Auburn, ME	98
Cedar Rapids, IA	85			Lexington–Fayette, KY	212
Champaign–Urbana–Rantoul, IL	200	Gadsden, AL	93	Lima, OH	131
Charleston, SC	303	Gainesville, FL	319	Lincoln, NE	108
		Galveston–Texas City, TX	265		
Charleston, WV	86	Gary–Hammond, IN	187	Little Rock–North Little Rock, AR	279
Charlotte–Gastonia–Rock Hill, NC–SC	270	Glens Falls, NY	47	Longview–Marshall, TX	179
				Lorain–Elyria, OH	53
Charlottesville, VA	96	Grand Forks, ND	12	Los Angeles–Long Beach, CA	327
Chattanooga, TN–GA	164	Grand Rapids, MI	166	Louisville, KY–IN	160
Chicago, IL	205	Great Falls, MT	111		
		Greeley, CO	186	Lowell, MA–NH	116
Chico, CA	165	Green Bay, WI	51	Lubbock, TX	316
Cincinnati, OH–KY–IN	181			Lynchburg, VA	66
Clarksville–Hopkinsville, TN–KY	90	Greensboro–Winston-Salem– High Point, NC	171	Macon–Warner Robins, GA	104
Cleveland, OH	241	Greenville–Spartanburg, SC	259	Madison, WI	102
Colorado Springs, CO	223	Hagerstown, MD	57		
		Hamilton–Middletown, OH	143	Manchester, NH	61
Columbia, MO	215	Harrisburg–Lebanon–Carlisle, PA	59	Mansfield, OH	219
Columbia, SC	307			McAllen–Edinburg–Mission, TX	128
Columbus, GA–AL	118	Hartford, CT	271	Medford, OR	88
Columbus, OH	226	Hickory, NC	99	Melbourne–Titusville–Palm Bay, FL	208
Corpus Christi, TX	281	Honolulu, HI	142		
		Houma–Thibodaux, LA	10	Memphis, TN–AR–MS	301
Cumberland, MD–WV	3	Houston, TX	304	Miami–Hialeah, FL	328
Dallas, TX	308			Middlesex–Somerset–Hunterdon, NJ	80
Danbury, CT	43	Huntington–Ashland, WV–KY–OH	74	Middletown, CT	67
Danville, VA	7	Huntsville, AL	157	Midland, TX	251
Davenport–Rock Island–Moline, IA–IL	126	Indianapolis, IN	192		
		Iowa City, IA	125	Milwaukee, WI	124
Dayton–Springfield, OH	244	Jackson, MI	199	Minneapolis–St. Paul, MN–WI	151
Daytona Beach, FL	284			Mobile, AL	306
Decatur, IL	149	Jackson, MS	225	Modesto, CA	245
Denver, CO	287	Jacksonville, FL	263	Monmouth–Ocean, NJ	116
Des Moines, IA	209	Jacksonville, NC	171		
		Janesville–Beloit, WI	133	Monroe, LA	168
Detroit, MI	314	Jersey City, NJ	293	Montgomery, AL	115
Dothan, AL	158			Muncie, IN	104
Dubuque, IA	49	Johnson City–Kingsport–Bristol, TN–VA	18	Muskegon, MI	311
Duluth, MN–WI	29			Nashua, NH	24

Metro Area	Places Rated Rank	Metro Area	Places Rated Rank	Metro Area	Places Rated Rank
Nashville, TN	184	Raleigh–Durham, NC	182	Springfield, MO	143
Nassau–Suffolk, NY	45	Reading, PA	36	Stamford, CT	127
New Bedford, MA	194	Redding, CA	143		
New Britain, CT	150	Reno, NV	235	State College, PA	39
New Haven–Meriden, CT	146			Steubenville–Weirton, OH–WV	17
		Richland–Kennewick–Pasco, WA	102	Stockton, CA	289
New London–Norwich, CT–RI	61	Richmond–Petersburg, VA	221	Syracuse, NY	79
New Orleans, LA	315	Riverside–San Bernardino, CA	298	Tacoma, WA	249
New York, NY	329	Roanoke, VA	106		
Newark, NJ	295	Rochester, MN	20	Tallahassee, FL	248
Niagara Falls, NY	101			Tampa–St. Petersburg–	
		Rochester, NY	147	Clearwater, FL	302
Norfolk–Virginia Beach–Newport		Rockford, IL	246	Terre Haute, IN	60
News, VA	188	Sacramento, CA	286	Texarkana, TX–Texarkana, AR	120
Norwalk, CT	56	Saginaw–Bay City–Midland, MI	218	Toledo, OH	189
Oakland, CA	309	St. Cloud, MN	4		
Ocala, FL	278			Topeka, KS	191
Odessa, TX	322	St. Joseph, MO	173	Trenton, NJ	257
		St. Louis, MO–IL	273	Tucson, AZ	290
Oklahoma City, OK	272	Salem, OR	195	Tulsa, OK	222
Olympia, WA	94	Salem–Gloucester, MA	31	Tuscaloosa, AL	195
Omaha, NE–IA	193	Salinas–Seaside–Monterey,			
Orange County, NY	112	CA	233	Tyler, TX	167
Orlando, FL	320			Utica–Rome, NY	10
		Salt Lake City–Ogden, UT	173	Vallejo–Fairfield–Napa, CA	169
Owensboro, KY	47	San Angelo, TX	204	Vancouver, WA	94
Oxnard–Ventura, CA	110	San Antonio, TX	261	Victoria, TX	226
Panama City, FL	283	San Diego, CA	231		
Parkersburg–Marietta, WV–OH	29	San Francisco, CA	318	Vineland–Millville–Bridgeton,	
Pascagoula, MS	52			NJ	240
		San Jose, CA	215	Visalia–Tulare–Porterville, CA	239
Pawtucket–Woonsocket–Attleboro,		Santa Barbara–Santa Maria–		Waco, TX	251
RI–MA	91	Lompoc, CA	201	Washington, DC–MD–VA	276
Pensacola, FL	297	Santa Cruz, CA	169	Waterbury, CT	108
Peoria, IL	155	Santa Rosa–Petaluma, CA	154		
Philadelphia, PA–NJ	214	Sarasota, FL	162	Waterloo–Cedar Falls, IA	81
Phoenix, AZ	269			Wausau, WI	22
		Savannah, GA	317	West Palm Beach–Boca Raton–	
Pine Bluff, AR	253	Scranton–Wilkes-Barre, PA	6	Delray Beach, FL	324
Pittsburgh, PA	78	Seattle, WA	254	Wheeling, WV–OH	1
Pittsfield, MA	65	Sharon, PA	8	Wichita, KS	250
Portland, ME	122	Sheboygan, WI	23		
Portland, OR	305			Wichita Falls, TX	255
		Sherman–Denison, TX	206	Williamsport, PA	25
Portsmouth–Dover–Rochester,		Shreveport, LA	261	Wilmington, DE–NJ–MD	234
NH–ME	27	Sioux City, IA–NE	97	Wilmington, NC	292
Poughkeepsie, NY	61	Sioux Falls, SD	44	Worcester, MA	77
Providence, RI	189	South Bend–Mishawaka, IN	207		
Provo–Orem, UT	28			Yakima, WA	232
Pueblo, CO	257	Spokane, WA	136	York, PA	21
		Springfield, IL	268	Youngstown–Warren, OH	161
Racine, WI	212	Springfield, MA	264	Yuba City, CA	255

![boxing gloves icon]

Place Profiles: Crime Rates in 329 Metro Areas

The following charts detail each metro area's rates for seven FBI Crime Index offenses: murder, forcible rape, robbery, aggravated assault, burglary, larceny-theft, and motor vehicle theft. These offenses are divided into violent and property crimes, and a total rate for each of these categories is also given.

All figures are from the FBI's *Crimes by County— 1982,* 1984. Two metro areas were not included in this

work: Anchorage, Alaska, and Burlington, Vermont. The crime rates given for Anchorage, therefore, are for the city of Anchorage, and those given for Burlington are the statewide averages. Both these metro areas' rates appear in parentheses.

A star preceding a metro area's name highlights that metro area as one of the top 25 places for safety from crime.

	Violent Crime Rates					Property Crime Rates						
	Murder	Forcible Rape	Robbery	Aggravated Assault	Total	Burglary	Larceny-Theft	Motor Vehicle Theft	Total	Places Rated Score	Places Rated Rank
Metro Area Average	10.0	39.2	298.6	314.7	663	1,669.5	3,436.3	554.3	5,660	1,229	—
Abilene, TX	11.7	55.2	116.3	233.4	417	1,205.7	3,557.6	301.2	5,065	923	156
Akron, OH	3.9	39.3	133.2	201.9	378	1,203.7	3,556.8	316.1	5,077	886	141
Albany, GA	17.1	81.1	116.0	203.9	418	1,830.1	3,465.7	223.5	5,519	970	175
Albany–Schenectady–Troy, NY	2.5	14.2	69.1	185.6	271	1,097.7	2,149.0	138.7	3,385	610	54
Albuquerque, NM	9.0	59.1	232.3	479.8	780	2,145.5	4,513.4	371.6	7,031	1,483	299
Alexandria, LA	10.0	15.0	55.8	205.3	286	1,270.0	2,936.4	202.5	4,409	727	87
Allentown–Bethlehem, PA–NJ	4.1	16.4	72.6	101.9	195	870.6	2,173.8	146.8	3,191	514	34
Alton–Granite City, IL	4.5	19.7	64.8	142.2	231	1,370.8	3,166.2	212.5	4,750	706	82
★ Altoona, PA	5.1	16.1	53.3	86.2	161	863.4	1,364.4	152.7	2,381	399	9
Amarillo, TX	13.4	28.9	125.0	324.3	492	1,907.6	3,601.4	305.1	5,814	1,073	220
Anaheim–Santa Ana, CA	4.1	30.0	181.1	200.3	416	1,863.7	3,346.6	466.5	5,677	983	183
Anchorage, AK	(11.6)	(83.0)	(252.6)	(226.3)	(574)	(1,291.1)	(4,615.3)	(588.1)	(6,495)	(1,223)	267
Anderson, IN	3.6	29.8	70.3	199.1	303	1,990.8	3,596.5	162.1	5,749	878	139
Anderson, SC	15.3	28.4	53.8	410.9	508	1,405.0	2,950.4	306.2	4,662	975	178
Ann Arbor, MI	2.4	48.3	99.0	336.6	486	1,326.9	4,064.8	418.3	5,810	1,067	217
Anniston, AL	8.2	24.5	132.4	537.9	703	1,253.1	2,749.1	223.3	4,225	1,125	238
Appleton–Oshkosh–Neenah, WI	1.4	12.6	16.7	75.4	106	922.1	3,160.0	102.0	4,184	525	38
Asheville, NC	7.3	13.3	52.7	147.2	221	885.1	2,386.2	185.4	3,457	566	45
Athens, GA	10.4	34.1	101.4	230.2	376	1,516.0	3,775.2	275.4	5,567	933	159
Atlanta, GA	12.5	52.9	264.3	369.0	699	1,929.6	3,693.4	469.2	6,092	1,308	274
Atlantic City, NJ	10.9	54.9	337.1	390.2	793	2,590.5	7,584.7	674.2	10,849	1,878	325
Augusta, GA–SC	11.6	41.3	99.0	294.2	446	1,588.2	2,434.7	237.9	4,261	872	137
Aurora–Elgin, IL	4.5	19.4	100.4	221.7	346	1,570.3	3,004.9	171.1	4,746	821	119
Austin, TX	13.7	48.9	131.2	186.9	381	1,976.8	4,402.0	300.4	6,679	1,049	210
Bakersfield, CA	14.7	50.7	269.8	453.7	789	2,407.9	4,750.8	562.7	7,721	1,561	312
Baltimore, MD	13.3	39.6	505.2	605.9	1,164	1,548.1	3,692.6	417.3	5,658	1,730	323
Bangor, ME	0.0	12.2	44.3	61.1	118	979.7	4,103.9	247.6	5,331	651	69
Baton Rouge, LA	14.1	43.4	187.7	638.0	883	2,178.3	4,281.1	363.1	6,823	1,565	313
Battle Creek, MI	4.3	30.2	124.4	302.7	462	1,751.9	3,762.0	182.6	5,697	1,031	203
Beaumont–Port Arthur, TX	10.6	43.5	212.3	524.8	791	1,762.1	3,116.5	336.2	5,215	1,313	275
★ Beaver County, PA	3.4	15.2	37.2	73.4	129	574.8	1,045.8	189.0	1,810	310	2
Bellingham, WA	3.7	22.1	19.3	196.2	241	1,554.8	3,968.1	313.2	5,836	825	123
Benton Harbor, MI	4.7	56.3	120.3	452.7	634	1,523.9	3,860.2	180.7	5,565	1,190	260
Bergen–Passaic, NJ	4.0	8.8	234.5	161.2	409	1,110.7	2,700.9	677.6	4,489	857	132
Billings, MT	0.9	22.6	77.7	153.7	255	1,274.7	3,937.0	335.4	5,547	810	113
Biloxi–Gulfport, MS	14.1	60.6	152.8	323.7	551	1,981.5	242.2	365.6	2,589	810	113
★ Binghamton, NY	1.5	11.3	25.3	56.3	94	774.3	2,272.4	157.1	3,204	415	16
Birmingham, AL	15.2	38.7	196.6	330.0	581	1,598.9	3,223.5	599.1	5,422	1,123	237
★ Bismarck, ND	1.2	11.0	13.4	30.5	56	604.4	2,783.4	176.7	3,565	413	13
Bloomington, IN	0.0	16.4	25.6	121.7	164	967.5	3,763.7	200.5	4,932	657	72
Bloomington–Normal, IL	3.3	15.8	45.8	171.5	236	1,207.3	3,033.3	122.4	4,363	673	75
Boise City, ID	2.8	23.8	52.6	324.2	403	1,329.5	3,211.2	223.5	4,764	880	140
Boston, MA	5.3	24.2	306.3	344.4	680	1,387.8	2,632.2	1,331.1	5,351	1,215	266
Boulder–Longmont, CO	2.0	32.9	54.1	334.7	424	1,480.7	4,865.3	296.7	6,643	1,088	224
Bradenton, FL	7.4	50.7	120.0	347.7	526	1,831.4	3,588.0	256.2	5,676	1,093	228
Brazoria, TX	15.9	24.4	53.2	172.8	266	1,130.6	3,676.0	214.1	5,021	768	100
Bremerton, WA	3.3	35.8	51.1	169.9	260	1,245.2	2,497.0	170.6	3,913	651	69
Bridgeport–Milford, CT	5.9	18.8	213.0	167.9	405	1,538.5	3,192.1	645.6	5,376	943	163
Bristol, CT	2.9	2.9	40.5	180.7	227	923.5	2,087.0	172.0	3,183	545	41
Brockton, MA	0.0	35.6	200.4	558.1	794	1,595.7	2,802.4	1,019.0	5,417	1,336	282
Brownsville–Harlingen, TX	10.2	32.1	72.1	309.1	424	1,888.3	3,024.9	589.2	5,502	974	177
Bryan–College Station, TX	12.9	38.7	96.2	235.1	383	1,690.3	4,288.2	350.2	6,329	1,016	197
Buffalo, NY	5.3	30.0	187.3	300.3	523	1,268.6	2,724.6	488.4	4,482	971	176
Burlington, NC	10.9	16.8	48.3	282.1	358	1,064.5	2,289.7	133.2	3,487	707	83
Burlington, VT	(1.6)	(29.2)	(17.7)	(59.2)	(108)	(1,277.7)	(2,354.1)	(229.3)	(3,861)	(494)	32
Canton, OH	4.2	27.2	107.7	144.8	284	1,077.4	2,292.5	287.1	3,657	650	68
Casper, WY	9.1	26.1	52.2	318.4	406	1,545.0	3,923.8	366.7	5,836	989	185
Cedar Rapids, IA	2.4	14.2	56.0	112.1	185	1,211.4	3,860.7	222.9	5,295	714	85

	Violent Crime Rates					Property Crime Rates				Places Rated Score	Places Rated Rank
	Murder	Forcible Rape	Robbery	Aggravated Assault	Total	Burglary	Larceny- Theft	Motor Vehicle Theft	Total		
Metro Area Average	**10.0**	**39.2**	**298.6**	**314.7**	**663**	**1,669.5**	**3,436.3**	**554.3**	**5,660**	**1,229**	**—**
Champaign–Urbana–Rantoul, IL	2.4	22.0	114.0	375.1	514	1,472.1	3,454.0	156.1	5,082	1,022	200
Charleston, SC	12.8	52.8	261.5	592.3	919	1,813.4	3,549.0	392.4	5,755	1,495	303
Charleston, WV	5.0	28.2	137.0	150.3	321	1,012.7	2,681.7	312.5	4,007	721	86
Charlotte–Gastonia–Rock Hill, NC–SC	9.6	30.2	142.0	513.1	695	1,793.0	3,739.4	252.7	5,785	1,273	270
Charlottesville, VA	15.4	18.9	54.0	184.2	273	738.6	3,916.9	180.8	4,836	756	96
Chattanooga, TN–GA	11.3	23.0	105.6	294.1	434	1,280.0	3,478.2	365.4	5,124	946	164
Chicago, IL	12.8	24.2	313.3	210.7	561	1,068.6	2,912.7	748.0	4,729	1,034	205
Chico, CA	6.6	44.4	69.6	265.7	386	1,842.0	3,544.8	218.0	5,605	947	165
Cincinnati, OH–KY–IN	6.0	33.4	166.7	275.0	481	1,280.1	3,427.2	262.1	4,969	978	181
Clarksville–Hopkinsville, TN–KY	11.9	25.0	98.9	247.2	383	1,171.2	2,194.2	167.4	3,533	736	90
Cleveland, OH	13.2	42.0	333.1	281.9	670	1,418.2	2,220.2	1,037.3	4,676	1,138	241
Colorado Springs, CO	4.3	61.2	150.5	256.1	472	1,812.6	4,001.0	328.9	6,143	1,086	223
Columbia, MO	5.9	26.7	78.0	290.4	401	1,736.2	4,740.4	159.0	6,636	1,065	215
Columbia, SC	11.8	56.7	219.0	646.5	934	1,667.7	3,802.2	427.4	5,897	1,524	307
Columbus, GA–AL	10.1	34.3	156.4	196.4	397	1,351.5	2,565.1	316.1	4,233	820	118
Columbus, OH	8.4	38.6	243.4	233.9	524	1,743.0	3,640.8	296.0	5,680	1,092	226
Corpus Christi, TX	15.1	46.8	158.6	423.3	644	2,135.7	4,251.8	527.7	6,915	1,335	281
★ Cumberland, MD–WV	0.9	19.2	18.3	75.1	114	501.6	1,676.7	61.3	2,240	337	3
Dallas, TX	17.9	66.3	310.2	378.5	773	2,317.8	4,730.8	507.7	7,556	1,529	308
Danbury, CT	2.7	24.2	57.2	118.5	203	1,088.5	2,104.4	256.5	3,449	548	43
★ Danville, VA	8.7	11.3	27.8	93.0	141	589.6	1,696.5	92.2	2,378	379	7
Davenport–Rock Island–Moline, IA–IL	1.8	22.6	100.6	244.4	369	1,270.1	3,206.2	165.3	4,642	834	126
Dayton–Springfield, OH	7.9	37.9	306.2	231.2	583	1,661.8	3,768.8	242.5	5,673	1,151	244
Daytona Beach, FL	8.8	57.1	173.4	431.2	671	2,223.4	4,218.1	327.4	6,769	1,347	284
Decatur, IL	1.5	19.0	104.8	203.5	329	1,900.7	3,667.7	113.9	5,682	897	149
Denver, CO	7.6	53.2	233.4	324.8	619	2,065.7	4,861.6	529.7	7,457	1,365	287
Des Moines, IA	5.2	28.1	107.4	199.9	341	1,524.3	5,212.2	294.8	7,031	1,044	209
Detroit, MI	14.0	48.7	462.5	344.2	869	2,211.9	3,748.0	1,213.7	7,174	1,587	314
Dothan, AL	6.5	15.5	76.7	434.0	533	1,235.2	2,579.0	156.6	3,971	930	158
Dubuque, IA	0.0	1.1	37.4	69.5	108	1,162.5	3,275.0	188.1	4,626	571	49
Duluth, MN–WI	3.0	21.4	25.9	51.1	101	956.9	2,696.9	216.9	3,871	488	29
East St. Louis–Belleville, IL	19.0	43.5	142.8	552.8	758	1,170.9	1,920.3	292.4	3,384	1,096	230
★ Eau Claire, WI	2.3	11.3	19.6	54.2	87	691.9	2,670.5	93.4	3,456	433	19
El Paso, TX	8.9	46.8	184.9	562.3	803	1,488.9	3,261.4	452.0	5,202	1,323	277
Elkhart–Goshen, IN	1.5	26.3	30.7	122.7	181	742.7	2,568.4	116.8	3,428	524	37
Elmira, NY	5.1	11.2	48.8	147.3	212	792.4	2,835.4	70.1	3,698	582	50
Enid, OK	12.1	19.6	72.3	182.4	286	1,627.7	3,700.0	254.7	5,582	845	130
Erie, PA	3.2	31.4	121.3	150.9	307	934.4	2,150.7	195.5	3,281	635	64
Eugene–Springfield, OR	5.1	35.6	93.0	115.2	249	1,602.1	4,424.1	228.6	6,255	874	138
Evansville, IN–KY	5.1	25.8	102.3	265.3	399	1,170.3	3,244.8	235.4	4,651	864	135
Fall River, MA–RI	1.3	17.9	106.8	271.3	397	1,493.2	2,492.4	647.0	4,633	861	134
Fargo–Moorhead, ND–MN	0.0	24.9	31.3	65.4	122	663.6	2,972.1	176.9	3,813	503	33
Fayetteville, NC	8.7	54.1	180.0	336.7	580	2,070.2	3,275.8	359.6	5,706	1,150	243
Fayetteville–Springdale, AR	4.0	24.1	37.2	103.6	169	1,085.1	2,474.9	200.1	3,760	545	41
Fitchburg–Leominster, MA	1.1	25.4	68.8	170.5	166	1,198.7	1,397.4	296.5	3,893	655	71
Flint, MI	8.5	56.7	234.0	630.8	930	2,488.9	4,614.3	305.7	7,409	1,671	320
Florence, AL	5.1	10.2	28.3	122.8	166	943.5	2,384.8	172.3	3,501	516	35
Florence, SC	7.0	41.7	168.7	585.1	803	1,707.5	3,305.5	306.0	5,319	1,334	280
Fort Collins–Loveland, CO	1.9	29.4	28.7	137.6	198	1,227.1	4,028.0	205.7	5,461	744	91
Fort Lauderdale–Hollywood– Pompano Beach, FL	13.7	46.0	368.2	376.6	805	2,190.1	4,514.0	613.8	7,318	1,536	310
Fort Myers, FL	5.4	35.1	150.2	226.1	417	1,301.5	2,253.2	150.6	3,705	787	107
Fort Pierce, FL	12.9	59.8	179.9	475.8	728	2,451.5	4,214.0	273.6	6,939	1,422	291
Fort Smith, AR–OK	7.3	31.6	49.9	145.4	234	1,221.2	2,797.7	267.1	4,286	663	73
Fort Walton Beach, FL	7.5	20.1	70.3	147.3	245	796.1	1,975.7	221.0	2,993	544	40
Fort Wayne, IN	7.3	27.2	120.0	110.7	265	822.1	3,377.7	243.3	4,443	710	84
Fort Worth–Arlington, TX	12.6	60.1	263.3	301.6	638	2,109.6	4,404.8	585.9	7,100	1,348	285
Fresno, CA	13.3	56.9	302.2	385.2	758	2,366.6	4,390.9	498.4	7,256	1,483	299

	Violent Crime Rates					Property Crime Rates				Places Rated Score	Places Rated Rank
	Murder	Forcible Rape	Robbery	Aggravated Assault	Total	Burglary	Larceny-Theft	Motor Vehicle Theft	Total		
Metro Area Average	10.0	39.2	298.6	314.7	663	1,669.5	3,436.3	554.3	5,660	1,229	—
Gadsden, AL	7.7	16.3	57.4	254.7	336	1,098.1	2,799.4	230.7	4,128	749	93
Gainesville, FL	10.5	78.8	164.9	680.4	935	2,025.8	4,965.8	246.5	7,238	1,658	319
Galveston–Texas City, TX	10.5	58.6	234.3	346.3	650	1,798.9	3,314.0	521.1	5,634	1,213	265
Gary–Hammond, IN	18.3	49.1	212.3	226.7	506	1,351.2	2,653.6	886.4	4,891	996	187
Glens Falls, NY	1.8	7.2	8.1	225.3	242	911.0	2,199.3	149.3	3,260	568	47
★ Grand Forks, ND	1.5	5.9	16.2	39.8	63	582.0	2,639.0	154.7	3,376	401	12
Grand Rapids, MI	5.7	45.8	125.8	265.3	443	1,310.8	3,588.5	194.9	5,094	952	166
Great Falls, MT	1.2	8.5	59.3	136.7	206	1,294.8	4,131.1	440.5	5,866	792	111
Greeley, CO	6.2	34.6	44.6	321.4	407	1,462.5	4,133.7	279.1	5,875	994	186
Green Bay, WI	0.6	3.9	29.7	84.5	119	734.5	3,754.3	157.9	4,647	583	51
Greensboro–Winston-Salem–High Point, NC	7.2	25.3	106.6	395.3	534	1,355.5	2,754.5	214.7	4,325	967	171
Greenville–Spartanburg, SC	7.6	41.1	101.3	524.2	674	1,468.3	3,352.8	288.7	5,110	1,185	259
Hagerstown, MD	5.2	13.1	47.1	194.4	260	694.7	2,883.7	98.5	3,677	627	57
Hamilton–Middletown, OH	3.1	29.0	106.6	224.0	363	1,486.2	3,596.6	208.2	5,291	892	143
Harrisburg–Lebanon–Carlisle, PA	3.8	20.8	116.2	130.2	271	974.4	2,453.5	149.9	3,578	629	59
Hartford, CT	8.0	27.7	366.4	246.6	649	1,637.9	3,849.3	820.0	6,307	1,279	271
Hickory, NC	8.6	10.6	45.1	366.1	430	1,163.7	2,046.1	141.1	3,351	765	99
Honolulu, HI	3.2	34.3	185.6	50.9	274	1,576.8	4,128.5	465.1	6,170	891	142
★ Houma–Thibodaux, LA	9.5	19.7	53.1	116.9	199	743.7	1,178.5	89.5	2,012	400	10
Houston, TX	28.9	58.7	486.9	218.5	793	2,545.5	3,104.1	1,405.6	7,055	1,499	304
Huntington–Ashland, WV–KY–OH	4.2	20.8	67.9	229.3	322	1,099.1	2,089.6	241.5	3,430	665	74
Huntsville, AL	8.5	32.4	107.5	187.6	336	1,410.0	4,128.4	344.9	5,883	924	157
Indianapolis, IN	8.0	46.6	216.1	220.8	492	1,448.4	3,177.0	462.6	5,088	1,000	192
Iowa City, IA	0.0	23.3	18.4	277.4	319	1,050.7	3,862.8	192.7	5,106	830	125
Jackson, MI	3.3	44.2	85.7	415.7	549	1,312.8	3,196.7	209.5	4,719	1,021	199
Jackson, MS	20.0	39.9	221.7	168.6	450	2,155.0	3,942.2	309.5	6,407	1,091	225
Jacksonville, FL	10.6	52.7	273.5	376.2	713	1,617.2	3,150.3	209.8	4,977	1,211	263
Jacksonville, NC	6.1	19.9	109.1	489.1	624	1,028.3	2,250.5	152.3	3,431	967	171
Janesville–Beloit, WI	1.4	20.2	72.0	174.2	268	1,430.4	4,292.7	178.5	5,902	858	133
Jersey City, NJ	13.2	32.9	498.5	306.0	851	1,875.5	2,717.4	1,239.7	5,833	1,434	293
★ Johnson City–Kingsport–Bristol, TN–VA	4.5	12.8	33.6	109.8	161	791.8	1,642.8	195.4	2,630	424	18
★ Johnstown, PA	2.3	7.5	16.2	153.5	180	614.4	1,010.1	108.6	1,733	353	5
Joliet, IL	6.5	15.5	101.4	268.9	392	1,315.2	2,776.8	354.6	4,447	837	129
Joplin, MO	3.1	10.9	38.9	161.7	215	1,103.4	2,844.3	185.8	4,134	628	58
Kalamazoo, MI	1.9	38.7	81.2	552.7	675	1,058.1	3,279.5	119.4	4,457	1,120	236
Kankakee, IL	6.8	18.4	170.3	247.7	443	1,632.2	3,463.7	231.2	5,327	976	179
Kansas City, KS	7.0	31.1	153.6	376.6	568	1,840.1	3,534.3	364.8	5,739	1,142	242
Kansas City, MO	11.6	49.8	331.8	469.5	863	1,932.1	3,658.9	457.2	6,048	1,468	296
Kenosha, WI	4.0	29.5	151.3	108.3	293	1,557.2	4,227.4	391.7	6,176	911	153
Killeen–Temple, TX	7.8	37.7	112.2	193.6	351	1,220.6	2,405.7	189.7	3,816	733	89
Knoxville, TN	6.8	26.5	110.0	124.7	268	1,242.5	1,840.3	456.0	3,539	622	55
★ Kokomo, IN	3.9	11.6	29.9	69.5	115	814.2	2,020.1	142.8	2,977	413	13
La Crosse, WI	2.2	8.7	12.0	105.8	129	1,045.7	4,272.1	151.6	5,469	676	76
Lafayette, IN	4.1	19.0	33.1	78.7	135	878.7	2,269.9	154.0	3,303	465	26
Lafayette, LA	11.3	40.9	134.5	418.5	605	1,398.7	2,556.9	291.6	4,247	1,030	202
Lake Charles, LA	11.5	32.8	111.0	375.7	531	1,792.8	3,547.6	279.0	5,619	1,093	228
Lake County, IL	3.9	19.6	134.3	212.1	370	1,150.9	3,142.4	231.5	4,525	822	120
Lakeland–Winter Haven, FL	10.3	57.3	154.1	580.3	802	1,621.5	3,808.2	278.2	5,708	1,373	288
★ Lancaster, PA	1.1	9.6	42.7	83.1	137	716.1	1,895.6	154.7	2,766	413	13
Lansing–East Lansing, MI	2.2	59.2	88.4	220.9	371	1,405.1	3,646.2	181.2	5,233	894	147
Laredo, TX	7.5	25.3	111.4	263.0	407	2,104.4	3,943.8	378.2	6,426	1,050	211
Las Cruces, NM	6.1	42.6	111.7	369.6	530	2,258.3	6,620.5	391.9	9,271	1,457	294
Las Vegas, NV	19.8	70.2	603.2	363.8	1,057	3,076.9	4,722.9	757.6	8,557	1,913	326
Lawrence, KS	2.9	30.7	65.7	258.5	358	1,747.0	4,582.1	268.8	6,598	1,018	198
Lawrence–Haverhill, MA–NH	2.5	15.7	93.2	314.0	426	1,586.9	2,371.98	877.3	4,836	909	152

	Violent Crime Rates					Property Crime Rates						
	Murder	Forcible Rape	Robbery	Aggravated Assault	Total	Burglary	Larceny-Theft	Motor Vehicle Theft	Total	Places Rated Score	Places Rated Rank
Metro Area Average	10.0	39.2	298.6	314.7	663	1,669.5	3,436.3	554.3	5,660	1,229	—
Lawton, OK	4.2	62.4	179.7	437.0	683	1,510.2	2,860.9	354.3	4,725	1,156	246
Lewiston–Auburn, ME	3.8	8.9	57.1	205.7	275	1,255.5	3,418.7	215.8	4,890	764	98
Lexington–Fayette, KY	12.6	30.5	147.0	263.8	454	1,547.3	4,144.8	318.6	6,011	1,055	212
Lima, OH	2.0	22.4	108.7	235.1	368	1,338.7	3,383.5	144.1	4,866	855	131
Lincoln, NE	1.0	25.6	50.6	149.4	227	1,146.8	4,270.6	207.7	5,625	789	108
Little Rock–North Little Rock, AR	10.3	57.8	216.0	404.1	688	1,868.5	4,148.4	381.2	6,398	1,328	279
Longview–Marshall, TX	21.6	41.3	111.4	277.3	452	1,650.1	3,221.7	376.7	5,249	976	179
Lorain–Elyria, OH	3.7	18.6	76.4	167.6	266	1,296.0	1,808.6	317.8	3,422	609	53
Los Angeles–Long Beach, CA	18.1	67.7	651.8	532.3	1,270	2,301.2	3,496.8	1,104.2	6,902	1,960	327
Louisville, KY–IN	6.5	28.2	222.9	175.4	433	1,534.2	3,159.1	350.5	5,044	937	160
Lowell, MA–NH	6.4	16.9	110.7	265.3	399	1,126.0	2,458.3	615.6	4,200	819	116
Lubbock, TX	11.4	70.3	143.2	615.7	841	2,479.6	4,790.1	400.2	7,670	1,608	316
Lynchburg, VA	4.8	21.9	34.3	191.3	252	909.9	2,876.5	121.4	3,908	643	66
Macon–Warner Robins, GA	9.9	27.5	91.6	214.8	344	1,075.8	3,007.2	304.6	4,388	783	104
Madison, WI	2.2	26.3	63.2	107.9	200	1,290.5	4,323.6	178.9	5,793	779	102
Manchester, NH	0.8	19.9	57.3	58.8	137	1,168.6	3,410.4	383.4	4,962	633	61
Mansfield, OH	4.6	11.4	139.2	434.9	590	1,532.2	3,049.2	235.0	4,816	1,072	219
McAllen–Edinburg–Mission, TX	5.0	25.2	41.4	324.4	396	1,566.7	2,577.1	275.4	4,399	836	128
Medford, OR	4.5	23.2	48.0	150.0	226	1,248.4	3,596.6	181.4	5,026	728	88
Melbourne–Titusville–Palm Bay, FL	5.8	45.5	84.2	351.8	487	1,613.7	3,626.4	280.2	5,520	1,039	208
Memphis, TN–AR–MS	15.4	83.6	492.0	303.9	895	2,013.0	3,306.6	608.3	5,928	1,488	301
Miami–Hialeah, FL	29.7	55.7	732.7	770.7	1,589	2,471.2	5,331.6	897.8	8,701	2,459	328
Middlesex–Somerset–Hunterdon, NJ	3.0	15.6	205.5	148.2	372	343.5	2,485.4	355.9	3,185	691	80
Middletown, CT	8.2	8.2	43.3	189.7	249	967.0	2,674.1	325.8	3,967	646	67
Midland, TX	18.0	42.8	74.4	465.3	601	1,998.6	3,029.5	623.0	5,651	1,166	251
Milwaukee, WI	5.4	17.8	165.1	126.6	315	1,129.7	3,684.0	301.1	5,115	826	124
Minneapolis–St. Paul, MN–WI	3.2	33.4	181.4	138.0	356	1,611.4	3,559.2	328.8	5,499	906	151
Mobile, AL	16.3	51.6	261.8	504.9	835	2,338.0	4,124.2	297.8	6,760	1,511	306
Modesto, CA	6.1	37.6	116.8	324.6	485	2,017.4	4,363.0	312.4	6,693	1,154	245
Monmouth–Ocean, NJ	2.6	24.4	94.8	233.0	355	1,176.3	3,204.0	266.0	4,646	819	116
Monroe, LA	8.4	37.8	52.5	443.9	543	1,247.6	2,712.2	186.9	4,147	957	168
Montgomery, AL	10.4	19.6	110.6	230.9	372	1,312.8	2,936.1	183.5	4,433	815	115
Muncie, IN	6.3	26.6	87.7	245.1	366	1,029.9	2,936.9	209.9	4,177	783	104
Muskegon, MI	2.6	43.8	138.6	674.4	859	2,002.6	4,596.4	179.2	6,778	1,537	311
★ Nashua, NH	0.7	18.1	41.0	46.5	106	1,006.9	2,263.1	186.8	3,457	452	24
Nashville, TN	11.9	44.5	215.7	209.3	481	1,533.6	3,193.4	303.4	5,030	984	184
Nassau–Suffolk, NY	2.5	8.9	113.4	86.9	212	998.1	2,169.4	375.1	3,543	566	45
New Bedford, MA	0.8	18.0	181.9	291.2	492	1,841.1	2,798.4	566.1	5,206	1,012	194
New Britain, CT	0.7	29.7	213.6	150.7	395	1,328.1	3,339.3	416.9	5,084	903	150
New Haven–Meriden, CT	5.3	23.8	221.2	122.6	373	1,499.4	3,142.7	554.2	5,196	893	146
New London–Norwich, CT–RI	2.9	29.2	72.9	147.8	253	1,054.5	2,502.6	249.5	3,807	633	61
New Orleans, LA	24.0	60.2	497.7	425.5	1,007	1,759.5	3,579.1	630.4	5,969	1,604	315
New York, NY	20.8	45.0	1,180.1	536.3	1,782	2,247.5	3,556.8	1,349.5	7,154	2,498	329
Newark, NJ	8.8	46.0	538.5	383.6	977	1,446.1	2,672.4	726.1	4,845	1,461	295
Niagara Falls, NY	1.8	24.9	137.9	174.6	339	1,218.9	2,844.5	295.4	4,359	775	101
Norfolk–Virginia Beach–Newport News, VA	9.8	39.4	203.1	227.5	480	1,240.8	3,689.0	237.5	5,167	997	188
Norwalk, CT	2.4	19.6	87.8	69.8	180	1,244.9	2,746.8	464.9	4,457	625	56
Oakland, CA	10.2	51.3	356.6	385.9	804	2,125.5	4,693.5	468.8	7,288	1,533	309
Ocala, FL	10.8	34.0	132.2	508.7	686	2,140.9	3,967.8	304.6	6,413	1,327	278
Odessa, TX	29.8	61.2	232.6	372.7	696	3,285.8	5,893.1	834.7	10,014	1,698	322
Oklahoma City, OK	12.6	59.4	240.9	342.4	655	2,205.8	3,439.6	773.4	6,419	1,297	272
Olympia, WA	1.6	41.3	40.6	145.8	229	1,477.9	3,579.6	170.0	5,228	752	94
Omaha, NE–IA	4.8	35.5	138.3	313.5	492	1,295.9	3,559.7	305.3	5,161	1,008	193
Orange County, NY	3.8	13.8	117.9	274.7	410	1,277.6	2,458.4	202.0	3,938	804	112
Orlando, FL	10.4	64.5	269.5	611.5	956	2,448.3	4,316.6	389.8	7,155	1,671	320
Owensboro, KY	4.6	19.7	41.7	86.9	153	1,274.6	2,684.7	195.8	4,155	568	47

	Violent Crime Rates					Property Crime Rates					Places Rated Score	Places Rated Rank
	Murder	Forcible Rape	Robbery	Aggravated Assault	Total	Burglary	Larceny-Theft	Motor Vehicle Theft	Total			
Metro Area Average	10.0	39.2	298.6	314.7	663	1,669.5	3,436.3	554.3	5,660	1,229	—
Oxnard–Ventura, CA	5.8	35.2	136.5	201.0	379	1,387.7	2,431.2	309.0	4,128	791	110
Panama City, FL	10.4	74.7	78.5	591.7	755	1,361.1	4,262.9	264.7	5,889	1,344	283
Parkersburg–Marietta, WV–OH	1.9	15.3	46.4	97.3	161	937.6	2,157.6	176.2	3,271	488	29
Pascagoula, MS	1.9	19.0	90.2	150.1	261	1,254.9	1,879.0	163.4	3,297	591	52
Pawtucket–Woonsocket–Attleboro, RI–MA	5.1	18.2	65.2	159.3	248	1,381.4	2,979.7	598.7	4,960	744	91
Pensacola, FL	8.1	56.8	177.9	635.9	879	1,899.3	3,678.7	352.7	5,931	1,472	297
Peoria, IL	4.9	25.6	121.3	322.2	474	1,258.0	3,069.4	147.2	4,475	921	155
Philadelphia, PA–NJ	10.1	31.5	320.3	265.9	628	1,245.9	2,483.6	579.9	4,309	1,059	214
Phoenix, AZ	8.5	40.1	193.7	297.3	540	2,084.6	4,767.9	427.3	7,280	1,268	269
Pine Bluff, AR	8.8	58.2	183.4	373.5	624	1,878.3	3,368.9	205.4	5,453	1,169	253
Pittsburgh, PA	4.5	21.2	226.9	142.2	395	900.4	1,552.8	461.7	2,915	687	78
Pittsfield, MA	0.0	42.4	41.7	170.2	254	1,370.1	2,206.3	256.4	3,833	638	65
Portland, ME	3.8	23.4	65.4	201.8	294	1,510.2	3,466.0	309.1	5,285	823	122
Portland, OR	5.9	58.8	319.8	371.7	756	2,453.0	4,603.9	424.9	7,482	1,504	305
Portsmouth–Dover–Rochester, NH–ME	4.5	7.9	36.3	69.8	119	900.8	2,457.3	207.0	3,565	475	27
Poughkeepsie, NY	2.0	7.7	114.9	192.5	317	1,016.0	1,999.1	140.5	3,156	633	61
Providence, RI	3.7	22.4	150.9	291.8	469	1,484.4	2,868.2	936.2	5,289	998	189
Provo–Orem, UT	1.3	6.9	25.5	91.6	125	501.6	2,943.8	149.5	3,595	485	28
Pueblo, CO	6.8	39.8	126.3	408.2	581	1,862.7	3,871.3	268.4	6,002	1,181	257
Racine, WI	3.4	18.2	130.5	330.5	483	1,588.5	3,971.3	160.7	5,721	1,055	212
Raleigh–Durham, NC	10.8	32.2	129.7	235.9	409	1,601.3	3,890.1	235.0	5,726	981	182
Reading, PA	2.6	14.7	104.6	126.3	248	797.5	1,794.7	148.9	2,741	522	36
Redding, CA	4.1	36.4	61.3	294.7	397	1,307.0	3,422.8	227.6	4,957	892	143
Reno, NV	7.5	69.3	221.2	206.2	504	1,823.7	3,921.9	367.4	6,113	1,116	235
Richland–Kennewick–Pasco, WA	6.8	24.3	44.6	203.6	279	1,159.8	3,591.6	240.7	4,992	779	102
Richmond–Petersburg, VA	12.3	37.9	237.5	224.7	512	1,692.9	3,696.9	247.1	5,637	1,076	221
Riverside–San Bernardino, CA	9.9	46.4	245.0	457.5	759	2,588.0	4,013.5	557.8	7,159	1,475	298
Roanoke, VA	7.9	13.7	107.3	122.7	252	1,304.0	3,815.9	200.9	5,321	784	106
★ Rochester, MN	0.0	5.4	37.5	46.0	89	809.3	2,537.1	137.0	3,483	437	20
Rochester, NY	4.3	21.5	142.8	215.5	384	1,276.7	3,569.7	248.9	5,095	894	147
Rockford, IL	4.6	22.8	181.1	334.4	543	1,871.8	4,058.8	204.9	6,136	1,156	246
Sacramento, CA	8.1	45.0	273.3	281.9	608	2,239.2	4,773.5	529.0	7,542	1,363	286
Saginaw–Bay City–Midland, MI	7.0	44.1	120.1	351.0	523	1,371.4	3,910.5	174.6	5,457	1,068	218
★ St. Cloud, MN	1.8	10.3	11.5	23.5	47	555.2	2,260.1	143.6	2,959	343	4
St. Joseph, MO	4.5	18.1	65.5	243.8	332	1,698.5	4,441.9	229.1	6,370	969	173
St. Louis, MO–IL	15.5	30.6	326.1	368.7	741	1,778.6	3,321.7	549.1	5,649	1,306	273
Salem, OR	3.2	33.2	80.7	282.9	400	1,592.8	4,302.0	243.3	6,138	1,014	195
Salem–Gloucester, MA	0.0	5.1	43.4	98.1	147	905.2	2,026.8	504.4	3,436	490	31
Salinas–Seaside–Monterey, CA	9.8	39.0	166.8	315.0	531	1,631.7	3,889.2	245.1	5,766	1,107	233
Salt Lake City–Ogden, UT	4.1	32.6	125.5	191.7	354	1,434.9	4,407.3	310.8	6,153	969	173
San Angelo, TX	5.5	42.7	63.5	383.2	495	1,368.6	3,685.3	321.9	5,376	1,032	204
San Antonio, TX	18.5	41.4	207.4	313.9	581	2,047.9	3,586.9	523.5	6,158	1,197	261
San Diego, CA	6.4	43.9	250.8	244.3	545	1,659.5	3,239.4	636.7	5,536	1,099	231
San Francisco, CA	9.9	51.5	548.6	358.0	968	1,625.1	4,282.9	606.2	6,514	1,619	318
San Jose, CA	4.5	49.7	191.0	185.7	431	1,590.7	4,336.6	410.0	6,337	1,065	215
Santa Barbara–Santa Maria–Lompoc, CA	4.8	36.8	102.3	295.1	439	1,569.1	4,029.8	269.2	5,868	1,026	201
Santa Cruz, CA	3.1	30.6	99.3	256.7	390	1,682.3	3,739.1	318.8	5,740	964	169
Santa Rosa–Petaluma, CA	3.6	34.5	87.3	218.8	344	1,595.7	3,763.0	319.1	5,678	912	154
Sarasota, FL	6.0	53.0	103.2	235.5	398	1,559.3	3,642.1	208.7	5,410	939	162
Savannah, GA	16.4	84.8	303.4	430.0	835	2,027.0	5,431.0	339.4	7,797	1,614	317
★ Scranton–Wilkes-Barre, PA	3.6	8.9	42.3	82.0	137	739.5	1,446.8	169.5	2,356	372	6
Seattle, WA	4.4	60.3	184.8	245.7	495	1,910.4	4,481.2	355.1	6,747	1,170	254
★ Sharon, PA	2.3	12.4	35.0	81.6	131	587.7	1,743.5	196.7	2,528	384	8
★ Sheboygan, WI	1.9	5.8	15.6	29.2	53	846.9	3,043.4	80.7	3,971	450	23
Sherman–Denison, TX	9.4	20.8	62.4	454.3	547	1,624.9	3,046.1	209.0	4,880	1,035	206
Shreveport, LA	15.6	45.9	146.2	427.6	635	1,533.7	3,753.0	327.4	5,614	1,197	261

	Violent Crime Rates					Property Crime Rates				Places Rated Score	Places Rated Rank
	Murder	Forcible Rape	Robbery	Aggravated Assault	Total	Burglary	Larceny-Theft	Motor Vehicle Theft	Total		
Metro Area Average	10.0	39.2	298.6	314.7	663	1,669.5	3,436.3	554.3	5,660	1,229	—
Sioux City, IA–NE	4.3	23.0	35.0	133.0	195	1,323.6	4,062.8	253.3	5,640	759	97
Sioux Falls, SD	0.9	18.1	29.9	103.2	152	849.1	3,034.2	153.9	4,037	556	44
South Bend–Mishawaka, IN	4.2	39.3	179.6	165.8	389	1,857.8	4,397.5	240.3	6,496	1,038	207
Spokane, WA	5.1	22.4	96.0	216.2	340	1,525.4	3,513.9	252.0	5,291	869	136
Springfield, IL	2.7	35.7	170.6	429.0	638	1,673.0	3,983.4	210.5	5,867	1,225	268
Springfield, MA	3.5	41.6	109.6	572.9	728	1,668.4	2,640.9	538.0	4,847	1,212	264
Springfield, MO	3.8	33.2	81.7	143.2	262	1,841.0	4,210.5	250.8	6,302	892	143
Stamford, CT	3.0	13.5	197.4	134.6	348	1,331.8	3,107.2	428.1	4,867	835	127
State College, PA	0.9	12.4	33.5	135.9	183	678.6	2,793.1	100.6	3,572	540	39
★ Steubenville–Weirton, OH–WV	2.7	5.5	66.6	114.1	189	767.8	1,345.7	178.9	2,292	418	17
Stockton, CA	19.5	44.4	250.2	309.4	624	2,366.4	4,929.1	417.9	7,713	1,395	289
Syracuse, NY	2.0	21.1	132.2	109.5	265	1,328.6	2,735.4	174.2	4,238	689	79
Tacoma, WA	5.3	67.3	157.8	306.3	537	2,196.7	3,729.4	329.8	6,256	1,162	249
Tallahassee, FL	9.9	54.7	110.4	426.8	602	1,721.8	3,630.8	243.9	5,597	1,161	248
Tampa–St. Petersburg–Clearwater, FL	8.9	61.1	231.1	569.1	870	2,037.7	3,894.5	298.6	6,231	1,493	302
Terre Haute, IN	0.8	15.8	60.9	133.4	211	1,456.0	2,433.3	303.5	4,193	630	60
Texarkana, TX–Texarkana, AR	4.2	20.2	52.3	284.1	361	1,191.0	3,214.0	204.8	4,610	822	120
Toledo, OH	4.1	38.4	238.0	161.1	442	1,583.4	3,615.5	361.5	5,560	998	189
Topeka, KS	3.8	29.3	139.3	250.7	423	1,826.8	3,740.1	194.1	5,761	999	191
Trenton, NJ	5.2	34.9	342.9	214.1	597	1,822.0	3,502.5	518.6	5,843	1,181	257
Tucson, AZ	9.5	55.7	189.6	387.3	642	2,223.0	4,962.8	395.9	7,582	1,400	290
Tulsa, OK	8.2	41.6	167.7	298.0	516	1,825.9	3,200.0	623.5	5,649	1,080	222
Tuscaloosa, AL	6.5	19.4	84.7	401.9	513	1,218.6	3,516.5	275.6	5,011	1,014	195
Tyler, TX	9.5	39.3	113.6	242.5	405	1,605.6	3,590.6	305.8	5,502	955	167
★ Utica–Rome, NY	1.9	8.1	41.3	60.8	112	984.8	1,773.3	123.2	2,881	400	10
Vallejo–Fairfield–Napa, CA	6.1	40.3	114.0	307.2	468	1,348.9	3,383.0	234.4	4,966	964	169
Vancouver, WA	4.5	37.8	66.6	138.7	248	1,628.1	3,184.0	227.5	5,040	752	94
Victoria, TX	8.1	39.2	85.1	329.5	462	2,301.3	3,716.7	282.3	6,300	1,092	226
Vineland–Millville–Bridgeton, NJ	6.7	18.7	135.8	334.3	496	2,026.8	4,003.6	366.4	6,397	1,135	240
Visalia–Tulare–Porterville, CA	13.2	31.1	103.5	394.3	542	1,917.3	3,649.3	334.3	5,901	1,132	239
Waco, TX	17.9	39.1	145.7	334.9	538	1,866.7	4,154.2	264.2	6,285	1,166	251
Washington, DC–MD–VA	10.3	40.7	454.1	274.7	780	1,365.9	3,589.5	413.8	5,369	1,317	276
Waterbury, CT	10.8	20.4	167.4	86.3	285	1,442.0	3,175.1	421.1	5,038	789	108
Waterloo–Cedar Falls, IA	1.9	14.8	51.2	141.3	209	1,213.7	3,502.8	187.0	4,904	700	81
★ Wausau, WI	0.0	16.4	23.4	99.7	140	532.7	2,407.9	87.2	3,028	442	22
West Palm Beach–Boca Raton–Delray Beach, FL	12.5	56.7	261.3	664.3	995	2,501.9	4,896.2	484.2	7,882	1,783	324
★ Wheeling, WV–OH	4.3	11.3	63.9	44.5	124	657.5	1,052.9	127.2	1,838	308	1
Wichita, KS	10.0	51.3	170.7	263.4	495	1,761.7	4,581.8	339.0	6,683	1,164	250
Wichita Falls, TX	14.6	58.5	203.4	305.0	582	1,794.1	3,787.6	389.8	5,972	1,179	255
★ Williamsport, PA	3.4	9.2	31.1	98.4	142	863.4	2,201.0	157.2	3,222	464	25
Wilmington, DE–NJ–MD	3.6	30.0	139.0	367.5	540	1,469.9	3,842.8	433.7	5,746	1,115	234
Wilmington, NC	7.6	37.8	149.3	522.5	717	2,162.7	4,575.7	316.5	7,055	1,423	292
Worcester, MA	2.5	24.9	109.5	181.8	319	1,281.0	1,935.5	395.0	3,611	680	77
Yakima, WA	4.5	50.5	116.3	278.0	449	1,637.6	4,692.1	237.8	6,568	1,106	232
★ York, PA	1.6	11.0	61.5	71.5	146	736.3	2,050.1	158.7	2,945	440	21
Youngstown–Warren, OH	5.5	21.5	167.4	350.6	545	1,285.3	2,268.6	371.7	3,926	938	161
Yuba City, CA	10.3	32.7	68.1	502.0	613	1,899.8	3,493.5	268.7	5,662	1,179	255

Et Cetera

CRIME ON THE DECLINE?

In 1980, the number of crimes reported to the FBI reached the highest level ever recorded in the bureau's 50-year history of collecting crime figures. Two years later, the numbers took another turn—this time for the better, with a 3 percent overall drop in the eight Index crimes from 1981.

Although it is far too early to conclude that crime is on the decline, officials at the FBI are expressing "cautious optimism" about the findings for 1982: murder down 7 percent, forcible rape down 5 percent, robbery 6 percent, burglary 9 percent, larceny-theft 1 percent, motor vehicle theft 2 percent, and arson 12 percent. The only Index crime whose incidence increased was aggravated assault, and that rise was just 1 percent. The rates of both violent and property crime declined by 4 percent. Overall rates for violent and property crime also fell by 5 percent each in the first six months of 1983, the FBI reported.

The National Crime Survey of the Bureau of Justice Statistics came to similar conclusions. The study, based on twice-yearly interviews with about 130,000 victims of crime, found a 7 percent decrease in serious crimes in 1983. Violent crime fell 10 percent and property crime 8 percent. This marked the second year in a row that the bureau's survey and the FBI reports both showed significant declines.

Despite the unanimity of the two studies, there has been controversy about the findings. Many criminologists are skeptical about lower statistics meaning less crime, pointing to flaws in both systems of gathering data. The FBI reports have been faulted for reflecting only crimes already reported to police and for the fact that their data come from local authorities, who may overreport or underreport for their own reasons. And although the Bureau of Justice Statistics survey overcomes these drawbacks by getting information directly from crime victims, it has been criticized because individual perceptions could skew the results; for instance, a citizen from a small town might describe a purse-snatching as a serious crime, whereas a big-city resident would be liable to dismiss it as part of urban life. Both organizations are presently reevaluating their methods in hopes of improving their reliability.

The real test of whether these studies do presage a downswing will be the pattern of crime rates in the next few years. Still, experts have not been loath to offer explanations for the small dip that has occurred. One is the aging of the baby-boom generation, leaving a smaller proportion of the population in the crime-prone range of ages 18 to 24. Another is the fact that citizens are taking a more active interest in the security of their neighborhoods. Also cited are the increasingly rigorous sentences sought by prosecutors and im-posed by judges, and the Justice Department's nation-wide campaign to impose stricter penalties on repeat offenders.

Crime Rates in the Metro Areas

Does this recent drop in crime mean that the 329 metro areas have significantly lower rates than previously? To find out, let's compare these rates with those of the metro areas in the 1981 edition of *Places Rated Almanac*, which used data for 1979. (A note of caution: For two reasons, any comparison of these two sets of data will be imperfect. First, as explained in the Introduction to this book, the names and boundaries of many metro areas have shifted since 1981, so that the exact counterpart of a place described in the earlier edition may no longer exist. Second, unlike the case in this edition, crime data were not available for all the 1981 metro areas; in those places the averages for all metro areas within the state were used.)

As we pointed out early in this chapter, it is unusual for a place's crime rate to alter very much from year to year—safe places tend to remain safe, and dangerous places dangerous. In general, this rule holds true for our 329 metro areas. Of the 15 metro areas that were ranked safest by the 1981 *Places Rated Almanac*, ten also appear in this edition's top 15:

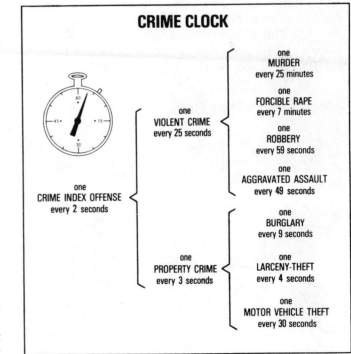

CRIME CLOCK

one
CRIME INDEX OFFENSE
every 2 seconds

one
VIOLENT CRIME
every 25 seconds

one
MURDER
every 25 minutes

one
FORCIBLE RAPE
every 7 minutes

one
ROBBERY
every 59 seconds

one
AGGRAVATED ASSAULT
every 49 seconds

one
PROPERTY CRIME
every 3 seconds

one
BURGLARY
every 9 seconds

one
LARCENY-THEFT
every 4 seconds

one
MOTOR VEHICLE THEFT
every 30 seconds

Source: FBI, *Uniform Crime Reports, 1982,* 1983.

Figures are for 1982.

Altoona, PA   Lancaster, PA
Binghamton, NY   St. Cloud, MN
Grand Forks, ND   Scranton–Wilkes-Barre, PA
Kokomo, IN   Utica–Rome, NY
Johnstown, PA   Wheeling, WV–OH

Likewise, 11 of 1981's fifteen most dangerous metro areas also number among the 15 most crime-ridden places in this edition:

Baltimore, MD   New York, NY
Gainesville, FL   Orlando, FL
Las Vegas, NV   San Francisco, CA
Los Angeles–Long   Savannah, GA
    Beach, CA   West Palm Beach–
Miami–Hialeah, FL   Boca Raton–Delray
New Orleans, LA   Beach, FL

There were, however, a few startling changes in overall rank. Those metro areas that lost the most ground in relative safety, dropping at least 149 places, were the following: Anniston, Alabama (from 74th to 238th); Brockton, Massachusetts (131st to 282nd); Laredo, Texas (62nd to 211th); Midland, Texas (70th to 251st); Odessa, Texas (169th to 322nd); and Sherman–Denison, Texas (52nd to 206th). Four of them owe their descent in the standings to higher violent crime rates: Anniston's rose by 54 percent, Brockton's by 86 percent, Odessa's by 83 percent, and Sherman–Denison's by a spectacular 141 percent. In Laredo and Midland, property crime rates that had jumped 43 percent and 56 percent, respectively, were the culprits.

Why do four Texas metro areas appear in this group? One possible explanation is the explosive growth that has taken place in the state, undermining the social fabric and placing unusual stress on communities and services.

Of those metro areas whose ranks improved since the last edition, only two recorded significantly large changes: Fort Myers, Florida, which went from 233rd place to 107th, and New London–Norwich, Connecticut–Rhode Island, which leapt from 172nd to 61st.

(Johnson City–Kingsport–Bristol, Tennessee–Virginia, and several New England metro areas also improved their rankings considerably, but these changes do not necessarily reflect a true drop in crime since the 1981 ranks of these places were based on state averages, individual metro area data being unavailable.) Fort Myers saw a 64 percent drop in its violent crime rate and a 35 percent dip in its property crime rate, while New London–Norwich recorded a 50 percent decline in violent crime and one of 31 percent in property crime over the same period.

Fort Myers's turnaround, according to the Lee County sheriff's office, was based on two community action programs, Crime Watch and CRIMESTOP. In Crime Watch, police officers train citizens in the basics of observation and reporting, teaching them what events to be suspicious of and which details they should note to help police track down a suspect. The CRIMESTOP program televises reenactments of unsolved felonies, filmed at the actual sites of the crimes, after which viewers who think they may have a lead are urged to call in. New London–Norwich, too, recently instituted programs that enlisted the aid of the community. Their success proves that citizen involvement is essential in fighting crime.

WHAT THE STATES SPEND TO FIGHT CRIME

If a state devotes a lot of money to law enforcement and criminal investigations, chances are that crime levels there are low—right?

Wrong. A close examination of justice expenditures and crime rates in the states reveals just the opposite. For example, Alaska, which leads the states in justice spending, has the ninth highest crime rate in the United States. And West Virginia, which devotes less of its budget to justice activities than all but two of the other 49 states, has the nation's lowest crime rate. In

Justice Spending in the States

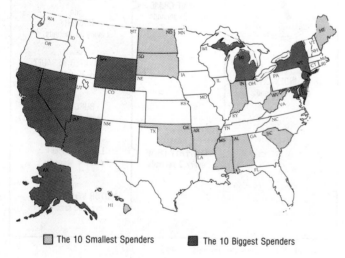

☐ The 10 Smallest Spenders   ■ The 10 Biggest Spenders

Crime in the States

☐ The 10 Most Crime-Free States   ■ The 10 Most Crime-Ridden States

Justice Spending and Crime Rate by State

State	Spending per Capita	Rank	Crime Rate	Rank	State	Spending per Capita	Rank	Crime Rate	Rank
Alabama	$ 65	44	4,134	40	Montana	$ 76	31	4,444	33
Alaska	275	1	6,265	9	Nebraska	78	30	4,019	42
Arizona	124	5	7,295	2	Nevada	150	3	8,104	1
Arkansas	48	50	3,479	44	New Hampshire	70	40	4,453	32
California	132	4	7,289	3	New Jersey	122	6	5,788	16
Colorado	98	16	6,861	6	New Mexico	95	18	5,608	18
Connecticut	93	21	5,808	15	New York	175	2	6,210	11
Delaware	121	7	6,341	8	North Carolina	80	28	4,225	38
Florida	104	15	7,192	4	North Dakota	61	46	2,777	49
Georgia	76	32	5,143	23	Ohio	81	26	5,098	24
Hawaii	108	14	6,981	5	Oklahoma	69	42	4,580	30
Idaho	73	37	4,114	41	Oregon	109	11	6,247	10
Illinois	109	12	5,082	25	Pennsylvania	89	22	3,453	45
Indiana	62	45	4,538	31	Rhode Island	98	17	5,601	19
Iowa	72	38	4,281	36	South Carolina	69	41	4,812	28
Kansas	75	36	4,942	26	South Dakota	66	43	2,960	47
Kentucky	75	34	3,082	46	Tennessee	75	35	3,878	43
Louisiana	93	19	5,212	21	Texas	70	39	5,711	17
Maine	58	47	4,200	39	Utah	79	29	5,302	20
Maryland	120	8	6,184	12	Vermont	76	33	5,163	22
Massachusetts	109	13	5,942	14	Virginia	88	23	4,256	37
Michigan	114	9	6,120	13	Washington	93	20	6,388	7
Minnesota	85	25	4,417	35	West Virginia	53	48	2,252	50
Mississippi	53	49	2,840	48	Wisconsin	87	24	4,439	34
Missouri	81	27	4,919	27	Wyoming	112	10	4,803	29

Source: Bureau of Justice Statistics, *Report to the Nation on Crime and Justice*, October 1983.

general, states with high expenditures have high crime rates, and those with low expenditures have low rates. This correlation indicates that states spend in response to crime rather than in hopes of preventing it.

However, other factors besides the crime rate may be at work. A state may owe a high justice expenditure to the fact that it attracts a great number of tourists and must therefore provide more police services, or to the fact that its criminal justice system is inefficient.

The table "Justice Spending and Crime Rate by State" shows how the states stack up in justice expenditures and crime rates. The figures on justice outlays come from the Bureau of Justice Statistics and are for 1979, the most recent year for which data are available. They represent the per capita amount a state spends each year on law enforcement, prosecution, public defense and adjudication, prisons and other forms of corrections, and such miscellaneous activities as victim compensation and criminal justice planning. The state crime rates, from the FBI *Uniform Crime Reports*, are also for 1979 to present a true comparison.

VICTIMS: ASKING FOR JUSTICE

Everybody wonders what to do about criminals. But only recently has a nationwide wave of anger and frustration addressed the question, What can be done to ease the problems of the victims of crime?

When you become a victim, you may also fall victim to social injustice, police callousness, court delays, and legal tangles. You may even get lost in the human services systems of the country if the crime leaves you hospitalized and unable to work.

Who Are the Victims?

According to the National Crime Survey of the Bureau of Justice Statistics for 1981, the number of crime victims has held fairly steady at an annual rate of about 35 victims per 1,000 people since 1973.

In 1981, men were victims of violent crime in 48 percent of cases, compared with 28 percent for women, and men were robbed or assaulted about twice as often as women. Blacks suffered greater numbers of crimes than whites—50 percent versus 35 percent—although offenders and their victims were generally of the same race.

For crimes of violence or theft, people between the ages of 12 and 24 had the highest victimization rates and those 65 or older the lowest. Members of families in the lowest income category (less than $3,000 a year) had the highest overall rate of victimization of any income group for crimes of violence, and unemployed persons were victimized more often than those who had jobs. The survey also found that victimization

State Aid to Victims of Crime

State	Financial Award	To Qualify, Victim Must . . .		
		Show Financial Need	Report to Police Within	File Claim Within
Alaska	$ 0–40,000	No	5 days	24 mo
California	100–23,000	Yes	*	12
Colorado	25– 1,500	No	3	6
Connecticut	100–10,000	No	5	24
Delaware	25–10,000	No	*	12
District of Columbia	0–25,000	Yes	7	6
Florida	0–10,000	Yes	3	12
Hawaii	0–10,000	No	*	18
Illinois	0–15,000	No	3	12
Indiana	100–10,000	No	2	3
Iowa	0– 2,000	No	1	6
Kansas	100–10,000	Yes	3	12
Kentucky	100–15,000	Yes	2	12
Louisiana	250–10,000	No	3	12
Maryland	100–45,000	Yes	2	6
Massachusetts	100–10,000	No	2	12
Michigan	100–15,000	Yes	2	1
Minnesota	100–25,000	No	5	12
Missouri	200–10,000	No	2	12
Montana	0–25,000	No	3	12
Nebraska	0–10,000	No	3	24
Nevada	100– 5,000	Yes	5	12
New Jersey	100–25,000	No	90	24
New Mexico	0–12,500	No	30	12
New York	0–20,000†	Yes	7	12
North Dakota	100–25,000	No	3	12
Ohio	0–25,000	No	3	12
Oklahoma	0–10,000	No	3	12
Oregon	250–23,000	No	3	6
Pennsylvania	100–25,000	No	3	12
Rhode Island	0–25,000	No	10	24
South Carolina	300–10,000	No	2	6
Tennessee	100–10,000	No	2	12
Texas	0–50,000	Yes	3	6
Virginia	100–10,000	Yes	2	6
Washington	200–15,000†	No	3	12
West Virginia	0–20,000	No	3	24
Wisconsin	0–12,000	No	5	24

Source: State Legislatures, November/December 1981, with additions from the National Organization of Victim Assistance.

*Must report, but no time limit specified.
†Plus unlimited medical expenses.

rates for violent crime were higher among residents of the central cities than among suburbanites or rural dwellers. In two thirds of all violent crimes in 1981, victims were assaulted by people they did not know.

Action for Victims

Most people say that the best way to help a crime victim is to catch the criminal. But it's hard to see how this helps victims who may be injured physically, suffering emotionally, and unable to take up their lives. A number of steps have recently been taken to offer victims more satisfaction.

In 1982, Congress responded to the growing con-

cern for victims' rights by passing the Victim and Witness Protection Act. This act imposes heavy penalties on those who threaten or intimidate a witness, instructs federal judges to study a crime's impact upon the victims before passing sentence, and requires many of those convicted to make restitution to their victims.

A restitution law was enacted at the federal level in 1982. Restitution takes three forms: service to the community, service to the victim, or financial payment. Someone found guilty of driving under the influence, for example, might be assigned to work a certain number of hours in a hospital emergency room, observing the results of drunk driving firsthand and also aiding the community. An offender might also be required to pay the victim a stipulated amount or to perform a service for the victim.

Thirty-seven states and the District of Columbia operate programs that compensate victims of violent crime (see the table "State Aid to Victims of Crime"). The funds distributed by the states come from a variety of sources. General revenues, fines, and penalties collected by the state are usually tapped for this purpose. Several states draw a small percentage of the salaries earned by offenders on work release or in prison, and others claim defendants' profits from the sale of books or films based on their criminal exploits.

Another move on behalf of victims was made in California in 1981, when Proposition 8—or Prop 8, as the victims' bill of rights is known—was passed into law by 56 percent of the vote. Some of its provisions were for the elimination of plea bargaining in felony cases, for longer sentences for habitual criminals, and for the admission of previously excluded evidence.

But Prop 8 has not worked the way it was intended. Some attorneys for accused criminals say Prop 8 has actually helped their clients, saving them from what ordinarily would have been convictions. Judges and prosecutors report that there is little evidence of greater number of convictions or of longer sentences. And court officials in some jurisdictions—notably Orange County—claim that the elimination of plea bargaining has aggravated the backlog of criminal cases.

LIFE BEHIND BARS

A cost of crime not often considered by the general public is the drain on society that occurs *after* the crime has been committed and *after* sentence has been passed—incarceration. Not only does society lose these convicts as full-time members of the work force, but it must also foot the ever-increasing bill for their imprisonment.

Prison Populations

As of 1983, there were approximately 432,000 inmates in America's 50 federal prisons, 600 state prisons, and 3,900 county and city jails. California, the nation's most populous state, also had the biggest prison population as of mid-1983—just over 37,000. Texas was a close second, its inmate population falling slightly below that mark, while New York (30,000) and Florida (28,000) ranked third and fourth.

If we look beyond prisons and consider all forms of correctional sanction, we find that 2.4 million people—more than 1 percent of the U.S. population—are under some correctional care, custody, or supervision. This figure translates to 1.2 percent of all adults over 18 and one in every 45 adult men.

The numbers are large—and getting larger. The nationwide prison population has doubled since 1973 and jumped by 23 percent since 1982. In 1972, the rate of incarceration across the country was 93 per 100,000 people; it was 177 per 100,000 in 1983, the highest such rate since the government began keeping records in 1925.

The following states, according to the Bureau of Justice Statistics, have seen staggering increases in their numbers of prisoners between the end of 1981 and the end of 1982: Alaska and North Dakota, 28 percent; Nevada, 25 percent; New Mexico, 23 percent; Oklahoma, 21 percent; and Hawaii, 18 percent. Since 1980, Arizona's inmate population has doubled.

Such increases may seem strange considering that the national crime rate has been declining since 1980. Most criminologists attribute them to recent changes made by state legislatures in sentencing. Nearly all states now require some sort of mandatory sentencing, which means that certain offenses automatically mean doing time. Increasing the length of minimum sen-

tences has also compounded the problem, as have the adoption in ten states of determinate sentencing (basing offenders' sentences on the seriousness of their crimes and on their records) and the straitening of parole-release laws in another dozen states.

Over the Limit

This trend has had immediate and obvious results. With record numbers of prisoners outstripping the resources of jails, inmates in prisons all over the country have been given makeshift cells in corridors, tents, trailers, and gymnasiums. Overcrowding has also meant, in many cases, the suspension of work and education programs for prisoners, leaving them almost exclusively confined to their cells. At San Quentin, California, where the official capacity of 2,700 inmates has been exceeded by 1,200, living conditions are so bad that its warden has described the state prison as a "time bomb."

This phrase might well apply to a great many other institutions, where the situation is such that guards cannot always protect inmates from each other. In 1980, for example, 39 percent of all deaths that occurred behind bars resulted from murder or "unknown causes," according to the Bureau of Justice Statistics. New York State (which includes the infamous Attica Correctional Facility) recorded 40 deaths from unknown causes, Texas 50 such deaths, and New Mexico 39 murders during that year.

FIREARMS AND CRIME

Although many claim that people rather than guns kill people, it is undisputable that the weapons most commonly used by murderers are firearms. In 1982, according to the FBI, 60 percent of all homicides were committed with either a handgun, shotgun, or rifle.

The handgun is often portrayed as the favorite weapon of the criminal. Easily concealed and extremely lethal, it was by far the most frequently used gun in 1982 homicides, being employed in 43 percent of all such deaths. In 1980, the FBI reported, handguns were used in some 220,000 robberies and 157,000 aggravated assaults. Sixty-six percent of law enforcement officers killed in that same year were slain with handguns. In fact, although handguns make up only 20 percent of the firearms in this country, they account for 90 percent of all firearms misuse, criminal or accidental.

Ownership of Guns

The table "Who Are the Firearms Owners?" provides a portrait of the Americans who own handguns or long guns (rifles or shotguns), based on a 1978 survey of 1,500 people. The majority of handgun owners in this study were white, male, 36 to 45 years old, graduates of technical or vocational schools, and residents of rural areas of the South. Self-avowed conservative Americans owned the greatest percentage of hand-

---

Death Row, U.S.A.

The same tough stance recently taken by the judiciary that has contributed to prison overcrowding has also meant a greater willingness to impose the death penalty. As of May 1984 there were 1,351 inmates awaiting execution in the United States, a 27 percent increase over 1982 and the greatest such total ever. Thirty-eight states had the death penalty in mid-1984.

Almost two thirds of those on death row at that time were in southern prisons, with Florida (214), Texas (172), and Georgia (115) reporting the highest totals. The western states recorded approximately another 20 percent of inmates sentenced to death, or 269 prisoners; 157 of these were imprisoned in California. The North Central states had about 11 percent of the total (143), and the northeastern states about 5 percent (62).

Of those 1,351 prisoners awaiting execution, according to the NAACP Legal Defense and Educational Fund, Inc., 701 were white, 562 black, 68 Hispanic, 15 American Indians, and four Asians (the race of one inmate was unknown to NAACP). Only 18 of them were women.

Who Are the Firearms Owners?

	"Does anyone living in this immediate household own a handgun or pistol or not?"			"How about a long gun—such as a rifle or shotgun—does anyone own one of those or not?"		
	Yes	No	Not Sure	Yes	No	Not Sure
National Average	**24%**	**72%**	**4%**	**36%**	**62%**	**3%**
Sex						
Male	29	67	4	43	55	2
Female	19	77	4	28	68	3
Race						
White	25	72	3	39	59	2
Black	23	69	9	20	75	5
Education						
Some grade school	21	72	6	23	72	5
Some high school	23	71	6	41	56	3
High school graduate	24	74	2	38	62	1
Technical/vocational	32	64	4	47	47	6
Some college	28	70	2	36	63	2
College graduate	22	73	5	28	68	4
Graduate/professional	20	72	8	42	54	4
Income						
Under $4,000	14	81	5	21	77	2
$4,000 to $6,999	21	76	2	23	75	1
$7,000 to $9,999	21	76	4	29	69	2
$10,000 to $12,999	21	78	1	37	62	1
$13,000 to $14,999	23	73	4	38	59	3
$15,000 to $19,999	24	74	2	40	59	1
$20,000 to $24,999	35	63	2	49	49	2
$25,000 and over	30	69	1	45	55	0
Age						
18 to 25 years	21	76	4	34	62	3
26 to 35 years	25	72	4	37	61	2
36 to 45 years	30	68	3	44	55	1
46 to 55 years	29	68	4	41	56	2
56 to 65 years	22	76	3	36	62	2
66 years and older	23	74	4	24	73	3
Community size						
Urban	23	72	6	29	68	3
Suburban	22	76	2	32	66	2
Rural	31	66	4	56	43	1
Region						
Northeast	15	84	1	31	69	0
Industrial	17	78	5	32	65	3
Midlands	16	83	1	38	61	1
South	41	50	9	39	56	5
Central	34	64	2	53	46	2
Pacific	19	80	2	25	74	2
Religion						
Protestant	29	66	5	40	57	3
Catholic	18	81	1	29	70	1
Jewish	11	89	0	20	80	0
Other	17	82	1	32	67	1
None	24	71	5	37	59	5
Politics						
Liberal	20	76	4	31	67	2
Moderate	25	73	3	38	60	2
Conservative	27	70	4	40	58	2

Source: Cambridge Reports, Inc., *An Analysis of Public Attitudes Toward Handgun Control,* 1978. Reprinted by permission.

guns (27 percent), but 20 percent of those people calling themselves liberals owned them, too.

In the case of long guns, the percentage of ownership rose with income up to $25,000 and then fell off slightly. This percentage was nearly twice as high among whites as among blacks, and was highest in rural areas of what the survey designated the Central region, among men between 36 and 45, and among those with technical or vocational degrees.

State Laws on Handguns

As of March 1982, thirty-six states had a constitutional provision allowing the ownership of handguns. But 41 of the states also had at least two requirements that had to be met before an adult could purchase or carry a handgun, such as undergoing a waiting period or obtaining a license or permit. In several states—Alaska, Kentucky, Nevada, and Oklahoma, for example—the restrictions were minimal, while in such states as Hawaii, Illinois, Massachusetts, and New York they were comprehensive.

Both statewide and national movements urging further control of the sale of handguns have been formed in recent years. Their members cite not only the roughly 11,000 Americans murdered each year by this weapon but also the 1,300 accidental fatalities and 10,000 suicides in which it is involved yearly. Proponents of further restrictions point to the success that legislation banning the sale of handguns has had in reducing murder rates in Boston, the District of Columbia, and South Carolina.

On the other side of the issue are sportsmen, hunters, collectors, and many other law-abiding citizens who use and own handguns. They claim that to disarm honest citizens through gun laws only stacks the odds more in favor of criminals who will not obey such laws.

DRIVING UNDER THE INFLUENCE

Not all criminals rob banks or commit murder; you might even be one yourself, if you drink and then drive. People who do so may not get caught every time they break the law, any more than speeders do, but they are criminals just the same. And when they do get caught, it's usually because their crime has had a devastating impact.

The Deadly Statistics

The damage done by those who drive under the influence adds up to some sobering figures: more than 25,000 deaths a year and $5 billion a year lost. Drunk drivers are estimated to cause between 50 percent and 90 percent of all traffic fatalities.

About one of every 50 drivers on the highway at any given time is likely to be legally drunk, and that proportion rises to one in ten on weekend nights. On an average day, intoxicated drivers kill 70 people, one every 20 minutes. Many of them don't think they are drunk—they just had a couple of drinks at a party, that's all.

To be considered legally drunk in most states, a person must have the equivalent of .10 percent alcohol in their blood. Someone who weighs about 150 pounds will attain that level with five drinks over two and a half hours. A drink, strictly defined, is the equivalent of one-half ounce of pure alcohol, found in one mixed drink, one 12-ounce can of beer, or one four-ounce glass of wine. To reach the .05 percent level, the upper limit set by some states, all it takes is three drinks within an hour and a half.

More than half of those persons charged with drunk driving are men between the ages of 18 and 40. The largest group arrested is men between the ages of 25 and 40, the second largest men between 18 and 25. And, although drivers under age 21 represent about 10 percent of all licensed drivers and drive only 9 percent of all vehicle miles driven, they account for fully 21 percent of alcohol-related fatalities.

U.S. Drinking Ages

Because of the large percentages of young people involved in such accidents, 29 of the 35 states that had lowered their drinking ages in the early 1970s have raised them again. The following information, dated June 1984, comes from the National Transportation Safety Board.

In 23 states, a person must be 21 years old to purchase or consume any alcoholic beverage (Nebraska's law will go into effect on July 1, 1985):

Alaska	Marlyland	Oklahoma
Arizona	Michigan	Oregon
Arkansas	Missouri	Pennsylvania
California	Nebraska	Rhode Island
Delaware	Nevada	Tennessee
Illinois	New Jersey	Utah
Indiana	New Mexico	Washington
Kentucky	North Dakota	

In 19 states, the legal minimum age for buying or consuming any alcoholic beverage is 18, 19, or 20:

Alabama (19)	Minnesota (19)
Connecticut (20)	Montana (19)
Florida (19)	New Hampshire (20)
Georgia (19)	New York (19)
Hawaii (18)	Texas (19)
Idaho (19)	Vermont (18)
Iowa (19)	West Virginia (19)
Louisiana (18)	Wisconsin (19)
Maine (20)	Wyoming (19)
Massachusetts (20)	

Three states allow only 3.2 percent beer to people under 21 (Colorado, Kansas, and South Dakota); in two places the legal minimum age for beer and table wine is 18, and 21 for fortified wine and distilled spirits (the District of Columbia and Mississippi); and three states require buyers to be at least 19 for beer and 21 for wine and distilled spirits (North Carolina, Ohio, and Virginia). In South Carolina a person must be at least 20 to purchase beer and wine, and 21 to buy distilled spirits.

In July 1984, a federal law was enacted to penalize states that allow drinking by people under 21; the bill would also reward states with mandatory sentences for drunk drivers. Both penalties and rewards are to be distributed in the form of federal highway funds.

Transportation:
Getting In, Out, & Around

Jaded travelers take for granted the vast networks of Interstate highways, airline routes, and Amtrak rails that lace up this country's different points. A look at a national map shows certain metro areas to be hubs with many highway, rail, and air-route spokes, while others appear as lesser intersections, removed from the mainstream of intercity travel.

Population size has something to do with an area's transportation assets, and so do the hazards of geography. There are 26 metro areas larger than Denver, for example, but because the Mile High City is plunked down at the edge of the Rocky Mountains halfway between Chicago and Southern California, and midway from Houston to Seattle, only five airports are busier than Denver's Stapleton International.

Intercity travel is only one part of the picture, of course. Some metro areas have efficient and inexpensive public transit systems relied on by hundreds of thousands of commuters each working day. In other metro areas, older fleets of transit buses with optimistic schedules lurch along routes that rarely reach any neighborhoods but those close to downtown. Still other metro areas have no public transit at all; their residents must get around by car, depending on expressways, commercial arteries, and residential streets.

GETTING AROUND TOWN

If you are moving to El Paso, can your family get by without a second car? If you are being transferred to your employer's headquarters in Cleveland, will it be more convenient to carpool or to use public transportation if you settle in the suburb of Shaker Heights? How much time might you need to spend each day getting to and from work? Becoming familiar with the local transportation features of a particular metro area will help you answer some of these questions.

The Commuting Life

Every weekday morning, in cities and towns all over the country, traffic trickles out of suburban streets, flows into arterial roads, and floods freeways to capacity with people bound for work. According to most transportation experts, the morning rush hour lasts 118 minutes, between 7:01 and 8:59. Most workers travel by automobile, alone; one out of five belongs to a car pool; and one out of 15 opts for public transit.

The evening rush hour lasts longer, 150 minutes, from 4:30 to 7:00. There are more traffic delays at this time than in the morning, when people so purposefully leave home and arrive at work in the shortest possible time. In the evening, many commuters stop for a drink, go shopping, run errands, or just dawdle. After all, one can't be fired for being late for supper. In fact, traffic experts say, even if you head straight home, the evening trip not only seems longer than the trip to work, it actually is—20 percent longer.

How much time do metro area dwellers spend going to and from work each day? To allow for the longer trip home in the evening, *Places Rated* multiplies the average journey-to-work figure by 2.2 to estimate the round-trip time in each of the metro areas. As you might suspect, daily commuting time increases with city size. Workers in Grand Forks, North Dakota, for instance, putting in 230 working days a year, spend about 110 hours commuting. New Yorkers spend 310 hours. The contrast between Grand Forks and New York, then, is more than one between a prairie college town and the nation's largest city. Based on commuting time alone, Grand Forkers have more free time than New Yorkers, the equivalent of five 40-hour weeks.

Getting to Work and Back

Shortest Commuting Time	Minutes per Day*	Longest Commuting Time	Minutes per Day*
1. Grand Forks, ND	28.6	1. New York, NY	81.0
2. Bismarck, ND	30.8	2. Nassau–Suffolk, NY	70.6
2. Rochester, MN	30.8	3. Washington, DC–MD–VA	64.5
4. Fargo–Moorhead, ND–MN	31.5	4. Monmouth–Ocean, NJ	64.0
4. Lawton, OK	31.5	5. Chicago, IL	63.8
6. Lafayette, IN	31.7	6. Houston, TX	58.5
6. Sheboygan, WI	31.7	7. Baltimore, MD	58.3
8. Appleton–Oshkosh–Neenah, WI	32.3	8. Jersey City, NJ	57.6
8. Sioux Falls, SD	32.3	9. Philadelphia, PA–NJ	56.3
10. Sioux City, IA–NE	32.6	10. New Orleans, LA	55.9
		10. Newark, NJ	55.9

Source (for journey-to-work figures): U.S. Bureau of the Census, *1980 Census of Population and Housing.*

Places Rated multiplies journey-to-work minutes by a factor of 2.2 to estimate round-trip daily commuting time.

Public Mass Transit

One reason for the long commute in big cities is the often onerous job of making linked transit trips to get to work. Nationally, the average duration of an *unlinked* transit trip—a direct route, with no transfers—is 15 minutes. But many big-city commuters have to make *linked* trips—driving to a park-and-ride lot; boarding a train, tram, or bus; and sometimes switching again before finally arriving at work.

Nevertheless, in larger cities where the tab for daily parking in a downtown garage tops ten dollars, where rush hour traffic jams approach grid-lock, where distances are long and time always seems short, public transit really counts. In three of our largest cities— Houston, Los Angeles, and Phoenix—daily driving over long distances is a way of life unrelieved by rapid public transit; taking the bus is the only alternative. In other places such as Atlanta, Washington, and San Francisco, large local bus fleets are complemented by rapid transit rail systems.

Depending on where they want to go, New York City commuters can choose from bus, heavy rail, light rail, commuter railroad, ferryboat, and even aerial tramway service. New York straphangers may not always enjoy their subway ride to work, but few among the jostled riders aboard a rocking, grimy IRT car would ever envy a Houston driver who has missed his or her exit on the Southwest Freeway at rush hour.

Metro Areas with No Public Transit

Anniston, AL	Jacksonville, NC
Bismarck, ND	Joplin, MO
Brazoria, TX	Kankakee, IL
Bryan–College Station, TX	Kokomo, IN
Burlington, NC	Las Cruces, NM
Casper, WY	Lawton, OK
Clarksville–Hopkinsville, TN–KY	Longview–Marshall, TX
Dothan, AL	Ocala, FL
Elkhart–Goshen, IN	Odessa, TX
Enid, OK	Pascagoula, MS
Fayetteville–Springdale, AR	Richland–Kennewick–Pasco, WA
Florence, AL	Sharon, PA
Fort Smith, AR–OK	Sherman–Denison, TX
Gadsden, AL	Texarkana, TX–Texarkana, AR
Great Falls, MT	Victoria, TX
Houma–Thibodaux, LA	Yuba City, CA
Huntsville, AL	

Source: *Places Rated* survey, April 1984.

The Mass Transit Quarter

Public transit is available in most cities, but it is an option passed up by 93 out of every 100 persons who commute to work because the operating schedule isn't convenient, the system doesn't reach the workplace, or because they prefer the freedom of their own car. In only 17 of the 945 cities with populations over 25,000 does at least one in four workers use public transit.

City	Commuters Using Public Transit
1. New York, NY	56%
2. San Francisco, CA	39
3. Washington, DC	38
4. Boston, MA	34
4. Jersey City, NJ	34
6. Chicago, IL	32
7. Philadelphia, PA	30
8. Cambridge, MA	28
8. Mount Vernon, NY	28
8. Oak Park, IL	28
8. Somerville, MA	28
12. Evanston, IL	27
13. Hoboken, NJ	26
13. Newark, NJ	26
15. Atlanta, GA	25
15. Baltimore, MD	25
15. Rockville Centre, NY	25

Source: U.S. Bureau of the Census, *1980 Census of Population and Housing.*

By Bus. In most cities, public transit and "the bus" are synonymous. Unlike rapid rail and trolley networks, a bus system requires no expensive construction, and routes can be easily changed to meet demand.

Each of the country's 1,022 public transit systems puts motor buses on the street, but transit systems do vary in size and type of operation. Several large systems—CTA (Chicago), Southern California RTD (Los Angeles), WMATA (Washington, D.C.), and NYCTA (New York), for example—operate more than 2,000 buses each, 24 hours a day, with less than one minute between buses on the heaviest routes during morning and evening rush hours. At the other extreme are the one- and two-bus "shoppers' specials" that run loops in the central business district of smaller metro areas.

On the Tracks. Although buses can meet the demand for public transit nearly everywhere, rail lines are more efficient in carrying large numbers of rush hour commuters in the major cities. Several kinds of rail service are available in the big metro areas, from rapid rail to trolley car to commuter train.

Rapid rail lines, owing to their exclusive rights-of-way, are unaffected by traffic jams. Their trains and trams not only carry hundreds of people, they carry them quickly: The average speed of buses during peak rush hour, nationwide, is 11.8 miles per hour. Rapid rail systems average more than 20 miles per hour. There are two types of rapid rail lines in use today in 15 metro areas: heavy rail, which accounts for 2.5 billion passenger trips in a year, and light rail, which accounts for 150 million passenger trips. Both are electrically powered, and both may be found in the same city.

Heavy rail systems—known locally as subways, elevated railways, or Els—have high-level platform stations. The cars are individually powered through the third rail, and are hitched together to form longer trains during rush hours. New York City's heavy rail system, composed of two separate networks, is the world's largest, with 6,263 cars traveling more than 450 miles of track; Philadelphia also has two systems. As of January 1984, ten U.S. metro areas have heavy rail systems:

Atlanta, GA	Oakland, CA
Boston, MA	Philadelphia, PA–NJ
Chicago, IL	(2 systems)
Cleveland, OH	San Francisco, CA
New York, NY	Seattle, WA
(2 systems)	Washington, DC–MD–VA

Light rail cars, powered by overhead electrical wires, travel at half the speed of heavy rail cars. Because their tracks are laid above ground, they are less expensive to build and therefore are the fastest-growing form of mass transit, currently being planned in 19 cities. Nine metro areas now have light rail transit:

Rating the Transit Supply

Totting up all of the local buses, rapid rail cars, and trolley coaches will give you the size of a metro area's transportation fleet, but that isn't an accurate measure of transit supply.

A better indicator can be found if you take the number of passengers that a fleet's vehicles can carry at one time, multiply that number by the miles the fleet runs up each day in service, and then divide by the number of people living in the metro area's urban part. The result is known as seat miles per capita.

In Madison, there are slightly more than six bus seats traveling one mile of route for every person in the Wisconsin capital's urbanized area, the best single-mode transit supply of any metro area. But the ultimate record for transportation supply goes to New York. If all vehicles were put in service at the same time, this metro area's multimode fleet would provide more than 23 seat miles for each resident. Not surprisingly, New York is the only city in the United States where a majority of commuters use public transit.

The Top 10 Metro Areas for Bus Transit Supply

Metro Area	Buses	Seat Miles per Capita
1. Madison, WI	193	6.02
2. Duluth, MN–WI	101	5.08
2. Santa Cruz, CA	94	5.08
4. Honolulu, HI	406	4.64
5. Portland, OR	649	4.21
6. Boulder–Longmont, CO	55	3.99
6. San Jose, CA	745	3.99
8. Portland, ME	63	3.92
9. Atlantic City, NJ	35	3.88
10. Minneapolis–St. Paul, MN–WI	1,012	3.77

The Top 10 Metro Areas for Bus and Rapid Rail Transit Supply

Metro Area	Seat Miles per Capita
1. New York, NY	23.49
2. San Francisco, CA	11.68
3. Washington, DC–MD–VA	8.81
4. Oakland, CA	7.18
5. Cleveland, OH	6.42
6. Seattle, WA	6.37
7. Boston, MA	5.60
8. Atlanta, GA	4.95
9. Chicago, IL	4.68
10. Philadelphia, PA–NJ	3.79

Source: Derived from U.S. Department of Transportation, Urban Mass Transportation Administration, *National Urban Mass Transportation Statistics—Section 15 Report,* 1984.

The average transit supply in the metro areas is 2.43 seat miles per capita.

Atlanta, GA	Newark, NJ
Boston, MA	Philadelphia, PA–NJ
Cleveland, OH	Pittsburgh, PA
Detroit, MI	San Francisco, CA
New Orleans, LA	

Trolley coaches are street car–type railways that travel on city streets with semiprivate or exclusive rights-of-way. They are a less efficient form of travel than rapid rail since the trams are at the mercy of automobile traffic and, in some cities, must stop for streetlights. Another disadvantage is that their routes cannot be altered. These systems have been largely replaced by bus; in fact, only five metro areas in the United States have trolley coach operations:

Boston, MA
Dayton–Springfield, OH
Philadelphia, PA–NJ
San Francisco, CA
Seattle, WA

Commuter railroads have been an important form of transportation from more distant suburbs to the central part of major cities since the nineteenth century. Using both locomotive-hauled and self-propelled passenger cars, this service is characterized by multitrip tickets, station-to-station fares, railroad employment practices, and usually only one or two stations in the central business district. Eighteen commuter railroads in 11 metro areas ferry more than a million commuters to and from work. The largest commuter railroad network, made up of seven firms, is found in New York and uses 2,500 cars to move 525,000 riders in a typical weekday. In Chicago, the next largest commuter railroad center, nine carriers operating 850 cars transport 290,000 workers in a typical day.

Freeway Traffic

Just as most metro area commuters have a car all to themselves on the way to work, most of them drive part of the way on a functionally classified urban freeway, that is, a divided highway with fully controlled access points. The extent to which a metro area is drawn tight by ribbons of freeway is governed by its land area and population. Los Angeles is regarded as a place overburdened with concrete, partly because so many of the innovations of limited-access, high-speed arterial road construction—ramps, trumpets, and cloverleafs—were seen early in Southern California.

In U.S. cities, the length of urban freeways amounts to 3.24 percent of the total road and street mileage. If you look at freeways in this way, Los Angeles may be undeserving of its reputation as the Freeway City since limited-access divided highways there make up only 2.3 percent of the total road mileage.

Nine metro areas have no freeways, and those that have them differ in the amount of traffic their freeways must accommodate. In 21 metro areas, traffic volume averages 90 percent or more of the capacity of the freeways. Most of these congested freeways are in major metro areas or in the East: Seven of the 21 are in the New York–Northern New Jersey–Long Island consolidated area. Surprisingly, traffic volume is also very heavy in some of the less populated metropolitan areas, including Olympia, Washington, and Anchorage, Alaska.

Most Congested Metro Areas

Allentown–Bethlehem, PA	Los Angeles–Long Beach, CA
Anchorage, AK	Middlesex–Somerset–
Atlanta, GA	Hunterdon, NJ
Austin, TX	Monmouth–Ocean, NJ
Bergen–Passaic, NJ	New Orleans, LA
Birmingham, AL	New York, NY
Cleveland, OH	Newark, NJ
Denver, CO	Olympia, WA
Detroit, MI	Orange County, NY
Houston, TX	San Antonio, TX
Jersey City, NJ	Wilmington, DE–NJ–MD

Traffic volume on the freeways in these metro areas averages 90% or more of design capacity.

INTERCITY TRAVEL

"You can't get there from here" is the punch line of the old joke about the lost city feller who asked directions of a bemused farmer. The line has little meaning in today's metropolitan areas, given the networks of well-traveled highways, railroads, and airways that connect these places.

Or does it? Obviously, you can neither take to the Interstate nor board a train if your destination is Anchorage or Honolulu. For that matter, you can't get to Bloomington, Indiana; Bremerton, Washington; or Burlington, North Carolina, by the same means. When it comes to intercity travel choices, some metro areas are better off than others.

Interstate Highways

When President Franklin Roosevelt idly penciled three east-west and five north-south lines on a U.S. map back in 1938 as part of a proposed national highway system, he probably had no idea that his drawing would be so important in determining whether many rural towns would grow and many others would decline. He envisioned a 34,000-mile network of multilane toll roads. Although the concept of collecting tolls was soon dropped by the Bureau of Public Roads, the basic routes on his map foresaw the Interstate Highway System, a river of economic life to cities and towns along the way and possibly a cause of stagnation for those that were bypassed.

The Interstate system is now an almost complete 42,500-mile road network, at least four traffic lanes wide, that spans 48 states and links together nearly every city with a population of more than 50,000. Still, 60 of our metro areas are not on the Interstate network. Even though Interstate routes account for only 1 percent of all road and street mileage in the United States, they carry 25 percent of all the traffic. As the car is the dominant means of intercity travel, so the dominant road is the Interstate.

On any given day, Americans drive more than 870 million miles on Interstate highways. Three out of ten of all those miles are logged in just four states: California, Illinois, Ohio, and Texas. The heaviest traffic can be found on the stretches of the Interstate system that are classified as urban. These cloverleafed freeways, spurs, and beltways in and around cities carry 55 percent of all the travel. The balance is borne by the long, often boringly straight rural routes that make up 77 percent of Interstate mileage.

Busiest Stretches of Interstate Highways

I–5, I–210, I–405, I–605 in Los Angeles, CA
I–5 in Seattle, WA
I–10, I–45, I–59, I–610 in Houston, TX
I–25 in Denver, CO
I–35E, I–635 in Dallas, TX
I–75 in Atlanta, GA
I–80, I–580 in Oakland, CA
I–80, I–380 in San Francisco, CA
I–90, I–94, I–290 in Chicago, IL
I–95 in New York, NY
I–280 in San Jose, CA
I–395 in Washington, DC–MD–VA

Loneliest Stretches of Interstate Highways

I–15 between Idaho Falls, ID, and Butte, MT
I–25 between Buffalo, WY, and Casper, WY
I–29 between Grand Forks, ND, and the Canadian border
I–29 between Sioux Falls, SD, and Fargo–Moorhead, ND
I–70 between Cove Fort, Utah, and the Colorado border
I–90 between Buffalo, WY, and Gillette, WY
I–91 between Derby Line, VT, and St. Johnsbury, VT
I–94 between Billings, MT, and the North Dakota border

According to the U.S. Department of Transportation, the busiest stretches on the Interstate carry 150,000 to 250,000 vehicles every 24 hours. The loneliest carry fewer than 2,500.

Decoding the Interstate System

The numbers in the middle of the red-white-and-blue, shield-shaped signs along the Interstate system were developed in 1957 by the American Association of State Highway Transportation Officials. There are 34 odd-numbered routes, which run north and south, and 27 even-numbered routes, which run east and west. The lowest-numbered routes are in the West and the South; I–5, for example, lies along the nation's West Coast and I–10 along the southern border.

In cities, these one- or two-digit numbers don't change as long as they are part of the major traffic stream. Beltways around the city, on the other hand, carry three numbers: the main route number with an even-numbered prefix. For example, I–495, an 88-mile-long route around Boston, and I–287, a 94-mile-long loop skirting New York City, are the two longest beltways in the Interstate system. If a main route carries an odd-numbered prefix (such as I–195 in Miami or I–780 in San Francisco), the route is a spur that connects with the main route at only one end.

Three-digit route numbers are never used twice in the same state. In New York, I–90 runs through Schenectady, Syracuse, Rochester, and Buffalo, and the beltways off this main route in those cities are numbered, respectively, I–890, I–690, I–490, and I–290. This rule isn't carried across state lines, however. Two cities on I–10 but in different states, Houston and New Orleans, have the identical beltway number of I–610.

Boarding Pass, Please

It's said in the South that when you die and are on your way to either heaven or hell, you'll have to make connections in Atlanta. Atlanta's airport, Hartsfield International, is the world's second busiest.

Like other airports that are reached by scheduled airlines, Hartsfield is a twentieth-century urban landmark in the same way the railroad station was a sign of the times in the late nineteenth century. Most of the 595 airports served by domestic carriers in the United States are quiet, even desolate places. But some, like Hartsfield, resemble self-contained cities, and last year 38 of these airports in the nation's large hubs handled 70 percent of the nearly 300 million people who boarded domestic flights. The busiest, Chicago's O'Hare International Airport, boarded more passengers than the 400 smallest U.S. airports combined.

Two hundred and forty-six metro areas have one airport with scheduled service, 19 have two airports, and two—Chicago and Los Angeles–Long Beach—have three. In one day, flights from these 290 airports average one for every 8,862 residents in metro areas that have access to passenger service.

The Busiest U.S. Airports

Airport	Annual Passengers
1. Chicago O'Hare International	42,873,000
2. Hartsfield International (Atlanta)	37,919,000
3. Los Angeles International	33,426,000
4. John F. Kennedy International (New York)	27,904,000
5. Dallas–Fort Worth Regional	26,783,000
6. Stapleton International (Denver)	25,247,000
7. San Francisco International	23,166,000
8. Miami International	19,321,000
9. La Guardia (New York)	18,183,000
10. Logan International (Boston)	17,848,000
11. Newark International	17,411,000
12. Lambert–St. Louis International	16,241,000
13. Honolulu International	15,261,000
14. Washington National (Washington, D.C.)	14,166,000
15. Houston Intercontinental	12,984,000

Source: Airport Operators Council International, 1984.

Figures represent the number of passengers arriving and departing at each airport every year.

You'll stand the best chance of dodging airport jams if you fly on Thursday afternoons and Saturday nights. The worst travel days used to be Fridays and Sundays. Now they are Tuesdays and Wednesdays because more people take advantage of special fares requiring midweek travel.

Riding the Rails

Sixty years ago, eight out of ten people who had to get from one city in the United States to another did it aboard a train. There were 20,000 different ones from which to choose, if you didn't care where you were going. The *Twentieth Century Limited, El Capitan, Blue Streak*—each had a unique, trademarked name. They still do—*Desert Wind, Sunset Limited, Empire Builder,*

Silver Palm—but today there are just 230 of them. Over the years, their share of the commercial passenger traffic has dwindled to 7 percent.

If passenger trains are ever to rise again, the renaissance will be due not to high gasoline prices and spot fuel shortages but to mounting congestion on intercity highways. California traffic experts, for example, foresee a four-hour automobile commute between San Jose and San Francisco by 1990. The railroads have a priceless asset: existing tracks and rights-of-way into the population centers of the nation.

The National Railroad Passenger Corporation, a profit-making body, was created by Congress to subsidize the passenger-carrying business of its member railroads. Better known as Amtrak, it began operation in 1971. Today it carries virtually all of the 25 million passengers who board intercity trains each year.

The passenger rails don't reach everywhere, however. Although Amtrak's timetable boasts stops at hundreds of cities and towns from Aberdeen, Maryland, to Yuma, Arizona, 166 of the 329 metro areas aren't on the route system. The metro areas bypassed include such large places as Tulsa, Louisville, and Des Moines.

On the average, there is a weekday Amtrak train for every 197,497 residents among the 163 metro areas with rail passenger service. Battle Creek, Michigan, ought to be as renowned for passenger trains as for breakfast cereal, since there are more Amtrak departures per capita here than in any other metro area: one for every 17,695 people per weekday. By far the biggest markets for train service are in the northeast quadrant of the United States. But the fastest-growing markets are on the West Coast, particularly for the two-hour-and-forty-minute run between Los Angeles and San Diego and for the six-hour San Francisco–Bakersfield route.

JUDGING TRANSPORTATION SUPPLY

When it comes to evaluating the supply of travel options in a metro area, a good measure is how many people can be served by a place's transit system and by the number of intercity travel choices. Would urban dwellers in Syracuse or San Angelo have a better chance of finding a seat on a bus? Which metro area airport—Atlanta's or Denver's—has more daily departures per local population?

In rating metro areas for transit supply, *Places Rated*'s approach is similar to that taken in the first edition of this book. As before, we examine three modes of transportation used between cities (Interstate highways, airplane, and passenger train) and one used locally (mass transit). A useful new scoring element introduced for this edition of *Places Rated Almanac* is the daily commute, the average time spent getting to and from work within a metro area. To arrive at a score for each metro area, these five criteria are compared with

The Busiest Two-Way Air Routes

Routes	Annual Passengers
1. Boston–New York City	4,220,250
2. New York City–Washington, D.C.	3,807,250
3. Los Angeles–New York City	2,453,920
4. Los Angeles–San Francisco	2,376,950
5. Chicago–New York City	2,332,640
6. Miami–New York City	1,658,080
7. New York City–San Francisco	1,458,660
8. Honolulu–Kahului, Maui	1,366,280
9. New York City–Pittsburgh	1,339,940
10. Fort Lauderdale–New York City	1,256,990
11. Las Vegas–Los Angeles	1,140,000
12. Detroit–New York City	983,010
13. Atlanta–New York City	964,580
14. Chicago–Los Angeles	936,520
15. Honolulu–Lihue, Kauai	924,830

Source: Air Transport Association of America, 1984.

The Busiest Amtrak Routes

Northeast Corridor*	Annual Passengers
1. New York–Philadelphia	2,400,000
2. Metroliners, Boston–New York–Washington	1,200,000
3. Harrisburg–Philadelphia	760,000
4. New Haven–Springfield, MA	260,000
Short Distance	
1. Los Angeles–San Diego	1,064,000
2. New York–Albany–Niagara Falls	841,000
3. Chicago–Detroit–Toledo	368,000
4. Chicago–St. Louis	274,000
5. Oakland–Bakersfield	221,000
Long Distance	
1. Chicago–Oakland–Los Angeles	725,000
2. New York–Florida	610,000
3. Los Angeles–Seattle	485,000
4. Chicago–New York–Boston	350,000
5. New York–New Orleans	250,000

Source: Amtrak, Ridership By Route, 1984.

*Another 6.1 million passengers a year travel various Amtrak routes along the Northeast Corridor not listed here.

the national metro area averages.

In the case of judging air service, some further adjustments were made in calculating a score for metro areas that are part of a Consolidated Metropolitan Statistical Area (see the Appendix for a list of CMSAs and component metro areas). Because major airports tend to serve a very wide geographical area and are able to accommodate large numbers of travelers, *Places Rated* considers the air service assets of CMSA component metro areas to be shared equally by all members of the CMSA, no matter which metro area the airport(s) may be located in.

Each metro area starts with a base score of zero, to which points are added according to the following indicators:

1. *Daily commute.* The time spent commuting to and from work is almost entirely unproductive—and unavoidable. To rate each

You're Better Off in Large Hubs

The Federal Aviation Administration (FAA) rates each metro area for its share of airline service by designating it as one of the following: large hub, medium hub, small hub, or non-hub.

A metro area is a . . .	if passengers leaving its airport(s) total . . .
large hub	1% or more
medium hub	0.25% to 0.99%
small hub	0.05% to 0.24%
non-hub	less than 0.05%
	of all U.S. airline passengers in a year.

There's one big advantage to living in a large hub besides having a wider choice of carriers with more frequent nonstop flights to more destinations: Flying between large hubs is cheaper.

The cost of an airline ticket into and out of Bismarck, North Dakota (a non-hub), or Charleston, West Virginia (a small hub), helps subsidize the same airline's small profit from a New York vacationer's air travel to Miami or a Los Angeles conventioneer's trip to Chicago. When airlines skirmish with bargain fares between large hubs, travelers in the smaller hubs end up paying part of the tab.

place for commuting time, the U.S. metro area average of 49.7 minutes is divided by the average minutes local workers spend in daily commuting. The result is then multiplied by 1,000. Consequently, the shorter the commuting time, the more points a metro area will receive. Workers in Houston, for instance, spend an average of 58.5 minutes commuting, which works out to 850 points, compared with an average time of only 28.6 minutes in Grand Forks, North Dakota. This daily commute results in a score that is more than twice Houston's.

2. *Mass transit.* Counting the number of motor buses and rapid rail cars in a metro area's transit system won't tell you enough about local transit performance. *Places Rated* instead adopts the urban mass transit industry's measure of *seat miles per capita*, which means the number of transit seats that travel one mile of transit route for each person in the urban core each day.

Among the 296 metro areas with public transit, the average number of seat miles per capita is 2.43. To rate each metro area for transit supply, the local seat mile figure is divided by this 2.43 average and multiplied by 1,000, with a maximum total of 5,000 points per metro area. Chicago's buses and

rapid rail cars provide 4.68 seat miles for each resident. The Second City therefore has a transit supply 1.926 times the metro area average, good for 1,926 points.

3. *Interstate highways.* There are an average of 1.438 main numbered routes for the 269 metro areas reached by the 42,500-mile Interstate system. To rate each metro area in this category, the number of routes in the metro area is divided by the average of 1.438 and multiplied by 1,000. Dallas is reached by four routes—I-20, I-30, I-35, and I-45; the Texas metro area therefore has 2.782 times the national average of Interstate routes, totaling 2,782 points.

4. *Airline flights.* For the 303 metro areas with access to airports with passenger service, the average number of residents per departing flight each day is 8,862. To rate each metro area, this average is divided by the local ratio of residents to departure, then multiplied by 1,000. (In the case of CMSA component metro areas, the ratio of residents per departure is arrived at by dividing the total number of departures in the CMSA by the total CMSA population. Each member metro area receives the same number of points.) The maximum score for each metro area is 3,000 points.

5. *Passenger train (Amtrak) departures.* The average number of residents per Amtrak departure each day for the 163 metro areas served by Amtrak is 197,497. To arrive at a score for each metro area, this average is divided by the local number of residents per daily train departure, then multiplied by 1,000, with a ceiling of 1,500 points.

Sample Comparison: New York, New York, and Houma–Thibodaux, Louisiana

A premier world port and trade center and a pair of cities in Louisiana bayou country are the best and worst metro areas, respectively, for transportation supply according to *Places Rated*'s criteria.

In Houma–Thibodaux, which comprises Lafourche and Terrebonne parishes, workers take 52.6 minutes to get to and from their jobs each day. Dividing 49.7 minutes, the national average round-trip commuting time for the metro areas, by 52.6 and multiplying by 1,000 yields a score of 945. There is no public transportation in this metro area, nor any Interstate highways linking it with other metro areas along the network.

And despite Houma–Thibodaux's population growth during the 1970s in the midst of the Louisiana oil and natural gas boom, it is served by only one airline. To board a plane for such destinations as Miami, Dallas, or Memphis means driving northeast on U.S. 90 for an hour or so to New Orleans International–Moisant Field. There are just four commuter flights per day out of Houma–Terrebonne Airport, or one flight for every 44,219 people in this small metro area. Houma–Thibodaux's score for this transportation asset is calculated by dividing 8,862, the national average of metro area residents per daily flight, by 44,219 and multiplying by 1,000; the result is 200 points. Amtrak service is also lacking, meaning that the total score for this metro area is the sum of its points for commuting time and air travel—1,145, the lowest of all 329 metro areas.

New York, in contrast, is the core of the country's largest metro complex: the New York–Northern New Jersey–Long Island consolidated area. Workers here spend an average of 81 minutes every day commuting, good for a score of only 614. Most of New York's commuters use public transit, and it is ironic that they spend so much time—the longest daily trip of any metro area—aboard the biggest transit system in the world. New York's 4,662 buses and 6,263 rapid rail cars provide a phenomenal 23.49 seats per mile of route for each resident. When divided by the national metro area average of 2.43 and multiplied by 1,000, this figure results in a score of 9,667, which is trimmed to the maximum number of points *Places Rated* allows for this category, 5,000.

Three Interstate highways reach the nation's largest city, giving it an additional 2,086 points after dividing 3 by 1.438, the national average of Interstate highways per metro area, and multiplying by 1,000. As part of the New York–Northern New Jersey–Long Island consolidated area, made up of 12 metro areas, New York is served by eight passenger airports: Allaire Field, Igor I. Sikorsky Memorial, John F. Kennedy International, La Guardia, Long Island–MacArthur, Newark International, Republic, and Stewart. There are a total of 1,229 airline flights out of these facilities each day, or one flight for every 14,271 people. This results in a score of 621 for air travel.

Amtrak's biggest hub in the United States is at Grand Central Station, in downtown Manhattan. Twenty-seven trains leave here every day, most of which reach other metro areas in the consolidated area, which means one train for every 649,604 people. This works out to a score of 304 when divided into the national average of one daily train for every 197,497 metro area residents and then multiplied by 1,000. The sum of New York's five scores is 8,625, the highest of any metro area in the United States.

Places Rated: Metro Areas Ranked for Transportation Supply

Determining a score for transportation means looking closely at a metro area's ability to accommodate the transportation needs of its residents, using the following criteria: (1) daily commute, (2) public transportation, (3) Interstate highways, (4) air service, and (5) passenger rail service.

Places that receive tie scores are given the same rank and are listed in alphabetical order.

Metro Areas from Best to Worst

Places Rated Rank	Places Rated Score	Places Rated Rank	Places Rated Score	Places Rated Rank	Places Rated Score
1. New York, NY	8,625	16. Boston, MA	6,801	31. Springfield, IL	6,172
2. Atlanta, GA	8,409	17. Reno, NV	6,767	32. Harrisburg–Lebanon–	
3. San Francisco, CA	8,299	18. Richmond–Petersburg, VA	6,680	Carlisle, PA	6,164
4. Washington, DC–MD–VA	8,236	19. Seattle, WA	6,634	33. Springfield, MA	6,159
5. Denver, CO	8,145	20. Boise City, ID	6,575	34. Charlotte–Gastonia–	
				Rock Hill, NC–SC	6,099
6. Chicago, IL	7,742			35. La Crosse, WI	6,096
7. Champaign–Urbana–					
Rantoul, IL	7,447	21. Albuquerque, NM	6,558	36. Madison, WI	6,084
8. Baltimore, MD	7,405	22. Raleigh–Durham, NC	6,544	37. Charlottesville, VA	6,041
9. Cleveland, OH	7,333	23. East St. Louis–Belleville, IL	6,539	38. Savannah, GA	5,958
10. Burlington, VT	7,146	24. Oakland, CA	6,430	39. Portland, OR	5,947
		25. Fargo–Moorhead, ND–MN	6,325	40. New Haven–Meriden, CT	5,938
11. Hartford, CT	7,120				
12. St. Louis, MO–IL	7,119	26. Billings, MT	6,285	41. Honolulu, HI	5,911
13. Boulder–Longmont, CO	7,108	27. Sioux Falls, SD	6,271	42. Philadelphia, PA–NJ	5,903
14. Syracuse, NY	6,951	28. Memphis, TN–AR–MS	6,247	43. Las Vegas, NV	5,900
15. Albany–Schenectady–		29. Salt Lake City–Ogden, UT	6,228	44. Bloomington–Normal, IL	5,889
Troy, NY	6,883	30. Dallas, TX	6,213	45. Orlando, FL	5,887

Places Rated Rank	Places Rated Score
46. Kansas City, MO	5,869
47. Columbia, SC	5,859
48. Gary–Hammond, IN	5,855
49. Omaha, NE–IA	5,806
50. Indianapolis, IN	5,804
51. Erie, PA	5,754
52. Cincinnati, OH–KY–IN	5,748
53. Redding, CA	5,727
54. Santa Barbara–Santa Maria–Lompoc, CA	5,662
55. South Bend–Mishawaka, IN	5,634
56. Lincoln, NE	5,618
57. Pittsburgh, PA	5,616
58. Bangor, ME	5,613
59. Jacksonville, FL	5,611
60. Minneapolis–St. Paul, MN-WI	5,606
61. Tampa–St. Petersburg–Clearwater, FL	5,588
62. Grand Forks, ND	5,587
63. Niagara Falls, NY	5,561
64. Lansing–East Lansing, MI	5,557
65. Spokane, WA	5,534
66. Tallahassee, FL	5,530
67. Des Moines, IA	5,521
68. San Diego, CA	5,489
69. Providence, RI	5,474
70. Charleston, WV	5,470
71. Louisville, KY–IN	5,420
72. Kalamazoo, MI	5,419
73. Fort Wayne, IN	5,416
74. San Antonio, TX	5,387
75. Buffalo, NY	5,384
76. Topeka, KS	5,348
77. Toledo, OH	5,323
78. Midland, TX	5,310
79. Eugene–Springfield, OR	5,293
80. Cedar Rapids, IA	5,270
81. Lafayette, LA	5,268
82. San Jose, CA	5,224
83. Duluth, MN–WI	5,205
84. Miami–Hialeah, FL	5,202
85. West Palm Beach–Boca Raton–Delray Beach, FL	5,201
86. Portland, ME	5,185
87. Birmingham, AL	5,177
88. Rochester, NY	5,165
89. Sacramento, CA	5,097
90. Anchorage, AK	5,091
91. Asheville, NC	5,086
92. Nashville, TN	5,030
93. Santa Cruz, CA	5,010
94. Kansas City, KS	5,006
95. Jersey City, NJ	4,982
96. Alton–Granite City, IL	4,975
97. Florence, SC	4,963
98. Lafayette, IN	4,956
99. Milwaukee, WI	4,945
100. Jackson, MS	4,917
101. Flint, MI	4,912
102. Lynchburg, VA	4,909
103. Amarillo, TX	4,902
104. New Britain, CT	4,900
105. Akron, OH	4,883
106. Detroit, MI	4,808
107. Jackson, MI	4,800
108. Trenton, NJ	4,786
109. Dayton–Springfield, OH	4,775
110. Pawtucket–Woonsocket–Attleboro, RI–MA	4,738
111. Salem, OR	4,732
112. Tacoma, WA	4,730
113. Phoenix, AZ	4,729
114. Tuscaloosa, AL	4,723
115. Richland–Kennewick–Pasco, WA	4,714
116. Battle Creek, MI	4,652
117. Joliet, IL	4,645
118. Middletown, CT	4,636
119. Houston, TX	4,626
120. Fall River, MA–RI	4,602
121. Manchester, NH	4,595
122. Utica–Rome, NY	4,592
123. Fort Myers, FL	4,583
124. New Orleans, LA	4,579
125. St. Cloud, MN	4,565
126. Provo–Orem, UT	4,546
127. Wilmington, DE–NJ–MD	4,532
128. Binghamton, NY	4,529
129. New London–Norwich, CT–RI	4,505
130. Bristol, CT	4,495
131. Kenosha, WI	4,473
132. Fort Worth–Arlington, TX	4,472
133. Oklahoma City, OK	4,459
134. Greensboro–Winston-Salem–High Point, NC	4,458
135. Stockton, CA	4,427
136. Casper, WY	4,410
137. Fayetteville, NC	4,402
138. Shreveport, LA	4,401
139. Parkersburg–Marietta, WV–OH	4,399
139. Rochester, MN	4,399
141. Tucson, AZ	4,397
142. Fresno, CA	4,388
143. Columbus, OH	4,364
144. Los Angeles–Long Beach, CA	4,345
145. Johnstown, PA	4,343
146. Muncie, IN	4,325
147. Sioux City, IA–NE	4,316
148. Bismarck, ND	4,303
149. Canton, OH	4,279
150. Knoxville, TN	4,273
151. Altoona, PA	4,246
152. Charleston, SC	4,207
153. Middlesex–Somerset–Hunterdon, NJ	4,198
154. Fort Lauderdale–Hollywood–Pompano Beach, FL	4,186
154. Little Rock–North Little Rock, AR	4,186
156. Elkhart–Goshen, IN	4,168
157. Poughkeepsie, NY	4,166
158. Salinas–Seaside–Monterey, CA	4,160
159. Lubbock, TX	4,158
160. Vallejo–Fairfield–Napa, CA	4,153
161. Vineland–Millville–Bridgeton, NJ	4,133
162. Daytona Beach, FL	4,117
163. Lima, OH	4,084
164. Olympia, WA	4,083
165. Lexington–Fayette, KY	4,080
166. Chico, CA	4,067
167. Abilene, TX	4,031
168. Huntington–Ashland, WV–KY–OH	4,001
169. Anaheim–Santa Ana, CA	3,954
170. Greenville–Spartanburg, SC	3,950
171. Aurora–Elgin, IL	3,943
172. Wichita, KS	3,933
173. Lancaster, PA	3,908
174. Davenport–Rock Island–Moline, IA–IL	3,907
175. Columbia, MO	3,893
176. Roanoke, VA	3,872
177. Decatur, IL	3,867
178. Springfield, MO	3,828
179. Lowell, MA–NH	3,820
180. Vancouver, WA	3,817
181. Brockton, MA	3,810
182. Bradenton, FL	3,805
183. Ocala, FL	3,798
184. Green Bay, WI	3,793
185. Bellingham, WA	3,776
186. Pittsfield, MA	3,759
187. Tulsa, OK	3,758
188. Great Falls, MT	3,747
189. Sarasota, FL	3,742
190. Yakima, WA	3,731
191. Bakersfield, CA	3,725
192. Cumberland, MD–WV	3,709
193. El Paso, TX	3,705
194. Scranton–Wilkes-Barre, PA	3,683
195. Austin, TX	3,670
196. Dubuque, IA	3,668
197. Worcester, MA	3,643
198. Lorain–Elyria, OH	3,629
199. Corpus Christi, TX	3,626
200. Monroe, LA	3,606
201. Fayetteville–Springdale, AR	3,581
202. Lawrence–Haverhill, MA–NH	3,575
203. Racine, WI	3,558
204. Atlantic City, NJ	3,556
205. Terre Haute, IN	3,550
206. Lake Charles, LA	3,549
207. Norwalk, CT	3,536
208. Gainesville, FL	3,527
209. Newark, NJ	3,514
210. Medford, OR	3,512
211. Bergen–Passaic, NJ	3,511
212. Montgomery, AL	3,509
213. Pueblo, CO	3,501
214. Evansville, IN–KY	3,496
214. Wausau, WI	3,496
216. Tyler, TX	3,460
217. Salem–Gloucester, MA	3,459
218. Sheboygan, WI	3,458

Places Rated Rank	Places Rated Score
219. Grand Rapids, MI	3,454
220. Kankakee, IL	3,444
221. Ann Arbor, MI	3,433
222. Hagerstown, MD	3,431
223. Galveston–Texas City, TX	3,423
224. Lake County, IL	3,422
225. Lakeland–Winter Haven, FL	3,412
226. Chattanooga, TN–GA	3,401
227. Colorado Springs, CO	3,389
228. Youngstown–Warren, OH	3,374
229. Muskegon, MI	3,353
230. Waterloo–Cedar Falls, IA	3,351
231. Mobile, AL	3,345
232. Hamilton–Middletown, OH	3,338
233. Baton Rouge, LA	3,329
234. Elmira, NY	3,324
235. Laredo, TX	3,322
236. Nashua, NH	3,320
237. Santa Rosa–Petaluma, CA	3,313
238. Orange County, NY	3,299
239. Appleton–Oshkosh–Neenah, WI	3,298
240. New Bedford, MA	3,219
241. Norfolk–Virginia Beach–Newport News, VA	3,215
242. Bridgeport–Milford, CT	3,197
242. Eau Claire, WI	3,197
244. Saginaw–Bay City–Midland, MI	3,186
245. Danville, VA	3,161
246. Macon–Warner Robins, GA	3,144
247. Riverside–San Bernardino, CA	3,141
248. Reading, PA	3,120
249. Brownsville–Harlingen, TX	3,119
250. Stamford, CT	3,110
251. Williamsport, PA	3,097
252. Visalia–Tulare–Porterville, CA	3,094
253. Fort Smith, AR–OK	3,092
253. Janesville–Beloit, WI	3,092
255. Anniston, AL	3,051

Places Rated Rank	Places Rated Score
256. Waco, TX	3,018
257. Columbus, GA–AL	2,995
258. Benton Harbor, MI	2,989
258. Las Cruces, NM	2,989
260. Rockford, IL	2,987
261. Peoria, IL	2,967
262. Beaver County, PA	2,960
263. Lewiston–Auburn, ME	2,941
264. San Angelo, TX	2,938
265. Lawrence, KS	2,931
266. Pensacola, FL	2,918
267. Wilmington, NC	2,904
268. Fort Walton Beach, FL	2,886
269. Allentown–Bethlehem, PA–NJ	2,881
270. Mansfield, OH	2,876
271. Anderson, IN	2,865
272. Killeen–Temple, TX	2,862
273. Wichita Falls, TX	2,793
274. Beaumont–Port Arthur, TX	2,782
275. Panama City, FL	2,778
276. Iowa City, IA	2,770
277. Yuba City, CA	2,768
278. State College, PA	2,740
279. Danbury, CT	2,715
280. Anderson, SC	2,707
281. Hickory, NC	2,703
282. Monmouth–Ocean, NJ	2,690
283. St. Joseph, MO	2,689
284. Longview–Marshall, TX	2,680
285. Huntsville, AL	2,661
286. Fort Collins–Loveland, CO	2,637
287. Melbourne–Titusville–Palm Bay, FL	2,560
288. Texarkana, TX–Texarkana, AR	2,537
289. Johnson City–Kingsport–Bristol, TN–VA	2,532
290. Albany, GA	2,531
291. Bryan–College Station, TX	2,530
292. Augusta, GA–SC	2,523

Places Rated Rank	Places Rated Score
293. Biloxi–Gulfport, MS	2,516
294. Wheeling, WV–OH	2,450
295. Alexandria, LA	2,444
296. Waterbury, CT	2,434
297. Victoria, TX	2,407
298. Brazoria, TX	2,391
299. Lawton, OK	2,366
300. Joplin, MO	2,335
301. Portsmouth–Dover–Rochester, NH–ME	2,321
302. Enid, OK	2,312
303. Owensboro, KY	2,273
304. York, PA	2,267
305. Fitchburg–Leominster, MA	2,244
306. Glens Falls, NY	2,241
307. Oxnard–Ventura, CA	2,238
308. Dothan, AL	2,232
309. Clarksville–Hopkinsville, TN–KY	2,226
310. Gadsden, AL	2,174
311. Fort Pierce, FL	2,143
312. Nassau–Suffolk, NY	2,119
313. McAllen–Edinburg–Mission, TX	2,117
314. Sharon, PA	2,017
315. Modesto, CA	2,000
316. Odessa, TX	1,944
317. Sherman–Denison, TX	1,922
318. Burlington, NC	1,910
319. Athens, GA	1,866
320. Kokomo, IN	1,817
321. Jacksonville, NC	1,780
322. Pascagoula, MS	1,750
323. Bloomington, IN	1,746
324. Pine Bluff, AR	1,671
325. Bremerton, WA	1,670
326. Greeley, CO	1,641
327. Steubenville–Weirton, OH–WV	1,532
328. Florence, AL	1,454
329. Houma–Thibodaux, LA	1,145

Metro Areas Listed Alphabetically

Metro Area	Places Rated Rank	Metro Area	Places Rated Rank	Metro Area	Places Rated Rank
Abilene, TX	167	Anniston, AL	255	Beaver County, PA	262
Akron, OH	105	Appleton–Oshkosh–Neenah, WI	239	Bellingham, WA	185
Albany, GA	290	Asheville, NC	91	Benton Harbor, MI	258
Albany–Schenectady–Troy, NY	15	Athens, GA	319	Bergen–Passaic, NJ	211
Albuquerque, NM	21	Atlanta, GA	2	Billings, MT	26
Alexandria, LA	295	Atlantic City, NJ	204	Biloxi–Gulfport, MS	293
Allentown–Bethlehem, PA–NJ	269	Augusta, GA–SC	292	Binghamton, NY	128
Alton–Granite City, IL	96	Aurora–Elgin, IL	171	Birmingham, AL	87
Altoona, PA	151	Austin, TX	195	Bismarck, ND	148
Amarillo, TX	103	Bakersfield, CA	191	Bloomington, IN	323
Anaheim–Santa Ana, CA	169	Baltimore, MD	8	Bloomington–Normal, IL	44
Anchorage, AK	90	Bangor, ME	58	Boise City, ID	20
Anderson, IN	271	Baton Rouge, LA	233	Boston, MA	16
Anderson, SC	280	Battle Creek, MI	116	Boulder–Longmont, CO	13
Ann Arbor, MI	221	Beaumont–Port Arthur, TX	274	Bradenton, FL	182

Metro Area	Places Rated Rank	Metro Area	Places Rated Rank	Metro Area	Places Rated Rank
Brazoria, TX	298	Florence, SC	97	Laredo, TX	235
Bremerton, WA	325	Fort Collins–Loveland, CO	286	Las Cruces, NM	258
Bridgeport–Milford, CT	242	Fort Lauderdale–Hollywood–		Las Vegas, NV	43
Bristol, CT	130	Pompano Beach, FL	154	Lawrence, KS	265
Brockton, MA	181	Fort Myers, FL	123	Lawrence–Haverhill, MA–NH	202
		Fort Pierce, FL	311		
Brownsville–Harlingen, TX	249			Lawton, OK	299
Bryan–College Station, TX	291	Fort Smith, AR–OK	253	Lewiston–Auburn, ME	263
Buffalo, NY	75	Fort Walton Beach, FL	268	Lexington–Fayette, KY	165
Burlington, NC	318	Fort Wayne, IN	73	Lima, OH	163
Burlington, VT	10	Fort Worth–Arlington, TX	132	Lincoln, NE	56
		Fresno, CA	142		
Canton, OH	149			Little Rock–North Little Rock, AR	154
Casper, WY	136	Gadsden, AL	310	Longview–Marshall, TX	284
Cedar Rapids, IA	80	Gainesville, FL	208	Lorain–Elyria, OH	198
Champaign–Urbana–Rantoul, IL	7	Galveston–Texas City, TX	223	Los Angeles–Long Beach, CA	144
Charleston, SC	152	Gary–Hammond, IN	48	Louisville, KY–IN	71
		Glens Falls, NY	306		
Charleston, WV	70			Lowell, MA–NH	179
Charlotte–Gastonia–Rock Hill, NC–SC	34	Grand Forks, ND	62	Lubbock, TX	159
Charlottesville, VA	37	Grand Rapids, MI	219	Lynchburg, VA	102
Chattanooga, TN–GA	226	Great Falls, MT	188	Macon–Warner Robins, GA	246
Chicago, IL	6	Greeley, CO	326	Madison, WI	36
		Green Bay, WI	184		
Chico, CA	166			Manchester, NH	121
Cincinnati, OH–KY–IN	52	Greensboro–Winston-Salem– High Point, NC	134	Mansfield, OH	270
Clarksville–Hopkinsville, TN–KY	309	Greenville–Spartanburg, SC	170	McAllen–Edinburg–Mission, TX	313
Cleveland, OH	9	Hagerstown, MD	222	Medford, OR	210
Colorado Springs, CO	227	Hamilton–Middletown, OH	232	Melbourne–Titusville–Palm Bay, FL	287
		Harrisburg–Lebanon–Carlisle, PA	32		
Columbia, MO	175	Hartford, CT	11	Memphis, TN–AR–MS	28
Columbia, SC	47	Hickory, NC	281	Miami–Hialeah, FL	84
Columbus, GA–AL	257	Honolulu, HI	41	Middlesex–Somerset–Hunterdon, NJ	153
Columbus, OH	143	Houma–Thibodaux, LA	329	Middletown, CT	118
Corpus Christi, TX	199	Houston, TX	119	Midland, TX	78
Cumberland, MD–WV	192	Huntington–Ashland, WV–KY–OH	168	Milwaukee, WI	99
Dallas, TX	30	Huntsville, AL	285	Minneapolis–St. Paul, MN–WI	60
Danbury, CT	279	Indianapolis, IN	50	Mobile, AL	231
Danville, VA	245	Iowa City, IA	276	Modesto, CA	315
Davenport–Rock Island–Moline, IA–IL	174	Jackson, MI	107	Monmouth–Ocean, NJ	282
		Jackson, MS	100	Monroe, LA	200
Dayton–Springfield, OH	109	Jacksonville, FL	59	Montgomery, AL	212
Daytona Beach, FL	162	Jacksonville, NC	321	Muncie, IN	146
Decatur, IL	177	Janesville–Beloit, WI	253	Muskegon, MI	229
Denver, CO	5	Jersey City, NJ	95	Nashua, NH	236
Des Moines, IA	67				
		Johnson City–Kingsport–Bristol, TN–VA	289	Nashville, TN	92
Detroit, MI	106	Johnstown, PA	145	Nassau-Suffolk, NY	312
Dothan, AL	308	Joliet, IL	117	New Bedford, MA	240
Dubuque, IA	196	Joplin, MO	300	New Britain, CT	104
Duluth, MN–WI	83	Kalamazoo, MI	72	New Haven–Meriden, CT	40
East St. Louis–Belleville, IL	23	Kankakee, IL	220		
		Kansas City, KS	94	New London–Norwich, CT–RI	129
Eau Claire, WI	242	Kansas City, MO	46	New Orleans, LA	124
El Paso, TX	193	Kenosha, WI	131	New York, NY	1
Elkhart–Goshen, IN	156	Killeen–Temple, TX	272	Newark, NJ	209
Elmira, NY	234			Niagara Falls, NY	63
Enid, OK	302	Knoxville, TN	150		
		Kokomo, IN	320	Norfolk–Virginia Beach–Newport News, VA	241
Erie, PA	51	La Crosse, WI	35	Norwalk, CT	207
Eugene–Springfield, OR	79	Lafayette, IN	98	Oakland, CA	24
Evansville, IN–KY	214	Lafayette, LA	81	Ocala, FL	183
Fall River, MA–RI	120			Odessa, TX	316
Fargo–Moorhead, ND–MN	25	Lake Charles, LA	206		
		Lake County, IL	224	Oklahoma City, OK	133
Fayetteville, NC	137	Lakeland–Winter Haven, FL	225	Olympia, WA	164
Fayetteville–Springdale, AR	201	Lancaster, PA	173	Omaha, NE–IA	49
Fitchburg–Leominster, MA	305	Lansing–East Lansing, MI	64	Orange County, NY	238
Flint, MI	101			Orlando, FL	45
Florence, AL	328				
				Owensboro, KY	303

Metro Area	Places Rated Rank	Metro Area	Places Rated Rank	Metro Area	Places Rated Rank
Oxnard–Ventura, CA	307	St. Joseph, MO	283	Tallahassee, FL	66
Panama City, FL	275	St. Louis, MO–IL	12	Tampa–St. Petersburg–	
Parkersburg–Marietta, WV–OH	139	Salem, OR	111	Clearwater, FL	61
Pascagoula, MS	322	Salem–Gloucester, MA	217	Terre Haute, IN	205
		Salinas–Seaside–Monterey, CA	158	Texarkana, TX–Texarkana, AR	288
Pawtucket–Woonsocket–Attleboro,				Toledo, OH	77
RI–MA	110	Salt Lake City–Ogden, UT	29		
Pensacola, FL	266	San Angelo, TX	264	Topeka, KS	76
Peoria, IL	261	San Antonio, TX	74	Trenton, NJ	108
Philadelphia, PA–NJ	42	San Diego, CA	68	Tucson, AZ	141
Phoenix, AZ	113	San Francisco, CA	3	Tulsa, OK	187
				Tuscaloosa, AL	114
Pine Bluff, AR	324	San Jose, CA	82		
Pittsburgh, PA	57	Santa Barbara–Santa Maria–		Tyler, TX	216
Pittsfield, MA	186	Lompoc, CA	54	Utica–Rome, NY	122
Portland, ME	86	Santa Cruz, CA	93	Vallejo–Fairfield–Napa, CA	160
Portland, OR	39	Santa Rosa–Petaluma, CA	237	Vancouver, WA	180
		Sarasota, FL	189	Victoria, TX	297
Portsmouth–Dover–Rochester,					
NH–ME	301	Savannah, GA	38	Vineland–Millville–Bridgeton, NJ	161
Poughkeepsie, NY	157	Scranton–Wilkes-Barre, PA	194	Visalia–Tulare–Porterville, CA	252
Providence, RI	69	Seattle, WA	19	Waco, TX	256
Provo–Orem, UT	126	Sharon, PA	314	Washington, DC–MD–VA	4
Pueblo, CO	213	Sheboygan, WI	218	Waterbury, CT	296
Racine, WI	203	Sherman–Denison, TX	317	Waterloo–Cedar Falls, IA	230
Raleigh–Durham, NC	22	Shreveport, LA	138	Wausau, WI	214
Reading, PA	248	Sioux City, IA–NE	147	West Palm Beach–Boca Raton–	
Redding, CA	53	Sioux Falls, SD	27	Delray Beach, FL	85
Reno, NV	17	South Bend–Mishawaka, IN	55	Wheeling, WV–OH	294
				Wichita, KS	172
Richland–Kennewick–Pasco, WA	115	Spokane, WA	65		
Richmond–Petersburg, VA	18	Springfield, IL	31	Wichita Falls, TX	273
Riverside–San Bernardino, CA	247	Springfield, MA	33	Williamsport, PA	251
Roanoke, VA	176	Springfield, MO	178	Wilmington, DE–NJ–MD	127
Rochester, MN	139	Stamford, CT ·	250	Wilmington, NC	267
				Worcester, MA	197
Rochester, NY	88	State College, PA	278		
Rockford, IL	260	Steubenville–Weirton, OH–WV	327	Yakima, WA	190
Sacramento, CA	89	Stockton, CA	135	York, PA	304
Saginaw–Bay City–Midland, MI	244	Syracuse, NY	14	Youngstown–Warren, OH	228
St. Cloud, MN	125	Tacoma, WA	112	Yuba City, CA	277

Place Profiles: Transportation Indicators in 329 Metro Areas

The following pages provide brief summaries of local commuting conditions, mass public transit, and options for intercity transportation in each of the 329 metro areas.

The sources for the information are the U.S. Department of Commerce, Bureau of the Census, *1980 Census of Population and Housing;* American Public Transit Association, *Transit Facts, 1982–1983,* and U.S. Department of Transportation, Urban Mass Transit Administration, *Directory of Regularly Scheduled, Fixed Route, Local Public Transportation Service,* 1981, *Directory of Regularly Scheduled, Fixed Route, Local Rural Public Transportation Service,* 1981, and *National Urban Mass Transportation Statistics—Section 15 Report,* 1984; U.S. Department of Transportation, Federal Highway Administration, unpublished Highway Performance Monitoring System data, 1984, and *Interstate System*

Route Log and Finder List, undated; Official Airline Guides, Inc., *Travel Planner,* Spring 1984, and U.S. Department of Transportation, Federal Aviation Administration, *Air Traffic Activity,* fiscal year 1983; and National Railroad Passenger Corporation, *Amtrak Timetable,* 1984.

The first entry in the profiles, Daily Commute, is the average number of minutes that workers in the metro area spend getting to and from work, regardless of the mode of transportation. These figures are the 1980 Census journey-to-work data for each metro area multiplied by 2.2 to represent a round-trip whose return half takes slightly longer than the first half.

Under the heading Public Transportation is the number of mass transit vehicles available during rush hour. Just below this figure appears the seat miles per capita, a measurement common in the transit industry, which is the number of transit seats that travel one mile of transit route daily for each person in the metro area's urban core. In metro areas with more than one mode of public transportation—such as Atlanta and San Francisco—this number is the total for all modes.

Descriptions of freeway traffic are derived from the Federal Highway Administration, which rates urban freeways for their level of service on a scale from "free-flowing" progressing through "flowout capacity" and ending at "congested." *Places Rated* adopts the following simplification, using the Federal Highway Administration's definition of a highway's full capacity as 2,000 vehicles per hour in one 12-foot-wide traffic lane: Freeway traffic is judged *very heavy* if the traffic volume is 90 percent or more of the freeway's capacity, *heavy* if the volume is 50 to 89 percent of capacity, *moderate* if the volume is 34 to 49 percent, and *light* if the volume is 33 percent or less. The entry None indicates a metro area with no freeways.

A major part of a metro area's freeway mileage comes from the beltways, spurs, and heavily traveled routes of the Interstate Highway System. But the 61 two-digit main routes are intercity travel assets, too. Accordingly, each main route in the system that reaches the metro area is listed.

The first item under the heading Air Service is the FAA's hub classification for the metro area: large hub, medium hub, small hub, or non-hub. In most CMSAs, the core metro area is designated a large hub, and other member metro areas are classified as part of that hub. Thus, the entry for Boulder–Longmont, Colorado, reads "Part of Denver hub." The airport's name is listed next. (Because of local boosterism, many airports have the word "international" in their title; the airport in Great Falls, Montana, for example, is named International but has no international flights.) The airport's three-letter identifier, recognized interna-

tionally, is enclosed in parentheses next to its title. Every airport in the world with scheduled service has a unique identifier. All airports, including those that *Places Rated* scores as part of the air service "pool" shared by members of a consolidated area, are listed under the metro area in which they are located. In four cases, however, airports are listed under two metro areas and credited to both. Two of these exceptions involve airports that straddle the boundaries of two metro areas (Dallas–Fort Worth Regional, listed under Dallas and Fort Worth, and Sarasota–Bradenton Airport, credited to both Bradenton and Sarasota); the other two are cases of airports located in one metro area but roughly equidistant from two metro areas (Akron–Canton Regional, located in Akron but also close to Canton, and Bradley International of Hartford, about 20 minutes away from both downtown Hartford and Springfield, Massachusetts).

For metro areas that neither have airports nor share them, the location of the nearest airport is given along with its distance and direction from the metro area. Also listed in this category are the number of airlines that serve the airport and the total number of flights departing each day. (*Places Rated* also counts air taxis, or carriers that fly passengers on small aircraft with fewer than 30 seats and a maximum payload of less than 7,500 pounds; and commuter carriers, which are air taxis that make at least five round-trips a week between two or more points under a published flight schedule.)

Finally, figures for Amtrak service are the number of passenger trains departing from the metro area on an average weekday. Metro areas that are part of CMSAs share in the number of Amtrak departures from the major city in the CMSA.

A star preceding a metro area's name highlights it as one of the top 25 places for transportation assets.

Metro Area	Daily Commute	Public Transportation	Freeway Traffic	Interstate Highways	Air Service	Amtrak Service	Places Rated Score	Places Rated Rank
Abilene, TX	34.8 min	17 city buses Seat miles/capita: 1.14	Light	I-20	Non-hub Abilene Municipal (ABI) 2 airlines, 18 flights/day	—	4,031	167
Akron, OH	43.8 min	135 city buses Seat miles/capita: 1.74	Heavy	I-76 I-77 I-80	Part of Cleveland hub Akron–Canton Regional (CAK) 6 airlines, 24 flights/day	—	4,883	105
Albany, GA	38.9 min	15 city buses Seat miles/capita: 1.13	Light	—	Non-hub Albany–Dougherty County (ABY) 2 airlines, 10 flights/day	—	2,531	290
★ Albany–Schenectady–Troy, NY	43.3 min	236 city buses Seat miles/capita: 3.21	Light	I-87 I-88 I-90	Medium hub Albany County (ALB) 13 airlines, 78 flights/day	11 trains/day	6,883	15
★ Albuquerque, NM	41.6 min	82 city buses Seat miles/capita: 1.31	Heavy	I-25 I-40	Medium hub Albuquerque International (ABQ) 16 airlines, 118 flights/day	2 trains/day	6,558	21
Alexandria, LA	37.8 min	16 city buses Seat miles/capita: 1.15	Light	—	Non-hub Esler Regional (ESF) 5 airlines, 10 flights/day	—	2,444	295

Metro Area	Daily Commute	Public Transportation	Freeway Traffic	Interstate Highways	Air Service	Amtrak Service	Places Rated Score	Places Rated Rank
Allentown–Bethlehem, PA–NJ	41.4 min	65 city buses Seat miles/capita: 1.14	Very heavy	I-78	Small hub Allentown–Bethlehem–Easton (ABE) 5 airlines, 37 flights/day	—	2,881	269
Alton–Granite City, IL	45.1 min	18 city buses Seat miles/capita: 1.35	Light	I-55 I-70	Part of St. Louis hub	6 trains/day	4,975	96
Altoona, PA	37.0 min	31 city buses Seat miles/capita: 2.62	Light	—	Non-hub Altoona–Blair County (AOO) 1 airline, 5 flights/day	4 trains/day	4,246	151
Amarillo, TX	37.8 min	39 city buses Seat miles/capita: 1.74	Moderate	I-27 I-40	Small hub Amarillo International (AMA) 6 airlines, 29 flights/day	—	4,902	103
Anaheim–Santa Ana, CA	51.9 min	497 city buses Seat miles/capita: 1.71	Heavy	I-5 I-10	Part of Los Angeles hub John Wayne–Orange County (SNA) 12 airlines, 66 flights/day	6 trains/day	3,954	169
Anchorage, AK	38.7 min	50 city buses Seat miles/capita: 1.96	Very heavy	—	Medium hub Anchorage International (ANC) 19 airlines, 185 flights/day	—	5,091	90
Anderson, IN	40.5 min	27 city buses Seat miles/capita: 2.29	Light	I-69	Nearest airport: Muncie, 20 miles NE	—	2,865	271
Anderson, SC	40.9 min	6 city buses Seat miles/capita: 1.45	Light	I-85	Non-hub Anderson County (AND) 1 airline, 3 flights/day	—	2,707	280
Ann Arbor, MI	41.4 min	47 city buses Seat miles/capita: 1.18	Moderate	I-94	Part of Detroit hub	5 trains/day	3,433	221
Anniston, AL	39.6 min	—	Light	—	Non-hub Anniston–Calhoun County (ANB) 1 airline, 4 flights/day	2 trains/day	3,051	255
Appleton–Oshkosh–Neenah, WI	32.3 min	58 city buses Seat miles/capita: 2.72	Heavy	—	Small hub Outagamie County (ATW) Wittman Field (OSH) 3 airlines, 21 flights/day	—	3,298	239
Asheville, NC	40.7 min	45 city buses Seat miles/capita: 2.93	Moderate	I-26 I-40	Small hub Asheville Regional (AVL) 4 airlines, 23 flights/day	—	5.086	91
Athens, GA	40.0 min	8 city buses Seat miles/capita: .85	None	—	Non-hub Athens Municipal (AHN) 1 airline, 4 flights/day	—	1,866	319
★ Atlanta, GA	54.3 min	885 city buses 120 rapid rail cars Seat miles/capita: 4.95	Very heavy	I-20 I-75 I-85	Large hub William B. Hartsfield–Atlanta International (ATL) 18 airlines, 765 flights/day	4 trains/day	8,409	2
Atlantic City, NJ	44.2 min	35 city buses Seat miles/capita: 3.88	Moderate	—	Non-hub Bader Field (AIY) Pomona Field (ACY) 5 airlines, 26 flights/day	—	3,556	204
Augusta, GA–SC	43.6 min	30 city buses Seat miles/capita: .80	Moderate	I-20	Small hub Bush Field (AGS) 4 airlines, 14 flights/day	—	2,523	292
Aurora–Elgin, IL	46.0 min	59 city buses Seat miles/capita: 1.48	Heavy	I-90	Part of Chicago hub	6 trains/day	3,943	171
Austin, TX	41.8 min	71 city buses Seat miles/capita: 1.25	Very heavy	I-35	Small hub Robert Mueller Municipal (AUS) 11 airlines, 77 flights/day	—	3,670	195
Bakersfield, CA	38.5 min	40 city buses Seat miles/capita: 1.20	Heavy	—	Non-hub Meadows Field (BFL) 6 airlines, 20 flights/day	4 trains/day	3,725	191
★ Baltimore, MD	58.3 min	900 city buses 2 commuter railroads Seat miles/capita: 3.42	Moderate	I-70 I-83 I-95 I-97	Medium hub Baltimore–Washington International (BWI) 26 airlines, 214 flights/day	31 trains/day	7,405	8
Bangor, ME	33.0 min	9 city buses Seat miles/capita: 1.00	Light	I-95	Small hub Bangor International (BGR) 4 airlines, 29 flights/day	—	5,613	58
Baton Rouge, LA	50.2 min	55 city buses Seat miles/capita: 1.04	Heavy	I-10 I-12	Small hub Baton Rouge Metropolitan–Ryan Field (BTR) 5 airlines, 29 flights/day	—	3,329	233
Battle Creek, MI	37.8 min	20 city buses Seat miles/capita: 1.71	Light	I-94	Small hub W. K. Kellogg Regional (BTL) 1 airline, 7 flights/day	8 trains/day	4,652	116

Metro Area	Daily Commute	Public Transportation	Freeway Traffic	Interstate Highways	Air Service	Amtrak Service	Places Rated Score	Places Rated Rank
Beaumont–Port Arthur, TX	42.5 min	33 city buses Seat miles/capita: .91	Light	I-10	Non-hub Jefferson County (BPT) 5 airlines, 23 flights/day	—	2,782	274
Beaver County, PA	44.7 min	13 city buses Seat miles/capita: .42	Heavy	—	Part of Pittsburgh hub Beaver County (BFP) 1 airline, 1 daily flight	—	2,960	262
Bellingham, WA	35.9 min	16 city buses Seat miles/capita: 2.71	Heavy	I-5	Non-hub Bellingham International (BLI) 1 airline, 7 flights/day	—	3,776	185
Benton Harbor, MI	36.5 min	2 city buses Seat miles/capita: .22	Light	I-94 I-96	Non-hub Ross Field (BEH) 1 airline, 3 flights/day	—	2,989	258
Bergen–Passaic, NJ	54.3 min	460 city buses Seat miles/capita: 2.37	Very heavy	I-80	Part of New York hub	—	3,511	211
Billings, MT	35.4 min	15 city buses Seat miles/capita: 1.19	Light	I-90 I-94	Small hub Billings Logan International (BIL) 5 airlines, 41 flights/day	—	6,285	26
Biloxi–Gulfport, MS	44.9 min	18 city buses Seat miles/capita: .67	Moderate	I-10	Non-hub Gulfport–Biloxi Regional (GPT) 1 airline, 9 flights/day	—	2,516	293
Binghamton, NY	38.3 min	39 city buses Seat miles/capita: 1.61	Light	I-81 I-88	Non-hub Edwin A. Link Field–Broom County (BGM) 8 airlines, 35 flights/day	—	4,529	128
Birmingham, AL	51.3 min	237 city buses Seat miles/capita: 2.61	Very heavy	I-20 I-59 I-65	Medium hub Birmingham Municipal (BHM) 9 airlines, 60 flights/day	2 trains/day	5,177	87
Bismarck, ND	30.8 min	—	Light	I-94	Non-hub Bismarck Municipal (BIS) 5 airlines, 18 flights/day	—	4,303	148
Bloomington, IN	38.1 min	4 city buses Seat miles/capita: .42	None	—	Non-hub Monroe County (BMG) 1 airline, 3 flights/day	—	1,746	323
Bloomington–Normal, IL	33.4 min	23 city buses Seat miles/capita: 1.86	Light	I-55 I-74	Non-hub Bloomington–Normal (BMI) 1 airline, 10 flights/day	6 trains/day	5,889	44
★ Boise City, ID	36.7 min	28 city buses Seat miles/capita: 1.38	Moderate	I-80	Small hub Boise Air Terminal (BOI) 10 airlines, 48 flights/day	2 trains/day	6,575	20
★ Boston, MA	51.7 min	1,115 city buses 796 rapid rail cars 50 trolley coaches 2 commuter railroads 2 ferry systems Seat miles/capita: 5.60	Heavy	I-90 I-93 I-95	Large hub General Edward Lawrence Logan International (BOS) 42 airlines, 404 flights/day	11 trains/day	6,801	16
★ Boulder–Longmont, CO	45.5 min	55 city buses Seat miles/capita: 3.99	Heavy	I-25	Part of Denver hub Boulder Municipal (WBU) 1 airline, 4 flights/day	—	7,108	13
Bradenton, FL	41.1 min	18 city buses Seat miles/capita: .81	Moderate	I-75	Small hub Sarasota–Bradenton (SRQ) 11 airlines, 62 flights/day	—	3,805	182
Brazoria, TX	50.6 min	—	Heavy	—	Part of Houston hub	—	2,391	298
Bremerton, WA	55.0 min	18 city buses Seat miles/capita: 1.86	Light	—	Nearest airport: Seattle, 52 miles SE	—	1,670	325
Bridgeport–Milford, CT	44.7 min	70 city buses Seat miles/capita: 1.13	Heavy	I-95	Part of New York hub Igor I. Sikorsky Memorial (BDR) 2 airlines, 17 flights/day	9 trains/day	3,197	242
Bristol, CT	42.2 min	3 city buses Seat miles/capita: .24	Heavy	I-84	Part of Hartford hub	—	4,495	130
Brockton, MA	51.0 min	45 city buses Seat miles/capita: 1.68	Heavy	I-95	Part of Boston hub	—	3,810	181
Brownsville–Harlingen, TX	35.9 min	24 city buses Seat miles/capita: 1.75	Light	—	Non-hub Harlingen (HRL) Brownsville–South Padre Island International (BRO) 5 airlines, 24 flights/day	—	3,119	249
Bryan–College Station, TX	33.4 min	—	None	—	Non-hub Easterwood Field (CLL) 3 airlines, 11 flights/day	—	2,530	291

Metro Area	Daily Commute	Public Transportation	Freeway Traffic	Interstate Highways	Air Service	Amtrak Service	Places Rated Score	Places Rated Rank
Buffalo, NY	42.9 min	393 city buses Seat miles/capita: 2.61	Moderate	I-90	Medium hub Greater Buffalo International (BUF) 12 airlines, 134 flights/day	11 trains/day	5,384	75
Burlington, NC	40.9 min	—	Heavy	I-85	Nearest airport: Greensboro, 32 miles W	—	1,910	318
★ Burlington, VT	38.1 min	18 city buses Seat miles/capita: 1.57	Light	I-89	Non-hub Burlington International (BTV) 8 airlines, 43 flights/day	2 trains/day	7,146	10
Canton, OH	40.9 min	60 city buses Seat miles/capita: 1.63	Heavy	I-77	Small hub Akron–Canton Regional (CAK) 6 airlines, 24 flights/day	4 trains/day	4,279	149
Casper, WY	39.8 min	—	Moderate	I-25	Non-hub Natrona County International (CPR) 6 airlines, 20 flights/day	—	4,410	136
Cedar Rapids, IA	36.3 min	45 city buses Seat miles/capita: 2.21	Light	I-80	Small hub Cedar Rapids Municipal (CID) 7 airlines, 44 flights/day	—	5,270	80
★ Champaign–Urbana–Rantoul, IL	33.7 min	51 city buses Seat miles/capita: 3.11	Moderate	I-57 I-72 I-74	Non-hub U. of Illinois–Willard (CMI) 4 airlines, 21 flights/day	2 trains/day	7,447	7
Charleston, SC	48.6 min	32 city buses Seat miles/capita: .65	Light	I-26	Small hub Charleston AFB International (CHS) 4 airlines, 35 flights/day	4 trains/day	4,207	152
Charleston, WV	47.5 min	83 city buses Seat miles/capita: 3.60	Moderate	I-64 I-77 I-79	Small hub Kanawha Airport (CRW) 6 airlines, 26 flights/day	—	5,470	70
Charlotte–Gastonia–Rock Hill, NC–SC	44.4 min	129 city buses Seat miles/capita: 1.88	Heavy	I-77 I-85	Medium hub Charlotte–Douglas International (CLT) 15 airlines, 264 flights/day	2 trains/day	6,099	34
Charlottesville, VA	42.0 min	12 city buses Seat miles/capita: 1.35	Light	I-64	Non-hub Charlottesville–Albemarle (CHO) 4 airlines, 27 flights/day	2 trains/day	6,041	37
Chattanooga, TN–GA	48.2 min	71 city buses 1 cable incline Seat miles/capita: 1.57	Heavy	I-24 I-75	Small hub Lovell Field (CHA) 4 airlines, 16 flights/day	—	3,401	226
★ Chicago, IL	63.8 min	2,420 city buses 1,100 rapid rail cars 7 commuter railroads 1 ferry system Seat miles/capita: 4.68	Heavy	I-55 I-57 I-80 I-90 I-94	Large hub Merrill C. Meigs (CGX) Chicago Midway (MDW) Chicago–O'Hare International (ORD) 42 airlines, 927 flights/day	21 trains/day	7,742	6
Chico, CA	35.4 min	8 city buses Seat miles/capita: 1.03	Heavy	—	Non-hub Chico Municipal (CIC) 3 airlines, 12 flights/day	2 trains/day	4,067	166
Cincinnati, OH–KY–IN	49.3 min	622 city buses 1 ferry system Seat miles/capita: 3.69	Heavy	I-71 I-74 I-75	Medium hub Greater Cincinnati International (CVG) 13 airlines, 168 flights/day	2 trains/day	5,748	52
Clarksville–Hopkinsville, TN–KY	36.7 min	—	None	I-24	Non-hub Outlaw Field (CKV) 1 airline, 3 flights/day	—	2,226	309
★ Cleveland, OH	51.5 min	1,016 city buses 171 rapid rail cars Seat miles/capita: 6.42	Very heavy	I-71 I-77 I-80 I-90	Large hub Burke–Lakefront (BKL) Cleveland–Hopkins International (CLE) 28 airlines, 211 flights/day	3 trains/day	7,333	9
Colorado Springs, CO	38.7 min	50 city buses Seat miles/capita: 1.20	Heavy	I-25	Small hub City of Colorado Springs Municipal (COS) 6 airlines, 32 flights/day	—	3,389	227
Columbia, MO	34.8 min	19 city buses Seat miles/capita: 1.94	Light	I-70	Non-hub Columbia Regional (COU) 3 airlines, 11 flights/day	—	3,893	175
Columbia, SC	44.4 min	40 city buses Seat miles/capita: .86	Moderate	I-20 I-26 I-77	Small hub Columbia Metropolitan (CAE) 5 airlines, 37 flights/day	4 trains/day	5,859	47

Metro Area	Daily Commute	Public Transportation	Freeway Traffic	Interstate Highways	Air Service	Amtrak Service	Places Rated Score	Places Rated Rank
Columbus, GA–AL	38.5 min	56 city buses Seat miles/capita: 1.73	Moderate	I-85	Small hub Columbus Metropolitan (CSG) 2 airlines, 8 flights/day	—	2,995	257
Columbus, OH	45.8 min	273 city buses Seat miles/capita: 2.06	Very heavy	I-70 I-71	Medium hub Port Columbus International (CMH) 17 airlines, 146 flights/day	—	4,364	143
Corpus Christi, TX	41.1 min	52 city buses 1 ferry system Seat miles/capita: 1.41	Moderate	I-37	Small hub Corpus Christi International (CRP) 5 airlines, 42 flights/day	—	3,626	199
Cumberland, MD–WV	39.6 min	10 city buses Seat miles/capita: 1.11	Light	—	Non-hub Cumberland Municipal (CBE) 1 airline, 6 flights/day	2 trains/day	3,709	192
Dallas, TX	52.8 min	582 city buses Seat miles/capita: 1.98	Heavy	I-20 I-30 I-35E I-45	Large hub Dallas–Fort Worth Regional (DFW) Dallas Love Field (DAL) 37 airlines, 554 flights/day	—	6,213	30
Danbury, CT	53.9 min	6 city buses Seat miles/capita: .42	Heavy	I-84	Part of New York hub	—	2,715	279
Danville, VA	43.3 min	6 city buses Seat miles/capita: .86	Light	—	Non-hub Danville Municipal (DAN) 1 airline, 2 flights/day	2 trains/day	3,161	245
Davenport– Rock Island– Moline, IA–IL	38.1 min	78 city buses Seat miles/capita: 1.82	Moderate	I-74 I-80	Small hub Quad-City (MLI) 6 airlines, 20 flights/day	—	3,907	174
Dayton– Springfield, OH	42.2 min	230 city buses 80 trolley coaches Seat miles/capita: 2.64	Very heavy	I-70 I-75	Medium hub James M. Cox–Dayton International (DAY) 9 airlines, 119 flights/day	—	4,775	109
Daytona Beach, FL	39.4 min	40 city buses Seat miles/capita: 1.56	Moderate	I-4 I-95	Small hub Daytona Beach Regional (DAB) 4 airlines, 24 flights/day	—	4,117	162
Decatur, IL	34.5 min	31 city buses Seat miles/capita: 1.91	Light	I-72	Non-hub Decatur (DEC) 1 airline, 14 flights/day	—	3,867	177
★ Denver, CO	48.6 min	671 city buses Seat miles/capita: 3.31	Very heavy	I-25 I-70 I-76	Large hub Stapleton International (DEN) 24 airlines, 533 flights/day	6 trains/day	8,145	5
Des Moines, IA	37.8 min	105 city buses Seat miles/capita: 2.62	Heavy	I-35 I-80	Small hub Des Moines Municipal (DSM) 9 airlines, 72 flights/day	—	5,521	67
Detroit, MI	51.3 min	1,347 city buses 2 commuter railroads Seat miles/capita: 2.36	Very heavy	I-75 I-94 I-96	Large hub Detroit City (DET) Detroit Metropolitan–Wayne County (DTW) 31 airlines, 308 flights/day	3 trains/day	4,808	106
Dothan, AL	38.5 min	—	Light	—	Non-hub Dothan (DHN) 2 airlines, 13 flights/day	—	2,232	308
Dubuque, IA	33.4 min	26 city buses 1 cable incline Seat miles/capita: 2.54	Moderate	—	Non-hub Dubuque Municipal (DBQ) 2 airlines, 12 flights/day	—	3,668	196
Duluth, MN–WI	38.9 min	101 city buses Seat miles/capita: 5.08	Moderate	I-35	Small hub Duluth International (DLH) 2 airlines, 12 flights/day	1 train daily	5,205	83
★ East St. Louis– Belleville, IL	45.1 min	56 city buses Seat miles/capita: 3.46	Heavy	I-55 I-64 I-70	Part of St. Louis hub	—	6,539	23
Eau Claire, WI	33.2 min	14 city buses Seat miles/capita: 1.29	Heavy	I-94	Non-hub Eau Claire County (EAU) 2 airlines, 7 flights/day	—	3,197	242
El Paso, TX	42.5 min	115 city buses Seat miles/capita: 1.69	Heavy	I-10	Medium hub El Paso International (ELP) 8 airlines, 62 flights/day	—	3,705	193
Elkhart–Goshen, IN	34.1 min	—	Light	I-80	Non-hub Elkhart Municipal (EKI) 1 airline, 8 flights/day	2 trains/day	4,168	156
Elmira, NY	36.3 min	17 city buses Seat miles/capita: 1.66	Light	—	Non-hub Elmira–Corning Regional (ELM) 4 airlines, 14 flights/day	—	3,324	234

Metro Area	Daily Commute	Public Transportation	Freeway Traffic	Interstate Highways	Air Service	Amtrak Service	Places Rated Score	Places Rated Rank
Enid, OK	33.9 min	—	Light	—	Non-hub Enid–Woodring Municipal (WDG) 1 airline, 6 flights/day	—	2,312	302
Erie, PA	37.6 min	77 city buses Seat miles/capita: 2.88	Moderate	I-79 I-90	Small hub Erie International (ERI) 2 airlines, 14 flights/day	2 trains/day	5,754	51
Eugene–Springfield, OR	38.7 min	80 city buses Seat miles/capita: 2.92	Moderate	I-5	Small hub Mahlon Sweet Field (EUG) 4 airlines, 21 flights/day	2 trains/day	5,293	79
Evansville, IN–KY	40.9 min	24 city buses Seat miles/capita: .89	Moderate	I-64	Small hub Evansville Dress Regional (EVV) 5 airlines, 38 flights/day	—	3,496	214
Fall River, MA–RI	42.2 min	41 city buses Seat miles/capita: 1.93	Moderate	I-95	Part of Providence hub	—	4,602	120
★ Fargo–Moorhead, ND–MN	31.5 min	29 city buses Seat miles/capita: 1.85	Moderate	I-29 I-94	Small hub Hector Field (FAR) 3 airlines, 17 flights/day	2 trains/day	6,325	25
Fayetteville, NC	38.1 min	26 city buses Seat miles/capita: .80	Heavy	I-95	Small hub Fayetteville Municipal–Grannis Field (FAY) 2 airlines, 16 flights/day	2 trains/day	4,402	137
Fayetteville–Springdale, AR	36.1 min	—	None	—	Non-hub Drake Field (FYV) 3 airlines, 25 flights/day	—	3,581	201
Fitchburg–Leominster, MA	39.4 min	8 city buses Seat miles/capita: .70	None	I-90	Nearest airport: Boston, 53 miles SE	—	2,244	305
Flint, MI	42.5 min	58 city buses Seat miles/capita: 1.16	Moderate	I-69 I-75	Small hub Bishop (FNT) 5 airlines, 19 flights/day	4 trains/day	4,912	101
Florence, AL	46.9 min	—	Light	—	Non-hub Muscle Shoals (MSL) 2 airlines, 6 flights/day	—	1,454	328
Florence, SC	41.4 min	3 city buses Seat miles/capita: .36	Light	I-20 I-95	Non-hub Florence City–County (FLO) 3 airlines, 9 flights/day	4 trains/day	4,963	97
Fort Collins–Loveland, CO	38.7 min	12 city buses Seat miles/capita: 1.02	Light	I-25	Non-hub Fort Collins–Loveland Municipal (FTO) 1 airline, 4 flights/day	—	2,637	286
Fort Lauderdale–Hollywood–Pompano Beach, FL	49.7 min	151 city buses Seat miles/capita: 1.00	Heavy	I-95	Part of Miami hub Fort Lauderdale–Hollywood International (FLL) 29 airlines, 150 flights/day	4 trains/day	4,186	154
Fort Myers, FL	45.5 min	15 city buses Seat miles/capita: .71	Moderate	I-75	Small hub Page Field (FMY) 11 airlines, 58 flights/day	—	4,583	123
Fort Pierce, FL	43.8 min	8 city buses Seat miles/capita: .76	Moderate	I-95	Nearest airport: West Palm Beach, 40 miles S	—	2,143	311
Fort Smith, AR–OK	41.4 min	—	Light	I-40	Non-hub Fort Smith Municipal (FSM) 4 airlines, 22 flights/day	—	3,092	253
Fort Walton Beach, FL	38.5 min	8 city buses Seat miles/capita: .62	Moderate	I-10	Non-hub Fort Walton Municipal (VPS) 4 airlines, 8 flights/day	—	2,886	268
Fort Wayne, IN	40.3 min	98 city buses Seat miles/capita: 2.76	Light	I-69	Small hub Fort Wayne Municipal–Baer Field (FWA) 4 airlines, 34 flights/day	4 trains/day	5,416	73
Fort Worth–Arlington, TX	48.4 min	135 city buses Seat miles/capita: .92	Heavy	I-20 I-35W	Part of Dallas hub Dallas–Fort Worth Regional (DFW) 33 airlines, 554 flights/day	—	4,472	132
Fresno, CA	40.5 min	103 city buses Seat miles/capita: 2.07	Heavy	—	Small hub Fresno Air Terminal (FAT) 11 airlines, 47 flights/day	4 trains/day	4,388	142
Gadsden, AL	43.8 min	—	Light	I-59	Non-hub Gadsden Municipal (GAD) 1 airline, 4 flights/day	—	2,174	310
Gainesville, FL	41.1 min	36 city buses Seat miles/capita: 2.31	Moderate	I-75	Non-hub Gainesville Regional (GNV) 3 airlines, 13 flights/day	—	3,527	208

Metro Area	Daily Commute	Public Transportation	Freeway Traffic	Interstate Highways	Air Service	Amtrak Service	Places Rated Score	Places Rated Rank
Galveston–Texas City, TX	46.2 min	15 city buses 1 ferry system Seat miles/capita: .59	Heavy	I-45	Part of Houston hub	—	3,423	223
Gary–Hammond, IN	49.7 min	121 city buses Seat miles/capita: 1.25	Heavy	I-65 I-80 I-90 I-94	Part of Chicago hub	4 trains/day	5,855	48
Glens Falls, NY	38.9 min	5 city buses Seat miles/capita: .65	Moderate	I-87	Nearest airport: Albany, 47 miles S	—	2,241	306
Grand Forks, ND	28.6 min	6 city buses Seat miles/capita: .76	Light	I-29	Non-hub Grand Forks International (GFK) 3 airlines, 10 flights/day	2 trains/day	5,587	62
Grand Rapids, MI	37.6 min	102 city buses Seat miles/capita: 1.81	Heavy	I-96	Small hub Kent County International (GRR) 7 airlines, 47 flights/day	—	3,454	219
Great Falls, MT	32.8 min	—	Light	I-15	Small hub Great Falls International (GTF) 4 airlines, 14 flights/day	—	3,747	188
Greeley, CO	41.4 min	10 city buses Seat miles/capita: 1.07	Light	—	Nearest airport: Denver, 50 miles SW	—	1,641	326
Green Bay, WI	33.4 min	26 city buses Seat miles/capita: 1.21	Light	I-43	Small hub Austin–Straubel Field (GRB) 5 airlines, 22 flights/day	—	3,793	184
Greensboro–Winston-Salem–High Point, NC	40.5 min	81 city buses Seat miles/capita: 1.22	Heavy	I-40 I-85	Medium hub Greensboro Regional (GSO) Smith Reynolds (INT) 8 airlines, 84 flights/day	2 trains/day	4,458	134
Greenville–Spartanburg, SC	41.1 min	23 city buses Seat miles/capita: .46	Light	I-26 I-85	Small hub Greenville–Spartanburg (GSP) 8 airlines, 30 flights/day	2 trains/day	3,950	170
Hagerstown, MD	46.6 min	14 city buses Seat miles/capita: 1.41	Light	I-70 I-81	Non-hub Washington County Regional (HGR) 2 airlines, 5 flights/day	—	3,431	222
Hamilton–Middletown, OH	42.9 min	25 city buses Seat miles/capita: .85	Light	I-75	Part of Cincinnati hub	2 trains/day	3,338	232
Harrisburg–Lebanon–Carlisle, PA	41.1 min	82 city buses Seat miles/capita: 1.96	Moderate	I-76 I-81 I-83	Small hub Harrisburg International–Olmsted Field (MDT) 7 airlines, 40 flights/day	4 trains/day	6,164	32
★ Hartford, CT	44.4 min	259 city buses Seat miles/capita: 3.38	Heavy	I-84 I-86 I-91	Medium hub Bradley International (BDL) 18 airlines, 117 flights/day	12 trains/day	7,120	11
Hickory, NC	38.1 min	8 city buses Seat miles/capita: .86	Moderate	I-40	Non-hub Hickory Municipal (HKY) 2 airlines, 8 flights/day	—	2,703	281
Honolulu, HI	49.7 min	406 city buses Seat miles/capita: 4.64	Heavy	I-1	Large hub Honolulu International (HNL) 29 airlines, 290 flights/day	—	5,911	41
Houma–Thibodaux, LA	52.6 min	—	None	—	Non-hub Houma–Terrebonne (HUM) 1 airline, 4 flights/day	—	1,145	329
Houston, TX	58.5 min	860 city buses Seat miles/capita: 2.37	Very heavy	I-10 I-45	Large hub William P. Hobby (HOU) Houston Intercontinental (IAH) 35 airlines, 493 flights/day	—	4,626	119
Huntington–Ashland, WV–KY–OH	44.7 min	34 city buses Seat miles/capita: 1.26	Light	I-64	Non-hub Tri-State–Walker-Long Field (HTS) 5 airlines, 19 flights/day	2 trains/day	4,001	168
Huntsville, AL	40.7 min	—	Moderate	—	Small hub Huntsville–Madison County (HSV) 4 airlines, 32 flights/day	—	2,661	285
Indianapolis, IN	46.9 min	227 city buses Seat miles/capita: 1.81	Heavy	I-65 I-69 I-70 I-74	Medium hub Indianapolis International (IND) 14 airlines, 138 flights/day	1 train daily	5,804	50
Iowa City, IA	34.8 min	14 city buses Seat miles/capita: 1.57	Light	I-80	Nearest airport: Cedar Rapids, 22 miles NW	—	2,770	276
Jackson, MI	39.6 min	33 city buses Seat miles/capita: 2.71	Moderate	I-94	Non-hub Jackson County–Reynolds Field (JXN) 1 airline, 4 flights/day	5 trains/day	4,800	107

Metro Area	Daily Commute	Public Transportation	Freeway Traffic	Interstate Highways	Air Service	Amtrak Service	Places Rated Score	Places Rated Rank
Jackson, MS	45.5 min	42 city buses Seat miles/capita: 1.06	Moderate	I-20 I-55	Small hub Allen C. Thompson Field (JAN) 6 airlines, 37 flights/day	2 trains/day	4,917	100
Jacksonville, FL	47.7 min	206 city buses Seat miles/capita: 2.29	Heavy	I-10 I-95	Medium hub Jacksonville International (JAX) 11 airlines, 93 flights/day	4 trains/day	5,611	59
Jacksonville, NC	33.9 min	—	Light	—	Non-hub Albert J. Ellis (OAJ) 1 airline, 4 flights/day	—	1,780	321
Janesville–Beloit, WI	34.5 min	12 city buses Seat miles/capita: 1.55	Moderate	I-90	Non-hub Rock County (JVL) 1 airline, 5 flights/day	—	3,092	253
Jersey City, NJ	57.6 min	225 city buses 1 commuter railroad Seat miles/capita: 2.69	Very heavy	I-78 I-80 I-95	Part of New York hub	—	4,982	95
Johnson City–Kingsport–Bristol, TN–VA	43.1 min	14 city buses Seat miles/capita: .42	Moderate	I-81	Small hub Tri-City (TRI) 5 airlines, 25 flights/day	—	2,532	289
Johnstown, PA	43.3 min	45 city buses 1 cable incline Seat miles/capita: 3.32	Light	—	Non-hub Johnstown–Cambria County (JST) 1 airline, 10 flights/day	2 trains/day	4,343	145
Joliet, IL	53.7 min	47 city buses Seat miles/capita: 1.87	Heavy	I-55 I-80	Part of Chicago hub	8 trains/day	4,645	117
Joplin, MO	36.5 min	—	Light	I-44	Non-hub Joplin Municipal (JLN) 3 airlines, 4 flights/day	—	2,335	300
Kalamazoo, MI	37.4 min	67 city buses Seat miles/capita: 2.88	Moderate	I-94	Small hub Kalamazoo Municipal (AZO) 3 airlines, 17 flights/day	7 trains/day	5,419	72
Kankakee, IL	39.8 min	—	Light	I-57	Nearest airport: Chicago, 50 miles NE	5 trains/day	3,444	220
Kansas City, KS	42.9 min	12 city buses Seat miles/capita: .15	Heavy	I-29 I-35 I-70	Part of Kansas City, MO, hub	—	5,006	94
Kansas City, MO	48.0 min	350 city buses Seat miles/capita: 2.55	Heavy	I-29 I-35 I-70	Large hub Kansas City International (MCI) Kansas City Downtown (MKC) 26 airlines, 208 flights/day	3 trains/day	5,869	46
Kenosha, WI	40.5 min	31 city buses Seat miles/capita: 2.41	Heavy	I-94	Part of Chicago hub	—	4,473	131
Killeen–Temple, TX	35.0 min	9 city buses Seat miles/capita: .81	Light	I-35	Non-hub Killeen Municipal (ILE) Draughon–Miller Municipal (TPL) 1 airline, 10 flights/day	—	2,862	272
Knoxville, TN	49.9 min	121 city buses Seat miles/capita: 2.83	Heavy	I-40 I-75	Small hub McGhee Tyson (TYS) 10 airlines, 46 flights/day	—	4,273	150
Kokomo, IN	33.7 min	—	Light	—	Non-hub Kokomo Municipal (OKK) 1 airline, 4 flights/day	—	1,817	320
La Crosse, WI	33.9 min	29 city buses Seat miles/capita: 2.84	Light	I-90	Non-hub La Crosse Municipal (LSE) 2 airlines, 13 flights/day	2 trains/day	6,096	35
Lafayette, IN	31.7 min	30 city buses Seat miles/capita: 2.19	Light	I-65	Non-hub Purdue University (LAF) 1 airline, 4 flights/day	2 trains/day	4,956	98
Lafayette, LA	47.7 min	22 city buses Seat miles/capita: 1.29	Moderate	I-10	Non-hub Lafayette Regional (LFT) 5 airlines, 91 flights/day	—	5,268	81
Lake Charles, LA	43.3	10 city buses Seat miles/capita: .54	Moderate	I-10	Non-hub Lake Charles Municipal (LCH) 3 airlines, 28 flights/day	—	3,549	206
Lake County, IL	53.2	38 city buses Seat miles/capita: .57	Heavy	I-94	Part of Chicago hub	—	3,422	224
Lakeland–Winter Haven, FL	42.9 min	4 city buses Seat miles/capita: .14	Moderate	I-4	Nearest airport: Tampa, 35 miles SW	6 trains/day	3,412	225
Lancaster, PA	37.4 min	38 city buses Seat miles/capita:1.61	Moderate	—	Non-hub Lancaster (LNS) 1 airline, 17 flights/day	12 trains/day	3,908	173

Metro Area	Daily Commute	Public Transportation	Freeway Traffic	Interstate Highways	Air Service	Amtrak Service	Places Rated Score	Places Rated Rank
Lansing–East Lansing, MI	39.6 min	76 city buses Seat miles/capita:1.99	Heavy	I-69 I-96	Small hub Capital City (LAN) 5 airlines, 28 flights/day	4 trains/day	5,557	64
Laredo, TX	37.2 min	20 city buses Seat miles/capita: 1.40	Light	I-35	Non-hub Laredo International (LRD) 3 airlines, 8 flights/day	—	3,322	235
Las Cruces, NM	37.6 min	—	Moderate	I-10 I-25	Non-hub Las Cruces–Crawford (LRU) 1 airline, 3 flights/day	—	2,989	258
Las Vegas, NV	41.6 min	25 city buses Seat miles/capita: .38	Moderate	I-15	Large hub McCarran International (LAS) 26 airlines, 255 flights/day	2 trains/day	5,900	43
Lawrence, KS	35.4 min	16 city buses Seat miles/capita: 2.02	Moderate	I-70	Nearest airport: Kansas City, MO, 35 miles NE	—	2,931	265
Lawrence–Haverhill, MA–NH	44.4 min	24 city buses Seat miles/capita: .76	Heavy	I-93	Part of Boston hub	—	3,575	202
Lawton, OK	31.5 min	—	Light	I-44	Non-hub Lawton Municipal (LAW) 1 airline, 10 flights/day	—	2,366	299
Lewiston–Auburn, ME	35.9 min	14 city buses Seat miles/capita: 1.33	Light	I-95	Non-hub Auburn–Lewiston Municipal (LEW) 1 airline, 3 flights/day	—	2,941	263
Lexington–Fayette, KY	40.5 min	52 city buses Seat miles/capita: 1.79	Heavy	I-64 I-75	Small hub Blue Grass (LEX) 6 airlines, 26 flights/day	—	4,080	165
Lima, OH	37.0 min	11 city buses Seat miles/capita: 1.05	Light	I-75	Non-hub Lima–Allen County (LIA) 1 airline, 2 flights/day	4 trains/day	4,084	163
Lincoln, NE	34.8 min	63 city buses Seat miles/capita: 2.39	Light	I-80	Small hub Lincoln Municipal (LNK) 4 airlines, 22 flights/day	4 trains/day	5,618	56
Little Rock–North Little Rock, AR	43.8 min	62 city buses Seat miles/capita: 1.40	Heavy	I-30 I-40	Small hub Adams Field (LIT) 7 airlines, 58 flights/day	—	4,186	154
Longview–Marshall, TX	38.7 min	—	Light	I-20	Non-hub Gregg County (GGG) 3 airlines, 12 flights/day	—	2,680	284
Lorain–Elyria, OH	42.0 min	9 city buses Seat miles/capita: .27	Heavy	I-80 I-90	Part of Cleveland hub	2 trains/day	3,629	198
Los Angeles–Long Beach, CA	53.5 min	3,465 city buses 1 commuter railroad 1 ferry system Seat miles/capita: 2.80	Very heavy	I-5 I-10	Large hub Burbank–Glendale–Pasadena (BUR) Long Beach–Daugherty Field (LGB) Los Angeles International (LAX) 61 airlines, 708 flights/day	13 trains/day	4,345	144
Louisville, KY–IN	48.6 min	318 city buses Seat miles/capita: 2.78	Heavy	I-64 I-65 I-71	Medium hub Standiford Field (SDF) 12 airlines, 126 flights/day	—	5,420	71
Lowell, MA–NH	47.3 min	36 city buses Seat miles/capita: 1.52	Heavy	I-95	Part of Boston hub	—	3,820	179
Lubbock, TX	35.9 min	42 city buses Seat miles/capita: 1.59	Light	I-27	Small hub Lubbock International (LBB) 5 airlines, 34 flights/day	—	4,158	159
Lynchburg, VA	35.6 min	26 city buses Seat miles/capita: 1.84	Light	—	Non-hub Lynchburg Municipal–Preston Glenn Field (LYN) 2 airlines, 20 flights/day	2 trains/day	4,909	102
Macon–Warner Robins, GA	42.9 min	22 city buses Seat miles/capita: .79	Heavy	I-16 I-75	Non-hub Lewis B. Wilson (MCN) 2 airlines, 8 flights/day	—	3,144	246
Madison, WI	39.6 min	193 city buses Seat miles/capita: 6.02	Moderate	I-90 I-94	Small hub Dane County Regional–Truax Field (MSN) 6 airlines, 35 flights/day	—	6,084	36
Manchester, NH	42.5 min	33 city buses Seat miles/capita: 2.14	Moderate	I-93	Non-hub Manchester (MHT) 4 airlines, 27 flights/day	—	4,595	121
Mansfield, OH	36.5 min	10 city buses Seat miles/capita: .84	Heavy	I-71	Non-hub Mansfield–Lahm Municipal (MFD) 1 airline, 7 flights/day	—	2,876	270

Metro Area	Daily Commute	Public Transportation	Freeway Traffic	Interstate Highways	Air Service	Amtrak Service	Places Rated Score	Places Rated Rank
McAllen–Edinburg–Mission, TX	37.6 min	24 city buses Seat miles/capita: 1.02	Light	—	Non-hub Miller International (MFE) 2 airlines, 12 flights/day	—	2,117	313
Medford, OR	36.7 min	5 city buses Seat miles/capita: .63	Light	I-5	Non-hub Medford–Jackson County (MRF) 4 airlines, 18 flights/day	—	3,512	210
Melbourne–Titusville–Palm Bay, FL	44.2 min	12 city buses Seat miles/capita: .38	Moderate	I-95	Small hub Melbourne Regional (MLB) 4 airlines, 18 flights/day	—	2,560	287
Memphis, TN–AR–MS	48.4 min	313 city buses Seat miles/capita: 2.69	Heavy	I-40 I-55	Medium hub Memphis International (MEM) 13 airlines, 236 flights/day	2 trains/day	6,247	28
Miami–Hialeah, FL	52.1 min	865 city buses Seat miles/capita: 3.58	Heavy	I-95	Large hub Miami International (MIA) 61 airlines, 381 flights/day	4 trains/day	5,202	84
Middlesex–Somerset–Hunterdon, NJ	53.9 min	310 city buses Seat miles/capita: 2.33	Very heavy	I-78 I-80	Part of New York hub	—	4,198	153
Middletown, CT	42.0 min	7 city buses Seat miles/capita: .57	Heavy	I-91	Part of Hartford hub	—	4,636	118
Midland, TX	35.9 min	6 city buses Seat miles/capita: .56	Moderate	I-20	Small hub Midland Regional (MAF) 8 airlines, 39 flights/day	—	5,310	78
Milwaukee, WI	42.7 min	631 city buses Seat miles/capita: 3.48	Heavy	I-43 I-94	Medium hub General Mitchell Field (MKE) 12 airlines, 125 flights/day	2 trains/day	4,945	99
Minneapolis–St. Paul, MN–WI	44.2 min	1,012 city buses Seat miles/capita: 3.77	Moderate	I-35 I-94	Large hub Minneapolis–St. Paul International (MSP) 23 airlines, 304 flights/day	3 trains/day	5,606	60
Mobile, AL	51.7 min	38 city buses Seat miles/capita: .86	Light	I-10 I-65	Small hub Bates Field (MOB) 7 airlines, 32 flights/day	—	3,345	231
Modesto, CA	36.7 min	20 city buses Seat miles/capita: .84	Heavy	—	Non-hub Modesto City–County (MOD) 4 airlines, 9 flights/day	—	2,000	315
Monmouth–Ocean, NJ	64.0 min	306 city buses Seat miles/capita: 2.40	Very heavy	—	Part of New York hub Allaire Field (ARX) 2 airlines, 10 flights/day	—	2,690	282
Monroe, LA	39.4 min	18 city buses Seat miles/capita: 1.07	Heavy	I-20	Non-hub Monroe Regional (MLU) 3 airlines, 19 flights/day	—	3,606	200
Montgomery, AL	44.7 min	35 city buses Seat miles/capita: 1.18	Moderate	I-65 I-85	Small hub Dannelly Field (MGM) 4 airlines, 16 flights/day	—	3,509	212
Muncie, IN	36.5 min	21 city buses Seat miles/capita: 1.53	Moderate	I-69	Non-hub Delaware County–Johnson Field (MIE) 1 airline, 2 flights/day	2 trains/day	4,325	146
Muskegon, MI	38.7 min	14 city buses Seat miles/capita: .88	Moderate	I-96	Non-hub Muskegon County (MKG) 2 airlines, 18 flights/day	—	3,353	229
Nashua, NH	43.6 min	1 city bus Seat miles/capita: .09	Heavy	I-93	Part of Boston hub	—	3,320	236
Nashville, TN	49.3 min	153 city buses Seat miles/capita: 1.97	Heavy	I-24 I-40 I-65	Medium hub Nashville Metropolitan (BNA) 13 airlines, 108 flights/day	—	5,030	92
Nassau–Suffolk, NY	70.6 min	940 city buses 1 commuter railroad Seat miles/capita: 1.19	Heavy	—	Part of New York hub Republic (FRG) Long Island–MacArthur (ISP) 11 airlines, 58 flights/day	—	2,119	312
New Bedford, MA	39.4 min	51 city buses Seat miles/capita: 2.55	Moderate	I-95	Non-hub New Bedford Municipal (EWB) 1 airline, 4 flights/day	—	3,219	240
New Britain, CT	38.9 min	20 city buses Seat miles/capita: .98	Heavy	I-84	Part of Hartford hub	11 trains/day	4,900	104
New Haven–Meriden, CT	42.9 min	130 city buses Seat miles/capita: 2.35	Heavy	I-91 I-95	Large hub Tweed–New Haven (HVN) 2 airlines, 52 flights/day	12 trains/day	5,938	40
New London–Norwich, CT–RI	40.3 min	24 city buses Seat miles/capita: 1.07	Heavy	I-95	Non-hub Groton–New London (GON) 3 airlines, 18 flights/day	11 trains/day	4,505	129

Metro Area	Daily Commute	Public Transportation	Freeway Traffic	Interstate Highways	Air Service	Amtrak Service	Places Rated Score	Places Rated Rank
New Orleans, LA	55.9 min	568 city buses 35 rapid rail cars 1 ferry system Seat miles/capita: 3.65	Very heavy	I-10	Large hub New Orleans International– Moisant Field (MSY) 23 airlines, 167 flights/day	2 trains/day	4,579	124
★ New York, NY	81.0 min	4,662 buses 6,263 rapid rail cars 2 ferry systems Seat miles/capita: 23.49	Very heavy	I-78 I-87 I-95	Large hub John F. Kennedy International (JFK) La Guardia (LGA) 87 airlines, 838 flights/day	27 trains/day	8,625	1
Newark, NJ	55.9 min	677 city buses 26 rapid rail cars Seat miles/capita: 2.44	Very heavy	I-95	Part of New York hub Newark International (EWR) 28 airlines, 304 flights/day	27 trains/day	3,514	209
Niagara Falls, NY	37.2 min	89 city buses Seat miles/capita: 2.61	Moderate	I-90	Part of Buffalo hub	6 trains/day	5,561	63
Norfolk–Virginia Beach–Newport News, VA	47.1 min	305 city buses Seat miles/capita: 1.85	Moderate	I-64	Medium hub Norfolk International (ORF) Patrick Henry International (PHF) 13 airlines, 92 flights/day	—	3,215	241
Norwalk, CT	54.1 min	39 city buses Seat miles/capita: 2.42	Heavy	I-95	Part of New York hub	—	3,536	207
★ Oakland, CA	56.3 min	886 city buses 439 rapid rail cars Seat miles/capita: 7.18	Heavy	I-80	Part of San Francisco hub Metropolitan Oakland International (OAK) 12 airlines, 118 flights/day	4 trains/day	6,430	24
Ocala, FL	42.5 min	—	Moderate	I-75	Non-hub Ocala Municipal–Jim Taylor Field (OCF) 1 airline, 6 flights/day	2 trains/day	3,798	183
Odessa, TX	39.8 min	—	Moderate	I-20	Nearest airport: Midland, 15 miles SW	—	1,944	316
Oklahoma City, OK	44.9 min	81 city buses Seat miles/capita: .80	Moderate	I-35 I-40 I-44	Medium hub Will Rogers World (OKC) 15 airlines, 91 flights/day	—	4,459	133
Olympia, WA	44.0 min	19 city buses Seat miles/capita: 1.84	Very heavy	I-5	Nearest airport: Seattle, 30 miles NE	4 trains/day	4,083	164
Omaha, NE–IA	38.7 min	223 city buses Seat miles/capita: 2.89	Moderate	I-80	Medium hub Eppley Airfield (OMA) 16 airlines, 85 flights/day	4 trains/day	5,806	49
Orange County, NY	53.5 min	5 city buses Seat miles/capita: .13	Very heavy	I-84 I-87	Part of New York hub Stewart (SWF) 1 airline, 2 flights/day	—	3,299	238
Orlando, FL	45.5 min	47 city buses Seat miles/capita: .54	Heavy	I-4	Medium hub Orlando International (MCO) 22 airlines, 188 flights/day	6 trains/day	5,887	45
Owensboro, KY	41.1 min	5 city buses Seat miles/capita: .58	Light	—	Non-hub Owensboro–Daviess County (OWB) 1 airline, 8 flights/day	—	2,273	303
Oxnard–Ventura, CA	51.0 min	50 city buses Seat miles/capita: .88	Heavy	—	Part of Los Angeles hub Oxnard (OXR) 2 airlines, 20 flights/day	2 trains/day	2,238	307
Panama City, FL	37.8 min	3 city buses Seat miles/capita: .25	None	—	Non-hub Panama City–Bay County (PFN) 2 airlines, 15 flights/day	—	2,778	275
Parkersburg–Marietta, WV–OH	43.6 min	9 city buses Seat miles/capita: .95	Light	I-77	Non-hub Wood County (PKB) 2 airlines, 12 flights/day	6 trains/day	4,399	139
Pascagoula, MS	47.1 min	—	Light	I-10	Nearest airport: Mobile, AL, 35 miles SW	—	1,750	322
Pawtucket–Woonsocket–Attleboro, RI–MA	40.9 min	100 city buses Seat miles/capita: 2.17	Moderate	I-95	Part of Providence hub	—	4,738	110
Pensacola, FL	43.8 min	28 city buses Seat miles/capita: .86	Moderate	I-10	Small hub Pensacola Municipal (PNS) 7 airlines, 24 flights/day	—	2,918	266
Peoria, IL	40.7 min	47 city buses Seat miles/capita: 1.20	Heavy	I-74	Small hub Greater Peoria (PIA) 5 airlines, 23 flights/day	—	2,967	261
Philadelphia, PA–NJ	56.3 min	1,534 city buses 808 rapid rail cars 174 trolley coaches 2 commuter railroads Seat miles/capita: 3.79	Heavy	I-76 I-95	Large hub North Philadelphia (PNE) Philadelphia International (PHL) 31 airlines, 360 flights/day	42 trains/day	5,903	42

Metro Area	Daily Commute	Public Transportation	Freeway Traffic	Interstate Highways	Air Service	Amtrak Service	Places Rated Score	Places Rated Rank
Phoenix, AZ	47.7 min	245 city buses Seat miles/capita: 1.16	Heavy	I-10 I-17	Large hub Phoenix Sky Harbor International (PHX) Scottsdale Municipal (SCF) 23 airlines, 265 flights/day	2 trains/day	4,729	113
Pine Bluff, AR	41.8 min	11 city buses Seat miles/capita: 1.17	Light	—	Nearest airport: Little Rock, 45 miles NW	—	1,671	324
Pittsburgh, PA	50.4 min	915 city buses 92 rapid rail cars 2 cable inclines Seat miles/capita: 3.80	Heavy	I-76 I-79	Large hub Allegheny County (AGC) Greater Pittsburgh International (PIT) 19 airlines, 368 flights/day	4 trains/day	5,616	57
Pittsfield, MA	33.2 min	16 city buses Seat miles/capita: 1.85	None	—	Nearest airport: Albany, NY, 45 miles NW	2 trains/day	3,759	186
Portland, ME	37.6 min	63 city buses 1 ferry system Seat miles/capita: 3.92	Moderate	I-95	Small hub Portland International Jetport (PWM) 5 airlines, 34 flights/day	—	5,185	86
Portland, OR	45.8 min	649 city buses Seat miles/capita: 4.21	Heavy	I-5 I-84	Medium hub Portland International (PDX) 19 airlines, 143 flights/day	5 trains/day	5,947	39
Portsmouth–Dover–Rochester, NH–ME	39.6 min	14 city buses Seat miles/capita: .90	Moderate	I-95	Nearest airport: Manchester, 47 miles W	—	2,321	301
Poughkeepsie, NY	49.5 min	23 city buses Seat miles/capita: 1.12	Heavy	I-97	Non-hub Dutchess County (POU) 5 airlines, 14 flights/day	13 trains/day	4,166	157
Providence, RI	39.6 min	178 city buses Seat miles/capita: 2.17	Moderate	I-84 I-95	Small hub Theodore Francis Green State (PVD) 9 airlines, 53 flights/day	11 trains/day	5,474	69
Provo–Orem, UT	38.3 min	60 city buses Seat miles/capita: 2.36	Moderate	I-15	Non-hub Provo Municipal (PVU) 1 airline, 2 flights/day	4 trains/day	4,546	126
Pueblo, CO	35.9 min	23 city buses Seat miles/capita: 1.40	Moderate	I-25	Non-hub Pueblo Memorial (PUB) 1 airline, 12 flights/day	—	3,501	213
Racine, WI	37.4 min	25 city buses Seat miles/capita: 1.40	Heavy	I-94	Part of Milwaukee hub	2 trains/day	3,558	203
★ Raleigh–Durham, NC	42.5 min	132 city buses Seat miles/capita: 2.42	Heavy	I-40 I-85	Medium hub Raleigh–Durham (RDU) 12 airlines, 100 flights/day	4 trains/day	6,544	22
Reading, PA	39.4 min	52 city buses Seat miles/capita: 2.00	Heavy	I-76	Non-hub Reading Municipal (RDG) 1 airline, 12 flights/day	—	3,120	248
Redding, CA	33.7 min	16 city buses Seat miles/capita: 2.02	Heavy	I-5	Non-hub Redding Municipal (RDD) 6 airlines, 16 flights/day	2 trains/day	5,727	53
★ Reno, NV	36.7 min	13 city buses Seat miles/capita: .53	Moderate	I-80	Medium hub Reno–Cannon International (RNO) 14 airlines, 73 flights/day	2 trains/day	6,767	17
Richland–Kennewick–Pasco, WA	46.6 min	—	Heavy	—	Non-hub Tri-Cities (PSC) 4 airlines, 35 flights/day	2 trains/day	4,714	115
★ Richmond–Petersburg, VA	48.8 min	222 city buses Seat miles/capita: 2.47	Heavy	I-64 I-85 I-95	Small hub Richard Evelyn Byrd International (RIC) 12 airlines, 91 flights/day	8 trains/day	6,680	18
Riverside–San Bernardino, CA	48.4 min	133 city buses Seat miles/capita: 1.26	Heavy	I-10	Part of Los Angeles hub Ontario International (ONT) Riverside Municipal (RAL) 17 airlines, 85 flights/day	4 trains/day	3,141	247
Roanoke, VA	52.4 min	35 city buses Seat miles/capita: 1.31	Heavy	I-81	Small hub Roanoke Regional (ROA) 2 airlines, 42 flights/day	—	3,872	176
Rochester, MN	30.8 min	10 city buses Seat miles/capita: 1.10	Light	I-90	Small hub Rochester Municipal (RST) 4 airlines, 17 flights/day	—	4,399	139
Rochester, NY	42.9 min	253 city buses Seat miles/capita: 2.78	Heavy	I-90	Medium hub Rochester–Monroe County (ROC) 10 airlines, 73 flights/day	8 trains/day	5,165	88

Metro Area	Daily Commute	Public Transportation	Freeway Traffic	Interstate Highways	Air Service	Amtrak Service	Places Rated Score	Places Rated Rank
Rockford, IL	37.2 min	50 city buses Seat miles/capita: 1.63	Light	I-90	Non-hub Greater Rockford (RFD) 1 airline, 9 flights/day	—	2,987	260
Sacramento, CA	42.7 min	238 city buses Seat miles/capita: 1.99	Heavy	I-5 I-80	Small hub Sacramento Metropolitan (SMF) 13 airlines, 80 flights/day	6 trains/day	5,097	89
Saginaw–Bay City–Midland, MI	39.4 min	106 city buses Seat miles/capita: 1.71	Moderate	I-75	Small hub Tri-City (MBS) 3 airlines, 25 flights/day	—	3,186	244
St. Cloud, MN	37.2 min	22 city buses Seat miles/capita: 2.51	Light	I-94	Nearest airport: Minneapolis, 68 miles SE	2 trains/day	4,565	125
St. Joseph, MO	37.0 min	19 city buses Seat miles/capita: 1.58	Light	I-29	Nearest airport: Kansas City, 30 miles SE	—	2,689	283
★ St. Louis, MO-IL	50.6 min	942 city buses Seat miles/capita. 3.47	Heavy	I-44 I-55 I-64 I-70	Large hub Lambert–St. Louis International (STL) 26 airlines, 383 flights/day	6 trains/day	7,119	12
Salem, OR	40.7 min	58 city buses Seat miles/capita: 2.85	Moderate	I-5	Non-hub McNary Field (SLE) 1 airline, 4 flights/day	2 trains/day	4,732	111
Salem–Gloucester, MA	52.1 min	34 city buses 1 commuter railroad Seat miles/capita: .88	Heavy	I-95	Part of Boston hub	—	3,459	217
Salinas–Seaside–Monterey, CA	36.1 min	52 city buses Seat miles/capita: 1.75	Heavy	—	Small hub Monterey Peninsula (MRY) 6 airlines, 23 flights/day	2 trains/day	4,160	158
Salt Lake City–Ogden, UT	44.2 min	307 city buses Seat miles/capita: 2.32	Heavy	I-15 I-80	Medium hub Salt Lake International (SLC) 13 airlines, 194 flights/day	4 trains/day	6,228	29
San Angelo, TX	34.5 min	15 city buses Seat miles/capita: 1.35	Moderate	—	Non-hub Mathis Field (SJT) 2 airlines, 9 flights/day	—	2,938	264
San Antonio, TX	44.9 min	454 city buses Seat miles/capita: 3.20	Very heavy	I-10 I-35 I-37	Medium hub San Antonio International (SAT) 14 airlines, 106 flights/day	—	5,387	74
San Diego, CA	43.1 min	516 city buses Seat miles/capita: 2.02	Heavy	I-5 I-8 I-15	Medium hub San Diego International–Lindbergh Field (SAN) 21 airlines, 142 flights/day	7 trains/day	5,489	68
★ San Francisco, CA	55.2 min	1,082 city buses 439 rapid rail cars 174 street cars 345 trolley coaches 4 ferry systems Seat miles/capita: 11.68	Heavy	I-80	Large hub San Francisco International (SFO) 36 airlines, 406 flights/day	7 trains/day	8,299	3
San Jose, CA	50.2 min	745 city buses Seat miles/capita: 3.99	Heavy	I-80	Part of San Francisco hub San Jose Municipal (SJC) 16 airlines, 92 flights/day	2 trains/day	5,224	82
Santa Barbara–Santa Maria–Lompoc, CA	36.1 min	76 city buses Seat miles/capita: 2.44	Heavy	—	Non-hub Santa Barbara Municipal (SBA) 8 airlines, 66 flights/day	2 trains/day	5,662	54
Santa Cruz, CA	48.6 min	94 city buses Seat miles/capita: 5.08	Heavy	—	Part of San Francisco hub	—	5,010	93
Santa Rosa–Petaluma, CA	49.9 min	21 city buses Seat miles/capita: 1.02	Heavy	—	Part of San Francisco hub	—	3,313	237
Sarasota, FL	38.9 min	15 city buses Seat miles/capita: .49	Moderate	I-75	Small hub Sarasota–Bradenton (SRQ) 11 airlines, 62 flights/day	—	3,742	189
Savannah, GA	47.1 min	63 city buses Seat miles/capita: 2.25	Moderate	I-16 I-95	Small hub Savannah International (SAV) 4 airlines, 27 flights/day	8 trains/day	5,958	38
Scranton–Wilkes-Barre, PA	40.9 min	102 city buses Seat miles/capita: 1.67	Moderate	I-81 I-84	Small hub Wilkes-Barre–Scranton International (AVP) 6 airlines, 32 flights/day	—	3,683	194
★ Seattle, WA	50.8 min	1,248 city buses 115 trolley coaches 1 ferry system Seat miles/capita: 6.37	Heavy	I-5 I-90	Large hub Henry M. Jackson International (SEA) 28 airlines, 254 flights/day	4 trains/day	6,634	19
Sharon, PA	37.6 min	—	Moderate	I-80	Nearest airport: Youngstown, OH, 10 miles W	—	2,017	314

Metro Area	Daily Commute	Public Transportation	Freeway Traffic	Interstate Highways	Air Service	Amtrak Service	Places Rated Score	Places Rated Rank
Sheboygan, WI	31.7 min	18 city buses Seat miles/capita: 2.05	Light	I-43	Non-hub Sheboygan County Memorial (SBM) 1 airline, 4 flights/day	—	3,458	218
Sherman–Denison, TX	40.5 min	—	Light	I-35	Nearest airport: Dallas, 65 miles SW	—	1,922	317
Shreveport, LA	43.6 min	57 city buses Seat miles/capita: 1.44	Moderate	I-20 I-49	Small hub Shreveport Regional (SHV) 5 airlines, 48 flights/day	—	4,401	138
Sioux City, IA–NE	32.6 min	34 city buses Seat miles/capita: 2.34	Moderate	I-29	Small hub Sioux City Municipal (SUX) 5 airlines, 15 flights/day	—	4,316	147
Sioux Falls, SD	32.3 min	31 city buses Seat miles/capita: 2.41	Moderate	I-29 I-90	Small hub Joe Foss Field (FSD) 7 airlines, 29 flights/day	—	6,271	27
South Bend–Mishawaka, IN	38.1 min	58 city buses Seat miles/capita: 1.71	Light	I-80	Small hub Michiana Regional (SBN) 4 airlines, 39 flights/day	2 trains/day	5,634	55
Spokane, WA	40.5 min	80 city buses Seat miles/capita: 2.00	Heavy	I-90	Medium hub Spokane International (GEG) 8 airlines, 63 flights/day	2 trains/day	5,534	65
Springfield, IL	38.1 min	42 city buses Seat miles/capita: 2.28	Moderate	I-55 I-72	Non-hub Capital (SPI) 3 airlines, 22 flights/day	6 trains/day	6,172	31
Springfield, MA	39.8 min	217 city buses Seat miles/capita: 2.86	Moderate	I-90 I-91	Medium hub Bradley International (BDL) 18 airlines, 117 flights/day	12 trains/day	6,159	33
Springfield, MO	39.2 min	36 city buses Seat miles/capita: 1.73	Moderate	I-44	Small hub Springfield Regional (SGF) 4 airlines, 27 flights/day	—	3,828	178
Stamford, CT	53.2 min	37 city buses Seat miles/capita: 1.35	Heavy	I-95	Part of New York hub	14 trains/day	3,110	250
State College, PA	38.1 min	18 city buses Seat miles/capita: 2.34	Light	—	Non-hub University Park (SCE) 1 airline, 6 flights/day	—	2,740	278
Steubenville–Weirton, OH–WV	42.2 min	10 city buses Seat miles/capita: .86	Light	—	Nearest airport: Pittsburgh, PA, 33 miles NE	—	1,532	327
Stockton, CA	38.5 min	53 city buses Seat miles/capita: 1.79	Heavy	I-5	Non-hub Stockton Metropolitan (SCK) 4 airlines, 8 flights/day	4 trains/day	4,427	135
★ Syracuse, NY	41.4 min	195 city buses Seat miles/capita: 3.43	Moderate	I-81 I-90	Medium hub Syracuse Hancock International (SYR) 11 airlines, 105 flights/day	10 trains/day	6,951	14
Tacoma, WA	47.1 min	191 city buses 115 trolley coaches Seat miles/capita: 3.25	Heavy	I-5	Part of Seattle hub	6 trains/day	4,730	112
Tallahassee, FL	40.9 min	46 city buses Seat miles/capita: 2.57	Moderate	I-10	Small hub Tallahassee Municipal (TLH) 8 airlines, 55 flights/day	—	5,530	66
Tampa–St. Petersburg–Clearwater, FL	45.1 min	214 city buses Seat miles/capita: 1.05	Heavy	I-4 I-75	Large hub Tampa International (TPA) St. Petersburg–Clearwater International (PIE) 25 airlines, 262 flights/day	10 trains/day	5,588	61
Terre Haute, IN	41.1 min	22 city buses Seat miles/capita: 1.96	Light	I-70	Non-hub Hulman Regional (HUF) 1 airline, 13 flights/day	—	3,550	205
Texarkana, TX–Texarkana, AR	40.9 min	—	Light	I-30	Non-hub Texarkana Municipal (TXK) 1 airline, 8 flights/day	—	2,537	288
Toledo, OH	39.4 min	211 city buses Seat miles/capita: 2.90	Heavy	I-75 I-80	Small hub Toledo Express (TOL) 9 airlines, 36 flights/day	3 trains/day	5,323	77
Topeka, KS	40.5 min	28 city buses Seat miles/capita: 1.48	Moderate	I-70	Non-hub Forbes Field (FOE) 3 airlines, 23 flights/day	2 trains/day	5,348	76
Trenton, NJ	47.7 min	93 city buses Seat miles/capita: 2.38	Moderate	I-95	Part of Philadelphia hub Mercer County (TTN) 2 airlines, 11 flights/day	43 trains/day	4,786	108

Metro Area	Daily Commute	Public Transportation	Freeway Traffic	Interstate Highways	Air Service	Amtrak Service	Places Rated Score	Places Rated Rank
Tucson, AZ	46.4 min	159 city buses Seat miles/capita: 2.35	Heavy	I-10 I-19	Medium hub Tucson International (TUS) 13 airlines, 58 flights/day	—	4,397	141
Tulsa, OK	44.7 min	95 city buses Seat miles/capita: 1.43	Moderate	I-44	Medium hub Tulsa International (TUL) 14 airlines, 101 flights/day	—	3,758	187
Tuscaloosa, AL	42.5 min	10 city buses Seat miles/capita: .67	Light	I-20 I-59	Non-hub Tuscaloosa Municipal (TCL) 2 airlines, 6 flights/day	2 trains/day	4,723	114
Tyler, TX	41.1 min	1 city bus Seat miles/capita: .09	Light	I-20	Non-hub Pounds Field (TYR) 3 airlines, 22 flights/day	—	3,460	216
Utica–Rome, NY	37.4 min	40 city buses Seat miles/capita: 1.72	Light	I-90	Non-hub Oneida County (UCA) 2 airlines, 13 flights/day	10 trains/day	4,592	122
Vallejo–Fairfield–Napa, CA	47.3 min	24 city buses Seat miles/capita: 1.24	Heavy	I-80	Part of San Francisco hub	2 trains/day	4,153	160
Vancouver, WA	48.4 min	25 city buses Seat miles/capita: .87	Heavy	I-5	Part of Portland hub	8 trains/day	3,817	180
Victoria, TX	44.4 min	—	Light	—	Non-hub Victoria Regional (VCT) 3 airlines, 10 flights/day	—	2,407	297
Vineland–Millville–Bridgeton, NJ	37.6 min	24 city buses Seat miles/capita: 1.80	Moderate	—	Part of Philadelphia hub	—	4,133	161
Visalia–Tulare–Porterville, CA	35.4 min	1 city bus Seat miles/capita: .11	Moderate	—	Non-hub Visalia Municipal (VIS) 1 airline, 4 flights/day	3 trains/day	3,094	252
Waco, TX	36.7 min	17 city buses Seat miles/capita: .84	Heavy	I-35	Non-hub Waco–Madison Cooper (ACT) 1 airline, 12 flights/day	—	3,018	256
★ Washington, DC–MD–VA	64.5 min	2,043 city buses 296 rapid rail cars Seat miles/capita: 8.81	Heavy	I-66 I-95	Large hub Dulles International (IAD) Washington National (DCA) 40 airlines, 408 flights/day	22 trains/day	8,236	4
Waterbury, CT	42.9 min	34 city buses Seat miles/capita: 1.41	Heavy	I-84	Nearest airport: New Haven, 30 miles SE	—	2,434	296
Waterloo–Cedar Falls, IA	33.4 min	22 city buses Seat miles/capita: 1.22	Light	—	Small hub Waterloo Municipal (ALO) 5 airlines, 25 flights/day	—	3,351	230
Wausau, WI	33.2 min	14 city buses Seat miles/capita: 1.76	Light	—	Non-hub Central Wisconsin (CWA) 2 airlines, 16 flights/day	—	3,496	214
West Palm Beach–Boca Raton–Delray Beach, FL	43.6 min	71 city buses Seat miles/capita: .97	Heavy	I-95	Medium hub Palm Beach International (PBI) 22 airlines, 104 flights/day	4 trains/day	5,201	85
Wheeling, WV–OH	45.5 min	21 city buses Seat miles/capita: 1.38	Moderate	I-70	Nearest airport: Pittsburgh, PA, 50 miles NE	—	2,450	294
Wichita, KS	39.4 min	74 city buses Seat miles/capita: 1.61	Heavy	I-35	Small hub Wichita Mid–Continent (ICT) 10 airlines, 61 flights/day	—	3,933	172
Wichita Falls, TX	34.8 min	8 city buses Seat miles/capita: .56	Very heavy	I-44	Non-hub Wichita Falls Municipal (SPS) 2 airlines, 6 flights/day	—	2,793	273
Williamsport, PA	38.7 min	18 city buses Seat miles/capita: 2.04	Light	—	Non-hub Williamsport–Lycoming County (IPT) 1 airline, 13 flights/day	—	3,097	251
Wilmington, DE–NJ–MD	45.5 min	100 city buses Seat miles/capita: 1.64	Very heavy	I-95	Part of Philadelphia hub Greater Wilmington–New Castle County (ILG) 1 airline, 5 flights/day	31 trains/day	4,532	127
Wilmington, NC	40.9 min	13 city buses Seat miles/capita: .98	Heavy	—	Non-hub New Hanover County (ILM) 3 airlines, 15 flights/day	—	2,904	267
Worcester, MA	41.1 min	61 city buses Seat miles/capita: 1.47	Heavy	I-90	Non-hub Worcester Municipal (ORH) 3 airlines, 7 flights/day	2 trains/day	3,643	197
Yakima, WA	37.8 min	16 city buses Seat miles/capita: 1.31	Moderate	I-82	Non-hub Yakima Air Terminal (YKM) 2 airlines, 23 flights/day	—	3,731	190

Metro Area	Daily Commute	Public Transportation	Freeway Traffic	Interstate Highways	Air Service	Amtrak Service	Places Rated Score	Places Rated Rank
York, PA	43.3 min	20 city buses Seat miles/capita: 1.03	Moderate	I-83	Nearest airport: Harrisburg, 25 miles NE	—	2,267	304
Youngstown–Warren, OH	40.9 min.	75 city buses Seat miles/capita: 1.30	Moderate	I-76 I-80	Small hub Youngstown Municipal (YNG) 4 airlines, 14 flights/day	—	3,374	228
Yuba City, CA	39.2 min	—	Moderate	—	Nearest airport: Sacramento, 35 miles SE	2 trains/day	2,768	277

Et Cetera

MAJOR U.S. AIRLINES

In the early days of U.S. commercial air travel, airlines made most of their money contracting with the Post Office Department to deliver mail, and an adventurous passenger was likely to spend the flight sitting on a pile of mail sacks. A coast-to-coast flight in 1926 took 32 hours, including 14 stops for refueling, and cost the passenger $400. Today that same flight takes a little less than six hours, at a price as low as $99.

Air travel is far more comfortable and efficient than it was in its barnstorming years. Compared with the 13 airlines that operated in 1926 and carried 6,000 passengers, there are now 30 U.S. certified carriers that carry more than 300 million passengers a year. They are ranked below by the number of miles they travel in service per month.

Major Airlines	Millions of Miles per Month	Aircraft
1. United	33.4	317
2. American	24.8	228
3. Eastern	25.1	260
4. Delta	23.7	220
5. Republic	13.9	163
6. TWA	11.5	150
7. USAir	10.7	120
8. Northwest	8.2	111
9. Continental	7.4	112
10. Western	7.3	72
11. Pan American	4.3	NA*

National Airlines		
1. Piedmont	7.5	73
2. Southwest	5.0	37
3. Frontier	4.8	53
4. Ozark	3.9	44
5. Pacific Southwest	3.0	31
6. AirCal	1.9	22

Large Regional Airlines		
1. People Express	4.5	20
2. New York Air	1.2	NA*
3. Northeastern	1.1	NA*
4. Muse Air	1.0	7
5. Empire	0.7	5
6. Jet America	0.6	3
7. Air Wisconsin	0.5	16

Alaskan and Hawaiian Airlines	Millions of Miles per Month	Aircraft
1. Alaska Airlines	2.2	NA*
2. Wien Air Alaska	1.4	10
3. Hawaiian	0.6	12
4. Aloha	0.4	8
5. Reeve Aleutian	0.1	6

Source: Federal Aviation Administration, *Statistical Handbook of Aviation*, 1984, and *Aviation Week and Space Technology*, July 30, 1984.

*Not available.

FERRYBOATS, CABLE CARS, AND INCLINES

Besides the ubiquitous bus and the different rail systems in larger cities are other types of vehicles operated by U.S. transit systems. Although these modes have little impact on total mass transit, they are by far the most fun to watch and ride, undeniably adding to a city's flavor.

San Francisco has the nation's only cable car system. In operation since the nineteenth century, the 41 cars are the only transit property in the National Register of Historic Places.

The largest transit vehicles in the United States are ferryboats, which range in size up to 380 feet and can carry as many as 2,500 passengers per trip. Eleven metro areas have ferryboat systems:

Boston, MA (2 systems)
Chicago, IL
Cincinnati, OH–KY–IN
Corpus Christi, TX
Galveston–Texas City, TX
Los Angeles–Long Beach, CA
New Orleans, LA
New York, NY (2 systems)
Portland, ME
San Francisco, CA (4 systems)
Seattle, WA

Four metro areas operate cog or cable incline cars that traverse steep hills:

Chattanooga, TN–GA: Lookout Mountain
Dubuque, IA: Fourth Street Elevator
Johnstown, PA: Johnstown-Westmont Incline
Pittsburgh, PA: Monongahela and Duquesne Heights

WHERE'S THE BUS (OR TRAM, OR STREET CAR)?

If you've got the fare and you know where your transit stops and where it's going, on a darkening and cold winter afternoon the quality of public transportation ultimately comes down to how long you have to stand around waiting for it. Basing our calculations on the assumption that all the vehicles of a transit system are in service and spaced evenly over each mile of their routes, *Places Rated* ranks the 35 largest such systems according to their waiting times.

In the first column of the table are detailed the different modes of transportation in the system. *Route miles* means the number of miles over which a system's fleet travels in service. If a bus or tram travels in only one direction within the right-of-way, each mile is counted once. If a vehicle travels in both directions, each mile is counted twice. For example, a mile of single track over which street cars operate in two directions represents two route miles.

Fleet age is simply the average number of years a transit system's collection of vehicles has been in service. The oldest fleets in the United States are the San Francisco Municipal Railway's historic cable cars (87 years old) and the charming street cars (62 years old) operated by the New Orleans Public Service Company. The transit vehicle with the shortest active life is the ever-present diesel-powered bus. By the time these roarers are finally scrapped—after an average of nine years on the street—their odometers may register more than 300,000 miles.

But just because a vehicle is old doesn't necessarily mean it's slow. The *average speed* (the average number of miles traveled per hour including frequent stops for passengers) is governed by local congestion on the roads. Seattle's METRO buses are more than twice as old as the Dallas Transit System's fleet, but they still move faster over their routes.

Headway is the distance between vehicles if they are spaced evenly over each mile of route; if you just miss a CTA bus in Chicago, for example, the next one should be only 1.18 miles behind. *Waiting time*, finally, represents the average amount of time you should have to wait for a ride given the number of vehicles in the system, their average speed, and their headway.

The transit systems are presented in order of their average waiting time for all modes of transportation, from shortest to longest. This average is a weighted average and is derived in the following way, using the NYCTA system as an example: The waiting time of 5.96 minutes for buses is multiplied by the number of buses (4,573) and then added to the product of the waiting time for rapid rail cars (0.57 minutes) and the number of cars (6,263). This sum (30,825) is then divided by the total number of transit vehicles within the system (10,836), which results in an average waiting time of 2.84 minutes, second best in this ranking.

Not all the figures for numbers of vehicles jibe with those presented in the Place Profiles. This is because the figures in the profiles are for the entire metro area—which might encompass more than one network —whereas the numbers in this table are for individual transit systems.

The 35 Largest Transit Systems Ranked by Waiting Time

System	Number of Vehicles	Route Miles	Fleet Age	Average Speed	Headway	Waiting Time
1. BART (San Francisco–Oakland)	450 rapid rail cars	142	9 yr	27.5 mph	0.63 mi	1.38 min
2. NYCTA/MTA (New York)	4,573 buses	1,841	9	8.1	0.81	5.96
	6,263 rapid rail cars	464	21	18.4	0.15	0.57
3. CTA (Chicago)	2,420 buses	1,428	10	10.1	1.18	7.01
	1,100 rapid rail cars	175	20	27.1	0.32	0.70
4. WMATA (Washington, D.C.)	2,043 buses	1,288	9	14.0	1.26	6.36
	296 rapid rail cars	78	5	17.9	0.53	1.77
5. San Francisco Municipal Railway	526 buses	445	11	9.6	1.69	10.58
	174 street cars	41	6	11.4	0.47	2.48
	345 trolley coaches	111	20	7.4	0.64	5.22
	41 cable cars	4	87	4.3	0.20	2.72
6. MBTA (Boston)	1,115 buses	1,420	9	12.7	2.55	12.03
	496 rapid rail cars	78	16	22.0	0.31	0.84
	300 street cars	59	22	15.1	0.39	1.56
	50 trolley coaches	32	14	12.8	1.28	6.00
7. Greater Cleveland RTA	1,016 buses	1,031	11	12.0	2.03	9.74
	100 rapid rail cars	38	24	31.0	0.76	1.47
	71 street cars	26	29	16.2	0.73	2.71
8. SORTA (Cincinnati)	528 buses	586	9	14.3	2.22	9.31
9. SEPTA (Philadelphia)	1,534 buses	2,006	9	10.1	2.62	15.54
	440 rapid rail cars	106	32	15.3	0.48	1.89
	368 street cars	176	27	9.3	0.96	6.24
	174 trolley coaches	42	14	8.0	0.48	3.62

System	Number of Vehicles	Route Miles	Fleet Age	Average Speed	Headway	Waiting Time
10. New Orleans Public Service	505 buses 35 street cars	507 13	8 yr 62	10.4 mph 8.7	2.01 mi 0.74	11.58 min 5.12
11. Santa Clara County Transit (San Jose)	745 buses	1,112	7	14.1	2.99	11.94
12. Kansas City (MO) Transit Authority	350 buses	481	9	13.6	2.75	12.22
13. MTA Harris County (Houston)	860 buses	1,372	7	13.9	3.19	13.77
14. Southern California RTD (Los Angeles)	2,960 buses	4,901	10	13.5	3.31	13.89
15. Baltimore MTA	900 buses	1,274	9	11.3	2.83	14.16
16. Dallas Transit System	582 buses	1,015	5	14.6	3.49	14.33
17. Metro Dade County Transit (Miami)	865 buses	1,404	8	12.6	3.25	14.76
18. Seattle METRO	1,027 buses 115 trolley coaches	1,940 108	11 5	19.1 18.6	3.78 1.88	15.96 8.05
19. Honolulu Department of Transportation	406 buses	796	10	14.7	3.92	15.48
20. SEMTA (Detroit)	1,346 buses	2,984	8	15.6	4.43	17.74
21. Bi-State Transit (St. Louis)	1,098 buses	2,131	8	12.8	3.88	17.78
22. Tri-County MTD (Portland, OR)	649 buses	1,367	9	16.2	4.21	18.05
23. MARTA (Atlanta)	885 buses 120 rapid rail cars	2,182 31	10 3	13.4 19.0	4.93 0.52	21.29 1.66
24. Memphis Area Transit	313 buses	759	13	14.7	4.85	19.80
25. Milwaukee Transit System	631 buses	1,344	12	12.6	4.26	20.29
26. Alameda County Transit (Oakland)	835 buses	2,170	11	14.4	5.20	21.36
27. PAT (Pittsburgh)	903 buses 92 street cars	2,369 52	10 37	13.2 14.9	5.25 1.13	23.85 4.55
28. MTC (Minneapolis–St. Paul)	1,012 buses	2,700	9	13.6	5.34	22.08
29. San Diego Transit Authority	341 buses	1,063	12	12.8	6.23	27.51
30. VIA MTS (San Antonio)	454 buses	1,482	8	14.0	6.53	27.98
31. River City Transit Authority (Louisville)	318 buses	995	6	13.3	6.26	28.23
32. Denver RTD	671 buses	2,850	6	16.5	8.49	35.89
33. Phoenix Transit	245 buses	1,208	10	16.6	9.86	38.17
34. Niagara Frontier Transit (Buffalo)	482 buses	1,882	12	10.9	7.81	42.99
35. Orange County Transit (Anaheim)	497 buses	2,959	6	14.4	11.91	46.70

Source: U.S. Department of Transportation, Urban Mass Transit Authority, *National Urban Mass Transportation Statistics—Section 15 Report,* 1984.

CONTRADICTORY RULES OF THE ROAD

Except for the national speed limit of 55 miles per hour imposed in 1974, each state regulates what its drivers can and cannot do. Consequently, driving across state boundaries can also mean a brush with contradictory traffic codes. Here are eight examples, with one caveat. The information comes from the National Committee on Uniform Traffic Laws, the National Highway Traffic Safety Administration, and the American Automobile Association's latest *Digest of Motor Laws,* but it may not reflect recent changes in the law.

Speed Limits. There are two kinds of speed limits—absolute and prima facie, a legal phrase meaning "at first view." If the speed limit of 55 is absolute, going 56 means breaking the law. If the speed limit of 55 is prima facie, however, going 56 or even 60 is merely apparent evidence of unreasonable and imprudent speed. Drivers may escape a fine if they can convince the traffic court that their speed was reasonable and safe in light of the highway's condition, traffic, and visibility. All or some speed limits in 16 states are prima facie:

Alabama	Michigan
Arizona	Minnesota
Arkansas	New Hampshire
California	Ohio
Colorado	Oregon
Connecticut	Rhode Island
Idaho	Texas
Massachusetts	Utah

Right and Left Turn on Red. In 1947, California became the first state to permit drivers to turn right on a red signal after a complete stop. The last was Massachusetts, in 1980. New York City now is the only major jurisdiction that prohibits the turn. According to the Federal Highway Administration, fewer accidents occur when drivers turn right on a red light than when they turn right on a green light. Furthermore, the rule saves each driver an average of 14 seconds at a turn, cuts gasoline consumption and exhaust emissions, and allows intersections to handle more traffic.

In the past five years, most states have enacted statutes permitting left turns on a red signal, but only after a complete stop and only from a one-way street into another one-way street. Fourteen places still prohibit turning left on red:

Arkansas	New Jersey
Connecticut	North Carolina
District of Columbia	Rhode Island
Kansas	South Carolina
Maine	Utah
Mississippi	Vermont
Missouri	Wyoming

The state of New York permits a left turn on red everywhere except New York City. Tennessee permits the turn when so marked by each city.

Child Restraints. Automobile accidents are the leading cause of death among young children. Because standard seat belts are not designed for very small children, and because these children are at greater risk in automobile accidents than adults, 41 states require the use of special restraints when driving with children who are less than preschool age. The nine states without such mandatory restraint laws are:

Alaska	Texas
Idaho	Utah
Iowa	Vermont
Louisiana	Wyoming
South Dakota	

Studded Tires. Most states allow drivers to mount studded snow tires on their automobiles for better traction during an icy winter. Because the carbide-tipped studs damage road surfaces, nine states prohibit their use:

Alabama	Mississippi
Hawaii	Texas
Illinois	Utah
Louisiana	Wisconsin
Minnesota	

Glass Tinting. Tinted automobile window glass is a frequently chosen factory option. Over the past five years, however, aftermarket application of black and gunmetal gray plastic sheeting to the inside of car windows has become extremely popular. Because it interferes with night vision, it is prohibited in all but 15 states:

Alaska	Montana
Arkansas	Nebraska
Connecticut	Nevada
Georgia	Oklahoma
Kentucky	South Carolina
Maine	South Dakota
Maryland	Wyoming
Missouri	

Audio Headsets. The issue here is whether the ears are as necessary for safe driving as the eyes. When you don't hear an ambulance siren, a ticket for failing to yield the right-of-way to an emergency vehicle is the likely consequence. But when you can't hear a train whistle or the air horn of an oncoming 18-wheeler, the

---

Rules of the Road Rated

If your travels take you to Massachusetts, you will find the oddest, most archaic, and most contradictory traffic laws in the United States. In Kansas, on the other hand, the most rational and up-to-date rules of the road have been on the books for years.

These judgments have been made by the National Committee on Uniform Traffic Laws, a semiofficial organization that publishes and continually revises the Uniform Vehicle Code (UVC), a complete set of motor laws designed as a model for the states. The committee—whose members are traffic court judges, state motor vehicle commissioners, and representatives of the automobile manufacturing and insurance industries—rates the states on how closely their statutes agree with the UVC. Complete agreement yields a score of 1,065.

States Ranked by Traffic Laws from Best to Worst

State	Score	State	Score
1. Kansas	932	26. Montana	586
2. Alabama	911	27. Arizona	579
3. South Carolina	862	28. Minnesota	576
4. Utah	852	29. Ohio	565
5. Idaho	837	30. Tennessee	560
6. North Dakota	833	31. Rhode Island	557
7. Georgia	827	32. Louisiana	538
8. Washington	812	33. Oregon	529
9. Pennsylvania	787	34. West Virginia	528
10. Illinois	775	35. Nevada	509
11. Colorado	747	36. South Dakota	461
12. Delaware	720	37. California	454
13. Maryland	717	38. Kentucky	448
14. Nebraska	714	39. Arkansas	434
15. Florida	711	40. Iowa	420
16. Hawaii	683	41. Connecticut	415
17. Texas	649	42. Michigan	405
18. New York	648	43. Maine	398
19. New Hampshire	630	43. Wisconsin	398
19. Vermont	630	45. North Carolina	344
21. Alaska	625	46. Mississippi	318
22. Wyoming	620	47. Virginia	315
23. Oklahoma	615	48. New Jersey	314
24. Indiana	600	49. Missouri	286
25. New Mexico	596	50. Massachusetts	253

Source: U.S. Department of Transportation, *Rules of the Road Rated*, 1981.

The District of Columbia was awarded 452 points for its traffic laws, a score that would place it 38th among the states.

result could be far more serious. Accordingly, 11 states prohibit the driver from wearing an audio headset:

Alaska	Minnesota
California	Pennsylvania
Florida	Rhode Island
Georgia	Virginia
Illinois	Washington
Massachusetts	

Motorcycle Helmets. The mileage fatality rate (deaths per 100 million miles) for motorcycle travel is five times that for auto travel, and the major cause is head injuries. Consequently, 41 states require motorcycle riders to wear helmets. Motorcyclists have challenged the law, but state courts have generally upheld it because it affects the biker's right to receive insurance compensation for injuries. Nine states, however, do not require protective headgear of any kind for motorcyclists and passengers:

California	Maine
Colorado	Nebraska
Connecticut	Rhode Island
Illinois	Washington
Iowa	

Mandatory Safety Inspections. Most states require regular inspection of automobiles to rid the highways of dangerous vehicles with bald tires, wobbly suspensions, smoky exhausts, and defective brakes and lights. But 13 states do not require regular examinations, although their state police may randomly pull cars over for roadside inspections:

Alabama	North Dakota
Florida	Ohio
Idaho	Oregon
Illinois	South Dakota
Indiana	Washington
Nebraska	Wisconsin
New Mexico	

Connecticut, Iowa, Kansas, Maryland, and Nevada require inspections only on newly registered cars or cars that are being sold. In Arizona, Colorado, and Georgia, regular inspections are mandatory only for exhaust emissions.

FINDING YOUR WAY ON THE INTERSTATE

By staying with a combination of Interstate routes, it is possible to drive from one metro area in the continental United States to almost any other without having to stop for a traffic light.

Five of the principal routes are more than 2,000 miles long. The longest, I–90, stretches 3,088 miles between downtown Boston and Seattle's waterfront. The next longest routes are I–80 (2,909 miles, from San Francisco to Hackensack, New Jersey), I–10 (2,460 miles along the nation's southern border, from Los Angeles to Jacksonville, Florida), I–40 (2,458 miles, from Barstow, California, to Smithfield, North Carolina), and I–70 (2,181 miles from Cove Fort, Utah, to Baltimore). Three of these routes, I–10, I–80, and I–90, cross the country from coast to coast, and I–40 nearly makes it.

Seven Interstate routes span the nation in a north-south direction, or nearly so: I–5 (1,382 miles, from San Diego to Bellingham, Washington), I–15 (1,431 miles, from San Diego to the Montana-Canada border), I–35 (1,572 miles from Laredo, Texas, to Duluth), I–55 (944 miles, from suburban New Orleans to Chicago), I–65 (887 miles, from Mobile, Alabama, to Gary–Hammond, Indiana), I–75 (1,742 miles, from Naples, Florida, to the Michigan-Canada border), and I–95 (1,857 miles, from the city of Miami to the Maine-Canada border).

The Interstate System: A Route Log and Finder List

Route	Total Mileage	Mileage by State		Selected Cities Served
I–4	132.10	Florida	132.10	Daytona Beach, Lakeland, Orlando, Tampa, Winter Haven
I–5	1,381.88	California	797.00	Anaheim, Los Angeles, Redding, Sacramento, San Diego, Santa Ana, Stockton
		Oregon	308.50	Eugene, Medford, Portland, Salem
		Washington	276.30	Bellingham, Olympia, Seattle, Tacoma, Vancouver
I–8	348.49	California	170.00	San Diego
		Arizona	178.49	Casa Grande, Yuma
I–10	2,460.29	California	242.50	Los Angeles, Riverside, San Bernardino
		Arizona	392.96	Phoenix, Tucson
		New Mexico	164.43	Las Cruces
		Texas	880.79	Beaumont, El Paso, Houston, San Antonio
		Louisiana	274.42	Baton Rouge, Lafayette, Lake Charles, New Orleans
		Mississippi	77.10	Biloxi, Gulfport, Pascagoula
		Alabama	66.20	Mobile
		Florida	361.89	Jacksonville, Pensacola, Tallahassee
I–12	85.59	Louisiana	85.59	Baton Rouge
I–15	1,430.95	California	288.10	Riverside, San Bernardino, San Diego
		Nevada	123.77	Las Vegas
		Arizona	29.35	Beaver Dam
		Utah	398.85	Ogden, Orem, Provo, Salt Lake City
		Idaho	195.87	Blackfoot, Idaho Falls, Pocatello
		Montana	395.01	Butte, Great Falls, Helena, Sweetgrass

Route	Total Mileage	Mileage by State		Selected Cities Served
I–16	165.41	Georgia	165.41	Macon, Savannah
I–17	145.67	Arizona	145.67	Flagstaff, Phoenix
I–19	63.13	Arizona	63.13	Tucson
I–20	1,537.17	Texas	634.54	Abilene, Arlington, Dallas, Fort Worth, Longview, Marshall, Midland, Odessa, Tyler
		Louisiana	189.87	Monroe, Shreveport
		Mississippi	154.50	Jackson, Meridian, Vicksburg
		Alabama	215.00	Anniston, Birmingham, Tuscaloosa
		Georgia	201.75	Atlanta, Augusta
		South Carolina	141.51	Columbia, Florence
I–24	316.52	Illinois	38.73	Vienna
		Kentucky	93.37	Hopkinsville
		Tennessee	180.30	Chattanooga, Clarksville, Nashville
		Georgia	4.12	—
I–25	1,060.62	New Mexico	460.76	Albuquerque, Las Cruces, Santa Fe
		Colorado	298.94	Colorado Springs, Denver, Fort Collins, Longmont, Pueblo
		Wyoming	300.92	Casper, Cheyenne
I–26	260.81	North Carolina	39.95	Asheville
		South Carolina	220.86	Charleston, Columbia, Spartanburg
I–27	124.38	Texas	124.38	Amarillo, Lubbock
I–29	752.34	Missouri	130.30	Kansas City, St. Joseph
		Iowa	151.81	Council Bluffs, Sioux City
		South Dakota	252.70	Sioux Falls
		North Dakota	217.53	Fargo, Grand Forks
I–30	336.78	Texas	193.70	Dallas, Texarkana
		Arkansas	143.08	Little Rock, Texarkana
I–35	1,572.39	Texas	503.82	Arlington, Austin, Dallas, Fort Worth, Laredo, San Antonio, Temple, Waco
		Oklahoma	235.96	Oklahoma City
		Kansas	235.60	Kansas City, Lawrence, Topeka, Wichita
		Missouri	114.80	Kansas City
		Iowa	218.51	Des Moines
		Minnesota	263.70	Albert Lea, Duluth, Minneapolis, St. Paul
I–37	142.96	Texas	142.96	Corpus Christi, San Antonio
I–40	2,458.14	California	154.60	Barstow, Needles
		Arizona	359.67	Flagstaff, Kingman
		New Mexico	374.11	Albuquerque, Gallup, Tucumcari
		Texas	177.00	Amarillo
		Oklahoma	331.03	Clinton, Oklahoma City
		Arkansas	284.80	Fort Smith, Little Rock
		Tennessee	451.60	Knoxville, Memphis, Nashville
		North Carolina	325.33	Asheville, Burlington, Durham, Greensboro, Hickory, Raleigh, Winston-Salem
I–43	119.58	Wisconsin	119.58	Green Bay, Milwaukee, Sheboygan
I–44	484.66	Oklahoma	193.86	Oklahoma City, Tulsa
		Missouri	290.80	Joplin, Springfield, St. Louis
I–45	284.99	Texas	284.99	Dallas, Galveston, Houston, Texas City
I–49	34.08	Louisiana	34.08	Alexandria
I–55	943.70	Louisiana	65.81	Hammond, La Place
		Mississippi	289.70	Grenada, Jackson, McComb
		Tennessee	12.20	Memphis
		Arkansas	72.22	Blytheville, West Memphis
		Missouri	209.20	Cape Girardeau, St. Louis
		Illinois	294.57	Bloomington, Chicago, East St. Louis, Joliet, Springfield
I–57	380.57	Missouri	22.00	—
		Illinois	358.57	Champaign, Chicago, Kankakee, Rantoul, Urbana
I–59	444.12	Louisiana	11.48	New Orleans, Slidell
		Mississippi	171.20	Hattiesburg, Laurel, Meridian
		Alabama	241.50	Birmingham, Gadsden, Tuscaloosa
		Georgia	19.94	—
I–64	929.33	Illinois	128.06	Belleville, East St. Louis
		Indiana	124.04	Evansville, New Albany
		Kentucky	191.70	Frankfort, Lexington, Louisville
		West Virginia	186.55	Charleston, Huntington
		Virginia	298.98	Charlottesville, Newport News, Norfolk, Richmond
I–65	887.38	Alabama	366.30	Birmingham, Mobile, Montgomery
		Tennessee	121.40	Nashville
		Kentucky	137.60	Bowling Green, Louisville
		Indiana	262.08	Gary, Indianapolis, Lafayette

(continued on page 216)

Interstate Highways

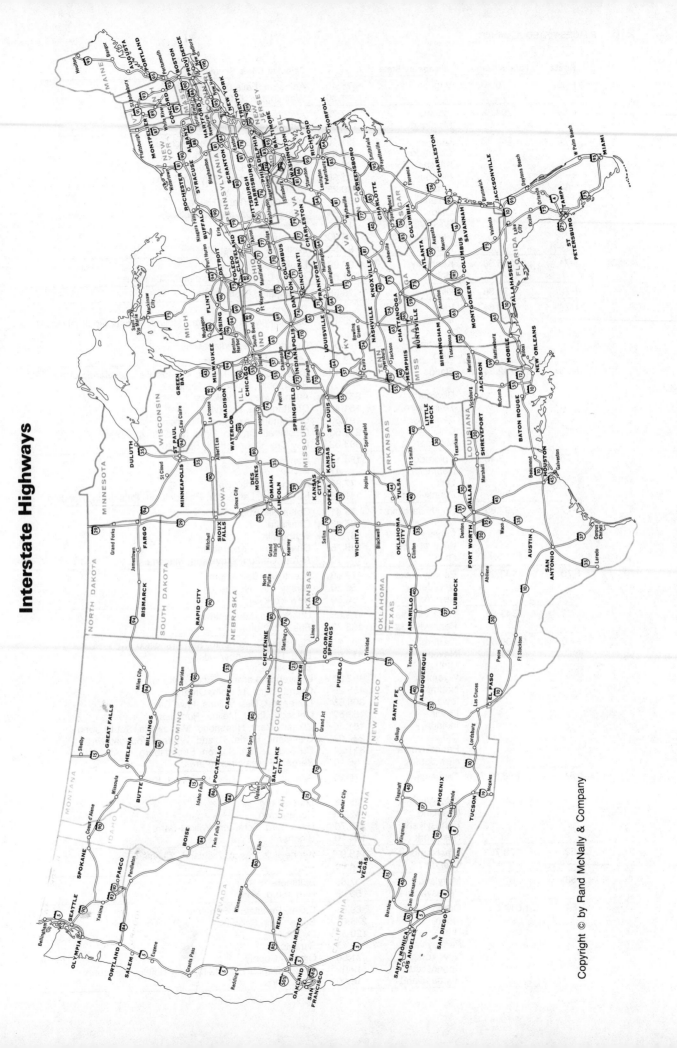

Route	Total Mileage	Mileage by State		Selected Cities Served
I–66	76.70	Virginia	75.40	Arlington, Falls Church
			1.30	Washington, D.C.
I–69	294.39	Indiana	157.79	Anderson, Fort Wayne, Indianapolis, Muncie
		Michigan	136.60	Battle Creek, Flint, Lansing
I–70	2,180.82	Utah	231.10	Cove Fort, Green River, Richfield
		Colorado	450.51	Denver, Grand Junction
		Kansas	424.20	Kansas City, Lawrence, Topeka
		Missouri	251.60	Columbia, Kansas City, St. Louis
		Illinois	160.25	East St. Louis
		Indiana	156.27	Indianapolis, Terre Haute
		Ohio	225.69	Columbus, Dayton, Springfield
		West Virginia	14.40	Wheeling
		Pennsylvania	169.30	Pittsburgh
		Maryland	97.50	Baltimore, Hagerstown
I–71	345.58	Kentucky	97.92	Louisville
		Ohio	247.66	Akron, Cincinnati, Cleveland, Columbus
I–72	78.68	Illinois	78.68	Champaign, Springfield
I–74	416.64	Iowa	5.42	Davenport
		Illinois	220.10	Bloomington, Champaign, Moline, Peoria, Rock Island, Urbana
		Indiana	171.87	Crawfordsville, Indianapolis
		Ohio	19.45	Cincinnati
I–75	1,742.34	Florida	429.19	Bradenton, Fort Myers, Gainesville, Lakeland, Ocala, St. Petersburg, Sarasota, Tampa
		Georgia	355.00	Atlanta, Macon, Valdosta
		Tennessee	161.40	Chattanooga, Knoxville
		Kentucky	191.60	Covington, Lexington, Richmond
		Ohio	211.53	Cincinnati, Dayton, Lima, Middletown, Toledo
		Michigan	393.62	Bay City, Detroit, Flint, Saginaw
I–76	618.48	Colorado	184.14	Denver
		Nebraska	2.47	—
		Ohio	77.82	Akron, Youngstown
		Pennsylvania	351.25	Harrisburg, Lancaster, Philadelphia, Pittsburgh, Reading
I–77	597.86	South Carolina	75.41	Columbia, Rock Hill
		North Carolina	105.43	Charlotte
		Virginia	67.17	Wytheville
		West Virginia	186.75	Charleston, Parkersburg
		Ohio	163.10	Akron, Canton, Cleveland, Marietta
I–78	143.39	Pennsylvania	76.69	Allentown, Bethlehem
		New Jersey	66.20	Jersey City, Newark
		New York	0.50	New York City
I–79	343.56	West Virginia	159.85	Charleston, Morgantown
		Pennsylvania	183.73	Erie, Pittsburgh
I–80	2,909.52	California	203.80	Oakland, Sacramento, San Francisco
		Nevada	410.66	Elko, Reno, Winnemucca
		Utah		Salt Lake City
		Wyoming	402.82	Cheyenne, Laramie, Rock Springs
		Nebraska	455.26	Grand Island, Lincoln, Omaha
		Iowa	306.55	Davenport, Des Moines, Iowa City
		Illinois	163.52	Chicago, Joliet, Moline, Rock Island
		Indiana	151.65	Elkhart, Gary, Hammond, Mishawaka, South Bend
		Ohio	237.07	Cleveland, Elyria, Toledo, Warren, Youngstown
		Pennsylvania	311.24	Du Bois, Milton, Sharon, Stroudsburg
		New Jersey	68.10	Bergen–Passaic metro area
I–81	856.08	Tennessee	75.30	Bristol, Johnson City, Kingsport, Knoxville
		Virginia	325.00	Bristol, Roanoke
		West Virginia	25.98	Martinsburg
		Maryland	12.00	Hagerstown
		Pennsylvania	233.70	Harrisburg, Scranton, Wilkes-Barre
		New York	184.10	Binghamton, Syracuse
I–82	128.77	Washington	113.97	Kennewick, Pasco, Richland, Yakima
		Oregon	14.80	—
I–83	87.56	Maryland	37.50	Baltimore
		Pennsylvania	50.06	Harrisburg, York
I–84	1,014.60	Oregon	369.01	Baker, Pendleton, Portland
		Idaho	275.61	Boise, Twin Falls
		Utah	120.53	Ogden
		Pennsylvania	49.75	Scranton
		New York	71.60	Orange County
		Connecticut	112.09	Bristol, Danbury, Hartford, New Britain, Waterbury
		Rhode Island	16.00	Providence

Route	Total Mileage	Mileage by State		Selected Cities Served
I-85	668.33	Alabama	80.10	Montgomery
		Georgia	178.94	Atlanta
		South Carolina	106.25	Anderson, Greenville, Spartanburg
		North Carolina	233.44	Burlington, Charlotte, Durham, Gastonia, Greensboro, High Point
		Virginia	69.60	Petersburg
I-86	38.75	Connecticut	30.69	Hartford
		Massachusetts	8.06	Sturbridge
I-87	333.30	New York	333.30	Albany, Glens Falls, New York City, Orange County, Poughkeepsie, Troy
I-88	117.28	New York	117.28	Binghamton, Schenectady
I-89	191.33	New Hampshire	60.94	Concord
		Vermont	130.39	Burlington, Montpelier
I-90	3,087.65	Washington	296.72	Seattle, Spokane
		Idaho	73.77	Coeur d'Alene, Kellogg
		Montana	551.20	Billings, Butte, Missoula
		Wyoming	208.78	Sheridan
		South Dakota	412.85	Rapid City, Sioux Falls
		Minnesota	275.58	Albert Lea, Rochester
		Wisconsin	187.17	Beloit, Janesville, La Crosse, Madison
		Illinois	112.98	Chicago, Elgin, Rockford
		Indiana	156.90	Elkhart, Gary, Hammond, Mishawaka, South Bend
		Ohio	244.13	Cleveland, Elyria, Lorain, Toledo
		Pennsylvania	46.60	Erie
		New York	386.77	Albany, Buffalo, Rochester, Rome, Schenectady, Syracuse, Troy, Utica
		Massachusetts	134.20	Boston, Pittsfield, Springfield, Worcester
I-91	290.70	Connecticut	57.98	Hartford, Meriden, Middletown, New Haven
		Massachusetts	54.92	Springfield
		Vermont	177.80	Brattleboro, St. Johnsbury
I-93	174.30	Massachusetts	31.37	Boston, Lawrence, Lowell
		New Hampshire	131.93	Concord, Manchester
		Vermont	11.00	St. Johnsbury
I-94	1,607.12	Montana	247.93	Billings, Miles City
		North Dakota	352.61	Bismarck, Fargo
		Minnesota	259.27	Minneapolis, Moorhead, St. Cloud, St. Paul
		Wisconsin	348.17	Eau Claire, Kenosha, Madison, Milwaukee, Racine
		Illinois	77.37	Chicago, Lake County
		Indiana	45.73	Gary, Hammond
		Michigan	276.04	Ann Arbor, Battle Creek, Benton Harbor, Detroit, Jackson, Kalamazoo
I-95	1,857.44	Florida	380.39	Boca Raton, Daytona Beach, Fort Lauderdale, Fort Pierce, Hialeah, Hollywood, Jacksonville, Melbourne, Miami, Palm Beach, Pompano Beach, Titusville, West Palm Beach
		Georgia	111.69	Savannah
		South Carolina	198.75	Florence
		North Carolina	181.22	Fayetteville
		Virginia	181.80	Arlington, Petersburg, Richmond
			0.12	Washington, D.C.
		Maryland	109.15	Baltimore
		Delaware	23.42	Wilmington
		Pennsylvania	51.94	Philadelphia
		New Jersey	74.20	Elizabeth, Newark, Trenton
		New York	23.25	New York City
		Connecticut	111.57	Bridgeport, Milford, New Haven, New London, Norwalk, Stamford
		Rhode Island	43.33	Providence
		Massachusetts	52.56	Attleboro, Boston
		New Hampshire	16.15	Portsmouth
		Maine	297.89	Augusta, Bangor, Portland
I-96	193.10	Michigan	193.10	Detroit, Grand Rapids, Lansing, Muskegon
I-97	1.90	Maryland	1.90	Washington, D.C., urban area

Source: U.S. Department of Transportation, *Interstate System Route Log and Finder List,* undated.

Education:
Where Schools Get Good Marks

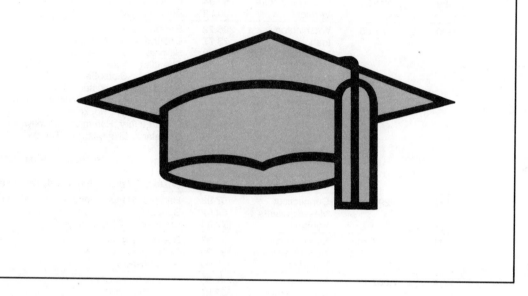

Nine months of the year, all day long, three of every ten Americans are either working for an educational institution or being taught in one. Supporting the public side of this endeavor takes billions of tax dollars, and recent reviews of whether the price is worth it have caused educators and parents to tangle.

Education isn't the sacred cow it once was. The achievement of high school students on most standardized tests is lower today than it was in 1957, when the launching of Sputnik also launched an urgent nationwide push to improve education. Among seventeen-year-olds tested in 1982, says a report by the National Commission on Excellence in Education, nearly 40 percent couldn't draw inferences from written material, only one fifth could write a persuasive essay, and only one third could solve a math problem requiring several steps.

Privately, parents and teachers each blame the other. Although parents say they trust teachers more than politicians, journalists, or business people, they don't give teachers high marks. Only half the public gave teachers a grade of B or better when asked in a 1984 Gallup poll to choose either A, B, C, D, or F. For their part, teachers are even stingier graders—only 21 percent gave parents a grade of B or higher.

As for education and the metro areas, two things are certain: (1) If there is one public service in which shoddy performance pushes families to change their address, it is the kind of education their children are getting in public schools, and (2) If schemes for improving the schools—such as merit pay for good teachers, longer days, smaller classes, and an extra month in the academic year—are to be tried, they will require money.

PUBLIC SCHOOLS AT THE ELEMENTARY AND SECONDARY LEVEL

The quality of the public schools usually tips the balance for a relocating family weighing a neighborhood's good and bad points. Too often, the choice is influenced by a real estate agent's hearsay that the schools are great or ought to be because the town's tax rate is high. Are there ways for parents to compare districts and schools within these districts more objectively? Definitely.

Shopping for a District

The smallest political unit in the United States has got to be the school district. In the 1930s, the country was fragmented into 128,000 of them. After decades of consolidations, they now number fewer than 16,000 and range in size from the giant New York City Public and Los Angeles Unified school districts to several hundred "paper" ones that don't operate schools themselves, busing children instead to other districts.

218

Moving into a metro area often means stepping into a thicket of school districts, each with its own politics, funding, philosophy, standards, curricula—and, yes, results. Since your tax dollars will help support the district, you'll want to investigate their differences with a consumer's eye. Visit the district principal or superintendent's office and consider several factors:

• A good district can give you a written philosophy or a statement of educational objectives approved within the last five years by the state board of education. If educational philosophy and objectives are explicit and under constant examination and review, then a district takes its mission seriously.

• The classroom teachers in the district should have not only a standard certificate but also (in 50 percent of the cases or better) at least a master's degree or equivalent in the subject they teach.

• Nationally, only 77 percent of ninth-graders finish high school. A district's holding power—that is, the percent of its ninth-grade pupils who stay in school and graduate—should be at least 90 percent.

• If 95 percent of a district's enrollment is in average daily attendance, that's a good indication of how closely parents and schools keep tabs on children. Nationally, the average daily attendance is 90 percent; in some districts, it is a good deal less.

• Beware of the professional revolving door. A high number of eligible teachers not getting tenure *might* mean that the district has tough standards; but it could also be a sign that the district cuts costs by hiring beginners and then refusing them tenure at the end of their probationary period. Under this scheme, it is possible for a child to progress from kindergarten through high school and have inexperienced, unfamiliar teachers each year.

Shopping for a School

Moving into a good school district won't necessarily mean that you'll find quality education in all of its schools. Get a district map of neighborhood boundaries for the schools as well as a list of Parent-Teacher Association (PTA) contacts. Talking with a local parent will save you time. Then visit the school's principal or the head guidance counselor to obtain specific information.

• A good high school should have one guidance counselor for every 200 students, and it should also have at least one full-time career counselor.

• Classroom size in high school should average no more than 30 students.

• The size of the senior class should range from 300 to 500 students. If the enrollment is much smaller than that, many worthwhile specialized courses won't be offered.

• A quality high school should offer four years of English, mathematics, and foreign languages; second-year courses in biology, astronomy, chemistry, and

The 40 Largest Public School Districts

Unit	Students Enrolled
1. New York City Public	924,123
2. Los Angeles Unified	540,903
3. City of Chicago	442,889
4. Dade County (Miami, FL)	224,580
5. Philadelphia City	213,980
6. Detroit City	208,656
7. Houston Independent School District	193,702
8. Broward County (Fort Lauderdale, FL)	127,758
9. Dallas Independent School District	127,584
10. Fairfax County (Fairfax, VA)	124,631
11. Baltimore City	123,376
12. Prince Georges County (Upper Marlboro, MD)	116,598
13. Memphis City	111,262
14. San Diego City Unified	110,904
15. Hillsborough County (Tampa, FL)	109,953
16. Duval County (Jacksonville, FL)	99,512
17. Jefferson County (Louisville, KY)	96,609
18. Montgomery County (Rockville, MD)	95,696
19. District of Columbia	94,975
20. Baltimore County (Towson, MD)	92,387
21. Clark County (Las Vegas, NV)	89,547
22. Milwaukee	86,312
23. Pinellas County (Clearwater, FL)	85,341
24. Orleans Parish (New Orleans, LA)	83,391
25. Orange County (Orlando, FL)	79,431
26. Jefferson County (Lakewood, CO)	77,274
27. De Kalb County (Decatur, GA)	76,114
28. Cleveland	75,796
29. Mecklenburg County–Charlotte City (Charlotte, NC)	72,756
30. Albuquerque	72,012
31. Columbus (Columbus, OH)	71,594
32. Atlanta City	69,977
33. Palm Beach County (West Palm Beach, FL)	69,855
34. Nashville–Davidson County (Nashville, TN)	67,437
35. Anne Arundel County (Annapolis, MD)	67,422
36. Fort Worth Independent School District	65,822
37. Boston	62,989
38. Mobile County (Mobile, AL)	62,641
39. Denver	62,438
40. Granite (Salt Lake City, UT)	62,129

Source: U.S. Department of Education, *Universe of Public School Districts*, 1984.

physics; college-preparatory courses in the humanities; at least one year of computer literacy; and Advanced Placement (AP) courses for college credit. (South Carolina recently became the first state to require all its high schools to offer AP courses.)

• A good high school averages ten National Merit Scholarship commendations a year; an excellent school averages 15 or more a year.

• Because one fifth of all four-year public colleges must accept every high school graduate within the state, regardless of program followed or grades earned, it is no longer noteworthy that most of a high school's graduating seniors go on to college. The question to ask is, Which colleges are accepting them—top-rated schools with tough admissions standards or open-admission institutions with no requirements but that the check be good and the diploma in hand?

Don't cross a high school off your list if it doesn't measure up on all of these points. A school can have all but one or two and still be a good one.

Many relocation experts advise their clients that the stability of a town is reflected best in its schools. If the high school is good, chances are that the schools at the lower levels will also be good. In choosing an elementary school or a junior high, again, ask questions of principals and other parents.

• In junior high schools—grades 7, 8, and 9—there should be special provision for both bright students and slow learners.

• In elementary schools, there should be a full-time librarian and a classroom-size library.

• Class size in elementary schools should average no more than 20 pupils.

If you can't investigate schools personally, you can still gauge their quality from afar. Among the standard albeit imperfect yardsticks are pupil/teacher ratio, the amount of money spent on educating one student, teacher salaries, and effort to support the public schools with tax revenue.

Pupil/Teacher Ratios

Teachers unions bargain as fiercely for smaller classes as they do for more money at contract-renegotiation time. Teaching classes with fewer pupils reduces professional stress, forestalling the gray hair that comes with the career. And such classes insure the need for more teachers at a time when enrollments aren't growing. In addition, testing shows that small classes do make a difference in a child's learning.

Imagine that a child in a typical classroom of 40 children scores at the modest 50th percentile (right in the middle) of an achievement test. The same child taught in a classroom of 15 or 20 would have scored at the 55th percentile; in a group of ten, at the 65th percentile; and a class of five, at the 75th percentile. A child in a group of 40, then, would score 25 percentile points higher if taught in a group of five students. These findings, based on research conducted since 1900 involving one million students, come from the Far West Laboratory for Educational Research and Development, in San Francisco.

Unfortunately, classes averaging five pupils are luxuries that public school districts can't afford. To reduce the average class size in metropolitan Cleveland by just one student would mean hiring 1,200 additional teachers and finding an extra $2.2 million to pay them each month; in metropolitan Dallas, the monthly payroll would climb by $3 million for 2,000 additional teachers.

The number of pupils for each full-time teacher is smaller in some metro areas than in others, and this ratio can be regarded as a rough indicator of how many children there are in a typical classroom, as well as how good an opportunity these children have to learn.

Metro Area Pupil/Teacher Ratios

Lowest		Highest	
1. Billings, MT	8.08	1. Vancouver, WA	20.52
2. Pittsfield, MA	10.72	2. Bremerton, WA	20.30
3. Trenton, NJ	11.07	3. Vallejo–Fairfield–	
4. Charlottesville,		Napa, CA	20.27
VA	11.15	4. Jacksonville, NC	20.17
5. Burlington, VT	11.43	5. Seattle, WA	20.15
6. Middlesex–		6. San Jose, CA	19.83
Somerset–		7. Las Vegas, NV	19.62
Hunterdon, NJ	11.73	8. Richland–	
7. Bristol, CT	11.74	Kennewick–	
7. Hartford, CT	11.74	Pasco, WA	19.59
7. Middletown, CT	11.74	9. Provo–Orem, UT	19.54
7. New Britain, CT	11.74	10. Dothan, AL	19.35

Source: U.S. Bureau of the Census, *Compendium of Public Employment,* forthcoming, and Market Data Retrieval, *National School Market Index,* 1983.

These figures are derived by dividing public school enrollment by the number of "instructional staff," a term that embraces not only teachers but also principals, librarians, guidance counselors, psychological counselors—in other words, everyone involved in teaching or the improvement of education.

The national metro area average for pupil/teacher ratio is 15.12.

The Cost of Educating One Pupil

Nassau–Suffolk, New York, spends more than three times as much money to educate one pupil as does Dothan, Alabama. Are children better schooled on Long Island? Or is public instruction accomplished more efficiently in southeastern Alabama? Neither, necessarily. There are many items hidden in a metro area's figures for expenses per student, items that either have nothing to do with education or reflect a special need of the metro area. In New York, there is the expense of salaries for security guards in Bronx school hallways; in Miami and Houston, of bilingual instruction for large Hispanic enrollments; in Anchorage, of high energy costs during a long heating season; in St. Louis, of busing children in and out of center-city schools. Living costs are another factor. Much of the difference between Dothan's outlay of $1,505 per student and Nassau–Suffolk's figure of $4,637 represents the gap between what it takes to live in the Northeast and the Deep South.

Just as the cost of educating one student varies between rich and poor states, so it varies between rich and poor districts *within* the states. For example, Odessa, in western Texas, spends almost twice as much money per student as El Paso, about 300 miles away. The variation between the richest school district and the poorest is widest in Georgia, according to a recent U.S. Department of Education survey. In Hawaii, which has the country's only statewide school district, there is no disparity at all. Dollars per pupil becomes a meaningful statistic when data for metro areas within the same state are compared.

Dollars Spent per Pupil in the Metro Areas

Most		Fewest	
1. Casper, WY	$4,870	1. Dothan, AL	$1,505
2. Middlesex–Somerset–Hunterdon, NJ	4,869	2. Gadsden, AL	1,537
		3. Montgomery, AL	1,561
3. Nassau–Suffolk, NY	4,637	4. Mobile, AL	1,606
4. San Francisco, CA	4,001	5. Anniston, AL	1,607
5. Rochester, NY	3,992	6. Clarksville–Hopkinsville, TN–KY	1,620
6. Poughkeepsie, NY	3,881	7. Tuscaloosa, AL	1,717
7. Trenton, NJ	3,873	8. Chattanooga, TN–GA	1,763
8. Anchorage, AK	3,843	9. Boise City, ID	1,772
9. Binghamton, NY	3,766	10. Johnson City–Kingsport–Bristol, TN–VA	1,776
10. Niagara Falls, NY	3,762		

Source: U.S. Bureau of the Census, *Compendium of Government Finance*, forthcoming, and Market Data Retrieval, *National School Market Index*, 1983.

The national metro area average for dollars spent per pupil is $2,861.

What Teachers Earn

Parents tend to think that teachers bail out of their profession because of burnout brought on by semester after semester of unruly and unmotivated pupils. Not entirely, say ex-teachers; it's mainly the money.

Their seventh- and eighth-grade pupils pull down $1.50 an hour for baby-sitting, teachers point out when they negotiate their contracts. If a teacher working five class periods were to be paid $1.50 per day for nothing more than watching over each child in an average-size classroom, he or she would earn $3,750 each month of the academic year. Yet teachers accomplish much more than keeping every five- to seventeen-year-old off the street. They teach them, too, throughout a long, arduous day. Therefore, the argument goes, teachers should be paid more.

Teaching requires formal preparation, certification, and a lifelong perfection of skills. Moreover, teacher earnings have suffered more from inflation than the earnings of other professionals: The average amount of money teachers earn today is no more than what they made in 1973, after adjustment to current dollars. Teachers in some districts can barely stay afloat. According to the National Education Association, classroom teachers who support families in some counties

Compulsory Education

Most state laws requiring school attendance until a specified age were passed near the beginning of the century and haven't changed much in the decades since. The span of compulsory attendance ranges from six years in Mississippi to 12 in Hawaii, Ohio, and Utah.

Place	Compulsory Attendance Age Range*
Alabama	Between 7 and 16
Alaska	Between 7 and 16
Arizona	Between 8 and 16
Arkansas	Between 7 and 15 (both inclusive)
California	Between 6 and 16
Colorado	Of 7 and under 16
Connecticut	Over 7 and under 16
Delaware	Between 6 and 16
District of Columbia	Between 7 and 16
Florida	Attained 7 but not 16
Georgia	Between 7th and 16th birthdays
Hawaii	At least 6 and not 18
Idaho	Of 7 but not 16
Illinois	Between 7 and 16
Indiana	Not less than 7, not more than 16
Iowa	Over 7 and under 16
Kansas	Of 7 and under 16
Kentucky	Of 7 and under 16
Louisiana	Between 7 and 15
Maine	Between 7th and 15th anniversaries
Maryland	Between 6 and 16
Massachusetts	Between 6 and 16
Michigan	Between 6 and 16
Minnesota	Between 7 and 16
Mississippi	From 7 to 13
Missouri	Between 7 and 16
Montana	Is 7, not yet reached 16th birthday
Nebraska	Not less than 7 nor more than 16
Nevada	Between 7 and 17
New Hampshire	Between 6 and 16
New Jersey	Between 6 and 16
New Mexico	Attained 6 and until attaining 17
New York	From 6 to 16
North Carolina	Between 7 and 16
North Dakota	Of 7 to 16
Ohio	Between 6 and 18
Oklahoma	Between 8 and 16
Oregon	Between 7 and 18
Pennsylvania	Not later than 8, until 17
Rhode Island	Completed 7 years of life, not completed 16 years of life
South Carolina	Of 7 to 16
South Dakota	Of 7 and not exceeding 16
Tennessee	Between 7 and 16
Texas	As much as 7, not more than 17
Utah	Between 6 and 18
Vermont	Between 7 and 16
Virginia	Reached 6th birthday, not passed the 17th birthday
Washington	Child 8 and under 15
West Virginia	Begin with the 7th birthday, continue to the 16th birthday
Wisconsin	Between 6 and 16
Wyoming	Between 7 and 16 inclusive

Source: U.S. Department of Education, *Digest of Education Statistics*, 1984.

*As stated in the state's compulsory attendance laws.

in the Deep South qualify for food stamps under certain conditions. On the other hand, in every one of America's metro areas teachers earn more than uniformed firemen and policemen. Some taxpayers and city managers point out that for nine months' work classroom teachers are the best paid of municipal employees.

The $2,000 difference between the monthly paychecks of Anchorage teachers and those in Wilmington may reflect the value taxpayers and city managers place on teachers as much as differences in the cost of living and average household income.

Metro Area Average Monthly Teacher Salaries

Highest		Lowest	
1. Anchorage, AK	$2,927	1. Wilmington, DE–NJ–MD	$ 929
2. Detroit, MI	2,609	2. Mobile, AL	1,063
3. Santa Barbara–Santa Maria–Lompoc, CA	2,517	3. Augusta, GA–SC	1,097
		4. Charleston, WV	1,134
4. Nassau–Suffolk, NY	2,494	5. Richmond–Petersburg, VA	1,152
5. Flint, MI	2,474	6. Macon–Warner Robins, GA	1,181
6. San Jose, CA	2,417		
7. Anaheim–Santa Ana, CA	2,416	7. Pascagoula, MS	1,199
8. San Diego, CA	2,369	8. Houma–Thibodaux, LA	1,202
9. Grand Forks, ND	2,344	9. Florence, SC	1,205
10. Ann Arbor, MI	2,327	9. Montgomery, AL	1,205

Source: U.S. Bureau of the Census, *Compendium of Public Employment*, forthcoming.

Figures represent the average paycheck for the 2,210,274 teachers in the metro areas in October 1982. It should be noted that different school districts pay their teachers over different time periods; some teachers have nine-month contracts, others ten-month contracts, and still others year-long contracts.

The national metro area average for monthly teacher salaries is $1,778.

Support Your Public Schools: The Effort Index

Along with the pupil/teacher ratio, the amount of effort a metro area devotes to supporting and improving neighborhood schools may be considered one of the most important reflections of the local quality of education. *Places Rated Almanac* gauges the level of this support by applying a formula to determine each place's effort index.

To calculate effort index, we look at how much revenue a place devotes to public schools relative to its need. Metro areas with many children in private schools, for example, have low public school budget needs, as do metro areas whose populations of school-age children are shrinking. A metro area's relative need is determined by dividing its total population by its public school enrollment and comparing this to the national average. (Nationally the ratio is 5.836 persons for every one in public school.) Finally, we divide this figure for need by the actual proportion of tax revenues given over to public schools as compared to the national average.

This formula (the creation of the Advisory Commission on Intergovernmental Relations) puts all metro areas on an equal footing, offering an effective way to compare them. If a metro's effort index is greater than 1.000, it is giving above-average support to its school system, whereas an index less than 1.000 indicates that the metro area is giving below-average support, possibly falling short of local needs.

Metro Area Effort Indexes

Lowest		Highest	
1. Richland–Kennewick–Pasco, WA	0.456	1. State College, PA	1.760
2. New York, NY	0.618	2. Middlesex–Somerset–Hunterdon, NJ	1.754
3. Anchorage, AK	0.692	3. Cumberland, MD–WV	1.667
4. Dothan, AL	0.699	4. Fort Pierce, FL	1.642
5. Pascagoula, MS	0.703	5. Davenport–Rock Island–Moline, IA–IL	1.627
6. Houma–Thibodaux, LA	0.710		
7. Visalia–Tulare–Porterville, CA	0.713	6. Salem, OR	1.605
8. Las Vegas, NV	0.720	7. Burlington, VT	1.575
9. Huntsville, AL	0.736	8. New London–Norwich, CT–RI	1.543
10. Tuscaloosa, AL	0.738	9. Bryan–College Station, TX	1.535
		10. Lancaster, PA	1.505

Source: U.S. Bureau of the Census, *Compendium of Government Finance*, forthcoming, and Market Data Retrieval, *National School Market Index*, 1983.

The national metro area average for effort index is 1.000.

FOR ONE IN NINE: PRIVATE SCHOOLS

A startling statistic about K–12 education in the United States since 1930 is the nearly 100 percent growth in the number of private schools in contrast to the 75 percent decline in the number of public schools. This isn't to say that public K–12 education is collapsing; most of the schools that have closed are rural one-room buildings. But the statistic does show that private schools have become a thriving alternative. During the 1970s, when school enrollments were dropping, private schools held on to more of their enrollment than did public schools, losing only 6 percent as compared with 11 percent for public schools. Today one out of nine school-age children attends a private or parochial school.

Recent research from the Department of Education shows that students in private high schools take more courses than their public school counterparts and that they take these courses in smaller classes. Critics of public education point out that because private institutions forego the smorgasbord of electives that public schools offer their students, graduates of private high schools have tougher basic courses on their transcripts and are better prepared for college study. (In fact, private school pupils score higher on average on the Scholastic Aptitude Tests than students in public schools.) Not for nothing are private schools a preferred educational option for many families, not all of whom are Catholic or well-to-do.

Most private schools are run by some religious group, accounting for 80 percent of all private schools. The remaining institutions tend to be small schools;

Private Schools in the Metro Areas

Whatever the reason for the steady enrollments in private school—the desire for religious training or for a more rigorous education—it is undeniable that private schools are a fixture on the American education scene. All of the 329 metro areas have at least one private K–12 school, and only 55 metro areas have fewer than ten. The 20 places below have the greatest proportion of private-school students among their school-age populations.

The 20 Metro Areas with the Highest Proportion of Students in Private School, K–12

Metro Area	Percent Students in Private School
1. Dubuque, IA	35.3%
2. New Orleans, LA	28.9
3. Owensboro, KY	25.0
4. Jersey City, NJ	24.8
4. New York, NY	24.8
6. Wilmington, DE–NJ–MD	23.7
7. St. Louis, MO–IL	22.9
8. Stamford, CT	22.8
9. San Francisco, CA	22.6
10. Erie, PA	22.5
11. Baltimore, MD	22.4
11. Trenton, NJ	22.4
13. West Palm Beach–Boca Raton– Delray Beach, FL	22.2
14. Wheeling, WV–OH	21.7
15. Cleveland, OH	21.3
16. Savannah, GA	21.0
17. Milwaukee, WI	20.9
18. Chicago, IL	20.5
19. Miami–Hialeah, FL	20.4
20. Bristol, CT	20.1

Source: Derived from Market Data Retrieval, *National School Market Index,* 1983.

they enroll only 16 percent of private school pupils. Among religiously affiliated schools, Catholic schools predominate in number and enrollment, but there are also substantial numbers of pupils in Baptist, Lutheran, Christian, Jewish, Seventh-Day Adventist, and Episcopal schools.

Private Schools and Enrollments

Type of School	Schools	Students
Catholic	9,660	3,190,687
Lutheran	1,533	219,963
Seventh-Day Adventist	1,092	82,609
Baptist	1,071	233,334
Christian	651	112,906
Jewish	399	85,231
Episcopal	315	76,973
Other sectarian	1,491	224,788
Nonsectarian	4,767	802,374
Total	20,979	5,028,865

Source: National Center for Education Statistics, unpublished data, 1984.

BEYOND HIGH SCHOOL: METRO AREA COLLEGES AND UNIVERSITIES

Educators like to say that schooling leads to just three things: more schooling, employment, or unemployment. When high school graduates go on to college or find jobs, the public education system is successful; if they do neither, the system is considered a flop. In fact, nearly half of metro area high school graduates enter college, and six out of ten of these begin their freshman year at an institution within 50 miles of home.

More than an Education

Everywhere from Abilene to Youngstown, chamber of commerce promotional brochures tout the diversity of local colleges and universities more frequently than other urban assets. And with good reason. Among the 12 million full-time college students in the United States, nine million are studying in metro areas. For 21 million other people, the typical location for their evening or weekend continuing education course is a local college classroom.

But colleges and universities contribute other things besides education. In smaller metro areas, a worthy theatre where a touring group of professional players can stage *Hamlet* or an auditorium where an orchestra and choir can perform *The Messiah* can often only be found at the local college campus. Colleges and universities are stable white-collar employers, too. In Gainesville, Florida; Lawrence, Kansas; and Tuscaloosa, Alabama, they are the major employer. Finally, there is the connection between research-oriented universities and healthy economies. Two prime examples are Stanford University's impetus to the growth of high-tech enterprises in San Jose and the Bay Area, and M.I.T.'s faculty and alumni who have started many thriving electronics firms along Route 128 outside of Boston.

Metro Area Higher Education Options

Although a metro area may have many colleges and students, it may not necessarily be the home of quality education. But if these colleges are of different kinds and offer different programs—that is, if they provide a number of academic options—then we can conclude that the metro area is meeting the varied needs of a community.

Just as a city's municipal bonds are rated for quality and safety using letter grades, so *Places Rated Almanac* has devised a similar method of assessing options in higher education. (The options rating for each metro area is shown in the Place Profiles later in the chapter.)

C-Rated Metro Areas. These metro areas offer limited options. There may either be no public colleges at all (as in Abilene, Texas), only two-year public colleges (as in Bremerton, Washington), or only four-year colleges that may not offer courses at night and on weekends for certification in trade and technical occupations, as most two-year colleges do.

B-Rated Metro Areas. The options found here can include private colleges and universities, but there must also be at least one public two-year college and one public four-year college to satisfy the demand for low-cost education, ranging from instruction in the trades and technical occupations to courses leading to a bachelor's degree.

A-Rated Metro Areas. In these metro areas there are at least two public junior colleges, two public four-year colleges, and a group of privately controlled colleges and universities, one or more of which must be highly selective in admitting students. Such private schools would appeal to students searching for smaller classes, more individual attention, and specialized courses.

AA-Rated Metro Areas. These metro areas have a full complement of professional schools in law, medicine, and business, as well as accredited art and music schools. For undergraduates, there are more than two public junior colleges and more than two public four-year colleges, plus a wide choice of private colleges.

The College-Educated Majority

The year 1967 was a good one for education. It marked the first time in history that the majority of Americans over 25 had the equivalent of a high school diploma. We won't be seeing a similar year for college, however. In spite of millions of full-time students enrolled in college, only one in six persons over 25 currently has at least 16 years of school, the equivalent of a college degree.

Persons over 25 with 16 or more years of schooling are the rule rather than the exception in only 14 of the 945 cities in the United States with populations over 25,000. Not surprisingly, ten have large university communities.

City	Percent of Population with 16 Years of Schooling
1. Chapel Hill, NC	68.7%
2. East Lansing, MI	65.4
3. Davis, CA	60.9
4. State College, PA	59.5
5. Ann Arbor, MI	56.2
5. Blacksburg, VA	56.2
7. College Station, TX	54.0
8. Berkeley, CA	52.3
9. Upper Arlington, OH	52.0
10. Shaker Heights, OH	50.6
11. Palo Alto, CA	54.0
11. Wilmette, IL	54.0
13. Rancho Palos Verdes, CA	51.2
14. Boulder, CO	50.5

Source: U.S. Bureau of the Census, *1980 Census of Population and Housing.*

AAA-Rated Metro Areas. The handful of top-rated metro areas are the ones with the richest and most varied mix of campuses. They boast of international student populations as well as large numbers of students drawn from everywhere in the country; of universities whose faculty divide their time between research and teaching both there and at other area institutions; of open-admissions junior colleges offering not just instruction in the trades and technical occupations but also traditional courses transferable for credit to senior colleges; of colleges that pool specialized classes, films, and library resources; of professional schools in law, medicine, business, engineering, science, music, and art; and of a wide variety of private colleges with unique cultural and religious programs. The only metro areas in the nation that meet these requirements are Boston, Chicago, Los Angeles–Long Beach, New York, Philadelphia, San Francisco, and Washington.

JUDGING EDUCATIONAL EFFORT AND OPPORTUNITIES

To measure the chances for quality education in the metro areas, *Places Rated* examines two sides of academic life that affect the community—the K–12 system, which includes public elementary, junior high, and high schools, and the local mix of public and private colleges and universities.

Public K–12 schools are rated by examining two critical factors. The first is the number of pupils for each full-time teacher, or the pupil/teacher ratio. If there is one thing on which parents and educators agree, it is that a child's opportunity to learn improves in small classes. The second factor is the local effort index. A creation of the Advisory Commission on Intergovernmental Relations, this figure indicates how much of a metro area's tax revenue is turned over to support and improve the public schools. Indirectly, the effort index also shows how strongly public schools compete for money with such other municipal services as parks and recreation, fire and police, streets, sanitation, and health care. Although a metro area's effort rating doesn't necessarily tell you how good the schools are, it does suggest how good the metro area's taxpayers expect them to be.

Places Rated's tack for scoring local higher education is based on the variety of academic options that can meet the differing needs of a community: night and weekend continuing education courses for people who work, full-time graduate courses in the professions, courses leading to occupational certification in junior colleges, and the traditional bachelor's degree curriculum offered in a four-year college.

Each metro area begins with a base score of zero, to which points are added according to the following indicators:

1. *Pupil/teacher ratio.* A metro area's number of pupils per full-time teacher in the public schools is divided into the national metro average for this ratio of 15.12. The result is multiplied by 1,000 and added to the score. In Dallas's six counties, for example, the 14.16 pupils for each full-time teacher earns the Texas metro area 1,068 points. There is a ceiling of 1,500 points in this category.

2. *Effort index.* This figure, which represents that portion of a metro area's revenue allotted to supporting and improving public schools, is multiplied by 1,000 and added to the score. Dallas's effort index of 0.951 means an additional 951 points. A ceiling of 1,500 points is also in effect for effort index.

3. *Academic options.* Each metro area earns points on the basis of its letter grade for options in higher education: 1,500 points for an AAA rating, given to those metro areas with the richest and most varied offerings; 1,250 points for AA; 1,000 points for A; 750 for B; and 500 for C.

Sample Comparison: Philadelphia, Pennsylvania– New Jersey, and Pascagoula, Mississippi

The country's best and worst metro areas for educational opportunities according to *Places Rated*'s scoring system are located in the Northeast and the Deep South, respectively.

The Philadelphia metro area is a multiple-county giant that straddles parts of Pennsylvania and New Jersey. In the category of K–12 quality, its marks exceed the national average, although they're not outstanding: its pupil/teacher ratio is 13.22, slightly better than the national metro area average of 15.12, and its effort index—its proportion of available tax income that goes to support local schools—is 1.137, just an eyelash above the national average of 1.000. Each of these figures is indexed against the appropriate national average and then multiplied by 1,000, resulting in a total of 2,281 points (1,144 for pupil/ teacher ratio and 1,137 for effort index). But Philadelphia's prodigious number of colleges and universities, offering a wide range of academic options, propels the metro area into first place. With its 46 four-year institutions and 21 two-year schools—among them the University of Pennsylvania, Temple University, Curtis Institute of Music, and Hahnemann Medical College— Philadelphia earns the highest rating possible in this

Spanking, Paddling, and Suspensions

During a given school year, one of every 30 pupils is spanked or paddled at least once, and one in 19 is suspended for breaking school rules. According to the Education Department's Office for Civil Rights, the states in which suspensions exceed the national average are all located east of the Mississippi River, with the exception of California. Paddling and spanking, typical forms of discipline in the elementary grades, are concentrated in the Southeast and adjacent southwestern states but are unheard of in New England.

States Reporting Corporal Punishment Exceeding National Average*

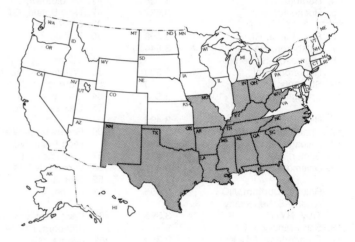

Source: National Center for Education Statistics, *Condition of Education*, 1984.

*The national average for corporal punishment is 3.5% of public elementary and secondary school enrollment. The shaded area of the map shows states exceeding this level.

category, AAA, good for 1,500 points. Its total score is 3,781.

At the other end of the scale is Pascagoula, a fast-growing county in the Gulf South. Its pupil/ teacher ratio is 15.15, which yields 998 points after being divided into the national average and then multiplied by 1,000. Its effort index of 0.703 is the fifth lowest among the metro areas and results in 703 points. Pascagoula is one of only two metro areas in the nation with no colleges, either two-year or four-year (the other is Bristol, Connecticut), and so receives no points for higher academic options. Its combined score for pupil/teacher ratio and effort index, then, remains its overall score: 1,701, putting it in last place among the metro areas.

Places Rated: Metro Areas Ranked for Educational Effort and Opportunities

The following criteria are used to rate a metro area for the educational opportunities it affords its residents: (1) pupil/teacher ratio in the public K–12 system, (2) effort index in K–12, and (3) academic options in higher education. Places that receive tie scores are given the same rank and listed alphabetically.

Metro Areas from Best to Worst

Places Rated Rank	Places Rated Score	Places Rated Rank	Places Rated Score	Places Rated Rank	Places Rated Score
1. Philadelphia, PA–NJ	3,781	44. Syracuse, NY	3,144	88. Waterbury, CT	2,995
2. Bergen–Passaic, NJ	3,653			90. Asheville, NC	2,990
3. Washington, DC–MD–VA	3,635	46. Jackson, MS	3,130		
4. Hartford, CT	3,628	47. Middletown, CT	3,128	90. Hagerstown, MD	2,990
5. Rochester, NY	3,582	47. New Britain, CT	3,128	92. New York, NY	2,984
		49. Chico, CA	3,126	93. Wichita, KS	2,981
6. Providence, RI	3,558	50. Buffalo, NY	3,121	94. Orlando, FL	2,976
7. Pittsburgh, PA	3,544			95. Bryan–College Station, TX	2,973
8. Middlesex–Somerset–Hunterdon, NJ	3,539	51. Eugene–Springfield, OR	3,118		
9. St. Louis, MO–IL	3,530	52. Wilmington, DE–NJ–MD	3,112	95. Portland, ME	2,973
10. Springfield, MA	3,525	53. Florence, SC	3,109	97. Alexandria, LA	2,972
		54. Lancaster, PA	3,097	97. Cleveland, OH	2,972
11. New Haven–Meriden, CT	3,495	55. Gainesville, FL	3,094	99. Utica–Rome, NY	2,970
12. Charlottesville, VA	3,489			100. Muncie, IN	2,965
13. Chicago, IL	3,486	56. Greensboro–Winston-Salem–High Point, NC	3,090		
14. Boston, MA	3,479	57. Springfield, IL	3,078	101. Eau Claire, WI	2,960
15. Baltimore, MD	3,471	58. Omaha, NE–IA	3,069	102. Kansas City, MO	2,949
		59. Detroit, MI	3,064	103. Alton–Granite City, IL	2,945
16. Raleigh–Durham, NC	3,455	60. Austin, TX	3,063	103. Lafayette, IN	2,945
17. Albany–Schenectady–Troy, NY	3,399			105. Danville, VA	2,943
18. San Francisco, CA	3,371	61. Pawtucket–Woonsocket–Attleboro, RI–MA	3,058		
19. Cumberland, MD–WV	3,363	62. Atlanta, GA	3,057	106. Phoenix, AZ	2,942
20. Newark, NJ	3,362	63. Binghamton, NY	3,052	107. Richmond–Petersburg, VA	2,940
		64. Fayetteville, NC	3,051	108. San Antonio, TX	2,938
21. Ann Arbor, MI	3,346	65. Jacksonville, FL	3,048	109. Bangor, ME	2,934
22. Portland, OR	3,343			110. Atlantic City, NJ	2,929
23. Burlington, VT	3,323	66. Madison, WI	3,047		
24. Trenton, NJ	3,311	67. Milwaukee, WI	3,044	111. Columbus, OH	2,928
25. Worcester, MA	3,299	67. Tampa–St. Petersburg–Clearwater, FL	3,044	112. Fort Smith, AR–OK	2,927
		69. Charlotte–Gastonia–Rock Hill, NC–SC	3,031	112. St. Joseph, MO	2,927
26. Tyler, TX	3,283	70. Bridgeport–Milford, CT	3,029	114. Johnson City–Kingsport–Bristol, TN	2,925
27. Salem, OR	3,278			115. Youngstown–Warren, OH	2,920
28. Houston, TX	3,271	70. Danbury, CT	3,029		
29. Dallas, TX	3,269	70. Norwalk, CT	3,029	116. Cincinnati, OH–KY–IN	2,918
30. Pittsfield, MA	3,264	70. Stamford, CT	3,029	116. Kenosha, WI	2,918
		74. Kansas City, KS	3,028	118. Augusta, GA–SC	2,915
31. New London–Norwich, CT–RI	3,244	74. Louisville, KY–IN	3,028	119. Pensacola, FL	2,914
32. Greenville–Spartanburg, SC	3,236			120. Columbia, SC	2,908
33. Nassau–Suffolk, NY	3,234	74. Reading, PA	3,028		
34. Scranton–Wilkes-Barre, PA	3,230	77. La Crosse, WI	3,027	120. Oklahoma City, OK	2,908
35. Harrisburg–Lebanon–Carlisle, PA	3,224	78. Albuquerque, NM	3,026	122. Williamsport, PA	2,906
		78. Portsmouth–Dover–Rochester, NH–ME	3,026	123. Kokomo, IN	2,904
35. West Palm Beach–Boca Raton–Delray Beach, FL	3,224	80. Sharon, PA	3,022	124. York, PA	2,903
37. Los Angeles–Long Beach, CA	3,195			125. Davenport–Rock Island–Moline, IL	2,901
38. State College, PA	3,169	81. Norfolk–Virginia Beach–Newport News, VA	3,014		
39. Killeen–Temple, TX	3,167	82. Minneapolis–St. Paul, MN–WI	3,013	126. Texarkana, TX–Texarkana, AR	2,899
40. Charleston, SC	3,164	83. Terre Haute, IN	3,012	127. Poughkeepsie, NY	2,898
		84. Billings, MT	3,008	128. Kalamazoo, MI	2,896
41. Fort Pierce, FL	3,154	85. Wheeling, WV–OH	3,002	129. Charleston, WV	2,894
42. Champaign–Urbana–Rantoul, IL	3,147			130. Lansing–East Lansing, MI	2,891
43. Denver, CO	3,145	86. Elmira, NY	3,000		
44. Allentown–Bethlehem, PA–NJ	3,144	87. Lakeland–Winter Haven, FL	2,998	131. Waterloo–Cedar Falls, IA	2,889
		88. New Orleans, LA	2,995	132. Miami–Hialeah, FL	2,879
				133. Lincoln, NE	2,878
				134. Wilmington, NC	2,876
				135. South Bend–Mishawaka, IN	2,874

Places Rated Rank	Places Rated Score	Places Rated Rank	Places Rated Score	Places Rated Rank	Places Rated Score
136. Bloomington, IN	2,873	193. Brockton, MA	2,729	251. Daytona Beach, FL	2,612
137. Joplin, MO	2,871	193. Fort Myers, FL	2,729	252. Santa Cruz, CA	2,611
137. Mansfield, OH	2,871	193. Salem–Gloucester, MA	2,729	253. Lake County, IL	2,607
139. Joliet, IL	2,868			254. Riverside–San Bernardino, CA	2,596
140. Waco, TX	2,867	196. Manchester, NH	2,728	255. Biloxi–Gulfport, MS	2,592
		196. Nashua, NH	2,728		
141. Ocala, FL	2,864	198. Hickory, NC	2,726	256. Boulder–Longmont, CO	2,587
142. Lexington–Fayette, KY	2,861	199. Roanoke, VA	2,723	257. Lorain–Elyria, OH	2,582
143. Shreveport, LA	2,858	200. Santa Rosa–Petaluma, CA	2,722	258. Little Rock–North Little Rock, AR	2,581
144. Kankakee, IL	2,855			259. Jersey City, NJ	2,574
145. Bloomington–Normal, IL	2,854	201. Grand Forks, ND	2,721	260. Bakersfield, CA	2,564
		201. Odessa, TX	2,721		
145. Greeley, CO	2,854	203. Santa Barbara–Santa Maria–Lompoc, CA	2,719	261. Albany, GA	2,560
147. Amarillo, TX	2,852	204. Brazoria, TX	2,718	262. Sheboygan, WI	2,557
147. Toledo, OH	2,852	205. Bradenton, FL	2,712	263. Pine Bluff, AR	2,554
149. Birmingham, AL	2,851			264. Tacoma, WA	2,546
150. Appleton–Oshkosh–Neenah, WI	2,844	206. Seattle, WA	2,710	265. Benton Harbor, MI	2,545
		207. San Jose, CA	2,709		
151. Anaheim–Santa Ana, CA	2,843	207. Springfield, MO	2,709	265. Lubbock, TX	2,545
152. Iowa City, IA	2,842	209. San Angelo, TX	2,707	267. Bremerton, WA	2,544
153. Corpus Christi, TX	2,840	210. Grand Rapids, MI	2,705	268. Niagara Falls, NY	2,538
154. Laredo, TX	2,827			269. Elkhart–Goshen, IN	2,537
155. Longview–Marshall, TX	2,816	211. Dubuque, IA	2,701	270. Beaver County, PA	2,535
		212. Lawrence, KS	2,700		
156. Melbourne–Titusville–Palm Bay, FL	2,814	213. Victoria, TX	2,696	271. Janesville–Beloit, WI	2,532
157. Fort Walton Beach, FL	2,809	214. Lewiston–Auburn, ME	2,694	272. Reno, NV	2,529
157. Galveston–Texas City, TX	2,809	215. Johnstown, PA	2,691	273. Gary–Hammond, IN	2,526
159. Memphis, TN–AR–MS	2,804			274. Huntington–Ashland, WV–KY–OH	2,525
160. Lynchburg, VA	2,803	216. Indianapolis, IN	2,690	275. Burlington, NC	2,519
		217. Bismarck, ND	2,686		
161. Fitchburg–Leominster, MA	2,799	218. Tucson, AZ	2,685	276. Flint, MI	2,511
162. Evansville, IN–KY	2,797	219. Decatur, IL	2,683	277. Fargo–Moorhead, ND–MN	2,506
162. Medford, OR	2,797	220. Rockford, IL	2,680	278. Parkersburg–Marietta, WV–OH	2,503
164. Topeka, KS	2,795			279. Honolulu, HI	2,502
165. San Diego, CA	2,794	221. Glens Falls, NY	2,674	279. St. Cloud, MN	2,502
		222. Sioux City, IA–NE	2,673		
166. Sacramento, CA	2,793	223. Steubenville–Weirton, OH–WV	2,672	281. Panama City, FL	2,500
167. Tallahassee, FL	2,790	224. Columbus, GA–AL	2,665	282. Vallejo–Fairfield–Napa, CA	2,498
168. Monmouth–Ocean, NJ	2,787	225. Clarksville–Hopkinsville, TN–KY	2,654	283. Owensboro, KY	2,491
169. Mobile, AL	2,779			283. Yakima, WA	2,491
170. Altoona, PA	2,778	225. Jackson, MI	2,654	285. Battle Creek, MI	2,483
		227. Pueblo, CO	2,653		
170. Bellingham, WA	2,778	228. Sherman–Denison, TX	2,652	286. El Paso, TX	2,479
172. Spokane, WA	2,774	229. Macon–Warner Robins, GA	2,651	286. Lawrence–Haverhill, MA–NH	2,479
173. Anderson, SC	2,772	229. Sioux Falls, SD	2,651	286. Lowell, MA–NH	2,479
173. Dayton–Springfield, OH	2,772			289. Redding, CA	2,471
173. Fort Wayne, IN	2,772	231. Athens, GA	2,646	290. Anderson, IN	2,469
		231. Jacksonville, NC	2,646		
173. Saginaw–Bay City–Midland, MI	2,772	231. Oakland, CA	2,646	291. Savannah, GA	2,456
177. Enid, OK	2,764	234. McAllen–Edinburg–Mission, TX	2,644	292. Casper, WY	2,453
178. Nashville, TN	2,763	235. Erie, PA	2,641	292. Monroe, LA	2,453
179. Knoxville, TN	2,761			294. Peoria, IL	2,452
180. Abilene, TX	2,757	236. Baton Rouge, LA	2,635	295. Fall River, MA–RI	2,439
		237. East St. Louis–Belleville, IL	2,630		
181. Canton, OH	2,754	237. Muskegon, MI	2,630	295. New Bedford, MA	2,439
181. Colorado Springs, CO	2,754	239. Lima, OH	2,629	295. Salinas–Seaside–Monterey, CA	2,439
181. Orange County, NY	2,754	240. Bristol, CT	2,628	298. Akron, OH	2,438
184. Wausau, WI	2,749			299. Florence, AL	2,427
185. Hamilton–Middletown, OH	2,747	240. Tulsa, OK	2,628	300. Midland, TX	2,416
		242. Fort Worth–Arlington, TX	2,627		
185. Vineland–Millville–Bridgeton, NJ	2,747	243. Sarasota, FL	2,626	301. Chattanooga, TN–GA	2,415
185. Wichita Falls, TX	2,747	244. Olympia, WA	2,625	302. Anchorage, AK	2,414
188. Beaumont–Port Arthur, TX	2,745	245. Green Bay, WI	2,622	303. Brownsville–Harlingen, TX	2,413
189. Great Falls, MT	2,737			303. Fort Collins–Loveland, CO	2,413
190. Las Cruces, NM	2,736	246. Cedar Rapids, IA	2,619	305. Fresno, CA	2,407
		246. Duluth, MN–WI	2,619		
191. Fort Lauderdale–Hollywood–Pompano Beach, FL	2,734	248. Provo–Orem, UT	2,618	306. Boise City, ID	2,391
192. Racine, WI	2,732	249. Modesto, CA	2,616	307. Tuscaloosa, AL	2,390
		250. Des Moines, IA	2,613		

Places Rated Rank	Places Rated Score	Places Rated Rank	Places Rated Score	Places Rated Rank	Places Rated Score
308. Montgomery, AL	2,388	316. Lafayette, LA	2,305	323. Stockton, CA	2,155
309. Yuba City, CA	2,387	317. Gadsden, AL	2,299	325. Rochester, MN	2,134
310. Columbia, MO	2,377	318. Huntsville, AL	2,257		
		319. Las Vegas, NV	2,241	326. Visalia–Tulare–Porterville, CA	2,128
311. Lawton, OK	2,375	320. Dothan, AL	2,230	327. Houma–Thibodaux, LA	1,995
312. Salt Lake City–Ogden, UT	2,340			328. Richland–Kennewick–Pasco, WA	1,728
313. Lake Charles, LA	2,336	321. Aurora–Elgin, IL	2,208	329. Pascagoula, MS	1,701
314. Fayetteville–Springdale, AR	2,334	322. Anniston, AL	2,189		
315. Vancouver, WA	2,332	323. Oxnard–Ventura, CA	2,155		

Metro Areas Listed Alphabetically

Metro Area	Places Rated Rank	Metro Area	Places Rated Rank	Metro Area	Places Rated Rank
Abilene, TX	180	Bridgeport–Milford, CT	70	Elkhart–Goshen, IN	269
Akron, OH	298	Bristol, CT	240	Elmira, NY	86
Albany, GA	261	Brockton, MA	193	Enid, OK	177
Albany–Schenectady–Troy, NY	17				
Albuquerque, NM	78	Brownsville–Harlingen, TX	303	Erie, PA	235
		Bryan–College Station, TX	95	Eugene–Springfield, OR	51
Alexandria, LA	97	Buffalo, NY	50	Evansville, IN–KY	162
Allentown–Bethlehem, PA–NJ	44	Burlington, NC	275	Fall River, MA–RI	295
Alton–Granite City, IL	103	Burlington, VT	23	Fargo–Moorhead, ND–MN	277
Altoona, PA	170				
Amarillo, TX	147	Canton, OH	181	Fayetteville, NC	64
		Casper, WY	292	Fayetteville–Springdale, AR	314
Anaheim–Santa Ana, CA	151	Cedar Rapids, IA	246	Fitchburg–Leominster, MA	161
Anchorage, AK	302	Champaign–Urbana–Rantoul, IL	42	Flint, MI	276
Anderson, IN	290	Charleston, SC	40	Florence, AL	299
Anderson, SC	173				
Ann Arbor, MI	21	Charleston, WV	129	Florence, SC	53
		Charlotte–Gastonia–Rock Hill, NC–SC	69	Fort Collins–Loveland, CO	303
Anniston, AL	322	Charlottesville, VA	12	Fort Lauderdale–Hollywood–Pompano Beach, FL	191
Appleton–Oshkosh–Neenah, WI	150	Chattanooga, TN–GA	301	Fort Myers, FL	193
Asheville, NC	90	Chicago, IL	13	Fort Pierce, FL	41
Athens, GA	231				
Atlanta, GA	62	Chico, CA	49	Fort Smith, AR–OK	112
		Cincinnati, OH–KY–IN	116	Fort Walton Beach, FL	157
Atlantic City, NJ	110	Clarksville–Hopkinsville, TN–KY	225	Fort Wayne, IN	173
Augusta, GA–SC	118	Cleveland, OH	97	Fort Worth–Arlington, TX	242
Aurora–Elgin, IL	321	Colorado Springs, CO	181	Fresno, CA	305
Austin, TX	60				
Bakersfield, CA	260	Columbia, MO	310	Gadsden, AL	317
		Columbia, SC	120	Gainesville, FL	55
Baltimore, MD	15	Columbus, GA–AL	224	Galveston–Texas City, TX	157
Bangor, ME	109	Columbus, OH	111	Gary–Hammond, IN	273
Baton Rouge, LA	236	Corpus Christi, TX	153	Glens Falls, NY	221
Battle Creek, MI	285				
Beaumont–Port Arthur, TX	188	Cumberland, MD–WV	19	Grand Forks, ND	201
		Dallas, TX	29	Grand Rapids, MI	210
Beaver County, PA	270	Danbury, CT	70	Great Falls, MT	189
Bellingham, WA	170	Danville, VA	105	Greeley, CO	145
Benton Harbor, MI	265	Davenport–Rock Island–Moline, IA–IL	125	Green Bay, WI	245
Bergen–Passaic, NJ	2				
Billings, MT	84	Dayton–Springfield, OH	173	Greensboro–Winston-Salem–High Point, NC	56
		Daytona Beach, FL	251	Greenville–Spartanburg, SC	32
Biloxi–Gulfport, MS	255	Decatur, IL	219	Hagerstown, MD	90
Binghamton, NY	63	Denver, CO	43	Hamilton–Middletown, OH	185
Birmingham, AL	149	Des Moines, IA	250	Harrisburg–Lebanon–Carlisle, PA	35
Bismarck, ND	217				
Bloomington, IN	136	Detroit, MI	59	Hartford, CT	4
		Dothan, AL	320	Hickory, NC	198
Bloomington–Normal, IL	145	Dubuque, IA	211	Honolulu, HI	279
Boise City, ID	306	Duluth, MN–WI	246	Houma–Thibodaux, LA	327
Boston, MA	14	East St. Louis–Belleville, IL	237	Houston, TX	28
Boulder–Longmont, CO	256				
Bradenton, FL	205	Eau Claire, WI	101	Huntington–Ashland, WV–KY–OH	274
		El Paso, TX	286	Huntsville, AL	318
Brazoria, TX	204				
Bremerton, WA	267				

Metro Area	Places Rated Rank	Metro Area	Places Rated Rank	Metro Area	Places Rated Rank
Indianapolis, IN	216	Milwaukee, WI	67	Rochester, MN	325
Iowa City, IA	152	Minneapolis–St. Paul, MN–WI	82		
Jackson, MI	225	Mobile, AL	169	Rochester, NY	5
		Modesto, CA	249	Rockford, IL	220
Jackson, MS	46	Monmouth–Ocean, NJ	168	Sacramento, CA	166
Jacksonville, FL	65			Saginaw–Bay City–Midland, MI	173
Jacksonville, NC	231	Monroe, LA	292	St. Cloud, MN	279
Janesville–Beloit, WI	271	Montgomery, AL	308		
Jersey City, NJ	259	Muncie, IN	100	St. Joseph, MO	112
		Muskegon, MI	237	St. Louis, MO–IL	9
Johnson City–Kingsport–Bristol, TN–VA	114	Nashua, NH	196	Salem, OR	27
				Salem–Gloucester, MA	193
Johnstown, PA	215	Nashville, TN	178	Salinas–Seaside–Monterey, CA	295
Joliet, IL	139	Nassau–Suffolk, NY	33		
Joplin, MO	137	New Bedford, MA	295	Salt Lake City–Ogden, UT	312
Kalamazoo, MI	128	New Britain, CT	47	San Angelo, TX	209
		New Haven–Meriden, CT	11	San Antonio, TX	108
Kankakee, IL	144			San Diego, CA	165
Kansas City, KS	74	New London–Norwich, CT–RI	31	San Francisco, CA	18
Kansas City, MO	102	New Orleans, LA	88		
Kenosha, WI	116	New York, NY	92	San Jose, CA	207
Killeen–Temple, TX	39	Newark, NJ	20	Santa Barbara–Santa Maria–	
		Niagara Falls, NY	268	Lompoc, CA	203
Knoxville, TN	179			Santa Cruz, CA	252
Kokomo, IN	123	Norfolk–Virginia Beach–		Santa Rosa–Petaluma, CA	200
La Crosse, WI	77	Newport News, VA	81	Sarasota, FL	243
Lafayette, IN	103	Norwalk, CT	70		
Lafayette, LA	316	Oakland, CA	231	Savannah, GA	291
		Ocala, FL	141	Scranton–Wilkes-Barre, PA	34
Lake Charles, LA	313	Odessa, TX	201	Seattle, WA	206
Lake County, IL	253			Sharon, PA	80
Lakeland–Winter Haven, FL	87	Oklahoma City, OK	120	Sheboygan, WI	262
Lancaster, PA	54	Olympia, WA	244		
Lansing–East Lansing, MI	130	Omaha, NE–IA	58	Sherman–Denison, TX	228
		Orange County, NY	181	Shreveport, LA	143
Laredo, TX	154	Orlando, FL	94	Sioux City, IA–NE	222
Las Cruces, NM	190			Sioux Falls, SD	229
Las Vegas, NV	319	Owensboro, KY	283	South Bend–Mishawaka, IN	135
Lawrence, KS	212	Oxnard–Ventura, CA	323		
Lawrence–Haverhill, MA–NH	286	Panama City, FL	281	Spokane, WA	172
		Parkersburg–Marietta, WV–OH	278	Springfield, IL	57
Lawton, OK	311	Pascagoula, MS	329	Springfield, MA	10
Lewiston–Auburn, ME	214			Springfield, MO	207
Lexington–Fayette, KY	142	Pawtucket–Woonsocket–Attleboro, RI–MA	61	Stamford, CT	70
Lima, OH	239	Pensacola, FL	119		
Lincoln, NE	133	Peoria, IL	294	State College, PA	38
		Philadelphia, PA–NJ	1	Steubenville–Weirton, OH–WV	223
Little Rock–North Little Rock, AR	258	Phoenix, AZ	106	Stockton, CA	323
Longview–Marshall, TX	155			Syracuse, NY	44
Lorain–Elyria, OH	257	Pine Bluff, AR	263	Tacoma, WA	264
Los Angeles–Long Beach, CA	37	Pittsburgh, PA	7		
Louisville, KY–IN	74	Pittsfield, MA	30	Tallahassee, FL	167
		Portland, ME	95	Tampa–St. Petersburg–	
Lowell, MA–NH	286	Portland, OR	22	Clearwater, FL	67
Lubbock, TX	265			Terre Haute, IN	83
Lynchburg, VA	160	Portsmouth–Dover–Rochester, NH–ME	78	Texarkana, TX–Texarkana, AR	126
Macon–Warner Robins, GA	229	Poughkeepsie, NY	127	Toledo, OH	147
Madison, WI	66	Providence, RI	6		
		Provo–Orem, UT	248	Topeka, KS	164
Manchester, NH	196	Pueblo, CO	227	Trenton, NJ	24
Mansfield, OH	137			Tucson, AZ	218
McAllen–Edinburg–Mission, TX	234	Racine, WI	192	Tulsa, OK	240
Medford, OR	162	Raleigh–Durham, NC	16	Tuscaloosa, AL	307
Melbourne–Titusville–Palm Bay, FL	156	Reading, PA	74		
		Redding, CA	289	Tyler, TX	26
Memphis, TN–AR–MS	159	Reno, NV	272	Utica–Rome, NY	99
Miami–Hialeah, FL	132			Vallejo–Fairfield–Napa, CA	282
Middlesex–Somerset–Hunterdon, NJ	8	Richland–Kennewick–Pasco, WA	328	Vancouver, WA	315
Middletown, CT	47	Richmond–Petersburg, VA	107	Victoria, TX	213
Midland, TX	300	Riverside–San Bernardino, CA	254		
		Roanoke, VA	199	Vineland–Millville–Bridgeton, NJ	185

Metro Area	Places Rated Rank	Metro Area	Places Rated Rank	Metro Area	Places Rated Rank
Visalia–Tulare–Porterville, CA	326	West Palm Beach–Boca Raton–Delray Beach, FL	35	Wilmington, NC	134
Waco, TX	140	Wheeling, WV–OH	85	Worcester, MA	25
Washington, DC–MD–VA	3	Wichita, KS	93		
Waterbury, CT	88			Yakima, WA	283
		Wichita Falls, TX	185	York, PA	124
Waterloo–Cedar Falls, IA	131	Williamsport, PA	122	Youngstown–Warren, OH	115
Wausau, WI	184	Wilmington, DE–NJ–MD	52	Yuba City, CA	309

Place Profiles: Educational Features of 329 Metro Areas

The following pages outline the main features of the educational landscape in U.S. metro areas: elementary and secondary (public and private schools) and colleges and universities (two- and four-year institutions, both public and private).

Besides the two factors used by *Places Rated Almanac* to rank the performance of public schools—pupil/teacher ratio and effort index for public-school support—information on dollars spent per pupil and average teacher salary are also given. The figures for salary represent the average monthly paycheck paid in October 1982 and have not been standardized to offset possible differences in the length of teachers' pay periods. Figures for New England County Metro Area Standards are used for New England metro areas. Hawaii's statewide averages are used for Honolulu. Figures for the number of private K–12 schools and their total enrollment are included under the heading

Private. The number of each metro area's institutions of higher education and their total enrollments are included under the heading Colleges and Universities.

Sources for K–12 data include: U.S. Bureau of the Census, *Compendium of Public Employment* and *Compendium of Government Finances*, both forthcoming as of November 1984. Data on the number of districts, school buildings, and enrollment of metro area public schools come from the National School Market Index, published annually by Market Data Retrieval, Westport, Connecticut, as do figures on metro area private schools and their enrollment. For higher education, the source is the National Center for Education Statistics, *Education Directory, Colleges and Universities, 1983–84*, 1984.

A star preceding a metro area's name highlights it as one of the top 25 places for educational effort and opportunities.

Abilene, TX
Elementary and Secondary
  Public: 5 districts, 42 schools, 20,409 pupils
    Pupil/Teacher Ratio: 13.29
    Dollars per Pupil: $1,960
    Average Teacher Salary: $1,651
    Effort Index: 1.119
  Private: 4 schools, 908 pupils
Colleges and Universities
  Two-year: None
  Four-year and Beyond: 2 private; 5,847 students
  Degree Options: C
Places Rated Score: 2,757
Places Rated Rank: 180

Akron, OH
Elementary and Secondary
  Public: 30 districts, 207 schools, 117,740 pupils
    Pupil/Teacher Ratio: 16.79
    Dollars per Pupil: $2,532
    Average Teacher Salary: $2,140
    Effort Index: 1.038

Private: 45 schools, 12,580 pupils
Colleges and Universities
  Two-year: None
  Four-year and Beyond: 1 private, 2 public; 47,719 students
  Degree Options: C
Places Rated Score: 2,438
Places Rated Rank: 298

Albany, GA
Elementary and Secondary
  Public: 2 districts, 36 schools, 22,840 pupils
    Pupil/Teacher Ratio: 14.70
    Dollars per Pupil: $1,977
    Average Teacher Salary: $1,305
    Effort Index: 0.781
  Private: 11 schools, 2,667 pupils
Colleges and Universities
  Two-year: 1 public; 1,884 students
  Four-year and Beyond: 1 public; 1,896 students
  Degree Options: B
Places Rated Score: 2,560
Places Rated Rank: 261

★ Albany–Schenectady–Troy, NY
Elementary and Secondary
  Public: 56 districts, 237 schools, 132,891 pupils
    Pupil/Teacher Ratio: 15.10
    Dollars per Pupil: $3,607
    Average Teacher Salary: $1,967
    Effort Index: 1.148
  Private: 112 schools, 22,742 pupils
Colleges and Universities
  Two-year: 3 private, 2 public; 13,812 students
  Four-year and Beyond: 8 private, 2 public; 41,853 students
  Degree Options: AA
Places Rated Score: 3,399
Places Rated Rank: 17

Albuquerque, NM
Elementary and Secondary
  Public: 1 district, 110 schools, 67,073 pupils
    Pupil/Teacher Ratio: 11.78
    Dollars per Pupil: $3,368
    Average Teacher Salary: $1,539
    Effort Index: 1.243

Private: 34 schools, 8,411 pupils
Colleges and Universities
Two-year: None
Four-year and Beyond: 1 private, 1
public; 25,864 students
Degree Options: C
Places Rated Score: 3,026
Places Rated Rank: 78

Alexandria, LA
Elementary and Secondary
Public: 1 district, 52 schools,
23,083 pupils
Pupil/Teacher Ratio: 12.28
Dollars per Pupil: $2,450
Average Teacher Salary: $1,354
Effort Index: 1.241
Private: 11 schools, 4,097 pupils
Colleges and Universities
Two-year: 1 public; 1,713 students
Four-year and Beyond: 1 private; 1,049
students
Degree Options: C
Places Rated Score: 2,972
Places Rated Rank: 97

Allentown–Bethlehem, PA–NJ
Elementary and Secondary
Public: 46 districts, 194 schools,
100,994 pupils
Pupil/Teacher Ratio: 13.79
Dollars per Pupil: $2,903
Average Teacher Salary: $1,733
Effort Index: 1.298
Private: 59 schools, 13,535 pupils
Colleges and Universities
Two-year: 2 private, 3 public; 9,978
students
Four-year and Beyond: 7 private; 15,355
students
Degree Options: B
Places Rated Score: 3,144
Places Rated Rank: 44

Alton–Granite City, IL
Elementary and Secondary
Public: 16 districts, 112 schools,
47,900 pupils
Pupil/Teacher Ratio: 15.80
Dollars per Pupil: $2,540
Average Teacher Salary: $1,778
Effort Index: 1.238
Private: 36 schools, 6,499 pupils
Colleges and Universities
Two-year: 1 public; 5,155 students
Four-year and Beyond: 1 public; 11,098
students
Degree Options: B
Places Rated Score: 2,945
Places Rated Rank: 103

Altoona, PA
Elementary and Secondary
Public: 7 districts, 42 schools,
23,064 pupils
Pupil/Teacher Ratio: 15.29
Dollars per Pupil: $2,389
Average Teacher Salary: $1,465
Effort Index: 1.289
Private: 19 schools, 3,579 pupils
Colleges and Universities
Two-year: 1 public; 2,428 students
Four-year and Beyond: None
Degree Options: C
Places Rated Score: 2,778
Places Rated Rank: 170

Amarillo, TX
Elementary and Secondary
Public: 5 districts, 58 schools,
32,704 pupils
Pupil/Teacher Ratio: 14.37
Dollars per Pupil: $2,624
Average Teacher Salary: $1,603
Effort Index: 1.050
Private: 12 schools, 1,939 pupils
Colleges and Universities
Two-year: 2 public; 7,121 students
Four-year and Beyond: 1 public; 6,805
students
Degree Options: B
Places Rated Score: 2,852
Places Rated Rank: 147

Anaheim–Santa Ana, CA
Elementary and Secondary
Public: 29 districts, 483 schools,
341,367 pupils
Pupil/Teacher Ratio: 19.11
Dollars per Pupil: $3,161
Average Teacher Salary: $2,416
Effort Index: 1.052
Private: 188 schools, 23,674 pupils
Colleges and Universities
Two-year: 7 public; 146,935 students
Four-year and Beyond: 6 private, 1
public; 32,331 students
Degree Options: A
Places Rated Score: 2,843
Places Rated Rank: 151

Anchorage, AK
Elementary and Secondary
Public: 1 district, 74 schools,
38,745 pupils
Pupil/Teacher Ratio: 15.55
Dollars per Pupil: $3,843
Average Teacher Salary: $2,927
Effort Index: 0.692
Private: 13 schools, 2,187 pupils
Colleges and Universities
Two-year: 1 public; 8,268 students
Four-year and Beyond: 1 private, 1
public; 4,252 students
Degree Options: B
Places Rated Score: 2,414
Places Rated Rank: 302

Anderson, IN
Elementary and Secondary
Public: 5 districts, 46 schools,
27,099 pupils
Pupil/Teacher Ratio: 16.55
Dollars per Pupil: $1,961
Average Teacher Salary: $1,600
Effort Index: 1.056
Private: 11 schools, 1,866 pupils
Colleges and Universities
Two-year: None
Four-year and Beyond: 1 private; 2,008
students
Degree Options: C
Places Rated Score: 2,469
Places Rated Rank: 290

Anderson, SC
Elementary and Secondary
Public: 5 districts, 50 schools,
27,437 pupils
Pupil/Teacher Ratio: 17.34
Dollars per Pupil: $1,801
Average Teacher Salary: $1,361
Effort Index: 1.400
Private: 17 schools, 1,469 pupils

Colleges and Universities
Two-year: None
Four-year and Beyond: 1 private; 1,048
students
Degree Options: C
Places Rated Score: 2,772
Places Rated Rank: 173

★ Ann Arbor, MI
Elementary and Secondary
Public: 10 districts, 80 schools,
40,532 pupils
Pupil/Teacher Ratio: 16.23
Dollars per Pupil: $3,574
Average Teacher Salary: $2,327
Effort Index: 1.414
Private: 33 schools, 4,615 pupils
Colleges and Universities
Two-year: 1 public; 8,247 students
Four-year and Beyond: 2 private, 2
public; 55,696 students
Degree Options: A
Places Rated Score: 3,346
Places Rated Rank: 21

Anniston, AL
Elementary and Secondary
Public: 5 districts, 34 schools,
22,146 pupils
Pupil/Teacher Ratio: 18.14
Dollars per Pupil: $1,607
Average Teacher Salary: $1,434
Effort Index: 0.855
Private: 5 schools, 1,594 pupils
Colleges and Universities
Two-year: None
Four-year and Beyond: 1 public; 6,284
students
Degree Options: C
Places Rated Score: 2,189
Places Rated Rank: 322

Appleton–Oshkosh–Neenah, WI
Elementary and Secondary
Public: 18 districts, 104 schools,
47,620 pupils
Pupil/Teacher Ratio: 15.63
Dollars per Pupil: $2,954
Average Teacher Salary: $1,800
Effort Index: 1.127
Private: 66 schools, 11,899 pupils
Colleges and Universities
Two-year: 1 public; 5,308 students
Four-year and Beyond: 1 private, 1
public; 11,750 students
Degree Options: B
Places Rated Score: 2,844
Places Rated Rank: 150

Asheville, NC
Elementary and Secondary
Public: 2 districts, 49 schools, 28,792
pupils
Pupil/Teacher Ratio: 14.86
Dollars per Pupil: $2,292
Average Teacher Salary: $1,458
Effort Index: 1.222
Private: 13 schools, 2,033 pupils
Colleges and Universities
Two-year: 3 private, 1 public; 3,499
students
Four-year and Beyond: 1 private, 1
public; 3,067 students
Degree Options: B
Places Rated Score: 2,990
Places Rated Rank: 90

Athens, GA
Elementary and Secondary
Public: 6 districts, 40 schools, 21,745 pupils
    Pupil/Teacher Ratio: 13.37
    Dollars per Pupil: $2,103
    Average Teacher Salary: $1,316
    Effort Index: 1.015
Private: 9 schools, 2,013 pupils
Colleges and Universities
Two-year: None
Four-year and Beyond: 1 public; 25,886 students
Degree Options: C
Places Rated Score: 2,646
Places Rated Rank: 231

Atlanta, GA
Elementary and Secondary
Public: 24 districts, 650 schools, 413,946 pupils
    Pupil/Teacher Ratio: 15.17
    Dollars per Pupil: $2,267
    Average Teacher Salary: $1,480
    Effort Index: 0.810
Private: 187 schools, 38,020 pupils
Colleges and Universities
Two-year: 2 private, 3 public; 23,517 students
Four-year and Beyond: 16 private, 4 public; 65,819 students
Degree Options: AA
Places Rated Score: 3,057
Places Rated Rank: 62

Atlantic City, NJ
Elementary and Secondary
Public: 42 districts, 111 schools, 45,374 pupils
    Pupil/Teacher Ratio: 12.75
    Dollars per Pupil: $3,596
    Average Teacher Salary: $2,038
    Effort Index: 0.993
Private: 33 schools, 8,784 pupils
Colleges and Universities
Two-year: 1 public; 3,591 students
Four-year and Beyond: 1 public; 5,056 students
Degree Options: B
Places Rated Score: 2,929
Places Rated Rank: 110

Augusta, GA–SC
Elementary and Secondary
Public: 4 districts, 110 schools, 61,991 pupils
    Pupil/Teacher Ratio: 13.25
    Dollars per Pupil: $2,235
    Average Teacher Salary: $1,097
    Effort Index: 1.024
Private: 41 schools, 7,442 pupils
Colleges and Universities
Two-year: 1 private, 1 public; 1,670 students
Four-year and Beyond: 1 private, 3 public; 8,769 students
Degree Options: B
Places Rated Score: 2,915
Places Rated Rank: 118

Aurora–Elgin, IL
Elementary and Secondary
Public: 15 districts, 142 schools, 86,769 pupils
    Pupil/Teacher Ratio: 17.80
    Dollars per Pupil: $2,218
    Average Teacher Salary: $1,950
    Effort Index: 0.858

Private: 47 schools, 11,199 pupils
Colleges and Universities
Two-year: 2 public; 12,673 students
Four-year and Beyond: 2 private; 1,728 students
Degree Options: C
Places Rated Score: 2,208
Places Rated Rank: 321

Austin, TX
Elementary and Secondary
Public: 21 districts, 160 schools, 94,921 pupils
    Pupil/Teacher Ratio: 12.36
    Dollars per Pupil: $2,815
    Average Teacher Salary: $1,584
    Effort Index: 1.090
Private: 36 schools, 6,865 pupils
Colleges and Universities
Two-year: 1 public; 15,362 students
Four-year and Beyond: 6 private, 1 public; 52,870 students
Degree Options: B
Places Rated Score: 3,063
Places Rated Rank: 60

Bakersfield, CA
Elementary and Secondary
Public: 49 districts, 168 schools, 80,367 pupils
    Pupil/Teacher Ratio: 15.79
    Dollars per Pupil: $3,441
    Average Teacher Salary: $2,114
    Effort Index: 0.856
Private: 36 schools, 5,690 pupils
Colleges and Universities
Two-year: 3 public; 15,465 students
Four-year and Beyond: 1 public; 3,641 students
Degree Options: B
Places Rated Score: 2,564
Places Rated Rank: 260

★ Baltimore, MD
Elementary and Secondary
Public: 6 districts, 532 schools, 336,231 pupils
    Pupil/Teacher Ratio: 13.75
    Dollars per Pupil: $3,208
    Average Teacher Salary: $2,079
    Effort Index: 1.121
Private: 228 schools, 96,745 pupils
Colleges and Universities
Two-year: 5 private, 4 public; 53,090 students
Four-year and Beyond: 10 private, 5 public; 58,339 students
Degree Options: AA
Places Rated Score: 3,471
Places Rated Rank: 15

Bangor, ME
Elementary and Secondary
Public: 9 districts, 34 schools, 13,138 pupils
    Pupil/Teacher Ratio: 13.79
    Dollars per Pupil: $2,048
    Average Teacher Salary: $1,396
    Effort Index: 1.088
Private: 8 schools, 1,187 pupils
Colleges and Universities
Two-year: 1 private, 1 public; 1,383 students
Four-year and Beyond: 1 private, 1 public; 13,150 students
Degree Options: B
Places Rated Score: 2,934
Places Rated Rank: 109

Baton Rouge, LA
Elementary and Secondary
Public: 4 districts, 154 schools, 86,188 pupils
    Pupil/Teacher Ratio: 14.09
    Dollars per Pupil: $2,651
    Average Teacher Salary: $1,800
    Effort Index: 1.062
Private: 57 schools, 17,493 pupils
Colleges and Universities
Two-year: None
Four-year and Beyond: 2 public; 40,225 students
Degree Options: C
Places Rated Score: 2,635
Places Rated Rank: 236

Battle Creek, MI
Elementary and Secondary
Public: 10 districts, 57 schools, 25,776 pupils
    Pupil/Teacher Ratio: 16.55
    Dollars per Pupil: $2,950
    Average Teacher Salary: $2,247
    Effort Index: 1.070
Private: 10 schools, 1,705 pupils
Colleges and Universities
Two-year: 1 public; 5,193 students
Four-year and Beyond: 1 private; 1,742 students
Degree Options: C
Places Rated Score: 2,483
Places Rated Rank: 285

Beaumont–Port Arthur, TX
Elementary and Secondary
Public: 17 districts, 126 schools, 72,795 pupils
    Pupil/Teacher Ratio: 12.92
    Dollars per Pupil: $2,843
    Average Teacher Salary: $1,679
    Effort Index: 1.075
Private: 21 schools, 4,187 pupils
Colleges and Universities
Two-year: None
Four-year and Beyond: 1 public; 14,638 students
Degree Options: C
Places Rated Score: 2,745
Places Rated Rank: 188

Beaver County, PA
Elementary and Secondary
Public: 15 districts, 60 schools, 33,905 pupils
    Pupil/Teacher Ratio: 15.99
    Dollars per Pupil: $2,574
    Average Teacher Salary: $1,691
    Effort Index: 1.089
Private: 14 schools, 3,101 pupils
Colleges and Universities
Two-year: 2 public; 3,829 students
Four-year and Beyond: 1 private; 1,267 students
Degree Options: C
Places Rated Score: 2,535
Places Rated Rank: 270

Bellingham, WA
Elementary and Secondary
Public: 7 districts, 43 schools, 17,974 pupils
    Pupil/Teacher Ratio: 18.40
    Dollars per Pupil: $2,919
    Average Teacher Salary: $1,984
    Effort Index: 1.206
Private: 9 schools, 1,680 pupils

Colleges and Universities
Two-year: 1 public; 1,920 students
Four-year and Beyond: 1 public; 9,352
students
Degree Options: B
Places Rated Score: 2,778
Places Rated Rank: 170

Benton Harbor, MI
Elementary and Secondary
Public: 14 districts, 70 schools,
34,784 pupils
Pupil/Teacher Ratio: 17.44
Dollars per Pupil: $2,662
Average Teacher Salary: $1,679
Effort Index: 1.178
Private: 28 schools, 4,736 pupils
Colleges and Universities
Two-year: 1 public; 2,977 students
Four-year and Beyond: 1 private; 2,851
students
Degree Options: C
Places Rated Score: 2,545
Places Rated Rank: 265

★ Bergen–Passaic, NJ
Elementary and Secondary
Public: 95 districts, 395 schools,
193,177 pupils
Pupil/Teacher Ratio: 11.98
Dollars per Pupil: $3,556
Average Teacher Salary: $2,210
Effort Index: 1.391
Private: 173 schools, 44,258 pupils
Colleges and Universities
Two-year: 3 private, 2 public; 19,637
students
Four-year and Beyond: 4 private, 2
public; 32,278 students
Degree Options: A
Places Rated Score: 3,653
Places Rated Rank: 2

Billings, MT
Elementary and Secondary
Public: 15 districts, 58 schools,
20,444 pupils
Pupil/Teacher Ratio: 8.08
Dollars per Pupil: $2,652
Average Teacher Salary: $2,220
Effort Index: 1.008
Private: 11 schools, 1,401 pupils
Colleges and Universities
Two-year: None
Four-year and Beyond: 1 private, 1
public; 4,565 students
Degree Options: C
Places Rated Score: 3,008
Places Rated Rank: 84

Biloxi–Gulfport, MS
Elementary and Secondary
Public: 7 districts, 54 schools,
29,521 pupils
Pupil/Teacher Ratio: 13.97
Dollars per Pupil: $1,898
Average Teacher Salary: $1,365
Effort Index: 1.010
Private: 6 schools, 662 pupils
Colleges and Universities
Two-year: 1 private; 792 students
Four-year and Beyond: None
Degree Options: C
Places Rated Score: 2,592
Places Rated Rank: 255

Binghamton, NY
Elementary and Secondary
Public: 18 districts, 76 schools,
47,894 pupils
Pupil/Teacher Ratio: 13.26
Dollars per Pupil: $3,766
Average Teacher Salary: $1,869
Effort Index: 1.161
Private: 24 schools, 4,520 pupils
Colleges and Universities
Two-year: 1 public; 6,833 students
Four-year and Beyond: 1 public; 11,725
students
Degree Options: B
Places Rated Score: 3,052
Places Rated Rank: 63

Birmingham, AL
Elementary and Secondary
Public: 18 districts, 295 schools,
155,371 pupils
Pupil/Teacher Ratio: 16.55
Dollars per Pupil: $1,832
Average Teacher Salary: $1,694
Effort Index: 0.937
Private: 54 schools, 11,697 pupils
Colleges and Universities
Two-year: 2 private, 2 public; 10,309
students
Four-year and Beyond: 4 private, 2
public; 23,117 students
Degree Options: A
Places Rated Score: 2,851
Places Rated Rank: 149

Bismarck, ND
Elementary and Secondary
Public: 23 districts, 51 schools,
14,436 pupils
Pupil/Teacher Ratio: 15.44
Dollars per Pupil: $3,118
Average Teacher Salary: $2,131
Effort Index: 1.207
Private: 10 schools, 2,050 pupils
Colleges and Universities
Two-year: 1 public; 2,346 students
Four-year and Beyond: 1 private; 1,121
students
Degree Options: C
Places Rated Score: 2,686
Places Rated Rank: 217

Bloomington, IN
Elementary and Secondary
Public: 2 districts, 28 schools,
13,580 pupils
Pupil/Teacher Ratio: 17.32
Dollars per Pupil: $2,151
Average Teacher Salary: $1,760
Effort Index: 1.503
Private: 7 schools, 505 pupils
Colleges and Universities
Two-year: None
Four-year and Beyond: 1 public; 32,711
students
Degree Options: C
Places Rated Score: 2,873
Places Rated Rank: 136

Bloomington–Normal, IL
Elementary and Secondary
Public: 13 districts, 52 schools,
18,670 pupils
Pupil/Teacher Ratio: 14.02
Dollars per Pupil: $2,605
Average Teacher Salary: $1,778
Effort Index: 1.275
Private: 9 schools, 2,261 pupils

Colleges and Universities
Two-year: None
Four-year and Beyond: 1 private, 1
public; 22,232 students
Degree Options: C
Places Rated Score: 2,854
Places Rated Rank: 145

Boise City, ID
Elementary and Secondary
Public: 3 districts, 64 schools,
34,750 pupils
Pupil/Teacher Ratio: 16.34
Dollars per Pupil: $1,772
Average Teacher Salary: $1,592
Effort Index: 0.966
Private: 13 schools, 1,928 pupils
Colleges and Universities
Two-year: None
Four-year and Beyond: 1 public; 11,092
students
Degree Options: C
Places Rated Score: 2,391
Places Rated Rank: 306

★ Boston, MA
Elementary and Secondary
Public: 109 districts, 775 schools,
404,095 pupils
Pupil/Teacher Ratio: 14.46
Dollars per Pupil: $2,707
Average Teacher Salary: $1,964
Effort Index: 0.933
Private: 308 schools, 75,926 pupils
Colleges and Universities
Two-year: 13 private, 6 public; 37,292
students
Four-year and Beyond: 31 private, 3
public; 186,445 students
Degree Options: AAA
Places Rated Score: 3,479
Places Rated Rank: 14

Boulder–Longmont, CO
Elementary and Secondary
Public: 2 districts, 70 schools,
35,658 pupils
Pupil/Teacher Ratio: 15.10
Dollars per Pupil: $2,773
Average Teacher Salary: $1,472
Effort Index: 1.085
Private: 16 schools, 2,182 pupils
Colleges and Universities
Two-year: None
Four-year and Beyond: 1 private, 1
public; 22,304 students
Degree Options: C
Places Rated Score: 2,587
Places Rated Rank: 256

Bradenton, FL
Elementary and Secondary
Public: 1 district, 31 schools,
21,229 pupils
Pupil/Teacher Ratio: 12.82
Dollars per Pupil: $3,045
Average Teacher Salary: $1,405
Effort Index: 1.033
Private: 13 schools, 2,313 pupils
Colleges and Universities
Two-year: 1 public; 6,604 students
Four-year and Beyond: None
Degree Options: C
Places Rated Score: 2,712
Places Rated Rank: 205

Brazoria, TX
Elementary and Secondary
Public: 8 districts, 56 schools,
35,985 pupils
    Pupil/Teacher Ratio: 13.85
    Dollars per Pupil: $2,927
    Average Teacher Salary: $1,667
    Effort Index: 1.126
Private: 2 schools, 217 pupils
Colleges and Universities
Two-year: 2 public; 7,412 students
Four-year and Beyond: None
Degree Options: C
Places Rated Score: 2,718
Places Rated Rank: 204

Bremerton, WA
Elementary and Secondary
Public: 5 districts, 50 schools,
29,068 pupils
    Pupil/Teacher Ratio: 20.30
    Dollars per Pupil: $2,662
    Average Teacher Salary: $1,941
    Effort Index: 1.299
Private: 11 schools, 1,422 pupils
Colleges and Universities
Two-year: 1 public; 5,338 students
Four-year and Beyond: None
Degree Options: C
Places Rated Score: 2,544
Places Rated Rank: 267

Bridgeport–Milford, CT
Elementary and Secondary
Public: 11 districts, 117 schools,
64,086 pupils
    Pupil/Teacher Ratio: 12.10
    Dollars per Pupil: $3,139
    Average Teacher Salary: $1,990
    Effort Index: 1.279
Private: 29 schools, 9,741 pupils
Colleges and Universities
Two-year: 1 public; 2,657 students
Four-year and Beyond: 4 private; 17,212
    students
Degree Options: C
Places Rated Score: 3,029
Places Rated Rank: 70

Bristol, CT
Elementary and Secondary
Public: 3 districts, 14 schools,
10,843 pupils
    Pupil/Teacher Ratio: 11.74
    Dollars per Pupil: $2,994
    Average Teacher Salary: $1,770
    Effort Index: 1.340
Private: 8 schools, 2,731 pupils
Colleges and Universities
Two-year: None
Four-year and Beyond: None
Degree Options: None
Places Rated Score: 2,628
Places Rated Rank: 240

Brockton, MA
Elementary and Secondary
Public: 9 districts, 52 schools,
32,321 pupils
    Pupil/Teacher Ratio: 14.46
    Dollars per Pupil: $2,707
    Average Teacher Salary: $1,964
    Effort Index: 0.933
Private: 22 schools, 3,272 pupils
Colleges and Universities
Two-year: 1 public; 7,174 students

Four-year and Beyond: 3 private, 2
public; 19,052 students
Degree Options: B
Places Rated Score: 2,729
Places Rated Rank: 193

Brownsville–Harlingen, TX
Elementary and Secondary
Public: 10 districts, 85 schools,
58,915 pupils
    Pupil/Teacher Ratio: 14.22
    Dollars per Pupil: $1,962
    Average Teacher Salary: $1,257
    Effort Index: 0.849
Private: 15 schools, 3,475 pupils
Colleges and Universities
Two-year: 2 public; 6,103 students
Four-year and Beyond: None
Degree Options: C
Places Rated Score: 2,413
Places Rated Rank: 303

Bryan–College Station, TX
Elementary and Secondary
Public: 2 districts, 19 schools,
14,175 pupils
    Pupil/Teacher Ratio: 15.54
    Dollars per Pupil: $2,274
    Average Teacher Salary: $1,497
    Effort Index: 1.535
Private: 7 schools, 993 pupils
Colleges and Universities
Two-year: None
Four-year and Beyond: 1 public; 36,127
    students
Degree Options: C
Places Rated Score: 2,973
Places Rated Rank: 95

Buffalo, NY
Elementary and Secondary
Public: 29 districts, 231 schools,
157,327 pupils
    Pupil/Teacher Ratio: 13.30
    Dollars per Pupil: $3,746
    Average Teacher Salary: $2,194
    Effort Index: 0.984
Private: 152 schools, 37,513 pupils
Colleges and Universities
Two-year: 4 private, 3 public; 19,953
    students
Four-year and Beyond: 4 private, 3
public; 46,422 students
Degree Options: A
Places Rated Score: 3,121
Places Rated Rank: 50

Burlington, NC
Elementary and Secondary
Public: 2 districts, 32 schools,
19,624 pupils
    Pupil/Teacher Ratio: 15.55
    Dollars per Pupil: $2,175
    Average Teacher Salary: $1,460
    Effort Index: 1.047
Private: 4 schools, 718 pupils
Colleges and Universities
Two-year: 1 public; 2,052 students
Four-year and Beyond: 1 private; 2,625
    students
Degree Options: C
Places Rated Score: 2,519
Places Rated Rank: 275

★ Burlington, VT
Elementary and Secondary
Public: 20 districts, 51 schools,
21,038 pupils
    Pupil/Teacher Ratio: 11.43
    Dollars per Pupil: $2,855
    Average Teacher Salary: $1,350
    Effort Index: 1.575
Private: 13 schools, 2,100 pupils
Colleges and Universities
Two-year: 1 private; 1,605 students
Four-year and Beyond: 3 private, 1
public; 14,104 students
Degree Options: C
Places Rated Score: 3,323
Places Rated Rank: 23

Canton, OH
Elementary and Secondary
Public: 20 districts, 139 schools,
76,607 pupils
    Pupil/Teacher Ratio: 17.09
    Dollars per Pupil: $2,185
    Average Teacher Salary: $1,669
    Effort Index: 1.119
Private: 29 schools, 8,475 pupils
Colleges and Universities
Two-year: 2 public; 4,868 students
Four-year and Beyond: 3 private; 3,003
    students
Degree Options: B
Places Rated Score: 2,754
Places Rated Rank: 181

Casper, WY
Elementary and Secondary
Public: 1 district, 34 schools,
14,002 pupils
    Pupil/Teacher Ratio: 14.51
    Dollars per Pupil: $4,870
    Average Teacher Salary: $2,243
    Effort Index: 0.911
Private: 4 schools, 843 pupils
Colleges and Universities
Two-year: 1 public; 3,475 students
Four-year and Beyond: None
Degree Options: C
Places Rated Score: 2,453
Places Rated Rank: 292

Cedar Rapids, IA
Elementary and Secondary
Public: 11 districts, 68 schools,
32,416 pupils
    Pupil/Teacher Ratio: 16.14
    Dollars per Pupil: $3,675
    Average Teacher Salary: $1,774
    Effort Index: 1.182
Private: 17 schools, 3,805 pupils
Colleges and Universities
Two-year: 1 public; 5,928 students
Four-year and Beyond: 3 private; 3,468
    students
Degree Options: C
Places Rated Score: 2,619
Places Rated Rank: 246

Champaign–Urbana–Rantoul, IL
Elementary and Secondary
Public: 17 districts, 58 schools,
23,544 pupils
    Pupil/Teacher Ratio: 13.86
    Dollars per Pupil: $3,193
    Average Teacher Salary: $1,736
    Effort Index: 1.306
Private: 5 schools, 1,210 pupils

Colleges and Universities
Two-year: 1 public; 8,441 students
Four-year and Beyond: 1 public; 34,914 students
Degree Options: B
Places Rated Score: 3,147
Places Rated Rank: 42

Charleston, SC
Elementary and Secondary
Public: 5 districts, 123 schools, 80,551 pupils
Pupil/Teacher Ratio: 14.71
Dollars per Pupil: $2,167
Average Teacher Salary: $1,388
Effort Index: 1.386
Private: 71 schools, 12,892 pupils
Colleges and Universities
Two-year: 1 private, 1 public; 6,468 students
Four-year and Beyond: 1 private, 3 public; 12,673 students
Degree Options: B
Places Rated Score: 3,164
Places Rated Rank: 40

Charleston, WV
Elementary and Secondary
Public: 2 districts, 140 schools, 48,709 pupils
Pupil/Teacher Ratio: 13.82
Dollars per Pupil: $2,483
Average Teacher Salary: $1,134
Effort Index: 1.300
Private: 18 schools, 2,383 pupils
Colleges and Universities
Two-year: None
Four-year and Beyond: 1 private, 2 public; 9,555 students
Degree Options: C
Places Rated Score: 2,894
Places Rated Rank: 129

Charlotte–Gastonia–Rock Hill, NC–SC
Elementary and Secondary
Public: 14 districts, 307 schools, 185,578 pupils
Pupil/Teacher Ratio: 14.68
Dollars per Pupil: $2,306
Average Teacher Salary: $1,475
Effort Index: 1.001
Private: 60 schools, 14,195 pupils
Colleges and Universities
Two-year: 2 private, 4 public; 26,761 students
Four-year and Beyond: 10 private, 2 public; 24,951 students
Degree Options: A
Places Rated Score: 3,031
Places Rated Rank: 69

★ Charlottesville, VA
Elementary and Secondary
Public: 4 districts, 43 schools, 17,734 pupils
Pupil/Teacher Ratio: 11.15
Dollars per Pupil: $2,695
Average Teacher Salary: $1,214
Effort Index: 1.383
Private: 18 schools, 2,600 pupils
Colleges and Universities
Two-year: 1 public; 3,348 students
Four-year and Beyond: 1 public; 17,118 students
Degree Options: B
Places Rated Score: 3,489
Places Rated Rank: 12

Chattanooga, TN–GA
Elementary and Secondary
Public: 9 districts, 156 schools, 75,934 pupils
Pupil/Teacher Ratio: 17.25
Dollars per Pupil: $1,763
Average Teacher Salary: $1,550
Effort Index: 0.788
Private: 45 schools, 9,931 pupils
Colleges and Universities
Two-year: 2 private, 1 public; 6,110 students
Four-year and Beyond: 3 private, 1 public; 13,087 students
Degree Options: B
Places Rated Score: 2,415
Places Rated Rank: 301

★ Chicago, IL
Elementary and Secondary
Public: 201 districts, 1,456 schools, 926,573 pupils
Pupil/Teacher Ratio: 16.21
Dollars per Pupil: $3,242
Average Teacher Salary: $1,995
Effort Index: 1.053
Private: 724 schools, 239,512 pupils
Colleges and Universities
Two-year: 4 private, 18 public; 181,436 students
Four-year and Beyond: 34 private, 3 public; 151,725 students
Degree Options: AAA
Places Rated Score: 3,486
Places Rated Rank: 13

Chico, CA
Elementary and Secondary
Public: 15 districts, 56 schools, 23,173 pupils
Pupil/Teacher Ratio: 14.18
Dollars per Pupil: $3,600
Average Teacher Salary: $1,986
Effort Index: 1.310
Private: 21 schools, 1,843 pupils
Colleges and Universities
Two-year: 1 public; 8,402 students
Four-year and Beyond: 1 public; 14,289 students
Degree Options: B
Places Rated Score: 3,126
Places Rated Rank: 49

Cincinnati, OH–KY–IN
Elementary and Secondary
Public: 59 districts, 394 schools, 233,481 pupils
Pupil/Teacher Ratio: 16.93
Dollars per Pupil: $2,456
Average Teacher Salary: $1,899
Effort Index: 1.025
Private: 174 schools, 55,195 pupils
Colleges and Universities
Two-year: 2 private, 3 public; 12,924 students
Four-year and Beyond: 7 private, 2 public; 53,468 students
Degree Options: A
Places Rated Score: 2,918
Places Rated Rank: 116

Clarksville–Hopkinsville, TN–KY
Elementary and Secondary
Public: 2 districts, 37 schools, 24,039 pupils
Pupil/Teacher Ratio: 15.93
Dollars per Pupil: $1,620

Average Teacher Salary: $1,536
Effort Index: 0.955
Private: 13 schools, 4,384 pupils
Colleges and Universities
Two-year: 1 public; 1,089 students
Four-year and Beyond: 1 public; 3,892 students
Degree Options: B
Places Rated Score: 2,654
Places Rated Rank: 225

Cleveland, OH
Elementary and Secondary
Public: 58 districts, 494 schools, 285,993 pupils
Pupil/Teacher Ratio: 16.10
Dollars per Pupil: $3,386
Average Teacher Salary: $1,890
Effort Index: 1.033
Private: 192 schools, 77,384 pupils
Colleges and Universities
Two-year: 3 private, 2 public; 66,614 students
Four-year and Beyond: 11 private, 1 public; 40,875 students
Degree Options: A
Places Rated Score: 2,972
Places Rated Rank: 97

Colorado Springs, CO
Elementary and Secondary
Public: 15 districts, 116 schools, 61,116 pupils
Pupil/Teacher Ratio: 15.52
Dollars per Pupil: $2,608
Average Teacher Salary: $1,615
Effort Index: 1.030
Private: 19 schools, 3,883 pupils
Colleges and Universities
Two-year: 2 private, 1 public; 7,079 students
Four-year and Beyond: 2 private, 1 public; 7,851 students
Degree Options: B
Places Rated Score: 2,754
Places Rated Rank: 181

Columbia, MO
Elementary and Secondary
Public: 6 districts, 33 schools, 14,520 pupils
Pupil/Teacher Ratio: 15.17
Dollars per Pupil: $2,136
Average Teacher Salary: $1,447
Effort Index: 0.880
Private: 11 schools, 930 pupils
Colleges and Universities
Two-year: None
Four-year and Beyond: 2 private, 1 public; 28,416 students
Degree Options: C
Places Rated Score: 2,377
Places Rated Rank: 310

Columbia, SC
Elementary and Secondary
Public: 7 districts, 114 schools, 75,648 pupils
Pupil/Teacher Ratio: 14.43
Dollars per Pupil: $2,367
Average Teacher Salary: $1,455
Effort Index: 1.110
Private: 60 schools, 8,637 pupils
Colleges and Universities
Two-year: 1 private, 1 public; 6,582 students

Four-year and Beyond: 4 private, 1
public; 28,358 students
Degree Options: B
Places Rated Score: 2,908
Places Rated Rank: 120

Columbus, GA–AL
Elementary and Secondary
Public: 5 districts, 85 schools,
41,771 pupils
Pupil/Teacher Ratio: 14.45
Dollars per Pupil: $2,022
Average Teacher Salary: $1,458
Effort Index: 0.869
Private: 21 schools, 2,928 pupils
Colleges and Universities
Two-year: 2 private, 1 public; 2,412
students
Four-year and Beyond: 1 public; 4,245
students
Degree Options: B
Places Rated Score: 2,665
Places Rated Rank: 224

Columbus, OH
Elementary and Secondary
Public: 54 districts, 423 schools,
225,330 pupils
Pupil/Teacher Ratio: 16.33
Dollars per Pupil: $2,406
Average Teacher Salary: $1,904
Effort Index: 1.002
Private: 79 schools, 21,892 pupils
Colleges and Universities
Two-year: 3 public; 11,990 students
Four-year and Beyond: 11 private, 2
public; 73,210 students
Degree Options: A
Places Rated Score: 2,928
Places Rated Rank: 111

Corpus Christi, TX
Elementary and Secondary
Public: 20 districts, 133 schools,
71,194 pupils
Pupil/Teacher Ratio: 13.03
Dollars per Pupil: $2,679
Average Teacher Salary: $1,259
Effort Index: 0.930
Private: 37 schools, 6,841 pupils
Colleges and Universities
Two-year: 1 public; 8,620 students
Four-year and Beyond: 1 public; 3,251
students
Degree Options: B
Places Rated Score: 2,840
Places Rated Rank: 153

★ Cumberland, MD–WV
Elementary and Secondary
Public: 2 districts, 45 schools,
18,798 pupils
Pupil/Teacher Ratio: 13.58
Dollars per Pupil: $3,013
Average Teacher Salary: $1,685
Effort Index: 1.667
Private: 9 schools, 1,832 pupils
Colleges and Universities
Two-year: 2 public; 3,097 students
Four-year and Beyond: 1 public; 3,654
students
Degree Options: B
Places Rated Score: 3,363
Places Rated Rank: 19

Dallas, TX
Elementary and Secondary
Public: 60 districts, 602 schools,
378,453 pupils
Pupil/Teacher Ratio: 14.16
Dollars per Pupil: $2,327
Average Teacher Salary: $1,471
Effort Index: 0.951
Private: 140 schools, 33,575 pupils
Colleges and Universities
Two-year: 2 private, 7 public; 51,164
students
Four-year and Beyond: 10 private, 3
public; 50,620 students
Degree Options: AA
Places Rated Score: 3,269
Places Rated Rank: 29

Danbury, CT
Elementary and Secondary
Public: 9 districts, 48 schools,
31,451 pupils
Pupil/Teacher Ratio: 12.10
Dollars per Pupil: $3,139
Average Teacher Salary: $1,990
Effort Index: 1.279
Private: 12 schools, 3,327 pupils
Colleges and Universities
Two-year: None
Four-year and Beyond: 1 public; 5,996
students
Degree Options: C
Places Rated Score: 3,029
Places Rated Rank: 70

Danville, VA
Elementary and Secondary
Public: 2 districts, 40 schools,
21,290 pupils
Pupil/Teacher Ratio: 13.74
Dollars per Pupil: $1,813
Average Teacher Salary: $1,485
Effort Index: 1.342
Private: 9 schools, 2,352 pupils
Colleges and Universities
Two-year: 1 public; 2,377 students
Four-year and Beyond: 1 private; 916
students
Degree Options: C
Places Rated Score: 2,943
Places Rated Rank: 105

Davenport–Rock Island–Moline, IA–IL
Elementary and Secondary
Public: 23 districts, 150 schools,
72,616 pupils
Pupil/Teacher Ratio: 16.78
Dollars per Pupil: $2,482
Average Teacher Salary: $1,923
Effort Index: 1.627
Private: 16 schools, 4,300 pupils
Colleges and Universities
Two-year: 3 public; 10,659 students
Four-year and Beyond: 3 private; 5,470
students
Degree Options: C
Places Rated Score: 2,901
Places Rated Rank: 125

Dayton–Springfield, OH
Elementary and Secondary
Public: 43 districts, 284 schools,
174,254 pupils
Pupil/Teacher Ratio: 15.88
Dollars per Pupil: $2,677

Average Teacher Salary: $1,823
Effort Index: 1.070
Private: 60 schools, 18,529 pupils
Colleges and Universities
Two-year: 2 private, 3 public; 24,998
students
Four-year and Beyond: 6 private, 1
public; 21,763 students
Degree Options: B
Places Rated Score: 2,772
Places Rated Rank: 173

Daytona Beach, FL
Elementary and Secondary
Public: 1 district, 56 schools,
36,076 pupils
Pupil/Teacher Ratio: 16.03
Dollars per Pupil: $3,314
Average Teacher Salary: $1,487
Effort Index: 1.169
Private: 23 schools, 4,556 pupils
Colleges and Universities
Two-year: 1 public; 7,793 students
Four-year and Beyond: 2 private; 4,534
students
Degree Options: C
Places Rated Score: 2,612
Places Rated Rank: 251

Decatur, IL
Elementary and Secondary
Public: 8 districts, 57 schools,
23,249 pupils
Pupil/Teacher Ratio: 15.14
Dollars per Pupil: $2,370
Average Teacher Salary: $1,945
Effort Index: 1.184
Private: 14 schools, 3,410 pupils
Colleges and Universities
Two-year: 1 public; 3,313 students
Four-year and Beyond: 1 private; 1,547
students
Degree Options: C
Places Rated Score: 2,683
Places Rated Rank: 219

Denver, CO
Elementary and Secondary
Public: 17 districts, 448 schools,
259,097 pupils
Pupil/Teacher Ratio: 15.42
Dollars per Pupil: $3,035
Average Teacher Salary: $1,849
Effort Index: 0.914
Private: 124 schools, 25,799 pupils
Colleges and Universities
Two-year: 1 private, 3 public; 22,551
students
Four-year and Beyond: 8 private, 4
public; 43,297 students
Degree Options: AA
Places Rated Score: 3,145
Places Rated Rank: 43

Des Moines, IA
Elementary and Secondary
Public: 22 districts, 159 schools,
66,749 pupils
Pupil/Teacher Ratio: 14.13
Dollars per Pupil: $2,928
Average Teacher Salary: $1,652
Effort Index: 1.043
Private: 25 schools, 5,900 pupils
Colleges and Universities
Two-year: 2 private, 1 public; 8,742
students

Four-year and Beyond: 6 private; 10,095
students
Degree Options: C
Places Rated Score: 2,613
Places Rated Rank: 250

Detroit, MI
Elementary and Secondary
Public: 111 districts, 1,288 schools,
827,764 pupils
Pupil/Teacher Ratio: 18.22
Dollars per Pupil: $3,236
Average Teacher Salary: $2,609
Effort Index: 0.984
Private: 410 schools, 118,345 pupils
Colleges and Universities
Two-year: 2 private, 8 public; 110,220
students
Four-year and Beyond: 14 private, 3
public; 74,030 students
Degree Options: AA
Places Rated Score: 3,064
Places Rated Rank: 59

Dothan, AL
Elementary and Secondary
Public: 5 districts, 41 schools,
26,430 pupils
Pupil/Teacher Ratio: 19.35
Dollars per Pupil: $1,505
Average Teacher Salary: $1,450
Effort Index: 0.699
Private: 8 schools, 2,673 pupils
Colleges and Universities
Two-year: 1 public; 1,971 students
Four-year and Beyond: 1 public; 1,570
students
Degree Options: B
Places Rated Score: 2,230
Places Rated Rank: 320

Dubuque, IA
Elementary and Secondary
Public: 2 districts, 30 schools,
14,798 pupils
Pupil/Teacher Ratio: 16.05
Dollars per Pupil: $2,800
Average Teacher Salary: $1,804
Effort Index: 1.259
Private: 24 schools, 8,079 pupils
Colleges and Universities
Two-year: None
Four-year and Beyond: 4 private; 4,318
students
Degree Options: C
Places Rated Score: 2,701
Places Rated Rank: 211

Duluth, MN–WI
Elementary and Secondary
Public: 21 districts, 110 schools,
45,894 pupils
Pupil/Teacher Ratio: 15.53
Dollars per Pupil: $3,438
Average Teacher Salary: $1,943
Effort Index: 0.895
Private: 19 schools, 2,747 pupils
Colleges and Universities
Two-year: 1 public; 3,724 students
Four-year and Beyond: 1 private, 2
public; 14,208 students
Degree Options: B
Places Rated Score: 2,619
Places Rated Rank: 246

East St. Louis–Belleville, IL
Elementary and Secondary
Public: 39 districts, 123 schools,
56,511 pupils
Pupil/Teacher Ratio: 17.13
Dollars per Pupil: $2,801
Average Teacher Salary: $1,888
Effort Index: 1.247
Private: 44 schools, 8,549 pupils
Colleges and Universities
Two-year: 2 public; 11,930 students
Four-year and Beyond: 1 private; 750
students
Degree Options: C
Places Rated Score: 2,630
Places Rated Rank: 237

Eau Claire, WI
Elementary and Secondary
Public: 11 districts, 54 schools,
21,198 pupils
Pupil/Teacher Ratio: 15.25
Dollars per Pupil: $3,417
Average Teacher Salary: $1,675
Effort Index: 1.219
Private: 28 schools, 3,847 pupils
Colleges and Universities
Two-year: 1 public; 3,146 students
Four-year and Beyond: 1 public; 10,883
students
Degree Options: B
Places Rated Score: 2,960
Places Rated Rank: 101

El Paso, TX
Elementary and Secondary
Public: 9 districts, 135 schools,
121,403 pupils
Pupil/Teacher Ratio: 16.40
Dollars per Pupil: $1,845
Average Teacher Salary: $1,496
Effort Index: 0.807
Private: 29 schools, 6,837 pupils
Colleges and Universities
Two-year: 1 public; 11,206 students
Four-year and Beyond: 1 public; 15,129
students
Degree Options: B
Places Rated Score: 2,479
Places Rated Rank: 286

Elkhart–Goshen, IN
Elementary and Secondary
Public: 7 districts, 58 schools,
26,780 pupils
Pupil/Teacher Ratio: 17.19
Dollars per Pupil: $2,276
Average Teacher Salary: $1,653
Effort Index: 1.157
Private: 18 schools, 2,534 pupils
Colleges and Universities
Two-year: None
Four-year and Beyond: 2 private; 1,113
students
Degree Options: C
Places Rated Score: 2,537
Places Rated Rank: 269

Elmira, NY
Elementary and Secondary
Public: 3 districts, 25 schools,
15,477 pupils
Pupil/Teacher Ratio: 11.89
Dollars per Pupil: $3,440
Average Teacher Salary: $1,865
Effort Index: 1.228
Private: 11 schools, 2,154 pupils

Colleges and Universities
Two-year: None
Four-year and Beyond: 1 private; 2,548
students
Degree Options: C
Places Rated Score: 3,000
Places Rated Rank: 86

Enid, OK
Elementary and Secondary
Public: 9 districts, 37 schools,
11,966 pupils
Pupil/Teacher Ratio: 13.18
Dollars per Pupil: $2,273
Average Teacher Salary: $1,495
Effort Index: 1.117
Private: 3 schools, 494 pupils
Colleges and Universities
Two-year: None
Four-year and Beyond: 1 private; 1,132
students
Degree Options: C
Places Rated Score: 2,764
Places Rated Rank: 177

Erie, PA
Elementary and Secondary
Public: 13 districts, 78 schools,
45,548 pupils
Pupil/Teacher Ratio: 15.88
Dollars per Pupil: $2,514
Average Teacher Salary: $1,684
Effort Index: 1.189
Private: 48 schools, 13,222 pupils
Colleges and Universities
Two-year: 2 private; 592 students
Four-year and Beyond: 3 private, 2
public; 13,849 students
Degree Options: C
Places Rated Score: 2,641
Places Rated Rank: 235

Eugene–Springfield, OR
Elementary and Secondary
Public: 16 districts, 112 schools,
44,088 pupils
Pupil/Teacher Ratio: 15.26
Dollars per Pupil: $4,060
Average Teacher Salary: $1,900
Effort Index: 1.377
Private: 26 schools, 2,921 pupils
Colleges and Universities
Two-year: 1 public; 7,748 students
Four-year and Beyond: 2 private, 1
public; 15,766 students
Degree Options: B
Places Rated Score: 3,118
Places Rated Rank: 51

Evansville, IN–KY
Elementary and Secondary
Public: 6 districts, 77 schools,
45,706 pupils
Pupil/Teacher Ratio: 17.39
Dollars per Pupil: $2,288
Average Teacher Salary: $1,816
Effort Index: 1.177
Private: 29 schools, 6,419 pupils
Colleges and Universities
Two-year: 1 private, 2 public; 3,086
students
Four-year and Beyond: 1 private, 1
public; 8,425 students
Degree Options: B
Places Rated Score: 2,797
Places Rated Rank: 162

Fall River, MA–RI
Elementary and Secondary
Public: 6 districts, 61 schools,
24,503 pupils
    Pupil/Teacher Ratio: 15.79
    Dollars per Pupil: $2,117
    Average Teacher Salary: $1,662
    Effort Index: 0.981
Private: 20 schools, 4,434 pupils
Colleges and Universities
Two-year: 1 public; 4,851 students
Four-year and Beyond: None
Degree Options: C
Places Rated Score: 2,439
Places Rated Rank: 295

Fargo–Moorhead, ND–MN
Elementary and Secondary
Public: 17 districts, 58 schools,
23,505 pupils
    Pupil/Teacher Ratio: 15.31
    Dollars per Pupil: $2,840
    Average Teacher Salary: $2,153
    Effort Index: 1.019
Private: 13 schools, 2,556 pupils
Colleges and Universities
Two-year: None
Four-year and Beyond: 1 private, 2
public; 19,119 students
Degree Options: C
Places Rated Score: 2,506
Places Rated Rank: 277

Fayetteville, NC
Elementary and Secondary
Public: 3 districts, 80 schools,
48,518 pupils
    Pupil/Teacher Ratio: 15.61
    Dollars per Pupil: $2,152
    Average Teacher Salary: $1,408
    Effort Index: 1.332
Private: 9 schools, 1,858 pupils
Colleges and Universities
Two-year: 1 private, 1 public; 6,172
students
Four-year and Beyond: 1 private, 1
public; 3,220 students
Degree Options: B
Places Rated Score: 3,051
Places Rated Rank: 64

Fayetteville–Springdale, AR
Elementary and Secondary
Public: 9 districts, 40 schools,
17,834 pupils
    Pupil/Teacher Ratio: 17.50
    Dollars per Pupil: $1,891
    Average Teacher Salary: $1,280
    Effort Index: 0.970
Private: 4 schools, 674 pupils
Colleges and Universities
Two-year: None
Four-year and Beyond: 1 public; 16,052
students
Degree Options: C
Places Rated Score: 2,334
Places Rated Rank: 314

Fitchburg–Leominster, MA
Elementary and Secondary
Public: 5 districts, 24 schools,
12,985 pupils
    Pupil/Teacher Ratio: 13.06
    Dollars per Pupil: $2,524
    Average Teacher Salary: $1,616
    Effort Index: 1.141
Private: 13 schools, 3,436 pupils

Colleges and Universities
Two-year: None
Four-year and Beyond: 1 public; 6,609
students
Degree Options: C
Places Rated Score: 2,799
Places Rated Rank: 161

Flint, MI
Elementary and Secondary
Public: 21 districts, 161 schools,
97,060 pupils
    Pupil/Teacher Ratio: 18.74
    Dollars per Pupil: $3,098
    Average Teacher Salary: $2,474
    Effort Index: 0.956
Private: 30 schools, 7,498 pupils
Colleges and Universities
Two-year: 1 private, 1 public; 12,627
students
Four-year and Beyond: 1 private, 1
public; 7,458 students
Degree Options: B
Places Rated Score: 2,511
Places Rated Rank: 276

Florence, AL
Elementary and Secondary
Public: 6 districts, 54 schools,
24,617 pupils
    Pupil/Teacher Ratio: 15.82
    Dollars per Pupil: $1,959
    Average Teacher Salary: $1,335
    Effort Index: 0.971
Private: 4 schools, 1,181 pupils
Colleges and Universities
Two-year: None
Four-year and Beyond: 1 private, 1
public; 5,395 students
Degree Options: C
Places Rated Score: 2,427
Places Rated Rank: 299

Florence, SC
Elementary and Secondary
Public: 5 districts, 42 schools,
23,523 pupils
    Pupil/Teacher Ratio: 14.40
    Dollars per Pupil: $1,905
    Average Teacher Salary: $1,205
    Effort Index: 1.309
Private: 20 schools, 2,765 pupils
Colleges and Universities
Two-year: 1 public; 2,324 students
Four-year and Beyond: 1 public; 2,911
students
Degree Options: B
Places Rated Score: 3,109
Places Rated Rank: 53

Fort Collins–Loveland, CO
Elementary and Secondary
Public: 3 districts, 62 schools,
26,250 pupils
    Pupil/Teacher Ratio: 15.11
    Dollars per Pupil: $2,768
    Average Teacher Salary: $1,521
    Effort Index: 0.912
Private: 10 schools, 1,396 pupils
Colleges and Universities
Two-year: None
Four-year and Beyond: 1 public; 18,909
students
Degree Options: C
Places Rated Score: 2,413
Places Rated Rank: 303

Fort Lauderdale–Hollywood–Pompano Beach, FL
Elementary and Secondary
Public: 1 district, 157 schools,
127,096 pupils
    Pupil/Teacher Ratio: 13.67
    Dollars per Pupil: $3,116
    Average Teacher Salary: $1,416
    Effort Index: 1.128
Private: 119 schools, 30,735 pupils
Colleges and Universities
Two-year: 1 private, 1 public; 23,736
students
Four-year and Beyond: 2 private; 6,498
students
Degree Options: C
Places Rated Score: 2,734
Places Rated Rank: 191

Fort Myers, FL
Elementary and Secondary
Public: 1 district, 46 schools,
30,800 pupils
    Pupil/Teacher Ratio: 13.19
    Dollars per Pupil: $3,183
    Average Teacher Salary: $1,382
    Effort Index: 1.083
Private: 17 schools, 4,155 pupils
Colleges and Universities
Two-year: 1 public; 5,647 students
Four-year and Beyond: None
Degree Options: C
Places Rated Score: 2,729
Places Rated Rank: 193

Fort Pierce, FL
Elementary and Secondary
Public: 2 districts, 31 schools,
23,513 pupils
    Pupil/Teacher Ratio: 13.11
    Dollars per Pupil: $3,670
    Average Teacher Salary: $1,514
    Effort Index: 1.642
Private: 21 schools, 3,817 pupils
Colleges and Universities
Two-year: 1 public; 5,894 students
Four-year and Beyond: None
Degree Options: C
Places Rated Score: 3,154
Places Rated Rank: 41

Fort Smith, AR–OK
Elementary and Secondary
Public: 24 districts, 83 schools,
30,773 pupils
    Pupil/Teacher Ratio: 14.25
    Dollars per Pupil: $1,922
    Average Teacher Salary: $1,376
    Effort Index: 1.366
Private: 9 schools, 1,460 pupils
Colleges and Universities
Two-year: 1 private, 1 public; 4,218
students
Four-year and Beyond: None
Degree Options: C
Places Rated Score: 2,927
Places Rated Rank: 112

Fort Walton Beach, FL
Elementary and Secondary
Public: 1 district, 35 schools,
23,413 pupils
    Pupil/Teacher Ratio: 14.01
    Dollars per Pupil: $2,558
    Average Teacher Salary: $1,215
    Effort Index: 1.230
Private: 4 schools, 688 pupils

Colleges and Universities
Two-year: 1 public; 3,638 students
Four-year and Beyond: None
Degree Options: C
Places Rated Score: 2,809
Places Rated Rank: 157

Fort Wayne, IN
Elementary and Secondary
Public: 20 districts, 108 schools,
62,034 pupils
Pupil/Teacher Ratio: 17.89
Dollars per Pupil: $2,382
Average Teacher Salary: $1,796
Effort Index: 1.177
Private: 57 schools, 14,576 pupils
Colleges and Universities
Two-year: 2 private, 1 public; 5,072
students
Four-year and Beyond: 4 private, 1
public; 12,953 students
Degree Options: B
Places Rated Score: 2,772
Places Rated Rank: 173

Fort Worth–Arlington, TX
Elementary and Secondary
Public: 36 districts, 313 schools,
189,145 pupils
Pupil/Teacher Ratio: 15.09
Dollars per Pupil: $2,300
Average Teacher Salary: $1,631
Effort Index: 0.875
Private: 57 schools, 12,362 pupils
Colleges and Universities
Two-year: 3 private, 1 public; 28,155
students
Four-year and Beyond: 5 private, 1
public; 35,195 students
Degree Options: B
Places Rated Score: 2,627
Places Rated Rank: 242

Fresno, CA
Elementary and Secondary
Public: 47 districts, 221 schools,
107,232 pupils
Pupil/Teacher Ratio: 18.11
Dollars per Pupil: $3,118
Average Teacher Salary: $1,905
Effort Index: 0.822
Private: 36 schools, 6,538 pupils
Colleges and Universities
Two-year: 3 public; 20,115 students
Four-year and Beyond: 3 private, 1
public; 17,503 students
Degree Options: B
Places Rated Score: 2,407
Places Rated Rank: 305

Gadsden, AL
Elementary and Secondary
Public: 3 districts, 40 schools,
18,850 pupils
Pupil/Teacher Ratio: 19.18
Dollars per Pupil: $1,537
Average Teacher Salary: $1,458
Effort Index: 1.011
Private: 6 schools, 1,187 pupils
Colleges and Universities
Two-year: 1 public; 3,572 students
Four-year and Beyond: None
Degree Options: C
Places Rated Score: 2,299
Places Rated Rank: 317

Gainesville, FL
Elementary and Secondary
Public: 2 districts, 41 schools,
25,331 pupils
Pupil/Teacher Ratio: 14.96
Dollars per Pupil: $3,239
Average Teacher Salary: $1,652
Effort Index: 1.333
Private: 26 schools, 2,691 pupils
Colleges and Universities
Two-year: 1 public; 7,354 students
Four-year and Beyond: 1 public; 34,252
students
Degree Options: B
Places Rated Score: 3,094
Places Rated Rank: 55

Galveston–Texas City, TX
Elementary and Secondary
Public: 9 districts, 67 schools,
51,418 pupils
Pupil/Teacher Ratio: 12.36
Dollars per Pupil: $2,906
Average Teacher Salary: $1,621
Effort Index: 0.835
Private: 17 schools, 2,889 pupils
Colleges and Universities
Two-year: 2 public; 4,946 students
Four-year and Beyond: 2 public; 2,245
students
Degree Options: B
Places Rated Score: 2,809
Places Rated Rank: 157

Gary–Hammond, IN
Elementary and Secondary
Public: 22 districts, 199 schools,
122,245 pupils
Pupil/Teacher Ratio: 17.16
Dollars per Pupil: $2,411
Average Teacher Salary: $1,786
Effort Index: 0.895
Private: 63 schools, 17,609 pupils
Colleges and Universities
Two-year: 1 public; 3,294 students
Four-year and Beyond: 1 private, 2
public; 13,885 students
Degree Options: B
Places Rated Score: 2,526
Places Rated Rank: 273

Glens Falls, NY
Elementary and Secondary
Public: 20 districts, 46 schools,
23,280 pupils
Pupil/Teacher Ratio: 13.19
Dollars per Pupil: $3,394
Average Teacher Salary: $1,911
Effort Index: 1.028
Private: 5 schools, 953 pupils
Colleges and Universities
Two-year: 1 public; 3,019 students
Four-year and Beyond: None
Degree Options: C
Places Rated Score: 2,674
Places Rated Rank: 221

Grand Forks, ND
Elementary and Secondary
Public: 8 districts, 27 schools,
10,583 pupils
Pupil/Teacher Ratio: 15.16
Dollars per Pupil: $2,758
Average Teacher Salary: $2,344
Effort Index: 1.224
Private: 4 schools, 614 pupils

Colleges and Universities
Two-year: None
Four-year and Beyond: 1 public; 10,905
students
Degree Options: C
Places Rated Score: 2,721
Places Rated Rank: 201

Grand Rapids, MI
Elementary and Secondary
Public: 28 districts, 138 schools,
114,119 pupils
Pupil/Teacher Ratio: 17.00
Dollars per Pupil: $2,739
Average Teacher Salary: $1,964 ·
Effort Index: 1.066
Private: 92 schools, 25,337 pupils
Colleges and Universities
Two-year: 1 private, 1 public; 13,718
students
Four-year and Beyond: 8 private, 1
public; 11,286 students
Degree Options: B
Places Rated Score: 2,705
Places Rated Rank: 210

Great Falls, MT
Elementary and Secondary
Public: 10 districts, 35 schools,
14,446 pupils
Pupil/Teacher Ratio: 14.94
Dollars per Pupil: $2,809
Average Teacher Salary: $1,897
Effort Index: 1.225
Private: 9 schools, 1,039 pupils
Colleges and Universities
Two-year: None
Four-year and Beyond: 1 private; 1,272
students
Degree Options: C
Places Rated Score: 2,737
Places Rated Rank: 189

Greeley, CO
Elementary and Secondary
Public: 12 districts, 56 schools,
20,679 pupils
Pupil/Teacher Ratio: 14.15
Dollars per Pupil: $3,177
Average Teacher Salary: $1,515
Effort Index: 1.036
Private: 7 schools, 610 pupils
Colleges and Universities
Two-year: 1 public; 5,302 students
Four-year and Beyond: 1 public; 9,671
students
Degree Options: B
Places Rated Score: 2,854
Places Rated Rank: 145

Green Bay, WI
Elementary and Secondary
Public: 8 districts, 60 schools, 32,192
pupils
Pupil/Teacher Ratio: 15.62
Dollars per Pupil: $3,188
Average Teacher Salary: $1,777
Effort Index: 0.904
Private: 35 schools, 7,863 pupils
Colleges and Universities
Two-year: 1 public; 5,540 students
Four-year and Beyond: 1 private, 1
public; 6,353 students
Degree Options: B
Places Rated Score: 2,622
Places Rated Rank: 245

Greensboro–Winston-Salem–High Point, NC
Elementary and Secondary
Public: 12 districts, 270 schools,
156,244 pupils
Pupil/Teacher Ratio: 15.03
Dollars per Pupil: $2,328
Average Teacher Salary: $1,520
Effort Index: 1.084
Private: 11 schools, 13,348 pupils
Colleges and Universities
Two-year: 4 private, 2 public; 9,575
students
Four-year and Beyond: 8 private, 4
public; 28,372 students
Degree Options: A
Places Rated Score: 3,090
Places Rated Rank: 56

Greenville–Spartanburg, SC
Elementary and Secondary
Public: 9 districts, 196 schools,
106,414 pupils
Pupil/Teacher Ratio: 14.54
Dollars per Pupil: $2,147
Average Teacher Salary: $1,376
Effort Index: 1.196
Private: 83 schools, 12,149 pupils
Colleges and Universities
Two-year: 4 private, 2 public; 10,515
students
Four-year and Beyond: 5 private, 2
public; 24,430 students
Degree Options: A
Places Rated Score: 3,236
Places Rated Rank: 32

Hagerstown, MD
Elementary and Secondary
Public: 1 district, 45 schools,
19,306 pupils
Pupil/Teacher Ratio: 14.09
Dollars per Pupil: $2,802
Average Teacher Salary: $1,891
Effort Index: 1.417
Private: 12 schools, 2,004 pupils
Colleges and Universities
Two-year: 1 private, 1 public; 2,772
students
Four-year and Beyond: None
Degree Options: C
Places Rated Score: 2,990
Places Rated Rank: 90

Hamilton–Middletown, OH
Elementary and Secondary
Public: 10 districts, 80 schools,
47,902 pupils
Pupil/Teacher Ratio: 16.91
Dollars per Pupil: $2,319
Average Teacher Salary: $1,619
Effort Index: 1.103
Private: 14 schools, 4,232 pupils
Colleges and Universities
Two-year: 2 public; 3,450 students
Four-year and Beyond: 1 public; 14,872
students
Degree Options: B
Places Rated Score: 2,747
Places Rated Rank: 185

Harrisburg–Lebanon–Carlisle, PA
Elementary and Secondary
Public: 29 districts, 185 schools,
95,696 pupils
Pupil/Teacher Ratio: 14.43
Dollars per Pupil: $2,617

Average Teacher Salary: $1,617
Effort Index: 1.176
Private: 65 schools, 11,877 pupils
Colleges and Universities
Two-year: 2 private, 2 public; 14,709
students
Four-year and Beyond: 5 private, 3
public; 14,234 students
Degree Options: A
Places Rated Score: 3,224
Places Rated Rank: 35

★ Hartford, CT
Elementary and Secondary
Public: 35 districts, 213 schools,
112,710 pupils
Pupil/Teacher Ratio: 11.74
Dollars per Pupil: $2,994
Average Teacher Salary: $1,770
Effort Index: 1.340
Private: 70 schools, 20,704 pupils
Colleges and Universities
Two-year: 1 private, 5 public; 16,751
students
Four-year and Beyond: 6 private, 3
public; 54,816 students
Degree Options: A
Places Rated Score: 3,628
Places Rated Rank: 4

Hickory, NC
Elementary and Secondary
Public: 5 districts, 72 schools,
38,819 pupils
Pupil/Teacher Ratio: 14.42
Dollars per Pupil: $2,169
Average Teacher Salary: $1,456
Effort Index: 1.177
Private: 8 schools, 1,247 pupils
Colleges and Universities
Two-year: 2 public; 4,382 students
Four-year and Beyond: 1 private; 1,382
students
Degree Options: C
Places Rated Score: 2,726
Places Rated Rank: 198

Honolulu, HI
Elementary and Secondary
Public: 1 district, 162 schools,
125,774 pupils
Pupil/Teacher Ratio: 24.77
Dollars per Pupil: $2,324
Average Teacher Salary: $2,003
Effort Index: 0.892
Private: 89 schools, 27,024 pupils
Colleges and Universities
Two-year: 4 public; 18,623 students
Four-year and Beyond: 4 private, 2
public; 27,473 students
Degree Options: A
Places Rated Score: 2,502
Places Rated Rank: 279

Houma–Thibodaux, LA
Elementary and Secondary
Public: 2 districts, 71 schools,
41,404 pupils
Pupil/Teacher Ratio: 19.27
Dollars per Pupil: $2,179
Average Teacher Salary: $1,202
Effort Index: 0.710
Private: 17 schools, 5,493 pupils
Colleges and Universities
Two-year: None

Four-year and Beyond: 1 public; 7,226
students
Degree Options: C
Places Rated Score: 1,995
Places Rated Rank: 327

Houston, TX
Elementary and Secondary
Public: 40 districts, 673 schools,
552,216 pupils
Pupil/Teacher Ratio: 14.30
Dollars per Pupil: $2,758
Average Teacher Salary: $1,557
Effort Index: 0.963
Private: 156 schools, 38,435 pupils
Colleges and Universities
Two-year: 5 public; 50,196 students
Four-year and Beyond: 7 private, 6
public; 69,740 students
Degree Options: AA
Places Rated Score: 3,271
Places Rated Rank: 28

Huntington–Ashland, WV–KY–OH
Elementary and Secondary
Public: 15 districts, 164 schools,
66,523 pupils
Pupil/Teacher Ratio: 15.84
Dollars per Pupil: $2,001
Average Teacher Salary: $1,529
Effort Index: 1.070
Private: 14 schools, 1,665 pupils
Colleges and Universities
Two-year: 1 private; 472 students
Four-year and Beyond: 1 private, 1
public; 12,189 students
Degree Options: C
Places Rated Score: 2,525
Places Rated Rank: 274

Huntsville, AL
Elementary and Secondary
Public: 2 districts, 57 schools,
37,671 pupils
Pupil/Teacher Ratio: 14.80
Dollars per Pupil: $1,863
Average Teacher Salary: $1,395
Effort Index: 0.736
Private: 18 schools, 3,953 pupils
Colleges and Universities
Two-year: None
Four-year and Beyond: 1 private, 2
public; 11,503 students
Degree Options: C
Places Rated Score: 2,257
Places Rated Rank: 318

Indianapolis, IN
Elementary and Secondary
Public: 44 districts, 341 schools,
216,048 pupils
Pupil/Teacher Ratio: 16.11
Dollars per Pupil: $2,345
Average Teacher Salary: $1,826
Effort Index: 1.001
Private: 106 schools, 25,506 pupils
Colleges and Universities
Two-year: 2 private, 1 public; 6,306
students
Four-year and Beyond: 6 private, 1
public; 32,400 students
Degree Options: B
Places Rated Score: 2,690
Places Rated Rank: 216

Iowa City, IA
Elementary and Secondary
Public: 4 districts, 27 schools, 10,402 pupils
  Pupil/Teacher Ratio: 15.62
  Dollars per Pupil: $2,687
  Average Teacher Salary: $1,696
  Effort Index: 1.374
Private: 4 schools, 354 pupils
Colleges and Universities
Two-year: None
Four-year and Beyond: 1 public; 28,948 students
Degree Options: C
Places Rated Score: 2,842
Places Rated Rank: 152

Jackson, MI
Elementary and Secondary
Public: 12 districts, 50 schools, 26,640 pupils
  Pupil/Teacher Ratio: 18.68
  Dollars per Pupil: $2,930
  Average Teacher Salary: $2,019
  Effort Index: 1.345
Private: 13 schools, 3,784 pupils
Colleges and Universities
Two-year: 1 public; 5,259 students
Four-year and Beyond: 1 private; 975 students
Degree Options: C
Places Rated Score: 2,654
Places Rated Rank: 225

Jackson, MS
Elementary and Secondary
Public: 8 districts, 104 schools, 59,282 pupils
  Pupil/Teacher Ratio: 14.64
  Dollars per Pupil: $2,446
  Average Teacher Salary: $1,237
  Effort Index: 1.097
Private: 42 schools, 13,338 pupils
Colleges and Universities
Two-year: 1 private, 2 public; 9,573 students
Four-year and Beyond: 6 private, 2 public; 14,231 students
Degree Options: A
Places Rated Score: 3,130
Places Rated Rank: 46

Jacksonville, FL
Elementary and Secondary
Public: 4 districts, 189 schools, 130,710 pupils
  Pupil/Teacher Ratio: 13.77
  Dollars per Pupil: $2,859
  Average Teacher Salary: $1,553
  Effort Index: 1.200
Private: 72 schools, 18,607 pupils
Colleges and Universities
Two-year: 1 public; 15,661 students
Four-year and Beyond: 4 private, 1 public; 11,308 students
Degree Options: B
Places Rated Score: 3,048
Places Rated Rank: 65

Jacksonville, NC
Elementary and Secondary
Public: 2 districts, 31 schools, 17,892 pupils
  Pupil/Teacher Ratio: 20.17
  Dollars per Pupil: $1,947
  Average Teacher Salary: $1,556
  Effort Index: 1.396

Private: 5 schools, 1,002 pupils
Colleges and Universities
Two-year: 1 public; 2,744 students
Four-year and Beyond: None
Degree Options: C
Places Rated Score: 2,646
Places Rated Rank: 231

Janesville–Beloit, WI
Elementary and Secondary
Public: 8 districts, 54 schools, 27,025 pupils
  Pupil/Teacher Ratio: 14.96
  Dollars per Pupil: $2,781
  Average Teacher Salary: $1,680
  Effort Index: 1.021
Private: 19 schools, 2,644 pupils
Colleges and Universities
Two-year: 1 public; 2,287 students
Four-year and Beyond: 1 private; 1,081 students
Degree Options: C
Places Rated Score: 2,532
Places Rated Rank: 271

Jersey City, NJ
Elementary and Secondary
Public: 13 districts, 100 schools, 76,503 pupils
  Pupil/Teacher Ratio: 13.34
  Dollars per Pupil: $3,041
  Average Teacher Salary: $1,863
  Effort Index: 0.941
Private: 75 schools, 25,231 pupils
Colleges and Universities
Two-year: None
Four-year and Beyond: 2 private, 1 public; 16,203 students
Degree Options: C
Places Rated Score: 2,574
Places Rated Rank: 259

Johnson City–Kingsport–Bristol, TN–VA
Elementary and Secondary
Public: 13 districts, 183 schools, 83,043 pupils
  Pupil/Teacher Ratio: 15.01
  Dollars per Pupil: $1,776
  Average Teacher Salary: $1,469
  Effort Index: 1.168
Private: 13 schools, 2,159 pupils
Colleges and Universities
Two-year: 2 public; 3,393 students
Four-year and Beyond: 5 private, 1 public; 11,968 students
Degree Options: B
Places Rated Score: 2,925
Places Rated Rank: 114

Johnstown, PA
Elementary and Secondary
Public: 24 districts, 81 schools, 42,464 pupils
  Pupil/Teacher Ratio: 16.13
  Dollars per Pupil: $2,435
  Average Teacher Salary: $1,562
  Effort Index: 1.253
Private: 29 schools, 6,299 pupils
Colleges and Universities
Two-year: 1 private; 541 students
Four-year and Beyond: 1 private, 1 public; 4,792 students
Degree Options: C
Places Rated Score: 2,691
Places Rated Rank: 215

Joliet, IL
Elementary and Secondary
Public: 42 districts, 139 schools, 70,341 pupils
  Pupil/Teacher Ratio: 16.00
  Dollars per Pupil: $2,701
  Average Teacher Salary: $1,746
  Effort Index: 1.173
Private: 43 schools, 9,929 pupils
Colleges and Universities
Two-year: 1 public; 11,078 students
Four-year and Beyond: 2 private, 1 public; 11,243 students
Degree Options: B
Places Rated Score: 2,868
Places Rated Rank: 139

Joplin, MO
Elementary and Secondary
Public: 12 districts, 67 schools, 23,734 pupils
  Pupil/Teacher Ratio: 15.70
  Dollars per Pupil: $2,077
  Average Teacher Salary: $1,386
  Effort Index: 1.409
Private: 10 schools, 1,236 pupils
Colleges and Universities
Two-year: None
Four-year and Beyond: 1 private, 1 public; 5,105 students
Degree Options: C
Places Rated Score: 2,871
Places Rated Rank: 137

Kalamazoo, MI
Elementary and Secondary
Public: 9 districts, 70 schools, 34,564 pupils
  Pupil/Teacher Ratio: 17.83
  Dollars per Pupil: $3,169
  Average Teacher Salary: $2,126
  Effort Index: 1.298
Private: 20 schools, 4,365 pupils
Colleges and Universities
Two-year: 1 public; 7,895 students
Four-year and Beyond: 2 private, 1 public; 22,385 students
Degree Options: B
Places Rated Score: 2,896
Places Rated Rank: 128

Kankakee, IL
Elementary and Secondary
Public: 13 districts, 45 schools, 18,713 pupils
  Pupil/Teacher Ratio: 16.52
  Dollars per Pupil: $2,742
  Average Teacher Salary: $1,745
  Effort Index: 1.440
Private: 12 schools, 2,724 pupils
Colleges and Universities
Two-year: 1 public; 3,589 students
Four-year and Beyond: 1 private; 1,907 students
Degree Options: C
Places Rated Score: 2,855
Places Rated Rank: 144

Kansas City, KS
Elementary and Secondary
Public: 19 districts, 220 schools, 93,531 pupils
  Pupil/Teacher Ratio: 12.91
  Dollars per Pupil: $2,812
  Average Teacher Salary: $1,596
  Effort Index: 1.107
Private: 48 schools, 11,656 pupils

Colleges and Universities
Two-year: 1 private, 2 public; 12,312
   students
Four-year and Beyond: 4 private, 1
   public; 3,850 students
Degree Options: B
Places Rated Score: 3,028
Places Rated Rank: 74

Kansas City, MO
Elementary and Secondary
Public: 37 districts, 284 schools,
   151,946 pupils
   Pupil/Teacher Ratio: 14.95
   Dollars per Pupil: $2,459
   Average Teacher Salary: $1,615
   Effort Index: 0.938
Private: 83 schools, 21,581 pupils
Colleges and Universities
Two-year: 1 private, 4 public; 15,448
   students
Four-year and Beyond: 10 private, 1
   public; 21,735 students
Degree Options: A
Places Rated Score: 2,949
Places Rated Rank: 102

Kenosha, WI
Elementary and Secondary
Public: 13 districts, 42 schools,
   21,514 pupils
   Pupil/Teacher Ratio: 14.62
   Dollars per Pupil: $3,633
   Average Teacher Salary: $2,166
   Effort Index: 1.133
Private: 20 schools, 3,623 pupils
Colleges and Universities
Two-year: 1 public; 6,938 students
Four-year and Beyond: 1 private, 1
   public; 7,226 students
Degree Options: B
Places Rated Score: 2,918
Places Rated Rank: 116

Killeen–Temple, TX
Elementary and Secondary
Public: 14 districts, 75 schools,
   38,831 pupils
   Pupil/Teacher Ratio: 12.95
   Dollars per Pupil: $2,745
   Average Teacher Salary: $1,335
   Effort Index: 1.589
Private: 4 schools, 600 pupils
Colleges and Universities
Two-year: 2 public; 7,614 students
Four-year and Beyond: 2 private; 1,636
   students
Degree Options: C
Places Rated Score: 3,167
Places Rated Rank: 39

Knoxville, TN
Elementary and Secondary
Public: 12 districts, 198 schools,
   101,464 pupils
   Pupil/Teacher Ratio: 15.76
   Dollars per Pupil: $1,842
   Average Teacher Salary: $1,396
   Effort Index: 1.052
Private: 21 schools, 3,792 pupils
Colleges and Universities
Two-year: 4 private, 1 public; 4,282
   students
Four-year and Beyond: 4 private, 1
   public; 30,224 students
Degree Options: B
Places Rated Score: 2,761
Places Rated Rank: 179

Kokomo, IN
Elementary and Secondary
Public: 7 districts, 38 schools,
   17,819 pupils
   Pupil/Teacher Ratio: 13.46
   Dollars per Pupil: $2,595
   Average Teacher Salary: $1,703
   Effort Index: 1.031
Private: 9 schools, 1,311 pupils
Colleges and Universities
Two-year: 1 public; 1,447 students
Four-year and Beyond: 1 public; 2,808
   students
Degree Options: B
Places Rated Score: 2,904
Places Rated Rank: 123

La Crosse, WI
Elementary and Secondary
Public: 5 districts, 29 schools,
   13,269 pupils
   Pupil/Teacher Ratio: 16.12
   Dollars per Pupil: $3,654
   Average Teacher Salary: $1,620
   Effort Index: 1.339
Private: 21 schools, 3,325 pupils
Colleges and Universities
Two-year: 1 public; 4,868 students
Four-year and Beyond: 1 private, 1
   public; 9,824 students
Degree Options: B
Places Rated Score: 3,027
Places Rated Rank: 77

Lafayette, IN
Elementary and Secondary
Public: 3 districts, 35 schools,
   17,425 pupils
   Pupil/Teacher Ratio: 16.52
   Dollars per Pupil: $2,359
   Average Teacher Salary: $1,786
   Effort Index: 1.280
Private: 10 schools, 804 pupils
Colleges and Universities
Two-year: 1 public; 1,482 students
Four-year and Beyond: 1 public; 32,635
   students
Degree Options: B
Places Rated Score: 2,945
Places Rated Rank: 103

Lafayette, LA
Elementary and Secondary
Public: 2 districts, 59 schools,
   36,075 pupils
   Pupil/Teacher Ratio: 14.66
   Dollars per Pupil: $1,801
   Average Teacher Salary: $1,625
   Effort Index: 0.774
Private: 21 schools, 6,164 pupils
Colleges and Universities
Two-year: None
Four-year and Beyond: 1 public; 15,702
   students
Degree Options: C
Places Rated Score: 2,305
Places Rated Rank: 316

Lake Charles, LA
Elementary and Secondary
Public: 1 district, 64 schools,
   32,682 pupils
   Pupil/Teacher Ratio: 16.50
   Dollars per Pupil: $2,644
   Average Teacher Salary: $1,589
   Effort Index: 0.920
Private: 5 schools, 607 pupils

Colleges and Universities
Two-year: None
Four-year and Beyond: 1 public; 7,270
   students
Degree Options: C
Places Rated Score: 2,336
Places Rated Rank: 313

Lake County, IL
Elementary and Secondary
Public: 51 districts, 167 schools,
   85,912 pupils
   Pupil/Teacher Ratio: 14.83
   Dollars per Pupil: $2,974
   Average Teacher Salary: $1,768
   Effort Index: 1.087
Private: 45 schools, 10,988 pupils
Colleges and Universities
Two-year: 1 public; 12,187 students
Four-year and Beyond: 8 private; 4,671
   students
Degree Options: C
Places Rated Score: 2,607
Places Rated Rank: 253

Lakeland–Winter Haven, FL
Elementary and Secondary
Public: 1 district, 96 schools,
   58,627 pupils
   Pupil/Teacher Ratio: 12.49
   Dollars per Pupil: $2,575
   Average Teacher Salary: $1,339
   Effort Index: 1.288
Private: 24 schools, 5,071 pupils
Colleges and Universities
Two-year: 1 private, 1 public; 5,501
   students
Four-year and Beyond: 4 private; 5,036
   students
Degree Options: C
Places Rated Score: 2,998
Places Rated Rank: 87

Lancaster, PA
Elementary and Secondary
Public: 17 districts, 125 schools, 58,972
   pupils
   Pupil/Teacher Ratio: 13.78
   Dollars per Pupil: $2,574
   Average Teacher Salary: $1,678
   Effort Index: 1.505
Private: 103 schools, 10,291 pupils
Colleges and Universities
Two-year: None
Four-year and Beyond: 4 private, 1
   public; 11,769 students
Degree Options: C
Places Rated Score: 3,097
Places Rated Rank: 54

Lansing–East Lansing, MI
Elementary and Secondary
Public: 25 districts, 167 schools,
   80,055 pupils
   Pupil/Teacher Ratio: 15.31
   Dollars per Pupil: $3,064
   Average Teacher Salary: $1,978
   Effort Index: 1.154
Private: 31 schools, 5,542 pupils
Colleges and Universities
Two-year: 1 public; 19,799 students
Four-year and Beyond: 3 private, 1
   public; 44,582 students
Degree Options: B
Places Rated Score: 2,891
Places Rated Rank: 130

Laredo, TX
Elementary and Secondary
Public: 4 districts, 39 schools,
28,747 pupils
    Pupil/Teacher Ratio: 13.77
    Dollars per Pupil: $2,522
    Average Teacher Salary: $1,277
    Effort Index: 0.979
Private: 9 schools, 2,566 pupils
Colleges and Universities
Two-year: 1 public; 3,546 students
Four-year and Beyond: 1 public; 900
    students
Degree Options: B
Places Rated Score: 2,827
Places Rated Rank: 154

Las Cruces, NM
Elementary and Secondary
Public: 3 districts, 38 schools,
20,862 pupils
    Pupil/Teacher Ratio: 11.93
    Dollars per Pupil: $2,795
    Average Teacher Salary: $1,496
    Effort Index: 0.968
Private: 9 schools, 792 pupils
Colleges and Universities
Two-year: None
Four-year and Beyond: 1 public; 13,395
    students
Degree Options: C
Places Rated Score: 2,736
Places Rated Rank: 190

Las Vegas, NV
Elementary and Secondary
Public: 1 district, 117 schools,
89,119 pupils
    Pupil/Teacher Ratio: 19.62
    Dollars per Pupil: $2,362
    Average Teacher Salary: $1,920
    Effort Index: 0.720
Private: 24 schools, 4,935 pupils
Colleges and Universities
Two-year: 1 public; 8,340 students
Four-year and Beyond: 1 public; 11,452
    students
Degree Options: B
Places Rated Score: 2,241
Places Rated Rank: 319

Lawrence, KS
Elementary and Secondary
Public: 3 districts, 28 schools,
8,659 pupils
    Pupil/Teacher Ratio: 15.80
    Dollars per Pupil: $2,372
    Average Teacher Salary: $1,571
    Effort Index: 0.993
Private: 3 schools, 356 pupils
Colleges and Universities
Two-year: 1 public; 879 students
Four-year and Beyond: 1 private, 1
    public; 25,239 students
Degree Options: B
Places Rated Score: 2,700
Places Rated Rank: 212

Lawrence–Haverhill, MA–NH
Elementary and Secondary
Public: 22 districts, 102 schools,
49,602 pupils
    Pupil/Teacher Ratio: 14.46
    Dollars per Pupil: $2,707
    Average Teacher Salary: $1,964
    Effort Index: 0.933
Private: 52 schools, 13,163 pupils

Colleges and Universities
Two-year: 1 public; 6,782 students
Four-year and Beyond: 1 private; 3,751
    students
Degree Options: C
Places Rated Score: 2,479
Places Rated Rank: 286

Lawton, OK
Elementary and Secondary
Public: 13 districts, 62 schools,
22,191 pupils
    Pupil/Teacher Ratio: 14.03
    Dollars per Pupil: $2,100
    Average Teacher Salary: $1,532
    Effort Index: 0.797
Private: 1 school, 157 pupils
Colleges and Universities
Two-year: None
Four-year and Beyond: 1 public; 5,497
    students
Degree Options: C
Places Rated Score: 2,375
Places Rated Rank: 311

Lewiston–Auburn, ME
Elementary and Secondary
Public: 9 districts, 29 schools,
17,838 pupils
    Pupil/Teacher Ratio: 14.91
    Dollars per Pupil: $1,826
    Average Teacher Salary: $1,288
    Effort Index: 1.180
Private: 11 schools, 1,853 pupils
Colleges and Universities
Two-year: 1 private, 1 public; 610
    students
Four-year and Beyond: 1 private; 1,452
    students
Degree Options: C
Places Rated Score: 2,694
Places Rated Rank: 214

Lexington–Fayette, KY
Elementary and Secondary
Public: 7 districts, 92 schools,
53,222 pupils
    Pupil/Teacher Ratio: 15.82
    Dollars per Pupil: $1,909
    Average Teacher Salary: $2,275
    Effort Index: 1.155
Private: 25 schools, 4,655 pupils
Colleges and Universities
Two-year: 2 private, 1 public; 22,930
    students
Four-year and Beyond: 5 private, 1
    public; 26,201 students
Degree Options: B
Places Rated Score: 2,861
Places Rated Rank: 142

Lima, OH
Elementary and Secondary
Public: 16 districts, 63 schools,
30,772 pupils
    Pupil/Teacher Ratio: 17.96
    Dollars per Pupil: $2,221
    Average Teacher Salary: $1,635
    Effort Index: 1.037
Private: 11 schools, 3,450 pupils
Colleges and Universities
Two-year: 1 private, 1 public; 4,023
    students
Four-year and Beyond: 1 private, 1
    public; 1,494 students
Degree Options: B
Places Rated Score: 2,629
Places Rated Rank: 239

Lincoln, NE
Elementary and Secondary
Public: 5 districts, 57 schools,
28,746 pupils
    Pupil/Teacher Ratio: 15.39
    Dollars per Pupil: $3,091
    Average Teacher Salary: $1,678
    Effort Index: 1.145
Private: 21 schools, 3,949 pupils
Colleges and Universities
Two-year: 1 public; 5,559 students
Four-year and Beyond: 2 private, 1
    public; 28,278 students
Degree Options: B
Places Rated Score: 2,878
Places Rated Rank: 133

Little Rock–North Little Rock, AR
Elementary and Secondary
Public: 20 districts, 165 schools,
85,435 pupils
    Pupil/Teacher Ratio: 16.08
    Dollars per Pupil: $1,977
    Average Teacher Salary: $1,416
    Effort Index: 1.141
Private: 39 schools, 9,287 pupils
Colleges and Universities
Two-year: 3 private; 1,285 students
Four-year and Beyond: 4 private, 3
    public; 18,666 students
Degree Options: C
Places Rated Score: 2,581
Places Rated Rank: 258

Longview–Marshall, TX
Elementary and Secondary
Public: 13 districts, 60 schools,
33,581 pupils
    Pupil/Teacher Ratio: 13.09
    Dollars per Pupil: $2,843
    Average Teacher Salary: $1,495
    Effort Index: 1.161
Private: 7 schools, 1,169 pupils
Colleges and Universities
Two-year: 1 public; 4,389 students
Four-year and Beyond: 3 private; 2,558
    students
Degree Options: C
Places Rated Score: 2,816
Places Rated Rank: 155

Lorain–Elyria, OH
Elementary and Secondary
Public: 16 districts, 95 schools,
54,937 pupils
    Pupil/Teacher Ratio: 17.15
    Dollars per Pupil: $2,456
    Average Teacher Salary: $1,699
    Effort Index: 1.200
Private: 24 schools, 7,553 pupils
Colleges and Universities
Two-year: 1 public; 6,692 students
Four-year and Beyond: 1 private; 2,809
    students
Degree Options: C
Places Rated Score: 2,582
Places Rated Rank: 257

Los Angeles–Long Beach, CA
Elementary and Secondary
Public: 81 districts, 1,601 schools,
1,237,707 pupils
    Pupil/Teacher Ratio: 18.84
    Dollars per Pupil: $3,259
    Average Teacher Salary: $2,213
    Effort Index: 0.892
Private: 920 schools, 211,540 pupils

Colleges and Universities
Two-year: 3 private, 22 public; 315,228 students
Four-year and Beyond: 43 private, 7 public; 250,435 students
Degree Options: AAA
Places Rated Score: 3,195
Places Rated Rank: 37

Louisville, KY–IN
Elementary and Secondary
Public: 12 districts, 249 schools, 206,974 pupils
Pupil/Teacher Ratio: 16.82
Dollars per Pupil: $2,114
Average Teacher Salary: $1,803
Effort Index: 1.129
Private: 133 schools, 35,873 pupils
Colleges and Universities
Two-year: 5 private, 2 public; 7,136 students
Four-year and Beyond: 4 private, 2 public; 30,406 students
Degree Options: A
Places Rated Score: 3,028
Places Rated Rank: 74

Lowell, MA–NH
Elementary and Secondary
Public: 7 districts, 66 schools, 39,615 pupils
Pupil/Teacher Ratio: 14.46
Dollars per Pupil: $2,707
Average Teacher Salary: $1,964
Effort Index: 0.933
Private: 30 schools, 5,597 pupils
Colleges and Universities
Two-year: None
Four-year and Beyond: 1 private, 1 public; 15,548 students
Degree Options: C
Places Rated Score: 2,479
Places Rated Rank: 286

Lubbock, TX
Elementary and Secondary
Public: 8 districts, 74 schools, 41,306 pupils
Pupil/Teacher Ratio: 15.91
Dollars per Pupil: $2,187
Average Teacher Salary: $1,495
Effort Index: 1.095
Private: 11 schools, 2,021 pupils
Colleges and Universities
Two-year: None
Four-year and Beyond: 1 private, 2 public; 24,344 students
Degree Options: C
Places Rated Score: 2,545
Places Rated Rank: 265

Lynchburg, VA
Elementary and Secondary
Public: 3 districts, 47 schools, 24,706 pupils
Pupil/Teacher Ratio: 14.64
Dollars per Pupil: $2,148
Average Teacher Salary: $1,449
Effort Index: 1.270
Private: 10 schools, 2,718 pupils
Colleges and Universities
Two-year: 1 public; 3,683 students
Four-year and Beyond: 3 private; 7,220 students
Degree Options: C
Places Rated Score: 2,803
Places Rated Rank: 160

Macon–Warner Robins, GA
Elementary and Secondary
Public: 5 districts, 86 schools, 49,020 pupils
Pupil/Teacher Ratio: 14.64
Dollars per Pupil: $2,037
Average Teacher Salary: $1,181
Effort Index: 0.868
Private: 22 schools, 6,530 pupils
Colleges and Universities
Two-year: 1 private, 1 public; 3,176 students
Four-year and Beyond: 2 private, 1 public; 4,685 students
Degree Options: B
Places Rated Score: 2,651
Places Rated Rank: 229

Madison, WI
Elementary and Secondary
Public: 16 districts, 105 schools, 50,909 pupils
Pupil/Teacher Ratio: 14.17
Dollars per Pupil: $3,580
Average Teacher Salary: $1,775
Effort Index: 1.230
Private: 31 schools, 5,102 pupils
Colleges and Universities
Two-year: 2 private, 1 public; 7,909 students
Four-year and Beyond: 1 private, 1 public; 42,980 students
Degree Options: B
Places Rated Score: 3,047
Places Rated Rank: 66

Manchester, NH
Elementary and Secondary
Public: 13 districts, 37 schools, 28,804 pupils
Pupil/Teacher Ratio: 13.98
Dollars per Pupil: $2,252
Average Teacher Salary: $1,478
Effort Index: 1.147
Private: 21 schools, 4,097 pupils
Colleges and Universities
Two-year: 1 private, 2 public; 2,692 students
Four-year and Beyond: 4 private; 9,399 students
Degree Options: C
Places Rated Score: 2,728
Places Rated Rank: 196

Mansfield, OH
Elementary and Secondary
Public: 10 districts, 54 schools, 26,355 pupils
Pupil/Teacher Ratio: 15.75
Dollars per Pupil: $2,359
Average Teacher Salary: $1,591
Effort Index: 1.161
Private: 9 schools, 2,335 pupils
Colleges and Universities
Two-year: 1 public; 1,962 students
Four-year and Beyond: 1 public; 1,095 students
Degree Options: B
Places Rated Score: 2,871
Places Rated Rank: 137

McAllen–Edinburg–Mission, TX
Elementary and Secondary
Public: 15 districts, 109 schools, 82,035 pupils
Pupil/Teacher Ratio: 12.09
Dollars per Pupil: $2,089

Average Teacher Salary: $1,375
Effort Index: 0.893
Private: 16 schools, 2,720 pupils
Colleges and Universities
Two-year: None
Four-year and Beyond: 1 public; 8,347 students
Degree Options: C
Places Rated Score: 2,644
Places Rated Rank: 234

Medford, OR
Elementary and Secondary
Public: 10 districts, 55 schools, 23,422 pupils
Pupil/Teacher Ratio: 14.26
Dollars per Pupil: $3,124
Average Teacher Salary: $1,731
Effort Index: 1.237
Private: 12 schools, 1,516 pupils
Colleges and Universities
Two-year: None
Four-year and Beyond: 1 public; 1,326 students
Degree Options: C
Places Rated Score: 2,797
Places Rated Rank: 162

Melbourne–Titusville–Palm Bay, FL
Elementary and Secondary
Public: 1 district, 62 schools, 44,524 pupils
Pupil/Teacher Ratio: 13.86
Dollars per Pupil: $3,153
Average Teacher Salary: $1,454
Effort Index: 1.223
Private: 25 schools, 5,276 pupils
Colleges and Universities
Two-year: 1 private, 1 public; 10,861 students
Four-year and Beyond: 1 private; 6,963 students
Degree Options: C
Places Rated Score: 2,814
Places Rated Rank: 156

Memphis, TN–AR–MS
Elementary and Secondary
Public: 10 districts, 239 schools, 163,121 pupils
Pupil/Teacher Ratio: 15.29
Dollars per Pupil: $1,792
Average Teacher Salary: $1,269
Effort Index: 0.815
Private: 100 schools, 28,963 pupils
Colleges and Universities
Two-year: 2 private, 2 public; 13,966 students
Four-year and Beyond: 8 private, 2 public; 27,593 students
Degree Options: A
Places Rated Score: 2,804
Places Rated Rank: 159

Miami–Hialeah, FL
Elementary and Secondary
Public: 1 district, 252 schools, 221,039 pupils
Pupil/Teacher Ratio: 15.96
Dollars per Pupil: $3,538
Average Teacher Salary: $1,790
Effort Index: 0.932
Private: 210 schools, 56,915 pupils
Colleges and Universities
Two-year: 4 private, 1 public; 39,237 students
Four-year and Beyond: 5 private, 3 public; 33,049 students

Degree Options: A
Places Rated Score: 2,879
Places Rated Rank: 132

★ **Middlesex–Somerset–Hunterdon, NJ**
Elementary and Secondary
Public: 71 districts, 294 schools, 146,784 pupils
Pupil/Teacher Ratio: 11.73
Dollars per Pupil: $4,869
Average Teacher Salary: $2,147
Effort Index: 1.754
Private: 30 schools, 4,556 pupils
Colleges and Universities
Two-year: 2 public; 17,411 students
Four-year and Beyond: 1 private, 1 public; 32,932 students
Degree Options: B
Places Rated Score: 3,539
Places Rated Rank: 8

Middletown, CT
Elementary and Secondary
Public: 5 districts, 29 schools, 10,997 pupils
Pupil/Teacher Ratio: 11.74
Dollars per Pupil: $2,994
Average Teacher Salary: $1,770
Effort Index: 1.340
Private: 11 schools, 2,769 pupils
Colleges and Universities
Two-year: 1 public; 2,986 students
Four-year and Beyond: 2 private; 3,158 students
Degree Options: C
Places Rated Score: 3,128
Places Rated Rank: 47

Midland, TX
Elementary and Secondary
Public: 2 districts, 28 schools, 17,166 pupils
Pupil/Teacher Ratio: 16.40
Dollars per Pupil: $2,921
Average Teacher Salary: $2,020
Effort Index: 0.994
Private: 4 schools, 1,674 pupils
Colleges and Universities
Two-year: 1 public; 3,346 students
Four-year and Beyond: None
Degree Options: C
Places Rated Score: 2,416
Places Rated Rank: 300

Milwaukee, WI
Elementary and Secondary
Public: 54 districts, 404 schools, 221,870 pupils
Pupil/Teacher Ratio: 14.73
Dollars per Pupil: $3,535
Average Teacher Salary: $2,163
Effort Index: 1.017
Private: 260 schools, 58,827 pupils
Colleges and Universities
Two-year: 1 private, 2 public; 28,774 students
Four-year and Beyond: 14 private, 1 public; 47,729 students
Degree Options: A
Places Rated Score: 3,044
Places Rated Rank: 67

Minneapolis–St. Paul, MN–WI
Elementary and Secondary
Public: 68 districts, 525 schools, 364,331 pupils
Pupil/Teacher Ratio: 17.20

Dollars per Pupil: $3,213
Average Teacher Salary: $2,095
Effort Index: 0.884
Private: 255 schools, 55,650 pupils
Colleges and Universities
Two-year: 5 private, 7 public; 32,096 students
Four-year and Beyond: 16 private, 2 public; 89,990 students
Degree Options: AA
Places Rated Score: 3,013
Places Rated Rank: 82

Mobile, AL
Elementary and Secondary
Public: 3 districts, 109 schools, 83,245 pupils
Pupil/Teacher Ratio: 15.37
Dollars per Pupil: $1,606
Average Teacher Salary: $1,063
Effort Index: 1.045
Private: 61 schools, 16,727 pupils
Colleges and Universities
Two-year: 2 public; 2,926 students
Four-year and Beyond: 3 private, 1 public; 11,448 students
Degree Options: B
Places Rated Score: 2,779
Places Rated Rank: 169

Modesto, CA
Elementary and Secondary
Public: 27 districts, 109 schools, 50,288 pupils
Pupil/Teacher Ratio: 15.95
Dollars per Pupil: $3,218
Average Teacher Salary: $1,929
Effort Index: 0.918
Private: 28 schools, 5,161 pupils
Colleges and Universities
Two-year: 1 public; 11,379 students
Four-year and Beyond: 1 public; 4,574 students
Degree Options: B
Places Rated Score: 2,616
Places Rated Rank: 249

Monmouth–Ocean, NJ
Elementary and Secondary
Public: 80 districts, 258 schools, 152,890 pupils
Pupil/Teacher Ratio: 13.02
Dollars per Pupil: $3,253
Average Teacher Salary: $2,044
Effort Index: 1.126
Private: 63 schools, 22,803 pupils
Colleges and Universities
Two-year: 2 public; 18,089 students
Four-year and Beyond: 4 private; 6,510 students
Degree Options: C
Places Rated Score: 2,787
Places Rated Rank: 168

Monroe, LA
Elementary and Secondary
Public: 2 districts, 53 schools, 28,504 pupils
Pupil/Teacher Ratio: 15.78
Dollars per Pupil: $1,988
Average Teacher Salary: $1,338
Effort Index: 0.995
Private: 12 schools, 3,266 pupils
Colleges and Universities
Two-year: None

Four-year and Beyond: 1 public; 11,075 students
Degree Options: C
Places Rated Score: 2,453
Places Rated Rank: 292

Montgomery, AL
Elementary and Secondary
Public: 4 districts, 76 schools, 52,897 pupils
Pupil/Teacher Ratio: 17.16
Dollars per Pupil: $1,561
Average Teacher Salary: $1,205
Effort Index: 1.007
Private: 34 schools, 7,706 pupils
Colleges and Universities
Two-year: None
Four-year and Beyond: 2 private; 2 public; 8,427 students
Degree Options: C
Places Rated Score: 2,388
Places Rated Rank: 308

Muncie, IN
Elementary and Secondary
Public: 7 districts, 44 schools, 22,574 pupils
Pupil/Teacher Ratio: 14.94
Dollars per Pupil: $2,183
Average Teacher Salary: $1,602
Effort Index: 1.203
Private: 6 schools, 836 pupils
Colleges and Universities
Two-year: 1 public; 2,194 students
Four-year and Beyond: 1 public; 18,208 students
Degree Options: B
Places Rated Score: 2,965
Places Rated Rank: 100

Muskegon, MI
Elementary and Secondary
Public: 12 districts, 70 schools, 30,721 pupils
Pupil/Teacher Ratio: 16.71
Dollars per Pupil: $2,966
Average Teacher Salary: $2,015
Effort Index: 1.225
Private: 18 schools, 3,398 pupils
Colleges and Universities
Two-year: 1 private, 1 public; 6,262 students
Four-year and Beyond: None
Degree Options: C
Places Rated Score: 2,630
Places Rated Rank: 237

Nashua, NH
Elementary and Secondary
Public: 7 districts, 33 schools, 19,359 pupils
Pupil/Teacher Ratio: 13.98
Dollars per Pupil: $2,252
Average Teacher Salary: $1,478
Effort Index: 1.147
Private: 21 schools, 4,794 pupils
Colleges and Universities
Two-year: 1 public; 1,160 students
Four-year and Beyond: 2 private; 3,272 students
Degree Options: C
Places Rated Score: 2,728
Places Rated Rank: 196

Nashville, TN
Elementary and Secondary
   Public: 11 districts, 264 schools, 145,834 pupils
      Pupil/Teacher Ratio: 17.20
      Dollars per Pupil: $1,782
      Average Teacher Salary: $1,877
      Effort Index: 0.884
   Private: 67 schools, 18,644 pupils
Colleges and Universities
   Two-year: 4 private, 1 public; 7,272 students
   Four-year and Beyond: 10 private, 1 public; 24,286 students
   Degree Options: A
Places Rated Score: 2,763
Places Rated Rank: 178

Nassau–Suffolk, NY
Elementary and Secondary
   Public: 128 districts, 672 schools, 393,369 pupils
      Pupil/Teacher Ratio: 13.33
      Dollars per Pupil: $4,637
      Average Teacher Salary: $2,494
      Effort Index: 1.099
   Private: 222 schools, 71,016 pupils
Colleges and Universities
   Two-year: 4 private, 5 public; 58,932 students
   Four-year and Beyond: 11 private, 3 public; 66,701 students
   Degree Options: A
Places Rated Score: 3,234
Places Rated Rank: 33

New Bedford, MA
Elementary and Secondary
   Public: 8 districts, 35 schools, 25,532 pupils
      Pupil/Teacher Ratio: 15.79
      Dollars per Pupil: $2,117
      Average Teacher Salary: $1,662
      Effort Index: 0.981
   Private: 11 schools, 2,443 pupils
Colleges and Universities
   Two-year: None
   Four-year and Beyond: 1 private, 1 public; 7,007 students
   Degree Options: C
Places Rated Score: 2,439
Places Rated Rank: 295

New Britain, CT
Elementary and Secondary
   Public: 4 districts, 36 schools, 19,490 pupils
      Pupil/Teacher Ratio: 11.74
      Dollars per Pupil: $2,994
      Average Teacher Salary: $1,770
      Effort Index: 1.340
   Private: 12 schools, 3,254 pupils
Colleges and Universities
   Two-year: 1 private; 383 students
   Four-year and Beyond: 1 public; 12,487 students
   Degree Options: C
Places Rated Score: 3,128
Places Rated Rank: 47

★ New Haven–Meriden, CT
Elementary and Secondary
   Public: 17 districts, 143 schools, 74,912 pupils
      Pupil/Teacher Ratio: 12.84
      Dollars per Pupil: $2,815

      Average Teacher Salary: $1,660
      Effort Index: 1.317
   Private: 49 schools, 12,552 pupils
Colleges and Universities
   Two-year: 1 private, 2 public; 3,656 students
   Four-year and Beyond: 5 private, 1 public; 32,683 students
   Degree Options: A
Places Rated Score: 3,495
Places Rated Rank: 11

New London–Norwich, CT–RI
Elementary and Secondary
   Public: 17 districts, 83 schools, 35,063 pupils
      Pupil/Teacher Ratio: 12.16
      Dollars per Pupil: $2,919
      Average Teacher Salary: $1,507
      Effort Index: 1.543
   Private: 14 schools, 4,308 pupils
Colleges and Universities
   Two-year: 1 private, 2 public; 5,159 students
   Four-year and Beyond: 1 private; 1,933 students
   Degree Options: C
Places Rated Score: 3,244
Places Rated Rank: 31

New Orleans, LA
Elementary and Secondary
   Public: 6 districts, 299 schools, 195,681 pupils
      Pupil/Teacher Ratio: 14.91
      Dollars per Pupil: $2,664
      Average Teacher Salary: $1,323
      Effort Index: 0.981
   Private: 205 schools, 79,407 pupils
Colleges and Universities
   Two-year: 1 private, 2 public; 9,709 students
   Four-year and Beyond: 9 private, 3 public; 42,117 students
   Degree Options: A
Places Rated Score: 2,995
Places Rated Rank: 88

New York, NY
Elementary and Secondary
   Public: 105 districts, 1,289 schools, 1,109,700 pupils
      Pupil/Teacher Ratio: 17.46
      Dollars per Pupil: $3,104
      Average Teacher Salary: $2,240
      Effort Index: 0.618
   Private: 1,025 schools, 366,038 pupils
Colleges and Universities
   Two-year: 30 private, 8 public; 74,567 students
   Four-year and Beyond: 95 private, 17 public; 357,769 students
   Degree Options: AAA
Places Rated Score: 2,984
Places Rated Rank: 92

★ Newark, NJ
Elementary and Secondary
   Public: 111 districts, 565 schools, 314,362 pupils
      Pupil/Teacher Ratio: 12.06
      Dollars per Pupil: $3,442
      Average Teacher Salary: $1,695
      Effort Index: 1.109
   Private: 221 schools, 53,452 pupils
Colleges and Universities

Two-year: 1 private, 2 public; 18,097 students
   Four-year and Beyond: 10 private, 4 public; 56,303 students
   Degree Options: A
Places Rated Score: 3,362
Places Rated Rank: 20

Niagara Falls, NY
Elementary and Secondary
   Public: 10 districts, 61 schools, 38,340 pupils
      Pupil/Teacher Ratio: 14.97
      Dollars per Pupil: $3,762
      Average Teacher Salary: $2,251
      Effort Index: 1.028
   Private: 29 schools, 5,364 pupils
Colleges and Universities
   Two-year: 1 public; 4,375 students
   Four-year and Beyond: 1 private; 3,825 students
   Degree Options: C
Places Rated Score: 2,538
Places Rated Rank: 268

Norfolk–Virginia Beach–Newport News, VA
Elementary and Secondary
   Public: 11 districts, 302 schools, 219,181 pupils
      Pupil/Teacher Ratio: 13.41
      Dollars per Pupil: $2,118
      Average Teacher Salary: $1,455
      Effort Index: 0.886
   Private: 109 schools, 23,891 pupils
Colleges and Universities
   Two-year: 3 public; 22,578 students
   Four-year and Beyond: 5 private, 4 public; 39,088 students
   Degree Options: A
Places Rated Score: 3,014
Places Rated Rank: 81

Norwalk, CT
Elementary and Secondary
   Public: 4 districts, 37 schools, 20,699 pupils
      Pupil/Teacher Ratio: 12.10
      Dollars per Pupil: $3,139
      Average Teacher Salary: $1,990
      Effort Index: 1.279
   Private: 16 schools, 2,364 pupils
Colleges and Universities
   Two-year: 2 public; 5,458 students
   Four-year and Beyond: 2 private; 65 students
   Degree Options: C
Places Rated Score: 3,029
Places Rated Rank: 70

Oakland, CA
Elementary and Secondary
   Public: 37 districts, 524 schools, 286,408 pupils
      Pupil/Teacher Ratio: 18.27
      Dollars per Pupil: $3,327
      Average Teacher Salary: $2,081
      Effort Index: 0.818
   Private: 243 schools, 42,318 pupils
Colleges and Universities
   Two-year: 1 private, 9 public; 96,895 students
   Four-year and Beyond: 19 private, 2 public; 48,920 students
   Degree Options: A
Places Rated Score: 2,646
Places Rated Rank: 231

Ocala, FL
Elementary and Secondary
Public: 1 district, 32 schools,
22,779 pupils
Pupil/Teacher Ratio: 13.67
Dollars per Pupil: $2,862
Average Teacher Salary: $1,506
Effort Index: 1.259
Private: 9 schools, 2,456 pupils
Colleges and Universities
Two-year: 1 public; 3,030 students
Four-year and Beyond: None
Degree Options: C
Places Rated Score: 2,864
Places Rated Rank: 141

Odessa, TX
Elementary and Secondary
Public: 1 district, 33 schools,
25,900 pupils
Pupil/Teacher Ratio: 14.84
Dollars per Pupil: $3,063
Average Teacher Salary: $1,842
Effort Index: 0.952
Private: 6 schools, 1,313 pupils
Colleges and Universities
Two-year: 1 public; 4,106 students
Four-year and Beyond: 3 private, 1
public; 3,658 students
Degree Options: B
Places Rated Score: 2,721
Places Rated Rank: 201

Oklahoma City, OK
Elementary and Secondary
Public: 60 districts, 346 schools,
159,822 pupils
Pupil/Teacher Ratio: 14.92
Dollars per Pupil: $2,365
Average Teacher Salary: $1,441
Effort Index: 0.895
Private: 35 schools, 9,206 pupils
Colleges and Universities
Two-year: 1 private, 4 public; 21,190
students
Four-year and Beyond: 7 private, 4
public; 44,425 students
Degree Options: A
Places Rated Score: 2,908
Places Rated Rank: 120

Olympia, WA
Elementary and Secondary
Public: 8 districts, 48 schools,
25,970 pupils
Pupil/Teacher Ratio: 18.96
Dollars per Pupil: $2,696
Average Teacher Salary: $1,949
Effort Index: 1.077
Private: 13 schools, 1,126 pupils
Colleges and Universities
Two-year: 1 public; 2,996 students
Four-year and Beyond: 1 private, 1
public; 3,128 students
Degree Options: B
Places Rated Score: 2,625
Places Rated Rank: 244

Omaha, NE–IA
Elementary and Secondary
Public: 24 districts, 226 schools,
105,152 pupils
Pupil/Teacher Ratio: 14.29
Dollars per Pupil: $2,904
Average Teacher Salary: $1,621
Effort Index: 1.011

Private: 71 schools, 17,769 pupils
Colleges and Universities
Two-year: 2 public; 9,561 students
Four-year and Beyond: 4 private, 2
public; 21,313 students
Degree Options: A
Places Rated Score: 3,069
Places Rated Rank: 58

Orange County, NY
Elementary and Secondary
Public: 17 districts, 81 schools,
50,795 pupils
Pupil/Teacher Ratio: 14.49
Dollars per Pupil: $3,720
Average Teacher Salary: $1,835
Effort Index: 1.210
Private: 31 schools, 6,434 pupils
Colleges and Universities
Two-year: 1 public; 5,425 students
Four-year and Beyond: 1 private; 1,038
students
Degree Options: C
Places Rated Score: 2,754
Places Rated Rank: 181

Orlando, FL
Elementary and Secondary
Public: 3 districts, 163 schools,
123,920 pupils
Pupil/Teacher Ratio: 12.97
Dollars per Pupil: $2,735
Average Teacher Salary: $1,601
Effort Index: 1.060
Private: 60 schools, 14,293 pupils
Colleges and Universities
Two-year: 2 public; 16,018 students
Four-year and Beyond: 3 private, 1
public; 18,848 students
Degree Options: B
Places Rated Score: 2,976
Places Rated Rank: 94

Owensboro, KY
Elementary and Secondary
Public: 2 districts, 29 schools,
13,225 pupils
Pupil/Teacher Ratio: 15.18
Dollars per Pupil: $2,060
Average Teacher Salary: $1,673
Effort Index: 0.995
Private: 17 schools, 4,415 pupils
Colleges and Universities
Two-year: 1 private; 274 students
Four-year and Beyond: 2 private; 1,813
students
Degree Options: C
Places Rated Score: 2,491
Places Rated Rank: 283

Oxnard–Ventura, CA
Elementary and Secondary
Public: 20 districts, 170 schools,
106,369 pupils
Pupil/Teacher Ratio: 19.18
Dollars per Pupil: $2,918
Average Teacher Salary: $2,297
Effort Index: 0.867
Private: 69 schools, 12,557 pupils
Colleges and Universities
Two-year: 2 public; 18,776 students
Four-year and Beyond: 1 private; 2,467
students
Degree Options: C
Places Rated Score: 2,155
Places Rated Rank: 323

Panama City, FL
Elementary and Secondary
Public: 1 district, 29 schools,
20,000 pupils
Pupil/Teacher Ratio: 12.92
Dollars per Pupil: $2,780
Average Teacher Salary: $1,455
Effort Index: 0.830
Private: 10 schools, 1,485 pupils
Colleges and Universities
Two-year: 1 public; 3,913 students
Four-year and Beyond: None
Degree Options: C
Places Rated Score: 2,500
Places Rated Rank: 281

Parkersburg–Marietta, WV–OH
Elementary and Secondary
Public: 8 districts, 83 schools,
31,332 pupils
Pupil/Teacher Ratio: 14.68
Dollars per Pupil: $2,155
Average Teacher Salary: $1,540
Effort Index: 0.973
Private: 12 schools, 1,305 pupils
Colleges and Universities
Two-year: 2 public; 4,184 students
Four-year and Beyond: 2 private; 1,713
students
Degree Options: C
Places Rated Score: 2,503
Places Rated Rank: 278

Pascagoula, MS
Elementary and Secondary
Public: 4 districts, 38 schools,
24,420 pupils
Pupil/Teacher Ratio: 15.15
Dollars per Pupil: $1,847
Average Teacher Salary: $1,199
Effort Index: 0.703
Private: 3 schools, 555 pupils
Colleges and Universities
Two-year: None
Four-year and Beyond: None
Degree Options: C
Places Rated Score: 1,701
Places Rated Rank: 329

Pawtucket–Woonsocket–Attleboro, RI–MA
Elementary and Secondary
Public: 14 districts, 100 schools,
48,612 pupils
Pupil/Teacher Ratio: 13.63
Dollars per Pupil: $2,850
Average Teacher Salary: $2,081
Effort Index: 1.449
Private: 23 schools, 6,071 pupils
Colleges and Universities
Two-year: None
Four-year and Beyond: 1 private; 6,582
students
Degree Options: C
Places Rated Score: 3,058
Places Rated Rank: 61

Pensacola, FL
Elementary and Secondary
Public: 2 districts, 86 schools,
52,995 pupils
Pupil/Teacher Ratio: 15.61
Dollars per Pupil: $3,161
Average Teacher Salary: $1,519
Effort Index: 1.195
Private: 31 schools, 7,632 pupils

Colleges and Universities
Two-year: 1 public; 8,659 students
Four-year and Beyond: 1 public; 5,294 students
Degree Options: B
Places Rated Score: 2,914
Places Rated Rank: 119

Peoria, IL

Elementary and Secondary
Public: 48 districts, 163 schools, 65,481 pupils
Pupil/Teacher Ratio: 16.72
Dollars per Pupil: $2,497
Average Teacher Salary: $1,849
Effort Index: 1.048
Private: 67 schools, 9,199 pupils
Colleges and Universities
Two-year: 1 private, 1 public; 13,809 students
Four-year and Beyond: 2 private; 6,164 students
Degree Options: C
Places Rated Score: 2,452
Places Rated Rank: 294

★ Philadelphia, PA–NJ

Elementary and Secondary
Public: 170 districts, 900 schools, 687,270 pupils
Pupil/Teacher Ratio: 13.22
Dollars per Pupil: $3,235
Average Teacher Salary: $1,975
Effort Index: 1.137
Private: 659 schools, 139,734 pupils
Colleges and Universities
Two-year: 15 private, 6 public; 69,670 students
Four-year and Beyond: 42 private, 4 public; 135,616 students
Degree Options: AAA
Places Rated Score: 3,781
Places Rated Rank: 1

Phoenix, AZ

Elementary and Secondary
Public: 55 districts, 366 schools, 274,189 pupils
Pupil/Teacher Ratio: 15.56
Dollars per Pupil: $2,781
Average Teacher Salary: $1,813
Effort Index: 0.970
Private: 203 schools, 31,952 pupils
Colleges and Universities
Two-year: 1 private, 6 public; 51,055 students
Four-year and Beyond: 8 private, 2 public; 61,754 students
Degree Options: A
Places Rated Score: 2,942
Places Rated Rank: 106

Pine Bluff, AR

Elementary and Secondary
Public: 9 districts, 45 schools, 17,976 pupils
Pupil/Teacher Ratio: 15.64
Dollars per Pupil: $1,876
Average Teacher Salary: $1,211
Effort Index: 1.088
Private: 4 schools, 761 pupils
Colleges and Universities
Two-year: None
Four-year and Beyond: 1 public; 2,731 students
Degree Options: C
Places Rated Score: 2,554
Places Rated Rank: 263

★ Pittsburgh, PA

Elementary and Secondary
Public: 80 districts, 631 schools, 322,010 pupils
Pupil/Teacher Ratio: 13.83
Dollars per Pupil: $3,079
Average Teacher Salary: $1,741
Effort Index: 1.201
Private: 284 schools, 62,150 pupils
Colleges and Universities
Two-year: 9 private, 10 public; 31,955 students
Four-year and Beyond: 11 private, 2 public; 63,201 students
Degree Options: AA
Places Rated Score: 3,544
Places Rated Rank: 7

Pittsfield, MA

Elementary and Secondary
Public: 8 districts, 38 schools, 15,043 pupils
Pupil/Teacher Ratio: 10.72
Dollars per Pupil: $2,660
Average Teacher Salary: $1,419
Effort Index: 1.354
Private: 17 schools, 2,730 pupils
Colleges and Universities
Two-year: 1 public; 1,988 students
Four-year and Beyond: 1 private; 129 students
Degree Options: C
Places Rated Score: 3,264
Places Rated Rank: 30

Portland, ME

Elementary and Secondary
Public: 14 districts, 85 schools, 31,218 pupils
Pupil/Teacher Ratio: 13.15
Dollars per Pupil: $2,074
Average Teacher Salary: $1,411
Effort Index: 1.073
Private: 23 schools, 3,412 pupils
Colleges and Universities
Two-year: 2 private, 1 public; 2,190 students
Four-year and Beyond: 3 private, 1 public; 13,238 students
Degree Options: B
Places Rated Score: 2,973
Places Rated Rank: 95

★ Portland, OR

Elementary and Secondary
Public: 62 districts, 385 schools, 184,007 pupils
Pupil/Teacher Ratio: 14.02
Dollars per Pupil: $3,904
Average Teacher Salary: $1,782
Effort Index: 1.265
. Private: 124 schools, 19,037 pupils
Colleges and Universities
Two-year: 2 private, 2 public; 12,752 students
Four-year and Beyond: 15 private, 2 public; 27,842 students
Degree Options: A
Places Rated Score: 3,343
Places Rated Rank: 22

★ Portsmouth–Dover–Rochester, NH–ME

Elementary and Secondary
Public: 19 districts, 50 schools, 35,512 pupils
Pupil/Teacher Ratio: 13.99

Dollars per Pupil: $3,096
Average Teacher Salary: $1,417
Effort Index: 1.195
Private: 17 schools, 3,782 pupils
Colleges and Universities
Two-year: 2 private, 1 public; 3,462 students
Four-year and Beyond: 1 public; 12,415 students
Degree Options: B
Places Rated Score: 3,026
Places Rated Rank: 78

Poughkeepsie, NY

Elementary and Secondary
Public: 14 districts, 69 schools, 42,926 pupils
Pupil/Teacher Ratio: 14.42
Dollars per Pupil: $3,881
Average Teacher Salary: $1,979
Effort Index: 1.349
Private: 34 schools, 6,120 pupils
Colleges and Universities
Two-year: 1 private, 1 public; 9,016 students
Four-year and Beyond: 3 private; 6,247 students
Degree Options: C
Places Rated Score: 2,898
Places Rated Rank: 127

★ Providence, RI

Elementary and Secondary
Public: 15 districts, 172 schools, 74,904 pupils
Pupil/Teacher Ratio: 13.63
Dollars per Pupil: $2,850
Average Teacher Salary: $2,081
Effort Index: 1.449
Private: 76 schools, 20,411 pupils
Colleges and Universities
Two-year: 1 public; 12,149 students
Four-year and Beyond: 10 private, 2 public; 54,731 students
Degree Options: A
Places Rated Score: 3,558
Places Rated Rank: 6

Provo–Orem, UT

Elementary and Secondary
Public: 3 districts, 90 schools, 51,790 pupils
Pupil/Teacher Ratio: 19.54
Dollars per Pupil: $2,009
Average Teacher Salary: $1,637
Effort Index: 1.094
Private: 3 schools, 433 pupils
Colleges and Universities
Two-year: 1 public; 5,593 students
Four-year and Beyond: 1 private; 29,695 students
Degree Options: B
Places Rated Score: 2,618
Places Rated Rank: 248

Pueblo, CO

Elementary and Secondary
Public: 2 districts, 50 schools, 24,889 pupils
Pupil/Teacher Ratio: 15.50
Dollars per Pupil: $2,742
Average Teacher Salary: $1,340
Effort Index: 0.927
Private: 7 schools, 675 pupils
Colleges and Universities
Two-year: 1 public; 1,064 students
Four-year and Beyond: 1 public; 5,432 students

Degree Options: B
Places Rated Score: 2,653
Places Rated Rank: 227

Racine, WI
Elementary and Secondary
Public: 12 districts, 54 schools,
30,634 pupils
Pupil/Teacher Ratio: 12.42
Dollars per Pupil: $2,821
Average Teacher Salary: $1,272
Effort Index: 1.015
Private: 37 schools, 6,888 pupils
Colleges and Universities
Two-year: None
Four-year and Beyond: 1 private; 60
students
Degree Options: C
Places Rated Score: 2,732
Places Rated Rank: 192

★ Raleigh–Durham, NC
Elementary and Secondary
Public: 7 districts, 155 schools,
94,583 pupils
Pupil/Teacher Ratio: 13.16
Dollars per Pupil: $2,440
Average Teacher Salary: $1,429
Effort Index: 1.056
Private: 38 schools, 8,129 pupils
Colleges and Universities
Two-year: 6 private, 2 public; 10,014
students
Four-year and Beyond: 5 private, 3
public; 64,077 students
Degree Options: AA
Places Rated Score: 3,455
Places Rated Rank: 16

Reading, PA
Elementary and Secondary
Public: 19 districts, 107 schools,
54,190 pupils
Pupil/Teacher Ratio: 14.02
Dollars per Pupil: $2,760
Average Teacher Salary: $1,656
Effort Index: 1.200
Private: 31 schools, 7,467 pupils
Colleges and Universities
Two-year: 2 public; 3,040 students
Four-year and Beyond: 2 private, 1
public; 8,742 students
Degree Options: B
Places Rated Score: 3,028
Places Rated Rank: 74

Redding, CA
Elementary and Secondary
Public: 28 districts, 63 schools,
22,774 pupils
Pupil/Teacher Ratio: 16.19
Dollars per Pupil: $3,631
Average Teacher Salary: $1,932
Effort Index: 1.037
Private: 19 schools, 2,391 pupils
Colleges and Universities
Two-year: 1 public; 9,462 students
Four-year and Beyond: None
Degree Options: C
Places Rated Score: 2,471
Places Rated Rank: 289

Reno, NV
Elementary and Secondary
Public: 1 district, 60 schools,
32,006 pupils
Pupil/Teacher Ratio: 14.96
Dollars per Pupil: $2,848

Average Teacher Salary: $1,654
Effort Index: 0.769
Private: 15 schools, 2,300 pupils
Colleges and Universities
Two-year: 1 public; 7,963 students
Four-year and Beyond: 2 private, 1
public; 9,976 students
Degree Options: B
Places Rated Score: 2,529
Places Rated Rank: 272

Richland–Kennewick–Pasco, WA
Elementary and Secondary
Public: 10 districts, 62 schools,
30,788 pupils
Pupil/Teacher Ratio: 19.59
Dollars per Pupil: $2,683
Average Teacher Salary: $1,868
Effort Index: 0.456
Private: 13 schools, 1,714 pupils
Colleges and Universities
Two-year: 1 public; 5,798 students
Four-year and Beyond: None
Degree Options: C
Places Rated Score: 1,728
Places Rated Rank: 328

Richmond–Petersburg, VA
Elementary and Secondary
Public: 13 districts, 233 schools,
139,400 pupils
Pupil/Teacher Ratio: 12.95
Dollars per Pupil: $2,421
Average Teacher Salary: $1,152
Effort Index: 1.023
Private: 51 schools, 10,833 pupils
Colleges and Universities
Two-year: 3 public; 15,229 students
Four-year and Beyond: 5 private, 2
public; 30,234 students
Degree Options: B
Places Rated Score: 2,940
Places Rated Rank: 107

Riverside–San Bernardino, CA
Elementary and Secondary
Public: 57 districts, 493 schools,
299,991 pupils
Pupil/Teacher Ratio: 18.98
Dollars per Pupil: $2,918
Average Teacher Salary: $2,141
Effort Index: 0.799
Private: 134 schools, 19,164 pupils
Colleges and Universities
Two-year: 8 public; 72,523 students
Four-year and Beyond: 3 private, 2
public; 17,745 students
Degree Options: A
Places Rated Score: 2,596
Places Rated Rank: 254

Roanoke, VA
Elementary and Secondary
Public: 4 districts, 75 schools,
39,208 pupils
Pupil/Teacher Ratio: 13.63
Dollars per Pupil: $2,291
Average Teacher Salary: $1,618
Effort Index: 1.114
Private: 10 schools, 1,855 pupils
Colleges and Universities
Two-year: 1 private, 1 public; 6,436
students
Four-year and Beyond: 1 private; 954
students
Degree Options: C
Places Rated Score: 2,723
Places Rated Rank: 199

Rochester, MN
Elementary and Secondary
Public: 5 districts, 31 schools,
18,685 pupils
Pupil/Teacher Ratio: 16.91
Dollars per Pupil: $2,635
Average Teacher Salary: $2,062
Effort Index: 0.740
Private: 11 schools, 2,203 pupils
Colleges and Universities
Two-year: 1 public; 3,278 students
Four-year and Beyond: 3 private; 1,196
students
Degree Options: C
Places Rated Score: 2,134
Places Rated Rank: 325

★ Rochester, NY
Elementary and Secondary
Public: 50 districts, 252 schools,
164,651 pupils
Pupil/Teacher Ratio: 12.69
Dollars per Pupil: $3,992
Average Teacher Salary: $2,190
Effort Index: 1.140
Private: 103 schools, 27,247 pupils
Colleges and Universities
Two-year: 4 private, 2 public; 14,507
students
Four-year and Beyond: 8 private, 2
public; 42,973 students
Degree Options: AA
Places Rated Score: 3,582
Places Rated Rank: 5

Rockford, IL
Elementary and Secondary
Public: 13 districts, 101 schools,
50,863 pupils
Pupil/Teacher Ratio: 14.81
Dollars per Pupil: $2,480
Average Teacher Salary: $1,830
Effort Index: 1.159
Private: 25 schools, 7,020 pupils
Colleges and Universities
Two-year: 1 public; 9,985 students
Four-year and Beyond: 1 private; 1,469
students
Degree Options: C
Places Rated Score: 2,680
Places Rated Rank: 220

Sacramento, CA
Elementary and Secondary
Public: 55 districts, 389 schools,
192,673 pupils
Pupil/Teacher Ratio: 17.10
Dollars per Pupil: $3,234
Average Teacher Salary: $2,028
Effort Index: 0.909
Private: 134 schools, 21,497 pupils
Colleges and Universities
Two-year: 1 private, 4 public; 55,970
students
Four-year and Beyond: 2 public; 40,992
students
Degree Options: A
Places Rated Score: 2,793
Places Rated Rank: 166

Saginaw–Bay City–Midland, MI
Elementary and Secondary
Public: 21 districts, 161 schools,
79,668 pupils
Pupil/Teacher Ratio: 17.72
Dollars per Pupil: $2,965
Average Teacher Salary: $2,086
Effort Index: 1.169

Private: 57 schools, 13,223 pupils
Colleges and Universities
  Two-year: 1 public; 10,279 students
  Four-year and Beyond: 1 private, 1
    public; 6,489 students
  Degree Options: B
Places Rated Score: 2,772
Places Rated Rank: 173

St. Cloud, MN
Elementary and Secondary
  Public: 16 districts, 64 schools,
    32,393 pupils
      Pupil/Teacher Ratio: 15.93
      Dollars per Pupil: $2,933
      Average Teacher Salary: $1,857
      Effort Index: 1.053
  Private: 32 schools, 6,807 pupils
Colleges and Universities
  Two-year: None
  Four-year and Beyond: 2 private, 1
    public; 15,845 students
  Degree Options: C
Places Rated Score: 2,502
Places Rated Rank: 279

St. Joseph, MO
Elementary and Secondary
  Public: 4 districts, 34 schools,
    14,277 pupils
      Pupil/Teacher Ratio: 15.14
      Dollars per Pupil: $2,321
      Average Teacher Salary: $1,368
      Effort Index: 1.428
  Private: 6 schools, 1,322 pupils
Colleges and Universities
  Two-year: None
  Four-year and Beyond: 1 public; 4,269
    students
  Degree Options: C
Places Rated Score: 2,927
Places Rated Rank: 112

★ St. Louis, MO–IL
Elementary and Secondary
  Public: 46 districts, 486 schools,
    280,749 pupils
      Pupil/Teacher Ratio: 15.23
      Dollars per Pupil: $2,955
      Average Teacher Salary: $1,837
      Effort Index: 1.287
  Private: 203 schools, 83,423 pupils
Colleges and Universities
  Two-year: 3 private, 5 public; 38,142
    students
  Four-year and Beyond: 21 private, 2
    public; 45,064 students
  Degree Options: AA
Places Rated Score: 3,530
Places Rated Rank: 9

Salem, OR
Elementary and Secondary
  Public: 40 districts, 120 schools,
    40,300 pupils
      Pupil/Teacher Ratio: 14.71
      Dollars per Pupil: $3,613
      Average Teacher Salary: $1,705
      Effort Index: 1.605
  Private: 47 schools, 5,833 pupils
Colleges and Universities
  Two-year: 1 public; 6,523 students
  Four-year and Beyond: 2 private, 1
    public; 4,598 students
  Degree Options: B
Places Rated Score: 3,278
Places Rated Rank: 27

Salem–Gloucester, MA
Elementary and Secondary
  Public: 15 districts, 79 schools,
    36,856 pupils
      Pupil/Teacher Ratio: 14.46
      Dollars per Pupil: $2,707
      Average Teacher Salary: $1,964
      Effort Index: 0.933
  Private: 32 schools, 6,774 pupils
Colleges and Universities
  Two-year: 2 private, 1 public; 5,656
    students
  Four-year and Beyond: 2 private, 1
    public; 10,336 students
  Degree Options: B
Places Rated Score: 2,729
Places Rated Rank: 193

Salinas–Seaside–Monterey, CA
Elementary and Secondary
  Public: 25 districts, 94 schools,
    48,591 pupils
      Pupil/Teacher Ratio: 15.98
      Dollars per Pupil: $3,520
      Average Teacher Salary: $1,961
      Effort Index: 0.993
  Private: 22 schools, 4,448 pupils
Colleges and Universities
  Two-year: 2 public; 14,221 students
  Four-year and Beyond: 1 private; 411
    students
  Degree Options: C
Places Rated Score: 2,439
Places Rated Rank: 295

Salt Lake City–Ogden, UT
Elementary and Secondary
  Public: 7 districts, 317 schools,
    211,280 pupils
      Pupil/Teacher Ratio: 19.24
      Dollars per Pupil: $2,183
      Average Teacher Salary: $1,707
      Effort Index: 0.804
  Private: 26 schools, 4,820 pupils
Colleges and Universities
  Two-year: 2 private, 1 public; 8,773
    students
  Four-year and Beyond: 1 private, 2
    public; 35,958 students
  Degree Options: B
Places Rated Score: 2,340
Places Rated Rank: 312

San Angelo, TX
Elementary and Secondary
  Public: 6 districts, 36 schools,
    15,482 pupils
      Pupil/Teacher Ratio: 14.22
      Dollars per Pupil: $2,009
      Average Teacher Salary: $1,546
      Effort Index: 1.143
  Private: 4 schools, 531 pupils
Colleges and Universities
  Two-year: None
  Four-year and Beyond: 1 public; 5,834
    students
  Degree Options: C
Places Rated Score: 2,707
Places Rated Rank: 209

San Antonio, TX
Elementary and Secondary
  Public: 2 districts, 312 schools,
    216,678 pupils
      Pupil/Teacher Ratio: 13.88
      Dollars per Pupil: $2,371

Average Teacher Salary: $1,486
Effort Index: 1.098
  Private: 86 schools, 22,383 pupils
Colleges and Universities
  Two-year: 2 public; 27,344 students
  Four-year and Beyond: 6 private, 1
    public; 20,985 students
  Degree Options: B
Places Rated Score: 2,938
Places Rated Rank: 108

San Diego, CA
Elementary and Secondary
  Public: 43 districts, 473 schools,
    309,642 pupils
      Pupil/Teacher Ratio: 18.90
      Dollars per Pupil: $3,271
      Average Teacher Salary: $2,369
      Effort Index: 0.994
  Private: 198 schools, 33,065 pupils
Colleges and Universities
  Two-year: 1 private, 7 public; 89,353
    students
  Four-year and Beyond: 9 private, 1
    public; 52,143 students
  Degree Options: A
Places Rated Score: 2,794
Places Rated Rank: 165

★ San Francisco, CA
Elementary and Secondary
  Public: 43 districts, 330 schools,
    166,566 pupils
      Pupil/Teacher Ratio: 15.98
      Dollars per Pupil: $4,001
      Average Teacher Salary: $2,181
      Effort Index: 0.925
  Private: 252 schools, 48,593 pupils
Colleges and Universities
  Two-year: 1 private, 6 public; 61,998
    students
  Four-year and Beyond: 20 private, 3
    public; 56,160 students
  Degree Options: AAA
Places Rated Score: 3,371
Places Rated Rank: 18

San Jose, CA
Elementary and Secondary
  Public: 33 districts, 343 schools,
    241,008 pupils
      Pupil/Teacher Ratio: 19.38
      Dollars per Pupil: $3,497
      Average Teacher Salary: $2,417
      Effort Index: 0.929
  Private: 99 schools, 11,946 pupils
Colleges and Universities
  Two-year: 4 private, 7 public; 87,550
    students
  Four-year and Beyond: 5 private, 1
    public; 48,108 students
  Degree Options: A
Places Rated Score: 2,709
Places Rated Rank: 207

Santa Barbara–Santa Maria–
Lompoc, CA
Elementary and Secondary
  Public: 23 districts, 92 schools,
    45,512 pupils
      Pupil/Teacher Ratio: 17.91
      Dollars per Pupil: $3,656
      Average Teacher Salary: $2,517
      Effort Index: 1.125
  Private: 39 schools, 7,050 pupils
Colleges and Universities
  Two-year: 2 public; 17,404 students

Four-year and Beyond: 3 private, 1
 public; 18,358 students
Degree Options: B
Places Rated Score: 2,719
Places Rated Rank: 203

Santa Cruz, CA
Elementary and Secondary
 Public: 10 districts, 53 schools,
 34,229 pupils
  Pupil/Teacher Ratio: 19.05
  Dollars per Pupil: $2,916
  Average Teacher Salary: $1,873
  Effort Index: 1.067
 Private: 29 schools, 3,977 pupils
Colleges and Universities
 Two-year: 1 public; 10,483 students
 Four-year and Beyond: 1 private, 1
  public; 7,326 students
 Degree Options: B
Places Rated Score: 2,611
Places Rated Rank: 252

Santa Rosa–Petaluma, CA
Elementary and Secondary
 Public: 6 districts, 77 schools,
 46,949 pupils
  Pupil/Teacher Ratio: 16.30
  Dollars per Pupil: $3,375
  Average Teacher Salary: $2,012
  Effort Index: 1.044
 Private: 24 schools, 4,276 pupils
Colleges and Universities
 Two-year: 1 public; 20,138 students
 Four-year and Beyond: 1 public; 6,664
  students
 Degree Options: B
Places Rated Score: 2,722
Places Rated Rank: 200

Sarasota, FL
Elementary and Secondary
 Public: 1 district, 28 schools,
 24,684 pupils
  Pupil/Teacher Ratio: 14.86
  Dollars per Pupil: $2,765
  Average Teacher Salary: $1,482
  Effort Index: 1.109
 Private: 19 schools, 3,065 pupils
Colleges and Universities
 Two-year: None
 Four-year and Beyond: 2 private; 624
  students
 Degree Options: C
Places Rated Score: 2,626
Places Rated Rank: 243

Savannah, GA
Elementary and Secondary
 Public: 2 districts, 62 schools,
 35,371 pupils
  Pupil/Teacher Ratio: 14.18
  Dollars per Pupil: $2,124
  Average Teacher Salary: $1,470
  Effort Index: 0.889
 Private: 27 schools, 9,410 pupils
Colleges and Universities
 Two-year: 1 private; 654 students
 Four-year and Beyond: 1 private, 2
  public; 5,559 students
 Degree Options: C
Places Rated Score: 2,456
Places Rated Rank: 291

Scranton–Wilkes-Barre, PA
Elementary and Secondary
 Public: 35 districts, 201 schools,
 108,967 pupils

 Pupil/Teacher Ratio: 14.55
 Dollars per Pupil: $2,559
 Average Teacher Salary: $1,567
 Effort Index: 1.441
Private: 93 schools, 19,490 pupils
Colleges and Universities
 Two-year: 4 private, 4 public; 14,919
  students
 Four-year and Beyond: 6 private, 2
  public; 22,969 students
 Degree Options: B
Places Rated Score: 3,230
Places Rated Rank: 34

Seattle, WA
Elementary and Secondary
 Public: 34 districts, 481 schools,
 267,266 pupils
  Pupil/Teacher Ratio: 20.15
  Dollars per Pupil: $2,917
  Average Teacher Salary: $2,211
  Effort Index: 0.959
 Private: 169 schools, 32,674 pupils
Colleges and Universities
 Two-year: 9 public; 49,769 students
 Four-year and Beyond: 9 private, 1
  public; 47,411 students
 Degree Options: A
Places Rated Score: 2,710
Places Rated Rank: 206

Sharon, PA
Elementary and Secondary
 Public: 12 districts, 47 schools,
 21,915 pupils
  Pupil/Teacher Ratio: 13.73
  Dollars per Pupil: $2,859
  Average Teacher Salary: $1,625
  Effort Index: 1.421
 Private: 12 schools, 2,179 pupils
Colleges and Universities
 Two-year: 1 public; 922 students
 Four-year and Beyond: 2 private; 3,007
  students
 Degree Options: C
Places Rated Score: 3,022
Places Rated Rank: 80

Sheboygan, WI
Elementary and Secondary
 Public: 9 districts, 45 schools,
 17,824 pupils
  Pupil/Teacher Ratio: 15.45
  Dollars per Pupil: $3,288
  Average Teacher Salary: $1,703
  Effort Index: 1.078
 Private: 24 schools, 3,465 pupils
Colleges and Universities
 Two-year: None
 Four-year and Beyond: 1 private; 809
  students
 Degree Options: C
Places Rated Score: 2,557
Places Rated Rank: 262

Sherman–Denison, TX
Elementary and Secondary
 Public: 13 districts, 45 schools,
 16,386 pupils
  Pupil/Teacher Ratio: 13.82
  Dollars per Pupil: $2,572
  Average Teacher Salary: $1,541
  Effort Index: 1.058
 Private: 4 schools, 358 pupils
Colleges and Universities
 Two-year: 1 public; 4,559 students

Four-year and Beyond: 1 private; 1,186
 students
Degree Options: C
Places Rated Score: 2,652
Places Rated Rank: 228

Shreveport, LA
Elementary and Secondary
 Public: 2 districts, 102 schools,
 62,370 pupils
  Pupil/Teacher Ratio: 13.41
  Dollars per Pupil: $2,523
  Average Teacher Salary: $1,539
  Effort Index: 0.980
 Private: 37 schools, 9,977 pupils
Colleges and Universities
 Two-year: 2 public; 2,157 students
 Four-year and Beyond: 1 private, 1
  public; 5,721 students
 Degree Options: B
Places Rated Score: 2,858
Places Rated Rank: 143

Sioux City, IA–NE
Elementary and Secondary
 Public: 9 districts, 56 schools,
 19,619 pupils
  Pupil/Teacher Ratio: 15.13
  Dollars per Pupil: $3,071
  Average Teacher Salary: $1,719
  Effort Index: 1.173
 Private: 15 schools, 3,383 pupils
Colleges and Universities
 Two-year: 1 public; 1,461 students
 Four-year and Beyond: 2 private; 2,513
  students
 Degree Options: C
Places Rated Score: 2,673
Places Rated Rank: 222

Sioux Falls, SD
Elementary and Secondary
 Public: 7 districts, 48 schools,
 18,502 pupils
  Pupil/Teacher Ratio: 14.28
  Dollars per Pupil: $2,280
  Average Teacher Salary: $1,313
  Effort Index: 1.092
 Private: 23 schools, 3,034 pupils
Colleges and Universities
 Two-year: 1 private; 364 students
 Four-year and Beyond: 3 private; 2,985
  students
 Degree Options: C
Places Rated Score: 2,651
Places Rated Rank: 229

South Bend–Mishawaka, IN
Elementary and Secondary
 Public: 5 districts, 67 schools,
 39,010 pupils
  Pupil/Teacher Ratio: 18.10
  Dollars per Pupil: $2,424
  Average Teacher Salary: $1,926
  Effort Index: 1.289
 Private: 29 schools, 8,625 pupils
Colleges and Universities
 Two-year: 1 private, 1 public; 2,626
  students
 Four-year and Beyond: 3 private, 1
  public; 17,389 students
 Degree Options: B
Places Rated Score: 2,874
Places Rated Rank: 135

Spokane, WA
Elementary and Secondary
  Public: 14 districts, 122 schools,
  61,742 pupils
    Pupil/Teacher Ratio: 18.93
    Dollars per Pupil: $2,601
    Average Teacher Salary: $1,940
    Effort Index: 1.225
  Private: 34 schools, 5,872 pupils
Colleges and Universities
  Two-year: 2 public; 14,621 students
  Four-year and Beyond: 2 private, 1
  public; 13,449 students
  Degree Options: B
Places Rated Score: 2,774
Places Rated Rank: 172

Springfield, IL
Elementary and Secondary
  Public: 15 districts, 69 schools,
  28,505 pupils
    Pupil/Teacher Ratio: 15.23
    Dollars per Pupil: $2,762
    Average Teacher Salary: $1,694
    Effort Index: 1.335
  Private: 29 schools, 6,922 pupils
Colleges and Universities
  Two-year: 1 private, 1 public; 7,509
  students
  Four-year and Beyond: 1 public; 3,327
  students
  Degree Options: B
Places Rated Score: 3,078
Places Rated Rank: 57

★ Springfield, MA
Elementary and Secondary
  Public: 20 districts, 153 schools,
  76,705 pupils
    Pupil/Teacher Ratio: 13.54
    Dollars per Pupil: $3,088
    Average Teacher Salary: $1,762
    Effort Index: 1.408
  Private: 64 schools, 15,734 pupils
Colleges and Universities
  Two-year: 1 private, 2 public; 12,634
  students
  Four-year and Beyond: 7 private, 1
  public; 20,040 students
  Degree Options: A
Places Rated Score: 3,525
Places Rated Rank: 10

Springfield, MO
Elementary and Secondary
  Public: 15 districts, 85 schools,
  36,564 pupils
    Pupil/Teacher Ratio: 15.36
    Dollars per Pupil: $1,921
    Average Teacher Salary: $1,454
    Effort Index: 1.224
  Private: 15 schools, 1,778 pupils
Colleges and Universities
  Two-year: 1 private, 1 public; 2,489
  students
  Four-year and Beyond: 4 private, 1
  public; 19,416 students
  Degree Options: C
Places Rated Score: 2,709
Places Rated Rank: 207

Stamford, CT
Elementary and Secondary
  Public: 4 districts, 42 schools,
  27,737 pupils
    Pupil/Teacher Ratio: 12.10
    Dollars per Pupil: $3,139
    Average Teacher Salary: $1,990

    Effort Index: 1.279
  Private: 35 schools, 8,234 pupils
Colleges and Universities
  Two-year: None
  Four-year and Beyond: 2 private; 66
  students
  Degree Options: C
Places Rated Score: 3,029
Places Rated Rank: 70

State College, PA
Elementary and Secondary
  Public: 4 districts, 31 schools,
  14,890 pupils
    Pupil/Teacher Ratio: 12.94
    Dollars per Pupil: $3,057
    Average Teacher Salary: $1,485
    Effort Index: 1.760
  Private: 10 schools, 1,034 pupils
Colleges and Universities
  Two-year: None
  Four-year and Beyond: 1 public; 36,162
  students
  Degree Options: C
Places Rated Score: 3,169
Places Rated Rank: 38

Steubenville–Weirton, OH–WV
Elementary and Secondary
  Public: 8 districts, 75 schools,
  29,262 pupils
    Pupil/Teacher Ratio: 15.38
    Dollars per Pupil: $2,376
    Average Teacher Salary: $1,631
    Effort Index: 1.189
  Private: 16 schools, 3,238 pupils
Colleges and Universities
  Two-year: 1 public; 1,789 students
  Four-year and Beyond: 2 private; 1,693
  students
  Degree Options: C
Places Rated Score: 2,672
Places Rated Rank: 223

Stockton, CA
Elementary and Secondary
  Public: 17 districts, 127 schools,
  66,565 pupils
    Pupil/Teacher Ratio: 18.17
    Dollars per Pupil: $3,177
    Average Teacher Salary: $2,113
    Effort Index: 0.823
  Private: 38 schools, 7,277 pupils
Colleges and Universities
  Two-year: 1 private; 265 students
  Four-year and Beyond: 1 private; 5,997
  students
  Degree Options: C
Places Rated Score: 2,155
Places Rated Rank: 323

Syracuse, NY
Elementary and Secondary
  Public: 37 districts, 194 schools,
  119,713 pupils
    Pupil/Teacher Ratio: 13.03
    Dollars per Pupil: $3,470
    Average Teacher Salary: $1,839
    Effort Index: 0.983
  Private: 55 schools, 12,319 pupils
Colleges and Universities
  Two-year: 3 private, 2 public; 12,802
  students
  Four-year and Beyond: 3 private, 3
  public; 36,262 students
  Degree Options: A
Places Rated Score: 3,144
Places Rated Rank: 44

Tacoma, WA
Elementary and Secondary
  Public: 15 districts, 187 schools,
  89,823 pupils
    Pupil/Teacher Ratio: 17.65
    Dollars per Pupil: $3,215
    Average Teacher Salary: $2,053
    Effort Index: 1.189
  Private: 32 schools, 6,452 pupils
Colleges and Universities
  Two-year: 1 public; 3,973 students
  Four-year and Beyond: 2 private; 7,782
  students
  Degree Options: C
Places Rated Score: 2,546
Places Rated Rank: 264

Tallahassee, FL
Elementary and Secondary
  Public: 2 districts, 49 schools,
  36,135 pupils
    Pupil/Teacher Ratio: 15.32
    Dollars per Pupil: $2,412
    Average Teacher Salary: $1,232
    Effort Index: 1.053
  Private: 19 schools, 5,728 pupils
Colleges and Universities
  Two-year: 1 public; 4,871 students
  Four-year and Beyond: 2 public; 26,847
  students
  Degree Options: B
Places Rated Score: 2,790
Places Rated Rank: 167

Tampa–St. Petersburg–Clearwater, FL
Elementary and Secondary
  Public: 4 districts, 283 schools, 224,517
  pupils
    Pupil/Teacher Ratio: 14.06
    Dollars per Pupil: $2,932
    Average Teacher Salary: $1,579
    Effort Index: 1.219
  Private: 158 schools, 34,380 pupils
Colleges and Universities
  Two-year: 3 private, 2 public; 31,361
  students
  Four-year and Beyond: 5 private, 1
  public; 35,492 students
  Degree Options: B
Places Rated Score: 3,044
Places Rated Rank: 67

Terre Haute, IN
Elementary and Secondary
  Public: 2 districts, 43 schools,
  23,053 pupils
    Pupil/Teacher Ratio: 17.79
    Dollars per Pupil: $2,445
    Average Teacher Salary: $1,634
    Effort Index: 1.412
  Private: 12 schools, 1,191 pupils
Colleges and Universities
  Two-year: 1 public; 1,559 students
  Four-year and Beyond: 2 private, 1
  public; 13,917 students
  Degree Options: B
Places Rated Score: 3,012
Places Rated Rank: 83

Texarkana, TX–Texarkana, AR
Elementary and Secondary
  Public: 18 districts, 58 schools,
  23,561 pupils
    Pupil/Teacher Ratio: 14.95
    Dollars per Pupil: $2,039
    Average Teacher Salary: $1,392
    Effort Index: 1.138

Private: 1 school, 182 pupils
Colleges and Universities
  Two-year: 1 public; 3,553 students
  Four-year and Beyond: 1 public; 1,142
  students
  Degree Options: B
Places Rated Score: 2,899
Places Rated Rank: 126

Toledo, OH
Elementary and Secondary
  Public: 25 districts, 191 schools,
  104,464 pupils
    Pupil/Teacher Ratio: 17.44
    Dollars per Pupil: $2,513
    Average Teacher Salary: $1,745
    Effort Index: 0.985
  Private: 69 schools, 21,583 pupils
Colleges and Universities
  Two-year: 1 private, 1 public; 4,918
  students
  Four-year and Beyond: 1 private, 3
  public; 39,882 students
  Degree Options: A
Places Rated Score: 2,852
Places Rated Rank: 147

Topeka, KS
Elementary and Secondary
  Public: 5 districts, 67 schools,
  25,335 pupils
    Pupil/Teacher Ratio: 14.30
    Dollars per Pupil: $3,404
    Average Teacher Salary: $1,330
    Effort Index: 1.237
  Private: 15 schools, 2,880 pupils
Colleges and Universities
  Two-year: None
  Four-year and Beyond: 1 public; 6,515
  students
  Degree Options: C
Places Rated Score: 2,795
Places Rated Rank: 164

★ Trenton, NJ
Elementary and Secondary
  Public: 11 districts, 89 schools,
  47,402 pupils
    Pupil/Teacher Ratio: 11.07
    Dollars per Pupil: $3,873
    Average Teacher Salary: $1,976
    Effort Index: 1.195
  Private: 49 schools, 13,701 pupils
Colleges and Universities
  Two-year: 1 public; 10,248 students
  Four-year and Beyond: 4 private, 2
  public; 26,496 students
  Degree Options: B
Places Rated Score: 3,311
Places Rated Rank: 24

Tucson, AZ
Elementary and Secondary
  Public: 14 districts, 160 schools,
  121,136 pupils
    Pupil/Teacher Ratio: 16.74
    Dollars per Pupil: $2,858
    Average Teacher Salary: $2,311
    Effort Index: 1.032
  Private: 79 schools, 10,329 pupils
Colleges and Universities
  Two-year: 1 public; 21,780 students
  Four-year and Beyond: 1 public; 30,669
  students
  Degree Options: B
Places Rated Score: 2,685
Places Rated Rank: 218

Tulsa, OK
Elementary and Secondary
  Public: 46 districts, 387 schools,
  126,163 pupils
    Pupil/Teacher Ratio: 17.33
    Dollars per Pupil: $2,421
    Average Teacher Salary: $1,666
    Effort Index: 1.006
  Private: 25 schools, 7,058 pupils
Colleges and Universities
  Two-year: 1 private, 2 public; 17,925
  students
  Four-year and Beyond: 2 private, 1
  public; 10,227 students
  Degree Options: B
Places Rated Score: 2,628
Places Rated Rank: 240

Tuscaloosa, AL
Elementary and Secondary
  Public: 2 districts, 42 schools,
  23,433 pupils
    Pupil/Teacher Ratio: 16.76
    Dollars per Pupil: $1,717
    Average Teacher Salary: $1,505
    Effort Index: 0.738
  Private: 4 schools, 1,752 pupils
Colleges and Universities
  Two-year: 1 public; 3,206 students
  Four-year and Beyond: 1 private, 1
  public; 16,510 students
  Degree Options: B
Places Rated Score: 2,390
Places Rated Rank: 307

Tyler, TX
Elementary and Secondary
  Public: 8 districts, 45 schools,
  25,265 pupils
    Pupil/Teacher Ratio: 14.07
    Dollars per Pupil: $2,666
    Average Teacher Salary: $1,476
    Effort Index: 1.458
  Private: 10 schools, 1,213 pupils
Colleges and Universities
  Two-year: 1 public; 7,217 students
  Four-year and Beyond: 1 private, 1
  public; 3,242 students
  Degree Options: B
Places Rated Score: 3,283
Places Rated Rank: 26

Utica–Rome, NY
Elementary and Secondary
  Public: 29 districts, 108 schools,
  56,738 pupils
    Pupil/Teacher Ratio: 13.75
    Dollars per Pupil: $3,380
    Average Teacher Salary: $1,812
    Effort Index: 1.120
  Private: 30 schools, 5,904 pupils
Colleges and Universities
  Two-year: 1 private, 2 public; 9,381
  students
  Four-year and Beyond: 3 private, 1
  public; 7,094 students
  Degree Options: B
Places Rated Score: 2,970
Places Rated Rank: 99

Vallejo–Fairfield–Napa, CA
Elementary and Secondary
  Public: 11 districts, 114 schools,
  61,260 pupils
    Pupil/Teacher Ratio: 20.27
    Dollars per Pupil: $3,023

  Average Teacher Salary: $2,076
    Effort Index: 1.002
  Private: 40 schools, 7,313 pupils
Colleges and Universities
  Two-year: 2 public; 16,040 students
  Four-year and Beyond: 1 private, 1
  public; 2,080 students
  Degree Options: B
Places Rated Score: 2,498
Places Rated Rank: 282

Vancouver, WA
Elementary and Secondary
  Public: 9 districts, 79 schools,
  42,405 pupils
    Pupil/Teacher Ratio: 20.52
    Dollars per Pupil: $2,543
    Average Teacher Salary: $2,007
    Effort Index: 1.095
  Private: 14 schools, 2,017 pupils
Colleges and Universities
  Two-year: 1 public; 5,731 students
  Four-year and Beyond: None
  Degree Options: C
Places Rated Score: 2,332
Places Rated Rank: 315

Victoria, TX
Elementary and Secondary
  Public: 4 districts, 30 schools,
  14,257 pupils
    Pupil/Teacher Ratio: 14.84
    Dollars per Pupil: $2,328
    Average Teacher Salary: $1,302
    Effort Index: 0.927
  Private: 6 schools, 687 pupils
Colleges and Universities
  Two-year: 1 public; 2,529 students
  Four-year and Beyond: 1 public; 936
  students
  Degree Options: B
Places Rated Score: 2,696
Places Rated Rank: 213

Vineland–Millville–Bridgeton, NJ
Elementary and Secondary
  Public: 16 districts, 59 schools,
  27,171 pupils
    Pupil/Teacher Ratio: 12.76
    Dollars per Pupil: $2,936
    Average Teacher Salary: $1,728
    Effort Index: 1.062
  Private: 16 schools, 3,398 pupils
Colleges and Universities
  Two-year: 1 public; 2,419 students
  Four-year and Beyond: None
  Degree Options: C
Places Rated Score: 2,747
Places Rated Rank: 185

Visalia–Tulare–Porterville, CA
Elementary and Secondary
  Public: 48 districts, 120 schools,
  59,887 pupils
    Pupil/Teacher Ratio: 16.52
    Dollars per Pupil: $2,861
    Average Teacher Salary: $1,865
    Effort Index: 0.713
  Private: 16 schools, 1,838 pupils
Colleges and Universities
  Two-year: 2 public; 9,317 students
  Four-year and Beyond: None
  Degree Options: C
Places Rated Score: 2,128
Places Rated Rank: 326

Waco, TX
Elementary and Secondary
Public: 18 districts, 75 schools, 28,704 pupils
   Pupil/Teacher Ratio: 13.68
   Dollars per Pupil: $2,362
   Average Teacher Salary: $1,462
   Effort Index: 1.261
Private: 13 schools, 2,191 pupils
Colleges and Universities
   Two-year: 2 public; 9,272 students
   Four-year and Beyond: 1 private; 467 students
   Degree Options: C
Places Rated Score: 2,867
Places Rated Rank: 140

★ Washington, DC–MD–VA
Elementary and Secondary
Public: 16 districts, 939 schools, 568,828 pupils
   Pupil/Teacher Ratio: 15.43
   Dollars per Pupil: $2,681
   Average Teacher Salary: $2,223
   Effort Index: 1.155
Private: 505 schools, 101,086 pupils
Colleges and Universities
   Two-year: 1 private, 6 public; 73,681 students
   Four-year and Beyond: 26 private, 5 public; 155,068 students
   Degree Options: AAA
Places Rated Score: 3,635
Places Rated Rank: 3

Waterbury, CT
Elementary and Secondary
Public: 9 districts, 65 schools, 31,717 pupils
   Pupil/Teacher Ratio: 12.84
   Dollars per Pupil: $2,815
   Average Teacher Salary: $1,660
   Effort Index: 1.317
Private: 15 schools, 6,077 pupils
Colleges and Universities
   Two-year: 2 public; 5,565 students
   Four-year and Beyond: 1 private; 1,484 students
   Degree Options: C
Places Rated Score: 2,995
Places Rated Rank: 88

Waterloo–Cedar Falls, IA
Elementary and Secondary
Public: 12 districts, 69 schools, 27,883 pupils
   Pupil/Teacher Ratio: 16.26
   Dollars per Pupil: $3,025
   Average Teacher Salary: $1,723
   Effort Index: 1.209
Private: 16 schools, 4,396 pupils
Colleges and Universities
   Two-year: 1 public; 1,897 students
   Four-year and Beyond: 1 private, 1 public; 11,437 students
   Degree Options: B
Places Rated Score: 2,889
Places Rated Rank: 131

Wausau, WI
Elementary and Secondary
Public: 8 districts, 39 schools, 17,931 pupils
   Pupil/Teacher Ratio: 14.30
   Dollars per Pupil: $3,241
   Average Teacher Salary: $1,583
   Effort Index: 1.192

Private: 22 schools, 4,012 pupils
Colleges and Universities
   Two-year: 1 public; 3,521 students
   Four-year and Beyond: None
   Degree Options: C
Places Rated Score: 2,749
Places Rated Rank: 184

West Palm Beach–Boca Raton–Delray Beach, FL
Elementary and Secondary
Public: 1 district, 91 schools, 70,243 pupils
   Pupil/Teacher Ratio: 12.36
   Dollars per Pupil: $3,471
   Average Teacher Salary: $1,402
   Effort Index: 1.250
Private: 79 schools, 20,120 pupils
Colleges and Universities
   Two-year: 1 public; 11,954 students
   Four-year and Beyond: 3 private, 1 public; 10,327 students
   Degree Options: B
Places Rated Score: 3,224
Places Rated Rank: 35

Wheeling, WV–OH
Elementary and Secondary
Public: 2 districts, 41 schools, 15,658 pupils
   Pupil/Teacher Ratio: 14.94
   Dollars per Pupil: $2,296
   Average Teacher Salary: $1,707
   Effort Index: 1.240
Private: 27 schools, 4,343 pupils
Colleges and Universities
   Two-year: 3 public; 5,775 students
   Four-year and Beyond: 1 private, 1 public; 3,503 students
   Degree Options: B
Places Rated Score: 3,002
Places Rated Rank: 85

Wichita, KS
Elementary and Secondary
Public: 19 districts, 182 schools, 71,777 pupils
   Pupil/Teacher Ratio: 12.54
   Dollars per Pupil: $2,702
   Average Teacher Salary: $1,435
   Effort Index: 1.025
Private: 35 schools, 8,513 pupils
Colleges and Universities
   Two-year: 1 public; 2,985 students
   Four-year and Beyond: 2 private, 1 public; 18,204 students
   Degree Options: B
Places Rated Score: 2,981
Places Rated Rank: 93

Wichita Falls, TX
Elementary and Secondary
Public: 5 districts, 43 schools, 21,165 pupils
   Pupil/Teacher Ratio: 12.52
   Dollars per Pupil: $2,231
   Average Teacher Salary: $1,479
   Effort Index: 1.039
Private: 7 schools, 1,067 pupils
Colleges and Universities
   Two-year: None
   Four-year and Beyond: 1 public; 4,818 students
   Degree Options: C
Places Rated Score: 2,747
Places Rated Rank: 185

Williamsport, PA
Elementary and Secondary
Public: 8 districts, 40 schools, 21,622 pupils
   Pupil/Teacher Ratio: 13.62
   Dollars per Pupil: $3,290
   Average Teacher Salary: $1,501
   Effort Index: 1.296
Private: 11 schools, 1,463 pupils
Colleges and Universities
   Two-year: 1 public; 3,701 students
   Four-year and Beyond: 1 private; 1,192 students
   Degree Options: C
Places Rated Score: 2,906
Places Rated Rank: 122

Wilmington, DE–NJ–MD
Elementary and Secondary
Public: 21 districts, 149 schools, 84,377 pupils
   Pupil/Teacher Ratio: 14.30
   Dollars per Pupil: $2,827
   Average Teacher Salary: $929
   Effort Index: 1.285
Private: 35 schools, 26,171 pupils
Colleges and Universities
   Two-year: 3 public; 7,198 students
   Four-year and Beyond: 2 private, 1 public; 21,561 students
   Degree Options: B
Places Rated Score: 3,112
Places Rated Rank: 52

Wilmington, NC
Elementary and Secondary
Public: 1 district, 30 schools, 19,888 pupils
   Pupil/Teacher Ratio: 14.91
   Dollars per Pupil: $2,404
   Average Teacher Salary: $1,442
   Effort Index: 1.265
Private: 11 schools, 1,589 pupils
Colleges and Universities
   Two-year: 1 public; 1,927 students
   Four-year and Beyond: 1 public; 5,766 students
   Degree Options: B
Places Rated Score: 2,876
Places Rated Rank: 134

★ Worcester, MA
Elementary and Secondary
Public: 33 districts, 154 schools, 65,992 pupils
   Pupil/Teacher Ratio: 13.06
   Dollars per Pupil: $2,524
   Average Teacher Salary: $1,616
   Effort Index: 1.141
Private: 51 schools, 12,162 pupils
Colleges and Universities
   Two-year: 3 private, 1 public; 7,281 students
   Four-year and Beyond: 7 private, 1 public; 21,756 students
   Degree Options: A
Places Rated Score: 3,299
Places Rated Rank: 25

Yakima, WA
Elementary and Secondary
Public: 15 districts, 77 schools, 34,259 pupils
   Pupil/Teacher Ratio: 17.96
   Dollars per Pupil: $2,618
   Average Teacher Salary: $1,940
   Effort Index: 1.149

Private: 16 schools, 2,162 pupils
Colleges and Universities
 Two-year: 1 public; 2,997 students
 Four-year and Beyond: 1 private; 292
  students
 Degree Options: C
Places Rated Score: 2,491
Places Rated Rank: 283

York, PA
Elementary and Secondary
 Public: 15 districts, 99 schools,
 50,225 pupils
  Pupil/Teacher Ratio: 14.47
  Dollars per Pupil: $2,297
  Average Teacher Salary: $1,600
  Effort Index: 1.359
 Private: 38 schools, 6,811 pupils
Colleges and Universities
 Two-year: 1 public; 1,341 students

Four-year and Beyond: 3 private; 6,565
 students
 Degree Options: C
Places Rated Score: 2,903
Places Rated Rank: 124

Youngstown–Warren, OH
Elementary and Secondary
 Public: 37 districts, 183 schools,
 94,885 pupils
  Pupil/Teacher Ratio: 16.48
  Dollars per Pupil: $2,404
  Average Teacher Salary: $1,728
  Effort Index: 1.253
 Private: 43 schools, 13,331 pupils
Colleges and Universities
 Two-year: 2 private, 1 public; 2,705
  students
 Four-year and Beyond: 1 public; 15,590
  students

Degree Options: B
Places Rated Score: 2,920
Places Rated Rank: 115

Yuba City, CA
Elementary and Secondary
 Public: 17 districts, 59 schools,
 20,293 pupils
  Pupil/Teacher Ratio: 17.21
  Dollars per Pupil: $3,727
  Average Teacher Salary: $1,888
  Effort Index: 1.009
 Private: 13 schools, 1,459 pupils
Colleges and Universities
 Two-year: 1 public; 8,192 students
 Four-year and Beyond: None
 Degree Options: C
Places Rated Score: 2,387
Places Rated Rank: 309

Et Cetera

SOLVING THE SAT PUZZLE . . . OR TRYING

After 17 years of unbroken decline, the average scores of students on the Scholastic Aptitude Tests (SAT), given by the College Entrance Examination Board (CEEB), bottomed out in 1980 and started slowly upward in 1982. "We now think that we have a trend," CEEB President George Hanford told the *Chronicle of Higher Education*. At the current rate of recovery, however, math scores won't match their 1963 high until the year 2000 and verbal scores not until well into the next century. Although CEEB officials don't know why the scores have risen recently, they do suggest that recent high school seniors have enjoyed better instruction in the lower grades and have taken more courses in high school than the students who graduated before them.

Two researchers pointed out in a 1982 issue of *Phi Delta Kappan* that SAT scores started declining 18 years after the 1945 atomic bomb tests and began rising 18 years after the United States suspended all but underground atomic testing in 1963. The steepest drops in scores occurred in states nearest the bomb detonations, especially Nevada and Utah; smaller declines occurred in the northeastern and southeastern states that were far from the proving grounds. According to these researchers, those who blame the drop in SAT scores on television viewing, the Vietnam War, the child-spacing effect, changes in the number and mix of students taking the test, and poorer performance of schools are overlooking the effects of atomic fallout on the cognitive abilities of children.

But in Texas two other scholars of SAT trends have a different theory. The states that have the records of the highest scores, they claim, are not those that spend the most money for education, nor those with a long

tradition of quality public education, but those with the coldest winters: Average scores from cold-weather states are consistently higher than scores from warm-weather states. They offer two explanations for the link between cold weather and high SAT scores: (1) research on thermal conditions and human behavior suggests that cool room temperatures reduce mistakes on tests, and (2) long winters force children to remain inside after school and on weekends, thereby favoring family interaction, which is critical for pupil achievement.

Nonsense, another researcher points out. If one were to rank the states by their average total SATs, one would be ranking the states by the percent of college-bound seniors who actually took the test. In general, the larger the group tested, the lower the average level of performance.

Average SAT Scores: The States Ranked

State	Percent of College-Bound Seniors Tested	Average Score		
		Verbal	Math	Total
1. Iowa	3%	519	570	1,089
2. South Dakota	3	520	566	1,086
3. North Dakota	3	500	554	1,054
4. Kansas	5	502	549	1,051
5. Utah	4	503	542	1,045
6. Nebraska	6	493	548	1,041
7. Montana	9	490	544	1,034
7. Wyoming	5	489	545	1,034
9. Minnesota	7	481	539	1,020
10. New Mexico	8	487	527	1,014
11. Oklahoma	5	484	525	1,009
11. Tennessee	8	486	523	1,009
13. Wisconsin	10	475	532	1,007
14. Arkansas	4	482	521	1,003
15. Kentucky	6	479	518	997

State	Percent of College-Bound Seniors Tested	Average Score Verbal	Math	Total
16. Idaho	7%	480	512	992
16. Mississippi	3	480	512	992
18. Colorado	17	468	514	982
19. Illinois	14	463	518	981
19. Missouri	11	469	512	981
21. Louisiana	5	472	508	980
22. Michigan	11	461	515	976
22. West Virginia	7	466	510	976
24. Alabama	6	467	503	970
25. Ohio	16	460	508	968
25. Washington	19	463	505	968
27. Nevada	17	442	489	931
27. New Hampshire	57	448	483	931
29. Alaska	30	443	471	914
30. Oregon	42	435	472	907
30. Vermont	54	437	470	907
32. Connecticut	69	436	468	904
33. Delaware	50	433	469	902
34. Maryland	50	429	469	898
35. California	38	421	476	897
36. Massachusetts	66	429	467	896
37. New York	62	424	470	894
37. Virginia	51	428	466	894
39. Maine	46	429	463	892
40. Florida	38	423	467	890
41. Pennsylvania	52	425	462	887
42. Rhode Island	61	424	461	885
43. New Jersey	65	418	458	876
44. Hawaii	47	395	474	869
45. Texas	32	413	453	866
46. Indiana	47	410	454	864
47. North Carolina	47	395	432	827
48. Georgia	49	392	430	822
49. South Carolina	49	384	419	803
50. Arizona	11	169	509	678

Source: College Entrance Examination Board, unpublished data, 1984.

CERTIFYING PUPILS . . .

In the late 1970s, parents became convinced that teachers were neglecting the primary subjects, particularly reading, writing, and mathematics. Moreover, it wasn't possible to tell from a report card just how well a child was doing in relation to other children. Students were being promoted from grade to grade regardless of accomplishment. The result: Elementary pupils and even high school graduates who couldn't read a newspaper, write an intelligent sentence, address a postcard, or balance a checkbook.

This concern about students being ill prepared for adulthood led to a movement among taxpayers for accountability, or the holding of school districts responsible for teaching basic skills. One form of accountability is mandatory competency testing, an exam taken by each pupil to certify whether he or she can actually read, write, and solve mathematical problems.

Competency testing is a sensitive issue among educators, many of whom have been embarrassed by the results. When the tests were first administered to

pupils in the Florida public schools in 1978, the results were shocking. Thirty-seven percent failed a reading test for which the passing score was two and a half years below their grade level. In Kansas in 1981, nearly four out of ten high school juniors scored below the minimum level for reading and mathematics.

Forty states employ competency tests mainly to identify students who need "remediation," a term that means tutoring or retaking a course. Twenty-one states, however, use the test to certify pupils for grade promotion in elementary school and for high school graduation.

Grade Promotion and High School Graduation: The 21 States That Certify Students

State	Test Required for: Grade Promotion	High School Graduation	First Graduating Class Assessed
Alabama		•	1985
Arizona		•	1976
Arkansas	•		
California	•	•	1979
Delaware		•	1981
Florida	•	•	1983
Georgia		•	1985
Hawaii		•	1983
Louisiana	•		1992
Maryland			1982
Nevada		•	1982
New Jersey		•	1985
New York		•	1979
North Carolina		•	1980
Oregon		•	1978
South Carolina	•	•	1990
Tennessee		•	1982
Texas		•	1986
Utah		•	1980
Vermont		•	1981
Virginia		•	1981

Source: Education Commission of the States, *States Activity—Minimum Competency Testing,* 1984.

. . . AND TESTING THE TEACHERS

Pupils in public schools aren't the only ones encountering competency tests. To identify candidates who have neither an aptitude for teaching nor skill in an academic discipline, 20 states require new teachers to take a competency test before they get their first license. Some of these states administer the test before the candidate enters a teacher-training program, while other states test the candidate after the training sequence but before the license is awarded.

That's not the end of teacher accountability. Thirty-nine states require teachers to renew their licenses, or become recertified, by taking continuing education courses. The renewal period is usually every three to five years, though some states allow longer periods based on the candidate's successful teaching experience. Thirty-four of these states will issue no lifetime licenses. Five states—Indiana, Michigan, Rhode Island, Texas, and Washington—have periodic renewal

Raising Standards: The New Basics

The National Commission on Excellence in Education recommends that all college-bound high school seniors be required to take at least 16 units of the New Basics before qualifying for their diplomas. The commission defines these New Basics as one year of computer science, two years of a foreign language, four years of English, three years of mathematics, three years of science, and three years of social studies.

In ranking the states by the number of such courses their legislatures or state boards of education require of college-bound seniors, only Texas and Virginia come close to the recommended standard.

Seven states—Colorado, Iowa, Maine, Massachusetts, Michigan, Nebraska, and Wyoming—have their own graduation requirements, determined by local boards, that do not necessarily conform to the New Basics formula.

High School Courses Required for Graduation: The States Ranked

State	New Basics Units	Computer	Foreign Language	English	Mathematics	Science	Social Studies	Physical Education	Electives	Effective Class of
1. Virginia	16.0		3.0	4.0	3.0	3.0	3.0	2.0	4.0	1985
2. Texas	15.5	1.0	2.0	4.0	3.0	3.0	2.5	2.0	3.0	1988
3. New Hampshire	14.0	0.5	3.0	4.0	2.0	2.0	2.5	1.25	4.0	1989
4. Louisiana	13.5	0.5		4.0	3.0	3.0	3.0	2.0	7.5	1990
4. Rhode Island	13.5	0.5	2.0	4.0	3.0	2.0	2.0		4.0	1988
6. Florida	13.0			4.0	3.0	3.0	3.0	1.0	9.0	1987
6. Missouri	13.0			4.0	3.0	3.0	3.0	1.0	8.0	1985
6. Pennsylvania	13.0			4.0	3.0	3.0	3.0	1.0		1989
6. Vermont	13.0			4.0	3.0	3.0	3.0	1.5		1989
10. Arkansas	12.0			4.0	2.0	3.0	3.0	1.0	6.5	1988
10. Connecticut	12.0			4.0	3.0	2.0	3.0	1.0	6.0	1988
10. Georgia	12.0	1.0		4.0	2.0	2.0	3.0	1.0	8.0	1988
10. Hawaii	12.0			4.0	2.0	2.0	4.0	1.5	6.0	1983
10. South Carolina	12.0			4.0	3.0	2.0	3.0	1.0	7.0	1987
15. Oregon	11.5		1.0	3.0	2.0	2.0	3.5	2.0	8.0	1988
15. South Dakota	11.5	0.5		4.0	2.0	2.0	3.0		8.0	1989
15. Wisconsin	11.5	0.5		4.0	2.0	2.0	3.0	2.0		1989
18. Alaska	11.0			4.0	2.0	2.0	3.0	1.0	9.0	1985
18. California	11.0		1.0	3.0	2.0	2.0	3.0	2.0		1987
18. Delaware	11.0			4.0	2.0	2.0	3.0	1.5	6.5	1987
18. Kansas	11.0			4.0	2.0	2.0	3.0	1.0	8.0	1988
18. Kentucky	11.0			4.0	3.0	2.0	2.0	1.0	7.0	1987
18. Maryland	11.0			4.0	2.0	2.0	3.0	1.0	8.0	*
18. North Dakota	11.0			4.0	2.0	2.0	3.0	1.0	5.0	1984
18. West Virginia	11.0		1.0	4.0	2.0	1.0	3.0	2.0	7.0	1985
26. Utah	10.5	0.5		3.0	2.0	2.0	3.0	2.0	9.0	1988
27. Alabama	10.0			4.0	2.0	1.0	3.0	3.5	6.5	1985
27. Arizona	10.0			4.0	2.0	2.0	2.0		9.5	1987
27. Idaho	10.0			4.0	2.0	2.0	2.0	1.5	6.0	1988
27. Indiana	10.0			4.0	2.0	2.0	2.0	1.5	8.0	1989
27. New Mexico	10.0			4.0	2.0	2.0	2.0	1.0	9.0	1987
27. North Carolina	10.0			4.0	2.0	2.0	2.0	1.0	9.0	1987
27. Oklahoma	10.0			4.0	2.0	2.0	2.0		10.0	1987
34. Tennessee	9.5			4.0	2.0	2.0	1.5	1.5	9.0	1987
34. Washington	9.5			3.0	2.0	2.0	2.5	2.0	5.5	1989
36. Illinois	9.0	1.0		3.0	2.0	1.0	2.0	4.5	2.25	1988
36. Minnesota	9.0			4.0	1.0	1.0	3.0	1.5	9.5	1982
36. Montana	9.0			4.0	2.0	1.0	2.0	1.0	10.0	1986
36. New Jersey	9.0			4.0	2.0	1.0	2.0	4.0	4.0	*
36. New York	9.0			4.0	1.0	1.0	3.0	0.5	8.5	*
41. Nevada	8.0			3.0	2.0	1.0	2.0	2.5	9.5	1986
41. Ohio	8.0			3.0	2.0	1.0	2.0	1.0	9.0	1988
43. Mississippi	7.5			3.0	1.0	1.0	2.5		8.5	*

Source: Places Rated rankings derived from Education Commission of the States, *Minimum High School Graduation Course Requirements in the States*, August 1984.

*Graduation requirements have been in effect for a number of years.

leading to life certificates, which are increasingly being linked to advanced professional training.

Testing the Teachers

State	Competency		Recertification	
	Test	Starting	Required	Every . . .
Alabama	Yes	1981	Yes	8–12 yr*
Alaska	No		Yes	5
Arizona	Yes	1980	Yes	6
Arkansas	Yes	1983	Yes	6–10*
California	Yes	1982	Yes	5
Colorado	Yes	1983	Yes	5
Connecticut	Yes	1985	No	
Delaware	Yes	1983	No	
Florida	Yes	1980	Yes	6
Georgia	Yes	1979	Yes	5–10*
Hawaii	No		No	
Idaho	No		No	
Illinois	No		No	
Indiana	No		Yes	5–10*
Iowa	No		Yes	6–10*
Kansas	No		Yes	3–5*
Kentucky	No		Yes	10
Louisiana	Yes	1979	No	
Maine	No		Yes	5
Maryland	No		Yes	5–10*
Massachusetts	No		No	
Michigan	No		Yes	6
Minnesota	No		Yes	5
Mississippi	Yes	1977	Yes	5–10*
Missouri	No		No	
Montana	No		Yes	5
Nebraska	No		Yes	3
Nevada	No		Yes	5–6*
New Hampshire	No		Yes	3
New Jersey	No		No	
New Mexico	Yes	1983	Yes	4–10*
New York	Yes	1984	No	
North Carolina	Yes	1981	Yes	5
North Dakota	No		Yes	5
Ohio	No		Yes	4–8*
Oklahoma	Yes	1982	Yes	5
Oregon	No		Yes	3–5*
Pennsylvania	No		Yes	6
Rhode Island	No		Yes	3–5*
South Carolina	Yes	1982	Yes	5
South Dakota	No		Yes	5
Tennessee	Yes	1981	Yes	10
Texas	Yes	1985	Yes	3–5*
Utah	No		Yes	5
Vermont	No		Yes	5
Virginia	Yes	1981	Yes	5
Washington	No		Yes	4
West Virginia	Yes	1985	Yes	3–5*
Wisconsin	No		No	
Wyoming	No		Yes	5–10*

Source: Education Commission of the States, Clearinghouse Notes, and Phi Delta Kappan, October 1984.

*Certification interval depends on years of successful teaching experience.

OUTSTANDING PUBLIC SECONDARY SCHOOLS

In 1983 and again in 1984, the Department of Education asked the chief education officer of each state to name the best public secondary schools in his or her state.

Of the nearly 1,000 schools so nominated, 354 have received official recognition for excellence in education. These schools had to pass a rigorous screening process, which included a careful look at curricula and academic achievement; inspection of buildings, classrooms, and facilities; informal observations of classes, lunch periods, and assemblies; and interviews with students, parents, teachers, and administrators. The evaluators, none of whom worked for the federal government, were specialists in public-school improvement and accreditation.

Two hundred seventy-five of these outstanding secondary schools are located in metro areas. The schools include 123 junior high schools (JHS), middle schools (MS), and intermediate schools (IS), as well as 152 high schools (HS).

The Best Secondary Schools in the Metro Areas

Akron, OH
Hudson HS, Hudson
Hudson JHS, Hudson
Perkins JHS, Akron

Albany–Schenectady–Troy, NY
Niskayuna HS, Schenectady

Albuquerque, NM
Albuquerque HS, Albuquerque
Hoover MS, Albuquerque
Jefferson MS, Albuquerque
Manzano HS, Albuquerque
Taft MS, Albuquerque
West Mesa HS, Albuquerque

Anaheim–Santa Ana, CA
Venado MS, Irvine

Ann Arbor, MI
Huron HS, Ann Arbor
Slauson IS, Ann Arbor

Atlanta, GA
Douglass HS, Atlanta
Garrett MS, Austell
Walton HS, Marietta

Austin, TX
Austin HS, Austin

Baton Rouge, LA
Baton Rouge HS, Baton Rouge
McKinley MS, Baton Rouge

Birmingham, AL
Bush MS, Birmingham
Homewood HS, Homewood
Homewood MS, Homewood
Mountain Brook HS, Mountain Brook

Boston, MA
Acton–Boxborough HS, Acton
Rockland JHS, Rockland

Bridgeport–Milford, CT
Flood IS, Stratford
Wooster IS, Stratford

Casper, WY
Walsh HS, Casper

Cedar Rapids, IA
Franklin JHS, Cedar Rapids
Linn-Mar JHS, Cedar Rapids
Washington HS, Cedar Rapids

Charleston, WV
Washington HS, Charleston

Charlotte–Gastonia–Rock Hill, NC–SC
Carmel JHS, Charlotte, NC
Rock Hill HS, Rock Hill, SC

Chicago, IL
Community HS North, Downers Grove
Glenbrook North HS, Northbrook
Glenbrook South HS, Glenview
Homewood-Flossmoor HS, Flossmoor
Medinah ES, Roselle
Old Orchard JHS, Skokie
Rich Township HS, Richton Park
Thomas JHS, Arlington Heights
York Community HS, Elmhurst

Cincinnati, OH–KY–IN
Harrison JHS, Harrison, OH
Indian Hill HS, Cincinnati
Princeton HS, Cincinnati
Princeton JHS, Cincinnati
Wyoming HS, Wyoming, OH

Cleveland, OH
Shaker Heights HS, Shaker Heights
Woodbury JHS, Shaker Heights

Colorado Springs, CO
Cheyenne Mountain HS, Colorado Springs
Holmes JHS, Colorado Springs

Columbia, SC
Irmo HS, Columbia
Spring Valley HS, Columbia
Wright MS, Columbia

Columbus, OH
Jones MS, Columbus

Dallas, TX
Richardson HS, Richardson

Dayton–Springfield, OH
Ankeny JHS, Beavercreek
Centerville HS, Centerville

Daytona Beach, FL
Mainland HS, Daytona Beach

Denver, CO
Carmody JHS, Lakewood
Mrachek MS, Aurora
Wheat Ridge HS, Wheat Ridge

Des Moines, IA
Indian Hills JHS, Des Moines
Valley HS, West Des Moines

Detroit, MI
Andover HS, Bloomfield Hills
Cass Technical HS, Detroit
Grosse Point South HS,
Grosse Point
Lahser HS, Bloomfield Hills
Southfield HS, Southfield

Eau Claire, WI
Memorial HS, Eau Claire

El Paso, TX
Desert View MS, El Paso

Eugene–Springfield, OR
Monroe MS, Eugene
Oaklea MS, Junction City
South Eugene HS, Eugene

Fargo–Moorhead, ND–MN
Franklin JHS, Fargo

**Fort Lauderdale–Hollywood–
Pompano Beach, FL**
South Plantation HS, Plantation

Fort Smith, AR–OK
Gans JHS, Muldrow, OK
Muldrow HS, Muldrow, OK
Southside HS, Fort Smith, AR

Gary–Hammond, IN
Valparaiso HS, Valparaiso
Westchester MS, Chesterton

Grand Rapids, MI
Northview HS, Grand Rapids
West Ottawa MS, Holland

Greenville–Spartanburg, SC
League MS, Greenville
Spartanburg Senior HS, Spar-
tanburg

Hartford, CT
Illing JHS, Manchester

Houma–Thibodaux, LA
Raceland JHS, Raceland

Houston, TX
Bellaire HS, Bellaire
Bleyl JHS, Houston
Stratford HS, Houston

Indianapolis, IN
Carmel HS, Carmel
Clay JHS, Carmel
Davis HS, Indianapolis
Lawrence North HS, India-
napolis
North Central HS, Indianapolis
Warren Central HS, India-
napolis
Westland MS, Indianapolis

Iowa City, IA
South East JHS, Iowa City

Jackson, MS
Clinton HS, Clinton

Jacksonville, FL
Gorris JHS, Jacksonville
Davis JHS, Jacksonville
Parker HS, Jacksonville
Ribault HS, Jacksonville

Kansas City, KS
Oregon Trail JHS, Olathe
Shawnee Mission South HS,
Shawnee Mission
Shawnee Mission West HS,
Shawnee Mission

Kansas City, MO
Blue Springs HS, Blue Springs
Lewis MS, Excelsior Springs

Lafayette, LA
Lafayette MS, Lafayette

Lake County, IL
Elm Place MS, Highland Park
Wilmot JHS, Deerfield

Lansing–East Lansing, MI
Okemos HS, Okemos

Las Vegas, NV
Cannon JHS, Las Vegas
Guinn JHS, Las Vegas

Lewiston–Auburn, ME
Auburn MS, Auburn

Lincoln, NE
East HS, Lincoln
Lincoln HS, Lincoln

**Los Angeles–Long Beach,
CA**
Artesia HS, Lakewood
Montebello MS, Montebello
Pioneer HS, Whittier
West HS, Torrance

Lynchburg, VA
Glass HS, Lynchburg

Madison, WI
LaFollette HS, Madison

Medford, OR
Crater HS, Central Point

**Melbourne–Titusville–
Palm Bay, FL**
Jefferson JHS, Merritt Island

Memphis, TN–AR–MS
Collierville MS, Collierville, TN
Snowden MS, Memphis

Miami–Hialeah, FL
American HS, Hialeah
Highland Oaks JHS, North
Miami Beach

Milwaukee, WI
Brown Deer HS, Brown Deer
Burroughs MS, Milwaukee
King HS, Milwaukee
Webster Transitional MS,
Cedarburg

Minneapolis–St. Paul, MN–WI
Edina HS, Edina, MN
Hopkins HS, Minnetonka, MN
Hopkins North JHS, Minneton-
ka, MN
Hopkins West JHS, Minneton-
ka, MN
Oak-Land JHS, Lake Elmo, MN
Richfield HS, Richfield, MN
Stillwater JHS, Stillwater, MN

Mobile, AL
Vigor HS, Prichard

Nassau–Suffolk, NY
Miller Place HS, Miller Place
Murphy JHS, Stony Brook
Northport HS, Northport
Shoreham–Wading River MS,
Shoreham

New Bedford, MA
New Bedford HS, New Bedford

New Haven–Meriden, CT
Amity Regional HS, Orange
Conte Arts MS, New Haven

New Orleans, LA
King HS, Metairie
Lakewood JHS, Luling

New York, NY
Blue Mountain MS, Peekskill
Bronx HS of Science, Bronx
Brooklyn Technical HS,
Brooklyn
Cardozo HS, Bayside
Edgemont HS, Scarsdale
Fox Lane MS, Bedford
New Rochelle HS, New Ro-
chelle
Scarsdale HS, Scarsdale
Stuyvesant HS, New York

**Norfolk–Virginia Beach–
Newport News, VA**
Dunbar-Erwin MS, Newport
News
Menchville HS, Newport News

Norwalk, CT
Middlebrook MS, Wilton
Wilton HS, Wilton

Oakland, CA
Alvarado MS, Union City
Logan HS, Union City

Oklahoma City, OK
Marshall HS, Oklahoma City
Millwood HS, Oklahoma City
Northeast HS, Oklahoma City

Olympia, WA
Jefferson MS, Olympia

Omaha, NE–IA
Arbor Heights JHS, Omaha
Burke HS, Omaha
Kirn JHS, Council Bluffs, IA
Millard North HS, Omaha
Millard South HS, Omaha
Westside HS, Omaha

**Pawtucket–Woonsocket–
Attleboro, RI–MA**
Lincoln HS, Lincoln, RI

Philadelphia, PA–NJ
Bala-Cynwyd MS, Bala-
Cynwyd, PA
Conestoga HS, Berwyn, PA
Harriton HS, Rosemont, PA
Radnor HS, Radnor, PA
Welsh Valley MS, Narberth, PA

Phoenix, AZ
Agua Fria Union HS, Avondale
Chandler HS, Chandler
Foston JHS, Mesa
Mesa HS, Mesa
Rhodes JHS, Mesa
Shea MS, Phoenix
Westwood HS, Mesa
Willis JHS, Chandler

Pine Bluff, AR
White Hall HS, Pine Bluff

Pittsburgh, PA
Mount Lebanon HS, Pittsburgh
Upper St. Clair HS, Pittsburgh

Portland, ME
Deering HS, Portland
King MS, Portland
Portland HS, Portland

Portland, OR
Cedar Park IS, Beaverton
Clackamas HS, Milwaukie
Lake Oswego HS, Lake
Oswego

Light MS, Portland
McLoughlin JHS, Milwaukie
Renne IS, Newburg
Sunset HS, Beaverton
West Linn HS, West Linn

**Portsmouth–Dover–
Rochester, NH–ME**
Exeter JHS, Exeter, NH

Providence, RI
Bain JHS, Cranston
East Greenwich HS, East
Greenwich
Western Hills JHS, Cranston

Provo–Orem, UT
Timpview HS, Provo

Raleigh–Durham, NC
Broughton HS, Raleigh
Enloe HS, Raleigh

Reno, NV
Reno HS, Reno
Swope MS, Reno

**Richland–Kennewick–Pasco,
WA**
Hanford HS, Richland
Pasco HS, Pasco

Richmond–Petersburg, VA
Hermitage HS, Richmond

**Riverside–San Bernardino,
CA**
Mission JHS, Riverside
Terrace Hills JHS, Grand
Terrace

Roanoke, VA
Breckinridge JHS, Roanoke
Cave Spring HS, Roanoke
Hidden Valley JHS, Roanoke

Rochester, MN
Adams JHS, Rochester

Rochester, NY
Greece Athena HS,
Rochester

St. Louis, MO–IL
Brentwood JHS, Brentwood,
MO
Ladue JHS, Ladue, MO
McCluer North HS, Florissant,
MO
Parkway West Senior HS,
Ballwin, MO
Patonville Heights MS,
Maryland Heights, MO
Watkins HS, St. Louis

Salt Lake City–Ogden, UT
Bountiful HS, Bountiful
Brighton HS, Salt Lake City
Butler MS, Salt Lake City
Eastmont MS, Sandy
Highland HS, Salt Lake City
South HS, Salt Lake City

San Antonio, TX
Churchill HS, San Antonio

San Diego, CA
Chula Vista HS, Chula Vista
Fallbrook Union HS, Fallbrook
Santana HS, Santee
Twin Peaks MS, Poway

San Francisco, CA
Borel MS, San Mateo
Crocker JHS, Hillsborough
Davidson MS, San Rafael
Lowell HS, San Francisco

San Jose, CA
Leyva JHS, San Jose

Seattle, WA
Lindbergh HS, Renton
Redmond HS, Redmond
Shorewood HS, Seattle

Shreveport, LA
Captain Shreve HS, Shreveport
Youree Drive MS, Shreveport

Spokane, WA
Sacajawea JHS, Spokane

Springfield, MO
Kickapoo HS, Springfield

Tacoma, WA
Curtis HS, Tacoma
Curtis JHS, Tacoma

Tampa–St. Petersburg–Clearwater, FL
Brandon HS, Brandon
Hollins HS, St. Petersburg
Largo MS, Largo

Toledo, OH
Arbor Hills JHS, Sylvania

Topeka, KS
Topeka West HS, Topeka

Tucson, AZ
Amphitheatre HS, Tucson
Utterback JHS, Tucson

Tulsa, OK
Washington HS, Tulsa

Vancouver, WA
Battle Ground HS, Battle
Ground

Washington, DC–MD–VA
Alice Deal JHS, Washington
Brookland JHS, Washington
George Mason HS, Falls
Church, VA

Hobson MS, Washington
Jefferson JHS, Washington
Williams HS, Alexandria, VA

Wheeling, WV–OH
Bridge Street JHS, Wheeling
Triadelphia JHS, Wheeling
Wheeling JHS, Wheeling
Wheeling Park HS, Wheeling

Wichita, KS
Horace Mann MS, Wichita

Wilmington, DE–NJ–MD
Brandywine HS, Wilmington

Source: U.S. Department of Education, press releases from the Secondary School Recognition Program, 1983 and 1984.

THE HIGH COST OF COLLEGE

Some say that in the future white-collar workplace, only those who have college degrees will get the nod for new slots in management training, or even entry-level jobs behind the counter or in the mail room. But coming up with four years of tuition and fees to help their children launch a career is breaking a lot of middle-income families. To go away to college and make it through in standard time, most students need at least two out of these three sources of money (aside from parental largesse): a scholarship, a student loan, and a part-time job.

The best way to cut costs at the very start is to do some sharp thinking when choosing a college. If you are planning on college, consider your options. You can:

• Live at home, enroll in a low-cost two-year college that offers courses good toward a bachelor's degree, and then transfer to a local four-year state college for your junior and senior years. This is the least expensive way to get a college education.

• Enroll in a public four-year college or university in your home state. The tuition will definitely be higher than that of a two-year college. And if you decide to live on campus, it will cost you $2,500 more per year than attending college while living at home.

• Enroll in a public college or university outside your home state. This will mean paying stiff tuition charges. But establishing legal residency could save you a significant amount. Tuitions in California public colleges, for example, are one fifth what you'd pay in several northeastern states.

• Register at a private college or university. This is the most expensive option, even if you live at home.

Private vs. Public Tuition

The costs for a room and daily meals on campus aren't much greater at private colleges than they are at state institutions. The average $16,400 extra that a student pays for choosing a private over a state college is entirely in the tuition.

Students at private colleges pay two thirds of the real cost of their education; the rest comes from gifts and earnings from the school's endowment. At state-run colleges, the student pays only one fifth of the real cost, the slack being taken up by state government money. But private colleges spend a great deal more to educate each student than do public colleges since they offer unique cultural and religious environments, smaller classes, and special programs not available at state schools. In paying more for tuition at a private school, the student often gets more.

Tuition, Room, and Board:
The Most Expensive Colleges and Universities

East	Total
1. Harvard University (Cambridge, MA)	$13,185
2. Barnard College (New York, NY)	13,165
3. Yale University (New Haven, CT)	13,160
4. Sarah Lawrence College (Bronxville, NY)	13,130
5. Princeton University (Princeton, NJ)	12,910
6. Smith College (Northampton, MA)	12,740
7. Bard College (Annandale-on-Hudson, NY)	12,680
8. Dartmouth College (Hanover, NH)	12,580
9. Tufts University (Medford, MA)	12,534
10. Brown University (Providence, RI)	12,495

South	Total
1. Tulane University of Louisiana (New Orleans, LA)	$10,450
2. Vanderbilt University (Nashville, TN)	10,071
3. Emory University (Atlanta, GA)	9,970
4. Duke University (Durham, NC)	9,969
5. Sweet Briar College (Sweet Briar, VA)	9,650
6. Hollins College (Hollins College, VA)	9,600
7. Southern Methodist University (Dallas, TX)	9,585
8. Randolph-Macon Woman's College (Lynchburg, VA)	9,580
9. University of Miami (Coral Gables, FL)	9,328
10. Rollins College (Winter Park, FL)	9,251

West	Total
1. Stanford University (Stanford, CA)	$12,839
2. Harvey Mudd College (Claremont, CA)	11,710
3. Scripps College (Claremont, CA)	11,460
4. University of Southern California (Los Angeles, CA)	11,350
5. Occidental College (Los Angeles, CA)	11,298
6. University of the Pacific (Stockton, CA)	11,297
7. Pomona College (Claremont, CA)	11,200
8. Pepperdine University (Malibu, CA)	11,064
9. Mills College (Oakland, CA)	10,500
10. University of Redlands (Redlands, CA)	10,375

Midwest	Total
1. Northwestern University (Evanston, IL)	$12,291
2. University of Chicago	12,136
3. Oberlin College (Oberlin, OH)	11,425
4. Washington University (St. Louis, MO)	11,320
5. Kenyon College (Gambier, OH)	10,500
6. Carleton College (Northfield, MN)	10,149
7. Denison University (Granville, OH)	10,020
7. Lake Forest College (Lake Forest, IL)	10,020
9. Case Western Reserve University (Cleveland, OH)	9,870
10. College of Wooster (Wooster, OH)	9,650

Source: National Center for Education Statistics, *Basic Student Charges, 1983–84,* 1984.

In-State and Out-of-State Tuition

Each fall, 300,000 freshmen head for colleges outside their home state. Half enroll in private schools, and the other half enter state colleges at which tuition for nonresidents often equals tuition they would pay at any private school. It isn't accidental that states showing net gains from the annual freshman migration have a good supply of private schools within their borders, or are noted for downhill skiing, or are simply located in the best parts of the Sun Belt. The states that lose the most students are found in the cold Midwest and Northeast.

The biggest dollar differences between in-state and out-of-state tuition are found at each of the California State University and Colleges 14 campuses, at each of the University of California's nine campuses, the three campuses of the University of Colorado, the University of Michigan's main campus, and the University of Vermont. At these 28 schools, nonresident tuition is at least $3,000 more than in-state tuition.

Paying the out-of-state tuition differential has been challenged in the courts by students claiming discrimination. Others simply change their legal residence by re-registering their cars in the new state and taking part-time jobs in which state taxes are withheld, thus qualifying for the lower rate.

The Annual Freshman Exchange

Losers	Outgoing Freshmen	Winners	Incoming Freshmen
1. New York	31,000	1. California	25,500
2. New Jersey	28,300	2. Massachusetts	20,800
3. Illinois	19,800	3. New York	18,500
4. Pennsylvania	16,400	4. Pennsylvania	17,400
5. Connecticut	13,700	5. Texas	14,500
6. Ohio	12,000	6. Florida	13,900

Source: National Center for Education Statistics, *Condition of Education,* 1984.

TOP-RANKED PH.D. PROGRAMS

The following rankings are derived from the five-volume *Assessment of Research-Doctorate Programs in the United States.* Institutions are ranked by the number of programs in five basic fields—physical sciences and

Basic Yearly Student Charges in Public Colleges by State

	Tuition	Room	Board	Total		Tuition	Room	Board	Total
U.S. Average	$870	$1,140	$1,250	$3,260	U.S. Average	$870	$1,140	$1,250	$3,260
1. Hawaii	340	900	900	2,140	26. Iowa	990	900	1,140	3,030
2. Mississippi	830	660	900	2,390	27. Wisconsin	990	1,080	1,110	3,180
3. Oklahoma	610	840	1,010	2,460	28. Alaska	600	920	1,760	3,280
4. North Dakota	850	600	1,070	2,520	29. Washington	810	1,160	1,330	3,300
5. New Mexico	770	880	880	2,530	30. Oregon	970	1,000	1,350	3,320
6. North Carolina	500	910	1,140	2,550	31. Minnesota	1,160	980	1,190	3,330
7. Arkansas	820	730	1,070	2,620	31. Virginia	980	1,150	1,200	3,330
8. Arizona	560	1,010	1,060	2,630	33. Nevada	850	1,190	1,340	3,380
9. Louisiana	690	980	980	2,650	34. Utah	880	970	1,540	3,390
10. Missouri	790	950	950	2,690	35. Illinois	880	1,220	1,300	3,400
10. Texas	420	1,040	1,230	2,690	36. Indiana	1,280	880	1,320	3,480
12. Kentucky	740	870	1,110	2,720	37. Colorado	1,020	1,100	1,430	3,550
13. Florida	730	1,030	1,020	2,780	38. Connecticut	870	1,520	1,370	3,760
14. Tennessee	750	960	1,100	2,810	39. Delaware	1,210	1,460	1,100	3,770
15. Kansas	860	910	1,050	2,820	40. Michigan	1,310	1,060	1,420	3,790
16. Alabama	880	800	1,150	2,830	41. New Jersey	1,130	1,420	1,260	3,810
17. South Dakota	1,120	830	950	2,900	42. Maine	1,430	1,290	1,290	4,010
18. Nebraska	1,000	830	1,080	2,910	43. Massachusetts	1,060	1,500	1,500	4,060
18. Wyoming	580	960	1,370	2,910	44. New York	1,240	1,460	1,380	4,080
20. California	280	1,280	1,430	2,990	45. Maryland	1,080	1,510	1,510	4,100
21. Georgia	860	880	1,260	3,000	46. Ohio	1,500	1,490	1,130	4,120
21. Montana	780	800	1,420	3,000	47. Pennsylvania	1,760	1,250	1,180	4,190
23. South Carolina	960	910	1,140	3,010	48. Rhode Island	1,180	1,560	1,560	4,300
24. Idaho	790	760	1,470	3,020	49. New Hampshire	1,810	1,350	1,330	4,490
24. West Virginia	600	1,150	1,270	3,020	50. Vermont	2,180	1,450	1,270	4,900

Source: National Center for Education Statistics, unpublished data, 1984.

mathematics, humanities, engineering, biological sciences, and social and behavioral sciences—that scored 60 or higher in reputation for "faculty quality." A rating of 50 represented the mean; a score of 75 would be considered exceptional.

The table "Top-Ranked Ph.D.-Granting Institutions" details how many programs in each field scored at least 60 points and also indicates how many of those programs also ranked at the higher level of 70 points or above. The entry Overall Score represents the total number of both these kinds of programs.

It's interesting to note that five of the top ten institutions for Ph.D. programs are also among the nation's most expensive places at which to get an education: Harvard, Princeton, Stanford, University of Chicago, and Yale.

Top-Ranked Ph.D.-Granting Institutions

| Institution | Programs Rated 60 or Above | | | | | | Programs Rated 70 or Above | Overall Score |
	Physics, Science, Mathematics	Humanities	Engineering	Biology	Social Science	Total		
1. University of California, Berkeley	6	9	4	4	7	30	15	45
2. Stanford University (Stanford, CA)	6	4	4	4	6	24	10	34
3. Harvard University (Cambridge, MA)	5	5	—	4	6	20	12	32
3. Yale University (New Haven, CT)	6	7	—	6	6	25	7	32
5. Massachusetts Institute of Technology (Cambridge, MA)	5	2	4	3	3	17	12	29
6. Princeton University (Princeton, NJ)	5	7	4	—	5	21	7	28
7. University of Chicago	5	4	—	4	7	20	7	27
8. University of California, Los Angeles	5	5	2	6	6	24	—	24
8. University of Michigan	2	6	3	4	6	21	3	24
8. University of Wisconsin	5	3	2	5	6	21	3	24
11. Columbia University (New York, NY)	5	6	—	4	6	21	2	23
12. Cornell University (Ithaca, NY)	6	6	3	4	3	22	1	23
13. University of Illinois (Champaign, IL)	4	2	4	4	3	17	2	19
14. University of Pennsylvania (Philadelphia, PA)	2	5	1	3	5	16	1	17
15. California Institute of Technology (Pasadena, CA)	4	—	4 *	1	—	9	6	15
16. University of Minnesota	3	—	2	2	4	11	2	13
16. University of Texas (Austin, TX)	3	3	3	2	2	13	—	13
18. University of North Carolina (Chapel Hill, NC)	2	3	—	2	4	11	—	11
18. Northwestern University (Evanston, IL)	1	1	3	1	5	11	—	11
20. University of Washington (Seattle, WA)	2	—	1	5	2	10	—	10

Source: David S. Webster, *Change*, May/June 1983; derived from *Assessment of Research-Doctorate Programs in the United States.*

The Arts:

Where the Cultural Action Is

Sure you want to escape from your gigantic metro area to a serene spot that's uncrowded, crime-free, and inexpensive. Who doesn't? So when the chance arrives, either in the form of a company relocation, a mid-life change, or retirement, you pack up and make your break. And you're delighted to find that rural or small-town life is all it's cracked up to be. There is a sense of cohesion, of continuity and tradition, of community spirit and neighborliness that you thought had died in America. You're happier than you've been in years.

For about four months.

Because in your rush to leave behind all the unpleasant and dangerous aspects of big-city life, you forgot the museum done in neoclassical stone that you passed twice each day in the crush of commuter traffic. You overlooked the several libraries offering not only books but also filmstrips and movies, records and tapes, and free lectures and exhibits. And then there were the big universities, three of them, that you tended to take for granted yet that provided so much for you and your family. And what about the symphony and the two repertory theatres?

You trot down to the public library in your new town, only to find a well-worn selection of fiction, mostly published in the fifties, and a few back issues of *Family Circle* and *Field & Stream.* You search for a theatre or musical event and find your only choice is a

concert stop by touring country-and-western performer Clyde McFritter and His Heavy Haulers.

Of all the categories that form the composite known as quality of life, the one called the arts is singularly and inevitably associated with big cities. Of course, this is true for some recreational facilities as well—professional sports teams, zoos, amusement parks. However, many of the most valuable recreational facilities, such as lakes, hiking trails, campgrounds, and national forests, are found far from cities; in fact, they *must* be far from cities. The arts alone are big-city phenomena. Therefore, it should come as no surprise that *Places Rated*'s top three metro areas for the arts are New York, Chicago, and Los Angeles, which are also our three most populous. Yet this is not to say that culture cannot be found in many smaller places in America. Although it's fairly safe to assume that the bigger a met is, the more cultural facilities it will have, there are interesting exceptions to this rule, as we will discover later in the chapter.

WHAT *ARE* THE ARTS, ANYWAY?

The answer to the question of what makes up art or the arts is simple: Nobody can agree. But even though people can't get together on a single definition, or on one thing that all art is, most people do concur that certain specific things are indeed included in the broad category called the arts. For example, the following two lists draw a distinction that most of us would recognize:

Definitely Art	Possibly Art
paintings, frescoes, murals	sidewalk drawing
ballet	break dancing
stained glass	monogrammed glasses
Placido Domingo	The Who
Chicago Symphony Orchestra	folk music, blues, jazz
Chinese bronzes	comic books

It is not within *Places Rated Almanac*'s purview to decide which, if any, of the items in the right-hand list are art. Rather, we choose to confine our survey of cultural amenities in the metro areas to items identical with or related to those in the first list, those which most people agree have artistic or cultural merit. Whether any or all of the items in the second list are art is a moot question today; most are controversial or dubious simply because they have not yet withstood the test of time. It can be argued that at least some of them may be considered folk art, which is increasingly popular and will be discussed in another section of this chapter.

The broad categories of cultural wealth that *Places Rated* has selected to survey include museums, fine arts radio and public television, universities, symphony orchestras, theatres, opera companies, dance troupes, and public libraries. Singly, each represents either an important facet of artistic achievement or the transmission of, or learning about, that achievement. Together, they reflect the cultural and intellectual tone of a metro area. Finally, their presence indicates a second layer of cultural life: the specialty shops catering to lovers of classical music or fine paintings and prints; the ethnic restaurants, literary clubs, and lecture societies that flourish in the atmosphere produced by artists, musicians, professors, and others of similar bent; perhaps even the kind of conversation made at a bridge party, cookout, or day at the beach.

MUSEUMS: CULTURAL STOREHOUSES

The artistic elements of city life might be broken down into two categories: performances and possessions. The performing arts and broadcasts that feature fine music or cultural fare belong in the first group. The collected arts, such as those found in museums, belong in the second.

A. Bartlett Giamatti, president of Yale University, once referred to museums and libraries as "institutions that mediate between the past and the future." Whether it is through a collection of artifacts in history museums, or the paintings and sculpture in an art museum, or the technologically entertaining displays in a science museum, these institutions give us an opportunity to benefit from the accomplishments of others and participate in a cultural life far beyond our own immediate experience.

The Arts and the Electronic Revolution

Even though most cultural facilities are found in big cities, a revolution in communication is under way that is making the arts accessible to those who live in remote rural areas. Even if you, as a recent refugee from a huge metro area, have given up live performances of the theatre, symphony, ballet, and opera, a whole world of artistic enjoyment is still available to you in your new home in small-town America. Recorded performances, both audio and visual, are available on cable television, public radio and television, and commercially sold cassettes.

What will this electronic revolution mean? Will videocassette recorders, cable television, satellite reception, and digital laser disks render the arts universal and homogeneous? A 1984 Harris poll reported that ownership of videocassette recorders has increased to 17 percent of Americans, many of them people who frequently attend arts performances; it concluded that a continuation of this trend "could become a threat instead of a boon to the arts." Will "cultural" cities become a thing of the past, totally replaced by broadcasting and recording sites?

Most arts lovers and critics think not. They make the point that a symphony in residence enriches a town just by being there—even when it's not performing or recording. Likewise, a community that is willing to support a theatre, dance company, or opera shows its dedication to the arts by the mere fact of this support, which reflects the community's values and priorities.

The first public museum in America was the Charleston Museum, still in existence, organized in 1773 by the Charleston, South Carolina, Library Society. Since that time, nearly 5,000 more museums have been established in this country; the number varies according to whose definition you use. A museum can be simply a collection of objects on view to the public on an occasional basis, or a treasure trove of artistic, scientific, or historic artifacts housed in a magnificent public building, looked after by hundreds of employees and supported by millions of dollars annually.

The most prevalent type of museum in the United States is the history museum. The greatest number can be found in the eastern half of the country. Approximately half of all museums are run by private, nonprofit organizations. Most museums in the country were started in the 1900s, with a huge escalation in the 1950s and 1960s, when more than a third of all museums existing today were built.

Since data on the operating and acquisitions budgets of museums are not available in all cases, determining a museum's relative size and scope is a problem. However, after reviewing data from the American Association of Museums (AAM) and the National Council on the Arts, *Places Rated* has prepared a basic set of requirements. To qualify for inclusion in this almanac, a museum first must comply with the AAM's official definition: "An organized and permanent non-profit institution, essentially educational or aesthetic in purpose, with professional staff, which owns and utilizes tangible objects, cares for them, and exhibits them to the public on some regular schedule." Furthermore, each museum must have a minimum of three curators, or equivalents, each in charge of an internal department or field. It must also have a regular publication and/or a library of 5,000 volumes or more, although this requirement is waived if the museum has five or more curators.

In all, 100 metro areas have museums that meet these requirements, and 13 metro areas have four or more qualifying museums. New York is far and away the leader in this category, with 18 major museums.

Major Museums: The Top 13 Metro Areas

Metro Area	Qualifying Museums	Metro Area	Qualifying Museums
1. New York, NY	18	8. Ann Arbor, MI	4
2. Washington, DC–MD–VA	10	8. Dallas, TX	4
		8. Detroit, MI	4
3. Boston, MA	6	8. Minneapolis–St. Paul, MN–WI	4
3. Chicago, IL	6		
3. Los Angeles–Long Beach, CA	6	8. New Haven–Meriden, CT	4
3. Philadelphia, PA–NJ	6	8. Seattle, WA	4
7. San Francisco, CA	5		

Source: American Association of Museums, *Official Museum Directory*, National Register Publishing Company, 1982.

TUNING IN TO CULTURE: PUBLIC TELEVISION AND FINE ARTS RADIO

When television channels were first allocated, certain of them were reserved by the Federal Communications Commission for nonprofit "educational" television stations, which were to be extensions of the classroom. Gradually the concept was broadened. "Educational television" became "public television," which grew to include all kinds of artistic and intellectual fare not readily available on commercial television: discussion programs, opera, symphony, Shakespeare, engrossing explanations of science and the universe, and creative and intellectually stimulating children's shows. The finest programs of the various stations were shared through a national network—the Public Broadcasting Service (PBS). And the audience increased.

During the month of March 1980, for example, A. C. Nielsen reported that more than 52 million U.S. households (68.2 percent of all American television-owning families) watched an average of 9 hours and 25 minutes of public television. The viewing time was an hour and a half longer than had been reported just two years before. And the total audience had doubled since 1975. Today, there are more than 290 U.S. public television stations broadcasting a total of more than 30,000 hours per week, nearly twice as many hours as a decade ago.

What are all these stations showing and their audiences so eagerly watching? In many cases, the arts. During the course of a television season, public television will broadcast performances of many major U.S. symphony orchestras, such as those of Boston, Los Angeles, Chicago, Minnesota, Cleveland, Philadelphia, Detroit, New York, and Washington, D.C. Also televised will be presentations by nearly every major dance company and choreographer, performances by major opera companies, and a wide range of theatre productions.

Virtually every metro area in the country has access to public television by way of cable, and 148 of 329 metro areas have at least one such station broadcasting from within their boundaries. Sixteen metro areas have two public TV stations, and two—New York and San Francisco—have three.

In addition to public television, many metro areas support their own public radio stations. These stations belong to the National Public Radio (NPR) network, sharing collectively programs that may originate in one station or another around the country. NPR, like PBS, is supported by the Corporation for Public Broadcasting, an independent federal agency that relies on matching grants to finance noncommercial broadcasting. Fine arts and public radio stations are found in 136 metro areas; 21 metro areas have two stations, and 12 have three or more:

Buffalo, NY (3)
Chicago, IL (3)
Columbus, OH (3)
Los Angeles–Long Beach, CA (4)
Louisville, KY–IN (3)
Madison, WI (3)

Minneapolis–St. Paul, MN–WI (3)
New York, NY (3)
Portland, OR (3)
San Francisco, CA (3)
Washington, DC–MD–VA (3)
Waterloo–Cedar Falls, IA (3)

COLLEGES AND UNIVERSITIES: CULTURAL MICROCOSMS

Although universities are primarily educational institutions, they are cultural microcosms as well. Within their walls, one can usually find a symphony orchestra, a dance company or two, at least one theatre, and a fine arts radio station and/or a culturally oriented television station. A large and prestigious university needs all these facilities.

These institutions offer many cultural advantages to the local resident. University-produced symphony concerts and plays are almost always much less expensive than their professional counterparts. Also, they are usually less crowded and are located where parking and crowds are less of a problem. Ask the people who live in medium-sized metro areas, such as Ann Arbor, Michigan; Madison, Wisconsin; Austin, Texas; or Raleigh–Durham, North Carolina, what helps make their localities so special. Before long, they'll mention the universities—and they don't have to be students to appreciate them.

All institutions of higher learning contribute to the

cultural level of a metro area, but the larger ones, with more students, will have more extensive and varied cultural facilities and programs. Furthermore, it seems obvious that schools offering degrees in the fine and performing arts will have more programs and events for the community's benefit. In an attempt to limit our survey to institutions making a special cultural contribution to the community, *Places Rated* therefore considers only four-year schools having undergraduate enrollments of 2,000 students or more and offering at least one degree in one of the following fields (not to be confused with arts *courses*, which almost all universities have): Art/Art History, Creative Writing, Dance, Drama/Theatre, Music, and Voice/Opera.

Qualifying colleges and universities are found in 205 metro areas, and 65 of these universities offer degrees in four or more of the named fields. There are 19 metro areas enjoying the cultural benefits of four or more qualifying universities, and an elite group of ten have five or more.

Fine Arts Universities: The Top 10 Metro Areas

Metro Area	Qualifying Universities	Metro Area	Qualifying Universities
1. New York, NY	12	7. Minneapolis–St. Paul, MN–WI	5
2. Boston, MA	11	7. New Orleans, LA	5
3. Chicago, IL	10	7. Norfolk–Virginia Beach–Newport News, VA	5
4. Philadelphia, PA–NJ	9	7. Providence, RI	5
4. Washington, DC–MD–VA	9		
6. Los Angeles–Long Beach, CA	8		

Source: Lovejoy's College Guide, 16th ed.

THE PERFORMING ARTS: SYMPHONY, THEATRE, OPERA, AND DANCE

To say that the American performing arts underwent a renaissance in the 1970s would be an understatement. More surprising has been the continued flourishing of the arts in the early 1980s, given the dramatic decline in government funding. In addition to increased corporate support, there has been an unparalleled interest on the part of individual Americans in participating in the arts, whether as professionals, amateurs, or spectators. Symphony attendance, for example, rose from 12.7 million in 1970 to 22 million in 1982; opera attendance, in the same period, from 4.6 million to 10.1 million. And according to a Harris poll released in late 1984, more Americans went to performances of theatre, dance, opera, and music in 1984 than in 1980. The biggest winners were ballet and opera, whose attendance rates jumped from 25 percent of the population in 1980 to 34 percent and 35 percent, respectively, in 1984. These gains in arts attendance occurred despite a drop in the amount of leisure time adult Americans have, from an average of 19.2 hours a week in 1980 to 18.1 hours a week in 1984.

Symphony Orchestras

Concerts by symphony orchestras in this country date back to a performance in 1731 in Charleston, South Carolina. More than 100 years later, in 1842, the New York Philharmonic became America's first organized symphony. Today, the American Symphony Orchestra League estimates that there are 1,500 orchestras in the United States and Canada, half of which are members of the league. Thirty-four orchestras are classified by the league as Major; that is, each has an annual operating income of more than $3.25 million. Four Major orchestras are located in Canada, and the rest are in the United States.

Performing Arts on Campus

If you live in a college town, you already have more cultural activities to choose from than someone who lives in a town without a college or university. But if your home also happens to be home to a school with one or more highly rated programs in the performing arts, the variety of offerings may amount to an arts Eden.

Listed below are the ten best schools in America for three of the performing arts according to *The Gourman Report*, which evaluates schools on the basis of the strength of departments and the academic performance of students.

The 10 Best Universities for Art

1. New York University (New York)
2. Harvard University (Cambridge, MA)
3. Princeton University (Princeton, NJ)
4. Yale University (New Haven, CT)
5. University of California, Berkeley
6. University of Chicago
7. University of Pennsylvania (Philadelphia)
8. Cornell University (Ithaca, NY)
9. Stanford University (Stanford, CA)
10. University of California, Los Angeles

The 10 Best Universities for Drama/Theatre

1. Northwestern University (Evanston, IL)
2. University of California, Los Angeles
3. Yale University (New Haven, CT)
4. Cornell University (Ithaca, NY)
5. Stanford University (Stanford, CA)
6. University of Denver
7. Indiana University (Bloomington)
8. University of Washington (Seattle)
9. University of Iowa (Iowa City)
10. Carnegie-Mellon (Pittsburgh, PA)

The 10 Best Universities for Music

1. Harvard University (Cambridge, MA)
2. Yale University (New Haven, CT)
3. University of California, Berkeley
4. University of California, Los Angeles
5. University of Chicago
6. University of Michigan (Ann Arbor)
7. University of Illinois (Urbana)
8. Princeton University (Princeton, NJ)
9. New York University (New York)
10. Columbia University (New York)

Source: Dr. Jack Gourman, The Gourman Report: A Rating of Undergraduate Programs in American and International Universities, 4th ed. National Education Standards (Los Angeles), 1984.

Major American Symphony Orchestras

Atlanta Symphony Orchestra
Baltimore Symphony Orchestra
Boston Symphony Orchestra
Buffalo Philharmonic Orchestra
Chicago Symphony Orchestra
Cincinnati Symphony Orchestra
Cleveland Orchestra
Dallas Symphony Orchestra
Denver Symphony Orchestra
Detroit Symphony Orchestra
Houston Symphony Orchestra
Indianapolis Symphony Orchestra
Los Angeles Philharmonic
Milwaukee Symphony Orchestra
Minnesota Orchestra (Minneapolis)
National Symphony Orchestra (Washington, D.C.)
New Orleans Philharmonic Symphony Orchestra
New York Philharmonic (New York City)
Oregon Symphony Orchestra (Portland)
Philadelphia Orchestra
Pittsburgh Symphony Orchestra
Rochester Philharmonic Orchestra (Rochester, NY)
St. Louis Symphony Orchestra
St. Paul Chamber Orchestra
San Antonio Symphony Orchestra
San Diego Symphony Orchestra
San Francisco Symphony
Seattle Symphony Orchestra
Syracuse Symphony Orchestra
Utah Symphony Orchestra (Salt Lake City)

Source: American Symphony Orchestra League, *Symphony Magazine,* Vol. 34, No. 6, December 1983.

The other categories of orchestras delineated by the league are Regional (those with annual budgets between $900,000 and $3.25 million), Metropolitan (with budgets between $250,000 and $900,000), Urban (with budgets between $115,000 and $250,000), Community (with budgets less than $115,000), College (composed exclusively of faculty and students of a college or university), and Youth (made up of junior high, high school, and/or college students and not exclusively affiliated with one educational institution).

Orchestras are far from uncommon in the metro areas; 257 claim at least one. Thirty-three of these places have four or more orchestras, and ten metro areas have six or more.

Symphony Orchestras: The Top 10 Metro Areas

Metro Area	Qualifying Orchestras	Metro Area	Qualifying Orchestras
1. New York, NY	21	6. Baltimore, MD	7
2. Los Angeles–Long Beach, CA	15	6. San Francisco, CA	7
3. Chicago, IL	14	8. Houston, TX	6
4. Boston, MA	10	8. Oakland, CA	6
5. Pittsburgh, PA	9	8. Seattle, WA	6

Source: American Symphony Orchestra League, *Symphony Magazine,* Vol. 34, No. 6, December 1983.

Repertory Theatre

Theatre has taken many forms in America over the years, from traditional Shakespearean plays, to vaudeville in the late 1800s and early 1900s, to musicals, to college and community productions. A profound change in American theatre occurred with the rise of the motion picture. From 1900 to 1920, the number of legitimate theatres in the country fell from 1,500 to 500. Yet, a rebound occurred during the prosperous 1920s on Broadway: 150 were added in 1920–21, and another 280 in 1927–28. Broadway reigned supreme from the late 1920s to the early 1950s, when "off-Broadway" productions started to appear in reaction to plays that many producers and theatregoers felt were too commercial and unartistic.

According to Peter Zeisler, in the introduction to *Theatre Profiles/3* (1977), "Until the 1950s, what professional theatre the American public saw was that which had been deemed 'successful' in London or New York. Professional theatre production was centered in New York, just as film and television is centered in California. Missouri could not see new work until it had been 'proved' in New York and, even then, not until it chugged into town as a 'road show'—often two years later. . . . Today, as much is going to New York as is coming from New York." *Theatre Profiles* is an annual publication of the Theatre Communications Group of New York City that lists all the repertory theatres in the country. Repertory theatres are those with a professional staff of actors in residence whose full-time job is acting. This differs of course from community theatres, whose actors are part-time, usually unpaid amateurs. In its survey of theatre in the metro areas, *Places Rated* includes only those theatres with annual budgets of $250,000 or more.

There are only 125 companies in the United States with such large budgets, and they are found in just 69 metro areas. Nineteen of these places have two or more qualifying companies; six have four or more.

Theatre: The Top 6 Metro Areas

Metro Area	Qualifying Theatres	Metro Area	Qualifying Theatres
1. New York, NY	21	4. Washington, DC–MD–VA	5
2. Chicago, IL	7	5. Los Angeles–Long Beach, CA	4
3. Minneapolis–St. Paul, MN–WI	6	5. Seattle, WA	4

Source: Theatre Communications Group, *Theatre Profiles/6,* New York, 1984.

Opera

Opera lovers boast that theirs is the greatest of the performing arts, for it combines orchestral and vocal music with theatre and often the dance. The first opera performed in America was the ballad opera *Flora, or Hob in the Well,* in 1735, at Charleston, South Carolina. The first grand opera was performed in 1825, at New York City's Park Theatre, Rossini's *Barber of Seville.* New York has continued to be the country's most important center for opera, but the art form has spread to all quadrants of the nation. From about 650 performing groups in 1969–70, opera expanded to nearly 1,000 groups in 1982, reaching an audience of more than ten million people.

Some of these performing groups are college and university workshops, whereas others are local clubs and choruses. But approximately 130 are companies with annual budgets exceeding $100,000. Full-scale opera productions using professional orchestras and bringing the world's leading singers to the stage are a costly business, and most metro areas haven't the resources or the audiences needed to support this performing art.

In surveying opera in the metropolitan areas, *Places Rated* relied on Opera America, an association of professional opera companies, and its *Profile: 1983,* which lists its members as of that year. The 68 opera companies that qualify by being so listed are fairly evenly distributed, with 59 metro areas having at least one company. Only eight metro areas have two or more opera companies:

Baltimore, MD (2)	New York, NY (3)
Boston, MA (2)	Philadelphia, PA–NJ (2)
Chicago, IL (2)	San Francisco, CA (2)
Houston, TX (2)	San Jose, CA (2)

Dance

Modern dance and ballet groups flourish throughout America. Ballet is most often found in big cities, but there are regional ballet associations with annual festivals in several parts of the country as well. The first was the Southeast Regional Ballet Festival Association, located in Atlanta, followed by similar groups in the Northeast and Southwest and on the West Coast. A tremendous boost to dance in this country came from the companies of Martha Graham, Merce Cunningham, and the Joffrey Ballet, and more lately from the "Dance in America" series on public television.

Many dance companies are small, because of the nature of the art form. Jazz and modern dance troupes, for example, seldom exceed ten dancers, and many "companies" are composed of between six and eight performers. To exclude these small companies purely on the basis of size would do an injustice to both the art form and the metro areas that are home to the troupes. Therefore, *Places Rated* has included even small groups and companies in its inventory of the arts, using *Dance Magazine Annual, '84* as a source.

Dance companies are one of the most common features on the American arts scene, numbering 400 shared among 133 metro areas. Of these places, 23 have five or more dance groups. The list below shows the metro areas with at least eight companies.

Dance Companies:
The Top 9 Metro Areas

Metro Area	Dance Companies
1. New York, NY	149
2. San Francisco, CA	22
3. Los Angeles–Long Beach, CA	20
4. Chicago, IL	18
5. Washington, DC–MD–VA	16
6. Philadelphia, PA–NJ	11
7. Boston, MA	9
7. Houston, TX	9
9. Oakland, CA	8

Source: Dance Magazine, Dance Magazine Annual, '84, 1983.

THE PUBLIC LIBRARY: SOMETHING FOR EVERYONE

Every metro area—no matter how small, poor, or isolated—has at least one public library. The public library is the one cultural facility that we have all experienced, regardless of educational background, income, or artistic enthusiasm. Besides books, most libraries also contain records, slides, filmstrips, magazines, and other items that may be used in the building or borrowed for free.

There are more than 8,500 public libraries in the United States, 5,500 of which are branch libraries of a city, county, or regional library system. When the libraries found on college campuses are included, the total comes to over 12,000. This figure, however, does not include the many thousands of libraries in elementary and high schools.

The largest public library system is the New York Public Library, which encompasses more than seven million volumes stored in 80 neighborhood branches. Yet, huge as it is, New York's library offers its citizens less than one volume per person. Although Boston has a smaller library (still impressive with almost five million volumes), it provides more than one and a half books per person. Buffalo's libraries supply nearly three and a half per person.

Public Libraries:
The 16 Metro Areas with the Most Volumes

Metro Area	Number of Volumes	Volumes per Capita
1. New York, NY	7,271,592	0.88
2. Boston, MA	4,916,277	1.75
3. Los Angeles–Long Beach, CA	4,602,998	0.62
4. Chicago, IL	4,383,710	0.72
5. Cleveland, OH	4,089,384	2.15
6. Buffalo, NY	3,467,124	3.41
7. Cincinnati, OH–KY–IN	3,332,926	2.38
8. Houston, TX	3,156,063	1.15
9. St. Louis, MO–IL	3,025,890	1.67
10. Philadelphia, PA–NJ	2,947,727	0.63
11. Detroit, MI	2,408,863	0.54
12. Honolulu, HI	2,241,156	2.94
13. Newark, NJ	2,231,560	1.19
14. Dallas, TX	2,105,231	1.08
15. Milwaukee, WI	2,096,002	1.50
16. Pittsburgh, PA	2,039,057	0.92

Source: R. R. Bowker, *American Library Directory,* 1983.

The number of volumes in a metro area's library tells only half the story of a place's reading habits; how much *use* those volumes get, or the library's circulation, is the other half. Circulation is expressed in terms of yearly checkouts. When we add that number to the number of library volumes and divide the sum by the population served by the library system, the result is what *Places Rated* calls the reading quotient, which may serve as a rough indicator of the reading habits of a given place. The reading quotients for the metro areas are given in the Place Profiles later in the chapter.

Most big cities have a reading quotient of between 3.0 and 5.0; the general metro area average is between 4.0 and 7.0. In the 12 metro areas that have reading quotients of 3.0 or lower, reading, at least as expressed in visits to and use of public libraries, is not a major pastime. But the 11 metro areas with reading quotients above 12.0 are places where the local libraries are used and used often.

Reading Quotients in the Metro Areas

Highest	Reading Quotient	Lowest	Reading Quotient
1. Bangor, ME	30.0	1. Canton, OH	2.0
2. Salem–Gloucester, MA	21.1	2. Binghamton, NY	2.1
3. Champaign–Urbana–Rantoul, IL	17.3	3. Longview–Marshall, TX	2.4
4. Pittsfield, MA	15.0	4. Fitchburg–Leominster, MA	2.6
5. Madison, WI	14.0	4. Fort Lauderdale–Hollywood–Pompano Beach, FL	2.6
6. Bloomington–Normal, IL	13.8	6. Biloxi–Gulfport, MS	2.7
7. Columbia, MO	13.7	7. Harrisburg–Lebanon–Carlisle, PA	2.8
7. Duluth, MN–WI	13.7	7. Williamsport, PA	2.8
9. Salinas–Seaside–Monterey, CA	13.2	9. Birmingham, AL	2.9
10. Bellingham, WA	12.3	10. Allentown–Bethlehem, PA–NJ	3.0
11. Salem, OR	12.2	10. Scranton–Wilkes-Barre, PA	3.0
		10. Wichita Falls, TX	3.0

Source: R. R. Bowker, *American Library Directory*, 1983, provided the information used to calculate the reading quotients.

What, if anything, can we surmise from the above tables? For one thing, it seems that the metro areas with the highest reading quotients tend to be small or medium-sized. Fairly heavy concentrations of avid readers are found in New England and the northern Midwest, whereas five of the metro areas with the lowest reading quotients are in the South. Climate may be a partial reason for differences in reading habits. Perhaps time spent reading increases as "ideal" outdoor weather decreases. This would explain the high reading quotients in the cold Midwest and New England, and generally lower scores in the South.

JUDGING SUPPLY OF CULTURAL FACILITIES

The nine categories of arts facilities we have described above include not hundreds but thousands of institutions throughout the country. To list all the facilities in each category for each metro area would require several books the size of this one. For example, the *Official Museum Directory* compiled by the American Association of Museums lists more than 3,000 museums in the United States; many are very specialized or are maintained by corporations for specific purposes. Many are very small and exist solely to make money or to serve as a tax shelter for those who own and operate them. Only a small portion are big enough in size and scope to be of real interest or importance to most people.

How can the significant institutions be winnowed out and used to assess the cultural climate of a place? Generally, we start by excluding institutions run for profit. Therefore, commercial television, commercial theatres and supper clubs, and libraries and museums that are appendages of corporations are not included. In addition, whenever possible, we rely on ratings and classifications devised and used by appropriate associations or accrediting bodies, such as the American Symphony Orchestra League and the American Association of Museums.

It can be argued that it is not possible to rank metro areas according to their cultural facilities with total fairness. Nevertheless, one can examine selected cultural variables and indicate their *supply* in the metro areas. We do not attempt here to judge the relative artistic merit of individual symphonies, museums, or operas but rather to indicate how they compare in size, frequency of performance, duration of broadcast, number of productions, and so forth.

In addition to the supply of the various facilities, *ease of access* to them is important. In a sense, the question is asked: How much of a thing can be used, seen, heard, enjoyed, visited, and how often, for how long, and how easily? Some facilities (museums, libraries, and fine arts radio stations, for example) have much more "use potential" than do others. Accordingly, their point potential is high.

In rating the metro areas for supply of cultural facilities, *Places Rated*'s approach is very similar to that taken in the first edition of this book. The nine categories of facilities are the same, although some adjustments have been made in how they are rated. One notable change was improving the criteria used to identify and evaluate universities for their cultural roles. Many more orchestras and dance companies are included.

A major new element is the addition of CMSA Access points, awarded in recognition of the fact that metro areas in close proximity tend to share certain major facilities such as airports, professional sports arenas, and outstanding health care facilities. In the case of the arts, each metro area that is part of a Consolidated Metropolitan Statistical Area (see the Appendix for a complete list) is eligible to receive bonus points for exceptional cultural facilities found in nearby metro areas, as explained in item 10 below.

Each metro area starts with a base score of zero, to which points are added according to the following indicators:

1. *Museums.* All museums meeting the basic criteria outlined earlier in this chapter receive a base score of 500 points. One hundred points is added to the score for each additional curator over the required minimum of three. The ceiling score for any museum is 2,000 points, which is quite

high. *Places Rated* believes that this high point potential accurately reflects the tremendous breadth of exhibits and collections of our major museums, as well as their accessibility to the general public.

2. *Fine arts and public radio.* Along with public television stations, these facilities offer an endless variety of cultural information and entertainment. Because of the scope of their subject matter and their extreme accessibility, their point potential is high. Radio stations receive from 200 to 500 points each, depending on their weekly broadcast time.

Weekly air time:	Points:
Less than 120 hours	200
120–140 hours	300
141–160 hours	400
More than 160 hours	500

If broadcast information is incomplete, stations receive the minimum 200 points.

3. *Public television.* Public television stations receive a constant score of 500 points each.

4. *Universities.* Four-year colleges and universities with enrollments of 2,000 students or more and offering at least one degree in the arts are eligible for points. The school's enrollment, divided by 100, is the number of points each institution contributes; universities have a point ceiling of 1,000.

5. *Symphony orchestras.* In this edition of *Places Rated Almanac,* from 100 to 500 points are awarded to each type of symphony orchestra recognized by the American Symphony Orchestra League. They are Major, Regional, Metropolitan, Urban, Community, College, and Youth. In the Place Profiles, four of the categories are readily identified by the number of stars that follow their names.

Type of orchestra:	Points:
Community, College, Youth	100
Urban (★)	200
Metropolitan (★★)	300
Regional (★★★)	400
Major (★★★★)	500

6. *Theatres.* Professional nonprofit repertory theatres listed in *Theatre Profiles/6* and having annual budgets of $250,000 or more receive points on the basis of their annual operating expenses. In the Place Profiles, the stars following a theatre's name indicate its budget level.

Annual budget:	Points:
Less than $1,000,000	100
$1,000,000 to $2,000,000 (★)	200
$2,000,000 to $3,000,000 (★★)	300
$3,000,000 to $4,000,000 (★★★)	400
$4,000,000 and over (★★★★)	500

7. *Opera companies.* Opera companies identified in Opera America's *Profile: 1983* as current and corresponding members receive a base score of 200 points. To this additional points are awarded according to the number of productions and performances. Some opera companies boast of many performances yet produce only two or three operas each season. To reflect this, the product of productions times performances is added to the base score. For example, the Mobile, Alabama, opera has three productions and ten performances. Thus its score is 200 plus 3 x 10, or 230 points. The ceiling for any opera company is 500 points.

8. *Dance companies. Places Rated* has identified 400 dance companies eligible for inclusion in the Place Profiles, drawing upon *Dance Magazine Annual, '84.* Each company so listed is awarded a minimum of 50 points. Additional points are awarded to some dance categories on the basis of the size of the troupe; one or two stars following a company's name in the Place Profiles indicate its troupe size and the number of points awarded. The ceiling for any dance company is 200 points.

Type of troupe:	Number of dancers:	Points:
All categories	No lower limit	50
Ethnic-Folk,		
Modern (★)	More than 15	100
Ballet (★)	More than 15	100
Ballet (★★)	40 or more	200

9. *Public libraries.* The points awarded for libraries are determined by their size as expressed in thousands of volumes. America's largest public library system is New York's, with 7,271,592 volumes. The New York metro area therefore receives 7,272 points for its libraries.

10. *CMSA Access.* Each of the 76 metro areas that is part of a Consolidated Metropolitan Statistical Area is eligible for bonus points based on certain outstanding or easily shared cultural facilities: major museums receiving 1,000 or more points; all public radio and television stations; four-star (Major) symphonies; theatres receiving one or more stars; all opera companies; and two-star dance companies. A place receives a bonus of 30 percent of the points accumulated by the *other* metro areas in the CMSA for these facilities; a metro area's *own* points are not considered in calculating its bonus. Thus, in the Detroit–Ann Arbor consolidated area, Ann Arbor receives 894 access points based on Detroit's 2,980 points for

Outstanding Cultural Assets

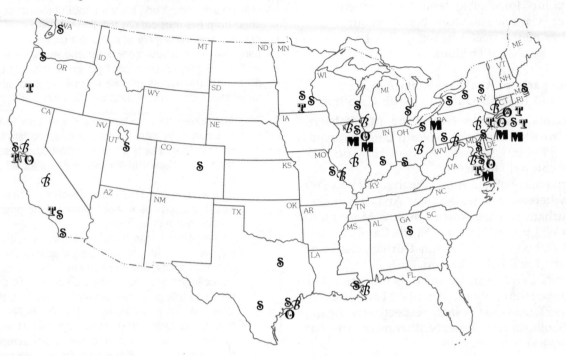

S   Major Symphony

ℬ   Best Ballet

O   Grand Opera

T   Outstanding Theatre

M   Elite Museum

America's Cultural Elite

In its inventory of the arts in America, *Places Rated* has compiled thousands of names of museums, symphony orchestras, theatres, operas, and ballet companies. But only a relative handful qualify as members of the cultural elite, receiving from *Places Rated* the maximum points for their respective categories.

The map shows, as might be expected, a large number of these institutions located in the Northeast. However, small pockets of cultural excellence also appear in the Midwest, Texas, and the West Coast. The symphony orchestras indicated on the map are the 30 Major symphonies listed on page 267.

Elite Museums

Below are the only museums in America that earn *Places Rated*'s highest possible score of 2,000 points:

American Museum of Natural History (New York, NY)
Art Institute of Chicago (Chicago, IL)
Cleveland Museum of Art (Cleveland, OH)
Field Museum of Natural History (Chicago, IL)
Metropolitan Museum of Art (New York, NY)
Smithsonian Institution (Washington, DC–MD–VA)

Outstanding Theatres

These theatres have annual operating budgets of more than $4 million, the highest in the country:

American Conservatory Theatre (San Francisco, CA)
Arena Stage (Washington, DC–MD–VA)
Circle in the Square (New York, NY)
Guthrie Theatre (Minneapolis–St. Paul, MN–WI)
Mark Taper Forum (Los Angeles–Long Beach, CA)
New York Shakespeare Festival (New York, NY)
Oregon Shakespeare Festival (Medford, OR)
Paper Mill Playhouse (Newark, NJ)

Grand Opera

The opera companies listed below were awarded the maximum number of points based on their number of productions and performances:

Houston Grand Opera (Houston, TX)
Lyric Opera of Chicago (Chicago, IL)
Metropolitan Opera (New York, NY)
New York City Opera (New York, NY)
San Francisco Opera (San Francisco, CA)
Washington Opera (Washington, DC–MD–VA)

Best Ballet Companies

The ballet companies that qualify for *Places Rated*'s highest rating with at least 40 dancers are the following:

American Ballet Theatre (New York, NY)
Ballet des Jeunes (Philadelphia, PA–NJ)
Bethesda Ballet Company (Washington, DC–MD–VA)
Columbus Theatre Ballet Association (Columbus, OH)
Crescent Ballet Company (New Orleans, LA)
Fresno Ballet (Fresno, CA)
Houston Ballet (Houston, TX)
Kasamon Ballet (Pittsburgh, PA)
Le Ballet Petit Dance Ensemble (Chicago, IL)
Rockford Company (Rockford, IL)
St. Charles Civic Ballet (St. Louis, MO–IL)
San Francisco Ballet (San Francisco, CA)
Springfield Ballet Company (Springfield, IL)

shared facilities, and Detroit receives a 750-point bonus thanks to Ann Arbor's total of 2,500 points for eligible facilities. Thirteen metro areas receive no access bonus because the other metro area(s) in the CMSA have none of the shared facilities.

Sample Comparison: Anaheim–Santa Ana, California, and Raleigh–Durham, North Carolina

Anaheim–Santa Ana ranks 49th in the arts; Raleigh–Durham, across the continent in North Carolina, ranks 47th. Only 98 points separate the two. How do they compare in cultural facilities?

In the inventory of museums, the first category, we see that whereas Anaheim–Santa Ana has none, Raleigh–Durham has the North Carolina Museum of Art (worth 600 points) and the North Carolina State Museum (1,000 points). So Raleigh–Durham chalks up an early lead, 1,600 points to zero.

The North Carolina metro area also has two fine arts and public radio stations, WSHA-FM and WUNC-FM, worth 500 and 300 points, respectively. Again, Anaheim–Santa Ana has none. Neither metro area has a public television station.

Both of our sample places do quite well as far as universities are concerned. Anaheim–Santa Ana is home to the Irvine branch of the University of California, worth 849 points, and the Fullerton campus of California State University, which contributes 1,000 points. Raleigh–Durham counters with Duke University (937 points) and the University of North Carolina at Chapel Hill (1,000 points). The standings for this scoring element are close, with Anaheim–Santa Ana raking in 1,849 points and Raleigh–Durham 1,937.

But in the next category, Symphony Orchestras, Anaheim–Santa Ana has the advantage. It earns 300 points for its one College and two Youth symphonies. Additionally, it receives 200 points for its Urban symphony and 300 points for its Metropolitan orchestra, the Orange County Pacific Symphony, for a total of 800 points. Raleigh–Durham comes up with only 500 points for its two symphonies, a Community orchestra (100 points) and a Regional one (400).

Each metro area has a repertory theatre. However, the South Coast Repertory Theatre in Anaheim–Santa Ana has a larger budget and therefore contributes more points (300) than does Raleigh–Durham's Playmakers Repertory Company (100). At this point the working total for our two places is 4,837 for Raleigh–Durham and 2,949 for Anaheim–Santa Ana.

There are no opera companies in these two metro areas. In supply of dance companies, they are fairly even. Neither has a major ballet, and the dance companies each does possess are rather small, adding only the minimum 50 points apiece. The three companies in Anaheim–Santa Ana yield 150 points, and the four in Raleigh–Durham 200.

New York, New York

"New York, New York, it's a wonderful town!" says the song from the musical *On the Town*. When it comes to the arts and the supply of cultural facilities, this certainly is true, for New York is far and away the winner in this category. Even a brief glance at this metro area's cultural assets reveals it to be the cultural capital of the United States, and perhaps the world:

- *Museums:* New York has no fewer than 18 major museums. Its total for museums alone is 17,600 points! That is only a few hundred points less than sixth-place Philadelphia's score for *all* cultural facilities.
- *Fine Arts Public Radio and Television:* New York has three stations in each category; no other metro area has as many.
- *Universities:* These cultural microcosms, the scoring element with perhaps the broadest cultural effect on a city, are plentiful here. Twelve qualifying colleges and universities contribute 10,017 points to this giant metro area—more than the total arts score posted by 15th-place Baltimore.
- *Symphony Orchestras:* New York has 21 symphony orchestras, including one Major symphony, one Regional symphony, and three Metropolitan symphonies.
- *Theatres:* Who knows the actual number of all the theatres in New York? The Big Apple has 21 that qualify for inclusion in *Places Rated Almanac*.
- *Opera Companies:* With three major professional opera companies, New York is far and away America's opera capital and one of the great opera centers of the world.
- *Dance Companies:* There are 149 dance companies in New York that meet *Places Rated*'s qualifications. Their total point contribution is 8,650, a figure greater than the overall arts score of 308 of the 329 metro areas.

These facilities, representing an unrivaled cornucopia of artistic and cultural riches, together with a library system of more than seven million volumes, combine to give the New York metro area a grand total of 56,745 points. Second-place Chicago, which earns 24,846 points, is not even close.

Public libraries, which represent the next-to-last category, are scored on the basis of their total volumes, with one point awarded for every 1,000 volumes. Anaheim–Santa Ana gains more points here since its library has 725,268 volumes (good for 725 points) compared with the 592,800 in Raleigh–Durham's (593 points). This disparity can be explained by the size of Anaheim–Santa Ana's population, which at 1,932,709 is nearly four times that of Raleigh–Durham's (561,222).

So far Raleigh–Durham is clearly in the lead, 5,730

to 3,824. Not only does it have more facilities; it also provides more relative to its size than does Anaheim–Santa Ana.

But adding in points for the tenth category, CMSA Access, nearly bridges the gap between the two metro areas. As part of the Los Angeles–Anaheim–Riverside consolidated area, Anaheim–Santa Ana is eligible for 30 percent of the total points earned for designated cultural facilities by the other three metro areas in the CMSA, which amounts to 1,808 points. This boosts Anaheim–Santa Ana's total score for the arts to 5,632 and puts it only two places behind Raleigh–Durham. Since Raleigh–Durham is not a member of a CMSA, it earns no points in this category.

Places Rated: Metro Areas Ranked for Supply of Cultural Facilities

Nine kinds of institutions or facilities are evaluated in arriving at a score for a metro area's cultural assets: (1) museums; (2) fine arts and public radio stations; (3) public television stations; (4) universities offering a degree or degrees in the arts; (5) symphony orchestras; (6) theatres; (7) opera companies; (8) dance companies; and (9) public libraries. Metro areas can also earn bonus points for shared facilities—major museums, public radio and television stations, major symphonies, certain theatres, operas, and selected dance companies—within their Consolidated Metropolitan Statistical Areas.

Places that receive tie scores are given the same rank and are listed in alphabetical order.

Metro Areas from Best to Worst

Places Rated Rank	Places Rated Score	Places Rated Rank	Places Rated Score	Places Rated Rank	Places Rated Score
1. New York, NY	56,745	31. Ann Arbor, MI	7,559	60. Louisville, KY–IN	4,916
2. Chicago, IL	24,846	31. Atlanta, GA	7,559		
3. Los Angeles–Long Beach, CA	23,567	33. Jersey City, NJ	7,420	61. Tucson, AZ	4,889
		34. Danbury, CT	7,415	62. Oklahoma City, OK	4,843
4. Washington, DC–MD–VA	21,701	35. Norwalk, CT	7,273	63. Miami–Hialeah, FL	4,837
5. Boston, MA	21,042			64. Albany–Schenectady– Troy, NY	4,655
		36. Honolulu, HI	7,168	65. Phoenix, AZ	4,573
6. Philadelphia, PA–NJ	17,270	37. Norfolk–Virginia Beach– Newport News, VA	7,087		
7. San Francisco, CA	14,226	38. Orange County, NY	6,987	66. Wilmington, DE–NJ–MD	4,545
8. Newark, NJ	14,224	39. Rochester, NY	6,956	67. Lincoln, NE	4,523
9. Cleveland, OH	12,679	40. Dayton–Springfield, OH	6,935	68. Albuquerque, NM	4,496
10. Minneapolis–St. Paul, MN–WI	11,714			69. Memphis, TN–AR–MS	4,486
		41. Columbus, OH	6,648	70. Sacramento, CA	4,483
11. Houston, TX	11,073	42. Fort Worth–Arlington, TX	6,466		
12. Pittsburgh, PA	11,069	43. San Jose, CA	6,446	71. Toledo, OH	4,389
13. Dallas, TX	10,438	44. Indianapolis, IN	6,348	72. Nashville, TN	4,342
14. Detroit, MI	10,389	45. Oakland, CA	6,162	73. Charlotte–Gastonia– Rock Hill, NC–SC	4,313
15. Baltimore, MD	9,788			74. Tacoma, WA	4,297
		46. Providence, RI	6,152	75. San Antonio, TX	4,295
16. Cincinnati, OH–KY–IN	9,688	47. Raleigh–Durham, NC	5,730		
17. Seattle, WA	9,577	48. Richmond–Petersburg, VA	5,697	76. Tulsa, OK	4,248
18. Bergen–Passaic, NJ	9,304	49. Anaheim–Santa Ana, CA	5,632	77. Baton Rouge, LA	4,237
19. St. Louis, MO–IL	8,896	50. Akron, OH	5,564	78. Lansing–East Lansing, MI	4,206
20. San Diego, CA	8,818			79. Greensboro–Winston-Salem– High Point, NC	4,188
		51. Kansas City, MO	5,553		
21. Milwaukee, WI	8,766	52. Salt Lake City–Ogden, UT	5,528	80. Gary–Hammond, IN	4,115
22. Nassau–Suffolk, NY	8,640	53. Austin, TX	5,355		
23. Buffalo, NY	8,567	54. Riverside–San Bernardino, CA	5,327	81. Birmingham, AL	3,958
24. Denver, CO	8,477	55. Portland, OR	5,160	82. Aurora–Elgin, IL	3,857
25. Bridgeport–Milford, CT	8,368			83. Kenosha, WI	3,844
		56. Madison, WI	5,123	84. El Paso, TX	3,800
26. Middlesex–Somerset– Hunterdon, NJ	8,058	57. Syracuse, NY	5,080	85. Omaha, NE–IA	3,787
27. New Orleans, LA	7,978	58. Tampa–St. Petersburg– Clearwater, FL	5,040		
28. Stamford, CT	7,865	59. Trenton, NJ	5,029	86. Santa Cruz, CA	3,748
29. New Haven–Meriden, CT	7,852			87. Lake County, IL	3,746
30. Monmouth–Ocean, NJ	7,563				

Places Rated Rank	Places Rated Score	Places Rated Rank	Places Rated Score	Places Rated Rank	Places Rated Score
88. Boulder–Longmont, CO	3,663	144. Jacksonville, FL	2,162	201. Pueblo, CO	1,307
89. Hartford, CT	3,616	145. Bloomington, IN	2,152	202. Bellingham, WA	1,302
90. Fresno, CA	3,596			203. San Angelo, TX	1,301
		146. Nashua, NH	2,122	204. Beaver County, PA	1,284
90. Lexington–Fayette, KY	3,596	147. Fargo–Moorhead, ND–MN	2,111	205. Lawton, OK	1,280
92. Athens, GA	3,546	147. Lawrence–Haverhill, MA–NH	2,111		
93. Springfield, MA	3,466	149. Vineland–Millville–Bridgeton, NJ	2,097	206. State College, PA	1,271
94. Santa Rosa–Petaluma, CA	3,457	150. Kalamazoo, MI	2,071	207. Roanoke, VA	1,263
95. Lubbock, TX	3,402			208. Greeley, CO	1,254
		151. Erie, PA	2,032	209. Amarillo, TX	1,235
96. Gainesville, FL	3,335	152. Fort Lauderdale–Hollywood–Pompano Beach, FL	2,027	210. McAllen–Edinburg–Mission, TX	1,231
97. Knoxville, TN	3,309	153. Bryan–College Station, TX	2,002		
98. Salem–Gloucester, MA	3,276	154. Brockton, MA	2,001	211. Terre Haute, IN	1,226
99. Grand Rapids, MI	3,255	155. Bangor, ME	1,995	212. Bakersfield, CA	1,222
100. Jackson, MS	3,209			213. Bismarck, ND	1,211
		156. Corpus Christi, TX	1,992	214. Racine, WI	1,171
101. Joliet, IL	3,177	157. Provo–Orem, UT	1,985	215. Kansas City, KS	1,167
102. Lawrence, KS	3,150	158. Springfield, IL	1,983		
103. Harrisburg–Lebanon–Carlisle, PA	3,083	159. Pensacola, FL	1,954	216. Appleton–Oshkosh–Neenah, WI	1,166
104. Lowell, MA–NH	3,057	160. Johnson City–Kingsport–Bristol, TN–VA	1,925	217. New London–Norwich, CT–RI	1,164
105. Waterloo–Cedar Falls, IA	3,000			218. Waco, TX	1,141
		161. Grand Forks, ND	1,921	219. Reading, PA	1,108
106. Charleston, SC	2,993	161. Huntsville, AL	1,921	220. Janesville–Beloit, WI	1,092
107. Spokane, WA	2,988	163. Fayetteville–Springdale, AR	1,915		
108. Wichita, KS	2,987	164. Evansville, IN–KY	1,876	221. Lynchburg, VA	1,079
109. Vallejo–Fairfield–Napa, CA	2,962	165. St. Cloud, MN	1,871	222. Wilmington, NC	1,077
110. West Palm Beach–Boca Raton–Delray Beach, FL	2,888			223. Elmira, NY	1,048
		166. Columbus, GA–AL	1,861	224. Augusta, GA–SC	1,047
111. Columbia, MO	2,882	167. Des Moines, IA	1,857	225. Rockford, IL	1,026
112. Fort Wayne, IN	2,846	168. Medford, OR	1,856		
113. Shreveport, LA	2,826	169. Scranton–Wilkes-Barre, PA	1,832	226. York, PA	1,022
114. Las Cruces, NM	2,804	170. Eau Claire, WI	1,807	227. Florence, AL	1,021
115. Youngstown–Warren, OH	2,797			228. Davenport–Rock Island–Moline, IA–IL	1,017
		171. Beaumont–Port Arthur, TX	1,795	229. Lancaster, PA	1,015
116. Oxnard–Ventura, CA	2,769	172. Worcester, MA	1,784	230. Salinas–Seaside–Monterey, CA	1,004
117. Santa Barbara–Santa Maria–Lompoc, CA	2,684	173. Lafayette, LA	1,772		
118. Orlando, FL	2,681	174. Mobile, AL	1,764	231. Abilene, TX	996
119. South Bend–Mishawaka, IN	2,672	175. Galveston–Texas City, TX	1,756	231. Yakima, WA	996
120. Eugene–Springfield, OR	2,631			233. Canton, OH	989
		176. Colorado Springs, CO	1,749	234. Niagara Falls, NY	966
121. Charleston, WV	2,605	177. Burlington, VT	1,741	235. Killeen–Temple, TX	920
122. Greenville–Spartanburg, SC	2,569	178. Saginaw–Bay City–Midland, MI	1,708		
123. Lorain–Elyria, OH	2,565	179. Chico, CA	1,647	236. Cedar Rapids, IA	904
124. Green Bay, WI	2,547	180. Springfield, MO	1,634	236. East St. Louis–Belleville, IL	904
125. Muncie, IN	2,498			238. St. Joseph, MO	879
		181. Topeka, KS	1,632	239. Utica–Rome, NY	858
126. Columbia, SC	2,489	182. Fort Collins–Loveland, CO	1,609	240. Redding, CA	845
127. Chattanooga, TN–GA	2,483	183. Binghamton, NY	1,599		
128. Boise City, ID	2,385	184. Las Vegas, NV	1,586	241. Fayetteville, NC	844
129. Duluth, MN–WI	2,377	185. Stockton, CA	1,579	242. Hagerstown, MD	825
130. Portland, ME	2,351			243. Sarasota, FL	817
		186. Vancouver, WA	1,557	244. Daytona Beach, FL	809
131. Anchorage, AK	2,346	187. Monroe, LA	1,528	245. Owensboro, KY	804
132. Allentown–Bethlehem, PA–NJ	2,333	188. Brazoria, TX	1,506		
133. Hamilton–Middletown, OH	2,316	189. Alton–Granite City, IL	1,487	246. Poughkeepsie, NY	785
134. Peoria, IL	2,294	190. Bloomington–Normal, IL	1,470	247. Billings, MT	778
135. Savannah, GA	2,262			248. Rochester, MN	769
		191. La Crosse, WI	1,466	249. New Bedford, MA	766
136. Iowa City, IA	2,255	192. Lake Charles, LA	1,456	250. Wausau, WI	761
137. Lafayette, IN	2,236	193. Macon–Warner Robins, GA	1,435		
138. Reno, NV	2,210	194. Tuscaloosa, AL	1,432	251. Panama City, FL	755
139. Champaign–Urbana–Rantoul, IL	2,203	195. Charlottesville, VA	1,422	252. Fall River, MA–RI	749
140. Huntington–Ashland, WV–KY–OH	2,195			253. Lewiston–Auburn, ME	736
		196. Sioux City, IA–NE	1,393	254. Middletown, CT	730
141. Tallahassee, FL	2,181	197. Asheville, NC	1,391	255. Houma–Thibodaux, LA	725
142. Little Rock–North Little Rock, AR	2,180	198. Montgomery, AL	1,374		
143. Flint, MI	2,163	199. New Britain, CT	1,360	256. Olympia, WA	708
		200. Lima, OH	1,352	257. Salem, OR	691
				258. Biloxi–Gulfport, MS	679

Places Rated Rank	Places Rated Score	Places Rated Rank	Places Rated Score	Places Rated Rank	Places Rated Score
259. Johnstown, PA	666	282. Cumberland, MD–WV	373	308. Portsmouth–Dover–Rochester, NH–ME	165
260. Modesto, CA	631	282. Pine Bluff, AR	373	309. Brownsville–Harlingen, TX	162
		284. Fort Pierce, FL	368	310. Pascagoula, MS	155
261. Florence, SC	628	285. Battle Creek, MI	354		
262. Atlantic City, NJ	621			311. Bradenton, FL	154
263. Glens Falls, NY	603	286. Elkhart–Goshen, IN	353	312. Gadsden, AL	153
264. Wichita Falls, TX	599	287. Dubuque, IA	340	313. Laredo, TX	150
265. Jacksonville, NC	567	288. Alexandria, LA	334	314. Steubenville–Weirton, OH–WV	147
		288. Longview–Marshall, TX	334	315. Fort Smith, AR–OK	145
266. Mansfield, OH	554	290. Jackson, MI	323		
267. Muskegon, MI	529			316. Burlington, NC	131
267. Richland–Kennewick–Pasco, WA	529	291. Waterbury, CT	318	317. Yuba City, CA	122
269. Bristol, CT	514	292. Lakeland–Winter Haven, FL	309	318. Dothan, AL	117
270. Visalia–Tulare–Porterville, CA	511	293. Casper, WY	303	319. Clarksville–Hopkinsville, TN–KY	111
		294. Decatur, IL	298	320. Parkersburg–Marietta, WV–OH	91
271. Pawtucket–Woonsocket–Attleboro, RI–MA	480	295. Kokomo, IN	285		
272. Manchester, NH	475			321. Fort Walton Beach, FL	87
273. Sioux Falls, SD	465	296. Fitchburg–Leominster, MA	270	321. Victoria, TX	87
274. Midland, TX	438	297. Anniston, AL	268	323. Danville, VA	85
275. Melbourne–Titusville–Palm Bay, FL	437	297. Sheboygan, WI	268	324. Joplin, MO	80
		299. Ocala, FL	266	325. Benton Harbor, MI	79
276. Anderson, IN	430	300. Odessa, TX	259		
277. Wheeling, WV–OH	422			326. Kankakee, IL	75
278. Tyler, TX	404	301. Altoona, PA	256	327. Sherman–Denison, TX	68
279. Great Falls, MT	401	302. Albany, GA	237	328. Texarkana, TX–Texarkana, AR	63
280. Bremerton, WA	382	303. Pittsfield, MA	228	329. Sharon, PA	52
		304. Enid, OK	215		
281. Fort Myers, FL	380	305. Williamsport, PA	196		
		306. Hickory, NC	188		
		307. Anderson, SC	169		

Metro Areas Listed Alphabetically

Metro Area	Places Rated Rank	Metro Area	Places Rated Rank	Metro Area	Places Rated Rank
Abilene, TX	231	Beaumont–Port Arthur, TX	171	Cedar Rapids, IA	236
Akron, OH	50			Champaign–Urbana–Rantoul, IL	139
Albany, GA	302	Beaver County, PA	204	Charleston, SC	106
Albany–Schenectady–Troy, NY	64	Bellingham, WA	202		
Albuquerque, NM	68	Benton Harbor, MI	325	Charleston, WV	121
		Bergen–Passaic, NJ	18	Charlotte–Gastonia–Rock Hill, NC–SC	73
Alexandria, LA	288	Billings, MT	247	Charlottesville, VA	195
Allentown–Bethlehem, PA–NJ	132			Chattanooga, TN–GA	127
Alton–Granite City, IL	189	Biloxi–Gulfport, MS	258	Chicago, IL	2
Altoona, PA	301	Binghamton, NY	183		
Amarillo, TX	209	Birmingham, AL	81	Chico, CA	179
		Bismarck, ND	213	Cincinnati, OH–KY–IN	16
Anaheim–Santa Ana, CA	49	Bloomington, IN	145	Clarksville–Hopkinsville, TN–KY	319
Anchorage, AK	131			Cleveland, OH	9
Anderson, IN	276	Bloomington–Normal, IL	190	Colorado Springs, CO	176
Anderson, SC	307	Boise City, ID	128		
Ann Arbor, MI	31	Boston, MA	5	Columbia, MO	126
		Boulder–Longmont, CO	88	Columbia, SC	125
Anniston, AL	297	Bradenton, FL	311	Columbus, GA–AL	166
Appleton–Oshkosh–Neenah, WI	216			Columbus, OH	41
Asheville, NC	197	Brazoria, TX	188	Corpus Christi, TX	156
Athens, GA	92	Bremerton, WA	280		
Atlanta, GA	31	Bridgeport–Milford, CT	25	Cumberland, MD–WV	282
		Bristol, CT	269	Dallas, TX	13
Atlantic City, NJ	262	Brockton, MA	154	Danbury, CT	34
Augusta, GA–SC	224			Danville, VA	323
Aurora–Elgin, IL	82	Brownsville–Harlingen, TX	309	Davenport–Rock Island–Moline, IA–IL	228
Austin, TX	53	Bryan–College Station, TX	153		
Bakersfield, CA	212	Buffalo, NY	23	Dayton–Springfield, OH	39
		Burlington, NC	316	Daytona Beach, FL	244
Baltimore, MD	15	Burlington, VT	177	Decatur, IL	294
Bangor, ME	155			Denver, CO	24
Baton Rouge, LA	77	Canton, OH	233		
Battle Creek, MI	285	Casper, WY	293		

Metro Area	Places Rated Rank	Metro Area	Places Rated Rank	Metro Area	Places Rated Rank
Des Moines, IA	167	Jersey City, NJ	33	Nashville, TN	72
				Nassau–Suffolk, NY	22
Detroit, MI	14	Johnson City–Kingsport–Bristol,		New Bedford, MA	249
Dothan, AL	318	TN–VA	160	New Britain, CT	199
Dubuque, IA	287	Johnstown, PA	259	New Haven–Meriden, CT	29
Duluth, MN–WI	129	Joliet, IL	101		
East St. Louis–Belleville, IL	236	Joplin, MO	324	New London–Norwich, CT–RI	217
		Kalamazoo, MI	150	New Orleans, LA	27
Eau Claire, WI	170			New York, NY	1
El Paso, TX	84	Kankakee, IL	326	Newark, NJ	8
Elkhart–Goshen, IN	286	Kansas City, KS	215	Niagara Falls, NY	234
Elmira, NY	223	Kansas City, MO	51		
Enid, OK	304	Kenosha, WI	83	Norfolk–Virginia Beach–	
		Killeen–Temple, TX	235	Newport News, VA	37
Erie, PA	151			Norwalk, CT	35
Eugene–Springfield, OR	120	Knoxville, TN	97	Oakland, CA	45
Evansville, IN–KY	164	Kokomo, IN	295	Ocala, FL	299
Fall River, MA–RI	252	La Crosse, WI	191	Odessa, TX	300
Fargo–Moorhead, ND–MN	147	Lafayette, IN	137		
		Lafayette, LA	173	Oklahoma City, OK	62
Fayetteville, NC	241			Olympia, WA	256
Fayetteville–Springdale, AR	163	Lake Charles, LA	192	Omaha, NE–IA	85
Fitchburg–Leominster, MA	296	Lake County, IL	87	Orange County, NY	38
Flint, MI	143	Lakeland–Winter Haven, FL	292	Orlando, FL	118
Florence, AL	227	Lancaster, PA	229		
		Lansing–East Lansing, MI	78	Owensboro, KY	245
Florence, SC	261			Oxnard–Ventura, CA	116
Fort Collins–Loveland, CO	182	Laredo, TX	313	Panama City, FL	251
Fort Lauderdale–Hollywood–		Las Cruces, NM	114	Parkersbury–Marietta, WV–OH	320
Pompano Beach, FL	152	Las Vegas, NV	184	Pascagoula, MS	310
Fort Myers, FL	281	Lawrence, KS	102		
Fort Pierce, FL	284	Lawrence–Haverhill, MA–NH	147	Pawtucket–Woonsocket–Attleboro,	
				RI–MA	271
Fort Smith, AR–OK	315	Lawton, OK	205	Pensacola, FL	159
Fort Walton Beach, FL	321	Lewiston–Auburn, ME	253	Peoria, IL	134
Fort Wayne, IN	112	Lexington–Fayette, KY	90	Philadelphia, PA–NJ	6
Fort Worth–Arlington, TX	42	Lima, OH	200	Phoenix, AZ	65
Fresno, CA	90	Lincoln, NE	67		
				Pine Bluff, AR	282
Gadsden, AL	312	Little Rock–North Little Rock, AR	142	Pittsburgh, PA	12
Gainesville, FL	96	Longview–Marshall, TX	288	Pittsfield, MA	303
Galveston–Texas City, TX	175	Lorain–Elyria, OH	123	Portland, ME	130
Gary–Hammond, IN	80	Los Angeles–Long Beach, CA	3	Portland, OR	55
Glens Falls, NY	263	Louisville, KY–IN	60		
				Portsmouth–Dover–Rochester,	
Grand Forks, ND	161	Lowell, MA–NH	104	NH–ME	308
Grand Rapids, MI	99	Lubbock, TX	95	Poughkeepsie, NY	246
Great Falls, MT	279	Lynchburg, VA	221	Providence, RI	46
Greeley, CO	208	Macon–Warner Robins, GA	193	Provo–Orem, UT	157
Green Bay, WI	124	Madison, WI	56	Pueblo, CO	201
Greensboro–Winston-Salem–		Manchester, NH	272	Racine, WI	214
High Point, NC	79	Mansfield, OH	266	Raleigh–Durham, NC	47
Greenville–Spartanburg, SC	122	McAllen–Edinburg–Mission, TX	210	Reading, PA	219
Hagerstown, MD	242	Medford, OR	168	Redding, CA	240
Hamilton–Middletown, OH	133	Melbourne–Titusville–Palm Bay, FL	275	Reno, NV	138
Harrisburg–Lebanon–Carlisle, PA	103				
		Memphis, TN–AR–MS	69	Richland–Kennewick–Pasco, WA	267
Hartford, CT	89	Miami–Hialeah, FL	63	Richmond–Petersburg, VA	48
Hickory, NC	306	Middlesex–Somerset–Hunterdon, NJ	26	Riverside–San Bernardino, CA	54
Honolulu, HI	36	Middletown, CT	254	Roanoke, VA	207
Houma–Thibodaux, LA	255	Midland, TX	274	Rochester, MN	248
Houston, TX	11				
		Milwaukee, WI	21	Rochester, NY	39
Huntington–Ashland, WV–KY–OH	140	Minneapolis–St. Paul, MN–WI	10	Rockford, IL	225
Huntsville, AL	161	Mobile, AL	174	Sacramento, CA	70
Indianapolis, IN	44	Modesto, CA	260	Saginaw–Bay City–Midland, MI	178
Iowa City, IA	136	Monmouth–Ocean, NJ	30	St. Cloud, MN	165
Jackson, MI	290				
		Monroe, LA	187	St. Joseph, MO	238
Jackson, MS	100	Montgomery, AL	198	St. Louis, MO–IL	19
Jacksonville, FL	144	Muncie, IN	125	Salem, OR	257
Jacksonville, NC	265	Muskegon, MI	267	Salem–Gloucester, MA	98
Janesville–Beloit, WI	220	Nashua, NH	146	Salinas–Seaside–Monterey, CA	230

Metro Area	Places Rated Rank	Metro Area	Places Rated Rank	Metro Area	Places Rated Rank
Salt Lake City–Ogden, UT	52	Springfield, MA	93	Vancouver, WA	186
San Angelo, TX	203	Springfield, MO	180	Victoria, TX	321
San Antonio, TX	75	Stamford, CT	28		
San Diego, CA	20			Vineland–Millville–	
San Francisco, CA	7	State College, PA	206	Bridgeton, NJ	149
		Steubenville–Weirton,		Visalia–Tulare–Porterville, CA	270
San Jose, CA	43	OH–WV	314	Waco, TX	218
Santa Barbara–Santa Maria–		Stockton, CA	185	Washington, DC–MD–VA	4
Lompoc, CA	117	Syracuse, NY	57	Waterbury, CT	291
Santa Cruz, CA	86	Tacoma, WA	74		
Santa Rosa–Petaluma, CA	94			Waterloo–Cedar Falls, IA	105
Sarasota, FL	243	Tallahassee, FL	141	Wausau, WI	250
		Tampa–St. Petersburg–		West Palm Beach–Boca Raton–	
Savannah, GA	135	Clearwater, FL	58	Delray Beach, FL	110
Scranton–Wilkes-Barre, PA	169	Terre Haute, IN	211	Wheeling, WV–OH	277
Seattle, WA	17	Texarkana, TX–Texarkana, AR	328	Wichita, KS	108
Sharon, PA	329	Toledo, OH	71		
Sheboygan, WI	297			Wichita Falls, TX	264
		Topeka, KS	181	Williamsport, PA	305
Sherman–Denison, TX	327	Trenton, NJ	59	Wilmington, DE–NJ–MD	66
Shreveport, LA	113	Tucson, AZ	61	Wilmington, NC	222
Sioux City, IA–NE	196	Tulsa, OK	76	Worcester, MA	172
Sioux Falls, SD	273	Tuscaloosa, AL	194		
South Bend–Mishawaka, IN	119			Yakima, WA	231
		Tyler, TX	278	York, PA	226
Spokane, WA	107	Utica–Rome, NY	239	Youngstown–Warren, OH	115
Springfield, IL	158	Vallejo–Fairfield–Napa, CA	109	Yuba City, CA	317

Place Profiles: Cultural Facilities of 329 Metro Areas

In the pages that follow, some of the cultural facilities of the 329 metropolitan areas are profiled. The information is derived from a number of sources: American Association of Museums, *Official Museum Directory*, National Register Publishing Company, 1982; Corporation for Public Broadcasting, *CPB Public Broadcasting Directory, 1983–84*, Washington, 1983, and unpublished data, 1984; *Lovejoy's College Guide*, 16th ed., and *College Blue Book*, 19th ed.; American Symphony Orchestra League, *Symphony Magazine*, Vol. 34, No. 6, December 1983; Theatre Communications Group, *Theatre Profiles/6*, New York, 1984; Opera America, *Profile: 1983*, Washington, 1984; *Dance Magazine, Dance Magazine Annual, '84*, 1983; and R. R. Bowker, *American Library Directory*, 1983.

Under the heading Museums are listed the institutions meeting the *Places Rated Almanac* guidelines. The number in parentheses following the museum's name shows the points awarded according to *Places Rated's* scoring criteria.

Fine arts and public radio stations are listed by their identifying call letters and dial number. East of the Mississippi River, call letters begin with a W; west of the Mississippi, they begin with a K. When such information is available, the station's broadcast radius and average weekly air time are also given. In many instances, a station's broadcast range is great enough that its programs may be received in metro areas other than the originating one. This is also the case with public television stations.

The colleges and universities named are the four-year institutions of higher learning that meet *Places Rated's* requirements: an undergraduate enrollment of 2,000 or more students, and degree programs in any of six arts-related courses of study. Each university's name is followed by the number of points it contributes to its metro area's score. A bullet (•) in an institution's listing means that it offers degrees in four of the six possible arts-related fields; two bullets indicate degree programs available in five or more fields.

Symphony orchestras listed are members of the American Symphony Orchestra League. Community, College, and Youth orchestras are listed by name only. Other categories recognized by the league may be identified by the stars appended to their names: ★ = Urban; ★★ = Metropolitan; ★★★ = Regional; ★★★★ = Major.

Only nonprofit professional theatres with an annual budget of $250,000 or more are included in the profiles. If a theatre's budget is $1 million or more, its budget range is indicated by the stars following its name: ★ = $1 million to $2 million; ★★ = $2 million to $3 million; ★★★ = $3 million to $4 million; ★★★★ = $4 million or more.

Opera companies that appear in the profiles are members of Opera America. Their names are accompanied by the yearly number of productions and performances. Four-star opera companies are those that receive the maximum number of points possible under *Places Rated*'s system.

If the name of a dance company does not indicate its principal artistic focus, the company's name is followed by a letter or letters in parentheses: B = ballet; E-F = ethnic-folk; J = jazz; and M = modern. Most dance companies have only a few full-time dancers; classical ballet typically requires the greatest number and jazz the smallest. In the profiles, larger dance companies are identified by a star or stars. A single star indicates 25 to 39 dancers for a ballet company and 15 or more dancers for an ethnic-folk or modern dance troupe. A ballet company that employs 40 or more dancers is indicated by two stars.

Circulation figures given for public libraries represent total number of annual checkouts. The reading quotient for each metro area is calculated by adding library volumes to circulation and dividing by population served (this is not always the same as the metro area population); an NA indicates that available data are insufficient for deriving the reading quotient.

A star preceding a metro area's name highlights it as one of the top 25 places for cultural facilities.

Abilene, TX
Universities:
  Abilene Christian University (350)
  Hardin-Simmons University (210)
Symphony Orchestras:
  Abilene Philharmonic★
Public Libraries:
  235,894 volumes; circulation 273,656
Reading Quotient: 4.6
Places Rated Score: 996
Places Rated Rank: 231

Akron, OH
Public Television:
  WEAO Channel 49
Universities:
  Kent State University (1,000)
  University of Akron (1,000)
Symphony Orchestras:
  Akron Symphony Orchestra★★
  Akron Youth Symphony
Dance Companies:
  Ohio Ballet
Public Libraries:
  1,073,099 volumes; circulation
  2,014,701
Reading Quotient: 7.1
CMSA Access: CLEVELAND–AKRON–
  LORAIN, OH (1,541)
Places Rated Score: 5,564
Places Rated Rank: 50

Albany, GA
Symphony Orchestras:
  Albany Symphony Orchestra
  (Community)
Public Libraries:
  136,882 volumes; circulation NA
Reading Quotient: NA
Places Rated Score: 237
Places Rated Rank: 302

Albany–Schenectady–Troy, NY
Museums:
  New York State Museum (700)
  Schenectady Museum (600)
Fine Arts and Public Radio:
  WAMC-FM 90.3 (110 mi; 84 hrs)
  WMHT-FM 89.1 (70 mi; 168 hrs)
Public Television:
  WMNT Channel 17
Universities:
  SUNY at Albany (1,000)
  Union College (200)

Symphony Orchestras:
  Albany Symphony Orchestra★★
  Empire State Youth Orchestra
Theatres:
  Capitol Repertory Company
Public Libraries:
  454,546 volumes; circulation 1,114,735
Reading Quotient: 7.6
Places Rated Score: 4,655
Places Rated Rank: 64

Albuquerque, NM
Museums:
  Albuquerque Museum (600)
  Maxwell Museum of Anthropology (900)
Fine Arts and Public Radio:
  KUNM-FM 90.1 (100 mi; 163 hrs)
Public Television:
  KNME Channel 22
Universities:
  University of Albuquerque (206)
  University of New Mexico (785)••
Symphony Orchestras:
  Albuquerque Youth Symphony
  Chamber Orchestra of Albuquerque
  (Community)
  New Mexico Symphony Orchestra★★★
Public Libraries:
  404,782 volumes; circulation 1,725,000
Reading Quotient: 5.2
Places Rated Score: 4,496
Places Rated Rank: 68

Alexandria, LA
Symphony Orchestras:
  Rapides Symphony Orchestra
  (Community)
Public Libraries:
  233,781 volumes; circulation 538,760
Reading Quotient: 5.7
Places Rated Score: 334
Places Rated Rank: 288

Allentown–Bethlehem, PA–NJ
Museums:
  Allentown Art Museum (500)
Public Television:
  WLVT Channel 39
Universities:
  Lafayette College (205)
  Lehigh University (432)
Symphony Orchestras:
  Allentown Symphony (Community)
Theatres:
  Pennsylvania Stage Company

Dance Companies:
  Ballet Guild of Lehigh Valley★
Public Libraries:
  395,750 volumes; circulation 1,324,584
Reading Quotient: 3.0
Places Rated Score: 2,333
Places Rated Rank: 132

Alton–Granite City, IL
Universities:
  Southern Illinois University, Edwardsville
  (602)
Public Libraries:
  217,464 volumes; circulation 463,767
Reading Quotient: 9.5
CMSA Access: ST. LOUIS–EAST ST.
  LOUIS–ALTON, MO–IL (668)
Places Rated Score: 1,487
Places Rated Rank: 189

Altoona, PA
Symphony Orchestras:
  Altoona Symphony Orchestra
  (Community)
Public Libraries:
  156,065 volumes; circulation 314,817
Reading Quotient: 6.7
Places Rated Score: 256
Places Rated Rank: 301

Amarillo, TX
Universities:
  West Texas State University (546)
Symphony Orchestras:
  Amarillo Symphony★★
Public Libraries:
  389,007 volumes; circulation 788,537
Reading Quotient: 7.6
Places Rated Score: 1,235
Places Rated Rank: 209

Anaheim–Santa Ana, CA
Universities:
  California State University, Fullerton
  (1,000)
  University of California, Irvine (849)
Symphony Orchestras:
  Chapman Symphony Orchestra
  (College)
  Orange County Pacific Symphony★★
  Orange County Youth Symphony
  Southeast Youth Symphony Orchestra
  Symphony West★
Theatres:
  South Coast Repertory Theatre★★

Dance Companies:
  Gloria Newman Dance Theatre (M)
  Matti Lascoe Dance Theatre
    Company (M)
  Penrod–Plastino Movement Theatre (M)
Public Libraries:
  725,268 volumes; circulation 2,197,160
Reading Quotient: 6.7
CMSA Access: Los Angeles–Anaheim–
  Riverside, CA (1,808)
Places Rated Score: 5,632
Places Rated Rank: 49

Anchorage, AK
Fine Arts and Public Radio:
  KSKA-FM 91.1 (147 hrs)
Public Television:
  KAKM Channel 7
Universities:
  University of Alaska (363)
Symphony Orchestras:
  Anchorage Symphony Orchestra
    (Community)
  Anchorage Youth Symphony
Theatres:
  Alaska Repertory Theatre★★
Opera Companies:
  Anchorage Civic Opera
    3 productions; 18 performances
Dance Companies:
  Anchorage Civic Ballet
Public Libraries:
  278,580 volumes; circulation 698,424
Reading Quotient: 5.2
Places Rated Score: 2,346
Places Rated Rank: 131

Anderson, IN
Symphony Orchestras:
  Anderson Symphony Orchestra
    (Community)
Public Libraries:
  330,252 volumes; circulation 371,515
Reading Quotient: 9.7
Places Rated Score: 430
Places Rated Rank: 276

Anderson, SC
Public Libraries:
  169,406 volumes; circulation 404,923
Reading Quotient: 4.3
Places Rated Score: 169
Places Rated Rank: 307

Ann Arbor, MI
Museums:
  Herbarium of the University of Michigan
    (1,000)
  Kelsey Museum of Ancient and
    Medieval Archeology (600)
  University of Michigan Museum of
    Anthropology (1,200)
  University of Michigan Museum of
    Zoology (500)
Fine Arts and Public Radio:
  WUOM-FM 91.7 (41 mi; 135 hrs)
Universities:
  Eastern Michigan University (1,000)
  University of Michigan (1,000)••
Symphony Orchestras:
  Ann Arbor Chamber Orchestra★
  Michigan Youth Orchestra
  University of Michigan Orchestra
Dance Companies:
  Ann Arbor Ballet Theatre★
  Ann Arbor Civic Ballet★
  Malini's Dances of India Troupe (E-F)

University of Michigan Dance
  Company (M)
Public Libraries:
  125,000 volumes; circulation 919,317
Reading Quotient: 7.9
CMSA Access: Detroit–Ann Arbor,
  MI (894)
Places Rated Score: 7,559
Places Rated Rank: 31

Anniston, AL
Theatres:
  Alabama Shakespeare Festival
Public Libraries:
  167,856 volumes; circulation 233,896
Reading Quotient: 3.4
Places Rated Score: 268
Places Rated Rank: 297

Appleton–Oshkosh–Neenah, WI
Universities:
  University of Wisconsin, Oshkosh (696)
Symphony Orchestras:
  Oshkosh Symphony Orchestra
    (Community)
Public Libraries:
  370,343 volumes; circulation 946,231
Reading Quotient: 11.3
Places Rated Score: 1,166
Places Rated Rank: 216

Asheville, NC
Fine Arts and Public Radio:
  WCQS-FM 88.5 (72 hrs)
Public Television:
  WUNF Channel 33
Universities:
  University of North Carolina, Asheville
    (227)
Symphony Orchestras:
  Asheville Symphony Orchestra ★
Public Libraries:
  264,023 volumes; circulation 726,126
Reading Quotient: 6.2
Places Rated Score: 1,391
Places Rated Rank: 197

Athens, GA
Museums:
  Clarke Heritage Foundation (500)
  University of Georgia Museum of Art
    (500)
  University of Georgia Museum of
    Natural History (800)
Public Television:
  WGTV Channel 8
Universities:
  University of Georgia (1,000)
Dance Companies:
  Athens Ballet Theatre
Public Libraries:
  195,937 volumes; circulation NA
Reading Quotient: NA
Places Rated Score: 3,546
Places Rated Rank: 92

Atlanta, GA
Museums:
  Fernbank Science Center (500)
  High Museum of Art (700)
Fine Arts and Public Radio:
  WABE-FM 90.1 (45 mi; 168 hrs)
  WCLK-FM 91.9 (20 mi; 168 hrs)
Public Television:
  WETV Channel 30
Universities:
  Clark College (204)
  Emory University (308)

Georgia State University (934)•
  Kennesaw College (413)
Symphony Orchestras:
  Atlanta Community Orchestra
  Atlanta Symphony Orchestra ★★★★
  Atlanta Symphony Youth Orchestra
  Atlanta–Emory Orchestra (College)
  Georgia State University Orchestra
Theatres:
  Academy Theatre
  Alliance Theatre Company/Atlanta
    Children's Theatre★★
Dance Companies:
  Atlanta Ballet
  Carl Ratcliff Dance Theatre (M)
  Gwinnett Ballet Theatre
  Ruth Mitchell Dance Company
Public Libraries:
  1,500,000 volumes; circulation
    4,500,000
Reading Quotient: 10.3
Places Rated Score: 7,559
Places Rated Rank: 31

Atlantic City, NJ
Universities:
  Stockton State College (494)
Dance Companies:
  Atlantic Contemporary Ballet Theatre
Public Libraries:
  76,851 volumes; circulation 115,533
Reading Quotient: 4.8
Places Rated Score: 621
Places Rated Rank: 262

Augusta, GA–SC
Universities:
  Augusta College (208)
Symphony Orchestras:
  Augusta Symphony Orchestra★
Opera Companies:
  Augusta Opera Association, Inc.
    2 productions; 4 performances
Dance Companies:
  Augusta Ballet Company
Public Libraries:
  380,788 volumes; circulation 771,571
Reading Quotient: 4.2
Places Rated Score: 1,047
Places Rated Rank: 224

Aurora–Elgin, IL
Symphony Orchestras:
  Elgin Area Youth Orchestra
  Elgin Symphony Orchestra★
  Fox River Symphony Orchestra
    (Community)
Public Libraries:
  411,122 volumes; circulation 1,067,685
Reading Quotient: 9.5
CMSA Access: Chicago–Gary–Lake
  County, IL–IN–WI (3,046)
Places Rated Score: 3,857
Places Rated Rank: 82

Austin, TX
Museums:
  Texas Memorial Museum (2,000)
Fine Arts and Public Radio:
  KUT-FM 90.5 (42 mi; 168 hrs)
Public Television:
  KLRU Channel 18
Universities:
  University of Texas (1,000)•
Symphony Orchestras:
  Austin Community Orchestra
  Austin Symphony Orchestra★★★

Dance Companies:
Austin Ballet Theatre
Ballet Austin
Sharir Dance Company (E-F)
Public Libraries:
704,652 volumes; circulation 2,066,326
Reading Quotient: 7.4
Places Rated Score: 5,355
Places Rated Rank: 53

Bakersfield, CA
Universities:
California State College, Bakersfield
(258)
Symphony Orchestras:
Bakersfield Symphony Orchestra★★
Public Libraries:
663,522 volumes; circulation 1,708,983
Reading Quotient: 5.6
Places Rated Score: 1,222
Places Rated Rank: 212

★ Baltimore, MD
Museums:
Baltimore Museum of Art (1,000)
Museum and Library of Maryland
History (700)
Walter's Art Gallery (600)
Fine Arts and Public Radio:
WBJC-FM 91.5 (39 mi; 164 hrs)
WEAA-FM 88.9 (40 mi; 165 hrs)
Public Television:
WMPS Channel 67
Universities:
Johns Hopkins University (225)
Morgan State University (362)
Towson State University (1,000)•
University of Maryland, Baltimore City
(487)
Symphony Orchestras:
Baltimore Symphony Orchestra★★★★
Gettysburg Symphony Orchestra
(Community)
Greater Baltimore Youth Orchestra
Hopkins Symphony Orchestra
(Community)
New Harbor Chamber Orchestra
(Community)
Peabody Symphony Orchestra (College)
UMBC Symphony
Theatres:
Center Stage★
Opera Companies:
Annapolis Opera, Inc.
3 productions; 13 performances
Baltimore Opera Company
5 productions; 15 performances
Dance Companies:
Ballet Theatre of Annapolis★
Baltimore Ballet
Towson State University Dance
Company (M)
Public Libraries:
1,900,197 volumes; circulation
2,124,114
Reading Quotient: 5.1
Places Rated Score: 9,788
Places Rated Rank: 15

Bangor, ME
Fine Arts and Public Radio:
WMEH-FM 90.9 (31 mi; 133 hrs)
Universities:
University of Maine, Orono (972)
Symphony Orchestras:
Bangor Symphony Orchestra★
Dance Companies:
Umo Dance Company (M)

Public Libraries:
472,840 volumes; circulation 461,334
Reading Quotient: 30.0
Places Rated Score: 1,995
Places Rated Rank: 155

Baton Rouge, LA
Museums:
Louisiana Arts and Science Center
(700)
Fine Arts and Public Radio:
WRKF-FM 89.3 (35 mi; 168 hrs)
Public Television:
WLPB Channel 27
Universities:
Louisiana State University and
Agriculture and Mechanical College
(1,000)
Southern University of Agriculture and
Mechanical College (693)
Symphony Orchestras:
Baton Rouge Symphony Orchestra★★
Dance Companies:
Baton Rouge Ballet Theatre★
Public Libraries:
443,983 volumes; circulation 1,429,408
Reading Quotient: 5.0
Places Rated Score: 4,237
Places Rated Rank: 77

Battle Creek, MI
Symphony Orchestras:
Battle Creek Symphony Orchestra★
Public Libraries:
154,446 volumes; circulation 417,752
Reading Quotient: 5.7
Places Rated Score: 354
Places Rated Rank: 285

Beaumont–Port Arthur, TX
Fine Arts and Public Radio:
KVLU-FM 91.3 (25 mi; 139 hrs)
Universities:
Lamar University (896)
Symphony Orchestras:
Beaumont Symphony Orchestra★
Dance Companies:
Beaumont Civic Ballet Company★
Public Libraries:
298,884 volumes; circulation NA
Reading Quotient: NA
Places Rated Score: 1,795
Places Rated Rank: 171

Beaver County, PA
Public Libraries:
31,955 volumes; circulation 95,941
Reading Quotient: 7.7
CMSA Access: PITTSBURGH–BEAVER
VALLEY, PA (1,252)
Places Rated Score: 1,284
Places Rated Rank: 204

Bellingham, WA
Universities:
Western Washington State College
(1,000)•
Public Libraries:
301,950 volumes; circulation 1,016,380
Reading Quotient: 12.3
Places Rated Score: 1,302
Places Rated Rank: 202

Benton Harbor, MI
Public Libraries:
78,796 volumes; circulation 64,099
Reading Quotient: 4.2
Places Rated Score: 79
Places Rated Rank: 325

★ Bergen–Passaic, NJ
Universities:
Fairleigh Dickinson University (658)
Ramapo College of New Jersey (430)
William Patterson College of New Jersey
(682)
Symphony Orchestras:
Bergen Philharmonic Orchestra
(Community)
Bergen Youth Orchestra
Garden State Chamber Orchestra
(Community)
New Jersey Philharmonic (Community)
Dance Companies:
Acanthus Ballet
Baron Ballet Company
Dance Inc's "Classical Jazz Theatre"
Irine Fokine Ballet Company
Joan Wolf Ballet Company
Public Libraries:
169,249 volumes; circulation 207,250
Reading Quotient: 7.3
CMSA Access: NEW YORK–NORTHERN
NEW JERSEY–LONG ISLAND, NY–NJ–
CT (6,715)
Places Rated Score: 9,304
Places Rated Rank: 18

Billings, MT
Fine Arts and Public Radio:
KEMC-FM 91.7 (131 hrs)
Symphony Orchestras:
Billings Symphony Orchestra★
Public Libraries:
277,995 volumes; circulation 583,000
Reading Quotient: 8.0
Places Rated Score: 778
Places Rated Rank: 247

Biloxi–Gulfport, MS
Public Television:
WMAH Channel 19
Public Libraries:
178,770 volumes; circulation 401,055
Reading Quotient: 2.7
Places Rated Score: 679
Places Rated Rank: 258

Binghamton, NY
Fine Arts and Public Radio:
WSKG-FM 89.3 (60 mi; 138 hrs)
Public Television:
WSKG Channel 46
Symphony Orchestras:
Binghamton Symphony and Choral
Society★
Binghamton Youth Symphony
Opera Companies:
Tri-Cities Opera Company, Inc.
3 productions; 12 performances
Public Libraries:
262,578 volumes; circulation 501,190
Reading Quotient: 2.1
Places Rated Score: 1,599
Places Rated Rank: 183

Birmingham, AL
Museums:
Birmingham Museum of Art (600)
Fine Arts and Public Radio:
WBHM-FM 90.3 (41 mi; 131 hrs)
Public Television:
WBIQ Channel 10
Universities:
University of Alabama, Birmingham
(624)
Samford University (214)

Symphony Orchestras:
Alabama Symphony Orchestra★★★
Alabama Youth Symphony
Dance Companies:
Ballet UAB★
Birmingham Creative Dance
Company (M)
State of Alabama Ballet
Public Libraries:
1,019,818 volumes; circulation
1,023,841
Reading Quotient: 2.9
Places Rated Score: 3,958
Places Rated Rank: 81

Bismarck, ND
Fine Arts and Public Radio:
WCND-FM 90.5 (80 mi; 129 hrs)
Public Television:
KBME Channel 3
Symphony Orchestras:
Bismarck–Mandan Symphony
Orchestra★
Public Libraries:
211,000 volumes; circulation 466,714
Reading Quotient: 5.8
Places Rated Score: 1,211
Places Rated Rank: 213

Bloomington, IN
Fine Arts and Public Radio:
WFIU-FM 103.7 (45 mi; 131 hrs)
Public Television:
WTIU Channel 30
Universities:
Indiana University (1,000)
Symphony Orchestras:
Bloomington Symphony Orchestra
(Community)
Indiana University Orchestra
Public Libraries:
152,000 volumes; circulation 572,318
Reading Quotient: 7.4
Places Rated Score: 2,152
Places Rated Rank: 145

Bloomington–Normal, IL
Fine Arts and Public Radio:
WGLT-FM 89.1 (35 mi; 133 hrs)
Universities:
Illinois State University (1,000)●
Symphony Orchestras:
Bloomington–Normal Symphony
(Community)
Public Libraries:
69,565 volumes; circulation 420,000
Reading Quotient: 13.8
Places Rated Score: 1,470
Places Rated Rank: 190

Boise City, ID
Museums:
Idaho State Historical Museum (500)
Public Television:
KAID Channel 4
Universities:
Boise State University (774)●
Symphony Orchestras:
Boise Philharmonic★★
Treasure Valley Youth Symphony
Public Libraries:
211,376 volumes; circulation 573,278
Reading Quotient: 7.7
Places Rated Score: 2,385
Places Rated Rank: 128

★ Boston, MA
Museums:
Botanical Museum of Harvard (700)
Fogg Art Museum (1,000)
Gray Herbarium (500)
Museum of Fine Arts (1,200)
Museum of Science (700)
Peabody Museum of Archeology and
Ethnology (500)
Fine Arts and Public Radio:
WBUR-FM 90.9 (100 mi; 165 hrs)
WGBH-FM 89.7 (90 mi; 168 hrs)
Public Television:
WEBX Channel 44
WGBH Channel 2
Universities:
Berklee College of Music (246)
Boston College (898)
Boston University (1,000)●
Brandeis University (249)
Framingham State College (312)
Harvard and Radcliffe Colleges (650)
Northeastern University (1,000)
Simmons College (192)
Tufts University (431)
University of Massachusetts (1,000)
Wellesley College (206)
Symphony Orchestras:
Boston Symphony Orchestra★★★★
Boston University/Tanglewood/Young
Artists Orchestra
Concord Orchestra (Community)
Greater Boston Youth Symphony
Handel and Haydn Society★★
Harvard–Radcliffe Orchestra
MIT Symphony Orchestra
Mystic Valley Orchestra (Community)
New England Symphony Orchestra
(Community)
Northeastern University Symphony
Theatres:
American Repertory Theatre★★
Boston Shakespeare Company
Huntington Theatre Company★
Opera Companies:
Opera Company of Boston
4 productions; 16 performances
Boston Lyric Opera
8 productions; 16 performances
Dance Companies:
Art of Black Dance and Music (E-F)
Beth Soll and Company (M)
Boston Ballet★
Boston Flamenco Ballet (E-F)
Concert Dance Company of Boston (M)
Mandala Folk Dance Ensemble (E-F)★
MIT Dance Company (M)
New England Dinosaur (M)
Ramon de los Reyes Spanish Dance
Theatre (E-F)
Public Libraries:
4,916,277 volumes; circulation
1,454,414
Reading Quotient: 11.3
Places Rated Score: 21,042
Places Rated Rank: 5

Boulder–Longmont, CO
Museums:
Boulder Historical Museum (500)
University of Colorado Museum (700)
Universities:
University of Colorado (1,000)●
Symphony Orchestras:
Boulder Chamber Orchestra
(Community)

Boulder Philharmonic★
Colorado Music Festival★★
Dance Companies:
Nancy Spanier Dance Theatre of
Colorado (M)
Public Libraries:
184,991 volumes; circulation 703,000
Reading Quotient: 8.3
CMSA Access: DENVER–BOULDER,
CO (628)
Places Rated Score: 3,663
Places Rated Rank: 88

Bradenton, FL
Public Libraries:
154,149 volumes; circulation 762,542
Reading Quotient: 5.8
Places Rated Score: 154
Places Rated Rank: 311

Brazoria, TX
Public Libraries:
215,523 volumes; circulation 588,992
Reading Quotient: 3.5
CMSA Access: HOUSTON–GALVESTON–
BRAZORIA, TX (1,290)
Places Rated Score: 1,506
Places Rated Rank: 188

Bremerton, WA
Symphony Orchestras:
Bremerton Symphony Orchestra
(Community)
Public Libraries:
282,227 volumes; circulation 905,114
Reading Quotient: 7.5
Places Rated Score: 382
Places Rated Rank: 280

★ Bridgeport–Milford, CT
Public Television:
WEDW Channel 49
Universities:
Fairfield University (283)
University of Bridgeport (305)
Symphony Orchestras:
Greater Bridgeport Symphony
Orchestra★
Public Libraries:
515,328 volumes; circulation 411,229
Reading Quotient: 6.5
CMSA Access: NEW YORK–NORTHERN
NEW JERSEY–LONG ISLAND, NY–NJ–
CT (6,565)
Places Rated Score: 8,368
Places Rated Rank: 25

Bristol, CT
Public Libraries:
140,000 volumes; circulation 201,659
Reading Quotient: 5.9
CMSA Access: HARTFORD–NEW
BRITAIN–MIDDLETOWN, CT (374)
Places Rated Score: 514
Places Rated Rank: 269

Brockton, MA
Public Libraries:
262,879 volumes; circulation 495,458
Reading Quotient: 7.9
CMSA Access: BOSTON–LAWRENCE–
SALEM, MA–NH (1,738)
Places Rated Score: 2,001
Places Rated Rank: 154

Brownsville–Harlingen, TX
Public Libraries:
   161,781 volumes; circulation
   274,166
Reading Quotient: 3.4
Places Rated Score: 162
Places Rated Rank: 309

Bryan–College Station, TX
Fine Arts and Public Radio:
   KAMU-FM 90.9 (16 mi; 128 hrs)
Public Television:
   KAMU Channel 15
Universities:
   Texas A&M University (1,000)
Symphony Orchestras:
   Brazos Valley Symphony Orchestra
   (Community)
Public Libraries:
   102,000 volumes; circulation 310,000
Reading Quotient: 4.2
Places Rated Score: 2,002
Places Rated Rank: 153

★ Buffalo, NY
Museums:
   Albright Knox Art Gallery (700)
   Buffalo Museum of Science (700)
Fine Arts and Public Radio:
   WBFO-FM 88.7 (22 mi; 168 hrs)
   WEBR-AM 970 (90 mi; 168 hrs)
   WNED-FM 94.5 (100 mi; 133 hrs)
Public Television:
   WNED Channel 17
Universities:
   SUNY at Buffalo (1,000)
Symphony Orchestras:
   Buffalo Philharmonic Orchestra★★★★
   Greater Buffalo Youth Orchestra
Theatres:
   Studio Arena Theatre★★
Public Libraries:
   3,467,124 volumes; circulation
   5,849,765
Reading Quotient: 9.2
Places Rated Score: 8,567
Places Rated Rank: 23

Burlington, NC
Public Libraries:
   131,082 volumes; circulation
   329,699
Reading Quotient: 3.5
Places Rated Score: 131
Places Rated Rank: 316

Burlington, VT
Public Television:
   WETK Channel 33
Universities:
   University of Vermont (768)
Symphony Orchestras:
   Vermont Symphony Orchestra★★
   Vermont Youth Orchestra
Public Libraries:
   73,000 volumes; circulation 180,000
Reading Quotient: 6.7
Places Rated Score: 1,741
Places Rated Rank: 177

Canton, OH
Symphony Orchestras:
   Canton Symphony Orchestra★★
   Canton Youth Symphony
Dance Companies:
   Canton Ballet Company

Public Libraries:
   539,309 volumes; circulation 2,071,389
Reading Quotient: 2.0
Places Rated Score: 989
Places Rated Rank: 233

Casper, WY
Symphony Orchestras:
   Casper Symphony Orchestra★
Public Libraries:
   103,260 volumes; circulation 307,827
Reading Quotient: 5.7
Places Rated Score: 303
Places Rated Rank: 293

Cedar Rapids, IA
Fine Arts and Public Radio:
   KCCK-FM 89.5 (25 mi; 126 hrs)
Symphony Orchestras:
   Cedar Rapids Symphony Orchestra★★
   Cedar Rapids Youth Symphony
Public Libraries:
   204,492 volumes; circulation 646,496
Reading Quotient: 7.7
Places Rated Score: 904
Places Rated Rank: 236

Champaign–Urbana–Rantoul, IL
Fine Arts and Public Radio:
   WILL-AM 580 (150 mi; 82 hrs)
   WILL-FM 90.9 (85 mi; 133 hrs)
Universities:
   University of Illinois (1,000)
Symphony Orchestras:
   Champaign County Youth Symphony
   Champaign–Urbana Symphony
   Orchestra★
Dance Companies:
   Beverly Blossom and Company (M)
Public Libraries:
   353,063 volumes; circulation 1,672,167
Reading Quotient: 17.3
Places Rated Score: 2,203
Places Rated Rank: 139

Charleston, SC
Museums:
   Charleston Museum (600)
Fine Arts and Public Radio:
   WSCI-FM 89.3 (100 mi; 130 hrs)
Public Television:
   WITV Channel 7
Universities:
   Baptist College (244)
   Charleston College (385)
Symphony Orchestras:
   Charleston Symphony Orchestra★★
Opera Companies:
   Spoletto Festival, U.S.A.
   3 productions; 9 performances
Dance Companies:
   Robert Ivey Ballet
Public Libraries:
   387,332 volumes; circulation 722,006
Reading Quotient: 4.0
Places Rated Score: 2,993
Places Rated Rank: 106

Charleston, WV
Museums:
   Sunrise Foundation (700)
Fine Arts and Public Radio:
   WVPN-FM 88.5 (50 mi; 132 hrs)
Universities:
   West Virginia State College (449)
Symphony Orchestras:
   Charleston Symphony Orchestra★★

Charleston Symphony Youth Orchestra
   Lilliput Orchestra (Community)
Dance Companies:
   Charleston Ballet★
   Charleston Ballet Company
Public Libraries:
   506,159 volumes; circulation 982,892
Reading Quotient: 6.9
Places Rated Score: 2,605
Places Rated Rank: 121

Charlotte–Gastonia–Rock Hill, NC–SC
Museums:
   Mint Museum of Art (500)
Fine Arts and Public Radio:
   WFAE-FM 90.7 (65 mi; 127 hrs)
Public Television:
   WTVI Channel 42
Universities:
   University of North Carolina, Charlotte
   (854)••
Symphony Orchestras:
   Charlotte Symphony Orchestra★★★
   Youth Symphony of the Carolinas
Opera Companies:
   Charlotte Opera Association
   3 productions; 6 performances
Dance Companies:
   Dance Gallery/Charlotte (M)
Public Libraries:
   1,391,441 volumes; circulation
   3,637,272
Reading Quotient: 6.5
Places Rated Score: 4,313
Places Rated Rank: 73

Charlottesville, VA
Universities:
   University of Virginia (1,000)
Symphony Orchestras:
   Charlottesville University Community
   Symphony
   Youth Orchestra of Charlottesville–
   Albemarle
Public Libraries:
   221,845 volumes; circulation 710,249
Reading Quotient: 6.9
Places Rated Score: 1,422
Places Rated Rank: 195

Chattanooga, TN–GA
Public Television:
   WTCI Channel 45
Universities:
   Tennessee Temple University (338)
   University of Tennessee, Chattanooga
   (754)
Symphony Orchestras:
   Chattanooga Symphony Orchestra★★
Opera Companies:
   Chattanooga Opera Association
   3 productions; 6 performances
Public Libraries:
   373,482 volumes; circulation 920,992
Reading Quotient: 4.5
Places Rated Score: 2,483
Places Rated Rank: 127

★ Chicago, IL
Museums:
   Art Institute of Chicago (2,000)
   Balzekas Museum of Lithuanian Culture
   (700)
   Chicago Historical Society (1,000)
   Field Museum of Natural History (2,000)
   Museum of Science and Industry
   (1,100)

Oriental Institute of the University of
Chicago (700)
Fine Arts and Public Radio:
WBEZ-FM 91.5 (100 mi; 162 hrs)
WFMT-FM 98.7 (150 mi; 168 hrs)
WNIB-FM 97.1 (45 mi; 168 hrs)
Public Television:
WTTW Channel 11
Universities:
Chicago State University (744)
De Paul University (516)
Loyola University (664)
Northeastern Illinois University (467)
Northwestern University (1,000)
Roosevelt University (668)
St. Xavier College (217)
University of Chicago (285)
University of Illinois (1,000)
Wheaton College (207)
Symphony Orchestras:
American Conservatory of Music
Orchestra (College)
Chicago Chamber Orchestra★
Chicago Pops Orchestra (Community)
Chicago String Ensemble (Community)
Chicago Symphony Orchestra★★★★
Chicago Symphony Wind Ensemble
(Community)
Civic Orchestra of Chicago (Youth)
Classical Youth Symphony
De Paul University Symphony
Evanston Symphony Orchestra
(Community)
Music of the Baroque★★
Orchestra of Illinois★★
Skokie Valley Symphony Orchestra
(Community)
Youth Symphony Orchestra of Greater
Chicago
Theatres:
Body Politic Theatre
Goodman Theatre★★
Northlight Repertory
Organic Theatre Company
Steppenwolf Theatre Company
Victory Gardens Theatre
Wisdom Bridge Theatre
Opera Companies:
Chicago Opera Theatre
3 productions; 18 performances
Lyric Opera of Chicago★★★★
8 productions; 62 performances
Dance Companies:
Akasha and Company (M)
American Dance Center Ballet
Company
Arve Connection Dance Company (M)
Chicago City Ballet★
Chicago Contemporary Dance
Theatre (M)
Chicago Dance Laboratory (M)
Chicago Dance Medium (M)
Chicago Repertory Dance
Ensemble (M)
Ensemble Español (E-F)
Gus Giordano Jazz Dance Chicago
Joel Hall Dancers (J)
Joseph Holmes Dance Theatre (M)
Le Ballet Petit Dance Ensemble★★
Margot Grimmer American Dance
Company
Mordine and Company (M)
Muntu Dance Theatre (E-F)★
Nana Solbrig and the Chicago Moving
Company (M)
Venetia Stifler and Concert Dance,
Inc. (M)

Public Libraries:
4,383,710 volumes; circulation
7,811,071
Reading Quotient: 4.1
CMSA Access: CHICAGO–GARY–LAKE
COUNTY, IL–IN–WI (90)
Places Rated Score: 24,846
Places Rated Rank: 2

Chico, CA
Fine Arts and Public Radio:
KCHO-FM 91.1 (130 mi; 152 hrs)
Universities:
California State University, Chico (1,000)
Public Libraries:
246,895 volumes; circulation 710,849
Reading Quotient: 6.2
Places Rated Score: 1,647
Places Rated Rank: 179

★ Cincinnati, OH–KY–IN
Museums:
Cincinnati Art Museum (700)
Cincinnati Historical Society (500)
Cincinnati Museum of Natural History
(500)
Fine Arts and Public Radio:
WGUC-FM 90.9 (50 mi; 164 hrs)
WVXU-FM 91.7 (30 mi; 168 hrs)
Public Television:
WCET Channel 48
Universities:
Northern Kentucky University (400)
University of Cincinnati (1,000)●
Xavier University (255)
Symphony Orchestras:
Cincinnati Symphony Orchestra★★★★
Cincinnati Youth Symphony Orchestra
Philharmonic and Concert Orchestras
(College)
Theatres:
Cincinnati Playhouse in the Park★
Opera Companies:
Cincinnati Opera Association
8 productions; 25 performances
Dance Companies:
Cheryl Wallace Dance Works (M)
Cincinnati/New Orleans City Ballet
Company★
Contemporary Dance Theatre (M)
Public Libraries:
3,332,926 volumes; circulation
6,166,548
Reading Quotient: 10.9
Places Rated Score: 9,688
Places Rated Rank: 16

Clarksville–Hopkinsville, TN–KY
Public Libraries:
110,701 volumes; circulation 568,257
Reading Quotient: 9.7
Places Rated Score: 111
Places Rated Rank: 319

★ Cleveland, OH
Museums:
Cleveland Museum of Art (2,000)
Cleveland Museum of Natural History
(1,400)
Western Reserve Historical Society
(800)
Public Television:
WVIZ Channel 25
Universities:
Case-Western Reserve University (394)●
Cleveland State University (1,000)
John Carroll University (260)

Symphony Orchestras:
Cleveland Institute of Music Youth
Orchestra
Cleveland Orchestra★★★★
Ohio Chamber Orchestra★★
Theatres:
Cleveland Playhouse★★
Great Lakes Shakespeare Festival★
Opera Companies:
Cleveland Opera
3 productions; 12 performances
Dance Companies:
Cleveland Ballet★
Cleveland State University Dance
Committee (M)★
Footpath Dance Company (M)
Hungarian Theatre and Dance
Company of Cleveland (E-F)★
North Coast Ballet Theatre
Shalhevet (E-F)
Public Libraries:
4,089,384 volumes; circulation
8,085,150
Reading Quotient: 10.2
CMSA Access: CLEVELAND–AKRON–
LORAIN, OH (150)
Places Rated Score: 12,679
Places Rated Rank: 9

Colorado Springs, CO
Museums:
Colorado Springs Fine Arts Center (500)
Universities:
University of Colorado, Colorado
Springs (203)
Symphony Orchestras:
Colorado Springs Symphony
Orchestra★★★
Opera Companies:
Colorado Opera Festival
2 productions; 6 performances
Dance Companies:
Rocky Mountain Ballet
Public Libraries:
383,644 volumes; circulation 1,001,448
Reading Quotient: 8.3
Places Rated Score: 1,749
Places Rated Rank: 176

Columbia, MO
Museums:
University of Missouri Museum of Art
and Archeology (800)
Fine Arts and Public Radio:
KBIA-FM 91.3 (80 mi; 133 hrs)
KOPN-FM 89.5 (40 mi; 160 hrs)
Universities:
University of Missouri (1,000)
Symphony Orchestras:
Missouri Symphony Orchestra
(Community)
Public Libraries:
282,245 volumes; circulation 1,505,191
Reading Quotient: 13.7
Places Rated Score: 2,882
Places Rated Rank: 111

Columbia, SC
Fine Arts and Public Radio:
WLTR-FM 91.3 (42 mi; 130 hrs)
Public Television:
WRLK Channel 35
Universities:
University of South Carolina (1,000)
Symphony Orchestras:
Columbia Youth Orchestra
Palmetto State Orchestra Association
(College)

Dance Companies:
    Columbia City Ballet★
Public Libraries:
    388,860 volumes; circulation 944,385
Reading Quotient: 5.7
Places Rated Score: 2,489
Places Rated Rank: 126

Columbus, GA–AL
Museums:
    Columbus Museum of Art and Science,
    Inc. (500)
Public Television:
    WJSP Channel 28
Universities:
    Columbus College (230)
Symphony Orchestras:
    Columbus Symphony Orchestra★
Public Libraries:
    431,118 volumes; circulation 701,436
Reading Quotient: 5.4
Places Rated Score: 1,861
Places Rated Rank: 166

Columbus, OH
Museums:
    Ohio Historical Center (500)
Fine Arts and Public Radio:
    WCBE-FM 90.5 (50 mi; 126 hrs)
    WOSU-AM 820 (95 mi; 91 hrs)
    WOSU-FM 89.7 (60 mi; 133 hrs)
Public Television:
    WOSU Channel 34
    WPBO Channel 42
Universities:
    Capital University (257)
    Denison University (310)●
    Ohio State University (1,000)●
    Ohio Wesleyan University (226)
Symphony Orchestras:
    Columbus Symphony Orchestra★★★
    Columbus Symphony Youth Orchestra
    Pro Musica Chamber Orchestra of
    Columbus★
Dance Companies:
    Allan Miles Ballet
    Ballet Metropolitan
    Columbus Theatre Ballet Association★★
    Dancentral (M)
    Les Danseurs Noir (J)
    Ohio State University Dance
    Company (M)★
    Zivili (E–F)★
Public Libraries:
    1,255,000 volumes; circulation 3,866,356
Reading Quotient: 6.0
Places Rated Score: 6,648
Places Rated Rank: 41

Corpus Christi, TX
Museums:
    Corpus Christi Museum (500)
Fine Arts and Public Radio:
    KKED-FM 90.3 (70 mi; 131 hrs)
Public Television:
    KEDT Channel 16
Symphony Orchestras:
    Corpus Christi Symphony Orchestra★★
Dance Companies:
    Corpus Christi Ballet Theatre★
Public Libraries:
    292,193 volumes; circulation 614,641
Reading Quotient: 3.8
Places Rated Score: 1,992
Places Rated Rank: 156

Cumberland, MD–WV
Universities:
    Frostburg State College (210)
Public Libraries:
    163,231 volumes; circulation 602,684
Reading Quotient: 9.6
Places Rated Score: 373
Places Rated Rank: 282

★ Dallas, TX
Museums:
    Dallas Historical Society (500)
    Dallas Museum of Fine Art (800)
    Dallas Museum of Natural History
    (1,100)
    International Museum of Cultures (500)
Fine Arts and Public Radio:
    KERA-FM 90.1 (60 mi; 163 hrs)
Public Television:
    KERA Channel 13
Universities:
    North Texas State University (1,000)
    Southern Methodist University (550)
    Texas Women's University (445)●
    University of Dallas (282)
Symphony Orchestras:
    AIMS Orchestra (College)
    Dallas Symphony Orchestra★★★★
    Greater Dallas Youth Orchestra
Theatres:
    Dallas Theatre Center★★★
    Theatre Three
Opera Companies:
    Dallas Opera
    6 productions; 23 performances
Dance Companies:
    American Dancing (E–F)★
    Dallas Ballet★
    Dallas Black Dance Theatre (M)★
    Dallas Metropolitan Ballet★
    Dancers Unlimited Repertory
    Company (M)
    Garland Ballet Association
    Plana Ballet Theatre
Public Libraries:
    2,105,231 volumes; circulation
    3,983,961
Reading Quotient: 5.9
CMSA Access: DALLAS–FORT WORTH,
    TX (68)
Places Rated Score: 10,438
Places Rated Rank: 13

Danbury, CT
Universities:
    Western Connecticut State College
    (274)
Symphony Orchestras:
    Connecticut Symphony Orchestra
    (Community)
    Ridgefield Orchestra (Community)
    Ridgefield Youth Orchestra
Public Libraries:
    126,132 volumes; circulation 334,518
Reading Quotient: 7.7
CMSA Access: NEW YORK–NORTHERN
    NEW JERSEY–LONG ISLAND, NY–NJ–
    CT (6,715)
Places Rated Score: 7,415
Places Rated Rank: 34

Danville, VA
Public Libraries:
    85,294 volumes; circulation 193,019
Reading Quotient: 6.1
Places Rated Score: 85
Places Rated Rank: 323

Davenport–Rock Island–Moline, IA–IL
Universities:
    St. Ambrose College (213)
Symphony Orchestras:
    Augustana College Symphony
    Tri-City Symphony Orchestra★★
    Tri-City Youth Symphony Orchestra
Public Libraries:
    304,064 volumes; circulation 600,000
Reading Quotient: 8.8
Places Rated Score: 1,017
Places Rated Rank: 228

Dayton–Springfield, OH
Museums:
    Dayton Art Institute (600)
    Dayton Museum of Natural History (900)
Public Television:
    WPTD Channel 16
    WPTO Channel 14
Universities:
    Central State University (219)
    University of Dayton (634)
    Wittenberg University (225)
    Wright State University (779)●
Symphony Orchestras:
    Allegro Chamber Players (Youth)
    Dayton Philharmonic Orchestra★★
    Dayton Philharmonic Youth Orchestra
    Springfield Symphony Orchestra★
Dance Companies:
    Antioch College Dance Ensemble (M)
    Dance Theatre Dayton
    Dayton Ballet
    Dayton Contemporary Dance
    Company (M)
    Sinclair Dance Ensemble (M)
Public Libraries:
    1,677,923 volumes; circulation
    5,652,877
Reading Quotient: 10.2
Places Rated Score: 6.,935
Places Rated Rank: 40

Daytona Beach, FL
Universities:
    Stetson University (200)
Dance Companies:
    Atlantic Dance Company
    Ballet Guild of Sanford–Seminole
    Rozak Dancers (E–F)
Public Libraries:
    458,802 volumes; circulation 1,716,516
Reading Quotient: 8.0
Places Rated Score: 809
Places Rated Rank: 244

Decatur, IL
Symphony Orchestras:
    Millikin–Decatur Civic Symphony
    (Community)
Public Libraries:
    197,955 volumes; circulation NA
Reading Quotient: NA
Places Rated Score: 298
Places Rated Rank: 294

★ Denver, CO
Museums:
    Colorado Historical Society (700)
    Denver Art Museum (800)
    Denver Museum of Natural History (800)
Fine Arts and Public Radio:
    KCFR-FM 90.1 (70 mi; 152 hrs)
Public Television:
    KRMA Channel 6

Universities:
  Metropolitan State College (637)
  University of Colorado, Denver (785)
  University of Denver (440)
Symphony Orchestras:
  Denver Chamber Orchestra
    (Community)
  Denver Symphony Orchestra★★★★
  Young Artists Orchestra of Denver
Theatres:
  Denver Center Theatre Company★★★
Opera Companies:
  Central City Opera House Association
    3 productions; 31 performances
Dance Companies:
  Changing Scene Dance Company (E-F)
  Cleo Parker Robinson Dance
    Ensemble (M)
  Colorado Ballet
  Premiere Dance Art Company (B)
Public Libraries:
  1,822,111 volumes; circulation NA
Reading Quotient: NA
Places Rated Score: 8,477
Places Rated Rank: 24

Des Moines, IA
Public Television:
  KDIN Channel 11
Universities:
  Drake University (586)●
Symphony Orchestras:
  Des Moines Community Orchestra
  Drake University Symphony Orchestra
  Greater Des Moines Youth Symphony
Opera Companies:
  Des Moines Metropolitan Opera
    3 productions; 16 performances
Dance Companies:
  Des Moines Ballet Company
Public Libraries:
  172,965 volumes; circulation 1,234,390
Reading Quotient: 7.4
Places Rated Score: 1,857
Places Rated Rank: 167

★ **Detroit, MI**
Museums:
  Cranbrook Institute of Science (800)
  Detroit Historical Museum (700)
  Detroit Institute of Arts (1,200)
  Greenfield Village/Ford Museum (800)
Fine Arts and Public Radio:
  WDET-FM 101.9 (35 mi; 168 hrs)
Public Television:
  WTVS Channel 56
Universities:
  University of Detroit (250)
  Wayne State University (1,000)
Symphony Orchestras:
  Allen Park Symphony (Community)
  Dearborn Symphony Orchestra★
  Detroit Symphony Orchestra★★★★
  Livonia Youth Symphony Society
Opera Companies:
  Michigan Opera Theatre
    4 productions; 20 performances
Dance Companies:
  Body Electric Company (E-F)
  Detroit City Ballet
  Michigan Ballet Theatre
  Northern Ballet Theatre of Livonia
  Nritya Sudha's Hindu Temple Rhythms
    (E-F)★
Public Libraries:
  2,408,863 volumes; circulation NA

Reading Quotient: NA
CMSA Access: DETROIT–ANN ARBOR,
  MI (750)
Places Rated Score: 10,389
Places Rated Rank: 14

Dothan, AL
Public Libraries:
  117,477 volumes; circulation 312,167
Reading Quotient: 5.8
Places Rated Score: 117
Places Rated Rank: 318

Dubuque, IA
Symphony Orchestras:
  Dubuque Symphony Orchestra★
Public Libraries:
  140,000 volumes; circulation 409,020
Reading Quotient: 8.5
Places Rated Score: 340
Places Rated Rank: 287

Duluth, MN–WI
Fine Arts and Public Radio:
  KUMD-FM 103.3 (60 mi; 136 hrs)
  WSCD-FM 92.9 (50 mi; 140 hrs)
Public Television:
  WDSE Channel 8
Universities:
  University of Minnesota (661)
Symphony Orchestras:
  Duluth–Superior Symphony Orchestra★★
Public Libraries:
  315,634 volumes; circulation 959,251
Reading Quotient: 13.7
Places Rated Score: 2,377
Places Rated Rank: 129

East St. Louis–Belleville, IL
Public Libraries:
  235,621 volumes; circulation 349,503
Reading Quotient: 6.0
CMSA Access: ST. LOUIS–EAST ST.
  LOUIS–ALTON, MO–IL (668)
Places Rated Score: 904
Places Rated Rank: 236

Eau Claire, WI
Public Television:
  WHWC Channel 28
Universities:
  University of Wisconsin, Eau Claire
    (942)
Symphony Orchestras:
  Chippewa Valley Symphony
    (Community)
  University of Wisconsin, Eau Claire,
    Symphony
Public Libraries:
  164,957 volumes; circulation 533,734
Reading Quotient: 13.6
Places Rated Score: 1,807
Places Rated Rank: 170

El Paso, TX
Museums:
  El Paso Museum of Art (600)
Fine Arts and Public Radio:
  KTEP-FM 88.5 (100 mi; 164 hrs)
Public Television:
  KCOS Channel 13
Universities:
  University of Texas, El Paso (1,000)
Symphony Orchestras:
  El Paso Symphony Orchestra★★
  El Paso Youth Symphony
  Irving Symphony Orchestra
    (Community)

University of Texas, El Paso, Symphony
Dance Companies:
  Antonio Triana–Ballet Español (E-F)
  Ballet El Paso
  Susan Francis Dancers (J)
Public Libraries:
  450,000 volumes; circulation 1,200,000
Reading Quotient: 3.8
Places Rated Score: 3,800
Places Rated Rank: 84

Elkhart–Goshen, IN
Symphony Orchestras:
  Elkhart Symphony Orchestra★
Public Libraries:
  153,109 volumes; circulation 412,881
Reading Quotient: 8.3
Places Rated Score: 353
Places Rated Rank: 286

Elmira, NY
Universities:
  Elmira College (293)
Symphony Orchestras:
  Elmira Symphony and Choral Society★
Dance Companies:
  Elmira Corning Ballet★
Public Libraries:
  455,196 volumes; circulation 412,712
Reading Quotient: 8.9
Places Rated Score: 1,048
Places Rated Rank: 223

Enid, OK
Symphony Orchestras:
  Enid–Phillips Symphony (Community)
Public Libraries:
  114,943 volumes; circulation 214,269
Reading Quotient: 5.2
Places Rated Score: 215
Places Rated Rank: 304

Erie, PA
Fine Arts and Public Radio:
  WQLN-FM 91.3 (NW PA; 126 hrs)
Public Television:
  WQLN Channel 54
Universities:
  Edinboro State College (442)
Symphony Orchestras:
  Erie Philharmonic Orchestra★★
  Erie Philharmonic Youth Orchestra
Public Libraries:
  390,000 volumes; circulation 1,308,199
Reading Quotient: 6.0
Places Rated Score: 2,032
Places Rated Rank: 151

Eugene–Springfield, OR
Fine Arts and Public Radio:
  KLCC-FM 89.7 (65 mi; 140 hrs)
  KWAX-FM 91.1 (58 mi; 133 hrs)
Universities:
  University of Oregon (1,000)●●
Symphony Orchestras:
  Eugene Symphony Orchestra★★
  Eugene Youth Symphony
Dance Companies:
  Concert Dance Theatre (M)★
  Dobre Folk Ensemble (E-F)★
  Eugene Ballet Company★
  Oslund and Company Dance (M)
Public Libraries:
  281,271 volumes; circulation 1,384,166
Reading Quotient: 11.4
Places Rated Score: 2,631
Places Rated Rank: 120

Evansville, IN–KY
Public Television:
  WNIN Channel 9
Universities:
  University of Evansville (294)
Symphony Orchestras:
  Evansville Philharmonic Orchestra★★
  University of Evansville Symphony
Public Libraries:
  681,710 volumes; circulation NA
Reading Quotient: NA
Places Rated Score: 1,876
Places Rated Rank: 164

Fall River, MA–RI
Symphony Orchestras:
  Greater Fall River Symphony Orchestra
    (Community)
Public Libraries:
  308,699 volumes; circulation 291,887
Reading Quotient: 6.0
CMSA Access: PROVIDENCE–PAWTUCKET–
  FALL RIVER, RI–MA (340)
Places Rated Score: 749
Places Rated Rank: 252

Fargo–Moorhead, ND–MN
Fine Arts and Public Radio:
  KDSU-FM 91.9 (90 mi; 134 hrs)
Public Television:
  KFME Channel 13
Universities:
  North Dakota State University (800)
Symphony Orchestras:
  Fargo–Moorhead Symphony Orchestra★
Public Libraries:
  311,196 volumes; circulation 410,000
Reading Quotient: 11.8
Places Rated Score: 2,111
Places Rated Rank: 147

Fayetteville, NC
Fine Arts and Public Radio:
  WFSS-FM 89.1 (65 mi; 126 hrs)
Universities:
  Pembroke State University (219)
Symphony Orchestras:
  Fayetteville Symphony Orchestra
    (Community)
Public Libraries:
  225,132 volumes; circulation 564,272
Reading Quotient: 3.2
Places Rated Score: 844
Places Rated Rank: 241

Fayetteville–Springdale, AR
Public Television:
  KAFT Channel 13
Universities:
  University of Arkansas (1,000)●
Symphony Orchestras:
  North Arkansas Symphony Orchestra★
Public Libraries:
  215,000 volumes; circulation 800,000
Reading Quotient: 6.8
Places Rated Score: 1,915
Places Rated Rank: 163

Fitchburg–Leominster, MA
Public Libraries:
  269,921 volumes; circulation 497,041
Reading Quotient: 2.6
Places Rated Score: 270
Places Rated Rank: 296

Flint, MI
Fine Arts and Public Radio:
  WFBE-FM 95.1 (17 mi; 130 hrs)
Public Television:
  WFUM Channel 28
Universities:
  University of Michigan, Flint (237)
Symphony Orchestras:
  Flint Community Music School
    Orchestra (College)
  Flint Symphony Orchestra★★★
Dance Companies:
  Dance Repertory Company
  Flint Ballet Theatre★
Public Libraries:
  475,604 volumes; circulation 898,907
Reading Quotient: 8.6
Places Rated Score: 2,163
Places Rated Rank: 143

Florence, AL
Public Television:
  WFIQ Channel 36
Universities:
  University of Northern Alabama (475)
Public Libraries:
  45,963 volumes; circulation 150,806
Reading Quotient: 4.3
Places Rated Score: 1,021
Places Rated Rank: 227

Florence, SC
Public Television:
  WJPM Channel 33
Public Libraries:
  128,156 volumes; circulation 355,893
Reading Quotient: 4.4
Places Rated Score: 628
Places Rated Rank: 261

Fort Collins–Loveland, CO
Fine Arts and Public Radio:
  KCSU-FM 90.9 (30 mi; 133 hrs)
Universities:
  Colorado State University (1,000)
Symphony Orchestras:
  Fort Collins Symphony Orchestra
    (Community)
Public Libraries:
  208,554 volumes; circulation 725,650
Reading Quotient: 8.0
Places Rated Score: 1,609
Places Rated Rank: 182

Fort Lauderdale–Hollywood–Pompano Beach, FL
Symphony Orchestras:
  Broward Community College Youth
    Symphony
  Broward Symphony Orchestra
    (Community)
  Florida Chamber Orchestra★★
  Fort Lauderdale Symphony Orchestra★★
Public Libraries:
  597,296 volumes; circulation 2,067,553
Reading Quotient: 2.6
CMSA Access: MIAMI–FORT LAUDERDALE,
  FL (630)
Places Rated Score: 2,027
Places Rated Rank: 152

Fort Myers, FL
Symphony Orchestras:
  Southwest Florida Symphony
    Orchestra★
Public Libraries:
  179,987 volumes; circulation 1,008,711
Reading Quotient: 5.4
Places Rated Score: 380
Places Rated Rank: 281

Fort Pierce, FL
Fine Arts and Public Radio:
  WQCS-FM 88.3 (40 mi; 126 hrs)
Public Libraries:
  67,500 volumes; circulation 337,500
Reading Quotient: 3.9
Places Rated Score: 368
Places Rated Rank: 284

Fort Smith, AR–OK
Symphony Orchestras:
  Fort Smith Symphony (Community)
Public Libraries:
  45,000 volumes; circulation 170,000
Reading Quotient: 6.7
Places Rated Score: 145
Places Rated Rank: 315

Fort Walton Beach, FL
Dance Companies:
  Fort Walton Beach Ballet Association
Public Libraries:
  36,755 volumes; circulation 118,032
Reading Quotient: 5.1
Places Rated Score: 87
Places Rated Rank: 321

Fort Wayne, IN
Universities:
  Indiana University–Purdue University at
    Fort Wayne (915)
Symphony Orchestras:
  Fort Wayne Philharmonic★★
Dance Companies:
  Fort Wayne Ballet★
  Fort Wayne Dance Collective (M)
Public Libraries:
  1,481,309 volumes; circulation
    1,755,443
Reading Quotient: 11.0
Places Rated Score: 2,846
Places Rated Rank: 112

Fort Worth–Arlington, TX
Museums:
  Amon Carter Museum of Western Art
    (500)
  Fort Worth Museum of Science and
    History (500)
  Kimball Art Museum (700)
Universities:
  Texas Christian University (664)●
  University of Texas, Arlington (1,000)
Symphony Orchestras:
  Fort Worth Civic Orchestra (Community)
  Fort Worth Symphony Orchestra★★★
  University of Texas, Arlington,
    Symphony
  Youth Orchestra of Greater Fort Worth
Opera Companies:
  Fort Worth Opera Association
    4 productions; 7 performances
Dance Companies:
  Ballet Concerto
  Fort Worth Ballet
  TCU Modern Dance Lab Company★
Public Libraries:
  973,187 volumes; circulation 3,271,279
Reading Quotient: 4.0
CMSA Access: DALLAS–FORT WORTH,
  TX (1,001)
Places Rated Score: 6,466
Places Rated Rank: 42

Fresno, CA
Fine Arts and Public Radio:
  KSJV-FM 91.5 (70 mi; 140 hrs)
  KVPR-FM 89.3 (85 mi; 126 hrs)

Public Television:
   KMTF Channel 18
Universities:
   California State University, Fresno
      (1,000)
Symphony Orchestras:
   Fresno Junior Philharmonic Orchestra
   Fresno Philharmonic Orchestra★★
Dance Companies:
   Fresno Ballet★★
Public Libraries:
   895,926 volumes; circulation 2,057,677
Reading Quotient: 5.7
Places Rated Score: 3,596
Places Rated Rank: 90

Gadsden, AL
Public Libraries:
   153,170 volumes; circulation 310,924
Reading Quotient: 4.5
Places Rated Score: 153
Places Rated Rank: 312

Gainesville, FL
Museums:
   Florida State Museum (1,000)
Fine Arts and Public Radio:
   WUFT-FM 89.1 (42 mi; 168 hrs)
Public Television:
   WUFT Channel 5
Universities:
   University of Florida (1,000)
Symphony Orchestras:
   University of Florida Symphony
      Orchestra
Theatres:
   Hippodrome Street Theatre
Dance Companies:
   Dance Alive!(B)
Public Libraries:
   85,437 volumes; circulation 752,513
Reading Quotient: 5.4
Places Rated Score: 3,335
Places Rated Rank: 96

Galveston–Texas City, TX
Symphony Orchestras:
   Galveston Symphony Orchestra
      (Community)
Public Libraries:
   366,013 volumes; circulation 334,873
Reading Quotient: 3.3
CMSA Access: HOUSTON–GALVESTON–
   BRAZORIA, TX (1,290)
Places Rated Score: 1,756
Places Rated Rank: 175

Gary–Hammond, IN
Symphony Orchestras:
   Northwest Indiana Symphony★
   Northwest Indiana Youth Orchestra
Public Libraries:
   768,715 volumes; circulation 1,002,000
Reading Quotient: 7.2
CMSA Access: CHICAGO–GARY–LAKE
   COUNTY, IL–IN–WI (3,046)
Places Rated Score: 4,115
Places Rated Rank: 80

Glens Falls, NY
Symphony Orchestras:
   Glens Falls Symphony Orchestra
      (Community)
Opera Companies:
   Lake George Opera Festival
      4 productions; 32 performances

Public Libraries:
   174,866 volumes; circulation 269,311
Reading Quotient: 9.6
Places Rated Score: 603
Places Rated Rank: 263

Grand Forks, ND
Fine Arts and Public Radio:
   KFJM-AM 1370 (75 mi; 91 hrs)
Public Television:
   KGFE Channel 2
Universities:
   University of North Dakota (1,000)
Symphony Orchestras:
   Greater Grand Forks Symphony
      (Community)
Public Libraries:
   120,695 volumes; circulation 374,755
Reading Quotient: 7.5
Places Rated Score: 1,921
Places Rated Rank: 161

Grand Rapids, MI
Museums:
   Grand Rapids Public Museum (600)
Public Television:
   WGVC Channel 35
Universities:
   Aquinas College (272)
   Calvin College (397)
   Grand Valley State College (366)
   Hope College (220)
Symphony Orchestras:
   Grand Rapids Symphony Orchestra★★★
   Grand Rapids Youth Symphony
Dance Companies:
   Grand Rapids Civic Ballet Company★
Public Libraries:
   300,000 volumes; circulation 1,878,000
Reading Quotient: 5.0
Places Rated Score: 3,255
Places Rated Rank: 99

Great Falls, MT
Symphony Orchestras:
   Great Falls Symphony Orchestra★
Public Libraries:
   201,152 volumes; circulation 510,791
Reading Quotient: 4.9
Places Rated Score: 401
Places Rated Rank: 279

Greeley, CO
Fine Arts and Public Radio:
   KUNC-FM 91.5 (50 mi; 132 hrs)
Universities:
   University of Northern Colorado (839)
Public Libraries:
   114,622 volumes; circulation 390,875
Reading Quotient: 7.6
Places Rated Score: 1,254
Places Rated Rank: 208

Green Bay, WI
Museums:
   Neville Public Museum (600)
Public Television:
   WPNE Channel 38
Universities:
   University of Wisconsin, Green Bay
      (899)
Symphony Orchestras:
   Green Bay Symphony Orchestra★
Public Libraries:
   347,926 volumes; circulation 1,255,375
Reading Quotient: 9.1
Places Rated Score: 2,547
Places Rated Rank: 124

**Greensboro–Winston-Salem–
High Point, NC**
Fine Arts and Public Radio:
   WFDD-FM 88.5 (40 mi; 126 hrs)
Public Television:
   WUNL Channel 26
Universities:
   University of North Carolina,
      Greensboro (823)••
   Wake Forest University (308)
Symphony Orchestras:
   Eastern Philharmonic Orchestra★★
   Greensboro Civic Orchestra
      (Community)
   Greensboro Symphony Orchestra★★
   Winston-Salem Symphony Orchestra★★
Theatres:
   North Carolina Shakespeare Festival
Dance Companies:
   North Carolina Dance Theatre
Public Libraries:
   1,106,807 volumes; circulation
      2,837,111
Reading Quotient: 7.0
Places Rated Score: 4,188
Places Rated Rank: 79

Greenville–Spartanburg, SC
Public Television:
   WNTV Channel 29
   WRET Channel 49
Universities:
   Furman University (238)
Symphony Orchestras:
   Carolina Youth Symphony
   Greenville Symphony Orchestra★
   Spartanburg Symphony Orchestra
      (Community)
Dance Companies:
   Carolina Ballet Theatre★★
Public Libraries:
   730,921 volumes; circulation 1,677,501
Reading Quotient: 5.0
Places Rated Score: 2,569
Places Rated Rank: 122

Hagerstown, MD
Public Television:
   WWPB Channel 31
Symphony Orchestras:
   Maryland Symphony Orchestra
      (Community)
Public Libraries:
   224,999 volumes; circulation 718,484
Reading Quotient: 8.3
Places Rated Score: 825
Places Rated Rank: 242

Hamilton–Middletown, OH
Universities:
   Miami University (1,000)
Symphony Orchestras:
   Hamilton–Fairfield Symphony
      (Community)
   Middletown Symphony Orchestra
      (Community)
Dance Companies:
   Miami University Dance Theatre (M)★
Public Libraries:
   235,919 volumes; circulation NA
Reading Quotient: NA
CMSA Access: CINCINNATI–HAMILTON,
   OH–KY–IN (780)
Places Rated Score: 2,316
Places Rated Rank: 133

Harrisburg–Lebanon–Carlisle, PA
Museums:
Pennsylvania Historical and Museum
Commission (700)
William Penn Memorial Museum (700)
Fine Arts and Public Radio:
WITF-FM 89.5 (50 mi; 131 hrs)
Public Television:
WITF Channel 33
Symphony Orchestras:
Harrisburg Symphony Orchestra★★
Harrisburg Youth Symphony Orchestra
Public Libraries:
482,949 volumes; circulation 1,169,069
Reading Quotient: 2.8
Places Rated Score: 3,083
Places Rated Rank: 103

Hartford, CT
Museums:
Wadsworth Atheneum (600)
Fine Arts and Public Radio:
WPBH-FM 90.5 (19 mi; 140 hrs)
Public Television:
WEDH Channel 24
Universities:
University of Hartford (401)
Symphony Orchestras:
Hartford Chamber Orchestra★★
Hartford Symphony Orchestra★★★
Hartford Symphony Orchestra (Youth)
Theatres:
Hartford Stage Company★
Opera Companies:
Connecticut Opera
4 productions; 12 performances
Dance Companies:
Connecticut Jazz Dance Company
Hartford Conservatory Modern Dance
Ensemble
Public Libraries:
466,653 volumes; circulation 547,866
Reading Quotient: 7.4
Places Rated Score: 3,616
Places Rated Rank: 89

Hickory, NC
Symphony Orchestras:
Western Piedmont Symphony
(Community)
Public Libraries:
87,917 volumes; circulation 177,346
Reading Quotient: 5.3
Places Rated Score: 188
Places Rated Rank: 306

Honolulu, HI
Museums:
Bernice Pauahi Bishop Museum (800)
Honolulu Academy of the Arts (800)
Fine Arts and Public Radio:
KHPR-FM 88.1 (50 mi; 168 hrs)
Public Television:
KHET Channel 11
KMEB Channel 10
Universities:
University of Hawaii (1,000)
Symphony Orchestras:
Honolulu Symphony Orchestra★★★
Theatres:
Honolulu Theatre for Youth
Opera Companies:
Hawaii Opera Theatre
3 productions; 9 performances
Dance Companies:
Ballet Hawaii
Dances We Dance Company (M)

Public Libraries:
2,241,156 volumes; circulation
5,200,000
Reading Quotient: 7.7
Places Rated Score: 7,168
Places Rated Rank: 36

Houma–Thibodaux, LA
Universities:
Nicholls State University (468)
Public Libraries:
256,983 volumes; circulation 407,258
Reading Quotient: 3.7
Places Rated Score: 725
Places Rated Rank: 255

★ Houston, TX
Museums:
Houston Museum of Natural Science
(1,100)
Museum of Fine Art (700)
Fine Arts and Public Radio:
KPFT-FM 90.1 (45 mi; 168 hrs)
KUHF-FM 88.7 (48 mi; 145 hrs)
Public Television:
KUHT Channel 8
Universities:
Houston Baptist University (222)
Rice University (245)
University of Houston (1,000)
Symphony Orchestras:
Clear Lake Symphony (Community)
Houston Pops Orchestra★★
Houston Symphony Orchestra★★★★
Houston Youth Symphony and Ballet
Symphony North of Houston
(Community)
Texas Chamber Orchestra★
Theatres:
Alley Theatre★★★
Opera Companies:
Houston Grand Opera★★★★
10 productions; 54 performances
Texas Opera Theatre
2 productions; 100 performances
Dance Companies:
Allegro Ballet of Houston
Delia Stewart Dance Company (J)
Discovery Dance Group
Encore Jazz Dancers
Greater Houston Civic Ballet Company★
Houston Ballet★★
Royal Ballet Theatre of Texas
Southwest Jazz Ballet Company
Space/Dance/Theatre
Public Libraries:
3,156,063 volumes; circulation
8,414,755
Reading Quotient: 3.8
Places Rated Score: 11,073
Places Rated Rank: 11

Huntington–Ashland, WV–KY–OH
Museums:
Huntington Galleries (500)
Public Television:
WPBY Channel 33
Universities:
Marshall University (835)
Symphony Orchestras:
Huntington Chamber Orchestra
(Community)
Public Libraries:
260,000 volumes; circulation 656,431
Reading Quotient: 8.6
Places Rated Score: 2,195
Places Rated Rank: 140

Huntsville, AL
Fine Arts and Public Radio:
WLRH-FM 89.3 (60 mi; 130 hrs)
Public Television:
WHIQ Channel 25
Universities:
University of Alabama, Huntsville (546)
Symphony Orchestras:
Huntsville Symphony Orchestra★
Huntsville Youth Orchestra
Dance Companies:
Huntsville Civic Ballet
Public Libraries:
225,170 volumes; circulation 461,000
Reading Quotient: 3.5
Places Rated Score: 1,921
Places Rated Rank: 161

Indianapolis, IN
Museums:
Children's Museum (500)
Indianapolis Museum of Art (900)
Fine Arts and Public Radio:
WAJC-FM 104.5 (65 mi; 126 hrs)
WIAN-FM 90.1 (27 mi; 162 hrs)
Public Television:
WFYI Channel 20
Universities:
Butler University (208)
Indiana University–Purdue University at
Indianapolis (919)
Symphony Orchestras:
Butler University Symphony Orchestra
Indianapolis Symphony Orchestra★★★★
Theatres:
Indiana Repertory Theatre★
Opera Companies:
Indianapolis Opera
3 productions; 6 performances
Dance Companies:
Dance Kaleidoscope (M)
Indianapolis Ballet Theatre
Public Libraries:
1,403,317 volumes; circulation
3,829,511
Reading Quotient: NA
Places Rated Score: 6,348
Places Rated Rank: 44

Iowa City, IA
Fine Arts and Public Radio:
KSUI-AM 910 (120 mi; 131 hrs)
KSUI-FM 9l.7 (70 mi; 134 hrs)
Public Television:
KIIN Channel 12
Universities:
University of Iowa (1,000)
Public Libraries:
155,000 volumes; circulation 487,000
Reading Quotient: 10.4
Places Rated Score: 2,255
Places Rated Rank: 136

Jackson, MI
Symphony Orchestras:
Jackson Symphony Orchestra
(Community)
Public Libraries:
222,550 volumes; circulation 685,322
Reading Quotient: 6.0
Places Rated Score: 323
Places Rated Rank: 290

Jackson, MS
Fine Arts and Public Radio:
WJSU-FM (126 hrs)

Public Television:
 WMAA Channel 29
Universities·
 Jackson State University (710)
 Mississippi College (143)
Symphony Orchestras:
 Jackson State University Orchestra
 Jackson Symphony Orchestra★★
 Jackson Symphony Youth Orchestra
Opera Companies:
 Mississippi Opera Association
  2 productions; 4 performances
Dance Companies:
 Ballet Mississippi
Public Libraries:
 797,748 volumes; circulation 1,268,369
Reading Quotient: 4.7
Places Rated Score: 3,209
Places Rated Rank: 100

Jacksonville, FL
Fine Arts and Public Radio:
 WJCT-FM 89.9 (125 mi; 133 hrs)
Public Television:
 WJCT Channel 7
Universities:
 Jacksonville University (302)•
Symphony Orchestras:
 Jacksonville Symphony Orchestra★★★
Dance Companies:
 Ballet Guild of Jacksonville★
 Florida Ballet at Jacksonville
 Jacksonville Ballet Theatre★
Public Libraries:
 410,433 volumes; circulation 2,026,528
Reading Quotient: 4.0
Places Rated Score: 2,162
Places Rated Rank: 144

Jacksonville, NC
Public Television:
 WUNM Channel 19
Public Libraries:
 67,000 volumes; circulation 300,000
Reading Quotient: 3.3
Places Rated Score: 567
Places Rated Rank: 265

Janesville–Beloit, WI
Universities:
 University of Wisconsin, Janesville (899)
Symphony Orchestras:
 Beloit–Janesville Symphony Orchestra
 (Community)
Public Libraries:
 92,535 volumes; circulation NA
Reading Quotient: NA
Places Rated Score: 1,092
Places Rated Rank: 220

Jersey City, NJ
Universities:
 Jersey City State College (461)
Public Libraries:
 243,777 volumes; circulation NA
Reading Quotient: NA
CMSA Access: NEW YORK–NORTHERN
 NEW JERSEY–LONG ISLAND, NY–NJ–
 CT (6,715)
Places Rated Score: 7,420
Places Rated Rank: 33

Johnson City–Kingsport–Bristol, TN–VA
Fine Arts and Public Radio:
 WETS-FM 89.5 (65 mi; 126 hrs)

Universities:
 East Tennessee State University (792)
Symphony Orchestras:
 Jackson Symphony Orchestra★
 Johnson City Symphony (Community)
 Kingsport Symphony Orchestra
 (Community)
Theatres:
 Barter Theatre★
Dance Companies:
 Bristol Ballet Company★
Public Libraries:
 133,162 volumes; circulation 371,312
Reading Quotient: 6.5
Places Rated Score: 1,925
Places Rated Rank: 160

Johnstown, PA
Universities:
 University of Pittsburgh, Johnstown
 (240)
Symphony Orchestras:
 Johnstown Symphony Orchestra★
 Johnstown Youth Symphony
Public Libraries:
 126,209 volumes; circulation NA
Reading Quotient: NA
Places Rated Score: 666
Places Rated Rank: 259

Joliet, IL
Public Libraries:
 130,588 volumes; circulation 245,685
Reading Quotient: 4.8
CMSA Access: CHICAGO–GARY–LAKE
 COUNTY, IL–IN–WI (3,046)
Places Rated Score: 3,177
Places Rated Rank: 101

Joplin, MO
Public Libraries:
 80,000 volumes; circulation NA
Reading Quotient: NA
Places Rated Score: 80
Places Rated Rank: 324

Kalamazoo, MI
Fine Arts and Public Radio:
 WMUK-FM 102.1 (33 mi; 127 hrs)
Universities:
 Western Michigan University (1,000)•
Symphony Orchestras:
 Kalamazoo Junior Symphony
 Kalamazoo Symphony Orchestra★★
Dance Companies:
 Kalamazoo Ballet Company★
Public Libraries:
 270,589 volumes; circulation 721,512
Reading Quotient: 8.0
Places Rated Score: 2,071
Places Rated Rank: 150

Kankakee, IL
Public Libraries:
 74,824 volumes; circulation 174,989
Reading Quotient: 8.3
Places Rated Score: 75
Places Rated Rank: 326

Kansas City, KS
Universities:
 Pittsburg State University (317)
Symphony Orchestras:
 Youth Symphony of Kansas City
Public Libraries:
 342,720 volumes; circulation 444,019

Reading Quotient: 4.6
CMSA Access: KANSAS CITY, MO–KANSAS
 CITY, KS (407)
Places Rated Score: 1,167
Places Rated Rank: 215

Kansas City, MO
Museums:
 Nelson/Atkins Museum of Fine Art (700)
Fine Arts and Public Radio:
 KCUR-FM 89.3 (45 mi; 136 hrs)
Public Television:
 KCPT Channel 19
Universities:
 Avila College (197)
 Central Missouri State University (816)
 University of Missouri, Kansas City (612)
Symphony Orchestras:
 Independence Symphony Orchestra
 (Community)
 Kansas City Symphony★★★
 Northland Symphony Orchestra
 (Community)
Theatres:
 Missouri Repertory Theatre★
Opera Companies:
 Lyric Opera of Kansas City
  6 productions; 26 performances
Dance Companies:
 Kansas City Ballet
Public Libraries:
 1,221,854 volumes; circulation 975,000
Reading Quotient: 7.4
Places Rated Score: 5,553
Places Rated Rank: 51

Kenosha, WI
Fine Arts and Public Radio:
 WGTD-FM 91.1 (129 hrs)
Universities:
 University of Wisconsin, Kenosha (281)
Symphony Orchestras:
 Kenosha Symphony (Community)
Public Libraries:
 207,038 volumes; circulation 719,926
Reading Quotient: 11.5
CMSA Access: CHICAGO–GARY–LAKE
 COUNTY, IL–IN–WI (2,956)
Places Rated Score: 3,844
Places Rated Rank: 83

Killeen–Temple, TX
Fine Arts and Public Radio:
 KNCT-FM 91.3 (8,846.5 sq mi; 131 hrs)
Public Television:
 KNCT Channel 46
Public Libraries:
 119,714 volumes; circulation NA
Reading Quotient: NA
Places Rated Score: 920
Places Rated Rank: 235

Knoxville, TN
Fine Arts and Public Radio:
 WUOT-FM 91.9 (41 mi; 168 hrs)
Public Television:
 WSJK Channel 2
Universities:
 University of Tennessee (1,000)
Symphony Orchestras:
 Knoxville Symphony Orchestra★★
 Knoxville Symphony Youth Orchestra
Dance Companies:
 Appalachian Ballet Company★
 Oak Ridge Civic Ballet Association★
 Tennessee Festival Ballet★

Public Libraries:
608,546 volumes; circulation 1,489,422
Reading Quotient: 6.6
Places Rated Score: 3,309
Places Rated Rank: 97

Kokomo, IN
Symphony Orchestras:
Kokomo Symphony Orchestra
(Community)
Public Libraries:
185,000 volumes; circulation 498,058
Reading Quotient: 7.2
Places Rated Score: 285
Places Rated Rank: 295

La Crosse, WI
Fine Arts and Public Radio:
WLSU-FM 88.9 (25 mi; 134 hrs)
Public Television:
WHLA Channel 31
Symphony Orchestras:
La Crosse Symphony Orchestra
(Community)
La Crosse Youth Symphony
Symphony School of America Orchestra
(Youth)
University of Wisconsin, La Crosse,
Symphony
Public Libraries:
265,737 volumes; circulation 206,843
Reading Quotient: 5.0
Places Rated Score: 1,466
Places Rated Rank: 191

Lafayette, IN
Museums:
Tippecanoe County Historical Museum
(600)
Fine Arts and Public Radio:
WBAA-AM 920 (65 mi; 126 hrs)
Universities:
Purdue University (1,000)
Symphony Orchestras:
Lafayette Symphony (Community)
Purdue University Symphony Orchestra
Public Libraries:
135,518 volumes; circulation 317,543
Reading Quotient: 4.5
Places Rated Score: 2,236
Places Rated Rank: 137

Lafayette, LA
Fine Arts and Public Radio:
KRVS-FM 88.7 (78 mi; 164 hrs)
Universities:
University of Southwestern Louisiana
(991)
Symphony Orchestras:
L'Orchestre (College)
Public Libraries:
180,864 volumes; circulation 558,469
Reading Quotient: 4.9
Places Rated Score: 1,772
Places Rated Rank: 173

Lake Charles, LA
Public Television:
KLTL Channel 18
Universities:
McNeese State University (470)
Symphony Orchestras:
Lake Charles Symphony Orchestra
(Community)
Dance Companies:
Lake Charles Ballet Joyeux
Lake Charles Civic Ballet Company★

Public Libraries:
235,695 volumes; circulation NA
Reading Quotient: NA
Places Rated Score: 1,456
Places Rated Rank: 192

Lake County, IL
Symphony Orchestras:
Flute and Fiddle Club Orchestra
(Community)
Waukegan Symphony Orchestra
(Community)
Public Libraries:
499,676 volumes; circulation 402,289
Reading Quotient: 7.6
CMSA Access: CHICAGO–GARY–LAKE
COUNTY, IL–IN–WI (3,046)
Places Rated Score: 3,746
Places Rated Rank: 87

Lakeland–Winter Haven, FL
Symphony Orchestras:
Lakeland Symphony Orchestra
(Community)
Winter Haven Youth Symphony
Public Libraries:
108,719 volumes; circulation 334,873
Reading Quotient: 8.5
Places Rated Score: 309
Places Rated Rank: 292

Lancaster, PA
Universities:
Franklin and Marshall College (206)
Millersville State College (459)
Public Libraries:
350,000 volumes; circulation 690,000
Reading Quotient: 2.8
Places Rated Score: 1,015
Places Rated Rank: 229

Lansing–East Lansing, MI
Museums:
Michigan State University Museum
(1,200)
Fine Arts and Public Radio:
WKAR-AM 870 (70 mi; 86 hrs)
WKAR-FM 90.5 (80 mi; 132 hrs)
Public Television:
WKAR Channel 23
Universities:
Michigan State University (1,000)
Symphony Orchestras:
Lansing Symphony Orchestra★★
Theatres:
Boarshead–Michigan Public Theatre
Opera Companies:
Opera Company of Greater Lansing
1 production; 2 performances
Dance Companies:
Lansing Ballet Company
Public Libraries:
354,226 volumes; circulation 771,212
Reading Quotient: 5.9
Places Rated Score: 4,206
Places Rated Rank: 78

Laredo, TX
Symphony Orchestras:
Laredo Philharmonic Orchestra
(Community)
Public Libraries:
50,152 volumes; circulation NA
Reading Quotient: NA
Places Rated Score: 150
Places Rated Rank: 313

Las Cruces, NM
Museums:
New Mexico State University Museum
(900)
Fine Arts and Public Radio:
KRWG-FM 90.7 (100 mi; 133 hrs)
Public Television:
KRWG Channel 22
Universities:
New Mexico State University (901)
Symphony Orchestras:
Las Cruces Symphony (Community)
Public Libraries:
103,282 volumes; circulation 235,535
Reading Quotient: 3.5
Places Rated Score: 2,804
Places Rated Rank: 114

Las Vegas, NV
Fine Arts and Public Radio:
KNPR-FM 89.5 (40 mi; 147 hrs)
Public Television:
KLVX Channel 10
Symphony Orchestras:
Las Vegas Chamber Symphony
Orchestra (Community)
Las Vegas Civic Symphony
(Community)
Dance Companies:
Nevada Dance Theatre
Public Libraries:
436,172 volumes; circulation 1,605,667
Reading Quotient: 5.3
Places Rated Score: 1,586
Places Rated Rank: 184

Lawrence, KS
Museums:
Spencer Museum of Art (600)
University of Kansas Systematics
Museums (1,000)
Fine Arts and Public Radio:
KANU-FM 91.5 (40 mi; 139 hrs)
Universities:
University of Kansas (1,000)●
Symphony Orchestras:
Lawrence Chamber Players
(Community)
Public Libraries:
150,000 volumes; circulation 426,000
Reading Quotient: 11.5
Places Rated Score: 3,150
Places Rated Rank: 102

Lawrence–Haverhill, MA–NH
Public Libraries:
373,017 volumes; circulation 325,794
Reading Quotient: 6.4
CMSA Access: BOSTON–LAWRENCE–
SALEM, MA–NH (1,738)
Places Rated Score: 2,111
Places Rated Rank: 147

Lawton, OK
Museums:
Museum of the Great Plains (700)
Universities:
Cameron University (282)
Symphony Orchestras:
Lawton Philharmonic Orchestra★
Public Libraries:
98,000 volumes; circulation 240,000
Reading Quotient: 3.1
Places Rated Score: 1,280
Places Rated Rank: 205

Lewiston–Auburn, ME
Public Television:
 WCBB Channel 10
Public Libraries:
 236,000 volumes; circulation 128,000
Reading Quotient: 5.8
Places Rated Score: 736
Places Rated Rank: 253

Lexington–Fayette, KY
Fine Arts and Public Radio:
 WBKY 91.3 (80 mi; 138 hrs)
Public Television:
 WKLE Channel 46
Universities:
 Kentucky State University (120)
 Eastern Kentucky University (1,000)
 University of Kentucky (1,000)
Symphony Orchestras:
 Central Kentucky Youth Orchestra
 Lexington Philharmonic Orchestra★★
Dance Companies:
 Lexington Ballet Company
Public Libraries:
 226,065 volumes; circulation 836,456
Reading Quotient: 5.1
Places Rated Score: 3,596
Places Rated Rank: 90

Lima, OH
Museums:
 Allen County Museum (700)
Universities:
 Ohio Northern University (218)
Symphony Orchestras:
 Lima Symphony Orchestra★
Public Libraries:
 234,312 volumes; circulation 476,950
Reading Quotient: 6.5
Places Rated Score: 1,352
Places Rated Rank: 200

Lincoln, NE
Museums:
 State Historical Museum (1,100)
 University of Nebraska State Museum
 (600)
Fine Arts and Public Radio:
 KUCV-FM 90.9 (60 mi; 131 hrs)
Public Television:
 KUON Channel 12
Universities:
 University of Nebraska (1,000)●
Symphony Orchestras:
 Lincoln Civic Orchestra (Community)
 Lincoln Symphony Orchestra★★
 Lincoln Youth Symphony Orchestra
 Nebraska Chamber Orchestra
 (Community)
Public Libraries:
 423,386 volumes; circulation 1,192,394
Reading Quotient: 8.4
Places Rated Score: 4,523
Places Rated Rank: 67

Little Rock–North Little Rock, AR
Public Television:
 KETS Channel 2
Universities:
 University of Arkansas, Little Rock
 (540)●
Symphony Orchestras:
 Arkansas Symphony Orchestra★★
Theatres:
 Arkansas Repertory Theatre

Opera Companies:
 The Arkansas Opera Theatre
 2 productions; 4 performances
Dance Companies:
 Ballet Arkansas
Public Libraries:
 481,860 volumes; circulation 704,965
Reading Quotient: 4.2
Places Rated Score: 2,180
Places Rated Rank: 142

Longview–Marshall, TX
Symphony Orchestras:
 Longview Symphony Orchestra
 (Community)
 Marshall Symphony Orchestra
 (Community)
Public Libraries:
 134,182 volumes; circulation 190,525
Reading Quotient: 2.4
Places Rated Score: 334
Places Rated Rank: 288

Lorain–Elyria, OH
Universities:
 Oberlin College (368)●
Dance Companies:
 Oberlin Dance Company (M)★
Public Libraries:
 406,057 volumes; circulation 940,772
Reading Quotient: 6.1
CMSA Access: CLEVELAND–AKRON–
 LORAIN, OH (1,691)
Places Rated Score: 2,565
Places Rated Rank: 123

★ Los Angeles–Long Beach, CA
Museums:
 California Museum of Science and
 Industry (600)
 J. Paul Getty Museum (500)
 Los Angeles County Museum of Art
 (1,000)
 Los Angeles State and County
 Arboretum (750)
 Natural History Museum of Los Angeles
 County (700)
 Southwest Museum (500)
Fine Arts and Public Radio:
 KLON-FM 88.1 (18 mi; 164 hrs)
 KPCC-FM 89.3 (30 mi; 131 hrs)
 KPFK-FM 90.7 (64 mi; 168 hrs)
 KUSC-FM 91.5 (32 mi; 168 hrs)
Public Television:
 KCET Channel 28
 KLCS Channel 58
Universities:
 California State Polytechnic University,
 Pomona (1,000)
 California State University, Long Beach
 (1,000)●
 California State University, Los Angeles
 (858)
 California State University, Northridge
 (1,000)
 Loyola Marymount University (372)
 Pepperdine University (217)
 UCLA (1,000)●
 University of Southern California
 (1,000)●
Symphony Orchestras:
 American Youth Symphony
 Glendale Symphony Orchestra★★
 Long Beach Symphony Orchestra★★★
 Los Angeles Chamber Orchestra★★★
 Los Angeles Philharmonic★★★★

Los Angeles Solo Repertory Orchestra
 (Community)
Loyola Marymount University Symphony
 Orchestra
New American Orchestra (Community)
Pasadena Chamber Orchestra★
Pasadena Symphony Orchestra★★
Pasadena Young Musicians Orchestra★
Pasadena Youth Symphony Orchestra
Symphony of the Verdugos
 (Community)
University of Southern California
 Symphony
Young Musicians Foundation Debut
 Orchestra
Theatres:
 Los Angeles Actor's Theatre
 Los Angeles Stage Company★
 Los Angeles Theatre Works
 Mark Taper Forum★★★★
Opera Companies:
 Los Angeles Opera Theatre
 3 productions; 9 performances
Dance Companies:
 Avaz International Dance Theatre (E-F)★
 Ballet Pacifica
 Bella Lewitzky Dance Company (M)
 Benn Howard Dance Company (M)
 Bethune Ballet
 Black Ballet Jazz, USA
 Elle Johnson Dance Company (M)
 Gene Maribaccio Ballet Company of
 Los Angeles
 "Koroyar" Folklore Ensemble (E-F)★
 Landrum Dance Theatre (J)
 Lola Montes and Her Spanish Dancers
 (E-F)
 Los Angeles Ballet★
 Margalit Dance Theatre Company (M)
 Newport Ballet
 Pasadena Dance Theatre (B)
 Rudy Perez Performance Ensemble (M)
 R'Wanda Lewis Afro-American Dance
 Company (E-F)
 Shale: Mary Jane Eisenberg Company
 TNR/The New Repertory (M)
 Valentina Oumansky Dramatic Dance
 Ensemble (M)
Public Libraries:
 4,602,998 volumes; circulation
 10,364,280
Reading Quotient: 4.9
CMSA Access: LOS ANGELES–ANAHEIM–
 RIVERSIDE, CA (340)
Places Rated Score: 23,567
Places Rated Rank: 3

Louisville, KY–IN
Fine Arts and Public Radio:
 WFPK-FM 91.9 (70 mi; 126 hrs)
 WFPL-FM 89.3 (70 mi; 132 hrs)
 WUOL-FM 90.5 (70 mi; 130 hrs)
Public Television:
 WKMJ Channel 68
 WKPC Channel 15
Universities:
 Bellarmine College (115)
 University of Louisville (488)
Symphony Orchestras:
 Louisville–Jefferson County Youth
 Orchestra
 Louisville Orchestra★★★
Theatres:
 Actor's Theatre of Louisville★★★
 Stage One

Opera Companies:
  Kentucky Opera Association
    4 productions; 11 performances
Dance Companies:
  Louisville Ballet
Public Libraries:
  1,119,771 volumes; circulation
    2,627,899
Reading Quotient: 5.5
Places Rated Score: 4,916
Places Rated Rank: 60

Lowell, MA–NH
Universities:
  University of Lowell (878)
Theatres:
  Merrimack Regional Theatre
Public Libraries:
  340,792 volumes; circulation 303,611
Reading Quotient: 6.8
CMSA Access: BOSTON–LAWRENCE–
  SALEM, MA–NH (1,738)
Places Rated Score: 3,057
Places Rated Rank: 104

Lubbock, TX
Museums:
  Texas Technical University Museum
    (1,300)
Public Television:
  KTXT Channel 5
Universities:
  Texas Tech University (1,000)
Symphony Orchestras:
  Lubbock Symphony Orchestra★★
Public Libraries:
  302,264 volumes; circulation NA
Reading Quotient: NA
Places Rated Score: 3,402
Places Rated Rank: 95

Lynchburg, VA
Universities:
  Liberty Baptist College (334)
  Lynchburg College (245)
  Washington and Lee University (300)
Symphony Orchestras:
  Lynchburg Symphony Orchestra
    (Community)
Public Libraries:
  99,546 volumes; circulation 239,291
Reading Quotient: 5.1
Places Rated Score: 1,079
Places Rated Rank: 221

Macon–Warner Robins, GA
Museums:
  Museum of Arts and Sciences (600)
Universities:
  Mercer University (350)●
Symphony Orchestras:
  Macon Symphony Orchestra
    (Community)
Dance Companies:
  Macon Ballet Company
Public Libraries:
  335,000 volumes; circulation 1,550,000
Reading Quotient: 7.5
Places Rated Score: 1,435
Places Rated Rank: 193

Madison, WI
Museums:
  Elvehjem Museum of Art (600)
  State Historical Society of Wisconsin
    (800)

Fine Arts and Public Radio:
  WERN-FM 88.7 (70 mi; 126 hrs)
  WHA-AM 970 (60 mi; 88 hrs)
  WORT-FM 89.9 (22 mi; 142 hrs)
Public Television:
  WHA Channel 21
Universities:
  University of Wisconsin (1,000)●
Symphony Orchestras:
  Madison Symphony Orchestra★★
  University of Wisconsin Symphony
  Wisconsin Chamber Orchestra
    (Community)
  Wisconsin Youth Symphony Orchestras
Dance Companies:
  Kanopy Dance Theatre (M)
  Wisconsin Dance Ensemble★
Public Libraries:
  572,909 volumes; circulation 1,945,587
Reading Quotient: 14.0
Places Rated Score: 5,123
Places Rated Rank: 56

Manchester, NH
Symphony Orchestras:
  New Hampshire Symphony Orchestra★
Public Libraries:
  274,684 volumes; circulation 931,178
Reading Quotient: 7.0
Places Rated Score: 475
Places Rated Rank: 272

Mansfield, OH
Symphony Orchestras:
  Mansfield Symphony Orchestra★
  Mansfield Symphony Youth Orchestra
Public Libraries:
  253,895 volumes; circulation 596,003
Reading Quotient: 6.5
Places Rated Score: 554
Places Rated Rank: 266

McAllen–Edinburg–Mission, TX
Universities:
  Pan American University (904)
Symphony Orchestras:
  Valley Symphony Orchestra
    (Community)
Dance Companies:
  Edinburg Dance Theatre
Public Libraries:
  176,607 volumes; circulation 620,359
Reading Quotient: 5.8
Places Rated Score: 1,231
Places Rated Rank: 210

Medford, OR
Public Television:
  KSYS Channel 8
Universities:
  Southern Oregon State College (393)
Symphony Orchestras:
  Peter Britt Gardens Music & Arts
    Festival★
Theatres:
  Oregon Shakespeare Festival★★★★
Public Libraries:
  263,159 volumes; circulation 1,018,741
Reading Quotient: 9.7
Places Rated Score: 1,856
Places Rated Rank: 168

Melbourne–Titusville–Palm Bay, FL
Symphony Orchestras:
  Brevard Symphony Orchestra★

Public Libraries:
  237,069 volumes; circulation 646,557
Reading Quotient: 5.4
Places Rated Score: 437
Places Rated Rank: 275

Memphis, TN–AR–MS
Museums:
  Memphis Pink Palace Museum (500)
Fine Arts and Public Radio:
  WKNO-FM 90.1 (120 mi; 126 hrs)
Public Television:
  WKNO Channel 10
Universities:
  Memphis State University (1,000)
Symphony Orchestras:
  Memphis Symphony Orchestra★★★
  Memphis Youth Symphony Orchestra
Theatres:
  Playhouse on the Square
Opera Companies:
  Opera Memphis
    4 productions; 8 performances
Public Libraries:
  1,354,000 volumes; circulation
    2,545,404
Reading Quotient: 4.9
Places Rated Score: 4,486
Places Rated Rank: 69

Miami–Hialeah, FL
Fine Arts and Public Radio:
  WLRN-FM 91.3 (34 mi; 164 hrs)
Public Television:
  WLRN Channel 17
  WPBT Channel 2
Universities:
  Barry University (168)
  University of Miami (1,000)●
Symphony Orchestras:
  Central Miami Youth Symphony
  Miami Beach Symphony Orchestra★★
  Miami Chamber Symphony (Community)
  South Florida Youth Symphony
Theatres:
  Coconut Grove Playhouse★
Opera Companies:
  Greater Miami Opera Association
    4 productions; 50 performances
Dance Companies:
  Miami Ballet★
Public Libraries:
  869,238 volumes; circulation 2,051,604
Reading Quotient: NA
Places Rated Score: 4,837
Places Rated Rank: 63

**Middlesex–Somerset–
Hunterdon, NJ**
Public Television:
  WNJB Channel 58
Universities:
  Douglass College (449)●
  Rutgers State University of New Jersey
    (225)
Theatres:
  Crossroads Theatre Company
  George Street Playhouse
Public Libraries:
  119,300 volumes; circulation 258,853
Reading Quotient: 8.0
CMSA Access: NEW YORK–NORTHERN
  NEW JERSEY–LONG ISLAND, NY–NJ–
  CT (6,565)
Places Rated Score: 8,058
Places Rated Rank: 26

Middletown, CT
Universities:
  Wesleyan University (256)
Public Libraries:
  99,766 volumes; circulation NA
Reading Quotient: NA
CMSA Access: HARTFORD–NEW
  BRITAIN–MIDDLETOWN, CT (374)
Places Rated Score: 730
Places Rated Rank: 254

Midland, TX
Symphony Orchestras:
  Midland–Odessa Symphony and
    Chorale★★
Public Libraries:
  138,472 volumes; circulation NA
Reading Quotient: NA
Places Rated Score: 438
Places Rated Rank: 274

★ Milwaukee, WI
Museums:
  Milwaukee Art Museum (600)
  Milwaukee County Historical Society
    (500)
  Milwaukee Public Museum (500)
Fine Arts and Public Radio:
  WUWM-FM 89.7 (metro Milwaukee;
    147 hrs)
  WYMS-FM 88.9 (20.5 mi; 126 hrs)
Public Television:
  WMVS Channel 10
  WMVT Channel 36
Universities:
  University of Wisconsin, Milwaukee
    (1,000)●
  Marquette University (793)
Symphony Orchestras:
  Milwaukee Symphony Orchestra★★★★
  Music for Youth
  Wisconsin Conservatory of Music
    Chamber Orchestra (College)
Theatres:
  Great American Children's Theatre
    Company
  Milwaukee Repertory Theatre★★
Opera Companies:
  Florentine Opera Company
    3 productions; 9 performances
Dance Companies:
  Bauer Dance Ensemble (M)
  JoJean Retrum Dance Company (J)
  Ko-Thi Dance Company (E-F)
  Milwaukee Ballet Company★
Public Libraries:
  2,096,002 volumes; circulation
    3,350,664
Reading Quotient: 5.3
Places Rated Score: 8,766
Places Rated Rank: 21

★ Minneapolis–St. Paul, MN–WI
Museums:
  Bell Museum of Natural History (1,100)
  Minneapolis Institute of Arts (800)
  Science Museum of Minnesota (600)
  Walker Art Center (600)
Fine Arts and Public Radio:
  KSJN–AM 1330 (40 mi; 131 hrs)
  KSJN–FM 91.1 (54 mi; 133 hrs)
  KUOM–AM 770 (86 mi; 48 hrs)
Public Television:
  KTCA Channel 2
  KTCI Channel 17
Universities:
  Bethel College (219)

College of St. Thomas (323)
  Gustavus Adolphus College (225)
  St. Olaf College (404)●
  University of Minnesota, Twin Cities
    (1,000)
Symphony Orchestras:
  Bloomington Symphony Orchestra
    (Community)
  Civic Orchestra of Minneapolis
    (Community)
  Minnesota Orchestra★★★★
  Minnesota Youth Orchestra
  St. Paul Chamber Orchestra★★★★
Theatres:
  Actor's Theatre of St. Paul
  Children's Theatre Company★★
  Cricket Theatre
  Guthrie Theatre★★★★
  Illusion Theatre
  Playwright's Center
Opera Companies:
  Minnesota Opera Company
    4 productions; 13 performances
Dance Companies:
  Ethnic Dance Theatre (E-F)★
  Minnesota Dance Theatre (M)★
  Minnesota Jazz Company
  Nancy Hauser Dance Company (M)
  New Dance Ensemble (M)
Public Libraries:
  1,541,423 volumes; circulation
    4,446,249
Reading Quotient: 9.4
Places Rated Score: 11,714
Places Rated Rank: 10

Mobile, AL
Fine Arts and Public Radio:
  WHIL-FM 91.3 (84 mi; 132 hrs)
Public Television:
  WEIQ Channel 42
Universities:
  University of South Alabama (609)
Opera Companies:
  Mobile Opera, Inc.
    3 productions; 10 performances
Public Libraries:
  124,585 volumes; circulation 944,514
Reading Quotient: 3.4
Places Rated Score: 1,764
Places Rated Rank: 174

Modesto, CA
Dance Companies:
  Central Valley Dance Company
  Modesto Civic Ballet Company★
Public Libraries:
  530,752 volumes; circulation 1,501,284
Reading Quotient: 7.6
Places Rated Score: 631
Places Rated Rank: 260

Monmouth–Ocean, NJ
Universities:
  Monmouth College (315)
Symphony Orchestras:
  Garden State Philharmonic Symphony
    Orchestra (Community)
  Garden State Philharmonic Youth
    Orchestra
  Monmouth Symphony Orchestra
    (Community)
Dance Companies:
  Shore Ballet Company★
  Dorothy Pons Dance Company (J)
Public Libraries:
  82,795 volumes; circulation NA

Reading Quotient: NA
CMSA Access: NEW YORK–NORTHERN
  NEW JERSEY–LONG ISLAND, NY–NJ–
  CT (6,715)
Places Rated Score: 7,563
Places Rated Rank: 30

Monroe, LA
Public Television:
  KLTM Channel 13
Universities:
  Northeast Louisiana University (767)
Public Libraries:
  257,740 volumes; circulation 680,611
Reading Quotient: 7.1
Places Rated Score: 1,528
Places Rated Rank: 187

Montgomery, AL
Fine Arts and Public Radio:
  WTSU-FM 89.9 (43 mi; 126 hrs)
Public Television:
  WAIQ Channel 26
Universities:
  Alabama State University (342)
Symphony Orchestras:
  Montgomery Symphony (Community)
Dance Companies:
  Montgomery Civic Ballet
Public Libraries:
  82,252 volumes; circulation NA
Reading Quotient: NA
Places Rated Score: 1,374
Places Rated Rank: 198

Muncie, IN
Fine Arts and Public Radio:
  WBST-FM 92.1 (15 mi; 163 hrs)
Public Television:
  WIPS Channel 49
Universities:
  Ball State University (1,000)
Symphony Orchestras:
  Muncie Symphony Orchestra★
Public Libraries:
  297,543 volumes; circulation 447,636
Reading Quotient: 9.3
Places Rated Score: 2,498
Places Rated Rank: 125

Muskegon, MI
Symphony Orchestras:
  West Shore Symphony Orchestra★
  West Shore Youth Symphony Orchestra
Public Libraries:
  229,086 volumes; circulation 546,159
Reading Quotient: 5.0
Places Rated Score: 529
Places Rated Rank: 267

Nashua, NH
Symphony Orchestras:
  Nashua Symphony Orchestra
    (Community)
Theatres:
  American Stage Festival
Public Libraries:
  184,119 volumes; circulation 523,648
Reading Quotient: 10.4
CMSA Access: BOSTON–LAWRENCE–
  SALEM, MA–NH (1,738)
Places Rated Score: 2,122
Places Rated Rank: 146

Nashville, TN
Museums:
  Country Music Hall of Fame (500)

Tennessee Botanical Gardens and Fine
Art Center (500)
Fine Arts and Public Radio:
WPLN-FM 90.3 (34 mi; 131 hrs)
Public Television:
WDCN Channel 8
Universities:
Middle Tennessee State University (824)
Vanderbilt University (541)
Symphony Orchestras:
Nashville Community Orchestra
Nashville Symphony Orchestra★★★
Nashville Youth Symphony
Dance Companies:
The Dancers' Studio Theatre Company
(J)
Public Libraries:
527,152 volumes; circulation 1,965,307
Reading Quotient: 5.2
Places Rated Score: 4,342
Places Rated Rank: 72

★ Nassau–Suffolk, NY
Universities:
Adelphi University (454)
Hofstra University (599)
Symphony Orchestras:
Great Neck Symphony (Community)
Nassau Symphony (Community)
Theatres:
Nassau Repertory Theatre
Dance Companies:
Eglevsky Ballet Company★
Long Island Dance Company (M)
New York Dance Theatre
Public Libraries:
372,035 volumes; circulation 11,993,867
Reading Quotient: 8.4
CMSA Access: NEW YORK–NORTHERN
NEW JERSEY–LONG ISLAND, NY–NJ–
CT (6,715)
Places Rated Score: 8,640
Places Rated Rank: 22

New Bedford, MA
Museums:
New Bedford Whaling Museum (500)
Symphony Orchestras:
New Bedford Symphony Orchestra
(Community)
Public Libraries:
165,539 volumes; circulation 407,388
Reading Quotient: 5.7
Places Rated Score: 766
Places Rated Rank: 249

New Britain, CT
Universities:
Central Connecticut State University
(660)
Symphony Orchestras:
New Britain Symphony Orchestra
(Community)
Public Libraries:
226,130 volumes; circulation 318,218
Reading Quotient: 7.5
CMSA Access: HARTFORD–NEW
BRITAIN–MIDDLETOWN, CT (374)
Places Rated Score: 1,360
Places Rated Rank: 199

New Haven–Meriden, CT
Museums:
New Haven Colony Historical Society
(600)

Peabody Museum of Natural History
(1,000)
Yale Center for British Art (500)
Yale University Art Gallery (900)
Public Television:
WEDY Channel 24
Universities:
Southern Connecticut State College
(660)
University of New Haven (753)
Yale University (613)●
Symphony Orchestras:
Chamber Orchestra of New England★
Meriden Symphony Orchestra★
New Haven Symphony Orchestra★★
Philharmonic Orchestra of Yale
University
Young Artists Philharmonic
Theatres:
Long Wharf Theatre★★
Yale Repertory Theatre★
Dance Companies:
Connecticut Ballet Company
Margo Knis Dance Ensemble (M)★
Margo Knis Jazz Dance Ensemble
Public Libraries:
726,403 volumes; circulation 666,376
Reading Quotient: 7.6
Places Rated Score: 7,852
Places Rated Rank: 29

New London–Norwich, CT–RI
Public Television:
WEDH Channel 53
Symphony Orchestras:
Eastern Connecticut Symphony★
Theatres:
O'Neill Theatre Center★★
Public Libraries:
164,000 volumes; circulation 301,000
Reading Quotient: 7.6
Places Rated Score: 1,164
Places Rated Rank: 217

New Orleans, LA
Museums:
Historic New Orleans Collection (600)
Louisiana State Museum (1,200)
New Orleans Museum of Art (700)
Fine Arts and Public Radio:
WWNO-FM 89.9 (70 mi; 133 hrs)
Public Television:
WYES Channel 12
Universities:
Loyola University (245)
Southeastern Louisiana University (899)
Tulane University of Louisiana (487)
University of New Orleans (820)
Xavier University of Louisiana (222)
Symphony Orchestras:
New Orleans Philharmonic Symphony
Orchestra★★★★
New Orleans Symphony Youth
Orchestra
Opera Companies:
New Orleans Opera Association
4 productions; 13 performances
Dance Companies:
Crescent Ballet Company★★
Delta Festival Ballet of New Orleans
New Orleans City/Cincinnati Ballet
Company★
Public Libraries:
802,934 volumes; circulation 1,176,304
Reading Quotient: 3.5
Places Rated Score: 7,978
Places Rated Rank: 27

★ New York, NY
Museums:
American Museum of Natural History
(2,000)
American Numismatic Society (800)
Brooklyn Art Museum (1,300)
Brooklyn Botanic Garden (1,200)
Brooklyn Children's Museum (600)
Cooper-Hewitt Museum of Design (500)
Hall of Science (500)
Hispanic Society of America (1,000)
Metropolitan Museum of Art (2,000)
Museum of the American Indian (900)
Museum of the City of New York (700)
Museum of Modern Art (900)
New York Botanical Gardens (1,300)
New York Historical Society (600)
Pierpont Morgan Library and Art
Museum (1,100)
Solomon R. Guggenheim Museum (600)
Staten Island Institute of Arts and
Sciences (600)
Whitney Museum of American Art
(1,000)
Fine Arts and Public Radio:
WBAI-FM 99.5 (60 mi; 168 hrs)
WNYC-AM 830 (115 hrs)
WNYC-FM 93.9 (35 mi; 168 hrs)
Public Television:
WNET Channel 13
WNYC Channel 31
WNYE Channel 25
Universities:
Barnard College (250)
Bernard Baruch College (1,000)
Brooklyn College (1,000)●
City College (1,000)●
Columbia University (1,000)
Fordham University (599)
Hunter College (940)
New York University (1,000)
Queens College (1,000)●
St. Johns University (1,000)
Staten Island College (564)
Yeshiva University (664)
Symphony Orchestras:
American Composers Orchestra★
American Symphony Orchestra★★★
Bronx Philharmonic (Community)
Bronx Symphony Orchestra
(Community)
Brooklyn Philharmonic Symphony
Orchestra★★
Camerata Youth Symphony
City Symphony of Westchester★★
Columbia University Orchestra
Doctors Orchestra Society of New York
(Community)
Downeast Chamber Orchestra (Youth)
Greenwich House Orchestra (College)
Independent School Orchestras (Youth)
Jupiter Symphony Orchestra★
Levite Symphony Orchestra
(Community)
Little Orchestra Society★★
New York Chamber Symphony
(Community)
New York Philharmonic★★★★
New York University Symphony
Orchestra
Staten Island Symphony (Community)
West End Symphony (Community)
Youth Symphony Orchestra of New York
Theatres:
The Acting Company★
American Jewish Theatre

American Place Theatre
Circle in the Square★★★★
Circle Repertory Company★
CSC Repertory
Empire State Institute for the Performing Arts
Ensemble Studio Theatre
First All Children's Theatre
INTAR
Mabou Mines
Manhattan Theatre Club★
Music-Theatre Group, Lenox Arts Center
New Dramatists
New Federal Theatre
New York Shakespeare Festival★★★★
Playwrights Horizons★★★
Puerto Rican Traveling Theatre Company
Repertorio Español
Roundabout Theatre Company★★
Theatre for the New City
Opera Companies:
  Chamber Opera Theatre of New York
    3 productions; 18 performances
  Metropolitan Opera★★★★
    23 productions; 210 performances
  New York City Opera★★★★
    19 productions; 134 performances
Dance Companies:*
  Alvin Ailey American Dance Theatre (M)★
  American Ballet Theatre★★
  American Ballet Theatre II★
  Bronx Dance Theatre★
  Chuck Davis Dance Company (E-F)★
  Dance Theatre of Harlem★
  Feld Ballet★
  Festival Dance Theatre★
  George Tomov Yugoslav Folkdance Ensemble (E-F)★
  Harkness Ballet of New York★
  Heritage Festivals (E-F)★
  Joffrey Ballet★
  Juilliard Dance Ensemble (M)★
  Martha Graham Dance Company (M)★
  Mayiri Armenian Folk Dance Group (E-F)★
  Metropolitan Opera Ballet★
  Paul Taylor Dance Company (M)★
  Pearl Lang Dance Company (M)★
  Philippine Dance Company of New York (E-F)★
  Polish American Folk Dance Company (E-F)★
  Twyla Tharp Dance (M)★
  U.S. Terpsichore★
  Westchester Ballet Company★
  Windmere Ballet Theatre★
Public Libraries:
  7,271,592 volumes; circulation NA
Reading Quotient: NA
CMSA Access: NEW YORK–NORTHERN NEW JERSEY–LONG ISLAND, NY–NJ–CT (1,596)
Places Rated Score: 56,745
Places Rated Rank: 1

---

*A total of 149 dance companies qualified for inclusion in New York's profile, but for reasons of space only those receiving one or two stars are listed.

★ **Newark, NJ**
Museums:
  Newark Museum (1,100)
Fine Arts and Public Radio:
  WBGO-FM 88.3 (40 mi; 164 hrs)
Public Television:
  WNJM Channel 50
Universities:
  Kean College of New Jersey (611)
  Montclair State College (750)
  Newark College of Arts and Sciences (331)
  Seton Hall (569)
Symphony Orchestras:
  New Jersey Symphony Orchestra★★★
  New Philharmonic of North West New Jersey (Community)
Theatres:
  New Jersey Shakespeare Festival
  Paper Mill Playhouse★★★★
  The Whole Theatre Company
Opera Companies:
  New Jersey State Opera
    3 productions; 3 performances
Dance Companies:
  Garden State Ballet★
  Judith Janus and Contemporary Dancers (M)
  New Jersey Ballet Company
  Newark Dance Theatre (J)
  Renate Booue Dance Company (M)
  Westminster Dance Theatre
Public Libraries:
  2,231,560 volumes; circulation 1,770,831
Reading Quotient: 10.5
CMSA Access: NEW YORK–NORTHERN NEW JERSEY–LONG ISLAND, NY–NJ–CT (5,872)
Places Rated Score: 14,224
Places Rated Rank: 8

Niagara Falls, NY
Public Libraries:
  186,056 volumes; circulation 298,317
Reading Quotient: 6.9
CMSA Access: BUFFALO–NIAGARA FALLS, NY (780)
Places Rated Score: 966
Places Rated Rank: 234

Norfolk–Virginia Beach–Newport News, VA
Museums:
  Chrysler Museum (700)
Fine Arts and Public Radio:
  WHRO-FM 89.5 (25 mi; 133 hrs)
Public Television:
  WHRO Channel 15
Universities:
  College of William and Mary (461)
  Hampton Institute (323)
  Norfolk State University (726)
  Old Dominion University (1,000)
  Virginia Commonwealth University (1,000)
Symphony Orchestras:
  Old Dominion University Symphony
  Peninsula Symphony of Virginia (Community)
  Virginia Beach Community Orchestra
  Virginia Beach Pops★
  Virginia Orchestra Group★★★
Theatres:
  Virginia Stage Company

Opera Companies:
  Virginia Opera Association
    7 productions; 38 performances
Dance Companies:
  Old Dominion University Ballet Company
Public Libraries:
  560,856 volumes; circulation 3,117,007
Reading Quotient: 5.3
Places Rated Score: 7,087
Places Rated Rank: 37

Norwalk, CT
Symphony Orchestras:
  Norwalk Symphony Orchestra (Community)
  Norwalk Youth Symphony
Theatres:
  Westport County Playhouse★
Dance Companies:
  Ballet Etudes Repertory Company
  Nikki Williams Dancers (J)
  Westport Dance Center (M)
Public Libraries:
  68,326 volumes; circulation 277,064
Reading Quotient: 4.5
CMSA Access: NEW YORK–NORTHERN NEW JERSEY–LONG ISLAND, NY–NJ–CT (6,655)
Places Rated Score: 7,273
Places Rated Rank: 35

Oakland, CA
Museums:
  Lawrence Hall of Science (600)
Universities:
  University of California, Berkeley (1,000)●
Symphony Orchestras:
  Berkeley Youth Orchestra
  Contra Costa Chamber Orchestra (Community)
  Diablo Youth Orchestra
  Oakland Symphony Orchestra★★★
  Oakland Symphony Youth Orchestra
  Young People's Symphony Orchestra
Theatres:
  Berkeley Repertory Theatre★
  Berkeley Shakespeare Festival
Dance Companies:
  Ballet Joyeux
  Berkeley Conservatory Ballet
  Dimensions Dance Theatre (E-F)
  Khadra International Folk Ballet (E-F)★
  Nancy Karp and Dancers (M)
  Oakland Ballet Company★
  Oakland Theatre of Dance
  Terry Meyers Dancers Company (M)
Public Libraries:
  748,377 volumes; circulation 1,618,201
Reading Quotient: 6.6
CMSA Access: SAN FRANCISCO–OAKLAND–SAN JOSE, CA (2,114)
Places Rated Score: 6,162
Places Rated Rank: 45

Ocala, FL
Symphony Orchestras:
  CFCC Aeolian Players (College)
Public Libraries:
  165,811 volumes; circulation 732,758
Reading Quotient: 4.3
Places Rated Score: 266
Places Rated Rank: 299

Odessa, TX
Symphony Orchestras:
  West Texas Youth Orchestra
Public Libraries:
  159,355 volumes; circulation 694,158
Reading Quotient: 7.4
Places Rated Score: 259
Places Rated Rank: 300

Oklahoma City, OK
Museums:
  Oklahoma Historical Society (600)
Public Television:
  KETA Channel 13
Universities:
  Central State University (1,000)
  Oklahoma City University (404)••
  University of Oklahoma (1,000)
Symphony Orchestras:
  Chamber Orchestra of Oklahoma
    (Community)
  Oklahoma City Junior Symphony
  Oklahoma Symphony Orchestra★★★
Dance Companies:
  Ballet Oklahoma★
  University of Oklahoma Ballet
Public Libraries:
  588,872 volumes; circulation 1,913,671
Reading Quotient: 4.2
Places Rated Score: 4,843
Places Rated Rank: 62

Olympia, WA
Symphony Orchestras:
  Olympia Symphony Orchestra
    (Community)
Public Libraries:
  607,803 volumes; circulation 1,981,858
Reading Quotient: 9.1
Places Rated Score: 708
Places Rated Rank: 256

Omaha, NE–IA
Museums:
  Joslyn Art Museum (1,200)
Fine Arts and Public Radio:
  KIOS-FM 91.5 (75 mi; 138 hrs)
  KVNO-FM 90.7 (50 mi; 140 hrs)
Universities:
  Creighton University (450)•
Symphony Orchestras:
  Omaha Area Youth Orchestras
  Omaha Symphony Orchestra★★★
Theatres:
  Nebraska Theatre Caravan
  Omaha Magic Theatre
Opera Companies:
  Opera Omaha, Inc.
    3 productions; 10 performances
Dance Companies:
  A Company of Dancers from Creighton
    University
Public Libraries:
  557,237 volumes; circulation 1,771,537
Reading Quotient: 7.1
Places Rated Score: 3,787
Places Rated Rank: 85

Orange County, NY
Symphony Orchestras:
  Orange County Symphony Orchestra
    (Community)
Public Libraries:
  172,166 volumes; circulation 256,682

Reading Quotient: NA
CMSA Access: NEW YORK–NORTHERN
  NEW JERSEY–LONG ISLAND, NY–NJ–
  CT (6,715)
Places Rated Score: 6,987
Places Rated Rank: 38

Orlando, FL
Fine Arts and Public Radio:
  WMFE-FM 90.7 (80 mi; 129 hrs)
Public Television:
  WMFE Channel 24
Universities:
  Rollins College (215)
Symphony Orchestras:
  Florida Symphony Orchestra★★★
  Florida Symphony Youth Orchestra
  University of Central Florida Community
    Symphony
Opera Companies:
  Orlando Opera Company
    3 productions; 7 performances
Dance Companies:
  Ballet Royal★
  Southern Ballet Theatre★
Public Libraries:
  644,525 volumes; circulation
    2,315,900
Reading Quotient: 6.2
Places Rated Score: 2,681
Places Rated Rank: 118

Owensboro, KY
Public Television:
  WKOH Channel 31
Symphony Orchestras:
  Owensboro Symphony Orchestra★
Public Libraries:
  103,914 volumes; circulation
    323,000
Reading Quotient: 5.0
Places Rated Score: 804
Places Rated Rank: 245

Oxnard–Ventura, CA
Symphony Orchestras:
  CLC Conejo Symphony Orchestra
    (Community)
  Ventura County Symphony Orchestra★
Public Libraries:
  560,927 volumes; circulation
    1,698,156
Reading Quotient: 7.1
CMSA Access: LOS ANGELES–ANAHEIM–
  RIVERSIDE, CA (1,908)
Places Rated Score: 2,769
Places Rated Rank: 116

Panama City, FL
Fine Arts and Public Radio:
  WKGC-AM 1480 (50 mi; 130 hrs)
  WKGC-FM 90.7 (50 mi; 140 hrs)
Public Libraries:
  154,596 volumes; circulation
    488,210
Reading Quotient: 4.3
Places Rated Score: 755
Places Rated Rank: 251

Parkersburg–Marietta, WV–OH
Public Libraries:
  91,150 volumes; circulation 258,962
Reading Quotient: 3.7
Places Rated Score: 91
Places Rated Rank: 320

Pascagoula, MS
Public Libraries:
  154,596 volumes; circulation 488,210
Reading Quotient: 4.3
Places Rated Score: 155
Places Rated Rank: 310

Pawtucket–Woonsocket–Attleboro, RI–MA
Public Libraries:
  239,500 volumes; circulation 300,000
Reading Quotient: 6.1
CMSA Access: PROVIDENCE–PAWTUCKET–
  FALL RIVER, RI–MA (240)
Places Rated Score: 480
Places Rated Rank: 271

Pensacola, FL
Fine Arts and Public Radio:
  WUWF-FM 88.1 (100 mi; 168 hrs)
Public Television:
  WSRE Channel 23
Universities:
  University of West Florida (535)
Symphony Orchestras:
  Greater Pensacola Symphony Orchestra
    (Community)
Public Libraries:
  318,766 volumes; circulation 1,231,903
Reading Quotient: 5.3
Places Rated Score: 1,954
Places Rated Rank: 159

Peoria, IL
Fine Arts and Public Radio:
  WCBU-FM 89.9 (34 mi; 150 hrs)
Public Television:
  WTVP Channel 47
Universities:
  Bradley University (459)
Symphony Orchestras:
  Central Illinois Youth Symphony
  Peoria Symphony Orchestra★★
Dance Companies:
  Peoria Civic Ballet
Public Libraries:
  485,000 volumes; circulation 900,000
Reading Quotient: 11.1
Places Rated Score: 2,294
Places Rated Rank: 134

★ Philadelphia, PA–NJ
Museums:
  Academy of Natural Sciences of
    Philadelphia (800)
  Franklin Institute of Science (500)
  Independence National Historical Park
    (500)
  Pennsylvania Academy of the Fine Arts
    (700)
  Philadelphia Museum of Art (900)
  University of Pennsylvania Museum
    (1,400)
Fine Arts and Public Radio:
  WUHY-FM 90.0 (35 mi; 131 hrs)
Public Television:
  WHVY Channel 12
  WNJS Channel 23
Universities:
  Beaver College (218)
  Bryn Mawr University (293)
  Cheyney State College (250)
  Glassboro State College (597)
  LaSalle College (382)

Temple University (1,000)•
University of Pennsylvania (972)•
Villanova University (630)
West Chester State College (628)
Symphony Orchestras:
  Concerto Soloists of Philadelphia★★
  New School of Music Orchestra
  Philadelphia Orchestra★★★★
  Philadelphia Youth Orchestra
  Temple University Symphony Orchestra
Theatres:
  Philadelphia Drama Guild★
Opera Companies:
  Opera Company of Philadelphia
    5 productions; 10 performances
  Pennsylvania Opera Theatre
    2 productions; 6 performances
Dance Companies:
  Agape Dancers (M)
  Ann Vaachon/Dance Candait (M)
  Arthur Hall's Afro-American Dance
    Ensemble★
  Ballet des Jeunes★★
  Camargo Ballet
  Germantown Dance Theatre
  Group Motion Dance Theatre (M)
  Philadanco/Philadelphia Dance
    Company (M)★
  Schuylkill Valley Regional Dance
    Company
  South Street Dance Company (M)
  Zero Moving Dance Company (M)
Public Libraries:
  2,947,727 volumes; circulation
    4,960,439
Reading Quotient: NA
CMSA Access: PHILADELPHIA–WILMINGTON–
  TRENTON, PA–NJ–DE–MD (690)
Places Rated Score: 17,270
Places Rated Rank: 6

Phoenix, AZ
Museums:
  Heard Museum (700)
  Phoenix Art Museum (500)
Fine Arts and Public Radio:
  KMCR-FM 91.5 (126 hrs)
Universities:
  Arizona State University (1,000)•
Symphony Orchestras:
  Phoenix College Orchestra
  Phoenix Symphony Orchestra★★★
  Phoenix Symphony Youth Orchestra
  Scottsdale Symphony Orchestra
    (Community)
  Sun City Symphony Orchestra
    (Community)
Dance Companies:
  Arizona Metropolitan Ballet
  Yelena Ballet and Dance Theatre
Public Libraries:
  1,173,000 volumes; circulation
    3,600,000
Reading Quotient: 5.8
Places Rated Score: 4,573
Places Rated Rank: 65

Pine Bluff, AR
Universities:
  University of Arkansas, Pine Bluff (255)
Public Libraries:
  117,923 volumes; circulation NA
Reading Quotient: NA
Places Rated Score: 373
Places Rated Rank: 282

★ Pittsburgh, PA
Museums:
  Buhl Planetarium and Institute of
    Popular Science (700)
  Carnegie Museum of Natural History
    (1,300)
  Museum of Art, Carnegie Institute (700)
Fine Arts and Public Radio:
  WDUG-FM 90.5 (35 mi; 133 hrs)
  WQED-FM 89.3 (60 mi; 139 hrs)
Public Television:
  WQED Channel 13
  WQEV Channel 16
Universities:
  California State College (442)
  Carnegie-Mellon University (408)
  Duquesne University (458)
  University of Pittsburgh (1,000)
Symphony Orchestras:
  American Youth Symphony and Chorus
  Duquesne University Symphony
  McKeesport Symphony Orchestra
    (Community)
  New Pittsburgh Chamber Orchestra
    (Community)
  Pittsburgh Civic Orchestra (Community)
  Pittsburgh Symphony Orchestra★★★★
  Pittsburgh Youth Symphony Orchestra
  Three Rivers Training Orchestra (Youth)
  University of Pittsburgh Orchestra
Theatres:
  Pittsburgh Public Theatre★★
Opera Companies:
  Pittsburgh Opera, Inc.
    6 productions; 12 performances
Dance Companies:
  American Dance Ensemble
  The Extension (J)
  Kasamon Ballet★★
  Pittsburgh Ballet Theatre★
  Pittsburgh Dance Alley (M)
  The Tamburitzanc (E-F)★
Public Libraries:
  2,039,057 volumes; circulation
    3,221,558
Reading Quotient: 3.5
Places Rated Score: 11,069
Places Rated Rank: 12

Pittsfield, MA
Dance Companies:
  Berkshire Ballet
Public Libraries:
  178,448 volumes; circulation 601,186
Reading Quotient: 15.0
Places Rated Score: 228
Places Rated Rank: 303

Portland, ME
Fine Arts and Public Radio:
  WMEA-FM 90.1 (58 mi; 133 hrs)
Public Television:
  WMEG Channel 26
Universities:
  University of Southern Maine (820)
Symphony Orchestras:
  Portland Symphony Orchestra★★
Theatres:
  Portland Stage Company
Dance Companies:
  Ram Island Dance Company (M)
Public Libraries:
  281,359 volumes; circulation 441,689
Reading Quotient: NA
Places Rated Score: 2,351
Places Rated Rank: 130

Portland, OR
Museums:
  Oregon Museum of Science and
    Industry (600)
Fine Arts and Public Radio:
  KBOO-FM 90.7 (30 mi; 168 hrs)
  KBPS-AM 1450 (30 mi; 126 hrs)
  KCAP-FM 91.5 (90 mi; 126 hrs)
Public Television:
  KOAP Channel 10
Universities:
  Portland State University (728)•
  University of Portland (200)
Symphony Orchestras:
  Oregon Symphony Orchestra★★★★
  Portland Youth Philharmonic Association
Opera Companies:
  Portland Opera Association
    4 productions; 12 performances
Public Libraries:
  1,184,232 volumes; circulation
    3,244,838
Reading Quotient: 7.5
Places Rated Score: 5,160
Places Rated Rank: 55

Portsmouth–Dover–Rochester, NH–ME
Theatres:
  Theatre by the Sea
Public Libraries:
  65,319 volumes; circulation NA
Reading Quotient: NA
Places Rated Score: 165
Places Rated Rank: 308

Poughkeepsie, NY
Universities:
  Vassar College (222)
Symphony Orchestras:
  Hudson Valley Philharmonic
    Orchestra★★
Dance Companies:
  Mid-Hudson Ballet Company
  Orange County Ballet Theatre
  Poughkeepsie Civic Ballet
Public Libraries:
  113,407 volumes; circulation 312,772
Reading Quotient: 5.1
Places Rated Score: 785
Places Rated Rank: 246

Providence, RI
Museums:
  Rhode Island Historical Society (700)
  Rhode Island School of Design Museum
    of Art (700)
Public Television:
  WSBE Channel 36
Universities:
  Brown University (523)
  Providence College (459)
  Rhode Island College (438)
  Roger Williams College (240)
  University of Rhode Island (852)
Symphony Orchestras:
  Brown University Orchestra
  Rhode Island Philharmonic Orchestra★★
  Rhode Island Philharmonic Youth
    Orchestra
  Young Peoples Symphony of Rhode
    Island
Theatres:
  Trinity Square Repertory Company★★
Dance Companies:
  State Ballet of Rhode Island★

Public Libraries:
739,773 volumes; circulation NA
Reading Quotient: NA
Places Rated Score: 6,152
Places Rated Rank: 46

Provo–Orem, UT
Fine Arts and Public Radio:
KBYU-FM 88.9 (150 mi; 140 hrs)
Public Television:
KBYU Channel 11
Universities:
Brigham Young University (1,000)
Symphony Orchestras:
Utah Valley Youth Symphony Orchestra
Public Libraries:
85,000 volumes; circulation NA
Reading Quotient: NA
Places Rated Score: 1,985
Places Rated Rank: 157

Pueblo, CO
Public Television:
KTSC Channel 8
Universities:
University of Southern Colorado (457)
Symphony Orchestras:
Pueblo Symphony Orchestra★
Public Libraries:
150,000 volumes; circulation 383,376
Reading Quotient: 4.2
Places Rated Score: 1,307
Places Rated Rank: 201

Racine, WI
Symphony Orchestras:
Racine Symphony Orchestra
(Community)
Public Libraries:
252,717 volumes; circulation 668,226
Reading Quotient: 5.3
CMSA Access: MILWAUKEE–RACINE,
WI (818)
Places Rated Score: 1,171
Places Rated Rank: 214

Raleigh–Durham, NC
Museums:
North Carolina Museum of Art (600)
North Carolina State Museum (1,000)
Fine Arts and Public Radio:
WSHA-FM 88.9 (18 mi; 168 hrs)
WUNC-FM 91.5 (135 hrs)
Universities:
Duke University (937)
University of North Carolina (1,000)
Symphony Orchestras:
Durham Symphony Orchestra
(Community)
North Carolina Symphony Orchestra★★★
Theatres:
Playmakers Repertory Company
Dance Companies:
Bryce Wagner Dance Project (M)
Concert Dancers of Raleigh
New Performers Dance Company (M)
Synergic Theatre/Delta Carnival (M)
Public Libraries:
592,800 volumes; circulation 1,803,578
Reading Quotient: 5.3
Places Rated Score: 5,730
Places Rated Rank: 47

Reading, PA
Universities:
Kutztown State College (568)

Symphony Orchestras:
Reading Symphony Orchestra★
Public Libraries:
339,786 volumes; circulation NA
Reading Quotient: NA
Places Rated Score: 1,108
Places Rated Rank: 219

Redding, CA
Public Television:
KIXE-TV Channel 9
Symphony Orchestras:
Shasta Symphony Orchestra
(Community)
Public Libraries:
245,426 volumes; circulation 480,034
Reading Quotient: 6.3
Places Rated Score: 845
Places Rated Rank: 240

Reno, NV
Museums:
Nevada Historical Society (500)
Fine Arts and Public Radio:
KUNR-FM 88.7 (49 mi; 133 hrs)
Universities:
University of Nevada (554)
Symphony Orchestras:
Reno Chamber Orchestra (Community)
Reno Philharmonic Association★
Opera Companies:
Nevada Opera Association
3 productions; 9 performances
Public Libraries:
328,831 volumes; circulation 931,178
Reading Quotient: 6.5
Places Rated Score: 2,210
Places Rated Rank: 138

Richland–Kennewick–Pasco, WA
Symphony Orchestras:
Mid-Columbia Symphony Orchestra★
Public Libraries:
328,688 volumes; circulation 797,489
Reading Quotient: 7.4
Places Rated Score: 529
Places Rated Rank: 267

Richmond–Petersburg, VA
Museums:
Association for the Preservation of
Virginia Antiquities (500)
Valentine Museum (600)
Virginia Museum of Fine Art (600)
Fine Arts and Public Radio:
WRFK-FM 106.5 (50 mi; 132 hrs)
Public Television:
WCVE Channel 23
WCVW Channel 57
Universities:
University of Richmond (247)
Virginia State University (456)
Symphony Orchestras:
Richmond Community Orchestra
Richmond Symphony Orchestra★★★
Richmond Symphony Youth Orchestra
Theatres:
Virginia Museum Theatre
Dance Companies:
Concert Ballet of Virginia★
Richmond Ballet Company
Public Libraries:
1,143,881 volumes; circulation
2,457,422
Reading Quotient: 8.2
Places Rated Score: 5,697
Places Rated Rank: 48

Riverside–San Bernardino, CA
Museums:
San Bernardino County Museum (800)
Fine Arts and Public Radio:
KVCR-FM 91.9 (18 mi; 126 hrs)
Public Television:
KVCR-TV Channel 24
Universities:
California State College, San Bernardino
(346)
University of California, Riverside (412)●
Symphony Orchestras:
Inland Empire Symphony Orchestra
(Community)
San Bernardino Chamber Orchestra
(College)
Dance Companies:
Concert Dance Theatre
Riverside Ballet Theatre
Public Libraries:
1,001,162 volumes; circulation
2,771,041
Reading Quotient: 5.0
CMSA Access: LOS ANGELES–ANAHEIM–
RIVERSIDE, CA (1,668)
Places Rated Score: 5,327
Places Rated Rank: 54

Roanoke, VA
Fine Arts and Public Radio:
WVTF-FM 89.1 (100 mi; 128 hrs)
Public Television:
WBCA Channel 15
Symphony Orchestras:
Roanoke Symphony Orchestra
Public Libraries:
363,216 volumes; circulation NA
Reading Quotient: NA
Places Rated Score: 1,263
Places Rated Rank: 207

Rochester, MN
Fine Arts and Public Radio:
KLSE-FM 91.7 (40 mi; 131 hrs)
Symphony Orchestras:
Rochester Symphony Orchestra★★
Public Libraries:
168,745 volumes; circulation 696,036
Reading Quotient: 9.4
Places Rated Score: 769
Places Rated Rank: 248

Rochester, NY
Museums:
International Museum of Photography
(500)
Rochester Museum and Science Center
(1,100)
Strong Museum (500)
Fine Arts and Public Radio:
WXXI-FM 91.5 (45 mi; 168 hrs)
Public Television:
WXXI Channel 21
Universities:
Nazareth College of Rochester (313)
SUNY at Brockport (646)●
SUNY at Geneseo (448)
University of Rochester (450)
Symphony Orchestras:
Brighton Symphony Orchestra
(Community)
Rochester Philharmonic Orchestra★★★★
Rochester Philharmonic Youth
Orchestra
Theatres:
Ge Va Theatre

Opera Companies:
Opera Theatre of Rochester
3 productions; 5 performances
Dance Companies:
Bucket Dance Company (M)
Public Libraries:
934,083 volumes; circulation 1,409,352
Reading Quotient: 9.7
Places Rated Score: 6,956
Places Rated Rank: 39

Rockford, IL
Symphony Orchestras:
Rockford Area Youth Symphony
Rockford Symphony Orchestra★★
Theatres:
New American Theatre
Dance Companies:
Rockford Company (B)★★
Public Libraries:
326,389 volumes; circulation 873,929
Reading Quotient: 8.6
Places Rated Score: 1,026
Places Rated Rank: 225

Sacramento, CA
Fine Arts and Public Radio:
KXPR-FM 90.9 (60 mi; 145 hrs)
Public Television:
KVIE Channel 6
Universities:
California State University, Sacramento
(1,000)●
Symphony Orchestras:
Camellia Symphony Orchestra
(Community)
Sacramento Symphony Orchestra★★★
Sacramento Youth Symphony
Opera Companies:
Sacramento Opera
2 productions; 4 performances
Dance Companies:
Capitol City Ballet
Sacramento Ballet
Theatre Ballet of Sacramento
Public Libraries:
1,625,000 volumes; circulation NA
Reading Quotient: NA
Places Rated Score: 4,483
Places Rated Rank: 70

Saginaw–Bay City–Midland, MI
Symphony Orchestras:
Midland Symphony Orchestra★★
Northwood Orchestra★
Saginaw Symphony Orchestra★★
Saginaw Symphony Youth Orchestra
Public Libraries:
808,165 volumes; circulation 2,074,128
Reading Quotient: 7.7
Places Rated Score: 1,708
Places Rated Rank: 178

St. Cloud, MN
Fine Arts and Public Radio:
KSJR-FM 91.1 (44 mi; 168 hrs)
Universities:
St. Cloud State University (952)
Symphony Orchestras:
St. Cloud Civic Orchestra (Community)
Public Libraries:
319,142 volumes; circulation 1,047,972
Reading Quotient: 5.2
Places Rated Score: 1,871
Places Rated Rank: 165

St. Joseph, MO
Museums:
St. Joseph Museum (500)
Symphony Orchestras:
St. Joseph Symphony Orchestra
(Community)
Public Libraries:
278,748 volumes; circulation 467,049
Reading Quotient: 7.6
Places Rated Score: 879
Places Rated Rank: 238

★ St. Louis, MO–IL
Museums:
Missouri Historical Society (500)
St. Louis Art Museum (800)
Fine Arts and Public Radio:
KWMU-FM 90.7 (100 mi; 168 hrs)
Public Television:
KETC Channel 9
Universities:
University of Missouri, St. Louis (1,000)
Washington University (945)●
Symphony Orchestras:
St. Louis Symphony Orchestra★★★★
St. Louis Symphony Youth Orchestra
Theatres:
Repertory Theatre of St. Louis★
Opera Companies:
Opera Theatre of St. Louis
5 productions; 25 performances
Dance Companies:
Metropolitan Ballet of St. Louis★
Mid-America Dance Company (M)
Missouri Concert Ballet Company
St. Charles Civic Ballet★★
St. Louis Civic Ballet
St. Louis Repertory Dancers (M)
Public Libraries:
3,025,890 volumes; circulation
8,639,769
Reading Quotient: 9.2
Places Rated Score: 8,896
Places Rated Rank: 19

Salem, OR
Public Television:
KVDO Channel 3
Public Libraries:
191,035 volumes; circulation 911,000
Reading Quotient: 12.2
Places Rated Score: 691
Places Rated Rank: 257

Salem–Gloucester, MA
Museums:
Peabody Museum of Salem (500)
Universities:
Salem State College (512)
Symphony Orchestras:
Cape Ann Symphony Orchestra
(Community)
Sinfonie-by-the-Sea (Community)
Dance Companies:
North Shore Civic Ballet
Public Libraries:
276,006 volumes; circulation 1,121,522
Reading Quotient: 21.1
CMSA Access: BOSTON–LAWRENCE–SALEM,
MA–NH (1,738)
Places Rated Score: 3,276
Places Rated Rank: 98

Salinas–Seaside–Monterey, CA
Fine Arts and Public Radio:
KUBO-FM 90.9 (40 mi; 140 hrs)

Symphony Orchestras:
Monterey County Symphony
Orchestra★★
Theatres:
El Teatro Campesino
Public Libraries:
304,040 volumes; circulation 1,136,685
Reading Quotient: 13.2
Places Rated Score: 1,004
Places Rated Rank: 230

Salt Lake City–Ogden, UT
Museums:
Utah Museum of Fine Art (600)
Utah Museum of Natural History (600)
Fine Arts and Public Radio:
KUER-FM 90.4 (65 mi; 126 hrs)
Public Television:
KUED Channel 7
Universities:
University of Utah (1,000)●
Symphony Orchestras:
Golden Spike Youth Symphony
Orchestra
Murray Symphony Orchestra
(Community)
Rocky Mountain Symphony
(Community)
Utah Symphony Orchestra★★★★
Utah Youth Symphony
Opera Companies:
Utah Opera Company
4 productions; 15 performances
Dance Companies:
Ballet West★
Public Libraries:
1,268,310 volumes; circulation
3,810,272
Reading Quotient: 5.0
Places Rated Score: 5,528
Places Rated Rank: 52

San Angelo, TX
Museums:
Fort Concho National Historic Landmark
(500)
Universities:
Angelo State University (425)
Symphony Orchestras:
San Angelo Symphony Orchestra★
Public Libraries:
175,903 volumes; circulation 452,696
Reading Quotient: 8.3
Places Rated Score: 1,301
Places Rated Rank: 203

San Antonio, TX
Museums:
San Antonio Museum of Art (600)
Public Television:
KLRN Channel 9
Universities:
Southwest Texas State University
(1,000)
Trinity University (238)
Symphony Orchestras:
San Antonio Symphony Orchestra★★★★
Youth Orchestras of San Antonio
Dance Companies:
San Antonio Ballet Company★
Texas Civic Ballet
Public Libraries:
1,207,133 volumes; circulation
2,217,603
Reading Quotient: 3.5
Places Rated Score: 4,295
Places Rated Rank: 75

★ San Diego, CA

Museums:
Natural History Museum (600)
San Diego Museum of Art (700)
San Diego Museum of Man (500)
Fine Arts and Public Radio:
KPBS-FM 89.5 (50 mi; 131 hrs)
Public Television:
KPBS Channel 15
Universities:
San Diego State University (1,000)
University of California, La Jolla (1,000)
University of San Diego (295)
Symphony Orchestras:
Jewish Community Center Symphony
  Orchestra (Community)
San Diego Symphony Orchestra★★★★
Heartland Youth Philharmonic
San Diego Youth Symphony
Theatres:
Old Globe Theatre★★★
San Diego Repertory Theatre
Opera Companies:
San Diego Opera
  8 productions; 30 performances
Dance Companies:
All That Jazz Dancers
California Ballet Company★
National Ballet of San Diego
Stage Seven Dance Theatre (B)★
Three's Company (M)
Victor Moreno Dance Theatre★
Public Libraries:
1,733,387 volumes; circulation
  4,235,888
Reading Quotient: 6.6
Places Rated Score: 8,818
Places Rated Rank: 20

★ San Francisco, CA

Museums:
Asian Art Museum of San Francisco
  (800)
California Academy of Sciences (1,200)
California Division of Mines and
  Geology (500)
California Historical Society (600)
Fine Arts Museum of San Francisco
  (900)
Fine Arts and Public Radio:
KALW-FM 91.7 (50 mi; 126 hrs)
KPFA-FM 94.1 (Bay Area; 168 hrs)
KQED-FM 88.5 (50 mi; 133 hrs)
Public Television:
KCSM Channel 60
KQEC Channel 32
KQED Channel 9
Universities:
San Francisco State University (1,000)●
University of San Francisco (282)
Symphony Orchestras:
Bay Area Women's Philharmonic
  (Community)
Chamber Symphony of San Francisco
  (Community)
San Francisco Chamber Players
  (Community)
San Francisco Conservatory of Music
  Orchestra (College)
San Francisco State University
  Symphony Orchestra
San Francisco Symphony★★★★
San Francisco Symphony Youth
  Orchestra
Theatres:
American Conservatory Theatre★★★★
Magic Theatre

One Act Theatre Company of San
  Francisco
Opera Companies:
San Francisco Opera★★★★
  14 productions; 101 performances
San Rafael–Marin Opera Company
  3 productions; 9 performances
Dance Companies:
Bagong Diwa Dance Company (E-F)
Ballet Theatre West
Bay Area Repertory Dance
  Company (M)
Christopher Beck and Company
  Dance/Theatre (M)
Dionysian Duncan Dancers (M)
Ed Mack Dance Studio Theatre (J)
Ethnic Music and Dance Ensemble
  (E-F)★
Jan Van Dyke and Dancers (M)
Margaret Jenkins Dance Company (M)
Marika Sakellariou Dance Company (M)
Marin Ballet★
Mixed Bag Productions (M)
Oberlin Dance Collective (M)
Peninsula Ballet Theatre★
Rosa Montoya Bailes Flamencos (E-F)
San Francisco Ballet★★
San Francisco Ballet Celeste
  International
Sarh Dances–Motion Arts Company (M)
Tance Johnson Dancers (M)
Theatre Ballet of San Francisco
Theatre Flamenco of San Francisco
  (E-F)
Westwood International Folk Ensemble
  (E-F)★
Public Libraries:
1,761,025 volumes; circulation
  2,470,091
Reading Quotient: 6.2
CMSA Access: SAN FRANCISCO–OAKLAND–
  SAN JOSE, CA (606)
Places Rated Score: 14,226
Places Rated Rank: 7

San Jose, CA

Public Television:
KTEH Channel 54
Universities:
San Jose University (1,000)
Stanford University (659)
Symphony Orchestras:
San Jose Symphony Orchestra★★
Theatres:
San Jose Repertory Company
Opera Companies:
Palo Alto Scholar Opera
  2 productions; 8 performances
San Jose Symphony Opera
  1 production; 3 performances
Dance Companies:
City Center Ballet of San Jose
Janlyn Dance Company (M)
Los Lupenos de San Jose (E-F)★
Margaret Wingrove and Dancers (M)
San Jose Dance Theatre★
Santa Clara Ballet Company
Public Libraries:
1,230,000 volumes; circulation
  2,300,000
Reading Quotient: 5.4
CMSA Access: SAN FRANCISCO–OAKLAND–
  SAN JOSE, CA (1,838)
Places Rated Score: 6,446
Places Rated Rank: 43

Santa Barbara–Santa Maria–Lompoc, CA

Museums:
Santa Barbara Museum of Natural
  History (800)
Universities:
University of California, Santa Barbara
  (1,000)●
Symphony Orchestras:
Santa Barbara Symphony Orchestra★★
Dance Companies:
Santa Barbara Ballet
Public Libraries:
533,679 volumes; circulation 1,807,736
Reading Quotient: 7.8
Places Rated Score: 2,684
Places Rated Rank: 117

Santa Cruz, CA

Fine Arts and Public Radio:
KUSP-FM 88.9 (155 hrs)
Universities:
University of California, Santa Cruz
  (633)
Symphony Orchestras:
Santa Cruz County Symphony★
Santa Cruz County Youth Symphony
Dance Companies:
Tandy Beal and Company (M)
Public Libraries:
311,000 volumes; circulation 975,000
Reading Quotient: 7.8
CMSA Access: SAN FRANCISCO–OAKLAND–
  SAN JOSE, CA (2,054)
Places Rated Score: 3,748
Places Rated Rank: 86

Santa Rosa–Petaluma, CA

Fine Arts and Public Radio:
KBBF-FM 89.1 (50 mi; 126 hrs)
Symphony Orchestras:
Santa Rosa Symphony★★
Sonoma County Junior Symphony
Dance Companies:
Ann Woodhead Dance Company (M)
Public Libraries:
622,954 volumes; circulation 1,635,000
Reading Quotient: 7.4
CMSA Access: SAN FRANCISCO–OAKLAND–
  SAN JOSE, CA (2,084)
Places Rated Score: 3,457
Places Rated Rank: 94

Sarasota, FL

Symphony Orchestras:
Florida West Coast Symphony
  Orchestra★★
Florida West Coast Youth Orchestra
Sarasota Community Orchestra
Theatres:
Asolo State Theatre★
Public Libraries:
117,000 volumes; circulation 687,543
Reading Quotient: 6.4
Places Rated Score: 817
Places Rated Rank: 243

Savannah, GA

Museums:
Old Fort Jackson (500)
Fine Arts and Public Radio:
WSVH 91.1 (90 mi; 127 hrs)
Public Television:
WVAN Channel 9
Universities:
Savannah State College (230)

Symphony Orchestras:
Savannah Symphony Orchestra★★
Dance Companies:
Savannah Ballet
Public Libraries:
382,224 volumes; circulation 960,522
Reading Quotient: 5.2
Places Rated Score: 2,262
Places Rated Rank: 135

Scranton–Wilkes-Barre, PA
Museums:
Everhart Museum of Natural History,
Science and Art (600)
Fine Arts and Public Radio:
WVIA-FM 89.9 (65 mi; 126 hrs)
Universities:
Marywood College (310)
Wilkes College (208)
Dance Companies:
Wilkes-Barre Ballet Theatre Company
Public Libraries:
363,572 volumes; circulation 285,293
Reading Quotient: 3.0
Places Rated Score: 1,832
Places Rated Rank: 169

★ Seattle, WA
Museums:
Museum of History and Industry (500)
Seattle Aquarium (500)
Seattle Art Museum (600)
Thomas Burke Memorial Washington
State Museum (1,000)
Fine Arts and Public Radio:
KUOW-FM 94.9 (40 mi; 156 hrs)
Public Television:
KCTS Channel 9
Universities:
Seattle Pacific University (212)
Seattle University (464)
University of Washington (1,000)●
Symphony Orchestras:
Bellevue Philharmonic Orchestra
(Community)
Northwest Chamber Orchestra★★
Olympic Youth Symphonies
Seattle Symphony Orchestra★★★★
Seattle Youth Symphony
Thalia Symphony and Chamber
Symphony (Community)
Theatres:
A Contemporary Theatre★
The Empty Space
Intiman Theatre Company
Seattle Repertory Theatre★★
Opera Companies:
Seattle Opera
5 productions; 25 performances
Dance Companies:
Cornish Dance Theatre
Kinetics Company (M)
Martha Nishitani Modern Dance
Company
Pacific Northwest Ballet★
Skinner Releasing Dance Company (M)
Public Libraries:
1,546,110 volumes; circulation
4,229,140
Reading Quotient: 11.7
CMSA Access: SEATTLE–TACOMA,
WA (330)
Places Rated Score: 9,577
Places Rated Rank: 17

Sharon, PA
Public Libraries:
52,400 volumes; circulation 76,000
Reading Quotient: 6.7
Places Rated Score: 52
Places Rated Rank: 329

Sheboygan, WI
Public Libraries:
267,711 volumes; circulation 917,733
Reading Quotient: 11.7
Places Rated Score: 268
Places Rated Rank: 297

Sherman–Denison, TX
Public Libraries:
68,357 volumes; circulation 324,108
Reading Quotient: 5.9
Places Rated Score: 68
Places Rated Rank: 327

Shreveport, LA
Public Television:
KLTS Channel 24
Universities:
Grambling State University (324)
Louisiana State University, Shreveport
(202)
Louisiana Technical University (855)
Symphony Orchestras:
Shreveport Symphony Orchestra★★
Opera Companies:
Shreveport Opera Association
5 productions; 12 performances
Dance Companies:
Ballet Lyrique★
Public Libraries:
284,739 volumes; circulation NA
Reading Quotient: NA
Places Rated Score: 2,826
Places Rated Rank: 113

Sioux City, IA–NE
Fine Arts and Public Radio:
KWIT 90.3 (100 mi; 133 hrs)
Public Television:
KSIN Channel 27
Symphony Orchestras:
Sioux City Symphony Orchestra★★
Siouxland Youth Symphony
Public Libraries:
192,946 volumes; circulation 478,440
Reading Quotient: 8.2
Places Rated Score: 1,393
Places Rated Rank: 196

Sioux Falls, SD
Symphony Orchestras:
South Dakota Symphony★★
Public Libraries:
164,818 volumes; circulation 540,539
Reading Quotient: 8.7
Places Rated Score: 465
Places Rated Rank: 273

South Bend–Mishawaka, IN
Public Television:
WNIT Channel 34
Universities:
Andrews University (200)
Indiana University, South Bend (392)
University of Notre Dame (715)
Symphony Orchestras:
South Bend Symphony Orchestra★★
Dance Companies:
Patchwork Dance Company (J)

Public Libraries:
514,756 volumes; circulation 1,747,716
Reading Quotient: 10
Places Rated Score: 2,672
Places Rated Rank: 119

Spokane, WA
Fine Arts and Public Radio:
KBPX-FM 91.1 (100 mi; 129 hrs)
Public Television:
KSPS Channel 7
Universities:
Eastern Washington University (734)●
Gonzaga University (221)
Symphony Orchestras:
Spokane Junior Symphony
Spokane Symphony Orchestra★★★
Dance Companies:
Spokane Ballet
Public Libraries:
683,396 volumes; circulation 2,307,961
Reading Quotient: 8.7
Places Rated Score: 2,988
Places Rated Rank: 107

Springfield, IL
Museums:
Illinois State Museum (850)
Fine Arts and Public Radio:
WSSR-FM 91.9 (50 mi; 145 hrs)
Symphony Orchestras:
Springfield Symphony Orchestra★
Dance Companies:
Springfield Ballet Company★★
Public Libraries:
333,133 volumes; circulation 837,784
Reading Quotient: 11.7
Places Rated Score: 1,983
Places Rated Rank: 158

Springfield, MA
Museums:
Museum of Fine Arts (500)
Springfield Science Museum (600)
Public Television:
WGBY Channel 57
Universities:
Westfield State College (290)
Symphony Orchestras:
Holyoke College Civic Orchestra
Springfield Symphony Orchestra★★★
Western Massachusetts Young People's
Symphony
Theatres:
Stage West
Dance Companies:
Amherst Ballet Theatre Company
Dance Gallery (M)
Pioneer Valley Ballet
Public Libraries:
726,410 volumes; circulation 963,394
Reading Quotient: 11.1
Places Rated Score: 3,466
Places Rated Rank: 93

Springfield, MO
Fine Arts and Public Radio:
KSMU-FM 91.1 (15 mi; 133 hrs)
Public Television:
KOZK Channel 21
Symphony Orchestras:
Southwest Missouri State University
Symphony
Springfield Symphony Orchestra★
Opera Companies:
Springfield Regional Opera
3 productions; 10 performances

Public Libraries:
   304,307 volumes; circulation 1,109,925
Reading Quotient: 7.7
Places Rated Score: 1,634
Places Rated Rank: 180

Stamford, CT
Symphony Orchestras:
   Connecticut Philharmonic Orchestra
      (Community)
   Greenwich Symphony Orchestra★
   Stamford Symphony Orchestra★
Theatres:
   Hartman Theatre★
Opera Companies:
   Stamford State Opera, Inc.
      3 productions; 3 performances
Public Libraries:
   364,123 volumes; circulation 677,775
Reading Quotient: 10.2
CMSA Access: NEW YORK–NORTHERN
NEW JERSEY–LONG ISLAND, NY–NJ–
CT (6,592)
Places Rated Score: 7,865
Places Rated Rank: 28

State College, PA
Universities:
   Pennsylvania State University (1,000)●
Symphony Orchestras:
   Nittany Valley Symphony (Community)
Dance Companies:
   Contemporary Dance Company (M)★
Public Libraries:
   71,003 volumes; circulation 268,290
Reading Quotient: 5.5
Places Rated Score: 1,271
Places Rated Rank: 206

Steubenville–Weirton, OH–WV
Public Libraries:
   146,637 volumes; circulation 360,209
Reading Quotient: 5.5
Places Rated Score: 147
Places Rated Rank: 314

Stockton, CA
Fine Arts and Public Radio:
   KUOP-FM 91.3 (70 mi; 153 hrs)
Universities:
   University of the Pacific (351)
Symphony Orchestras:
   Stockton Symphony★★
Dance Companies:
   San Joaquin Ballet
Public Libraries:
   478,266 volumes; circulation 1,110,919
Reading Quotient: 4.8
Places Rated Score: 1,579
Places Rated Rank: 185

Syracuse, NY
Museums:
   Everson Museum of Art (500)
Fine Arts and Public Radio:
   WCNY-FM 91.3 (60 mi; 154 hrs)
Public Television:
   WCNY Channel 24
Universities:
   Colgate University (260)
   SUNY at Oswego (669)
   Syracuse University (1,000)
Symphony Orchestras:
   Onondaga Civic Symphony Orchestra
      (Community)
   Syracuse Symphony Orchestra★★★★
   Syracuse Symphony Youth Orchestra

Theatres:
   Syracuse Stage★
Opera Companies:
   Opera Theatre of Syracuse
      3 productions; 6 performances
Public Libraries:
   632,534 volumes; circulation 1,063,057
Reading Quotient: 3.7
Places Rated Score: 5,080
Places Rated Rank: 57

Tacoma, WA
Museums:
   Puget Sound Museum of Natural History
      (700)
Fine Arts and Public Radio:
   KPLU-FM 88.5 (76 mi; 138 hrs)
   KTOY-FM 91.7 (30 mi; 138 hrs)
Public Television:
   KTPS Channel 28
Universities:
   Pacific Lutheran University (269)
   University of Puget Sound (278)
Symphony Orchestras:
   Tacoma Symphony Orchestra★★
   Tacoma Youth Symphony
Theatres:
   Tacoma Actors Guild
Dance Companies:
   Balletacoma★
   Tacoma Performance Dance Company★
Public Libraries:
   282,256 volumes; circulation 1,107,650
Reading Quotient: 4.5
CMSA Access: SEATTLE–TACOMA,
WA (968)
Places Rated Score: 4,297
Places Rated Rank: 74

Tallahassee, FL
Fine Arts and Public Radio:
   WFSU-FM 90.5 (35 mi; 140 hrs)
Public Television:
   WFSU Channel 11
Universities:
   Florida State University (1,000)●
Symphony Orchestras:
   Florida State University Symphony
Dance Companies:
   Dance Arts Guild of Tallahassee
   Tallahassee Civic Ballet
Public Libraries:
   181,219 volumes; circulation 644,958
Reading Quotient: 5.3
Places Rated Score: 2,181
Places Rated Rank: 141

Tampa–St. Petersburg–
Clearwater, FL
Fine Arts and Public Radio:
   WUSF-FM 89.7 (47 mi; 148 hrs)
Public Television:
   WEDU Channel 3
   WUSF Channel 16
Universities:
   University of South Florida (1,000)●
   University of Tampa (158)
Symphony Orchestras:
   Florida Gulf Coast Symphony★★★
   Pinellas Youth Symphony
   St. Petersburg Community Symphony
Opera Companies:
   Florida Opera West, Inc.
      3 productions; 4 performances
Dance Companies:
   City Center Ballet, Inc.★
   Dancemakers (J)

Firethorn (M)
   Florida Ballet Theatre★
   Tampa Ballet★
Public Libraries:
   1,270,096 volumes; circulation
      3,781,383
Reading Quotient: 5.2
Places Rated Score: 5,040
Places Rated Rank: 58

Terre Haute, IN
Universities:
   Indiana State University (938)
Symphony Orchestras:
   Terre Haute Symphony★
Public Libraries:
   88,247 volumes; circulation 702,624
Reading Quotient: 7.1
Places Rated Score: 1,226
Places Rated Rank: 211

Texarkana, TX–Texarkana, AR
Public Libraries:
   63,072 volumes; circulation 160,547
Reading Quotient: 4.3
Places Rated Score: 63
Places Rated Rank: 328

Toledo, OH
Museums:
   Toledo Museum of Art (700)
Fine Arts and Public Radio:
   WGTE-FM 91.3 (45 mi; 135 hrs)
Public Television:
   WGTE Channel 30
Universities:
   University of Toledo (1,000)
Symphony Orchestras:
   Toledo Symphony Orchestra★★★
   Toledo Youth Orchestra
Dance Companies:
   Cassandra Civic Ballet Company
   Toledo Ballet★
   Valois Company of Dancers (M)
Public Libraries:
   1,188,510 volumes; circulation
      3,783,282
Reading Quotient: 10.5
Places Rated Score: 4,389
Places Rated Rank: 71

Topeka, KS
Public Television:
   KTWU Channel 11
Universities:
   Emporia State University (362)
   Washburn University of Topeka (488)
Public Libraries:
   281,934 volumes; circulation 958,317
Reading Quotient: 10.7
Places Rated Score: 1,632
Places Rated Rank: 181

Trenton, NJ
Museums:
   New Jersey State Museum (1,200)
Fine Arts and Public Radio:
   WWFM-FM 89.1 (11 mi; 130 hrs)
Public Television:
   WNJT Channel 52
Universities:
   Princeton University (446)
   Rider College (333)
Theatres:
   McCarter Theatre Company★★
Dance Companies:
   Princeton Ballet Society★

Public Libraries:
  630,820 volumes; circulation 924,584
Reading Quotient: 7.7
CMSA Access: PHILADELPHIA–WILMINGTON–
  TRENTON, PA–NJ–DE–MD (1,219)
Places Rated Score: 5,029
Places Rated Rank: 59

Tucson, AZ
Museums:
  Arizona Heritage Center (500)
  Sonora Desert Museum (600)
Fine Arts and Public Radio:
  KUAT-AM 1550 (65 mi; 84 hrs)
  KUAT-FM 90.5 (60 mi; 126 hrs)
Public Television:
  KUAT Channel 6
Universities:
  University of Arizona (1,000)•
Symphony Orchestras:
  Tucson Symphony Orchestra★★★★
Theatres:
  Arizona Theatre Company★
Opera Companies:
  Arizona Opera Company
    3 productions; 11 performances
Dance Companies:
  Tucson Metropolitan Ballet★
  Territory Dance Theatre (M)
Public Libraries:
  698,800 volumes; circulation 3,600,000
Reading Quotient: 7.6
Places Rated Score: 4,889
Places Rated Rank: 61

Tulsa, OK
Museums:
  Gilcrease Institute of American History
    and Art (500)
  Philbrook Art Center (500)
Fine Arts and Public Radio:
  KWGS-FM 89.5 (30 mi; 145 hrs)
Public Television:
  KOED Channel 4
Universities:
  Oral Roberts University (304)
  University of Tulsa (413)
Symphony Orchestras:
  Oklahoma Sinfonia and Chorale★
  Tulsa Philharmonic Orchestra★★★
  Tulsa Youth Symphony Orchestra
Theatres:
  American Theatre Company
Opera Companies:
  Tulsa Opera
    3 productions; 9 performances
Dance Companies:
  Tulsa Ballet Theatre★
Public Libraries:
  503,824 volumes; circulation 1,760,920
Reading Quotient: 4.9
Places Rated Score: 4,248
Places Rated Rank: 76

Tuscaloosa, AL
Fine Arts and Public Radio:
  WUAL-FM 91.5 (80 mi; 138 hrs)
Universities:
  University of Alabama (1,000)
Public Libraries:
  132,000 volumes; circulation 463,213
Reading Quotient: 4.4
Places Rated Score: 1,432
Places Rated Rank: 194

Tyler, TX
Symphony Orchestras:
  East Texas Symphony Orchestra★
  Tyler Youth Symphony Orchestra
Public Libraries:
  104,396 volumes; circulation 325,000
Reading Quotient: 5.7
Places Rated Score: 404
Places Rated Rank: 278

Utica–Rome, NY
Museums:
  Munson/Williams/Proctor Institute of Art
    (500)
Symphony Orchestras:
  Utica Symphony Orchestra★
Public Libraries:
  158,030 volumes; circulation 251,566
Reading Quotient: 2.5
Places Rated Score: 858
Places Rated Rank: 239

Vallejo–Fairfield–Napa, CA
Symphony Orchestras:
  Napa Valley Symphony Association★
Public Libraries:
  587,966 volumes; circulation 1,413,471
Reading Quotient: 6.3
CMSA Access: SAN FRANCISCO–OAKLAND–
  SAN JOSE, CA (2,174)
Places Rated Score: 2,962
Places Rated Rank: 109

Vancouver, WA
Museums:
  Clark County Historical Museum (600)
Public Libraries:
  312,762 volumes; circulation 1,291,533
Reading Quotient: 7.4
CMSA Access: PORTLAND–VANCOUVER,
  OR–WA (644)
Places Rated Score: 1,557
Places Rated Rank: 186

Victoria, TX
Public Libraries:
  87,000 volumes; circulation NA
Reading Quotient: NA
Places Rated Score: 87
Places Rated Rank: 321

Vineland–Millville–Bridgeton, NJ
Public Libraries:
  187,568 volumes; circulation 329,523
Reading Quotient: 5.3
CMSA Access: PHILADELPHIA–WILMINGTON–
  TRENTON, PA–NJ–DE–MD (1,909)
Places Rated Score: 2,097
Places Rated Rank: 149

Visalia–Tulare–Porterville, CA
Public Libraries:
  510,987 volumes; circulation 931,044
Reading Quotient: 6.3
Places Rated Score: 511
Places Rated Rank: 270

Waco, TX
Universities:
  Baylor University (873)
Symphony Orchestras:
  Waco Symphony Orchestra
    (Community)
Public Libraries:
  168,350 volumes; circulation 578,255
Reading Quotient: 4.4
Places Rated Score: 1,141
Places Rated Rank: 218

★ Washington, DC–MD–VA
Museums:
  Daughters of the American Revolution
    Museum (600)
  Freer Gallery of Art (600)
  Library of Congress Collections (600)
  National Archives (700)
  National Gallery of Art (1,600)
  National Museum of American Art
    (1,100)
  National Museum of Natural History
    (900)
  National Portrait Gallery (900)
  Smithsonian Institution (including Air
    and Space Museum) (2,000)
  U.S. Marine Corps Museum (800)
Fine Arts and Public Radio:
  WAMU-FM 88.5 (50 mi; 168 hrs)
  WETA-FM 90.9 (125 mi; 138 hrs)
  WPFW-FM 89.3 (100 mi; 168 hrs)
Public Television:
  WETA Channel 26
  WHMM Channel 32
Universities:
  American University (453)
  Bowie State College (288)
  Catholic University (259)
  George Mason University (625)
  George Washington University (740)•
  Georgetown University (524)
  Howard University (565)
  University of D.C. (400)
  University of Maryland (1,000)•
Symphony Orchestras:
  D.C. Youth Orchestra
  Georgetown Symphony (Community)
  Handel Festival Orchestra★
  National Symphony Orchestra★★★★
Theatres:
  Arena Stage★★★★
  Folger Theatre★
  Living Stage Theatre Company
  New Playwright's Theatre
  Round House Theatre
Opera Companies:
  Washington Opera★★★★
    8 productions; 63 performances
Dance Companies:
  African Heritage Dancers and
    Drummers (E-F)★
  Ava-Teri Dance Theatre (M)
  Bethesda Ballet Company★★
  Capitol Ballet Company
  Center Dance Ensemble (M)
  Dance Exchange (M)
  Fairfax Ballet Company
  Kinor Dance Company (E-F)
  Maida Withers and The Dance
    Construction Company (M)
  Maryland Dance Theatre (M)
  Montgomery Ballet Company
  Murray Spalding Dance Theatre (M)
  Perle/Bloom and Company (M)
  Prochotsky Ballet Theatre
  Richard Cunningham Dance
    Company (M)
  Washington Ballet
Public Libraries:
  1,346,723 volumes; circulation
    1,487,009
Reading Quotient: 4.4
Places Rated Score: 21,701
Places Rated Rank: 4

Waterbury, CT
Symphony Orchestras:
  Waterbury Symphony Orchestra
    (Community)

Dance Companies:
  Nutmeg Ballet Company
Public Libraries:
  167,852 volumes; circulation
  179,988
Reading Quotient: 3.4
Places Rated Score: 318
Places Rated Rank: 291

Waterloo–Cedar Falls, IA
Fine Arts and Public Radio:
  KBBG-FM 88.1 (60 mi; 138 hrs)
  KHKE-FM 89.5 (42 mi; 131 hrs)
  KUNI-FM 90.9 (74 mi; 168 hrs)
Public Television
  KRIN Channel 32
Universities:
  University of Northern Iowa (820)
Symphony Orchestras:
  Waterloo–Cedar Falls Symphony
  Orchestra★
Public Libraries:
  380,243 volumes; circulation 1,202,664
Reading Quotient: 8.5
Places Rated Score: 3,000
Places Rated Rank: 105

Wausau, WI
Public Television:
  WHRM Channel 20
Public Libraries:
  261,415 volumes; circulation 766,030
Reading Quotient: 9.3
Places Rated Score: 761
Places Rated Rank: 250

West Palm Beach–Boca Raton–Delray Beach, FL
Fine Arts and Public Radio:
  WHRS-FM 90.7 (50 mi; 126 hrs)
Public Television:
  WHRS Channel 42
Universities:
  Florida Atlantic University (830)
Symphony Orchestras:
  Greater Palm Beach Symphony★★
  Boca Raton Symphony Orchestra★
Theatres:
  Caldwell Playhouse
Opera Companies:
  Palm Beach Opera, Inc.
  2 productions; 4 performances
Public Libraries:
  449,559 volumes; circulation 2,136,233
Reading Quotient: 5.4
Places Rated Score: 2,888
Places Rated Rank: 110

Wheeling, WV–OH
Symphony Orchestras:
  Wheeling Symphony Orchestra★★
Public Libraries:
  121,760 volumes; circulation 213,000
Reading Quotient: 5.5
Places Rated Score: 422
Places Rated Rank: 277

Wichita, KS
Fine Arts and Public Radio:
  KMUW-FM 89.1 (40 mi; 165 hrs)

Public Television:
  KPTS Channel 8
Universities:
  Wichita State University (860)••
Symphony Orchestras:
  Wichita State University Symphony
  Orchestra
  Wichita Symphony Orchestra★★★
  Wichita Youth Orchestra
Dance Companies:
  Mid-America Dance Company (M)
Public Libraries:
  476,906 volumes; circulation 1,139,428
Reading Quotient: 5.9
Places Rated Score: 2,987
Places Rated Rank: 108

Wichita Falls, TX
Universities:
  Midwestern State University (241)
Symphony Orchestras:
  Wichita Falls Symphony Orchestra★
Dance Companies:
  Wichita Falls Ballet Theatre
Public Libraries:
  108,247 volumes; circulation 169,456
Reading Quotient: 3.0
Places Rated Score: 599
Places Rated Rank: 264

Williamsport, PA
Symphony Orchestras:
  Susquehanna Valley Symphony
  Orchestra (Community)
Public Libraries:
  96,013 volumes; circulation 240,688
Reading Quotient: 2.8
Places Rated Score: 196
Places Rated Rank: 305

Wilmington, DE–NJ–MD
Museums:
  Hagley Museum (600)
Universities:
  University of Delaware (1,000)
Symphony Orchestras:
  Delaware Symphony Orchestra★★
Theatres:
  Delaware Theatre Company
Public Libraries:
  635,627 volumes; circulation 1,593,392
Reading Quotient: 5.6
CMSA Access: PHILADELPHIA–
  WILMINGTON–TRENTON, PA–NJ–DE–
  MD (1,909)
Places Rated Score: 4,545
Places Rated Rank: 66

Wilmington, NC
Public Television:
  WUNJ Channel 39
Universities:
  University of North Carolina, Wilmington
  (406)
Public Libraries:
  171,165 volumes; circulation 355,620
Reading Quotient: 5.1
Places Rated Score: 1,077
Places Rated Rank: 222

Worcester, MA
Museums:
  Worcester Art Museum (800)
Universities:
  Clark University (203)
Theatres:
  Worcester Foothills Theatre Company
Dance Companies:
  Pyramid Dance Company (M)
Public Libraries:
  631,307 volumes; circulation 904,278
Reading Quotient: 9.5
Places Rated Score: 1,784
Places Rated Rank: 172

Yakima, WA
Public Television:
  KXVE Channel 47
Symphony Orchestras:
  Yakima Symphony Orchestra
  (Community)
  Yakima Youth Orchestra
Public Libraries:
  296,189 volumes; circulation 870,154
Reading Quotient: 6.9
Places Rated Score: 996
Places Rated Rank: 231

York, PA
Museums:
  Historical Society of York County (500)
Symphony Orchestras:
  York Junior Symphony
  York Symphony Association★
  York Youth Symphony
Public Libraries:
  122,000 volumes; circulation 330,000
Reading Quotient: 4.1
Places Rated Score: 1,022
Places Rated Rank: 226

Youngstown–Warren, OH
Fine Arts and Public Radio:
  WYSO-FM 91.3 (60 mi; 162 hrs)
Universities:
  Youngstown State University (990)
Symphony Orchestras:
  Dana Symphony Orchestra (College)
  Warren Chamber Orchestra
  (Community)
  Youngstown Symphony Orchestra
  (Youth)
Dance Companies:
  Ballet Midwest
  Ballet Western Reserve
Public Libraries:
  906,848 volumes; circulation 430,444
Reading Quotient: 5.4
Places Rated Score: 2,797
Places Rated Rank: 115

Yuba City, CA
Public Libraries:
  122,101 volumes; circulation 231,133
Reading Quotient: 6.7
Places Rated Score: 122
Places Rated Rank: 317

Et Cetera

A DAVID AND GOLIATH PROPOSITION

Show us the biggest metro areas and we'll show you the best places to live for the arts: New York, Chicago, Los Angeles, Washington, D.C., and Boston. The fairly consistent relationship between a metro area's size and its supply of cultural facilities might lead you to believe that such places as Bangor, Maine, and Bloomington, Indiana—both with populations under 100,000 and ranking 155th and 145th, respectively, in the arts—must resign themselves to being cultural underdogs. But think again.

Pick On Someone Your Own Size

What would happen if Bangor and Bloomington, remembering the old playground maxim, were to say to New York, "Go pick on someone your own size"? By grouping metro areas according to their populations, we are able to explore which ones have a large supply of cultural assets relative to their size and which might be considered culturally deficient. *Places Rated* divides the metro areas into four competitive population groups, based on criteria established by the federal government.

The following lists show how the metro areas rank in the arts when they are measured against similarly sized places.

Metro Areas and the Arts: Some Size Comparisons

Largest Metro Areas
(Population 1,000,000 or More)

Best Metro Areas	Places Rated Score	Worst Metro Areas	Places Rated Score
1. New York, NY	56,745	1. Fort Lauderdale–Hollywood–Pompano Beach, FL	2,027
2. Chicago, IL	24,846	2. San Antonio, TX	4,295
3. Los Angeles–Long Beach, CA	23,567	3. Sacramento, CA	4,483
4. Washington, DC–MD–VA	21,701	4. Phoenix, AZ	4,573
5. Boston, MA	21,042	5. Miami–Hialeah, FL	4,837
6. Philadelphia, PA–NJ	17,270	6. Tampa–St. Petersburg–Clearwater, FL	5,040
7. San Francisco, CA	14,226	7. Portland, OR	5,160
8. Newark, NJ	14,224	8. Riverside–San Bernardino, CA	5,327
9. Cleveland, OH	12,679	9. Anaheim–Santa Ana, CA	5,632
10. Minneapolis–St. Paul, MN–WI	11,714	10. Oakland, CA	6,162

Medium-Sized Metro Areas
(Population 250,000 to 1,000,000)

Best Metro Areas	Places Rated Score	Worst Metro Areas	Places Rated Score
1. Bridgeport–Milford, CT	8.368	1. Lakeland–Winter Haven, FL	309
2. Middlesex–Somerset–Hunterdon, NJ	8,058	2. Melbourne–Titusville–Palm Bay, FL	437
3. New Haven–Meriden, CT	7,852	3. Pawtucket–Woonsocket–Attleboro, RI–MA	480
4. Monmouth–Ocean, NJ	7,563	4. Atlantic City, NJ	621
5. Ann Arbor, MI	7,559	5. Modesto, CA	631
6. Jersey City, NJ	7,420	6. Johnstown, PA	666
7. Honolulu, HI	7,168	7. Daytona Beach, FL	809
8. Orange County, NY	6,987	8. Utica–Rome, NY	858
9. Rochester, NY	6,956	9. East St. Louis–Belleville, IL	904
10. Dayton–Springfield, OH	6,935	10. Canton, OH	989

Small Metro Areas
(Population 100,000 to 250,000)

Best Metro Areas	Places Rated Score	Worst Metro Areas	Places Rated Score
1. Stamford, CT	7,865	1. Sharon, PA	52
2. Danbury, CT	7,415	2. Texarkana, TX–Texarkana, AR	63
3. Norwalk, CT	7,273	3. Kankakee, IL	75
4. Lincoln, NE	4,523	4. Benton Harbor, MI	79
5. Kenosha, WI	3,844	5. Joplin, MO	80
6. Santa Cruz, CA	3,748	6. Danville, VA	85
7. Boulder–Longmont, CO	3,663	7. Fort Walton Beach, FL	87
8. Athens, GA	3,546	8. Parkersburg–Marietta, WV–OH	91
9. Lubbock, TX	3,402	9. Clarksville–Hopkinsville, TN–KY	111
10. Gainesville, FL	3,335	10. Dothan, AL	117

Smallest Metro Areas
(Population Less than 100,000)

Best Metro Areas	Places Rated Score	Worst Metro Areas	Places Rated Score
1. Lawrence, KS	3,150	1. Sherman–Denison, TX	68
2. Las Cruces, NM	2,804	2. Victoria, TX	87
3. Iowa City, IA	2,255	3. Burlington, NC	131
4. Bloomington, IN	2,152	4. Laredo, TX	150
5. Bryan–College Station, TX	2,002	5. Enid, OK	215
6. Bangor, ME	1,995	6. Pittsfield, MA	228
7. Grand Forks, ND	1,921	7. Fitchburg–Leominster, MA	270
8. La Crosse, WI	1,466	8. Casper, WY	303
9. San Angelo, TX	1,301	9. Dubuque, IA	340
10. Bismarck, ND	1,211	10. Pine Bluff, AR	373

Going one step further, there is a way that metro areas with populations below 100,000 can stand up to and even defeat arts giants like New York and Chicago. It's the culture per capita score, the weapon with which small places can bring metropolitan Goliaths to their knees.

Determining Culture per Capita

Applying the culture per capita scoring system will prove to a transferring executive who loves the arts or to a retired theatergoer that a move to the Great Plains

Apples and Oranges

Critics might call it comparing apples to oranges, but applying the per capita scoring principles to the metro area of your choice can result in interesting and some-times upsetting conclusions.

Casper, Wyoming, and Enid, Oklahoma, for in-stance, should be delighted to discover where their per capita scores rank them in relation to Chicago and Los Angeles–Long Beach.

Here is a sample of what might be found when the per capita scores of smaller places are compared with those of the cultural leaders.

Per Capita Comparisons: A Sampler

Metro Area	Per Capita Score	Overall Arts Rank
Boston, MA	750	5
New York, NY	685	1
Washington, DC–MD–VA	668	4
Casper, WY	422	293
Pine Bluff, AR	411	282
Chicago, IL	410	2
Dubuque, IA	363	287
Enid, OK	342	304
Los Angeles–Long Beach, CA	315	3

does not mean leaving all that wonderful entertain-ment back home in the big city. Of course, the largest places will still have the most resources, but per capita, places like Bryan–College Station, Texas; Grand Forks, North Dakota; and Lawrence, Kansas, make quite an effort—in fact, might be considered overachievers—in providing their citizens with culture and art.

To evaluate a metro area in terms of cultural facilities per capita, each metro area's *Places Rated* score is divided by its population. This number is then multiplied by 100,000 to do away with the decimal point; the resulting number is the score. For example, New York's overall arts score of 56,745 is divided by the metro area population of 8,274,961, yielding .00680. Multiplying this figure by 100,000 results in a culture per capita score of 680 for New York.

When we compare the 329 metro areas on the basis of culture per capita, the usual megalopolitan leaders fade from view, and Bangor, Bloomington, Grand Forks, and Lawrence have their chance to shine.

Culture per Capita: The Top 20 Metro Areas

Metro Area	Per Capita Score	Metro Area	Per Capita Score
1. Norwalk, CT	5,741	12. Orange County, NY	2,691
2. Lawrence, KS	4,657	13. Bangor, ME	2,377
3. Danbury, CT	4,352	14. Lincoln, NE	2,345
4. Stamford, CT	3,955	15. Bloomington, IN	2,178
5. Kenosha, WI	3,122	16. Bryan–College Station, TX	2,139
6. Las Cruces, NM	2,911	17. Santa Cruz, CA	1,992
7. Grand Forks, ND	2,906	18. Bridgeport–Milford, CT	1,980
8. Columbia, MO	2,871	19. Gainesville, FL	1,946
9. Ann Arbor, MI	2,855	20. Muncie, IN	1,943
10. Iowa City, IA	2,760		
11. Athens, GA	2,727		

A closer look at the top 20 places for culture per capita reveals that although the largest metro areas are absent from the list, they do have far-reaching effects, even on per capita scores. Eight of the 20 metro areas are actually components of Consolidated Metropolitan Statistical Areas (CMSAs) and draw much of their strength from the metro areas of New York, Chicago, Detroit, and San Francisco. As a matter of fact, the

high-ranking Connecticut metro areas of Norwalk, Danbury, and Stamford each receive more than 6,000 bonus points as part of the New York–Northern New Jersey–Long Island consolidated area.

By disregarding all metro areas with CMSA access, we can discover which are meeting the cultural needs of their populations on their own.

The 21 Best Non-CMSA Metro Areas in Culture per Capita

Metro Area	Per Capita Score	Metro Area	Per Capita Score
1. Lawrence, KS	4,657	13. Fayetteville–Springdale, AR	1,906
2. Las Cruces, NM	2,911	14. Waterloo–Cedar Falls, IA	1,843
3. Grand Forks, ND	2,906	15. Lafayette, IN	1,837
4. Columbia, MO	2,871	16. La Crosse, WI	1,610
5. Iowa City, IA	2,760	17. Lubbock, TX	1,608
6. Athens, GA	2,727	18. Madison, WI	1,583
7. Bangor, ME	2,377	19. New Haven–Meriden, CT	1,569
8. Lincoln, NE	2,345	20. Fargo–Moorhead, ND–MN	1,534
9. Bloomington, IN	2,178	20. San Angelo, TX	1,534
10. Bryan–College Station, TX	2,139		
11. Gainesville, FL	1,946		
12. Muncie, IN	1,943		

What sparks these smaller metro areas to achieve in the arts? Just as every metro area exists for a different reason, so the local types of support for the arts also differ. In centers for manufacturing and retail trade, this support may be in the form of grants and endow-ments; in agricultural areas, it may come from individ-uals. With the exception of La Crosse, Wisconsin, the metro areas listed above all have one source of aid in common: Each is home to a university offering majors in the performing arts. As with nearly every college or university, support for the arts runs high both within the walls of the school and in the community itself.

FOLK ART IN AMERICA

Folk art is where you find it. And in one form or another—be it music, ethnic food traditions, games, sayings, rhymes, crafts, or simple street pastimes—that's just about everywhere you care to look.

Interest in folk art currently is greater than it has ever been in America, as shown by the remarkable upsurge in the number of folk festivals throughout the country. Many of these festivals are ethnic in origin. The Midwest has numerous festivals celebrating the customs of such places as Germany, Sweden, Norway, Poland, and Lithuania. In the East, similar festivals honoring the Greeks, Italians, and Portuguese are common. Almost every state has at least one gathering of Scottish clans. Black Americans celebrate their history in the traditional musical forms of ballads, blues, and gospel songs. In New Orleans, these old oral traditions combine with instrumentation and more modern city blues to create the world-renowned sound of New Orleans jazz.

Some festivals center on events. There are festivals celebrating the harvest, the making of wine, the departure of fishing fleets, or the butchering of whales. Some festivals are religious; others honor national or local heroes; still others reflect the livelihood of a region, such as the logging festivals of the Northwest,

and the steam-thresher revivals of the Great Plains.

The list of festivals that follows has been compiled with the help of the National Council for the Traditional Arts, in Washington, D.C., and the various folk arts coordinators at the state level. In choosing these festivals, careful attention was paid to include only those faithful to the traditional folk arts. Size and duration of the festivals were considered, as was breadth of appeal. However, some of the biggest festivals were excluded because of their commercial orientation. Finally, whenever possible, we included festivals that occur at different times of the year and at different locations in each state. In many instances a phone number has been included after the festival name to provide further information to those interested.

In most cases, the reader can get a good idea of what each festival is like simply from the festival's name. When the nature of the festival is not obvious, a short explanation is provided. Almost all of the festivals on the list provide music and food—either free or for a nominal charge—in addition to the main event.

Selected Folk Festivals, by State

ALABAMA
Mobile Jazz Festival
Mobile
Early May   (205) 343-4420

Tennessee Valley Old Time Fiddlers
   Convention
Athens
Early October   (205) 837-4235

ALASKA
Little Norway Festival
Petersburg
Mid-May   (907) 772-3646

ARIZONA
"Tucson Meet Yourself"
A celebration of traditions of the Southwest
Tucson
2nd weekend in October

WA:K Annual Pow Wow
Authentic Indian ceremonies and crafts fair
Tucson
Early to mid-March

ARKANSAS
Arkansas Folk Festival
Traditional music, bluegrass
Mountain View
Mid-April   (501) 269-3851

"Back in the Hills" Antique Show and Folklife
   Fair
Crafts, demonstrations, games
War Eagle (near Hindsville)
Early May   (501) 789-5398

CALIFORNIA
Fiesta de la Primavera
Mexican mariachi bands and Spanish
   dancers
Old Town, San Diego
Mid-May   (714) 297-2219

Ghost Mountain Bluegrass Festival
Pollock Pines
Late May   (916) 487-9761

COLORADO
Colorado State Fair
Crafts, music, Western skills competition
Pueblo
Late August

Rocky Mountain Bluegrass Festival
Henderson
Late August   (303) 771-2410

CONNECTICUT
Danbury State Fair
Danbury State Fairgrounds
Mid-July   (203) 748-3535

DELAWARE
Delaware State Fair
Harrington
3rd week in July   (302) 398-3269

DISTRICT OF COLUMBIA
Festival of American Folk Life
Sponsored by the Smithsonian Institution
Washington Monument grounds
Early October   (202) 381-6532

FLORIDA
Florida Folk Festival
Native American folklore, crafts,
   demonstrations
White Springs
3rd week in May   (904) 397-2192

Pioneer Days Festival
Traditional music, arts and crafts
Pine Castle Center of the Arts, Orlando
Last weekend in October   (305) 855-7461

GEORGIA
Chattahoochee Folk Festival
Columbus
Last week in September   (404) 323-3617

Georgia Sea Island Festival
Music of the Georgia coast
St. Simons Island
Mid-August   (912) 265-9545

HAWAII
King Kamehameha Celebration
Traditional Hawaiian dances, storytelling
Honolulu
Early June   (808) 548-4512

IDAHO
National Oldtime Fiddlers Contest
Weiser
Mid-June   (208) 549-0452

ILLINOIS
International Folk Fair
Celebration of Chicago's ethnic diversity
Chicago
October   (312) 744-3315

Pilsen Community *Fiesta del Sol*
Hispanic neighborhood celebration
Chicago
August   (312) 666-2663

Southern Illinois Folk Festival
Emphasis on Indian and German-American
   traditions
Du Quoin
Late September   (618) 542-5484

INDIANA
Annual Duneland Folk Festival
Chesterton and Porter
Mid-July   (219) 926-7561

Annual Indiana Fiddlers Gathering
Battleground
Early September

Bean Blossom Festival
Bill Monroe's famous bluegrass festival
Bean Blossom
Mid-June

IOWA
Council Bluffs Old-Time Country Music
   Contest
Council Bluffs
Late August   (712) 366-1136

Midwest Old Settlers and Threshers Reunion
Antique farm machinery, demonstrations,
    music
Mount Pleasant
Late August   (319) 385-8937

Nordic Fest
One of the largest Norwegian-American
    celebrations in the country
Decorah
Late July   (319) 382-4147

KANSAS
After Harvest Czech Festival
Wilson
3rd week in July   (913) 658-2965

National Flat-Picking Championship
Guitar-playing competition
Winfield
Fall   (316) 221-3250

Smoky Hill River Festival
Crafts, children's games
Salina
Mid-June   (913) 827-4640

KENTUCKY
Celebration of Traditional Music
Berea
Late October   (606) 986-9341

Kentucky Folklife Celebration
Traditional mountain music and dances
Louisville
Early June

LOUISIANA
Baton Rouge Blues Festival
Mostly black blues and gospel
Baton Rouge
Late April   (504) 344-8558

Cajun Music Festival
Food, music
Lafayette
3rd week in September

Lagniappe on the Bayou
Cajun-Creole celebration
Chauvin
Mid-October   (504) 594-5859

New Orleans Jazz and Heritage Festival
New Orleans
Mid-April   (504) 522-4786

MAINE
Annual Fishermen's Festival
Blessing of the fleet, nautical contests
Boothbay Harbor
Late March   (207) 633-4232

Heritage Days
Community celebration
Bath
Early July   (207) 443-9751

MARYLAND
Colonial Highland Gathering
Scottish games, music, dances
Fair Hill
Early June   (302) 731-5100

MASSACHUSETTS
Feast of St. Anthony
Italian religious feast
Boston (North End)
July   (617) 742-9547

St. Peter's Fiesta
Italian-Portuguese fishing celebration
Gloucester
3rd week in June   (617) 283-1601

MICHIGAN
Ann Arbor Council of Traditional Music and
    Dance
Ann Arbor
Early September

Wheatland Bluegrass and Old Time Music
    Festival
Remus
Early September

MINNESOTA
Forestville Arts and Crafts Festival
Forestville State Park, Preston
Early June   (507) 765-2219

Laskiainen
Finnish celebration: logging, games, music
Palo–Markham
1st weekend in February

Paul Bunyan Festival
Brainerd
Late September   (218) 829-0097

MISSISSIPPI
Delta Blues Festival
Black blues, spirituals
Greenville
Early September   (601) 335-3523

Northeast Mississippi Blues and Gospel
    Festival
Traditional black music
Rust College, Holly Springs
Late September

MISSOURI
Frontier Folklife Festival
St. Louis
Mid-September

Missouri State Fiddling Championship
Columbia
Late August

Mountain Folks Music Festival
Music of the Ozarks
Silver Dollar City, Branson
Mid-June   (417) 338-2611

MONTANA
Homesteaders Days
Hot Springs
Mid-June   (406) 741-3494

NEBRASKA
Camp Creek Antique Machinery and
    Threshing Show
Old farm machinery, music, games, crafts
Waverly
3rd weekend in July

Kolachs Days
Czech celebration
Verdigre
Mid-June   (402) 668-2266

Wilber Czech Festival
Wilber
Early August   (402) 821-2283

NEVADA
Basque Festival
Elko
Early July

NEW HAMPSHIRE
Annual League of New Hampshire
    Craftsman's Fair
Carpentry, musical instruments, stained
    glass
Mount Sunapee State Park, Newbury
1st week in August   (603) 224-3375

Canterbury Fair
Canterbury Center
Late July

New Hampshire Folk Festival
Concord
Last Sunday in August   (603) 224-2508

NEW JERSEY
Middletown Folk Festival
Middletown
Mid-June   (201) 291-9200

New Jersey Folk Festival at Douglass
    College
New Brunswick
Late April   (201) 745-0077

NEW MEXICO
Feria de Artesanos
Arts and crafts show
Albuquerque
Late August

Indian Market
Native American crafts show
Santa Fe
Late August   (505) 983-5220

Jickarilla Apache Tribal Fair
Dulce
Mid-July

Shalako Dance
Authentic religious ceremony
Zuni Pueblo
1st week in December   (505) 782-4481

NEW YORK
Berkshire Mountains Bluegrass Festival
Ancram and Hillsdale
Late July   (617) 492-0415

Festival of North Country Folklife
Robert Moses State Park, Massena
Early August

Scampagnata Folcloristica Italiana
Italian-American celebration
ARTPARK, Lewiston
Late June

NORTH CAROLINA
Annual Mountain Dance and Folk Festival
Asheville
Early August   (704) 254-1981

Bascom Lamar Lunsford Mountain Music
    and Dance Festival
One of the oldest folk festivals in America
Mars Hill
Early October   (704) 689-1330

World Champion Old Time Fiddlers
    Convention
Union Grove
1st week in April   (704) 539-4934

NORTH DAKOTA
North Dakota Roughrider Days
Dickinson
Early July   (701) 225-5115

OHIO

Gambier Folk Festival
Kenyon College, Gambier
Late October   (614) 427-4875

Kent State Folk Festival
Kent
Late February

OKLAHOMA

American Indian Exposition
Anadarko
Mid-August   (405) 247-3424

Grant's Annual Bluegrass and Oldtime
    Festival
Salt Creek Park, Hugo
Early August   (405) 326-5598

World Series of Fiddling and Bluegrass
    Festival
Powderhorn Park, Langley
Late August   (405) 732-3964

OREGON

State of Jefferson Days
Historic celebration
Klamath Falls
3 weekends in August   (503) 884-5193

Willamette Valley Folk Festival
University of Oregon, Eugene
Mid-May   (503) 686-4373

PENNSYLVANIA

Brandywine Mountain Music Convention
Concordville
Mid- to late July   (302) 654-3930

Goshenhoppen Folk Festival
Small authentic Pennsylvania Dutch festival
East Greenville
2nd weekend in August   (215) 754-6013

Harvest Days Festival
Landis Valley Farm Museum
Lancaster
Early October   (717) 569-0401

Pittsburgh Folk Festival
Multi-ethnic celebration
Pittsburgh
Memorial Day weekend   (412) 227-6812

RHODE ISLAND

Annual Usquepaug Johnnycake Festival
Historic festival
Richmond–South Kingstown
Late October

Blessing of the Fleet Festival
Newport
Late July   (401) 847-1600

Cranberry Festival of the Tomaquag Indians
Exeter
Early October   (401) 539-7795

SOUTH CAROLINA

Lee County Cotton Pickin Festival
Square dances, cotton picking, gospel music
Bishopville
Mid-October   (803) 484-5302

Piccolo Spoletto Traditional Music Festival
One of the best festivals for fine arts
    lovers
Charleston
Late May–early June

SOUTH DAKOTA

Black Hills Bluegrass Festival
Nemo
July

Black Hills Steam Show and Threshing Bee
Antique farm machinery, music
Sturgis
Mid-August

South Dakota and Open Fiddling Contest
Yankton
3rd week in September   (605) 665-7290

Steam Threshing Jamboree
Madison
3rd week in August

TENNESSEE

National Storytelling Festival
Jonesboro
Mid-September   (615) 753-2171

Tennessee Grassroots Days
Centennial Park, Nashville
Late September–early October
    (615) 331-0602

Uncle Dave Macon Days
Traditional music and crafts
Murfreesboro
Early to mid-September   (615) 898-2300

TEXAS

Annual Border Festival
Music, crafts, Mexican rodeo
El Paso
Early October   (915) 543-7780

Texas Folklife Festival
Mexican and native American folklore,
    crafts
San Antonio
Late July   (512) 226-7651

UTAH

Festival of the American West
Logan
Early August   (801) 750-1145

Southern Utah Folklife Festival
Springdale
Early September   (801) 328-9681

VERMONT

"Midsummer"
Traditional music, games, dances
Montpelier
Mid-July   (802) 229-9408

Tunbridge Fair
Tunbridge
September

VIRGINIA

Blue Ridge Folklife Festival
Ferrum College, Ferrum
Late October   (703) 365-2121

Sara–Maybelle Carter Memorial Festival
Abingdon
Late July–early August   (703) 386-9480

WASHINGTON

The Festival of American Fiddle Tunes
Port Townsend
Late June–early July   (206) 385-5021

Northwest Regional Folklife Festival
Seattle
3rd week in May   (206) 625-5050

WEST VIRGINIA

Augusta Festival
Elkins
Early August   (304) 636-0006

Vandalia Gathering
Traditional music, storytelling
State Capitol, Charleston
3rd week in May   (304) 348-0220

WISCONSIN

Lakefront Summerfest
Multi-ethnic celebration
Summerfest Grounds, Milwaukee
Weekends, July-September
    (414) 273-2680

Polka Festival
Merrill
Mid-June   (715) 536-2974

Swiss Volksfest
Swiss-American celebration
New Glarus
Early August   (608) 527-2095

WYOMING

Cheyenne Frontier Days
Rodeo, horse racing, covered wagons
Cheyenne
3rd week in July   (307) 634-3321

Wyoming State Fiddle Contest
Shoshoni
Memorial Day weekend

YWCA Ethnic Fest
Rock Springs
Mid-May

HITTING THE BOOKS

In which states do people read the most? Where do they read the least? Where are the greatest concentrations of books found? Which state spends the most money per capita on its libraries, and which spends the least?

Circulation rate is one way to find out which are America's "readingest" states. Library circulation rates —that is, annual number of checkouts per resident— indicate both how much people read and how successful local libraries are in serving their communities. According to R. R. Bowker's *American Library Directory*, the annual per capita circulation rate in the United States ranges from a low of 1.71 books per person in Mississippi to a high of 9.15 books per person in Iowa.

Library Circulation Rates in the States

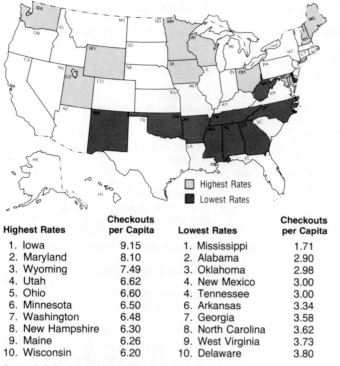

☐ Highest Rates
■ Lowest Rates

Highest Rates	Checkouts per Capita	Lowest Rates	Checkouts per Capita
1. Iowa	9.15	1. Mississippi	1.71
2. Maryland	8.10	2. Alabama	2.90
3. Wyoming	7.49	3. Oklahoma	2.98
4. Utah	6.62	4. New Mexico	3.00
5. Ohio	6.60	4. Tennessee	3.00
6. Minnesota	6.50	6. Arkansas	3.34
7. Washington	6.48	7. Georgia	3.58
8. New Hampshire	6.30	8. North Carolina	3.62
9. Maine	6.26	9. West Virginia	3.73
10. Wisconsin	6.20	10. Delaware	3.80

Source: R. R. Bowker, *American Library Directory,* 1983.

Listed above are states with circulation rates higher than 6.00 and lower than 4.00.

Do circulation rates reflect the availability of library volumes, or does the number of public library books reveal the importance that people in an area attach to collecting and disseminating knowledge? In any event, it is interesting to note that the two states providing the greatest number of public library volumes per capita—Maine and New Hampshire—are also among the states with the highest circulation rates, whereas four of the five states with the fewest library volumes per capita are among those with the lowest circulation rates.

Per Capita Library Holdings in the States

Most Books	Volumes per Capita	Fewest Books	Volumes per Capita
1. Maine	4.67	1. South Carolina	1.30
2. New Hampshire	4.60	2. Oklahoma	1.33
3. Massachusetts	4.54	3. Tennessee	1.40
4. Vermont	4.01	4. Alabama	1.45
		4. North Carolina	1.45

Source: R. R. Bowker, *American Library Directory,* 1983.

Another reflection of how important a region considers its libraries is its annual library expenditures, since library services are often among the first to be cut when a community is looking for ways to reduce

expenses. Wyoming leads the states in this category, spending an average of $16.21 per person per year on its libraries; Arkansas spends the least, only $2.94 per person.

Library Expenditures in the States

Biggest Spenders	Dollars per Capita per Year	Smallest Spenders	Dollars per Capita per Year
1. Wyoming	$16.21	1. Arkansas	$2.94
2. New York	15.42	2. South Carolina	4.01
3. Maryland	12.69	3. Alabama	4.67
4. Connecticut	12.49	4. Tennessee	4.79
5. Iowa	11.93	5. Kentucky	5.00
6. Washington	11.71		
7. Hawaii	11.70		

Source: R. R. Bowker, *American Library Directory,* 1983.

A LIBRARY WITH A SURPLUS?

A growing problem in the nation's capital, besides the budget deficit and the national debt, is one of space: many government museums and libraries are running out of room for the mountains of publicly owned artifacts and relics, according to a 1984 issue of *U.S. News & World Report.*

The Smithsonian Institution, nicknamed the Nation's Attic, has only enough room in its dozen museums open to the public for 1 percent of its possessions. After conducting its first total inventory in 1983 (the project took five years), it discovered 100 million items it didn't know it had. Among the Smithsonian's treasure troves are thousands of preserved fish and birds, which have been laid to rest in liquid-filled bottles and trays. In 20 aircraft hangars outside Washington that are owned by the institution rest spare parts for its antique planes: rotary piston engines, fabric-covered wooden wings, and old propellers and fuselages. There is also a special section housing 10,000 American Indian pots from the nineteenth century.

The National Archives, whose most famous documents are the Declaration of Independence and the Constitution, also has a few other pieces of paper lying around, to wit: three billion documents, five million still pictures, 91 million feet of movie film, and 11 million maps.

The Library of Congress, in the true tradition of great libraries the world over, has a good deal more under its roof than books. But it has some of those, too: 20 million, which sit on 535 *miles* of shelf space. It also has ten million prints and photographs, three million musical scores, 3.8 million maps, 47,000 atlases, and 400,000 newspapers. So you think you've got storage problems?

Recreation:

The Best Places to Play

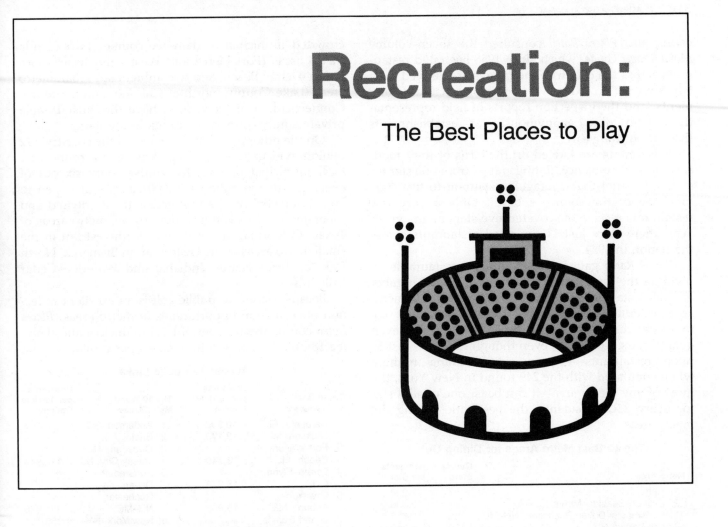

After "Where's that?", the question that chamber of commerce brochure writers find people ask most often about an unfamiliar place is "Is there anything to do there?" No matter where they live, Americans want to make the most of their leisure time. Not for nothing are billions spent each year on everything from video games to insulated jogging clothes, from season tickets at the ballpark to European vacations, from down-filled sleeping bags to graphite fishing rods.

But not everyone can take advantage of the myriad opportunities for recreation. A ski trip to Aspen or a golf weekend at Hilton Head Island is too costly for most people's budgets, and even a backpacking trip in a national park where entrance fees and camping charges are nominal might be out of the question due to the dollars and time it takes to get there and back.

Fortunately, there are many other things to do that are inexpensive and close by. Movies, golf, bowling, and even good restaurants are available nearly every-place in the country; in fact, people living in smaller metro areas usually have better access to these than residents of bigger metro areas. On the other hand, urban crowd pleasers such as zoos, family theme parks, professional sports arenas, and racetracks en-hance leisure living in larger places. For some of us, convenient outdoor recreation in a national forest or along a wild and scenic river is a lucky geographical circumstance; the protected outdoors is a part of the landscape just as developed urban land is. *Places Rated Almanac* looks at each of these kinds of recreation in finding the best places to play in the United States.

COMMON DENOMINATORS

For scuba diving, the coasts of Florida, California, and Hawaii are your best bets. When it comes to skiing on powdery snow, certain parts of the country are better suited than others because of local topography and climate. The weather and the winds turn other areas into premier places for soaring in gliders. But there are certain kinds of recreation that you can find every-where: dining out at a quality restaurant, a round of weekend golf, bowling at a local tenpin center, or moviegoing at a downtown picture palace or a subur-ban shopping mall.

Food, Glorious Food

If you're among the one in ten people who enjoys getting out of the house at least once a week for dinner, you might as well go to a worthwhile eatery instead of a portion-controlled Casa de la Maison where distantly prepared frozen packages of beef Wellington and veal *cordon bleu* are microwaved, dished out, and priced at ten times what the restaurant paid for them.

To determine the best metro areas in America for

eating out, *Places Rated* consulted the seven-volume *Mobil Travel Guide,* which since 1958 has rated restaurants across the country. The ratings are derived from two sources: an extensive review of consumer comments, and the inspection reports of field representatives who dine anonymously at establishments throughout the year.

Restaurants are judged on the basis of their food, service, and ambience. Ratings range from one star for a "good, better-than-average" restaurant to five stars for "one of the country's best." Only a very few restaurants receive the coveted five stars in any given year; there were just 11 top-rated restaurants across the nation in 1984.

Places Rated gauges access to good restaurants by dividing the resident population by the total number of quality stars awarded by *Mobil Travel Guide* to metro area restaurants. Four one-star restaurants and one three-star restaurant, for example, would yield seven quality stars. Therefore, even though Reno has just 39 rated restaurants—not an overwhelming number when compared with the 249 found in New York, the most of any metro area—it can boast one quality star for every 2,226 residents, the best ratio among the metro areas.

The 12 Best Metro Areas for Dining Out

Metro Area	Quality Stars	Residents per Star
1. Reno, NV	87	2,226
2. Salinas–Seaside–Monterey, CA	87	3,338
3. Portsmouth–Dover–Rochester, NH–ME	52	3,672
4. Las Vegas, NV	109	4,249
5. Glens Falls, NY	22	4,984
6. San Francisco, CA	286	5,030
7. Rochester, MN	18	5,111
8. Atlantic City, NJ	53	5,215
9. Fort Myers, FL	36	5,702
10. Portland, ME	32	6,057
11. Burlington, VT	18	6,406
12. Salem–Gloucester, MA	38	6,797

Source: Rand McNally & Company, *Mobil Travel Guide* (7 vols.), 1984.

Sixteen metro areas have no restaurants awarded quality ratings by *Mobil Travel Guide:* Anderson, IN; Anderson, SC; Brazoria, TX; Burlington, NC; Danville, VA; Gadsden, AL; Hamilton–Middletown, OH; Houma–Thibodaux, LA; Jacksonville, NC; Jersey City, NJ; Muncie, IN; Panama City, FL; Texarkana, TX–Texarkana, AR; Tyler, TX; Waterbury, CT; and Yakima, WA.

Public Golf Links

Certainly golf is a common denominator; the game is played in every U.S. metro area, including Anchorage, Alaska. You've got three options when it comes to finding a local golf course on an idle, sunny weekend: the private equity course, which is typically part of a country club open only to members and their guests; daily-fee operations open to all players; and city-built and -operated courses, again open to everyone.

If you're a golfer who can afford to join a private country club with an 18-hole course, you've got one big advantage aside from all the dances and dinners you're paying dues for: You belong to the fortunate 14 percent of golfers who don't have to wait to tee off at a

crowded municipal or daily-fee course. Two Florida metro areas (Fort Pierce and West Palm Beach–Boca Raton–Delray Beach) and two affluent suburban metro areas (Lake County, north of Chicago, and Stamford, Connecticut, near New York) have the most 18-hole private equity courses per capita in the nation.

On the other hand, if you're one of the country's 12 million avid golfers who regularly play a round at a local municipal or daily-fee course, only six out of every ten of the nation's 12,000 courses are open to you. Interestingly, the best access to city-owned and -operated courses is not in the upscale metro areas of Texas, California, or the Pacific Northwest but in the small metro areas of the Heartland, in Bismarck, North Dakota; Terre Haute, Indiana; and Waterloo–Cedar Falls, Iowa.

Because access to public golf is an excellent reflection of recreation opportunities in metro areas, *Places Rated* counts the number of local municipal and daily-fee 18-hole (or equivalent) courses per capita.

Access to Public Links

The 10 Best Metro Areas	Residents per 18-Hole Course	The 10 Worst Metro Areas	Residents per 18-Hole Course
1. Sarasota, FL	10,932	1. Anderson, SC	*
2. Jackson, MI	13,173	2. Bristol, CT	*
3. Fort Walton Beach, FL	13,740	3. Gadsden, AL	*
4. Lorain–Elyria, OH	15,273	4. Jersey City, NJ	1,113,944
5. Lewiston–Auburn, ME	16,938	5. Portsmouth–Dover–Rochester, NH–ME	381,876
6. Grand Rapids, MI	16,949	6. New York, NY	359,781
7. Benton Harbor, MI	17,128	7. Houma–Thibodaux, LA	353,752
8. Kenosha, WI	17,591	8. Montgomery, AL	272,867
9. Rochester, MN	18,401	9. Hagerstown, MD	226,172
10. Kalamazoo, MI	18,468	10. Texarkana, TX–Texarkana, AR	226,134

Source: National Golf Foundation, unpublished administrative records, 1984.

The national average for public golf is 23,177 residents per 18-hole course.

*These metro areas have no public golf courses.

Tenpin Bowling

In "Rip Van Winkle," Washington Irving compared the sound of a hardwood ball striking hardwood pins to an ominous clap of thunder. This short story first appeared in 1819, a few years before the sport moved indoors to lanes built in the larger American cities for bowlers, typically Germans, who wanted to play year-round. Bowling has been around a long, long time indeed, and, in all its variations—skittles, fivepins, ninepins, tenpins, candlepins, duckpins—is probably played by more of the world's people than any other game, with the possible exception of soccer.

Nearly 70 million people in the United States take a turn each year at tenpins, the dominant bowling variation. But if the 8,500 bowling centers in this country had to depend solely on this kind of casual participation, many might quickly convert to tanning salons or microcomputer showrooms for a steadier income. The credit for keeping bowling alleys in business goes to such highly organized competitive associations as the American Bowling Congress (ABC), to which 4.5 million men belong, and the Women's International Bowling Congress, with 3.9 million female members, which promote frequent tournaments throughout the country.

Ninety-nine percent of the tenpin bowling centers in this country are certified by the ABC for tournament competition. To rate metro areas for access to tenpin bowling, *Places Rated* compares the number of lanes with the local population. Metro areas that lead the country in this common denominator are typically smaller, blue-collar metro areas in the Frost Belt, where indoor sports and active teams thrive.

Access to Tenpin Bowling

The 10 Best Metro Areas	Residents per Lane	The 10 Worst Metro Areas	Residents per Lane
1. Green Bay, WI	487	1. Boston, MA	16,313
2. Milwaukee, WI	489	2. Portland, ME	13,845
3. Daytona Beach, FL	520	3. Birmingham, AL	6,596
4. Appleton–Oshkosh–Neenah, WI	540	4. Galveston–Texas City, TX	6,123
5. Ocala, FL	572	5. Jackson, MS	5,839
6. Kalamazoo, MI	625	6. Fresno, CA	5,306
7. Elmira, NY	660	7. Laredo, TX	4,962
8. Davenport–Rock Island–Moline, IA–IL	676	8. McAllen–Edinburg–Mission, TX	4,720
9. Canton, OH	679	9. Springfield, IL	4,694
10. Erie, PA	682	10. Florence, SC	4,590

Source: American Bowling Congress, unpublished data, 1984.

The national average for tenpin bowling lanes is one for every 1,556 people.

Moviegoing

Does anyone remember when John Huston won two Academy Awards—best director and best screenplay —for *The Treasure of Sierra Madre?* And his father, Walter, was named best supporting actor for his performance as the grizzled old prospector in the same film? The year was 1948. Jane Wyman won an Oscar that year, too, for her role in *Johnny Belinda; Hamlet* got best picture, and its star, Laurence Olivier, was named best actor.

Thirty plus years ago, moviegoing was the American thing to do of an evening, any evening. Spilled popcorn was regularly swept up from the aisles between shows, the next John Wayne or Spencer Tracy film was announced on a large easel near the candy counter in the lobby, ushers in uniform took you to your seat with a red-lensed flashlight, and you always got a Fox Movietone or Pathé newsreel with the film. There were 18,631 motion picture theaters in 1948, most of them small neighborhood houses, with a few downtown palaces for premieres and first-run screenings. Never again would there be so many, for 1948 also marked the commercial appearance of television.

Today there are fewer than 8,000 commercial four-wall (as opposed to drive-in) movie theaters in the United States. If you adjust for ticket-price inflation, paid attendance has declined from $4.1 billion in the late 1940s to $1.1 billion in the last few years.

Places Rated divides a metro area's population by the number of four-wall theaters to determine local access to movies. Many of these establishments may be of the multiscreen, Cinema Six variety found in suburban shopping malls, but most are still the single-screen Bijou or Strand kind of neighborhood theater.

Access to Movie Theaters

The 10 Best Metro Areas	Residents per Theater	The 10 Worst Metro Areas	Residents per Theater
1. Grand Forks, ND	11,017	1. Utica–Rome, NY	160,090
2. Killeen–Temple, TX	13,416	2. Scranton–Wilkes-Barre, PA	104,114
3. Des Moines, IA	14,137	3. Pittsfield, MA	83,490
4. Charlottesville, VA	14,196	4. Lowell, MA–NH	81,047
5. San Francisco, CA	15,039	5. Niagara Falls, NY	75,785
6. Bellingham, WA	15,243	6. Washington, DC–MD–VA	73,882
7. Abilene, TX	15,847	7. Bristol, CT	73,762
8. Salinas–Seaside–Monterey, CA	16,136	8. Louisville, KY–IN	73,597
9. Iowa City, IA	16,343	9. Lancaster, PA	72,469
10. Eau Claire, WI	16,367	10. Chattanooga, TN–GA	71,090

Source: Derived from the U.S. Bureau of the Census, *1977 Census of Selected Service Establishments*, 1981, and *County Business Patterns*, 1983–1984.

The national average is 24,580 residents per theater.

CROWD PLEASERS

At different times of the year, a resident of the Los Angeles–Long Beach metro area can view the animals at the Los Angeles Zoo; sample the varied offerings at Marineland of the Pacific and the Universal Studios Tour; watch auto racing at the Long Beach Grand Prix; bet on the horses at two racetracks; or take in professional baseball, football, basketball, and hockey, as well as NCAA Division I competition.

Few metro areas have as varied a supply of crowd pleasers as Los Angeles–Long Beach, but some of these opportunities are common in many of the larger metro areas. From Disneyland in Anaheim to New York's Bronx Zoo, these assets offer Americans interesting ways to spend their leisure time.

Seeing the Animals: Zoos and Aquariums

The two best metro areas for seeing the animals are Chicago and San Diego. Each has not one but two of the country's top-ranked zoological parks. Altogether, 114 metro areas have at least one zoo. The idea that zoos enhance people's lives is a European one that flourishes especially well in America's Midwest. Besides Chicago's two great zoos, the Cincinnati, Cleveland, Detroit, Milwaukee, and St. Louis zoological parks are among the best in the United States. It is not coincidental that the working-class citizens of these cities can trace their roots to European countries—particularly Germany—that also have great zoos.

"Postage-stamp collecting" is the name that zookeepers give to the assembling of colorful animal specimens without regard to whether the animals would fit and thrive in a zoo's limited space. This was once a sure way of drawing more patrons and carving out a reputation as an outstanding institution. Today, professionally run zoos have fewer species on exhibit but more specimens of each. The standard phylogenetic exhibits (grouping African lions with Bengal tigers, timber wolves with hyenas) are being replaced with ecological displays (wildlife in desert or mountain environments) and behavioral exhibits (hibernation, burrowing, nocturnalism) that group specimens more creatively and openly.

This isn't to say that zoos no longer maintain large, diverse collections, for the best American zoos are those with the biggest animal populations. But today the benchmark of a zoo's quality isn't simply how many animals it can keep or breed; just as important is how creatively and naturally the animals are exhibited.

Fifteen American zoos are visited by at least a million people each year. All of them are city- or society-owned, and several are so well known that they attract many tourists.

The 15 Most Popular Zoos

	Visitors per Year
1. Lincoln Park Zoo (Chicago)	4,800,000
2. National Zoological Park (Washington, D.C.)	3,300,000
3. San Diego Zoo	3,000,000
4. Bronx Zoo (New York)	2,000,000
4. Forest Park Zoo (St. Louis)	2,000,000
6. Houston Zoological Gardens	1,800,000
7. Brookfield Zoo (Brookfield, IL)	1,700,000
8. Los Angeles Zoo	1,414,000
9. Wild Animal Park (San Diego)	1,300,000
10. Honolulu Zoo	1,100,000
10. Milwaukee County Zoo	1,100,000
10. Philadelphia Zoological Gardens	1,100,000
13. Denver Zoological Gardens	1,000,000
13. Minnesota Zoological Gardens (Minneapolis)	1,000,000
13. San Antonio Zoo and Aquarium	1,000,000

Source: American Association of Zoological Parks and Aquariums, *Zoological Parks and Aquariums in the Americas, 1982–83,* 1983.

Aquariums are far less common than zoos in the United States; in fact, only ten of the 329 metro areas can boast one: Baltimore, Boston, Chicago, Cleveland, Dallas, Honolulu, New York, San Francisco, Seattle, and Tacoma. Not surprisingly, seven of these metro areas are found in states with ocean coastlines. Unlike the great zoological parks, which are run municipally or by societies, some of the best aquariums (including Boston's New England Aquarium) are owned and operated for profit by private firms.

Family Theme Parks

The person who started it all was Walter Elias Disney; his creation was Disneyland. Because he ignored such time-honored features as a waterfront location and games of chance and skill, the amusement park industry viewed his 180-acre playland skeptically when it opened in Anaheim, California, in 1954. Disney's purpose was to use his famous cartoon characters and feature films as themes to structure a family-centered park more carefully than such parks as Chicago's Riverview or Ocean Park in Santa Monica, places avoided by families because of their tawdriness and cheap, carny atmosphere. That he succeeded is obvious; today, Disneyland and Walt Disney World in Florida—which includes the Magic Kingdom, opened in 1971, and Epcot Center, opened in 1982—together attract more than 22 million people a year.

Of the nearly 100 parks in the United States that market themselves as family theme parks, there are 25 that each draw more than one million visitors a year. Twenty-two metro areas have at least one theme park with this many annual visitors. These extremely popular parks are located near or in large metro areas, but they aren't havens for locals in the way that traditional parks such as Elitch Gardens in Denver, Salt Lake City's Lagoon Amusement Park, or Lake Pontchartrain Beach in New Orleans still are. Rather, theme parks are nationally advertised vacation-industry attractions.

Two "vacation" states—California and Florida—have ten of the top 25 theme parks, attracting more than half of the country's annual 75 million theme-park visitors. In these states, some parks' owners have chosen their locations strategically. The Orlando metro area, for example, is home not only to Walt Disney World & Epcot Center but also Sea World of Florida, which located there to take advantage of Disney World's draw. In Southern California, Knott's Berry Farm, a traditional roadside attraction since 1920, converted to theme-park format and joined Sea World of California and Six Flags Magic Mountain in trying to capitalize on Disneyland's crowds.

The Auto-Racing Circuit

America's celebrated love affair with fast cars started in Providence, Rhode Island, where the first automobile track race was sponsored in 1896. The affair hasn't ended, at least not for cars that hit 200 miles an hour on oval tracks. Last year, the 250,000 reserved seats for the Indianapolis 500 were sold out weeks before the race, in most instances at $55 per ticket. Whether on a "short eight" crash track in rural Oregon or a banked concrete oval in the Deep South, auto racing in all its variations draws millions each year.

Of the 1,100 auto racetracks in the United States, only a fraction are sanctioned by one or more of the three leading racing organizations: NASCAR, SCCA, and USAC. NASCAR, the National Association for Stock Car Racing, sanctions late-model and modified stock-car racing; SCCA, the Sports Car Club of America, has jurisdiction over sports-car events; and USAC, the United States Automobile Club, sanctions Indy, dirt-car, sprint-car, midget, and late-model racing.

Among the 58 metro areas with sanctioned tracks,

The 25 Most Popular Theme Parks

Park (Opening Year)	Operating Schedule	Annual Visitors	Park (Opening Year)	Operating Schedule	Annual Visitors
1. **Walt Disney World & Epcot Center** (1971)—Orlando, FL	365 days	12,560,000	14. **Opryland USA** (1972) Nashville, TN	140 days	2,290,000
2. **Disneyland** (1954) Anaheim, CA	303 days	10,420,000	15. **Six Flags Over Georgia** (1967)—Atlanta, GA	148 days	2,180,000
3. **Knott's Berry Farm** (1920) Buena Park, CA	365 days	4,000,000	16. **Busch Gardens—The Old Country** (1975) Williamsburg, VA	137 days	1,920,000
4. **Universal Studios Tour** (1964)—Los Angeles, CA	365 days	3,450,000	17. **Marriott's Great America** (1976)—Santa Clara, CA	141 days	1,760,000
5. **Busch Gardens—The Dark Continent** (1959)—Tampa, FL	365 days	3,080,000	18. **Astroworld** (1968) Houston, TX	159 days	1,660,000
6. **Sea World of Florida** (1973) Orlando, FL	365 days	3,000,000	19. **Hersheypark** (1907) Hershey, PA	120 days	1,480,000
7. **Six Flags Great Adventure** (1974)—Jackson, NJ	163 days	2,760,000	20. **Worlds of Fun** (1973) Kansas City, MO	140 days	1,400,000
8. **Cedar Point** (1960) Sandusky, OH	119 days	2,630,000	21. **Sea World of Ohio** (1970) Aurora, OH	100 days	1,170,000
9. **Kings Island** (1972) Cincinnati, OH	126 days	2,601,000	22. **Six Flags Over Mid-America** (1971)—St. Louis, MO	140 days	1,120,000
10. **Six Flags Magic Mountain** (1971)—Valencia, CA	185 days	2,570,000	23. **Carowinds** (1973) Charlotte, NC	121 days	1,113,000
11. **Sea World of California** (1964)—San Diego, CA	365 days	2,560,000	24. **Cypress Gardens** (1936) Winter Haven, FL	365 days	1,112,000
12. **Six Flags Great America** (1976)—Gurnee, IL	120 days	2,370,000	25. **Kings Dominion** (1975) Richmond, VA	121 days	1,011,000
13. **Six Flags Over Texas** (1961) Arlington, TX	146 days	2,330,000			

Source: Kings Entertainment Company, 1984, and Merrill Lynch, *Theme Park Industry Survey,* 1983.

Indianapolis deserves its title of automobile-racing center. Besides the famous Brickyard—the Indianapolis Motor Speedway—the Hoosier capital has three other sanctioned tracks. Nine other metro areas have two tracks: Colorado Springs, Colorado; Flint, Michigan; Greensboro–Winston-Salem–High Point, North Carolina; Johnson City–Kingsport–Bristol, Tennessee–Virginia; Las Vegas; Nassau–Suffolk, New York; Portland, Oregon; Richmond–Petersburg, Virginia; and Seattle.

Pari-Mutuel Betting: Win, Place, or Show Payoffs

The biggest spectator sport in the United States is pari-mutuel racing at the track. Based on a system in which the players who bet on the first-, second-, and third-place finishers share the total amount of money bet, pari-mutuel racing draws nearly 100 million people each year. Eighty-six metro areas offer pari-mutuel betting.

Thoroughbred racing dominates the American racing scene. There are 4,967 days of racing at the country's 83 Thoroughbred tracks, exclusive of county fairs. The ten listed nearby draw the biggest daily crowds. Number 10, Ak-Sar-Ben (Nebraska spelled backwards), is an 85-day, nonprofit civic meet held near downtown Omaha that usually attracts more than a million racegoers. In the Los Angeles–Long Beach metro area, Santa Anita Park's two-part season draws close to four million spectators. Aqueduct's three-part season is one of the longest in Thoroughbred racing, and although attendance has fallen over the years, the track still draws more spectators than do the New York Yankees across town in the Bronx.

Standardbred horses are entered in harness racing; jockeys ride behind the horses in small, two-wheeled carts. Harness racing competes with Thoroughbred racing for the racegoer's wager in 13 states. Its annual following at the track is a good deal smaller than that of Thoroughbred racing (45 million versus 26 million racegoers). However, in Delaware, upstate New York, Michigan, and the Chicago environs, pacing and trotting races attract more bettors and a greater cash total in bets than their Thoroughbred competition, and in Canada they outdraw Thoroughbred races two to one.

The country cousin of the more citified and patrician Thoroughbred contests, quarter-horse racing usually takes place at state and county fairs. It gets its name from the wide-open quarter-mile sprint the horses run on the track. Sixteen states permit betting on quarter-horse races, usually on mixed programs with Thoroughbred races. The sport is more popular in the West and Northwest than in any other region.

Dog racing evolved from the early sport of coursing, in which two greyhounds were released together in pursuit of a hare. Modern greyhound racing stems from a 1904 coursing contest held in South Dakota. Its sponsor, Owen Patrick Smith, developed a strong distaste for the killing of hares and spent the next 15 years adapting a mechanical lure to the inside rail of an oval track. The lure now resembles a rabbit and moves around the track on an electric rail. Since greyhounds chase by sight rather than scent, it has proven to be effective.

Of the country's 45 greyhound tracks, there are ten that account for half of dog racing's 23 million annual

The 10 Most Popular Thoroughbred Tracks

Track	Average Daily Attendance	Average Bet
1. Santa Anita Park (Arcadia, CA)	32,013	$163
2. Hollywood Park (Inglewood, CA)	28,891	180
3. Saratoga (Saratoga Springs, NY)	26,644	112
4. Oaklawn Jockey Club (Hot Springs, AR)	23,271	129
5. Del Mar (Del Mar, CA)	19,584	167
6. Belmont Park (Elmont, NY)	19,530	177
7. Aqueduct (New York)	14,749	204
8. Meadowlands (East Rutherford, NJ)	14,233	151
9. Gulfstream Park (Hallandale, FL)	14,074	151
10. Ak-Sar-Ben (Omaha)	13,655	118

Source: *Daily Racing Form*, March 26, 1984, and Thoroughbred Racing Associations of North America, Inc., *Directory and Record Book*, 1984.

The 10 Most Popular Harness Tracks

Track	Average Daily Attendance	Average Bet
1. Meadowlands (East Rutherford, NJ)	16,010	$145
2. Sportsman's Park (Cicero, IL)	8,988	132
3. Roosevelt Raceway (Westbury, NY)	7,873	168
4. Hollywood Park (Inglewood, CA)	7,805	127
5. Hawthorne (Cicero, IL)	7,179	150
6. Yonkers Raceway (Yonkers, NY)	6,441	204
7. Maywood Park (Maywood, IL)	6,135	139
8. Los Alamitos (Cypress, CA)	5,499	150
9. Pompano Park (Pompano Beach, FL)	5,492	88
10. Hazel Park (Hazel Park, MI)	5,200	140

Source: U.S. Trotting Association, *Trotting and Pacing Guide*, 1984.

The 10 Most Popular Greyhound Tracks

Track	Average Daily Attendance	Average Bet
1. Wonderland (Revere, MA)	1,247,653	$119
2. Southland Greyhound Park (West Memphis, AR)	1,189,108	108
3. Lincoln Greyhound Park (Lincoln, RI)	1,159,070	101
4. St. Petersburg Kennel Club (St. Petersburg)	1,045,078	92
5. Hollywood Greyhound Track (Hallandale, FL)	1,043,201	108
6. Wheeling Downs Greyhound Park (Wheeling, WV)	929,243	118
7. Plainfield Greyhound Park (Plainfield, CT)	867,773	131
8. Biscayne Greyhound Park (Miami, FL)	832,963	125
9. Tampa Greyhound Park (Tampa)	749,318	114
10. Mobile Greyhound Park (Mobile)	728,305	106

Source: American Greyhound Track Operators Association, *Directory*, 1984.

attendance. Wonderland is a ten-minute subway ride from downtown Boston. Plainfield Greyhound Park, near Hartford, is Connecticut's sole pari-mutuel racetrack. The only place where people in western Tennessee, northern Mississippi, and northeastern Arkansas can make a legal bet is at Southland Greyhound Park, on the Arkansas side of the Mississippi River, near Memphis.

Rooting for the Home Team

A frequent topic of discussion on talk shows, in bars, and at work is where the "good" sports towns are. The question is usually argued from one of two perspectives: whether a town has teams with winning records, or whether fans turn out to root for the teams. These two trends are often linked: Over the regular seasons, the clubs with the best attendance usually also have had some of the best records.

Another way to find the best sports towns is to measure the access that a metro area's fans have to regular-season games. "Game seats per capita" is an elementary measurement used most often in professional sports franchising and marketing, especially at expansion time. This figure is found by multiplying the number of home games played by all the teams in a metro area (for example, 81 baseball; 41 basketball; 8 football) by the combined seating capacity of the teams' playing arenas and then dividing that number by the metro area's population.

Professional Sports. In arriving at a figure for game seats per capita at professional sporting events, *Places Rated* surveyed each of the 132 metro areas with major-league or minor-league teams in any of four sports: baseball, basketball, football, and hockey. For example, the number of regular-season football games played by the Indianapolis Colts multiplied by the Hoosier Dome's capacity is 480,000. The same calculations yield a figure of 1,037,000 for NBA Pacers basketball and Checkers minor-league hockey games played in Market Square Arena, and 995,918 for Indians minor-league baseball games played at Bush Stadium. The sum of these four figures divided by Indianapolis's metro area population is 2.154, or a little more than two game seats for everyone in the eight-county metro area. Other metro areas have better averages, and in each of them the presence of a baseball team, with its large stadium and long playing season, makes a good deal of difference.

The New York State metro area of Glens Falls has the highest figure for game seats per capita of any metro area due to its White Sox baseball team and Adirondack Reds hockey club, both minor league, combined with its population of 109,649. But if you're interested in major-league sports, consider Denver: Its NBA Nuggets, USFL Gold, and NFL Broncos—as well as minor-league baseball and hockey teams—give it the best game-seats rating of metro areas with major-league clubs.

Access to Professional Sports: The Top 15 Metro Areas

Metro Area	Game Seats per Capita	Metro Area	Game Seats per Capita
1. Glens Falls, NY*	9.421	9. Cleveland, OH	3.926
2. Denver, CO	5.890	10. Milwaukee, WI	3.824
3. Kansas City, MO	5.030	11. Hagerstown, MD*	3.714
4. Honolulu, HI*	4.721	12. San Francisco, CA	3.484
5. Billings, MT*	4.716		
6. Buffalo, NY	4.608	13. Burlington, VT*	3.460
7. Seattle, WA	4.405	14. Cincinnati, OH–KY–IN	3.369
8. Fort Worth–Arlington, TX	4.161	15. Portland, ME*	3.304

Source: Derived from professional sports media guides.

One hundred thirty-two metro areas have professional sports teams.

*These metro areas have only minor-league teams.

Collegiate Sports. Among the biggest crowd pleasers around are the varsity teams fielded by American colleges and universities. The cream of those is generally found among the teams classified Division I (split into Divisions I–A and I–AA for football only) by the National Collegiate Athletic Association (NCAA). Eligibility for this division is based on the quality of a school's typical opponent, or "schedule strength," and game attendance figures.

Nearly 37 million fans attended the 3,224 regular-season games played by the 649 colleges and universities with varsity football teams in 1983. Although the 189 Division I–A and I–AA teams played only one third of these games, they drew 83 percent of the attendance that year. Basketball is even more widely available. Some 32 million fans came out for the 16,108 regular-season and tournament games played by the 1,266 schools that had men's varsity basketball teams in 1983. The 274 NCAA Division I teams played one quarter of these games, yet they accounted for 65 percent of total attendance.

Division I football or basketball is on view in 150 of

Average Ticket Prices for Professional Sports

Baseball
Highest: $6.75 (Baltimore Orioles, Milwaukee Brewers, New York Yankees)
Lowest: $4.00 (Toronto Blue Jays)

Basketball
Highest: $15.50 (Los Angeles Lakers)
Lowest: $6.60 (Indiana Pacers)

Football
Highest: $17.75 (Los Angeles Raiders, San Diego Chargers)
Lowest: $10.75 (Cincinnati Bengals)

Hockey
Highest: $16.84 (New York Islanders)
Lowest: $8.50 (Buffalo Sabres)

Source: H. L. Klein, *People and Properties,* 1984.
Prices are for the 1983 season.

---

the 329 metro areas, from the Cowboys of Hardin-Simmons in Abilene to the Penguins of Youngstown State. Using game seats per capita as the criterion, the best metro area for NCAA Division I football and basketball is Lawrence, Kansas. The number of University of Kansas Jayhawks games played at home multiplied by the seating capacities of Memorial Stadium (football) and Allen Fieldhouse (basketball) yield a figure of 465,498, or almost seven game seats for everyone in town and in surrounding Douglas County.

Access to NCAA Division I Sports: The Top 15 Metro Areas

Metro Area	Game Seats per Capita	Metro Area	Game Seats per Capita
1. Lawrence, KS	6.882	9. Tuscaloosa, AL	3.752
2. Iowa City, IA	5.863	10. Fayetteville–Springdale, AR	3.533
3. Columbia, MO	5.212		
4. Bloomington, IN	4.953	11. Champaign–Urbana–Rantoul, IL	3.357
5. Bryan–College Station, TX	4.888	12. Las Cruces, NM	3.341
6. State College, PA	4.545	13. Ann Arbor, MI	3.264
7. Lafayette, IN	4.351	14. Gainesville, FL	3.011
8. Athens, GA	4.131	15. Charlottesville, VA	2.902

Source: National Collegiate Athletic Association, *NCAA Basketball* and *NCAA Football,* 1984.

One hundred fifty metro areas have NCAA Division I football or basketball teams.

OUTDOOR RECREATION ASSETS

To many people, recreation is not something that takes place within four walls or in the middle of a crowded city. Instead, it means turning to the open spaces for fishing, boating, swimming, hiking, running, picnicking, or getting away from it all. Just as some metro areas have more to offer in urban recreation, others undeniably are richer in access to the great outdoors.

Coastlines and Inland Water

Sooners boast that Oklahoma has so many impounded lakes of every size that if you were to tip the state to the south a bit, the water would flow out and flood Texas for a good while. And Maryland crabbers point out to newcomers that the true length of estuarine shore reached by the Chesapeake Bay's tide would total more than 8,000 miles if all the bends and kinks were straightened out.

You'll spot inland water in nine out of ten of America's metro areas. Aside from being a basic necessity of life, water can be a scenic and recreational amenity if there is enough of it to fish in, boat on, and swim in if the temperature is right. Where would Reno be without Lake Tahoe?

Or Nassau–Suffolk, New York, without Long Island Sound? Four of every five Americans today are congregated together in metro areas within 100 miles of an ocean or Great Lakes coastline; by the end of the decade, the U.S. Department of the Interior predicts, three of every four will live within 50 miles of a coastline. Ocean or Great Lakes coastlines form part of the peripheries of 84 metro areas and 100 percent of one, Honolulu.

Large Areas of Inland Water

Metro Area	Inland Water Area	Percent of Total Surface Area
1. Galveston–Texas City, TX	265 sq mi	66%
2. New Orleans, LA	1,265	53
3. Jersey City, NJ	16	34
4. Melbourne–Titusville–Palm Bay, FL	299	30
5. Brownsville–Harlingen, TX	263	29
5. Burlington, VT	132	29
5. Salt Lake City–Ogden, UT	478	29
8. West Palm Beach–Boca Raton–Delray Beach, FL	555	28
9. Fort Myers, FL	220	27
10. Houma–Thibodaux, LA	633	25
10. San Francisco, CA	250	25
12. Nassau–Suffolk, NY	290	24
13. Portland, ME	113	20
14. Bremerton, WA	77	19
14. Wilmington, NC	34	19

Source: U.S. Bureau of the Census, Area Measurements, Series G-20, 1962–67.

Inland water area includes ponds and lakes of surface area greater than 40 acres; streams, canals, and rivers if width is one eighth of a mile or greater; water area along irregular Great Lakes and ocean coastlines, if bays, inlets, and estuaries are between one and ten miles wide.

National Forests, Parks, and Wildlife Refuges

Some of the most popular outdoor activities—driving for pleasure, walking, picnicking, sight-seeing, bird watching, nature walking, and fishing—would probably be even more enjoyable in the country's splendid system of national forests, parks, and wildlife refuges.

There are 155 national forests and 19 national grasslands on 191 million acres in the United States. The main purpose of the National Forest System is silviculture: growing wood, harvesting it carefully, and preserving naturally beautiful areas. Within the forest system are more than a quarter of a million miles of roads, built not only for loggers but for everyone. They lead to a wide variety of recreation outlets: ski resorts, marinas, fishing lakes and streams, hiking trails, and campgrounds.

In contrast to the National Forest System, the National Park System is meant expressly for recreation. The founding of Yellowstone National Park in 1872 marked the beginning of the oldest and now the largest national park system in the world. It comprises 334 national parks, preserves, monuments, memorials, battlefields, seashores, riverways, and trails that together cover some 79 million acres.

Whereas the National Park System acts to keep irreplaceable geographical and historical treasures in the public domain, the national wildlife refuges protect native flora and fauna from people. There are 413 of these remarkable sanctuaries throughout the country,

embracing more than 87 million acres. Most of them are open to the public for a variety of wildlife activities, particularly photography and nature observation. In certain of the refuges and at irregular times, fishing and hunting are permitted, depending on the size of the wild populations. Although the majority of the nation's wildlife refuges are located in open, sometimes remote country, they aren't exclusively a rural amenity. Several can be found within metropolitan areas, such as the Nisqually National Wildlife Refuge in Olympia, Washington, and San Pablo Bay National Wildlife Refuge in the California metro area of Santa Rosa–Petaluma.

JUDGING RECREATIONAL OPPORTUNITIES

Is there more to do in Houston than in Dallas? How do the California rivals of Los Angeles and San Francisco compare for recreation? Or Jacksonville and Tampa–St. Pete? To answer these questions, Places Rated Almanac examines three categories of assets—Common Denominators (quality restaurants, golf, bowling, and movies), Crowd Pleasers (zoos, aquariums, theme parks, automobile racing, pari-mutuel betting, and professional and collegiate sports), and Outdoor Recreation Assets (miles of coastline, inland water area,

Outdoor Recreation Assets: 17 Outstanding Metro Areas

Metro Area	Coastline (mi)	Inland Water Area (sq mi)	Acres in National Parks, Forests, Wildlife Refuges
Anchorage, AK	90	36.0	275,000
Bellingham, WA	—	53.7	841,958
Brownsville–Harlingen, TX	31	262.9	45,451
Eugene–Springfield, OR	30	48.1	1,416,153
Fort Collins–Loveland, CO	—	29.7	766,568
Galveston–Texas City, TX	25	165.0	—
Houma–Thibodaux, LA	79	632.8	—
Melbourne–Titusville–Palm Bay, FL	72	299.0	35,733
Miami–Hialeah, FL	84	67.1	605,117
New Orleans, LA	75	1,265.2	32,948
Provo–Orem, UT	—	126.9	485,642
Salt Lake City–Ogden, UT	—	477.5	201,480
San Francisco, CA	75	249.6	127,278
Santa Barbara–Santa Maria–Lompoc, CA	78	7.5	754,425
Seattle, WA	70	89.1	966,533
Tacoma, WA	15	113.1	365,990
Visalia–Tulare–Porterville, CA	—	3.0	1,403,459

Listed above in alphabetical order are the metro areas earning the maximum 2,000 points for their supply of Outdoor Recreation Assets. (See the section "Judging Recreational Opportunities," below, for an explanation of how Places Rated points are calculated.)

and acreage in national forests, parks, and wildlife refuges).

In rating the metro areas for their recreational opportunities, *Places Rated* has introduced a number of elements that were not included in the first edition of this book. In the Common Denominators category, access to good restaurants has replaced access to neighborhood bars. The Crowd Pleasers category has been expanded to include minor-league teams and NCAA Division I basketball and football. The all-new category of Outdoor Recreation Assets provides a more well rounded view of an area's leisure-time options.

Like the chapters on health care, transportation, and the arts, this chapter's rating system now allows for bonus points to be awarded to metro areas that are part of a Consolidated Metropolitan Statistical Area (a complete list is in the Appendix). CMSA Access points are *Places Rated*'s way of recognizing that certain outstanding facilities can be enjoyed by people within a relatively wide radius. In the case of recreation, each metro area that is part of a CMSA is eligible to receive points for the Crowd Pleasers assets located in neighboring metro areas, as explained in item 15 below.

In the categories of Common Denominators and Crowd Pleasers, metro areas are awarded points not for their number of facilities but rather for how available these facilities are to residents. Access to these different events is given a rating of AA, A, B, or C (AA indicating the best access and C the worst), and those ratings mean a certain number of points for the metro area: 400 for an AA rating, 300 for A, 200 for B, and 100 for C. The exceptions to this rule—zoos, aquariums, and auto racing—are explained below. For Outdoor Recreation Assets, metro areas earn points according to a different system, also delineated below.

Each metro area starts with a base score of zero, to which points are added according to the following criteria:

1. *Good restaurants.*

A metro area gets a rating of:	If there is one quality star for every:
AA	14,000 or fewer people
A	14,001–20,000 people
B	20,001–32,500 people
C	32,501 or more people

2. *Public golf courses.*

A metro area gets a rating of:	If there is one 18-hole course for every:
AA	20,000 or fewer people
A	20,001–25,000 people
B	25,001–40,000 people
C	40,001 or more people

3. *Certified tenpin bowling lanes.*

A metro area gets a rating of:	If there is one lane for every:
AA	950 or fewer people
A	951–1,300 people
B	1,301–3,000 people
C	3,001 or more people

4. *Movie theaters.*

A metro area gets a rating of:	If there is one theater for every:
AA	25,000 or fewer people
A	25,001–32,500 people
B	32,501–45,000 people
C	45,001 or more people

5. *Zoos.* Metro areas with zoos are rated by criteria based on the size of their collections as listed in the directory of member zoos of the American Association of Zoological Parks and Aquariums.

A metro area gets a rating of:	If the collections in its zoo(s) include:
AA	1,500 or more specimens, of which 500 are mammals of at least 250 species, and its annual operating budget exceeds $4 million
A	750 to 1,499 specimens, of which 300 are mammals of at least 150 species, and its annual operating budget falls between $1.5 and $3.9 million
B	300 to 749 specimens, of which 150 are mammals of at least 50 species, and its annual operating budget falls between $750,000 and $1.49 million
C	Fewer than 300 specimens, and its annual operating budget is less than $749,999

These standards apply to the total collections of *all* the zoos in a metro area.

6. *Aquariums.* Ten metro areas receive an A rating for having an aquarium certified by the American Association of Zoological Parks and Aquariums.

7. *Family theme parks.* Theme parks drawing more than one million visitors per year are awarded points as follows:

A metro area gets a rating of:	If there is one open day for every:
AA	4,500 or fewer people
A	4,501–6,500 people
B	6,501–10,000 people
C	10,001 or more people

8. *Auto racing.* Metro areas earn points for having one or more sanctioned speedways as follows: AA for four speedways, A for three speedways, B for two speedways, and C for one speedway.

9. *Pari-mutuel betting.* Tracks for Thoroughbred, harness, and greyhound racing, as well as jai alai frontons, are scored as follows:

A metro area gets a rating of:	If there is one racing/open day for every:
AA	2,000 or fewer people
A	2,001–3,500 people
B	3,501–9,500 people
C	9,501 or more people

A Baseball Odyssey

Quick—What major-league baseball team is descended from the old Beaneaters? It's not the Boston Red Sox; in fact, it's not even an American League team. It's the Atlanta Braves.

This is just one of many odd and intriguing changes major-league teams have undergone since 1876, when eight professional clubs joined forces to form the National League. Twenty-five years later, in 1901, the American League began play, also with eight teams. Since that time, many of the teams have changed names and moved from one city to another, and the leagues have expanded the number of franchises. The list below shows which of today's American League (AL) and National League (NL) teams have moved to another city and/or changed their name since their founding date.*

Atlanta Braves (NL)—*1876*, began as Boston Red Caps; *1883*, renamed Beaneaters; *1907*, renamed Doves; *1909*, renamed Pilgrims; *1936*, renamed Bees; *1941*, renamed Braves; *1953*, moved to Milwaukee and renamed Milwaukee Braves; *1966*, moved to Atlanta and renamed Atlanta Braves.

Baltimore Orioles (AL)—*1901*, began as Milwaukee Brewers; *1902*, moved to St. Louis and renamed St. Louis Browns; *1954*, moved to Baltimore and renamed Baltimore Orioles.

Boston Red Sox (AL)—*1901*, began as Somersets; *1905*, renamed Puritans; *1907*, renamed Red Sox.

California Angels (AL)—*1961*, began as Los Angeles Angels; *1965*, renamed California Angels.

Chicago Cubs (NL)—*1876*, began as White Stockings; *1894*, renamed Colts; *1898*, renamed Orphans; *1899*, renamed Cubs.

Cleveland Indians (AL)—*1901*, began as Bronchos; *1902*, renamed Blues; *1905*, renamed Naps; *1912*, renamed Molly McGuires; *1914*, renamed Indians.

Houston Astros (NL)—*1962*, began as Houston Colt .45's; *1964*, renamed Astros.

Los Angeles Dodgers (NL)—*1890*, began as Brooklyn Bridegrooms; *1898*, renamed Superbas; *1911*, renamed Dodgers; *1958*, moved to Los Angeles and renamed Los Angeles Dodgers.

Milwaukee Brewers (AL)—*1969*, began as Seattle Pilots; *1970*, moved to Milwaukee and renamed Milwaukee Brewers.

Minnesota Twins (AL)—*1901*, began as Washington Senators; *1960*, moved to Minneapolis–St. Paul and renamed Minnesota Twins.

New York Yankees (AL)—*1901*, began as Baltimore Orioles; *1903*, moved to New York and renamed New York Highlanders; *1912*, renamed Yankees.

Oakland A's (AL)—*1901*, began as Philadelphia Athletics; *1955*, moved to Kansas City and renamed Kansas City Athletics; *1968*, moved to Oakland and renamed Oakland Athletics; *1974*, renamed Oakland A's.

Pittsburgh Pirates (NL)—*1887*, began as Alleghenys; *1890*, renamed Innocents; *1891*, renamed Pirates.

San Francisco Giants (NL)—*1879*, began as Troy (NY) Trojans; *1883*, moved to New York City and renamed New York Gothams; *1886*, renamed Giants; *1958*, moved to San Francisco and renamed San Francisco Giants.

Texas Rangers (AL)—*1961*, began as Washington Senators; *1971*, moved to Arlington and renamed Texas Rangers.

Source: Joseph L. Reichler, ed., *Baseball Encyclopedia*, 1982.

*The Cincinnati Reds (NL, 1876), Philadelphia Phillies (NL, 1883), St. Louis Cardinals (NL, 1892), Chicago White Sox (AL, 1901), Detroit Tigers (AL, 1901), New York Mets (NL, 1962), Kansas City Royals (AL, 1969), Montreal Expos (NL, 1969), San Diego Padres (NL, 1969), Seattle Mariners (AL, 1977), and Toronto Blue Jays (AL, 1977) have neither changed their name nor moved.

---

10. *Professional sports.*

A metro area gets a rating of:	If local major- and minor-league teams provide:
AA	2.500 or more game seats per capita
A	1.500–2.499 game seats per capita
B	.750–1.499 game seats per capita
C	.749 or fewer game seats per capita

11. *NCAA Division I football and basketball.*

A metro area gets a rating of:	If local NCAA Division I teams provide:
AA	1.500 or more game seats per capita
A	.700–1.499 game seats per capita
B	.300–.699 game seats per capita
C	.299 or fewer game seats per capita

12. *Coastlines.* Each mile of general coastline, whether on the ocean or on the Great Lakes, gets 10 points. For example, the 84 miles of Atlantic coastline east of Miami–Hialeah earn the Florida metro area 840 points.

13. *Inland water area.* The percent of a metro area's total surface area that is classified as inland water is multiplied by 50. In Chicago, 9.6 of the 1,902 square miles of surface area are inland water. That works out to 0.5 percent inland water, or 25 points.

14. *National forests, parks, and wildlife refuges.* The percent of a metro area's total acreage that is set aside for national forests, parks, or wildlife refuges is multiplied by 50. Seattle has more than 2,704,640 total acres, 35.74 percent of which composes the Mount Baker and Snoqualmie national forests (966,533 acres), giving the Washington metro area 1,787 points.

15. *CMSA Access.* The 76 metro areas that are part of America's 22 CMSA complexes are eligible for bonus points based on the total number of points amassed for Crowd Pleasers by the other metro areas in its

CMSA. A metro area's own points are not considered in calculating its access bonus.

A metro area gets a rating of:	If points for Crowd Pleasers earned by CMSA partner(s) total:
AA	1,000 or more
A	700–999
B	400–699
C	100–399

Four eligible metro areas receive no access bonus because the other area or areas in their CMSA have no Crowd Pleasers.

To maintain relative parity among the three major recreation categories—Common Denominators, Crowd Pleasers, and Outdoor Recreation Assets—a ceiling of 2,000 points is applied to the total for outdoor assets (items 12, 13, and 14 above).

Sample Comparison: Seattle, Washington, and Danville, Virginia

As it did in the first edition of *Places Rated Almanac,* Seattle wins top honors among the metro areas for recreational facilities. Danville—which did not exist as a metro area in 1981—finishes next to last, with just more than a tenth of the points earned by Seattle.

The Washington metro area receives either A or B ratings for all its Common Denominators, adding up to 1,000 points for this category. Its Crowd Pleasers are equally impressive: There is a premier AA-rated zoo, Woodland Park; an A-rated aquarium; and supplies of auto racing and pari-mutuel betting that earn B and C ratings, respectively. Seattle's ratio of game seats to local residents ranks seventh among the 132 metro areas with major- and minor-league professional sports. The AL Mariners, NFL Seahawks, and NBA SuperSonics play a total of 130 home games in the Kingdome; and 25 miles north of downtown, the Everett Giants, a San Francisco Giants farm club, play 37 baseball games in Memorial Stadium. Although the University of Washington Huskies play the only NCAA Division I basketball and football games in town, the crowds at Husky Stadium and Edmundson Fieldhouse on the west bank of Lake Washington add to Seattle's reputation as a partisan sports town. The

access to all these Crowd Pleasers earns Seattle a hefty 1,500 points for this category.

Manufactured recreation amenities tend to crop up with population density; that's an elementary marketing rule. But no other populous metro area has as splendid a combination of outdoor recreation endowments as Seattle. For openers, there's a 70-mile shoreline frontage on Puget Sound and nearly 90 square miles of inland water, including giant Lake Washington and suburban Lake Sammamish. An hour's drive east on I-90 will get you to several challenging Cascade ski slopes in the midst of Snoqualmie National Forest. North on I-5 and then east on state roads is a big chunk of Mount Baker National Forest. Taken together, these natural facilities earn Seattle 2,000 points, the maximum for Outdoor Recreation Assets. Seattle also is eligible for a bonus of 300 points because it shares the Crowd Pleasers of nearby Tacoma, its partner in the Seattle–Tacoma consolidated area. The total recreation score for Seattle, then, is 4,800.

Danville, in contrast, ranks 328th in recreation outlets. There are no restaurants here rated for quality by the *Mobil Travel Guide,* nor are there any municipal golf courses. On the other hand, the 27 holes of daily-fee golf and 46 lanes of tenpin bowling give the Virginia metro area respectable B ratings in both those categories. The supply of movie theaters is good for only a C rating, bringing Danville's total for Common Denominators to 500 points. In Crowd Pleasers, the metro area comes up empty; it has no zoos, aquariums, theme parks, racetracks, not even a Class A Carolina League baseball team like the ones in Lynchburg and Roanoke.

Although Danville's natural setting east of the Blue Ridge Mountains is pleasant, there are no large lakes for water sports in surrounding Pittsylvania County; the metro area's one tenth of a square mile of inland water is good for just 1 point. Likewise, there are no acres set aside as national parks, national forests, or national wildlife refuges. Danville's 1 point for outdoor recreation, added to its previous total of 500 points, yields a recreation score of 501. The only metro area to score lower is Gadsden, Alabama, with 300 points.

Places Rated: Metro Areas Ranked for Recreational Opportunities

Fourteen criteria are used to rate a metro area's supply of recreation assets: (1) good restaurants, (2) public golf courses, (3) certified lanes for tenpin bowling, (4) movie theaters, (5) zoos, (6) aquariums, (7) family theme parks, (8) sanctioned automobile racetracks, (9) pari-mutuel betting attractions, (10) major- and minor-league professional sports teams, (11) NCAA Division I football and basketball teams, (12) miles of ocean or Great Lakes coastline, (13) inland water, and (14) national forests, national parks, or national wildlife refuges. The 76 metro areas that belong to a Consolidated Metropolitan Statistical Area can also earn points for shared recreation assets found in other metro areas within that consolidated area. Metro areas that receive tie scores are given the same rank and listed alphabetically.

Metro Areas from Best to Worst

Places Rated Rank	Places Rated Score	Places Rated Rank	Places Rated Score	Places Rated Rank	Places Rated Score
1. Seattle, WA	4,800	47. Houma–Thibodaux, LA	2,700	96. Saginaw–Bay City–Midland, MI	2,059
2. San Francisco, CA	4,600	48. Wilmington, NC	2,668	97. Fort Pierce, FL	2,058
3. Miami–Hialeah, FL	4,300	49. Muskegon, MI	2,666	98. Billings, MT	2,046
4. Fort Collins–Loveland, CO	4,200	50. Rochester, NY	2,659	99. Kansas City, MO	2,043
5. Boulder–Longmont, CO	4,012	51. Akron, OH	2,632	100. Corpus Christi, TX	2,037
6. Fort Myers, FL	4,005	52. Albuquerque, NM	2,612	101. Roanoke, VA	2,036
7. Tacoma, WA	4,000	53. Charleston, SC	2,561	102. Tulsa, OK	2,024
8. Las Vegas, NV	3,996	54. Sarasota, FL	2,535	103. Columbus, OH	2,020
9. Daytona Beach, FL	3,967	55. Portland, OR	2,532	104. Racine, WI	2,016
10. Los Angeles–Long Beach, CA	3,948	56. Knoxville, TN	2,514	105. Fall River, MA–RI	2,005
11. Salt Lake City–Ogden, UT	3,900	57. Lakeland–Winter Haven, FL	2,513	106. Memphis, TN–AR–MS	1,994
12. Melbourne–Titusville–Palm Bay, FL	3,800	58. Detroit, MI	2,483	107. Bloomington, IN	1,990
13. West Palm Beach–Boca Raton–Delray Beach, FL	3,772	59. Phoenix, AZ	2,472	108. Philadelphia, PA–NJ	1,979
14. Nassau–Suffolk, NY	3,705	60. Fort Lauderdale–Hollywood–Pompano Beach, FL	2,455	109. Omaha, NE–IA	1,977
15. Honolulu, HI	3,703	61. Cincinnati, OH–KY–IN	2,451	110. Bremerton, WA	1,973
16. New York, NY	3,579	62. Buffalo, NY	2,441	111. San Jose, CA	1,964
17. Monmouth–Ocean, NJ	3,544	63. Lake County, IL	2,435	112. Pascagoula, MS	1,956
18. New Orleans, LA	3,500	64. Redding, CA	2,424	113. La Crosse, WI	1,953
19. Eugene–Springfield, OR	3,400	65. Oakland, CA	2,394	114. Toledo, OH	1,952
20. Portland, ME	3,366	66. Reno, NV	2,386	115. Madison, WI	1,944
21. Burlington, VT	3,357	67. Colorado Springs, CO	2,375	116. Richmond–Petersburg, VA	1,943
22. San Diego, CA	3,347	68. Fort Worth–Arlington, TX	2,366	117. Louisville, KY–IN	1,942
23. Cleveland, OH	3,300	69. Denver, CO	2,324	118. Gary–Hammond, IN	1,940
23. Provo-Orem, UT	3,300	70. Appleton–Oshkosh–Neenah, WI	2,315	119. Tallahassee, FL	1,936
23. Santa Barbara–Santa Maria–Lompoc, CA	3,300	71. Dallas, TX	2,310	120. Jackson, MI	1,933
26. Bellingham, WA	3,200	72. Sacramento, CA	2,306	121. Green Bay, WI	1,925
27. Salinas–Seaside–Monterey, CA	3,179	73. Ann Arbor, MI	2,288	122. Wilmington, DE–NJ–MD	1,923
28. Anaheim–Santa Ana, CA	3,156	74. New London–Norwich, CT–RI	2,281	123. Davenport–Rock Island–Moline, IA–IL	1,920
29. Tucson, AZ	3,131	75. Norwalk, CT	2,268	124. Bergen–Passaic, NJ	1,918
30. Duluth, MN–WI	3,107	76. Providence, RI	2,263	124. Riverside–San Bernardino, CA	1,918
31. Ocala, FL	3,095	77. Santa Rosa–Petaluma, CA	2,255	126. Bridgeport–Milford, CT	1,913
32. Boston, MA	3,066	78. St. Louis, MO–IL	2,243	127. Grand Rapids, MI	1,909
33. Anchorage, AK	3,000	79. Savannah, GA	2,237	128. Indianapolis, IN	1,906
33. Brownsville–Harlingen, TX	3,000	80. Salem–Gloucester, MA	2,234	129. Waterloo–Cedar Falls, IA	1,900
33. Galveston–Texas City, TX	3,000	81. Kenosha, WI	2,224	130. Glens Falls, NY	1,883
36. Fresno, CA	2,984	82. Clarksville–Hopkinsville, TN–KY	2,219	131. Lawrence–Haverhill, MA–NH	1,879
37. Norfolk–Virginia Beach–Newport News, VA	2,964	83. Great Falls, MT	2,176	132. Niagara Falls, NY	1,873
38. Tampa–St. Petersburg–Clearwater, FL	2,943	84. Mobile, AL	2,164	132. Salem, OR	1,873
39. Baltimore, MD	2,925	85. Kalamazoo, MI	2,163	134. Orange County, NY	1,866
40. Milwaukee, WI	2,902	86. Pensacola, FL	2,160	135. Lake Charles, LA	1,855
41. Jacksonville, FL	2,884	87. Minneapolis–St. Paul, MN–WI	2,158	136. Lewiston–Auburn, ME	1,853
42. Orlando, FL	2,881	88. Johnson City–Kingsport–Bristol, TN–VA	2,155	137. Nashville, TN	1,849
43. Chicago, IL	2,856	89. Bangor, ME	2,148	138. Houston, TX	1,825
44. Syracuse, NY	2,851	90. Pittsburgh, PA	2,145	139. South Bend–Mishawaka, IN	1,819
45. Visalia–Tulare–Porterville, CA	2,800	91. Yakima, WA	2,140	140. Newark, NJ	1,818
46. Atlantic City, NJ	2,711	92. Oxnard–Ventura, CA	2,135	141. Lafayette, IN	1,814
		93. Biloxi–Gulfport, MS	2,106	142. Beaumont–Port Arthur, TX	1,813
		94. Fort Walton Beach, FL	2,092	143. Lincoln, NE	1,804
		95. Panama City, FL	2,089	144. Des Moines, IA	1,802
				145. Aurora–Elgin, IL	1,800

Places Rated Rank	Places Rated Score	Places Rated Rank	Places Rated Score	Places Rated Rank	Places Rated Score
146. Hartford, CT	1,790	202. Pawtucket–Woonsocket– Attleboro, RI–MA	1,513	258. Brockton, MA	1,217
147. Lawton, OK	1,757	203. Brazoria, TX	1,512	258. New Britain, CT	1,217
148. Lawrence, KS	1,752	204. San Antonio, TX	1,509	260. Columbus, GA–AL	1,214
149. Utica–Rome, NY	1,750	205. Wichita, KS	1,508		
150. Oklahoma City, OK	1,742			261. Altoona, PA	1,210
		206. Iowa City, IA	1,506	262. Macon–Warner Robins, GA	1,204
151. Springfield, MO	1,737	207. Rochester, MN	1,503	262. Richland–Kennewick– Pasco, WA	1,204
152. Fort Smith, AR–OK	1,736	208. Midland, TX	1,502	264. Enid, OK	1,200
153. Lafayette, LA	1,734	209. Cedar Rapids, IA	1,501	264. State College, PA	1,200
154. Stamford, CT	1,729	210. Hagerstown, MD	1,491		
155. Binghamton, NY	1,722			266. Jacksonville, NC	1,177
		211. Columbia, SC	1,484	267. Anniston, AL	1,165
156. Fort Wayne, IN	1,711	212. Beaver County, PA	1,480	268. Canton, OH	1,157
157. Charlottesville, VA	1,704	213. Benton Harbor, MI	1,477	269. Parkersburg–Marietta, WV–OH	1,148
158. Santa Cruz, CA	1,703	214. Vineland–Millville–Bridgeton, NJ	1,474	270. Lancaster, PA	1,147
159. Lubbock, TX	1,702	215. Vancouver, WA	1,464		
160. Champaign–Urbana– Rantoul, IL	1,700			271. Topeka, KS	1,141
		216. Little Rock–North Little Rock, AR	1,462	272. San Angelo, TX	1,136
161. Fayetteville–Springdale, AR	1,695	217. Steubenville–Weirton, OH–WV	1,460	273. Mansfield, OH	1,133
162. Peoria, IL	1,688	218. Olympia, WA	1,451	274. Lowell, MA–NH	1,129
163. Middletown, CT	1,682	219. New Bedford, MA	1,450	275. Wichita Falls, TX	1,126
164. Boise City, ID	1,672	220. Lynchburg, VA	1,439		
165. Poughkeepsie, NY	1,670			276. Dayton–Springfield, OH	1,122
		221. Casper, WY	1,435	277. Kankakee, IL	1,119
166. Wausau, WI	1,654	222. Lima, OH	1,428	278. Allentown–Bethlehem, PA–NJ	1,117
167. Greensboro–Winston-Salem– High Point, NC	1,651	222. Muncie, IN	1,428	279. Montgomery, AL	1,112
168. Battle Creek, MI	1,648	224. Jackson, MS	1,427	280. Amarillo, TX	1,109
169. Trenton, NJ	1,646	225. Pittsfield, MA	1,420		
170. Joliet, IL	1,636			281. El Paso, TX	1,101
		226. Medford, OR	1,416	282. Sharon, PA	1,100
171. Bismarck, ND	1,630	227. Fargo–Moorhead, ND–MN	1,414	283. Tuscaloosa, AL	1,090
171. Stockton, CA	1,630	228. Baton Rouge, LA	1,413	284. Huntsville, AL	1,075
173. Evansville, IN–KY	1,622	228. Bryan–College Station, TX	1,413	285. Austin, TX	1,063
174. Pueblo, CO	1,619	230. Greenville–Spartanburg, SC	1,410		
175. Albany–Schenectady– Troy, NY	1,617	230. Victoria, TX	1,410	286. McAllen–Edinburg–Mission, TX	1,059
		232. Abilene, TX	1,405	287. Kansas City, KS	1,045
176. Janesville–Beloit, WI	1,615	233. Lexington–Fayette, KY	1,403	288. Cumberland, MD–WV	1,036
177. East St. Louis–Belleville, IL	1,610	234. Terre Haute, IN	1,401	289. Elkhart–Goshen, IN	1,023
178. Lansing–East Lansing, MI	1,609	235. Eau Claire, WI	1,397	290. Alexandria, LA	1,018
178. Las Cruces, NM	1,609				
180. Raleigh–Durham, NC	1,606	236. Portsmouth–Dover–Rochester, NH–ME	1,390	291. Athens, GA	1,001
		237. Shreveport, LA	1,389	291. Jersey City, NJ	1,001
181. Bloomington–Normal, IL	1,605	238. Scranton–Wilkes-Barre, PA	1,386	293. Kokomo, IN	1,000
182. Hamilton–Middletown, OH	1,604	239. Atlanta, GA	1,362	294. Florence, AL	994
182. New Haven–Meriden, CT	1,604	240. Sioux City, IA–NE	1,359	295. Waterbury, CT	946
184. Lorain–Elyria, OH	1,602				
185. Elmira, NY	1,600	241. Flint, MI	1,355	296. Sherman–Denison, TX	937
		242. Bradenton, FL	1,349	297. Rockford, IL	933
186. Middlesex–Somerset– Hunterdon, NJ	1,596	243. Erie, PA	1,340	298. Killeen–Temple, TX	931
187. Dubuque, IA	1,587	244. Columbia, MO	1,331	299. Yuba City, CA	918
188. Washington, DC–MD–VA	1,578	245. Youngstown–Warren, OH	1,327	300. Augusta, GA–SC	913
189. Danbury, CT	1,572				
189. St. Cloud, MN	1,572	246. Sioux Falls, SD	1,324	301. Worcester, MA	910
		247. Sheyboygan, WI	1,316	302. Johnstown, PA	903
191. Bakersfield, CA	1,568	248. Grand Forks, ND	1,304	303. Odessa, TX	900
192. Vallejo–Fairfield–Napa, CA	1,559	249. Alton–Granite City, IL	1,280	304. Albany, GA	859
193. Reading, PA	1,549	250. Wheeling, WV–OH	1,271	305. Owensboro, KY	852
194. Chico, CA	1,543				
195. Asheville, NC	1,542	251. St. Joseph, MO	1,265	306. Charleston, WV	844
		252. Waco, TX	1,248	307. York, PA	842
196. Monroe, LA	1,541	253. Chattanooga, TN–GA	1,238	308. Huntington–Ashland, WV–KY–OH	840
197. Springfield, IL	1,536	254. Gainesville, FL	1,237	309. Anderson, IN	838
198. Harrisburg–Lebanon– Carlisle, PA	1,532	255. Charlotte–Gastonia–Rock Hill, NC–SC	1,236	310. Manchester, NH	837
199. Nashua, NH	1,523				
200. Spokane, WA	1,517	256. Birmingham, AL	1,234	311. Longview–Marshall, TX	834
		257. Decatur, IL	1,222	312. Modesto, CA	833
201. Springfield, MA	1,514			313. Joplin, MO	801
				314. Florence, SC	800

Places Rated Rank	Places Rated Score	Places Rated Rank	Places Rated Score	Places Rated Rank	Places Rated Score
315. Hickory, NC	797	320. Williamsport, PA	726	325. Texarkana, TX–Texarkana, AR	669
316. Pine Bluff, AR	793	321. Dothan, AL	714	326. Tyler, TX	631
317. Fitchburg–Leominster, MA	790	322. Fayetteville, NC	709	327. Anderson, SC	613
318. Bristol, CT	777	323. Laredo, TX	702	328. Danville, VA	501
319. Greeley, CO	739	324. Burlington, NC	701	329. Gadsden, AL	300

Metro Areas Listed Alphabetically

Metro Area	Places Rated Rank	Metro Area	Places Rated Rank	Metro Area	Places Rated Rank
Abilene, TX	232	Brownsville–Harlingen, TX	33	Fargo–Moorhead, ND–MN	227
Akron, OH	51	Bryan–College Station, TX	228		
Albany, GA	304	Buffalo, NY	62	Fayetteville, NC	322
Albany–Schenectady–Troy, NY	175	Burlington, NC	324	Fayetteville–Springdale, AR	161
Albuquerque, NM	52	Burlington, VT	21	Fitchburg–Leominster, MA	327
				Flint, MI	241
Alexandria, LA	290	Canton, OH	268	Florence, AL	294
Allentown–Bethlehem, PA–NJ	278	Casper, WY	221		
Alton–Granite City, IL	249	Cedar Rapids, IA	209	Florence, SC	314
Altoona, PA	261	Champaign–Urbana–Rantoul, IL	160	Fort Collins–Loveland, CO	4
Amarillo, TX	280	Charleston, SC	53	Fort Lauderdale–Hollywood–Pompano Beach, FL	60
Anaheim–Santa Ana, CA	28	Charleston, WV	306	Fort Myers, FL	6
Anchorage, AK	33	Charlotte–Gastonia–Rock Hill, NC–SC	255	Fort Pierce, FL	97
Anderson, IN	309	Charlottesville, VA	157		
Anderson, SC	327	Chattanooga, TN–GA	253	Fort Smith, AR–OK	152
Ann Arbor, MI	73	Chicago, IL	43	Fort Walton Beach, FL	94
				Fort Wayne, IN	156
Anniston, AL	267	Chico, CA	194	Fort Worth–Arlington, TX	68
Appleton–Oshkosh–Neenah, WI	70	Cincinnati, OH–KY–IN	61	Fresno, CA	36
Asheville, NC	195	Clarksville–Hopkinsville, TN–KY	82		
Athens, GA	291	Cleveland, OH	23	Gadsden, AL	329
Atlanta, GA	239	Colorado Springs, CO	67	Gainesville, FL	254
				Galveston–Texas City, TX	33
Atlantic City, NJ	46	Columbia, MO	244	Gary–Hammond, IN	118
Augusta, GA–SC	300	Columbia, SC	211	Glens Falls, NY	130
Aurora–Elgin, IL	145	Columbus, GA–AL	260		
Austin, TX	285	Columbus, OH	103	Grand Forks, ND	248
Bakersfield, CA	191	Corpus Christi, TX	100	Grand Rapids, MI	127
				Great Falls, MT	83
Baltimore, MD	39	Cumberland, MD–WV	288	Greeley, CO	319
Bangor, ME	89	Dallas, TX	71	Green Bay, WI	121
Baton Rouge, LA	228	Danbury, CT	189		
Battle Creek, MI	168	Danville, VA	328	Greensboro–Winston-Salem–High Point, NC	167
Beaumont–Port Arthur, TX	142	Davenport–Rock Island–Moline, IA–IL	123	Greenville–Spartanburg, SC	230
Beaver County, PA	212			Hagerstown, MD	210
Bellingham, WA	26	Dayton–Springfield, OH	276	Hamilton–Middletown, OH	182
Benton Harbor, MI	213	Daytona Beach, FL	9	Harrisburg–Lebanon–Carlisle, PA	198
Bergen–Passaic, NJ	124	Decatur, IL	257		
Billings, MT	98	Denver, CO	69	Hartford, CT	146
		Des Moines, IA	144	Hickory, NC	315
Biloxi–Gulfport, MS	93			Honolulu, HI	15
Binghamton, NY	155	Detroit, MI	58	Houma–Thibodaux, LA	47
Birmingham, AL	256	Dothan, AL	321	Houston, TX	138
Bismarck, ND	171	Dubuque, IA	187		
Bloomington, IN	107	Duluth, MN–WI	30	Huntington–Ashland, WV–KY–OH	308
		East St. Louis–Belleville, IL	177	Huntsville, AL	284
Bloomington–Normal, IL	181			Indianapolis, IN	128
Boise City, ID	164	Eau Claire, WI	235	Iowa City, IA	206
Boston, MA	32	El Paso, TX	281	Jackson, MI	120
Boulder–Longmont, CO	5	Elkhart–Goshen, IN	289		
Bradenton, FL	242	Elmira, NY	185	Jackson, MS	224
		Enid, OK	264	Jacksonville, FL	41
Brazoria, TX	203			Jacksonville, NC	266
Bremerton, WA	110	Erie, PA	243	Janesville–Beloit, WI	176
Bridgeport–Milford, CT	126	Eugene–Springfield, OR	19	Jersey City, NJ	291
Bristol, CT	318	Evansville, IN–KY	173		
Brockton, MA	258	Fall River, MA–RI	105	Johnson City–Kingsport–Bristol, TN–VA	88

Metro Area	Places Rated Rank	Metro Area	Rank Places Rank	Metro Area	Places Rated Rank
Johnstown, PA	302	New Haven–Meriden, CT	182	San Francisco, CA	2
Joliet, IL	170			San Jose, CA	111
Joplin, MO	313	New London–Norwich, CT–RI	74	Santa Barbara–Santa Maria–	
Kalamazoo, MI	85	New Orleans, LA	18	Lompoc, CA	23
		New York, NY	16	Santa Cruz, CA	158
Kankakee, IL	277	Newark, NJ	140	Santa Rosa–Petaluma, CA	77
Kansas City, KS	287	Niagara Falls, NY	132	Sarasota, FL	54
Kansas City, MO	99				
Kenosha, WI	81	Norfolk–Virginia Beach–		Savannah, GA	79
Killeen–Temple, TX	298	Newport News, VA	37	Scranton–Wilkes-Barre, PA	238
		Norwalk, CT	75	Seattle, WA	1
Knoxville, TN	56	Oakland, CA	65	Sharon, PA	282
Kokomo, IN	293	Ocala, FL	31	Sheboygan, WI	247
La Crosse, WI	113	Odessa, TX	303	Sherman–Denison, TX	296
Lafayette, IN	141			Shreveport, LA	237
Lafayette, LA	153	Oklahoma City, OK	150	Sioux City, IA–NE	240
		Olympia, WA	218	Sioux Falls, SD	246
Lake Charles, LA	135	Omaha, NE–IA	109	South Bend–Mishawaka, IN	139
Lake County, IL	63	Orange County, NY	134		
Lakeland–Winter Haven, FL	57	Orlando, FL	42	Spokane, WA	200
Lancaster, PA	270			Springfield, IL	197
Lansing–East Lansing, MI	178	Owensboro, KY	305	Springfield, MA	201
		Oxnard–Ventura, CA	92	Springfield, MO	151
Laredo, TX	323	Panama City, FL	95	Stamford, CT	154
Las Cruces, NM	178	Parkersburg–Marietta, WV–OH	269		
Las Vegas, NV	8	Pascagoula, MS	112	State College, PA	264
Lawrence, KS	148			Steubenville–Weirton, OH–WV	217
Lawrence–Haverhill, MA–NH	131	Pawtucket–Woonsocket–		Stockton, CA	171
		Attleboro, RI–MA	202	Syracuse, NY	44
Lawton, OK	147	Pensacola, FL	86	Tacoma, WA	7
Lewiston–Auburn, ME	136	Peoria, IL	162		
Lexington–Fayette, KY	233	Philadelphia, PA–NJ	108	Tallahassee, FL	119
Lima, OH	222	Phoenix, AZ	59	Tampa–St. Petersburg–	
Lincoln, NE	143			Clearwater, FL	38
		Pine Bluff, AR	316	Terre Haute, IN	234
Little Rock–North Little Rock, AR	216	Pittsburgh, PA	90	Texarkana, TX–Texarkana, AR	325
Longview–Marshall, TX	311	Pittsfield, MA	225	Toledo, OH	114
Lorain–Elyria, OH	184	Portland, ME	20		
Los Angeles–Long Beach, CA	10	Portland, OR	55	Topeka, KS	271
Louisville, KY–IN	117			Trenton, NJ	169
		Portsmouth–Dover–		Tucson, AZ	29
Lowell, MA–NH	274	Rochester, NH–ME	236	Tulsa, OK	102
Lubbock, TX	159	Poughkeepsie, NY	165	Tuscaloosa, AL	283
Lynchburg, VA	220	Providence, RI	76		
Macon–Warner Robins, GA	262	Provo–Orem, UT	23	Tyler, TX	326
Madison, WI	115	Pueblo, CO	174	Utica–Rome, NY	149
				Vallejo–Fairfield–Napa, CA	192
Manchester, NH	310	Racine, WI	104	Vancouver, WA	215
Mansfield, OH	273	Raleigh–Durham, NC	180	Victoria, TX	230
McAllen–Edinburg–Mission, TX	286	Reading, PA	193		
Medford, OR	226	Redding, CA	64	Vineland–Millville–Bridgeton, NJ	214
Melbourne–Titusville–Palm Bay, FL	12	Reno, NV	66	Visalia–Tulare–Porterville, CA	45
				Waco, TX	252
Memphis, TN–AR–MS	106	Richland–Kennewick–Pasco, WA	262	Washington, DC–MD–VA	188
Miami–Hialeah, FL	3	Richmond–Petersburg, VA	116	Waterbury, CT	295
Middlesex–Somerset–Hunterdon, NJ	186	Riverside–San Bernardino, CA	124		
Middletown, CT	163	Roanoke, VA	101	Waterloo–Cedar Falls, IA	129
Midland, TX	208	Rochester, MN	207	Wausau, WI	166
		Rochester, NY	50	West Palm Beach–Boca Raton–	
Milwaukee, WI	40	Rockford, IL	297	Delray Beach, FL	13
Minneapolis–St. Paul, MN–WI	87	Sacramento, CA	72	Wheeling, WV–OH	250
Mobile, AL	84	Saginaw–Bay City–Midland, MI	96	Wichita, KS	205
Modesto, CA	312	St. Cloud, MN	189		
Monmouth–Ocean, NJ	17	St. Joseph, MO	251	Wichita Falls, TX	275
		St. Louis, MO–IL	78	Williamsport, PA	320
Monroe, LA	196	Salem, OR	132	Wilmington, DE–NJ–MD	122
Montgomery, AL	279	Salem–Gloucester, MA	80	Wilmington, NC	48
Muncie, IN	222	Salinas–Seaside–Monterey, CA	27	Worcester, MA	301
Muskegon, MI	49				
Nashua, NH	199	Salt Lake City–Ogden, UT	11	Yakima, WA	91
		San Angelo, TX	272	York, PA	307
Nashville, TN	137	San Antonio, TX	204	Youngstown–Warren, OH	245
Nassau–Suffolk, NY	14	San Diego, CA	22	Yuba City, CA	299
New Bedford, MA	219				
New Britain, CT	258				

The following profiles are a selective catalogue of recreation features in each metro area.

The profiles begin with the category Common Denominators, specific options for urban recreation that ought to be available everywhere; the access rating for each item is shown in the right-hand column. The Good Restaurants entry tells how many restaurants at each quality level are in a metro area ("4 ★★" means, for example, that the place has four two-star restaurants). An NA indicates that the *Mobil Travel Guide* does not rate restaurants in that area.

The Crowd Pleasers category lists local zoos, aquariums, theme parks, automobile racecourses (along with sanctioning organization), and pari-mutuel betting attractions. Also included are the days per year that theme parks and pari-mutuel tracks are open along with their access rating. Under the heading Professional Sports, the names of major- and minor-league baseball, basketball, football, and hockey teams are given along with the total game seats per capita and access rating. Major-league team names are in capital letters. Local colleges and universities that field NCAA Division I teams in football and/or basketball are also listed, with separate total game seats per capita and access rating. If the school has only a basketball *or* football team at the Division I level, the team's name is followed by (b) or (f).

The third category, Outdoor Recreation Assets, counts the metro area's number of miles of ocean or Great Lakes coastline, its square miles of inland water, and the acreage for all national forests, parks, and wildlife refuges located there. The figures for inland water come from a series of U.S. Census Bureau geographic reports from the 1960s (still the best source for measurement of water surface areas in each of the nation's metropolitan counties). Ponds and lakes are counted if their surface areas are 40 acres or more; streams, canals, and rivers are also counted if their width is one eighth of a mile or more. The water area along irregular Great Lakes and ocean coastlines is counted, too, if the bays, inlets, and estuaries are between one and ten miles in width. Lengths of ocean and Great Lakes coastlines are estimated from state totals measured by the National Oceanic and Atmospheric Administration. A number of abbreviations are used in this section:

The figure in parentheses beside each major heading represents the number of *Places Rated* points awarded the metro area for assets in that category. If the metro area is part of a CMSA complex and receives bonus points for shared recreation assets, the number of access points is shown in parentheses following the name of the consolidated area. A star preceding a metro area's name highlights it as one of the top 25 places for recreation.

Information comes from these sources: American Association of Zoological Parks and Aquariums, *Zoological Parks and Aquariums in the Americas, 1982–1983,* 1983; American Baseball League, unpublished data, 1984; American Bowling Congress, unpublished data, 1984; American Greyhound Track Operators Association, *Directory,* 1984; American Hockey League, *Media Guide,* 1984; Brown Publishing Company, *National Speedway Directory,* 1984; Central Hockey League, *Media Guide,* 1984; Continental Basketball Association, unpublished data, 1984; Daily Racing Form, March 26, 1984; International Hockey League, *Media Guide,* 1984; Kings Entertainment Company, 1984; Merrill Lynch, *Theme Park Industry Survey,* 1983; National Association of Collegiate Directors of Athletics, *The 1983–1984 National Directory of College Athletics,* 1983; National Association of Professional Baseball Leagues, unpublished data, 1984; National Basketball Association, *Media Guide,* 1983; National Collegiate Athletic Association, *National Collegiate Championships,* 1984, *NCAA Basketball,* 1984, and *NCAA Football,* 1984; National Football League, unpublished data, 1984; National Golf Foundation, unpublished administrative records, 1984; National Hockey League, unpublished data, 1984; National League of Professional Baseball Teams, unpublished data, 1984; Rand McNally & Company, *Mobil Travel Guide* (7 vols.), 1984; Thoroughbred Racing Associations of North America, Inc., *Directory and Record Book,* 1983; U.S. Department of Agriculture, Forest Service, *Land Areas of the National Forest System,* 1984; U.S. Department of Commerce: Bureau of the Census, *Area Measurements, Series G-20,* 1962–1967, *County Business Patterns,* 1983–1984, *1977 Census of Selected Service Establishments,* 1981, and National Oceanic and Atmospheric Administration, *The Coastline of the United States,* 1975; U.S. Department of the Interior: Fish and Wildlife Service, unpublished master deed listing, 1984, and National Park Service, *Index to the National Park System and Related Areas,* 1983, and unpublished master deed listing, 1984; United States Football League, unpublished data, 1984; and U.S. Trotting Association, *Trotting and Pacing Guide,* 1984.

NF	National Forest	NP	National Park
NHP	National Historic Park	NRA	National Recreation Area
NHS	National Historic Site	NSR	National Scenic River
NMP	National Military Park	NS	National Seashore
NM	National Monument	NWR	National Wildlife Refuge

Rating | | Rating

Abilene, TX
Common Denominators (1,000)
- Good Restaurants: 1 ★, 2 ★★ — **B**
- Golf Courses: 4 private; 1 municipal — **C**
- Bowling Lanes: 108 — **A**
- Movie Theaters: 7 — **AA**

Crowd Pleasers (400)
- Zoos: Abilene Zoological Gardens — **C**
- NCAA Division I: .914 game seats per capita — **A**
  Hardin-Simmons Cowboys (b)

Outdoor Recreation Assets (5)
- Inland Water Area: 2.9 square miles

Places Rated Score: 1,405   Places Rated Rank: 232

Akron, OH
Common Denominators (1,200)
- Good Restaurants: 1 ★, 4 ★★, 1 ★★★★ — **C**
- Golf Courses: 10 private; 28.5 daily fee; 2.5 municipal — **AA**
- Bowling Lanes: 804 — **AA**
- Movie Theaters: 22 — **A**

Crowd Pleasers (800)
- Zoos: Akron Children's Zoo — **C**
- Theme Parks: Sea World of Ohio (100 days) — **B**
- Auto Racing: Nelson Ledges (SCCA) — **C**
- Pari-mutuel Betting: Northfield Harness (89 days) — **B**
- NCAA Division I: .667 game seats per capita — **B**
  Kent State Golden Flashes, University of Akron Zips

Outdoor Recreation Assets (232)
- Inland Water Area: 17 square miles
- National Forests, Parks, Wildlife Refuges:
  Cuyahoga Valley NRA (16,074 acres)

CMSA Access: CLEVELAND–AKRON–LORAIN, OH (400)
Places Rated Score: 2,632   Places Rated Rank: 51

Albany, GA
Common Denominators (700)
- Good Restaurants: 1 ★★ — **C**
- Golf Courses: 2.5 private; 1 municipal — **C**
- Bowling Lanes: 78 — **B**
- Movie Theaters: 4 — **A**

Crowd Pleasers (100)
- Zoos: Chehaw Wild Animal Park — **C**

Outdoor Recreation Assets (59)
- Inland Water Area: 8.1 square miles

Places Rated Score: 859   Places Rated Rank: 304

Albany–Schenectady–Troy, NY
Common Denominators (1,100)
- Good Restaurants: 10 ★★, 8 ★★★ — **A**
- Golf Courses: 18 private; 15.5 daily fee; 6.5 municipal — **A**
- Bowling Lanes: 1,000 — **AA**
- Movie Theaters: 18 — **C**

Crowd Pleasers (400)
- Pari-mutuel Betting: Saratoga (harness, 202 days; Thoroughbred, 24 days) — **B**
- Professional Sports: .595 game seats per capita — **C**
  Albany A's (baseball), Patroons (basketball)
- NCAA Division I: .039 game seats per capita — **C**
  Siena College Indians (b)

Outdoor Recreation Assets (117)
- Inland Water Area: 71.8 square miles
- National Forests, Parks, Wildlife Refuges:
  Saratoga NHP (2,605 acres)

Places Rated Score: 1,617   Places Rated Rank: 175

Albuquerque, NM
Common Denominators (1,000)
- Good Restaurants: 1★, 5 ★★, 3 ★★★ — **B**
- Golf Courses: 6.5 private; 1 daily fee; 3.5 municipal — **C**
- Bowling Lanes: 300 — **A**
- Movie Theaters: 18 — **AA**

Crowd Pleasers (1,100)
- Zoos: Rio Grande Zoological Park — **A**
- Auto Racing: Seven Flags Raceway (NASCAR) — **C**
- Pari-mutuel Betting: New Mexico State Fair (Thoroughbred, 17 days) — **C**
- Professional Sports: 2.101 game seats per capita — **A**
  Dukes (baseball), Silvers (basketball)
- NCAA Division I: .889 game seats per capita — **A**
  University of New Mexico Lobos

Outdoor Recreation Assets (512)
- National Forest, Parks, Wildlife Refuges:
  Cibola NF (76,588 acres)

Places Rated Score: 2,612   Places Rated Rank: 52

Alexandria, LA
Common Denominators (500)
- Good Restaurants: 1 ★★★ — **C**
- Golf Courses: 2.5 private; 1 daily fee — **C**
- Bowling Lanes: 40 — **C**
- Movie Theaters: 4 — **B**

Crowd Pleasers (100)
- Zoos: Alexandria Zoological Park — **C**

Outdoor Recreation Assets (418)
- Inland Water Area: 8.6 square miles
- National Forests, Parks, Wildlife Refuges:
  Kisatchie NF (101,221 acres)

Places Rated Score: 1,018   Places Rated Rank: 290

Allentown–Bethlehem, PA–NJ
Common Denominators (800)
- Good Restaurants: 2 ★, 1 ★★★, 1 ★★★★ — **C**
- Golf Courses: 13 private; 7.5 daily fee; 2 municipal — **B**
- Bowling Lanes: 600 — **A**
- Movie Theaters: 17 — **B**

Crowd Pleasers (200)
- NCAA Division I: .373 game seats per capita — **B**
  Lafayette College Leopards, Lehigh Engineers

Outdoor Recreation Assets (117)
- Inland Water Area: 2.2 square miles
- National Forests, Parks, Wildlife Refuges:
  Appalachian Trail (4,079 acres)
  Delaware NSR (368 acres)
  Delaware Water Gap NRA (16,066 acres)

Places Rated Score: 1,117   Places Rated Rank: 278

Alton–Granite City, IL
Common Denominators (800)
- Good Restaurants: 1 ★★ — **C**
- Golf Courses: 4.5 private; 3 daily fee; 2 municipal — **B**
- Bowling Lanes: 272 — **A**
- Movie Theaters: 6 — **B**

Outdoor Recreation Assets (80)
- Inland Water Area: 17.6 square miles

CMSA Access: ST. LOUIS–EAST ST. LOUIS–ALTON, MO–IL (400)
Places Rated Score: 1,280   Places Rated Rank: 249

Altoona, PA
Common Denominators (1,200)
- Good Restaurants: 2 ★★, 2 ★★★ — **AA**
- Golf Courses: 3 private; 3 daily fee — **B**
- Bowling Lanes: 133 — **A**
- Movie Theaters: 5 — **A**

Outdoor Recreation Assets (10)
- Inland Water Area: .2 square miles
- National Forests, Parks, Wildlife Refuges:
  Allegheny Portage NHS (517 acres)

Places Rated Score: 1,210   Places Rated Rank: 261

Amarillo, TX
Common Denominators (1,000)
- Good Restaurants: 1 ★, 3 ★★ — **B**
- Golf Courses: 4 private; 2 daily fee; 2 municipal — **B**
- Bowling Lanes: 112 — **B**
- Movie Theaters: 7 — **AA**

Rating

Outdoor Recreation Assets (109)
  Inland Water Area: 25.9 square miles
  National Forests, Parks, Wildlife Refuges:
    Alibates Flint Quarries NM (1,079 acres)
    Buffalo Lake NWR (7,664 acres)
    Lake Meredith NRA (23,379 acres)
Places Rated Score: 1,109   Places Rated Rank: 280

Anaheim–Santa Ana, CA
Common Denominators (800)
  Good Restaurants: 2 ★, 33 ★★, 26 ★★★, 2 ★★★★   AA
  Golf Courses: 16 private; 11 daily fee; 7 municipal   C
  Bowling Lanes: 1,182   B
  Movie Theaters: 38   C
Crowd Pleasers (1,000)
  Theme Parks: AA
    Disneyland (303 days)
    Knott's Berry Farm (365 days)
    Six Flags Magic Mountain (185 days)
  Pari-mutuel Betting: C
    Los Alamitos (harness, 19 days; Thoroughbred,
    13 days)
  Professional Sports: 3.108 game seats per capita   AA
    CALIFORNIA ANGELS (baseball), LOS
    ANGELES RAMS (football)
  NCAA Division I: .076 game seats per capita   C
    Fullerton State Titans, University of
    California (Irvine) Anteaters (b)
Outdoor Recreation Assets (956)
  Pacific Coastline: 40 miles
  Inland Water Area: 3.9 square miles
  National Forests, Parks, Wildlife Refuges:
    Cleveland NF (54,281 acres)
CMSA Access: LOS ANGELES–ANAHEIM–
  RIVERSIDE, CA (400)
Places Rated Score: 3,156   Places Rated Rank: 28

Anchorage, AK
Common Denominators (900)
  Good Restaurants: NA   A
  Golf Courses: 1 private; 1 daily fee   C
  Bowling Lanes: 160   A
  Movie Theaters: 5   B
Crowd Pleasers (100)
  Zoos: Alaska Zoo   C
Outdoor Recreation Assets (2,000)
  Pacific Coastline: 90 miles
  Inland Water Area: 36 square miles
  National Forests, Parks, Wildlife Refuges:
    Chugach NF (275,000 acres)
Places Rated Score: 3,000   Places Rated Rank: 33

Anderson, IN
Common Denominators (700)
  Golf Courses: 4.5 private; 1.5 daily fee; 1   B
    municipal
  Bowling Lanes: 160   AA
  Movie Theaters: 3   C
Outdoor Recreation Assets (138)
  Inland Water Area: 12.5 square miles
Places Rated Score: 838   Places Rated Rank: 309

Anderson, SC
Common Denominators (300)
  Golf Courses: 5 private   —
  Bowling Lanes: 32   C
  Movie Theaters: 3   B
Crowd Pleasers (300)
  Professional Sports: 2.162 game seats per capita   A
    Braves (baseball)
Outdoor Recreation Assets (13)
  Inland Water Area: 1.9 square miles
Places Rated Score: 613   Places Rated Rank: 327

Rating

Ann Arbor, MI
Common Denominators (1,400)
  Good Restaurants: 4 ★, 6 ★★, 1 ★★★   AA
  Golf Courses: 7 private; 5.5 daily fee; 3 municipal   AA
  Bowling Lanes: 318   AA
  Movie Theaters: 7   B
Crowd Pleasers (400)
  NCAA Division I: 3.264 game seats per capita   AA
    Eastern Michigan Hurons, University of Michigan
    Wolverines
Outdoor Recreation Assets (88)
  Inland Water Area: 12.5 square miles
CMSA Access: DETROIT–ANN ARBOR, MI (400)
Places Rated Score: 2,288   Places Rated Rank: 73

Anniston, AL
Common Denominators (900)
  Good Restaurants: 1 ★★★   C
  Golf Courses: 3 private; 2 daily fee; 0.5 municipal   B
  Bowling Lanes: 44   B
  Movie Theaters: 5   AA
Outdoor Recreation Assets (265)
  Inland Water Area: 1.2 square miles
  National Forests, Parks, Wildlife Refuges:
    Talladega NF (19,985 acres)
Places Rated Score: 1,165   Places Rated Rank: 267

Appleton–Oshkosh–Neenah, WI
Common Denominators (1,300)
  Good Restaurants: 5 ★★, 2 ★★★   A
  Golf Courses: 6 private; 11.5 daily fee; 2 municipal AA
  Bowling Lanes: 540   AA
  Movie Theaters: 8   B
Crowd Pleasers (300)
  Professional Sports: 1.531 game seats per capita   A
    Foxes (baseball), Wisconsin Fliers (basketball)
Outdoor Recreation Assets (715)
  Inland Water Area: 202.9 square miles
Places Rated Score: 2,315   Places Rated Rank: 70

Asheville, NC
Common Denominators (700)
  Good Restaurants: 1 ★, 1 ★★★   C
  Golf Courses: 5 private; 1.5 daily fee; 2 municipal   B
  Bowling Lanes: 48   C
  Movie Theaters: 6   A
Crowd Pleasers (400)
  Auto Racing: Asheville (NASCAR)   C
  Professional Sports: 1.566 game seats per capita   A
    Tourists (baseball)
Outdoor Recreation Assets (442)
  Inland Water Area: .8 square miles
  National Forests, Parks, Wildlife Refuges:
    Blue Ridge Parkway (5,411 acres)
    Pisgah NF (31,390 acres)
Places Rated Score: 1,542   Places Rated Rank: 195

Athens, GA
Common Denominators (600)
  Good Restaurants: 1 ★   C
  Golf Courses: 1.5 private; 2 daily fee; 1 municipal   B
  Bowling Lanes: 36   C
  Movie Theaters: 4   B
Crowd Pleasers (400)
  NCAA Division I: 4.131 game seats per capita   AA
    University of Georgia Bulldogs
Outdoor Recreation Assets (1)
  National Forests, Parks, Wildlife Refuges:
    Oconee NF (112 acres)
Places Rated Score: 1,001   Places Rated Rank: 291

Atlanta, GA
Common Denominators (600)
  Good Restaurants: 1 ★, 19 ★★, 20 ★★★, 1 ★★★★   B

	Rating
Golf Courses: 45.5 private; 14 daily fee; 9 municipal	C
Bowling Lanes: 656	C
Movie Theaters: 64	B

Crowd Pleasers (700)
Theme Parks: Six Flags Over Georgia (148 days)	C
Auto Racing: Atlanta International (NASCAR)	C
Professional Sports: 2.534 game seats per capita	AA

BRAVES (baseball), HAWKS (basketball), FALCONS (football)
NCAA Division I: .212 game seats per capita	C

Georgia Tech Yellow Jackets, Georgia State Panthers (b)

Outdoor Recreation Assets (62)
Inland Water Area: 50.2 square miles
National Forests, Parks, Wildlife Refuges:
Chattahoochee River NRA (5,968 acres)
Kennesaw Mountain National Battlefield Park (2,884 acres)
Martin Luther King, Jr., NHS (8 acres)
Places Rated Score: 1,362   Places Rated Rank: 239

Atlantic City, NJ
Common Denominators (1,200)
Good Restaurants: 1 ★, 12 ★★, 8 ★★★, 1 ★★★★	AA
Golf Courses: 6 private; 6.5 daily fee; 0.5 municipal	A
Bowling Lanes: 90	C
Movie Theaters: 27	AA

Crowd Pleasers (400)
Pari-mutuel Betting: Atlantic City (harness, 145 days; Thoroughbred, 93 days)	AA

Outdoor Recreation Assets (1,111)
Atlantic Coastline: 52 miles
Inland Water Area: 67.2 square miles
National Forests, Parks, Wildlife Refuges:
Brigantine NWR (19,840 acres)
Places Rated Score: 2,711   Places Rated Rank: 46

Augusta, GA–SC
Common Denominators (800)
Good Restaurants: 1 ★★	C
Golf Courses: 12 private; 3.5 daily fee; 1 municipal	B
Bowling Lanes: 158	B
Movie Theaters: 11	A

Outdoor Recreation Assets (113)
Inland Water Area: 35 square miles
National Forests, Parks, Wildlife Refuges:
Sumter NF (6,021 acres)
Places Rated Score: 913   Places Rated Rank: 300

Aurora–Elgin, IL
Common Denominators (1,400)
Good Restaurants: 6 ★, 9 ★★, 4 ★★★	AA
Golf Courses: 3.5 private; 3 daily fee; 6 municipal	A
Bowling Lanes: 346	AA
Movie Theaters: 12	A

CMSA Access: CHICAGO–GARY–LAKE COUNTY, IL–IN–WI (400)
Places Rated Score: 1,800   Places Rated Rank: 145

Austin, TX
Common Denominators (700)
Good Restaurants: 2 ★, 3 ★★, 1 ★★★	C
Golf Courses: 11.5 private; 5 daily fee; 3 municipal	B
Bowling Lanes: 254	B
Movie Theaters: 16	B

Crowd Pleasers (300)
NCAA Division I: 1.096 game seats per capita	A

University of Texas Longhorns

Outdoor Recreation Assets (63)
Inland Water Area: 35.3 square miles
Places Rated Score: 1,063   Places Rated Rank: 285

Bakersfield, CA
Common Denominators (1,000)
	Rating
Good Restaurants: 1 ★, 4 ★★, 2 ★★★	B
Golf Courses: 4.5 private; 7 daily fee; 4 municipal	A
Bowling Lanes: 204	B
Movie Theaters: 15	A

Crowd Pleasers (200)
Professional Sports: .781 game seats per capita	B

Dodgers (baseball)

Outdoor Recreation Assets (368)
Inland Water Area: 19.6 square miles
National Forests, Parks, Wildlife Refuges:
Kern–Pixley NWR (10,618 acres)
Los Padres NF (64,803 acres)
Sequoia NF (294,917 acres)
Places Rated Score: 1,568   Places Rated Rank: 191

Baltimore, MD
Common Denominators (600)
Good Restaurants: 9 ★, 10 ★★, 10 ★★★	C
Golf Courses: 32.5 private; 4 daily fee; 8.5 municipal	C
Bowling Lanes: 983	B
Movie Theaters: 62	B

Crowd Pleasers (1,100)
Zoos: Baltimore Zoo	A
Aquariums: National Aquarium in Baltimore	A
Pari-mutuel Betting:	C

Pimlico (Thoroughbred, 76 days)
Trimonium (Thoroughbred, 42 days)
Professional Sports: 2.347 game seats per capita	A

ORIOLES (baseball), STARS (football), Skipjacks (hockey)
NCAA Division I: .140 game seats per capita	C

Towson State Tigers (b), U.S. Naval Academy Midshipmen, University of Baltimore Super Bees (b)

Outdoor Recreation Assets (1,225)
Chesapeake Bay Coastline: 96 miles
Inland Water Area: 137.9 square miles
National Forests, Parks, Wildlife Refuges:
Fort McHenry NM (43 acres)
Hampton NHS (59 acres)
National Capital Park (432 acres)
Susquehanna NWR (4 acres)
Places Rated Score: 2,925   Places Rated Rank: 39

Bangor, ME
Common Denominators (1,200)
Good Restaurants: 1 ★, 3 ★★, 1 ★★★	AA
Golf Courses: 3.5 daily fee; 1 municipal	AA
Bowling Lanes: 20	C
Movie Theaters: 3	A

Crowd Pleasers (600)
Pari-mutuel Betting: Bangor Raceway (harness, 37 days)	A
NCAA Division I: .971 game seats per capita	A

University of Maine Black Bears

Outdoor Recreation Assets (348)
Inland Water Area: 25.3 square miles
Places Rated Score: 2,148   Places Rated Rank: 89

Baton Rouge, LA
Common Denominators (700)
Good Restaurants: 6 ★★, 5 ★★★, 2 ★★★★	A
Golf Courses: 9.5 private; 4 municipal	C
Bowling Lanes: 160	C
Movie Theaters: 14	B

Crowd Pleasers (500)
Zoos: Greater Baton Rouge Zoo	B
NCAA Division I: 1.145 game seats per capita	

Louisiana State Fighting Tigers

Outdoor Recreation Assets (213)
Inland Water Area: 68.4 square miles
Places Rated Score: 1,413   Places Rated Rank: 228

	Rating

Battle Creek, MI
Common Denominators (1,500)
Good Restaurants: 1 ★, 3 ★★, 1 ★★★ — **A**
Golf Courses: 6 private; 5.5 daily fee; 1.5
  municipal — **AA**
Bowling Lanes: 202 — **AA**
Movie Theaters: 7 — **AA**
Crowd Pleasers (100)
Zoos: Binder Park Zoo — **C**
Outdoor Recreation Assets (48)
Inland Water Area: 6.9 square miles
Places Rated Score: 1,648   Places Rated Rank: 168

Beaumont–Port Arthur, TX
Common Denominators (600)
Good Restaurants: 2 ★, 3 ★★★ — **C**
Golf Courses: 7.5 private; 2.5 daily fee; 3 — **B**
  municipal
Bowling Lanes: 122 — **C**
Movie Theaters: 11 — **B**
Crowd Pleasers (400)
Professional Sports: .815 game seats per capita — **B**
  Golden Gators (baseball)
NCAA Division I: .401 game seats per capita — **B**
  Lamar Cardinals
Outdoor Recreation Assets (813)
Gulf of Mexico Coastline: 32 miles
Inland Water Area: 72.3 square miles
National Forests, Parks, Wildlife Refuges:
  Big Thicket National Preserve (41,730 acres)
  McFaddin NWR (41,682 acres)
  Texas Point NWR (8,952 acres)
Places Rated Score: 1,813   Places Rated Rank: 142

Beaver County, PA
Common Denominators (1,000)
Good Restaurants: 1 ★★★ — **C**
Golf Courses: 4 private; 5.5 daily fee — **A**
Bowling Lanes: 242 — **AA**
Movie Theaters: 5 — **B**
Outdoor Recreation Assets (80)
Inland Water Area: 7 square miles
CMSA Access: PITTSBURGH–BEAVER VALLEY, PA (400)
Places Rated Score: 1,480   Places Rated Rank: 212

Bellingham, WA
Common Denominators (1,100)
Good Restaurants: 2 ★★, 1 ★★★ — **A**
Golf Courses: 2 private; 1.5 daily fee; 1 municipal — **B**
Bowling Lanes: 76 — **B**
Movie Theaters: 7 — **AA**
Crowd Pleasers (100)
Professional Sports: .416 game seats per capita — **C**
  Mariners (baseball)
Outdoor Recreation Assets (2,000)
Inland Water Area: 53.7 square miles
National Forests, Parks, Wildlife Refuges:
  Mount Baker NF (452,909 acres)
  North Cascades NP (281,413 acres)
  Ross Lake NRA (107,633 acres)
  San Juan Island NWR (3 acres)
Places Rated Score: 3,200   Places Rated Rank: 26

Benton Harbor, MI
Common Denominators (1,000)
Good Restaurants: 1 ★, 1 ★★, 1 ★★★ — **B**
Golf Courses: 4.5 private; 9 daily fee; 1 municipal — **AA**
Bowling Lanes: 114 — **B**
Movie Theaters: 4 — **B**
Outdoor Recreation Assets (477)
Great Lakes Coastline: 44 miles
Inland Water Area: 4.3 square miles
Places Rated Score: 1,477   Places Rated Rank: 213

Bergen–Passaic, NJ
Common Denominators (600)
Good Restaurants: 3 ★, 9 ★★, 6 ★★★ — **C**
Golf Courses: 17 private; 4.5 daily fee; 6.5 — **C**
  municipal
Bowling Lanes: 858 — **B**
Movie Theaters: 36 — **B**
Crowd Pleasers (700)
Zoos: — **C**
  Bergen County Wildlife Center
  Van Saun Park Zoo
Pari-mutuel Betting: Meadowlands (harness, 185 — **B**
  days; Thoroughbred, 99 days)
Professional Sports: 1.654 game seats per capita — **A**
  NETS (basketball), GENERALS, GIANTS
  (football), DEVILS (hockey)
NCAA Division I: .013 game seats per capita — **C**
  Fairleigh Dickinson Knights (b)
Outdoor Recreation Assets (218)
Inland Water Area: 18.1 square miles
National Forests, Parks, Wildlife Refuges:
  Appalachian Trail (255 acres)
CMSA Access: NEW YORK–NORTHERN NEW
  JERSEY–LONG ISLAND, NY–NJ–CT (400)
Places Rated Score: 1,918   Places Rated Rank: 124

Billings, MT
Common Denominators (1,300)
Good Restaurants: 1 ★, 4 ★★, 1 ★★★ — **AA**
Golf Courses: 3.5 private; 1.5 daily fee — **B**
Bowling Lanes: 100 — **A**
Movie Theaters: 5 — **AA**
Crowd Pleasers (700)
Pari-mutuel Betting: Yellowstone Exhibition — **A**
  (Thoroughbred, 38 days)
Professional Sports: 4.716 game seats per capita — **AA**
  Mustangs (baseball), Montana Magic (hockey)
Outdoor Recreation Assets (46)
Inland Water Area: 24.1 square miles
Places Rated Score: 2,046   Places Rated Rank: 98

Biloxi–Gulfport, MS
Common Denominators (1,100)
Good Restaurants: 3 ★, 8 ★★, 2 ★★★ — **AA**
Golf Courses: 4.5 private; 5 daily fee — **A**
Bowling Lanes: 188 — **B**
Movie Theaters: 5 — **B**
Outdoor Recreation Assets (1,006)
Gulf of Mexico Coastline: 30 miles
Inland Water Area: 22.4 square miles
National Forests, Parks, Wildlife Refuges:
  De Soto NF (61,389 acres)
  Gulf Islands NS (19,997 acres)
Places Rated Score: 2,106   Places Rated Rank: 93

Binghamton, NY
Common Denominators (1,500)
Good Restaurants: 1 ★, 2 ★★, 4 ★★★ — **A**
Golf Courses: 4.5 private; 8 daily fee; 3 municipal — **AA**
Bowling Lanes: 364 — **AA**
Movie Theaters: 12 — **AA**
Crowd Pleasers (200)
Zoos: Ross Park Zoo — **C**
Professional Sports: .737 game seats per capita — **C**
  Whalers (hockey)
Outdoor Recreation Assets (22)
Inland Water Area: 5.5 square miles
Places Rated Score: 1,722   Places Rated Rank: 155

Birmingham, AL
Common Denominators (400)
Good Restaurants: 7 ★★, 4 ★★★ — **C**
Golf Courses: 20 private; 5 daily fee; 5 — **C**
  municipal
Bowling Lanes: 134 — **C**

	Rating
Movie Theaters: 19	C
Crowd Pleasers (800)	
Zoos: Birmingham Zoo	B
Auto Racing: Birmingham International (NASCAR)	C
Professional Sports: 1.692 game seats per capita	A
Barons (baseball), STALLIONS (football)	
NCAA Division I: .618 game seats per capita	B
Samford University Bulldogs (b), University of	
Alabama Blazers (b)	
Outdoor Recreation Assets (34)	
Inland Water Area: 27.5 square miles	
National Forests, Parks, Wildlife Refuges:	
Watercress NWR (7 acres)	
Places Rated Score: 1,234	Places Rated Rank: 256

Bismarck, ND

	Rating
Common Denominators (1,400)	
Good Restaurants: 5 ★★	AA
Golf Courses: 1 private; 2.5 municipal	A
Bowling Lanes: 100	AA
Movie Theaters: 3	A
Crowd Pleasers (100)	
Zoos: Dakota Zoo	C
Outdoor Recreation Assets (130)	
Inland Water Area: 73.5 square miles	
National Forests, Parks, Wildlife Refuges:	
Canfield Lake NWR (3 acres)	
Florence Lake NWR (1,468 acres)	
Long Lake NWR (10,330 acres)	
Places Rated Score: 1,630	Places Rated Rank: 171

Bloomington, IN

	Rating
Common Denominators (1,100)	
Good Restaurants: 2 ★★★	A
Golf Courses: 2 private; 1 daily fee; 1 municipal	B
Bowling Lanes: 42	B
Movie Theaters: 5	AA
Crowd Pleasers (400)	
NCAA Division I: 4.953 game seats per capita	AA
Indiana University Fightin' Hoosiers	
Outdoor Recreation Assets (490)	
Inland Water Area: 9.1 square miles	
National Forests, Parks, Wildlife Refuges:	
Hoosier NF (18,317 acres)	
Places Rated Score: 1,990	Places Rated Rank: 107

Bloomington–Normal, IL

	Rating
Common Denominators (1,100)	
Good Restaurants: 1 ★, 2 ★★	B
Golf Courses: 2.5 private; 1.5 daily fee; 2	A
municipal	
Bowling Lanes: 104	A
Movie Theaters: 4	A
Crowd Pleasers (500)	
Zoos: Miller Park Zoo	C
NCAA Division I: 1.502 game seats per capita	AA
Illinois State Redbirds	
Outdoor Recreation Assets (5)	
Inland Water Area: 1.1 square miles	
Places Rated Score: 1,605	Places Rated Rank: 181

Boise City, ID

	Rating
Common Denominators (800)	
Good Restaurants: 2 ★, 1 ★★★	C
Golf Courses: 4 private; 2.5 daily fee; 0.5	B
municipal	
Bowling Lanes: 122	B
Movie Theaters: 6	A
Crowd Pleasers (800)	
Zoos: Boise City Zoo	C
Pari-mutuel Betting: Les Bois Park	A
(Thoroughbred, 51 days)	
NCAA Division I: 1.522 game seats per capita	AA
Boise State Broncos	
Outdoor Recreation Assets (72)	
Inland Water Area: 8.6 square miles	

	Rating
National Forests, Parks, Wildlife Refuges:	
Boise NF (4,211 acres)	
Places Rated Score: 1,672	Places Rated Rank: 164

Boston, MA

	Rating
Common Denominators (800)	
Good Restaurants: 21 ★, 34 ★★, 15 ★★★, 3 ★★★★	A
Golf Courses: 32 private; 21.5 daily fee; 11.5	C
municipal	
Bowling Lanes: 172	C
Movie Theaters: 94	A
Crowd Pleasers (1,300)	
Zoos:	A
Franklin Park Zoo	
Stone Zoo	
Aquariums: New England Aquarium	A
Pari-mutuel Betting:	A
Foxboro Raceway (harness, 288 days)	
Raynham (greyhound, 135 days)	
Suffolk Downs (Thoroughbred, 244 days)	
Wonderland (greyhound, 310 days)	
Professional Sports: 1.575 game seats per capita	A
RED SOX (baseball), CELTICS (basketball),	
PATRIOTS (football), BRUINS (hockey)	
NCAA Division I: .275 game seats per capita	C
Boston College Eagles, Boston University	
Terriers, Harvard Crimson, Northeastern	
University Huskies	
Outdoor Recreation Assets (666)	
Atlantic Coastline: 41 miles	
Inland Water Area: 87.8 square miles	
National Forests, Parks, Wildlife Refuges:	
Adams NHS (9 acres)	
Boston NHP (41 acres)	
Frederick Law Olmstead NHS (2 acres)	
Great Meadows NWR (1,526 acres)	
John F. Kennedy NHS (0.09 acres)	
Longfellow NHS (2 acres)	
Minute Man NHP (712 acres)	
Oxbow NWR (662 acres)	
Saugus Iron Works NHS (9 acres)	
CMSA Access: BOSTON–LAWRENCE–SALEM, MA–NH (300)	
Places Rated Score: 3,066	Places Rated Rank: 32

★ Boulder–Longmont, CO

	Rating
Common Denominators (1,300)	
Good Restaurants: 4 ★★, 2 ★★★, 2 ★★★★	AA
Golf Courses: 2 private; 1.5 daily fee; 2.5	B
municipal	
Bowling Lanes: 142	A
Movie Theaters: 8	AA
Crowd Pleasers (500)	
Auto Racing: Colorado National (NASCAR)	C
NCAA Division I: 2.141 game seats per capita	AA
University of Colorado Buffalos	
Outdoor Recreation Assets (1,812)	
Inland Water Area: 9.7 square miles	
National Forests, Parks, Wildlife Refuges:	
Rocky Mountain NP (27,259 acres)	
Roosevelt NF (138,624 acres)	
CMSA Access: DENVER–BOULDER, CO (400)	
Places Rated Score: 4,012	Places Rated Rank: 5

Bradenton, FL

	Rating
Common Denominators (800)	
Good Restaurants: 1 ★, 1 ★★	C
Golf Courses: 2.5 private; 3 daily fee; 1 municipal	A
Bowling Lanes: 64	B
Movie Theaters: 4	B
Outdoor Recreation Assets (549)	
Gulf of Mexico Coastline: 24 miles	
Inland Water Area: 46 square miles	
National Forests, Parks, Wildlife Refuges:	
DeSoto National Monument (25 acres)	
Passage Key NWR (36 acres)	
Places Rated Score: 1,349	Places Rated Rank: 242

	Rating

Brazoria, TX
Common Denominators (400)
  Golf Courses: 3.5 private; 0.5 daily fee; 1   **C**
    municipal
  Bowling Lanes: 68   **B**
  Movie Theaters: 3   **C**
Outdoor Recreation Assets (812)
  Gulf of Mexico Coastline: 35 miles
  Inland Water Area: 79.8 square miles
  National Forests, Parks, Wildlife Refuges:
    Brazoria NWR (10,361 acres)
    San Bernard NWR (21,783 acres)
CMSA Access: HOUSTON–GALVESTON–BRAZORIA, TX (300)
Places Rated Score: 1,512   Places Rated Rank: 203

Bremerton, WA
Common Denominators (700)
  Good Restaurants: 1 ★★★   **C**
  Golf Courses: 2 private; 2 daily fee; 1 municipal   **B**
  Bowling Lanes: 68   **B**
  Movie Theaters: 4   **B**
Outdoor Recreation Assets (1,273)
  Puget Sound Coastline: 30 miles
  Inland Water Area: 76.5 square miles
Places Rated Score: 1,973   Places Rated Rank: 110

Bridgeport–Milford, CT
Common Denominators (600)
  Good Restaurants: 1 ★, 5 ★★, 1 ★★★   **B**
  Golf Courses: 6.5 private; 1 daily fee; 2.5   **C**
    municipal
  Bowling Lanes: 260   **B**
  Movie Theaters: 9   **C**
Crowd Pleasers (600)
  Zoos: Beardsley Zoological Gardens   **C**
  Pari-mutuel Betting: **AA**
    Bridgeport Jai Alai (187 days)
    Milford Jai Alai (177 days)
  NCAA Division I: .089 game seats per capita   **C**
    Fairfield University Stags (b)
Outdoor Recreation Assets (313)
  Atlantic Coastline: 17 miles
  Inland Water Area: 7.9 square miles
CMSA Access: NEW YORK–NORTHERN NEW
  JERSEY–LONG ISLAND, NY–NJ–CT (400)
Places Rated Score: 1,913   Places Rated Rank: 126

Bristol, CT
Common Denominators (400)
  Good Restaurants: 1 ★   **C**
  Golf Courses: 1 private   **—**
  Bowling Lanes: 40   **B**
  Movie Theaters: 1   **C**
Outdoor Recreation Assets (77)
  Inland Water Area: 1.2 square miles
CMSA Access: HARTFORD–NEW BRITAIN–
  MIDDLETOWN, CT (300)
Places Rated Score: 777   Places Rated Rank: 318

Brockton, MA
Common Denominators (600)
  Good Restaurants: 1 ★★   **C**
  Golf Courses: 1.5 private; 3 daily fee; 1 municipal   **B**
  Bowling Lanes: 56   **C**
  Movie Theaters: 5   **B**
Crowd Pleasers (100)
  Professional Sports: .451 game seats per capita   **C**
    Bay State Bombardiers (b)
Outdoor Recreation Assets (117)
  Inland Water Area: 3.5 square miles
CMSA Access: BOSTON–LAWRENCE–SALEM, MA–NH (400)
Places Rated Score: 1,217   Places Rated Rank: 258

Brownsville–Harlingen, TX
Common Denominators (700)
  Good Restaurants: 2 ★, 3 ★★, 2 ★★★   **A**

	Rating

  Golf Courses: 3 private; 3 daily fee; 1.5 municipal   **B**
  Bowling Lanes: 52   **C**
  Movie Theaters: 4   **C**
Crowd Pleasers (300)
  Zoos: Gladys Porter Zoo   **A**
Outdoor Recreation Assets (2,000)
  Gulf of Mexico Coastline: 31 miles
  Inland Water Area: 262.9 square miles
  National Forests, Parks, Wildlife Refuges:
    Laguna Atascosa NWR (44,940 acres)
    Lower Rio Grande Valley NWR (511 acres)
Places Rated Score: 3,000   Places Rated Rank: 33

Bryan–College Station, TX
Common Denominators (1,000)
  Good Restaurants: 2 ★, 1 ★★   **B**
  Golf Courses: 1 private; 1 daily fee; 1 municipal   **B**
  Bowling Lanes: 38   **B**
  Movie Theaters: 4   **AA**
Crowd Pleasers (400)
  NCAA Division I: 4.888 game seats per capita   **AA**
    Texas A & M Aggies
Outdoor Recreation Assets (13)
  Inland Water Area: 1.5 square miles
Places Rated Score: 1,413   Places Rated Rank: 228

Buffalo, NY
Common Denominators (900)
  Good Restaurants: 1 ★, 6 ★★, 8 ★★★   **B**
  Golf Courses: 13 private; 7.5 daily fee; 9 municipal   **B**
  Bowling Lanes: 1,272   **AA**
  Movie Theaters: 21   **C**
Crowd Pleasers (1,100)
  Zoos: Buffalo Zoological Gardens   **A**
  Auto Racing: Holland International (NASCAR)   **C**
  Pari-mutuel Betting: Buffalo Raceway (harness,   **B**
    143 days)
  Professional Sports: 4.608 game seats per capita   **AA**
    Bisons (baseball), BILLS (football), SABRES
    (hockey)
  NCAA Division I: .023 game seats per capita   **C**
    Canisius College Golden Griffins (b)
Outdoor Recreation Assets (341)
  Great Lakes Coastline: 29 miles
  Inland Water Area: 10.6 square miles
  National Forests, Parks, Wildlife Refuges:
    Theodore Roosevelt Inaugural NHS (1 acre)
CMSA Access: BUFFALO–NIAGARA FALLS, NY (100)
Places Rated Score: 2,441   Places Rated Rank: 62

Burlington, NC
Common Denominators (700)
  Golf Courses: 2 private; 4 daily fee; 1 municipal   **AA**
  Bowling Lanes: 32   **C**
  Movie Theaters: 3   **B**
Outdoor Recreation Assets (1)
  Inland Water Area: .1 square miles
Places Rated Score: 701   Places Rated Rank: 324

★ Burlington, VT
Common Denominators (1,200)
  Good Restaurants: 1 ★, 4 ★★, 3 ★★★   **AA**
  Golf Courses: 1 private; 3.5 daily fee   **A**
  Bowling Lanes: 78   **B**
  Movie Theaters: 4   **A**
Crowd Pleasers (700)
  Auto Racing: Catamount International (NASCAR)   **C**
  Professional Sports: 3.460 game seats per capita   **AA**
    Reds (baseball)
  NCAA Division I: .358 game seats per capita   **B**
    University of Vermont Catamounts (b)
Outdoor Recreation Assets (1,457)
  Inland Water Area: 132.3 square miles
Places Rated Score: 3,357   Places Rated Rank: 21

Rating

Canton, OH
Common Denominators (1,100)
Good Restaurants: 4 ★★, 1 ★★★   C
Golf Courses: 6 private; 17 daily fee   AA
Bowling Lanes: 596   AA
Movie Theaters: 10   B
Outdoor Recreation Assets (57)
Inland Water Area: 11.1 square miles
Places Rated Score: 1,157   Places Rated Rank: 268

Casper, WY
Common Denominators (1,000)
Good Restaurants: 1 ★★   C
Golf Courses: 2 private; 0.5 daily fee; 1 municipal   B
Bowling Lanes: 70   A
Movie Theaters: 3   AA
Crowd Pleasers (400)
Professional Sports: 3.076 game seats per capita   AA
Wildcats (basketball)
Outdoor Recreation Assets (35)
Inland Water Area: 26.7 square miles
National Forests, Parks, Wildlife Refuges:
Medicine Bow NF (5,614 acres)
Pathfinder NWR (1,535 acres)
Places Rated Score: 1,435   Places Rated Rank: 221

Cedar Rapids, IA
Common Denominators (1,100)
Good Restaurants: 2 ★★   C
Golf Courses: 2.5 private; 3 daily fee; 3.5 municipal   AA
Bowling Lanes: 194   AA
Movie Theaters: 5   B
Crowd Pleasers (400)
Auto Racing: Hawkeye Downs (NASCAR)   C
Professional Sports: 2.474 game seats per capita   A
Reds (baseball)
Outdoor Recreation Assets (1)
Inland Water Area: .2 square miles
Places Rated Score: 1,501   Places Rated Rank: 209

Champaign–Urbana–Rantoul, IL
Common Denominators (1,300)
Good Restaurants: 1 ★, 6 ★★, 3 ★★★   AA
Golf Courses: 4 private; 2 daily fee; 2 municipal   B
Bowling Lanes: 128   A
Movie Theaters: 8   AA
Crowd Pleasers (400)
NCAA Division I: 3.357 game seats per capita   AA
University of Illinois Fighting Illini
Places Rated Score: 1,700   Places Rated Rank: 160

Charleston, SC
Common Denominators (900)
Good Restaurants: 1 ★, 2 ★★, 6 ★★★   A
Golf Courses: 12.5 private; 5.5 daily fee; 1 municipal   B
Bowling Lanes: 256   B
Movie Theaters: 12   B
Crowd Pleasers (400)
Professional Sports: 1.004 game seats per capita   B
Royals (baseball)
NCAA Division I: .494 game seats per capita   B
Baptist College Buccaneers (b), The Citadel Bulldogs
Outdoor Recreation Assets (1,261)
Atlantic Coastline: 75 miles
Inland Water Area: 217.1 square miles
National Forests, Parks, Wildlife Refuges:
Cape Romain NWR (34,049 acres)
Fort Sumter NM (67 acres)
Francis Marion NF (250,005 acres)
Santee NWR (2 acres)
Places Rated Score: 2,561   Places Rated Rank: 53

Rating

Charleston, WV
Common Denominators (800)
Good Restaurants: 3 ★★, 2 ★★★   B
Golf Courses: 5 private; 2 daily fee; 2 municipal   B
Bowling Lanes: 128   B
Movie Theaters: 7   B
Outdoor Recreation Assets (44)
Inland Water Area: 11.1 square miles
Places Rated Score: 844   Places Rated Rank: 306

Charlotte–Gastonia–Rock Hill, NC–SC
Common Denominators (600)
Good Restaurants: 3 ★★, 2 ★★★   C
Golf Courses: 21.5 private; 15.5 daily fee; 2.5 municipal   B
Bowling Lanes: 356   B
Movie Theaters: 20   C
Crowd Pleasers (600)
Theme Parks: Carowinds (121 days)   B
Auto Racing: Charlotte (SCCA, NASCAR)   C
Professional Sports: .754 game seats per capita   B
Charlotte O's, Gastonia Expos (baseball)
NCAA Division I: .207 game seats per capita   C
Davidson College Wildcats, University of North Carolina 49ers (b)
Outdoor Recreation Assets (36)
Inland Water Area: 20.2 square miles
National Forests, Parks, Wildlife Refuges:
Kings Mountain NMP (2,529 acres)
Places Rated Score: 1,236   Places Rated Rank: 255

Charlottesville, VA
Common Denominators (1,100)
Good Restaurants: 2 ★★, 3 ★★★   AA
Golf Courses: 3.5 private; 1 municipal   C
Bowling Lanes: 40   B
Movie Theaters: 8   AA
Crowd Pleasers (400)
NCAA Division I: 2.902 game seats per capita   AA
University of Virginia Cavaliers
Outdoor Recreation Assets (204)
Inland Water Area: .3 square miles
National Forests, Parks, Wildlife Refuges:
Appalachian Trail (926 acres)
Shenandoah NP (29,786 acres)
Places Rated Score: 1,704   Places Rated Rank: 157

Chattanooga, TN–GA
Common Denominators (700)
Good Restaurants: 4 ★, 8 ★★, 3 ★★★   A
Golf Courses: 8 private; 3.5 daily fee; 1.5 municipal   C
Bowling Lanes: 152   B
Movie Theaters: 6   C
Crowd Pleasers (400)
Professional Sports: 1.369 game seats per capita   B
Lookouts (baseball)
NCAA Division I: .465 game seats per capita   B
University of Tennessee Moccasins
Outdoor Recreation Assets (138)
Inland Water Area: 45.3 square miles
National Forests, Parks, Wildlife Refuges:
Chickamauga and Chattanooga NMP (8,085 acres)
Places Rated Score: 1,238   Places Rated Rank: 253

Chicago, IL
Common Denominators (1,000)
Good Restaurants: 18 ★, 94 ★★, 34 ★★★, 7 ★★★★, 2 ★★★★★   A
Golf Courses: 49 private; 59 daily fee; 33 municipal   A
Bowling Lanes: 4,328   B
Movie Theaters: 145   B

	Rating

Crowd Pleasers (1,100)
Zoos: **AA**
  Brookfield Zoo
  Lincoln Park Zoo
Aquariums: Shedd Aquarium **A**
Pari-mutuel Betting: **C**
  Arlington Park (Thoroughbred, 109 days)
  Associates (harness, 21 days)
  Egyptian Trotting (21 days)
  Hawthorne (harness, 48 days; Thoroughbred, 85 days)
  Maywood Park (harness, 76 days)
  Sportsman's Park (Thoroughbred, 75 days)
  Suburban Downs (harness, 48 days)
  Washington Park (harness, 27 days)
Professional Sports: 1.403 game seats per capita **B**
  CUBS, WHITE SOX (baseball), BULLS (basketball), BEARS (football), BLACK HAWKS (hockey)
NCAA Division I: .109 game seats per capita **C**
  DePaul University Blue Demons (b), Loyola University Ramblers (b), Northwestern University Wildcats, University of Illinois Flames (b)
Outdoor Recreation Assets (356)
Great Lakes Coastline: 33 miles
Inland Water Area: 9.6 square miles
National Forests, Parks, Wildlife Refuges:
  Chicago Portage NHS (91 acres)
CMSA Access: CHICAGO–GARY–LAKE COUNTY, IL–IN–WI (400)
Places Rated Score: 2,856   Places Rated Rank: 43

Chico, CA
Common Denominators (900)
Good Restaurants: 1 ★★★ **C**
Golf Courses: 1 private; 1 daily fee; 2 municipal **B**
Bowling Lanes: 74 **B**
Movie Theaters: 7 **AA**
Outdoor Recreation Assets (643)
Inland Water Area: 6.8 square miles
National Forests, Parks, Wildlife Refuges:
  Lassen NF (49,239 acres)
  Plumas NF (81,972 acres)
Places Rated Score: 1,543   Places Rated Rank: 194

Cincinnati, OH–KY–IN
Common Denominators (1,100)
Good Restaurants: 3 ★, 20 ★★, 21 ★★★, 2 ★★★★, 1 ★★★★★ **AA**
Golf Courses: 24.5 private; 10.5 daily fee; 16.5 municipal **B**
Bowling Lanes: 1,260 **A**
Movie Theaters: 43 **B**
Crowd Pleasers (1,200)
Zoos: Cincinnati Zoo **A**
Theme Parks: Kings Island (126 days) **C**
Pari-mutuel Betting: **A**
  Latonia (Thoroughbred, 131 days)
  Latonia Trots (67 days)
  Lebanon Raceway (harness, 65 days)
  Miami Valley Trotting (61 days)
  River Downs (Thoroughbred, 117 days)
Professional Sports: 3.369 game seats per capita **AA**
  REDS (baseball), BENGALS (football)
NCAA Division I: .291 game seats per capita **C**
  University of Cincinnati Bearcats, Xavier Musketeers (b)
Outdoor Recreation Assets (51)
Inland Water Area: 21.8 square miles
National Forests, Parks, Wildlife Refuges:
  William Howard Taft NHS (3 acres)
CMSA Access: CINCINNATI–HAMILTON, OH–KY–IN (100)
Places Rated Score: 2,451   Places Rated Rank: 61

Clarksville–Hopkinsville, TN–KY
Common Denominators (700)
Good Restaurants: 1 ★, 1 ★★★ **C**

	Rating

Golf Courses: 3.5 private; 2 municipal **B**
Bowling Lanes: 72 **B**
Movie Theaters: 4 **B**
Crowd Pleasers (300)
NCAA Division I: 1.111 game seats per capita **A**
  Austin Peay Governors
Outdoor Recreation Assets (1,219)
Inland Water Area: 4.8 square miles
National Forests, Parks, Wildlife Refuges:
  Cherokee NF (193,640 acres)
Places Rated Score: 2,219   Places Rated Rank: 82

★ Cleveland, OH
Common Denominators (1,200)
Good Restaurants: 3 ★, 24 ★★, 8 ★★★ **B**
Golf Courses: 27 private; 37 daily fee; 12 municipal **A**
Bowling Lanes: 2,076 **AA**
Movie Theaters: 63 **A**
Crowd Pleasers (1,200)
Zoos: Cleveland Metroparks Zoo **A**
Aquariums: Cleveland Aquarium **A**
Pari-mutuel Betting: Thistledown (Thoroughbred, 94 days) **C**
Professional Sports: 3.926 game seats per capita **AA**
  INDIANS (baseball), CAVALIERS (basketball), BROWNS (football)
NCAA Division I: .021 game seats per capita **C**
  Cleveland State Vikings (b)
Outdoor Recreation Assets (600)
Great Lakes Coastline: 56 miles
Inland Water Area: 2.1 square miles
National Forests, Parks, Wildlife Refuges:
  Cuyahoga Valley NRA (6,469 acres)
CMSA Access: CLEVELAND–AKRON–LORAIN, OH (300)
Places Rated Score: 3,300   Places Rated Rank: 23

Colorado Springs, CO
Common Denominators (1,200)
Good Restaurants: 3 ★, 6 ★★, 4 ★★★ **AA**
Golf Courses: 11.5 private; 1.5 daily fee; 2.5 municipal **B**
Bowling Lanes: 310 **A**
Movie Theaters: 11 **A**
Crowd Pleasers (800)
Zoos: Cheyenne Mountain Zoo **A**
Auto Racing: **B**
  Pikes Peak Hill Climb (SCCA)
  Colorado Springs International (NASCAR)
Pari-mutuel Betting: Rocky Mountain Greyhound Park (72 days) **B**
NCAA Division I: 1.006 game seats per capita **A**
  U.S. Air Force Academy Falcons
Outdoor Recreation Assets (375)
Inland Water Area: 2.1 square miles
National Forests, Parks, Wildlife Refuges:
  Pike NF (100,726 acres)
Places Rated Score: 2,375   Places Rated Rank: 67

Columbia, MO
Common Denominators (900)
Good Restaurants: 2 ★, 1 ★★ **B**
Golf Courses: 2.5 private; 1 daily fee; 2 municipal **B**
Bowling Lanes: 24 **C**
Movie Theaters: 6 **AA**
Crowd Pleasers (400)
NCAA Division I: 5.212 game seats per capita **AA**
  University of Missouri Tigers
Outdoor Recreation Assets (31)
Inland Water Area: 4.2 square miles
Places Rated Score: 1,331   Places Rated Rank: 244

Columbia, SC
Common Denominators (600)
Good Restaurants: 2 ★, 1 ★★ **C**
Golf Courses: 8.5 private; 4 daily fee; 1 municipal **B**

	Rating
Bowling Lanes: 140	B
Movie Theaters: 9	C

Crowd Pleasers (600)
- Zoos: Riverbanks Zoological Park — B
- Professional Sports: .702 game seats per capita — C
  Pros (baseball)
- NCAA Division I: 1.276 game seats per capita — A
  University of South Carolina Gamecocks

Outdoor Recreation Assets (284)
- Inland Water Area: 59.9 square miles
- National Forests, Parks, Wildlife Refuges:
  Congaree Swamp NM (15,138 acres)

Places Rated Score: 1,484 — Places Rated Rank: 211

Columbus, GA–AL
Common Denominators (900)
- Good Restaurants: 2 ★★★ — C
- Golf Courses: 4.5 private; 1 daily fee; 2 municipal — B
- Bowling Lanes: 172 — A
- Movie Theaters: 8 — A

Crowd Pleasers (300)
- Professional Sports: 1.831 game seats per capita — A
  Astros (baseball)

Outdoor Recreation Assets (14)
- Inland Water Area: 3 square miles

Places Rated Score: 1,214 — Places Rated Rank: 260

Columbus, OH
Common Denominators (1,100)
- Good Restaurants: 2 ★, 10 ★★, 6 ★★★ — B
- Golf Courses: 23 private, 26.5 daily fee; 5 — A
  municipal
- Bowling Lanes: 1,260 — A
- Movie Theaters: 41 — A

Crowd Pleasers (900)
- Zoos: Columbus Zoological Gardens — A
- Pari-mutuel Betting: — B
  Beulah Racetrack (Thoroughbred, 22 days)
  MARA (harness, 60 days)
  Scioto Downs (harness, 61 days)
- Professional Sports: .844 game seats per capita — B
  Clippers (baseball)
- NCAA Division I: .467 game seats per capita — B
  Ohio State Buckeyes

Outdoor Recreation Assets (20)
- Inland Water Area: 14.3 square miles

Places Rated Score: 2,020 — Places Rated Rank: 103

Corpus Christi, TX
Common Denominators (900)
- Good Restaurants: 3 ★, 3 ★★, 1 ★★★ — B
- Golf Courses: 5 private; 2 daily fee; 2 municipal — B
- Bowling Lanes: 172 — B
- Movie Theaters: 11 — A

Outdoor Recreation Assets (1,137)
- Gulf of Mexico Coastline: 25 miles
- Inland Water Area: 273.3 square miles

Places Rated Score: 2,037 — Places Rated Rank: 100

Cumberland, MD–WV
Common Denominators (1,000)
- Good Restaurants: 1 ★★, 1 ★★★ — AA
- Golf Courses: 2 private; 1 daily fee — C
- Bowling Lanes: 54 — B
- Movie Theaters: 4 — A

Outdoor Recreation Assets (36)
- National Forests, Parks, Wildlife Refuges:
  Chesapeake and Ohio Canal NHP (3,494 acres)

Places Rated Score: 1,036 — Places Rated Rank: 288

Dallas, TX
Common Denominators (700)
- Good Restaurants: 12 ★, 9 ★★, 15 ★★★, 3 ★★★★ — B
- Golf Courses: 33 private; 4.5 daily fee; — C
  15 municipal

	Rating
Bowling Lanes: 672	B
Movie Theaters: 54	B

Crowd Pleasers (1,100)
- Zoos: Dallas Zoo — A
- Aquariums: Dallas Aquarium — A
- Professional Sports: 2.331 game seats per capita — A
  MAVERICKS (basketball), COWBOYS (football)
- NCAA Division I: .347 game seats per capita — B
  North Texas State Mean Green, Southern
  Methodist Mustangs

Outdoor Recreation Assets (110)
- Inland Water Area: 98.8 square miles

CMSA Access: DALLAS–FORT WORTH, TX (400)

Places Rated Score: 2,310 — Places Rated Rank: 71

Danbury, CT
Common Denominators (1,000)
- Good Restaurants: 1 ★, 2 ★★, 3 ★★★ — AA
- Golf Courses: 3.5 private; 1 daily fee; 1.5 — B
  municipal
- Bowling Lanes: 70 — B
- Movie Theaters: 5 — B

Outdoor Recreation Assets (172)
- Inland Water Area: 9.9 square miles

CMSA Access: NEW YORK–NORTHERN NEW JERSEY–
  LONG ISLAND, NY–NJ–CT (400)

Places Rated Score: 1,572 — Places Rated Rank: 189

Danville, VA
Common Denominators (500)
- Golf Courses: 4 private; 1.5 daily fee — B
- Bowling Lanes: 46 — B
- Movie Theaters: 2 — C

Outdoor Recreation Assets (1)
- Inland Water Area: .1 square miles

Places Rated Score: 501 — Places Rated Rank: 328

Davenport–Rock Island–Moline, IA–IL
Common Denominators (1,400)
- Good Restaurants: 2 ★, 8 ★★, 1 ★★★ — A
- Golf Courses: 8 private; 3.5 daily fee; 7 municipal — A
- Bowling Lanes: 568 — AA
- Movie Theaters: 16 — AA

Crowd Pleasers (400)
- Zoos: Weed Park Zoo — C
- Professional Sports: 1.550 game seats per capita — A
  Quad City Cubs (baseball)

Outdoor Recreation Assets (120)
- Inland Water Area: 40.3 square miles
- National Forests, Parks, Wildlife Refuges:
  Upper Mississippi NWR (398 acres)

Places Rated Score: 1,920 — Places Rated Rank: 123

Dayton–Springfield, OH
Common Denominators (900)
- Good Restaurants: 5 ★★, 2 ★★★, 2 ★★★★ — C
- Golf Courses: 16.5 private; 6.5 daily fee; — B
  11 municipal
- Bowling Lanes: 1,118 — AA
- Movie Theaters: 25 — B

Crowd Pleasers (200)
- Zoos: — C
  Animal Fair
  Dayton Museum of Natural History
- NCAA Division I: .186 game seats per capita — C
  University of Dayton Flyers (b)

Outdoor Recreation Assets (22)
- Inland Water Area: 7.4 square miles

Places Rated Score: 1,122 — Places Rated Rank: 276

★ Daytona Beach, FL
Common Denominators (1,600)
- Good Restaurants: 1 ★, 7 ★★, 4 ★★★ — AA
- Golf Courses: 2 private; 9.5 daily fee; 3 municipal — AA
- Bowling Lanes: 498 — AA
- Movie Theaters: 11 — AA

	Rating
Crowd Pleasers (900)	
Auto Racing: Daytona International (SCCA, NASCAR)	C
Pari-mutuel Betting:	AA
Daytona Beach Kennel Club (106 days)	
Volusia Jai Alai (181 days)	
Professional Sports: 1.270 game seats per capita	B
Astros (baseball)	
NCAA Division I: .477 game seats per capita	B
Bethune-Cookman Wildcats, Stetson University	
Hatters (b)	

Outdoor Recreation Assets (1,467)
Atlantic Coastline: 49 miles
Inland Water Area: 145 square miles
National Forests, Parks, Wildlife Refuges:
  Canaveral NS (28,148 acres)
  Lake Woodruff NWR (18,225 acres)
Places Rated Score: 3,967   Places Rated Rank: 9

Decatur, IL

Common Denominators (1,100)	
Good Restaurants: 3 **	B
Golf Courses: 2 private; 0.5 daily fee; 3 municipal	A
Bowling Lanes: 156	AA
Movie Theaters: 3	B
Crowd Pleasers (100)	
Zoos: Scoville Farm Zoo	C

Outdoor Recreation Assets (22)
Inland Water Area: 2.6 square miles
Places Rated Score: 1,222   Places Rated Rank: 257

Denver, CO

Common Denominators (1,100)	
Good Restaurants: 5 *, 18 **, 9 ***, 1 ****	A
Golf Courses: 18.5 private; 4 daily fee; 16 municipal	B
Bowling Lanes: 1,332	
Movie Theaters: 47	
Crowd Pleasers (1,000)	
Zoos: Denver Zoological Gardens	A
Auto Racing: Continental Divide (SCCA)	C
Pari-mutuel Betting:	B
Centennial (Thoroughbred, 117 days)	
Mile High Kennel Club (72 days)	
Professional Sports: 5.890 game seats per capita	AA
Bears (baseball), NUGGETS (basketball), GOLD, BRONCOS (football), Colorado Flames (hockey)	

Outdoor Recreation Assets (24)
Inland Water Area: 18.3 square miles
CMSA Access: DENVER–BOULDER, CO (200)
Places Rated Score: 2,324   Places Rated Rank: 69

Des Moines, IA

Common Denominators (1,200)	
Good Restaurants: 2 *, 7 **	B
Golf Courses: 8.5 private; 6.5 daily fee; 4.5 municipal	A
Bowling Lanes: 266	A
Movie Theaters: 26	AA
Crowd Pleasers (600)	
Professional Sports: 1.592 game seats per capita	A
Cubs (baseball)	
NCAA Division I: .722 game seats per capita	A
Drake University Bulldogs	

Outdoor Recreation Assets (2)
Inland Water Area: .8 square miles
Places Rated Score: 1,802   Places Rated Rank: 144

Detroit, MI

Common Denominators (700)	
Good Restaurants: 11 *, 35 **, 6 ***, 1 ****	C
Golf Courses: 40 private; 78 daily fee; 26 municipal	B
Bowling Lanes: 4,517	A
Movie Theaters: 80	C

	Rating
Crowd Pleasers (1,000)	
Zoos:	AA
Belle Isle Zoo and Aquarium	
Detroit Zoological Park	
Auto Racing: Mount Clemens Race Track (NASCAR)	C
Pari-mutuel Betting:	C
Detroit Race Course (Thoroughbred, 90 days)	
Hazel Park (harness, 84 days; Thoroughbred, 108 days)	
Northville Downs (harness, 78 days)	
Wolverine Raceway (harness, 84 days)	
Professional Sports: 1.538 game seats per capita	A
TIGERS (baseball), Spirits, PISTONS (basketball), LIONS (football), RED WINGS (hockey)	
NCAA Division I: .029 game seats per capita	C
University of Detroit Titans (b)	

Outdoor Recreation Assets (583)
Great Lakes Coastline: 48 miles
Inland Water Area: 92.9 square miles
CMSA Access: DETROIT–ANN ARBOR, MI (200)
Places Rated Score: 2,483   Places Rated Rank: 58

Dothan, AL

Common Denominators (700)	
Good Restaurants: 1 **, 1 ***	B
Golf Courses: 3 private; 1 daily fee	C
Bowling Lanes: 56	B
Movie Theaters: 3	B

Outdoor Recreation Assets (14)
Inland Water Area: 3.3 square miles
Places Rated Score: 714   Places Rated Rank: 321

Dubuque, IA

Common Denominators (1,500)	
Good Restaurants: 4 **	AA
Golf Courses: 2.5 private; 1 daily fee; 1.5 municipal	A
Bowling Lanes: 132	AA
Movie Theaters: 5	AA

Outdoor Recreation Assets (87)
Inland Water Area: 9.8 square miles
National Forests, Parks, Wildlife Refuges:
  Upper Mississippi NWR (476 acres)
Places Rated Score: 1,587   Places Rated Rank: 187

Duluth, MN–WI

Common Denominators (1,500)	
Good Restaurants: 1 *, 8 **, 2 ***	AA
Golf Courses: 4 private; 2 daily fee; 5.5 municipal	A
Bowling Lanes: 284	AA
Movie Theaters: 14	AA
Crowd Pleasers (100)	
Zoos: Duluth Zoological Gardens	C

Outdoor Recreation Assets (1,507)
Great Lakes Coastline: 36 miles
Inland Water Area: 656.1 square miles
National Forests, Parks, Wildlife Refuges:
  Superior NF (670,753 acres)
Places Rated Score: 3,107   Places Rated Rank: 30

East St. Louis–Belleville, IL

Common Denominators (800)	
Good Restaurants: 1 **, 1 ***	C
Golf Courses: 3 private; 6 daily fee; 1 municipal	B
Bowling Lanes: 242	A
Movie Theaters: 9	B
Crowd Pleasers (400)	
Pari-mutuel Betting: Fairmount Park (Thoroughbred, 165 days)	AA

Outdoor Recreation Assets (10)
Inland Water Area: 2.3 square miles
CMSA Access: St. Louis–East St. Louis–Alton, MO–IL (400)
Places Rated Score: 1,610   Places Rated Rank: 177

Rating

Eau Claire, WI
Common Denominators (1,300)
- Good Restaurants: 2 ★, 4 ★★, 1 ★★★ — AA
- Golf Courses: 2.5 private; 2 daily fee — B
- Bowling Lanes: 128 — A
- Movie Theaters: 8 — AA

Outdoor Recreation Assets (97)
- Inland Water Area: 32.1 square miles

Places Rated Score: 1,397   Places Rated Rank: 235

El Paso, TX
Common Denominators (500)
- Golf Courses: 5 private; 2.5 municipal — C
- Bowling Lanes: 262 — B
- Movie Theaters: 12 — B

Crowd Pleasers (600)
- Zoos: El Paso Zoological Park — C
- Professional Sports: .992 game seats per capita — B
  Diablos (baseball)
- NCAA Division I: .877 game seats per capita — A
  University of Texas Miners

Outdoor Recreation Assets (1)
- National Forests, Parks, Wildlife Refuges:
  Chamizal National Memorial (55 acres)

Places Rated Score: 1,101   Places Rated Rank: 281

Elkhart–Goshen, IN
Common Denominators (1,000)
- Good Restaurants: 1 ★, 1 ★★, 1 ★★★ — B
- Golf Courses: 3 private; 1.5 daily fee; 1.5 — B
  municipal
- Bowling Lanes: 148 — AA
- Movie Theaters: 4 — B

Outdoor Recreation Assets (23)
- Inland Water Area: 2.1 square miles

Places Rated Score: 1,023   Places Rated Rank: 289

Elmira, NY
Common Denominators (1,300)
- Good Restaurants: 1 ★, 2 ★★, 1 ★★★★ — AA
- Golf Courses: 1 private; 3.5 daily fee; 1 municipal — AA
- Bowling Lanes: 148 — AA
- Movie Theaters: 2 — C

Crowd Pleasers (300)
- Professional Sports: 1.985 game seats per capita — A
  Suns (baseball)

Places Rated Score: 1,600   Places Rated Rank: 185

Enid, OK
Common Denominators (1,200)
- Good Restaurants: 1 ★, 1 ★★★ — A
- Golf Courses: 1 private; 0.5 daily fee — C
- Bowling Lanes: 68 — AA
- Movie Theaters: 3 — AA

Places Rated Score: 1,200   Places Rated Rank: 264

Erie, PA
Common Denominators (1,200)
- Good Restaurants: 1 ★, 2 ★★ — C
- Golf Courses: 4 private; 7 daily fee; 3.5 municipal — AA
- Bowling Lanes: 410 — AA
- Movie Theaters: 9 — A

Crowd Pleasers (100)
- Zoos: Erie Zoo — C

Outdoor Recreation Assets (40)
- Inland Water Area: 6.4 square miles

Places Rated Score: 1,340   Places Rated Rank: 243

★ Eugene–Springfield, OR
Common Denominators (900)
- Good Restaurants: 2 ★, 4 ★★, 3 ★★★ — A
- Golf Courses: 2.5 private; 4.5 daily fee; 0.5 — B
  municipal
- Bowling Lanes: 166 — B
- Movie Theaters: 8 — B

Crowd Pleasers (500)
- Professional Sports: .860 game seats per capita — B
  Emeralds (baseball)
- NCAA Division I: 1.235 game seats per capita — A
  University of Oregon Ducks

Outdoor Recreation Assets (2,000)
- Pacific Coastline: 30 miles
- Inland Water Area: 48.1 square miles
- National Forests, Parks, Wildlife Refuges:
  Oregon Islands NWR (6 acres)
  Siuslaw NF (242,790 acres)
  Umpqua NF (151,588 acres)
  Willamette NF (1,021,769 acres)

Places Rated Score: 3,400   Places Rated Rank: 19

Evansville, IN–KY
Common Denominators (700)
- Good Restaurants: 2 ★★, 1 ★★★ — C
- Golf Courses: 5 private; 3.5 daily fee; 3 municipal — B
- Bowling Lanes: 184 — B
- Movie Theaters: 8 — B

Crowd Pleasers (800)
- Zoos: Mesker Park Zoo — C
- Pari-mutuel Betting: — A
  Audubon Raceway (harness, 46 days)
  Ellis Park (Thoroughbred, 59 days)
- Professional Sports: 1.477 game seats per capita — B
  Triplets (baseball)
- NCAA Division I: .579 game seats per capita — B
  University of Evansville Purple Aces (b)

Outdoor Recreation Assets (122)
- Inland Water Area: 36 square miles

Places Rated Score: 1,622   Places Rated Rank: 173

Fall River, MA–RI
Common Denominators (700)
- Good Restaurants: 1 ★★ — C
- Golf Courses: 2.5 private; 1.5 daily fee — C
- Bowling Lanes: 64 — B
- Movie Theaters: 5 — A

Outdoor Recreation Assets (1,005)
- Atlantic Coastline: 18 miles
- Inland Water Area: 27.9 square miles

CMSA Access: PROVIDENCE–PAWTUCKET–
FALL RIVER, RI–MA (300)

Places Rated Score: 2,005   Places Rated Rank: 105

Fargo–Moorhead, ND–MN
Common Denominators (1,400)
- Good Restaurants: 2 ★, 3 ★★ — A
- Golf Courses: 3.5 private; 1.5 daily fee; 2.5 — A
  municipal
- Bowling Lanes: 154 — AA
- Movie Theaters: 6 — AA

Outdoor Recreation Assets (14)
- Inland Water Area: 7.7 square miles

Places Rated Score: 1,414   Places Rated Rank: 227

Fayetteville, NC
Common Denominators (700)
- Good Restaurants: 1 ★★ — C
- Golf Courses: 5 private; 3 daily fee — B
- Bowling Lanes: 192 — A
- Movie Theaters: 4 — C

Outdoor Recreation Assets (9)
- Inland Water Area: 1.2 square miles

Places Rated Score: 709   Places Rated Rank: 322

Fayetteville–Springdale, AR
Common Denominators (1,100)
- Good Restaurants: 1 ★, 1 ★★, 1 ★★★ — A
- Golf Courses: 1 private; 2 daily fee — B
- Bowling Lanes: 92 — A
- Movie Theaters: 4 — A

	Rating
Crowd Pleasers (400)	
NCAA Division I: 3.533 game seats per capita	**AA**
University of Arkansas Razorbacks	
Outdoor Recreation Assets (195)	
Inland Water Area: .8 square miles	
National Forests, Parks, Wildlife Refuges:	
Ozark NF (23,247 acres)	
Places Rated Score: 1,695	**Places Rated Rank: 161**

Fitchburg–Leominster, MA

	Rating
Common Denominators (400)	
Good Restaurants: 1★★★	**B**
Golf Courses: 1 private; 3 daily fee	**A**
Movie Theaters: 2	**C**
Outdoor Recreation Assets (190)	
Inland Water Area: 6.8 square miles	
Places Rated Score: 790	**Places Rated Rank: 317**

Flint, MI

	Rating
Common Denominators (1,000)	
Good Restaurants: 1 ★, 1 ★★, 1 ★★★	**C**
Golf Courses: 10 private; 8 daily fee; 4 municipal	**A**
Bowling Lanes: 612	**AA**
Movie Theaters: 12	**B**
Crowd Pleasers (300)	
Auto Racing:	**B**
Auto City (NASCAR)	
Waterford Hills (SCCA)	
Professional Sports: .390 game seats per capita	**C**
Generals (hockey)	
Outdoor Recreation Assets (55)	
Inland Water Area: 7 square miles	
Places Rated Score: 1,355	**Places Rated Rank: 241**

Florence, AL

	Rating
Common Denominators (600)	
Good Restaurants: 3 ★★	**B**
Golf Courses: 4.5 private; 0.5 daily fee; 2.5 municipal	**B**
Bowling Lanes: 36	**C**
Movie Theaters: 3	**C**
Outdoor Recreation Assets (394)	
Inland Water Area: 92.1 square miles	
National Forests, Parks, Wildlife Refuges:	
Natchez Trace Parkway (4,176 acres)	
Places Rated Score: 994	**Places Rated Rank: 294**

Florence, SC

	Rating
Common Denominators (400)	
Golf Courses: 5 private; 1 daily fee	**C**
Bowling Lanes: 24	**C**
Movie Theaters: 3	**B**
Crowd Pleasers (400)	
Auto Racing: Darlington Raceway (NASCAR)	**C**
Professional Sports: 2.446 game seats per capita	**A**
Blue Jays (baseball)	
Places Rated Score: 800	**Places Rated Rank: 314**

★ Fort Collins–Loveland, CO

	Rating
Common Denominators (1,400)	
Good Restaurants: 1 ★, 4 ★★, 4 ★★★	**AA**
Golf Courses: 2 private; 3.5 municipal	**B**
Bowling Lanes: 160	**AA**
Movie Theaters: 6	**AA**
Crowd Pleasers (800)	
Pari-mutuel Betting: Cloverleaf Kennel Club (69 days)	**AA**
NCAA Division I: 1.877 game seats per capita	**AA**
Colorado State Rams	
Outdoor Recreation Assets (2,000)	
Inland Water Area: 29.7 square miles	
National Forests, Parks, Wildlife Refuges:	
Rocky Mountain NP (143,434 acres)	
Roosevelt NF (623,134 acres)	
Places Rated Score: 4,200	**Places Rated Rank: 4**

Fort Lauderdale–Hollywood–Pompano Beach, FL

	Rating
Common Denominators (1,200)	
Good Restaurants: 9 ★, 16 ★★, 21 ★★★, 1 ★★★★	**AA**
Golf Courses: 20 private; 25 daily fee; 4 municipal	**A**
Bowling Lanes: 802	**A**
Movie Theaters: 23	**B**
Crowd Pleasers (600)	
Zoos: Markham Park Zoo	**C**
Pari-mutuel Betting:	**AA**
Dania Jai Alai (290 days)	
Gulfstream Park (Thoroughbred, 50 days)	
Hollywood Greyhound Track (105 days)	
Pompano Park (harness, 108 days)	
Professional Sports: .538 game seats per capita	**C**
Yankees (baseball)	
Outdoor Recreation Assets (255)	
Atlantic Coastline: 25 miles	
Inland Water Area: 1.3 square miles	
CMSA Access: MIAMI–FORT LAUDERDALE, FL (400)	
Places Rated Score: 2,455	**Places Rated Rank: 60**

★ Fort Myers, FL

	Rating
Common Denominators (1,500)	
Good Restaurants: 7 ★, 10 ★★, 3 ★★★	**AA**
Golf Courses: 8.5 private; 9 daily fee; 2 municipal	**AA**
Bowling Lanes: 266	**AA**
Movie Theaters: 7	**A**
Crowd Pleasers (700)	
Pari-mutuel Betting: Naples–Fort Myers Kennel Club (109 days)	**AA**
Professional Sports: 1.849 game seats per capita	**A**
Royals (baseball)	
Outdoor Recreation Assets (1,805)	
Gulf of Mexico Coastline: 38 miles	
Inland Water Area: 220 square miles	
National Forests, Parks, Wildlife Refuges:	
Caloosahatchee NWR (140 acres)	
J.N. "Ding" Darling NWR (4,960 acres)	
Matlacha Pass NWR (231 acres)	
Pine Island NWR (404 acres)	
Places Rated Score: 4,005	**Places Rated Rank: 6**

Fort Pierce, FL

	Rating
Common Denominators (900)	
Good Restaurants: 2 ★★	**C**
Golf Courses: 12 private; 6 daily fee	**AA**
Bowling Lanes: 92	**B**
Movie Theaters: 4	**B**
Crowd Pleasers (400)	
Pari-mutuel Betting: Fort Pierce Jai Alai (180 days)	**AA**
Outdoor Recreation Assets (758)	
Atlantic Coastline: 45 miles	
Inland Water Area: 68.4 square miles	
National Forests, Parks, Wildlife Refuges:	
Hobe Sound NWR (960 acres)	
Places Rated Score: 2,058	**Places Rated Rank: 97**

Fort Smith, AR–OK

	Rating
Common Denominators (1,200)	
Good Restaurants: 1 ★, 3 ★★, 1 ★★★	**A**
Golf Courses: 2.5 private; 4.5 daily fee; 1 municipal	**AA**
Bowling Lanes: 96	**B**
Movie Theaters: 6	**A**
Outdoor Recreation Assets (536)	
Inland Water Area: 37.8 square miles	
National Forests, Parks, Wildlife Refuges:	
Fort Smith NHS (23 acres)	
Ouachita NF (15,128 acres)	
Ozark NF (84,547 acres)	
Places Rated Score: 1,736	**Places Rated Rank: 152**

Fort Walton Beach, FL

	Rating
Common Denominators (1,400)	
Good Restaurants: 4 ★★, 1 ★★★	**AA**

	Rating
Golf Courses: 2.5 private; 6.5 daily fee; 1.5 municipal	AA
Bowling Lanes: 92	A
Movie Theaters: 4	A

Outdoor Recreation Assets (692)
   Gulf of Mexico Coastline: 24 miles
   Inland Water Area: 58.7 square miles
   National Forests, Parks, Wildlife Refuges:
      Choctawhatchee NF (675 acres)
      Gulf Islands NS (15,910 acres)

Places Rated Score: 2,092   Places Rated Rank: 94

Fort Wayne, IN
Common Denominators (1,300)

	Rating
Good Restaurants: 2 ★★, 1 ★★★, 1 ★★★★	B
Golf Courses: 5 private; 11 daily fee; 1 municipal	AA
Bowling Lanes: 428	AA
Movie Theaters: 13	A

Crowd Pleasers: (400)

	Rating
Zoos: Fort Wayne Children's Zoo	C
Auto Racing: Allen County Memorial Coliseum (USAC)	C
Professional Sports: .906 game seats per capita Komets (hockey)	B

Outdoor Recreation Assets (11)
   Inland Water Area: 2.9 square miles

Places Rated Score: 1,711   Places Rated Rank: 156

Fort Worth–Arlington, TX
Common Denominators (800)

	Rating
Good Restaurants: 5 ★, 21 ★★, 5 ★★★	A
Golf Courses: 20 private; 1 daily fee; 8 municipal	C
Bowling Lanes: 404	B
Movie Theaters: 29	B

Crowd Pleasers (1,100)

	Rating
Zoos: Fort Worth Zoological Park	A
Theme Parks: Six Flags Over Texas (146 days)	B
Professional Sports: 4.161 game seats per capita TEXAS RANGERS (baseball)	AA
NCAA Division I: .466 game seats per capita Texas Christian Horned Frogs, University of Texas Mavericks	B

Outdoor Recreation Assets (66)
   Inland Water Area: 33 square miles
CMSA Access: DALLAS–FORT WORTH, TX (400)

Places Rated Score: 2,366   Places Rated Rank: 68

Fresno, CA
Common Denominators (700)

	Rating
Good Restaurants: 4 ★★, 1 ★★★	C
Golf Courses: 6 private; 5.5 daily fee; 2 municipal	B
Bowling Lanes: 97	C
Movie Theaters: 20	A

Crowd Pleasers (500)

	Rating
Zoos: Roeding Park Zoo	B
Professional Sports: .354 game seats per capita Giants (baseball)	C
NCAA Division I: .456 game seats per capita California State Bulldogs	B

Outdoor Recreation Assets (1,784)
   Inland Water Area: 37.6 square miles
   National Forests, Parks, Wildlife Refuges:
      Kings Canyon NP (354,828 acres)
      Sequoia NF (130,641 acres)
      Sierra NF (855,231 acres)

Places Rated Score: 2,984   Places Rated Rank: 36

Gadsden, AL
Common Denominators (300)

	Rating
Golf Courses: 4 private	—
Bowling Lanes: 32	C
Movie Theaters: 3	B

Places Rated Score: 300   Places Rated Rank: 329

Gainesville, FL
Common Denominators (500)

	Rating
Good Restaurants: 2 ★, 1 ★★★	C
Golf Courses: 3 private; 1.5 daily fee	C
Bowling Lanes: 56	C
Movie Theaters: 5	B

Crowd Pleasers (500)

	Rating
Zoos: Santa Fe Teaching Zoo Skye Hye Zoological Park	C
NCAA Division I: 3.011 game seats per capita University of Florida Gators	AA

Outdoor Recreation Assets (237)
   Inland Water Area: 56.6 square miles

Places Rated Score: 1,237   Places Rated Rank: 254

Galveston–Texas City, TX
Common Denominators (700)

	Rating
Good Restaurants: 1 ★, 2 ★★, 2 ★★★	A
Golf Courses: 3.5 private; 2 daily fee; 2 municipal	B
Bowling Lanes: 32	C
Movie Theaters: 3	C

Outdoor Recreation Assets (2,000)
   Gulf of Mexico Coastline: 25 miles
   Inland Water Area: 165 square miles
CMSA Access: HOUSTON–GALVESTON–BRAZORIA, TX (300)

Places Rated Score: 3,000   Places Rated Rank: 33

Gary–Hammond, IN
Common Denominators (1,000)

	Rating
Good Restaurants: 3 ★, 4 ★★, 3 ★★★	B
Golf Courses: 7 private; 14.5 daily fee; 4 municipal	A
Bowling Lanes: 617	A
Movie Theaters: 16	B

Crowd Pleasers (100)

	Rating
NCAA Division I: .087 game seats per capita Valparaiso Crusaders (b)	C

Outdoor Recreation Assets (440)
   Great Lakes Coastline: 32 miles
   Inland Water Area: 5 square miles
   National Forests, Parks, Wildlife Refuges:
      Indiana Dunes National Lakeshore (10,948 acres)
CMSA Access: CHICAGO–GARY–LAKE COUNTY, IL–IN–WI (400)

Places Rated Score: 1,940   Places Rated Rank: 118

Glens Falls, NY
Common Denominators (1,300)

	Rating
Good Restaurants: 2 ★, 4 ★★, 4 ★★★	AA
Golf Courses: 1 private; 5 daily fee	AA
Bowling Lanes: 146	AA
Movie Theaters: 2	C

Crowd Pleasers (400)

	Rating
Professional Sports: 9.421 game seats per capita White Sox (baseball), Adirondack Reds (hockey)	AA

Outdoor Recreation Assets (183)
   Inland Water Area: 63 square miles

Places Rated Score: 1,883   Places Rated Rank: 130

Grand Forks, ND
Common Denominators (1,300)

	Rating
Good Restaurants: 1 ★, 1 ★★	B
Golf Courses: 1.5 private; 1.5 daily fee; 1 municipal	AA
Bowling Lanes: 54	A
Movie Theaters: 6	AA

Outdoor Recreation Assets (4)
   National Forests, Parks, Wildlife Refuges:
      Kelly's Slough NWR (680 acres)

Places Rated Score: 1,304   Places Rated Rank: 248

Grand Rapids, MI
Common Denominators (1,400)

	Rating
Good Restaurants: 5 ★, 17 ★★, 4 ★★★, 1 ★★★★	AA

	Rating
Golf Courses: 9 private; 33.5 daily fee; 2 municipal	**AA**
Bowling Lanes: 674	**AA**
Movie Theaters: 16	**B**

Crowd Pleasers (200)

Zoos: John Ball Zoological Gardens	**B**

Outdoor Recreation Assets (309)

Great Lakes Coastline: 24 miles
Inland Water Area: 19.6 square miles

Places Rated Score: 1,909   Places Rated Rank: 127

Great Falls, MT
Common Denominators (1,400)

Good Restaurants: 3 ★★	**AA**
Golf Courses: 1 private; 1.5 municipal	**B**
Bowling Lanes: 114	**AA**
Movie Theaters: 4	**AA**

Crowd Pleasers (200)

Professional Sports: 1.490 game seats per capita	**B**
Dodgers (baseball)	

Outdoor Recreation Assets (576)

Inland Water Area: 12.4 square miles
National Forests, Parks, Wildlife Refuges:
   Benton Lake NWR (11,955 acres)
   Lewis and Clark NF (197,103 acres)

Places Rated Score: 2,176   Places Rated Rank: 83

Greeley, CO
Common Denominators (700)

Good Restaurants: 1 ★, 1 ★★★	**B**
Golf Courses: 2 private; 1 municipal	**C**
Bowling Lanes: 78	**B**
Movie Theaters: 3	**B**

Outdoor Recreation Assets (39)

Inland Water Area: 31.5 square miles

Places Rated Score: 739   Places Rated Rank: 319

Green Bay, WI
Common Denominators (1,300)

Good Restaurants: 1 ★, 4 ★★	**A**
Golf Courses: 1 private; 6.5 daily fee; 1 municipal	**AA**
Bowling Lanes: 360	**AA**
Movie Theaters: 5	**B**

Crowd Pleasers (400)

Professional Sports: 1.282 game seats per capita	**B**
PACKERS (football)	
NCAA Division I: .445 game seats per capita	**B**
University of Wisconsin Phoenix (b)	

Outdoor Recreation Assets (225)

Great Lakes Coastline: 18 miles
Inland Water Area: 4.7 square miles

Places Rated Score: 1,925   Places Rated Rank: 121

Greensboro–Winston-Salem–High Point, NC
Common Denominators (800)

Good Restaurants: 2 ★★	**C**
Golf Courses: 19 private; 20 daily fee; 9 municipal	**AA**
Bowling Lanes: 314	**B**
Movie Theaters: 12	**C**

Crowd Pleasers (800)

Zoos: North Carolina Zoological Park	**B**
Auto Racing:	**B**
Bowman Gray Stadium (NASCAR)	
Caraway (NASCAR)	
Professional Sports: 1.200 game seats per capita	**B**
Greensboro Hornets, Winston-Salem Spirits (baseball)	
NCAA Division I: .524 game seats per capita	**B**
North Carolina A & T Aggies, Wake Forest Demon Deacons	

Outdoor Recreation Assets (51)

Inland Water Area: 19.3 square miles
National Forests, Parks, Wildlife Refuges:
   Guilford Courthouse NMP (220 acres)
   Uwharrie NF (9,807 acres)

Places Rated Score: 1,651   Places Rated Rank: 167

	Rating

Greenville–Spartanburg, SC
Common Denominators (700)

Good Restaurants: 3 ★★, 1 ★★★	**C**
Golf Courses: 12 private; 12.5 daily fee	**B**
Bowling Lanes: 234	**B**
Movie Theaters: 16	**B**

Crowd Pleasers (700)

Zoos: Greenville Zoo	**C**
Auto Racing: Greenville–Pickens Speedway (NASCAR)	**C**
Professional Sports: 1.344 game seats per capita	**B**
Greenville Braves, Spartanburg Suns (baseball)	
NCAA Division I: 1.004 game seats per capita	**A**
Clemson Tigers, Furman Paladins	

Outdoor Recreation Assets (10)

Inland Water Area: 4.3 square miles

Places Rated Score: 1,410   Places Rated Rank: 230

Hagerstown, MD
Common Denominators (800)

Good Restaurants: 1 ★, 2 ★★	**B**
Golf Courses: 2 private; 0.5 municipal	**C**
Bowling Lanes: 42	**B**
Movie Theaters: 4	**A**

Crowd Pleasers (400)

Professional Sports: 3.714 game seats per capita	**AA**
Suns (baseball)	

Outdoor Recreation Assets (291)

Inland Water Area: 12.1 square miles
National Forests, Parks, Wildlife Refuges:
   Antietam National Battlefield (1,764 acres)
   Appalachian Trail (22 acres)
   Catoctin Mountain Park (75 acres)
   Chesapeake and Ohio Canal NHP (6,557 acres)
   Harper's Ferry NHP (765 acres)

Places Rated Score: 1,491   Places Rated Rank: 210

Hamilton–Middletown, OH
Common Denominators (900)

Golf Courses: 4.5 private; 6.5 daily fee; 4 municipal	**AA**
Bowling Lanes: 236	**A**
Movie Theaters: 6	**B**

Crowd Pleasers (300)

NCAA Division I: .750 game seats per capita	**A**
Miami University Redskins	

Outdoor Recreation Assets (4)

Inland Water Area: .4 square miles

CMSA Access: CINCINNATI–HAMILTON, OH–KY–IN (400)

Places Rated Score: 1,604   Places Rated Rank: 182

Harrisburg–Lebanon–Carlisle, PA
Common Denominators (800)

Good Restaurants: 4 ★★, 1 ★★★	**C**
Golf Courses: 10 private; 13 daily fee; 2 municipal	**A**
Bowling Lanes: 496	**A**
Movie Theaters: 9	**C**

Crowd Pleasers (600)

Theme Parks: Hersheypark (120 days)	**A**
Pari-mutuel Betting: Penn National (Thoroughbred, 92 days)	**B**
Professional Sports: .525 game seats per capita	**C**
Hershey Bears (hockey)	

Outdoor Recreation Assets (132)

Inland Water Area: 32.6 square miles
National Forests, Parks, Wildlife Refuges:
   Appalachian Trail (8,363 acres)

Places Rated Score: 1,532   Places Rated Rank: 198

Hartford, CT
Common Denominators (1,000)

Good Restaurants: 1 ★, 7 ★★, 6 ★★★, 1 ★★★★	**A**
Golf Courses: 15 private; 13.5 daily fee; 5.5 municipal	**A**
Bowling Lanes: 386	**B**
Movie Theaters: 17	**B**

Rating

Crowd Pleasers (600)
Zoos: Children's Zoo **C**
Pari-mutuel Betting: Hartford Jai Alai (300 days) **A**
Professional Sports: .848 game seats per capita **B**
WHALERS (hockey)
Outdoor Recreation Assets (90)
Inland Water Area: 19.4 square miles
CMSA Access: HARTFORD–NEW BRITAIN–
MIDDLETOWN, CT (100)
Places Rated Score: 1,790   Places Rated Rank: 146

Hickory, NC
Common Denominators (600)
Good Restaurants: 1 ★★ **C**
Golf Courses: 5.5 private; 4.5 daily fee **B**
Bowling Lanes: 80 **B**
Movie Theaters: 3 **C**
Crowd Pleasers (100)
Auto Racing: Hickory (NASCAR) **C**
Outdoor Recreation Assets (97)
Inland Water Area: 22.6 square miles
Places Rated Score: 797   Places Rated Rank: 315

★ **Honolulu, HI**
Common Denominators (1,000)
Good Restaurants: NA **A**
Golf Courses: 11 private; 10 daily fee; 3.5 **B**
municipal
Bowling Lanes: 534 **B**
Movie Theaters: 29 **A**
Crowd Pleasers (1,200)
Zoos: Honolulu Zoo **A**
Aquariums: Waikiki Aquarium **A**
Professional Sports: 4.721 game seats per capita **AA**
Islanders (baseball)
NCAA Division I: .457 game seats per capita **B**
University of Hawaii Rainbow Warriors
Outdoor Recreation Assets (1,503)
Pacific Coastline: 135 miles
Inland Water Area: 15.2 square miles
National Forests, Parks, Wildlife Refuges:
Hawaiian Islands NWR (1,907 acres)
Places Rated Score: 3,703   Places Rated Rank: 15

Houma–Thibodaux, LA
Common Denominators (500)
Golf Courses: 2 private; 0.5 daily fee **C**
Bowling Lanes: 70 **B**
Movie Theaters: 4 **B**
Crowd Pleasers (200)
NCAA Division I: .612 game seats per capita **B**
Nicholls State Colonels
Outdoor Recreation Assets (2,000)
Gulf of Mexico Coastline: 79 miles
Inland Water Area: 632.8 square miles
Places Rated Score: 2,700   Places Rated Rank: 47

Houston, TX
Common Denominators (800)
Good Restaurants: 8 ★, 26 ★★, 31 ★★★, 1 ★★★★ **A**
Golf Courses: 50 private; 9.5 daily fee; 7 municipal **C**
Bowling Lanes: 1,190 **B**
Movie Theaters: 67 **B**
Crowd Pleasers (900)
Zoos: Houston Zoological Gardens **A**
Theme Parks: Astroworld (159 days) **C**
Professional Sports: 1.764 game seats per capita **A**
ASTROS (baseball), ROCKETS (basketball),
GAMBLERS, OILERS (football)
NCAA Division I: .323 game seats per capita **B**
Houston Baptist Huskies (b), Rice Owls, Texas
Southern Tigers (b), University of Houston
Cougars
Outdoor Recreation Assets (125)
Inland Water Area: 57.6 square miles

Rating

National Forests, Parks, Wildlife Refuges:
Big Thicket National Preserve (1,348 acres)
Sam Houston NF (47,358 acres)
Places Rated Score: 1,825   Places Rated Rank: 138

Huntington–Ashland, WV–KY–OH
Common Denominators (600)
Good Restaurants: 2 ★★★ **C**
Golf Courses: 4.5 private; 7.5 daily fee; 0.5 **B**
municipal
Bowling Lanes: 146 **B**
Movie Theaters: 5 **C**
Crowd Pleasers (200)
NCAA Division I: .664 game seats per capita **B**
Marshall Thundering Herd
Outdoor Recreation Assets (40)
Inland Water Area: 17.1 square miles
Places Rated Score: 840   Places Rated Rank: 308

Huntsville, AL
Common Denominators (900)
Good Restaurants: 4 ★★, 1 ★★★ **A**
Golf Courses: 3.5 private; 2.5 daily fee; 2 **B**
municipal
Bowling Lanes: 118 **B**
Movie Theaters: 6 **B**
Crowd Pleasers (100)
Auto Racing: Huntsville International (NASCAR) **C**
Outdoor Recreation Assets (75)
Inland Water Area: 7.4 square miles
National Forests, Parks, Wildlife Refuges:
Wheeler NWR (3,019 acres)
Places Rated Score: 1,075   Places Rated Rank: 284

Indianapolis, IN
Common Denominators (900)
Good Restaurants: 2 ★, 6 ★★ 4 ★★★, 2 ★★★★ **C**
Golf Courses: 21 private; 15.5 daily fee; 11.5 **B**
municipal
Bowling Lanes: 1,084 **A**
Movie Theaters: 36 **A**
Crowd Pleasers (1,000)
Zoos: Indianapolis Zoo **C**
Auto Racing: **AA**
Indiana State Fairgrounds (USAC)
Indianapolis Motor Speedway (USAC)
Indianapolis Raceway (SCCA, USAC)
Speedrome (USAC)
Professional Sports: 2.154 game seats per capita **A**
Indians (baseball), PACERS (basketball),
COLTS (football), Checkers (hockey)
NCAA Division I: .167 game seats per capita **C**
Butler University Bulldogs (b)
Outdoor Recreation Assets (6)
Inland Water Area: 3.8 square miles
Places Rated Score: 1,906   Places Rated Rank: 128

Iowa City, IA
Common Denominators (1,100)
Good Restaurants: 2 ★★ **B**
Golf Courses: 0.5 private; 1.5 daily fee; 1 **A**
municipal
Bowling Lanes: 56 **B**
Movie Theaters: 5 **AA**
Crowd Pleasers (400)
NCAA Division I: 5.863 game seats per capita **AA**
University of Iowa Hawkeyes
Outdoor Recreation Assets (6)
Inland Water Area: .7 square miles
Places Rated Score: 1,506   Places Rated Rank: 206

Jackson, MI
Common Denominators (1,300)
Good Restaurants: 1 ★, 3 ★★ **B**
Golf Courses: 3.5 private; 9.5 daily fee; 2 **AA**
municipal

Rating

Bowling Lanes: 180 — **AA**
Movie Theaters: 6 — **A**
Crowd Pleasers (500)
Auto Racing: Michigan International (NASCAR) — **C**
Pari-mutuel Betting: Jackson Raceway (harness, 141 days) — **AA**
Outdoor Recreation Assets (133)
Inland Water Area: 18.8 square miles
Places Rated Score: 1,933   Places Rated Rank: 120

Jackson, MS
Common Denominators (700)
Good Restaurants: 3 ★, 8 ★★, 3 ★★★ — **AA**
Golf Courses: 11.5 private; 1 daily fee; 2 municipal — **C**
Bowling Lanes: 62 — **C**
Movie Theaters: 7 — **C**
Crowd Pleasers (700)
Zoos: Jackson Zoological Park — **B**
Professional Sports: .977 game seats per capita — **B**
Mets (baseball)
NCAA Division I: .807 game seats per capita — **A**
Jackson State Tigers
Outdoor Recreation Assets (27)
Inland Water Area: 1.2 square miles
National Forests, Parks, Wildlife Refuges:
Natchez Trace Parkway (7,352 acres)
Places Rated Score: 1,427   Places Rated Rank: 224

Jacksonville, FL
Common Denominators (800)
Good Restaurants: 1 ★, 5 ★★, 5 ★★★ — **B**
Golf Courses: 19.5 private; 8 daily fee; 2.5 municipal — **B**
Bowling Lanes: 452 — **B**
Movie Theaters: 20 — **B**
Crowd Pleasers (900)
Zoos: Jacksonville Zoological Park — **B**
Pari-mutuel Betting: — **A**
Bayard Greyhound Park (150 days)
Jacksonville Kennel Club (84 days)
Orange Park Kennel Club (77 days)
Professional Sports: 1.636 game seats per capita — **A**
Suns (baseball), BULLS (football)
NCAA Division I: .180 game seats per capita — **C**
University of Jacksonville Dolphins (b)
Outdoor Recreation Assets (1,184)
Atlantic Coastline: 80 miles
Inland Water Area: 201.6 square miles
National Forests, Parks, Wildlife Refuges:
Castillo de San Marcos NM (21 acres)
Fort Caroline National Memorial (132 acres)
Fort Matanzas NM (299 acres)
Places Rated Score: 2,884   Places Rated Rank: 41

Jacksonville, NC
Common Denominators (500)
Golf Courses: 3 private; 1 daily fee — **C**
Bowling Lanes: 48 — **B**
Movie Theaters: 3 — **B**
Outdoor Recreation Assets (677)
Atlantic Coastline: 30 miles
Inland Water Area: 57.6 square miles
Places Rated Score: 1,177   Places Rated Rank: 266

Janesville–Beloit, WI
Common Denominators (1,300)
Good Restaurants: 2 ★, 4 ★★ — **AA**
Golf Courses: 2.5 private; 2 daily fee; 2.5 municipal — **A**
Bowling Lanes: 186 — **AA**
Movie Theaters: 4 — **B**
Crowd Pleasers (300)
Professional Sports: 1.908 game seats per capita — **A**
Brewers (baseball)
Outdoor Recreation Assets (15)
Inland Water Area: 2.1 square miles
Places Rated Score: 1,615   Places Rated Rank: 176

Jersey City, NJ
Common Denominators (500)
Golf Courses: 0.5 daily fee — **C**
Bowling Lanes: 320 — **B**
Movie Theaters: 17 — **B**
Crowd Pleasers (100)
NCAA Division I: .075 game seats per capita — **C**
St. Peter's College Peacocks (b)
Outdoor Recreation Assets (1)
National Forests, Parks, Wildlife Refuges:
Statue of Liberty NM (45 acres)
CMSA Access: NEW YORK–NORTHERN NEW JERSEY–LONG ISLAND, NY–NJ–CT (400)
Places Rated Score: 1,001   Places Rated Rank: 291

Johnson City–Kingsport–Bristol, TN–VA
Common Denominators (1,000)
Good Restaurants: 6 ★★, 5 ★★★ — **A**
Golf Courses: 4 private; 5 daily fee; 4 municipal — **B**
Bowling Lanes: 156 — **B**
Movie Theaters: 17 — **A**
Crowd Pleasers (400)
Auto Racing: — **B**
Bristol International (NASCAR)
Kingsport International (NASCAR)
Professional Sports: .582 game seats per capita — **C**
Bristol Tigers, Johnson City Cardinals, Kingsport Mets (baseball)
NCAA Division I: .288 game seats per capita — **C**
East Tennessee State Buccaneers
Outdoor Recreation Assets (755)
Inland Water Area: 40.8 square miles
National Forests, Parks, Wildlife Refuges:
Appalachian Trail (966 acres)
Cherokee NF (193,640 acres)
Jefferson NF (55,961 acres)
Places Rated Score: 2,155   Places Rated Rank: 88

Johnstown, PA
Common Denominators (800)
Good Restaurants: 1 ★, 1 ★★★ — **C**
Golf Courses: 4.5 private; 6 daily fee; 0.5 municipal — **B**
Bowling Lanes: 172 — **B**
Movie Theaters: 10 — **A**
Crowd Pleasers (100)
NCAA Division I: .197 game seats per capita — **C**
St. Francis College Red Flash (b)
Outdoor Recreation Assets (3)
Inland Water Area: .1 square miles
National Forests, Parks, Wildlife Refuges:
Allegheny Portage Railroad NHS (330 acres)
Appalachian Trail (79 acres)
Johnstown Flood National Memorial (164 acres)
Places Rated Score: 903   Places Rated Rank: 302

Joliet, IL
Common Denominators (1,000)
Good Restaurants: 1 ★, 1 ★★, 2 ★★★ — **C**
Golf Courses: 6 private; 9.5 daily fee; 3 municipal — **AA**
Bowling Lanes: 268 — **A**
Movie Theaters: 9 — **B**
Crowd Pleasers (200)
Pari-mutuel Betting: Balmoral Park (Thoroughbred, 61 days) — **B**
Outdoor Recreation Assets (36)
Inland Water Area: 9 square miles
CMSA Access: CHICAGO–GARY–LAKE COUNTY, IL–IN–WI (400)
Places Rated Score: 1,636   Places Rated Rank: 170

Joplin, MO
Common Denominators (800)
Good Restaurants: 2 ★★★ — **B**
Golf Courses: 3.5 private; 2 municipal — **B**
Bowling Lanes: 82 — **B**
Movie Theaters: 3 — **B**

Rating

Outdoor Recreation Assets (1)
National Forests, Parks, Wildlife Refuges:
George Washington Carver NM (210 acres)
Places Rated Score: 801   Places Rated Rank: 313

Kalamazoo, MI
Common Denominators (1,500)
Good Restaurants: 2 ★, 3 ★★, 2 ★★★   A
Golf Courses: 4 private; 9 daily fee; 2.5 municipal   AA
Bowling Lanes: 340   AA
Movie Theaters: 10   AA
Crowd Pleasers (500)
Professional Sports: .965 game seats per capita   B
Wings (hockey)
NCAA Division I: 1.093 game seats per capita   A
Western Michigan Broncos
Outdoor Recreation Assets (163)
Inland Water Area: 18.3 square miles
Places Rated Score: 2,163   Places Rated Rank: 85

Kankakee, IL
Common Denominators (1,100)
Good Restaurants: 1 ★★, 1 ★★★   B
Golf Courses: 1 private; 5 daily fee; 0.5 municipal   AA
Bowling Lanes: 96   A
Movie Theaters: 3   B
Outdoor Recreation Assets (19)
Inland Water Area: 2.6 square miles
Places Rated Score: 1,119   Places Rated Rank: 277

Kansas City, KS
Common Denominators (700)
Good Restaurants: 2 ★★, 3 ★★★   C
Golf Courses: 15.5 private; 2.5 daily fee;   B
5 municipal
Bowling Lanes: 370   B
Movie Theaters: 14   B
Outdoor Recreation Assets (45)
Inland Water Area: 15.1 square miles
CMSA Access: KANSAS CITY, MO–KANSAS CITY, KS (300)
Places Rated Score: 1,045   Places Rated Rank: 287

Kansas City, MO
Common Denominators (1,200)
Good Restaurants: 2 ★, 18 ★★, 14 ★★★, 3 ★★★★   AA
Golf Courses: 9 private; 13 daily fee; 6.5 municipal   B
Bowling Lanes: 668   B
Movie Theaters: 37   AA
Crowd Pleasers (800)
Zoos: Swope Park Zoo   B
Theme Parks: Worlds of Fun (140 days)   B
Professional Sports: 5.030 game seats per capita   AA
ROYALS (baseball), KINGS (basketball),
CHIEFS (football)
Outdoor Recreation Assets (43)
Inland Water Area: 28.4 square miles
Places Rated Score: 2,043   Places Rated Rank: 99

Kenosha, WI
Common Denominators (1,300)
Good Restaurants: 1 ★, 1 ★★, 1 ★★★   B
Golf Courses: 1 private; 4 daily fee; 3 municipal   AA
Bowling Lanes: 148   AA
Movie Theaters: 4   A
Crowd Pleasers (300)
Professional Sports: 1.990 game seats per capita   A
Twins (baseball)
Outdoor Recreation Assets (224)
Great Lakes Coastline: 12 miles
Inland Water Area: 5.7 square miles
CMSA Access: CHICAGO–GARY–LAKE COUNTY,
IL–IN–WI (400)
Places Rated Score: 2,224   Places Rated Rank: 81

Killeen–Temple, TX
Common Denominators (900)
Good Restaurants: 2 ★, 1 ★★★   C
Golf Courses: 4.5 private; 1.5 daily fee; 2   B
municipal
Bowling Lanes: 84   B
Movie Theaters: 16   AA
Outdoor Recreation Assets (31)
Inland Water Area: 13.2 square miles
Places Rated Score: 931   Places Rated Rank: 298

Knoxville, TN
Common Denominators (900)
Good Restaurants: 7 ★★, 5 ★★★, 1 ★★★★   A
Golf Courses: 7 private; 12 daily fee; 2 municipal   B
Bowling Lanes: 196   B
Movie Theaters: 14   B
Crowd Pleasers (700)
Zoos: Knoxville Zoological Park   B
Professional Sports: 1.032 game seats per capita   B
Blue Jays (baseball)
NCAA Division I: 1.098 game seats per capita   A
University of Tennessee Volunteers
Outdoor Recreation Assets (914)
Inland Water Area: 149.1 square miles
National Forests, Parks, Wildlife Refuges:
Appalachian Trail (640 acres)
Great Smoky Mountains NP (225,193 acres)
Places Rated Score: 2,514   Places Rated Rank: 56

Kokomo, IN
Common Denominators (900)
Good Restaurants: 1 ★★   C
Golf Courses: 1 private; 3 daily fee; 1 municipal   AA
Bowling Lanes: 72   B
Movie Theaters: 3   B
Crowd Pleasers (100)
Auto Racing: Kokomo Speedway (USAC)   C
Places Rated Score: 1,000   Places Rated Rank: 293

La Crosse, WI
Common Denominators (1,500)
Good Restaurants: 1 ★, 1 ★★, 2 ★★★   AA
Golf Courses: 1 private; 2.5 daily fee   A
Bowling Lanes: 96   AA
Movie Theaters: 4   AA
Outdoor Recreation Assets (453)
Inland Water Area: 23.2 square miles
National Forests, Parks, Wildlife Refuges:
Upper Mississippi River NWR (11,666 acres)
Places Rated Score: 1,953   Places Rated Rank: 113

Lafayette, IN
Common Denominators (1,300)
Good Restaurants: 2 ★★, 1 ★★★   A
Golf Courses: 2.5 private; 3 daily fee; 1 municipal   A
Bowling Lanes: 104   A
Movie Theaters: 5   AA
Crowd Pleasers (500)
Zoos: Columbian Park Zoo   C
NCAA Division I: 4.351 game seats per capita   AA
Purdue Boilermakers
Outdoor Recreation Assets (14)
Inland Water Area: 1.4 square miles
Places Rated Score: 1,814   Places Rated Rank: 141

Lafayette, LA
Common Denominators (700)
Good Restaurants: 3 ★★, 7 ★★★   AA
Golf Courses: 2 private; 2 municipal   C
Bowling Lanes: 56   C
Movie Theaters: 4   C
Crowd Pleasers (700)
Pari-mutuel Betting: Evangeline Downs   AA
(Thoroughbred, 109 days)

	Rating
NCAA Division I: 1.312 game seats per capita	**A**
Southwestern Louisiana Ragin' Cajuns	

Outdoor Recreation Assets (334)
  Inland Water Area: 68 square miles
Places Rated Score: 1,734   Places Rated Rank: 153

Lake Charles, LA
Common Denominators (1,100)	
Good Restaurants: 1 ***	**C**
Golf Courses: 2 private; 1 daily fee; 2 municipal	**A**
Bowling Lanes: 76	**AA**
Movie Theaters: 6	**A**
Crowd Pleasers (700)	
Pari-mutuel Betting: Delta Downs (Thoroughbred, 105 days)	**AA**
NCAA Division I: 1.103 game seats per capita McNeese State Cowboys	**A**

Outdoor Recreation Assets (55)
  Inland Water Area: 12 square miles
Places Rated Score: 1,855   Places Rated Rank: 135

Lake County, IL
Common Denominators (1,200)	
Good Restaurants: 3 *, 6 **, 1 ***	**B**
Golf Courses: 23 private; 10.5 daily fee; 9.5 municipal	**AA**
Bowling Lanes: 322	**A**
Movie Theaters: 15	**A**
Crowd Pleasers (400)	
Theme Parks: Six Flags Great America (120 days)	**AA**

Outdoor Recreation Assets (435)
  Great Lakes Coastline: 25 miles
  Inland Water Area: 16.8 square miles
CMSA Access: Chicago–Gary–Lake County, IL–IN–WI (400)
Places Rated Score: 2,435   Places Rated Rank: 63

Lakeland–Winter Haven, FL
Common Denominators (1,300)	
Good Restaurants: 2 **, 6 ***, 1 ****	**AA**
Golf Courses: 6.5 private; 9 daily fee; 3.5 municipal	**AA**
Bowling Lanes: 206	**B**
Movie Theaters: 11	**A**
Crowd Pleasers (700)	
Theme Parks: Cypress Gardens (365 days)	**AA**
Professional Sports: 2.383 game seats per capita Lakeland Tigers, Winter Haven Red Sox (baseball)	**A**

Outdoor Recreation Assets (513)
  Inland Water Area: 187.2 square miles
Places Rated Score: 2,513   Places Rated Rank: 57

Lancaster, PA
Common Denominators (900)	
Good Restaurants: 4 *, 6 **, 1 ***, 1 ****	**A**
Golf Courses: 4.5 private; 5 daily fee	**B**
Bowling Lanes: 284	**A**
Movie Theaters: 5	**C**
Crowd Pleasers (100)	
Professional Sports: .214 game seats per capita Lightning (basketball)	**C**

Outdoor Recreation Assets (147)
  Inland Water Area: 27.9 square miles
Places Rated Score: 1,147   Places Rated Rank: 270

Lansing–East Lansing, MI
Common Denominators (1,200)	
Good Restaurants: 2 *, 4 **, 3 ***	**B**
Golf Courses: 2.5 private; 18 daily fee; 2.5 municipal	**AA**
Bowling Lanes: 440	**A**
Movie Theaters: 14	**A**
Crowd Pleasers (400)	
Zoos: Potter Park Zoo	**C**

	Rating
NCAA Division I: 1.215 game seats per capita	**A**
Michigan State Spartans	

Outdoor Recreation Assets (9)
  Inland Water Area: 3.1 square miles
Places Rated Score: 1,609   Places Rated Rank: 178

Laredo, TX
Common Denominators (700)	
Good Restaurants: 1 *, 3 **	**A**
Golf Courses: 1 private; 1 municipal	**C**
Bowling Lanes: 20	**C**
Movie Theaters: 3	**B**

Outdoor Recreation Assets (2)
  Inland Water Area: 1.4 square miles
Places Rated Score: 702   Places Rated Rank: 323

Las Cruces, NM
Common Denominators (1,100)	
Good Restaurants: 2 **, 1 ***	**AA**
Golf Courses: 5 private; 2 daily fee	**B**
Bowling Lanes: 50	**B**
Movie Theaters: 3	**A**
Crowd Pleasers (400)	
NCAA Division I: 3.341 game seats per capita New Mexico State Aggies	**AA**

Outdoor Recreation Assets (109)
  National Forests, Parks, Wildlife Refuges:
    San Andres NWR (2 acres)
    White Sands NM (53,059 acres)
Places Rated Score: 1,609   Places Rated Rank: 178

★ Las Vegas, NV
Common Denominators (1,300)	
Good Restaurants: 4 *, 16 **, 23 ***, 1 ****	**AA**
Golf Courses: 2 private; 7 daily fee; 2.5 municipal	**B**
Bowling Lanes: 400	**A**
Movie Theaters: 27	**AA**
Crowd Pleasers (1,100)	
Zoos: Las Vegas Valley Zoo	**C**
Auto Racing:	**B**
Caesar's Palace Grand Prix (SCCA)	
Craig Road Speedway (NASCAR)	
Pari-mutuel Betting: MGM Grand Jai Alai (365 days)	**AA**
Professional Sports: 1.457 game seats per capita Stars (baseball)	**B**
NCAA Division I: .524 game seats per capita University of Nevada Rebels	**B**

Outdoor Recreation Assets (1,596)
  Inland Water Area: 209.8 square miles
  National Forests, Parks, Wildlife Refuges:
    Desert NWR (828,766 acres)
    Lake Mead NRA (588,785 acres)
    Moapa Valley NWR (11 acres)
    Toiyabe NF (58,040 acres)
Places Rated Score: 3,996   Places Rated Rank: 8

Lawrence, KS
Common Denominators (1,300)	
Good Restaurants: 1 **	**C**
Golf Courses: 1 private; 2.5 daily fee	**AA**
Bowling Lanes: 80	**AA**
Movie Theaters: 4	**AA**
Crowd Pleasers (400)	
NCAA Division I: 6.882 game seats per capita University of Kansas Jayhawks	**AA**

Outdoor Recreation Assets (52)
  Inland Water Area: 3.2 square miles
Places Rated Score: 1,752   Places Rated Rank: 148

Lawrence–Haverhill, MA–NH
Common Denominators (600)	
Good Restaurants: 3 **, 5 ***	**A**
Golf Courses: 2.5 private; 7.5 daily fee	**B**
Movie Theaters: 7	**C**

	Rating
Crowd Pleasers (400)	
Pari-mutuel Betting:	**AA**
Rockingham (Thoroughbred, 143 days)	
Seabrook Greyhound Park (144 days)	
Outdoor Recreation Assets (479)	
Atlantic Coastline: 13 miles	
Inland Water Area: 27.8 square miles	
National Forests, Parks, Wildlife Refuges:	
Parker River NWR (2,321 acres)	

CMSA Access: BOSTON–LAWRENCE–SALEM, MA–NH (400)
Places Rated Score: 1,879   Places Rated Rank: 131

Lawton, OK

Common Denominators (1,300)	
Good Restaurants: 3 ★, 5 ★★, 1 ★★★	**AA**
Golf Courses: 2 private; 1 daily fee; 1 municipal	**B**
Bowling Lanes: 154	**AA**
Movie Theaters: 4	**A**
Outdoor Recreation Assets (457)	
Inland Water Area: 5.4 square miles	
National Forests, Parks, Wildlife Refuges:	
Wichita Mountains NWR (59,019 acres)	

Places Rated Score: 1,757   Places Rated Rank: 147

Lewiston–Auburn, ME

Common Denominators (1,200)	
Good Restaurants: 3 ★★	**A**
Golf Courses: 5 daily fee	**AA**
Bowling Lanes: 32	**B**
Movie Theaters: 3	**A**
Crowd Pleasers (400)	
Pari-mutuel Betting: Lewiston Raceway (harness,	**AA**
81 days)	
Outdoor Recreation Assets (253)	
Inland Water Area: 12.1 square miles	

Places Rated Score: 1,853   Places Rated Rank: 136

Lexington–Fayette, KY

Common Denominators (800)	
Good Restaurants: 4 ★★, 2 ★★★, 2 ★★★★	**A**
Golf Courses: 9 private; 6 daily fee; 1 municipal	**B**
Bowling Lanes: 168	**B**
Movie Theaters: 6	**C**
Crowd Pleasers (600)	
Pari-mutuel Betting:	**B**
Keeneland (Thoroughbred, 32 days)	
The Red Mile (harness, 52 days)	
NCAA Division I: 1.834 game seats per capita	**AA**
University of Kentucky Wildcats	
Outdoor Recreation Assets (3)	
Inland Water Area: .8 square miles	

Places Rated Score: 1,403   Places Rated Rank: 233

Lima, OH

Common Denominators (1,300)	
Good Restaurants: 2 ★★★	**B**
Golf Courses: 3.5 private; 6 daily fee	**AA**
Bowling Lanes: 182	**AA**
Movie Theaters: 6	**A**
Crowd Pleasers (100)	
Professional Sports: .614 game seats per capita	**C**
Ohio Mixers (basketball)	
Outdoor Recreation Assets (28)	
Inland Water Area: 4.5 square miles	

Places Rated Score: 1,428   Places Rated Rank: 222

Lincoln, NE

Common Denominators (1,100)	
Good Restaurants: 1 ★, 1 ★★, 2 ★★★	**B**
Golf Courses: 2 private; 1 daily fee; 3 municipal	**B**
Bowling Lanes: 164	**A**
Movie Theaters: 8	**AA**
Crowd Pleasers (700)	
Zoos: Folsom Children's Zoo	**C**
Pari-mutuel Betting: Nebraska State Fair	**B**
(Thoroughbred, 43 days)	

	Rating
NCAA Division I: 2.657 game seats per capita	**AA**
University of Nebraska Cornhuskers	
Outdoor Recreation Assets (4)	
Inland Water Area: .6 square miles	

Places Rated Score: 1,804   Places Rated Rank: 143

Little Rock–North Little Rock, AR

Common Denominators (800)	
Good Restaurants: 2 ★, 3 ★★, 1 ★★★, 1 ★★★★	**B**
Golf Courses: 13 private; 3 daily fee; 4.5 municipal	**B**
Bowling Lanes: 202	**B**
Movie Theaters: 12	**B**
Crowd Pleasers (400)	
Zoos: Little Rock Zoological Park	**C**
Professional Sports: .874 game seats per capita	**B**
Arkansas Travelers (baseball)	
NCAA Division I: .066 game seats per capita	**C**
University of Arkansas Trojans (b)	
Outdoor Recreation Assets (262)	
Inland Water Area: 69.6 square miles	
National Forests, Parks, Wildlife Refuges:	
Ouachita NF (53,357 acres)	

Places Rated Score: 1,462   Places Rated Rank: 216

Longview–Marshall, TX

Common Denominators (800)	
Good Restaurants: 2 ★, 2 ★★	**B**
Golf Courses: 4.5 private; 2.5 daily fee	**B**
Bowling Lanes: 80	**B**
Movie Theaters: 4	**B**
Outdoor Recreation Assets (34)	
Inland Water Area: 8.1 square miles	

Places Rated Score: 834   Places Rated Rank: 311

Lorain–Elyria, OH

Common Denominators (1,000)	
Good Restaurants: 1 ★, 2 ★★	**C**
Golf Courses: 6 private; 17 daily fee; 1 municipal	**AA**
Bowling Lanes: 332	**AA**
Movie Theaters: 6	**C**
Outdoor Recreation Assets (202)	
Great Lakes Coastline: 20 miles	
Inland Water Area: .2 square miles	

CMSA Access: CLEVELAND–AKRON–LORAIN, OH (400)
Places Rated Score: 1,602   Places Rated Rank: 184

★ Los Angeles–Long Beach, CA

Common Denominators (700)	
Good Restaurants: 2 ★, 46 ★★, 29 ★★★, 4 ★★★★	**C**
Golf Courses: 31.5 private; 8 daily fee;	**C**
34.5 municipal	
Bowling Lanes: 2,809	**B**
Movie Theaters: 269	**A**
Crowd Pleasers (1,000)	
Zoos: Los Angeles Zoo	**AA**
Theme Parks:	**C**
Marineland of the Pacific (300 days)	
Universal Studios Tour (365 days)	
Auto Racing: Long Beach Grand Prix (SCCA)	**C**
Pari-mutuel Betting:	**C**
Hollywood Park (harness, 53 days;	
Thoroughbred, 98 days)	
Santa Anita Park (Thoroughbred, 121 days)	
Professional Sports: 1.002 game seats per capita	**B**
DODGERS (baseball), CLIPPERS, LAKERS	
(basketball), EXPRESS, RAIDERS (football),	
KINGS (hockey)	
NCAA Division I: .255 game seats per capita	**C**
Long Beach State 49ers, Loyola	
Marymount University Lions (b), Pepperdine	
University Waves (b), University of California	
Bruins, University of Southern	
California Trojans	
Outdoor Recreation Assets (1,848)	
Pacific Coastline: 55 miles	
Inland Water Area: 11.1 square miles	

	Rating
National Forests, Parks, Wildlife Refuges:	
Angeles NF (642,260 acres)	
Santa Monica Mountains NRA (26,734 acres)	
CMSA Access: LOS ANGELES–ANAHEIM– RIVERSIDE, CA (400)	
Places Rated Score: 3,948 Places Rated Rank: 10	

Louisville, KY–IN
Common Denominators (800)
Good Restaurants: 1 ★, 6 ★★, 7 ★★★, 1 ★★★★	B
Golf Courses: 15 private; 5 daily fee; 8 municipal	B
Bowling Lanes: 958	A
Movie Theaters: 13	C

Crowd Pleasers (1,100)
Zoos: Louisville Zoological Gardens	A
Pari-mutuel Betting:	B
Churchill Downs (Thoroughbred, 117 days)	
Louisville Downs (harness, 153 days)	
Professional Sports: 2.558 game seats per capita	AA
Redbirds (baseball), Catbirds (basketball)	
NCAA Division I: .422 game seats per capita	B
University of Louisville Cardinals	

Outdoor Recreation Assets (42)
Inland Water Area: 19.3 square miles
Places Rated Score: 1,942   Places Rated Rank: 117

Lowell, MA–NH
Common Denominators (600)
Good Restaurants: 1 ★★	C
Golf Courses: 2 private; 3.5 daily fee	B
Bowling Lanes: 104	B
Movie Theaters: 3	C

Outdoor Recreation Assets (129)
Inland Water Area: 5.6 square miles
National Forests, Parks, Wildlife Refuges:
Lowell NHP (4 acres)
CMSA Access: BOSTON–LAWRENCE–SALEM, MA–NH (400)
Places Rated Score: 1,129   Places Rated Rank: 274

Lubbock, TX
Common Denominators (1,300)
Good Restaurants: 1 ★, 5 ★★, 4 ★★★	AA
Golf Courses: 3 private; 0.5 daily fee; 3 municipal	B
Bowling Lanes: 152	A
Movie Theaters: 11	AA

Crowd Pleasers (400)
| NCAA Division I: 1.725 game seats per capita | AA |
| Texas Tech Red Raiders | |

Outdoor Recreation Assets (2)
Inland Water Area: .3 square miles
National Forests, Parks, Wildlife Refuges:
Lower Rio Grande Valley NWR (118 acres)
Places Rated Score: 1,702   Places Rated Rank: 159

Lynchburg, VA
Common Denominators (700)
Good Restaurants: 1 ★★, 2 ★★★	A
Golf Courses: 4 private; 1 daily fee	C
Bowling Lanes: 64	B
Movie Theaters: 3	C

Crowd Pleasers (300)
| Professional Sports: 2.081 game seats per capita | A |
| Mets (baseball) | |

Outdoor Recreation Assets (439)
Inland Water Area: .7 square miles
National Forests, Parks, Wildlife Refuges:
Blue Ridge Parkway (2,037 acres)
George Washington NF (55,587 acres)
Places Rated Score: 1,439   Places Rated Rank: 220

Macon–Warner Robins, GA
Common Denominators (500)
Good Restaurants: 2 ★★, 1 ★★★	C
Golf Courses: 8.5 private; 0.5 daily fee; 1.5 municipal	C
Bowling Lanes: 100	B

	Rating
Movie Theaters: 5	C

Crowd Pleasers (400)
Professional Sports: 1.093 game seats per capita	B
Pirates (baseball)	
NCAA Division I: .444 game seats per capita	B
Mercer University Bears (b)	

Outdoor Recreation Assets (304)
Inland Water Area: .1 square miles
National Forests, Parks, Wildlife Refuges:
Ocmulgee NM (683 acres)
Oconee NF (16,570 acres)
Piedmont NWR (28,503 acres)
Places Rated Score: 1,204   Places Rated Rank: 262

Madison, WI
Common Denominators (1,000)
Good Restaurants: 3 ★, 5 ★★	B
Golf Courses: 3.5 private; 6 daily fee; 3.5 municipal	A
Bowling Lanes: 386	AA
Movie Theaters: 7	C

Crowd Pleasers (800)
Zoos: Henry Vilas Park Zoo	B
Professional Sports: .849 game seats per capita	B
Muskies (baseball)	
NCAA Division I: 1.711 game seats per capita	AA
University of Wisconsin Badgers	

Outdoor Recreation Assets (144)
Inland Water Area: 34.7 square miles
Places Rated Score: 1,944   Places Rated Rank: 115

Manchester, NH
Common Denominators (700)
Good Restaurants: 2 ★★, 1 ★★★	A
Golf Courses: 1 daily fee; 1 municipal	B
Movie Theaters: 3	B

Outdoor Recreation Assets (137)
Inland Water Area: 6.5 square miles
Places Rated Score: 837   Places Rated Rank: 310

Mansfield, OH
Common Denominators (1,000)
Good Restaurants: 1 ★★, 2 ★★★	A
Golf Courses: 2 private; 3 daily fee	B
Bowling Lanes: 134	A
Movie Theaters: 3	B

Crowd Pleasers (100)
| Auto Racing: Mid-Ohio Racetrack (SCCA) | C |

Outdoor Recreation Assets (33)
Inland Water Area: 3.3 square miles
Places Rated Score: 1,133   Places Rated Rank: 273

McAllen–Edinburg–Mission, TX
Common Denominators (900)
Good Restaurants: 3 ★, 9 ★★	AA
Golf Courses: 1 private; 2 daily fee; 3 municipal	B
Bowling Lanes: 60	C
Movie Theaters: 8	B

Crowd Pleasers (100)
| NCAA Division I: .229 game seats per capita | C |
| Pan American University Broncs (b) | |

Outdoor Recreation Assets (59)
Inland Water Area: 12.4 square miles
National Forests, Parks, Wildlife Refuges:
Santa Anna NWR (3,769 acres)
Places Rated Score: 1,059   Places Rated Rank: 286

Medford, OR
Common Denominators (1,100)
Good Restaurants: 4 ★★, 2 ★★★	AA
Golf Courses: 1.5 private; 0.5 daily fee; 0.5 municipal	C
Bowling Lanes: 74	B
Movie Theaters: 7	AA

Crowd Pleasers (300)
| Auto Racing: Medford Raceway (NASCAR) | C |

	Rating
Professional Sports: .838 game seats per capita	**B**
A's (baseball)	
Outdoor Recreation Assets (16)	
Inland Water Area: 9 square miles	
Places Rated Score: 1,416 Places Rated Rank: 226	

★ Melbourne–Titusville–Palm Bay, FL
Common Denominators (1,400)

	Rating
Good Restaurants: 1 ★, 8 ★★, 1 ★★★	**AA**
Golf Courses: 4.5 private; 4 daily fee; 3 municipal	**A**
Bowling Lanes: 196	**A**
Movie Theaters: 12	**AA**

Crowd Pleasers (400)

	Rating
Pari-mutuel Betting: Melbourne Sports Palace	**AA**
(jai alai, 150 days)	

Outdoor Recreation Assets (2,000)
Atlantic Coastline: 72 miles
Inland Water Area: 299 square miles
National Forests, Parks, Wildlife Refuges:
  Canaveral NS (29,479 acres)
  St. John's NWR (6,254 acres)
Places Rated Score: 3,800   Places Rated Rank: 12

Memphis, TN–AR–MS
Common Denominators (800)

	Rating
Good Restaurants: 7 ★★, 5 ★★★	**B**
Golf Courses: 19 private; 1 daily fee;	**C**
9 municipal	
Bowling Lanes: 384	**B**
Movie Theaters: 30	**A**

Crowd Pleasers (1,000)

	Rating
Zoos: Memphis Zoo and Aquarium	**A**
Pari-mutuel Betting: Southland Greyhound Park	**B**
(136 days)	
Professional Sports: 1.294 game seats per capita	**A**
Chicks (baseball), SHOWBOATS (football)	
NCAA Division I: .434 game seats per capita	**B**
Memphis State Tigers	

Outdoor Recreation Assets (194)
Inland Water Area: 80.8 square miles
National Forests, Parks, Wildlife Refuges:
  Lower Hatchie NWR (346 acres)
  Wapanocca NWR (5,484 acres)
Places Rated Score: 1,994   Places Rated Rank: 106

★ Miami–Hialeah, FL
Common Denominators (1,100)

	Rating
Good Restaurants: 8 ★, 16 ★★, 15 ★★★, 2 ★★★★,	**A**
1 ★★★★★	
Golf Courses: 16.5 private; 12.5 daily fee;	**B**
8 municipal	
Bowling Lanes: 654	**B**
Movie Theaters: 69	**AA**

Crowd Pleasers (1,000)

	Rating
Zoos: Miami Metro Zoo	**A**
Pari-mutuel Betting:	**A**
Biscayne Greyhound Park (102 days)	
Calder (Thoroughbred, 189 days)	
Flagler Greyhound Park (104 days)	
Hialeah (Thoroughbred, 50 days)	
Miami Jai Alai (242 days)	
Professional Sports: .800 game seats per capita	**B**
Marlins (baseball), DOLPHINS (football)	
NCAA Division I: .321 game seats per capita	**B**
University of Miami Hurricanes (f)	

Outdoor Recreation Assets (2,000)
Atlantic Coastline: 84 miles
Inland Water Area: 67.1 square miles
National Forests, Parks, Wildlife Refuges:
  Big Cypress National Preserve (18,628 acres)
  Biscayne NP (170,773 acres)
  Everglades NP (415,716 acres)
CMSA Access: MIAMI–FORT LAUDERDALE, FL (200)
Places Rated Score: 4,300   Places Rated Rank: 3

Middlesex–Somerset–Hunterdon, NJ
Common Denominators (900)

	Rating
Good Restaurants: 2 ★, 10 ★★, 1 ★★★	**C**
Golf Courses: 12 private; 8.5 daily fee;	**B**
5.5 municipal	
Bowling Lanes: 640	**A**
Movie Theaters: 29	**A**

Crowd Pleasers (200)

	Rating
NCAA Division I: .660 game seats per capita	**B**
Rutgers Scarlet Knights	

Outdoor Recreation Assets (96)
Atlantic Coastline: 6 miles
Inland Water Area: 7.3 square miles
National Forests, Parks, Wildlife Refuges:
  Morristown NHP (188 acres)
CMSA Access: NEW YORK–NORTHERN NEW
  JERSEY–LONG ISLAND, NY–NJ–CT (400)
Places Rated Score: 1,596   Places Rated Rank: 186

Middletown, CT
Common Denominators (1,200)

	Rating
Good Restaurants: 1 ★★★	**B**
Golf Courses: 3.5 daily fee	**AA**
Bowling Lanes: 46	**B**
Movie Theaters: 4	**AA**

Outdoor Recreation Assets (182)
Inland Water Area: 7.7 square miles
CMSA Access: HARTFORD–NEW BRITAIN–
  MIDDLETOWN, CT (300)
Places Rated Score: 1,682   Places Rated Rank: 163

Midland, TX
Common Denominators (1,200)

	Rating
Good Restaurants: 1 ★, 1 ★★	**B**
Golf Courses: 2 private; 1.5 municipal	**B**
Bowling Lanes: 106	**AA**
Movie Theaters: 5	**AA**

Crowd Pleasers (300)

	Rating
Professional Sports: 2.477 game seats per capita	**A**
Cubs (baseball)	

Outdoor Recreation Assets (2)
Inland Water Area: .3 square miles
Places Rated Score: 1,502   Places Rated Rank: 208

Milwaukee, WI
Common Denominators (1,200)

	Rating
Good Restaurants: 1 ★, 21 ★★, 10 ★★★, 2 ★★★★	**A**
Golf Courses: 17 private; 18.5 daily fee;	**B**
12.5 municipal	
Bowling Lanes: 2,864	**AA**
Movie Theaters: 43	**A**

Crowd Pleasers (1,000)

	Rating
Zoos: Milwaukee County Zoo	**AA**
Auto Racing: Road America (SCCA)	**C**
Professional Sports: 3.824 game seats per capita	**AA**
BREWERS (baseball), BUCKS (basketball),	
Admirals (hockey)	
NCAA Division I: .103 game seats per capita	**C**
Marquette Warriors (b)	

Outdoor Recreation Assets (602)
Great Lakes Coastline: 49 miles
Inland Water Area: 32.6 square miles
CMSA Access: MILWAUKEE–RACINE, WI (100)
Places Rated Score: 2,902   Places Rated Rank: 40

Minneapolis–St. Paul, MN–WI
Common Denominators (1,000)

	Rating
Good Restaurants: 19 ★, 40 ★★, 16 ★★★, 1 ★★★★	**A**
Golf Courses: 29.5 private; 28 daily fee;	**B**
22 municipal	
Bowling Lanes: 1,886	**A**
Movie Theaters: 56	**B**

Crowd Pleasers (900)

	Rating
Zoos:	**AA**
Como Zoo	
Minnesota Zoological Gardens	

	Rating

Professional Sports: 2.613 game seats per capita **AA**
TWINS (baseball), VIKINGS (football), NORTH
STARS (hockey)
NCAA Division I: .248 game seats per capita **C**
University of Minnesota Golden Gophers
Outdoor Recreation Assets (258)
Inland Water Area: 240.8 square miles
National Forests, Parks, Wildlife Refuges:
Lower St. Croix NSR (5,178 acres)
St. Croix NSR (5,673 acres)
Places Rated Score: 2,158   Places Rated Rank: 87

Mobile, AL

Common Denominators (800)
Good Restaurants: 3 ★★, 5 ★★★ **B**
Golf Courses: 9 private; 3 daily fee; 3 municipal **B**
Bowling Lanes: 160 **B**
Movie Theaters: 10 **B**
Crowd Pleasers (600)
Auto Racing: Mobile International (NASCAR) **C**
Pari-mutuel Betting: Mobile Greyhound Park **AA**
(286 days)
NCAA Division I: .299 game seats per capita **C**
University of South Alabama Jaguars (b)
Outdoor Recreation Assets (764)
Gulf of Mexico Coastline: 53 miles
Inland Water Area: 128.9 square miles
National Forests, Parks, Wildlife Refuges:
Bon Secour NWR (2,168 acres)
Places Rated Score: 2,164   Places Rated Rank: 84

Modesto, CA

Common Denominators (700)
Good Restaurants: 2 ★★ **C**
Golf Courses: 2 private; 1.5 daily fee; **C**
1.5 municipal
Bowling Lanes: 106 **B**
Movie Theaters: 9 **A**
Crowd Pleasers (100)
Professional Sports: .658 game seats per capita **C**
A's (baseball)
Outdoor Recreation Assets (33)
Inland Water Area: 10 square miles
Places Rated Score: 833   Places Rated Rank: 312

★ Monmouth–Ocean, NJ

Common Denominators (1,000)
Good Restaurants: 3 ★, 17 ★★, 3 ★★★ **A**
Golf Courses: 13.5 private; 7 daily fee; 6 municipal **B**
Bowling Lanes: 540 **B**
Movie Theaters: 28 **A**
Crowd Pleasers (700)
Theme Parks: Six Flags Great Adventure **A**
(163 days)
Pari-mutuel Betting: **A**
Freehold Raceway (harness, 148 days)
Monmouth Park (Thoroughbred, 110 days)
NCAA Division I: .043 game seats per capita **C**
Monmouth College Hawks (b)
Outdoor Recreation Assets (1,444)
Atlantic Coastline: 80 miles
Inland Water Area: 124.8 square miles
National Forests, Parks, Wildlife Refuges:
Barnegat NWR (7,427 acres)
Brigantine NWR (256 acres)
Gateway NRA (4,169 acres)
CMSA Access: NEW YORK–NORTHERN NEW
JERSEY–LONG ISLAND, NY–NJ–CT (400)
Places Rated Score: 3,544   Places Rated Rank: 17

Monroe, LA

Common Denominators (800)
Good Restaurants: 1 ★★, 2 ★★★ **A**
Golf Courses: 2.5 private; 2 municipal **B**
Bowling Lanes: 72 **B**
Movie Theaters: 2 **C**

	Rating

Crowd Pleasers (600)
Zoos: Louisiana Purchase Gardens and Zoo **A**
NCAA Division I: 1.465 game seats per capita **A**
Northeast Louisiana Indians
Outdoor Recreation Assets (141)
Inland Water Area: 5.4 square miles
National Forests, Parks, Wildlife Refuges:
D'Arbonne NWR (7,859 acres)
Places Rated Score: 1,541   Places Rated Rank: 196

Montgomery, AL

Common Denominators (700)
Good Restaurants: 5 ★★★ **A**
Golf Courses: 11 private; 1 municipal **C**
Bowling Lanes: 88 **C**
Movie Theaters: 7 **B**
Crowd Pleasers (300)
Zoos: Montgomery Zoo **B**
NCAA Division I: .172 game seats per capita **C**
Alabama State Hornets (b)
Outdoor Recreation Assets (112)
Inland Water Area: 45.1 square miles
Places Rated Score: 1,112   Places Rated Rank: 279

Muncie, IN

Common Denominators (1,100)
Golf Courses: 2 private; 4.5 daily fee **AA**
Bowling Lanes: 180 **AA**
Movie Theaters: 5 **A**
Crowd Pleasers (300)
NCAA Division I: 1.342 game seats per capita **A**
Ball State Cardinals
Outdoor Recreation Assets (28)
Inland Water Area: 2.2 square miles
Places Rated Score: 1,428   Places Rated Rank: 222

Muskegon, MI

Common Denominators (1,500)
Good Restaurants: 3 ★, 4 ★★ **A**
Golf Courses: 4 private; 5 daily fee; 1 municipal **AA**
Bowling Lanes: 228 **AA**
Movie Theaters: 7 **AA**
Crowd Pleasers (200)
Professional Sports: 1.285 game seats per capita **B**
Mohawks (hockey)
Outdoor Recreation Assets (966)
Great Lakes Coastline: 30 miles
Inland Water Area: 17.6 square miles
National Forests, Parks, Wildlife Refuges:
Manistee NF (12,500 acres)
Places Rated Score: 2,666   Places Rated Rank: 49

Nashua, NH

Common Denominators (700)
Good Restaurants: 3 ★★ **B**
Golf Courses: 1 private; 4 daily fee **A**
Bowling Lanes: 40 **C**
Movie Theaters: 3 **C**
Crowd Pleasers (400)
Professional Sports: 3.192 game seats per capita **AA**
Pirates (baseball)
Outdoor Recreation Assets (23)
Inland Water Area: 1.2 square miles
CMSA Access: BOSTON–LAWRENCE–SALEM, MA–NH (400)
Places Rated Score: 1,523   Places Rated Rank: 199

Nashville, TN

Common Denominators (1,000)
Good Restaurants: 4 ★, 5 ★★, 9 ★★★, 3 ★★★★ **A**
Golf Courses: 15.5 private; 3 daily fee; **B**
9.5 municipal
Bowling Lanes: 426 **B**
Movie Theaters: 27 **A**
Crowd Pleasers (800)
Theme Parks: Opryland USA (140 days) **A**

Rating

Professional Sports: 1.330 game seats per capita **B**
    Sounds (baseball)
    NCAA Division I: .991 game seats per capita **A**
    Middle Tennessee State Blue Raiders,
    Tennessee State Tigers, Vanderbilt
    Commodores
Outdoor Recreation Assets (49)
    Inland Water Area: 37.3 square miles
    National Forests, Parks, Wildlife Refuges:
    Natchez Trace Parkway (1,132 acres)
    Stones River National Battlefield (351 acres)
Places Rated Score: 1,849   Places Rated Rank: 137

★ Nassau–Suffolk, NY
Common Denominators (1,200)
    Good Restaurants: 6 ★, 44 ★★, 23 ★★★ **A**
    Golf Courses: 59 private; 14.5 daily fee; **B**
    23 municipal
    Bowling Lanes: 2,137 **A**
    Movie Theaters: 122 **AA**
Crowd Pleasers (500)
    Auto Racing: **B**
    Islip (NASCAR)
    Riverhead (NASCAR)
    Pari-mutuel Betting: **C**
    Belmont Park (Thoroughbred, 108 days)
    Roosevelt Raceway (harness, 158 days)
    Professional Sports: .249 game seats per capita **C**
    ISLANDERS (hockey)
    NCAA Division I: .021 game seats per capita **C**
    Hofstra Flying Dutchmen (b)
Outdoor Recreation Assets (1,605)
    Atlantic Coastline: 170 miles
    Inland Water Area: 89.6 square miles
    National Forests, Parks, Wildlife Refuges:
    Amagansett NWR (36 acres)
    Conscience Point NWR (60 acres)
    E.A. Norton NWR (187 acres)
    Fire Island NS (18,606 acres)
    Oyster Bay NWR (3,204 acres)
    Sagamore Hill NHS (78 acres)
    Seatuck NWR (183 acres)
    Target Rock NWR (80 acres)
    Wertheim NWR (2,235 acres)
CMSA Access: NEW YORK–NORTHERN NEW
    JERSEY–LONG ISLAND, NY–NJ–CT (400)
Places Rated Score: 3,705   Places Rated Rank: 14

New Bedford, MA
Common Denominators (600)
    Good Restaurants: 2 ★, 1 ★★ **C**
    Golf Courses: 1.5 private; 0.5 daily fee; **C**
    1 municipal
    Bowling Lanes: 84 **B**
    Movie Theaters: 5 **B**
Crowd Pleasers (100)
    Zoos: Buttonwood Park Zoo **C**
Outdoor Recreation Assets (750)
    Atlantic Coastline: 26 miles
    Inland Water Area: 20.4 square miles
Places Rated Score: 1,450   Places Rated Rank: 219

New Britain, CT
Common Denominators (700)
    Good Restaurants: 2 ★★ **C**
    Golf Courses: 2 daily fee; 1.5 municipal **B**
    Bowling Lanes: 92 **B**
    Movie Theaters: 4 **B**
Crowd Pleasers (300)
    Professional Sports: 1.722 game seats per capita **A**
    Red Sox (baseball)
Outdoor Recreation Assets (17)
    Inland Water Area: .3 square miles
CMSA Access: HARTFORD–NEW BRITAIN–
    MIDDLETOWN, CT (200)
Places Rated Score: 1,217   Places Rated Rank: 258

New Haven–Meriden, CT
Common Denominators (800)
    Good Restaurants: 3 ★, 6 ★★ **C**
    Golf Courses: 11 private; 2 daily fee; 3 municipal **C**
    Bowling Lanes: 304 **B**
    Movie Theaters: 22 **AA**
Crowd Pleasers (400)
    Professional Sports: .450 game seats per capita **C**
    Nighthawks (hockey)
    NCAA Division I: .901 game seats per capita **A**
    Yale Bulldogs
Outdoor Recreation Assets (404)
    Atlantic Coastline: 30 miles
    Inland Water Area: 8.7 square miles
Places Rated Score: 1,604   Places Rated Rank: 182

New London–Norwich, CT–RI
Common Denominators (1,000)
    Good Restaurants: 2 ★, 2 ★★, 2 ★★★ **B**
    Golf Courses: 4 private; 3 daily fee; 2 municipal **B**
    Bowling Lanes: 172 **B**
    Movie Theaters: 11 **AA**
Crowd Pleasers (600)
    Zoos: Moran Nature Center and Zoo **C**
    Auto Racing: Stafford (NASCAR) **C**
    Pari-mutuel Betting: Plainfield Greyhound Park **AA**
    (212 days)
Outdoor Recreation Assets (681)
    Atlantic Coastline: 35 miles
    Inland Water Area: 33.4 square miles
Places Rated Score: 2,281   Places Rated Rank: 74

★ New Orleans, LA
Common Denominators (800)
    Good Restaurants: 8 ★, 16 ★★, 18 ★★★, 7 ★★★★ **AA**
    Golf Courses: 17.5 private; 4.5 daily fee; **C**
    6 municipal
    Bowling Lanes: 406 **C**
    Movie Theaters: 29 **B**
Crowd Pleasers (700)
    Zoos: Audubon Park Zoo **A**
    Pari-mutuel Betting: **B**
    Fair Grounds (Thoroughbred, 97 days)
    Jefferson Downs (Thoroughbred, 137 days)
    Professional Sports: .463 game seats per capita **C**
    SAINTS (football)
    NCAA Division I: .116 game seats per capita **C**
    Tulane Green Wave, University of New Orleans
    Privateers (b)
Outdoor Recreation Assets (2,000)
    Gulf of Mexico Coastline: 75 miles
    Inland Water Area: 1,265.2 square miles
    National Forests, Parks, Wildlife Refuges:
    Boguechito NWR (16,792 acres)
    Breton NWR (8,402 acres)
    Jean Lafitte NHP (7,754 acres)
Places Rated Score: 3,500   Places Rated Rank: 18

★ New York, NY
Common Denominators (1,000)
    Good Restaurants: 41 ★, 118 ★★, 81 ★★★, 8 ★★★★, **A**
    1 ★★★★★
    Golf Courses: 49 private; 3 daily fee; 20 municipal **C**
    Bowling Lanes: 2,824 **B**
    Movie Theaters: 356 **AA**
Crowd Pleasers (1,100)
    Zoos: **AA**
    Bronx Zoo
    Staten Island Zoo
    Aquariums: New York Aquarium **A**
    Pari-mutuel Betting: **C**
    Aqueduct (Thoroughbred, 176 days)
    Yonkers Raceway (harness, 77 days)
    Professional Sports: 1.340 game seats per capita **B**
    METS, YANKEES (baseball), KNICKER-
    BOCKERS (basketball), JETS (football),
    RANGERS (hockey)

	Rating
NCAA Division I: .047 game seats per capita	C

Brooklyn College Kingsmen (b), Columbia University Lions, Fordham Rams (b), Iona College Gaels (b), Long Island University (Brooklyn) Blackbirds (b), Manhattan College Jaspers (b), St. Francis College Terriers (b), Wagner College Seahawks (b)

Outdoor Recreation Assets (1,079)
Atlantic Coastline: 27 miles
Inland Water Area: 149.8 square miles
National Forests, Parks, Wildlife Refuges:
Appalachian Trail (960 acres)
Castle Clinton NM (1 acre)
Federal Hall NM (0.45 acres)
Gateway NRA (21,715 acres)
General Grant National Memorial (0.76 acres)
Hamilton Grange National Memorial (0.71 acres)
Statue of Liberty NM (13 acres)
Theodore Roosevelt Birthplace NHS (0.11 acres)
CMSA Access: NEW YORK–NORTHERN NEW JERSEY–LONG ISLAND, NY–NJ–CT (400)
Places Rated Score: 3,579   Places Rated Rank: 16

Newark, NJ

Common Denominators (700)

	Rating
Good Restaurants: 4 ★, 6 ★★, 10 ★★★, 1 ★★★★	C
Golf Courses: 36 private; 7 daily fee; 13.5 municipal	C
Bowling Lanes: 1,077	B
Movie Theaters: 69	A

Crowd Pleasers (300)

	Rating
Zoos: Turtle Back Zoo	B
NCAA Division I: .022 game seats per capita	C

Seton Hall Pirates (b)

Outdoor Recreation Assets (418)
Inland Water Area: 25 square miles
National Forests, Parks, Wildlife Refuges:
Appalachian Trail (3,211 acres)
Delaware NSR (684 acres)
Delaware Water Gap NRA (37,398 acres)
Edison NHS (21 acres)
Great Swamp NWR (6,792 acres)
Morristown NHP (1,488 acres)
CMSA Access: NEW YORK–NORTHERN NEW JERSEY–LONG ISLAND, NY–NJ–CT (400)
Places Rated Score: 1,818   Places Rated Rank: 140

Niagara Falls, NY

Common Denominators (900)

	Rating
Good Restaurants: 5 ★★, 1 ★★★	A
Golf Courses: 3.5 private; 3 daily fee; 4 municipal	A
Bowling Lanes: 88	B
Movie Theaters: 3	C

Crowd Pleasers (200)

	Rating
Professional Sports: .699 game seats per capita	C

White Sox (baseball)

	Rating
NCAA Division I: .212 game seats per capita	C

Niagara University Purple Eagles (b)

Outdoor Recreation Assets (373)
Great Lakes Coastline: 31 miles
Inland Water Area: 6.6 square miles
CMSA Access: BUFFALO–NIAGARA FALLS, NY (400)
Places Rated Score: 1,873   Places Rated Rank: 132

Norfolk–Virginia Beach–Newport News, VA

Common Denominators (800)

	Rating
Good Restaurants: 13 ★★, 17 ★★★, 1 ★★★★	A
Golf Courses: 10 private; 5.5 daily fee; 6 municipal	C
Bowling Lanes: 708	B
Movie Theaters: 35	B

Crowd Pleasers (600)

	Rating
Zoos: Lafayette Zoological Park	C
Theme Parks: Busch Gardens–The Old Country (137 days)	B
Auto Racing: Langley Speedway (NASCAR)	C

	Rating
Professional Sports: .613 game seats per capita	C

Peninsula Pilots, Tidewater Tides (baseball)

	Rating
NCAA Division I: .299 game seats per capita	C

Old Dominion Monarchs (b), William and Mary Indians

Outdoor Recreation Assets (1,564)
Atlantic Coastline: 69 miles
Inland Water Area: 151.1 square miles
National Forests, Parks, Wildlife Refuges:
Back Bay NWR (4,589 acres)
Colonial NHP (8,814 acres)
Great Dismal Swamp NWR (77,733 acres)
Jamestown NHS (21 acres)
Mackay Island NWR (874 acres)
Nansemond NWR (208 acres)
Plum Tree Island NWR (3,276 acres)
Yorktown National Cemetery (3 acres)
Places Rated Score: 2,964   Places Rated Rank: 37

Norwalk, CT

Common Denominators (1,300)

	Rating
Good Restaurants: 2 ★, 5 ★★	AA
Golf Courses: 3.5 private; 2 municipal	B
Bowling Lanes: 104	
Movie Theaters: 9	AA

Outdoor Recreation Assets (568)
Atlantic Coastline: 9 miles
Inland Water Area: 8.5 square miles
CMSA Access: NEW YORK–NORTHERN NEW JERSEY–LONG ISLAND, NY–NJ–CT (400)
Places Rated Score: 2,268   Places Rated Rank: 75

Oakland, CA

Common Denominators (600)

	Rating
Good Restaurants: 1 ★, 14 ★★, 3 ★★★, 1 ★★★★	C
Golf Courses: 14 private; 11.5 daily fee; 8.5 municipal	C
Bowling Lanes: 1,036	B
Movie Theaters: 50	B

Crowd Pleasers (800)

	Rating
Zoos:	B

Knowland Park Zoo
Oakland Baby Zoo

	Rating
Pari-mutuel Betting: Golden Gate Fields (Thoroughbred, 100 days)	C
Professional Sports: 2.898 game seats per capita	AA

A'S (baseball), GOLDEN STATE WARRIORS (basketball), INVADERS (football)

	Rating
NCAA Division I: .267 game seats per capita	C

St. Mary's College Gaels (b), University of California Golden Bears

Outdoor Recreation Assets (594)
Inland Water Area: 157.4 square miles
National Forests, Parks, Wildlife Refuges:
Antioch Dunes NWR (55 acres)
Eugene O'Neill NHS (13 acres)
John Muir NHS (9 acres)
San Francisco Bay NWR (10,620 acres)
CMSA Access: SAN FRANCISCO–OAKLAND–SAN JOSE, CA (400)
Places Rated Score: 2,394   Places Rated Rank: 65

Ocala, FL

Common Denominators (1,300)

	Rating
Good Restaurants: 2 ★, 2 ★★	B
Golf Courses: 2 private; 2.5 daily fee; 1.5 municipal	A
Bowling Lanes: 214	AA
Movie Theaters: 5	AA

Crowd Pleasers (300)

	Rating
Pari-mutuel Betting: Ocala Jai Alai (60 days)	A

Outdoor Recreation Assets (1,495)
Inland Water Area: 52.5 square miles
National Forests, Parks, Wildlife Refuges:
Ocala NF (274,383 acres)
Places Rated Score: 3,095   Places Rated Rank: 31

Rating

Odessa, TX
Common Denominators (900)
- Good Restaurants: 3 ★★ — **A**
- Golf Courses: 2 private; 1 daily fee — **C**
- Bowling Lanes: 80 — **B**
- Movie Theaters: 4 — **A**

Places Rated Score: 900   Places Rated Rank: 303

Oklahoma City, OK
Common Denominators (1,000)
- Good Restaurants: 4 ★, 10 ★★, 10 ★★★, 1 ★★★★ — **A**
- Golf Courses: 10.5 private; 6 daily fee; 11.5 municipal — **B**
- Bowling Lanes: 494 — **B**
- Movie Theaters: 27 — **A**

Crowd Pleasers (700)
- Zoos: Oklahoma City Zoo — **A**
- Professional Sports: .984 game seats per capita — **B**
  89ers (baseball)
- NCAA Division I: .599 game seats per capita — **B**
  University of Oklahoma Sooners

Outdoor Recreation Assets (42)
- Inland Water Area: 35.7 square miles

Places Rated Score: 1,742   Places Rated Rank: 150

Olympia, WA
Common Denominators (1,000)
- Good Restaurants: 2 ★★ — **B**
- Golf Courses: 1 private; 4 daily fee — **A**
- Bowling Lanes: 80 — **B**
- Movie Theaters: 4 — **A**

Outdoor Recreation Assets (451)
- Puget Sound Coastline: 10 miles
- Inland Water Area: 47 square miles
- National Forests, Parks, Wildlife Refuges:
  Nisqually NWR (1,985 acres)
  Olympic NF (10 acres)
  Snoqualmie NF (612 acres)

Places Rated Score: 1,451   Places Rated Rank: 218

Omaha, NE–IA
Common Denominators (1,100)
- Good Restaurants: 1 ★, 9 ★★, 8 ★★★ — **AA**
- Golf Courses: 10.5 private; 3.5 daily fee; 7.5 municipal — **B**
- Bowling Lanes: 606 — **A**
- Movie Theaters: 18 — **B**

Crowd Pleasers (800)
- Zoos: Henry Doorly Zoo — **B**
- Pari-mutuel Betting: Ak-Sar-Ben (Thoroughbred, 85 days) — **B**
- Professional Sports: 1.974 game seats per capita — **A**
  Royals (baseball)
- NCAA Division I: .222 game seats per capita — **C**
  Creighton University Bluejays (b)

Outdoor Recreation Assets (77)
- Inland Water Area: 29.5 square miles
- National Forests, Parks, Wildlife Refuges:
  De Soto NWR (4,324 acres)

Places Rated Score: 1,977   Places Rated Rank: 109

Orange County, NY
Common Denominators (1,000)
- Good Restaurants: 4 ★, 4 ★★, 1 ★★★ — **A**
- Golf Courses: 7.5 private; 5 daily fee; 1 municipal — **B**
- Bowling Lanes: 232 — **A**
- Movie Theaters: 6 — **B**

Crowd Pleasers (300)
- NCAA Division I: .978 game seats per capita — **A**
  U.S. Military Academy Cadets

Outdoor Recreation Assets (166)
- Inland Water Area: 13.4 square miles
- National Forests, Parks, Wildlife Refuges:
  Appalachian Trail (2,422 acres)
  Upper Delaware NSR (6,559 acres)

CMSA Access: NEW YORK–NORTHERN NEW JERSEY–LONG ISLAND, NY–NJ–CT (400)
Places Rated Score: 1,866   Places Rated Rank: 134

Orlando, FL
Common Denominators (1,300)
- Good Restaurants: 5 ★, 17 ★★, 10 ★★★, 2 ★★★★ — **AA**
- Golf Courses: 8 private; 25.5 daily fee; 7 municipal — **AA**
- Bowling Lanes: 570 — **A**
- Movie Theaters: 19 — **B**

Crowd Pleasers (1,000)
- Zoos: Central Florida Zoological Park — **C**
- Theme Parks: — **AA**
  Sea World of Florida (365 days)
  Walt Disney World & Epcot Center (365 days)
- Pari-mutuel Betting: — **A**
  Sanford–Orlando Kennel Club (106 days)
  Seminole Greyhound Park (105 days)
- Professional Sports: 1.268 game seats per capita — **B**
  Twins (baseball), RENEGADES (football)

Outdoor Recreation Assets (581)
- Inland Water Area: 297.1 square miles

Places Rated Score: 2,881   Places Rated Rank: 42

Owensboro, KY
Common Denominators (700)
- Good Restaurants: 1 ★★ — **C**
- Golf Courses: 2 private; 0.5 daily fee; 1.5 municipal — **B**
- Bowling Lanes: 36 — **B**
- Movie Theaters: 2 — **B**

Outdoor Recreation Assets (152)
- Inland Water Area: 14.1 square miles

Places Rated Score: 852   Places Rated Rank: 305

Oxnard–Ventura, CA
Common Denominators (1,000)
- Good Restaurants: 12 ★★, 5 ★★★ — **AA**
- Golf Courses: 3.5 private; 4.5 daily fee; 4 municipal — **B**
- Bowling Lanes: 236 — **B**
- Movie Theaters: 15 — **B**

Outdoor Recreation Assets (735)
- Pacific Coastline: 37 miles
- Inland Water Area: 1.5 square miles
- National Forests, Parks, Wildlife Refuges:
  Angeles NF (1,473 acres)
  Channel Islands NP (9,905 acres)
  Hopper Mountain NWR (1,871 acres)
  Los Padres NF (556,632 acres)
  Santa Monica Mountains NRA (17,165 acres)

CMSA Access: LOS ANGELES–ANAHEIM–RIVERSIDE, CA (400)
Places Rated Score: 2,135   Places Rated Rank: 92

Panama City, FL
Common Denominators (900)
- Golf Courses: 3.5 private; 2.5 daily fee — **A**
- Bowling Lanes: 56 — **B**
- Movie Theaters: 4 — **AA**

Outdoor Recreation Assets (1,189)
- Gulf of Mexico Coastline: 44 miles
- Inland Water Area: 113.6 square miles

Places Rated Score: 2,089   Places Rated Rank: 95

Parkersburg–Marietta, WV–OH
Common Denominators (1,100)
- Good Restaurants: 1 ★★, 2 ★★★ — **A**
- Golf Courses: 2 private; 6 daily fee — **AA**
- Bowling Lanes: 71 — **B**
- Movie Theaters: 4 — **B**

Outdoor Recreation Assets (48)
- Inland Water Area: 9.6 square miles

Places Rated Score: 1,148   Places Rated Rank: 269

Rating

Pascagoula, MS
Common Denominators (1,000)
Good Restaurants: 1 ★, 2 ★★, 1 ★★★   **B**
Golf Courses: 1.5 private; 3 daily fee;   **A**
  0.5 municipal
Bowling Lanes: 40   **B**
Movie Theaters: 4   **A**
Outdoor Recreation Assets (956)
Gulf of Mexico Coastline: 25 miles
Inland Water Area: 25.3 square miles
National Forests, Parks, Wildlife Refuges:
  Gulf Islands NS (49,873 acres)
Places Rated Score: 1,956   Places Rated Rank: 112

Pawtucket–Woonsocket–Attleboro, RI–MA
Common Denominators (700)
Good Restaurants: 1 ★   **C**
Golf Courses: 4.5 private; 8.5 daily fee   **A**
Bowling Lanes: 72   **C**
Movie Theaters: 8   **B**
Crowd Pleasers (600)
Pari-mutuel Betting: Lincoln Greyhound Park   **AA**
  (248 days)
Professional Sports: 1.323 game seats per capita   **B**
  Red Sox (baseball)
Outdoor Recreation Assets (113)
Inland Water Area: 7 square miles
National Forests, Parks, Wildlife Refuges:
  Trustom Pond NWR (579 acres)
CMSA Access: PROVIDENCE–PAWTUCKET–
  FALL RIVER, RI–MA (100)
Places Rated Score: 1,513   Places Rated Rank: 202

Pensacola, FL
Common Denominators (700)
Good Restaurants: 2 ★★★   **C**
Golf Courses: 6 private; 5 daily fee; 1 municipal   **B**
Bowling Lanes: 186   **B**
Movie Theaters: 7   **B**
Crowd Pleasers (400)
Auto Racing: Five Flags (NASCAR)   **C**
Pari-mutuel Betting: Pensacola Greyhound Park   **A**
  (104 days)
Outdoor Recreation Assets (1,060)
Gulf of Mexico Coastline: 43 miles
Inland Water Area: 212.2 square miles
Places Rated Score: 2,160   Places Rated Rank: 86

Peoria, IL
Common Denominators (1,100)
Good Restaurants: 2 ★★, 1 ★★★   **C**
Golf Courses: 6 private; 4.5 daily fee;   **A**
  6.5 municipal
Bowling Lanes: 439   **AA**
Movie Theaters: 13   **A**
Crowd Pleasers (500)
Zoos: Glen Oak Zoo   **C**
Professional Sports: 1.886 game seats per capita   **A**
  Chiefs (baseball), Prancers (hockey)
NCAA Division I: .259 game seats per capita   **C**
  Bradley University Braves (b)
Outdoor Recreation Assets (88)
Inland Water Area: 31.8 square miles
Places Rated Score: 1,688   Places Rated Rank: 162

Philadelphia, PA–NJ
Common Denominators (700)
Good Restaurants: 27 ★, 54 ★★, 18 ★★★, 4 ★★★★,   **B**
  1 ★★★★★
Golf Courses: 67.5 private; 48 daily fee;   **B**
  13 municipal
Bowling Lanes: 1,756   **B**
Movie Theaters: 98   **C**
Crowd Pleasers (900)
Zoos: Philadelphia Zoological Gardens   **AA**

Rating

Pari-mutuel Betting: **C**
  Continental (Thoroughbred, 135 days)
  Keystone (Thoroughbred, 135 days)
  Liberty Bell (harness, 135 days)
  William Penn (harness, 87 days)
Professional Sports: 1.574 game seats per capita   **A**
  PHILLIES (baseball), 76ERS (basketball),
  EAGLES (football), FLYERS (hockey)
NCAA Division I: .205 game seats per capita   **C**
  Drexel Dragons (b), LaSalle College Explorers
  (b), St. Joseph Hawks (b), Temple Owls,
  University of Pennsylvania Quakers, Villanova
  Wildcats (b)
Outdoor Recreation Assets (79)
Inland Water Area: 50.1 square miles
National Forests, Parks, Wildlife Refuges:
  Brigantine NWR (97 acres)
  Edgar Allen Poe House NHS (0.52 acres)
  Hopewell Village NHS (320 acres)
  Independence NHP (2,814 acres)
  Thaddeus Kosciuszko NM (0.02 acres)
  Valley Forge NHP (2,988 acres)
CMSA Access: PHILADELPHIA–WILMINGTON–
  TRENTON, PA–NJ–DE–MD (300)
Places Rated Score: 1,979   Places Rated Rank: 108

Phoenix, AZ
Common Denominators (800)
Good Restaurants: 2 ★, 18 ★★, 12 ★★★, 3 ★★★★   **A**
Golf Courses: 29.5 private; 23 daily fee;   **B**
  6 municipal
Bowling Lanes: 820   **B**
Movie Theaters: 33   **C**
Crowd Pleasers (1,100)
Zoos: Phoenix Zoo   **A**
Auto Racing: Phoenix International (NASCAR)   **C**
Pari-mutuel Betting:
  Phoenix Greyhound Park (294 days)
  Turf Paradise (Thoroughbred, 158 days)
Professional Sports: 1.174 game seats per capita   **B**
  Giants (baseball), SUNS (basketball),
  ARIZONA WRANGLERS (football)
NCAA Division I: .356 game seats per capita   **B**
  Arizona State Sun Devils
Outdoor Recreation Assets (572)
Inland Water Area: 14.9 square miles
National Forests, Parks, Wildlife Refuges:
  Tonto NF (658,436 acres)
Places Rated Score: 2,472   Places Rated Rank: 59

Pine Bluff, AR
Common Denominators (600)
Good Restaurants: 1 ★   **C**
Golf Courses: 2 private; 1 municipal   **C**
Bowling Lanes: 68   **A**
Movie Theaters: 2   **C**
Outdoor Recreation Assets (193)
Inland Water Area: 34.1 square miles
Places Rated Score: 793   Places Rated Rank: 316

Pittsburgh, PA
Common Denominators (1,000)
Good Restaurants: 2 ★, 11 ★★, 22 ★★★   **B**
Golf Courses: 40 private; 44 daily fee;   **B**
  6.5 municipal
Bowling Lanes: 1,656   **A**
Movie Theaters: 71   **A**
Crowd Pleasers (1,100)
Zoos: **AA**
  Pittsburgh Aviary
  Pittsburgh Zoo
Pari-mutuel Betting: **B**
  Mountain Laurel (harness, 248 days)
  The Meadows (harness, 63 days)

	Rating
Professional Sports: 2.470 game seats per capita	**A**
PIRATES (baseball), STEELERS (football), PENGUINS (hockey)	
NCAA Division I: .358 game seats per capita	**B**
Duquesne Dukes (b), Robert Morris College Colonials (b), University of Pittsburgh Panthers	

Outdoor Recreation Assets (45)
Inland Water Area: 28.1 square miles
National Forests, Parks, Wildlife Refuges:
Fort Necessity National Battlefield (903 acres)
Friendship Hill NHS (661 acres)
Places Rated Score: 2,145   Places Rated Rank: 90

Pittsfield, MA

	Rating
Common Denominators (1,100)	
Good Restaurants: 1 ★★, 2 ★★★	**AA**
Golf Courses: 4 private; 4 daily fee	**AA**
Bowling Lanes: 58	**B**
Movie Theaters: 1	**C**
Crowd Pleasers (200)	
Pari-mutuel Betting:	**B**
Berkshire Downs (Thoroughbred, 6 days)	
Great Barrington (Thoroughbred, 16 days)	

Outdoor Recreation Assets (120)
Inland Water Area: 5.5 square miles
Places Rated Score: 1,420   Places Rated Rank: 225

★ Portland, ME

	Rating
Common Denominators (1,200)	
Good Restaurants: 3 ★, 13 ★★, 1 ★★★	**AA**
Golf Courses: 4 private; 5 daily fee; 2.5 municipal	**AA**
Bowling Lanes: 14	**C**
Movie Theaters: 7	**A**
Crowd Pleasers (800)	
Pari-mutuel Betting: Scarborough Downs (harness, 123 days)	**AA**
Professional Sports: 3.304 game seats per capita	**AA**
Maine Guides (baseball), Maine Mariners (hockey)	

Outdoor Recreation Assets (1,366)
Atlantic Coastline: 36 miles
Inland Water Area: 112.7 square miles
National Forests, Parks, Wildlife Refuges:
Rachel Carson NWR (144 acres)
Places Rated Score: 3,366   Places Rated Rank: 20

Portland, OR

	Rating
Common Denominators (1,100)	
Good Restaurants: 13 ★, 26 ★★, 19 ★★★	**AA**
Golf Courses: 9.5 private; 16.5 daily fee; 4 municipal	**B**
Bowling Lanes: 744	**B**
Movie Theaters: 44	**A**
Crowd Pleasers (1,100)	
Zoos: Washington Park Zoo	**A**
Auto Racing:	**B**
Portland International (SCCA)	
Rose City (NASCAR)	
Pari-mutuel Betting:	**B**
Multnomah Kennel Club (80 days)	
Portland Meadows (Thoroughbred, 92 days)	
Professional Sports: 2.425 game seats per capita	**A**
Beavers (baseball), TRAIL BLAZERS (basketball), BREAKERS (football)	
NCAA Division I: .027 game seats per capita	**C**
Portland State Vikings (b)	

Outdoor Recreation Assets (332)
Inland Water Area: 46.4 square miles
National Forests, Parks, Wildlife Refuges:
Eagle Creek NWR (166 acres)
McLoughlin House NHS (0.63 acres)
Mount Hood NF (72,415 acres)
Siuslaw NF (25,440 acres)
Willamette NF (856 acres)
Places Rated Score: 2,532   Places Rated Rank: 55

Portsmouth–Dover–Rochester, NH–ME

	Rating
Common Denominators (700)	
Good Restaurants: 3 ★, 17 ★★, 5 ★★★	**AA**
Golf Courses: 0.5 daily fee	**C**
Bowling Lanes: 58	**C**
Movie Theaters: 4	**C**
Crowd Pleasers (200)	
NCAA Division I: .592 game seats per capita	**B**
University of New Hampshire Wildcats	

Outdoor Recreation Assets (490)
Atlantic Coastline: 26 miles
Inland Water Area: 24.6 square miles
National Forests, Parks, Wildlife Refuges:
Rachel Carson NWR (1,748 acres)
Places Rated Score: 1,390   Places Rated Rank: 236

Poughkeepsie, NY

	Rating
Common Denominators (1,400)	
Good Restaurants: 6 ★★, 3 ★★★, 1 ★★★★, 1 ★★★★★	**AA**
Golf Courses: 5.5 private; 5 daily fee; 3.5 municipal	**AA**
Bowling Lanes: 328	**AA**
Movie Theaters: 6	**B**
Crowd Pleasers (100)	
NCAA Division I: .159 game seats per capita	**C**
Marist College Red Foxes (b)	

Outdoor Recreation Assets (170)
Inland Water Area: 20.7 square miles
National Forests, Parks, Wildlife Refuges:
Appalachian Trail (3,619 acres)
Eleanor Roosevelt NHS (181 acres)
Home of Franklin D. Roosevelt NHS (264 acres)
Vanderbilt Mansion NHS (212 acres)
Places Rated Score: 1,670   Places Rated Rank: 165

Providence, RI

	Rating
Common Denominators (800)	
Good Restaurants: 1 ★, 3 ★★, 5 ★★★	**B**
Golf Courses: 9.5 private; 9.5 daily fee; 1.5 municipal	**B**
Bowling Lanes: 234	**B**
Movie Theaters: 16	**B**
Crowd Pleasers (300)	
Zoos: Roger Williams Park Zoo	**C**
NCAA Division I: .477 game seats per capita	**B**
Brown Bruins, Providence College Friars (b)	

Outdoor Recreation Assets (963)
Atlantic Coastline: 12 miles
Inland Water Area: 103.6 square miles
National Forests, Parks, Wildlife Refuges:
Roger Williams National Memorial (5 acres)
CMSA Access: PROVIDENCE–PAWTUCKET–FALL
RIVER, RI–MA (200)
Places Rated Score: 2,263   Places Rated Rank: 76

★ Provo–Orem, UT

	Rating
Common Denominators (900)	
Good Restaurants: 1 ★★	**C**
Golf Courses: 3 private; 0.5 daily fee; 3.5 municipal	**B**
Bowling Lanes: 104	**B**
Movie Theaters: 9	**AA**
Crowd Pleasers (400)	
NCAA Division I: 2.843 game seats per capita	**AA**
Brigham Young Cougars	

Outdoor Recreation Assets (2,000)
Inland Water Area: 126.9 square miles
National Forests, Parks, Wildlife Refuges:
Ashley NF (3,885 acres)
Manti-La Sal NF (91,292 acres)
Timpanogos Cave NM (250 acres)
Uinta NF (390,215 acres)
Places Rated Score: 3,300   Places Rated Rank: 23

Rating

Pueblo, CO
Common Denominators (1,100)
Good Restaurants: 1 ★, 3 ★★	A
Golf Courses: 1 private; 1.5 daily fee; 1.5 municipal	B
Bowling Lanes: 118	A
Movie Theaters: 5	A

Crowd Pleasers (500)
Auto Racing: Pueblo Motorsports (SCCA)	C
Pari-mutuel Betting: Pueblo Greyhound Park (74 days)	AA

Outdoor Recreation Assets (19)
Inland Water Area: 8.8 square miles
Places Rated Score: 1,619   Places Rated Rank: 174

Racine, WI
Common Denominators (1,300)
Good Restaurants: 4 ★, 1 ★★, 1 ★★★	A
Golf Courses: 2 private; 2 daily fee; 4 municipal	AA
Bowling Lanes: 224	AA
Movie Theaters: 4	B

Crowd Pleasers (100)
Zoos: Racine Zoological Garden	C

Outdoor Recreation Assets (216)
Great Lakes Coastline: 12 miles
Inland Water Area: 6.4 square miles
CMSA Access: MILWAUKEE–RACINE, WI (400)
Places Rated Score: 2,016   Places Rated Rank: 104

Raleigh–Durham, NC
Common Denominators (1,100)
Good Restaurants: 1 ★, 2 ★★, 6 ★★★	B
Golf Courses: 14.5 private; 15.5 daily fee	A
Bowling Lanes: 236	B
Movie Theaters: 34	AA

Crowd Pleasers (500)
Professional Sports: .624 game seats per capita Durham Bulls (baseball)	C
NCAA Division I: 1.826 game seats per capita Duke Blue Devils, North Carolina State Wolfpack, University of North Carolina Tarheels	AA

Outdoor Recreation Assets (6)
Inland Water Area: 2.5 square miles
Places Rated Score: 1,606   Places Rated Rank: 180

Reading, PA
Common Denominators (1,200)
Good Restaurants: 2 ★, 1 ★★, 1 ★★★, 2 ★★★★	B
Golf Courses: 5 private; 11 daily fee	AA
Bowling Lanes: 270	A
Movie Theaters: 11	A

Crowd Pleasers (300)
Professional Sports: 1.837 game seats per capita Phillies (baseball)	A

Outdoor Recreation Assets (49)
Inland Water Area: 1.9 square miles
National Forests, Parks, Wildlife Refuges:
Appalachian Trail (3,703 acres)
Hopewell Village NHS (529 acres)
Places Rated Score: 1,549   Places Rated Rank: 193

Redding, CA
Common Denominators (800)
Good Restaurants: 1 ★, 1 ★★	C
Golf Courses: 2.5 private; 1.5 daily fee	B
Bowling Lanes: 76	B
Movie Theaters: 4	A

Crowd Pleasers (100)
Auto Racing: Shasta (NASCAR)	C

Outdoor Recreation Assets (1,524)
Inland Water Area: 62.8 square miles
National Forests, Parks, Wildlife Refuges:
Lassen NF (149,931 acres)
Lassen Volcanic NP (4,200 acres)
Shasta NF (471,224 acres)

Trinity NF (30,626 acres)
Whiskeytown–Shasta–Trinity NRA (42,488 acres)
Places Rated Score: 2,424   Places Rated Rank: 64

Reno, NV
Common Denominators (1,400)
Good Restaurants: 8 ★, 16 ★★, 13 ★★★, 2 ★★★★	AA
Golf Courses: 1 private; 2 daily fee; 3.5 municipal	A
Bowling Lanes: 166	A
Movie Theaters: 8	AA

Crowd Pleasers (500)
Professional Sports: 1.627 game seats per capita Padres (baseball)	A
NCAA Division I: .697 game seats per capita University of Nevada Wolf Pack	B

Outdoor Recreation Assets (486)
Inland Water Area: 232.9 square miles
National Forests, Parks, Wildlife Refuges:
Anaho Island NWR (248 acres)
Sheldon NWR (187,200 acres)
Toiyabe NF (56,087 acres)
Places Rated Score: 2,386   Places Rated Rank: 66

Richland–Kennewick–Pasco, WA
Common Denominators (900)
Good Restaurants: 1 ★★	C
Golf Courses: 2 private; 3.5 daily fee; 1 municipal	A
Bowling Lanes: 132	A
Movie Theaters: 4	B

Crowd Pleasers (200)
Professional Sports: .768 game seats per capita Tri-Cities Triplets (baseball)	B

Outdoor Recreation Assets (104)
Inland Water Area: 61.3 square miles
Places Rated Score: 1,204   Places Rated Rank: 262

Richmond–Petersburg, VA
Common Denominators (900)
Good Restaurants: 2 ★, 7 ★★, 3 ★★★	B
Golf Courses: 14.5 private; 11.5 daily fee	B
Bowling Lanes: 330	B
Movie Theaters: 26	A

Crowd Pleasers (900)
Theme Parks: Kings Dominion (121 days)	A
Auto Racing:	B
Richmond Fairgrounds (NASCAR) Southside Speedway (NASCAR)	
Professional Sports: .873 game seats per capita Braves (baseball)	B
NCAA Division I: .498 game seats per capita University of Richmond Spiders, Virginia Commonwealth University Rams (b)	B

Outdoor Recreation Assets (143)
Inland Water Area: 78.2 square miles
National Forests, Parks, Wildlife Refuges:
Harrison Lake NWR (445 acres)
Maggie L. Walker NHS (1.28 acres)
Petersburg National Battlefield (1,524 acres)
Poplar Grove National Cemetery (9 acres)
Presquile NWR (1,329 acres)
Richmond National Battlefield Park (771 acres)
Places Rated Score: 1,943   Places Rated Rank: 116

Riverside–San Bernardino, CA
Common Denominators (900)
Good Restaurants: 4 ★, 19 ★★, 14 ★★★.	A
Golf Courses: 49.5 private; 30 daily fee; 5 municipal	B
Bowling Lanes: 956	B
Movie Theaters: 37	B

Crowd Pleasers (200)
Zoos: Living Desert Reserve	C
Auto Racing: Riverside International (NASCAR, SCCA)	C

Rating

Outdoor Recreation Assets (418)
Inland Water Area: 108.1 square miles
National Forests, Parks, Wildlife Refuges:
Angeles NF (10,129 acres)
Cleveland NF (77,977 acres)
Death Valley NM (85,152 acres)
Joshua Tree NM (556,995 acres)
San Bernardino NF (658,645 acres)
CMSA Access: LOS ANGELES–ANAHEIM–
RIVERSIDE, CA (400)
Places Rated Score: 1,918   Places Rated Rank: 124

Roanoke, VA
Common Denominators (1,000)
Good Restaurants: 1 ★★, 1 ★★★, 1 ★★★★   B
Golf Courses: 6.5 private; 2.5 daily fee   C
Bowling Lanes: 202   A
Movie Theaters: 13   AA
Crowd Pleasers (200)
Professional Sports: 1.270 game seats per capita   B
Salem Redbirds (baseball)
Outdoor Recreation Assets (836)
Inland Water Area: 1.2 square miles
National Forests, Parks, Wildlife Refuges:
Appalachian Trail (3,458 acres)
Blue Ridge Parkway (5,661 acres)
George Washington NF (13,520 acres)
Jefferson NF (67,819 acres)
Places Rated Score: 2,036   Places Rated Rank: 101

Rochester, MN
Common Denominators (1,500)
Good Restaurants: 3 ★, 3 ★★, 3 ★★★   AA
Golf Courses: 1 private; 2 daily fee; 3 municipal   AA
Bowling Lanes: 72   A
Movie Theaters: 5   AA
Outdoor Recreation Assets (3)
Inland Water Area: .4 square miles
Places Rated Score: 1,503   Places Rated Rank: 207

Rochester, NY
Common Denominators (1,200)
Good Restaurants: 3 ★, 22 ★★, 17 ★★★, 1 ★★★★   AA
Golf Courses: 17 private; 26.5 daily fee;   A
5 municipal
Bowling Lanes: 1,260   AA
Movie Theaters: 19   C
Crowd Pleasers (500)
Auto Racing: Spencer Speedway (NASCAR)   C
Pari-mutuel Betting: Finger Lakes (Thoroughbred,   B
153 days)
Professional Sports: 1.236 game seats per capita   B
Red Wings (baseball), Americans (hockey)
Outdoor Recreation Assets (959)
Great Lakes Coastline: 90 miles
Inland Water Area: 34.5 square miles
Places Rated Score: 2,659   Places Rated Rank: 50

Rockford, IL
Common Denominators (800)
Good Restaurants: 4 ★★   C
Golf Courses: 4 private; 6.5 municipal   B
Bowling Lanes: 422   AA
Movie Theaters: 6   C
Crowd Pleasers (100)
Auto Racing: Blackhawk Farms Raceway (SCCA)   C
Outdoor Recreation Assets (33)
Inland Water Area: 5.2 square miles
Places Rated Score: 933   Places Rated Rank: 297

Sacramento, CA
Common Denominators (700)
Good Restaurants: 3 ★, 7 ★★, 5 ★★★   C
Golf Courses: 11.5 private; 11.5 daily fee;   B
6.5 municipal

Rating

Bowling Lanes: 554   B
Movie Theaters: 29   B
Crowd Pleasers (200)
Zoos: Sacramento Zoo   C
Pari-mutuel Betting: C
California State Fair (Thoroughbred, 14 days)
Golden Bear Raceway (harness, 35 days)
Outdoor Recreation Assets (1,406)
Inland Water Area: 174.5 square miles
National Forests, Parks, Wildlife Refuges:
Eldorado NF (539,658 acres)
Tahoe NF (269,335 acres)
Places Rated Score: 2,306   Places Rated Rank: 72

Saginaw–Bay City–Midland, MI
Common Denominators (1,200)
Good Restaurants: 3 ★, 6 ★★, 4 ★★★   A
Golf Courses: 5.5 private; 15 daily fee;   AA
2.5 municipal
Bowling Lanes: 560   AA
Movie Theaters: 9   C
Crowd Pleasers (400)
Zoos: Saginaw Children's Zoo   C
Auto Racing: Dixie (NASCAR)   C
Pari-mutuel Betting: Saginaw Valley Trotting   B
(67 days)
Outdoor Recreation Assets (459)
Great Lakes Coastline: 40 miles
Inland Water Area: 7.2 square miles
National Forests, Parks, Wildlife Refuges:
Shiawassee NWR (8,984 acres)
Places Rated Score: 2,059   Places Rated Rank: 96

St. Cloud, MN
Common Denominators (1,300)
Good Restaurants: 2 ★★   C
Golf Courses: 1.5 private; 5 daily fee;   AA
1 municipal
Bowling Lanes: 174   AA
Movie Theaters: 7   AA
Outdoor Recreation Assets (272)
Inland Water Area: 72.8 square miles
National Forests, Parks, Wildlife Refuges:
Sherburne NWR (29,406 acres)
Places Rated Score: 1,572   Places Rated Rank: 189

St. Joseph, MO
Common Denominators (1,200)
Good Restaurants: 1 ★★, 1 ★★★   A
Golf Courses: 2 private; 1 municipal   C
Bowling Lanes: 106   AA
Movie Theaters: 4   AA
Outdoor Recreation Assets (65)
Inland Water Area: 5.3 square miles
Places Rated Score: 1,265   Places Rated Rank: 251

St. Louis, MO–IL
Common Denominators (800)
Good Restaurants: 1 ★, 13 ★★, 14 ★★★, 3 ★★★★,   B
1 ★★★★★
Golf Courses: 22.5 private; 16 daily fee;   C
2.5 municipal
Bowling Lanes: 1,244   B
Movie Theaters: 67   A
Crowd Pleasers (1,100)
Zoos: Forest Park Zoo   AA
Theme Parks: Six Flags Over Mid-America   C
(140 days)
Auto Racing: Mid-America Raceway (SCCA)   C
Professional Sports: 2.884 game seats per capita   AA
CARDINALS (baseball, football), BLUES
(hockey)
NCAA Division I: .036 game seats per capita   C
St. Louis Billikens (b)

	Rating
Outdoor Recreation Assets (143)	
Inland Water Area: 77.2 square miles	
National Forests, Parks, Wildlife Refuges:	
Jefferson National Expansion Memorial NHS	
(91 acres)	
CMSA Access: ST. LOUIS–EAST ST. LOUIS–	
ALTON, MO–IL (200)	
Places Rated Score: 2,243 Places Rated Rank: 78	

Salem, OR
Common Denominators (900)
Good Restaurants: 1 ★, 2 ★★	C
Golf Courses: 2 private; 5.5 daily fee	B
Bowling Lanes: 160	B
Movie Theaters: 11	AA

Crowd Pleasers (100)
Professional Sports: .370 game seats per capita	C
Angels (baseball)	

Outdoor Recreation Assets (873)
Inland Water Area: 14 square miles
National Forests, Parks, Wildlife Refuges:
  Ankeny NWR (2,796 acres)
  Baskett Slough NWR (2,492 acres)
  Mount Hood NF (65,872 acres)
  Willamette NF (135,004 acres)
Places Rated Score: 1,873   Places Rated Rank: 132

Salem–Gloucester, MA
Common Denominators (900)
Good Restaurants: 6 ★, 10 ★★, 4 ★★★	AA
Golf Courses: 7 private; 3 daily fee; 1.5 municipal	B
Movie Theaters: 8	A

Outdoor Recreation Assets (934)
Atlantic Coastline: 33 miles
Inland Water Area: 22.3 square miles
National Forests, Parks, Wildlife Refuges:
  Parker River NWR (2,330 acres)
  Salem Maritime NHS (9 acres)
  Thatcher Island NWR (22 acres)
CMSA Access: BOSTON–LAWRENCE–SALEM, MA–NH (400)
Places Rated Score: 2,234   Places Rated Rank: 80

Salinas–Seaside–Monterey, CA
Common Denominators (1,300)
Good Restaurants: 7 ★, 11 ★★, 14 ★★★, 4 ★★★★	AA
Golf Courses: 10 private; 7.5 daily fee; 2 municipal	A
Bowling Lanes: 136	B
Movie Theaters: 18	AA

Crowd Pleasers (300)
Auto Racing: Laguna Seca (NASCAR, SCCA)	C
Professional Sports: .844 game seats per capita	B
Salinas Spurs (baseball)	

Outdoor Recreation Assets (1,579)
Pacific Coastline: 85 miles
Inland Water Area: 3 square miles
National Forests, Parks, Wildlife Refuges:
  Los Padres NF (304,578 acres)
  Pinnacles NM (1,283 acres)
  Salinas River NWR (364 acres)
Places Rated Score: 3,179   Places Rated Rank: 27

★ Salt Lake City–Ogden, UT
Common Denominators (1,000)
Good Restaurants: 6 ★, 10 ★★, 3 ★★★, 1 ★★★★	B
Golf Courses: 11 private; 5.5 daily fee; 10.5 municipal	B
Bowling Lanes: 574	B
Movie Theaters: 45	AA

Crowd Pleasers (900)
Zoos:	A
Hogle Zoological Garden	
Tracy Aviary	
Professional Sports: 1.845 game seats per capita	A
Gulls (baseball), JAZZ (basketball), Golden	
Eagles (hockey)	

	Rating
NCAA Division I: .717 game seats per capita	A
University of Utah Utes, Utah State Aggies	

Outdoor Recreation Assets (2,000)
Inland Water Area: 477.5 square miles
National Forests, Parks, Wildlife Refuges:
  Cache NF (67,554 acres)
  Wasatch NF (133,926 acres)
Places Rated Score: 3,900   Places Rated Rank: 11

San Angelo, TX
Common Denominators (1,100)
Good Restaurants: 1 ★, 1 ★★	B
Golf Courses: 1 private; 1 daily fee; 0.5 municipal	B
Bowling Lanes: 68	A
Movie Theaters: 4	AA

Outdoor Recreation Assets (36)
Inland Water Area: 10.9 square miles
Places Rated Score: 1,136   Places Rated Rank: 272

San Antonio, TX
Common Denominators (900)
Good Restaurants: 11 ★, 15 ★★, 7 ★★★, 2 ★★★★	A
Golf Courses: 13.5 private; 2 daily fee; 5.5 municipal	C
Bowling Lanes: 660	B
Movie Theaters: 33	A

Crowd Pleasers (600)
Zoos: San Antonio Zoo and Aquarium	A
Professional Sports: 1.095 game seats per capita	B
Dodgers (baseball), SPURS (basketball), GUNSLINGERS (football)	
NCAA Division I: .055 game seats per capita	C
University of Texas Roadrunners (b)	

Outdoor Recreation Assets (9)
Inland Water Area: 3.7 square miles
National Forests, Parks, Wildlife Refuges:
  San Antonio Missions NHP (463 acres)
Places Rated Score: 1,509   Places Rated Rank: 204

★ San Diego, CA
Common Denominators (900)
Good Restaurants: 3 ★, 38 ★★, 14 ★★★	A
Golf Courses: 17.5 private; 24 daily fee; 6 municipal	B
Bowling Lanes: 928	B
Movie Theaters: 56	B

Crowd Pleasers (1,300)
Zoos:	AA
San Diego Zoo	
Wild Animal Park	
Theme Parks: Sea World of California (365 days)	A
Pari-mutuel Betting: Del Mar (Thoroughbred, 43 days)	C
Professional Sports: 2.762 game seats per capita	AA
PADRES (baseball), CHARGERS (football)	
NCAA Division I: .264 game seats per capita	C
San Diego State Aztecs, U.S. International University Soaring Gulls (b), University of San Diego Toreros (b)	

Outdoor Recreation Assets (1,147)
Pacific Coastline: 55 miles
Inland Water Area: 52.2 square miles
National Forests, Parks, Wildlife Refuges:
  Cabrillo NM (144 acres)
  Cleveland NF (288,125 acres)
  Tijuana Slough NWR (407 acres)
Places Rated Score: 3,347   Places Rated Rank: 22

★ San Francisco, CA
Common Denominators (1,100)
Good Restaurants: 2 ★, 34 ★★, 52 ★★★, 15 ★★★★, 2 ★★★★★	AA
Golf Courses: 15 private; 4 daily fee; 6 municipal	C
Bowling Lanes: 572	B
Movie Theaters: 99	AA

Rating   Rating

Crowd Pleasers (1,100)
Zoos: San Francisco Zoological Gardens   A
Aquariums: Steinhart Aquarium   A
Pari-mutuel Betting: Bay Meadows (Thoroughbred,   C
111 days)
Professional Sports: 3.484 game seats per capita   AA
GIANTS (baseball), 49ERS (football)
Outdoor Recreation Assets (2,000)
Pacific Coastline: 75 miles
Inland Water Area: 249.6 square miles
National Forests, Parks, Wildlife Refuges:
Farallon NWR (91 acres)
Fort Point NHS (29 acres)
Golden Gate NRA (60,788 acres)
Muir Woods NM (554 acres)
Point Reyes NS (63,953 acres)
San Francisco Bay NWR (1,863 acres)
CMSA Access: SAN FRANCISCO–OAKLAND–
SAN JOSE, CA (400)
Places Rated Score: 4,600   Places Rated Rank: 2

San Jose, CA
Common Denominators (800)
Good Restaurants: 2 ★, 11 ★★, 7 ★★★   B
Golf Courses: 8.5 private; 7.5 daily fee;   C
6.5 municipal
Bowling Lanes: 648   B
Movie Theaters: 46   A
Crowd Pleasers (700)
Zoos: C
Applegate Zoo
San Jose Baby Zoo
Theme Parks: Marriott's Great America (141 days)   B
Auto Racing: San Jose Fairgrounds (NASCAR)   C
Professional Sports: .281 game seats per capita   C
Bees (baseball)
NCAA Division I: .568 game seats per capita   B
San Jose State Spartans, Stanford University
Cardinals, University of Santa Clara Broncos (b)
Outdoor Recreation Assets (64)
Inland Water Area: 11.6 square miles
National Forests, Parks, Wildlife Refuges:
San Francisco NWR (3,156 acres)
CMSA Access: SAN FRANCISCO–OAKLAND–
SAN JOSE, CA (400)
Places Rated Score: 1,964   Places Rated Rank: 111

★ Santa Barbara–Santa Maria–Lompoc, CA
Common Denominators (1,100)
Good Restaurants: 2 ★, 10 ★★, 4 ★★★   AA
Golf Courses: 7 private; 2.5 daily fee; 1 municipal   C
Bowling Lanes: 164   B
Movie Theaters: 13   AA
Crowd Pleasers (200)
Zoos: Santa Barbara Zoological Gardens   C
NCAA Division I: .131 game seats per capita   C
University of California Gauchos (b)
Outdoor Recreation Assets (2,000)
Pacific Coastline: 78 miles
Inland Water Area: 7.5 square miles
National Forests, Parks, Wildlife Refuges:
Channel Islands NP (125,539 acres)
Los Padres NF (628,886 acres)
Places Rated Score: 3,300   Places Rated Rank: 23

Santa Cruz, CA
Common Denominators (800)
Good Restaurants: 2 ★★   C
Golf Courses: 3 daily fee; 1 municipal   B
Bowling Lanes: 60   B
Movie Theaters: 11   AA
Crowd Pleasers (100)
Auto Racing: Watsonville Fairgrounds (NASCAR)   C

Outdoor Recreation Assets (403)
Pacific Coastline: 40 miles
Inland Water Area: .1 square miles
CMSA Access: SAN FRANCISCO–OAKLAND–
SAN JOSE, CA (400)
Places Rated Score: 1,703   Places Rated Rank: 158

Santa Rosa–Petaluma, CA
Common Denominators (1,100)
Good Restaurants: 8 ★★, 6 ★★★   AA
Golf Courses: 2 private; 3.5 daily fee;   B
3.5 municipal
Bowling Lanes: 186   B
Movie Theaters: 10   A
Crowd Pleasers (300)
Auto Racing: Sears Point International (NASCAR,   C
SCCA)
Pari-mutuel Betting: Sonoma County Fair   C
(Thoroughbred, 13 days)
Professional Sports: .514 game seats per capita   C
Santa Rosa Redwood Pioneers (baseball)
Outdoor Recreation Assets (455)
Pacific Coastline: 44 miles
Inland Water Area: 4.5 square miles
National Forests, Parks, Wildlife Refuges:
San Pablo Bay NWR (249 acres)
CMSA Access: SAN FRANCISCO–OAKLAND–
SAN JOSE, CA (400)
Places Rated Score: 2,255   Places Rated Rank: 77

Sarasota, FL
Common Denominators (1,500)
Good Restaurants: 5 ★, 3 ★★, 5 ★★★   AA
Golf Courses: 7 private; 16.5 daily fee; 2 municipal   AA
Bowling Lanes: 204   A
Movie Theaters: 9   AA
Crowd Pleasers (400)
Pari-mutuel Betting: Sarasota Kennel Club   A
(101 days)
Professional Sports: .402 game seats per capita   C
Stingers (basketball)
Outdoor Recreation Assets (635)
Gulf of Mexico Coastline: 35 miles
Inland Water Area: 32.7 square miles
Places Rated Score: 2,535   Places Rated Rank: 54

Savannah, GA
Common Denominators (900)
Good Restaurants: 1 ★, 4 ★★, 2 ★★★   A
Golf Courses: 5 private; 1.5 daily fee; 1 municipal   C
Bowling Lanes: 116   B
Movie Theaters: 8   A
Crowd Pleasers (500)
Auto Racing: Roebling Road (SCCA)   C
Professional Sports: 2.514 game seats per capita   AA
Cardinals (baseball)
Outdoor Recreation Assets (837)
Atlantic Coastline: 30 miles
Inland Water Area: 57 square miles
National Forests, Parks, Wildlife Refuges:
Fort Pulaski NM (5,623 acres)
Savannah NWR (11,499 acres)
Wassaw NWR (10,050 acres)
Places Rated Score: 2,237   Places Rated Rank: 79

Scranton–Wilkes-Barre, PA
Common Denominators (900)
Good Restaurants: 5 ★, 2 ★★   C
Golf Courses: 12 private; 25 daily fee;   AA
1.5 municipal
Bowling Lanes: 600   A
Movie Theaters: 7   C
Crowd Pleasers (400)
Zoos: Nay Aug Zoo   C
Auto Racing: Pocono International (NASCAR,   C
SCCA)

	Rating
Pari-mutuel Betting: Pocono Downs (harness, 150 days)	B
Outdoor Recreation Assets (86)	
Inland Water Area: 35.4 square miles	
National Forests, Parks, Wildlife Refuges:	
Delaware NSR (372 acres)	
Delaware Water Gap NRA (6,662 acres)	
Places Rated Score: 1,386 Places Rated Rank: 238	

★ Seattle, WA

	Rating
Common Denominators (1,000)	
Good Restaurants: 5 ★, 22 ★★, 14 ★★★, 2 ★★★★	A
Golf Courses: 17 private; 14 daily fee; 10.5 municipal	B
Bowling Lanes: 916	B
Movie Theaters: 56	A
Crowd Pleasers (1,500)	
Zoos: Woodland Park Zoo	AA
Aquariums: Seattle Aquarium	A
Auto Racing:	B
Evergreen Speedway (NASCAR)	
Seattle International (SCCA)	
Pari-mutuel Betting: Longacres (Thoroughbred, 131 days)	C
Professional Sports: 4.405 game seats per capita	AA
Everett Giants, MARINERS (baseball),	
SUPERSONICS (basketball), SEAHAWKS	
(football)	
NCAA Division I: .259 game seats per capita	C
University of Washington Huskies	
Outdoor Recreation Assets (2,000)	
Puget Sound Coastline: 70 miles	
Inland Water Area: 89.1 square miles	
National Forests, Parks, Wildlife Refuges:	
Mount Baker NF (462,209 acres)	
Snoqualmie NF (504,324 acres)	
CMSA Access: SEATTLE–TACOMA, WA (300)	
Places Rated Score: 4,800 Places Rated Rank: 1	

Sharon, PA

	Rating
Common Denominators (1,100)	
Good Restaurants: 2 ★★	B
Golf Courses: 3.5 private; 6.5 daily fee	AA
Bowling Lanes: 150	AA
Movie Theaters: 2	C
Places Rated Score: 1,100 Places Rated Rank: 282	

Sheboygan, WI

	Rating
Common Denominators (1,000)	
Good Restaurants: 1 ★★	C
Golf Courses: 1 private; 3 daily fee	A
Bowling Lanes: 150	AA
Movie Theaters: 3	B
Outdoor Recreation Assets (316)	
Great Lakes Coastline: 29 miles	
Inland Water Area: 2.7 square miles	
Places Rated Score: 1,316 Places Rated Rank: 247	

Sherman–Denison, TX

	Rating
Common Denominators (700)	
Good Restaurants: 1 ★★★	B
Golf Courses: 3 private; 0.5 daily fee; 0.5 municipal	C
Bowling Lanes: 40	B
Movie Theaters: 2	B
Outdoor Recreation Assets (237)	
Inland Water Area: 44.2 square miles	
Places Rated Score: 937 Places Rated Rank: 296	

Shreveport, LA

	Rating
Common Denominators (700)	
Good Restaurants: 5 ★★, 3 ★★★	A
Golf Courses: 5.5 private; 1 daily fee; 2.5 municipal	C
Bowling Lanes: 114	B
Movie Theaters: 5	C

	Rating
Crowd Pleasers (500)	
Pari-mutuel Betting: Louisiana Downs (Thoroughbred, 125 days)	A
Professional Sports: .612 game seats per capita Captains (baseball)	C
NCAA Division I: .136 game seats per capita Centenary College Gentlemen (b)	C
Outdoor Recreation Assets (189)	
Inland Water Area: 65.6 square miles	
Places Rated Score: 1,389 Places Rated Rank: 237	

Sioux City, IA–NE

	Rating
Common Denominators (1,000)	
Good Restaurants: 1 ★, 2 ★★	B
Golf Courses: 4.5 private; 1.5 daily fee; 1 municipal	B
Bowling Lanes: 106	A
Movie Theaters: 4	A
Crowd Pleasers (300)	
Pari-mutuel Betting: Akotad Park (Thoroughbred, 37 days)	A
Outdoor Recreation Assets (59)	
Inland Water Area: 13.4 square miles	
Places Rated Score: 1,359 Places Rated Rank: 240	

Sioux Falls, SD

	Rating
Common Denominators (1,200)	
Good Restaurants: 1 ★, 2 ★★	B
Golf Courses: 3 private; 0.5 daily fee; 2 municipal	B
Bowling Lanes: 182	AA
Movie Theaters: 5	AA
Crowd Pleasers (100)	
Zoos: Great Plains Zoo	C
Outdoor Recreation Assets (24)	
Inland Water Area: 3.9 square miles	
Places Rated Score: 1,324 Places Rated Rank: 246	

South Bend–Mishawaka, IN

	Rating
Common Denominators (1,200)	
Good Restaurants: 1 ★, 5 ★★, 3 ★★★	AA
Golf Courses: 4.5 private; 2 daily fee; 3 municipal	B
Bowling Lanes: 312	AA
Movie Theaters: 6	B
Crowd Pleasers (600)	
Zoos: Potawatomi Park Zoo	B
NCAA Division I: 1.833 game seats per capita University of Notre Dame Fighting Irish	AA
Outdoor Recreation Assets (19)	
Inland Water Area: 1.7 square miles	
Places Rated Score: 1,819 Places Rated Rank: 139	

Spokane, WA

	Rating
Common Denominators (900)	
Good Restaurants: 1 ★, 5 ★★, 3 ★★★	A
Golf Courses: 2 private; 2 daily fee; 5 municipal	B
Bowling Lanes: 256	A
Movie Theaters: 5	C
Crowd Pleasers (500)	
Zoos: Walk in the Wild	C
Pari-mutuel Betting: Playfair Race Course (Thoroughbred, 98 days)	A
NCAA Division I: .152 game seats per capita Gonzaga Zags (b)	C
Outdoor Recreation Assets (117)	
Inland Water Area: 18.6 square miles	
National Forests, Parks, Wildlife Refuges:	
Turnbull NWR (14,489 acres)	
Places Rated Score: 1,517 Places Rated Rank: 200	

Springfield, IL

	Rating
Common Denominators (1,100)	
Good Restaurants: 2 ★, 3 ★★, 5 ★★★	AA
Golf Courses: 3 private; 1.5 daily fee; 2.5 municipal	B
Bowling Lanes: 40	C
Movie Theaters: 10	AA

	Rating

Crowd Pleasers (400)
Zoos: Henson C. Robinson Children's Zoo — **C**
Professional Sports: 1.864 game seats per capita — **A**
    Cardinals (baseball)
Outdoor Recreation Assets (36)
Inland Water Area: 8.5 square miles
National Forests, Parks, Wildlife Refuges:
    Lincoln Home NHS (12 acres)
Places Rated Score: 1,536   Places Rated Rank: 197

Springfield, MA
Common Denominators (800)
Good Restaurants: 2 ★, 4 ★★, 4 ★★★ — **B**
Golf Courses: 9 private; 12.5 daily fee; 4 municipal — **A**
Bowling Lanes: 192 — **B**
Movie Theaters: 10 — **C**
Crowd Pleasers (600)
Theme Parks: Riverside (120 days) — **AA**
Pari-mutuel Betting: Northampton (Thoroughbred, — **C**
    10 days)
Professional Sports: .576 game seats per capita — **C**
    Indians (hockey)
Outdoor Recreation Assets (114)
Inland Water Area: 13.4 square miles
National Forests, Parks, Wildlife Refuges:
    Springfield Armory NHS (55 acres)
Places Rated Score: 1,514   Places Rated Rank: 201

Springfield, MO
Common Denominators (1,000)
Good Restaurants: 2 ★★, 3 ★★★ — **A**
Golf Courses: 4 private; 2 daily fee; 2 municipal — **B**
Bowling Lanes: 140 — **B**
Movie Theaters: 7 — **A**
Crowd Pleasers (400)
Zoos: Dickerson Park Zoo — **C**
NCAA Division I: .713 game seats per capita — **A**
    Southwest Missouri State Bears
Outdoor Recreation Assets (337)
Inland Water Area: .6 square miles
National Forests, Parks, Wildlife Refuges:
    Mark Twain NF (51,327 acres)
    Wilson's Creek National Battlefield (1,749 acres)
Places Rated Score: 1,737   Places Rated Rank: 151

Stamford, CT
Common Denominators (1,000)
Good Restaurants: 2 ★, 4 ★★, 1 ★★★ — **A**
Golf Courses: 9.5 private; 2 municipal — **C**
Bowling Lanes: 80 — **B**
Movie Theaters: 9 — **AA**
Outdoor Recreation Assets (329)
Atlantic Coastline: 11 miles
Inland Water Area: 5.6 square miles
CMSA Access: New York–Northern New Jersey–
    Long Island, NY–NJ–CT (400)
Places Rated Score: 1,729   Places Rated Rank: 154

State College, PA
Common Denominators (800)
Good Restaurants: 1 ★★, 1 ★★★ — **B**
Golf Courses: 3 private; 3 daily fee — **A**
Bowling Lanes: 55 — **B**
Movie Theaters: 2 — **C**
Crowd Pleasers (400)
NCAA Division I: 4.545 game seats per capita — **AA**
    Pennsylvania State Nittany Lions
Places Rated Score: 1,200   Places Rated Rank: 264

Steubenville–Weirton, OH–WV
Common Denominators (1,000)
Good Restaurants: 1 ★ — **C**
Golf Courses: 4.5 private; 4 daily fee; — **A**
    0.5 municipal
Bowling Lanes: 118 — **A**
Movie Theaters: 6 — **A**

Crowd Pleasers (400)
Pari-mutuel Betting: Waterford Park — **AA**
    (Thoroughbred, 151 days)
Outdoor Recreation Assets (60)
Inland Water Area: 7 square miles
Places Rated Score: 1,460   Places Rated Rank: 217

Stockton, CA
Common Denominators (800)
Good Restaurants: 1 ★, 2 ★★, 1 ★★★ — **C**
Golf Courses: 6 private; 2 daily fee; 3 municipal — **B**
Bowling Lanes: 170 — **B**
Movie Theaters: 11 — **A**
Crowd Pleasers (800)
Auto Racing: Stockton 99 (NASCAR) — **C**
Pari-mutuel Betting: Ruidoso Downs — **B**
    (Thoroughbred, 74 days)
Professional Sports: 1.572 game seats per capita — **A**
    Lodi Crushers, Stockton Mudville Nine
    (baseball)
NCAA Division I: .619 game seats per capita — **B**
    University of the Pacific Tigers
Outdoor Recreation Assets (30)
Inland Water Area: 8.5 square miles
Places Rated Score: 1,630   Places Rated Rank: 171

Syracuse, NY
Common Denominators (1,600)
Good Restaurants: 2 ★, 17 ★★, 10 ★★★ — **AA**
Golf Courses: 16 private; 25.5 daily fee; — **AA**
    2 municipal
Bowling Lanes: 764 — **AA**
Movie Theaters: 28 — **AA**
Crowd Pleasers (700)
Zoos: Burnet Park Zoo — **C**
Auto Racing: Shangri-La (NASCAR) — **C**
Professional Sports: 1.143 game seats per capita — **B**
    Chiefs (baseball)
NCAA Division I: .739 game seats per capita — **A**
    Colgate University Red Raiders, Syracuse
    University Orangemen
Outdoor Recreation Assets (551)
Great Lakes Coastline: 36 miles
Inland Water Area: 91.5 square miles
Places Rated Score: 2,851   Places Rated Rank: 44

★ Tacoma, WA
Common Denominators (900)
Good Restaurants: 2 ★, 2 ★★, 4 ★★★ — **B**
Golf Courses: 6.5 private; 6 daily fee; — **B**
    2.5 municipal
Bowling Lanes: 344 — **B**
Movie Theaters: 17 — **A**
Crowd Pleasers (700)
Zoos: Point Defiance Zoo — **B**
Aquarium: Point Defiance Aquarium — **A**
Professional Sports: 1.186 game seats per capita — **B**
    Tigers (baseball)
Outdoor Recreation Assets (2,000)
Puget Sound Coastline: 15 miles
Inland Water Area: 113.1 square miles
National Forests, Parks, Wildlife Refuges:
    Mount Rainier NP (235,239 acres)
    Nisqually NWR (813 acres)
    Snoqualmie NF (129,938 acres)
CMSA Access: Seattle–Tacoma, WA (400)
Places Rated Score: 4,000   Places Rated Rank: 7

Tallahassee, FL
Common Denominators (700)
Good Restaurants: 2 ★★, 1 ★★★ — **B**
Golf Courses: 4.5 private; 2 daily fee; — **B**
    0.5 municipal
Bowling Lanes: 44 — **C**
Movie Theaters: 5 — **B**

Rating

Crowd Pleasers (400)
- NCAA Division I: 3.305 game seats per capita — **AA**
  Florida A & M Rattlers, Florida State Seminoles

Outdoor Recreation Assets (836)
- Inland Water Area: 36.5 square miles
- National Forests, Parks, Wildlife Refuges:
  Apalachicola NF (104,405 acres)

Places Rated Score: 1,936   Places Rated Rank: 119

Tampa–St. Petersburg–Clearwater, FL

Common Denominators (900)
- Good Restaurants: 26 ★, 21 ★★, 6 ★★★, 4 ★★★★ — **A**
- Golf Courses: 27.5 private; 38 daily fee; 5 municipal — **A**
- Bowling Lanes: 1,042 — **B**
- Movie Theaters: 30 — **C**

Crowd Pleasers (1,000)
- Theme Parks: Busch Gardens—The Dark Continent (365 days) — **AA**
- Pari-mutuel Betting: — **A**
  St. Petersburg Kennel Club (101 days)
  Tampa Bay Downs (Thoroughbred, 80 days)
  Tampa Greyhound Park (104 days)
  Tampa Jai Alai (150 days)
- Professional Sports: 1.479 game seats per capita — **B**
  Tampa Tarpons, St. Petersburg Cardinals (baseball), BANDITS, BUCCANEERS (football)
- NCAA Division I: .040 game seats per capita — **C**
  University of South Florida Bulls (b)

Outdoor Recreation Assets (1,043)
- Gulf of Mexico Coastline: 78 miles
- Inland Water Area: 122.8 square miles
- National Forests, Parks, Wildlife Refuges:
  Chassahowitzka NWR (6,707 acres)
  Egmont Key NWR (328 acres)
  Pinellas NWR (15 acres)

Places Rated Score: 2,943   Places Rated Rank: 38

Terre Haute, IN

Common Denominators (1,000)
- Good Restaurants: 1 ★, 1 ★★ — **C**
- Golf Courses: 1.5 private; 0.5 daily fee; 3.5 municipal — **A**
- Bowling Lanes: 144 — **A**
- Movie Theaters: 5 — **A**

Crowd Pleasers (400)
- NCAA Division I: 1.715 game seats per capita — **AA**
  Indiana State Sycamores

Outdoor Recreation Assets (1)
- Inland Water Area: .1 square miles

Places Rated Score: 1,401   Places Rated Rank: 234

Texarkana, TX–Texarkana, AR

Common Denominators (500)
- Golf Courses: 2 private; 0.5 daily fee — **C**
- Bowling Lanes: 78 — **B**
- Movie Theaters: 3 — **B**

Outdoor Recreation Assets (169)
- Inland Water Area: 51 square miles

Places Rated Score: 669   Places Rated Rank: 325

Toledo, OH

Common Denominators (900)
- Good Restaurants: 2 ★, 11 ★★, 2 ★★★ — **B**
- Golf Courses: 8.5 private; 8 daily fee; 4 municipal — **B**
- Bowling Lanes: 610 — **A**
- Movie Theaters: 17 — **B**

Crowd Pleasers (800)
- Zoos: Toledo Zoological Gardens — **A**
- Pari-mutuel Betting: Raceway Park (harness, 61 days) — **C**
- Professional Sports: 1.48 game seats per capita — **B**
  Mud Hens (baseball), Goaldiggers (hockey)

Rating

- NCAA Division I: .654 game seats per capita — **B**
  Bowling Green State Falcons, University of Toledo Rockets

Outdoor Recreation Assets (252)
- Great Lakes Coastline: 19 miles
- Inland Water Area: 9.7 square miles
- National Forests, Parks, Wildlife Refuges:
  Cedar Point NWR (2,445 acres)
  Ottawa NWR (2,078 acres)
  West Sister Island NWR (82 acres)

Places Rated Score: 1,952   Places Rated Rank: 114

Topeka, KS

Common Denominators (900)
- Good Restaurants: 1 ★★ — **C**
- Golf Courses: 4 private; 0.5 daily fee; 2.5 municipal — **B**
- Bowling Lanes: 152 — **A**
- Movie Theaters: 6 — **A**

Crowd Pleasers (200)
- Zoos: Topeka Zoological Park — **B**

Outdoor Recreation Assets (41)
- Inland Water Area: 4.5 square miles

Places Rated Score: 1,141   Places Rated Rank: 271

Trenton, NJ

Common Denominators (800)
- Good Restaurants: 1 ★, 5 ★★ — **B**
- Golf Courses: 7 private; 2 daily fee; 2 municipal — **B**
- Bowling Lanes: 268 — **A**
- Movie Theaters: 6 — **C**

Crowd Pleasers (400)
- Auto Racing: New Egypt Speedway (NASCAR) — **C**
- NCAA Division I: 1.154 game seats per capita — **A**
  Princeton Tigers, Rider College Broncs (b)

Outdoor Recreation Assets (46)
- Inland Water Area: 2.1 square miles

CMSA Access: PHILADELPHIA–WILMINGTON–TRENTON, PA–NJ–DE–MD (400)

Places Rated Score: 1,646   Places Rated Rank: 169

Tucson, AZ

Common Denominators (900)
- Good Restaurants: 5 ★★, 1 ★★★★, 1 ★★★★★ — **B**
- Golf Courses: 7 private; 5 daily fee; 6 municipal — **B**
- Bowling Lanes: 340 — **B**
- Movie Theaters: 17 — **A**

Crowd Pleasers (1,200)
- Zoos: — **A**
  Gene Reid Zoological Gardens
  Arizona-Sonora Desert Museum
- Pari-mutuel Betting: Tucson Greyhound Park (235 days) — **A**
- Professional Sports: 1.287 game seats per capita — **A**
  Toros (baseball)
- NCAA Division I: .886 game seats per capita — **A**
  University of Arizona Wildcats

Outdoor Recreation Assets (1,031)
- Inland Water Area: 1.1 square miles
- National Forests, Parks, Wildlife Refuges:
  Cabeza Prieta NWR (416,210 acres)
  Coronado NF (382,093 acres)
  Organ Pipe Cactus NM (330,479 acres)
  Saguaro NM (83,337 acres)

Places Rated Score: 3,131   Places Rated Rank: 29

Tulsa, OK

Common Denominators (1,100)
- Good Restaurants: 1 ★, 14 ★★, 9 ★★★ — **AA**
- Golf Courses: 9.5 private; 5 daily fee; 6 municipal — **B**
- Bowling Lanes: 368 — **B**
- Movie Theaters: 22 — **A**

Crowd Pleasers (800)
- Zoos: Tulsa Zoological Park — **B**
- Auto Racing: Hallett Racing Circuit (SCCA) — **C**

	Rating
Professional Sports: 1.637 game seats per capita Drillers (baseball), OUTLAWS (football), Oilers (hockey)	A
NCAA Division I: .620 game seats per capita University of Tulsa Golden Hurricane, Oral Roberts Titans (b)	B
Outdoor Recreation Assets (124)	
Inland Water Area: 123.7 square miles	

Places Rated Score: 2,024 — Places Rated Rank: 102

Tuscaloosa, AL

Common Denominators (600)	
Good Restaurants: 1 ★★, 1 ★★★	B
Golf Courses: 5 private; 1 daily fee	C
Bowling Lanes: 64	B
Movie Theaters: 3	C
Crowd Pleasers (400)	
NCAA Division I: 3.752 game seats per capita University of Alabama Crimson Tide	AA
Outdoor Recreation Assets (90)	
Inland Water Area: 10.6 square miles	
National Forests, Parks, Wildlife Refuges:	
Talladega NF (8,562 acres)	

Places Rated Rank: 283

Tyler, TX

Common Denominators (500)	
Golf Courses: 5.5 private; 2 daily fee	B
Bowling Lanes: 32	C
Movie Theaters: 3	B
Crowd Pleasers (100)	
Zoos: Caldwell Children's Zoo	C
Outdoor Recreation Assets (31)	
Inland Water Area: 5.7 square miles	

Places Rated Score: 631 — Places Rated Rank: 326

Utica–Rome, NY

Common Denominators (1,300)	
Good Restaurants: 1 ★, 8 ★★, 5 ★★★	AA
Golf Courses: 11.5 private; 14.5 daily fee; 1.5 municipal	AA
Bowling Lanes: 408	AA
Movie Theaters: 2	C
Crowd Pleasers (300)	
Zoos: Utica Zoo	C
Professional Sports: .712 game seats per capita Utica Blue Sox, Twin Falls Mets (baseball)	C
NCAA Division I: .122 game seats per capita Utica College Pioneers (b)	C
Outdoor Recreation Assets (150)	
Inland Water Area: 78.9 square miles	
National Forests, Parks, Wildlife Refuges:	
Fort Stanwix NM (16 acres)	

Places Rated Score: 1,750 — Places Rated Rank: 149

Vallejo–Fairfield–Napa, CA

Common Denominators (800)	
Good Restaurants: 3 ★, 7 ★★, 4 ★★★, 2 ★★★★	AA
Golf Courses: 5.5 private; 1.5 daily fee; 2 municipal	C
Bowling Lanes: 144	B
Movie Theaters: 7	C
Crowd Pleasers (100)	
Pari-mutuel Betting: Solano County Fair (Thoroughbred, 12 days)	C
Outdoor Recreation Assets (259)	
Inland Water Area: 81.7 square miles	
CMSA Access: SAN FRANCISCO–OAKLAND– SAN JOSE, CA (400)	

Places Rated Score: 1,559 — Places Rated Rank: 192

Vancouver, WA

Common Denominators (800)	
Good Restaurants: 1 ★, 1 ★★, 1 ★★★	B
Golf Courses: 2 private; 2 daily fee	C

	Rating
Bowling Lanes: 132	B
Movie Theaters: 6	A
Outdoor Recreation Assets (264)	
Inland Water Area: 31 square miles	
National Forests, Parks, Wildlife Refuges:	
Fort Vancouver NHS (209 acres)	
Gifford Pinchot NF (1,150 acres)	
CMSA Access: PORTLAND–VANCOUVER, OR–WA (400)	

Places Rated Score: 1,464 — Places Rated Rank: 215

Victoria, TX

Common Denominators (1,300)	
Good Restaurants: 1 ★★, 1 ★★★	AA
Golf Courses: 0.5 private; 1 municipal	B
Bowling Lanes: 58	A
Movie Theaters: 3	AA
Crowd Pleasers (100)	
Zoos: Texas Zoo	C
Outdoor Recreation Assets (10)	
Inland Water Area: 1.8 square miles	

Places Rated Score: 1,410 — Places Rated Rank: 230

Vineland–Millville–Bridgeton, NJ

Common Denominators (600)	
Good Restaurants: 1 ★★	C
Golf Courses: 1 daily fee	C
Bowling Lanes: 72	B
Movie Theaters: 4	B
Crowd Pleasers (100)	
Zoos: Cohanzick Zoo	C
Outdoor Recreation Assets (374)	
Atlantic Coastline: 30 miles	
Inland Water Area: 7.4 square miles	
CMSA Access: PHILADELPHIA–WILMINGTON– TRENTON, PA–NJ–DE–MD (400)	

Places Rated Score: 1,474 — Places Rated Rank: 214

Visalia–Tulare–Porterville, CA

Common Denominators (700)	
Good Restaurants: 1 ★	C
Golf Courses: 1 private; 4.5 daily fee; 1.5 municipal	B
Bowling Lanes: 132	B
Movie Theaters: 6	B
Crowd Pleasers (100)	
Professional Sports: .399 game seats per capita Visalia Oaks (baseball)	C
Outdoor Recreation Assets (2,000)	
Inland Water Area: 3 square miles	
National Forests, Parks, Wildlife Refuges:	
Blue Ridge NWR (577 acres)	
Inyo NF (190,574 acres)	
Kings Canyon NP (105,252 acres)	
Pixley NWR (5,147 acres)	
Sequoia NF (700,135 acres)	
Sequoia NP (401,774 acres)	

Places Rated Score: 2,800 — Places Rated Rank: 45

Waco, TX

Common Denominators (700)	
Good Restaurants: 3 ★★, 1 ★★★	A
Golf Courses: 4 private; 1 daily fee; 1 municipal	C
Bowling Lanes: 56	C
Movie Theaters: 5	B
Crowd Pleasers (500)	
Zoos: Central Texas Zoo	C
NCAA Division I: 2.120 game seats per capita Baylor Bears	AA
Outdoor Recreation Assets (48)	
Inland Water Area: 9.8 square miles	

Places Rated Score: 1,248 — Places Rated Rank: 252

Washington, DC–MD–VA

Common Denominators (600)	
Good Restaurants: 10 ★, 42 ★★, 30 ★★★, 6 ★★★★	A
Golf Courses: 59 private; 9 daily fee; 19 municipal	C

	Rating
Bowling Lanes: 1,032	C
Movie Theaters: 44	C

Crowd Pleasers (700)

Zoos: National Zoological Park	AA
Pari-mutuel Betting:	C

Bowie (Thoroughbred, 114 days)
Freestate (harness, 85 days)
Laurel (Thoroughbred, 75 days)
Rosecroft (harness, 85 days)

Professional Sports: .499 game seats per capita	C

Prince William Pirates (baseball), BULLETS (basketball), REDSKINS (football), CAPITALS (hockey)

NCAA Division I: .215 game seats per capita	C

American University Eagles (b), George Mason University Patriots (b), George Washington University Colonials (b), Georgetown University Hoyas (b), Howard University Bisons, University of Maryland Terps

Outdoor Recreation Assets (278)

Inland Water Area: 129 square miles
National Forests, Parks, Wildlife Refuges:
Antietam National Battlefield (0.22 acres)
Appalachian Trail (1,061 acres)
Battleground National Cemetery (1 acre)
Catoctin Mountain Park (5,694 acres)
Chesapeake and Ohio Canal NHP (4,761 acres)
Clara Barton NHS (9 acres)
Ford's Theatre NHS (0.29 acres)
Fort Washington Park (341 acres)
Frederick Douglass Home (8 acres)
Fredericksburg and Spotsylvania County
    Battlefields NMP (84 acres)
George Washington Parkway (7,045 acres)
Greenbelt Park (1,176 acres)
Harpers Ferry NHP (370 acres)
John F. Kennedy Center for the Performing Arts
    (18 acres)
Lincoln Memorial (164 acres)
Lyndon B. Johnson Memorial Grove (17 acres)
Manassas National Battlefield Park (3,021 acres)
Marumsco NWR (63 acres)
Mason Neck NWR (1,131 acres)
Monocacy National Battlefield (422 acres)
National Capital Parks (6,036 acres)
National Mall (146 acres)
Piscataway Park (4,210 acres)
Presquile NWR (1,329 acres)
Prince William Forest Park (17,410 acres)
Robert E. Lee Memorial (28 acres)
Rock Creek Park (1,754 acres)
Theodore Roosevelt Island (89 acres)
Thomas Jefferson Memorial (18 acres)
Thomas Stone NHS (322 acres)
Washington Monument (106 acres)
White House (18 acres)
Wolf Trap Farm Park for the Performing Arts
    (130 acres)

Places Rated Score: 1,578   Places Rated Rank: 188

Waterbury, CT

Common Denominators (600)

Golf Courses: 2 private; 2 municipal	C
Bowling Lanes: 126	B
Movie Theaters: 7	A

Crowd Pleasers (300)

Professional Sports: 1.708 game seats per capita	A

Angels (baseball)

Outdoor Recreation Assets (46)

Inland Water Area: 2.1 square miles
Places Rated Score: 946   Places Rated Rank: 295

Waterloo–Cedar Falls, IA

Common Denominators (1,300)

Good Restaurants: 2 ★★, 1 ★★★	B

	Rating
Golf Courses: 3.5 private; 1 daily fee;	AA
5.5 municipal	
Bowling Lanes: 182	AA
Movie Theaters: 6	A

Crowd Pleasers (600)

Professional Sports: 2.365 game seats per capita	A

Waterloo Indians (baseball)

NCAA Division I: .755 game seats per capita	A

University of Northern Iowa Panthers
Places Rated Score: 1,900   Places Rated Rank: 129

Wausau, WI

Common Denominators (1,300)

Good Restaurants: 1 ★, 4 ★★	AA
Golf Courses: 1 private; 2.5 daily fee	B
Bowling Lanes: 118	AA
Movie Theaters: 4	A

Crowd Pleasers (300)

Professional Sports: 1.573 game seats per capita	A

Timbers (baseball)

Outdoor Recreation Assets (54)

Inland Water Area: 16.7 square miles
Places Rated Score: 1,654   Places Rated Rank: 166

★ West Palm Beach–Boca Raton–Delray Beach, FL

Common Denominators (1,300)

Good Restaurants: 8 ★, 12 ★★, 5 ★★★, 1 ★★★★,	AA
1 ★★★★★	
Golf Courses: 62.5 private; 14.5 daily fee;	AA
5.5 municipal	
Bowling Lanes: 420	A
Movie Theaters: 16	B

Crowd Pleasers (600)

Zoos: Dreher Park Zoo	C
Auto Racing: Moroso Motorsports (SCCA)	C
Pari-mutuel Betting:	A

Palm Beach Kennel Club (114 days)
West Palm Beach Fronton (155 days)

Professional Sports: .633 game seats per capita	C

West Palm Beach Expos (baseball)

Outdoor Recreation Assets (1,872)

Atlantic Coastline: 47 miles
Inland Water Area: 555 square miles
National Forests, Parks, Wildlife Refuges:
Loxahatchee NWR (2,550 acres)
Places Rated Score: 3,772   Places Rated Rank: 13

Wheeling, WV–OH

Common Denominators (700)

Good Restaurants: 1 ★, 2 ★★	C
Golf Courses: 3 private; 0.5 daily fee;	B
2.5 municipal	
Bowling Lanes: 118	B
Movie Theaters: 5	B

Crowd Pleasers (500)

Zoos: Oglebay's Good Zoo	C
Pari-mutuel Betting: Wheeling Downs Greyhound	AA
Park (303 days)	

Outdoor Recreation Assets (71)

Inland Water Area: 13.5 square miles
Places Rated Score: 1,271   Places Rated Rank: 250

Wichita, KS

Common Denominators (700)

Good Restaurants: 1 ★★, 3 ★★★	C
Golf Courses: 6 private; 5 daily fee; 4 municipal	B
Bowling Lanes: 414	A
Movie Theaters: 9	C

Crowd Pleasers (800)

Zoos: Sedgwick County Zoo	A
Professional Sports: 1.404 game seats per capita	B

Aeros (baseball)

NCAA Division I: .720 game seats per capita	A

Wichita State Shockers

Rating

Outdoor Recreation Assets (8)
Inland Water Area: 4.2 square miles
Places Rated Score: 1,508   Places Rated Rank: 205

Wichita Falls, TX
Common Denominators (1,100)
Good Restaurants: 3 ★★   **B**
Golf Courses: 3.5 private; 0.5 daily fee;   **B**
2 municipal
Bowling Lanes: 100   **A**
Movie Theaters: 5   **AA**
Outdoor Recreation Assets (26)
Inland Water Area: 3.1 square miles
Places Rated Score: 1,126   Places Rated Rank: 275

Williamsport, PA
Common Denominators (700)
Good Restaurants: 1 ★★, 1 ★★★   **B**
Golf Courses: 1 private; 1 municipal   **C**
Bowling Lanes: 96   **A**
Movie Theaters: 2   **C**
Outdoor Recreation Assets (26)
Inland Water Area: 6.5 square miles
Places Rated Score: 726   Places Rated Rank: 320

Wilmington, DE–NJ–MD
Common Denominators (800)
Good Restaurants: 4 ★★, 1 ★★★   **C**
Golf Courses: 11.5 private; 5.5 daily fee;   **B**
2 municipal
Bowling Lanes: 444   **A**
Movie Theaters: 16   **B**
Crowd Pleasers (400)
Zoos: Brandywine Zoo   **C**
Pari-mutuel Betting: Brandywine (harness,   **B**
139 days)
NCAA Division I: .294 game seats per capita   **C**
University of Delaware Blue Hens
Outdoor Recreation Assets (323)
Inland Water Area: 68 square miles
National Forests, Parks, Wildlife Refuges:
Supawna Meadow NWR (1,716 acres)
CMSA Access: PHILADELPHIA–WILMINGTON–
TRENTON, PA–NJ–DE–MD (400)
Places Rated Score: 1,923   Places Rated Rank: 122

Wilmington, NC
Common Denominators (1,200)
Good Restaurants: 3 ★★, 1 ★★★   **AA**
Golf Courses: 4 private; 1 daily fee; 1 municipal   **B**
Bowling Lanes: 50   **B**
Movie Theaters: 5   **AA**
Crowd Pleasers (300)
NCAA Division I: .766 game seats per capita   **A**
University of North Carolina Seahawks (b)
Outdoor Recreation Assets (1,168)
Atlantic Coastline: 26 miles
Inland Water Area: 33.6 square miles
Places Rated Score: 2,668   Places Rated Rank: 48

Worcester, MA
Common Denominators (600)
Good Restaurants: 3 ★★, 2 ★★★   **C**
Golf Courses: 3.5 private; 8.5 daily fee;   **A**
2 municipal

Rating

Bowling Lanes: 126   **C**
Movie Theaters: 6   **C**
Crowd Pleasers (100)
NCAA Division I: .194 game seats per capita   **C**
Holy Cross Crusaders
Outdoor Recreation Assets (210)
Inland Water Area: 29.1 square miles
Places Rated Score: 910   Places Rated Rank: 301

Yakima, WA
Common Denominators (800)
Golf Courses: 3 private; 2 daily fee   **C**
Bowling Lanes: 142   **A**
Movie Theaters: 8   **AA**
Crowd Pleasers (400)
Auto Racing: Yakima Speedway (NASCAR)   **C**
Pari-mutuel Betting: Yakima Meadows   **A**
(Thoroughbred, 84 days)
Outdoor Recreation Assets (940)
Inland Water Area: 15.3 square miles
National Forests, Parks, Wildlife Refuges:
Gifford Pinchot NF (37,552 acres)
Snoqualmie NF (466,801 acres)
Toppenish NWR (1,763 acres)
Places Rated Score: 2,140   Places Rated Rank: 91

York, PA
Common Denominators (800)
Good Restaurants: 5 ★★, 2 ★★★   **B**
Golf Courses: 5.5 private; 8.5 daily fee   **A**
Bowling Lanes: 332   **A**
Movie Theaters: 7   **C**
Outdoor Recreation Assets (42)
Inland Water Area: 5.1 square miles
National Forests, Parks, Wildlife Refuges:
Eisenhower NHS (690 acres)
Gettysburg National Cemetery (21 acres)
Gettysburg NMP (3,689 acres)
Places Rated Score: 842   Places Rated Rank: 307

Youngstown–Warren, OH
Common Denominators (1,100)
Good Restaurants: 1 ★, 4 ★★, 2 ★★★   **C**
Golf Courses: 6.5 private; 20 daily fee;   **AA**
2.5 municipal
Bowling Lanes: 606   **AA**
Movie Theaters: 13   **B**
Crowd Pleasers (100)
NCAA Division I: .297 game seats per capita   **C**
Youngstown State Penguins
Outdoor Recreation Assets (127)
Inland Water Area: 26.1 square miles
Places Rated Score: 1,327   Places Rated Rank: 245

Yuba City, CA
Common Denominators (600)
Good Restaurants: 1 ★   **C**
Golf Courses: 1 private; 1.5 daily fee   **B**
Movie Theaters: 4   **A**
Outdoor Recreation Assets (318)
Inland Water Area: 9.6 square miles
National Forests, Parks, Wildlife Refuges:
Plumas NF (23,885 acres)
Tahoe NF (20,494 acres)
Places Rated Score: 918   Places Rated Rank: 299

Et Cetera

WHERE ARE THE BEST SPORTS TOWNS?

There are as many ways to determine the best sports towns in America as there are sports fans. Earlier in this chapter, *Places Rated* looked at major spectator sports from the point of view of the fan's ease of access and on this basis found the best metro areas to be Glens Falls, New York; Denver; and Kansas City, Missouri.

Obviously, though, being able to attend a game easily is not the only thing a fan aspires to. Rooting for the home team is fun, but rooting for a *winning* home team is ecstasy. In the lists that follow, *Places Rated* looks at the metro areas to find which have the winningest teams.

Major-League Title Towns

For baseball fans in the mid-1970s, the place to be was Oakland, California, as the A's hauled in three straight World Series championships. In the 1960s, football fans found a warm welcome in frosty Green Bay, where the Packers took five NFL Championships over a seven-year span. And if basketball is your sport, you won't go far wrong anytime if you back the Boston Celtics, winners of more titles than any other team in NBA history.

Our survey of metro areas with major professional championships looks at the winners in four team sports: baseball, football, basketball, and ice hockey. In the cases of baseball and ice hockey, we include the winners of the World Series (since 1903) and Stanley Cup (since 1894), respectively. For football and basketball, we include the Super Bowl and NBA Championship winners as well as the champions of the predecessors of the modern NFL (the National Football League, 1933–1969, and American Football League, 1960–1969) and the NBA (the Basketball Association of America, 1947–1949). The NFL and AFL champions of 1966, 1967, and 1968 met in the Super Bowls of 1967, 1968, and 1969, before the formation of the modern NFL; for those years, we name the winners of both the individual league championships and the Super Bowl.

If a team has changed names or towns, we list it with the name and in the town where it played at the time it won the championship in question.

Professional Championships in the Metro Areas

Anaheim–Santa Ana, CA
NFL Championship: Los Angeles Rams, 1951

Baltimore, MD
World Series: Orioles, 1966, 1970, 1983
Super Bowl: Colts, 1971
NFL Championship: Colts, 1958, 1959, 1968
BAA Championship: Bullets, 1948

Boston, MA
World Series: Somersets, 1903; Pilgrims, 1911; Red Sox, 1912, 1914, 1915, 1916, 1918

NBA Championship: Celtics, 1957, 1959, 1960, 1961, 1962, 1963, 1964, 1965, 1966, 1968, 1969, 1974, 1976, 1981, 1984
Stanley Cup: Bruins, 1929, 1939, 1941, 1970, 1972

Buffalo, NY
AFL Championship: Bills, 1964, 1965

Chicago, IL
World Series: White Sox, 1906, 1917; Cubs, 1907, 1908
NFL Championship: Bears, 1933, 1940, 1941, 1943, 1946, 1963; Cardinals, 1947
Stanley Cup: Black Hawks, 1934, 1938, 1961

Cincinnati, OH–KY–IN
World Series: Reds, 1919, 1940, 1975, 1976

Cleveland, OH
World Series: Indians, 1920, 1948
NFL Championship: Rams, 1945; Browns, 1950, 1954, 1955, 1964

Dallas, TX
Super Bowl: Cowboys, 1972, 1978
AFL Championship: Texans, 1962

Detroit, MI
World Series: Tigers, 1935, 1945, 1968, 1984
NFL Championship: Lions, 1935, 1952, 1953, 1957
Stanley Cup: Red Wings, 1936, 1937, 1943, 1950, 1952, 1954, 1955

Green Bay, WI
Super Bowl: Packers, 1967, 1968
NFL Championship: Packers, 1936, 1937, 1939, 1944, 1961, 1962, 1965, 1966, 1967

Houston, TX
AFL Championship: Oilers, 1960, 1961

Kansas City, MO
Super Bowl: Chiefs, 1970
AFL Championship: Chiefs, 1966, 1969

Los Angeles–Long Beach, CA
World Series: Dodgers, 1959, 1963, 1965, 1981
Super Bowl: Raiders, 1984
NFL Championship: Rams, 1951
NBA Championship: Lakers, 1972, 1980, 1982

Miami–Hialeah, FL
Super Bowl: Dolphins, 1973, 1974

Milwaukee, WI
World Series: Braves, 1957
NBA Championship: Bucks, 1971

Minneapolis–St. Paul, MN–WI
NFL Championship: Minnesota Vikings, 1969
BAA Championship: Minneapolis Lakers, 1949
NBA Championship: Minneapolis Lakers, 1950, 1952, 1953, 1954

Nassau–Suffolk, NY
Stanley Cup: New York Islanders, 1980, 1981, 1982, 1983

New York, NY
World Series: Giants, 1905, 1921, 1922, 1933, 1954; Yankees, 1923, 1927, 1928, 1932, 1936, 1937, 1938, 1939, 1941, 1943, 1947, 1949, 1950, 1951, 1952, 1953, 1956, 1958, 1961, 1962, 1977, 1978; Brooklyn Dodgers, 1955; Mets, 1969
Super Bowl: Jets, 1969
AFL Championship: Jets, 1968
NFL Championship: Giants, 1934, 1938, 1944, 1956
NBA Championship: Knickerbockers, 1970, 1973
Stanley Cup: Rangers, 1928, 1933, 1940

Oakland, CA
World Series: Athletics, 1972, 1973; A's, 1974
Super Bowl: Raiders, 1977, 1981
AFL Championship: Raiders, 1967
NBA Championship: Golden State Warriors, 1975

Philadelphia, PA–NJ
World Series: Athletics, 1910, 1911, 1913, 1929, 1930; Phillies, 1980
NFL Championship: Eagles, 1948, 1949, 1960
BAA Championship: Warriors, 1947
NBA Championship: Warriors, 1956; 76ers, 1967, 1983
Stanley Cup: Flyers, 1974, 1975

Pittsburgh, PA
World Series: Pirates, 1909, 1925, 1960, 1971, 1979
Super Bowl: Steelers, 1975, 1976, 1979, 1980

Portland, OR
NBA Championship: Trail Blazers, 1977

Rochester, NY
NBA Championship: Royals, 1951

St. Louis, MO–IL
World Series: Cardinals, 1926, 1931, 1934, 1942, 1944, 1946, 1964, 1967, 1982
NBA Championship: Hawks, 1958

San Diego, CA
AFL Championship: Chargers, 1963

San Francisco, CA
Super Bowl: 49ers, 1982

Seattle, WA
NBA Championship: SuperSonics, 1979
Stanley Cup: Metropolitans, 1917

Syracuse, NY
NBA Championship: Nationals, 1955

Washington, DC–MD–VA
World Series: Senators, 1924
Super Bowl: Redskins, 1983
NFL Championship: Redskins, 1937, 1942
NBA Championship: Bullets, 1978

Source: Official league histories.

Collegiate Title Towns

The 1984–1985 academic year marks the 103rd season of college athletic championships that began all the way back when Harvard University's J. S. Clark captured the first singles title in college tennis in 1883. Founded in 1906, the National Collegiate Athletic Association (NCAA) began administering collegiate athletic championships in 1921, beginning with its first outdoor track meet. In 1981, the association initiated women's championships. Some 600 colleges and universities have been named national champion in each of the NCAA's three divisions over the years. What follows is a list of the 45 metro area locations of the Division I champions for the past five years.

Many NCAA sports, such as basketball and volleyball, have both men's and women's championships. An M or W after the sport indicates whether the title was in men's or women's competition. Sports such as baseball, football, and wrestling are played at the championship level by men only, whereas field hockey and softball championships are for women only; accordingly, no M or W designation is given. Ski teams are coed.

NCAA Championships in the Metro Areas

Alton–Granite City, IL
Southern Illinois University, Edwardsville: Soccer (M), 1979

Anaheim–Santa Ana, CA
California State University, Fullerton: Baseball, 1984
University of California, Irvine: Water Polo, 1982

Athens, GA
University of Georgia: Football (Division I–A), 1980

Austin, TX
University of Texas: Baseball, 1983; Swimming and Diving (M), 1981; Swimming and Diving (W), 1984

Baltimore, MD
Johns Hopkins University: Lacrosse (M), 1980, 1984

Bloomington, IN
Indiana University: Basketball (M), 1981; Soccer (M), 1982, 1983, 1984

Boise City, ID
Boise State University: Football (Division I–AA), 1980

Boulder–Longmont, CO
University of Colorado: Skiing, 1982

Bryan–College Station, TX
Texas A & M University: Softball, 1983

Burlington, VT
University of Vermont: Skiing, 1980

Charlottesville, VA
University of Virginia: Cross-Country Track (W), 1981, 1982

Pro Sports Franchising

All the 88 major-league professional sports teams in the United States play at home in only 38 of the country's 329 metro areas. The greatest number of franchises, six, is found in the Los Angeles–Long Beach metro area.

In professional sports marketing, the largest metro areas are the ones that get the teams. In such places as Los Angeles–Long Beach, local governments can afford to underwrite stadiums and arenas, and ticket-buying fans can be found in the greatest number. But what about a small major-league metro area, such as Green Bay? The Packers are one of the oldest franchises in the NFL. The team divides its eight regular-season home games between Milwaukee's County Stadium and Lambeau Field in Green Bay. The Pack is also the only municipally owned team in professional sports; therefore, it is the only club whose owners can't threaten to move it.

There are large metro areas, however, that either have no professional sports franchises or could support more teams than they already do. The owners of major-league baseball's 26 franchises appointed a committee in 1983 to identify likely places that could put together publicly financed stadiums and blue-ribbon groups of prospective owners. Nine cities were mentioned for expansion: Denver, Phoenix, Washington, Miami, Buffalo, New Orleans, Indianapolis, Vancouver, and Tampa. Milwaukee has expressed interest in a hockey team. But while it may be true, as some studies show, that big-time professional football could easily expand into eight more cities and major-league baseball into six, the number of franchises is strictly controlled by owners. In fact, this control is so powerful that professional sports has been called the only unregulated monopoly allowed to operate in the United States. If there is to be any expansion, it probably will occur at a glacial rate because club owners, like classic monopolists, do not care for the idea of anyone encroaching on their territorial rights.

Dallas, TX
Southern Methodist University: Outdoor Track (M), 1983

Denver, CO
University of Denver: Gymnastics (W), 1983

Detroit, MI
Wayne State University: Fencing (M), 1980, 1982, 1983, 1984; Fencing (W), 1982, 1984

El Paso, TX
University of Texas, El Paso: Cross-Country Track (M), 1980, 1981, 1984; Outdoor Track (M), 1980, 1981, 1982

Eugene–Springfield, OR
University of Oregon: Cross-Country Track (W), 1984; Outdoor Track (M), 1984

Fort Worth–Arlington, TX
Texas Christian University: Golf (W), 1983

Gainesville, FL
University of Florida: Swimming and Diving (M), 1983, 1984; Swimming and Diving (W), 1982

Grand Forks, ND
University of North Dakota: Ice Hockey, 1980, 1982

Greenville–Spartanburg, SC
Clemson University: Football (Division I–A), 1981

Honolulu, HI
University of Hawaii: Volleyball (W), 1982

Houston, TX
University of Houston: Golf (M), 1982, 1984

Iowa City, IA
University of Iowa: Wrestling, 1980, 1981, 1982, 1983, 1984

Lincoln, NE
University of Nebraska: Gymnastics (M), 1980, 1981, 1982, 1983, 1984

Los Angeles–Long Beach, CA
California State University, Northridge: Gymnastics (W), 1982
University of California, Los Angeles: Softball, 1982; Swimming and Diving (M), 1982; Tennis (M), 1982, 1984; Volleyball (M), 1981, 1982, 1983
University of Southern California: Basketball (W), 1983, 1984; Outdoor Track (W), 1982, 1983; Tennis (W), 1983; Volleyball (W), 1983

Louisville, KY–IN
University of Louisville: Basketball (M), 1980

Madison, WI
University of Wisconsin: Cross-Country Track (M), 1982; Ice Hockey, 1981, 1983

Miami–Hialeah, FL
University of Miami: Baseball, 1982; Football (Division I–A), 1983; Golf (W), 1984

Norfolk–Virginia Beach–Newport News, VA
Old Dominion University: Field Hockey, 1982, 1983, 1984

Oakland, CA
University of California, Berkeley: Swimming and Diving (M), 1980

Philadelphia, PA–NJ
Temple University: Lacrosse (W), 1984
University of Pennsylvania: Fencing (M), 1981

Phoenix, AZ
Arizona State University: Baseball, 1981

Provo–Orem, UT
Brigham Young University: Golf (M), 1981

Raleigh–Durham, NC
North Carolina State University: Basketball (M), 1983
University of North Carolina: Basketball (M), 1982; Lacrosse (M), 1981, 1982; Soccer (W), 1982

A Football Odyssey

The first NFL franchise in Cleveland, Ohio, belonged not to the Browns but to the Rams, who played such opponents as the Brooklyn Dodgers, Chicago Cardinals, and Pittsburgh Pirates back in the 1930s.

Organized professional football as we know it today began to take shape in 1922 with the establishment of the National Football League, although the early teams seem ragtag in comparison to the computerized juggernauts of the 1980s. Through a series of splits and mergers with other leagues over the years, the NFL has remained the dominant pro football organization, and presently consists of 28 teams. The list below recaps which of today's NFL teams have moved to another city and/or changed their name since their founding date.*

Detroit Lions—*1930*, began as the NFL Portsmouth (OH) Spartans; *1934*, moved to Detroit and renamed Detroit Lions.

Indianapolis Colts—*1952*, defunct Dallas Texans of the All-America Football Conference moved to Baltimore, renamed Baltimore Colts, and joined the NFL; *1983*, moved to Indianapolis and renamed Indianapolis Colts.

Kansas City Chiefs—*1959*, began as the Dallas Texans of the American Football League; *1963*, moved to Kansas City and renamed Kansas City Chiefs; *1970*, joined NFL.

Los Angeles Raiders—*1959*, began as Oakland Raiders of the American Football League; *1970*, joined NFL; *1982*, moved to Los Angeles and renamed Los Angeles Raiders.

Los Angeles Rams—*1937*, began as Cleveland Rams; *1946*, moved to Los Angeles and renamed Los Angeles Rams.

New England Patriots—*1959*, began as Boston Patriots of the American Football League; *1970*, joined NFL; *1971*, renamed New England Patriots.

New York Jets—*1959*, began as New York Titans of the American Football League; *1963*, renamed New York Jets; *1970*, joined NFL.

St. Louis Cardinals—*1913*, began as Racine Avenue (Chicago) Cardinals; *1922*, renamed Chicago Cardinals; *1960*, moved to St. Louis and renamed St. Louis Cardinals.

San Diego Chargers—*1959*, franchised as the AFL Los Angeles Chargers; *1961*, moved to San Diego and renamed San Diego Chargers; *1970*, joined NFL.

Washington Redskins—*1932*, began as Boston Braves; *1933*, renamed Boston Redskins; *1937*, moved to Washington and renamed Washington Redskins.

Source: NFL Properties, NFL Record and Fact Book, 1984.

*The Chicago Bears (1922), Green Bay Packers (1922), New York Giants (1925), Philadelphia Eagles (1933), Pittsburgh Steelers (1933), Dallas Cowboys (1960), Minnesota Vikings (1960), Atlanta Falcons (1965), New Orleans Saints (1966), Seattle Seahawks (1974), and Tampa Bay Buccaneers (1974) began as NFL teams and have neither moved nor changed their team name.

The Cleveland Browns (1946) and San Francisco 49ers (1946) are former All-America Football Conference teams that joined the NFL in 1949.

The Buffalo Bills (1959), Denver Broncos (1959), Houston Oilers (1959), Miami Dolphins (1965), and Cincinnati Bengals (1967) are former American Football League franchises that merged with the NFL in 1970.

Salt Lake City–Ogden, UT
University of Utah: Skiing, 1981, 1983, 1984

San Francisco, CA
University of San Francisco: Soccer (M), 1980

San Jose, CA
Stanford University: Tennis (M), 1980, 1981; Tennis (W), 1982, 1984; Swimming and Diving (W), 1983; Water Polo (M), 1980, 1981

State College, PA
Pennsylvania State University: Fencing (W), 1983; Football (Division I–A), 1982

Syracuse, NY
Syracuse University: Lacrosse (M), 1983

Tallahassee, FL
Florida State University: Outdoor Track (W), 1984

Tucson, AZ
University of Arizona: Baseball, 1980

Tulsa, OK
University of Tulsa: Golf (W), 1982

Tuscaloosa, AL
University of Alabama: Football (Division I–A), 1979

Washington, DC–MD–VA
Georgetown University: Basketball (M), 1984

Wilmington, DE–NJ–MD
University of Delaware: Lacrosse (W), 1983

Source: National Collegiate Athletic Association, *College Champions,* 1984.

In Division I–A Football, the NCAA recognizes as unofficial national champion the team selected each year by the Associated Press poll of sportswriters and the United Press International poll of coaches.

LEGAL HOLIDAYS

Properly speaking, there aren't any national holidays in the United States. A day off on Independence Day, Thanksgiving, or Christmas comes by the grace of state legislatures rather than a presidential proclamation or an act of Congress.

The only thing "national" about your holiday calendar is the nine days off given to everyone who works for the federal government: Christmas, Independence Day, Labor Day, New Year's Day, Thanksgiving, and four Mondays—Columbus Day, Memorial Day, Veterans Day, and Washington's Birthday—that were approved in 1968 to create predictable long weekends. Beginning in 1986, Martin Luther King Day will be observed on the third Monday of January, increasing the number of federal holidays to ten.

Although lawmakers in many states have since adopted these same days as legal holidays for their local constituencies, many have not. In 1978, for instance, the federal government moved Veterans Day from the second Monday in November back to its original date, November 11, because few states wanted to be completely in step with Washington's calendar.

The Civil War era gave us more events and heroes to honor with holidays than any other period in American history. However, they aren't all celebrated nationwide. Just as no former secessionist state takes notice of Lincoln's birthday, so none of the Union states honors Robert E. Lee's birthday. Memorial Day, a date originally created to mourn those who died for the Union cause, isn't observed in Alabama, Mississippi, or South Carolina. Those states, as well as Florida, Georgia, Kentucky, and Louisiana, celebrate Confederate Memorial Day instead. So if the calendars of some states have more holidays on them than others, it reflects which local heroes and events their lawmakers think worthy of commemoration.

For traveling salespeople who have found themselves all dressed up with no place to go in Boston on Evacuation Day or in Omaha on Arbor Day, and for anyone who wonders whether there are more long weekends in Florida than in California or Texas, we present a comprehensive list of days, fixed and movable, that are legal holidays somewhere in the United States.

An American List of Days

JANUARY

Fixed Dates

January 1, New Year's Day: All states
January 8, Battle of New Orleans Day: Louisiana
January 15, Martin Luther King Day: Connecticut, District of Columbia, Florida, Illinois, Kentucky, Louisiana, Maryland, Massachusetts, Michigan, New Jersey, Pennsylvania, South Carolina
January 19, Robert E. Lee's Birthday: Arkansas, Florida, Georgia, Kentucky, Louisiana, South Carolina
January 30, Franklin D. Roosevelt Day: Kentucky

Movable Feasts

Third Sunday, Martin Luther King Day: New York
Third Monday, Martin Luther King Day: Ohio
Robert E. Lee's Birthday: Alabama, Mississippi
Lee-Jackson Day: Virginia

FEBRUARY

Fixed Dates

February 12, Lincoln's Birthday: Alaska, California, Colorado, Connecticut, Florida, Illinois, Indiana, Iowa, Kansas, Kentucky, Maryland, Missouri, Montana, New Jersey, New Mexico, New York, Utah, Vermont, Washington, West Virginia
February 19, Robert E. Lee Day: Kentucky

Movable Feasts

First Monday, Lincoln's Birthday: Delaware, Oregon
Second Monday, Lincoln Day: Arizona
Third Monday, Washington's Birthday: All states
Tuesday before Ash Wednesday, Mardi Gras: Alabama, Florida (some counties), Louisiana (some parishes)

MARCH

Fixed Dates

March 2, Texas Independence Day: Texas
March 17, Evacuation Day: Massachusetts (Suffolk County only)
March 20, Youth Day: Oklahoma
March 25, Maryland Day: Maryland
March 26, Prince Jonah Kuhio Kalanianaole Day: Hawaii

Movable Feasts

First Tuesday, Town Meeting Day: Vermont
Two days before Easter, Good Friday: Connecticut, Delaware, Florida, Hawaii, Indiana, Louisiana, Maryland, New Jersey, North Dakota, Pennsylvania, Tennessee, Wisconsin (11 A.M.–3 P.M.)
One day after Easter, Easter Monday: North Carolina
Last Monday, Seward's Day: Alaska

APRIL

Fixed Dates

April 2, Pascua Florida Day: Florida
April 3, Arbor Day: Arizona

April 13, Thomas Jefferson's Birthday: Alabama, Oklahoma
April 21, San Jacinto Day: Texas
April 22, Arbor Day: Delaware, Nebraska
  Oklahoma Day: Oklahoma
April 26, Confederate Memorial Day: Florida, Georgia

Movable Feasts

Third Monday, Patriot's Day: Maine, Massachusetts
Fourth Monday, Fast Day: New Hampshire
Last Monday, Confederate Memorial Day: Alabama, Mississippi
Last Friday, Arbor Day: Utah

MAY

Fixed Dates

May 1, Bird Day: Oklahoma
May 4, Rhode Island Independence Day: Rhode Island
May 8, Truman Day: Missouri
May 10, Confederate Memorial Day: South Carolina
May 11, Minnesota Day: Minnesota
May 20, Mecklenburg Independence Day: North Carolina
May 25, Memorial Day: New Mexico, South Dakota, Vermont
May 30, Memorial Day: Delaware, Illinois, Maryland, New Hampshire

Movable Feasts

First Tuesday after first Monday, Primary Election Day: Indiana
Second Sunday, Mother's Day: Arizona, Oklahoma
Last Monday, Memorial Day: All states except Alabama, Mississippi, South Carolina, and those celebrating on May 30

JUNE

Fixed Dates

June 3, Jefferson Davis's Birthday: Florida, Georgia, South Carolina
  Confederate Memorial Day: Kentucky, Louisiana
June 9, Senior Citizens Day: Oklahoma
June 11, King Kamehameha I Day: Hawaii
June 14, Flag Day: Pennsylvania
June 15, Separation Day: Delaware
June 17, Bunker Hill Day: Massachusetts (Suffolk County only)
June 19, Emancipation Day: Texas
June 20, West Virginia Day: West Virginia

Movable Feasts

First Monday, Jefferson Davis's Birthday: Alabama, Mississippi
Second Sunday, Flag Day: New York
Third Sunday, Father's Day: Arizona

JULY

Fixed Dates

July 4, Independence Day: All states
July 24, Pioneer Day: Utah

Movable Feasts: None

AUGUST

Fixed Dates

August 16, Bennington Battle Day: Vermont
August 27, Lyndon B. Johnson's Birthday: Texas
August 30, Huey P. Long Day: Louisiana

Movable Feasts

First Sunday, American Family Day: Arizona, Minnesota
First Monday, Colorado Day: Colorado
Second Monday, Victory Day: Rhode Island
Third Friday, Admission Day: Hawaii

SEPTEMBER

Fixed Dates

September 9, Admission Day: California
September 12, Defenders' Day: Maryland
September 16, Cherokee Strip Day: Oklahoma

Movable Feasts

First Monday, Labor Day: All states
First Tuesday, Primary Election Day: Wisconsin
Second Tuesday, Primary Election Day: Wyoming
First Saturday after full moon, Indian Day: Oklahoma

OCTOBER

Fixed Dates

October 10, Oklahoma Historical Day: Oklahoma
October 12, Columbus Day: Maryland
October 18, Alaska Day: Alaska
October 31, Nevada Day: Nevada

Movable Feasts

Second Monday, Columbus Day: All states except Alaska, Iowa, Maryland, Michigan, Mississippi, Nevada, North Carolina, North Dakota, Oregon, South Carolina, Washington
Fourth Monday, Veterans Day: Arkansas, Montana, North Carolina, Utah

NOVEMBER

Fixed Dates

November 1, All Saints' Day: Louisiana
November 4, Will Rogers Day: Oklahoma
November 11, Veterans Day: All states except those celebrating in October
November 29, Nellie Tayloe Ross's Birthday: Wyoming

Movable Feasts

First Tuesday after first Monday, General Election Day: Arkansas, California, Colorado, District of Columbia, Delaware, Florida, Hawaii, Idaho, Illinois, Kentucky, Louisiana, Maryland, Missouri, Montana, New Jersey, New York, Oklahoma, Pennsylvania, Rhode Island, South Carolina, Tennessee, Texas, Virginia, West Virginia, Wisconsin, Wyoming

DECEMBER

Fixed Dates

December 7, Delaware Day: Delaware
December 10, Wyoming Day: Wyoming
December 25, Christmas: All states

Movable Feasts: None

LEGALIZED GAMBLING IN THE STATES

None of the 50 states has legalized gambling. What 46 of them do is to make certain forms of gambling legitimate and to authorize the state's right to run them as profitable enterprises, a right they steadfastly withhold from others. Nevada's constitution prohibits lotteries not because they are another form of gambling but because they would compete with the state's cut from casino gambling. A bettor who places twenty dollars on a horse with a bookie would break the law in New York or California—the number-one and number-two horse-racing states—just as he or she would anywhere else.

States permit certain forms of gambling to raise revenue. Seven states—California, Connecticut, Florida, Illinois, Massachusetts, New Jersey, and New York—each take in more money from lotteries or pari-mutuel betting on horses and dogs than Nevada does from its amusement tax on the tables, slot machines, sports-card betting shops, jai alai matches, and occasional horse races combined.

Another reason states sanction certain forms of gambling is to reduce illegal betting by offering comparable alternatives. But it is very difficult for states to raise money through legal gambling and control illegal operations at the same time. The illicit forms of gam-

Legalized Gambling by State

State	Horse Racing	Off-Track Betting	Dog Racing	Jai Alai	Lotteries	Bingo	Raffles	Casinos	Numbers	Sports Betting
Alabama			•				•			
Alaska						•	•			
Arizona	•	*	•		•	•	•			
Arkansas	•		•							
California	•						•			
Colorado	•	•	•		•	•	•			
Connecticut		•	•	•	•	•	•		•	
Delaware	•				•	•	•		•	*
Florida	•		•	•		•	•			
Georgia							•			
Hawaii										
Idaho	•									
Illinois	•	•			•	•			•	
Indiana										
Iowa	*		*			•	•			
Kansas						•				
Kentucky	•	•								
Louisiana	•	•								
Maine	•				•	•	•			
Maryland	•				•	•	•		•	
Massachusetts	•	•	•		•	•	•		•	
Michigan	•				•	•	•		•	
Minnesota	*					•				
Mississippi						•				
Missouri						•				
Montana	•					•	•			•
Nebraska	•					•	•			
Nevada	•	•	•	•		•		•	•	•
New Hampshire	•	•	•		•	•	•		•	
New Jersey	•				•	•	•	•	•	
New Mexico	•					•	•			
New York	•	•			•	•				
North Carolina						•				
North Dakota						•				
Ohio	•				•	•			•	
Oklahoma	*	*				•	•			
Oregon	•		•			•	•			
Pennsylvania	•	•			•	•			•	
Rhode Island	•	•	•	•	•	•			•	
South Carolina						•				
South Dakota	•		•			•	•			
Tennessee						•				
Texas						•				
Utah										
Vermont	•				•	•	•			
Virginia						•	•			
Washington	•	•			•	•	•			•
West Virginia	•		•			•	•			
Wisconsin						•				
Wyoming	•					•	•			

Source: National Association of State Racing Commissioners, 1984, and Public Gaming Research Institute, 1984.

• Indicates legal and operating.

*Indicates legal but not now operating.

Propositions for state lotteries in California, Missouri, Oregon, and West Virginia were approved by voters in November 1984. Missouri voters also approved horse racing.

bling are usually more popular: The payoff from an illegal bookmaking shop, floating dice and card games, or the numbers game is greater than that from sanctioned operations because there is no government takeout, and because the winnings are hidden from the tax collector. The stories about bookmakers setting up shop next door to New York City Off-Track Betting parlors are true, just as illegal numbers games still thrive in Massachusetts and New Jersey, two states with daily numbers games of their own.

WHAT IT TAKES FOR THE BEST SKIING

If you were to draw a line on a map of the United States separating states with the best conditions for skiing from those with poor conditions or no facilities, the result would be a jagged northward arc. It would begin in the Great Smoky Mountains of North Carolina and run due north to Lake Erie, west to the foothills of the Rockies, and then south along the Rocky Mountain cordillera to northern New Mexico and Arizona. Next it would reappear in the California Sierra Nevada, dropping southwest to end in the San Bernardino National Forest an hour and a half out of Los Angeles. Although there are ski areas south of this imaginary curve, the ideal conditions are north of it: rolling, rugged terrain and predictable winter weather that everyone except skiers would call bad.

By definition, a ski area is a hill or mountain with some form of developed trails and lift machinery. Usually there is a lodge for meals and overnight stays. If the area is large and popular, there is also après-ski —nighttime entertainment that can range from music to movies to disco—that to many skiers is as critical as fresh snow and challenging runs.

Of the 587 U.S. ski areas, more than half are found in eight northeastern and Great Lakes states—Massachusetts, Michigan, Minnesota, New Hampshire, New York, Pennsylvania, Vermont, and Wisconsin—because of harsh, long winters and large, recreation-hungry urban populations.

But if you're a skier with time and money, skiing Hanley's Happy Hill in Pennsylvania, Little Switzerland in Wisconsin, or even Vermont's Killington or Stowe isn't quite the same as skiing "destination" areas in the West such as Aspen, Park City, or Jackson Hole. Ski areas are where you find them, but the best *skiing* is in the highest part of the country: the Rocky Mountain West and the Sierra Nevada near Lake Tahoe.

The above statement is not purely a matter of opinion. According to ski-industry surveys, most of the eight to ten million skiers in the United States are of intermediate ability, tending toward advanced. If they could ski anywhere, they would choose areas that enhance their ability; that is, places with high mountains, great vertical rises, long runs, and heavy powder

The 15 Busiest Ski Areas

America's busiest ski areas, determined by a measurement known as a ski occasion (one ascent and descent of the mountain by a skier), are all located within national forests.

Ski Area	Ski Occasions
1. Mammoth Mountain, CA	1,536,214
2. Breckenridge, CO	763,200
3. Steamboat, CO	743,200
4. Keystone, CO	732,200
5. Snowmass, CO	679,800
6. Copper Mountain, CO	651,800
7. Taos Ski Valley, NM	624,235
8. Mount Bachelor, OR	603,918
9. Crystal Mountain, WA	600,000
10. Santa Fe Ski Area, NM	590,000
11. Alta, UT	533,536
12. Snow Summit, CA	503,571
13. Sugarbush Valley, VT	501,000
14. Bald Mountain, ID	444,227
15. Snowbird, UT	415,111

Source: U.S. Forest Service, *National Forest Recreation Use Reports*, 1984.

snowfalls that begin early in winter and last into spring. You'll find more of these qualities within short drives of Denver, Boulder, Reno, Salt Lake City, Seattle, Tacoma, and Spokane than anywhere else.

The 10 States with the Most Ski Areas

State	Ski Areas
1. New York	63
2. Wisconsin	48
3. Michigan	42
4. Colorado	41
5. California	37
5. Pennsylvania	37
7. New Hampshire	31
8. Vermont	28
9. Massachusetts	26
10. Minnesota	25

Source: Inter-Ski Services, Inc., *The White Book of Ski Areas*, 1983.

Vertical Rise . . .

The perpendicular distance from the base to the highest skiable point on a hill or mountain is a ski area's "vertical." Utah's 14 ski areas average 1,826 feet, whereas Alabama's single ski area has a rise of only 150 feet. Although vertical rise has little to do with the quality of the trails, it is a good indication of length of the runs and the mountain's challenge. More than one optimistic ski-area promoter has stretched the distance a bit—some, allegedly, by measuring from the top of the tallest tree on the crest to the surface of the highway below the base lodge.

The 9 Greatest Vertical Rises

Ski Area	Height
1. Jackson Hole, WY	4,139 ft
2. Aspen Highlands, CO	3,800
3. High Wallowas, OR	3,700
4. Heavenly Valley, CA	3,600
4. Snowmass, CO	3,600
4. Steamboat, CO	3,600
7. Timberline, OR	3,500
8. Sun Valley, ID	3,400
9. Beaver Creek, CO	3,340

Source: Inter-Ski Services, Inc., *The White Book of Ski Areas*, 1983.

. . . and Longest Runs . . .

The highest vertical is found at Wyoming's Jackson Hole, but the longest ski run is at Killington, in Vermont. The longest run is the longest continuous trail on the mountain, from the top to the runout, which is usually in the base lodge's parking lot.

The 9 Longest Ski Runs

Ski Area	Length
1. Killington, VT	10.2 mi
2. Jackson Hole, WY	7.0
3. Heavenly Valley, CA	5.5
3. Taos Ski Valley, NM	5.5
5. Mission Ridge, WA	5.0
6. Okemo Mountain, VT	4.5
6. Stowe, VT	4.5
6. Vail, CO	4.5
9. Stratton, VT	4.0

Source: Inter-Ski Services, Inc., *The White Book of Ski Areas*, 1983.

. . . and Lift Capacities

A ski area's lift capacity is the number of people that can be moved up the mountain in one hour. Lifts can be elementary rope or cable tows, bars (T-bars, J-bars, pomalifts, or platterpulls), chairs, trams, or gondolas. Whatever the mix of lifts at a ski resort, the total lift capacity is a good indication of how developed the ski area is and often of how efficient the lift lines are. Twenty-five U.S. ski areas have lift capacities of at least 15,000 skiers per hour, and ten of these can move 20,000 or more up the mountain every hour.

The 10 Best Ski Areas for Lift Capacity

Ski Area	Skiers per Hour
1. Mammoth Mountain, CA	36,000
2. Squaw Valley, CA	27,100
3. Heavenly Valley, CA	26,500
4. Killington, VT	22,800
5. Sun Valley, ID	22,204
6. Steamboat, CO	22,000
7. Vail, CO	21,430
8. Afton Alps, MN	20,000
8. Brandywine, OH	20,000
8. Wilmot Mountain, WI	20,000

Source: Inter-Ski Services, Inc., *The White Book of Ski Areas*, 1983.

Economics:

Living Costs, Incomes, Taxes, Jobs

In the detached view of some economists, we humans are little more than living resources continually searching for our highest valued use. After all, we switch jobs readily if the money is right. We'll change careers, too, if the prospects are more promising. And we may risk these changes even if it means packing up and moving far away.

For Americans, this is nothing new. Over three centuries our ancestors redistributed themselves as much for the main chance as for elbowroom. In the 1700s they jostled each other in steerage during the long ocean passage to the New World. Around 1800, they climbed aboard creaking wagons in Pennsylvania to make the hard, one-way trip to the Northwest Territory, where farmland was opening up. In this century they bundled their things together and trucked away from southern sharecropped farms for an hourly wage in Detroit automobile factories.

We are still at it, for similar reasons. Periodic Census Bureau surveys find that most people who quit one state for another are either tracking down a better job (or *any* job, period), being transferred by their employer, or fleeing high taxes and day-to-day living costs. By now, everyone knows that the southern and western states were the preferred destinations during the 1970s. If the consensus of public and private forecasters is correct, the migration to the sun will continue into the twenty-first century.

But not every Sun Belt metro area is an unbridled boomtown. Many are saddled with sunset industries. Some suffer recessions more deeply than the rest of the country and consistently bounce back more slowly. Others, owing to their rapid population growth, are now experiencing rapidly climbing living costs. Nor are all Frost Belt metro areas going under or even languishing. Having endured the collapse of their historic industries in recent years, many are now making up for lost time. Some currently enjoy the lowest unemployment rates in the nation and have enviable track records for income growth and job expansion.

"Money's no problem," an accountant will tell you. "Lack of money. . . now *that's* a problem." As is the case for most people, your short-term economic frets probably center on the price of hamburger, jeans, laundry detergent, or haircuts. Over the long run, your concerns may focus on tax bites, jobs, and boosting your income at least to the level where it beats inflation.

LOCAL LIVING COSTS

Get ready for some surprising answers should you ask experts why and how much living costs vary among metro areas.

Some home economists argue that the only accu-

371

rate way to compare expenses in different metro areas is to trundle a shopping cart around each place and fill it with the packaged goods you'd regularly consume; check the asking prices for homes in the Sunday paper's real estate section; call the gas and electric utility for the cost of residential service; and find out from the tax office just how homes are assessed and when the bill comes due. According to this theory, when you add up the costs of all these items and budget the amount over 12 months, you've got a rough idea of how much annual income you'd need in each metro area.

But after months of pondering such topics as the tastiness of food and physical standards of housing, a committee appointed in 1980 by the U.S. Department of Labor to recommend better ways to measure living costs threw in the towel. Given the infinite variety of consumer preferences, they reported, the only acceptable way to pin down why life in one city was more expensive than in another was to focus on climate's effect on clothing costs and home heating bills.

According to one national clothing retailer, however, the cost difference between a double-knit Sun Belt wardrobe and a woolen Frost Belt wardrobe complete with down-filled outerwear can amount to less than 1 percent of a household's annual budget. As for the comparative costs of keeping warm in Duluth's winter and staying cool in Waco's summer, often the only difference is the season during which local residents pay most of the bill.

One consulting firm that specializes in relocating transferred employees adopts a simple rule of thumb. In its experience, 80 percent of the difference in living costs between metro areas typically comes down to two items: the price of housing and the direct taxes people may encounter in their new area. The other 20 percent comes from local prices for consumer packaged goods and personal services.

To gauge living costs in each metro area, *Places Rated* compares the costs of housing, food, and miscellaneous goods and services against a national yardstick of 100. We also borrow a weighting rule from government surveys, which states that a middle-class family spends 33 percent of its income on homeownership expenses, 30 percent on services, and 17 percent on food. (The remaining 20 percent goes for transportation and health care.)

Housing. By *Places Rated* estimates, the average metro area housing costs for utilities, property taxes, and paying off a 25-year, 12 percent mortgage on an existing single-family house after making a one-quarter down payment are $8,340 a year. (For a more detailed analysis of homeownership costs, see the chapter "Housing: Affording the American Dream," pp. 70–116.) Using $8,340 as a norm equal to 100, the housing cost index in Stamford, Connecticut, is 283, while in Joplin, Missouri, it is 62.

Homeownership Costs in the Metro Areas

Lowest Costs	Cost Index (U.S. Avg. = 100)	Highest Costs	Cost Index (U.S. Avg. = 100)
1. Joplin, MO	62	1. Stamford, CT	283
2. Brownsville–Harlingen, TX	64	2. Norwalk, CT	242
2. McAllen–Edinburg–Mission, TX	64	3. San Francisco, CA	206
4. Gadsden, AL	65	4. Honolulu, HI	204
5. Anniston, AL	66	5. Anaheim–Santa Ana, CA	192
6. Terre Haute, IN	66	5. San Jose, CA	192
7. St. Joseph, MO	67	7. Santa Barbara–Santa Maria–Lompoc, CA	186
8. Anderson, IN	68	8. Bergen–Passaic, NJ	175
8. Danville, VA	68	9. Danbury, CT	173
8. Dothan, AL	68	9. San Diego, CA	173

Source: Places Rated figures, based on average homeownership costs as calculated in the chapter "Housing: Affording the American Dream."

Food. Every three months, the American Chamber of Commerce Researchers Association (ACCRA) prices a carefully selected list of consumer goods and services with the consumption habits of a typical middle-management executive's family in mind. This survey measures relative price levels in more than 200 participating cities, as compared with the national average of 100 for all the cities.

Twenty-seven items are on ACCRA's food list, including meats, fresh produce, dairy products, bread, and a variety of packaged food from frozen orange juice and coffee, to number-303 cans of sweet peas and tomatoes, to an 18-ounce box of Post Toasties. When ACCRA's survey results are applied to the metro areas, we find the lowest food costs in Springfield, Illinois, and the highest, not surprisingly, in Anchorage, Alaska.

Food Prices in the Metro Areas

Lowest Prices	Cost Index (U.S. Avg. = 100)	Highest Prices	Cost Index (U.S. Avg. = 100)
1. Springfield, IL	87	1. Anchorage, AK	139
2. Canton, OH	89	2. Honolulu, HI	125†
3. Columbia, MO	91	3. New York, NY	112
3. Dubuque, IA	91	4. Billings, MT	110
3. Joplin, MO	91	4. Bridgeport–Milford, CT	110*
6. Davenport–Rock Island–Moline, IA–IL	92*	4. Bristol, CT	110*
6. Fort Smith, AR–OK	92	4. Casper, WY	110
6. Greensboro–Winston-Salem–High Point, NC	92	4. Danbury, CT	110*
6. Hickory, NC	92	4. Eugene–Springfield, OR	110*
6. Sioux City, IA–NE	92*	4. Hartford, CT	110
		4. Middletown, CT	110*
		4. New Britain, CT	110*
		4. New Haven–Meriden, CT	110*
		4. Stamford, CT	110*
		4. Waterbury, CT	110*

Source: American Chamber of Commerce Researchers Association, "Inter-City Cost of Living Index," first quarter, 1984.

*Figures derived from prices in nearest metro area or city due to lack of data for metro area itself.

†Honolulu's figure is based on a cost-of-living premium for food awarded federal government employees living in Hawaii.

Miscellaneous Goods and Services. Eating out at McDonald's, Pizza Hut, or Kentucky Fried Chicken is a service on ACCRA's shopping list. So are cash-and-carry charges for dry cleaning a man's two-piece suit, visiting a barber for a basic haircut (no styling), and visiting a beauty salon for a shampoo, trim, and blow-dry. ACCRA's list also includes a six-ounce tube of Crest, an 11-ounce bottle of Johnson's Baby Shampoo, a can of Wilson tennis balls, a number-9 standard edition of Parker Brothers Monopoly, and a six-pack of 12-ounce Schlitz or Budweiser beer.

Anchorage again tops the metro areas in this category of living costs, while metro areas in the Mid-South and Midwest enjoy the lowest prices.

Miscellaneous Goods and Services Prices in the Metro Areas

Lowest Prices	Cost Index (U.S. Avg. = 100)	Highest Prices	Cost Index (U.S. Avg. = 100)
1. Jacksonville, NC	89*	1. Anchorage, AK	138
2. Anniston, AL	90*	2. Honolulu, HI	125†
2. Gadsden, AL	90	3. Oakland, CA	120*
4. Canton, OH	91	3. San Francisco, CA	120
4. Fort Wayne, IN	91	3. Santa Rosa–Petaluma, CA	120*
4. Pine Bluff, AR	91*		
7. Anderson, SC	92*	6. New York, NY	114
7. Burlington, NC	92	7. Bremerton, WA	112*
7. Dothan, AL	92	7. Olympia, WA	112*
7. Elkhart–Goshen, IN	92*	7. Portland, OR	112
		7. Seattle, WA	112*
7. Florence, SC	92*	7. Tacoma, WA	112
7. Indianapolis, IN	92	7. Vancouver, WA	112*
7. Kokomo, IN	92*	13. Reno, NV	111
7. Lafayette, IN	92*	14. Fresno, CA	110
7. South Bend–Mishawaka, IN	92	14. Las Vegas, NV	110
		14. Modesto, CA	110
7. Steubenville–Weirton, OH–WV	92		

Source: American Chamber of Commerce Researchers Association, "Inter-City Cost of Living Index," first quarter, 1984.

*Figures derived from prices in nearest metro area or city due to lack of data for metro area itself.

†Honolulu's figure is based on a cost-of-living premium for miscellaneous goods awarded federal government employees living in Hawaii.

SCRAPING BY ON $33,121 A YEAR

If budgeting the costs of all the things your household needs will give you a rough idea of how much income you'll have to earn to pay for it all, then you might ask whether average household incomes in different parts of the country indicate local living costs. For the most part, they do. According to a recent U.S. Labor Department report, two thirds of the difference in personal incomes between, say, Atlanta and Seattle reflects their different costs of living; the other third reflects their different employers, worker skills, and prevailing wages. (See "Income and Expenses: A Close Connection" on page 374 for more on this subject.)

Households aren't always made up of families. According to the 1984 Census Bureau survey on living arrangements, one quarter of all households are composed either of one person or of several people unrelated to one another (including two million POSSLQs: Persons of Opposite Sex Sharing Living Quarters). There are 12 million single-parent households with at least one child present, and two million of them are headed by men. The rest of the households comprise married couples, some with children, some childless, and some whose children have scattered from the nest.

Like being married 1.2 times and having 2.5 children in the bargain, 2.8 persons per household is an odd statistic. Yet that's roughly what you get when you divide the population of U.S. metro areas by the number of metro area households (figures are from the Rand McNally *1984 Commercial Atlas & Marketing Guide*).

When it comes to a statistic like per capita personal income in a given place, we know the textbook definition, but we also know that a corporate marketing vice president pulling down $100,000 a year plus five field hands earning $10,000 apiece doesn't really add up to six persons with average earnings of $25,000 each. Nonetheless, whether we talk of social phenomena, the stock market, or the strengths of major-league pitchers, we can seldom sidestep statistical averages.

To determine average household incomes in each of the 329 metro areas, *Places Rated Almanac* starts with per capita personal income. This includes not only paychecks but also money from such sources as interest and dividends, rents, alimony, and pensions—in short, the gross sum that you would record on your income tax return before claiming deductions. Per capita personal incomes are then multiplied by 2.8, the average number of persons in a metro area household. The average household income for all U.S. metro areas is currently $33,121, ranging from $51,601 in Anchorage to $16,478 in McAllen–Edinburg–Mission, in historically poor southernmost Texas.

Average Household Incomes in the Metro Areas

Highest		Lowest	
1. Anchorage, AK	$51,601	1. McAllen–Edinburg–Mission, TX	$16,478
2. San Francisco, CA	47,967	2. Laredo, TX	17,287
3. Bridgeport–Milford, CT	47,258	3. Brownsville–Harlingen, TX	17,903
3. Danbury, CT	47,258	4. Provo–Orem, UT	18,390
3. Norwalk, CT	47,258	5. Las Cruces, NM	21,641
3. Stamford, CT	47,258	6. Bloomington, IN	21,851
7. Midland, TX	46,458	7. El Paso, TX	21,929
8. Casper, WY	43,388	8. Anniston, AL	22,254
9. Bergen–Passaic, NJ	43,240	9. Fayetteville, NC	22,291
10. Nassau–Suffolk, NY	43,075	10. Jacksonville, NC	22,358

Source: U.S. Bureau of Economic Analysis, *Survey of Current Business*, April 1984.

The national metro area average for household income is $33,121.

Income and Expenses: A Close Connection

It may be true, as one Roman philosopher claimed, that money has no odor, but it does have a recognizable pattern: High incomes are usually found where the cost of living is high, and low incomes where living is cheap.

By "cost of living," *Places Rated* means the income required for homeownership, food, and miscellaneous goods and services. Each of these criteria is multiplied by a number that reflects its percentage of a middle-class family's income. Thus we multiply the cost index for homeownership, which consumes one third of an average budget, by 33; the index for food by 17; and the index for miscellaneous goods by 30. The total is then divided by 80, the sum of the three weighted numbers, to represent the overall cost of living.

Five of the 15 metro areas with the highest cost indexes also place among the top metro areas for income, including several in Connecticut. And five of the places where it's cheapest to live—some of them in Alabama and North Carolina—have among the lowest incomes. (A list of highest and lowest household incomes is on page 373.)

Household Income in the Metro Areas

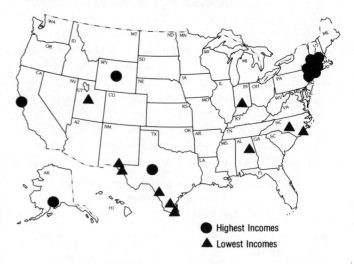

● Highest Incomes
▲ Lowest Incomes

Overall Cost of Living in the Metro Areas

Lowest Costs	Cost Index (U.S. Avg. = 100)	Highest Costs	Cost Index (U.S. Avg. = 100)
1. Joplin, MO	80	1. Stamford, CT	179
2. Anniston, AL	81	2. Oxnard–	
2. Gadsden, AL	81	Ventura, CA	177
4. Anderson, SC	83	3. Norwalk, CT	162
4. Dothan, AL	83	4. Honolulu, HI	158
		5. San Francisco, CA	153
6. Brownsville–			
Harlingen, TX	84	6. Anchorage, AK	142
6. Florence, AL	84	7. San Jose, CA	140
6. Jacksonville, NC	84	8. Anaheim–	
6. Pine Bluff, AR	84	Santa Ana, CA	139
6. St. Joseph, MO	84	9. Santa Barbara–	
		Santa Maria–	
6. South Bend–		Lompoc, CA	136
Mishawaka, IN	84	10. Bergen–Passaic, NJ	135
12. Burlington, NC	85		
12. Fayetteville, NC	85	11. Danbury, CT	133
12. McAllen–Edinburg–		11. New York, NY	133
Mission, TX	85	11. Newark, NJ	133
12. Texarkana, TX–		11. Oakland, CA	133
Texarkana, AR	85	15. Santa Rosa–	
		Petaluma, CA	132

Cost of Living in the Metro Areas

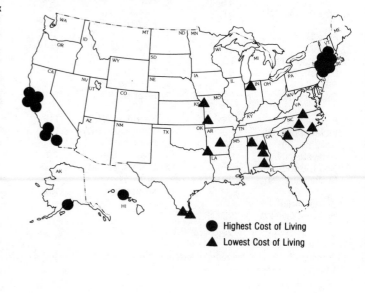

● Highest Cost of Living
▲ Lowest Cost of Living

TAXES: ONE OF LIFE'S CERTAINTIES

In a calendar year, May 1 marks the mythical Tax Freedom Day on which we stop handing over all of our earnings to federal, state, and local tax collectors and begin pocketing that money for ourselves. Looking at it another way, we spend two hours and 40 minutes of every eight-hour working day earning enough money to pay taxes, according to the District of Columbia–based Tax Foundation, and that amounts to $24 a day for each employed person.

No matter where you live, Social Security taxes hit you with the same impact. So can federal personal income taxes. But state and local taxes differ tremendously. To determine the relative tax bite among metro areas, *Places Rated* focuses on the two most common direct levies: state personal income taxes and state sales taxes. Based on a metro area's average household income, state income taxes are estimated for a two-paycheck couple with one child, filing either a joint or a combined separate return (whichever would result in the smaller amount of taxes owed in each state), after taking typical exemptions and deductions. The taxes that a family pays throughout the year in the store on retail sales are also based on the household's average income, using the optional general sales tax table found in the tax return mailed to taxpayers each year by the Internal Revenue Service.

As a percentage of average household incomes, state income and sales taxes take some of the biggest bites from household incomes in the District of Columbia, Massachusetts, Michigan, Minnesota, New York, Oregon, Utah, and Wisconsin. In Connecticut, Florida, New Hampshire, New Mexico, Texas, and Wyoming, the bite is smallest. And in Alaska and New Hampshire, there is no bite at all.

The Bite State Taxes Take from Household Income

Smallest Bites		Biggest Bites	
1. Anchorage, AK	0%	1. Washington, DC–MD–VA	5.66%
1. Manchester, NH	0	2. Honolulu, HI	5.38
1. Nashua, NH	0	3. Nassau–Suffolk, NY	5.18
1. Portsmouth–Dover–Rochester, NH–ME	0	4. Minneapolis–St. Paul, MN–WI	5.08
5. Las Cruces, NM	0.62	5. Rochester, MN	5.04
6. Brazoria, TX	0.72	6. Provo–Orem, UT	4.85
6. Lubbock, TX	0.72	7. Milwaukee, WI	4.83
8. Corpus Christi, TX	0.73	8. Salt Lake City–Ogden, UT	4.82
8. Sherman–Denison, TX	0.73	9. Portland, OR	4.70
10. Killeen–Temple, TX	0.74	10. Madison, WI	4.69
10. Texarkana, TX–Texarkana, AR	0.74		
10. Waco, TX	0.74		

Source: Derived from Advisory Commission on Intergovernmental Relations, "Tax Burdens for Families Residing in the Largest City in Each State," 1984.

WEATHERING THE RECESSION: JOB AND INCOME TRACK RECORDS

New Year's Day 1978 didn't seem to be a particularly notable date in the history of the American economy. Some 75 million residents of metro areas, the highest number ever, had a job to go back to after the holidays; the energy crisis was all but forgotten; food prices were creeping upward.

But over the next 60 months, something happened that was unforeseen by sanguine and cautious business forecasters alike. Not only did the nation experience ruinous inflation, we also suffered back-to-back business slumps far worse than any since the Great Depression.

Not all metro areas were equally stricken. Between 1978 and 1982, consumer prices rose 47.95 percent. Personal income growth in 103 metro areas either kept abreast of or outpaced that figure; incomes in 226 metro areas, however, lagged. During the same period, 167 metro areas outran the economy's job-formation record, while 162 metro areas fell behind it, with 74 of these actually losing jobs.

Clearly, some places hardly felt the recession, whereas others took it on the chin. And some of the latter group still haven't fully recovered. Let's look at their track records in income and job growth over the 60-month period from the relative flush times of January 1978 through the recession's onset, depth, and "official" end in November-December of 1982.

Income Growth

The cost of living has a broader meaning than the estimate based on pushing a shopping cart around a metro area and pricing its theater tickets, oil changes, T-shirts, shampoo, and other consumer packaged goods and services. Nationally, it is a measurement of what dollars can buy at different times.

Using the U.S. Bureau of Labor Statistics price index for city consumers fixed at 100 for the base year 1967, the cost of living started at 60 in 1920, dropped to 42 by 1940, rebounded to 116 in 1970, and had skyrocketed to 310 by August 1984. Clearly, inflation plays a big role in the nation's cost of living. Not for nothing are the dollar amounts of everything from pension checks, union wages, and apartment rents tied to the cost-of-living index.

Are you better off today than you were a few years ago? This familiar refrain is sounded during political

Tax Facts

- A typical family earning $25,000 a year pays nearly 20 percent of its income in sales and income taxes to federal, state, and local collectors. For a family earning $50,000, these same taxes take 27 percent. Families in the $75,000-and-over bracket are stuck with a tax bite of 40 percent.
- The median federal tax bite (income and Social Security taxes) is almost six times that of the median state-local sales and income tax bite. For the family earning $25,000 a year, taxes imposed by Washington take 16.6 percent of family income, whereas state-local taxes subtract 2.8 percent. For families earning $50,000, the figures are 23.2 percent and 3.6 percent, respectively.
- Usually the lowest family tax burdens are found in metro areas with unique revenue advantages. Families living in Anchorage, Casper, Las Vegas, and New Orleans shoulder light tax burdens because their home states tap revenue from outsiders—severance taxes and mineral royalties from mining and lumber companies in Alaska, Louisiana, and Wyoming, and amusement and sales taxes from visiting gamblers in Nevada.
- Alaska and New Hampshire are the only states in which residents pay no sales taxes or income taxes. And living in Alaska carries an additional benefit: Each resident receives an annual check from the state's $5.5 billion permanent fund, a savings account from oil and gas fees and royalty payments from North Slope drillers. In 1984, the bonus amounted to $358 per person.

campaigns, which invariably focus on the twin issues of income and joblessness. If voters are disheartened by paltry rises in their real income, then the politician looking to stay in office may be in trouble. And metro areas can be in trouble, too, if local personal incomes don't stay ahead of inflation. When consumers have no money to spend, a litany of trouble begins: Retail stores close up for lack of trade; real estate investments aren't sure things; property crime increases; and municipal services are cut.

Personal Income Growth in the Metro Areas

Greatest	Growth, 1978–82	Least	Growth, 1978–82
1. Lafayette, LA	76.22%	1. Williamsport, PA	20.24%
2. Enid, OK	65.91	2. Kokomo, IN	21.00
3. Jacksonville, NC	61.84	3. Eugene– Springfield, OR	24.33
4. Midland, TX	60.56	4. Flint, MI	25.49
5. Bryan–College Station, TX	60.35	5. Elkhart– Goshen, IN	26.03
6. Atlantic City, NJ	59.84	6. Texarkana, TX– Texarkana, AR	26.39
7. Oklahoma City, OK	59.48	7. Redding, CA	26.60
8. New London– Norwich, CT–RI	58.43	8. Steubenville– Weirton, OH–WV	26.67
9. Boulder– Longmont, CO	58.27	9. Detroit, MI	27.24
10. Colorado Springs, CO	58.05	10. Anderson, IN	27.67

Source: U.S. Bureau of Economic Analysis, unpublished metro area personal income data for 1978–82, 1984.

The national metro area average for income growth is 43.34%.

Job Expansion

In the midst of the back-to-back recessions of 1980 and 1981–82, it was easy to wonder whether we would ever again hear the buzz saws shriek in Oregon sawmills or the whistles signal a shift change in Pennsylvania ironworks; indeed, whether we would ever again see large numbers of workers troop past the gates of low-tech factories in full production.

Michigan, Indiana, Ohio, and Illinois were particularly hard hit. Between 1980 and 1982, nearly 100,000 jobs disappeared in these four states due to the slump in domestic automobile production and its effect on nearby employers. For every 10,000 jobs lost at Chrysler, Ford, and General Motors, an additional 20,000 were lost in other industries, including 4,500 in iron and steel, 2,500 in wholesale trade, and 900 in business services.

A look at the metro areas with the greatest loss of jobs between the flush times of early 1978 and the recession that bottomed out in November 1982 shows a group lumped in the Rust Bowl section of the United States. Here, in the graying, muscle-bound, blue-collar metro areas of the Great Lakes, firms that produce autos, steel, tires, and machinery predominate.

In contrast, metro areas with the biggest expansion in jobs during the same period were smaller metro areas that either benefited from a rise in light-manufacturing employment—particularly in electronics and instrument firms—or in petroleum refining or other energy production. Atlantic City owes its rebirth to amusement services.

Job Growth in the Metro Areas

Greatest	Growth, 1978–82	Least	Growth, 1978–82
1. Portsmouth– Dover–Rochester, NH–ME	62.51%	1. Beaver County, PA	−22.73%
2. Fort Pierce, FL	54.05	2. Syracuse, NY	−22.15
3. Bryan–College Station, TX	52.53	3. Anderson, IN	−20.47
4. Lafayette, LA	48.25	4. Kokomo, IN	−17.89
5. Midland, TX	47.62	5. Peoria, IL	−16.28
6. Atlantic City, NJ	46.69	6. Benton Harbor, MI	−15.87
7. Ocala, FL	39.38	7. Lorain–Elyria, OH	−15.36
8. Orlando, FL	38.53	8. Flint, MI	−15.30
9. Colorado Springs, CO	38.49	8. Muskegon, MI	−15.30
10. West Palm Beach–Boca Raton–Delray Beach, FL	38.48	10. Battle Creek, MI	−14.97

Source: U.S. Bureau of Labor Statistics, unpublished ES–202 records, 1984.

The national metro area average for job growth is 9.45%.

JUDGING PERSONAL ECONOMIC OUTLOOK

If the annual income in your household is $30,000, would you be better off in Dallas or Denver when it comes to paying state sales and income taxes? If you're out of work, would you find the prospects for landing a job more promising in Seattle or San Francisco? Even if you think you've found a likely metro area with a record of rapid job expansion and a modest tax bite, can you still afford to live and work there given the local costs for housing, groceries, and clothing?

To help you answer these questions, *Places Rated* compares five factors in each metro area: average household income, state sales and income tax bite, costs of living (a scoring element introduced in this edition), and recent five-year rates for income growth and job expansion. Figures for these last two factors also represent a change from the 1981 *Places Rated Almanac*, in which we presented projections for growth rather than actual trends.

Each metro area starts with a base score of zero, to which points are added according to the following indicators:

1. *Average household income adjusted for taxes and living costs.* The average annual household income is reduced by the estimated dollars paid out in state sales and income taxes at that income level. After-tax income is then divided by the local cost-of-living index (see page 374 for an explanation of how costs for housing, food, and miscellaneous items are combined to calculate a metro area's overall cost-of-living index). For example, Chicago's household income after taxes—$35,422—is divided by its cost-of-living index of 115. The result is multiplied by 10 and added to the

base score of zero; in Chicago's case, this works out to 3,080 points.

2. *Income growth.* The local growth rate for personal income over the five-year period between January 1978 and December 1982 (the latest available figures) is multiplied by 50 and added to the score.

3. *Job growth.* The percentage of growth in local number of jobs between January 1978 and December 1982 is multiplied by 50 and added to the total.

Sample Comparison: Midland, Texas, and Eugene–Springfield, Oregon

The two areas compared here for cost of living, household income, tax bite, and the impact of the last recession illustrate not just the economic extremes among the 329 metro areas but also how *Places Rated's* scoring method has changed since 1981, when both places were rated in the book's first edition.

Financially, people do quite well in Midland. In 1981, the small metro area in the Permian oil basin of West Texas was ranked 29th of 277 metro areas, mainly

An Occupational Directory

Using "white collar" or "blue collar" to differentiate between a job that deals either with information or things, is physical or mental, clean or messy, salaried or nonsalaried, high-paying or low-paying, seasonal or year-round, skilled or unskilled, unionized or professional, is somewhat imprecise.

According to U.S. Standard Occupational Classification (SOC) definitions, white-collar jobs include professional and technical workers, managers and administrators, sales workers, and clerical workers. Blue-collar occupations include craftsworkers, operatives, drivers, and nonfarm laborers.

But a quick look at some of the white-collar clerical job titles shows that many of them can be as unskilled, nonsalaried, and seasonal as jobs in the laboring category, while many blue-collar craftsworker jobs can be as skilled, salaried, and highly paid as those in the professional and technical category.

The SOC also identifies two other categories of occupations: service workers and farm workers. Service jobs include police and health-service, food-service, and child-care workers; farmers, farm laborers, and farm managers compose the farm workers category.

White Collar

Professional and Technical
Accountants
Computer specialists
Engineers
Health technologists and technicians
Lawyers and judges
Librarians, archivists, and curators
Life and physical scientists
Personnel and labor relations workers
Physicians, dentists, and related practitioners
Registered nurses, dietitians, and therapists
Religious workers
Research workers
Social scientists
Social and recreation workers
Teachers
Technicians (except health)
Vocational and educational counselors
Writers, artists, and entertainers

Managers and Administrators (Except Farm)
Bank officers and financial managers
Building managers and superintendents
Buyers, wholesale and retail trade
Health administrators
Office managers
Officials and administrators
Restaurant, cafeteria, and bar managers
Sales managers
School administrators

Sales Workers
Hucksters and peddlers
Insurance agents, brokers, and underwriters
Real estate agents and brokers
Retail store sales clerks
Stock and bond sales agents
Sales representatives
Salespeople

Clerical Workers
Bank tellers
Billing clerks
Bookkeepers
Cashiers
Clerical supervisors
Counter clerks, except food
Estimators and investigators
File clerks
Insurance adjusters, examiners, and investigators
Postal clerks and mail carriers
Receptionists
Secretaries
Shipping and receiving clerks
Statistical clerks
Stenographers
Stock clerks and storekeepers
Telephone operators
Typists and office-machine operators

Blue Collar

Craftsworkers
Carpenters
Construction craftsworkers
Machinists and job-setters
Metalcraft workers
Mechanics
Other craftsworkers
Print craftsworkers

Operatives (Except Transport)
Assemblers
Checkers, examiners, and inspectors of manufactured goods
Cutters

Dressmakers and seamstresses, except factory
Garage workers and gas station attendants
Laundry and dry-cleaning operatives
Machine operatives
Meat cutters and butchers
Miners
Packers and wrappers
Painters of manufactured goods
Precision machine operatives
Punch and stamping press operatives
Sewers and stitchers

Textile operatives
Welders and flame cutters

Transport Equipment Operatives
Bus drivers
Delivery and route workers
Forklift and tow motor operators
Taxi drivers and chauffeurs
Truck drivers

Laborers (Except Farm)
Construction laborers
Freight, material, and stock handlers
Gardeners and groundskeepers

Source: U.S. Standard Occupational Classification.

because of its high personal income, light tax bite, and rosy outlook for personal income and jobs through the end of the decade. Little has changed. Midland's average household income—$46,458—ranks first in Texas and seventh in the country. The Texas tax bite is just as forgiving now as it was in 1981. There are no levies on personal income nor any on interest and dividends, and while no one is forgiven retail sales taxes, these take only $291 out of average household incomes. When Midland's after-tax household income is divided by its cost-of-living index of 101, the result is 457.1; multiplying this figure by 10 yields 4,571 points.

Instead of looking at the forecast for job and income growth over the rest of the decade, as we did in the 1981 edition, *Places Rated* now examines actual growth over the latest five-year period for which data are available. From 1978 through 1982, the number of workers on the payroll of Midland's employers increased by nearly 47.62 percent. Personal income also shot up, by 60.56 percent, during that time. Not all of the growth came from the oil patch. Midland also produces semiconductors and is a thriving service center in an otherwise empty part of Texas. Multiplying Midland's percentages for job and income growth by 50 yields 5,409 points. This total, when added to the 4,571 points for adjusted household income, earns for Midland the highest score of any metro area, 9,980 points.

In contrast, Eugene–Springfield's economics rating plunged from 44th in *Places Rated*'s 1981 edition to the very bottom in this edition, basically because of recession. If there is one area in the United States where the local economy depends on a vulnerable industry, it is the timbered parts of the Pacific Northwest. Between 1978 and 1982, some 8,317 jobs departed from Eugene–Springfield. Some say these jobs, mainly in logging and in saw and planing mills, may never return. Even though home building has turned around, the Pacific Northwest lumber industry hasn't, due to stiff price competition from Canadian and southeastern producers. Job losses and shorter hours severely dampened household income growth here, too. Multiplying the sum of Eugene–Springfield's percentages for income growth (24.33) and job loss (−8.98) by 50 works out to only 768 points.

Oregon is one of five states that do not collect sales taxes. But what it passes up at the store, it collects every April 15 from residents filing their income tax returns. Accordingly, Eugene–Springfield's average $25,698 household income figure is reduced by $1,102, to reflect the Oregon personal income tax bite. Dividing after-tax income by the cost-of-living index of 108 and then multiplying by 10 yields 2,277 points. Adding this to the 768 points earned for income and job growth gives the Oregon metro area a score of 3,045, putting it in 329th place.

Places Rated: Metro Areas Ranked for Personal Economic Outlook

Places Rated Almanac focuses on three major criteria to rank metro areas for their economic promise: (1) average household income adjusted for taxes and living costs, (2) rate of income growth, and (3) rate of job expansion. Places that receive tie scores are given the same rank and are listed in alphabetical order.

Metro Areas from Best to Worst

Places Rated Rank	Places Rated Score	Places Rated Rank	Places Rated Score	Places Rated Rank	Places Rated Score
1. Midland, TX	9,980	13. Colorado Springs, CO	7,699	26. Bridgeport–Milford, CT	7,197
2. Lafayette, LA	9,702	14. Anchorage, AK	7,668	27. Fort Myers, FL	7,166
3. Portsmouth–Dover–Rochester, NH–ME	8,367	15. Abilene, TX	7,633	28. Denver, CO	7,164
4. Enid, OK	8,268	16. Victoria, TX	7,599	29. Fort Lauderdale–Hollywood–Pompano Beach, FL	7,136
5. Oklahoma City, OK	8,119	17. Odessa, TX	7,565	30. Boulder–Longmont, CO	7,127
6. Atlantic City, NJ	8,107	18. Houston, TX	7,464		
7. Bryan–College Station, TX	8,040	19. Austin, TX	7,439	31. Tulsa, OK	7,115
8. West Palm Beach–Boca Raton–Delray Beach, FL	7,992	20. Bradenton, FL	7,437	32. Manchester, NH	7,101
9. Fort Pierce, FL	7,973	21. Orlando, FL	7,413	33. Melbourne–Titusville–Palm Bay, FL	7,089
10. San Angelo, TX	7,720	22. Nassau–Suffolk, NY	7,371	34. Danbury, CT	7,060
		23. Tyler, TX	7,327	34. Ocala, FL	7,060
		24. San Jose, CA	7,270		
11. Sarasota, FL	7,715	25. Tampa–St. Petersburg–Clearwater, FL	7,256	36. Nashua, NH	6,962
12. Dallas, TX	7,710			37. Brockton, MA	6,900

Places Rated Rank	Places Rated Score	Places Rated Rank	Places Rated Score	Places Rated Rank	Places Rated Score
38. Longview–Marshall, TX	6,898	98. Beaumont–Port Arthur, TX	6,019	154. Champaign–Urbana–	
39. San Antonio, TX	6,873	98. Bismarck, ND	6,019	Rantoul, IL	5,485
40. Fort Worth–Arlington, TX	6,862	100. Bergen–Passaic, NJ	6,016	155. Pittsfield, MA	5,483
41. Wichita Falls, TX	6,805	101. St. Joseph, MO	5,991	156. New Haven–Meriden, CT	5,478
42. Poughkeepsie, NY	6,746	102. Nashville, TN	5,938	157. Topeka, KS	5,464
43. Burlington, VT	6,726	103. Springfield, MO	5,932	158. Oakland, CA	5,457
44. Corpus Christi, TX	6,690	104. Lubbock, TX	5,923	159. Dothan, AL	5,453
45. New London–Norwich, CT–RI	6,672	105. Billings, MT	5,913	160. Madison, WI	5,448
46. Houma–Thibodaux, LA	6,662	106. Seattle, WA	5,901	161. Greeley, CO	5,443
47. Lowell, MA–NH	6,651	107. Lake Charles, LA	5,872	162. Augusta, GA–SC	5,431
48. Fort Collins–Loveland, CO	6,631	108. Richmond–Petersburg, VA	5,870	163. Louisville, KY–IN	5,402
49. Daytona Beach, FL	6,592	109. Norfolk–Virginia Beach–		164. Wilmington, NC	5,390
50. Shreveport, LA	6,585	Newport News, VA	5,866	165. Springfield, IL	5,384
		110. Albany–Schenectady–			
51. Bristol, CT	6,527	Troy, NY	5,864	166. Eau Claire, WI	5,348
51. Lawrence–Haverhill, MA–NH	6,527			167. Des Moines, IA	5,346
53. New Britain, CT	6,470	111. Bloomington–Normal, IL	5,863	168. Las Cruces, NM	5,341
54. New Orleans, LA	6,453	112. Omaha, NE–IA	5,853	169. New York, NY	5,338
55. Norwalk, CT	6,432	113. Minneapolis–St. Paul, MN–WI	5,843	170. Santa Cruz, CA	5,335
		114. Miami–Hialeah, FL	5,840		
56. Phoenix, AZ	6,415	115. Orange County, NY	5,822	171. Richland–Kennewick–	
57. Huntsville, AL	6,412			Pasco, WA	5,326
58. Raleigh–Durham, NC	6,405	116. Santa Barbara–Santa		172. Joplin, MO	5,324
59. Jacksonville, NC	6,386	Maria–Lompoc, CA	5,821	173. Harrisburg–Lebanon–	
60. Boston, MA	6,363	117. Vallejo–Fairfield–Napa, CA	5,819	Carlisle, PA	5,322
		118. Biloxi–Gulfport, MS	5,801	174. Los Angeles–Long	
61. Fort Walton Beach, FL	6,342	119. St. Louis, MO–IL	5,800	Beach, CA	5,316
62. Killeen–Temple, TX	6,331	120. Alton–Granite City, IL	5,795	175. Sacramento, CA	5,309
63. Middlesex–Somerset–					
Hunterdon, NJ	6,324	121. Trenton, NJ	5,772	176. Chico, CA	5,307
64. Atlanta, GA	6,315	122. Lake County, IL	5,755	177. Springfield, MA	5,289
65. Salem–Gloucester, MA	6,309	123. Fresno, CA	5,746	178. Roanoke, VA	5,287
		124. Gainesville, FL	5,739	179. Columbia, SC	5,279
66. Baton Rouge, LA	6,308	124. McAllen–Edinburg–		180. Appleton–Oshkosh–	
67. Hartford, CT	6,307	Mission, TX	5,739	Neenah, WI	5,275
67. Middletown, CT	6,307				
69. Rochester, NY	6,304	126. Albuquerque, NM	5,727	181. Little Rock–	
70. Casper, WY	6,303	127. Santa Rosa–Petaluma, CA	5,703	North Little Rock, AR	5,273
		128. Newark, NJ	5,690	182. Cincinnati, OH–KY–IN	5,270
71. Waco, TX	6,259	129. Burlington, NC	5,680	183. Laredo, TX	5,264
72. Lexington–Fayette, KY	6,245	130. Reno, NV	5,677	184. Pittsburgh, PA	5,261
73. Amarillo, TX	6,241			185. Charleston, WV	5,257
74. Anaheim–Santa Ana, CA	6,220	131. Stockton, CA	5,672		
75. Sherman–Denison, TX	6,213	132. Bremerton, WA	5,671	186. Fayetteville, NC	5,255
		132. Charlotte–Gastonia–		187. Alexandria, LA	5,254
76. Portland, ME	6,186	Rock Hill, NC–SC	5,671	188. Albany, GA	5,250
77. Wilmington, DE–NJ–MD	6,174	134. Macon–Warner Robins, GA	5,659	189. Utica–Rome, NY	5,226
78. Kansas City, KS	6,166	135. Salinas–Seaside–		190. Evansville, IN–KY	5,206
79. Stamford, CT	6,158	Monterey, CA	5,656		
80. Monmouth–Ocean, NJ	6,154			191. Chicago, IL	5,205
		135. Waterbury, CT	5,656	192. Greensboro–Winston–	
81. Tucson, AZ	6,147	137. Green Bay, WI	5,650	Salem–High Point, NC	5,204
82. Jacksonville, FL	6,139	138. La Crosse, WI	5,648	192. Sioux Falls, SD	5,204
83. East St. Louis–Belleville, IL	6,113	139. Grand Forks, ND	5,646	194. Asheville, NC	5,196
84. Lawton, OK	6,105	140. Philadelphia, PA–NJ	5,638	195. Athens, GA	5,193
85. Rochester, MN	6,099				
		141. Binghamton, NY	5,614	196. Honolulu, HI	5,187
86. Panama City, FL	6,083	142. Fargo–Moorhead, ND–MN	5,594	196. Parkersburg–Marietta,	
87. Washington, DC–MD–VA	6,072	142. Lakeland–Winter Haven, FL	5,594	WV–OH	5,187
88. San Francisco, CA	6,063	144. Savannah, GA	5,591	198. Jackson, MS	5,186
89. Owensboro, KY	6,062	145. Reading, PA	5,587	199. Kenosha, WI	5,176
90. Bakersfield, CA	6,056			200. Bangor, ME	5,172
		146. Kankakee, IL	5,579		
91. Charlottesville, VA	6,055	147. Visalia–Tulare–Porterville, CA	5,563	201. Glens Falls, NY	5,166
92. Wichita, KS	6,036	148. Knoxville, TN	5,537	202. Columbus, OH	5,165
93. Las Vegas, NV	6,035	148. Monroe, LA	5,537	202. Iowa City, IA	5,165
94. Pensacola, FL	6,029	150. Oxnard–Ventura, CA	5,514	204. Memphis, TN–AR–MS	5,160
95. Galveston–Texas City, TX	6,026			205. Pawtucket–Woonsocket–	
		151. Baltimore, MD	5,503	Attleboro, RI–MA	5,154
96. Tallahassee, FL	6,021	152. San Diego, CA	5,489		
97. Brazoria, TX	6,020	153. St. Cloud, MN	5,488	205. Providence, RI	5,154

Places Rated Rank	Places Rated Score	Places Rated Rank	Places Rated Score	Places Rated Rank	Places Rated Score
207. Charleston, SC	5,153	246. Birmingham, AL	4,843	289. Huntington–Ashland, WV–KY–OH	4,383
208. Columbia, MO	5,147	247. Florence, SC	4,842	290. Janesville–Beloit, WI	4,371
209. Lancaster, PA	5,120	248. Bloomington, IN	4,829		
210. Modesto, CA	5,107	249. Elmira, NY	4,813	291. Terre Haute, IN	4,353
		250. Columbus, GA–AL	4,812	292. Akron, OH	4,350
211. Fitchburg–Leominster, MA	5,098			293. Lafayette, IN	4,333
212. Allentown–Bethlehem, PA–NJ	5,097	251. Kalamazoo, MI	4,794	294. Lima, OH	4,313
212. Aurora–Elgin, IL	5,097	252. Texarkana, TX–Texarkana, AR	4,772	295. Wausau, WI	4,300
214. Indianapolis, IN	5,082	253. Sheboygan, WI	4,765		
215. El Paso, TX	5,080	254. Lansing–East Lansing, MI	4,747	296. Erie, PA	4,299
		255. Cumberland, MD–WV	4,741	297. Decatur, IL	4,274
216. South Bend–Mishawaka, IN	5,056			298. Anderson, SC	4,262
217. Buffalo, NY	5,047	256. Wheeling, WV–OH	4,740	299. Bellingham, WA	4,247
218. Worcester, MA	5,040	257. Anniston, AL	4,730	299. Pine Bluff, AR	4,247
219. Vineland–Millville–Bridgeton, NJ	5,023	258. Hickory, NC	4,728		
220. Greenville–Spartanburg, SC	5,012	259. Spokane, WA	4,722	301. Altoona, PA	4,230
		260. Great Falls, MT	4,697	302. Gadsden, AL	4,220
221. Cedar Rapids, IA	5,009			303. Elkhart–Goshen, IN	4,214
222. Davenport–Rock Island–Moline, IA–IL	4,997	261. Yuba City, CA	4,694	304. Fort Wayne, IN	4,195
223. Yakima, WA	4,986	262. State College, PA	4,677	305. Johnstown, PA	4,181
224. Milwaukee, WI	4,982	263. Sioux City, IA–NE	4,648		
225. Brownsville–Harlingen, TX	4,968	264. Pueblo, CO	4,646	306. Peoria, IL	4,073
		265. Boise City, ID	4,633	307. Sharon, PA	4,055
226. York, PA	4,946			308. Battle Creek, MI	4,008
227. Salt Lake City–Ogden, UT	4,942	266. Fayetteville–Springdale, AR	4,631	309. Muncie, IN	3,980
228. New Bedford, MA	4,937	266. Joliet, IL	4,631	310. Dubuque, IA	3,949
229. Lynchburg, VA	4,926	268. Hamilton–Middletown, OH	4,618		
230. Riverside–San Bernardino, CA	4,923	269. Rockford, IL	4,592	311. Duluth, MN–WI	3,922
		270. Ann Arbor, MI	4,579	312. Detroit, MI	3,904
231. Olympia, WA	4,912			313. Youngstown–Warren, OH	3,894
232. Lincoln, NE	4,908	271. Lawrence, KS	4,573	314. Salem, OR	3,835
233. Scranton–Wilkes-Barre, PA	4,907	272. Vancouver, WA	4,571	315. Gary–Hammond, IN	3,826
234. Johnson City–Kingsport–Bristol, TN–VA	4,903	273. Mobile, AL	4,565		
235. Tuscaloosa, AL	4,900	274. Portland, OR	4,535	316. Jackson, MI	3,822
		275. Toledo, OH	4,534	317. Steubenville–Weirton, OH–WV	3,744
236. Montgomery, AL	4,892	276. Dayton–Springfield, OH	4,532	318. Flint, MI	3,724
237. Jersey City, NJ	4,889	277. Florence, AL	4,492	319. Saginaw–Bay City–Midland, MI	3,709
238. Tacoma, WA	4,887	278. Danville, VA	4,491	320. Muskegon, MI	3,708
239. Fall River, MA–RI	4,884	278. Pascagoula, MS	4,491		
240. Clarksville–Hopkinsville, TN–KY	4,880	280. Chattanooga, TN–GA	4,487	321. Medford, OR	3,692
241. Cleveland, OH	4,879			322. Benton Harbor, MI	3,635
242. Kansas City, MO	4,865	281. Hagerstown, MD	4,477	323. Provo–Orem, UT	3,459
243. Fort Smith, AR–OK	4,849	282. Syracuse, NY	4,474	324. Kokomo, IN	3,429
244. Grand Rapids, MI	4,848	283. Niagara Falls, NY	4,463	325. Anderson, IN	3,370
245. Canton, OH	4,847	284. Redding, CA	4,459		
		285. Lewiston–Auburn, ME	4,444	326. Lorain–Elyria, OH	3,301
		286. Racine, WI	4,415	327. Williamsport, PA	3,288
		287. Waterloo–Cedar Falls, IA	4,407	328. Beaver County, PA	3,119
		288. Mansfield, OH	4,386	329. Eugene–Springfield, OR	3,045

Metro Areas Listed Alphabetically

Metro Area	Places Rated Rank	Metro Area	Places Rated Rank	Metro Area	Places Rated Rank
Abilene, TX	15	Anaheim–Santa Ana, CA	74	Atlantic City, NJ	6
Akron, OH	292	Anchorage, AK	14	Augusta, GA–SC	162
Albany, GA	188	Anderson, IN	325	Aurora–Elgin, IL	212
Albany–Schenectady–Troy, NY	110	Anderson, SC	298	Austin, TX	19
Albuquerque, NM	126	Ann Arbor, MI	270	Bakersfield, CA	90
Alexandria, LA	187	Anniston, AL	257	Baltimore, MD	151
Allentown–Bethlehem, PA–NJ	212	Appleton–Oshkosh–Neenah, WI	180	Bangor, ME	200
Alton–Granite City, IL	120	Asheville, NC	194	Baton Rouge, LA	66
Altoona, PA	301	Athens, GA	195	Battle Creek, MI	308
Amarillo, TX	73	Atlanta, GA	64	Beaumont–Port Arthur, TX	98

Metro Area	Places Rated Rank	Metro Area	Places Rated Rank	Metro Area	Places Rated Rank
Beaver County, PA	328	Eau Claire, WI	166	Kankakee, IL	146
Bellingham, WA	299	El Paso, TX	215	Kansas City, KS	78
Benton Harbor, MI	322	Elkhart–Goshen, IN	303	Kansas City, MO	242
Bergen–Passaic, NJ	100	Elmira, NY	249	Kenosha, WI	199
Billings, MT	105	Enid, OK	4	Killeen–Temple, TX	62
Biloxi–Gulfport, MS	118	Erie, PA	296	Knoxville, TN	148
Binghamton, NY	141	Eugene–Springfield, OR	329	Kokomo, IN	324
Birmingham, AL	246	Evansville, IN–KY	190	La Crosse, WI	138
Bismarck, ND	98	Fall River, MA–RI	239	Lafayette, IN	293
Bloomington, IN	248	Fargo–Moorhead, ND–MN	142	Lafayette, LA	2
Bloomington–Normal, IL	111	Fayetteville, NC	186	Lake Charles, LA	107
Boise City, ID	265	Fayetteville–Springdale, AR	266	Lake County, IL	122
Boston, MA	60	Fitchburg–Leominster, MA	211	Lakeland–Winter Haven, FL	142
Boulder–Longmont, CO	30	Flint, MI	318	Lancaster, PA	209
Bradenton, FL	20	Florence, AL	277	Lansing–East Lansing, MI	254
Brazoria, TX	97	Florence, SC	247	Laredo, TX	183
Bremerton, WA	132	Fort Collins–Loveland, CO	48	Las Cruces, NM	168
Bridgeport–Milford, CT	26	Fort Lauderdale–Hollywood–Pompano Beach, FL	29	Las Vegas, NV	93
Bristol, CT	51			Lawrence, KS	271
Brockton, MA	37	Fort Myers, FL	27	Lawrence–Haverhill, MA–NH	51
		Fort Pierce, FL	9		
Brownsville–Harlingen, TX	225			Lawton, OK	84
Bryan–College Station, TX	7	Fort Smith, AR–OK	243	Lewiston–Auburn, ME	285
Buffalo, NY	217	Fort Walton Beach, FL	61	Lexington–Fayette, KY	72
Burlington, NC	129	Fort Wayne, IN	304	Lima, OH	294
Burlington, VT	43	Fort Worth–Arlington, TX	40	Lincoln, NE	232
		Fresno, CA	123		
Canton, OH	245			Little Rock–North Little Rock, AR	181
Casper, WY	70	Gadsden, AL	302	Longview–Marshall, TX	38
Cedar Rapids, IA	221	Gainesville, FL	124	Lorain–Elyria, OH	326
Champaign–Urbana–Rantoul, IL	154	Galveston–Texas City, TX	95	Los Angeles–Long Beach, CA	174
		Gary–Hammond, IN	315	Louisville, KY–IN	163
Charleston, SC	207	Glens Falls, NY	201		
				Lowell, MA–NH	47
Charleston, WV	185	Grand Forks, ND	139	Lubbock, TX	104
Charlotte–Gastonia–Rock Hill, NC–SC	132	Grand Rapids, MI	244	Lynchburg, VA	229
		Great Falls, MT	260	Macon–Warner Robins, GA	134
Charlottesville, VA	91	Greeley, CO	161	Madison, WI	160
Chattanooga, TN–GA	280	Green Bay, WI	137		
Chicago, IL	191			Manchester, NH	32
		Greensboro–Winston-Salem–High Point, NC	192	Mansfield, OH	288
Chico, CA	176			McAllen–Edinburg–Mission, TX	124
Cincinnati, OH–KY–IN	182	Greenville–Spartanburg, SC	220	Medford, OR	321
Clarksville–Hopkinsville, TN–KY	240	Hagerstown, MD	281	Melbourne–Titusville–Palm Bay, FL	33
Cleveland, OH	241	Hamilton–Middletown, OH	268		
Colorado Springs, CO	13	Harrisburg–Lebanon–Carlisle, PA	173	Memphis, TN–AR–MS	204
				Miami–Hialeah, FL	114
Columbia, MO	208	Hartford, CT	67	Middlesex–Somerset–Hunterdon, NJ	63
Columbia, SC	179	Hickory, NC	258	Middletown, CT	67
Columbus, GA–AL	250	Honolulu, HI	196	Midland, TX	1
Columbus, OH	202	Houma–Thibodaux, LA	46		
Corpus Christi, TX	44	Houston, TX	18	Milwaukee, WI	224
				Minneapolis–St. Paul, MN–WI	113
Cumberland, MD–WV	255	Huntington–Ashland, WV–KY–OH	289	Mobile, AL	273
Dallas, TX	12	Huntsville, AL	57	Modesto, CA	210
Danbury, CT	34	Indianapolis, IN	214	Monmouth–Ocean, NJ	80
Danville, VA	278	Iowa City, IA	202		
Davenport–Rock Island–Moline, IA–IL	222	Jackson, MI	316	Monroe, LA	148
				Montgomery, AL	236
Dayton–Springfield, OH	276	Jackson, MS	198	Muncie, IN	309
Daytona Beach, FL	49	Jacksonville, FL	82	Muskegon, MI	320
Decatur, IL	297	Jacksonville, NC	59	Nashua, NH	36
Denver, CO	28	Janesville–Beloit, WI	290		
Des Moines, IA	167	Jersey City, NJ	237	Nashville, TN	102
				Nassau–Suffolk, NY	22
Detroit, MI	312	Johnson City–Kingsport–Bristol, TN–VA	234	New Bedford, MA	228
Dothan, AL	159	Johnstown, PA	305	New Britain, CT	53
Dubuque, IA	310	Joliet, IL	266	New Haven–Meriden, CT	156
Duluth, MN–WI	311	Joplin, MO	172	New London–Norwich, CT–RI	45
East St. Louis–Belleville, IL	83	Kalamazoo, MI	251	New Orleans, LA	54

Metro Area	Places Rated Rank	Metro Area	Places Rated Rank	Metro Area	Places Rated Rank
New York, NY	169	Richland–Kennewick–Pasco, WA	171	State College, PA	262
Newark, NJ	128	Richmond–Petersburg, VA	108	Steubenville–Weirton, OH–WV	317
Niagara Falls, NY	283	Riverside–San Bernardino, CA	230	Stockton, CA	131
		Roanoke, VA	178	Syracuse, NY	282
Norfolk–Virginia Beach–Newport News, VA	109	Rochester, MN	85	Tacoma, WA	238
Norwalk, CT	55	Rochester, NY	69	Tallahassee, FL	96
Oakland, CA	158	Rockford, IL	269	Tampa–St. Petersburg–Clearwater, FL	25
Ocala, FL	34	Sacramento, CA	175	Terre Haute, IN	291
Odessa, TX	17	Saginaw–Bay City–Midland, MI	319	Texarkana, TX–Texarkana, AR	252
		St. Cloud, MN	153	Toledo, OH	275
Oklahoma City, OK	5				
Olympia, WA	231	St. Joseph, MO	101	Topeka, KS	157
Omaha, NE–IA	112	St. Louis, MO–IL	119	Trenton, NJ	121
Orange County, NY	115	Salem, OR	314	Tucson, AZ	81
Orlando, FL	21	Salem–Gloucester, MA	65	Tulsa, OK	31
		Salinas–Seaside–Monterey, CA	135	Tuscaloosa, AL	235
Owensboro, KY	89				
Oxnard–Ventura, CA	150	Salt Lake City–Ogden, UT	227	Tyler, TX	23
Panama City, FL	86	San Angelo, TX	10	Utica–Rome, NY	189
Parkersburg–Marietta, WV–OH	196	San Antonio, TX	39	Vallejo–Fairfield–Napa, CA	117
Pascagoula, MS	278	San Diego, CA	152	Vancouver, WA	272
		San Francisco, CA	88	Victoria, TX	16
Pawtucket–Woonsocket–Attleboro, RI–MA	205	San Jose, CA	24	Vineland–Millville–Bridgeton, NJ	219
Pensacola, FL	94	Santa Barbara–Santa Maria–Lompoc, CA	116	Visalia–Tulare–Porterville, CA	147
Peoria, IL	306	Santa Cruz, CA	170	Waco, TX	71
Philadelphia, PA–NJ	140	Santa Rosa–Petaluma, CA	127	Washington, DC–MD–VA	87
Phoenix, AZ	56	Sarasota, FL	11	Waterbury, CT	135
Pine Bluff, AR	299				
Pittsburgh, PA	184	Savannah, GA	144	Waterloo–Cedar Falls, IA	287
Pittsfield, MA	155	Scranton–Wilkes-Barre, PA	233	Wausau, WI	295
Portland, ME	76	Seattle, WA	106	West Palm Beach–Boca Raton–Delray Beach, FL	8
Portland, OR	274	Sharon, PA	307	Wheeling, WV–OH	256
		Sheboygan, WI	253	Wichita, KS	92
Portsmouth–Dover–Rochester, NH–ME	3	Sherman–Denison, TX	75		
Poughkeepsie, NY	42	Shreveport, LA	50	Wichita Falls, TX	41
Providence, RI	205	Sioux City, IA–NE	263	Williamsport, PA	327
Provo–Orem, UT	323	Sioux Falls, SD	192	Wilmington, DE–NJ–MD	77
Pueblo, CO	264	South Bend–Mishawaka, IN	216	Wilmington, NC	164
				Worcester, MA	218
Racine, WI	286	Spokane, WA	259		
Raleigh–Durham, NC	58	Springfield, IL	165	Yakima, WA	223
Reading, PA	145	Springfield, MA	177	York, PA	226
Redding, CA	284	Springfield, MO	103	Youngstown–Warren, OH	313
Reno, NV	130	Stamford, CT	79	Yuba City, CA	261

Place Profiles: Economic Life in 329 Metro Areas

The following profiles highlight certain economic features in the metro areas. These include the factors used to rank the metro areas—indexes for the costs of housing, food, and miscellaneous goods and services (the last given under the entry Other); household income; local tax bite; income growth; and job growth —along with information about white- and blue-collar workers, cyclical threat of unemployment (see pages 408–409 for more about this), and goods produced.

The information comes from these sources: American Chamber of Commerce Researchers Association,

"Inter-City Cost of Living Index," first quarter, 1984; U.S. Department of Commerce, Bureau of the Census, *1980 Census of Population and Housing,* and Bureau of Economic Analysis, "County and Metropolitan Area Personal Income," *Survey of Current Business,* May 1984; Commerce Clearing House, *State Tax Guide,* 1984, and Internal Revenue Service, *Your Individual Income Tax,* 1984; U.S. Department of Labor, Bureau of Labor Statistics Employment and Earnings branch, unpublished data, 1984.

New England metro area figures for household

income and for recent five-year growth in personal income and jobs are derived from New England County Metropolitan Area figures.

Asterisks beside figures for cost indexes of food and miscellaneous goods indicate that these numbers were derived from prices in the nearest metro area or city, since information was not available for the metro area in question. Honolulu's figures for these indexes were based on cost-of-living premiums paid to government employees in Hawaii.

A star preceding a metro area's name highlights it as one of the top 25 places for economic outlook.

Metro Area	Living Costs (U.S. Avg.=100)	Average Household Income and Taxes	Occupations (U.S. Avg.=100)	Five-Year Growth Income and Jobs	Places Rated Score	Places Rated Rank
★ Abilene, TX	Housing: 74 Food: 104 Other: 97	Income: $32,262 Taxes: $235 Bite: 0.73%	Blue-Collar Index: 105 White-Collar Index: 95 Unemployment Threat: Moderate	Income: 52.45% Jobs: 28.24%	7,633	15
	Goods: Food products, musical instruments, women's sportswear, tire retreads, candy, ice cream, fishing tackle, cotton, cattle					
Akron, OH	Housing: 98 Food: 103 Other: 100	Income: $29,560 Taxes: $832 Bite: 2.81%	Blue-Collar Index: 106 White-Collar Index: 94 Unemployment Threat: Moderate	Income: 35.10% Jobs: −5.56%	4,350	292
	Goods: Rubber and rubber products, rubberized fabric, fishing tackle, surgical instruments, clay, storm windows, chemicals					
Albany, GA	Housing: 88 Food: 99 Other: 98	Income: $24,234 Taxes: $856 Bite: 3.53%	Blue-Collar Index: 109 White-Collar Index: 91 Unemployment Threat: Moderate	Income: 43.41% Jobs: 11.84%	5,250	188
	Goods: Textile products, paper, rubber and plastic products, thread, golf clubs, cartons, pecans, peanuts					
Albany–Schenectady–Troy, NY	Housing: 95 Food: 99 Other: 98	Income: $31,458 Taxes: $1,304 Bite: 4.15%	Blue-Collar Index: 92 White-Collar Index: 108 Unemployment Threat: Low	Income: 48.63% Jobs: 6.48%	5,864	110
	Goods: Pork products, sausage, paper, men's shirts, billiard balls, electrical equipment and appliances, motors and generators, axle grease, steam and gas turbines, blankets					
Albuquerque, NM	Housing: 101 Food: 99* Other: 100*	Income: $29,753 Taxes: $248 Bite: 0.83%	Blue-Collar Index: 90 White-Collar Index: 110 Unemployment Threat: Low	Income: 42.69% Jobs: 12.84%	5,727	126
	Goods: Neon and electric signs, hardware, machine tools, stone, clay					
Alexandria, LA	Housing: 70 Food: 107 Other: 101	Income: $23,078 Taxes: $220 Bite: 0.95%	Blue-Collar Index: 106 White-Collar Index: 94 Unemployment Threat: Moderate	Income: 48.32% Jobs: 5.39%	5,254	187
	Goods: Fabricated metal, sashes and doors, valves, corn, sugarcane, meat products, lumber and wood products (especially furniture and wood flooring)					
Allentown–Bethlehem, PA–NJ	Housing: 99 Food: 99* Other: 106*	Income: $31,856 Taxes: $954 Bite: 2.99%	Blue-Collar Index: 120 White-Collar Index: 80 Unemployment Threat: High	Income: 42.57% Jobs: −1.22%	5,097	212
	Goods: Steel and primary metals, electrical appliances, autos, trucks, buses, textiles, blasting powder, hats, marine pumps					
Alton–Granite City, IL	Housing: 78 Food: 95* Other: 101*	Income: $30,680 Taxes: $994 Bite: 3.24%	Blue-Collar Index: 113 White-Collar Index: 87 Unemployment Threat: Moderate	Income: 38.71% Jobs: 11.22%	5,795	120
	Goods: Coal mining, railway equipment, corn syrup, firebrick, tar and creosote					
Altoona, PA	Housing: 74 Food: 98 Other: 100	Income: $24,181 Taxes: $747 Bite: 3.09%	Blue-Collar Index: 121 White-Collar Index: 79 Unemployment Threat: High	Income: 39.04% Jobs: −7.10%	4,230	301
	Goods: Candy, potato chips, meat and meat products, dairy products, paper, locomotives, shuttlecocks, copper and aluminum tubes, bathing suits					
Amarillo, TX	Housing: 78 Food: 103 Other: 104	Income: $32,452 Taxes: $235 Bite: 0.72%	Blue-Collar Index: 106 White-Collar Index: 94 Unemployment Threat: Moderate	Income: 41.15% Jobs: 14.39%	6,241	73
	Goods: Flour, wheat, corn, sorghum, clothing, lumber, printing, carbon black, helium, zinc					
Anaheim–Santa Ana, CA	Housing: 192 Food: 95 Other: 105	Income: $38,996 Taxes: $1,387 Bite: 3.56%	Blue-Collar Index: 92 White-Collar Index: 108 Unemployment Threat: Low	Income: 48.32% Jobs: 21.97%	6,220	74
	Goods: Computer components, fire alarms, electric meters, hand tools, aircraft parts, mobile homes					

Metro Area	Living Costs (U.S. Avg.=100)	Average Household Income and Taxes	Occupations (U.S. Avg.=100)	Five-Year Growth Income and Jobs	Places Rated Score	Places Rated Rank
★ Anchorage, AK	Housing: 146 Food: 139 Other: 138	Income: $51,601 Taxes: None Bite: None	Blue-Collar Index: 84 White-Collar Index: 116 Unemployment Threat: Low	Income: 51.44% Jobs: 29.24%	7,668	14
	Goods: Printing and publishing, seafood, lumber and wood products, furs					
Anderson, IN	Housing: 68 Food: 96* Other: 99*	Income: $26,765 Taxes: $883 Bite: 3.30%	Blue-Collar Index: 126 White-Collar Index: 74 Unemployment Threat: High	Income: 27.67% Jobs: −20.47%	3,370	325
	Goods: Auto electrical equipment, glass and brick, clay, pumps, playground equipment					
Anderson, SC	Housing: 69 Food: 95* Other: 92*	Income: $23,038 Taxes: $727 Bite: 3.16%	Blue-Collar Index: 134 White-Collar Index: 66 Unemployment Threat: High	Income: 34.53% Jobs: −3.06%	4,262	298
	Goods: Lumber, textiles, vacuum cleaners, waxing machines, fiberglass					
Ann Arbor, MI	Housing: 132 Food: 100* Other: 102*	Income: $32,556 Taxes: $1,530 Bite: 4.70%	Blue-Collar Index: 89 White-Collar Index: 111 Unemployment Threat: Low	Income: 32.96% Jobs: 4.19%	4,579	270
	Goods: Transportation equipment, bearings and springs, precision instruments, drill heads, awnings, cameras					
Anniston, AL	Housing: 66 Food: 94* Other: 90*	Income: $22,254 Taxes: $714 Bite: 3.21%	Blue-Collar Index: 120 White-Collar Index: 80 Unemployment Threat: High	Income: 38.73% Jobs: 2.69%	4,730	257
	Goods: Textiles, shirts, cloth, cast-iron pipe and other metals, fire hydrants, refrigerators					
Appleton–Oshkosh–Neenah, WI	Housing: 94 Food: 94 Other: 102	Income: $30,444 Taxes: $1,362 Bite: 4.47%	Blue-Collar Index: 115 White-Collar Index: 85 Unemployment Threat: Moderate	Income: 39.02% Jobs: 6.53%	5,275	180
	Goods: Paper, paper products, farm machinery, wire, canned food, garbage trucks, autos, overalls, plastic buoys					
Asheville, NC	Housing: 81 Food: 93* Other: 93*	Income: $25,990 Taxes: $964 Bite: 3.71%	Blue-Collar Index: 115 White-Collar Index: 85 Unemployment Threat: Moderate	Income: 41.43% Jobs: 5.62%	5,196	194
	Goods: Electrical equipment, textiles (especially nylon, rayon, and cotton), baby food, dresses, cigarette paper, burley tobacco					
Athens, GA	Housing: 80 Food: 96 Other: 99	Income: $23,251 Taxes: $808 Bite: 3.48%	Blue-Collar Index: 106 White-Collar Index: 94 Unemployment Threat: Moderate	Income: 39.00% Jobs: 15.54%	5,193	195
	Goods: Hosiery, tapestries, fertilizer, overalls, clocks, electric motors					
Atlanta, GA	Housing: 100 Food: 104 Other: 100	Income: $32,452 Taxes: $1,239 Bite: 3.82%	Blue-Collar Index: 75 White-Collar Index: 125 Unemployment Threat: Low	Income: 44.10% Jobs: 20.40%	6,315	64
	Goods: Automobiles, airplanes, candy, cottonseed oil, flour, printing and publishing, furniture					
★ Atlantic City, NJ	Housing: 133 Food: 108* Other: 105*	Income: $33,424 Taxes: $898 Bite: 2.69%	Blue-Collar Index: 100 White-Collar Index: 100 Unemployment Threat: Moderate	Income: 59.84% Jobs: 46.69%	8,107	6
	Goods: Clothing, bottles and glassware, rubber and plastics, saltwater taffy, reed furniture, baby carriages, distilling					
Augusta, GA–SC	Housing: 75 Food: 98 Other: 97	Income: $25,813 Taxes: $917 Bite: 3.55%	Blue-Collar Index: 110 White-Collar Index: 90 Unemployment Threat: Moderate	Income: 44.93% Jobs: 7.12%	5,431	162
	Goods: Cotton textiles and cloth, rayon, fertilizer, brick and tile					
Aurora–Elgin, IL	Housing: 125 Food: 100* Other: 106*	Income: $35,552 Taxes: $1,121 Bite: 3.15%	Blue-Collar Index: 112 White-Collar Index: 88 Unemployment Threat: Moderate	Income: 40.89% Jobs: 0.11%	5,097	212
	Goods: Railroad coaches, sand and gravel, furniture, skirts and shirts, street sweepers, watches					
★ Austin, TX	Housing: 106 Food: 105* Other: 95*	Income: $31,497 Taxes: $225 Bite: 0.71%	Blue-Collar Index: 88 White-Collar Index: 112 Unemployment Threat: Low	Income: 51.60% Jobs: 35.85%	7,439	19
	Goods: Electrical instruments, semiconductors, furniture, turkeys, dairy products, fiberglass boats					
Bakersfield, CA	Housing: 97 Food: 98 Other: 109	Income: $28,958 Taxes: $800 Bite: 2.76%	Blue-Collar Index: 106 White-Collar Index: 94 Unemployment Threat: Moderate	Income: 43.26% Jobs: 22.64%	6,056	90
	Goods: Oil-well tools, paint, pumps, fruit, potatoes, wheat, rubber and plastic goods, guitars					

Metro Area	Living Costs (U.S. Avg.=100)	Average Household Income and Taxes	Occupations (U.S. Avg.=100)	Five-Year Growth Income and Jobs	Places Rated Score	Places Rated Rank
Baltimore, MD	Housing: 110 Food: 99* Other: 106*	Income: $32,368 Taxes: $1,267 Bite: 3.91%	Blue-Collar Index: 98 White-Collar Index: 102 Unemployment Threat: Low	Income: 44.52% Jobs: 6.86%	5,503	151
	Goods: Electrical appliances, iron and steel, copper, wire and cable, ships, spices and flavorings					
Bangor, ME	Housing: 87 Food: 94* Other: 97*	Income: $24,256 Taxes: $646 Bite: 2.66%	Blue-Collar Index: 96 White-Collar Index: 104 Unemployment Threat: Low	Income: 42.37% Jobs: 9.76%	5,172	200
	Goods: Writing paper, lumber, canoes, potato chips, shoes					
Baton Rouge, LA	Housing: 97 Food: 98 Other: 95	Income: $30,867 Taxes: $319 Bite: 1.03%	Blue-Collar Index: 103 White-Collar Index: 97 Unemployment Threat: Moderate	Income: 47.48% Jobs: 15.05%	6,308	66
	Goods: Petrochemicals, acids, alcohol, coke, soda ash, synthetic rubber					
Battle Creek, MI	Housing: 76 Food: 95* Other: 106*	Income: $29,868 Taxes: $1,387 Bite: 4.64%	Blue-Collar Index: 116 White-Collar Index: 84 Unemployment Threat: High	Income: 32.53% Jobs: −14.97%	4,008	308
	Goods: Breakfast cereals, pumps, auto valves, steel and wire					
Beaumont– Port Arthur, TX	Housing: 75 Food: 104 Other: 107	Income: $33,398 Taxes: $235 Bite: 0.70%	Blue-Collar Index: 120 White-Collar Index: 80 Unemployment Threat: High	Income: 45.41% Jobs: 3.64%	6,019	98
	Goods: Petrochemicals, ships, oil-well equipment, wood products, rice, agricultural equipment					
Beaver County, PA	Housing: 94 Food: 107 Other: 106	Income: $27,695 Taxes: $837 Bite: 3.02%	Blue-Collar Index: 126 White-Collar Index: 74 Unemployment Threat: High	Income: 31.93% Jobs: −22.73%	3,119	328
	Goods: Steel tubing, ceramics, paint, cork, coal					
Bellingham, WA	Housing: 100 Food: 109* Other: 106*	Income: $27,140 Taxes: $443 Bite: 1.63%	Blue-Collar Index: 106 White-Collar Index: 94 Unemployment Threat: Moderate	Income: 31.34% Jobs: 2.25%	4,247	299
	Goods: Salmon packing, shingles, paper, cement, frozen food					
Benton Harbor, MI	Housing: 81 Food: 99 Other: 104	Income: $27,401 Taxes: $1,268 Bite: 4.63%	Blue-Collar Index: 114 White-Collar Index: 86 Unemployment Threat: Moderate	Income: 32.36% Jobs: −15.87%	3,635	322
	Goods: Washing machines, fruit packing, recreational vehicles, steel castings, vacuum pumps					
Bergen– Passaic, NJ	Housing: 175 Food: 108* Other: 105*	Income: $43,240 Taxes: $1,201 Bite: 2.78%	Blue-Collar Index: 94 White-Collar Index: 106 Unemployment Threat: Low	Income: 49.18% Jobs: 8.86%	6,016	100
	Goods: Scales, bowling balls, precision instruments, light fixtures, auto seat covers, freight cars, underwear					
Billings, MT	Housing: 100 Food: 110 Other: 104	Income: $31,592 Taxes: $759 Bite: 2.40%	Blue-Collar Index: 97 White-Collar Index: 103 Unemployment Threat: Low	Income: 41.44% Jobs: 17.51%	5,913	105
	Goods: Sugar, flour, beets, wheat, beans, beef, refined oil, printing, metal ornaments					
Biloxi– Gulfport, MS	Housing: 77 Food: 107* Other: 95*	Income: $23,274 Taxes: $558 Bite: 2.40%	Blue-Collar Index: 107 White-Collar Index: 93 Unemployment Threat: Moderate	Income: 46.70% Jobs: 18.84%	5,801	118
	Goods: Cat food, seafood canning, wood building products, clothing, tents and awnings, ships and boats					
Binghamton, NY	Housing: 99 Food: 96 Other: 104	Income: $30,318 Taxes: $1,234 Bite: 4.07%	Blue-Collar Index: 101 White-Collar Index: 99 Unemployment Threat: Moderate	Income: 48.23% Jobs: 5.89%	5,614	141
	Goods: Electrical equipment, instruments, shoes, photographic goods, stereo equipment, fast-freezer units, flexible shafting					
Birmingham, AL	Housing: 82 Food: 95 Other: 108	Income: $27,835 Taxes: $876 Bite: 3.15%	Blue-Collar Index: 105 White-Collar Index: 95 Unemployment Threat: Moderate	Income: 37.40% Jobs: 2.70%	4,843	245
	Goods: Primary metals (especially iron and steel), pipes and plates, stoves, caskets, truck trailers, airplanes					
Bismarck, ND	Housing: 100 Food: 100* Other: 96*	Income: $32,077 Taxes: $468 Bite: 1.46%	Blue-Collar Index: 88 White-Collar Index: 112 Unemployment Threat: Low	Income: 42.47% Jobs: 14.05%	6,019	98
	Goods: Farm machinery, woodworking, printing, food processing					

Metro Area	Living Costs (U.S. Avg.=100)	Average Household Income and Taxes	Occupations (U.S. Avg.=100)	Five-Year Growth Income and Jobs	Places Rated Score	Places Rated Rank
Bloomington, IN	Housing: 85 Food: 95 Other: 102	Income: $21,851 Taxes: $796 Bite: 3.64%	Blue-Collar Index: 91 White-Collar Index: 109 Unemployment Threat: Low	Income: 39.43% Jobs: 12.35%	4,829	248
	Goods: Radios, televisions, railroad ties, elevators, printing and publishing, limestone					
Bloomington–Normal, IL	Housing: 104 Food: 105* Other: 98*	Income: $30,713 Taxes: $995 Bite: 3.24%	Blue-Collar Index: 91 White-Collar Index: 109 Unemployment Threat: Low	Income: 42.29% Jobs: 16.69%	5,863	111
	Goods: Vacuum cleaners, farm machinery, feeds, dairy products					
Boise City, ID	Housing: 99 Food: 104* Other: 99*	Income: $30,736 Taxes: $1,406 Bite: 4.57%	Blue-Collar Index: 88 White-Collar Index: 112 Unemployment Threat: Low	Income: 31.56% Jobs: 2.44%	4,633	265
	Goods: Machinery, lumber and wood products, food (especially potatoes and grain)					
Boston, MA	Housing: 139 Food: 94* Other: 97*	Income: $36,644 Taxes: $1,695 Bite: 4.63%	Blue-Collar Index: 89 White-Collar Index: 111 Unemployment Threat: Low	Income: 53.86% Jobs: 12.08%	6,363	60
	Goods: Computers, missiles and missile-guidance systems, ships, shoes and boots, medical and navigational instruments, textile products; nation's foremost fishing port and wool market					
Boulder–Longmont, CO	Housing: 143 Food: 105 Other: 102	Income: $35,599 Taxes: $870 Bite: 2.44%	Blue-Collar Index: 90 White-Collar Index: 110 Unemployment Threat: Low	Income: 58.27% Jobs: 26.38%	7,127	30
	Goods: Copy machines, space hardware, electronic equipment, backpacks					
★ Bradenton, FL	Housing: 99 Food: 97* Other: 101*	Income: $30,831 Taxes: $324 Bite: 1.05%	Blue-Collar Index: 103 White-Collar Index: 97 Unemployment Threat: Moderate	Income: 52.72% Jobs: 34.38%	7,437	20
	Goods: Fresh vegetables, flowers, soft drinks, bottles, transportation equipment					
Brazoria, TX	Housing: 101 Food: 103* Other: 107*	Income: $31,055 Taxes: $225 Bite: 0.72%	Blue-Collar Index: 120 White-Collar Index: 80 Unemployment Threat: High	Income: 42.94% Jobs: 18.18%	6,020	97
	Goods: Chemical oil and gas production, cotton, rice and soybeans					
Bremerton, WA	Housing: 109 Food: 103* Other: 112*	Income: $32,631 Taxes: $506 Bite: 1.55%	Blue-Collar Index: 107 White-Collar Index: 93 Unemployment Threat: Moderate	Income: 38.87% Jobs: 15.60%	5,671	132
	Goods: Shipbuilding, meat packing, lumber, dairy products					
Bridgeport–Milford, CT	Housing: 161 Food: 110* Other: 103*	Income: $47,258 Taxes: $546 Bite: 1.16%	Blue-Collar Index: 104 White-Collar Index: 96 Unemployment Threat: Moderate	Income: 53.37% Jobs: 17.60%	7,197	26
	Goods: Airplane engines, firearms, ammunition, knives, adding machines, girdles, helicopters					
Bristol, CT	Housing: 120 Food: 110* Other: 103*	Income: $37,565 Taxes: $477 Bite: 1.27%	Blue-Collar Index: 120 White-Collar Index: 80 Unemployment Threat: High	Income: 52.28% Jobs: 12.04%	6,527	51
	Goods: Screw machine products, glass cutters, knives, sporting equipment, ball bearings, watches					
Brockton, MA	Housing: 99 Food: 94* Other: 97*	Income: $36,644 Taxes: $1,695 Bite: 4.63%	Blue-Collar Index: 106 White-Collar Index: 94 Unemployment Threat: Moderate	Income: 53.86% Jobs: 12.08%	6,900	37
	Goods: Shoe welts, soles and heels, garments, boxes, machine tools					
Brownsville–Harlingen, TX	Housing: 64 Food: 99 Other: 98	Income: $17,903 Taxes: $146 Bite: 0.82%	Blue-Collar Index: 111 White-Collar Index: 89 Unemployment Threat: Moderate	Income: 41.05% Jobs: 16.03%	4,968	225
	Goods: Palm-leaf hats, clothing, cotton bandages					
★ Bryan–College Station, TX	Housing: 99 Food: 103* Other: 100*	Income: $24,156 Taxes: $192 Bite: 0.79%	Blue-Collar Index: 92 White-Collar Index: 108 Unemployment Threat: Low	Income: 60.35% Jobs: 52.53%	8,040	7
	Goods: Cotton gins, aluminum windows, concrete blocks, printing and publishing, corn, cotton, cattle, poultry					
Buffalo, NY	Housing: 97 Food: 104 Other: 97	Income: $31,248 Taxes: $1,291 Bite: 4.13%	Blue-Collar Index: 104 White-Collar Index: 96 Unemployment Threat: Moderate	Income: 42.38% Jobs: −2.57%	5,047	217
	Goods: Steel, steel rolling and finishing, cast metals, aircraft parts, electrical goods					
Burlington, NC	Housing: 74 Food: 96 Other: 92	Income: $26,662 Taxes: $1,007 Bite: 3.78%	Blue-Collar Index: 127 White-Collar Index: 73 Unemployment Threat: High	Income: 42.97% Jobs: 10.26%	5,680	129
	Goods: Textiles, apparel, electrical goods, tobacco products, lumber					

Metro Area	Living Costs (U.S. Avg.=100)	Average Household Income and Taxes	Occupations (U.S. Avg.=100)	Five-Year Growth Income and Jobs	Places Rated Score	Places Rated Rank
Burlington, VT	Housing: 116 Food: 99* Other: 98*	Income: $29,582 Taxes: $935 Bite: 3.16%	Blue-Collar Index: 89 White-Collar Index: 111 Unemployment Threat: Low	Income: 51.67% Jobs: 28.79%	6,726	43
	Goods: Machine guns, maple furniture, kitchen equipment, printing and publishing, computer parts					
Canton, OH	Housing: 88 Food: 89 Other: 91	Income: $29,089 Taxes: $818 Bite: 2.81%	Blue-Collar Index: 118 White-Collar Index: 82 Unemployment Threat: High	Income: 37.53% Jobs: −4.14%	4,847	245
	Goods: Ball and roller bearings, safes, locks, office equipment, gasoline and diesel engines, electric sweepers					
Casper, WY	Housing: 118 Food: 110 Other: 106	Income: $43,389 Taxes: $302 Bite: 0.70%	Blue-Collar Index: 106 White-Collar Index: 94 Unemployment Threat: Moderate	Income: 37.38% Jobs: 11.74%	6,303	70
	Goods: Mining, food processing, bottling, ships, oil					
Cedar Rapids, IA	Housing: 93 Food: 94 Other: 97	Income: $33,166 Taxes: $1,131 Bite: 3.41%	Blue-Collar Index: 105 White-Collar Index: 95 Unemployment Threat: Moderate	Income: 35.25% Jobs: −2.52%	5,009	221
	Goods: Cereal grains, syrups, dairy products, radio and electronic equipment, road machinery, cranes, gravel crushers					
Champaign–Urbana–Rantoul, IL	Housing: 103 Food: 96 Other: 102	Income: $26,695 Taxes: $875 Bite: 3.28%	Blue-Collar Index: 86 White-Collar Index: 114 Unemployment Threat: Low	Income: 39.26% Jobs: 19.33%	5,485	154
	Goods: Paper cups, bleacher seats, railroad registers, soybean oil					
Charleston, SC	Housing: 89 Food: 95* Other: 102*	Income: $24,038 Taxes: $779 Bite: 3.24%	Blue-Collar Index: 107 White-Collar Index: 93 Unemployment Threat: Moderate	Income: 43.23% Jobs: 10.87%	5,153	207
	Goods: Pulp and paper, baking powder, machinery, textiles and apparel, creosoted timber, canned oysters					
Charleston, WV	Housing: 93 Food: 108 Other: 101	Income: $30,775 Taxes: $994 Bite: 3.23%	Blue-Collar Index: 102 White-Collar Index: 98 Unemployment Threat: Moderate	Income: 36.74% Jobs: 8.24%	5,257	185
	Goods: Flat glass, mining equipment, chemicals, coal, oil, bricks, armored cars					
Charlotte–Gastonia–Rock Hill, NC–SC	Housing: 86 Food: 93 Other: 93	Income: $28,904 Taxes: $1,121 Bite: 3.88%	Blue-Collar Index: 115 White-Collar Index: 85 Unemployment Threat: Moderate	Income: 41.29% Jobs: 10.39%	5,671	132
	Goods: Hosiery, yarn, cotton textiles, farm implements, flour, detergents, rope, iron pipe, meat products, chlorine					
Charlottesville, VA	Housing: 114 Food: 103* Other: 102*	Income: $28,468 Taxes: $1,019 Bite: 3.58%	Blue-Collar Index: 91 White-Collar Index: 109 Unemployment Threat: Low	Income: 50.31% Jobs: 19.50%	6,055	91
	Goods: Telephone and telegraph apparatus, semiconductors, ice cream, soft drinks					
Chattanooga, TN–GA	Housing: 74 Food: 98 Other: 97	Income: $25,782 Taxes: $314 Bite: 1.22%	Blue-Collar Index: 114 White-Collar Index: 86 Unemployment Threat: Moderate	Income: 32.68% Jobs: −0.82%	4,487	280
	Goods: Carpets, food and beverages, auto seat covers, textiles, fabricated metal products					
Chicago, IL	Housing: 131 Food: 100 Other: 106	Income: $36,593 Taxes: $1,171 Bite: 3.20%	Blue-Collar Index: 98 White-Collar Index: 102 Unemployment Threat: Low	Income: 37.01% Jobs: 5.48%	5,205	191
	Goods: Meat products, radios, televisions, musical instruments, candy, furniture, diesel engines, auto accessories					
Chico, CA	Housing: 103 Food: 99* Other: 100*	Income: $26,863 Taxes: $699 Bite: 2.60%	Blue-Collar Index: 97 White-Collar Index: 103 Unemployment Threat: Low	Income: 37.25% Jobs: 17.09%	5,307	176
	Goods: Pruning saws, almonds, conveyers, fruit drying					
Cincinnati, OH–KY–IN	Housing: 98 Food: 102* Other: 96*	Income: $31,427 Taxes: $902 Bite: 2.87%	Blue-Collar Index: 104 White-Collar Index: 96 Unemployment Threat: Moderate	Income: 38.72% Jobs: 4.37%	5,270	182
	Goods: Machine tools, robots, chemicals, soap, refrigerators, bread, beverages, transportation equipment					
Clarksville–Hopkinsville, TN–KY	Housing: 72 Food: 98* Other: 102*	Income: $22,884 Taxes: $299 Bite: 1.31%	Blue-Collar Index: 112 White-Collar Index: 88 Unemployment Threat: Moderate	Income: 38.71% Jobs: 8.14%	4,880	240
	Goods: Shoes, cowboy boots, cigars, meat, snuff, hogsheads, appliance parts					

Metro Area	Living Costs (U.S. Avg.=100)	Average Household Income and Taxes	Occupations (U.S. Avg.=100)	Five-Year Growth Income and Jobs	Places Rated Score	Places Rated Rank
Cleveland, OH	Housing: 110 Food: 99 Other: 105	Income: $35,720 Taxes: $1,067 Bite: 2.99%	Blue-Collar Index: 104 White-Collar Index: 96 Unemployment Threat: Moderate	Income: 37.41% Jobs: −5.21%	4,879	241
	Goods: Machine tools, nuts and bolts, iron and steel, auto parts, paints and lacquers, chemicals					
★ Colorado Springs, CO	Housing: 102 Food: 102 Other: 97	Income: $29,380 Taxes: $660 Bite: 2.25%	Blue-Collar Index: 95 White-Collar Index: 105 Unemployment Threat: Low	Income: 58.05% Jobs: 38.49%	7,699	13
	Goods: Electronic components, shell fuses, animal vaccines, brooms, engine mounts, motors, instruments					
Columbia, MO	Housing: 92 Food: 91 Other: 94	Income: $25,813 Taxes: $631 Bite: 2.44%	Blue-Collar Index: 81 White-Collar Index: 119 Unemployment Threat: Low	Income: 38.94% Jobs: 9.83%	5,147	208
	Goods: Electronic products, pool tables, plastic pipe, printing and publishing, corn, wheat, oats					
Columbia, SC	Housing: 90 Food: 95* Other: 102*	Income: $26,838 Taxes: $909 Bite: 3.39%	Blue-Collar Index: 93 White-Collar Index: 107 Unemployment Threat: Low	Income: 41.75% Jobs: 9.82%	5,279	179
	Goods: Cameras, microcomputers, cotton textiles, fertilizer, chemicals					
Columbus, GA–AL	Housing: 70 Food: 103 Other: 99	Income: $23,962 Taxes: $846 Bite: 3.53%	Blue-Collar Index: 109 White-Collar Index: 91 Unemployment Threat: Moderate	Income: 38.48% Jobs: 5.23%	4,812	250
	Goods: Bricks, hand tools, textiles, cast iron, farm implements					
Columbus, OH	Housing: 97 Food: 100 Other: 99	Income: $29,761 Taxes: $838 Bite: 2.82%	Blue-Collar Index: 96 White-Collar Index: 104 Unemployment Threat: Low	Income: 38.94% Jobs: 5.35%	5,165	202
	Goods: Refrigerators, ranges, auto parts, roller bearings, meat products, stone, airplanes					
Corpus Christi, TX	Housing: 83 Food: 104 Other: 104	Income: $29,229 Taxes: $214 Bite: 0.73%	Blue-Collar Index: 109 White-Collar Index: 91 Unemployment Threat: Moderate	Income: 50.44% Jobs: 22.29%	6,690	44
	Goods: Oil, chemicals, grain, cotton, soda ash, zinc, chlorine, shrimp					
Cumberland, MD–WV	Housing: 73 Food: 98* Other: 102*	Income: $23,369 Taxes: $869 Bite: 3.72%	Blue-Collar Index: 118 White-Collar Index: 82 Unemployment Threat: High	Income: 39.61% Jobs: 4.65%	4,741	255
	Goods: Railroad equipment, beer, macaroni, underwear, glassware					
★ Dallas, TX	Housing: 112 Food: 105* Other: 105*	Income: $38,769 Taxes: $265 Bite: 0.68%	Blue-Collar Index: 93 White-Collar Index: 107 Unemployment Threat: Low	Income: 53.40% Jobs: 29.51%	7,710	12
	Goods: Aluminum doors and windows, oil, gas, wall coverings, food products, frozen foods, potato and corn chips, tools and dies, jigs, farm and construction machinery and equipment, wooden truck trailers, lumber, printing, handbags, concrete					
Danbury, CT	Housing: 173 Food: 110* Other: 103*	Income: $47,258 Taxes: $546 Bite: 1.16%	Blue-Collar Index: 98 White-Collar Index: 102 Unemployment Threat: Low	Income: 53.37% Jobs: 17.60%	7,060	34
	Goods: Surgical instruments, hat-making machinery, aluminum foil, railroad-testing equipment, aircraft parts, electrical products					
Danville, VA	Housing: 68 Food: 100* Other: 98*	Income: $22,758 Taxes: $775 Bite: 3.41%	Blue-Collar Index: 135 White-Collar Index: 65 Unemployment Threat: High	Income: 37.65% Jobs: 1.05%	4,491	278
	Goods: Truck tires, broad silk, tobacco, mattresses, fertilizer					
Davenport–Rock Island–Moline, IA–IL	Housing: 97 Food: 92* Other: 97*	Income: $32,402 Taxes: $1,167 Bite: 3.60%	Blue-Collar Index: 110 White-Collar Index: 90 Unemployment Threat: Moderate	Income: 36.90% Jobs: −2.04%	4,997	222
	Goods: Farm tractors, cookies, cast metal, macaroni, candy					
Dayton–Springfield, OH	Housing: 92 Food: 105 Other: 97	Income: $30,232 Taxes: $865 Bite: 2.86%	Blue-Collar Index: 103 White-Collar Index: 97 Unemployment Threat: Moderate	Income: 34.69% Jobs: −4.60%	4,532	276
	Goods: Cash registers, computers, aircraft parts, bicycles, rubber and plastics, industrial belts, paper and paper-making machinery					
Daytona Beach, FL	Housing: 86 Food: 102 Other: 108	Income: $27,255 Taxes: $295 Bite: 1.08%	Blue-Collar Index: 97 White-Collar Index: 103 Unemployment Threat: Low	Income: 49.39% Jobs: 27.43%	6,592	49
	Goods: Electronic components, transportation equipment, fabricated metals, truck farming					

Metro Area	Living Costs (U.S. Avg.=100)	Average Household Income and Taxes	Occupations (U.S. Avg.=100)	Five-Year Growth Income and Jobs	Places Rated Score	Places Rated Rank
Decatur, IL	Housing: 89 Food: 96* Other: 102*	Income: $30,663 Taxes: $993 Bite: 3.24%	Blue-Collar Index: 110 White-Collar Index: 90 Unemployment Threat: Moderate	Income: 33.71% Jobs: −10.68%	4,274	297
	Goods: Earth movers, carburetors, pumps, valves, tanks, corn, soybeans					
Denver, CO	Housing: 129 Food: 104 Other: 103	Income: $39,099 Taxes: $1,002 Bite: 2.56%	Blue-Collar Index: 91 White-Collar Index: 109 Unemployment Threat: Low	Income: 53.38% Jobs: 23.07%	7,164	28
	Goods: Beer, mining and farm machinery, coffee roasters, meat products, stone and clay products, printing and publishing					
Des Moines, IA	Housing: 96 Food: 93* Other: 100*	Income: $34,622 Taxes: $1,205 Bite: 3.48%	Blue-Collar Index: 91 White-Collar Index: 109 Unemployment Threat: Low	Income: 38.08% Jobs: −0.06%	5,346	167
	Goods: Refrigerators, tires, crackers, biscuits, meat products, farming implements, printing and publishing					
Detroit, MI	Housing: 102 Food: 100* Other: 102*	Income: $33,858 Taxes: $1,589 Bite: 4.69%	Blue-Collar Index: 105 White-Collar Index: 95 Unemployment Threat: Moderate	Income: 27.24% Jobs: −12.44%	3,904	312
	Goods: Autos and auto products, ranges and heating devices, paper, twine, bolts and screws, ball bearings, boilers, ships					
Dothan, AL	Housing: 68 Food: 97 Other: 92	Income: $24,024 Taxes: $769 Bite: 3.20%	Blue-Collar Index: 114 White-Collar Index: 86 Unemployment Threat: Moderate	Income: 45.18% Jobs: 7.85%	5,453	159
	Goods: Fertilizer, hosiery, vaults, mirrors, toys, steel tubing, pajamas, cooking oil					
Dubuque, IA	Housing: 96 Food: 91 Other: 101	Income: $28,904 Taxes: $935 Bite: 3.23%	Blue-Collar Index: 113 White-Collar Index: 87 Unemployment Threat: Moderate	Income: 27.95% Jobs: −6.63%	3,949	310
	Goods: Furniture, cabinets, caskets, tractors, meat products					
Duluth, MN–WI	Housing: 72 Food: 100 Other: 95	Income: $26,712 Taxes: $1,124 Bite: 4.21%	Blue-Collar Index: 110 White-Collar Index: 90 Unemployment Threat: Moderate	Income: 30.10% Jobs: −10.49%	3,922	311
	Goods: Fish, frozen and canned food, mining and construction equipment, lumber, peat, farm tractors					
East St. Louis–Belleville, IL	Housing: 78 Food: 95* Other: 100*	Income: $28,176 Taxes: $923 Bite: 3.28%	Blue-Collar Index: 109 White-Collar Index: 91 Unemployment Threat: Moderate	Income: 39.82% Jobs: 21.88%	6,113	83
	Goods: Plumbers' supplies, rubber reclaiming, roofing materials, paint, stoves, drinking fountains					
Eau Claire, WI	Housing: 85 Food: 96* Other: 102*	Income: $25,388 Taxes: $1,029 Bite: 4.05%	Blue-Collar Index: 103 White-Collar Index: 97 Unemployment Threat: Moderate	Income: 43.10% Jobs: 12.05%	5,348	166
	Goods: Tires, inner tubes, golf carts, beer, dairy products, pressure cookers, sawmill and railroad equipment					
El Paso, TX	Housing: 88 Food: 96 Other: 101	Income: $21,930 Taxes: $170 Bite: 0.78%	Blue-Collar Index: 105 White-Collar Index: 95 Unemployment Threat: Moderate	Income: 43.26% Jobs: 12.52%	5,080	215
	Goods: Clothing, cattle, pecans, rice, maize, feeds, copper, sulfur, bricks and cement					
Elkhart–Goshen, IN	Housing: 79 Food: 97* Other: 92*	Income: $29,417 Taxes: $959 Bite: 3.26%	Blue-Collar Index: 120 White-Collar Index: 80 Unemployment Threat: High	Income: 26.03% Jobs: −6.43%	4,214	303
	Goods: Band instruments, mobile homes, burlap bags, lightning rods, pharmaceuticals					
Elmira, NY	Housing: 85 Food: 100* Other: 94*	Income: $27,683 Taxes: $1,055 Bite: 3.81%	Blue-Collar Index: 105 White-Collar Index: 95 Unemployment Threat: Moderate	Income: 43.96% Jobs: −5.58%	4,813	249
	Goods: Gliders, prefabricated homes, trucks, fire-fighting equipment, hydrants					
★ Enid, OK	Housing: 82 Food: 100* Other: 94*	Income: $36,198 Taxes: $920 Bite: 2.54%	Blue-Collar Index: 112 White-Collar Index: 88 Unemployment Threat: Moderate	Income: 65.91% Jobs: 21.06%	8,268	4
	Goods: Oil refining, well-drilling and farm machinery, dairy products					
Erie, PA	Housing: 93 Food: 101 Other: 104	Income: $28,129 Taxes: $860 Bite: 3.06%	Blue-Collar Index: 114 White-Collar Index: 86 Unemployment Threat: Moderate	Income: 37.37% Jobs: −6.47%	4,299	296
	Goods: Gas engines, electric locomotives, wringers, turbines, pipes, tools, vises					

Metro Area	Living Costs (U.S. Avg.=100)	Average Household Income and Taxes	Occupations (U.S. Avg.=100)	Five-Year Growth Income and Jobs	Places Rated Score	Places Rated Rank
Eugene– Springfield, OR	Housing: 112 Food: 110* Other: 103*	Income: $25,698 Taxes: $1,102 Bite: 4.29%	Blue-Collar Index: 102 White-Collar Index: 98 Unemployment Threat: Moderate	Income: 24.33% Jobs: −8.98%	3,045	329
	Goods: Plywood, canned fruits and vegetables, meat products, grass seed, sheep, poultry					
Evansville, IN–KY	Housing: 81 Food: 104 Other: 94	Income: $30,181 Taxes: $991 Bite: 3.28%	Blue-Collar Index: 118 White-Collar Index: 82 Unemployment Threat: High	Income: 37.24% Jobs: 2.73%	5,206	190
	Goods: Appliances, aluminum, vegetables, baby food, chemicals, plastics					
Fall River, MA–RI	Housing: 108 Food: 94* Other: 97*	Income: $27,591 Taxes: $1,198 Bites: 4.34%	Blue-Collar Index: 125 White-Collar Index: 75 Unemployment Threat: High	Income: 43.46% Jobs: 1.96%	4,884	239
	Goods: Dresses, suits, sportswear, thread, yarn, light fixtures, rubber goods					
Fargo– Moorhead, ND–MN	Housing: 98 Food: 100* Other: 96*	Income: $30,094 Taxes: $424 Bite: 1.41%	Blue-Collar Index: 91 White-Collar Index: 109 Unemployment Threat: Low	Income: 35.95% Jobs: 15.38%	5,594	142
	Goods: Luggage, fur coats, neon signs, meat and dairy products, jewelry					
Fayetteville, NC	Housing: 75 Food: 96* Other: 95*	Income: $22,291 Taxes: $800 Bite: 3.59%	Blue-Collar Index: 105 White-Collar Index: 95 Unemployment Threat: Moderate	Income: 42.75% Jobs: 12.94%	5,255	186
	Goods: Tobacco loopers, feeds, tires, lace, dolls, asphalt, plywood					
Fayetteville– Springdale, AR	Housing: 80 Food: 101 Other: 98	Income: $23,251 Taxes: $562 Bite: 2.42%	Blue-Collar Index: 108 White-Collar Index: 92 Unemployment Threat: Moderate	Income: 37.89% Jobs: 4.88%	4,631	266
	Goods: Electric organs, wagons, poultry packing, pipe fittings, sporting goods					
Fitchburg– Leominster, MA	Housing: 99 Food: 94* Other: 97*	Income: $29,375 Taxes: $1,292 Bite: 4.40%	Blue-Collar Index: 115 White-Collar Index: 85 Unemployment Threat: Moderate	Income: 44.94% Jobs: −0.87%	5,098	211
	Goods: Turbines, paper, saws and knives, handbags and luggage, shoes, hardware					
Flint, MI	Housing: 86 Food: 100 Other: 102	Income: $32,000 Taxes: $1,454 Bite: 4.68%	Blue-Collar Index: 124 White-Collar Index: 76 Unemployment Threat: High	Income: 25.49% Jobs: −15.30%	3,724	318
	Goods: Pickup trucks, autos, recreational vehicles, plumbing fixtures, structural steel, tents					
Florence, AL	Housing: 71 Food: 93* Other: 93*	Income: $24,595 Taxes: $783 Bite: 3.18%	Blue-Collar Index: 122 White-Collar Index: 78 Unemployment Threat: High	Income: 34.23% Jobs: −1.09%	4,492	277
	Goods: Primary metals (especially aluminum), chlorides, fertilizer, textiles					
Florence, SC	Housing: 78 Food: 95* Other: 92*	Income: $22,498 Taxes: $706 Bite: 3.14%	Blue-Collar Index: 113 White-Collar Index: 87 Unemployment Threat: Moderate	Income: 41.34% Jobs: 5.40%	4,842	247
	Goods: Welding equipment, mobile radios, fertilizer, clothing, furniture					
Fort Collins– Loveland, CO	Housing: 119 Food: 103 Other: 102	Income: $29,487 Taxes: $365 Bite: 2.25%	Blue-Collar Index: 97 White-Collar Index: 103 Unemployment Threat: Low	Income: 54.75% Jobs: 24.44%	6,631	48
	Goods: Dental appliances, instruments, pine timber, lamb, sugar, beets					
Fort Lauderdale– Hollywood– Pompano Beach, FL	Housing: 130 Food: 99 Other: 98	Income: $36,655 Taxes: $365 Bite: 1.00%	Blue-Collar Index: 94 White-Collar Index: 106 Unemployment Threat: Low	Income: 51.03% Jobs: 26.30%	7,136	29
	Goods: Electronic components, fiberglass, aircraft fittings, boats, oranges					
Fort Myers, FL	Housing: 111 Food: 97* Other: 101*	Income: $30,786 Taxes: $324 Bite: 1.05%	Blue-Collar Index: 100 White-Collar Index: 100 Unemployment Threat: Moderate	Income: 48.18% Jobs: 36.55%	7,166	27
	Goods: Concrete blocks, surgical and medical supplies, boats, fruits and vegetables					
★ Fort Pierce, FL	Housing: 106 Food: 102* Other: 108*	Income: $28,792 Taxes: $310 Bite: 1.08%	Blue-Collar Index: 106 White-Collar Index: 94 Unemployment Threat: Moderate	Income: 51.67% Jobs: 54.05%	7,973	9
	Goods: Barrels, plastic pipe, boats, fertilizer, fruit canning					
Fort Smith, AR–OK	Housing: 69 Food: 92 Other: 101	Income: $24,405 Taxes: $610 Bite: 2.50%	Blue-Collar Index: 119 White-Collar Index: 81 Unemployment Threat: High	Income: 40.54% Jobs: 1.10%	4,849	243
	Goods: Refrigerators, air conditioners, kitchen cabinets, caskets, food processing					

Metro Area	Living Costs (U.S. Avg.=100)	Average Household Income and Taxes	Occupations (U.S. Avg.=100)	Five-Year Growth Income and Jobs	Places Rated Score	Places Rated Rank
Fort Walton Beach, FL	Housing: 91 Food: 98* Other: 96*	Income: $25,466 Taxes: $280 Bite: 1.10%	Blue-Collar Index: 98 White-Collar Index: 102 Unemployment Threat: Low	Income: 49.64% Jobs: 23.62%	6,342	61
	Goods: Fish, beverages, pine lumber					
Fort Wayne, IN	Housing: 81 Food: 94 Other: 91	Income: $29,182 Taxes: $954 Bite: 3.27%	Blue-Collar Index: 101 White-Collar Index: 99 Unemployment Threat: Moderate	Income: 28.16% Jobs: −8.41%	4,195	304
	Goods: Televisions, radios, auto axles, mobile homes, public-address systems, pistons, gasoline pumps					
Fort Worth–Arlington, TX	Housing: 95 Food: 105 Other: 105	Income: $33,384 Taxes: $235 Bite: 0.70%	Blue-Collar Index: 104 White-Collar Index: 96 Unemployment Threat: Moderate	Income: 47.84% Jobs: 23.75%	6,862	40
	Goods: Pharmaceuticals, oil and gas, aluminum, steel, titanium and brass forgings, salad dressing, pickles, preserves, jams and jellies, grain, leather, electronic and computer parts, printed circuit boards, antennae and cables, wire, soap					
Fresno, CA	Housing: 111 Food: 98* Other: 110*	Income: $30,047 Taxes: $864 Bite: 2.88%	Blue-Collar Index: 98 White-Collar Index: 102 Unemployment Threat: Low	Income: 41.18% Jobs: 19.70%	5,746	123
	Goods: Wines, dried fruits, poultry, feeds, olive oil, vending machines, plastics					
Gadsden, AL	Housing: 65 Food: 94 Other: 90	Income: $23,136 Taxes: $735 Bite: 3.18%	Blue-Collar Index: 126 White-Collar Index: 74 Unemployment Threat: High	Income: 35.59% Jobs: −6.51%	4,220	302
	Goods: Food products, iron, wire, coat hangers, ammunition fuses, knives					
Gainesville, FL	Housing: 89 Food: 98 Other: 99	Income: $22,756 Taxes: $265 Bite: 1.16%	Blue-Collar Index: 85 White-Collar Index: 115 Unemployment Threat: Moderate	Income: 44.38% Jobs: 23.05%	5,739	124
	Goods: Electronic tubes, tung oil, petrochemicals, lumber, meat products					
Galveston–Texas City, TX	Housing: 93 Food: 103* Other: 107*	Income: $34,208 Taxes: $245 Bite: 0.72%	Blue-Collar Index: 108 White-Collar Index: 92 Unemployment Threat: Moderate	Income: 47.57% Jobs: 5.02%	6,026	95
	Goods: Petrochemicals, barges, pleasure craft, packing plants, dry docks, fish					
Gary–Hammond, IN	Housing: 92 Food: 100* Other: 106*	Income: $29,669 Taxes: $965 Bite: 3.25%	Blue-Collar Index: 123 White-Collar Index: 77 Unemployment Threat: High	Income: 30.48% Jobs: −11.94%	3,826	315
	Goods: Steel, tinplate, axles, coke, sulfates, bridges, railroad cars, autos, jet engines, light fixtures					
Glens Falls, NY	Housing: 85 Food: 99* Other: 98*	Income: $25,539 Taxes: $927 Bite: 3.63%	Blue-Collar Index: 111 White-Collar Index: 89 Unemployment Threat: Moderate	Income: 44.69% Jobs: 5.69%	5,166	201
	Goods: Book paper, color pigments, lace, shirts and dresses					
Grand Forks, ND	Housing: 95 Food: 100* Other: 96*	Income: $26,636 Taxes: $349 Bite: 1.31%	Blue-Collar Index: 94 White-Collar Index: 106 Unemployment Threat: Low	Income: 43.31% Jobs: 14.85%	5,646	139
	Goods: Flour, potato products, beet sugar, wheat, livestock					
Grand Rapids, MI	Housing: 93 Food: 95* Other: 105*	Income: $29,915 Taxes: $1,389 Bite: 4.64%	Blue-Collar Index: 111 White-Collar Index: 89 Unemployment Threat: Moderate	Income: 33.85% Jobs: 4.89%	4,848	244
	Goods: Furniture, typewriters, calculators, welding equipment, bathroom fixtures, varnishes, lacquers					
Great Falls, MT	Housing: 86 Food: 108 Other: 102	Income: $28,120 Taxes: $632 Bite: 2.25%	Blue-Collar Index: 92 White-Collar Index: 108 Unemployment Threat: Low	Income: 39.18% Jobs: −1.91%	4,697	260
	Goods: Wheat, barley, oats, hay, linseed oil, copper and zinc, livestock					
Greeley, CO	Housing: 99 Food: 103* Other: 102*	Income: $29,151 Taxes: $653 Bite: 2.24%	Blue-Collar Index: 108 White-Collar Index: 92 Unemployment Threat: Moderate	Income: 42.17% Jobs: 10.26%	5,443	161
	Goods: Sugar, soft drinks, meat products, potatoes and potato sorters					
Green Bay, WI	Housing: 101 Food: 95 Other: 95	Income: $30,282 Taxes: $1,352 Bite: 4.46%	Blue-Collar Index: 104 White-Collar Index: 96 Unemployment Threat: Moderate	Income: 43.02% Jobs: 10.34%	5,650	137
	Goods: Paper, tissue paper, cheese, fish, cranes, gloves, fertilizer					

Metro Area	Living Costs (U.S. Avg.=100)	Average Household Income and Taxes	Occupations (U.S. Avg.=100)	Five-Year Growth Income and Jobs	Places Rated Score	Places Rated Rank
Greensboro–Winston-Salem–High Point, NC	Housing: 85 Food: 92 Other: 104	Income: $29,450 Taxes: $1,147 Bite: 3.89%	Blue-Collar Index: 118 White-Collar Index: 82 Unemployment Threat: High	Income: 38.50% Jobs: 5.36%	5,204	192
	Goods: Wood furniture, loom reeds, burial vaults, cellophane, cigarettes, cotton goods, hosiery					
Greenville–Spartanburg, SC	Housing: 76 Food: 95 Other: 102	Income: $26,152 Taxes: $879 Bite: 3.36%	Blue-Collar Index: 122 White-Collar Index: 78 Unemployment Threat: High	Income: 40.22% Jobs: 3.85%	5,012	220
	Goods: Textiles, cotton, mill supplies, chemicals, timber, clothing					
Hagerstown, MD	Housing: 93 Food: 99* Other: 106*	Income: $26,880 Taxes: $1,020 Bite: 3.79%	Blue-Collar Index: 120 White-Collar Index: 80 Unemployment Threat: High	Income: 38.21% Jobs: −0.91%	4,477	281
	Goods: Pipe organs, dresses, dust collectors, cold-storage doors, mayonnaise					
Hamilton–Middletown, OH	Housing: 99 Food: 102* Other: 96*	Income: $28,448 Taxes: $799 Bite: 2.81%	Blue-Collar Index: 110 White-Collar Index: 90 Unemployment Threat: Moderate	Income: 36.45% Jobs: 0.05%	4,618	268
	Goods: Safes, printing presses, oil tanks, paper, coke, cast metals					
Harrisburg–Lebanon–Carlisle, PA	Housing: 95 Food: 98 Other: 106	Income: $31,447 Taxes: $945 Bite: 3.01%	Blue-Collar Index: 102 White-Collar Index: 98 Unemployment Threat: Moderate	Income: 42.24% Jobs: 3.21%	5,322	173
	Goods: Meat and dairy products, steel, road machinery, cotton clothing					
Hartford, CT	Housing: 140 Food: 110 Other: 103	Income: $37,565 Taxes: $477 Bite: 1.27%	Blue-Collar Index: 93 White-Collar Index: 107 Unemployment Threat: Low	Income: 52.28% Jobs: 12.04%	6,307	67
	Goods: Airplane engines, propellers, revolvers, tobacco, dishwashers, machine tools, glass-making machines					
Hickory, NC	Housing: 81 Food: 92 Other: 99	Income: $25,203 Taxes: $931 Bite: 3.69%	Blue-Collar Index: 139 White-Collar Index: 61 Unemployment Threat: High	Income: 35.97% Jobs: 4.65%	4,728	258
	Goods: Hosiery, twine, clotheslines, wagons, soft drinks					
Honolulu, HI	Housing: 204 Food: 125 Other: 125	Income: $33,964 Taxes: $1,828 Bite: 5.38%	Blue-Collar Index: 90 White-Collar Index: 110 Unemployment Threat: Low	Income: 39.55% Jobs: 23.52%	5,187	196
	Goods: Pineapples, pineapple products, sugar, clothing, awnings, tents, fish, cement					
Houma–Thibodaux, LA	Housing: 85 Food: 104* Other: 101*	Income: $29,350 Taxes: $296 Bite: 1.01%	Blue-Collar Index: 124 White-Collar Index: 76 Unemployment Threat: High	Income: 52.95% Jobs: 19.12%	6,662	46
	Goods: Shrimp, oysters, crabs, sugar products, oil and gas, sugarcane					
★ Houston, TX	Housing: 117 Food: 103 Other: 107	Income: $39,558 Taxes: $265 Bite: 0.67%	Blue-Collar Index: 100 White-Collar Index: 100 Unemployment Threat: Moderate	Income: 50.35% Jobs: 27.49%	7,464	18
	Goods: Oil-field equipment, synthetic rubber, fertilizer, refineries, steel, pulp and paper, rice mills					
Huntington–Ashland, WV–OH–KY	Housing: 80 Food: 103 Other: 94	Income: $24,307 Taxes: $744 Bite: 3.06%	Blue-Collar Index: 113 White-Collar Index: 87 Unemployment Threat: Moderate	Income: 32.78% Jobs: 2.52%	4,383	289
	Goods: Glass, dye, stoves, auto bumpers, insulators					
Huntsville, AL	Housing: 75 Food: 93 Other: 93	Income: $30,470 Taxes: $968 Bite: 3.18%	Blue-Collar Index: 94 White-Collar Index: 106 Unemployment Threat: Low	Income: 47.03% Jobs: 12.26%	6,412	57
	Goods: Telephones, acoustic instruments, rockets, boats, trailers, cotton clothing					
Indianapolis, IN	Housing: 84 Food: 96 Other: 92	Income: $31,461 Taxes: $1,021 Bite: 3.25%	Blue-Collar Index: 103 White-Collar Index: 97 Unemployment Threat: Moderate	Income: 34.07% Jobs: −0.08%	5,082	214
	Goods: Automotive products, electrical equipment, heavy machinery, drugs					
Iowa City, IA	Housing: 113 Food: 93 Other: 101	Income: $28,904 Taxes: $935 Bite: 3.23%	Blue-Collar Index: 82 White-Collar Index: 118 Unemployment Threat: Low	Income: 38.75% Jobs: 10.76%	5,165	202
	Goods: Brushes, toothpaste, adhesive paper, foam rubber					
Jackson, MI	Housing: 81 Food: 100 Other: 99	Income: $27,580 Taxes: $1,276 Bite: 4.63%	Blue-Collar Index: 113 White-Collar Index: 87 Unemployment Threat: Moderate	Income: 30.27% Jobs: −11.01%	3,822	316
	Goods: Grinding wheels, air conditioners, extracts and flavorings, auto and aircraft parts					

Metro Area	Living Costs (U.S. Avg.=100)	Average Household Income and Taxes	Occupations (U.S. Avg.=100)	Five-Year Growth Income and Jobs	Places Rated Score	Places Rated Rank
Jackson, MS	Housing: 87 Food: 107* Other: 95*	Income: $27,499 Taxes: $683 Bite: 2.48%	Blue-Collar Index: 95 White-Collar Index: 105 Unemployment Threat: Low	Income: 38.01% Jobs: 8.66%	5,186	198
	Goods: Cottonseed oil, furniture, desks, caskets, incubators, hydraulic aircraft and missile parts, work clothes					
Jacksonville, FL	Housing: 79 Food: 97 Other: 103	Income: $29,352 Taxes: $310 Bite: 1.06%	Blue-Collar Index: 99 White-Collar Index: 101 Unemployment Threat: Low	Income: 44.37% Jobs: 15.27%	6,139	82
	Goods: Pulp and paper, ships, food products					
Jacksonville, NC	Housing: 73 Food: 95* Other: 89*	Income: $22,358 Taxes: $802 Bite: 3.59%	Blue-Collar Index: 112 White-Collar Index: 88 Unemployment Threat: Moderate	Income: 61.84% Jobs: 14.55%	6,386	59
	Goods: Tobacco products, lumber, boats					
Janesville–Beloit, WI	Housing: 89 Food: 94 Other: 94	Income: $28,375 Taxes: $1,225 Bite: 4.32%	Blue-Collar Index: 118 White-Collar Index: 82 Unemployment Threat: High	Income: 30.95% Jobs: −2.56%	4,371	290
	Goods: Fountain pens, machine tools, church furniture, room dividers					
Jersey City, NJ	Housing: 106 Food: 108* Other: 105*	Income: $32,004 Taxes: $864 Bite: 2.70%	Blue-Collar Index: 113 White-Collar Index: 87 Unemployment Threat: Moderate	Income: 41.81% Jobs: −2.79%	4,889	237
	Goods: Soap, cork, cosmetics, macaroni, egg noodles, slippers and sandals					
Johnson City–Kingsport–Bristol, TN–VA	Housing: 73 Food: 98* Other: 107*	Income: $23,531 Taxes: $299 Bite: 1.27%	Blue-Collar Index: 122 White-Collar Index: 78 Unemployment Threat: High	Income: 40.32% Jobs: 6.68%	4,903	234
	Goods: Chemicals, electrical products, silk and rayon textiles, hosiery, bricks, cheese, cigarette filters, hardwood flooring					
Johnstown, PA	Housing: 78 Food: 98* Other: 100*	Income: $25,514 Taxes: $776 Bite: 3.04%	Blue-Collar Index: 124 White-Collar Index: 76 Unemployment Threat: High	Income: 37.89% Jobs: −8.68%	4,181	305
	Goods: Mining equipment, girdles, mattresses, soft drinks					
Joliet, IL	Housing: 112 Food: 101* Other: 106*	Income: $30,590 Taxes: $992 Bite: 3.24%	Blue-Collar Index: 114 White-Collar Index: 86 Unemployment Threat: Moderate	Income: 30.60% Jobs: 6.70%	4,631	266
	Goods: Wallpaper, earth-moving equipment, firebrick, barrels					
Joplin, MO	Housing: 62 Food: 91 Other: 94	Income: $23,517 Taxes: $567 Bite: 2.41%	Blue-Collar Index: 118 White-Collar Index: 82 Unemployment Threat: High	Income: 42.33% Jobs: 6.77%	5,324	172
	Goods: Furniture, dog food, explosives, engraving and typesetting equipment, store fixtures					
Kalamazoo, MI	Housing: 95 Food: 95 Other: 105	Income: $31,276 Taxes: $1,462 Bite: 4.67%	Blue-Collar Index: 104 White-Collar Index: 96 Unemployment Threat: Moderate	Income: 35.86% Jobs: −0.21%	4,794	251
	Goods: Paper, silos, fishing tackle, furnace blowers, printing ink, guitars and banjos, drugs					
Kankakee, IL	Housing: 87 Food: 99* Other: 104*	Income: $30,022 Taxes: $978 Bite: 3.26%	Blue-Collar Index: 115 White-Collar Index: 85 Unemployment Threat: Moderate	Income: 40.74% Jobs: 10.34%	5,579	146
	Goods: Industrial batteries, soybeans, corn products, water heaters, farming implements, hydraulic tools					
Kansas City, KS	Housing: 97 Food: 102 Other: 105	Income: $37,268 Taxes: $1,021 Bite: 2.74%	Blue-Collar Index: 93 White-Collar Index: 107 Unemployment Threat: Low	Income: 39.56% Jobs: 11.98%	6,166	78
	Goods: Fiberglass, tile, autos, soap, meat packing					
Kansas City, MO	Housing: 85 Food: 102* Other: 105*	Income: $30,783 Taxes: $789 Bite: 2.56%	Blue-Collar Index: 102 White-Collar Index: 98 Unemployment Threat: Moderate	Income: 37.41% Jobs: −2.60%	4,865	242
	Goods: Ammunition, autos and trucks, greeting cards, valve fittings, tile and brick, work garments					
Kenosha, WI	Housing: 102 Food: 94* Other: 94*	Income: $31,752 Taxes: $1,442 Bite: 4.54%	Blue-Collar Index: 120 White-Collar Index: 80 Unemployment Threat: High	Income: 41.01% Jobs: 0.01%	5,176	199
	Goods: Autos, musical instruments, tools, wire, rope, underwear, fire-fighting equipment, cranberries					

Metro Area	Living Costs (U.S. Avg.=100)	Average Household Income and Taxes	Occupations (U.S. Avg.=100)	Five-Year Growth Income and Jobs	Places Rated Score	Places Rated Rank
Killeen–Temple, TX	Housing: 77￼Food: 100￼Other: 93	Income: $25,810￼Taxes: $192￼Bite: 0.74%	Blue-Collar Index: 104￼White-Collar Index: 96￼Unemployment Threat: Moderate	Income: 52.26%￼Jobs: 16.13%	6,331	62
	Goods: School desks and chairs, theater seats, farm machinery, plastics					
Knoxville, TN	Housing: 80￼Food: 98￼Other: 107	Income: $26,454￼Taxes: $329￼Bite: 1.24%	Blue-Collar Index: 105￼White-Collar Index: 95￼Unemployment Threat: Moderate	Income: 42.91%￼Jobs: 12.25%	5,537	148
	Goods: Hosiery, burley tobacco, chemicals, rolled aluminum, cast metals, marble, soft coal					
Kokomo, IN	Housing: 79￼Food: 96*￼Other: 92*	Income: $29,439￼Taxes: $959￼Bite: 3.26%	Blue-Collar Index: 125￼White-Collar Index: 75￼Unemployment Threat: High	Income: 21.00%￼Jobs: −17.89%	3,429	324
	Goods: Electric signs, radios, playground equipment, auto transmissions, high-performance alloys					
La Crosse, WI	Housing: 100￼Food: 97￼Other: 93	Income: $28,554￼Taxes: $1,235￼Bite: 4.33%	Blue-Collar Index: 104￼White-Collar Index: 96￼Unemployment Threat: Moderate	Income: 44.88%￼Jobs: 11.76%	5,648	138
	Goods: Beer, dairy pumps, rubber boots, gauges, sheet metal, cast metals					
Lafayette, IN	Housing: 93￼Food: 96*￼Other: 92*	Income: $26,146￼Taxes: $1,173￼Bite: 4.48%	Blue-Collar Index: 94￼White-Collar Index: 106￼Unemployment Threat: Low	Income: 36.38%￼Jobs: −3.42%	4,333	293
	Goods: Soap, tools and gears, electric meters, meat products, aluminum, drugs					
★ Lafayette, LA	Housing: 103￼Food: 106￼Other: 101	Income: $36,089￼Taxes: $261￼Bite: 0.70%	Blue-Collar Index: 97￼White-Collar Index: 103￼Unemployment Threat: Low	Income: 76.22%￼Jobs: 48.25%	9,702	2
	Goods: Coffee roasters, aluminum windows, rice, sugar, corn, dairy products					
Lake Charles, LA	Housing: 83￼Food: 104￼Other: 101	Income: $29,288￼Taxes: $296￼Bite: 1.01%	Blue-Collar Index: 119￼White-Collar Index: 81￼Unemployment Threat: High	Income: 45.44%￼Jobs: 10.31%	5,872	107
	Goods: Ammonia, chlorine, soda ash, coke, gasoline, synthetic rubber, plastics					
Lake County, IL	Housing: 159￼Food: 101*￼Other: 106*	Income: $38,912￼Taxes: $1,228￼Bite: 3.16%	Blue-Collar Index: 75￼White-Collar Index: 125￼Unemployment Threat: Low	Income: 38.47%￼Jobs: 17.29%	5,755	122
	Goods: Asbestos, gypsum products, outboard motors, candy, machine tools, brass casting, pharmaceutical manufacturing					
Lakeland–Winter Haven, FL	Housing: 80￼Food: 97￼Other: 101	Income: $25,833￼Taxes: $280￼Bite: 1.08%	Blue-Collar Index: 112￼White-Collar Index: 88￼Unemployment Threat: Moderate	Income: 39.98%￼Jobs: 15.74%	5,594	142
	Goods: Citrus fruits, fertilizer, ceramic tile, beverages					
Lancaster, PA	Housing: 103￼Food: 99￼Other: 106	Income: $30,248￼Taxes: $918￼Bite: 3.03%	Blue-Collar Index: 122￼White-Collar Index: 78￼Unemployment Threat: High	Income: 39.65%￼Jobs: 5.81%	5,120	209
	Goods: Electric razors, ball bearings, boilers, tin cans, asbestos belting, shoes					
Lansing–East Lansing, MI	Housing: 95￼Food: 100￼Other: 100	Income: $30,439￼Taxes: $1,425￼Bite: 4.68%	Blue-Collar Index: 100￼White-Collar Index: 100￼Unemployment Threat: Moderate	Income: 34.96%￼Jobs: 0.76%	4,747	254
	Goods: Autos, auto wheels, tools and dies, aerial-photography equipment					
Laredo, TX	Housing: 74￼Food: 100*￼Other: 100*	Income: $17,287￼Taxes: $146￼Bite: 0.84%	Blue-Collar Index: 101￼White-Collar Index: 99￼Unemployment Threat: Moderate	Income: 46.51%￼Jobs: 20.24%	5,264	183
	Goods: Cattle, vegetables, citrus fruits, coal, natural gas, oil					
Las Cruces, NM	Housing: 83￼Food: 96*￼Other: 101*	Income: $21,641￼Taxes: $134￼Bite: 0.62%	Blue-Collar Index: 108￼White-Collar Index: 92￼Unemployment Threat: Moderate	Income: 43.29%￼Jobs: 17.29%	5,341	168
	Goods: Cottonseed oil, alfalfa, melons, livestock					
Las Vegas, NV	Housing: 119￼Food: 101￼Other: 110	Income: $32,626￼Taxes: $331￼Bite: 1.01%	Blue-Collar Index: 93￼White-Collar Index: 107￼Unemployment Threat: Low	Income: 36.99%￼Jobs: 26.04%	6,035	93
	Goods: Printing and publishing, foods, primary metals					
Lawrence, KS	Housing: 90￼Food: 102￼Other: 103	Income: $24,836￼Taxes: $585￼Bite: 2.36%	Blue-Collar Index: 91￼White-Collar Index: 109￼Unemployment Threat: Low	Income: 40.37%￼Jobs: 1.10%	4,573	271
	Goods: Pipe organs, creameries, milled alfalfa					

Metro Area	Living Costs (U.S. Avg.=100)	Average Household Income and Taxes	Occupations (U.S. Avg.=100)	Five-Year Growth Income and Jobs	Places Rated Score	Places Rated Rank
Lawrence–Haverhill, MA–NH	Housing: 125 Food: 94* Other: 97*	Income: $36,644 Taxes: $1,695 Bite: 4.63%	Blue-Collar Index: 109 White-Collar Index: 91 Unemployment Threat: Moderate	Income: 53.86% Jobs: 12.08%	6,527	51
	Goods: Gym lockers, paper boxes, textiles, electronic equipment, mattresses, cans					
Lawton, OK	Housing: 70 Food: 108* Other: 101*	Income: $23,775 Taxes: $409 Bite: 1.72%	Blue-Collar Index: 102 White-Collar Index: 98 Unemployment Threat: Moderate	Income: 52.30% Jobs: 17.88%	6,105	84
	Goods: Men's hats and slacks, cement, tile, greenhouses, hatcheries, cattle, wheat					
Lewiston–Auburn, ME	Housing: 82 Food: 94* Other: 97*	Income: $24,447 Taxes: $653 Bite: 2.67%	Blue-Collar Index: 123 White-Collar Index: 77 Unemployment Threat: High	Income: 36.27% Jobs: −0.26%	4,444	285
	Goods: Shoes and boots, belting, leather and plastic soles and heels, cotton, rayon, woolen goods					
Lexington–Fayette, KY	Housing: 100 Food: 97 Other: 101	Income: $30,570 Taxes: $924 Bite: 3.02%	Blue-Collar Index: 95 White-Collar Index: 105 Unemployment Threat: Low	Income: 45.94% Jobs: 19.68%	6,245	72
	Goods: Crop dryers, whiskey, tobacco, electric typewriters, neon signs, parachutes, peanut butter					
Lima, OH	Housing: 84 Food: 99 Other: 96	Income: $28,445 Taxes: $799 Bite: 2.81%	Blue-Collar Index: 125 White-Collar Index: 75 Unemployment Threat: High	Income: 32.28% Jobs: −6.11%	4,313	294
	Goods: School buses, ambulances, hearses, auto engines, aircraft parts, power shovels, cranes and derricks, stone, neon signs					
Lincoln, NE	Housing: 99 Food: 97 Other: 99	Income: $30,514 Taxes: $734 Bite: 2.41%	Blue-Collar Index: 94 White-Collar Index: 106 Unemployment Threat: Low	Income: 32.87% Jobs: 5.13%	4,908	232
	Goods: Flour and feed mills, meat products, office supplies, motor scooters, wax					
Little Rock–North Little Rock, AR	Housing: 87 Food: 100 Other: 104	Income: $28,686 Taxes: $779 Bite: 2.72%	Blue-Collar Index: 102 White-Collar Index: 98 Unemployment Threat: Moderate	Income: 39.81% Jobs: 7.51%	5,273	181
	Goods: Light bulbs, cameras, teletype machinery, fertilizer, cottonseed products, meat products					
Longview–Marshall, TX	Housing: 79 Food: 102* Other: 104*	Income: $30,159 Taxes: $225 Bite: 0.75%	Blue-Collar Index: 118 White-Collar Index: 82 Unemployment Threat: High	Income: 50.41% Jobs: 23.17%	6,898	38
	Goods: Road-building equipment, beer, plastics, mufflers, pruning saws, attic fans, valve regulators					
Lorain–Elyria, OH	Housing: 100 Food: 99* Other: 106*	Income: $27,700 Taxes: $764 Bite: 2.76%	Blue-Collar Index: 121 White-Collar Index: 79 Unemployment Threat: High	Income: 28.56% Jobs: −15.36%	3,301	326
	Goods: Cars and trucks, machine tools, plasterboard, primary metals					
Los Angeles–Long Beach, CA	Housing: 166 Food: 95* Other: 105*	Income: $36,624 Taxes: $1,237 Bite: 3.38%	Blue-Collar Index: 100 White-Collar Index: 100 Unemployment Threat: Moderate	Income: 44.04% Jobs: 6.98%	5,316	174
	Goods: Aircraft, missiles, electronic components, lumber and wood products, clothing, computers					
Louisville, KY–IN	Housing: 82 Food: 97 Other: 97	Income: $29,621 Taxes: $880 Bite: 2.97%	Blue-Collar Index: 107 White-Collar Index: 93 Unemployment Threat: Moderate	Income: 37.32% Jobs: 7.56%	5,402	163
	Goods: Electrical appliances, auto bodies, beer, biscuits, tanks, baseball bats, whiskey, cigarettes, racehorses					
Lowell, MA–NH	Housing: 116 Food: 94* Other: 97*	Income: $36,644 Taxes: $1,695 Bite: 4.63%	Blue-Collar Index: 110 White-Collar Index: 90 Unemployment Threat: Moderate	Income: 53.86% Jobs: 12.08%	6,651	47
	Goods: Textiles, yarns and threads, textile machinery, knitwear, wire and cable, printing, computers					
Lubbock, TX	Housing: 84 Food: 102 Other: 103	Income: $29,523 Taxes: $214 Bite: 0.72%	Blue-Collar Index: 97 White-Collar Index: 103 Unemployment Threat: Low	Income: 47.74% Jobs: 9.01%	5,923	104
	Goods: Dairy products, poultry, grain, livestock, cotton					
Lynchburg, VA	Housing: 83 Food: 100* Other: 98*	Income: $26,124 Taxes: $919 Bite: 3.52%	Blue-Collar Index: 113 White-Collar Index: 87 Unemployment Threat: High	Income: 40.17% Jobs: 3.56%	4,926	229
	Goods: Batteries, nuclear reactors, furniture, overalls, hosiery, shoes, chemicals					

Metro Area	Living Costs (U.S. Avg.=100)	Average Household Income and Taxes	Occupations (U.S. Avg.=100)	Five-Year Growth Income and Jobs	Places Rated Score	Places Rated Rank
Macon–Warner Robins, GA	Housing: 75 Food: 101 Other: 96	Income: $26,944 Taxes: $972 Bite: 3.61%	Blue-Collar Index: 106 White-Collar Index: 94 Unemployment Threat: Moderate	Income: 46.69% Jobs: 7.46%	5,659	134
	Goods: Cottonseed oil, flour, pulp wood, cardboard containers, ceramics, overalls, drugs					
Madison, WI	Housing: 119 Food: 94* Other: 102*	Income: $33,569 Taxes: $1,574 Bite: 4.69%	Blue-Collar Index: 82 White-Collar Index: 118 Unemployment Threat: Low	Income: 40.95% Jobs: 8.21%	5,448	160
	Goods: Hot dogs, sausages, dry-cell batteries, farm machinery, lenses, printing and publishing					
Manchester, NH	Housing: 118 Food: 94* Other: 97*	Income: $32,245 Taxes: None Bite: None	Blue-Collar Index: 106 White-Collar Index: 94 Unemployment Threat: Moderate	Income: 49.04% Jobs: 31.57%	7,101	32
	Goods: Knitting and textile machinery, textiles and clothing, boots and shoes, electronic components, lumber and wood products					
Mansfield, OH	Housing: 83 Food: 99* Other: 98*	Income: $27,594 Taxes: $761 Bite: 2.76%	Blue-Collar Index: 121 White-Collar Index: 79 Unemployment Threat: High	Income: 33.55% Jobs: −4.16%	4,386	288
	Goods: Instruments, fire alarms, thermostats, generators, gasoline engines, tires, steel tubes					
McAllen–Edinburg–Mission, TX	Housing: 64 Food: 100 Other: 100	Income: $16,478 Taxes: $146 Bite: 0.89%	Blue-Collar Index: 110 White-Collar Index: 90 Unemployment Threat: Moderate	Income: 48.69% Jobs: 27.67%	5,739	124
	Goods: Grapefruit, oranges, clothing, ready-mix concrete, oil, natural gas					
Medford, OR	Housing: 108 Food: 109* Other: 103*	Income: $24,699 Taxes: $1,046 Bite: 4.23%	Blue-Collar Index: 103 White-Collar Index: 97 Unemployment Threat: Moderate	Income: 29.08% Jobs: 0.12%	3,692	321
	Goods: Lumber, raisins, wine					
Melbourne–Titusville–Palm Bay, FL	Housing: 105 Food: 102* Other: 108*	Income: $29,646 Taxes: $310 Bite: 1.05%	Blue-Collar Index: 95 White-Collar Index: 105 Unemployment Threat: Low	Income: 49.80% Jobs: 36.11%	7,089	33
	Goods: Electrical equipment, transportation equipment, seafood, citrus fruit					
Memphis, TN–AR–MS	Housing: 84 Food: 103 Other: 97	Income: $27,910 Taxes: $329 Bite: 1.18%	Blue-Collar Index: 101 White-Collar Index: 99 Unemployment Threat: Moderate	Income: 38.21% Jobs: 5.67%	5,160	204
	Goods: Farm machinery, truck trailers, drugs, paper, furniture, feeds, cosmetics, cotton, lumber					
Miami–Hialeah, FL	Housing: 123 Food: 96 Other: 107	Income: $32,808 Taxes: $338 Bite: 1.03%	Blue-Collar Index: 96 White-Collar Index: 104 Unemployment Threat: Low	Income: 43.64% Jobs: 14.65%	5,840	114
	Goods: Clothing, drugs, mattresses, water heaters, shutters, ships					
Middlesex–Somerset–Hunterdon, NJ	Housing: 146 Food: 108* Other: 105*	Income: $40,205 Taxes: $1,121 Bite: 2.79%	Blue-Collar Index: 97 White-Collar Index: 103 Unemployment Threat: Low	Income: 49.65% Jobs: 13.28%	6,324	63
	Goods: Adhesive bandages, baby powder, baby products, paper machinery, wire, needles, auto parts					
Middletown, CT	Housing: 140 Food: 110* Other: 103*	Income: $37,565 Taxes: $477 Bite: 1.27%	Blue-Collar Index: 89 White-Collar Index: 111 Unemployment Threat: Low	Income: 52.28% Jobs: 12.04%	6,307	67
	Goods: Jet engines, leather gaskets, office supplies, brake linings					
★ Midland, TX	Housing: 104 Food: 103* Other: 97*	Income: $46,458 Taxes: $291 Bite: 0.63%	Blue-Collar Index: 96 White-Collar Index: 104 Unemployment Threat: Low	Income: 60.56% Jobs: 47.62%	9,980	1
	Goods: Machinery, oil-field supplies, electrical components, boats, printing and publishing					
Milwaukee, WI	Housing: 122 Food: 94* Other: 94*	Income: $35,272 Taxes: $1,703 Bite: 4.83%	Blue-Collar Index: 106 White-Collar Index: 94 Unemployment Threat: Moderate	Income: 40.33% Jobs: −4.03%	4,982	224
	Goods: Engines, auto frames, truck bodies, beer, heavy pumping machinery, mine shovels, outboard motors, motorcycles, earphones, cheese, sausage					
Minneapolis–St. Paul, MN–WI	Housing: 115 Food: 96 Other: 95	Income: $35,871 Taxes: $1,822 Bite: 5.08%	Blue-Collar Index: 94 White-Collar Index: 106 Unemployment Threat: Low	Income: 42.52% Jobs: 8.22%	5,843	113
	Goods: Computers, lawn mowers, sprinklers, dairy products, canned and frozen food, grains, flour, cereals, farm machinery					

Metro Area	Living Costs (U.S. Avg.=100)	Average Household Income and Taxes	Occupations (U.S. Avg.=100)	Five-Year Growth Income and Jobs	Places Rated Score	Places Rated Rank
Mobile, AL	Housing: 80 Food: 97 Other: 99	Income: $24,839 Taxes: $789 Bite: 3.18%	Blue-Collar Index: 111 White-Collar Index: 89 Unemployment Threat: Moderate	Income: 37.49% Jobs: 0.95%	4,565	273
	Goods: Pitch pine, petrochemicals, wood furniture, ships and barges					
Modesto, CA	Housing: 103 Food: 98* Other: 110*	Income: $29,641 Taxes: $829 Bite: 2.80%	Blue-Collar Index: 110 White-Collar Index: 90 Unemployment Threat: Moderate	Income: 36.86% Jobs: 10.40%	5,107	210
	Goods: Meat, poultry, dairy products, wine, olive oil, nuts, fruit, crates and bags, dehydrators					
Monmouth–Ocean, NJ	Housing: 140 Food: 108* Other: 105*	Income: $34,367 Taxes: $933 Bite: 2.71%	Blue-Collar Index: 94 White-Collar Index: 106 Unemployment Threat: Low	Income: 49.81% Jobs: 17.55%	6,154	80
	Goods: Venetian blinds, televisions, candy, clothing					
Monroe, LA	Housing: 74 Food: 104* Other: 101*	Income: $24,906 Taxes: $243 Bite: 0.98%	Blue-Collar Index: 102 White-Collar Index: 98 Unemployment Threat: Moderate	Income: 46.32% Jobs: 10.22%	5,537	148
	Goods: Paper, boxes, beverages, awnings, ink, bricks					
Montgomery, AL	Housing: 81 Food: 100 Other: 98	Income: $26,827 Taxes: $851 Bite: 3.17%	Blue-Collar Index: 99 White-Collar Index: 101 Unemployment Threat: High	Income: 36.62% Jobs: 4.13%	4,892	236
	Goods: Canned food, syrup, soft drinks, pickles, clothing, air conditioners					
Muncie, IN	Housing: 70 Food: 96 Other: 99	Income: $25,032 Taxes: $829 Bite: 3.31%	Blue-Collar Index: 110 White-Collar Index: 90 Unemployment Threat: Moderate	Income: 33.65% Jobs: −10.33%	3,980	309
	Goods: Auto parts, jet-engine parts, wire, fencing, fruit jars, lawn mowers					
Muskegon, MI	Housing: 77 Food: 99* Other: 104*	Income: $26,438 Taxes: $1,227 Bite: 4.64%	Blue-Collar Index: 118 White-Collar Index: 82 Unemployment Threat: High	Income: 34.65% Jobs: −15.30%	3,708	320
	Goods: Iron castings, auto and airplane engines, furniture, boilers, bearings, bowling and billiard balls, chlorine gas					
Nashua, NH	Housing: 129 Food: 94* Other: 97*	Income: $32,245 Taxes: None Bite: None	Blue-Collar Index: 103 White-Collar Index: 97 Unemployment Threat: Moderate	Income: 49.04% Jobs: 31.57%	6,962	36
	Goods: Paper, pulp, electronic components, molding machinery, caskets, greeting cards, beer, disinfectants, bronze and brass products					
Nashville, TN	Housing: 94 Food: 99 Other: 99	Income: $28,641 Taxes: $344 Bite: 1.20%	Blue-Collar Index: 102 White-Collar Index: 98 Unemployment Threat: Moderate	Income: 41.30% Jobs: 19.12%	5,938	102
	Goods: Boats and barges, coffee, spices, cereals, printing and publishing, hosiery, bridges, electronic equipment					
★ Nassau–Suffolk, NY	Housing: 134 Food: 101* Other: 103*	Income: $43,075 Taxes: $2,230 Bite: 5.18%	Blue-Collar Index: 90 White-Collar Index: 110 Unemployment Threat: Low	Income: 56.31% Jobs: 20.07%	7,371	22
	Goods: Aircraft, computers, fabricated metals, salad dressing, ticket punchers, pianos					
New Bedford, MA	Housing: 97 Food: 100* Other: 100*	Income: $27,591 Taxes: $1,198 Bite: 4.34%	Blue-Collar Index: 123 White-Collar Index: 77 Unemployment Threat: High	Income: 43.46% Jobs: 1.96%	4,937	228
	Goods: Golf balls, fish, mortar-shell casings, ball bearings, instant color film, cotton and silk goods, tire fabric					
New Britain, CT	Housing: 126 Food: 110* Other: 103*	Income: $37,565 Taxes: $477 Bite: 1.27%	Blue-Collar Index: 113 White-Collar Index: 87 Unemployment Threat: Moderate	Income: 52.28% Jobs: 12.04%	6,470	53
	Goods: Automatic doors, machine tools, hand tools, chucks, specialty meats					
New Haven–Meriden, CT	Housing: 137 Food: 110* Other: 103*	Income: $34,364 Taxes: $458 Bite: 1.33%	Blue-Collar Index: 98 White-Collar Index: 102 Unemployment Threat: Low	Income: 47.49% Jobs: 5.08%	5,478	156
	Goods: Firearms, ammunition, tools, clocks and watches, lamps, silverware, airplane parts, oil filters, telephones, cutlery, chocolate					
New London–Norwich, CT–RI	Housing: 123 Food: 100* Other: 103*	Income: $32,922 Taxes: $438 Bite: 1.29%	Blue-Collar Index: 109 White-Collar Index: 91 Unemployment Threat: Moderate	Income: 58.43% Jobs: 16.48%	6,672	45
	Goods: Submarines, ships, safety razors, toothpaste, underwear, engines and turbines					

Metro Area	Living Costs (U.S. Avg.=100)	Average Household Income and Taxes	Occupations (U.S. Avg.=100)	Five-Year Growth Income and Jobs	Places Rated Score	Places Rated Rank
New Orleans, LA	Housing: 102 Food: 98 Other: 98	Income: $32,704 Taxes: $346 Bite: 1.06%	Blue-Collar Index: 99 White-Collar Index: 101 Unemployment Threat: Low	Income: 52.66% Jobs: 11.68%	6,453	54
	Goods: Ships and barges, molasses and syrups, beer, burlap, roofing, luggage, clothing, asbestos					
New York, NY	Housing: 160 Food: 112 Other: 114	Income: $36,047 Taxes: $1,637 Bite: 4.54%	Blue-Collar Index: 88 White-Collar Index: 112 Unemployment Threat: Moderate	Income: 46.85% Jobs: 8.16%	5,338	169
	Goods: Clothing, printing and publishing, metal and machine-shop products, chemicals, paint, textiles, foods, beverages					
Newark, NJ	Housing: 171 Food: 108 Other: 105	Income: $38,279 Taxes: $1,056 Bite: 2.76%	Blue-Collar Index: 96 White-Collar Index: 104 Unemployment Threat: Low	Income: 50.55% Jobs: 7.29%	5,690	128
	Goods: Paint, varnish, perfume, cosmetics, liquor, gold, silver, electrical machinery					
Niagara Falls, NY	Housing: 92 Food: 104* Other: 97*	Income: $29,123 Taxes: $1,151 Bite: 3.95%	Blue-Collar Index: 118 White-Collar Index: 82 Unemployment Threat: High	Income: 40.82% Jobs: −9.84%	4,463	283
	Goods: Abrasives, record players, business forms, helicopters, paint					
Norfolk–Virginia Beach–Newport News, VA	Housing: 103 Food: 102 Other: 100	Income: $29,375 Taxes: $1,054 Bite: 3.59%	Blue-Collar Index: 103 White-Collar Index: 97 Unemployment Threat: Moderate	Income: 49.38% Jobs: 12.41%	5,866	109
	Goods: Ships, beverages, candy, peanuts, lawn mowers, electric motors, woodworking machinery, printing, furniture					
Norwalk, CT	Housing: 242 Food: 110* Other: 103*	Income: $47,258 Taxes: $546 Bite: 1.16%	Blue-Collar Index: 83 White-Collar Index: 117 Unemployment Threat: Low	Income: 53.37% Jobs: 17.60%	6,432	55
	Goods: Astronomic instruments, electric signals, office machines, duplicators, bathrobes, boats, oysters and lobsters, X-ray tubes					
Oakland, CA	Housing: 157 Food: 108* Other: 120*	Income: $38,279 Taxes: $1,345 Bite: 3.51%	Blue-Collar Index: 93 White-Collar Index: 107 Unemployment Threat: Low	Income: 45.00% Jobs: 8.60%	5,457	158
	Goods: Glass, aluminum, electric cable, cement, rubber goods, wheat, barley, paper products, publishing, clothing, candy, household products, oil, gas					
Ocala, FL	Housing: 81 Food: 97* Other: 101*	Income: $23,777 Taxes: $265 Bite: 1.11%	Blue-Collar Index: 108 White-Collar Index: 92 Unemployment Threat: Moderate	Income: 50.70% Jobs: 39.38%	7,060	34
	Goods: Meat and meat products, citrus fruits, frozen foods, drugs, air compressors, air-purification machinery, electronic equipment, lumber					
★ Odessa, TX	Housing: 80 Food: 103 Other: 97	Income: $34,591 Taxes: $245 Bite: 0.71%	Blue-Collar Index: 117 White-Collar Index: 83 Unemployment Threat: High	Income: 50.38% Jobs: 25.44%	7,565	17
	Goods: Oil-field supplies, elevators, welding equipment, brass, cattle, sheep, petrochemicals					
★ Oklahoma City, OK	Housing: 86 Food: 100 Other: 94	Income: $35,773 Taxes: $894 Bite: 2.50%	Blue-Collar Index: 99 White-Collar Index: 101 Unemployment Threat: Low	Income: 59.48% Jobs: 27.09%	8,119	5
	Goods: Aircraft, fabricated metal, computers, clothing, oil-field equipment, crude oil					
Olympia, WA	Housing: 99 Food: 103* Other: 112*	Income: $30,467 Taxes: $458 Bite: 1.59%	Blue-Collar Index: 91 White-Collar Index: 109 Unemployment Threat: Low	Income: 29.84% Jobs: 11.25%	4,912	231
	Goods: Shingles, belting, beer, oysters, farm machinery					
Omaha, NE–IA	Housing: 85 Food: 97* Other: 99*	Income: $31,912 Taxes: $784 Bite: 2.46%	Blue-Collar Index: 94 White-Collar Index: 106 Unemployment Threat: Low	Income: 41.05% Jobs: 9.07%	5,853	112
	Goods: Beer, paint and varnish, ball bearings, farm machinery, electric signs, dairy products, grain, feeds, livestock					
Orange County, NY	Housing: 122 Food: 101 Other: 103	Income: $30,218 Taxes: $1,227 Bite: 4.06%	Blue-Collar Index: 103 White-Collar Index: 97 Unemployment Threat: Moderate	Income: 49.29% Jobs: 14.44%	5,822	115
	Goods: Shirts, hats, boxes, purses, imitation leather, radio parts					
★ Orlando, FL	Housing: 98 Food: 102* Other: 108*	Income: $29,896 Taxes: $310 Bite: 1.04%	Blue-Collar Index: 95 White-Collar Index: 105 Unemployment Threat: Moderate	Income: 52.27% Jobs: 38.53%	7,413	21
	Goods: Missiles, candy, coffee, orange-juice concentrate, yachts					

Metro Area	Living Costs (U.S. Avg.=100)	Average Household Income and Taxes	Occupations (U.S. Avg.=100)	Five-Year Growth Income and Jobs	Places Rated Score	Places Rated Rank
Owensboro, KY	Housing: 81 Food: 104* Other: 94*	Income: $28,708 Taxes: $852 Bite: 2.97%	Blue-Collar Index: 116 White-Collar Index: 84 Unemployment Threat: High	Income: 40.55% Jobs: 19.48%	6,062	89
	Goods: Whiskey, cheese, canned foods, flour, oil, meat and poultry, radio tubes, cigars					
Oxnard–Ventura, CA	Housing: 168 Food: 101* Other: 104*	Income: $32,304 Taxes: $984 Bite: 3.05%	Blue-Collar Index: 97 White-Collar Index: 103 Unemployment Threat: Low	Income: 43.91% Jobs: 18.18%	5,514	150
	Goods: Aircraft components, trailers, seafood, tomatoes, petroleum products, electronic components					
Panama City, FL	Housing: 76 Food: 98* Other: 96*	Income: $24,570 Taxes: $280 Bite: 1.14%	Blue-Collar Index: 100 White-Collar Index: 100 Unemployment Threat: Moderate	Income: 45.57% Jobs: 20.88%	6,083	86
	Goods: Paper and paperboard, lawn mowers, boats, cypress shingles, cabinets					
Parkersburg–Marietta, WV–OH	Housing: 80 Food: 103* Other: 94*	Income: $26,852 Taxes: $836 Bite: 3.11%	Blue-Collar Index: 115 White-Collar Index: 85 Unemployment Threat: Moderate	Income: 37.31% Jobs: 8.61%	5,187	196
	Goods: Steel castings, nylon, fiberglass, plastics, glass tubing					
Pascagoula, MS	Housing: 75 Food: 107* Other: 95*	Income: $25,410 Taxes: $620 Bite: 2.44%	Blue-Collar Index: 117 White-Collar Index: 83 Unemployment Threat: High	Income: 44.09% Jobs: −9.99%	4,491	278
	Goods: Ships, paper bags, boxes, underwear, bricks, fertilizer, petrochemicals					
Pawtucket–Woonsocket–Attleboro, RI–MA	Housing: 113 Food: 100* Other: 100*	Income: $30,094 Taxes: $1,003 Bite: 3.33%	Blue-Collar Index: 130 White-Collar Index: 70 Unemployment Threat: High	Income: 43.96% Jobs: 3.72%	5,154	205
	Goods: Thread, lace, fiberglass, toys, wire and cable, gold and silver plate, nuclear fuel, jewelry					
Pensacola, FL	Housing: 78 Food: 98 Other: 96	Income: $25,032 Taxes: $280 Bite: 1.12%	Blue-Collar Index: 104 White-Collar Index: 96 Unemployment Threat: Moderate	Income: 48.11% Jobs: 16.85%	6,029	94
	Goods: Fertilizer, nylon, tar, creosote, wallboard					
Peoria, IL	Housing: 101 Food: 105 Other: 98	Income: $35,552 Taxes: $1,074 Bite: 3.20%	Blue-Collar Index: 108 White-Collar Index: 92 Unemployment Threat: Moderate	Income: 29.46% Jobs: −16.28%	4,073	306
	Goods: Bulldozers, earth-movers, castings, oil burners, beer and liquor, caskets					
Philadelphia, PA–NJ	Housing: 100 Food: 98* Other: 106*	Income: $33,449 Taxes: $1,001 Bite: 2.99%	Blue-Collar Index: 101 White-Collar Index: 99 Unemployment Threat: Moderate	Income: 44.64% Jobs: 4.50%	5,638	140
	Goods: Machinery, printing and publishing, drugs					
Phoenix, AZ	Housing: 107 Food: 105 Other: 108	Income: $31,041 Taxes: $1,019 Bite: 3.28%	Blue-Collar Index: 96 White-Collar Index: 104 Unemployment Threat: Low	Income: 45.18% Jobs: 27.00%	6,415	56
	Goods: Aircraft parts, radios, publishing, beer and liquor, fruit juices, pickles and olives, sugar					
Pine Bluff, AR	Housing: 68 Food: 102* Other: 91*	Income: $23,108 Taxes: $558 Bite: 2.41%	Blue-Collar Index: 115 White-Collar Index: 85 Unemployment Threat: Moderate	Income: 32.15% Jobs: −0.89%	4,247	299
	Goods: Towboats, cotton-picking equipment, paper bags, newsprint, transformers, beef, pork, rice, soybeans					
Pittsburgh, PA	Housing: 97 Food: 107* Other: 107*	Income: $32,934 Taxes: $990 Bite: 3.01%	Blue-Collar Index: 105 White-Collar Index: 95 Unemployment Threat: Moderate	Income: 44.83% Jobs: −1.64%	5,261	184
	Goods: Steel, iron, aluminum, rolling-mill machinery, coke, oil, foods, plate glass, chemicals					
Pittsfield, MA	Housing: 94 Food: 94* Other: 97*	Income: $30,537 Taxes: $1,358 Bite: 4.45%	Blue-Collar Index: 101 White-Collar Index: 99 Unemployment Threat: Moderate	Income: 49.07% Jobs: −0.83%	5,483	155
	Goods: Plastics, paper, electrical products, missiles					
Portland, ME	Housing: 97 Food: 94* Other: 97*	Income: $30,794 Taxes: $999 Bite: 3.24%	Blue-Collar Index: 99 White-Collar Index: 101 Unemployment Threat: Low	Income: 46.99% Jobs: 14.66%	6,186	76
	Goods: Paper and wooden boxes, shoes and boots, threads and yarn, potato chips, burial cases, fish packing					
Portland, OR	Housing: 119 Food: 106 Other: 112	Income: $33,020 Taxes: $1,553 Bite: 4.70%	Blue-Collar Index: 97 White-Collar Index: 103 Unemployment Threat: Low	Income: 32.64% Jobs: 2.85%	4,535	274
	Goods: Instruments, ships, fuel stokers, lumber, furniture, paper, woolen products					

Metro Area	Living Costs (U.S. Avg.=100)	Average Household Income and Taxes	Occupations (U.S. Avg.=100)	Five-Year Growth Income and Jobs	Places Rated Score	Places Rated Rank
★ Portsmouth–Dover–Rochester, NH–ME	Housing: 119 Food: 94* Other: 97*	Income: $30,170 Taxes: None Bite: None	Blue-Collar Index: 112 White-Collar Index: 88 Unemployment Threat: Moderate	Income: 47.36% Jobs: 62.51%	8,367	3
	Goods: Microwave parts, tools and dies, drinks, buttons, reaming tools					
Poughkeepsie, NY	Housing: 120 Food: 101* Other: 103*	Income: $34,616 Taxes: $1,537 Bite: 4.44%	Blue-Collar Index: 93 White-Collar Index: 107 Unemployment Threat: Low	Income: 55.84% Jobs: 18.94%	6,746	42
	Goods: Cream separators, milking equipment, business machines, electrical insulators, lingerie, precision gauges					
Providence, RI	Housing: 111 Food: 100* Other: 100*	Income: $30,094 Taxes: $1,003 Bite: 3.33%	Blue-Collar Index: 112 White-Collar Index: 88 Unemployment Threat: Moderate	Income: 43.96% Jobs: 3.72%	5,154	205
	Goods: Valves, jewelry, machine tools, woolens and worsteds, plastics, electronic parts					
Provo–Orem, UT	Housing: 112 Food: 100 Other: 105	Income: $18,390 Taxes: $892 Bite: 4.85%	Blue-Collar Index: 106 White-Collar Index: 94 Unemployment Threat: Moderate	Income: 29.52% Jobs: 6.96%	3,459	323
	Goods: Pig iron, cast iron, women's clothing, steel pipes, tanks, sporting goods					
Pueblo, CO	Housing: 80 Food: 100 Other: 96	Income: $27,499 Taxes: $601 Bite: 2.19%	Blue-Collar Index: 108 White-Collar Index: 92 Unemployment Threat: Moderate	Income: 40.46% Jobs: −7.31%	4,646	264
	Goods: Iron, steel, aluminum, auto pistons, storm sashes, brooms, tents, saddles, beer					
Racine, WI	Housing: 107 Food: 95* Other: 99*	Income: $31,511 Taxes: $1,427 Bite: 4.53%	Blue-Collar Index: 118 White-Collar Index: 82 Unemployment Threat: High	Income: 33.23% Jobs: −4.49%	4,415	286
	Goods: Floor and furniture waxes, playing cards, lawn mowers, luggage, tractors, books					
Raleigh–Durham, NC	Housing: 99 Food: 96 Other: 95	Income: $30,489 Taxes: $1,209 Bite: 3.97%	Blue-Collar Index: 88 White-Collar Index: 112 Unemployment Threat: Low	Income: 45.95% Jobs: 21.76%	6,405	58
	Goods: Cigarettes, tobacco products, textiles, generators, pillowcases, steel tanks, surgical instruments, hosiery					
Reading, PA	Housing: 91 Food: 98* Other: 106*	Income: $32,449 Taxes: $979 Bite: 3.02%	Blue-Collar Index: 122 White-Collar Index: 78 Unemployment Threat: High	Income: 44.50% Jobs: 3.02%	5,587	145
	Goods: Auto frames, hardware, lace machines, optical goods, steel alloys, women's underwear					
Redding, CA	Housing: 103 Food: 99* Other: 100*	Income: $26,348 Taxes: $679 Bite: 2.58%	Blue-Collar Index: 99 White-Collar Index: 101 Unemployment Threat: Low	Income: 26.60% Jobs: 11.75%	4,459	284
	Goods: Timber, wood products, beverage bottling					
Reno, NV	Housing: 149 Food: 102 Other: 111	Income: $38,472 Taxes: $374 Bite: 0.97%	Blue-Collar Index: 91 White-Collar Index: 109 Unemployment Threat: Low	Income: 32.32% Jobs: 20.26%	5,677	130
	Goods: Microwave equipment, suntan lotion, valves, labeling devices					
Richland–Kennewick–Pasco, WA	Housing: 101 Food: 100 Other: 99	Income: $32,404 Taxes: $506 Bite: 1.56%	Blue-Collar Index: 102 White-Collar Index: 98 Unemployment Threat: Moderate	Income: 30.03% Jobs: 12.69%	5,326	171
	Goods: Chemicals, foods, printing and publishing					
Richmond–Petersburg, VA	Housing: 100 Food: 103 Other: 102	Income: $33,510 Taxes: $1,248 Bite: 3.72%	Blue-Collar Index: 99 White-Collar Index: 101 Unemployment Threat: Low	Income: 44.80% Jobs: 8.71%	5,870	108
	Goods: Cigarettes, cigars, pipe and chewing tobacco, fountain pens, luggage, nylon, cellophane, drugs, peanuts, railroad-car bearings					
Riverside–San Bernardino, CA	Housing: 117 Food: 99 Other: 102	Income: $28,257 Taxes: $771 Bite: 2.73%	Blue-Collar Index: 106 White-Collar Index: 94 Unemployment Threat: Moderate	Income: 37.19% Jobs: 10.38%	4,923	230
	Goods: Orchard heaters, wire-tying machinery, primary metals, tree protectors, citrus fruits					
Roanoke, VA	Housing: 90 Food: 100 Other: 98	Income: $29,094 Taxes: $1,083 Bite: 3.62%	Blue-Collar Index: 102 White-Collar Index: 98 Unemployment Threat: Moderate	Income: 41.72% Jobs: 5.05%	5,287	178
	Goods: Locks, hydraulic drills, fiberglass, electronic components, textiles					
Rochester, MN	Housing: 110 Food: 96 Other: 102	Income: $35,344 Taxes: $1,781 Bite: 5.04%	Blue-Collar Index: 82 White-Collar Index: 118 Unemployment Threat: Low	Income: 45.08% Jobs: 12.36%	6,099	85
	Goods: Phonographs, silos, hospital supplies, beverages, foods, home pasteurizers					

Metro Area	Living Costs (U.S. Avg.=100)	Average Household Income and Taxes	Occupations (U.S. Avg.=100)	Five-Year Growth Income and Jobs	Places Rated Score	Places Rated Rank
Rochester, NY	Housing: 103 Food: 104* Other: 97*	Income: $34,896 Taxes: $1,556 Bite: 4.46%	Blue-Collar Index: 103 White-Collar Index: 97 Unemployment Threat: Moderate	Income: 50.32% Jobs: 9.74%	6,304	69
	Goods: Cameras, optical equipment, photographic film, enameled steel tanks, dental supplies, carburetors, thermometers, electrical components					
Rockford, IL	Housing: 91 Food: 99 Other: 104	Income: $31,483 Taxes: $1,012 Bite: 3.21%	Blue-Collar Index: 115 White-Collar Index: 85 Unemployment Threat: Moderate	Income: 32.06% Jobs: −2.41%	4,592	269
	Goods: Farm machinery, sports equipment, wire goods, pet food					
Sacramento, CA	Housing: 118 Food: 104 Other: 107	Income: $31,292 Taxes: $920 Bite: 2.94%	Blue-Collar Index: 89 White-Collar Index: 111 Unemployment Threat: Low	Income: 35.40% Jobs: 16.06%	5,309	175
	Goods: Rockets, guided missiles, olives, frozen foods, rice, polishers, mining equipment, lumber					
Saginaw–Bay City–Midland, MI	Housing: 88 Food: 100* Other: 102*	Income: $29,181 Taxes: $1,357 Bite: 4.65%	Blue-Collar Index: 116 White-Collar Index: 84 Unemployment Threat: High	Income: 28.83% Jobs: −12.62%	3,709	319
	Goods: Auto parts, power steering, chemicals, washtubs, aluminum, brass, iron					
St. Cloud, MN	Housing: 87 Food: 94 Other: 95	Income: $23,954 Taxes: $930 Bite: 3.88%	Blue-Collar Index: 108 White-Collar Index: 92 Unemployment Threat: Moderate	Income: 41.85% Jobs: 17.31%	5,488	153
	Goods: Dairy products, livestock, poultry, grain, floor sanders, truck bodies, sporting goods					
St. Joseph, MO	Housing: 67 Food: 96 Other: 97	Income: $28,073 Taxes: $709 Bite: 2.53%	Blue-Collar Index: 113 White-Collar Index: 87 Unemployment Threat: Moderate	Income: 48.58% Jobs: 6.09%	5,991	101
	Goods: Pet food, flour, paper, paper and wooden boxes, leather goods, clothing					
St. Louis, MO–IL	Housing: 91 Food: 95 Other: 101	Income: $34,546 Taxes: $916 Bite: 2.65%	Blue-Collar Index: 100 White-Collar Index: 100 Unemployment Threat: Moderate	Income: 42.39% Jobs: 3.55%	5,800	119
	Goods: Auto assembly, jet aircraft, railroad cars, space capsules, beer, hardware, shoes, pet food, clay, limestone, iron and steel					
Salem, OR	Housing: 100 Food: 109 Other: 103	Income: $26,213 Taxes: $1,132 Bite: 4.32%	Blue-Collar Index: 98 White-Collar Index: 102 Unemployment Threat: Low	Income: 30.39% Jobs: −2.39%	3,835	314
	Goods: Fruits and vegetables, juices, paper, wooden boxes, lumber, tin cans, woolens					
Salem–Gloucester, MA	Housing: 139 Food: 103 Other: 100	Income: $36,643 Taxes: $1,695 Bite: 4.63%	Blue-Collar Index: 102 White-Collar Index: 98 Unemployment Threat: Moderate	Income: 53.86% Jobs: 12.08%	6,309	65
	Goods: Fish packing, glue, ink, light bulbs, candy, cookware, mattresses					
Salinas–Seaside–Monterey, CA	Housing: 166 Food: 97* Other: 101*	Income: $36,439 Taxes: $1,226 Bite: 3.36%	Blue-Collar Index: 96 White-Collar Index: 104 Unemployment Threat: Low	Income: 38.18% Jobs: 19.49%	5,656	135
	Goods: Tires, pumps, electrical fixtures, chocolate milk, lettuce, beans, peas, strawberries					
Salt Lake City–Ogden, UT	Housing: 113 Food: 96 Other: 100	Income: $27,076 Taxes: $1,305 Bite: 4.82%	Blue-Collar Index: 100 White-Collar Index: 100 Unemployment Threat: Moderate	Income: 37.01% Jobs: 12.74%	4,942	227
	Goods: Surgical and medical supplies, mining, smelting, missiles, petroleum products					
★ San Angelo, TX	Housing: 76 Food: 102* Other: 97*	Income: $32,326 Taxes: $235 Bite: 0.73%	Blue-Collar Index: 106 White-Collar Index: 94 Unemployment Threat: Moderate	Income: 56.33% Jobs: 25.96%	7,720	10
	Goods: Wool and mohair, meat, grain, cotton, leather goods, surgical sutures					
San Antonio, TX	Housing: 83 Food: 99 Other: 96	Income: $28,367 Taxes: $214 Bite: 0.75%	Blue-Collar Index: 100 White-Collar Index: 100 Unemployment Threat: Moderate	Income: 52.94% Jobs: 22.65%	6,873	39
	Goods: Beer, flour, soap, candy, batteries, metal containers, shortening, oil					
San Diego, CA	Housing: 173 Food: 97 Other: 101	Income: $32,586 Taxes: $997 Bite: 3.06%	Blue-Collar Index: 93 White-Collar Index: 107 Unemployment Threat: Low	Income: 44.37% Jobs: 16.82%	5,489	152
	Goods: Computers, golf carts, bamboo, wines, acoustical equipment, caskets, missiles, parachutes, ships					
San Francisco, CA	Housing: 206 Food: 108 Other: 120	Income: $47,966 Taxes: $2,030 Bite: 4.23%	Blue-Collar Index: 81 White-Collar Index: 119 Unemployment Threat: Low	Income: 48.69% Jobs: 12.53%	6,063	88
	Goods: Dehydrated fruits and vegetables, canning, sheet metal, sugarcane products, paper, pulp, printing and publishing, clothing, tools, electronic parts, ships					

Metro Area	Living Costs (U.S. Avg.=100)	Average Household Income and Taxes	Occupations (U.S. Avg.=100)	Five-Year Growth Income and Jobs	Places Rated Score	Places Rated Rank
★ San Jose, CA	Housing: 192 Food: 101 Other: 104	Income: $41,994 Taxes: $1,594 Bite: 3.80%	Blue-Collar Index: 93 White-Collar Index: 107 Unemployment Threat: Low	Income: 57.98% Jobs: 29.70%	7,270	24
	Goods: Computers, electronic components, food canning, wine, beer, berries, atomic generating equipment					
Santa Barbara–Santa Maria–Lompoc, CA	Housing: 186 Food: 95* Other: 105*	Income: $36,501 Taxes: $1,230 Bite: 3.37%	Blue-Collar Index: 91 White-Collar Index: 109 Unemployment Threat: Low	Income: 51.19% Jobs: 13.37%	5,821	116
	Goods: Aircraft parts, electrical products, gimcracks, meat products, frozen foods, phonograph records, oil					
Santa Cruz, CA	Housing: 171 Food: 101* Other: 104*	Income: $32,608 Taxes: $998 Bite: 3.06%	Blue-Collar Index: 95 White-Collar Index: 105 Unemployment Threat: Low	Income: 41.49% Jobs: 16.95%	5,335	170
	Goods: Limes, chewing gum, wine, wire, lumber and wood products, electrical products					
Santa Rosa–Petaluma, CA	Housing: 155 Food: 108* Other: 120*	Income: $31,743 Taxes: $941 Bite: 2.96%	Blue-Collar Index: 98 White-Collar Index: 102 Unemployment Threat: Low	Income: 44.77% Jobs: 22.63%	5,703	127
	Goods: Wine, optical goods, macaroni, dairy products, fruits					
★ Sarasota, FL	Housing: 115 Food: 97* Other: 100*	Income: $39,474 Taxes: $378 Bite: 0.96%	Blue-Collar Index: 94 White-Collar Index: 106 Unemployment Threat: Low	Income: 51.56% Jobs: 28.98%	7,715	11
	Goods: Boats, citrus fruits, celery, mobile homes, electrical equipment					
Savannah, GA	Housing: 83 Food: 97* Other: 103*	Income: $27,359 Taxes: $989 Bite: 3.61%	Blue-Collar Index: 109 White-Collar Index: 91 Unemployment Threat: Moderate	Income: 44.73% Jobs: 10.38%	5,591	144
	Goods: Ships, fish, timber, asphalt, airplanes, plywood, sugar, paper bags					
Scranton–Wilkes-Barre, PA	Housing: 80 Food: 101 Other: 102	Income: $26,532 Taxes: $812 Bite: 3.06%	Blue-Collar Index: 119 White-Collar Index: 81 Unemployment Threat: High	Income: 43.19% Jobs: −0.36%	4,907	233
	Goods: Shoes, artillery shells, swimming pools, wire rope, pencils, rayon, silk, chewing gum, television tubes					
Seattle, WA	Housing: 122 Food: 103* Other: 112*	Income: $37,069 Taxes: $546 Bite: 1.47%	Blue-Collar Index: 95 White-Collar Index: 105 Unemployment Threat: Low	Income: 39.24% Jobs: 14.71%	5,901	106
	Goods: Commercial and military jet aircraft, fisheries, electronic components, lumber					
Sharon, PA	Housing: 80 Food: 107* Other: 106*	Income: $26,392 Taxes: $809 Bite: 3.07%	Blue-Collar Index: 123 White-Collar Index: 77 Unemployment Threat: High	Income: 35.00% Jobs: −7.76%	4,055	307
	Goods: Railroad tank cars, chains, pipes and tubes					
Sheboygan, WI	Housing: 97 Food: 96* Other: 95*	Income: $30,923 Taxes: $1,391 Bite: 4.50%	Blue-Collar Index: 124 White-Collar Index: 76 Unemployment Threat: High	Income: 39.22% Jobs: −5.45%	4,765	253
	Goods: Bratwurst, sausage, enamelware, clothes, brooms, cheese					
Sherman–Denison, TX	Housing: 69 Food: 105 Other: 93	Income: $29,386 Taxes: $214 Bite: 0.73%	Blue-Collar Index: 118 White-Collar Index: 82 Unemployment Threat: High	Income: 49.65% Jobs: 6.77%	6,213	75
	Goods: Medical supplies, earth augers, cotton and wool clothing, flour, soybeans, margarine, meat					
Shreveport, LA	Housing: 78 Food: 104 Other: 105	Income: $30,817 Taxes: $319 Bite: 1.04%	Blue-Collar Index: 109 White-Collar Index: 91 Unemployment Threat: Moderate	Income: 54.97% Jobs: 11.84%	6,585	50
	Goods: Chain saws, cast metals, electrical equipment, sheet metal, feeds, lumber and wood products					
Sioux City, IA–NE	Housing: 78 Food: 92* Other: 97*	Income: $29,565 Taxes: $961 Bite: 3.25%	Blue-Collar Index: 104 White-Collar Index: 96 Unemployment Threat: Moderate	Income: 32.60% Jobs: −4.64%	4,648	263
	Goods: Autos, fishing tackle, forklifts, popcorn, radios, stock feeds					
Sioux Falls, SD	Housing: 96 Food: 96 Other: 105	Income: $31,377 Taxes: $350 Bite: 1.12%	Blue-Collar Index: 98 White-Collar Index: 102 Unemployment Threat: Low	Income: 35.08% Jobs: 6.31%	5,204	192
	Goods: Meat, bakery products, granite, sash weights, microwave appliances, dairy products					

Metro Area	Living Costs (U.S. Avg.=100)	Average Household Income and Taxes	Occupations (U.S. Avg.=100)	Five-Year Growth Income and Jobs	Places Rated Score	Places Rated Rank
South Bend–Mishawaka, IN	Housing: 71 Food: 97 Other: 92	Income: $29,604 Taxes: $963 Bite: 3.25%	Blue-Collar Index: 106 White-Collar Index: 94 Unemployment Threat: Moderate	Income: 36.44% Jobs: −3.51%	5,056	216
	Goods: Power transmission equipment, plastic-coated fabric, pajamas, varnish, auto equipment, machine tools					
Spokane, WA	Housing: 83 Food: 104* Other: 99*	Income: $27,549 Taxes: $443 Bite: 1.61%	Blue-Collar Index: 96 White-Collar Index: 104 Unemployment Threat: Low	Income: 32.40% Jobs: 3.75%	4,722	259
	Goods: Silver, lead, zinc, aluminum, magnesium, clay, cement products, flour, feeds, cereals					
Springfield, IL	Housing: 95 Food: 87 Other: 96	Income: $32,790 Taxes: $1,056 Bite: 3.22%	Blue-Collar Index: 84 White-Collar Index: 116 Unemployment Threat: Low	Income: 34.95% Jobs: 5.22%	5,384	165
	Goods: Road tractors, heavy machinery, radio parts, yeast, electrical meters, cereal products					
Springfield, MA	Housing: 96 Food: 94* Other: 96*	Income: $29,327 Taxes: $1,290 Bite: 4.40%	Blue-Collar Index: 107 White-Collar Index: 93 Unemployment Threat: Moderate	Income: 45.15% Jobs: 2.23%	5,289	177
	Goods: Women's underwear, plastic tile, surgical dressings, matches, firearms, envelopes					
Springfield, MO	Housing: 76 Food: 95 Other: 95	Income: $27,266 Taxes: $677 Bite: 2.48%	Blue-Collar Index: 105 White-Collar Index: 95 Unemployment Threat: Moderate	Income: 45.56% Jobs: 11.95%	5,932	103
	Goods: Typewriters, paper cups, furniture, eggs, milk, flour, meat					
Stamford, CT	Housing: 283 Food: 110* Other: 103*	Income: $47,258 Taxes: $546 Bite: 1.16%	Blue-Collar Index: 79 White-Collar Index: 121 Unemployment Threat: Low	Income: 53.37% Jobs: 17.60%	6,158	79
	Goods: Plastics, ball bearings, postage meters, electric shavers, X-ray tubes, ships					
State College, PA	Housing: 101 Food: 98* Other: 100*	Income: $23,270 Taxes: $714 Bite: 3.07%	Blue-Collar Index: 96 White-Collar Index: 104 Unemployment Threat: Low	Income: 43.52% Jobs: 4.91%	4,677	262
	Goods: Dairy, poultry, grain					
Steubenville–Weirton, OH–WV	Housing: 79 Food: 100* Other: 92*	Income: $27,823 Taxes: $768 Bite: 2.76%	Blue-Collar Index: 132 White-Collar Index: 68 Unemployment Threat: High	Income: 26.67% Jobs: −13.27%	3,744	317
	Goods: Iron, steel, ferrous alloys, fireclay, coke, tar, tinplate containers, petrochemicals					
Stockton, CA	Housing: 102 Food: 98* Other: 99*	Income: $30,713 Taxes: $894 Bite: 2.91%	Blue-Collar Index: 107 White-Collar Index: 93 Unemployment Threat: Moderate	Income: 39.54% Jobs: 14.27%	5,672	131
	Goods: Auto windshields, glass containers, plows, paving machinery, cereal products, ships					
Syracuse, NY	Housing: 92 Food: 100 Other: 94	Income: $30,114 Taxes: $1,221 Bite: 4.05%	Blue-Collar Index: 100 White-Collar Index: 100 Unemployment Threat: Moderate	Income: 50.15% Jobs: −22.15%	4,474	282
	Goods: Telephone equipment, roller bearings, soda ash, purses, china, wax candles, washing machines, electronic components					
Tacoma, WA	Housing: 93 Food: 103 Other: 112	Income: $28,683 Taxes: $464 Bite: 1.62%	Blue-Collar Index: 104 White-Collar Index: 96 Unemployment Threat: Moderate	Income: 34.70% Jobs: 7.71%	4,887	238
	Goods: Railroad-car wheels, meat, fish, flour, copper, gold, aluminum, ships					
Tallahassee, FL	Housing: 96 Food: 99 Other: 96	Income: $24,144 Taxes: $280 Bite: 1.16%	Blue-Collar Index: 77 White-Collar Index: 123 Unemployment Threat: Low	Income: 45.36% Jobs: 25.82%	6,021	96
	Goods: Crates, boxes, boats, pine extracts, feed, insecticides, sweet potatoes					
★ Tampa–St. Petersburg–Clearwater, FL	Housing: 89 Food: 96* Other: 101*	Income: $29,890 Taxes: $310 Bite: 1.04%	Blue-Collar Index: 80 White-Collar Index: 120 Unemployment Threat: Low	Income: 52.61% Jobs: 30.23%	7,256	25
	Goods: Cigars, cigar boxes, beer, macaroni, brooms, ceramics, phosphate					
Terre Haute, IN	Housing: 66 Food: 95* Other: 102*	Income: $26,244 Taxes: $872 Bite: 3.32%	Blue-Collar Index: 111 White-Collar Index: 89 Unemployment Threat: Moderate	Income: 33.21% Jobs: −5.16%	4,353	291
	Goods: Phonograph records, picnic boxes, coolers, baking powder, antibiotics, heavy road machinery					
Texarkana, TX–Texarkana, AR	Housing: 69 Food: 104 Other: 91	Income: $25,947 Taxes: $192 Bite: 0.74%	Blue-Collar Index: 115 White-Collar Index: 85 Unemployment Threat: Moderate	Income: 26.39% Jobs: 8.45%	4,772	252
	Goods: Mobile homes, tires, blue jeans, pulp, wood and paper, battery cases					

Metro Area	Living Costs (U.S. Avg.=100)	Average Household Income and Taxes	Occupations (U.S. Avg.=100)	Five-Year Growth Income and Jobs	Places Rated Score	Places Rated Rank
Toledo, OH	Housing: 93 Food: 100* Other: 103*	Income: $30,497 Taxes: $873 Bite: 2.86%	Blue-Collar Index: 107 White-Collar Index: 93 Unemployment Threat: Moderate	Income: 33.53% Jobs: −3.31%	4,534	275
	Goods: Auto axles, drive shafts, glass, spark plugs, die castings, gypsum, atomizers					
Topeka, KS	Housing: 85 Food: 102* Other: 105*	Income: $33,199 Taxes: $864 Bite: 2.60%	Blue-Collar Index: 96 White-Collar Index: 104 Unemployment Threat: Low	Income: 40.97% Jobs: 0.94%	5,464	157
	Goods: Serum, tires, cast metals, printing and publishing, flour mills, meat, poultry, egg packing					
Trenton, NJ	Housing: 127 Food: 108* Other: 105*	Income: $36,520 Taxes: $999 Bite: 2.74%	Blue-Collar Index: 89 White-Collar Index: 111 Unemployment Threat: Low	Income: 49.08% Jobs: 4.59%	5,772	121
	Goods: Refrigerated showcases, light bulbs, rubber goods, purses, auto-body hardware, pottery					
Tucson, AZ	Housing: 102 Food: 101 Other: 105	Income: $27,913 Taxes: $834 Bite: 2.99%	Blue-Collar Index: 96 White-Collar Index: 104 Unemployment Threat: Low	Income: 47.46% Jobs: 22.89%	6,147	81
	Goods: Air conditioners, missiles, airplane instruments, ammunition, dental tools, women's clothing, cotton, grain, cattle					
Tulsa, OK	Housing: 90 Food: 106 Other: 104	Income: $35,700 Taxes: $891 Bite: 2.50%	Blue-Collar Index: 103 White-Collar Index: 97 Unemployment Threat: Moderate	Income: 50.98% Jobs: 21.01%	7,115	31
	Goods: Oil, petroleum products, meats, feeds, fishing rods, natural gas, boilers, burners					
Tuscaloosa, AL	Housing: 78 Food: 105 Other: 102	Income: $23,531 Taxes: $745 Bite: 3.17%	Blue-Collar Index: 105 White-Collar Index: 95 Unemployment Threat: Moderate	Income: 43.41% Jobs: 5.59%	4,900	235
	Goods: Truck bodies, tires, monuments, fishing lures, fertilizer					
★ Tyler, TX	Housing: 88 Food: 102 Other: 104	Income: $32,930 Taxes: $235 Bite: 0.71%	Blue-Collar Index: 111 White-Collar Index: 89 Unemployment Threat: Moderate	Income: 56.23% Jobs: 22.89%	7,327	23
	Goods: Battery cases, baskets, soil pipe, cast metals, water heaters					
Utica–Rome, NY	Housing: 81 Food: 100* Other: 99*	Income: $27,305 Taxes: $1,035 Bite: 3.79%	Blue-Collar Index: 106 White-Collar Index: 94 Unemployment Threat: Moderate	Income: 47.11% Jobs: 0.29%	5,226	189
	Goods: Golf clubs, fishing tackle, copper products, furnaces, magnesium castings, mufflers					
Vallejo–Fairfield–Napa, CA	Housing: 126 Food: 108* Other: 100*	Income: $31,578 Taxes: $933 Bite: 2.95%	Blue-Collar Index: 104 White-Collar Index: 96 Unemployment Threat: Moderate	Income: 43.14% Jobs: 18.53%	5,819	117
	Goods: Wine, flour, window screens, athletic equipment, sheet metal					
Vancouver, WA	Housing: 108 Food: 106* Other: 112*	Income: $28,767 Taxes: $464 Bite: 1.61%	Blue-Collar Index: 111 White-Collar Index: 89 Unemployment Threat: Moderate	Income: 31.79% Jobs: 7.70%	4,571	272
	Goods: Beer, pulp and paper, chemicals, brick, aluminum, lumber, paint, salmon, poultry					
★ Victoria, TX	Housing: 86 Food: 103 Other: 104	Income: $32,824 Taxes: $235 Bite: 0.72%	Blue-Collar Index: 117 White-Collar Index: 83 Unemployment Threat: High	Income: 55.17% Jobs: 28.92%	7,599	16
	Goods: Boats, chemicals, concrete, cotton compresses					
Vineland–Millville–Bridgeton, NJ	Housing: 87 Food: 108* Other: 105*	Income: $28,050 Taxes: $749 Bite: 2.67%	Blue-Collar Index: 123 White-Collar Index: 77 Unemployment Threat: High	Income: 46.93% Jobs: −2.18%	5,023	219
	Goods: Fireworks, glassware, candy, fruit and dairy products					
Visalia–Tulare–Porterville, CA	Housing: 93 Food: 99 Other: 100	Income: $25,804 Taxes: $730 Bite: 2.83%	Blue-Collar Index: 109 White-Collar Index: 91 Unemployment Threat: Moderate	Income: 36.90% Jobs: 22.67%	5,563	147
	Goods: Wine, carpet, transformers, fruit canning, electronic equipment					
Waco, TX	Housing: 73 Food: 108* Other: 100*	Income: $28,837 Taxes: $214 Bite: 0.74%	Blue-Collar Index: 108 White-Collar Index: 92 Unemployment Threat: Moderate	Income: 50.44% Jobs: 11.83%	6,259	71
	Goods: Work clothes, brooms, patio furniture, venetian blinds, asbestos					
Washington, DC–MD–VA	Housing: 165 Food: 107 Other: 107	Income: $41,888 Taxes: $2,371 Bite: 5.66%	Blue-Collar Index: 75 White-Collar Index: 125 Unemployment Threat: Low	Income: 47.67% Jobs: 13.44%	6,072	87
	Goods: Printing and publishing, bakery goods, sausage, paper, paint, sewer pipe, textiles, railroad refrigerator cars					

Metro Area	Living Costs (U.S. Avg.=100)	Average Household Income and Taxes	Occupations (U.S. Avg.=100)	Five-Year Growth Income and Jobs	Places Rated Score	Places Rated Rank
Waterbury, CT	Housing: 120 Food: 110* Other: 103*	Income: $34,364 Taxes: $458 Bite: 1.33%	Blue-Collar Index: 113 White-Collar Index: 87 Unemployment Threat: Moderate	Income: 47.49% Jobs: 5.08%	5,656	135
	Goods: Brass and copper goods, clocks and watches, women's underwear, toys, tools, wire					
Waterloo–Cedar Falls, IA	Housing: 94 Food: 98* Other: 95*	Income: $30,881 Taxes: $1,025 Bite: 3.32%	Blue-Collar Index: 112 White-Collar Index: 88 Unemployment Threat: Moderate	Income: 33.91% Jobs: −8.63%	4,407	287
	Goods: Farm tractors, athletic uniforms, refrigerators, meat, cereal and grain					
Wausau, WI	Housing: 92 Food: 96 Other: 95	Income: $26,168 Taxes: $1,086 Bite: 4.15%	Blue-Collar Index: 113 White-Collar Index: 87 Unemployment Threat: Moderate	Income: 35.14% Jobs: −2.51%	4,300	295
	Goods: Roofing granules, raincoats, snowplows, nameplates, sashes, granite monuments					
★ West Palm Beach–Boca Raton–Delray Beach, FL	Housing: 126 Food: 106 Other: 108	Income: $39,620 Taxes: $378 Bite: 0.95%	Blue-Collar Index: 96 White-Collar Index: 104 Unemployment Threat: Low	Income: 53.12% Jobs: 38.48%	7,992	8
	Goods: Aircraft equipment, transistors, tools and dies, fishing tackle					
Wheeling, WV–OH	Housing: 79 Food: 102* Other: 94*	Income: $27,594 Taxes: $859 Bite: 3.11%	Blue-Collar Index: 120 White-Collar Index: 80 Unemployment Threat: High	Income: 34.96% Jobs: 0.44%	4,740	256
	Goods: Metal stamping, garbage cans, washtubs, toys, brass, tinplate					
Wichita, KS	Housing: 85 Food: 101* Other: 103*	Income: $34,812 Taxes: $917 Bite: 2.63%	Blue-Collar Index: 107 White-Collar Index: 93 Unemployment Threat: Moderate	Income: 46.00% Jobs: 3.37%	6,036	92
	Goods: Airplanes, household appliances, oil, wheat, grain, meat					
Wichita Falls, TX	Housing: 77 Food: 108 Other: 101	Income: $33,877 Taxes: $235 Bite: 0.69%	Blue-Collar Index: 112 White-Collar Index: 88 Unemployment Threat: Moderate	Income: 57.64% Jobs: 6.11%	6,805	41
	Goods: Float glass, cotton gins, oil-field machinery, surgical dressings, beef, electrical equipment					
Williamsport, PA	Housing: 87 Food: 101* Other: 102*	Income: $26,317 Taxes: $807 Bite: 3.07%	Blue-Collar Index: 122 White-Collar Index: 78 Unemployment Threat: High	Income: 20.24% Jobs: −7.62%	3,288	327
	Goods: Crepe paper, airplane and marine engines, stainless steel, wire rope, flashbulbs					
Wilmington, DE–NJ–MD	Housing: 95 Food: 103* Other: 103*	Income: $33,927 Taxes: $1,358 Bite: 4.00%	Blue-Collar Index: 100 White-Collar Index: 100 Unemployment Threat: Moderate	Income: 44.89% Jobs: 13.44%	6,174	77
	Goods: Chemicals, explosives, leather goods, cork, floor coverings, ships, iron, barges, yachts					
Wilmington, NC	Housing: 82 Food: 97 Other: 98	Income: $26,633 Taxes: $1,005 Bite: 3.77%	Blue-Collar Index: 111 White-Collar Index: 89 Unemployment Threat: Moderate	Income: 41.38% Jobs: 10.09%	5,390	164
	Goods: Scrap iron, heavy machinery, paper, creosote, synthetic fibers, chemicals					
Worcester, MA	Housing: 104 Food: 94 Other: 97	Income: $29,374 Taxes: $1,292 Bite: 4.40%	Blue-Collar Index: 103 White-Collar Index: 97 Unemployment Threat: Moderate	Income: 44.94% Jobs: −0.87%	5,040	218
	Goods: Abrasives and grinding wheels, woolens and worsteds, machine tools, knives, firearms, thread, brushes					
Yakima, WA	Housing: 77 Food: 104 Other: 99	Income: $26,972 Taxes: $443 Bite: 1.64%	Blue-Collar Index: 109 White-Collar Index: 91 Unemployment Threat: Moderate	Income: 31.89% Jobs: 9.53%	4,986	223
	Goods: Wine, canvas goods, lumber, dried fruit, fruit sizers, sprayers, farm machinery					
York, PA	Housing: 100 Food: 98 Other: 102	Income: $28,985 Taxes: $879 Bite: 3.03%	Blue-Collar Index: 125 White-Collar Index: 75 Unemployment Threat: High	Income: 40.01% Jobs: 2.69%	4,946	226
	Goods: Hydraulic turbines, pretzels, furniture, refrigerating and air-conditioning equipment					
Youngstown–Warren, OH	Housing: 84 Food: 100 Other: 93	Income: $28,960 Taxes: $814 Bite: 2.81%	Blue-Collar Index: 122 White-Collar Index: 78 Unemployment Threat: High	Income: 30.30% Jobs: −14.27%	3,894	313
	Goods: Iron, steel, sheet metal and tubing, limestone, auto parts, fire extinguishers, ball bearings					
Yuba City, CA	Housing: 94 Food: 99* Other: 100*	Income: $27,501 Taxes: $724 Bite: 2.63%	Blue-Collar Index: 103 White-Collar Index: 97 Unemployment Threat: Moderate	Income: 30.46% Jobs: 8.21%	4,694	261
	Goods: Concrete pipe, seed cleaners, fruit canning					

WHERE THE MILLIONAIRES ARE

Figures compiled by the U.S. Trust Company in 1980 will make you think twice about the frowsy housewife in front of you in the supermarket checkout line: There are an estimated 574,300 millionaires in the United States, and not all of them live in Beverly Hills and Palm Beach.

The Gettys, Hunts, and Hearsts are where you would expect to find them, monitoring their empires from California, Texas, and New York. These states—along with Florida, Illinois, New Jersey, Ohio, Pennsylvania, Connecticut, and Michigan—have the greatest number of millionaires. But surprisingly, when the number of millionaires is related to the population of the state, the list looks quite different. Idaho, North Dakota, and Maine lead in terms of millionaires per 100,000 population, mainly because of the high land value and sparse population common in most agricultural states. California, Texas, and New York rank substantially lower because of their denser populations.

Millionaires per 100,000: The States Ranked

State	Millionaires per 100,000 Population	State	Millionaires per 100,000 Population
1. Idaho	2,621	26. Oklahoma	205
2. North Dakota	914	27. Mississippi	194
3. Maine	696	28. South Carolina	189
4. Nebraska	686	29. North Carolina	187
5. Minnesota	574	30. Michigan	171
6. Iowa	462	31. Washington	169
7. Indiana	453	32. California	163
8. Wisconsin	452	33. Texas	162
9. Montana	390	34. Alabama	161
10. New Jersey	389	34. Rhode Island	161
11. Connecticut	387	36. Virginia	153
12. Delaware	343	37. Pennsylvania	148
13. New York	319	38. Kentucky	146
14. Massachusetts	315	38. Louisiana	146
15. Illinois	311	40. South Dakota	136
16. Florida	303	41. Missouri	123
17. Kansas	293	42. Arizona	115
18. Ohio	289	43. Oregon	102
19. Tennessee	288	44. New Hampshire	97
20. Hawaii	269	45. Maryland/D.C.	86
21. Colorado	267	46. West Virginia	65
22. Vermont	239	47. Utah	56
23. Alaska	223	48. Arkansas	44
23. New Mexico	223	49. Nevada	35
25. Georgia	209	50. Wyoming	29

Source: U.S. Trust Company of New York, 1980 National Wealth Survey.

EXPENSIVE NEIGHBORHOODS: WHERE MONEY INCOME IS HIGHEST

Just as incomes are higher in metro areas than in the rural countryside, so are they higher in certain suburbs within a metro area. Among all the 7,749 incorporated cities, towns, boroughs, villages, and other places in the United States that have populations over 2,500, per capita money incomes in 75 metro area suburbs are at least two and a half times the national average of $7,298.

Where is the highest figure found? Not in tony Beverly Hills, Lake Forest, nor Chevy Chase. It's in Hunters Creek Village, out on Memorial Drive west of Houston, where average per capita income is a comfortable $32,859 a year.

The 34 Metro Areas with the Most Affluent Suburbs

Albany–Schenectady–Troy, NY
Schaghticoke

Anaheim–Santa Ana, CA
Newport Beach

Bergen–Passaic, NJ
Saddle River

Birmingham, AL
Mountain Brook

Chicago, IL
Barrington Hills
Flossmoor
Glencoe
Inverness
Kenilworth
Oak Brook
Olympia Fields
Winnetka

Cincinnati, OH–KY–IN
Amberly
Village of Indian Hill

Cleveland, OH
Pepper Pike

Dallas, TX
Highland Park

Denver, CO
Cherry Hills

Detroit, MI
Bloomfield
Franklin
Grosse Pointe Farms
Grosse Pointe Shores

Houston, TX
Bunker Hill Village
Hunters Creek Village
Piney Point Village

Kansas City, KS
Mission Hills

Lake County, IL
Lake Forest
Lincolnshire
Riverwoods

Los Angeles–Long Beach, CA
Beverly Hills
Marina Del Rey
Palos Verdes Estates
Rolling Hills Estates
San Marino
Woodside

Miami–Hialeah, FL
Bal Harbour
Key Biscayne

Milwaukee, WI
Elm Grove
Fox Point

Minneapolis–St. Paul, MN–WI
North Oaks

Nashville, TN
Belle Meade
Forest Hills

Nassau–Suffolk, NY
East Hills
Flower Hill
Great Neck Estates
Kings Point
Lloyd Harbor
Muttontown
Old Westbury
Sands Point
Scarsdale

New York, NY
Bronxville

Newark, NJ
Harding
Millburn

Oklahoma City, OK
Nichols Hills

Pittsburgh, PA
Fox Chapel

Riverside–San Bernardino, CA
Rancho Mirage

Saginaw–Bay City–Midland, MI
Spaulding

St. Louis, MO–IL
Frontenac
Ladue
Town and Country

San Diego, CA
Rancho Santa Fe

San Francisco, CA
Atherton
Hillsborough
Portola Valley
Ross
Sausalito
Tiburon

San Jose, CA
Los Altos Hills

Seattle, WA
Clyde Hill
Medina

Stamford, CT
Darien
New Canaan
Toledo, OH
Ottawa Hills

Washington, DC–MD–VA
Chevy Chase Section Four
West Palm Beach–Boca
Raton–Delray Beach, FL
Palm Beach

Source: U.S. Bureau of the Census, *1980 Census of Population and Housing.*

THE TAXMAN COMETH

Question: Where in America can you find rock-bottom property taxes, no sales taxes, no taxes on any of your sources of income, no niggling nickel-and-dime fees for registering a car or taking out a license to catch largemouth bass, and no inheritance taxes for your heirs to pay?

Answer: Dream on. This ideal tax haven would have to combine the low property taxes of Louisiana, New Hampshire's absence of retail sales taxes, South Dakota's forgiveness of taxes on personal income, South Carolina's light licensing fees, and Nevada's lack of estate taxes. Unfortunately, you just can't find all these wonderful tax breaks in one state.

Most Americans don't object to governments raising money through taxes, according to 1983 polls conducted by the Advisory Commission on Intergovernmental Relations. What they do object to is the effect certain levies have on their lives. Although federal income taxes take the same bite whether you live in New Bedford, New Orleans, or New York, state taxes can differ dramatically around the country. Sales taxes, excise taxes, license taxes, income taxes, property taxes, death taxes, gift taxes, severance taxes, and head taxes are just some of the forms that state taxes take. Depending on where you live, you may encounter all of them or only a few.

Property Taxes. Taxes on land and the buildings on it—whether they are homes, farms, industrial plants, or commercial buildings—are the biggest source of cash for local governments. They are imposed not by states but by the 13,527 cities, townships, counties, school districts, sanitary districts, hospital districts, and other assessing jurisdictions in the nation. The states' role is to specify the maximum rate on the market value of the property, or a percentage of it, as the legal standard for local assessors to follow. The local assessor determines the value to be taxed. If you think the valuation is too high, you have a limited right of appeal.

You can't escape property taxes in any state except Alaska (where you must be over 65 to take advantage of that break), but you can find significantly low rates in certain parts of the country. Nationally, the average bills on homes amount to 1.25 percent of their market value, whereas the average bills in Alabama, Arizona, Hawaii, Louisiana, and West Virginia are based on less than half that rate.

Sales Taxes. If Americans had a choice of raising income taxes or raising sales taxes, they would overwhelmingly opt for the latter, according to recent polls. Sometimes called retail taxes or consumption taxes, sales taxes are collected at the retail level on the purchase of goods. After property taxes, they account for the second largest source of revenue for state and local governments.

Among the states, the average sales tax is 5 percent. If you're living in Connecticut, you're paying the nation's highest state rate: 7.5 percent. But the highest rate paid by anyone in the country is the 8.5 percent levied on retail purchases in New York City's five boroughs, a rate created in 1975 to help the city stay afloat.

Five states—Alaska, Delaware, Montana, New Hampshire, and Oregon—collect no sales taxes at all. To a four-person family, this could mean a savings of hundreds of dollars. But you can avoid paying almost that much in states where such basics as food, medicine, and clothing are excluded from any sales tax.

Personal Income Taxes. When the first federal income tax went into effect in 1913, two states—Mississippi and Wisconsin—were already collecting income taxes on their own. It was only during the 1920s and 1930s that the majority of states began to raise cash by tapping personal incomes. Today, 40 states impose the tax; two (New Hampshire and Tennessee) apply it only to income from interest and dividends; one (Connecticut) applies it only to income from capital gains and dividends; and seven (Alaska, Florida, Nevada, South Dakota, Texas, Washington, and Wyoming) don't tax incomes at all.

License Taxes. These usually are enacted as flat fees for regulating a certain kind of privilege. For example, you'll pay a license tax on the family car for the right to use it on public highways; you'll buy a fishing license for the privilege of trolling for trout at the lake main-

---

Taxing the Necessities

You'll pay sales tax on groceries in . . .

Alabama	Mississippi	South Carolina
Arkansas	Missouri	South Dakota
Georgia	Nebraska	Tennessee
Hawaii	New Mexico	Utah
Idaho	North Carolina	Virginia
Kansas	Oklahoma	Wyoming
Michigan		

And sales tax on medicine in . . .

Arizona	Michigan	Utah
Arkansas	Mississippi	Vermont
Georgia	Missouri	Virginia
Hawaii	New Mexico	

But NO sales tax on clothes in . . .

Massachusetts	New Jersey
Minnesota	Rhode Island

And NO sales tax, period, in . . .

Alaska	New Hampshire
Delaware	Oregon
Montana	

Source: Commerce Clearing House, *State Tax Guide,* 1984.

Comparing Direct Tax Burdens: The States Ranked

State	Per Capita Burden	Percent of U.S. Average	State	Per Capita Burden	Percent of U.S. Average
1. New Hampshire	$ 77	15.12%	26. North Carolina	$450	88.28%
2. Alaska	197	38.72	27. Kansas	456	89.57
3. Montana	285	55.97	28. Oregon	457	89.63
4. Texas	300	58.89	29. Louisiana	459	90.21
5. Florida	320	62.84	30. Oklahoma	460	90.30
6. Nevada	362	70.98	31. Georgia	483	94.85
7. Vermont	363	71.36	32. Pennsylvania	505	99.17
8. Tennessee	367	72.15	33. Michigan	510	100.20
9. Connecticut	371	72.87	34. Colorado	511	100.31
10. South Dakota	376	73.86	35. Iowa	517	101.60
11. North Dakota	380	74.56	36. Illinois	523	102.82
12. Arkansas	401	78.77	37. Washington	528	103.82
12. New Jersey	401	78.77	38. Utah	535	105.20
14. Ohio	421	82.70	39. Delaware	545	107.15
15. Mississippi	424	83.22	40. Arizona	549	107.77
16. Alabama	434	85.23	41. New Mexico	556	109.19
17. Missouri	436	85.57	42. Massachusetts	565	110.88
18. Idaho	438	86.09	43. Virginia	575	112.81
19. Maine	439	86.10	44. Minnesota	605	118.78
20. Nebraska	440	86.41	45. Wisconsin	611	119.97
21. Indiana	443	87.02	46. Wyoming	622	122.23
22. South Carolina	446	87.53	47. Maryland	662	129.91
22. West Virginia	446	87.53	48. California	691	135.62
24. Kentucky	447	87.67	49. New York	788	154.65
25. Rhode Island	449	88.20	50. Hawaii	982	192.80

Source: Derived from the Advisory Commission on Intergovernmental Relations, *Tax Capacity of the Fifty States*, 1983.

Direct taxes include taxes on personal income, general sales, gasoline, driver's licenses, and automobile registration fees. The U.S. average per capita burden is $509.

tained by the state; you'll need a retail license to serve up beer and wine at the roadhouse you've just bought. Together, these license taxes and fees make up a small part of a state's revenues. Of all the states, Wyoming gets the most money per capita from the various taxes on driving a car, and New York—surprisingly—the least. Alaska's taxes on hunting and fishing privileges are the steepest in the country, Indiana's the lightest. If you're going to open a bar in Alaska or West Virginia, you can expect to shell out the highest license fees in the nation, whereas in Hawaii, Nevada, Wisconsin, and Wyoming, you'd pay nothing.

Excise Taxes. In most states, when you return from an errand having bought a tankful of gas for the family car, a bottle of gin, and a pack of cigarettes, you've also just paid excise taxes. Excise taxes are related to sales taxes but are different in that they are levied only on specific items. Gasoline at the pump, for example, is taxed in every state at a higher rate than the local sales tax rate (excise taxes on gasoline are heaviest in Wyoming, lightest in Texas). Tobacco and alcohol, too, are big targets for excise taxes, usually at rates that suggest social disapproval. In fact, taxes on cigarettes and liquor are popularly called sin taxes.

Estate and Inheritance Taxes. Death duties, as they are called sometimes, are taxes imposed when any kind of real property is transferred at death. They are imposed on the dead person's estate under the Federal Estate Tax, and in most states they take the form of inheritance taxes on the beneficiaries of the estate.

The philosophy underlying estate and inheritance taxes is that heirs should be required to pay a tax on additions to their wealth that they receive as an inheritance. To make the laws stick, however, gift taxes are also levied. Otherwise, property could be passed on tax-free by the owner in anticipation of death. Even though death and gift taxes are minor sources of revenue, several states—California, Connecticut, Iowa, New Jersey, and Pennsylvania—take greater pains to tap this source than the others.

GOLDEN TRIANGLES, RESEARCH TRIANGLES

One of the few areas in the nation left untouched by the Great Depression was the humid East Texas oil fields, where the Lone Star State's most famous gusher, at Spindletop Hill, began pumping atop a salt-dome formation near Beaumont in 1901. Over the years, companies the likes of Gulf, Union, Texaco, and Mobil have put up sprawling tank farms and refineries to process a seemingly endless outpour of oil.

Bounded by three cities—Beaumont, Port Arthur, and Orange—the area is known as the Golden Triangle. Among Texas's 28 metro areas, it ranks second from the bottom in percentage of people who are college graduates, but seventh highest in personal income. In no other metro area in the state is there a greater portion of people with blue-collar jobs. Yet despite the Golden Triangle's history of prosperity, even during the flush times of 1983–84 the unemployment rate here didn't drop below 12 percent.

Northeast some 1,000 miles is an area bordered by North Carolina's capital, Raleigh, and two nearby cities, Chapel Hill and Durham. In their midst is Research Triangle Park, a 5,500-acre chunk of pinelands tenanted by think tanks and white-smock research firms. The Research Triangle, as the three cities together have come to be called, is as different from East Texas as it is from nearby metro areas dominated by low-wage jobs in textile, furniture, and cigarette factories. Here you'll find North Carolina's highest portion of people with college degrees, white-collar jobs, and high personal incomes. You'll also find one of the nation's lowest unemployment rates.

Two rules on which labor economists agree are that a factory job producing durable and nondurable goods is anything but durable, and that a job in construction seldom rests on solid ground. In each of the seven business recessions that have hit the United States since the end of World War II, blue-collar workers have been the principal job losers.

During the 1974 recession, one of every three metro areas experienced sharp increases in unemployment because of large numbers of blue-collar workers who punched time clocks, whether in automobile plants in the Great Lakes states, in Pacific Northwest lumber mills, in factories that produced iron and steel in the Ohio Valley, or in petrochemical refineries in the Gulf South.

Nor was the Sun Belt immune. Orlando, Miami, and several other Florida metro areas experienced sharp increases in their numbers of jobless. So did Phoenix. A large number of building tradespeople were caught when the vacation- and retirement-home construction boom fizzled in mid-decade.

It hasn't been any different during the latest slumps of 1980 and 1981–82. Every section of the country had its share of hard times, but the stories that came out of muscle-bound metro areas—places with the largest numbers of blue-collar workers, who for the most part build the homes and make the goods that consumers buy in confident times—were the saddest.

Just as metro areas can be rated for features as diverse as their climates, the quality of their restaurants, and their supply of public golf courses, so can they be rated for how vulnerable they are to high unemployment during a business slump. It can be said that the cyclical threat of unemployment is:

- *High* if blue-collar workers represent 40 percent or more of the total of white-collar and blue-collar workers in the metro area

- *Moderate* if blue-collar workers represent from 34 percent to 39 percent of the total of white-collar and blue-collar workers in the metro area
- *Low* if blue-collar workers represent 33 percent or less of the total of white-collar and blue-collar workers in the metro area

In the 329 metropolitan areas, the unemployment threat is high in 64, moderate in 162, and low in 103. (See the Place Profiles earlier in this chapter for the unemployment threat in each metro area.)

Unemployment Threat in the Metro Areas

Highest	Blue-Collar Workers as Percent of Total Workforce
1. Hickory, NC	60.04%
2. Danville, VA	57.45
3. Anderson, SC	56.41
4. Steubenville–Weirton, OH–WV	54.97
5. Pawtucket–Woonsocket–Attleboro, RI–MA	53.61
6. Burlington, NC	51.90
7. Anderson, IN	51.52
8. Gadsden, AL	51.49
9. Beaver County, PA	51.21
10. Fall River, MA–RI	50.77
Lowest	
1. Lake County, IL	17.42%
2. Atlanta, GA	17.86
3. Washington, DC–MD–VA	17.90
4. Tallahassee, FL	19.16
5. Stamford, CT	20.06
6. Tampa–St. Petersburg–Clearwater, FL	21.18
7. San Francisco, CA	21.58
8. Columbia, MO	21.70
9. Iowa City, IA	22.62
10. Madison, WI	22.65

Source: Derived from the U.S. Bureau of the Census, *1980 Census of Population and Housing*.

COLLECTING UNEMPLOYMENT

If you are laid off or fired, or if you leave your job because of unusual circumstances such as your religious beliefs, the threat of sexual harassment, or illness, you are eligible for weekly cash benefits under local unemployment insurance programs. Unlike qualifying for food stamps or fuel assistance, to receive unemployment benefits you do not have to prove need; you must only show that you are involuntarily out of work. In Southern California, actors and aerospace workers queue up for weekly checks; in New York, so do longshoremen and advertising executives.

The unemployment insurance program, established in 1935 as part of the Social Security Act, is run jointly by the federal and state governments and covers nearly all nonfarm workers. The program was designed to provide both people and the local economy with partial replacement of wages and purchasing power during short periods of joblessness.

The amount of your unemployment check is related to how much you were earning before you became

Unemployment Can Be Debilitating, Dangerous, and Deadly

Psychologists and physicians have long noted evidence of depression, anxiety, aggression, insomnia, loss of self-esteem, and marital problems among their patients who are out of work. The damage to the U.S. economy caused by the consecutive business slumps of 1980 and 1981–82 has been estimated at billions of dollars in lost output, but the costs to the jobless are still being totaled long after the start of the recovery.

According to M. Harvey Brenner, a Johns Hopkins University researcher who has studied the effects of business cycles on the nation's health, hard economic times are always followed by increases in the numbers of illnesses, crimes, and deaths. Based on the U.S. population in 1980, Dr. Brenner concludes that a 10 percent rise in unemployment (from 10 percent unemployment to 11 percent, for example) would result in:

> 5,885 more admissions to mental institutions
> 403,830 more criminal arrests, including
>   8,078 for fraud and embezzlement
>   4,919 for aggravated assault
> 24,450 more deaths, including
>   17,392 from heart disease and stroke
>   409 from cirrhosis
>   403 homicides
>   189 suicides

Source: U.S. Congress, Joint Economic Committee, Committee Prints 98–198 and 98–200, June 1984.

State	Legal Range of Payments	Average Weekly Check	Average Duration
Hawaii	$5–$188	$129.82	15 wks
Idaho	45–173	116.45	15
Illinois	50–209	146.01	19
Indiana	40–141	94.24	14
Iowa	22–176	137.26	15
Kansas	43–175	128.05	15
Kentucky	22–140	116.01	16
Louisiana	10–205	144.75	17
Maine	22–208	101.40	15
Maryland	25–175	116.14	16
Massachusetts	14–278	115.36	16
Michigan	55–197	154.38	17
Minnesota	52–198	137.08	17
Mississippi	30–115	79.72	14
Missouri	14–105	93.72	14
Montana	42–171	122.11	14
Nebraska	12–120	96.73	13
Nevada	16–162	116.00	15
New Hampshire	26–141	95.37	9
New Jersey	20–170	120.09	17
New Mexico	29–145	105.49	17
New York	40–180	98.88	20
North Carolina	15–166	104.02	11
North Dakota	60–185	127.61	14
Ohio	10–233	143.59	18
Oklahoma	16–197	137.22	12
Oregon	47–204	117.48	18
Pennsylvania	35–222	146.38	18
Rhode Island	37–194	107.67	15
South Carolina	21–125	93.83	12
South Dakota	28–129	109.53	13
Tennessee	30–115	87.02	15
Texas	27–182	126.91	12
Utah	46–186	129.68	16
Vermont	18–146	107.42	15
Virginia	54–150	108.17	11
Washington	51–185	130.68	18
West Virginia	18–225	129.58	16
Wisconsin	37–196	136.62	16
Wyoming	20–183	136.56	13

Source: U.S. Department of Labor, Employment and Training Administration, 1984.

unemployed, subject to a ceiling. Of the possible payments allowed by law, those paid to workers with families in Alaska, Connecticut, Massachusetts, Ohio, and West Virginia are the highest in the country; those in Arizona, Missouri, Mississippi, and Tennessee are the lowest.

Most states limit eligibility to 26 weeks, although the limit is 30 weeks in Massachusetts and Washington and 28 weeks in West Virginia. Alaska, California, Connecticut, and Oregon continue benefits beyond 26 weeks if the state suffers high unemployment. Hawaii will pay benefits beyond 26 weeks if a man-made disaster creates high unemployment. During steep business slumps countrywide, the Federal-State Extended Compensation Program lengthens the time of eligibility another 13 weeks.

Unemployment Insurance Benefits by State

State	Legal Range of Payments	Average Weekly Check	Average Duration
Alabama	$22–$120	$ 80.24	13 wks
Alaska	34–228	130.25	15
Arizona	40–115	100.10	16
Arkansas	40–154	96.06	13
California	30–166	99.87	18
Colorado	25–206	140.83	12
Connecticut	15–252	122.47	13
Delaware	20–165	98.04	14
Florida	10–150	95.28	13
Georgia	27–125	96.39	11

WHAT AND WHERE THE JOBS WILL BE BY 1995

Projections from the Bureau of Labor Statistics show the number of workers rising from 102 million in 1982, the base year for the projections, to between 125 million and 130 million in 1995. But technological and social changes mean that some jobs will go begging, others will be overcrowded, and still others will be obsolete.

Half of all the additional jobs will be found in only 40 of the thousands of possible occupations. Nearly all of these 40 jobs will require no extensive training, and only ten will require a college degree. The fastest-growing occupations, on the other hand, aren't found on the list that will add the most jobs over the period. These occupations are mainly in the health, data processing, or business services fields, and all of them will undoubtedly require extensive training.

Fewer people are expected to compete for many other jobs over the period, either because the occupations are becoming technologically obsolete (such as stenographers and telephone switchboard operators) or because they are found in dying industries (railroad conductors and brake operators).

The Top 40 Job Gainers, 1982–1995

Occupation	Growth in Thousands	Occupation	Growth in Thousands
1. Janitors and sextons	779	21. Licensed practical nurses	220
2. Cashiers	744	22. Computer-systems analysts	217
3. Secretaries	719	23. Electrical engineers	209
4. General office clerks	696	24. Computer programmers	205
5. Salesclerks	685	25. General maintenance repairers	193
6. Registered nurses	642	26. Helpers in trades	190
7. Waiters and waitresses	562	27. Receptionists	189
8. Kindergarten and elementary teachers	511	28. Electricians	173
9. Truck drivers	425	29. Physicians	163
10. Nursing aides and orderlies	423	30. Clerical supervisors	162
11. Technical sales representatives	386	31. Computer operators	160
12. Accountants and auditors	344	31. Nontechnical sales representatives	160
13. Automotive mechanics	324	33. Lawyers	159
14. Supervisors of blue-collar workers	319	34. Stockroom and warehouse clerks	156
15. Kitchen helpers	305	35. Typists	155
16. Guards and doorkeepers	300	36. Delivery and route workers	153
17. Fast-food restaurant workers	297	37. Bookkeepers	152
18. Retail-store managers	292	38. Restaurant cooks	149
19. Carpenters	247	39. Bank tellers	142
20. Electrical and electronic technicians	222	40. Short-order and fast-food cooks	141

Source: U.S. Bureau of Labor Statistics, *Monthly Labor Review*, November 1983.

WHAT IT TAKES TO JOIN THE *FORTUNE* CLUB

Imagine how long it would take to squander an inheritance of $1,686.7 billion. Even if you were to spend or give away $1 million of your endowment each day, it would take you 4,621 years—and 35 days. In 1983, the combined sales of the 500 industrial companies rated the nation's largest by *Fortune* magazine reached that figure, the largest annual total recorded by *Fortune* since it began compiling its list in 1955.

There are three basic requirements for admission to

Fortune's elite club of the top 500 corporations in the country:

- The firm must derive more than half its revenues from manufacturing or mining or both. Several large companies, most recently the Barnes Group (1982 rank: 484), have been dropped from the list because the portion of their sales coming from producer goods dropped below 50 percent.
- The firm's stock must be publicly traded rather than privately held, so that its financial records can be examined by anyone. Three companies, Cone Mills, Dan River, and Geosource, went private after a period of public ownership; consequently, they were ousted from the directory.
- The firm must ring up an annual sales total that places it among the top 500. For a quarter of a century, Detroit's General Motors reigned as the largest American industrial corporation. Since 1980, however, the first spot has been occupied by New York City's Exxon Corporation. In that year, Exxon also became the first company in *Fortune*'s directory to do more than 12 figures ($100 billion) in business. By 1983, Exxon's sales had declined to $88.6 billion.

Since 1970, there have been remarkable southerly and westerly shifts in the locations of corporate headquarters of the top 500. Atlanta, the home of Coca-Cola since the turn of the century, is now on the home office letterhead of six other firms on *Fortune*'s list. The number of high-tech members based in California's Silicon Valley (otherwise known as San Jose) has jumped from two to eight. Only 59 of the 500 had their headquarters in the Sun Belt in 1970; today, the number has more than doubled to 131.

Below are the 111 metro areas that were headquarters of one or more Fortune 500 firms as of 1983, along with the companies located there. (Twenty-three Fortune 500 companies are not included; their home offices aren't located within any metro area.) The companies are listed in order of their sales rank in the 500, which is given in parentheses. Exxon, in New York City, is ranked first; Tandem Computers, in Cupertino, California (the San Jose metro area), is number 500.

Fortune 500 Metro Areas

Akron, OH
Goodyear Tire & Rubber (32)
Firestone Tire & Rubber (95)
B. F. Goodrich (125)
General Tire & Rubber (168)

Albany–Schenectady–Troy, NY
Mohasco (393)

Allentown–Bethlehem, PA–NJ
Bethlehem Steel (69)

Air Products & Chemicals (212)
Mack Trucks (259)

Anaheim–Santa Ana, CA
Baker International (192)
Smith International (375)

Ann Arbor, MI
Hoover Universal (351)

Appleton–Oshkosh–Neenah, WI
Kimberly-Clark (120)

Atlanta, GA
Coca-Cola (48)
Georgia-Pacific (51)
Gold Kist (238)
National Service Industries (311)
Fuqua Industries (367)
Oxford Industries (450)
Royal Crown Companies (459)

Austin, TX
Tracor (495)

Baltimore, MD
Crown Central Petroleum (208)
Black & Decker Manufacturing (265)
Easco (457)

Battle Creek, MI
Kellogg (158)

Benton Harbor, MI
Whirlpool (147)
Clark Equipment (327)

Bergen–Passaic, NJ
CPC International (90)
American Cyanamid (107)
Kidde (161)
Ingersoll-Rand (165)
Union Camp (204)
Becton Dickinson (273)
BOC (282)
Thomas J. Lipton (293)
Federal Paper Board (423)
Prentice-Hall (477)

Birmingham, AL
Vulcan Materials (339)

Boise City, ID
Boise Cascade (113)

Boston, MA
Raytheon (59)
Digital Equipment (84)
Gillette (169)
Cabot (224)
Polaroid (256)
General Cinema (312)
EG&G (318)
Data General (335)
M/A-Com (395)
Dennison Manufacturing (399)
Foxboro (442)
Prime Computer (451)

Bridgeport–Milford, CT
General Electric (10)
Warnaco (456)

Buffalo, NY
Agway (98)

Canton, OH
Timken (310)
Hoover (387)
Diebold (483)

Charlotte–Gastonia–Rock Hill, NC–SC
Nucor (439)

Chattanooga, TN–GA
Dorsey (482)

Chicago, IL
Standard Oil of Indiana (8)
Dart & Kraft (33)
Beatrice Foods (36)
Consolidated Foods (49)
Motorola (81)
Esmark (88)
IC Industries (96)

International Harvester (104)
Borg-Warner (106)
FMC (110)
Inland Steel (127)
Abbott Laboratories (137)
Quaker Oats (146)
Swift Independent (152)
McGraw-Edison (175)
Northwest Industries (183)
Baxter Travenol Laboratories (191)
Gould (198)
National Can (210)
U.S. Gypsum (215)
Tribune (218)
R. R. Donnelley & Sons (226)
Morton Thiokol (231)
Marmon Group (235)
International Minerals & Chemical (237)
Zenith Radio (246)
Brunswick (260)
Square D (269)
G. D. Searle (296)
Hartmarx (304)
Interlake (332)
Dean Foods (333)
CBI Industries (337)
Household Manufacturing (340)
Lubrizol (343)
Outboard Marine (344)
Bell & Howell (379)
Nalco Chemical (389)
Stone Container (391)
Wm. Wrigley Jr. (414)
AM International (427)
Illinois Tool Works (455)
Amsted Industries (458)
Roper (462)
Ceco (469)
Pittway (491)
Masonite (499)

Cincinnati, OH–KY–IN
Procter & Gamble (22)
Cincinnati Milacron (433)
Eagle-Picher Industries (443)
Palm Beach (467)

Cleveland, OH
Standard Oil of Ohio (25)
TRW (63)
Eaton (138)
Republic Steel (145)
White Consolidated Industries (178)
Sherwin-Williams (184)
Parker Hannifin (289)
Midland-Ross (360)
American Greetings (369)
Scott & Fetzer (397)
Ferro (401)

Columbus, OH
Anchor Hocking (349)
Worthington Industries (475)

Dallas, TX
Texas Instruments (77)
LTV (78)
Diamond Shamrock (89)
Dresser Industries (112)
American Petrofina (176)
National Gypsum (270)
Mitchell Energy & Development (305)
Tyler (306)
Lafarge (324)
E-Systems (338)

Business Climates: How the States Stack Up

Does it make a difference where in the country a company makes its products? According to Alexander Grant & Company, a national accounting firm, it may matter a great deal.

In 1983, the Chicago-based firm surveyed state manufacturing associations for their views on 22 local economic factors they deemed necessary for business success. These included labor cost, productivity, unionization, and energy costs, plus such considerations under local government control as taxes, debts, welfare expenditures, and environmental regulations.

States that had flexible environmental controls, laws that kept organized labor in check, and the lowest taxes, welfare aid, and debts received the highest scores and were judged the most favorable places to do business.

A comparison of the growth in manufacturing jobs in each of the states over the past five years shows that the Alexander Grant ratings have some validity. With the exception of South Dakota, all of the states ranked among the top ten for business climate experienced strong gains. All of the states in the bottom ten either held their own or lost ground.

The States Ranked for Business Climate

State	Score	State	Score
1. Florida	79.4	26. New Hampshire	48.7
2. South Dakota	76.5	27. Maryland	48.6
3. North Dakota	74.0	28. New Mexico	48.1
4. Nebraska	71.1	29. New Jersey	47.2
5. Arizona	70.8	30. California	42.9
6. Texas	68.8	31. Iowa	42.6
7. Mississippi	66.8	32. Wyoming	41.8
8. Utah	66.3	33. Massachusetts	40.7
9. Arkansas	65.9	34. Connecticut	38.6
9. North Carolina	65.9	35. Vermont	37.8
11. Kansas	65.6	36. Delaware	37.7
12. Virginia	65.1	37. Maine	37.6
13. Georgia	65.0	38. Washington	34.5
14. Tennessee	60.6	39. New York	33.7
15. South Carolina	60.5	40. West Virginia	32.8
16. Louisiana	59.0	41. Pennsylvania	32.2
17. Idaho	58.7	42. Wisconsin	32.1
18. Colorado	58.2	43. Minnesota	29.4
19. Alabama	57.4	44. Illinois	29.3
20. Montana	57.0	45. Rhode Island	26.3
21. Oklahoma	56.9	46. Ohio	23.3
22. Missouri	56.6	47. Oregon	21.3
23. Nevada	55.0	48. Michigan	11.8
24. Kentucky	50.1		
25. Indiana	49.8		

Source: Alexander Grant & Company, *General Manufacturing Business Climates,* 1984.

Alaska and Hawaii are not included because their economies were considered too different from those of the other states for comparison.

Dr Pepper (432)
Trinity Industries (465)
Holly (484)

Danbury, CT
Union Carbide (37)
Lone Star Industries (313)
Bangor Punta (438)

Davenport–Rock Island–Moline, IA–IL
Deere (92)

Dayton–Springfield, OH
NCR (101)
Mead (149)
Dayco (371)

Decatur, IL
Archer-Daniels-Midland (83)
A. E. Staley Manufacturing (207)

Denver, CO
Manville (199)
Adolph Coors (278)
Storage Technology (322)

Des Moines, IA
Meredith (479)

Detroit, MI
General Motors (2)
Ford Motor (4)
Chrysler (21)
Burroughs (82)
American Motors (105)
Fruehauf (173)
Masco (286)
Ex-Cell-O (308)
Federal-Mogul (363)
Frederick & Herrud (377)
Michigan Milk Producers Association (430)
Guardian Industries (468)

Elkhart–Goshen, IN
Miles Laboratories (277)
Coachmen Industries (463)

Erie, PA
Hammermill Paper (214)

Fayetteville–Springdale, AR
Tyson Foods (407)

Fort Wayne, IN
Central Soya (200)

Greeley, CO
Monfort of Colorado (250)

Green Bay, WI
Fort Howard Paper (347)

Greensboro–Winston-Salem–High Point, NC
R. J. Reynolds Industries (23)
Burlington Industries (133)
Blue Bell (258)

Greenville–Spartanburg, SC
Riegel Textile (498)

Hamilton–Middletown, OH
Armco (87)

Harrisburg–Lebanon–Carlisle, PA
Hershey Foods (202)
AMP (228)
Harsco (331)

Hartford, CT
United Technologies (18)
Emhart (205)
Coleco Industries (410)
Dexter (431)

Honolulu, HI
Pacific Resources (225)

Houston, TX
Shell Oil (13)
Tenneco (19)
Coastal (58)
Pennzoil (163)
Cooper Industries (190)
Superior Oil (196)
Anderson Clayton (244)
Hughes Tool (267)
Cameron Iron Works (307)
Big Three Industries (385)

Huntington–Ashland, WV–KY–OH
Ashland Oil (45)

Indianapolis, IN
Eli Lilly (130)
Stokely–Van Camp (444)

Jacksonville, FL
Charter (61)

Kalamazoo, MI
Upjohn (182)

Kankakee, IL
Roper (462)

Kansas City, MO
Interstate Bakeries (388)

Kenosha, WI
Snap-on Tools (474)

La Crosse, WI
G. Heileman Brewing (268)
Trane (284)

Lake County, IL
CF Industries (328)

Lancaster, PA
Armstrong World Industries (240)

Los Angeles–Long Beach, CA
Atlantic Richfield (12)
Occidental Petroleum (14)
Getty Oil (24)
Unocal (31)
Lockheed (50)
Litton Industries (74)
Carnation (116)
Northrop (123)
Teledyne (135)
Tosco (153)
Times Mirror (154)
Lear Siegler (236)
Mattel (248)
Avery International (341)
NI Industries (368)
Smith International (375)

Louisville, KY
Brown-Forman Distillers (406)

Lowell, MA–NH
Wang Laboratories (227)

Melbourne–Titusville–Palm Bay, FL
Harris (201)

Memphis, TN–AR–MS
Federal Co. (275)

Miami–Hialeah, FL
Knight-Ridder Newspapers (234)

Middlesex–Somerset–Hunterdon, NJ
Johnson & Johnson (57)
American Hoechst (213)

Milwaukee, WI
Johnson Controls (251)
Allis-Chalmers (253)
Rexnord (342)
A. O. Smith (330)
Pabst Brewing (376)
Briggs & Stratton (403)
Bucyrus-Erie (434)
Universal Foods (448)

Minneapolis–St. Paul, MN–WI
Minnesota Mining & Manufacturing (47)
Honeywell (60)
General Mills (62)
Control Data (76)
Pillsbury (102)
Land O'Lakes (121)
Farmers' Union Central Exchange (243)
International Multifoods (274)
Bemis (373)
Economics Laboratory (384)
Deluxe Check Printers (400)
MEI (402)
H. B. Fuller (493)

Muncie, IN
Ball (315)

Muskegon, MI
Sealed Power (494)

Nashua, NH
Sanders Associates (415)
Nashua (426)

Nashville, TN
Genesco (394)

Nassau–Suffolk, NY
Grumman (167)

New Britain, CT
Stanley Works (298)

New Haven–Meriden, CT
Uniroyal (180)
Insilco (381)
Armstrong Rubber (411)
Echlin (428)
Harvey Hubbell (490)

New Orleans, LA
Louisiana Land & Exploration (257)

New York, NY
Exxon (1)
Mobil (3)
IBM (5)
Texaco (6)
ITT (20)
AT & T Technologies (26)
Philip Morris (35)
Amerada Hess (39)
Union Pacific (40)
General Foods (41)
PepsiCo (44)
W. R. Grace (53)
Sperry (66)
Gulf & Western Industries (67)
Colgate-Palmolive (72)
American Home Products (73)
American Brands (79)
International Paper (80)
Borden (85)
Time Inc. (91)
Bristol-Myers (93)
North American Philips (97)
Pfizer (99)
United Brands (109)
Warner Communications (114)

Celanese (122)
Avon Products (131)
Norton Simon (136)
St. Regis (141)
Penn Central (151)
Revlon (159)
National Distillers & Chemical (166)
American Standard (170)
J. P. Stevens (186)
Ogden (187)
Sterling Drug (188)
SCM (193)
Colt Industries (219)
Lever Brothers (223)
Asarco (229)
Westvaco (232)
Joseph E. Seagram & Sons (233)
NL Industries (239)
Witco Chemical (245)
McGraw-Hill (255)
Amstar (264)
New York Times (281)
Dover (292)
Crane (294)
Phelps Dodge (300)
General Instrument (302)
AMF (303)
Cluett Peabody (325)
Dow Jones (326)
Todd Shipyards (345)
Freeport-McMoRan (346)
Kane-Miller (353)
Capital Cities Communications (356)
Inspiration Resources (357)
Reichhold Chemicals (362)
Sun Chemical (364)
Newmont Mining (370)
GAF (374)
Collins & Aikman (378)
Harcourt Brace Jovanovich (392)
M. Lowenstein (412)
ACF Industries (416)
Handy & Harman (418)
Revere Copper & Brass (452)
American Bakeries (460)
United Merchants & Manufacturers (464)
International Flavors & Fragrances (470)
Phillips-Van Heusen (473)
Ametek (478)
Bairnco (486)
Macmillan (489)

Newark, NJ
Allied (29)
Nabisco Brands (56)
Merck (124)
Warner-Lambert (128)
Englehard (174)
Schering-Plough (194)
BASF Wyandotte (285)

Norwalk, CT
General Electric (10)
Richardson-Vicks (276)
Perkin-Elmer (291)

Oakland, CA
Kaiser Aluminum & Chemical (140)
Clorox (314)

Oklahoma City, OK
Kerr-McGee (108)
Wilson Foods (171)

Omaha, NE–IA
ConAgra (162)

Peoria, IL
Caterpillar Tractor (64)

Philadelphia, PA–NJ
Sun (17)
Campbell Soup (119)
SmithKline Beckman
  (126)
Scott Paper (156)
Rohm & Haas (189)
Crown Cork & Seal (254)
Pennwalt (301)
Westmoreland Coal (437)

Phoenix, AZ
Southwest Forest Industries
  (380)

Pittsburgh, PA
Gulf Oil (11)
U.S. Steel (15)
Westinghouse Electric (34)
Rockwell International (43)
Aluminum Co. of America (65)
H. J. Heinz (100)
PPG Industries (103)
National Intergroup (132)
Allegheny International (160)
Koppers (221)
Mobay Chemical (252)
Cyclops (290)
Wheeling-Pittsburgh Steel
  (352)
Joy Manufacturing (390)
H. H. Robertson (436)

Portland, OR
Tektronix (263)
Louisiana-Pacific (279)
Willamette Industries (287)
Hyster (497)

**Portsmouth–Dover–Rochester,
NH–ME**
Tyco Laboratories (419)

Providence, RI
Textron (134)

Reading, PA
VF (280)

Richmond–Petersburg, VA
Reynolds Metals (118)
Ethyl (197)
James River Corp. of Virginia
  (209)
A. H. Robins (429)
Media General (453)

**Riverside–San Bernardino,
CA**
Fleetwood Enterprises (329)
Kaiser Steel (396)

Rochester, NY
Eastman Kodak (30)
Gannett (203)
Sybron (404)
Bausch & Lomb (424)

Rockford, IL
Sunstrand (316)

**Saginaw–Bay City–
Midland, MI**
Dow Chemical (28)
Dow Corning (355)

St. Louis, MO–IL
McDonnell Douglas (42)
General Dynamics (46)
Monsanto (52)
Anheuser-Busch (55)
Ralston Purina (71)
Emerson Electric (111)
Interco (150)
Chromalloy American (297)
Kellwood (421)

San Antonio, TX
Datapoint (440)
Harte-Hanks Communications
  (485)

San Diego, CA
Signal Companies (54)
Rohr Industries (425)

San Francisco, CA
Standard Oil of California (9)

Kaiser Aluminum & Chemical
  (140)
Levi Strauss (143)
Crown Zellerbach (144)
Alumax (230)
Clorox (314)
Potlatch (317)
Kaiser Steel (396)
Raychem (413)
Shaklee (441)
Liquid Air (471)
Cooper Labs (476)

San Jose, CA
Hewlett-Packard (75)
National Semiconductor (261)
Intel (272)
Apple Computer (299)
Amdahl (350)
Varian Associates (358)
ROLM (454)
Tandem Computers (500)

Savannah, GA
Gulfstream Aerospace (417)
Savannah Foods & Industries
  (461)

Seattle, WA
Boeing (27)
PACCAR (242)

Springfield, MO
Mid-America Dairymen (247)

Stamford, CT
Xerox (38)
Continental Group (68)
Champion International (86)
American Can (117)
Combustion Engineering (129)
Singer (155)
AMAX (164)
Avco (179)
Olin (185)
Chesebrough-Pond's (206)
Pitney Bowes (211)
General Signal (220)
Great Northern Nekoosa (222)
Stauffer Chemical (249)

U.S. Industries (283)
Lone Star Industries (313)
Peabody International (481)
Moore McCormack Resources
  (496)

Stockton, CA
Sun-Diamond Growers of
  California (447)

Syracuse, NY
Agway (98)

Tacoma, WA
Weyerhaeuser (70)

**Tampa–St. Petersburg–
Clearwater, FL**
Jim Walter (181)

Toledo, OH
Owens-Illinois (115)
Dana (139)
Owens-Corning Fiberglas (142)
Libbey-Owens-Ford (266)
Champion Spark Plug (354)
Sheller-Globe (405)

Tulsa, OK
Phillips Petroleum (16)
Williams Companies (172)
Mapco (177)

Washington, DC–MD–VA
Martin Marietta (94)
Fairchild Industries (321)
Washington Post (323)

Waterbury, CT
Scovill (366)

Wichita, KS
Cessna Aircraft (445)

Wilmington, DE–NJ–MD
E. I. du Pont de Nemours (7)
Hercules (148)
NVF (295)

Worcester, MA
Norton (271)
Data General (335)
Idle Wild Foods (398)

Source: Fortune, "The 500: The Fortune Directory of the Largest U.S. Industrial Corporations," April 30, 1984, © 1984 Time Inc.

Putting It All Together:

Finding the Best Places to Live in America

When it comes to rating the livability of different places, there are three basic viewpoints: One says you can't do it; the second says you can but shouldn't; and the third says that you can, as long as you make it clear what your yardsticks are and go on to use them consistently.

Obviously, *Places Rated* subscribes to the third theory. Now comes the time when we summarize the findings of all the previous chapters and attempt to discern general patterns of desirability in America by ranking the metro areas for their overall showing in the nine categories.

In the first edition of *Places Rated Almanac*, this chapter aroused a great deal of controversy, and joy and ire as well. One major source of criticism stemmed from the erroneous impression that *Places Rated* knew (maybe even selected) beforehand which places would score well and which wouldn't. This was not the case. In each chapter, certain relevant data sets and source materials were chosen for being accurate, comprehensive, and important to metropolitan living. Most of the data were obtained from various agencies of the federal government; professional associations, nonprofit organizations, and a few specialized corporations were also tapped. *Places Rated* used no source with a particular bias for or against any region, state, or city. Next, the authors devised scoring systems, awarding points for factors that most people agree are desirable or beneficial, and occasionally subtracting points for factors generally agreed to be undesirable or harmful.

Throughout, we have concentrated as much as possible on what is good rather than bad about metropolitan living. All 329 metro areas are examined and run through the scoring systems in exactly the same manner, using exactly the same data sets. Due to the complexity of the information and the large size of our metropolitan universe, the outcome for any given chapter—and certainly the book as a whole—was virtually impossible to predict.

Places Rated's nine categories for quality of life include some scored on facilities (health care, education, recreation, transportation, arts) and some scored on indicators (crime, housing, economics). Generally speaking, the smaller metro areas rank better on the indicators (usually having lower crime rates and less expensive housing, for example), while their larger cousins score higher on the facilities. Because of *Places Rated*'s strong emphasis on facilities, the larger metro areas are perhaps favored, but overall the scoring system seems to reflect the tastes and preferences of a great number of Americans.

In reviewing the findings of this or any other chapter, be sure to note the close groupings of scores. With such close results, ranking metro areas from first to 329th may give the impression of greater differences between them than actually exist. Any ranking of 50th or higher, for example, places a metro area in the top 15 percent of all American metro areas for that category, certainly an excellent showing.

SOME GENERAL OBSERVATIONS

Before proceeding to the overall rankings, we would like to note a few broad patterns that we have seen emerge during our work on the almanac over the past eight years.

• Although there have been a few noteworthy changes in some ranking categories from one edition to the next, most places showed remarkably little change in all categories and in their final standing.

• Places that show dramatic recent population growth and economic promise also tend to have crime rates that are very high. This is particularly true of Sun Belt metro areas.

• Despite the gloom-and-doom predictions made in recent decades about the death of the older eastern cities, it is now clear that many of the oldest and largest metro areas in the East are among the most desirable places to live in America. Not only did our cities not die, they are undergoing a rejuvenation unparalleled in our history.

• In the previous edition of *Places Rated Almanac* we reported a new phenomenon of demographic migration in America from large metro areas to rural areas. But this trend has slowed almost to a halt in the intervening years, which perhaps is both cause and effect of the rebirth of many of our big cities.

• America's so-called cities of the future—found mostly in the Sun Belt regions of the Southeast, the Gulf, and the Southwest—have not as yet developed into metro areas with the most promising quality-of-life indicators. Some, such as Miami, Houston, and Los Angeles, are beset with severe social problems (many due to changes resulting from great influxes of immigrants) that will undoubtedly affect them adversely in the near future.

FINDING THE BEST PLACES TO LIVE IN AMERICA

In 1970 the Urban Institute, located in Washington, D.C., rated 18 major American cities for livability according to such diverse factors as unemployment rates, crime rates, and per capita contributions to charity. Their method for determining the best all-around city (it was Minneapolis, by the way) was very

---

For Those Who Read This Chapter First

Those of you who have skipped ahead to "see how it all comes out" may be surprised by many of the final results listed in the cumulative table on pages 420–429. If you are curious about why a metro area receives a rank in a particular category, consult the explanation of the scoring system in the appropriate chapter; each chapter uses different criteria and a somewhat different method of combining them.

Using San Diego as an example may help to review how all the rankings are arrived at. How does this popular Southern California vacation spot end up in 33rd place behind such metro areas as Buffalo, New York, and Providence, Rhode Island?

San Diego certainly beats out the northern metro areas when it comes to climate. Its coastal location and abundance of sunshine combine to give it one of the most mild, even climates in the country. Since *Places Rated* uses mildness as its chief criterion for ranking the metro areas for climate, San Diego finishes third best in this category, behind only Oakland and San Francisco.

In housing, however, it does very poorly, placing 321st, largely because of high property taxes, expensive utilities, and an average price tag for a single-family house that is the seventh highest among the metro areas. *Places Rated*'s standards for housing are strictly economic and do not take into account aesthetics or comfort.

San Diego's showing in health care facilities is excellent—it ranks 31st and has an impressive supply of teaching hospitals, medical schools, and other amenities. Offsetting this are fairly high rates of violent and property crime that place it 231st for personal safety.

In two other categories—education and economics—San Diego earns middling marks. For its effort to support schools at the K–12 level and provide a broad range of options at the college level, it ranks 165th. And the economic promise for the individual here—which is rated on the basis of household income and taxes, cost of living, and local job and income growth—is just above average, at 152nd place.

But in the remaining three categories, San Diego performs quite well. It ranks 68th in transportation, rated in terms of how well a variety of transit modes accommodates the metro area population. Such assets as zoos, a theme park, several professional and collegiate sports teams, and a huge national forest help boost the California metro area to a 22nd-place finish in recreation, which is scored for both manufactured and natural facilities. In the arts, San Diego finishes 20th due to its variety of museums, symphony orchestras, and dance companies, to name a few of *Places Rated*'s criteria for this category.

One final caveat: It should be remembered that throughout *Places Rated Almanac* the unit of comparison is the metro area rather than the city.

simple: The ranks for each city for each of the factors were added together for a cumulative score.

Places Rated's method, in this edition and the previous one, is similar to the Urban Institute's. Every metro area's ranks for each of the nine factors—climate, housing, health care and environment, crime, transportation, education, the arts, recreation, and economics—are totaled. Albuquerque, New Mexico, for example, ranks 30th in climate, 218th in housing, 60th in health care, 299th in safety from crime, 21st in transportation, 78th in education, 68th in the arts, 52nd in recreation, and 126th in economics. The total of these ranks— 30 + 218 + 60 + 299 + 21 + 78 + 68 + 52 + 126—equals 952. Because this system is based on ranks, the lower the cumulative score, the better the metro area is judged to be all-around. (Albuquerque places 22nd overall among the metro areas.) The list below highlights the metro areas that rise to the top as the best places to live in America.

America's Top 50 Metro Areas

Metro Area	Cumulative Score
1. Pittsburgh, PA	716
2. Boston, MA	752
3. Raleigh–Durham, NC	753
4. Philadelphia, PA–NJ	774
4. San Francisco, CA	774
6. Nassau–Suffolk, NY	786
7. Louisville, KY–IN	840
8. St. Louis, MO–IL	845
9. Rochester, NY	860
10. Norwalk, CT	889
11. Dallas, TX	898
12. Seattle, WA	919
13. Atlanta, GA	921
14. Knoxville, TN	928
15. Buffalo, NY	931
16. Baltimore, MD	932
17. Washington, DC–MD–VA	933
18. Cincinnati, OH–KY–IN	938
19. Albany–Schenectady–Troy, NY	941
19. Burlington, VT	941
21. Syracuse, NY	950
22. Albuquerque, NM	952
23. Harrisburg–Lebanon–Carlisle, PA	957
24. Richmond–Petersburg, VA	960
25. New York, NY	965
26. Providence, RI	966
27. Chicago, IL	968
28. Middlesex–Somerset–Hunterdon, NJ	975
29. Denver, CO	977
30. Cleveland, OH	988
31. Charlottesville, VA	999
32. New Haven–Meriden, CT	1,009
33. San Diego, CA	1,013
34. Wilmington, DE–NJ–MD	1,014
35. Asheville, NC	1,016
36. Los Angeles–Long Beach, CA	1,021
37. Omaha, NE–IA	1,022
38. Bridgeport–Milford, CT	1,026

Metro Area	Cumulative Score
39. Norfolk–Virginia Beach–Newport News, VA	1,028
40. Greensboro–Winston-Salem–High Point, NC	1,030
41. Anaheim–Santa Ana, CA	1,035
42. Bergen–Passaic, NJ	1,060
43. San Jose, CA	1,062
44. Nashville, TN	1,066
45. Tampa–St. Petersburg–Clearwater, FL	1,069
46. Johnson City–Kingsport–Bristol, TN–VA	1,070
47. Oklahoma City, OK	1,076
48. Monmouth–Ocean, NJ	1,091
49. Jacksonville, FL	1,092
50. Stamford, CT	1,094

In many respects, the list of the top 50 metro areas in this second edition of *Places Rated Almanac* closely resembles that of the first edition. Although their rankings have changed somewhat, 33 of the metro areas were in the top 50 before. Seventeen places have dropped from the list this time around, but only two—Utica–Rome, New York, and Evansville, Indiana–Kentucky—dropped below 100th place.

Of the 17 newcomers to the top 50, five are metro areas that were not independently ranked in *Places Rated*'s first edition: Bergen–Passaic, New Jersey; Burlington, Vermont; Charlottesville, Virginia; Middlesex–Somerset–Hunterdon, New Jersey; and Monmouth–Ocean, New Jersey. (Burlington and Charlottesville were non-metropolitan at that time; parts of the other three were in other metro areas.)

Four metro areas that ranked 109th or worse in the first edition of *Places Rated* improved their position dramatically by moving into the top 50: Johnson City–Kingsport–Bristol, Tennessee–Virginia; Norfolk–Virginia Beach–Newport News, Virginia; Norwalk, Connecticut; and Wilmington, Delaware–New Jersey–Maryland.

Why have the rankings changed? As mentioned in the introduction to the book, there are many possible reasons. A new set of boundaries is one, for only about half of the metro areas are exactly the same geographical entities that were rated in the first edition. The Norfolk–Virginia Beach–Newport News metro area, which moved up to 39th place, is a combination of parts of two former metro areas: Norfolk–Virginia Beach–Portsmouth, Virginia–North Carolina, and Newport News–Hampton, Virginia, which ranked 115th and 77th, respectively, in our earlier edition.

More recent data is of course another factor that could cause changes in ratings, but this in and of itself has generally not made any marked difference in the overall standing of a metro area. More meaningful have been new scoring criteria, either in the factors being considered or in the weightings given those factors, as discussed in detail in each chapter. Many metro areas, notably formerly top-ranked Atlanta, saw

Consistency Counts

Many of *Places Rated*'s high-ranking metro areas are combinations of superior and dismal rankings in the individual categories. New York City is the classic example of an uneven performance. The Big Apple has no less than three first-place finishes: health care, transportation, and the arts. Anyone who knows New York can appreciate these rankings, too. But what of its miserable showings in housing (312th) and crime (329th)? High housing and real estate costs and dangerous streets could, for many people, cancel out the wonderful facilities that this supercity has to offer.

Places Rated decided to seek out those metro areas that show steady strength in *all* the categories, even though they might not have any dramatic first-place showings. We scanned, in vain, for places with no rankings below 150th. Since we struck out with this stringent standard, we looked for those with no ranks lower than 200th. Even with this more liberal guideline, we came up with just a handful of metro areas that showed consistent strength in all nine of the *Places Rated* categories.

Super-Solid Metro Areas

Metro Area (Overall Rank)	Highest Rank	Lowest Rank
Asheville, NC (35)	Climate (25)	Arts (197)
Cincinnati, OH–KY–IN (18)	Arts (16)	Housing (191)
Greensboro–Winston-Salem–High Point, NC (40)	Climate (54)	Economics (192)
Harrisburg–Lebanon–Carlisle, PA (23)	Transportation (32)	Recreation (198)
Knoxville, TN (14)	Climate (26)	Education (179)
Louisville, KY–IN (7)	Health Care (48)	Economics (163)
Nashville, TN (44)	Health Care (61)	Crime (184)
Pittsburgh, PA (1)	Education (7)	Housing (186)
Raleigh–Durham, NC (3)	Health Care (13)	Housing (198)

Interestingly, all these super-solid metro areas are found in roughly the same geographic area, stretching from the Ohio Valley in the north to the Piedmont and Appalachian regions of the Mid-South.

Somewhat disappointed at the small number of extremely solid metro areas, we went through the final grid again and selected those places with only one rank below 200th. The list of runners-up follows.

Solid Metro Areas

Metro Area (Overall Rank)	Highest Rank	Lowest Rank
Albany–Schenectady–Troy, NY (19)	Transportation (15)	Climate (250)
Alton–Granite City, IL (75)	Housing (52)	Recreation (249)
Binghamton, NY (68)	Crime (16)	Housing (202)
Buffalo, NY (15)	Arts (23)	Economics (217)
Charlottesville, VA (31)	Education (12)	Housing (263)
Evansville, IN–KY (140)	Housing (78)	Transportation (214)
Middlesex–Somerset–Hunterdon, NJ (28)	Education (8)	Housing (306)
New Haven–Meriden, CT (32)	Education (11)	Housing (299)
Oklahoma City, OK (47)	Economics (5)	Crime (272)
Omaha, NE–IA (36)	Health Care (26)	Climate (276)
Portland, ME (55)	Recreation (20)	Climate (240)
Roanoke, VA (87)	Climate (33)	Arts (207)
Rochester, NY (9)	Education (5)	Housing (233)
St. Louis, MO–IL (8)	Education (9)	Crime (273)
Springfield, IL (93)	Transportation (31)	Crime (268)
Syracuse, NY (21)	Transportation (14)	Economics (282)
Wilmington, DE–NJ–MD (34)	Education (52)	Crime (234)

Does this kind of consistency count? It certainly does: Of all these 26 solid and super-solid metro areas, only six fail to make it into *Places Rated*'s list of the 50 best places to live in America.

their rankings in the Recreation chapter change noticeably because of the many innovations made in that scoring system. Atlanta's recreation ranking fell from 28th to 239th, due in part to the addition of the major category Outdoor Recreation Assets to the chapter, improving the position of many other metro areas in relation to Atlanta, which receives few points in that category.

Also, the CMSA Access effect has been highly significant. For the first time, *Places Rated* has taken into account certain shared assets in health care, transportation, the arts, and recreation by crediting metro areas that are part of America's 22 Consolidated Metropolitan Statistical Areas with additional points. The CMSA Access effect is the major reason Nassau–Suffolk, New York, moved from 48th in *Places Rated*'s first edition to sixth place in this one. Norwalk, Connecticut, jumped from 148th place to tenth, and Wilmington, Delaware–New Jersey–Maryland, from 109th

to 34th. In all, 25 metro areas in our top 50 benefit to one degree or another from CMSA Access.

The majority of metro areas that perform best overall in this edition are located east of the Mississippi. Not only that, many are found in the northeastern quadrant of the country. The states of New York, New Jersey, and Connecticut are especially strong in highly ranked places, as is the multistate region of the Ohio Valley. The South and the West (excluding California), despite significant population growth in the last 20 years and generally favorable economic indicators, are still underrepresented in *Places Rated*'s list of top places.

As previously mentioned, the scoring systems used in some of the chapters—particularly those dealing with supply of various facilities—tend to favor bigger metro areas over smaller ones. Twenty-seven of the top 50 metro areas are therefore also among the 50 largest metro areas. There are, however, some note-

Solid and Super-Solid Metro Areas

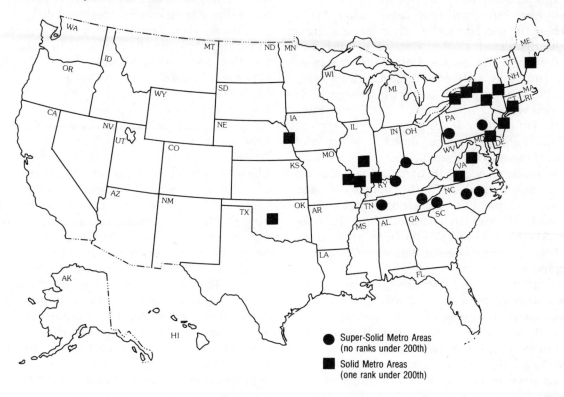

Super-Solid Metro Areas
(no ranks under 200th)

Solid Metro Areas
(one rank under 200th)

worthy exceptions. Third-place Raleigh–Durham, for example, is 74th in size. Tiny Norwalk, which ranks tenth overall, is 258th in size, and Burlington, Vermont, a brand-new metro area in a state previously unrepresented in *Places Rated*, ranks 19th overall in desirability but only 274th in population.

These small and medium-sized metro areas tend to have consistently good rankings in every category (Raleigh–Durham ranks 58th or better in six categories and no worse than 198th in any), whereas the large metro areas can show considerable inconsistency. A good example is fourth-ranked San Francisco, which finishes tenth or better in five categories yet scrapes bottom in housing costs (327th) and safety from crime (318th). Seventeenth-place Washington earns four rankings of sixth or better, but it too falters in housing (314th) and crime (276th). And 27th-ranked Chicago achieves four ranks above 14th but finishes 295th in housing costs and 205th in safety from crime.

The prime example of across-the-board strength in a large metropolitan area is Pittsburgh, which emerges as the best place to live in *Places Rated*'s comprehensive survey of metropolitan America.

AND THE WINNER IS . . .

Pittsburgh, Pennsylvania, which ranked fourth in the first edition of *Places Rated Almanac*, has climbed to the top of the list in this second edition. Many people who perhaps have a stereotyped and outdated image of a smoky, noisy, blast furnace of a city may be surprised

at this. But Pittsburgh shows great strength in the social indicators and is remarkably like a small town in many respects, despite its great size. Values are traditional and simple, neighborhoods tight yet friendly.

Pittsburgh's strengths lie as much in what it doesn't have as in what it does. Our number-one metro area heads an elite group of only nine places that have no rankings of 200th or worse in any of *Places Rated*'s nine major categories. Although its population of nearly 2.3 million people (about 450,000 in the city of Pittsburgh itself) places it tenth in population overall, the metro area ranks 78th in safety from crime, in the upper 24 percent of all metro areas as far as personal safety is concerned. Most comparably sized metro areas cannot even approach this level. Atlanta, the 12th largest metro area, ranks 274th in safety from crime, Baltimore (11th in population) 323rd, and Houston (eighth in population) 304th. Another odious fact of life in most large metro areas is the high cost of housing. A housing rank of 186th means Pittsburgh is in the 56th percentile, just under the midpoint. Several other large metro areas that also rank among the ten best overall have far higher housing prices: Boston ranks 300th, for example, and Nassau–Suffolk 298th.

Located at the confluence of the Allegheny and Monongahela rivers, which together form the Ohio River, Pittsburgh since the mid-1700s has provided a vital link between the interior waterways of the East and the Mississippi. These navigable waterways gave the city access to vast reserves of both coal and iron ore, which led to its growth as a foundry center.

Pittsburgh probably reached its zenith as the Steel City in the years during and immediately after World War II. Then, in the late 1940s, civic leaders grew increasingly distressed at the amount of dirt and smoke in their city. The problem of pollution was so severe, in fact, that architect Frank Lloyd Wright, when asked to suggest a solution for the city, gave his answer in two words: "Abandon it." But Pittsburgh's leaders were not dismayed. An urban redevelopment program was initiated that regulated industry and included strict measures for smoke control. The result, in the 1980s, is a smoke-free city of tall office buildings set in a stunning natural setting of rugged hills and river valleys, with plenty of recreational parks and a fine waterfront. The Golden Triangle, where the Allegheny joins the Monongahela, is the heart of the city's business district, with scores of handsome buildings and skyscrapers.

This manufacturing and commercial center in the southwest corner of the state still relies on primary metals as an important part of its economy, but in recent years there has been a dramatic shift away from heavy manufacturing to light assembly and commercial and service industries. A large number of major corporations have headquarters in Pittsburgh. As of 1984, Pittsburgh was home to 15 Fortune 500 corporations, which ranks it fifth among U.S. metro areas, after New York; Chicago; Stamford, Connecticut; and Los Angeles–Long Beach. Nonetheless, this metro area ranks only 184th in economic outlook. About a third of the work force is still blue collar, and the threat of unemployment is moderate. Although personal income has increased by nearly 45 percent in recent years, the job market has declined slightly.

Despite its reputation as a workingman's town, Pittsburgh has big-city strength in many important facilities. The metro area ranks seventh in education; it is home to several fine universities, such as Carnegie-Mellon and the University of Pittsburgh, and claims two of the nation's top secondary schools, Mount Lebanon High School and Upper St. Clair High School. An array of cultural amenities including the Pittsburgh Symphony Orchestra, Pittsburgh Ballet Theatre, Pittsburgh Opera, and the Carnegie Museum of Natural History and Museum of Art helps the Steel City capture a 12th-place ranking in the arts. Pittsburgh's 14th-place finish in health care derives from its full range of medical facilities and an excellent hospitalization/insurance costs index.

There's more to the Pittsburgh metro area than the central city. Surrounding towns like Mount Lebanon (pop. 34,414) and Monroeville (pop. 30,977) offer suburban living styles. Bethel Park (pop. 34,755) remains an exclusive, and expensive, suburb catering to upper-echelon executives and their families. Beaver County, Pennsylvania, though officially a separate metro area, is included in the greater Pittsburgh CMSA. Here is an area for those who prefer country living within a reasonable commute of downtown.

Pluses: Across-the-board strength in nearly all categories; excellent rankings in education, health care, and the arts.

Minuses: Middling rankings for housing costs and economic indicators.

Putting It All Together: Cumulative Scores and Overall Ranks of 329 Metro Areas

The following table shows the rank of every metro area for each of *Places Rated*'s nine categories. The sum of these—the cumulative score—is also shown, as is the overall rank. For example, Albuquerque's cumulative score of 952 ranks it 22nd overall among the 329 metro areas. As in the game of golf, the lower the cumulative score, the better. The best possible score would be 9, meaning a first-place rank in all nine categories.

Metro Area	Climate & Terrain	Housing	Health Care & Environment	Crime	Transportation	Education	The Arts	Recreation	Economics	Cumulative Score	Overall Rank
Abilene, TX	200	33	320	156	167	180	231	232	15	1,534	168
Akron, OH	105	190	73	141	105	298	50	51	292	1,305	97
Albany, GA	257	129	226	175	290	261	302	304	188	2,132	325
Albany–Schenectady–Troy, NY	250	171	85	54	15	17	64	175	110	941	19

Metro Area	Climate & Terrain	Housing	Health Care & Environment	Crime	Transportation	Education	The Arts	Recreation	Economics	Cumulative Score	Overall Rank
Albuquerque, NM	30	218	60	299	21	78	68	52	126	952	22
Alexandria, LA	203	18	218	87	295	97	288	290	187	1,683	232
Allentown–Bethlehem, PA–NJ	129	205	224	34	269	44	132	278	212	1,527	162
Alton–Granite City, IL	173	52	143	82	96	103	189	249	120	1,207	75
Altoona, PA	124	32	288	9	151	170	301	261	301	1,637	210
Amarillo, TX	68	58	213	220	103	147	209	280	73	1,371	115
Anaheim–Santa Ana, CA	5	324	52	183	169	151	49	28	74	1,035	41
Anchorage, AK	324	307	235	267	90	302	131	33	14	1,703	242
Anderson, IN	185	9	248	139	271	290	276	309	325	2,052	320
Anderson, SC	85	14	168	178	280	173	307	327	298	1,830	283
Ann Arbor, MI	155	296	32	217	221	21	31	73	270	1,316	101
Anniston, AL	127	6	236	238	255	322	297	267	257	2,005	316
Appleton–Oshkosh–Neenah, WI	302	165	164	38	239	150	216	70	180	1,524	161
Asheville, NC	25	76	103	45	91	90	197	195	194	1,016	35
Athens, GA	76	71	233	159	319	231	92	291	195	1,667	224
Atlanta, GA	24	210	15	274	2	62	31	239	64	921	13
Atlantic City, NJ	61	297	221	325	204	110	262	46	6	1,532	166
Augusta, GA–SC	184	39	65	137	292	118	224	300	162	1,521	157
Aurora–Elgin, IL	253	286	104	119	171	321	82	145	212	1,693	238
Austin, TX	282	242	181	210	195	60	53	285	19	1,527	162
Bakersfield, CA	127	181	289	312	191	260	212	191	90	1,853	290
Baltimore, MD	119	250	12	323	8	15	15	39	151	932	16
Bangor, ME	272	124	182	69	58	109	155	89	200	1,258	85
Baton Rouge, LA	286	182	304	313	233	236	77	228	66	1,925	306
Battle Creek, MI	189	42	153	203	116	285	285	168	308	1,749	258
Beaumont–Port Arthur, TX	290	38	228	275	274	188	171	142	98	1,704	243
Beaver County, PA	88	163	159	2	262	270	204	212	328	1,688	235
Bellingham, WA	15	211	319	123	185	170	202	26	299	1,550	173
Benton Harbor, MI	120	84	250	260	258	265	325	213	322	2,097	324
Bergen–Passaic, NJ	129	322	22	132	211	2	18	124	100	1,060	42
Billings, MT	271	209	275	113	26	84	247	98	105	1,428	135
Biloxi–Gulfport, MS	93	48	286	113	293	255	258	93	118	1,557	178
Binghamton, NY	146	202	137	16	128	63	183	155	141	1,171	68
Birmingham, AL	66	86	72	237	87	149	81	256	246	1,280	90
Bismarck, ND	327	214	176	13	148	217	213	171	98	1,577	187
Bloomington, IN	134	104	193	72	323	136	145	107	248	1,462	144
Bloomington–Normal, IL	239	237	172	75	44	145	190	181	111	1,394	120
Boise City, ID	83	195	281	140	20	306	128	164	265	1,582	190
Boston, MA	56	300	3	266	16	14	5	32	60	752	2
Boulder–Longmont, CO	265	305	144	224	13	256	88	5	30	1,330	104

Metro Area	Climate & Terrain	Housing	Health Care & Environment	Crime	Transportation	Education	The Arts	Recreation	Economics	Cumulative Score	Overall Rank
Bradenton, FL	277	199	307	228	182	205	311	242	20	1,971	311
Brazoria, TX	290	219	287	100	298	204	188	203	97	1,886	298
Bremerton, WA	12	249	312	69	325	267	280	110	132	1,756	263
Bridgeport–Milford, CT	34	313	27	163	242	70	25	126	26	1,026	38
Bristol, CT	207	280	141	41	130	240	269	318	51	1,677	228
Brockton, MA	105	203	151	282	181	193	154	258	37	1,564	180
Brownsville–Harlingen, TX	277	3	328	177	249	303	309	33	225	1,904	300
Bryan–College Station, TX	305	197	218	197	291	95	153	228	7	1,691	237
Buffalo, NY	112	180	36	176	75	50	23	62	217	931	15
Burlington, NC	45	29	140	83	318	275	316	324	129	1,659	221
Burlington, VT	305	267	63	32	10	23	177	21	43	941	19
Canton, OH	105	128	285	68	149	181	233	268	245	1,662	222
Casper, WY	299	270	302	185	136	292	293	221	70	2,068	322
Cedar Rapids, IA	283	156	162	85	80	246	236	209	221	1,678	230
Champaign–Urbana–Rantoul, IL	195	234	211	200	7	42	139	160	154	1,342	107
Charleston, SC	115	134	81	303	152	40	106	53	207	1,191	70
Charleston, WV	53	160	201	86	70	129	121	306	185	1,311	100
Charlotte–Gastonia–Rock Hill, NC–SC	38	116	139	270	34	69	73	255	132	1,126	58
Charlottesville, VA	58	263	90	96	37	12	195	157	91	999	31
Chattanooga, TN–GA	103	30	251	164	226	301	127	253	280	1,735	254
Chicago, IL	211	295	2	205	6	13	2	43	191	968	27
Chico, CA	72	232	318	165	166	49	179	194	176	1,551	174
Cincinnati, OH–KY–IN	93	191	46	181	52	116	16	61	182	938	18
Clarksville–Hopkinsville, TN–KY	159	22	283	90	309	225	319	82	240	1,729	251
Cleveland, OH	101	251	16	241	9	97	9	23	241	988	30
Colorado Springs, CO	191	224	198	223	227	181	176	67	13	1,500	151
Columbia, MO	168	150	54	215	175	310	111	244	208	1,635	208
Columbia, SC	191	140	86	307	47	120	126	211	179	1,407	127
Columbus, GA–AL	206	17	164	118	257	224	166	260	250	1,662	222
Columbus, OH	134	185	62	226	143	111	41	103	202	1,207	75
Corpus Christi, TX	310	96	280	281	199	153	156	100	44	1,619	205
Cumberland, MD–WV	85	24	185	3	192	19	282	288	255	1,333	106
Dallas, TX	159	256	20	308	30	29	13	71	12	898	11
Danbury, CT	115	320	40	43	279	70	34	189	34	1,124	57
Danville, VA	157	11	241	7	245	105	323	328	278	1,695	239
Davenport, Rock Island–Moline, IA–IL	277	182	115	126	174	125	228	123	222	1,572	183
Dayton–Springfield, OH	159	145	43	244	109	173	40	276	276	1,465	146
Daytona Beach, FL	124	118	197	284	162	251	244	9	49	1,438	138

Metro Area	Climate & Terrain	Housing	Health Care & Environment	Crime	Transportation	Education	The Arts	Recreation	Economics	Cumulative Score	Overall Rank
Decatur, IL	246	133	191	149	177	219	294	257	297	1,963	310
Denver, CO	200	293	28	287	5	43	24	69	28	977	29
Des Moines, IA	274	177	96	209	67	250	167	144	167	1,551	174
Detroit, MI	176	227	7	314	106	59	14	58	312	1,273	89
Dothan, AL	314	10	241	158	308	320	318	321	159	2,149	326
Dubuque, IA	292	176	218	49	196	211	287	187	310	1,926	307
Duluth, MN–WI	326	23	109	29	83	246	129	30	311	1,286	92
East St. Louis–Belleville, IL	173	53	284	230	23	237	236	177	83	1,496	149
Eau Claire, WI	322	108	178	19	242	101	170	235	166	1,541	170
El Paso, TX	83	130	263	277	193	286	84	281	215	1,812	280
Elkhart–Goshen, IN	200	59	237	37	156	269	286	289	303	1,836	287
Elmira, NY	258	108	253	50	234	86	223	185	249	1,646	216
Enid, OK	263	88	222	130	302	177	304	264	4	1,754	261
Erie, PA	70	151	262	64	51	235	151	243	296	1,523	160
Eugene–Springfield, OR	18	259	258	138	79	51	120	19	329	1,271	88
Evansville, IN–KY	146	78	180	135	214	162	164	173	190	1,442	140
Fall River, MA–RI	40	248	153	134	120	295	252	105	239	1,586	191
Fargo–Moorhead, ND–MN	328	192	150	33	25	277	147	227	142	1,521	157
Fayetteville, NC	124	36	158	243	137	64	241	322	186	1,511	154
Fayetteville–Springdale, AR	148	69	240	41	201	314	163	161	266	1,603	198
Fitchburg–Leominster, MA	221	200	216	71	305	161	296	317	211	1,998	314
Flint, MI	170	119	196	320	101	276	143	241	318	1,884	296
Florence, AL	155	21	232	35	328	299	227	294	277	1,868	293
Florence, SC	144	54	169	280	97	53	261	314	247	1,619	205
Fort Collins–Loveland, CO	234	276	193	91	286	303	182	4	48	1,617	204
Fort Lauderdale–Hollywood–Pompano Beach, FL	111	294	97	310	154	191	152	60	29	1,398	123
Fort Myers, FL	313	255	257	107	123	193	281	6	27	1,562	179
Fort Pierce, FL	75	243	264	291	311	41	284	97	9	1,615	202
Fort Smith, AR–OK	244	15	278	73	253	112	315	152	243	1,685	233
Fort Walton Beach, FL	176	141	274	40	268	157	321	94	61	1,532	166
Fort Wayne, IN	217	77	126	84	73	173	112	156	304	1,322	102
Fort Worth–Arlington, TX	188	174	132	285	132	242	42	68	40	1,303	96
Fresno, CA	129	254	298	299	142	305	90	36	123	1,676	227
Gadsden, AL	191	4	223	93	310	317	312	329	302	2,081	323
Gainesville, FL	298	132	69	319	208	55	96	254	124	1,555	176
Galveston–Texas City, TX	20	153	84	265	223	157	175	33	95	1,205	74
Gary–Hammond, IN	240	146	89	187	48	273	80	118	315	1,496	149
Glens Falls, NY	250	112	329	47	306	221	263	130	201	1,859	291
Grand Forks, ND	329	169	117	12	62	201	161	248	139	1,438	138
Grand Rapids, MI	214	159	93	166	219	210	99	127	244	1,531	165

Metro Area	Climate & Terrain	Housing	Health Care & Environment	Crime	Transportation	Education	The Arts	Recreation	Economics	Cumulative Score	Overall Rank
Great Falls, MT	295	114	214	111	188	189	279	83	260	1,733	252
Greeley, CO	234	194	202	186	326	145	208	319	161	1,975	312
Green Bay, WI	308	220	151	51	184	245	124	121	137	1,541	170
Greensboro–Winston-Salem–High Point, NC	54	106	71	171	134	56	79	167	192	1,030	40
Greenville–Spartanburg, SC	32	41	94	259	170	32	122	230	220	1,200	72
Hagerstown, MD	118	152	169	57	222	90	242	210	281	1,541	170
Hamilton–Middletown, OH	164	196	113	143	232	185	133	182	268	1,616	203
Harrisburg–Lebanon–Carlisle, PA	140	168	49	59	32	35	103	198	173	957	23
Hartford, CT	207	302	30	271	11	4	89	146	67	1,127	59
Hickory, NC	56	82	138	99	281	198	306	315	258	1,733	252
Honolulu, HI	22	326	92	142	41	279	36	15	196	1,149	63
Houma–Thibodaux, LA	286	110	247	10	329	327	255	47	46	1,657	220
Houston, TX	288	269	34	304	119	28	11	138	18	1,209	77
Huntington–Ashland, WV–KY–OH	46	65	157	74	168	274	140	308	289	1,521	157
Huntsville, AL	79	37	208	157	285	318	161	284	57	1,586	191
Indianapolis, IN	138	101	44	192	50	216	44	128	214	1,127	59
Iowa City, IA	283	260	38	125	276	152	136	206	202	1,678	230
Jackson, MI	204	85	209	199	107	225	290	120	316	1,755	262
Jackson, MS	293	122	66	225	100	46	100	224	198	1,374	116
Jacksonville, FL	266	64	108	263	59	65	144	41	82	1,092	49
Jacksonville, NC	121	26	189	171	321	231	265	266	59	1,649	219
Janesville–Beloit, WI	260	136	203	133	253	271	220	176	290	1,942	308
Jersey City, NJ	76	241	67	293	95	259	33	291	237	1,592	195
Johnson City–Kingsport–Bristol, TN–VA	29	27	111	18	289	114	160	88	234	1,070	46
Johnstown, PA	154	55	193	5	145	215	259	302	305	1,633	207
Joliet, IL	248	258	127	129	117	139	101	170	266	1,555	176
Joplin, MO	99	1	271	58	300	137	324	313	172	1,675	226
Kalamazoo, MI	189	172	129	236	72	128	150	85	251	1,412	128
Kankakee, IL	240	120	231	179	220	144	326	277	146	1,883	295
Kansas City, KS	148	189	70	242	94	74	215	287	78	1,397	122
Kansas City, MO	148	107	55	296	46	102	51	99	242	1,146	62
Kenosha, WI	229	226	125	153	131	116	83	81	199	1,343	108
Killeen–Temple, TX	309	49	291	89	272	39	235	298	62	1,644	215
Knoxville, TN	26	72	145	55	150	179	97	56	148	928	14
Kokomo, IN	216	63	237	13	320	123	295	293	324	1,884	296
La Crosse, WI	311	207	207	76	35	77	191	113	138	1,355	111
Lafayette, IN	231	157	216	26	98	103	137	141	293	1,402	124
Lafayette, LA	285	230	256	202	81	316	173	153	2	1,698	240
Lake Charles, LA	255	94	311	228	206	313	192	135	107	1,841	288

Metro Area	Climate & Terrain	Housing	Health Care & Environment	Crime	Transportation	Education	The Arts	Recreation	Economics	Cumulative Score	Overall Rank
Lake County, IL	211	311	99	120	224	253	87	63	122	**1,490**	148
Lakeland–Winter Haven, FL	319	68	309	288	225	87	292	57	142	**1,787**	272
Lancaster, PA	129	236	116	13	173	54	229	270	209	**1,429**	136
Lansing–East Lansing, MI	246	170	88	147	64	130	78	178	254	**1,355**	111
Laredo, TX	288	28	279	211	235	154	313	323	183	**2,014**	318
Las Cruces, NM	144	98	246	294	258	190	114	178	168	**1,690**	236
Las Vegas, NV	140	274	290	326	43	319	184	8	93	**1,677**	228
Lawrence, KS	214	138	224	198	265	212	102	148	271	**1,772**	270
Lawrence–Haverhill, MA–NH	151	287	105	152	202	286	147	131	51	**1,512**	155
Lawton, OK	248	19	276	246	299	311	205	147	84	**1,835**	285
Lewiston–Auburn, ME	234	90	186	98	263	214	253	136	285	**1,759**	264
Lexington–Fayette, KY	48	212	59	212	165	142	90	233	72	**1,233**	81
Lima, OH	199	99	188	131	163	239	200	222	294	**1,735**	254
Lincoln, NE	300	201	183	108	56	133	67	143	232	**1,423**	133
Little Rock–North Little Rock, AR	227	123	58	279	154	258	142	216	181	**1,638**	212
Longview–Marshall, TX	223	62	268	179	284	155	288	311	38	**1,808**	278
Lorain–Elyria, OH	101	206	119	53	198	257	123	184	326	**1,567**	182
Los Angeles–Long Beach, CA	5	316	5	327	144	37	3	10	174	**1,021**	36
Louisville, KY–IN	60	87	48	160	71	74	60	117	163	**840**	7
Lowell, MA–NH	191	266	123	116	179	286	104	274	47	**1,586**	191
Lubbock, TX	71	100	153	316	159	265	95	159	104	**1,422**	132
Lynchburg, VA	42	97	191	66	102	160	221	220	229	**1,328**	103
Macon–Warner Robins, GA	273	34	241	104	246	229	193	262	134	**1,716**	248
Madison, WI	307	273	45	102	36	66	56	115	160	**1,160**	65
Manchester, NH	296	272	190	61	121	196	272	310	32	**1,750**	260
Mansfield, OH	134	91	313	219	270	137	266	273	288	**1,991**	313
McAllen–Edinburg–Mission, TX	323	2	296	128	313	234	210	286	124	**1,916**	304
Medford, OR	67	246	317	88	210	162	168	226	321	**1,805**	277
Melbourne–Titusville–Palm Bay, FL	98	240	266	208	287	156	275	12	33	**1,575**	185
Memphis, TN–AR–MS	211	102	51	301	28	159	69	106	204	**1,231**	80
Miami–Hialeah, FL	49	285	41	328	84	132	63	3	114	**1,099**	52
Middlesex–Somerset–Hunterdon, NJ	129	306	24	80	153	8	26	186	63	**975**	28
Middletown, CT	82	302	156	67	118	47	254	163	67	**1,256**	84
Midland, TX	72	238	327	251	78	300	274	208	1	**1,749**	258
Milwaukee, WI	264	282	17	124	99	67	21	40	224	**1,138**	61
Minneapolis–St. Paul, MN–WI	320	264	11	151	60	82	10	87	113	**1,098**	51
Mobile, AL	275	75	80	306	231	169	174	84	273	**1,667**	224

Metro Area	Climate & Terrain	Housing	Health Care & Environment	Crime	Transportation	Education	The Arts	Recreation	Economics	Cumulative Score	Overall Rank
Modesto, CA	43	235	301	245	315	249	260	312	210	2,170	327
Monmouth–Ocean, NJ	61	304	33	116	282	168	30	17	80	1,091	48
Monroe, LA	269	31	308	168	200	292	187	196	148	1,799	276
Montgomery, AL	240	81	166	115	212	308	198	279	236	1,835	285
Muncie, IN	185	16	147	104	146	100	125	222	309	1,354	110
Muskegon, MI	99	45	205	311	229	237	267	49	320	1,762	266
Nashua, NH	172	292	146	24	236	196	146	199	36	1,447	141
Nashville, TN	79	161	61	184	92	178	72	137	102	1,066	44
Nassau–Suffolk, NY	31	298	9	45	312	33	22	14	22	786	6
New Bedford, MA	40	184	265	194	240	295	249	219	228	1,914	303
New Britain, CT	207	289	98	150	104	47	199	258	53	1,405	126
New Haven–Meriden, CT	96	299	50	146	40	11	29	182	156	1,009	32
New London–Norwich, CT–RI	96	284	254	61	129	31	217	74	45	1,191	70
New Orleans, LA	226	225	25	315	124	88	27	18	54	1,102	53
New York, NY	44	312	1	329	1	92	1	16	169	965	25
Newark, NJ	76	318	8	295	209	20	8	140	128	1,202	73
Niagara Falls, NY	142	149	269	101	63	268	234	132	283	1,641	213
Norfolk–Virginia Beach–Newport News, VA	50	229	56	188	241	81	37	37	109	1,028	39
Norwalk, CT	34	328	29	56	207	70	35	75	55	889	10
Oakland, CA	1	310	39	309	24	231	45	65	158	1,182	69
Ocala, FL	316	80	273	278	183	141	299	31	34	1,635	208
Odessa, TX	72	70	294	322	316	201	300	303	17	1,895	299
Oklahoma City, OK	142	117	75	272	133	120	62	150	5	1,076	47
Olympia, WA	21	203	306	94	164	244	256	218	231	1,737	256
Omaha, NE–IA	277	113	26	193	49	58	85	109	112	1,022	37
Orange County, NY	217	281	79	112	238	181	38	134	115	1,395	121
Orlando, FL	266	193	184	320	45	94	118	42	21	1,283	91
Owensboro, KY	196	82	173	47	303	283	245	305	89	1,723	250
Oxnard–Ventura, CA	4	317	118	110	307	323	116	92	150	1,537	169
Panama City, FL	176	44	325	283	275	281	251	95	86	1,816	281
Parkersburg–Marietta, WV–OH	59	67	215	29	139	278	320	269	196	1,572	183
Pascagoula, MS	93	35	241	52	322	329	310	112	278	1,772	270
Pawtucket–Woonsocket–Attleboro, RI–MA	88	261	114	91	110	61	271	202	205	1,403	125
Pensacola, FL	176	51	252	297	266	119	159	86	94	1,500	151
Peoria, IL	233	217	107	155	261	294	134	162	306	1,869	294
Philadelphia, PA–NJ	52	207	4	214	42	1	6	108	140	774	4
Phoenix, AZ	176	244	77	269	113	106	65	59	56	1,165	67
Pine Bluff, AR	262	8	277	253	324	263	282	316	299	2,234	328

Metro Area	Climate & Terrain	Housing	Health Care & Environment	Crime	Transportation	Education	The Arts	Recreation	Economics	Cumulative Score	Overall Rank
Pittsburgh, PA	88	186	14	78	57	7	12	90	184	716	1
Pittsfield, MA	244	162	206	65	186	30	303	225	155	1,576	186
Portland, ME	240	187	163	122	86	95	130	20	76	1,119	55
Portland, OR	16	275	76	305	39	22	55	55	274	1,117	54
Portsmouth–Dover–Rochester, NH–ME	255	277	237	27	301	78	308	236	3	1,722	249
Poughkeepsie, NY	237	278	299	61	157	127	246	165	42	1,612	201
Providence, RI	88	253	34	189	69	6	46	76	205	966	26
Provo–Orem, UT	223	257	326	28	126	248	157	23	323	1,711	247
Pueblo, CO	227	66	277	257	213	227	201	174	264	1,906	301
Racine, WI	229	245	148	212	203	192	214	104	286	1,833	284
Raleigh–Durham, NC	37	198	13	182	22	16	47	180	58	753	3
Reading, PA	65	144	110	36	248	74	219	193	145	1,234	82
Redding, CA	27	231	315	143	53	289	240	64	284	1,646	216
Reno, NV	182	308	229	235	17	272	138	66	130	1,577	187
Richland–Kennewick–Pasco, WA	27	222	314	102	115	328	267	262	171	1,808	278
Richmond–Petersburg, VA	92	213	37	221	18	107	48	116	108	960	24
Riverside–San Bernardino, CA	61	268	42	298	247	254	54	124	230	1,578	189
Roanoke, VA	33	137	133	106	176	199	207	101	178	1,270	87
Rochester, MN	317	252	18	20	139	325	248	207	85	1,611	200
Rochester, NY	176	233	53	147	88	5	39	50	69	860	9
Rockford, IL	260	142	142	246	260	220	225	297	269	2,061	321
Sacramento, CA	103	271	135	286	89	166	70	72	175	1,367	113
Saginaw–Bay City–Midland, MI	210	131	136	218	244	173	178	96	319	1,705	244
St. Cloud, MN	324	121	234	4	125	279	165	189	153	1,594	196
St. Joseph, MO	252	7	322	173	283	112	238	251	101	1,739	257
St. Louis, MO–IL	173	143	19	273	12	9	19	78	119	845	8
Salem, OR	23	216	187	195	111	27	257	132	314	1,462	144
Salem–Gloucester, MA	38	301	100	31	217	193	98	80	65	1,123	56
Salinas–Seaside–Monterey, CA	9	315	300	233	158	295	230	27	135	1,702	241
Salt Lake City–Ogden, UT	168	262	74	173	29	312	52	11	227	1,308	99
San Angelo, TX	237	40	321	204	264	209	203	272	10	1,760	265
San Antonio, TX	300	93	91	261	74	108	75	204	39	1,245	83
San Diego, CA	3	321	31	231	68	165	20	22	152	1,013	33
San Francisco, CA	1	327	10	318	3	18	7	2	88	774	4
San Jose, CA	8	325	47	215	82	207	43	111	24	1,062	43
Santa Barbara–Santa Maria–Lompoc, CA	7	323	261	201	54	203	117	23	116	1,305	97
Santa Cruz, CA	9	319	134	169	93	252	86	158	170	1,390	119

Metro Area	Climate & Terrain	Housing	Health Care & Environment	Crime	Transportation	Education	The Arts	Recreation	Economics	Cumulative Score	Overall Rank
Santa Rosa–Petaluma, CA	19	309	128	154	237	200	94	77	127	1,345	109
Sarasota, FL	303	265	177	162	189	243	243	54	11	1,647	218
Savannah, GA	164	92	122	317	38	291	135	79	144	1,382	118
Scranton–Wilkes–Barre, PA	105	73	101	6	194	34	169	238	233	1,153	64
Seattle, WA	12	283	21	254	19	206	17	1	106	919	12
Sharon, PA	113	73	203	8	314	80	329	282	307	1,709	245
Sheboygan, WI	275	188	241	23	218	262	297	247	253	2,004	315
Sherman–Denison, TX	196	13	292	206	317	228	327	296	75	1,950	309
Shreveport, LA	220	57	82	261	138	143	113	237	50	1,301	95
Sioux City, IA–NE	304	56	161	97	147	222	196	240	263	1,686	234
Sioux Falls, SD	321	175	130	44	27	229	273	246	192	1,637	210
South Bend–Mishawaka, IN	157	20	167	207	55	135	119	139	216	1,215	78
Spokane, WA	110	95	272	136	65	172	107	200	259	1,416	130
Springfield, IL	196	167	57	268	31	57	158	197	165	1,296	93
Springfield, MA	270	179	200	264	33	10	93	201	177	1,427	134
Springfield, MO	159	43	249	143	178	207	180	151	103	1,413	129
Stamford, CT	34	329	23	127	250	70	28	154	79	1,094	50
State College, PA	105	221	230	39	278	38	206	264	262	1,643	214
Steubenville–Weirton, OH–WV	164	61	270	17	327	223	314	217	317	1,910	302
Stockton, CA	55	223	304	289	135	323	185	171	131	1,816	281
Syracuse, NY	151	148	131	79	14	44	57	44	282	950	21
Tacoma, WA	12	155	258	249	112	264	74	7	238	1,369	114
Tallahassee, FL	296	178	297	248	66	167	141	119	96	1,608	199
Tampa–St. Petersburg–Clearwater, FL	277	135	106	302	61	67	58	38	25	1,069	45
Terre Haute, IN	138	5	281	60	205	83	211	234	291	1,508	153
Texarkana, TX–Texarkana, AR	258	12	303	120	288	126	328	325	252	2,012	317
Toledo, OH	204	153	68	189	77	147	71	114	275	1,298	94
Topeka, KS	222	111	112	191	76	164	181	271	157	1,485	147
Trenton, NJ	46	291	87	257	108	24	59	169	121	1,162	66
Tucson, AZ	87	228	95	290	141	218	61	29	81	1,230	79
Tulsa, OK	185	139	78	222	187	240	76	102	31	1,260	86
Tuscaloosa, AL	254	50	210	195	114	307	194	283	235	1,842	289
Tyler, TX	223	127	211	167	216	26	278	326	23	1,597	197
Utica–Rome, NY	151	79	293	10	122	99	239	149	189	1,331	105
Vallejo–Fairfield–Napa, CA	11	288	124	169	160	282	109	192	117	1,452	142
Vancouver, WA	16	247	266	94	180	315	186	215	272	1,791	274
Victoria, TX	314	114	316	226	297	213	321	230	16	2,047	319
Vineland–Millville–Bridgeton, NJ	61	126	174	240	161	185	149	214	219	1,529	164

Metro Area	Climate & Terrain	Housing	Health Care & Environment	Crime	Transportation	Education	The Arts	Recreation	Economics	Cumulative Score	Overall Rank
Visalia–Tulare–Porterville, CA	163	157	324	239	252	326	270	45	147	**1,923**	305
Waco, TX	293	25	260	251	256	140	218	252	71	**1,766**	268
Washington, DC–MD–VA	51	314	6	276	4	3	4	188	87	**933**	17
Waterbury, CT	115	279	102	108	296	88	291	295	135	**1,709**	245
Waterloo–Cedar Falls, IA	312	166	149	81	230	131	105	129	287	**1,590**	194
Wausau, WI	317	147	169	22	214	184	250	166	295	**1,764**	267
West Palm Beach–Boca Raton–Delray Beach, FL	217	290	295	324	85	35	110	13	8	**1,377**	117
Wheeling, WV–OH	164	60	179	1	294	85	277	250	256	**1,566**	181
Wichita, KS	231	105	175	250	172	93	108	205	92	**1,431**	137
Wichita Falls, TX	268	46	255	255	273	185	264	275	41	**1,862**	292
Williamsport, PA	134	125	160	25	251	122	305	320	327	**1,769**	269
Wilmington, DE–NJ–MD	81	173	82	234	127	52	66	122	77	**1,014**	34
Wilmington, NC	121	89	120	292	267	134	222	48	164	**1,457**	143
Worcester, MA	123	239	64	77	197	25	172	301	218	**1,416**	130
Yakima, WA	182	47	310	232	190	283	231	91	223	**1,789**	273
York, PA	170	215	199	21	304	124	226	307	226	**1,792**	275
Youngstown–Warren, OH	113	103	121	161	228	115	115	245	313	**1,514**	156
Yuba City, CA	69	164	323	255	277	309	317	299	261	**2,274**	329

Et Cetera

AMERICA'S CHOICE METRO AREAS

After feeding stacks of data through nine different scoring systems and comparing the final rankings, *Places Rated* can now point to the very best of the 329 metro areas. But because statistics alone rarely tell the whole story, in this section of the chapter we offer brief prose sketches of the 20 metro areas that follow first-place Pittsburgh (Pittsburgh is described on pages 419–420). Even this small and select slice of *Places Rated*'s universe—which includes places in upstate New York, the South, and the California coast—will surprise you with its diversity.

★ **Boston, MA** (2)
Population: 2,805,911   Population Rank: 7

Boston, also known as the Hub and the Athens of America, takes second place in *Places Rated*'s overall ranking of American metro areas.

Boston's historic importance to the early days of the republic, unrivaled by any other city except Philadelphia, is known to every schoolchild. Here was the stage for the Boston Tea Party, Paul Revere's famous ride, and the battles of Lexington and Concord. What is usually surprising to the newcomer to New England is how compressed the distances are: From downtown Boston (pop. 562,994) out to Concord (pop. 6,400) is only 18 miles, and the perfect way to see the historic landmarks in the heart of the city is on foot, since most sites are within a brisk 20-minute walk.

As early as the mid-1600s, Boston's harbor contributed to making the city a center of trading for the New World. Many Yankee families who invested in shipping became wealthy early on, and some spent their fortunes not only on huge mansions on Beacon Hill and in Back Bay but on supporting the arts and letters as well. Soon Boston's reputation as a center of learning and culture was established—a reputation reflected today in its outstanding rankings in the arts (fifth) and education (14th).

Fine museums, symphony, opera, theatre, and dance—a wide array of these is available to residents and visitors alike. And no other metro area for its size has as many first-rate universities. Heading the list is of course Harvard, founded in 1636, when John Harvard donated his library to the new school that had been founded in Cambridge. Wellesley, M.I.T., Tufts, Northeastern, Boston College, and Boston University are also located here. The creativity and intellectual talent that issue continually from these fine schools are Boston's most precious resources. Polaroid, Digital Equipment Corporation, Wang, and a host of other high-tech electronic enterprises had their origins in Boston's prestigious universities. The ring of space-age corporations that encircles the city on Route 128 is at the heart of Boston's current economic boom and low unemployment rate. The many top-ranked medical schools help explain the metro area's tremendous health care facilities (ranked third among the metro areas) and New England's constant contributions to medical science.

Like many other major metro areas, Boston is a collection of diverse towns, each contributing to the general tone of the area but each with its own identity and charm. North of the city are places like Lynn (pop. 78,471), Revere (pop. 42,423), and Chelsea (pop. 25,431)—industrial towns with historical significance now primarily engaged in manufacturing. To the south are Braintree (pop. 36,337) and Quincy (pop. 84,743), the hometown of John Adams, John Quincy Adams, and John Hancock; and Plymouth (pop. 7,232), landing site of the *Mayflower*.

But what of the sections and neighborhoods within Boston? They, too, are diverse, each with their own ethnic composition and local economy. As the Industrial Revolution took hold in the New World, the earliest and most numerous immigrant group was the Irish, and they still play perhaps the most important role in the city. The Irish enclaves in Boston are South Boston and Charlestown. Both of these are predominantly working-class, blue-collar residential neighborhoods which are so tightly knit that they are sometimes cool, even hostile, to strangers and any outside interference.

The North End is home to many of Boston's Italian-Americans, the second most populous ethnic group. Here, on the northern tip of the stubby peninsula that is downtown Boston, the visitor can walk through the crowded, intimate streets lined with small shops selling pasta, meats, vegetables, wines, pastries, espresso, and cookware, and hear nothing but Italian spoken, sung, and shouted.

And then there is Beacon Hill, that stalwart monument to the old-time Yankee aristocracy. This rolling rise of ground behind the State House is where Boston's elite make their homes. The streets are still brick, and the houses are stately Georgian and Regency three- or four-story mansions, many of them converted into apartments or condominiums. Henry James once called Beacon Hill's Mount Vernon Street "the only respectable street in America."

Boston is where it all began for the United States. And perhaps, if the technological revolution continues unabated, Boston, ironically, will be the cradle of the second great revolution, 200 years after the first.

Pluses: Abundant historic and ethnic charm; outstanding health care facilities; top-notch educational and performing arts assets.

Minuses: Very high housing costs (300th) and high crime rate (266th).

★ **Raleigh–Durham, NC** (3)
Population: 561,222   Population Rank: 74

How did this midsize metro area with a total population of just over half a million wind up at the top of the list along with Pittsburgh (pop. 2,218,870) and Boston (pop. 2,805,911)?

Simple: Raleigh–Durham has a lot going for it. A center of learning, a capital of one of America's most varied and promising states, a research center, the southeastern mecca for high-tech industry and development, and a beautiful, genteel place to live—the more you find out about this Piedmont metro area, the less surprising it is that Raleigh–Durham is one of America's most livable metro areas.

About half its population is divided among Raleigh (pop. 150,255), Durham (pop. 100,538), and Chapel Hill (pop. 32,421). The remainder is scattered in small towns and suburbs in Durham, Wake, Orange, and Franklin counties. The metro area is multidimensional and spread out among many towns, giving it an open, relaxed, and rural feel. Each of the three main cities is home to a major university—Raleigh contains North Carolina State University; Durham is the site of Duke; and Chapel Hill is where the main campus of the University of North Carolina, the oldest state university in the nation, was established.

Raleigh, founded in 1792 and named for Sir Walter Raleigh, the British soldier and explorer, is encircled by a beltway studded with plants, shopping malls, and office buildings. The downtown section centers on Capitol Square. The capitol, which replaced the original (it burned in 1831), is Greek Revival in style and striking in its simplicity. Nearby are the Governor's Mansion and the Oakwood Historic District, a neighborhood of old frame houses that have been restored and that command handsome real estate prices. Besides the capitol area, perhaps the greatest attraction is North Carolina State University, NCAA Division I basketball champions in 1983. It's a large school (more than 21,000 students) that offers undergraduate and graduate courses in more than 90 fields of study. Still, what impresses many visitors to Raleigh is the manageable size, friendly spirit, and intimacy of this seat of government, business, and learning.

The city of Durham is tied inextricably to the Duke family, founders of the American Tobacco Company in the 1880s. Sensing that cigarettes might be more than just a passing fad, the Dukes began mass-producing and packaging them during the last part of the century. Almost overnight, the company and the family reaped a huge fortune. In 1924 James B. Duke contributed a considerable portion of that fortune to establish Duke University, which remains one of the most prestigious universities in the nation, with a renowned medical center.

In contrast to the Gothic stone of Duke are the many tobacco warehouses and textile mills that still form a cornerstone of the local economy. Residents can smell the pungent aroma of raw tobacco leaf all over the city, and trucks and freight cars filled with the raw material and finished product bustle in and out of town continually. In recent decades, Durham has diversified its economic base, relying increasingly on service industries and high-tech manufacturing.

The tone and charm of Chapel Hill, the smallest of the three major cities in the metro area, reflect the fact that it was founded not as a commercial or manufacturing site but as a home for a state university. And this university-town flavor is evident everywhere in Chapel Hill, from the tweedy campus clothing and tobacco shops to the snug eateries and boutiques, the raucous night spots, and the quiet splendor of the campus itself, which encompasses 3,900 acres and more than 200 buildings. The quads, walkways, and tree-covered knolls of the campus are famous for a dazzling variety of plants and trees.

One recent development that undoubtedly has had much to do with Raleigh–Durham's high ranking was the selection in the late 1950s of Durham County as the site of Research Triangle Park, a planned research center that is now sometimes referred to as a miniature version of Boston in the fields of scientific and medical research and high-tech entrepreneurship.

Pluses: A good showing in nearly every category; mild, temperate climate (37th), plus excellent rankings in health care facilities (13th), education (16th), and transportation (22nd).

Minuses: Mediocre rankings in housing costs (198th) and crime (182nd).

★ Philadelphia, PA–NJ (4)
Population: 4,716,818   Population Rank: 4

Philadelphia, a huge and historic metro area, has much to recommend it. Founded as a Quaker colony in 1682 by William Penn, the central city (pop. 1,688,210) retains Quaker ideals of public service and social progress. It is still headquarters of many artistic, philosophic, dramatic, musical, and scientific societies. Among these are the Pennsylvania Academy of the Fine Arts, the Academy of Natural Sciences of Philadelphia, the American Philosophical Society, and the Franklin Institute of Science. Philadelphia's symphony orchestra is one of the elite performing ensembles in the world. It and the many area art and history museums, as well as 46 four-year colleges and universities (among them the University of Pennsylvania, Temple, Bryn Mawr, Drexel, Villanova, and St. Joseph's), all contribute to the metro area's rich cultural life. It's no surprise, then, that Philadelphia took first place in education and ranked sixth in the arts among *Places Rated*'s metro areas. The fine medical schools and hospitals that are a natural by-product of first-rate universities help establish Philadelphia's rank of fourth for health care options.

In addition to these impressive big-city blessings, however, is a more intimate side to the City of Brotherly Love. Philadelphia's neighborhoods, so well defined they act as mini-cities within the big one, are a key to understanding not only the physical place that is Philadelphia but its social and historical structure as well. Natives tend to tell you they're from Kingsessing, Northern Liberties, Strawberry Mansion, Brewerytown, Manayunk, or any one of the many Philadelphia neighborhoods. Urban renovation is currently and quickly transforming blighted sections of the city into resurgent neighborhoods while preserving the wonderful buildings and historic sections at their heart. In Manayunk, a textile center once referred to as the Manchester of America, countless solid-stone mill buildings became mostly vacant over the past 50 years with the decline of the textile industry in the Northeast. Now artists and designers are taking over the abandoned buildings and setting up studios. The old residents, primarily descendants of the Italian, Irish, Polish, and German immigrants who came over to run the looms, also remain in Manayunk, loyal to one another and to their neighborhood.

Another area that mirrors what's happening in Philadelphia is Society Hill. An old city quarter just south of Independence Hall, this once fashionable district had become a dismal island of poverty. Now its restored historic buildings attract top dollars. One of the driving forces behind this creative urban rehabbing is the Greater Philadelphia Partnership, which puts old homes and buildings back into use by practically giving them to prospective owners and residents along with grants for rehabilitating them. This style of urban renewal results in a high proportion of owner-occupied housing, which then leads to increased neighborhood pride, lower crime rates, and greater social stability.

Philadelphia is located in southeastern Pennsylvania between the Delaware and Schuylkill rivers, about 100 miles upstream from the mouth of the Delaware River at Delaware Bay. The land is low-lying and level, with a few rolling hills. The nearby Atlantic Coast to the east and the Appalachian Mountains to the west shield the area from temperature extremes both winter and summer, though summers can be muggy and hot.

Outlying parts of the metro area include places rich in history and scenic beauty, such as Swarthmore (pop. 5,950), home of Swarthmore College, founded in 1864 by the Society of Friends; Chester (pop. 45,794), settled in 1643 by the Swedish Trading Company; Valley Forge National Historical Park, a memorial to the trials of the Continental Army; and New Hope (pop. 1,473) in charming Bucks County, where Washington crossed the Delaware and where artists and writers have now settled, giving the area a reputation as an art center. These are all residential communities where one can enjoy the lushness and quaintness of the countryside while still being near the city.

Pluses: Top rankings in education, the arts, and health care; many landmarks of early American history; mild four-season climate (52nd).

Minuses: Below-average rankings for housing costs (207th) and crime (214th).

★ **San Francisco, CA** (4)
  Population: 1,488,871   Population Rank: 26

San Francisco is probably America's most beautiful metro area. Its extremely high rankings in climate (first among the metro areas) and recreation (second) reflect its spectacular environment. Situated on the tip of a narrow peninsula that separates San Francisco Bay from the Pacific Ocean, the city of San Francisco (pop. 678,974) is surrounded by cool ocean waters. Many of the buildings in San Francisco are white or cream-colored, giving the impression that this city is Mediterranean. It isn't, of course, but the climate is. San Francisco's location in a temperate latitude in the path of Pacific winds provides the metro area with the mildest climate in America—and perhaps even in the world. The only aspect of the climate that could be considered a drawback is the fog. Rising currents of hot summer air from the San Joaquin Valley draw cold ocean air in through the bay, causing an almost daily intrusion of fog. Still, National Weather Service statistics show San Francisco getting 66 of every possible 100 hours of sunshine.

The Bay Area's environmental blessings don't end with the weather. San Francisco is a city of parks and gardens, including the magnificent Golden Gate Park, 1,017 acres stretching from the ocean to the center of the city. Golden Gate National Recreation Area, which includes most of the San Francisco shoreline, the Marin County coast, and the islands of Angel and Alcatraz, is evidence of San Francisco's resolve to keep thousands of acres of natural beauty intact for future generations. Quality restaurants and great spectator sports are among San Francisco's other top recreational amenities.

San Francisco ranks third among the metro areas in transportation, and some people consider its most famous mode of transit, the cable car, to be another form of recreation. The metro area garners high marks

in health care (tenth) and the arts (seventh) as well; in all, it has a rank of tenth or better in five of *Places Rated*'s nine categories. Such elite performing arts groups as the San Francisco Symphony, the American Conservatory Theatre, San Francisco Opera, and San Francisco Ballet make this one of America's premier cultural centers. In contrast with its high marks in climate, health, arts, recreation, and transportation, however, San Francisco ranks very near the bottom of *Places Rated*'s list in housing (327th) and crime (318th). These poor showings are due to a high population density, caused in turn by the city's other attractive features. Housing in nearly all segments of the metro area is expensive and hard to find.

Like most major metropolitan areas, San Francisco is not one homogeneous city but a collection of neighborhoods. Chinatown, the city's best-known ethnic neighborhood, is the largest Asian community outside the Orient. The North Beach section, now famous for its nightlife, remains a close-knit, traditional Italian neighborhood replete with religious festivals, a glorious Columbus Day celebration, and scores of first-rate Italian restaurants and coffeehouses. The Mission district, home of many Mexican-Americans, borders on the Castro and Polk Street neighborhoods, center of the city's influential gay population. The Sunset district, with the Pacific Ocean on the west and Golden Gate Park on the north, and Richmond, a somewhat cooler and foggier area, both provide more traditional, middle-class, single-family residential options. Two sections of the city itself cater almost exclusively to the establishment: the financial district, which houses the Bank of America (the world's biggest bank), many brokerage houses, and most of the city's law firms; and Nob Hill, the domain of the wealthy and upwardly mobile.

The San Francisco metro area includes San Francisco County itself, San Mateo County to the south, and Marin County to the north (just across the Golden Gate Bridge), one of the most coveted residential counties in the United States. Real estate prices there prove it. In Sausalito (pop. 7,338), a famous artists' colony with a distinct maritime flavor, many residents live in barge-type houseboats decorated with gingerbread woodwork, stained-glass windows, and innumerable flowerpots. Tiburon (pop. 6,685) features steep hills lined with homes that command spectacular views of the bay and the city across it.

Pluses: America's mildest climate; great natural beauty; outstanding cultural and recreational assets.

Minuses: Housing prices are out of sight; high crime rate.

★ **Nassau–Suffolk, NY** (6)
  Population: 2,605,813   Population Rank: 9

East of the New York City boroughs of Brooklyn and Queens on Long Island lies a metro area that presents an interesting paradox. On one hand, Nassau–Suffolk serves New York, sending thousands of commuters daily into "the city" and providing weekend and vacation retreats for thousands of New Yorkers. Yet Nassau–Suffolk also exists for itself, deliberately determining its own facilities, industries, and way of life. The variety of activities, both commercial and recreational, is stunning.

Hardly a category of contemporary life is free of the contrasts that characterize the metro area. Residential Long Island includes apartment complexes, suburban single-family homes, estates, and summer cottages. Large urban industries like Grumman Aerospace Corporation (in Bethpage, pop. 29,900) and Brookhaven National Laboratory (in Upton) are countered by Long Island's agricultural and fishing industries. Recreational facilities range from the 17,000-seat Nassau Veterans Memorial Coliseum (in Hempstead, pop. 40,404) and Roosevelt Raceway (in Westbury, pop. 13,871) to the sand and surf of Jones Beach State Park and the unspoiled beauty of Fire Island National Seashore.

Part of this contrast is simply between the two counties. Nassau County, closer to New York City, is a bedroom county, with suburbs, stores, and recreational facilities responding to the pulse of a high-energy population eager to pay for goods and services while expecting the most for its money. Residential areas are tightly packed but maintained with the pride of those who have spent hard-earned money on choice real estate. Suffolk County, with its committed detachment from the frenzy of New York and the intensity of Nassau, lures many to its blend of rural farms, fishing villages, elegant mansions, art colonies, sedate old towns, and lazy, endless stretches of shoreline. The ultimate withdrawal is Montauk Point, 120 miles from New York City. Montauk Lighthouse, nearly 200 years old, marks the easternmost tip of Long Island. Suffolk County offers sanctuaries for the elite who want to get away from it all, with their own kind or alone, to visit such spots as the old whaling village of Sag Harbor (pop. 2,581) or to put down roots in places like the harbor town of Northport (pop. 7,651).

Because of its proximity to New York City (and because of its predominantly middle- and upper-class residents and visitors), Nassau–Suffolk's housing costs are quite high, giving it a very low housing rank (298th), but its ranks in health (ninth), arts (22nd), and education (33rd) all benefit for the same reason.

Both counties are changing from summer vacation spots to year-round residential communities. This trend is perhaps most notable in Long Beach, located just a short distance from Manhattan on Nassau County's south shore, where post–World War II deterioration, run-down housing, and high crime are being brought under control by new, carefully designed housing, stores, and public buildings.

Pluses: Proximity to New York City means good ranks in the arts, education, recreation, and health care facilities.

Minuses: Very high housing costs; very low ranking in transportation (312th).

★ Louisville, KY–IN (7)
Population: 956,756   Population Rank: 44

Mint juleps in frosted silver cups, paddle-wheel races on the Ohio, and Thoroughbreds steaming after a sunrise workout may all seem out of place in the hurry-up world of the eighties, but these are a way of life in Louisville, Kentucky (pop. 298,840), heart of the seventh-ranked metro area in the United States. One of the nine super-solid metro areas that earn no *Places Rated* ranking below 200th, Louisville (pronounced LOO-vull by natives) is a metro area in step with the present while preserving its past.

Ongoing maintenance of historic sites, such as Farmington and Locust Grove, is a poignant reminder of Louisville's gracious heritage. Other points of interest include Butchertown, which houses Bakery Square, antique shops, and the home of Thomas A. Edison; the restored downtown districts of Old Louisville and West Main Street; and Churchill Downs, first opened in May of 1875 and home of the annual Kentucky Derby.

Hand in hand with a reverence for history goes Louisville's commitment to the arts, evident in its ranking of 60th in this category. The Actor's Theatre of Louisville has received national recognition for its dedication to the promotion of new plays and rising playwrights and actors; the Louisville Children's Theatre is recognized for exemplary children's theatre in the Southeast; and Stage One was honored by an invitation to perform at the Kennedy Center. Louisville also supports two symphony orchestras, the Louisville Ballet, and the Kentucky Opera Association. In addition to many small historical museums, there are tours through the businesses that have made Louisville famous—Old Fitzgerald and Joseph E. Seagram Sons distilleries, Philip Morris, Louisville Stoneware Company, and Hillerich & Bradsby's Slugger Park.

Even though it produces the world's best baseball bats, bourbon, and racehorses, Louisville's economy is in a transitional phase. Some companies are closing their Louisville facilities. Still, Louisville's rank of 163rd in economic promise lands it precisely in the middle of the 329 metro areas. Also to the metro area's credit are the building and restoration efforts in the downtown area that are creating accommodations for business and pleasure.

Due to a recent focus on improving the quality of public schools and a good mix of degree options, Louisville ranks 74th in education. It does, however, face problems common to many school systems in the South and Southeast: overcrowded classroooms, low teacher salaries, and racial tension.

For a metro area with a population approaching the million mark, Louisville's ranks for housing costs (87th) and crime rate (160th) are surprisingly good. Its lack of inner-city congestion may help keep these two regrettable aspects of city living under control. This metro area, which spans seven counties in Kentucky and Indiana, is spread over farms, small towns, and cities where the people are friendly and hardworking. Out here in the towns of Shepherdsville (pop. 4,454), La Grange (pop. 2,971), and Shelbyville (pop. 5,329), and over the bridge in New Albany, Indiana (pop. 37,103), homes are available and affordable.

Louisville's high ranking of 48th for health care facilities goes deeper than its three teaching hospitals and the University of Louisville School of Medicine. November of 1984 saw the second successful implant of an artificial human heart, at the Humana Heart Institution International. The medical resources here are recognized as some of the best in the country.

On the first Saturday in May, just before the world's best Thoroughbreds run for the roses, the whole of Churchill Downs stands and sings "My Old Kentucky Home" while the rest of the world watches and listens. And for that moment the world understands the pride Louisvillians have in their city, their home, and their heritage.

Pluses: Good rankings in housing, health care facilities, the arts, and education; moderate climate, with four distinct seasons.

Minuses: Economy in a transitional phase; average crime rate; average recreation facilities.

★ St. Louis, MO–IL (8)
Population: 1,808,621   Population Rank: 19

Just the mention of St. Louis brings a myriad of responses: Gateway Arch, St. Louis Cardinals, Six Flags Over Mid-America, Anheuser-Busch, St. Louis Zoo, St. Louis *Post-Dispatch*. Names like T. S. Eliot, Stan Musial, Lewis and Clark, Eugene Field, Dred Scott, William Webster, and Yogi Berra are further reminders of the diversity of *Places Rated*'s eighth-ranked metro area. Sports, entertainment, the arts, and industry all flourish here.

St. Louis (pop. 453,085) began as a center for trade on the mighty Mississippi and grew into a hub for national and international commerce. One of the world's largest markets for wool, lumber, and pharmaceuticals, St. Louis is also an important producer of shoes, beer, aircraft, and basic metals. Nine Fortune 500 companies including McDonnell Douglas, Monsanto, Anheuser-Busch, and Ralston Purina have headquarters in St. Louis.

Receiving a number-12 rank among the metro areas for its transit supply, St. Louis maintains its historic position as a major transportation center. River traffic still thrives as cargo-loaded barges drift from one end of the river to the other. Truck transport also abounds; a network of Interstate highways flows through St. Louis, connecting East with West and North with South. Lambert–St. Louis International Airport offers the same convenience for travelers and air freight.

An innovative voluntary desegregation program is improving the racial balance of area schools. The metro area ranks ninth for education, due mostly to its above-average effort in supporting public schools and its many options in higher learning: St. Louis proudly claims Washington University, St. Louis University, and the St. Louis campus of the University of Missouri among its numerous institutions. And six of its secondary schools were judged outstanding by the Department of Education's Secondary School Recognition Program.

St. Louis is often called the City of Neighborhoods, and rightly so. Descendants of the German immigrants who flocked to St. Louis in the mid-1800s populate many of the neighborhoods. The Central West End, with its grand turn-of-the-century brick and stucco homes, antique shops, boutiques, restaurants, sidewalk cafés, and lanterned streets, reflects St. Louis's rich heritage. Laclede's Landing, a renovation of old warehouses along the riverfront just north of Gateway Arch, provides an exciting array of activities day and night with its numerous restaurants, music-filled pubs, and specialty shops.

St. Louis County has its own blend of old (Webster Groves, pop. 23,097, and Kirkwood, pop. 27,987) and new (Westwood, pop. 319, and Chesterfield, pop. 800), offering a variety of housing from traditional neighborhoods to attractive subdivisions and conveniently located condominiums. The gracious homes of Clayton (pop. 14,273), the St. Louis county seat, vie in charm with the luxurious estate settings of Ladue (pop. 9,376). Homeowning costs are slightly lower than average in the St. Louis metro area, which ranks 143rd in this *Places Rated* category.

There is obviously a lot that is right about this high-ranking metro area, but what is wrong? First, the summers can be insufferably hot, with temperatures climbing above 90 degrees Fahrenheit more often than not. No wonder the ice-cream cone was introduced here! Second, as with nearly every major city, the crime rate is high, ranked 273rd among the 329 metro areas. But St. Louis is a city of determination and resilience: When parts of the city were declared blighted urban areas, it demolished and rebuilt; when business slumped and the economic outlook was poor, St. Louis created facilities to attract tourists and conventioneers. This city of grace, tradition, and charm is a testament to the words of one of its most colorful sons, Yogi Berra, who exclaimed, "The game isn't over till it's over."

Pluses: Ranks high in transportation, education, and health care; full spectrum of cultural facilities, for an arts rank of 19th.

Minuses: Often dangerously hot summers; high crime rate.

★ Rochester, NY (9)
Population: 971,230   Population Rank: 43

Rochester (pop. 241,741) is the namesake city of a five-county metro area encompassing rich fruit-orchard and truck-gardening country on the southern

Large and Small Metro Areas

Places Rated Almanac's top 50 metro areas include 24 with a population of more than one million, 21 between 250,000 and one million in size, and only five with a population of less than 250,000, despite the fact that there are more small metro areas (170) than medium-sized (119) or large (40).

The large metropolitan areas undoubtedly offer a number of advantages: economic diversity, the chance for personal achievement, a wide range of cultural and recreational facilities, and freedom for diverse life-styles. But the flip side of this is often high crime rates, high living costs, a sense of personal insignificance, and restricted access to the natural environment.

Many people who live in large metro areas actually prefer smaller places but feel compelled for economic reasons to stay near the big city. These people might do well to look at some of *Places Rated*'s high-ranking medium and small metro areas as the ideal compromise between big-city strengths and the more manageable, even intimate life-style associated with smaller places. To assist you in evaluating the relative merits of large, medium, and small metro areas, we present the top places in each category.

America's Best Large Metro Areas
(Population 1,000,000 or more)

Metro Area	Cumulative Score
1. Pittsburgh, PA	716
2. Boston, MA	752
3. Philadelphia, PA–NJ	774
3. San Francisco, CA	774
5. Nassau–Suffolk, NY	786
6. St. Louis, MO–IL	845
7. Dallas, TX	898
8. Seattle, WA	919
9. Atlanta, GA	921
10. Buffalo, NY	931
11. Baltimore, MD	932
12. Washington, DC–MD–VA	933
13. Cincinnati, OH–KY–IN	938
14. New York, NY	965
15. Chicago, IL	968
16. Denver, CO	977
17. Cleveland, OH	988
18. San Diego, CA	1,013
19. Los Angeles–Long Beach, CA	1,021
20. San Jose, CA	1,062

America's Best Medium-Sized Metro Areas
(Population 250,000 to 1,000,000)

Metro Area	Cumulative Score
1. Raleigh–Durham, NC	753
2. Louisville, KY–IN	840
3. Rochester, NY	860
4. Knoxville, TN	928
5. Albany–Schenectady–Troy, NY	941
6. Syracuse, NY	950
7. Albuquerque, NM	952
8. Harrisburg–Lebanon–Carlisle, PA	957
9. Richmond–Petersburg, VA	960
10. Providence, RI	966
11. Middlesex–Somerset–Hunterdon, NJ	975
12. New Haven–Meriden, CT	1,009
13. Wilmington, DE–NJ–MD	1,014
14. Omaha, NE–IA	1,022
15. Bridgeport–Milford, CT	1,026
16. Greensboro–Winston-Salem–High Point, NC	1,030
17. Nashville, TN	1,066
18. Johnson City–Kingsport–Bristol, TN–VA	1,070
19. Oklahoma City, OK	1,076
20. Monmouth–Ocean, NJ	1,091

America's Best Small Metro Areas
(Population Less than 250,000)

Metro Area	Cumulative Score
1. Norwalk, CT	889
2. Burlington, VT	941
3. Charlottesville, VA	999
4. Asheville, NC	1,016
5. Stamford, CT	1,094
6. Portland, ME	1,119
7. Danbury, CT	1,124
8. Galveston–Texas City, TX	1,205
9. South Bend–Mishawaka, IN	1,215
10. Middletown, CT	1,256
11. Bangor, ME	1,258
12. Roanoke, VA	1,270
13. Springfield, IL	1,296
14. Lynchburg, VA	1,328
15. Boulder–Longmont, CO	1,330
16. Cumberland, MD–WV	1,333
17. Champaign–Urbana–Rantoul, IL	1,342
18. Kenosha, WI	1,343
19. Muncie, IN	1,354
20. La Crosse, WI	1,355

shore of Lake Ontario. One of its early nicknames was Flour City, an obvious if uninspired one for a town that dealt largely in milling wheat. As with many other New York State communities, Rochester's fortunes were closely tied to the opening of the Erie Canal in the early 1820s. With the Genesee River as an inland gateway, Rochester linked Lake Ontario ports with those on the canal, that famous east-west water route connecting the Great Lakes with the Hudson River and Atlantic Ocean. Thus established as a commercial center, Rochester became the flour-milling capital of the nation, relying on the wheat grown in the Genesee Valley.

Flour milling dominated the town until just after the Civil War, when horticultural ventures in flowers, ornamental shrubbery, and other nursery items were introduced to the region. Accordingly, Flour City became known as Flower City, a name eclipsed when a new industry sprang up, started by a young inventor named George Eastman.

Few figures in American industry can rival George Eastman, the father of modern photography, in creative genius. In the 1880s, while still in his thirties, he discovered the dry-plate process for taking pictures, which vastly simplified the more cumbersome wet-plate process. Soon after, he developed the same chemicals on a transparent strip of celluloid, and so was born roll film. This, coupled with his introduction of the Kodak hand-held camera in 1888, made photography an inexpensive, convenient hobby within the reach of most Americans. The Eastman Kodak Company grew impressively over the years, with profound effects and benefits for the city of Rochester, for Eastman was a philanthropist and educator as well as an inventor. Thus, Rochester received an estimated $100 million from the Kodak corporation to support the University of Rochester, the Eastman School of Music, Rochester Institute of Technology, and a host of other charitable and educational institutions.

Today Rochester, which ranks a solid 69th in economics, is in the midst of a high-tech boom. In addition to Kodak (30th in *Fortune* magazine's 1984 list of leading industrial corporations), the city has become well known for the manufacture of office equipment, gear-grinding machinery, optical equipment, and dental tools. Other Fortune 500 companies headquartered in the metro area are Sybron and Bausch & Lomb.

The metro area's high ranking in recreation (50th) owes much to its natural setting. The city of Rochester is gateway to New York's Finger Lakes region, and the metro area is dotted with small cities such as Canandaigua (pop. 10,419), a resort located on the westernmost of the Finger Lakes; and Geneva (pop. 15,133), a fisherman's mecca on Seneca Lake. Recreational boating is popular both on Irondequoit Bay and the Genesee River. Beaches and parks line the river and lakeshore, providing additional outdoor recreation for Rochester's pleasant summertimes and falls.

Rochester ranks 39th in the arts and provides artistic and cultural variety for residents, including performances by the Rochester Philharmonic Orchestra, one of America's major symphonies, and the Opera Theatre of Rochester. Its fifth-place rank in education reflects an emphasis on quality nurtured by pioneers such as George Eastman.

Pluses: Nice mix of cultural, recreational, and educational facilities; pleasant summers.

Minuses: Rather long, snowy winters; cloudy; above-average housing costs (233rd).

★ **Norwalk, CT** (10)
Population: 126,692   Population Rank: 258

For many travelers, Norwalk, Connecticut, is an exit on the Connecticut Turnpike; to many commuters, Norwalk is a parking lot and a train station. But as its tenth-place ranking indicates, this dark-horse metro area is more than a stopover between Wall Street and home. Norwalk lies on Long Island Sound just an hour's drive from New York City and all it has to offer. A major factor contributing to Norwalk's leap from 148th place in the first edition of *Places Rated Almanac* to its present high status is its membership in the New York–Northern New Jersey–Long Island CMSA, which benefited its rankings in both the arts and recreational opportunities substantially.

The city of Norwalk (pop. 77,767) is surrounded by fashionable, affluent residential towns. Because of this, Norwalk's appeal might appear to be in its surroundings. In fact, Norwalk has its own history and identity. Founded in 1651, this pre–Revolutionary War settlement was an industrial center producing clocks, nails, and paper. Today Norwalk focuses on manufacturing astronomic instruments, aircraft radar equipment, electric components, chemicals, and plastics, and is also becoming a research and development center. Economic opportunities are good in the metro area, resulting in a solid 55th-place ranking.

A city of contrasts, Norwalk claims both the best and the worst in terms of available housing. Some of the area's finest residential sections are here, including comfortable Rowayton and Silvermine. On the other hand, South Norwalk is fighting a high crime rate and inadequate housing. It is heartening to note, however, that the late 1970s saw a trend toward the renovation of run-down Victorian homes in this section, and more recently a proposed waterfront revival.

Two neighboring communities that enhance the Norwalk metro area are Wilton (pop. 6,500) and Westport (pop. 25,290)—bedroom suburbs, like Norwalk, that send commuters daily into New York City. Wilton supports some of the finest public schools in the nation and has a two-acre residential zoning ordinance that keeps most of the old clapboard homes in wooded seclusion. Through landscaping and careful commercial architecture, great care is taken to preserve an "authentic" New England appearance.

Westport is best described as a strictly residential town. With its borders along Long Island Sound, it offers a full repertoire of real estate for those who can afford it: from posh estates and quiet retreats for harried New York executives to homes and cottages by the shore for seasonal vacationers and the yachting rich. Saugatuck, in south Westport, is rich in nautical flavor, sporting seaside homes, yacht clubs, and marinas. Downtown, the Boston Post Road is alive with restaurants, night spots, theatre, specialty and antique shops, and branches of the larger New York stores.

This combination of quietly elegant New England and the proximity of New York City gives Norwalk a desirability that leads to the second highest housing costs among the metro areas, behind only Stamford, Connecticut.

Pluses: Located near New York, it has access to all of that city's cultural, recreational, and medical facilities; rich in history and New England charm.

Minuses: Housing costs are extremely high (328th).

★ Dallas, TX (11)
Population: 1,957,378   Population Rank: 14

Dallas, rising out of the rolling plains of the cattle country of north-central Texas, has an aura about it that transcends guidebook descriptions or secondhand recounting. In the city proper (pop. 904,078), big skyscrapers—almost none more than 20 years old—soar from the gentle hills as a stark monument to the money, power, and growth of Texas. Dallas is big, growing, strong, rich, fast, tough, snazzy.

Not hundreds but thousands of millionaires live in the Dallas metro area, either on the Texas plains outside town, within walled estates in the affluent sections of the city or its suburbs, or in new high-rise condos. More than a third of all Texas bank deposits are made in Dallas or neighboring Fort Worth, and Dallas has the third largest number of million-dollar businesses in the nation. Beef and oil are still big industries, but Dallas is increasingly becoming a center of service industries and light manufacturing; it is also a world leader in the production of precision electronic equipment, aircraft, and defense hardware. All of this is indicative of Dallas's 12th-place ranking for economic growth and promise.

Despite the cowboy image projected by the city's history and by the popular TV show *Dallas*, a visitor walking one of the main streets in April might be hard-pressed to tell Dallas from Chicago. Smart shops, catering to every taste and income, reveal the city as one of the country's three leading fashion markets. Add to this the Dallas Symphony Orchestra, the Dallas Theatre Center (the only Frank Lloyd Wright public theatre), and the Dallas Museum of Natural History and you begin to see why this metro area scored so well in the arts (13th). The presence of several major universities helps Dallas achieve its rankings in health (20th) and education (29th).

Dallas has its weak spots, too. Housing is not reasonably priced, as it is in Austin and other Texas metro areas. The climate is enjoyable in every season except summer, which is long and very hot; air-conditioning in cars and homes is a must. Dallas's poorest showing is in safety from crime, where the fast-growing metro area ranks 308th.

Pluses: Vigorous, energetic atmosphere; outstanding rankings in economics, the arts, and health care.

Minuses: Very high crime rate; high housing costs (256th).

★ Seattle, WA (12)
Population: 1,607,469   Population Rank: 23

Imagine a city of a half million people nestled between a huge marine bay and a 20-mile-long freshwater lake.

To the east and the west of this city are two major mountain chains dominating the horizons and providing spectacular sunrises and sunsets. Forests of fir, cedar, and spruce cover the city's rolling hills. In the harbor, hundreds of fishing boats arrive and depart daily, depositing salmon and king crab onto the docks, while farther out are anchored ocean-going freighters bound for Anchorage, Honolulu, Yokohama, and Hong Kong.

Welcome to Seattle, center of one of America's youngest metro areas, which in recent years has placed near the top of every list that has ranked American cities or metro areas. Seattle has been recognized for its stable social situation, unrivaled recreational facilities, beautiful location, and very mild climate. True, Seattle is not as safe as it used to be, with crime rates on the rise. Also, its low housing score (283rd) reflects its high real estate costs—perhaps an indication of low supply and high demand for housing. An extensive bus system, ferryboats, and the first public monorail combine to give this metro area a transportation ranking of 19th.

Until gold was struck in the Yukon Territory at the turn of the century, Seattle was a sleepy little lumber and cannery town. Thousands of people poured northward into the Yukon and Alaska with the gold rush, and whether going by land or by sea, their point of embarkation was Seattle. In the years since, Seattle has remained the chief link between the mainland and Alaska, and now the Orient. The metro area is also a major manufacturing center for the aerospace industry, with facilities devoted not only to the construction of jet aircraft (Boeing is headquartered here), but to spacecraft and missiles. The metro area ranks 106th in terms of job opportunities and economic outlook.

Situated between the Cascade and Olympic mountain ranges and bounded by Puget Sound, Seattle is within easy reach of many wilderness areas. This, combined with its outstanding array of other assets—from fine restaurants to exciting professional sports—helps explain its emergence as *Places Rated*'s premier recreational spot. Seattle also enjoys an international reputation in the arts (it ranks 17th among the metro areas), with the Seattle Symphony Orchestra, Pacific Northwest Ballet, and Seattle Repertory Theatre among the outstanding performing groups. The Seattle Opera's annual presentation of Wagner's *Ring* cycle draws performers and spectators from around the world.

Closely linked to a breathtaking natural setting is a climate that is best characterized as mild maritime. Directly in the path of the Pacific westerly winds, Seattle is constantly bathed by warm, moist ocean air. The cold air from the Arctic and interior regions is blocked by the eastern Cascades. The net effect of this airborne ocean bath is a mildness that has earned Seattle a 12th-place rank in climate.

To the north of Seattle is Everett (pop. 54,413), a major fishing port. Other surrounding towns like Bellevue (pop. 73,903), Renton (pop. 30,612), and Riverton Heights (pop. 33,500) offer suburban living for residents of the metro area who prefer the less crowded, country setting in the woods of the Pacific Northwest. And yet, even in downtown Seattle, amid the skyscrapers, the Kingdome, and the Space Needle, the impression a visitor gets is of mountains, forests, and water.

Pluses: Outstanding recreational assets in a beautiful natural setting; high rankings in the arts (17th) and health care facilities (21st).

Minuses: High housing costs; growing crime rate.

★ **Atlanta, GA** (13)
Population: 2,138,231   ˄ Population Rank: 12

"If you want to go to heaven you'll have to go by way of Atlanta." This saying reflects the importance of Hartsfield International Airport, which is partly responsible for the Atlanta metro area's number-two ranking in transportation. The airport boasts a spanking-clean pedestrian tunnel in which travelers can hear taped directions to color-coded concourses leading to various airlines.

The theme of modern efficiency is prevalent throughout Atlanta. In many ways, it is no longer a traditional southern city. Many businesses have transplanted their corporate headquarters to the area over the past two decades, followed by multitudes of young professionals from the North and West. Because of its central location and urban opportunities, Atlanta also attracts many young people from the Southeast. This blend of new residents gives the city an unusual mix of rural and urban, down-home and uptown. Along with the business expansion have come new and varied facilities for housing, shopping, and entertainment. There are places to live and things to do for the most diversified tastes.

Adjacent to the central city is the upscale residential district of Buckhead. Miles of beautifully landscaped, elegant estates remind one of Atlanta's affluence. The Coca-Cola fortune is perhaps the best known made in Atlanta but certainly not the only one. Sandy Springs (pop. 20,300), a fairly new suburb, reflects the prosperity of a city on the move.

Many southerners are devoted to maintaining tradition, and Atlanta holds its own in the arts (31st) and education (62nd). Ample health care facilities are another benefit of big-city status, and Atlanta ranks 15th in this category. A high crime rate, perhaps a byproduct of the city's sudden growth, is Atlanta's main problem, giving the metro area a crime rank of 274th.

Pluses: Exciting blend of old and new; mild climate (24th); excellent facilities for health care, arts, and transportation.

Minuses: High crime rate; below-average showing in recreation (239th) and housing costs (210th).

★ **Knoxville, TN** (14)
Population: 565,970   Population Rank: 73

What do dogwoods, power plants, symphonies, and funnel cakes have in common? Knoxville. These and other diverse entities have coexisted here, linking the pioneer past with an industrial present and a technological future. Located at the foothills of the scenic East Tennessee Appalachian Mountains, the city of Knoxville (pop. 175,045) was the last outpost for supplies needed by westward-bound pioneers from the Southeast. Currently, Knoxville reflects a continuing prosperity in farming, industry, and culture. Tobacco and produce markets are an active part of the local economy. Energy, a resounding theme of the recent Knoxville World's Fair, is more than a topic of conversation here: The headquarters of the Tennessee Valley Authority and Oak Ridge atomic energy complex are responsible for much of the area's growth.

Although not outstanding in any *Places Rated* category (its best rank is 26th, for its mild climate), this Mid-South metro area performs consistently well in all of them, joining the elite group of only nine metro areas with no rankings below 200th. Its good rankings in housing costs (72nd) and safety from crime (55th) set it apart from most of the other top-ranking places. Yet cultural, educational, and recreational amenities are readily available.

The University of Tennessee is a major asset, offering not only programs in the arts and sciences but also the Clarence Brown Theatre, whose season runs from January through June. "Shakespeare to the Schools" is a special outreach program designed to entertain and enlighten students unable to attend on-site theatre productions. The Knoxville area supports the Knoxville Symphony Orchestra and the Appalachian Ballet Company, along with its renowned Dogwood Arts Festival every spring.

Geographic location is a real plus for Knoxville. To the west is gently rolling fertile farmland; to the east are the mountains, with isolated hamlets, winding mountain roads, and breathtaking views. Nearby Gatlinburg (pop. 3,210) is the headquarters for Great Smoky Mountains National Park, where the seasons are reflected in the vibrant greens and pinks of spring and the reds, oranges, and yellows of fall, making it a major tourist attraction.

Pluses: Solid performance in nearly every category; splendid natural surroundings.

Minuses: Could do better in health care (145th), education (179th), and economics (148th).

★ **Buffalo, NY** (15)
Population: 1,015,472   Population Rank: 40

Probably the most widely known fact about Buffalo is that it gets a lot of snow, about 90 inches of it every year. Keeping highways, city streets, and airport runways clear during the winter is a major challenge; on at least one recent occasion, Buffalo had to borrow more sophisticated snow-removal equipment from Toronto to find the pavement at Greater Buffalo International Airport. In spite of the snow, this hearty city not only survives but continues to function in all its urban responsibilities. A solid metro area, it ranks below 200th in only one *Places Rated* category.

Buffalo is situated on gently rolling terrain at the southern end of the Niagara River, which separates the United States from Canada and joins Lake Erie and Lake Ontario. The river as a border affords both countries the benefits of tourism and electrical power from Niagara Falls. Buffalo has long been a manufacturing center. Steel and grain mills combine with farms and orchards to produce the freight for its impressive transport systems. These include one of the country's largest railroad centers: two passenger and 15 freight terminals process more than 25,000 trains per year. Buffalo has capitalized on its strategic location by developing ports on the Erie Canal, which opened in 1825, and on the St. Lawrence Seaway, which opened in 1959.

Two large institutions, the State University of New York at Buffalo and State University of New York College at Buffalo, which between them serve more than 35,000 students, provide higher education in Buffalo. Health care facilities are top-notch, and cultural opportunities abound. Studio Arena Theatre offers a full September-to-June season of dramatic performances, focusing on contemporary American productions. The Buffalo Philharmonic Orchestra provides notable symphonic and pops performances. Other assets include the Buffalo Museum of Science, the South Park Botanical Gardens, and the Buffalo Zoological Gardens; three professional sports teams and the Buffalo Raceway contribute to the metro area's creditable 62nd-place showing in recreation.

Pluses: Solid performance in almost every category, with strongest rankings in arts (23rd), health care (36th), and education (50th).

Minuses: Below-average economic picture (217th); snowy climate (not for the faint of heart).

★ Baltimore, MD (16)

Population: 2,199,531   Population Rank: 11

Baltimore—located on the world's largest estuary, city of the spice and crab trade, of endless seafood and German-American meals, home of Edgar Allan Poe, Babe Ruth, and H. L. Mencken—dominates this six-county metro area, which, not surprisingly, bumps nearby Washington from 16th place. In keeping with its past as a major port city and shipbuilding center, the metro area receives its highest category rank (eighth) in transportation. It is also the terminus of the Baltimore and Ohio Railroad, the nation's first.

Like many of the metro areas included in *Places Rated*'s list of the best places to live, Baltimore is an old eastern city that's been through hard times but is now undergoing an urban renaissance. At Harborplace,

Baltimore's renovated inner harbor, the U.S.S. *Constellation* docks, and shoppers browse through stores and cafés while admiring the restored buildings of the area. In its first year open to the public, Harborplace had more visitors than Disney World; with the revenues collected, the restoration process was accelerated and broadened.

Baltimore (pop. 786,775) is renowned for its many sections of distinct ethnic and historic flavor. Parts of these neighborhoods are filled with Victorian brick row houses with scrubbed white steps. More affluent neighborhoods include Roland Park, Homeland, and Mount Washington. The metro area ranks relatively poorly for its homeownership costs (250th), partly because of the expensive housing in suburban neighborhoods like Green Spring Valley and nearby towns like Hill Farm and Hunt Valley. Maryland's capital, Annapolis (pop. 31,740), is also part of this historic metro area.

Baltimore excels in most big-city amenities, with such institutions as Johns Hopkins University (with its outstanding medical center), the U.S. Naval Academy, and the Baltimore Symphony Orchestra contributing to high rankings in health care (12th), education (15th), and the arts (15th). Baltimore enjoys a solid 39th-place ranking for recreation, despite the recent defection of the NFL Colts to Indianapolis.

Pluses: Interesting and historic blend of North and South; strong performance in almost every *Places Rated* category.

Minuses: Above-average housing costs; very poor ranking in safety from crime (323rd).

★ Washington, DC–MD–VA (17)

Population: 3,250,822   Population   Rank: 6

Home-away-from-hometown, U.S.A., is Washington, D.C. (pop. 638,432), center of this 17th-ranked metro area. Its highly transient population reflects the influences of government and tourism. Politicians are drawn to the District of Columbia by necessity and Yuppies by choice. For the young aggressive professional and the politician, Washington is the place to be; there is *everything* to do here. Not only does Washington exceed most cities in its amount of cultural, educational, and recreational resources but also in the quality of what it has to offer. This excellence is apparent in Washington's architecture. The lack of skyscrapers is immediately obvious and pleasing, and there are spectacular views in every direction, the Capitol and the Washington Monument commanding the most notice.

Washington is a city of culture and learning: Performing arts, libraries, and museums earn this metro area a fourth-place ranking in the arts. It also boasts outstanding ranks in education (third), transportation (fourth), and health care (sixth).

Overall, housing in Washington is expensive and scarce, giving the metro area a rank of 314th for housing. Housing for the city's native and predominantly black population is depressed and spread throughout the district. The large percentage of disadvantaged urban dwellers and a high crime rate are major problems for the city. Housing for middle-class and wealthy people is expensive and located in well-defined neighborhoods, some very exclusive. One such neighborhood is Georgetown, which has fine homes and diverse restaurants and nightlife.

Outside the District of Columbia but very much a part of the Washington metro area are numerous communities in Virginia and Maryland. To the west and south are Alexandria (pop. 103,217), Arlington (pop. 152,700), Fairfax (pop. 19,390), and Springfield (pop. 12,500). Many of the young adults who work in Washington make their homes in the Virginia suburbs. Farther out is Leesburg (pop. 8,357), representative of Virginia's horse country. To the north and east of Washington is Maryland, where exclusive Chevy Chase (pop. 12,232), Silver Spring (pop. 72,893), Gaithersburg (pop. 26,424), and College Park (pop. 23,614, home of the University of Maryland) provide other suburban living options.

Pluses: An area of international reputation; outstanding array of major cultural, educational, and medical facilities; mild climate (51st).

Minuses: Very high housing costs (314th) and crime rate (276th).

★ Cincinnati, OH–KY–IN (18)
Population: 1,401,491   Population Rank: 28

Like Pittsburgh, its sister river city to the east, and Louisville to the west, Cincinnati grew and prospered early because of its excellent location on the Ohio River. As river traffic declined in the period after the Civil War and more goods were moved by railroad, Cincinnati diversified, becoming a manufacturing and rail center. Today, the Queen City (pop. 385,457) is the bituminous coal center of the United States and the world's largest inland coal port. Manufacturing is the major industrial activity in Cincinnati; goods produced range from soap and playing cards to radar equipment, machine tools, and truck and car bodies.

Cincinnati's rolling hills and river valley provide lush surroundings for suburban communities like Covington, Kentucky (pop. 46,563), and they accent the city's handsome downtown buildings and active riverfront area. You can still tour the river on a sternwheeler: Cincinnati is the home port of the *Delta Queen* and many other steamboats. The center of town is Fountain Square, where each October the city celebrates Oktoberfest Zinzinnati, a festival handed down through several generations of German immigrants. The Cincinnati Zoo is another recreational asset; one of the world's finest, it has an excellent reputation for raising endangered species, such as the white Bengal tiger.

Cincinnati is home to major universities, a repertory theatre, a ballet, and an operatic company, as well as a renowned symphony orchestra. These, in addition to its fine museums, help explain the metro area's high rank (16th) in the arts. Cincinnati is one of the few metro areas with no *Places Rated* rankings lower than 200th in any category. It is gifted with a mild climate, a relatively low crime rate for a city its size, and good health care, transportation, and recreational facilities.

Will Rogers claimed he always judged a town by its chili. He would have liked Cincinnati very much. Not at all like its hot and spicy Texas counterpart, Cincinnati chili is sweet, made with beans, cheese, and even pasta. You can have your Cincinnati chili plain, or two-way, or three-way, or four-way. . . . It's just another of the pleasant surprises you'll find in this Heartland metro area.

Pluses: Solid all-around performer, with outstanding cultural assets; easy access to scenic bluegrass country.

Minuses: Below-average rankings for housing costs (191st) and economics (182nd).

★ Albany–Schenectady–Troy, NY (19)
Population: 835,880   Population Rank: 55

This three-city metro area in the Hudson River–Catskill Mountain region of New York State is not glamorous. But like other upstate New York metro areas, it is solid, safe, culturally sound, and has a plentiful supply of facilities and services in education, arts, and transportation.

Albany (pop. 101,727), as capital of the state, is fraught with political drama. The Empire State Plaza, a new and dramatic collection of handsome buildings on a hundred-acre tract of land, houses state offices as well as the New York State Museum and the New York State Modern Art Collection. Albany became important to U.S. trade beginning with the 1825 opening of the Erie Canal, linking the upper Midwest with the ocean ports of the East. Now the home of many manufacturers, Albany retains its historic feel as a capital city and trade center.

Some of General Electric's largest factories and research complexes are located in the active manufacturing center of Schenectady (pop. 67,972). Schenectady has one of the highest ratios of Ph.D.s per capita in the nation. A town of many two-family houses with walk-up front porches supporting roofs on round pillars, Schenectady also features the Historic Stockade Area with its elegant nineteenth-century homes. Union College, one of the finest private colleges in the state, forms part of the triad of major universities that gives the metro area its *Places Rated* rank of 17th in education (the other two are State University of New York at Albany and Rensselaer Polytechnic Institute in Troy, the nation's oldest private technical school).

Troy (pop. 56,638) is primarily a manufacturing town and has undergone a decline in recent years due to the general falling-off of the U.S. textile industry.

The three main cities of this metro area are complemented by some interesting smaller towns. In Amsterdam (pop. 21,872) one can see the only section of the Erie Canal that remains unchanged since the canal was built. Also on display is a building style that reflects an early Dutch heritage, a style common to the area. The Victorian resort city of Saratoga Springs (pop. 23,906), north of Albany, is home of the famous Saratoga Race Track, National Museum of Racing, Saratoga Performing Arts Center, and Yaddo (a 400-acre estate converted into a retreat for artists and writers).

Pluses: Strong showing in transportation (15th) and education (17th), with stable social indicators (ranks 54th in safety from crime).

Minuses: Harsh winters (mildness ranking 250th); mediocre ranking in recreation (175th); solid but unexciting.

★ Burlington, VT (19)
Population: 115,308   Population Rank: 274

Burlington is the sole metropolitan representative for Vermont, that upright state (in many ways) nestled between New England and the Adirondacks, where maple syrup, cheese, wood products, and ski resorts abound. Vermont in the last century was a veritable patchwork of dairy farms and orchards. But increasingly since 1900 the small farmers and fruit growers went broke and abandoned the countryside, allowing the dense northern forests to cover the fields and pastures. Thus, until this edition of *Places Rated Almanac*, the Green Mountain State had no metro areas at all. It is still America's most rural state; the greatest percentage of its population is outside urban areas.

The tiny Burlington metro area is located on the eastern shore of Lake Champlain. It is a scenic setting, and area residents take full advantage of the huge lake (430 square miles) for fishing and boating. The city of Burlington (pop. 37,712) has a large marina for private boats. There are docking facilities for oceangoing vessels, too, since Lake Champlain is connected to the St. Lawrence Seaway by the Richelieu River, which makes Burlington a seaport.

The Adirondack Mountains to the west and the Green Mountains to the east provide some shelter from severe storms, but Burlington is not without its rugged spells of weather. In winter, invading Arctic air from Hudson Bay causes intense cold snaps. The cold winters are primarily responsible for Burlington's lowest rank, a climate placing of 305th.

But in all other categories except housing (267th), Burlington shines. Ranks in health care (63rd) and the arts (177th) are surprisingly strong for a metro area as small and remote as this one. The low crime rate (32nd) simply reflects the general trend of the smaller New England metro areas, which have always been remarkably crime-free. Burlington's rankings in education (23rd), transportation (tenth), and recreation (21st) all help boost it toward the top. And finally, the

economic outlook (43rd) for this city that manufactures missile components and data processing equipment as well as steel and wood products is as bright as the view at sunset across Lake Champlain from Battery Park in downtown Burlington.

Pluses: Small, unspoiled area with much to offer.

Minuses: Rigorous winters; somewhat remote; confirmed urbanites might be uncomfortable here.

★ Syracuse, NY (21)
Population: 642,971   Population Rank: 64

Syracuse is one of four upstate New York metro areas to make *Places Rated*'s top 25, and like Buffalo, Albany–Schenectady–Troy, and Rochester, ranks 200th or below in only one category (economics, in which it places 282nd).

Syracuse (pop. 170,105) is truly an all-American city, founded in the eighteenth century and growing and prospering through the twentieth. Local companies produce pharmaceuticals and china as well as electronic, air-conditioning, missile, and radar equipment. It is also an active city: Hardy Syracusans, undaunted by the 109 inches of snow that fall annually, take advantage of year-round offerings in recreation. Home to the Burnet Park Zoo and the Syracuse University Orangemen and dotted with many beautiful lakes (including the Finger Lakes), the metro area ranks 44th in leisure amenities. The century-old New York State Fair also takes place here each year, drawing fairgoers from New England and the Midwest.

Culturally, this metro area has it all. Syracuse Stage is the only professional theatre in central New York State and works with the drama department at Syracuse University to provide a quality theatre experience. In addition, there are the Syracuse Symphony Orchestra, the Everson Museum of Art, and the Opera Theatre of Syracuse, all of which chip in toward Syracuse's 57th-place ranking in the arts.

Education is a high priority in the area, which has well-recognized public schools and an enviable selection of colleges and universities, among them Colgate University and the State University College of Forestry. The result is an impressive standing of 44th for Syracuse in education.

Syracuse also happens to be one of the nation's leading test markets for new products since the characteristics of its population so closely resemble the national norms. Perhaps this "average" population can be traced to the area's well-mixed heritage, evident in the names of towns, streets, and waterways: Chittenango, Oswego, Marcellus, Skaneateles, Oneida, Liverpool, Cicero, Euclid, and Syracuse itself.

Pluses: Seems to have many of the advantages and few of the disadvantages of a major metropolitan city; strongest showings in transportation (14th), education, recreation, and the arts.

Minuses: Poor standing in economics (282nd); snowy, rigorous climate (151st).

MAKING THE RANKINGS WORK FOR YOU

At the spring 1984 meeting of the Association of American Geographers in Washington, D.C., a paper was read that drew more inquiries from the press and the public than any other in the association's 80-year history. "Rating America's Cities," by Prof. Robert M. Pierce of the State University of New York at Cortland, looked into what would happen if individual preferences were incorporated into the findings of the first edition of *Places Rated Almanac*. Pierce had asked 1,100 people in New York State to rank the almanac's nine dimensions of urban living according to their own preferences. Economics, climate, crime, and housing were thought most important by the people surveyed, whereas transportation and the arts were considered least important.

When Pierce reranked the 277 metro areas surveyed in the 1981 *Places Rated Almanac* according to these preferences, the list that emerged differed somewhat from *Places Rated*'s overall ranking. Atlanta, which came out first in *Places Rated*, ranked tenth in Pierce's study, while Greensboro–Winston-Salem–High Point, North Carolina (ranked third by *Places Rated*), finished first. Some rankings differed dramatically: The New York metro area, ranked 26th by *Places Rated*, fell to 156th in Pierce's list, and Kokomo, Indiana, leaped from 182nd to 75th.

Which ranking is "better"? It all depends—on who you are and what you're looking for. Although *Places Rated* can decide on diverse and comparable standards for metropolitan living and then suggest which of 329 metro areas come closest to these standards, finding the right spot is ultimately a matter of personal choice. (If you think you would prefer non-metropolitan living, for example, or are looking for a good place to retire, you might also want to consult *Places Rated Retirement Guide*, which rates and ranks 107 places for retirement living, most of them non-metropolitan.)

Using *Places Rated Almanac*, you can put together a custom-made list of metro areas that reflects your own personal preferences. There are two ways to make this job easy. One is to choose and consider only the metro areas that rank in the top 50 in the quality-of-life factor most important to you, be it climate, housing, crime, or whatever. Another way is to consider only the metro areas located in the region of the country you prefer. You may wish to add a certain category's rank to your total score twice if it is especially important to you; this will have the effect of further penalizing places that do poorly in that category.

What follows are three examples of how you can make *Places Rated*'s rankings work for you.

In 1982, Heidrick & Struggles, a national executive search firm, surveyed 2,000 senior managers whose names had appeared in the *Wall Street Journal*'s "Who's News" section over a 12-month period. The typical senior manager was forty-seven years old, white, and male; pulled down $173,000 a year; had one or more advanced degrees; worked 57 hours a week; was on the road 25 percent of the time; and was married to his first wife, who didn't work. If these senior managers were offered a job in another city, the survey showed, their prime considerations would be climate, cultural amenities, recreation opportunities, and economic outlook. The list below shows which of the 329 metro areas come to the fore when we add together the *Places Rated* rankings for these four categories.

The Best Metro Areas for Mobile Managers
(Combined Rankings for Climate, Arts, Recreation, and Economics)

Metro Area	Combined Ranking
1. Nassau–Suffolk, NY	89
2. San Francisco, CA	98
3. Seattle, WA	136
4. Boston, MA	153
5. Anaheim–Santa Ana, CA	156
6. San Jose, CA	186
7. Monmouth–Ocean, NJ	188
8. Los Angeles–Long Beach, CA	192
9. San Diego, CA	197
10. Norwalk, CT	199
11. Bridgeport–Milford, CT	211
12. Miami–Hialeah, FL	229
13. New York, NY	230
14. Norfolk–Virginia Beach–Newport News, VA	233
15. Dallas, TX	255
16. Tucson, AZ	258
17. Santa Barbara–Santa Maria–Lompoc, CA	263
18. Honolulu, HI	269
18. Oakland, CA	269
20. Salem–Gloucester, MA	281

So much for the preferences of top managers. What about their subordinates with families—might they have different priorities? The same year that managers were surveyed, the Fantus Company, a site-location consultant to business clients, polled engineers who subscribed to *Industrial Research and Development* magazine for the standards they would use in judging a city as a place to live. Their concerns had more to do with family than those of mobile senior managers. The factor most often cited was housing cost (64 percent), followed by climate (51 percent), education (30 percent), and recreational opportunities (25 percent). Using their percent responses to weight the *Places Rated* ranks for housing, climate, education, and recreation, an interesting list emerges.

The Best Metro Areas for Transferred Families
(Weighted Rankings for Housing, Climate, Education, and Recreation)

Metro Area	Combined Ranking
1. San Francisco, CA	581
2. Los Angeles–Long Beach, CA	667
3. Eugene–Springfield, OR	686
4. Nassau–Suffolk, NY	692
5. Boston, MA	753
6. Portland, OR	754
7. Charleston, SC	780
8. Baltimore, MD	829

Metro Area	Combined Ranking		Metro Area	Combined Ranking
9. Johnson City–Kingsport–Bristol, TN–VA	831		6. Boston, MA	347
10. Pittsburgh, PA	846		7. Middlesex–Somerset–Hunterdon, NJ	352
			8. Dallas, TX	363
11. Syracuse, NY	850		9. San Jose, CA	364
12. Philadelphia, PA–NJ	861		10. Washington, DC–MD–VA	371
13. Albuquerque, NM	867			
14. Norfolk–Virginia Beach–Newport News, VA	874		10. Atlanta, GA	371
15. Providence, RI	892		12. Richmond–Petersburg, VA	395
			13. Seattle, WA	396
16. St. Louis, MO–IL	905		14. Nassau–Suffolk, NY	401
17. Buffalo, NY	915		15. Philadelphia, PA–NJ	402
18. Rochester, NY	926			
19. Louisville, KY–IN	968		16. Chicago, IL	404
20. Miami–Hialeah, FL	993		17. Honolulu, HI	415
			18. San Francisco, CA	418
			19. St. Louis, MO–IL	423
			20. Salt Lake City–Ogden, UT	481

Now, what about a person who is just starting out? Suppose you are finishing college and are ready to launch a career in your chosen field, wherever the opportunity happens to be. You do have certain preferences, however. You don't want a place that's too small, and you're also interested in a low crime rate, good transportation facilities, a range of cultural activities, and promising economic opportunities. How will you narrow down the field to find which of the many metro areas might be best? Looking at the *Places Rated* rankings for crime, transportation, arts, and economics for places over a half million population could be a good way to start.

The Best Metro Areas for Career Starters
(Combined Rankings for Crime, Transportation, Arts, and Economics)

Metro Area	Combined Ranking
1. Raleigh–Durham, NC	309
2. Pittsburgh, PA	331
3. Minneapolis–St. Paul, MN–WI	334
4. Rochester, NY	343
5. Denver, CO	344

By now it should be apparent that the task of finding the best place for you can be as simple or as complicated as you wish. The person who enjoys numbers has been supplied with enough figures to turn the whole process into a never-ending parlor game in which various factors can be weighted, added, or deleted to fit individual needs. In fact, if you were to weight each of *Places Rated*'s nine factors differently on a scale of one to ten—rather than equally, as we have done in this book—you would come up with more than two and a half *billion* possible combinations.

Nonmathematicians may simply want to add up and compare the scores of the ten or 20 metro areas that sound most attractive to them. Remember, finding the ideal spot is a matter of personal choice. *Places Rated Almanac* does not pretend to be the final arbiter of the best and worst metro areas; rather, it is designed to serve as an instrument that you can fine-tune and adjust to help you find the kind of place where you want to live.

Appendix

Consolidated Metropolitan Statistical Areas (CMSAs) & Their Primary Metropolitan Statistical Area (PMSA) Components

**Boston–Lawrence–
Salem, MA–NH**
Boston, MA
Brockton, MA
Lawrence–Haverhill, MA–NH
Lowell, MA–NH
Nashua, NH
Salem–Gloucester, MA

Buffalo–Niagara Falls, NY
Buffalo, NY
Niagara Falls, NY

**Chicago–Gary–Lake County,
IL–IN–WI**
Aurora–Elgin, IL
Chicago, IL
Gary–Hammond, IN
Joliet, IL
Kenosha, WI
Lake County, IL

Cincinnati–Hamilton, OH–KY–IN
Cincinnati, OH–KY–IN
Hamilton–Middletown, OH

Cleveland–Akron–Lorain, OH
Akron, OH
Cleveland, OH
Lorain–Elyria, OH

Dallas–Fort Worth, TX
Dallas, TX
Fort Worth–Arlington, TX

Denver–Boulder, CO
Boulder–Longmont, CO
Denver, CO

Detroit–Ann Arbor, MI
Ann Arbor, MI
Detroit, MI

**Hartford–New Britain–
Middletown, CT**
Bristol, CT
Hartford, CT
Middletown, CT
New Britain, CT

Houston–Galveston–Brazoria, TX
Brazoria, TX
Galveston–Texas City, TX
Houston, TX

Kansas City, MO–Kansas City, KS
Kansas City, KS
Kansas City, MO

**Los Angeles–Anaheim–
Riverside, CA**
Anaheim–Santa Ana, CA
Los Angeles–Long Beach, CA
Oxnard–Ventura, CA
Riverside–San Bernardino, CA

Miami–Fort Lauderdale, FL
Fort Lauderdale–Hollywood–Pompano
   Beach, FL
Miami–Hialeah, FL

Milwaukee–Racine, WI
Milwaukee, WI
Racine, WI

**New York–Northern New Jersey–
Long Island, NY–NJ–CT**
Bergen–Passaic, NJ
Bridgeport–Milford, CT
Danbury, CT
Jersey City, NJ
Middlesex–Somerset–Hunterdon, NJ
Monmouth–Ocean, NJ
Nassau–Suffolk, NY
New York, NY
Newark, NJ

Norwalk, CT
Orange County, NY
Stamford, CT

**Philadelphia–Wilmington–Trenton,
PA–NJ–DE–MD**
Philadelphia, PA–NJ
Trenton, NJ
Vineland–Millville–Bridgeton, NJ
Wilmington, DE–NJ–MD

Pittsburgh–Beaver Valley, PA
Beaver County, PA
Pittsburgh, PA

Portland–Vancouver, OR–WA
Portland, OR
Vancouver, WA

**Providence–Pawtucket–Fall River,
RI–MA**
Fall River, MA–RI
Pawtucket–Woonsocket–
   Attleboro, RI–MA
Providence, RI

**St. Louis–East St. Louis–Alton,
MO–IL**
Alton–Granite City, IL
East St. Louis–Belleville, IL
St. Louis, MO–IL

**San Francisco–Oakland–
San Jose, CA**
Oakland, CA
San Francisco, CA
San Jose, CA
Santa Cruz, CA
Santa Rosa–Petaluma, CA
Vallejo–Fairfield–Napa, CA

Seattle–Tacoma, WA
Seattle, WA
Tacoma, WA

Metro Areas by State*

Alabama
Anniston
Birmingham
Columbus (GA–AL)
Dothan
Florence
Gadsden
Huntsville
Mobile
Montgomery
Tuscaloosa

Alaska
Anchorage

Arizona
Phoenix
Tucson

Arkansas
Fayetteville–Springdale
Fort Smith (AR–OK)
Little Rock–North Little Rock
Memphis (TN–AR–MS)
Pine Bluff
Texarkana (TX)–Texarkana (AR)

California
Anaheim–Santa Ana
Bakersfield
Chico
Fresno
Los Angeles–Long Beach
Modesto
Oakland
Oxnard–Ventura
Redding
Riverside–San Bernardino
Sacramento
Salinas–Seaside–Monterey
San Diego
San Francisco
San Jose
Santa Barbara–Santa Maria–Lompoc
Santa Cruz
Santa Rosa–Petaluma
Stockton
Vallejo–Fairfield–Napa
Visalia–Tulare–Porterville
Yuba City

Colorado
Boulder–Longmont
Colorado Springs
Denver
Fort Collins–Loveland
Greeley
Pueblo

Connecticut
Bridgeport–Milford
Bristol
Danbury
Hartford
Middletown
New Britain
New Haven–Meriden
New London–Norwich (CT–RI)
Norwalk
Stamford
Waterbury

Delaware
Wilmington (DE–NJ–MD)

District of Columbia
Washington (DC–MD–VA)

Florida
Bradenton
Daytona Beach
Fort Lauderdale–Hollywood–Pompano Beach
Fort Myers
Fort Pierce
Fort Walton Beach
Gainesville
Jacksonville
Lakeland–Winter Haven
Melbourne–Titusville–Palm Bay
Miami–Hialeah
Ocala
Orlando
Panama City
Pensacola
Sarasota
Tallahassee
Tampa–St. Petersburg–Clearwater
West Palm Beach–Boca Raton–Delray Beach

Georgia
Albany
Athens
Atlanta
Augusta (GA–SC)
Chattanooga (TN–GA)
Columbus (GA–AL)
Macon–Warner Robins
Savannah

Hawaii
Honolulu

Idaho
Boise City

Illinois
Alton–Granite City
Aurora–Elgin
Bloomington–Normal
Champaign–Urbana–Rantoul
Chicago
Davenport–Rock Island–Moline (IA–IL)
Decatur
East St. Louis–Belleville
Joliet
Kankakee
Lake County
Peoria
Rockford
St. Louis (MO–IL)
Springfield

Indiana
Anderson
Bloomington
Cincinnati (OH–KY–IN)
Elkhart–Goshen
Evansville (IN–KY)
Fort Wayne
Gary–Hammond
Indianapolis
Kokomo
Lafayette
Louisville (KY–IN)
Muncie
South Bend–Mishawaka
Terre Haute

Iowa
Cedar Rapids
Davenport–Rock Island–Moline (IA–IL)
Des Moines
Dubuque
Iowa City
Omaha (NE–IA)
Sioux City (IA–NE)
Waterloo–Cedar Falls

Kansas
Kansas City
Lawrence
Topeka
Wichita

Kentucky
Cincinnati (OH–KY–IN)
Clarksville–Hopkinsville (TN–KY)
Evansville (IN–KY)
Huntington–Ashland (WV–KY–OH)
Lexington–Fayette
Louisville (KY–IN)
Owensboro

Louisiana
Alexandria
Baton Rouge
Houma–Thibodaux
Lafayette
Lake Charles
Monroe
New Orleans
Shreveport

Maine
Bangor
Lewiston–Auburn
Portland
Portsmouth–Dover–Rochester (NH–ME)

Maryland
Baltimore
Cumberland (MD–WV)
Hagerstown
Washington (DC–MD–VA)
Wilmington (DE–NJ–MD)

Massachusetts
Boston
Brockton
Fall River (MA–RI)
Fitchburg–Leominster
Lawrence–Haverhill (MA–NH)
Lowell (MA–NH)
New Bedford
Pawtucket–Woonsocket–Attleboro (RI–MA)
Pittsfield
Salem–Gloucester
Springfield
Worcester

Michigan
Ann Arbor
Battle Creek
Benton Harbor
Detroit
Flint
Grand Rapids
Jackson
Kalamazoo
Lansing–East Lansing
Muskegon
Saginaw–Bay City–Midland

Minnesota
Duluth (MN–WI)
Fargo–Moorhead (ND–MN)
Minneapolis–St. Paul (MN–WI)
Rochester
St. Cloud

Mississippi
Biloxi–Gulfport
Jackson
Memphis (TN–AR–MS)
Pascagoula

Missouri
Columbia
Joplin
Kansas City
St. Joseph
St. Louis (MO–IL)
Springfield

Montana
Billings
Great Falls

Nebraska
Lincoln
Omaha (NE–IA)
Sioux City (IA–NE)

Nevada
Las Vegas
Reno

New Hampshire
Lawrence–Haverhill (MA–NH)
Lowell (MA–NH)
Manchester
Nashua
Portsmouth–Dover–Rochester (NH–ME)

New Jersey
Allentown–Bethlehem (PA–NJ)
Atlantic City
Bergen–Passaic
Jersey City
Middlesex–Somerset–Hunterdon
Monmouth–Ocean
Newark
Philadelphia (PA–NJ)
Trenton
Vineland–Millville–Bridgeton
Wilmington (DE–NJ–MD)

New Mexico
Albuquerque
Las Cruces

---

*Many metro areas include parts of two or more states; these are listed under every state in which they have a component county.

New York
Albany–Schenectady–Troy
Binghamton
Buffalo
Elmira
Glens Falls
Nassau–Suffolk
New York
Niagara Falls
Orange County
Poughkeepsie
Rochester
Syracuse
Utica–Rome

North Carolina
Asheville
Burlington
Charlotte–Gastonia–Rock Hill
  (NC–SC)
Fayetteville
Greensboro–Winston-Salem–
  High Point
Hickory
Jacksonville
Raleigh–Durham
Wilmington

North Dakota
Bismarck
Fargo–Moorhead (ND–MN)
Grand Forks

Ohio
Akron
Canton
Cincinnati (OH–KY–IN)
Cleveland
Columbus
Dayton–Springfield
Hamilton–Middletown
Huntington–Ashland
  (WV–KY–OH)
Lima
Lorain–Elyria
Mansfield
Parkersburg–Marietta (WV–OH)
Steubenville–Weirton (OH–WV)
Toledo

Wheeling (WV–OH)
Youngstown–Warren

Oklahoma
Enid
Fort Smith (AR–OK)
Lawton
Oklahoma City
Tulsa

Oregon
Eugene–Springfield
Medford
Portland
Salem

Pennsylvania
Allentown–Bethlehem (PA–NJ)
Altoona
Beaver County
Erie
Harrisburg–Lebanon–Carlisle
Johnstown
Lancaster
Philadelphia (PA–NJ)
Pittsburgh
Reading
Scranton–Wilkes-Barre
Sharon
State College
Williamsport
York

Rhode Island
Fall River (MA–RI)
New London–Norwich (CT–RI)
Pawtucket–Woonsocket–
  Attleboro (RI–MA)
Providence

South Carolina
Anderson
Augusta (GA–SC)
Charleston
Charlotte–Gastonia–Rock Hill
  (NC–SC)
Columbia
Florence
Greenville–Spartanburg

South Dakota
Sioux Falls

Tennessee
Chattanooga (TN–GA)
Clarksville–Hopkinsville (TN–KY)
Johnson City–Kingsport–Bristol
  (TN–VA)
Knoxville
Memphis (TN–AR–MS)
Nashville

Texas
Abilene
Amarillo
Austin
Beaumont–Port Arthur
Brazoria
Brownsville–Harlingen
Bryan–College Station
Corpus Christi
Dallas
El Paso
Fort Worth–Arlington
Galveston–Texas City
Houston
Killeen–Temple
Laredo
Longview–Marshall
Lubbock
McAllen–Edinburg–Mission
Midland
Odessa
San Angelo
San Antonio
Sherman–Denison
Texarkana (TX)–Texarkana
  (AR)
Tyler
Victoria
Waco
Wichita Falls

Utah
Provo–Orem
Salt Lake City–Ogden

Vermont
Burlington

Virginia
Charlottesville
Danville
Johnson City–Kingsport–Bristol
  (TN–VA)
Lynchburg
Norfolk–Virginia Beach–
  Newport News
Richmond–Petersburg
Roanoke
Washington (DC–MD–VA)

Washington
Bellingham
Bremerton
Olympia
Richland–Kennewick–Pasco
Seattle
Spokane
Tacoma
Vancouver
Yakima

West Virginia
Charleston
Cumberland (MD–WV)
Huntington–Ashland
  (WV–KY–OH)
Parkersburg–Marietta (WV–OH)
Steubenville–Weirton (OH–WV)
Wheeling (WV–OH)

Wisconsin
Appleton–Oshkosh–Neenah
Duluth (MN–WI)
Eau Claire
Green Bay
Janesville–Beloit
Kenosha
La Crosse
Madison
Milwaukee
Minneapolis–St. Paul (MN–WI)
Racine
Sheboygan
Wausau

Wyoming
Casper

List of Tables, Maps, & Diagrams

ABOUT THE AUTHORS

The first appearance of *Places Rated Almanac,* in 1981, created much excitement and controversy. Authors Richard Boyer and David Savageau were featured on the *Today* show and appeared on the *David Susskind Show,* the *CBS Evening News,* and numerous local television and radio programs. In 1983 they collaborated on the highly successful *Places Rated Retirement Guide,* which rates and ranks 107 places, many of them non-metropolitan areas, for retirement living.

Richard Boyer writes both fiction and nonfiction. In addition to co-authoring *Places Rated Almanac* and *Places Rated Retirement Guide,* he is author of three novels, including *Billingsgate Shoal* (winner of the Mystery Writers of America's Edgar award for Best Mystery Novel of 1982) and *The Penny Ferry,* both published by Houghton Mifflin Company. Formerly of Chicago and Boston, Mr. Boyer, upon completion of the first edition of *Places Rated Almanac,* followed the book's advice for selecting good places to live and now resides in Asheville, North Carolina.

David Savageau, since the first publication of *Places Rated Almanac,* has made public appearances throughout the country discussing the inexhaustible topic of quality of life. Mr. Savageau is principal-in-charge of Pre-LOCATION, a personal relocation consulting firm. Over the previous 15 years, he and his wife, Karyl, have lived successively in Denver, St. Louis, Indianapolis, and Boston. They now make their home in Gloucester, Massachusetts.